Catalogue of prints and drawings in the British Museum: Division I. Political and personal satires

British Museum. Dept. of Prints and Drawings,
Frederic George Stephens, M Dorothy George

CATALOGUE OF
POLITICAL AND PERSONAL
SATIRES

POLITENESS.

You be D__m'd   Vous etes une Bete

With Porter Rost Beef & Plumb Pudding well cramd   The poor Meagre Frenchman such Language dont suit.
Jack Englyn declares that Mons.ʳ may be D__d *POLITENESS.* So he Grins Indignation & calls him a Brute.

Pub.ᵈ by H Humphrey S.ᵗ James Street

The earliest representations in the British Museum
of the typical John Bull

Nᵒˢ 5611-12

CATALOGUE OF
POLITICAL AND PERSONAL
SATIRES

PRESERVED IN THE DEPARTMENT OF
PRINTS AND DRAWINGS IN
THE BRITISH MUSEUM

VOL. V

1771–1783

By

MARY DOROTHY GEORGE
LITT.D.

PRINTED BY ORDER OF THE TRUSTEES

1935

Sold at
THE BRITISH MUSEUM *and by*
BERNARD QUARITCH 11 *Grafton Street London W* 1
HUMPHREY MILFORD *Oxford University Press London E C* 4
KEGAN PAUL, TRUBNER & Co Lᴛᴅ
38 *Great Russell Street London W C.* 1

PRINTED IN GREAT BRITAIN

CONTENTS

The Frontispiece gives the earliest representations in the British Museum of the typical John Bull, Nos. 5611, 5612.

PREFACE

THE Catalogue of the Collection of Prints of Political and Personal Satire in the British Museum was begun by Mr. Frederic George Stephens during the Keepership of Mr. G W Reid Five volumes by Mr. Stephens, covering events of the years 1320 to 1770, were published between 1870 and 1883, as follows·

    I.   Nos. 1–1235 (Years 1320–1689).   1870.
    II.   Nos. 1236–2015 (Years 1689–1733).   1873.
   III. Part 1. Nos 2016–3116 (Years 1734–1750). 1877.
   III. Part ii. Nos. 3117–3804 (Years 1751–1760) 1877.
   IV.   Nos. 3805–4838 (Years 1761–1770). 1883.

In 1868 the Trustees purchased the large collection made by Mr Edward Hawkins, F.R S. (Keeper of the Antiquities from 1826 until his death in 1867), and from Volume III onwards Mr. Hawkins's notes formed the basis for many of the descriptions.

These volumes contain a mine of information in illustration of public opinion in relation to the events recorded, and offer most valuable material to the historian. It is regrettable that Mr. Stephens, who lived until 1907, was not entrusted with the continuance of a work for which he was peculiarly well fitted That the work was appreciated is shown by the fact that the first volume is out of print, and that comparatively small stocks remain of Vols. II–IV.

Mr. Stephens, of whom an appreciative notice appeared in the second supplement of the *Dictionary of National Biography*, studied at the Royal Academy Schools, was an original member of the Pre-Raphaelite Brotherhood, and an occasional exhibitor until 1854. His handsome features as a youth were used by Ford Madox Brown for the Christ in his 'Christ washing St. Peter's Feet', and by Millais for Ferdinand in his 'Ferdinand and Ariel' (1849).

Several portraits, including a study for the Christ, were privately printed in 1920 for the author's son, Lt.-Col H. F Stephens, R.E., in a volume entitled *Frederic George Stephens: Twenty-four reproductions of pictures and drawings from his collection*, with notes by J B Manson.

Mr. Stephens gradually gave up painting for history and criticism, acting as art critic of the *Athenaeum* between 1861 and 1901, and writing various shorter books, such as a *Life of D. G. Rossetti*, 1894, in addition to his Museum Catalogue.

In 1930 the Trustees decided that the work should be resumed, and the Museum was fortunate in securing the services of Dr Dorothy George, whose powers of careful research and clear exposition had been well shown in her book on *London Life in the XVIIIth Century* (1925).

The present volume is of particular interest as covering the years of the American Revolution, and it is greatly to be hoped that the present author may have the opportunity of carrying the catalogue in succeeding volumes up to the Reform Bill of 1832, so that the classical period of English caricature may be adequately covered

The general title of the earlier volumes 'Catalogue of Political and Personal Satires' has been kept as a matter of convenience in a continuation, though 'Catalogue of Prints of Political and Personal Satire' might have been a more accurate description. The catalogue is based on the separate series of 'Political and Personal Satires' in the Department of Prints and Drawings. It does not profess to include all prints of this category which may be scattered under masters and engravers in the departmental collections, though it does do so to some extent. Nor does it profess to include prints in the Museum Library, though again numerous examples are admitted. To have attained completeness in these respects would have delayed the production of a single volume for a lifetime.

Since the printing of the text a collection of caricatures mounted in twelve volumes referred to in the catalogue as B M.L , Tab. 524, has been transferred from the General Library to the Print Room.

Dr. George wishes to express her thanks for the help given her by Miss B Cobb, Miss Julie Hubrecht, Mr. Randall Davies, Mr. Archibald Doubleday, Mr Walter T. Spencer, and Mr Minto Wilson. She is especially indebted to Miss Cobb for her translations from the Dutch.

October, 1934.   A M. HIND.

NOTES ON THE METHOD FOLLOWED IN
THE PRESENT VOLUME

WITH some modifications the method used is that of the earlier volumes The prints are first described and then elucidated, in complicated and elaborate prints the explanation is incorporated in the description for the sake of clearness and brevity The titles are uniformly given in capitals, the inscriptions on the plate and the publication lines in italics These inscriptions are transcribed in full, except in a very few instances where the fact of omission is made clear. Where there is no title an explanatory caption is supplied, unless the original title has been discovered; in both cases this heading is enclosed in square brackets, in the latter case with a note of origin The dimensions are those of the subject, not the plate, unless otherwise stated, the first being the upright, the second the horizontal measurement. This reverses the order followed in the earlier volumes, where the horizontal dimension preceded the vertical. Left and right (unqualified) denote the left and right of the spectator

The terms used in describing the processes of the prints (*engraving, woodcut, aquatint,* or *mezzotint*) do not call for explanation in a work such as the present. But it should be stated that *woodcut* serves for both woodcut and wood-engraving, and that *engraving* is used to include line-engraving, etching and stipple-engraving. Etching and engraving are very often used in combination at the period dealt with, and to decide whether a particular print is mainly etched or mainly engraved is in a very great number of cases almost impossible, while stipple is the combination of both etching and engraving in a dotted manner.

The prints are numbered in continuation of the numbers in the earlier volumes. Close copies or slightly altered states have the number of the original followed by the letter A (or A, B, C, &c) No distinction is made between different states unless there has been some essential alteration in the engraving or lettering. The addition of a press-mark indicates that the print is in the British Museum Library, not in the Print Department. A few prints have been described from reproductions or from the catalogues of other public collections; these have no serial number.

The chief deviation from the method of Mr. Stephens is in the arrangement of the prints according to the date of their publication instead of under the date of the event illustrated. Further notes on this method are given at the beginning of the Introduction. As monthly magazines were normally published on the first day of the month following that advertised on their title the prints are so dated; e g. a print from the December number of a magazine is dated 1 January of the following year The indexes depend on this arrangement and illustrate (inter alia) the fluctuating fame of individuals, and the varying output of artists and printsellers. The small subject index is complementary to the cross-references in the text it is intended to show broadly, from year to year, what were the chief subjects of public interest and the favourite objects of satire, and also, as far as possible, to give references to those subjects which are most sought after by students For the sake of completeness and consistency it was necessary to include in the text the titles of the prints later than 1770 which Mr. Stephens had antedated, with their original number, and to index them as completely as the prints described in this volume The numbers are arranged in the index in the chronological order in which the titles occur in this volume. Some of the prints described in earlier volumes remain to be dealt with in a later volume. By the arrangement here adopted prints can be traced either from the index of titles or from the date of publication. An asterisk in the index of persons and of titles denotes a foreign print.

A few prints of the year 1770 which had been accidentally omitted from Volume IV have been included in this volume.

PUBLISHED WORKS REFERRED TO IN THE CATALOGUE BY ABBREVIATIONS

Andrews	= W. L Andrews, *Essay on the Portraiture of the American Revolutionary War.* New York, 1896.
Chaloner Smith	= J. Chaloner Smith, *British Mezzotinto Portraits,* 1883.
De Vinck	= *Bibliothèque Nationale, Inventaire Analytique par F -L Bruel de la Collection de Vinck.* Tome 1. *Ancien Régime* Paris, 1909.
Hart	= C. H. Hart, *Engraved Portraits of Washington* Grolier Club, New York, 1904
Frankau	= Julia Frankau, *John Raphael Smith, his Life and Work.* 1902
G W G	= *Genuine Works of Mr. James Gillray.* Published T M'Lean, 1830
Grego, Gillray	= *James Gillray, the Caricaturist, with the History of his Life and Times* Ed. T Wright [1873]
Grego, Rowlandson	= Joseph Grego, *Rowlandson the Caricaturist* Two vols. 1880
Muller	= F. Muller, *De Nederlandsche Geschiedenis in Platen,* Amsterdam, 2ᵈᵉ deel 1876, 77
Paston	= 'George Paston' [pseudonym for Miss E M Symonds], *Social Caricature in the Eighteenth Century.* 1905.

Russell   = Charles E. Russell, *English Mezzotint Portraits and their States* 1926

Thieme-Becker   = U. Thieme, F. Becker, F. C Willis und H. Vollmer, *Allgemeines Lexikon der bildenden Künstler*. Leipzig, 1907, &c (in progress).

Stauffer   = D M. Stauffer, *American Engravers upon Copper and Steel* Two vols Grolier Club, New York, 1907

Van Stolk   = G van Rijn, Atlas van Stolk, *Katalogus der Historie-Spot- en Zinne-prenten betrekkelijk de Geschiedenis van Nederland, verzameld door A van Stolk, Cz*. Vol vii, Amsterdam, 1901.

FURTHER ABBREVIATIONS USED IN THE DESCRIPTIONS

B M L = British Museum Library
H L = Half length
T Q L. = Three-quarter length
W.L. = Whole length
l = left
r = right
pl. = plate

INTRODUCTION

THE fifth volume of the Catalogue continues the description of satirical prints from the end of 1770, where it was left by Mr Stephens, to the end of 1783. His method has been followed with certain modifications described at the end of the preface The system of arranging prints according to 'the date of the earliest event directly illustrated' is in fact impossible to follow consistently and involves placing prints before their date of publication. For instance, a print on the Jacobite rising of 1745 (No. 1156) has been dated [10 June 1688] because it contains an allusion to the supposed spurious birth of Charles Edward's father.[1] These prints are strictly topical, their significance and interpretation depend on the date of publication, and this, thanks to Hogarth's Act,[2] is in most cases engraved on the plate. Chronologically arranged, they show in a remarkable way the *tempo* of political life, the fluctuations and inter-action of opinion and propaganda There is scarcely a political or diplomatic question which they do not illustrate, often from an unaccustomed angle: they illuminate the psychological strands in what Maitland calls the seamless web of history.

The strictly chronological order has been applied only to political satires. The prints fall into two categories, political and non-political, the latter being classed as personal in accordance with the title of the Catalogue. This group includes social satires and non-political prints in general As the political prints exclude the purely historical print (e g prints after West's *Death of Wolfe*, so opposed in spirit to Gillray's *Death of the Great Wolf*, a caricature of West's picture), so the personal and social satires exclude *genre* except where it is humorous or cautionary, and therefore a satire on manners or morals. Though most of the prints fall clearly into one or other category there are some which may be considered either political or personal, these are impossible to classify with rigorous consistency.

But the value of these personal prints for social history depends upon a knowledge of their date, they are therefore arranged in years, though within each year chronological order has been waived in favour of arrange-ment by series, by artist, or by subject, overlapping categories which cannot be strictly observed Taken together, the sequence of political and social prints reflects, as nothing else does, the changing and elusive spirit of the period. At the same time, a traditional symbolism and the recurrence of the same theme from age to age show how strong was the power of tradition, even in this art, so essentially of the moment.

The thirteen years covered by this volume saw a change in the manner of pictorial satire and a great development in its political importance. These developments were closely inter-related and can scarcely be dis-cussed separately, they were due to the interaction of aesthetic and political causes, and they are the more marked since in 1771 political satire was at a low ebb, while during 1782–3 it was at the highest point yet reached.

---

[1] This is an extreme case and the seeker after prints on the '45 would be unlikely to discover it But it is less misleading than the frequent placing of prints one, two, or more years before the date of publication
[2] 8 Geo. II, cap 13.

A third influence on the character and output of prints was that of the printsellers: the humorous print had become an important object of commerce and even of export; it follows that a period of political deadness such as the one beginning in 1771 tends to produce a decline in the number of political prints with a corresponding increase in personal and social satires

The change in the character of pictorial satire between 1771 and 1783 is, broadly speaking, the progressive superseding of the old-fashioned 'emblematical' or 'hieroglyphical' print, intricate and complicated, often depending on a key or explanation, by the caricature or satire dependent on expressive drawing, irony, wit, or humour, embodied in a design which makes an immediate appeal to the eye The development is mainly due to the early work of Gillray and Rowlandson, with whom Mortimer must be associated from his influence on this phase of English caricature. The two types merge, and correspond to a distinction which can be traced in pictorial satire from an early date, the older type continued to exist and its influence is not yet exhausted The newer manner was described in 1784 as 'comic history painting'[1] and there is no doubt that it owed something to the new vogue for history painting which both influenced the art of the caricaturists and was itself a subject of caricature. The change in design was closely associated with a change in technique: the superseding of engraving (or etching), heavily cross-hatched and conceived as a design in black and white, by the light etching intended to be coloured by hand. A few of the prints of the '50's and '60's are coloured, but the colouring is partial and crude. The proportion of coloured prints progressively increases [2] In the earlier prints persons were usually represented conventionally, to be identified by some attribute or by words issuing from the mouth (a device which was by no means given up). For instance, Lord Holland was almost invariably a fox (as was Charles Fox at the beginning of his career); Gillray and his abler contemporaries draw a portrait of Fox, more or less caricatured, the varying emotions which the theme requires being rendered with much expressiveness When he is a fox, much is made of the cunning and rapacity of the animal.

The appearance of the typical John Bull of Gillray, a stout citizen or farmer wearing top-boots, is significant of the change. He is as characteristic of the newer manner as Britannia is of the old and appears first (though without his name) in a print of 1779 by Nixon or Gillray (No. 5611), afterwards copied, improved, and entitled John Bull by Gillray in a print of uncertain date (No 5612) [3] For some time, however, it appeared as if John Bull might have had a serious rival in Jack English (or England),[4] a sailor generally successful and gallant, whereas John Bull is often plundered and bemused, as in No. 6227, where he is the deluded keeper of the Crown Inn. In No. 6210 by Gillray he is a stout and disconsolate man, and in No. 5860, probably relating to Yorktown, he is a plainly dressed

---

[1] *The Court and City Magazine*, July 1784, perhaps the only issue (copy in the Print Room) containing two coloured plates. 'Comic history painting' is distinguished from 'the *Burlesque* or what the Italians call *Caricatura*', the plates being described as an example of each kind; the difference, however, is scarcely perceptible. Nothing is said of the old emblematical print
[2] No. 3019 (1748) was advertised 'price 6d. plain, 1s. coloured', *General Advertiser*, 17 May 1748 No 3091 (1750) was sold at the same prices J. Langham (see Index of Printsellers) was a 'Print Colourer', see No. 6042
[3] Both original and copy reproduced in the frontispiece
[4] The verses describing John Bull in No 5612 call him Jack English

and despairing citizen The type, though it had appeared, was by no means established. John Bull is often a bull (Nos. 5636, 5640, 5645, 5687) as he had been in 1762 (No. 3907) and was in 1790 in a print by Gillray, once a mastiff (No 5569). Earlier references to John Bull in these satires derived more or less directly from Arbuthnot's pamphlets: he is associated with his sister Peg (Scotland) and is cheated by Sawney (Bute), as in Nos. 3904, 3906 (1762). A similar adaptation of Arbuthnot's fable is ascribed to Townshend with a set of verses attributed to Fox (No 6005)

Other names given by Arbuthnot continue to be used: Lewis Baboon (Louis Bourbon) and Nic Frog frequently, Don Strut occasionally (No. 5541). Lewis Baboon, or France, or the typical Frenchman as the case may be, is habitually a French petit-maître, Spain (or Don Diego or Don Strut) is almost always a Spanish don in quasi-Elizabethan dress with ruff, slashed doublet, and hose A similar convention for Frenchmen and Spaniards was used in Dutch prints. The United Provinces are represented by a rough peasant or burgher whose dress is almost that of 'the down-right Hollander' described by Goldsmith in 1755: 'one of the rudest figures in nature; upon a head of lank hair he wears a half-cocked narrow hat laced with black ribbon; no coat but seven waistcoats, and nine pair of breeches, so that his hips reach almost to his armpits'. The hat had become high-crowned and circular with a narrow brim

America is a combination of noble savage and amazon (as in No 5225), sometimes the Red Indian, sometimes the amazon prevails, occasionally a male Red Indian grasps a scalping-knife. Generally 'Miss America' (No. 6173) holds, or grasps at, the cap of Liberty on a staff or spear. The Phrygian cap of Liberty was a common object in pictorial satire from the days of Wilkes (a classic example being his portrait by Hogarth); it appears as early as 1741 in a print against Walpole by Gravelot (No 2439). The earlier convention was a circular wide-brimmed hat as in No. 1921 (1733) Just such a hat on the spear of Freedom appears in Dutch prints *circa* 1780 (Nos. 5718, 5730, 6292). The satires of Gillray and others on the *bonnet rouge* with the tricolour cockade appear to have increased the discredit into which this symbol was falling It should be noted that in the typical emblematical print England, France, Spain, and America were commonly represented by their respective animals, as in Nos. 6004, 6229, and in No. 5581 (a French print). In Dutch prints a dog generally takes the place of the British lion, while the Dutch lion of Dutch prints, who usually holds the seven arrows of the United Netherlands, appears as a dog in English prints. Britannia and the Dutch Maid (No 6292) have a certain resemblance.

The character of pictorial satire and caricature was also influenced by the work of the amateur. Incorrect and expressive drawing contrasted with the stereotyped correctness of the professional engraver who turned out figures of Britannia and Time for trade cards as well as for satires Hogarth complained of this when he called caricature 'the lowest part of the art of painting and sculpture',[1] and this attitude explains the dedication (doubtless ironical) of one state of *The Bench* (No 3662) to the 'Honble Coll T   s .d'[2] when he engraved on a separate plate an account of the difference between Character and Caricatura.[3]

[1] J B Nichols, *Anecdotes of William Hogarth*, 1833, pp. 66–7.
[2] Viscount Townshend, see Index of Artists.
[3] Caricatura 'is, or ought to be, totally devoid of every stroke that hath a tendency

The outstanding case of the persistence of an ancient theme, treated
in a traditional manner, is that of the *Danse Macabre*.[1] In this volume
Nos. 5172, 5326, 5441, 5513, 6128 are in the vein of the Dance of Death.
The subject of a grossly fat man supporting his own stomach in a wheel-
barrow dates from at least 1510 and was afterwards used to caricature
Luther and General Galas. There are two instances of it in the Catalogue,
Nos. 5433 and 6358.

The development of the art of caricature owed much to the greater
intensity of political life under the influence of the increased activity of
the Opposition owing to events in America, combined with the demand
for parliamentary and administrative reform. The publication of the
debates in the daily newspapers added greatly to the actuality of pictorial
satire, which shows how closely these debates were followed. The increasing importance of the satirical print during the period covered by the
present volume is evident, both in reflecting the spirit of the times and in
throwing light on that elusive thing—the mind of the common man, and
from its effectiveness as propaganda. As an influence on the public mind
the print had largely taken the place of the ballad, which in Walpole's time
still had considerable political importance.[2] It reached a public largely
untouched by the newspaper and the pamphlet, and indeed it made graphic
the contentions of the pamphleteers, while it seems that a print may have
suggested ideas to Junius himself (No. 4868). The pamphleteers also used
satirical prints as frontispieces to their works, and on occasion increased
their effects by selling the plates separately (No. 4839). In estimating their
effect it must be remembered that thousands gazed at them in the shop-
windows, that they were pasted up in clubs, workshops, taverns, and ale-
houses, and were exported in large numbers.[3]

During the American War the foreign circulation of prints was of great
importance, and the tendency of English political prints was in marked
contrast to those on the Napoleonic War. It was a characteristic of
English pictorial satire (at least until the fall of North's Ministry in 1782)
to be almost exclusively anti-ministerial: prints which in England were
merely factious seemed seditious or worse on the Continent. Not only
were ministerialists by convention regarded as placemen and pensioners
while the Opposition were Patriots, but the Opposition claimed a licence
of speech which they did not allow to the Government. Walpole, deplor-
ing, in 1770, the licence of the press, sees no remedy, since 'Ministers are
and ought to be lawful game, yet the law could not except them as proper

to good drawing . . . all the humourous effects of the fashionable manner of Caraca-
turing chiefly depend on the surprize we are under at finding ourselves caught with
every sort of Similitude in objects absolutely remote in their kind.'

[1] See Francis Douce, *The Dance of Death*, 1833.

[2] *Political Ballads illustrating the Administration of Sir Robert Walpole*, ed.
M. Percival, 1916. But the writer of a pamphlet on Sacheverell (1710) gives 'the
chief means by which the lower order of Whigs attack a political Adversary' as
'the Print, the Canto or Doggrell poem' and 'the Libell' (i.e. the pamphlet). Quoted
Wright, *Hist. of Caricature and Grotesque*, 1865, p. 412.

[3] Wendeborn (for twenty years an intelligent observer of London life) was told
by an eminent printseller that he sold great quantities of goods in the country, in
Scotland, Ireland, the East and West Indies, America, and other parts of the
world; that caricature prints went in great numbers to Germany, and thence to
the adjacent countries. He explains Hogarth's Act, noting that in Germany the
words published as the Act directs were often taken to mean published by express
order of parliament. *A View of England towards the close of the eighteenth century*,
1791, i. 190, ii. 213-16. (Author's trans.)

to be abused'.[1] The same one-sided licence was claimed in debate: Barré (in 1782), having demanded and obtained an apology from North for a remark which he considered unwarranted, 'attempted to demonstrate that every member possessed a right to use with impunity the most severe epithets towards a public functionary, though that right was not reciprocal'.[2] The same attitude was extended to pictorial satirists, who, if ministerial, were included in '*The Hungry Mob of Etchers and Scribblers*' (No. 3844). The mob of etchers was a small one: the obloquy encountered by Hogarth for *The Times* (No. 3970) will be remembered, while Mr. Stephens records (besides *The Times*) only one print which can be called an apology for Bute.[3] The *Morning Herald* anticipated (30 March 1782) that the advent of a popular Ministry would bring ruin to the print-shops.

But while the prints, up to a point, represent the attitude of the Opposition, they also reflect public opinion: they were for sale and they had to be popular. Thus during the American War a number of prints directed against France, Spain, and still more against Holland were by no means consistent with Opposition policy. Similarly, the significance of many of the No-Popery prints before and after the Gordon Riots is an interesting problem,[4] but they do not reflect the opinion of either party in Parliament. It may be said that the opinion represented is mainly that of London, but that opinion had then a high degree of political importance which was increased by the wide distribution of the prints.

The importance of the foreign circulation of prints can be illustrated at a number of points by the copying of English prints in America, Holland, and France and by the occasional copying of foreign prints in England. The Opposition having espoused the cause of America, English prints made admirable enemy-propaganda, while conversely French and Dutch prints, being anti-British, were copied in England. Foreign prints were also issued with fictitious English publication lines (e.g. No. 4958, pp. 289, 494). Portraiture was also used in France as in England for propagandist purposes, portraits of Franklin with appropriate symbols and inscriptions were multiplied (e.g. No. 5691).

There is reason to suspect that a well-known series of propagandist portraits, ostensibly of English origin, usually described as portraits of officers in the American War, are of foreign, probably French, origin (see No. 5290, &c.). Besides the twelve usually included in the series, four others are here suggested as belonging to it: Franklin (No. 5407), Paul Jones (No. 5561), George III (No. 5582), General Eliott (No. 6034). Some have French inscriptions, of all there appear to have been poor copies published in Augsburg, and all (including the German copies) have English publication lines, fictitious if this theory is correct, as probably are most of the artists' names. Most of the portraits appear to be imaginary and by the same artist who signs the plates of the two Howes 'Corbutt', the name used by R. Purcell, supposed to have died in poverty and disrepute *c.* 1766. Some of these plates show a distinct resemblance to the work of Purcell, suggesting that when he disappeared he went abroad and was afterwards employed on this series, probably in Paris. Purcell is known also as a caricaturist, and a French satirical print of 1778 is by 'Corbut' (p. 286).

---

[1] *Memoirs of the Reign of George III*, 1845, iv, p. 168.
[2] Wraxall, *Memoirs*, 1884, i, p. 368.
[3] The attacks on Bute in this volume can be counted from the number of times his name occurs in the index; he is never anything but a villain.
[4] Cf. below, p. xxiii.

The other artist suggested for one of the series is Brookshaw (No. 5561), who from about 1772 was working in Paris, and from 1779 in Brussels and Amsterdam. Only portraits which have a clearly political character are included in the catalogue; a striking instance is the portrait of Washington added to a London reprint of an American pamphlet (No. 5641).

A particularly interesting example of reciprocal copying is connected with Dixon's *The Oracle* (No. 5225), evidently intended as a protest against the punitive measures under discussion in 1774 Time with a magic lantern shows, to Britannia, Scotia, Hibernia and America, Discord being put to flight by Concord, Liberty, Commerce, Truth and Justice It does not appear to have been noticed that this is the origin of a well-known print by Guttanen of Nuremberg with the title *The Tea-Tax-Tempest or the Anglo-American Revolution* (No. 5490). America (reversed) is exactly as in Dixon's print, the other three have been transformed into Europe, Asia, and Africa. Time displays to them the triumph of America and the humiliation of British soldiers, apparently at Saratoga. A French copy (No 5491) was published, and also an English copy in which the humiliating allusions are made clearer by words issuing from the mouth of Time (No 6190).

A set of Dutch prints of 1780 affords further instances of this reciprocal copying An English No-Popery print (No 5702) appears to be taken from a Dutch original (No. 5712). A Dutch print (No. 5722) has a crude English copy: it depicts (*inter alia*) Lord George Gordon and London in flames. A Dutch engraver of small skill wishing to represent (in 1781) 'English Lords and Noblemen in the Parliament Assembly' (No. 5839) copied them from two English plates ridiculing the fashions of 1773 (Nos. 5169, 5170)

A magazine illustration of 1778 (No. 5472), showing the humiliation of England, the decay of British trade, the enrichment of France, Spain, and Holland at England's expense, and pillorying the two Howes for inactivity in America, had a whole progeny of copies, American, Dutch, and French, a translation of the English explanatory text being used. Paul Revere was a copier of English prints, including the one just mentioned A print of 1772 (No.4940), showing for purposes of faction the supposed humiliation of England by Spain, was copied in 1774 by Revere to damage British prestige. American prints were rare or there would doubtless have been English copies An interesting example is the famous print of the Boston Massacre, which was copied three times in England[1] to illustrate two English editions of the inflammatory *Short Narrative of the Horrid Massacre in Boston* . . . and an account of the affair in *The Freeholders Magazine* (Nos. 4378, 4378 A (p. 2), 4839). Another example of the reprinting in England of an inflammatory American pamphlet with the addition of a frontispiece is No. 5641.

By the close of the period covered by this volume, if not earlier, pictorial satire was recognized as peculiarly an English art and an English weapon Archenholtz, who writes as an eyewitness of events in London between 1771 and 1784, remarks, 'il faut compter au nombre des privilèges de cette nation, la liberté de faire des gravures satiriques, qui tournent en ridicule les ennemis du jour Le François les chansonne, le Hollandois plus pesant frappe des médailles; l'Anglois a choisi la gravure, comme le

[1] Mr W B Goodwin of Hartford, Connecticut, conjecturally identifies No 4839 with the print after Pelham, one of the only two known impressions of which is in the possession of the American Antiquarian Society

plus propre à donner de la publicité à la satire.'[1] In 1742 Gray, writing to Chute in Florence remarking on the present vogue for political satire in England, suggests that he should find and dispatch an Italian artist who should visit Holland on the way to learn taste.[2] The Dutch prints in this volume show a marked deterioration from the days when the English had learnt in the school of Romeyn de Hooghe.

POLITICAL SATIRES 1771–1783.

1771 opened ostensibly in the state of political excitement which appeared to have become normal and which depended largely on the supposed influence of Bute and the Princess Dowager of Wales The City Patriots, the Wilkites, and Junius fanned the flame. But the reaction had already begun. the attempt of the Opposition backed by Junius to rouse the country against the Ministry by accusing them of corrupt subservience to Spain (Nos. 4849, 4857, &c) was a failure. A new and famous phase in the vendetta between Wilkes and parliament arose over the question of the publication of debates. Important as the consequences were, at the time it was little more than an episode in the quarrel, and was so treated in pictorial satire (No. 4852) In spite of a riot (No. 4850) this factitious excitement could not check the growing political apathy. The failure of the clamour for war with Spain and the divisions among the Opposition increased the reaction. In the public mind these divisions centred in the quarrel between Wilkes and Horne and the consequent disruption of the City Patriots. The quarrel figures largely in the prints, neither the accusation that it was promoted by the Ministry (see No. 4868, anticipating *Junius*) nor the glorification of the City Patriots in the Tower (No. 4864, &c) could avert the decline in their political credit, correctly anticipated in No 4887 Wilkes's diminished repute was probably increased by his association with the gambling assurances on the sex of d'Éon (No 4870 &c.)

Dejection and disillusionment among the supporters of the Opposition are reflected in No 4955 (1772), remarkable as appearing in the *Town and Country Magazine*, which had been among the more inflammatory periodicals. There is a general tendency to revert to conventional attacks on governmental corruption (e g Nos 4877, 4885) with Bute and Mansfield playing their accustomed parts Two altered plates (Nos. 5126, 5127), from the *Political Magazine* of 1767 and 1768, suggest a bankruptcy of ideas among the Opposition Other interests of 1772–3 are the financial crisis (Nos. 4947, 4961), India (No 5101, &c.), and the Partition of Poland (No. 4957) During these years George III is usually depicted asleep (as in No. 4957), or in some way neglectful of his country's interests (e.g. No. 4883).

The prints are of especial value in showing the stereotypes formed of leading politicians at different times. This aspect of Fox's career is of peculiar interest from the importance he attached to his 'darling popularity'.[3] He began under the cloud of his father's reputation and his own

---

[1] Archenholtz, *Tableau de l'Angleterre*, Bruxelles, 1788, i, pp 149–50 (tr from *England und Italien*) Cf Boyer-Brun, *Hist des caricatures de la révolte des Français*, 1792, p 7 'Les Italiens, qui ont presque tout inventé dans les Arts, ont fait les premiers des Caricatures Les Anglois se sont appropriés ce genre en l'imitant. Les Français ont marché dans cette carrière sur les traces des Italiens et des Anglois.'

[2] *Letters*, ed. D C Tovey, i, p 108 At about this time the caricatures of Ghezzi were copied in England.   [3] See below, p xxvi

politics. His first appearance was at the age of eight in *The Sturdy Beggar*, No. 3579 (1757), a satire on the reversionary sinecures obtained by Henry Fox for his sons. In the same year in *The Bawd of the Nation or the Way to grow rich* (No. 3636) he and Stephen prophetically help their father to squander a fortune acquired at the country's expense. In No 5223 (1774) the two young men, in bondage to the Devil, rob their father to pay their gaming debts The great interest taken in his career from 1771 is noticeable—he is at first the leading macaroni, petit-maître, and enemy of liberty (No. 4892, &c.),[1] but in 1773 (No. 5113) he is shown making a secret compact with the gouty Chatham, to whom he is apparently dictating terms When, in 1774, he 'commenced patriot' in good earnest his appearances in the Catalogue for some years become fewer.

In 1774 American affairs reappear in the Catalogue The prints on the American Revolution are of great interest in illuminating the difficult and controversial question of public opinion in England in relation to the war. As in America, 'the Revolution was in the minds and hearts of the people'.[2] in England the struggle was against the minority in parliament who identified the cause of the Americans with Whig politics in general and with their own opposition to the authority of the Crown in particular. The prints being anti-ministerial are naturally pro-American. That this was on the whole a popular attitude in London is borne out by the press[3] and by the attitude of the City Corporation. It was the cause of an active and able minority[4] backed by the prestige of the great Whig families (though hampered by their disunion) and by the influence of dissent. Secondly, this opinion prevailed and the war came to an end less because of Yorktown[5] than because of the state of mind of the country, influenced by failure, by the extreme unpopularity of the Ministry, and by an active propaganda which is graphically represented in these prints. This pro-American attitude had an incalculable effect on American and Continental opinion; it hardened the king's heart and convinced him that the Opposition was factiously regardless of the country's interests. Finally, reaction was inevitable, and the attitude of the Opposition to the war was probably one cause of the growing unpopularity of the Ministry after North's fall—the prints certainly suggest this, e g. Nos. 6029, 6229.

The prints bring out the great influence on the American Revolution of the series of crises connected with Wilkes the villains here as in America are Bute and Mansfield, who are joined by North, Sandwich, and Germain America in these prints, as in much contemporary literature, is the land of liberty and virtue, England that of corruption and slavery—Liberty taking flight to America being a familiar theme (No 5580).

The strong feeling against episcopacy which was so potent and so inflammatory in America had its counterpart in England under the combined influence of dissent, of American opinion, of the attitude of the bench of

[1] Cf 'The Grand Defaulter's celebrated cub spent, not long ago, a whole week at the gaming table. He allowed himself no respite but when he went home to get a clean shirt What a hopeful legislator!' *Oxford Magazine*, vi, p 151, April 1771.

[2] John Adams, quoted Schlesinger, *New Viewpoints in American History*, 1922, p. 162

[3] F. J Hinkhouse, *Preliminaries of the American Revolution as seen in the English Press, 1763–1775*. 1926

[4] Cf Wraxall, *Memoirs*, 1884, pp 100–1, 'With the two exceptions of Johnson and of Gibbon . all the eminent or shining talents of the country, led on by Burke, were marshalled in support of the Colonies '

[5] Cf. Washington's letters after Yorktown.

bishops to the war and of the Anglican Church towards the doctrines of Locke and the sacred right of rebellion.[1] An interesting print, *An attempt to land a Bishop in America* (No. 4227 (1769)), illustrates the pre-war attitude of America and of many in England towards this controversial question. The association of episcopacy and popery, common in the seventeenth century, survived in New England and significantly reappears in these prints (Nos. 5228, 6209, &c.). The bigotry which culminated in the Gordon Riots owed much, first to the allegations against Bute (No. 4841), then to the passions roused by the Quebec Act as well as to the influence of American affairs in general. The treatment of Boston was compared with that of 'the French Roman Catholick town of Quebec' (No. 5286).

Two contentions of the Opposition were in the highest degree comforting to the enemy: one that it was impossible that England should win and that the war would end not only in defeat but ruin, the other, that victory if achieved would mean the end of liberty in England. These contentions are expressed directly and indirectly in the prints, which are in a high degree defeatist and as significant for the events they omit as for those they record. But the most effective war propaganda is the creation of an atmosphere of hate, therefore Indian atrocities and the representation of George III as a cruel tyrant are found in English pictorial satire as in revolutionary literature in America (Nos. 5470, 5631, &c.). The great difficulty of obtaining recruits in England was undoubtedly influenced by the unpopularity of the war in general and by a number of anti-recruiting satires, No. 5295 especially being of a deadly effectiveness.

1774-5 are concerned with the measures against the Colonies which followed the Boston Tea-party (No. 5226). The Quebec Act, though not punitive, roused the most opposition in England as in America. This was the beginning of those denunciations of George III for breaking his Coronation Oath (No. 5227)[2] which (presumably) bore fruit in his fatal opposition to Catholic Emancipation. In 1775 every political print relates to America; they are few, probably owing to the feeling of bewildered uncertainty which is apparent in contemporary letters and memoirs. During 1775 Sayer published a series of mezzotints remarkable for their knowledge of events in America, which were in fact the subject of innumerable paragraphs in the newspapers (p. 169, Nos. 5241, 5284, pp. 196, 197). Bowles also introduced the tarring and feathering of a commissioner of customs into his series of mezzotints (No. 5232). Here again, the doubts and uncertainties of opinion are reflected in the partly ironic, partly humorous, attitude towards the doings of the American patriots. Nos. 5286, 5287 have more political importance: they are comprehensive statements of pro-American propaganda in its cruder and more extreme forms.

Till the disasters of Saratoga and Trenton, 1776-7 were years of success for the British. 1776 is noteworthy for two of the few anti-American satires, one a crude and ill-timed print on the American entrenchments near Boston (No. 5329), which incidentally illustrates the fact that at the

---

[1] See Van Tyne, 'Influence of the Clergy and of religious and sectarian forces on the American Revolution,' *Am. Hist. Rev.* xix, pp. 44 ff. Cf. also James Murray's *Impartial History of the present War* . . . [1779-80], ii, p. 109: 'All the jargon of Sir Robert Filmer was retailed in several pulpits.'

[2] Cf. a letter from Philadelphia of July 1775, 'Majesty has fallen so low as to be known by no other appellation but that of perjured tyrant, a popish villain who has broke his coronation oath'. *Home Office Papers*, iii, p. 248. See below, pp. xxii, xxiii.

INTRODUCTION

beginning of the war Putnam was the best known (in England) of the American commanders The *Westminster Magazine*, completely changing its attitude, published *The Parricide, A Sketch of modern Patriotism* (No 5334), in which Fox appears for the first time as an active patriot. The occupation of Philadelphia occasioned a third anti-American print— *The Flight of the Congress* (No. 5401). By this time the Howes had roused suspicion and dislike in England, for their failure to follow up successes in some circles, for their Whig opinions in others, combined with their alleged desire to prolong the war for the perquisites and pleasures of high command. In America they were regarded with distrust by the loyalists and with contempt by the Whigs. They were thus included in the series of propagandist American portraits[1] in silent contrast to American officers (Nos. 5405, 5406).

The year 1778 marks a crisis in the struggle war-weariness in America (in spite of Saratoga) had reached a dangerous point. North's Conciliatory Propositions and the pending French alliance gave propaganda in America a new intensity which had its counterpart in England. *The Closet* (No. 5470) is an almost incredibly violent attack on the king, the Ministry, and the conduct of the war. It is the most explicit expression among the prints of the theory (widely held in America) of the perversion of the constitution by a tyrannical system, centred in the King's closet and directed by Bute, which had led directly to failure and atrocities Burgoyne and Simon Frazer are held up to contempt for the disaster of Saratoga; Indian braves are enjoying a cannibal feast upon the American prisoners who surrendered at the Cedars (May 1776) in accordance with baseless allegations in America.[2]

North's belated and ill-timed Conciliatory Propositions (No. 5473, &c.), which had a uniformly bad reception in England, must be judged by the fears which they roused in America and in France. When the Bills with North's speech were distributed from Howe's headquarters Governor Johnson of Maryland was warned that 'it will prove more dangerous to our cause than ten thousand of their best troops'. The French, in spite of the alliance, dreaded above everything a reconciliation between England and America and did their best to impugn the good faith of the Proposi- tions, representing them as a proof that England had recognized her defeat.[3] In England their reception was all that extreme patriots in America and the war party in France could desire They were represented as humiliating, even by Whigs, the Opposition could hardly oppose the concessions but denounced them as specious and deceitful and poured scorn on the choice of the Commissioners The first print on the subject (No. 5472) so exactly fitted the needs of enemy propaganda that it was copied for circulation in America in 1778 and again, by Revere, in 1780, and had a succession of

[1] See above, p xv.
[2] Captain Sullivan, one of the prisoners, wrote, 4 August 1776, from Montreal to his brother the general, a member of Congress, calling 'Almighty God to witness that not a man living could have used more humanity than Captain Forster did after the surrender   and whoever says the contrary,   he is an enemy to peace and a fallacious disturber of mankind. What reason they can give for not redeeming us I cannot conceive, if they are wrongly informed that the affair of the Cedars was a massacre, why do they not rather fulfil the cartel than let their hostages remain in the hands of a merciless enemy, or do they regard their troops only while the heavens make them victorious?' Stedman, *Hist of the American War*, 1794, i, p 172
[3] P. G. Davidson, 'Whig Propagandists of the American Revolution', *American Hist. Rev*, Apr 1934

xx

Dutch and French copies (Nos. 5726, 5726 A, B, and C, p. 451).[1] No. 5473 shows the Commissioners' kneeling obsequiously before America, enthroned and seated on bales of commerce destined for England's commercial rivals; they confess to tyranny and the commission of atrocities, while the concessions are represented as inspired by fear, and intended to deceive. No. 5487 shows the Commissioners making deceitful overtures to the Colonies in the guise of a zebra who is about to be saddled with the Stamp Act. The diplomatic tension in America before the Commissioners left America, having been obstructed and ridiculed in every way, as they had been ridiculed in England (Nos. 5474, 5475), is illustrated by a French satire (p. 286) representing England humiliated and despoiled of her trade as in No. 5472 and by another French satire on the Propositions (p 289) To this year also belongs Guttanen's engraving (No. 5490) copied without acknowledgement from Dixon

The scurrilous attacks on Wesley provoked by his attitude to the war reached a climax in 1778 and bear witness to the effect of his pamphlet *A Calm Address to our American Colonies*. They are here represented by the frontispieces to a succession of pamphlets in verse, probably by William Combe (Nos. 5493-6). The prints symbolize also the attacks by other writers: Wesley is sold to North and is charged with having changed the attitude of the common people to the war.[2] The *odium theologicum* which inflamed the contest is shown in attacks on the Anglican clergy, more especially on bishops and above all on Archbishop Markham (see index).

The No-Popery agitation which had been roused by the Quebec Act was given new stimulus by the Catholic Relief Act of 1778 The result was the formation of the Protestant Association, which carried on an active propaganda leading to the Gordon Riots. This propaganda, discoverable in forgotten pamphlets and in the newspapers, was also expressed in prints, some of which were probably paid for by the Association. But the theme was both traditional and popular and in Gillray it found a new expressiveness. The first in the Catalogue is No. 5489, representing the king's entertainment by Lord Petre.

When England and France were at last openly at war (July 1778) the attitude to the war changed its character; the prints in a broad view support the statement that 'before France declared herself the protectress of America the British nation hardly considered itself at war'.[3] The first event of the war with France (apart from some captures in the Channel) was the battle of Ushant on 27 July 1778, a date which was to become a political gibe directed against Keppel,[4] and frequently recurring in these prints The unfortunate consequences of the battle and of the two courts martial to which it gave rise are fully displayed in these prints, in which

[1] See p. xvi.

[2] Cf Camden to Chatham, Feb 1775· 'I am grieved to hear that the landed interest is almost altogether hostile to America, though the common people hold the war in abhorrence and the merchants and traders for obvious reasons are against it.' Chatham, *Corr* iv, p 123

[3] J Andrews, *Hist of the late War*, 1786, iii, p 220

[4] The significance is well illustrated in a clever dialogue by Mrs. Thrale written in August 1779: Johnson to W. W Pepys ' . . . Would you declaim upon the happiness of sound health to Beauclerc? Would you talk to your friend (sneeringly) Keppel of the twenty-seventh of July? Burke: Mr Keppel might be talked to concerning the Business of that Day, Dr Johnson, and often is, without any Diminution of that Self Complacency, which in Good men ever attends the performance of their Duty, however unsuccessful the event.' *Bulletin of the John Rylands Library*, Jan. 1932.

the spreading poison of faction in the Navy can be graphically traced (No. 5536, &c). The hatred which Sandwich (Jemmy Twitcher) had incurred by the betrayal of Wilkes was rekindled; Sir Hugh Palliser became a symbol of iniquity. Gibbon wrote (6 Apr. 1779) of Keppel's trial 'the whole stream of all men, and all parties, runs one way. Sir Hugh is disgraced, ruined, &c , &c ' The exploitation of the affair by the Whigs,[1] it can scarcely be doubted, tended in the end to their discomfiture (No. 5992, &c).

An increase in the number of political satires in 1779 reflects the growing strength and bitterness of the Opposition in spite of the difficulties of opposing a war with the Bourbon powers. A parody of the Birthday Ode (No. 5540) anticipates the *Probationary Odes* but in a more savage spirit. The attitude to the king is significant, by 1778 he was a cruel and obstinate tyrant (Nos 5470, 5549),[2] his portrait as an oriental despot was evidently popular, there are four versions of it (5546, &c) besides a copy in 1784. Decaying trade and an obstinate king are the theme of No. 5574, with a significant dedication to Washington.

The chief event of 1779 was the threat of invasion when the combined French and Spanish fleets were in command of the Channel. This evoked prints whose intention was patriotic (Nos. 5554–5), but the recruiting in London which was the result of this great danger was a subject of ridicule (Nos. 5551–2), as had been the raising of regiments by subscription after Saratoga. The exploit of Paul Jones is the subject of a number of prints in which he figures as a hero (see index), foreign prints show how damaging was his achievement to British prestige. The situation in Ireland was becoming increasingly threatening and is the subject of a print of great interest (No. 5572) from the light it throws on the volunteer and non-importation movement. Holland as a selfish and hostile neutral (a traditional subject in these prints in every war since Utrecht) first appears in No. 5557, a print which illustrates incidentally the help which England then expected from Russia.

Religious bigotry and an attack on the Catholic Relief Act of 1778 are comprehensively expressed in No. 5534, in which the direct action of the Scots against Popish chapels, &c , in Glasgow and Edinburgh is held up for imitation by the English, while the Beast of Rome absolves the king from his Coronation Oath.[3]

In 1779–80 Fox reached the zenith of his popularity after his duel with Adam (No. 5575) and the founding of the Westminster Association (Feb. 1780), which nominated him their candidate for Westminster (to be elected without expense) The prints of 1780 reflect the intense violence of politics apparently increased by British successes in America. The standard theme of ministerial corruption and treachery dominates many prints. The County Associations, County Petitions, and Committees of Correspondence for securing parliamentary and administrative reform as a means to the reduction of the power of the Crown and peace with America are the

---

[1] The best discussion is in *Sandwich Papers*, ii, 1933, Navy Records Society, ed G R Barnes and J. H Owen, unfortunately not published until the elucidation of No 5536, &c , was in print

[2] The changed attitude was noted in 1779 by an observant and moderate loyalist living in London "The Ministry were formerly charged with the mischiefs of the public measures, but now the evil begins to be drawn from the Crown, and the King is said to be the author and promoter of the system, even in some sense against the sense of his servants ' H. C van Shaack, *Life of Peter van Shaack*, New York, 1842, p 240.   [3] See above, p xix

subject of a number of satires (see index under Reform) Several prints associate the Protestant Association and Petition, sponsored by Lord George Gordon, with the County Associations and Petitions, to the detriment of the latter (Nos. 5633, 5649, &c) The excitement connected with the Associations roused fears of civil war which soon subsided [1] The overthrow of the Ministry is prophetically depicted in Nos 5640 and 5645; North, Sandwich, and Germain are threatened with the block (Nos 5660, &c) *Prerogative's Defeat or Liberties Triumph* (No. 5659) illustrates Dunning's famous motion. But the attacks on King, Ministry, and Church are interspersed with patriotic prints; the achievements of the Navy were a powerful counter-attraction to the misdeeds of the Ministry Rodney was especially popular, he was known to be an enemy of Sandwich[2] and believed to be the protégé of the King (No. 5673).

The No-Popery agitation which led up to the Gordon Riots is well illustrated in these prints; its association with the American War has received scant attention. It was combined with allegations of Popery against the Church of England, much of it was directed against the King. It must be considered in relation to the attacks on the Quebec Act and on bishops and it indicates a strain of opinion, especially in London, similar to that which was exploited with such effect in New England. In February 1780, when the excitement over the County Petitions was at its height, Almon published a print (No. 5631) in which George III shares a cannibal feast with Red Indians while a bishop, probably Markham, hurries up followed by a sailor carrying scalping-knives and crucifixes. A little later the king as *The Royal Ass* (No 5669) is led to Rome by Bute and Markham In No. 5670 (as the *Mangy Whelp*) he is taken to the same destination by Father Peters. In No 5671 the influence over the King of the 'Invisible Junto' (Bute, North, Mansfield, and the Devil) is outweighed by the Bible in a print dedicated to 'the truly honourable Lord George Gordon' After as before the Riots Gordon is the Protestant Hero (see index). No. 5678 was evidently timed to coincide with the much-advertised mass meeting in St. George's Fields (No 5694). This, like Nos. 5534, 5643, is a print in the spirit of the Popish Plot of a century earlier George III and North make a combined attack on the Constitution and on Protestantism, urged on by the Pope and a swarm of devils In No. 5680 (June 10) the King, in monkish robes, kneels before a crucifix on an altar, while the Protestant Petition lies torn on the floor, destined for ignominious usage. This is remarkable from its date, showing that the torrent of propaganda was scarcely checked by the riots. It was indeed diverted to showing that the Protestant Association was not responsible for the Riots (No. 5679, p. 408) Of all the prints relating to the riots one only (No 5685) throws the blame on Protestant bigotry. The culprits are the ruffians of the underworld (No. 5679, &c) or the Papists (No 5841), while the Government is accused of fostering the riots in order to introduce a military despotism (cf. Nos. 5682, 5683, 5687). The hidden hand or foreign enemy, the subject of much official investigation (*State Papers Domestic*), is represented here only ironically in a Dutch print and its English copy (Nos. 5722, 5723), an omission not without significance

---

[1] Cf Gibbon, 7 Feb. 1780, 'I think the rumours of a Civil War subside every day petitions are thought less formidable . .' *Letters*, ed Prothero, I, p 375
[2] The Abbé Morellet wrote from France to Shelburne, 4 Apr 1780, commenting on Rodney's victory of St Vincent (No 5658, &c), 'Je suis fort fâché de voir employer ainsi les membres de l'Opposition.' *Lettres de l'Abbé Morellet*, Paris, 1898

While the Lord Mayor deservedly is harshly dealt with (No. 5688, &c.), Gordon continues to be a hero.

These prints support the indications that the political reaction which followed the Gordon Riots had in fact begun before them, and that it was chiefly caused by the methods of the County Associations and Committees of Correspondence which Walpole feared portended civil war (No 5645). In view of the traditional attitude of pictorial satire[1] attacks on the Opposition are of especial significance. *Opposition Defeated* (No 5644) is noteworthy for its early association of Fox and the Prince of Wales in designs on the Crown. The check to political excitement caused by the Riots was probably increased by the taking of Charleston (a blow to the Opposition and significantly absent from these prints except for a hostile allusion in No. 5699), which would have meant complete disaster to Washington but for the arrival of Rochambeau (No 5706) and the French fleet

At the end of 1780 the chief interest was in the critical relations between England and Holland. The King's manifesto of 20 December was a virtual declaration of war, war was popular in general for reasons which are well illustrated in the prints of Nic Frog (Holland) as a greedy neutral (No 5557, &c.), but it was violently attacked by the Opposition. The chaotic state of opinion in Holland is described rather than depicted in a set of Dutch prints (No. 5712, &c.), fourteen of which were copied on a small scale and combined in one plate (No. 5728) published with the explanations issued with the originals and forming a fair-sized pamphlet, one of the many with which the Republic was deluged at this time. They are markedly inferior in design and effectiveness to the better English prints of the period, a reversal of the relative positions of the two countries in the earlier part of the century [2] They show the divided aims, delays, and uncertainties of Dutch policy, torn between the Patriots and the Orangists, and encumbered by the complexities of the constitution. Economic motives were dominant and conflicting, and were further complicated by the conflicting counsels of the English, French, Russian, and Spanish diplomats at The Hague, not to mention the American envoy. Appeals to the traditional resentment at the Navigation Acts and the rancour associated with the name of Cromwell (No 5729, &c) were added to arguments in behalf of economic self-sufficiency and naval prestige. The prints show also the exaggerated hopes which were entertained of the Armed Neutrality (No. 5714, &c), and incidentally, how great was the impression made in the Republic by the Gordon Riots (No. 5728, &c). Especially interesting is the multiplication of copies of No 5726[3] showing the (unrealized) expectations of securing a large share in the commerce of America which England had previously monopolized No. 5733[4] shows the real reason for the declaration of war as fear of the Armed Neutrality, while the pretext was the draft treaty with Congress discovered among the papers of Laurens

The declaration was in fact nicely timed to forestall the adherence of the United Provinces to the Neutral League, and was highly successful As neutrals the Dutch had been of great service to America and France, as combatants they were to become the real losers by the war and to compensate England for her losses. This was foretold in an Orangist

---

[1] See above, p xiv.   [2] See above, p xvii, n. 2.
[3] See above, pp. xvi, xx
[4] A print not recorded by Muller; it appears to be absent from the Collection Van Stolk.

print (No. 5712) and deplored in another Dutch print on the peace (No. 6292). The protest against the war with the Republic by the Opposition peers was the subject of a Dutch print with a fictitious English publication line (p. 494).

In 1781 a decline in the hopes of the Opposition, due to the continuation of the political reaction, some military successes (Nos. 5827, 5828, &c), and the popularity of the Dutch war (No 5827, &c.), is shown in a fall in the number of political prints. The capture of St. Eustatius by Rodney was the focus of excitement (No. 5837) and a great blow to the patriots (No. 5923) Rodney's high-handed conduct on the island was a subject of heated controversy. The case against him is amusingly illustrated in No. 5842 By-elections in London and Bristol receive attention; an American candidate at Bristol evoked two anti-American satires (Nos. 5832, 5833) Suddenly the situation was altered by the surrender of Cornwallis (No. 5855, &c.) After the Christmas recess the Ministry were clearly doomed The prints are defeatist in character, and military disasters, actual and anticipated, are symbolically depicted (Nos. 5959, 5961). The Opposition exulted at defeat with effects which are probably to be traced in the trend of opinion during 1782–3 [1]

At the beginning of 1782 the chief topics were North's budget and pending ministerial change, the protagonists being Fox and North. *Banco to the Knave* (No. 5972) depicts the exultation of the new ministers, Fox the chief winner; the scene is a faro bank at Brooks's which had been a source of income to Fox during 1781, a fact which was to be used against the new Ministry in connexion with the recall of Rodney.

The immediate importance given to Pitt in these prints is of great interest. from the beginning, like Fox, he is his father's son. In *The War of Posts* (No. 5984), though not a Minister, he is the chief opponent of the old gang and holds a sheaf of thunderbolts inscribed 'The Lightning of my Father'. As soon as the 'War of Posts' was over the most striking change is in the growing unpopularity of ministers and especially of Fox. The first charge was that of republicanism (No 5987, &c), probably due to Fox's imprudent conversation at Brooks's and elsewhere and his avowed intention of striking a blow at the power of the Crown. If the verses attached to No. 6005 are rightly attributed to Fox they would appear to show an attempt to counter the effect of these allegations of republicanism. The new Ministry was visibly losing popularity when the news of the battle of The Saints arrived; Rodney was recalled in the moment of victory to be replaced by Pigot, the purely political appointment of an inadequate officer. Gillray illustrated with deadly effect the allegations that the appointment was to enable him to pay his gaming debts to Fox (No. 5997). There were better reasons for condemning it; the state of public feeling and the scandalous talk of the town are well illustrated in Gillray's four satires (No. 5992, &c). Gibbon wrote (29 May), 'Every person of every party is provoked with our new Governors for taking the truncheon from the hand of a victorious Admiral, in whose place they have sent a Commander without experience or abilities.'

Another failure of the new Ministry was Shelburne's scheme for 'arming the people' on principles similar to those of the Irish Volunteers. This

[1] Loughborough wrote to Lord Carlisle on the attitude of the Opposition towards Yorktown 'It is strange that they should never learn that to show exultation in a public calamity makes them odious and aids those they are attacking ' Hist MSS. Comm. *Carlisle MSS.*, p. 539.

had a bad reception and was dropped. Sheridan wrote naïvely to Thomas Grenville (26 May), 'The arming plan don't seem to take at all '[1] It was attacked by Gillray in *Malagrida and Conspirators consulting the Ghost of Oliver Cromwell* (No 6006). Fox lost credit by the treatment of the Dutch of his proposals for a separate peace (No. 6014). The Dutch refusal was a blow to ministerial prestige but fortunate for the country, as the terms eventually obtained (No 6292) were much better than those offered by Fox, which included acceptance of free navigation under the terms of the Armed Neutrality.

Fox's resignation on the death of Rockingham was a further blow to his popularity,[2] the 'darling popularity'[3] which all knew to be so important to 'the Man of the People'. There are many prints on this resignation: Gillray depicts him running back to his gaming at Brooks's as a sole source of sustenance, after an ignominious quarrel with Shelburne (No 6013). Sayers's first political satire depicts Fox and Burke outside the gates of Paradise (No 6011), one of several applications of *Paradise Lost* to this situation. The prints entirely support Temple's warning to Fox 'that the people would not stand by him in his attempt to quit upon private grounds, which from their nature would appear to be a quarrel for offices, not a public measure'.[4] Burke was also ridiculed by Gillray for his resignation in an amusing print in the worst of taste, *Cincinnatus in Retirement* (No. 6026), in which he appears for the first time as an Irish jesuit. Shelburne was not spared, he is represented as the triumphant conspirator who has ejected Fox from office (Nos 6012, 6018, &c) It was evident that his Ministry was unlikely to last (No. 6023). The prints by Gillray and Sayers of Fox, Burke, Barré, and Shelburne have a cruel effectiveness, while the misdeeds of North's Ministry still recur in pictorial satire (e g Nos. 6024, 6033).

Prints on the defence of Gibraltar are a relief from the prevailing political acrimony. The preparations for the great combined attack which the Bourbon powers regarded as invincible are the subject of a print by Gillray in which Spain and Holland are admirably travestied as Don Quixote and Sancho Panza (No 6025). The confidence of the enemy powers is illustrated by one of the propagandist series of mezzotint portraits[5] (represented by an Augsburg copy) in which Eliott points in dismay to the bombardment (No 6034) Eliott's heroic and successful defence is the subject of Nos. 6035–8. The dramatic character of the two great successes in the West Indies and in the Mediterranean which changed the international situation increased the unpopularity of the Ministry: they produced a wave of patriotic feeling (Nos 6040, 6043) unsympathetic to the consistent defeatism of Fox and his friends during North's Ministry; this is illustrated by more attacks on Fox, especially Nos. 6029, 6030.

The year 1783 opens with the peace negotiations approaching finality and with the imminent fall of Shelburne. It was common form in English eighteenth-century politics to denounce the terms of peace, but in 1783 the attacks were by comparison moderate The recent successes had

---

[1] Buckingham, *Courts and Cabinets of George III*, 1, p. 32
[2] Temple to Thomas Grenville, 4 July 1782. 'My opinion with all whom I have seen, is that Fox has undone himself with the public. . . ' Ibid 1, p. 52.
[3] Cf Burke on Fox's India Bill, 'He has put to hazard his ease, his security, his interest, his power, even his darling popularity for the benefit of a people he has never seen ' *Parl Hist* xxiii, p 1384 Lady Sarah Napier, Fox's cousin, uses the same phrase
[4] Buckingham, *op. cit*, p. 51   [5] See above, p xv.

removed a sense of humiliation (cf. No 6040) and it was recognized that the terms were better than might have been expected While addresses were being received approving the preliminaries signed on 20 January, Fox and North had agreed to turn out the Ministry by a combined attack on these terms After a number of prints on the peace (not all completely unfavourable, No. 6172 taking a realistic view of the situation), the Coalition first appears in No 6176, *Shelburne Badger'd and Fox'd*. The defeat of North had been the subject of prints depicting conflicts between the fox and the badger (North): the violent change of attitude is stressed in a number of prints on the united action of the fox and the badger (No. 6186, &c). The great number of prints on the Coalition shows, as nothing else can, the measure of its unpopularity (e g No 6217) and must have done much to increase it; they must be studied in relation to the earlier prints. Though a case can be made for the Coalition, it seems clear that the popular indignation was not only genuine but natural,[1] though it was of course exploited.

The prints of 1782 had shown Fox and North in violent conflict for the fruits of office; now they were shown in an unholy compact to enjoy them (e.g. No. 6225). The whole case against the coalition at its most exaggerated is displayed in these satires.[2] According to Lecky 'the conduct of North was more blamed than that of Fox'. The evidence of the prints is that the reverse is true, so far as the public mind was concerned, even allowing for the fact that Fox was better copy and was treated unsparingly by Gillray and Sayers. In a number of prints Fox is sly and triumphant, North bewildered, notably in the famous *Coalition Medal* (No. 6183) Fox drives the coach, North is content to get up behind (No. 6226). Quotations from Fox's speeches were illustrated with damaging effect (Nos 6187, 6207). His attitude to the Crown was clearly unpopular (No. 6239, &c), especially in combination with his association with the Prince of Wales (Nos. 6231, 6266) In No. 6237 he is the executioner of a crowned goose (the King), while North and the Prince of Wales caper for joy. His poverty on resigning office in July 1782, when he appeared, even to his friends, to be living at the expense of Perdita Robinson (No. 6117), was highly damaging, and lent colour to the innumerable accusations that office meant plunder as much as power Even on 30 March 1783 the new French Ambassador wrote to Vergennes, 'Le Ministre populaire (Monsieur Fox) est un étrange Ministre des Affaires Étrangères; et lorsqu'il aura perdu sa popularité, ce qui s'achemine beaucoup, je ne sais ce qui lui restera '[3]

These satires, and many others, helped to prepare the public mind for the reception of the two India Bills, when Fox, as Carlo Khan, was represented as the emperor of the East appropriating the sovereignty of the king and the powers, profits, and patronage of the East India Company (No 6276, &c) The attack on the India Bills is one of many instances where the Opposition were able to raise a clamour by exploiting a popular cry. Lord Eldon wrote in his MS. *Anecdote Book*, 'Fox said that *Sayer's* caricatures had done him more mischief than the debates in Parliament and the works of the press. The prints of Carlo Khan [No 6276], Fox

---

[1] Cf E M Wrong's excellent little *Hist of England, 1688–1815*, 1927, p 182 The alliance 'is said to have shocked the nation, but it is hard to believe that England had suddenly become so squeamish'

[2] Walpole wrote, 25 April 1783, expressing doubts of the duration of the Coalition 'If satiric prints could dispatch them, they would be dead in their cradle, there are enough to hang a room.' *Letters*, xii, p 436

Quoted, Fitzmaurice, *Life of Shelburne*, 1912, p. 269 n.

running away with the India House [No. 6271], Fox and Burke quitting Paradise. .[No. 6011], and many other of these publications, had certainly a vast affect upon the public.'[1] Pictorial satires show in a remarkable way the movements of public clamour, which, if stirred up by the Opposition, were usually sufficient to induce the dropping or withdrawal of the unpopular measure In this case the Opposition had the support of the Crown, and exploited the clamour to justify first the dismissal of the Ministry and then a dissolution. But this could hardly have been done without the unpopularity acquired by Fox and Pitt's popularity based on the Chatham legend, while Fox never wholly escaped from the discredit attaching to the son of the 'public Defaulter of unaccounted millions' (No 4842, &c) Fox, like Lord Holland, is represented in many prints as the fox deceiving the geese, the fox greedy for the grapes of office (cf No 6213). In proportion as Fox became unpopular, the King became popular and is represented as an injured prince (No 5970, &c) instead of as the tyrant of 1778–9. The back-stairs influence of the King over the India Bill, which earlier in the reign would have been a potent cry, was neutralized by the relations between Fox, the Prince of Wales, and the King as well as by the unpopularity of the Coalition.

The volume ends with the dismissal of the Coalition (Nos 6283–6291). There is only one exception to the contempt with which the ejected Ministry and the India Bills are treated, No 6291. It strikes the defeatist note which had become unpopular (cf. No. 6229) The tenor of the prints is in direct contrast to the confidence of the Foxites that their speedy return to power was certain. The real turning-point of the reign was the end of the general election of 1784, but the arrangement of the Catalogue demands that it should end with the end of a calendar year, in 1783 this coincides with the Christmas recess which afforded a breathing-space in the contest of Fox and Pitt

Many subjects dealt with in the political satires have scarcely been touched on here: notably prints on Scottish, Irish, and Indian affairs.[2] The Irish Volunteers and Grattan's Parliament are the subject of one or two interesting prints Scotland is either a pernicious influence, personified in Bute or represented by a thistle, or, in No-Popery prints, the saviour of Britain. The close following of parliamentary debates becomes increasingly noteworthy during 1782–3 (e g. No 5979). Elections do not figure largely. they had less significance when the Government secured a majority, instead of a majority securing a Government. Certain elections, however, were of great significance, especially Westminster elections (No. 5699, &c). The defeat of Keppel at Windsor and his triumphant return for Surrey are the subject of several prints A very interesting print depicts the election of two nabobs for Shaftesbury in 1774 (No. 5341); though fantastic it is substantially true There are portraits in the collection which though slightly caricatured are admirably characteristic. This is especially the case with Sayers's set of portraits primarily of members of parliament speaking in the debates of 1782 (Nos 6052–77)

PERSONAL SATIRES

In a period when political and social life were inextricably mixed, when politics were personal and social to an extreme degree, and were also a preoccupation of all classes, the line between political and personal satires

[1] Twiss, *Life of Eldon*, 1. 162. [2] See Subject Index.

is naturally vague and fluctuating; almost all references to the Fox family for instance may be regarded as in some degree political. Even prints on the sex of d'Eon (Nos. 4870-4873, &c.) had a political significance from his association with Wilkes, though the part he had played as a secret agent of Spain and France was unknown. The popular portraits of characters in 'low life'[1] had often a political colour: Sam House was a leading Foxite, Jeffery Dunstan was chosen during the Westminster Election of 1784 to typify the less creditable supporters of Fox. A very favourite character in print-shops, the Chevalier Descazeaux (No. 5067), was, in the opinion of a French visitor in 1765, selected for ridicule and patronage because he was the embodiment of the Frenchman of English caricature. poor, vain, and absurd [2]

Thus the personal prints supplement the political prints at many points, and many which now appear to be impersonal social satires were doubtless based on the gossip and scandal of the day. They belong to a small world when notabilities were known by sight to most of the town, partly owing to the display in the print-shop windows Darly's series of Macaronies, which takes the chief place among the personal satires of 1771-2, especially has this intimate character, partly because many were after drawings by amateurs of their acquaintances. It is a guide to the celebrities of the day. In the absence of contemporary inscriptions (not always correct) only a few can now be identified with certainty, as for instance when a hint in the title is confirmed by a portrait *The Miniature Macaroni* is Cosway, *A Temple Macaroni* is Lord Temple.

Darly's series of larger plates (1776-8) is more general in character, but probably many if not most conceal personal allusions, e g a print in the *Dance of Death* tradition (No. 5441) depicts Mrs. Macaulay 'painting her cheeks'—to quote Dr Johnson An ostensible illustration to *Joseph Andrews* appears to be directed against Lady Harrington (No. 5522). A set of three prints (Nos. 5376, 5430, 5435) ostensibly by 'Dicky Sneer' or 'R.S.', an elegant young man appearing in all three, relates to some joke or piece of gossip, and R S. (perhaps identical with the R S of Nos 5452, 5453, 4778, &c.) may, it is here suggested, be Richard Sheridan.[3]

The series of *vis-à-vis* portraits illustrating a chronicle of scandal which was the chief feature of the *Town and Country Magazine* is said to have been compiled by the editor, Archibald Hamilton Junior, with the help of a Mr. Caracioli,[4] presumably on information from different contributors— they appear to vary considerably in authenticity. It has been suggested

[1] Cf Goldsmith's account of the print-shop, 'Here, thought I, the painter only reflects the public voice   . But, guess my surprise when I came to examine this depository of noted faces! All distinctions were levelled here, as in the grave, and I could not but regard it as a catacomb of real merit The brickdust man took up as much room as the truncheoned hero, and the judge was elbowed by the thief-taker; quacks, pimps, and buffoons increased the group, and noted stallions only made room for more noted strumpets ' *Citizen of the World*, Letter 109, 1761

[2] Grosley, *Londres*, 1770, 1, pp 173 ff. Cf. *The Connoisseur*, No 25 (1754), 'A little Frenchman, commonly known by the name of Count, and whose figure has long been stuck up in the windows of the print-shops, was always remarkable for the meanness, and the same time foppery of his appearance '

[3] See pp 274, 313 The difference in manner may be due to the etcher, or R.S. may have been responsible for the idea only, *invenit* connoting sometimes a sketch, sometimes a verbal description A certain resemblance to early portraits of Sheridan (in the Dicky Sneer set) lends colour to the guess, as does the fact that Nos 4778, 4779 are scenes at Bath

[4] E H W Meyerstein, *Life of Chatterton*, p 404 n

that Chatterton may have been responsible for the scandalous one on Walpole and Mrs. Clive (No 4362) [1] Like the macaroni prints, they have been immortalized by Goldsmith and Sheridan [2] Most of them have been identified by H Bleackley in *Notes and Queries*;[3] a few of those left unidentified are here elucidated, and his conclusions have not invariably been accepted. In the first few years (1769–71) many of these had a political character which was violently anti-ministerial This gradually disappears and the attitude to politicians is neutral with sometimes a slight governmental bias. The heads in most cases are conventionally drawn and have little value as portraits The plates and text were used, a month later, in the *Hibernian Magazine*

Several printsellers published humorous mezzotints, the best known being those of Carington Bowles (Bowles and Carver from 1793), who issued a series which came out at more or less regular intervals over a period of many years. The firm was noted for selling prints many years after the date of publication,[4] impressions were taken after the plates had become very worn, and the dates have usually been scraped from the print or, in later issues, burnished from the plate. Those in the collection lettered *Bowles and Carver's Caricatures*, in two volumes dated 1820, are all coloured, and it is possible that the collection was made about that time. They are numbered serially, and from impressions that are both numbered and dated the dates of other numbered prints can be approximately ascertained.[5] Such prints were advertised as 'Half Sheet Size Metzotintos (commonly called Postures) Fourteen inches high by Ten wide, one shilling each, Plain, Two shillings, Coloured'.[6] The series chiefly consisted of humorous prints, some were cautionary, some were portraits, some were pure *genre*. The draughtsmen and engravers were generally anonymous The humorous prints included in this volume appear in general to be social rather than personal satires, but many are topical and also personal, and there are doubtless many personal allusions which cannot now be discovered The Bowles shop in St. Paul's Church Yard was well known and is illustrated in two prints in his series (Nos 3758 (1774), 6352).

The series seems to represent City taste, and they are significantly different from Darly's series, partly the work of men of fashion, and intended for the Court end of the town. Favourite subjects are satires on Roman Catholicism (some in the guise of illustrations to Sheridan's *Duenna*) and on the rich clergy, both probably influenced by the spirit fostered by the contest with the Colonies. Lawyers and doctors are also ridiculed. Street scenes and satires on costume are frequent. Courtesans and (from 1778) camp scenes are favourite subjects When the subject verges on politics the treatment is humorous and in the manner of social rather than political satire Cases in point are two prints on the Coin Act (Nos 3759, 4534 (1774)), a tarring and feathering scene in America repre-

[1] E H. W Meyerstein, *Life of Chatterton*, p 272.
[2] Mrs. Hardcastle says, ' All I can do is to enjoy London at second-hand. I take care to know every *tête-à-tête* from the Scandalous Magazine,' *She Stoops to Conquer*, ii (1773) Snake says of Mrs. Clackit, 'Nay, I have more than once traced her causing a *tête-à-tête* in the *Town and Country Magazine*, when the parties, perhaps, had never seen each other's face before in the course of their lives,' *School for Scandal*, i i (1775)
[3] Tenth series, vol. iv, pp 242, 342-4, 462-4, 522-3 (1905).
[4] Angelo, *Reminiscences*, 1904, i, p. 308
[5] See Appendix, p 786
[6] Laurie and Whittle's catalogue, 1795, quoted Chaloner Smith, iv, p 1753 This catalogue included many prints published by Bowles.

senting an actual incident (No 5232, and p 169), a print on the formation
of the Coalition (No. 6348), and one on the proclamation of peace (No
6351). Other publishers issued similar humorous mezzotints, notably
John Bowles, William Humphrey, and Sayer and Bennett. The series of
Laurie and Whittle belongs to a later period and his prints are sentimental
rather than humorous

Among standard subjects of humour that of the 'cit' is perhaps pre-
eminent, especially among prints issued by the printsellers of the west
end of the town His country box, his horsemanship, his appearances in
the Park, his Sunday excursions, his guzzling at City feasts were all popular
subjects of pictorial satire and are all depicted in this volume, notably by
Bunbury and St. George Mansergh. This theme merges into the equally
traditional one of the tradesman or artisan who spends his time discussing
the affairs of the nation, on which there are several prints.

Grose enumerates the subjects which 'will always ensure the suffrages
of the vulgar'. These include ridicule of the supposedly typical Scot,
Irishman, Welshman, and Frenchman, all represented in this volume,
especially the Frenchman He is lean and hungry but dressed in shabby
finery, and is generally contrasted with a plainly dressed well-fed Englishman, the classic example being Hogarth's *Calais Gate* This was a favourite
subject of Gillray (Nos 5612,[1] 5790). Grose continues, 'Of this kind are
professional allusions: a physician and apothecary are lawful game by
prescription, a tailor by trade, and a mayor, alderman, or churchwarden
ex-officio'. All are represented here except the churchwarden, whose
place is taken by the parish clerk. The medical profession is dealt with
on the whole not unkindly in these prints (cf Nos. 5457, 6347, 6350), but
there is an interesting caricature by William Austin of Dr William
Hunter, the great anatomist, detected in the act of body-snatching (No
5119). The theme of the quack merges into that of the physician; quacks
ridiculed by name in this volume are John Hill of *The Hilliad*, Dr. Graham,
Buzaglo, and the mountebank Katterfelto

Literature, in the present volume, is represented pre-eminently by
Dr. Johnson. He is twice satirized by Gillray for his *Lives of the Poets*
(Nos. 6103, 6328). In Bunbury's *Chop House* (No 5922) there is a recognizable portrait of Johnson talking to Boswell, his cudgel-like stick beside
him. The likeness to Johnson in one of the figures in Rowlandson's
Rotation Office (No. 5273) is striking, and supports the probability that
the office is that of Saunders Welch, at which Johnson attended for a whole
winter. In a group by Mortimer (No. 6357), probably representing men
of letters, artists, and actors, Johnson is a central figure He has been
identified as one of the figures in a popular political satire (Nos 5479–
81), and there are one or two allusions to his political pamphlets. It has
already been suggested that Sheridan may appear in three prints of 1776–7,
during 1783 he appears in political prints Lord Lyttelton and his *Dialogues
of the Dead* are clearly the subject of No. 5122 by William Austin. Chatterton is dragged into a political print with seeming irrelevance (No 6291).
There is an amusing caricature of Voltaire by Orde, and Alfieri appears to
be the subject of No 6315

Some interesting Cambridge satires and caricatures are due to Bunbury
of Clare, Orde of Kings, Topham of Trinity, and to an unknown who
produced a set of three prints in 1773 (Nos. 5187–9)[2]

[1] See frontispiece.
[2] No 5189 was attributed to Bearblock in the Catalogue by the Cambridge

Most of the personal (and some of the political) satires are valuable material for the history of costume, including of course those which are direct satires on extravagant fashions. Many of the macaroni prints are incidentally satires on costumes: the macaroni manner of dress seems to have been the last flare up of ornate and elaborate masculine dress before the advent of the plainer fashions often attributed to the French Revolution. These had, however, already appeared and were introduced into France by the *Anglomanes* The macaroni fashions also mark the departure from the typical eighteenth-century men's dress the full-skirted coats, sleeves with wide cuffs, flapped waistcoats and high-quartered shoes were displaced by a dress which, though ornate in material and trimming, is more close-fitting and simpler in silhouette. The enormous club of hair was one of the most characteristic features of macaroni dress (e.g. No. 5008). The short-lived fashion of the large Artois shoe-buckle and the enormous button prevailed in 1777 but appears to have been rapidly killed by ridicule (No. 5432, &c.). The fashion for wearing riding-dress with a round high-crowned hat instead of the looped or cocked hat is caricatured in 1781.

In women's dress monstrous hairdressing was a favourite subject of satire. The pyramid of *c.* 1770-2 was different in shape from the inverted pyramid of 1776-7, whose broad plateau suggested to the satirists the notion of a woman's head-dress decorated with scenes and ornament of all sorts, including military operations (No 5330) The wearing of ostrich feathers in the hair was also a recurring subject of satire and was denounced as a moral offence (No 5370). After the tight waists (No. 5444), 'cork rumps' (No 5381), and exaggerated hair-dressing of 1776-7, women's dress became plainer, and masculine fashions of a military cut influenced costume during the period of militia camps from 1778 (e g No 5600).

The prints illustrate life and manners sometimes incidentally, for instance when they show the arrangement of a shop or the interior of a coffee-house or tavern, sometimes directly, in satires on changing fashions. Hieroglyphic letters afford evidence on popular pronunciation: Nos 5658, 5677 indicate the habitual addition of an aspirate but not its omission. A similar Irish letter (No 5542) is sound as to aspirates but gives 'deuce' as the appropriate symbol for the word juice. Some light is thrown on the history of words, the word 'bore', in its origin a fashionable coterie word, is illustrated in No 6147 Cartoon is used for a political satire in No. 5288, a humorous anticipation of a much later usage. Gillray calls his typical Irishman Paddy (No. 5605), anticipating by a year the earliest instance recorded in the *Oxford English Dictionary*. The older word, Teague, which Paddy displaced, is used in No 5644.

The collection of personal and social satires (taken together with the political satires) is sufficiently large and representative to enable the popular humour of the time to be to some extent recorded and classified. The most immediately striking thing is perhaps the passion for personal scandal and the ruthlessness with which it was exploited. This went together with censoriousness on things, such as fashions in dress, which involved manners rather than morals Similarly, in political satires, certain gibes in the worst of taste were constantly repeated, as indeed they were in parliament the tragic death of Miss Ray was used as a gibe against Lord Sand-

Antiquarian Society of an exhibition of Cambridge caricatures at the Fitzwilliam Museum in 1908 But this was on the assumption that the date was *c* 1800 James Bearblock, afterwards a fellow of King's, graduated B A in 1789, M A in 1792

wich; Germain is inevitably labelled Minden. The attacks on the Princess
Dowager of Wales were virulent, as in the print in the *Political Register*
commented on by Walpole;[1] they chiefly occur in Volume IV, but in
No. 4852 she is 'The Pell Mell Jezebel'. A device to protect the publishers
of libellous satires appears to have lapsed as they grew bolder through
immunity. This was the confusion of personalities,[2] said by Walpole to
have been used in *The Turnstile* (No. 3608) to cover the identity of the
Prince of Wales, 'pretended to be Lord Lincoln'. In No 4960 North and
Sir George Macartney seem to have been deliberately confused. In No.
4946 a red herring appears to have been drawn across the identity of the
Queen of Denmark (the sister of George III). There is no similar instance
in this volume after 1772

The age of humanitarianism had begun, but its influence in these satires
is slight, favourite and competing themes being political corruption, the
nabob and the rich, vulgar, and pretentious citizen. There are allusions to
the period of distress owing to high prices and a commercial crisis in
1772–3, but they are political or personal (e g. Nos. 4938, 5016) There is
one incidental allusion to the grievance of Enclosure Acts (No. 5236).
Allusions to distress and bad trade owing to the war were definitely political
(e g. No. 5574) Social injustice is, however, the theme of No. 5275.
Burthens of Plenty (No 5433), which to-day seems clearly directed against
extremes of wealth and poverty, was probably intended more as a satire
on gluttony, in an almost medieval spirit,[3] or was perhaps a personal satire
against some noted City guzzler (cf. No. 6314) Nos 6347 and 6350,
The Benevolent Physician, are sentimental rather than humanitarian[4]
There was certainly sympathy for the sailor or soldier on half-pay or
maimed and for the poor clergy, but in most of the prints on such subjects
the intention seems to be to attack the Government, or the placeman, or
the rich clergy, or to check recruiting. A very telling and genuinely sympathetic print on the soldier on half-pay (No. 6170) attacks a notorious
grievance without political rancour. Such was the preoccupation with
politics that subjects which would now be dealt with from the social or
economic standpoint were treated as political. This was especially the
case with prints on the clergy[5] Poverty and unemployment are treated as
a subject of comedy by Gillray (No. 5938) and a chained gang of convicts
is treated with equal lack of sympathy by Dighton (No. 5957). The
general attitude is that poverty and hunger are peculiarly the lot of the
Frenchman in his shabby finery. An imitation of Hogarth's *Harlot's
Progress* brought up to date (Nos. 5808–13) shows an actual improvement
in the treatment of unfortunate women since 1734.

ARTISTS.

The artists whose work is contained in this volume are recorded in the
index, which throws some light on their varying output from year to year.
Many of the prints are the work of those who for good reasons preferred
to remain anonymous, many are by the nameless engravers who worked for

[1] *Memoirs of the Reign of George III*, 1845, iii, p. 199
[2] Cf. the device used by Churchill in *The Ghost*, where Mansfield is first pilloried
without being named and then mentioned as another person, Sandwich is first
attacked as Lothario and then appears as a separate person under his own name.
[3] See above, p xiv.
[4] They are included only because they are companion prints to Nos. 3797, 3798
on *The Rapacious Quack*.   [5] See above, pp. xviii, xix

the printsellers often from sketches or 'hints' provided by amateurs The volume opens in the transition period between the death of Hogarth and the early work of Gillray and Rowlandson and their followers Between 1767 and 1774–5 political satire was almost restricted to illustrations in magazines.

During the early 'seventies humorous prints are chiefly to be found in the various series issued by the printsellers, among whom Matthew Darly is outstanding. Darly specialized in engraving and publishing the work of amateurs · caricature was a fashionable hobby and one which for obvious reasons was exploited by the drawing-masters and teachers of etching who were also engravers and printsellers The fashion was stimulated by the vogue of Townshend in political satire and of Bunbury in social satire. After 1770, Darly, who had been the chief publisher of political prints during the 'fifties and 'sixties, devoted himself almost entirely to personal and social satires, in which, especially during 1771–2, macaronies took a leading part In general these were engraved by himself from the designs of 'Ladies, Gentlemen, Artists, &c' (Nos. 4710, 4985), or, according to another title-page, were 'design'd by the greatest personages, artists, &c ' (No 5005) The engraved page which was placed after the title-page of these three volumes[1] illustrates the way in which the amateur was encouraged.

'Comic Humour, Caricatures, &c

'In a series of Drol Prints, consisting of Heads, Figures, Conversations and Satires upon the follies of the Age Design'd by several Ladies, Gentlemen and the most Humourous Artists &c Pub[d] by M Darly Engraver, and Printseller at No 39 near York Buildings Strand, London, where Gentlemen and Ladies may have Copper plates prepared and Varnished for etching Ladies to whom the fumes of the Aqua Fortis are Noxious may have their Plates carefully Bit, and proved, and may be attended at their own Houses, and have ev'ry necessary instruction in any part of Engraving, Etching, Dry Needle, Metzotinto &c ... Ladies and Gentlemen sending their Designs may have them neatly etch'd and printed for their own private Amusement at the most reasonable rates, or if for publication, shall have evry grateful return and acknowledgment for any Comic Design, Descriptive hints in writing (not political) shall have due Honor shewn 'em & be Immediately Drawn and Executed. ...'

The exclusion of politics is significant and marks an exceptional phase in the history of English caricature [2]

Bunbury was, at first, the leading contributor to this series His importance is indicated both by the priority given to his work (Nos. 4668, 4670, &c.) and by the words 'Where may be had all the works of Mr. Bunbury &c.' appended to the publication line of, e g., No 4918 Darly, however, soon lost Bunbury as a client, from about 1772 James and Charles Bretherton were for some years the chief engravers of his work. Other engravers of plates after Bunbury described in this volume were J. R. Smith, Dickinson, Baldrey, and Rowlandson. The precocity of Charles Bretherton is noteworthy: in 1772, aged twelve, he etched five plates, four, and perhaps the fifth, being after Bunbury

An amateur closely associated with Bunbury is Charles Loraine Smith,

[1] The volumes catalogued on pp 38–41, 70–80. This advertisement is not included in the volumes in the B.M. collection but is transcribed from a volume in the possession (1934) of Mr. W T Spencer of New Oxford Street
[2] See above, p. xvii.

better known for the sporting subjects of his later life. He is probably the C.L S. of Nos. 4734, 4742, and 6147, and the C. Smith of 4752. His work resembles that of Bunbury, though less competent he had a gift for the slightly caricatured and expressive portrait which Bunbury lacked, and No. 6193, attributed to Bunbury by Walter Sichel, has more resemblance to the work of Smith as shown in Nos 5983, 6125 (both supposed to have been engraved by Bartolozzi), and 6147. Two sketches by Smith, *Posting in Ireland*[1] and *Posting in Scotland*, were engraved by Gillray in 1805.

Other amateurs whose work was published by Darly were Edward Topham (afterwards the editor of *The World* and a favourite subject of caricature by Gillray and others), R. St. George Mansergh,[2] and Thomas Orde Orde, afterwards Lord Bolton, had a gift for portraiture as appears from the three plates described in this volume; No. 5510 is a particularly interesting satire on King's College, Cambridge. Two at least of his plates[3] and probably the others were issued privately, not published. Coplestone Warre Bamfylde illustrated Anstey's *Election Ball*. Other amateurs, represented in this volume by one or more prints, are Sir Edward Newenham, Lord de Ferrars, Elizabeth Gulston, Lady Craven, Captain Grose, Captain Minshull, and Captain Morse, the last an exhibitor of portraits at the R.A It has already been suggested that Sheridan may have designed several prints.[4] The attributions to Townshend in this volume are based on resemblance to his not very distinctive manner or on newspaper allegations. A print which does not suggest the amateur is attributed to the notorious Leonard McNally.

One of the few professional artists whose work in caricature can be identified during the early 'seventies is William Austin, whose manner is very distinctive Like Darly, he was a noted drawing-master, a teacher of etching, and a publisher of prints.[5] That he was a rival of Darly is indicated in No 5318 A caricature by him of Chatham and Charles Fox (No 5113) is particularly noteworthy Some of Robert Dighton's earlier and less-known work is included in this volume.

The humorous mezzotints, issued by several printsellers, like Darly's series, bridge the transition from the period of Hogarth to that of Gillray. In the well-known series of Carington Bowles[6] the artists were generally anonymous, but it includes (in this volume) many plates after Collet, a follower of Hogarth, several drawn and engraved by J. R. Smith, several after Robert Dighton, three after S. H. Grimm, one after Earlom, and one (at least) by Philip Dawe. Dawe engraved a number of caricatures in mezzotint, these probably include a set of five on the American Revolution

---

[1] Reproduced in colour in Fuchs and Kraemer, *Die Karicatur der Europaischer Volker*, 1904-6

[2] Probably Richard St George Mansergh of Headfort (m Mary Stepney), who was killed in the Irish Rebellion, 1797. He was the son of James Mansergh, who married Mary St George of Headfort (Burke, *Hist of the Landed Gentry*, 1847) He is perhaps identical with the Colonel Mansergh St George, wounded in the American War, who drew for the Ladies of Llangollen in 1788 'striking likenesses' of 'Poor Rousseau'. He and his wife were travelling with Miss Stepney (*Hamwood Papers*, ed Mrs G H Bell, 1930, pp. 74, 115) *A View in America in 1778* (No 5482) resembles Mansergh's manner

[3] They are in Richard Bull's collection of the work of 'honorary engravers' now in the Print Room   [4] See above, p. xxix.

[5] Austin at George Street, Hanover Square, appears in T Mortimer's *Universal Director*, 1763, as 'Drawing Master, Teacher of Etching and Author of a Specimen for sketching Landscapes in a new and easy manner and of The Complete Drawing Book This Artist imports foreign prints, drawings, and etchings' Darly is not included in his directory   [6] See Appendix

published by Sayer and Bennet, 1774-5 (see p. 169, No 5241, &c). Two important political mezzotints (not caricatures) by John Dixon are included in this volume.

Aquatint first appears in this Catalogue in 1776 (No. 5381). Paul Sandby, whose earlier caricatures had been directed against Hogarth, reappears after an interval of many years with two aquatints on Vestris (Nos 5908, 5909). Though Sandby has a small place in these volumes he is well known for his charming landscapes and scenes of social life. His drawings of the encampments in Hyde Park in 1780 are of historical interest. The dancing of Vestris was the subject of several charming aquatinted designs, two of which are attributed to Nathaniel or George Dance and Bartolozzi.

A new period in English caricature begins *c*. 1780 with the early work of Gillray and Rowlandson. It was anticipated by the work of J. H. Mortimer, whose influence on both artists was marked; his combination of fantasy, caricature, and the grand manner marks the beginning of a new school It is to be noted as early as 1768 in *The Reviewer's Cave*, No. 4247.[1] Angelo attests the admiration evoked by his facility in drawing monsters and caricatures [2] After his early and sudden death in 1779 designs from his sketches were engraved by several artists (Nos 5780, 5781, 6356-8), and it is possible that some of the early work of Gillray was based on his designs (cf. Nos. 5523, 5524, 5609). His *Iphigenia's late procession from Kingston to Bristol* (No. 5362) is sometimes attributed to Gillray John Boyne appears also to have been directly influenced by Mortimer, conspicuously so in *Banditti* (No 6281)

There is considerable doubt as to the authenticity of some of the earlier plates attributed to Gillray · he had several manners, and appears sometimes to have taken pains to conceal his authorship. There is reason to suspect his hand in a number of plates in this volume not attributed to him With one exception (No 5912) all the prints here catalogued as by Gillray are anonymous or pseudonymous, and while some of the initials or names used by him may indicate those who supplied him with ideas or sketches, others seem to be due to a peculiar secretiveness or obscure sense of humour,[3] possibly, of course, to engagements to printsellers. In *Returning from Brookes's* (1784) he concealed his style under an assumed amateurish incompetence,[4] and in varying degrees and manners he would appear to have done the same in several prints described in this volume As he afterwards used the signature of James Sayers, so, there is reason to suspect, he may in 1782 and 1783 have used those of Edward Topham and Thomas Colley. He was in close relations with John Nixon, a semi-amateur, and an imitator of both Rowlandson and Gillray, whose early work in this volume raises certain problems No 5616 is signed *J N. fecit* but appears to be a Gillray. *Politeness* (No 5611), signed *J N fecit et Inv^t 1779*, has some resemblance to Gillray's manner and was copied by Gillray in a print (No 5612) reissued by Humphrey from St. James's Street, that is, not before 1797. The question of authorship is of especial interest as the subject is Gillray's typical John Bull in top-boots, who, according to

---

[1] Mr Stephens attributes this to de Loutherbourg, who, however, did not come to England till 1771 No 4247 is actually a different state from that described in the text, and is inscribed in an old hand 'etch'd by Mortimer'.

[2] *Reminiscences*, 1904, p. 108.

[3] Cf a portrait (not caricature) of the Duchess of York published by H. Humphrey 10 Apr 1792, signed *Charlott Zethen designet et fecit*.

[4] *Real Character*, see p 408, is similar in manner to *Returning from Brookes's*, suggesting the concealed authorship of Gillray.

H. M. Broadley, did not appear until 1809.[1] Mr Hawkins attributes Nos. 5998 and 6113 (Nos 5999 and 6122 appear to be by the same artist) to 'Hixon'. Their manner resembles (though not conclusively) that of Nixon, suggesting a misreading of H. for N There was, however, an engraver Robert Hixon, whose trade card (c. 1792) is in the Banks Collection (D 2, 2164).

The work of Thomas Colley, a caricaturist unmentioned in books of reference, seems to be confined to the years 1780-3. It has a crude and simple naiveté both of drawing and sentiment which is both effective and attractive; he takes a special pleasure in naval victories, and his drawing of ships suggests that he had been to sea, probably in the navy. His manner is very individual but lends itself to imitation, and there seems to be a pseudo-Colley with more skill who imitates his manner and uses his signature. Several of the prints of this hypothetical imitator suggest the hand of Gillray, notably Nos 6233, 6237, 6252 If the theory here put forward is correct, the true Colley had a singular absence of political rancour (e.g. Nos. 6043, 6170) quite incompatible with No. 6237. Certain prints signed *E T.* (Topham) also suggest an imitation of Topham by Gillray.

The political work of James Sayers begins in 1782. His technique is amateurish and his line feeble, but his designs (notably the famous Carlo Khan, No. 6276) have a political effectiveness which approaches that of Gillray and gave him instant fame. His prints of 1783 and 1784 appear to have impressed contemporaries more than anything done at that time by Gillray, though they have none of his masterly and expressive drawing. His portraits (Nos. 6052–77) are valuable as likenesses and most useful in identifying the subjects of political caricature William Dent[2] was a caricaturist whose prints, according to Angelo, were admired, presumably for their political effect. This, however, depended chiefly on his scurrilous and indecent abuse of individuals; aesthetically his work is less than valueless, his feeble and incorrect drawing and scratchy technique are amateurish with none of the merits of the amateur He is probably to be regarded as an inferior follower of Sayers The greater part of his work is after 1783

PRINTSELLERS AND PUBLISHERS.

The index includes artists who occasionally published their own work (e.g Rowlandson and Paul Sandby) and booksellers whose imprint is on the plates which they had engraved for books and magazines, some of whom (e.g. Almon) also published an occasional print The outstanding printsellers in this volume who specialized in caricatures and humorous art are the two firms of Bowles, Matthew Darly, William Humphrey and the afterwards famous Hannah Humphrey, Sayer (or Sayer and Bennet), Wilkinson, Holland, and Mrs. Darchery.

The early history of the two ancient and closely associated firms of Bowles, one of St. Paul's Churchyard, the other of Cornhill, is confused, but during the period covered by this volume it is clear. By 1709 (when they jointly published a map)[3] both firms were in existence, Thomas 'Next the Chapter House in St. Paul's Churchyard', John at the Black Horse in Cornhill John Bowles of Cornhill (? John II) was in partnership

[1] *Pearson's Magazine,* 1909
[2] A William Dent was a merchant whose address in a *London Directory* of 1784 was Garraway's Coffee House
[3] H. R Plomer, *Dictionary of Booksellers,* 1932

with his son from 1754 to *c.* 1764 when the style of the firm was John Bowles and Son According to Chaloner Smith[1] the son died in 1762, according to Plomer he went into the business of his uncle Thomas (? Thomas II) in 1764, when Thomas died (8th April 1767) John bought the business for this son (Carington), so that the style Carington Bowles[2] dates only from 1767 though older plates were reissued with his imprint. Carington died intestate in 1793 and was succeeded by his son Carington, who continued the firm from that date as Bowles and Carver. This shop at the old address was still, *c.* 1830, exhibiting 'obsolete plates' of the days of the South Sea Bubble.[3] When the houses in the City were numbered (in and after 1766) Carington's shop became 69 St Paul's Churchyard and John's 13 Cornhill. John died in 1779 and his business was carried on by Wilkinson, but not at the old address. Prints of both shops are listed in this volume, Nos. 5220 (1773), 3758 (1774), 6352 (c 1783).

Robert Sayer was a rival of Bowles who succeeded to the very ancient business of the Overton family at the Golden Buck in Fleet Street. His partnership with Bennet, which according to Chaloner Smith was from 1775 to 1778, appears to have lasted from 1774 to 1782 (see index). Sayer reissued a number of Darly's plates (see No. 5173, &c.). He died at Bath, 29 June 1794, aged 69, and was succeeded by Laurie in partnership with Whittle. Plates in the Carington Bowles series of mezzotints also appear in Laurie and Whittle's catalogue of 1795.[4]

Matthew Darly was the chief publisher of satirical prints from the 'fifties, when he was in partnership with C. Edwards at the Acorn in the Strand, to *c.* 1779 After abjuring political subjects[5] from about 1771 he admitted in 1778 a few political satires to his series, one of the most interesting of which (No. 5473) bears his own holograph signature instead of the usual *MD* His activities dwindle after 1778 and disappear in 1781. During 1780 his publications were again chiefly political. The close association of Mary Darly with her husband has obscured her activities as a publisher, probably also as an artist In this volume she is represented by the title-page (No. 5369), dedicated to Garrick and perhaps designed by herself, which was prefixed to the large composite volume of Darly's caricatures. But in the 'sixties she published or sold many prints at Ryder's Court, Leicester Fields (also like the Strand shop known as The Acorn), see (e g) Nos. 3817, 3818, 3912, 3919, 3937, 3992, 4071. In 1763 she published a guide to the art of drawing caricatures (copy in Print Room) from Ryder's Court, with sixty small plates, all apparently by herself, except for pl. 20, by or after Townshend, a version of No. 3371 without its background [6] The book was sold by herself at the Ryder's Court address Her portrait by her husband appeared in 1772 as *The female Conoisseur* (No. 4692) in Darly's series. There are two portraits of Darly (Nos. 4632, 5367) and two prints of his shop in the Strand (Nos 4701, 5318).

The dwindling activities and final disappearance of Matt Darly coincide with the growing importance of the shops of the two Humphreys, probably

---

[1] *Op. cit*, vol 1, p 1   [2] See Appendix
[3] Angelo, *Reminiscences*, 1904, vol i, p 308.
[4] Chaloner Smith, iv, p. 1753 n
[5] See above, p xxxiv. He published one political print in 1771, No 4879
[6] This was the first of the series of cards said to have been invented by Townshend, it was said by Walpole to have had 'amazing vent'. *Memoires of the last ten Years of the Reign of George II*, 1822, ii, p. 68. See No 3342.

brother and sister: William of the Strand and Hannah of Bond Street (of St. James's Street from 1797), both associated with the new period of pictorial satire. Both firms reissued prints published by Darly; Darly had published two of Gillray's earliest plates, but William Humphrey was the chief publisher of his early work. The close association of the two men is illustrated in No. 5912, where Gillray acknowledges Humphrey as his superior in the art of etching. Another of the Humphrey family who also published Gillray's work was G. Humphrey of 48 Long Acre, whose imprint first appears in 1783. He is perhaps identical with the G. Humphrey who etched (c. 1780) a portrait of Dr. Benjamin Buckler which he inscribed (in 1813) 'My first etching' (No. 5756). He was perhaps the father of Miss Humphrey's nephew George, who helped her at St. James's Street and at her death succeeded to her business. The Mrs. Humphrey who published No. 5526 (1778) would appear from the address to be the wife of William; Hannah, though often styled by courtesy Mrs., seems never to have used the title on her prints.

Other printsellers who filled the gap left by Darly and supplied an increasing demand for political prints were Holland, Mrs. Darchery, and T. Cornell of Bruton Street. The last must be connected with 'the woman who keeps the print-shop in Bruton Street, who', according to Walpole, 'says she has engraved all the drawings that are sent her, and that she gets by them, one with another, ten pounds apiece' [1]

William Richardson of this volume was probably the father of the better known W. Richardson who issued a catalogue in 1792 saying that he had taken over his father's business. Another publisher of note is John Smith of Cheapside (formerly the *Hogarth's Head*), whose portrait occurs in No. 5530. Other notable printsellers who are represented by a few prints in this volume include Darling, Turner, Thane, Torré (famed as a pyrotechnist), and Seago. All these as well as Smith and William Austin are included in one or other of the three portrait groups of dealers in prints listed in the *B.M. Catalogue of Engraved British Portraits*, vol v. Austin, though a printseller, publisher, and dealer in prints, appears in this volume only as an artist and as the subject of a satirical print. It is probable, however, that he published and sold the prints by himself in this volume of the Catalogue.

M. DOROTHY GEORGE

[1] *Letters*, xii, p. 436 (Apr. 1783)

CATALOGUE OF
POLITICAL AND PERSONAL SATIRES
1770–1783
(Nos. 4839–6360)

The Power of the Mighty hath no Foundation
but in the Opinion of the People.

HOBBES, *Behemoth*

ADDENDA TO VOL. IV

1770

4839 THE FRUITS OF ARBITRARY POWER; OR THE BLOODY MASSACRE, PERPETRATED IN KING-STREET, BOSTON, BY A PARTY OF THE XXIXTH REGT.

Printed for and sold by W. Bingley, in Newgate-Street, Price 6d.

Engraving A larger version of Paul Revere's celebrated print better drawn and with minor differences. Seven soldiers (r) urged on by an officer with a drawn sword fire at a crowd of citizens (l), three of whom lie dead or dying, a fourth is carried off wounded. The soldiers are surrounded with smoke, some of which is intended to emerge from the Custom House, the building immediately behind them and on the extreme r The architectural background depicts King Street, Boston. In the foreground is a dog *Butchers' Hall* and *Custom Hou*[se] are inscribed on the façade of the house as in Revere's print but his 'G R ' is omitted. Instead of Revere's waxing crescent moon there is a waning moon After the (printed) title is printed, *In which Mess. Sam Grey, Sam Maverick, James Caldwell, Crispus Attucks, Patrick Carr were killed Six others were wounded, two of them* [*Christopher Monk and John Clark*] *mortally* This inscription, with slight differences, appears beneath the verses on Revere's print. The same verses[2] are here printed in two columns instead of three, and on the l. and r margins of the verses is an etched design; on the l. a skull and crossbones within a wreath, beneath it is printed, *How long shall they utter and speak hard things? and all the workers of Iniquity boast themselves? They break in pieces thy people, O Lord, and afflict thine Heritage. Ps xciv. 4, 5.* On the r , enclosed in a circle, a flash of lightning emerges from clouds and strikes two broken swords, in the centre of the clouds is a cap of liberty irradiated ; beneath is printed, *They slay the Widows and the Stranger, and murder the Fatherless. Yet they say, The Lord shall not see: Neither shall the God of Jacob regard it. Ps. xciv. 6, 7*

For the so-called Boston Massacre on 5 March 1770 see Van Tyne, *Causes of the War of Independence*, 1921, pp. 285-90. See also *A Fair Account of the late Unhappy Disturbance at Boston* . . London, 1770 (B.M L. 8175. b. 78), which controverts the inflammatory *Short Narrative . . .* (see below); Walpole, *Memoirs of the Reign of George III*, 1845, iv, p. 120. 'It was shown clearly at the trial that the soldiers had endured threats, gibes, insults, and actual violence before they fired in what they believed was self-defence.' Van Tyne, p 289

This plate, folded, was used as a frontispiece to an English reprint of *A Short Narrative of the Horrid Massacre in Boston . . . Boston, printed by order of the Town . . . and re-printed for W. Bingley in Newgate Street, London, 1770.* The Museum copy is inscribed in MS. 'Presented by Thomas Hollis[3] Esq. May 14, 1770' (B.M.L. 1061. h. 11) The impression

---

[1] In Revere's print there is an apostrophe.

[2] In Revere's version *Preston* (the captain) is printed 'P——n' and *venal Courts*, 'venal C——ts '

[3] Hollis wrote of the 'Boston Massacre' 'the business of *White Rose* is to inflame everywhere'. *Memoirs*, 1780, p 379

in the Print Department has not been folded, Bingley doubtless selling separate prints.

Revere's practice of copying English prints and the correction in his plate of the astronomical error in the drawing of the moon suggest that this was not copied from Revere. The origin of both was, perhaps, the plate of the 'massacre' engraved after a drawing by Henry Pelham, which Pelham accused Revere of copying in a letter of 29 March, 1770: ' . . after being at the great Trouble and Expence of making a design paying for paper, printing &c., find myself in the most ungenerous Manner deprived, not only of any proposed Advantage, but even of the expence I have been at, as truly as if you had plundered me on the highway.' *Copley-Pelham Letters*, Mass. Hist Soc. Collections 71, 1914, p 83; see also pp 84, 86, and Stauffer, 1. p. 206. For the Revere, often reproduced, e g. M Waldman, *Americana*, 1926, frontispiece, see Stauffer, No. 2675. $9\frac{1}{16} \times 8\frac{5}{8}$ in. Pl. $13\frac{7}{8} \times 9\frac{13}{16}$ in.

For another version of this design from the *Freeholder's Magazine* for May 1770 (1 June) see No. 4378. The subject is a narrower upright than No 4839 or the Revere, showing more sky and more ground. There are no inscriptions on the houses. Reproduced Andrews, *Portraiture*, p. 28

A third version, 4378 A, apparently copied from No. 4378, and with the same titles, has additions. a dog as in No 4839 (and the Revere) and an inscription on the house farthest r. of *G.R.* (?) *Boston* It is the frontispiece to another English reprint of the *Short Narrative* . *Re-printed for E. and C. Dilly in the Poultry; and J. Almon in Piccadilly.* 1770. $5\frac{15}{16} \times 4\frac{1}{8}$ in. B.M.L., E. 2235/1.

4840 THE HUMOURS OF A FAIR. [1 Sept. 1770]

Engrav'd for the Gentlemans Museum, and Grand Imperial Magazine.

Engraving. The original drawing for this, attributed to Hayman, is described in No. 4428. The engraving is in reverse The scene is a fair outside the gate of St James's Palace, in which the King's friends are satirized as showmen; the principal booth displays the sign of a boot (for Bute) and a flag inscribed *The Death of Brittannia with y^e Farce of Liberty.*

$4 \times 6\frac{5}{16}$ in.

4841 A GAME AT SKITTLES. [1 Oct. 1770]

Engraving. From the *London Museum*, 11. 131. Bute, standing in profile to the r. on the bank of the Tiber, is about to throw a ball at nine skittles on the opposite side of the river The ball is inscribed *The Pretender*, the skittles represent the King and Queen and their seven children: two have royal crowns, six others have royal coronets, and one is surmounted by the Prince of Wales's feathers. In the background is a view of Rome, far from topographically or architecturally correct, but showing St Peter's with its Piazza. In the foreground broken columns and fragments of masonry lie on the ground. Bute wears a Scots cap and a tartan plaid over a court suit; at his knee is the Garter ribbon. At his feet lies a rosary.

Beneath the design is engraved,

> *Treason & He to Rome are fled,*
> *There let him live without restraint;*
> *And, when the Spurious Monarch's dead,*
> *Let him be made a Roman Saint*   *J. S. Hall*

This satire is described under No 4457, but incorrectly, as Mr. Stephens had not seen it Bute went to the Continent in 1768, visiting Italy, and returning to England in 1771. Cf. Chatham's attack on Bute, 2 March, 1770: 'the secret influence of an invisible power, . . . who, notwithstanding he was abroad, was at this moment as potent as ever', *Parl. Hist.* xvi. 842.

$4 \times 6\frac{7}{16}$ in.

4842 THE INFERNAL SLOOP, CHASING THE GOOD SHIP BRITANNIA. [1 Nov. 1770]

Engraved for the Gentleman's Museum, & Grand Imperial Magazine.

Engraving The *Britannia* in full sail, fleeing before another ship (l.) manned by devils; a boat (r), with five oarsmen and a steersman, tows the *Britannia*; there are rocks in the foreground (r.) The figures are on a minute scale, with large inscribed labels issuing from them

A shot from the Infernal Sloop has just broken the Union flag from its staff in the stern Next it stands Bute, saying· *Let her Sink to the Dee'l, I'll have my will!* The rest of the crew of the *Britannia* (l. to r.) are: Lord Holland, with a fox's head, saying: *Oh! What will be come now of my Unaccounted Millions* Holland had been styled in the City petition of 1769 'the public defaulter of unaccounted millions', see No. 4296. Lord Mansfield, in Judge's wig and gown, says: *'tis ye Cursed Licentiousness of the Press that weighs us Down.* Jeremiah Dyson, as a negro, says to Mansfield: *Oh! Masters, Masters, what will you do for me your poor Mungo now.* For Dyson as Mungo see No. 4267. Lord Sandwich, holding a curved cricket bat, says: *d——n em they'll Twitcher my Notches* (an allusion to his fame as a cricketer and his nickname of Jemmy Twitcher from the *Beggar's Opera*). A small figure standing on bales inscribed *National Debt* and *Pensions* says. *Keep to my Plannings and you'll be Safe Enough*; he resembles Grafton rather than North, who succeeded Grafton as First Lord of the Treasury on 28 Jan. 1770. Crouching behind bales inscribed *Places and Pensions* is the very unpopular Duke of Bedford, identified by his words, *Oh Mercy on Bloomsbury Jack.* In the bow, standing on a bale inscribed *Stamp Act*, a man with outstretched arms says *Arrah we shall be Drown'd on them Curst American Rocks*; he is evidently Lord Hillsborough, Secretary of State for the Colonies and an Irishman Sitting astride the bowsprit is a man in a legal wig, saying *if She Sinks I'll be Justice of Water instead of Air.* He is probably Sir Fletcher Norton, appointed Chief Justice in Eyre of His Majesty's forests south of the Trent immediately after defending Mansfield's conduct in the Wilkes case in the Commons on 1 Feb. 1768, and elected Speaker in Jan. 1770, generally satirized as Sir Bull-face Double Fee. See Nos. 4238, 4462, and index. Possibly he is Eyre, the Recorder, see No. 4843. The men in the boat are rowing hard, the steersman says. *Pull like Men my Boys well [sic] keep her up yet.* Two of the oarsmen say: *Ah Jack we made ye Foe Fly when Pit had the Helm*, and *if we keep sober & Resolv'd we may bring her into Harbour Yet.*

The *Britannia* is so heavily laden with bales inscribed *Secret Services, National Debt, Pensions, Places, Reversions,* and *Stamp Act* that she is low in the water; the sea is rough and the 'American Rocks' are near. For other allusions to the Stamp Act see No. 5487, &c.

$4 \times 6\frac{1}{4}$ in

3

4843 THE COURT OF ALDERMEN [c. 1770]

S. Sparrow sculp.

Engraving Probably from a magazine The Lord Mayor is seated in a raised chair at the head of the table, aldermen in furred gowns sit on both sides of the table The six Aldermen on his r. wear laurel wreaths, over the head of each of the seven seated on his l. dangles a noose of rope In the Lord Mayor's hand is a paper, *Grant for Pressing*, a noose hangs over his head Immediately below him a clerk is writing at the table. In the foreground a hangman bows hat in hand to the alderman sitting on the extreme r , at the near end of the row on the Lord Mayor's l.; in his l. hand is a rope; from his pocket protrudes a broadside headed by a cut of a man hanging from a gibbet He says: *I am a Servant to Mr. All-man Shockspar and shall be glad to serve you*

This appears to represent the inquiry into the conduct of the Recorder, Sir James Eyre, for refusing to attend the presentation to the king of the City Remonstrance on 23 May, 1770 The actual proceedings took place at a meeting of the Common Council on 27 Sept 1770 A vote of censure was moved, being voted for by six aldermen and fifty-one commoners, against seven aldermen and eighty-eight commoners. The proceedings were published at length in the Wilkite magazines, see *London Museum*, ii 410 ff , Sharpe, *London and the Kingdom*, 1895, iii 101

Among the six Wilkite aldermen on the r of the chair Wilkes is speaking; he says: *You may Nash your teeth, Mr. Alderman, but we shall carry it Plumb in spite of your Kites and Blackbirds we will have the foolish Lad broke for neglect of Duty* William Nash, Samuel Plumbe, Sir Robert Kite, John Bird, and Sir Robert Ladbroke were anti-Wilkite aldermen Another alderman is saying· *He must let out his large House in Lincoln's Inn Fields to lodgers* (the Recorder lived in Lincoln's Inn Fields).

Four of the seven aldermen of the court party are speaking; they say (l. to r.): *They seem all to be out of their Heads; He's a man of Honor & a Gentleman* (the speaker is identified by Mr. Hawkins as Harley, the leader of the Court party in the City); a man with the head and pointed beard of Shakespeare to indicate that he is Alderman John Shakespeare says. *I should not like to dangle in my own Manufacture*, the last, seated on the outside, and identified by Mr. Hawkins as Sir Robert Ladbroke, says: *No Body will ever regard our Resolutions* For Ladbroke see No 4379

The Lord Mayor is Barlow Trecothick, who held office between the death of Beckford on 21 June, 1770 and the election of Brass Crosby on 9 November As was customary, he had backed a Press Warrant issued by the Lords of the Admiralty to enable it to be executed within the precincts of the City A man impressed on this warrant was brought on 26 October before Wilkes, who was sitting at Guildhall as a Justice of the Peace for the City. Wilkes discharged the man on the ground that Press Warrants were illegal by Magna Carta. *London Museum*, ii. 491 ff., *Ann Reg.* xiii 161, 162, Sharpe, op. cit. iii. 106 For Sir James Eyre and his obsequiousness to the Court see No 4408.

$3\frac{5}{8} \times 5\frac{7}{8}$ in

4844 CANDIDATES TO SUCCEED TOM TURLIS. [1770]

Engraving. Probably from a magazine Two groups of persons who are candidates for the place of hangman. Inscribed labels issue from the persons of four of them. Two men sit side by side on a settee, wearing curiously shaped crowns or coronets, one (l.) shaped like a wall. The former holds a paper inscribed *To J——e G——m* showing that he is Justice Gillam, who ordered the soldiers to fire on the Wilkite mob outside the King's Bench Prison on 10 May 1768 (see No. 4201). He says: *Everyone knows my abilities as a Man-killer* His companion says · *Let the Place be held by Commission and let the two Kennedies & my self, be Lords Commissioners of the Rope.* Behind, and to the l. of the settee three persons stand together. A rough-looking man, flourishing a stick says: *I wont accept of ye Office without a Peerage to Support its Dignity.* Next him is a Judge in wig and robes

On the r., their backs to a window, stand three men; Sir Fletcher Norton in his Speaker's robes, and the horns which indicate that he is 'Sir Bullface Double Fee', see Nos 4238, 4462, and index, says: *B——n S——h has spoil'd ye Trade, if Murderers were to be hang'd ye Place might be worth accept^{ce}* He stands between the two Kennedy brothers and is alluding to the reprieve (for transportation) of one of them, the other having been acquitted *B——n S——h* may be intended for Sir Sidney Stafford Smythe, a baron of the Exchequer. This reprieve was for the murder of a watchman in a drunken brawl, and was believed to be due to the influence of the young men's sister, Polly or Kitty Kennedy, see Nos 4399, 4463, 5095. It was made a political question by Parson Horne and others, see Walpole, *Memoirs of the Reign of George IV*, 1845, iv. 110-11; Stephens, *Memoirs of Horne Tooke*, i. 185.

The print appears to derive from a paragraph in the *Oxford Magazine* for March 1770 (iv, p 113) reporting that Turlis the hangman had informed the Lord Mayor that 'he will sooner resign his place than burn the City Remonstrance' [of 14 Mar. 1770] There was no order for burning the Remonstrance which was voted by the House of Commons on 19 March to be an unwarrantable and dangerous petition. Sharpe, *London and the Kingdom* See also No 4380.

$3\frac{1}{2} \times 5\frac{11}{16}$ in.

4845 THE TRIAL OF THE D. OF C, [Cumberland] AND LADY G——R [Grosvenor] FOR CRIM. CON.   [1770]

Engraving Probably from a magazine. One of several satires on the trial of the Duke of Cumberland on a suit for crim con. on 5 July 1770 in the King's Bench A judge on a raised seat, plaintiff and defendants, witnesses or spectators stand below, surrounding a rectangular barrier within which is a table, at which a clerk is writing Four counsel stand within the barrier, two to the r. of the judge, two to his l

The Judge (Mansfield) sits, his l. forefinger raised, listening with a stern expression to the remarks addressed to him In the centre, in back view, stands Lord Grosvenor, wearing a tie-wig with horns, to which he points, saying: *I only want to know for a Certainty whether I am entitled to this Head Dress.* On the l in profile to the r. stand Lady Grosvenor, holding out a fan, and Cumberland She says: *My case shall be laid before this Court, and I can have nothing to fear from an Upright Judge*; he says: *I can do no Wrong.* Behind him on the extreme l. is a woman wearing a hood and holding a fan She says · *It was a Pity to disturb them when they were going to Prince Making.* One of the counsel on the Judge's r. says: *If her L——d, has not bedded with her these two years She cannot be with Child, but she may be with Prince.* The two counsel on the other side say : *The Lady acted upon Revolution Principles She is strongly attached to the Present Family, and,*

There is no actual Proof of Adultery. A man in back view says: *The Youth wanted a Sop in Pan* A cook, on the extreme r., says, laughing: *How his —— R——y [sic] H—n — ss will be Roasted and Basted.*

See Nos. 4400, 4401, 4402 and the references there given.

$3\frac{3}{4} \times 6\frac{3}{4}$ in

4846 [MACKLIN.] [? 1770[1]]

Engraving Macklin as Shylock supports on his shoulders Shakespeare who holds out a book in his r hand, a pen in his l Macklin leans to the l holding out in his r hand a pair of scales, in his l a knife. Behind are Tragedy and Comedy. Tragedy (l), a draped woman holding a dagger, appears despondent, Comedy (r.) holding a mask, looks with contemptuous amusement at Macklin. Shakespeare is irradiated Beneath the design is engraved,

> *Immortal Shakespear! Child of Heaven & fire,*
> *The more we sink him rises still the higher:*
> *E'en thro'* THIS *Vehicle the Bard can pass*
> *Like Mecca's Prophet—mounted on an* ASS.

For Macklin see Nos 5175, 5203.

4847 THE FEMALE COTERIE AT THE ELECTION OF ONE OF THE MALE MEMBERS OF THEIR SOCIETY [c. 1770]

Engraving Probably from a magazine A number of ladies (eleven in all) sit at a table at the head of which is their president or chairman They are balloting for the admission of a member, according to the 'Authentic Rules of the Female Coterie' printed in the *Gentleman's Magazine,* 1770, p. 414, by which ladies balloted for men and men for ladies The president sits in a raised chair, a hammer in her r. hand; she says: *M'' Driver the New Member shall be admitted & duly return'd by me the proper Officer if upon examination he comes up to the Standard* Remarks from other ladies (l to r) are· *I hold up my hand for M'' Driver, if it had not been for him, several Noble Families would have been extinct that have now a numerous Issue; The ability of every Candidate ought to be strictly Examined; The Gentleman to be elected into this Society shall not be Husband to any of us; No our plan is to supply the deficiency of Husbands, I move for the Admission of M'' Driver as a Member. He has a promising Leg, an happy Assurance, & to crown the whole he is an Irishman, Lady H——n [Harrington] has her Reasons for not suffering M'' Driver to return to Ireland, but she must not Engross him all to herself* The lady on the President's right is writing in a large book On the table are writing materials, books, one being *Essay on Man,* a bottle marked *Eau de Vie,* a tray with coffee-pot, cups, &c.

For the Coterie, a ladies' club formed in 1770, see 'A Georgian Ladies' Club', in *Times Literary Supplement,* 11 Aug. 1932, which is largely based on MSS in the Public Record Office, Chancery Masters' Papers filed in the Suit C. 10 | 110 | 35. See also Nos. 4472 (and references there given), 5065, 5425

$3\frac{3}{4} \times 5\frac{3}{4}$ in.

[1] Mr. Hawkins has written on the print *Lond Mus. Ap. 1770,* but it is not in the B.M L copy of the magazine, which does contain, p 207 (Apr. 1770), a portrait of Macklin as Shylock by Lodge, inscribed, *This is the Jew, That Shakespeare drew.* The print is also inconsistent with a laudatory 'Account of the Life and Genius of Mr. Charles Macklin', ibid , pp. 288–90

THE PEACE-MAKERS.　　　　　See No. 4416 [1 Jan. 1771]
From the *London Museum*. On the Falkland Islands

THE PRESENT EMPEROR OF GERMANY RECEIVING PETI-
TIONS FROM, AND REDRESSING THE GRIEVANCES OF THE
MEANEST OF HIS SUBJECTS .. HOW HAPPY WOULD OTHER
PRINCES BE COULD THEY, OR—WOULD THEY DO THE
SAME.　　　　　See No. 4388 [1 Jan. 1771]
From the *Oxford Magazine*.

4848 A CONFERENCE IN THE SHADES.　　　[1 Feb. 1771]
Woodcut. From the *Town and Country Magazine*, iii 36 It illustrates
*A Conference in the Shades between the Duke of Bedford and Arthur Beard-
more Esq* Bedford (l), wearing the insignia of the Garter, holds out his
arms in an attitude of despair Beardmore, wearing a long livery gown
and with the cap of liberty on a staff, holds out to him a paper inscribed in
large letters *Magna Ch[ar]ta*, pointing with a monitory finger. Bedford
died 14 Jan., Beardmore, a Wilkite Common Councilman, died 18 Jan In
the dialogue they discuss without heat the political situation, the quarrel
between Wilkes and Horne, &c. See No 4861, &c.
$3\frac{3}{4} \times 5\frac{3}{4}$ in.

THE FATE OF CITY REM——CES.　　See No. 4387 [1 Feb. 1771]
Engraving From the *Oxford Magazine*, vi 12. George III giving the
Petitions and Remonstrances of his subjects to the little Prince of Wales
who has asked for paper for a kite.

THE SAWYERS DEMOLISHING THE TEMPLE OF LIBERTY.
　　　　　See No. 4431 [1 Feb. 1771]
Engraving. From the *Oxford Magazine*, vi 28. Bute, Lord Mansfield,
and Fletcher Norton demolishing the Temple of Liberty.

DIEU ET MON DROIT　　　　See No. 4423 [1 Feb. 1771]
AVITO VIRET HONORE

Frontispiece to *Political Register*, 1771. Ministerial misdeeds since
1763. The second title is Bute's motto.

4849 THE CONVENTION MAKERS. VOL. 3, No. 6. [1 Mar. 1771]
Engraving. From the *Town and Country Magazine*, iii. 80. The interior
of a room; a picture called *A Convention*, depicting the Convention between
England and Spain on the Falkland Islands, is falling from a broken

---

[1] No. 5134, published in 1773, satirizes the events of January 1771, and illustrates *Baratariana*, first published April–May 1771.

7

cornice inscribed *National Honour*, onto four prostrate figures Two other men hasten in alarm from the picture   *Londinia* (l), wearing a mural crown and carrying a shield with the arms of the City, points out the catastrophe to the Lord Mayor and two other men Britannia and Justice with a sword and spear enter threateningly from a door (r.). Bute looks through a window with a face of alarm *Magna Charta* which hangs on the wall is obscured by a large cobweb. From an overturned inkpot on the floor flows a stream inscribed *The Road from Rochford to ye Tower*. On the floor are also a crown, a broken anchor, inscribed *Tory Administration*, two books, one being *Places and Pensions Ledger Vol. 22*.

In the picture, three figures stand on the seashore: an Englishman inscribed *Submission*, with his hat under his arm, takes the hand of a Spaniard, inscribed *Reluctance*, who turns his back A third figure, *Indemnity*, waves a ragged cloth perhaps intended for a map of the Falkland Islands, and representing England's claim to an indemnity from Spain scattered to the winds

The convention between England and Spain was signed on 22 Jan 1771 by Rochford as Secretary of State, and Masserano the Spanish Ambassador. Spain disavowed the seizure of Port Egmont, but stipulated that its restoration should not affect Spain's claim to sovereignty over the Islands which she had always (ineffectively) asserted These satisfactory terms were the result of the fall of Choiseul, and the successful diplomacy of Harris at Madrid, which prevented war with Spain and France They were violently attacked by the Opposition, and especially by Chatham See Winstanley, *Chatham and the Whig Opposition*, 1912, pp 407 ff.; *Ann. Reg.* 1771, pp. 46–53, 238; Junius' letter of 30 Jan. 1771, answered by Johnson's *Thoughts on the late transactions respecting Falkland's Islands*, *Cambridge Hist of the Br Empire*, 1. 698 ff See also Nos 4415–19, 4856, 4857, 4897, 4934, 4935, 4940.

$4\frac{1}{4} \times 7$ in.

THE BUTTON MAKERS ADJUSTING THEIR DIFFERENCES.

See No. 4417 [1 Mar. 1771]

Engraving From the *Oxford Magazine*, vi 56 A conference between the kings of England and Spain over the Falkland Islands, the Princess Dowager of Wales is accused of having been bribed by the king of Spain to influence her son in Spain's favour.

TWITCHER'S ADVOCATE

See No. 4426 [1 Mar. 1771]

Dr. W. Scott or 'Anti-Sejanus'.

4850 VIRTUE DISGRAC'D MARCH 1771　　　[1 Apr 1771]
VICE TRIUMPHANT MARCH 1771
Design'd and Engrav'd for the Political Register.

Engraving From the *Political Register*, viii. 127. A design in two compartments. Above is 'Virtue' imprisoned in the Tower A head looks from each of two barred windows At the gate stand Britannia and Liberty; above their heads are cherubs in an arch of clouds.

This represents the imprisonment of Crosby, the Lord Mayor, and Alderman Oliver. See Nos. 4852–4, 4860, 4864, 4938.

In the lower compartment Westminster magistrates and constables stand on the steps of a portico, surmounted by clouds and two demons protecting 'Vice', the House of Commons The two foremost figures are wearing the portcullis badge of the arms of the City of Westminster suspended from their necks, one holds a paper inscribed *Riot Act*. Behind are constables with staves, behind again figures in the doorway, one with a staff.

This represents the serious riot at Westminster on 27 March, when the Lord Mayor went from the Mansion House to the House of Commons where he was committed to the Tower The badges were worn by the magistrates on Sir John Fielding's request 'for greater safety and effectiveness in suppressing riots . .' *Public Advertiser*, 16 Dec 1665 and 8 Sept. 1766. See Manchée, *Westminster City Fathers*, p 256, for a photograph of a badge. For the riot see *Ann Reg.* 1771, p. 85; *Corr. of George III*, ed. Fortescue, ii. 245. For the unpopularity of the House of Commons cf. No 4869, &c.

$6 \times 3\frac{5}{8}$ in.

4851 SIR GEORGE SAVILE BART. [1 Apr 1771]

J. Lodge sculp.

Engraving. *London Museum*, iii 197 Bust portrait of Savile looking to the l. in an oval Beneath the oval is an ornamental group of rolled documents, one is inscribed *The Calder Navigation*, another *Nullum Tempus*. Beneath these are engraved

> *A Wit's a Feather, & a Chief's a Rod,*
> *An honest Man's the noblest Work of God*
> > Pope

Savile introduced (1768 and 1769) the *Nullum Tempus* Bill for securing the land of a subject after sixty years' possession from any dormant right of the Crown, which was the outcome of the suit between Sir James Lowther and Portland, see Nos 4895, 5136 He was also active in procuring the Act of 1769 (9 Geo. III, c. 71) for extending the navigation of the River Calder and for restoring the damage done by floods. See *Commons' Journals*, xxxii, pp 223-4. See No 4981.

A companion portrait to No. 4856.

Oval $3\frac{7}{8} \times 3\frac{1}{8}$ in.   B.M.L , P.P. 5435 c

4852 AN EXACT REPRESENTATION OF THE SEVEN MALE-FACTORS THAT WHERE [sic] EXECUTED AT TOWER HILL ON APRIL 5, 1771 F[OR TREASON][1] TO THEIR COUNTREY.

Pub. by the Inventor J. Williams according to act of Parliament, April 10, 1771.

Etching Two carts conveying malefactors, after the manner of the usual procession to Tyburn, with a crowd of spectators in the foreground. Spectators also look from windows The victims have numbers which refer to explanatory notes beneath the print: *Nº 1 Lord Bloody scrol. Nº 2 Alderman contract the Citys great Curse Nº 3 Lord Hellish Facts a Lover of Arbitrary Power &c. &c 2ᵈ Curt Nº 1 Gray Goose a Lawyer*

[1] The letters in brackets appear to have been erased from the plate and then filled in with a pen.

9

of infamous practices in any Court N° *2 Col¹ Bluster remarkable for nothing but the murder of an innocent Woman.* N° *3 Jemmy Twitcher.* N° *4 Cocking George one that never kept his Word with any on[e].* Labels issue from the mouths of the victims and the spectators Each cart has a parson without a number; in the first cart (l) he has a halter round his neck and is saying: *Lying & Perjury & Deciet are my chief supports.* He is Dr. W Scott, *Twitcher's Advocate,* see No. 4426. No. 1, Lord Barrington, says *Oh! I hear the murderd Allen call me to Account Oh! St. Georges Fields.* No 2, Alderman Harley· *Oh! I have wrongd my Countrey & decievd my Fellow Citizens Oh! that I had been but Honest.* No. 3, Lord Halifax. *General Warrants and every oppressive measure against my country makes me repent Oh the cursed Jezebel* [the Princess Dowager of Wales].

In the second cart (r) the clergyman, Parson Horne, is saying: *my poor father used to say G— Damn ye Jacky never be seen to keep bad comp^y for fear you shoud come to be Hangd* He holds a paper on which is inscribed *I think.* No 1, de Grey, in Judge's wig and gown, says: *I have betrayd my Friend robd my country, been led by the nose by that infernal B——h Jezebel Carlton, Oh me* No 2, Luttrell, says: *Arabella, poor Arabella Bolton! pray for your murderer Oh I am a damd Villian* [sic] No 4, Onslow: *little did I think I shoud be pitted with such a parcel of Shake-Bags rascals Oh! that I had still been a hearty Cock* No 3, Sandwich *I never since I have been Jemmy Twitcher have been in such Wicked & bad Company no not I*

Spectators from the windows address the victims L. to r : *Remember St. George's Fields effectual murthers; Cocking George you dont Die Game; Take care Panurge the Halters Round your neck* (this is addressed to Dr. W. Scott, the parson, the reputed author of letters to the Press defending Sandwich, signed *Panurge* and *Cinna), Here's a General Warrant for Ye ye Dogs; it is a pity he should escape he's such a double rogue, What! the Vicar of Brentford* [Horne] *are you doing duty there twil be your turn soon.* Members of the crowd in the foreground (l. to r.) say: *Miss Bolton's Curses on the Wretch, We could pick out a score more T——s* [Traitors obliterated] *to their Countrey; I think the Lawyer becomes a Cart and a Halter; I thought George* [Onslow] *had been better fed he's well trim'd; The Alderman had better minded Tare and Trett; Jemmy Twitcher false to his God, his King, his country & his Friend* [Wilkes] An Irishman says. *By Jasus God if such varmint would be in Ireland to be hang'd for we woud stone 'em to death with Brick Bats; The Colonel shoud have been hangd at Brentford, Look at Double faced Jack the Parson of B,*[rentford]; *Hanging's too good for that Rogue the Alderman; They have lived too Long* A soldier, in the uniform of the foot-guards & holding a musket, says: *Damn the soldier that Draws a Trigger to oblige any Comander against an Englishman; Oh there's Tom Patts the Chicken Butcher's son I thought he would be hangd ere now; What! Cocking George. Il' lay you the Long Odds you die as great a dunghill as you have livd I say done first, Damn the Brentford Vicar they must hang him soon for he's a Villian in disguise* A woman says: *I thought the Pellmell Jezebel* [half erased but legible] *woud come to this*

On 5 April such a procession in which two carts were preceded by a hearse went to Tower Hill attended by the mob. The figures in the carts were of pasteboard, nearly life-size, hanging from gallows, with names on their backs L——d B——n; Ld H——x, Alderman H.; L——ll the Usurper; D—G—y; Jemmy Twitcher; Cocking George. They were burnt on Tower Hill and shortly afterwards their 'dying speeches' were sold in the streets *Gent. Mag.* 1771, p. 188; *Ann. Reg* 1771, p. 91.

The occasion of the demonstration was the imprisonment of the Lord
Mayor and Oliver in the Tower (see Nos. 4850, 4853, &c.), and on the same
day the L M. was taken before de Grey who refused a writ of *Habeas
Corpus* and re-committed him to the Tower. But except for the effigies of
de Grey and Onslow (who started the action in the Commons against the
printing of debates, see No. 4855), this satire is chiefly concerned with other
and earlier aspects of the struggle between Wilkes and the City on one
side and Court, Ministry, and Commons on the other Barrington is
pilloried for his connexion with the 'Massacre of St. George's Fields', see
No. 4196; 'Bloody Scrol' is a quotation from Wilkes's justification of his
libel on the offending letter (written by Weymouth, not Barrington):[1] 'I
thought it my duty to bring to light that bloody scroll.' *Parl. Hist.* XVI. 543;
Halifax for the general warrant of 1763, see Nos 4050, 4203. Harley was
the chief supporter of the Court among the aldermen, and as candidate
for the City had defeated Wilkes in the election of 1768; see Nos. 4069,
4190, 4213, 4235, 4269 For Luttrell, the Middlesex Election, and the
alleged seduction of Arabella Bolton, see Nos. 4284, 4285, 4971. Sandwich
was hated for his treachery to Wilkes over the *Essay on Woman*; the satires
relating to him are numerous, see No 4075 and Vol IV pp cxi–cxii, and
index to this volume. For the Princess Dowager of Wales see Nos. 3846,
3847, 4425, 4874, &c. The quarrel between Wilkes and Horne absorbed
popular attention in the early months of 1771 See Walpole, *Letters*,
VIII 7, 27–8, 44 and Nos 4861, 4862, 4863, 4867, 4879, 5102, 5127.
$11\frac{7}{8} \times 6\frac{1}{2}$ in.

4853 THE LORD MAYOR AND ALDERMAN OLIVER IN THE
TOWER. [1 May 1771]

Engrav'd for the Oxford Magazine.

Engraving From the *Oxford Magazine*, VI 136 Brass Crosby the Lord
Mayor and Alderman Oliver seated at a table on which are rolled documents. *Charters of the City of London, Bill of Rights, Mag[na] Chart[a]*
The L M says *We are imprisoned for doing our duty, therefore Captivity is
honourable.* Oliver says: *Our conduct is approv'd can the rulers at St.
Stephens say as much?* A warder in beefeater's dress by the door says. *In
1745 the Scots were sent here for rebelling, these Gentlemen are committed
for their L—y—lty.* For this well-known episode in the struggle which
secured the publication of parliamentary debates see Walpole's *Letters*,
VIII 16–20, 24–6; *Corr. of George III*, ed. Fortescue, ii. 232 ff. Crosby
remained in the Tower from 27 Mar. till the prorogation on 8 May See
Nos 4850, 4852, 4854, 4857, 4860, 4864, 4880
Reproduced, *Social England*, ed Traill, 1904, v 475.
$3\frac{5}{8} \times 5\frac{7}{8}$ in.

4854 THE RIGHT HONBLE BRASS CROSBY ESQR LORD MAYOR,
AND RICHD OLIVER ESQR, ALDERMAN OF LONDON.

[1 May 1771]

Engraving. From the *Town and Country Magazine*, III. 193. Portraits
(W L) commemorating the committal to the Tower by the House of

[1] 'Twas W——h urged th 'enforcing his commands;
'Twas B——n that gave th 'exciting pay, See No. 4196.

Commons of Crosby and Oliver Crosby (l) holds in his l hand a long staff resting on the ground on which is the cap of liberty. Oliver's r hand also holds the staff. See No 4853, &c

$4\frac{5}{8} \times 3\frac{3}{8}$ in.

4855 LITTLE COCKING GEORGE. [1 May 1771]

Woodcut From the *Town and County Magazine*, iii. 196. A man (W.L.) holds a fighting cock in both hands Above his head is printed *Cock a doodle-doo*. George Onslow was known as little Cocking George, and is described in the accompanying text as 'the great champion of *privilege* and cock-fighting'. He was burnt in effigy, 5 April 1771, as the originator of the proceedings against the printers for the publication of parliamentary debates, see No. 4852. He complained, 8 Feb 1771, 'Sometimes I am held up as a villain; sometimes I am held up as an idiot; and sometimes as both. To-day they call me *little Cocking George*. They will find Sir, I am a cock they will not easily beat.' Cavendish, *Debates*, ii. 257. Cf. No 6065.

4856 EARL OF ROCHFORD. [1 May 1771]

J. Lodge sculp

Engraving From the *London Museum*, iii 253 Bust portrait of Rochford in an oval, almost full face. Beneath the oval is a rolled document inscribed *Convention with Spain, 1771* Beneath this is engraved,

> Man may escape from Rope & Gun,
> But Infamy he ne'er can Shun
>
> Gay

Rochford carried on with ability and success the negotiations leading to the unpopular Convention with Spain of 14 Jan 1771, see No. 4849 A companion portrait to No. 4851

Oval, $3\frac{3}{4} \times 3\frac{1}{4}$. B.M.L., P.P. 5435 c.

4857 THE POLITICIAN.

Done from the original Drawing by S H Grimm Printed for S. Sledge Printseller, in Henrietta Street Covent Garden. Publish'd as the Act directs 2ᵈ May 1771.

Engraving A man wearing spectacles and of repulsive appearance with a gaping toothless mouth, sits draped in a sheet, while a French hair-dresser (his nationality indicated by his bag-wig and ruffles) applies tongs to his hair, and appears to be whispering in his ear. At this, or on account of the Speaker's Warrant dated 27 Mar. 1771, to the Lieutenant of the Tower to receive the Lord Mayor into custody, which he holds in his hand, the Politician starts in alarm In the centre over the fire-place is an oval picture of Don Quixote tilting at a windmill On the l hangs a map of the Iberian Peninsula, on the r one of the British Isles Hanging from a stool to the floor is *An Accurate Map of Falkland Iˢ* over which a dog and cat are fighting. On the floor are also a *Letter to the Premier*, a *Last dying Speech*, *A new Song on Liberty* (torn), a bundle of *Junius's Letters* and another of *Votes*. Open on a secretaire-bookcase is a *History of the Constitution with my own Remarks*, apparently in course of composition. A bust of *Oliver Cromwell* is on the top of the book-case.

A caricature portrait of Lord North; though he is generally treated in satire, c. 1771, as a tool of Bute and Grafton, Junius had particularly attacked him in his letter of 30 Jan 1771, as taking 'the whole upon himself' For the Falkland Islands see Nos. 4415–19, 4849, &c., in which the Ministry and the King are accused of corrupt subservience to Spain, a charge without foundation: see the negotiations with Spain in *Cal. II O. Papers*, 1770–2, pp. 65–6, 84–5, 104–7, 190, 193, 200, 209, 573, Lord Malmesbury's *Diaries and Correspondence*, 1844, 1, pp 58–78, *Letters of Hume*, ed. Greig, 1932, 11 240 ff.

$9\frac{1}{8} \times 12\frac{1}{2}$ in

4858 THE NATIONAL UNION 1771. [1 June 1771]

Design'd and Engrav'd for the Political Register.

Engraving From the *Political Register*, viii. 255. A man, standing on a bank, holds the staff of a large Union flag which is wrapped round a group of six standing figures who are poorly characterized, but are presumably patriots One is Lord Chatham, holding a crutch, beside him stands a judge in wig and robes who is probably Lord Camden

$5\frac{7}{8} \times 3\frac{7}{8}$ in.

4859 THE YOUNG HEIR AMONG BAD COUNCELLORS, OR THE LION BETRAY'D. [1 June 1771]

Engraving From the *Oxford Magazine*, vi 176. George III, as a lion, blindfolded and in chains, sits on a low platform surrounded by his counsellors, whose advice is inscribed on labels coming from their heads. These are (l. to r): Sandwich (Jemmy Twitcher) with goat's legs, holding a cricket-bat and wearing a cricketing cap on the top of which rests an anchor to show that he is First Lord of the Admiralty He says: *Be advised by me and I'll give them a twitcher*.[1] A dog with the letter N resting on his head to show that he is Lord North, holds the chain riveted on the lion's right paw, saying: *Be guided by me and go North about*; with one leg, which terminates in a barbed point, he is stabbing the lion's breast, blood gushes out and is being drunk by rats. North's other leg is in a jack boot, emblem of the supposed influence of Bute, see No. 3860, &c. The Duke of Grafton, standing behind the lion, caricatured but not travestied as an animal, says: *Shall a Lion regard the barking of Dogs*. (This favourable treatment is due to the fact that the caricaturist had not anticipated Grafton's appointment as Lord Privy Seal on 8 June 1771.) Lord Mansfield in judge's wig and robes and holding a book, says: *Let us put our own Laws in full force.* Fletcher Norton (Sir Bull-face Double Fee) in his Speaker's robes, with horns and talons for fingers, says: *I'll defend you as long as it is my Interer* [sic] In front of him stands Charles Fox as a young fox, wearing a bag-wig, his right hand, thrust through a muff, holds the ace of clubs, his left foot is in a dice-box, and two dice are on the ground beside him, he is looking through a single-eye glass; these emblems show his fondness for gambling and for French fashions The lion is saying: *I know you are all my friends and will take care of my Estate.*

The accompanying text explains that, owing to the influence of 'a north country servant' the king's present ministers are Jacobites, and that he has

---

[1] Twitcher is dialect for a severe blow. *O.F.D.* See No. 4877.

'discarded with contempt the descendants of those whose ancestors' brought his family into possession of their estates. An indication of the Whig creed that 'Revolution families' had a hereditary claim to office. Cf No 4303.

$5\frac{3}{8} \times 3\frac{13}{16}$ in

4860 THE PRINTERS BEFORE A COMMITTEE OF THE ROBIN-HOOD SOCIETY. [1 June 1771]

Engraving. From the *Oxford Magazine*, vi 161 Sir Fletcher Norton the Speaker, wearing horns in allusion to his nick-name, Sir Bull-face Double Fee, is seated in his robes behind a barrier inscribed *St Stephens Bar*; with three members of the house on his r hand, and three on his l Before the bar, facing the Speaker, stand two printers, one stands on the *General Evening [Post]*, the other on the *St. James Chronicle*. The former asks. *Is it agreeable to Magna Chaita that a Man should be a Judge in his own Cause?* The other says: *If my Trial is coming on I beg I may be on the Jury as well as my Opponent.*

An incident in the struggle between the House of Commons on one side and the Press and the City on the other, over the publication of parliamentary debates See a letter to the Speaker from Evans, printer of the *London Packet*, *Political Register*, x 229, *Ann. Reg* 1771, 183–93, *Cal. H.O. Papers, 1770–1772*, pp 223–4; A. Stephens, *Memoirs of Horne Tooke*, 1 323–51; F Bourne, *English Newspapers*, 1 209 ff., *Corr. of George III*, ed Fortescue, 11. 219–20 The printers were summoned to attend the House on 14 March; those who did so were reprimanded on their knees, Wheble and Miller refused to attend, being supported by Wilkes, Brass Crosby the Lord Mayor, and Oliver, whose well-known defiance of the House led to the imprisonment of the two latter in the Tower, see 4850, &c Baldwin of the *Whitehall Evening Post*, Bladon of the *General Evening Post*, and Wright, apologized at the bar of the House and were discharged

The Commons are pilloried as the Robin Hood Society, a debating society of tradesmen, &c, which had long been a stock subject of ridicule, see Nos 3260 (probably suggested by an article by Fielding in the *Covent Garden Journal*, 28 Jan, 1 Feb 1752), 3539, 6331. See also Nos. 4850, 4852–4, 4864.

$3\frac{9}{16} \times 5\frac{7}{8}$ in

4861 THE DOUBLE DISCOVERY [1 June 1771]

Woodcut. From the *Town and Country Magazine*, iii. 262 A flying demon holds the level beam of a pair of scales, on which stand Wilkes (l.) and Parson Horne (r.). Each stands in the attitude of a fencer, thrusting at the other with an outstretched goose-quill; neither has the advantage. Wilkes wears a bag-wig, Horne is in parson's gown and bands The demon says: *nicely pois'd indeed.* The print illustrates 'The Balance of Honour and Patriotism, or a Dialogue between Mr. H—— and Mr. ——, in which the Demon of Discord very properly interferes'. The dialogue ends with Horne's expressing a wish 'that you, good Mr. Devil, had been conducting me to H——ll, before Malagrida [Shelburne] had persuaded me to engage in this d——n'd controversy'.

One of a number of satires on the quarrel between Wilkes and Horne which began in November 1770 and was carried on by letters in the Press between 14 Jan and 10 July 1771. See *Stephens, Memoirs of Horne Tooke*, i. 176 ff. These satires accuse Horne of being inspired by the Devil, Ministers, &c. See Nos. 4852, 4863, 4866, 4868, 4886, 4948, 4967, 5104, 5129. An interesting indication of the distrust inspired by Shelburne then in the Opposition, and concerned at its weakness, of which this quarrel was one manifestation. Fitzmaurice, *Shelburne*, 1912, i. 423, 437. Cf. Nos. 4152, 4375.

$6\frac{1}{8} \times 4\frac{1}{4}$ in.

4862 THE TRIAL OF M. D'EON BY A JURY OF MATRONS.

No. 15 [1 June 1771]

Etching. From the *Town and Country Magazine*, iii. 249 The Chevalier d'Eon (l.), wearing a military hat and the order of St Louis round his neck, stands, partly draped, on a pedestal before a jury of twelve ladies (r.) who are to decide upon his sex, a matter which has for several weeks deeply engaged 'the polite and stock-jobbing world'. The accompanying text indicates the identity of the jury: Lady Har——n. [Harrington.], L——y R——d [Rochford?], L——y T—sh—d [Townshend], L——y G——r. [Grosvenor], L——y Sarah B——y [Bunbury], L——y Lig——r [Ligonier], L——y R——y [Rodney?]. The D. of N. [Northumberland?] They pronounced the matter doubtful

For D'Eon see Nos. 4308, 4865, &c.

This plate was used in the *Hibernian Magazine*, i 263 (July 1771).

$3\frac{7}{8} \times 6\frac{3}{8}$ in

4863 A PART OF THE NEW COMMITY OF INQUIRY

Price 6ᵈ.   [c. June 1771]

Etching with verses engraved beneath. Round a circular table draped with a cloth sit the devil (centre), the Pope (l.), and Horne (r.); engraved labels issue from their mouths. By Horne is an inkstand, and the table is spread with letters he is supposed to have written at the dictation of his two counsellors. He is saying: *My Dʳ Friend Satan if Wilkes should undecieve 'm* His l hand rests on a partly written letter· *Jesuits Hall June 1, 1771 Sʳ* . . .

The devil says to Horne: *I'll Insure you yᵉ P—n—ss D——gr, Bte, & N——th's* [Princess Dowager, Bute and North's] *favʳˢ and all my Frᵈˢ at Court.* The Pope says· *And I'll give you absolution for all, past Present & to come.*

Papers on the table are inscribed *To Jnᵒ Wilkes Esqʳ;* . . . *But I hope I have escap'd the infection* . . .; *To Lord N——th My lord I shall persue such measures as will be to Your interest in opposing W——kes Your &c. P H——rn* On the ground, peeping from beneath the table-cloth, an imp is writing on a scroll: . . . *is now to support the cause of my Master and yᵉ M—n—try*

The letter to Wilkes is quoted from the unfortunate letter from Horne to Wilkes of 3 Jan. 1766 in which he deprecated his clerical orders, adding apologetically, 'It is true I have suffered the infectious hand of a bishop to be waved over me; whose imposition like the sop given to Judas, is only a signal for the devil to enter . . . I hope I have escaped the contagion . . . if you should at any time discover the black spot under the tongue, pray kindly assist me to conquer the prejudices of education and profession'

This letter was published by Wilkes during their quarrel A Stephens, *Memoirs of Horne Tooke*, i 76
Beneath the design verses are engraved,

> *Good People I Pray, give atten^{n} this way,*
> *Don't be frightn'd to see us together,*
> *The best will be Friends, for to serve their own ends,*
> *And their sentim^{ts} change as the Weather.*

> *God Keep us from Sin, witho^{ut} & within,*
> *unTill [sic] certain of absolution,*
> *Which I have obtain'd, & thorowly gain'd,*
> *So a Fig for the Constitution.*

> *The Bishop's soft hand, his lawn Sleev's or Band,*
> *Cou'd never polute or defile me,*
> *If you think I am Wrong, look under my Tongue,*
> *And see if the Rogue has beguil'd me.*

> *It was Satan my Friend did ye Pope recomend,*
> *And they both of them swear to be trusty,*
> *So I'll try once again, my Old Friends & my Pen,*
> *For all Esqr Wilkes is so Rusty*

> *With fresh showers of Lyes I'll the Nation suprize,*
> *Nay the Devil shall stager to hear it,*
> *The infernals shall say, give H——n but his way,*
> *And he'll out Lye us all never fear it.*

For other satires on the quarrel between Wilkes and Horne see No. 4861, &c. For its political results see Walpole, *Memoirs of George III,* 1845, iv, pp. 308, 325.

$7\frac{1}{2} \times 8\frac{1}{2}$ in. Pl. $12 \times 8\frac{3}{4}$ in.

4864 BRITANNIA CONGRATULATING THE RIGHT HON. BRASS CROSBY, ESQ; LORD-MAYOR, AND MR. ALDERMAN OLIVER, ON THEIR RELEASEMENT FROM THE TOWER, AT THE RISING OF PARLIAMENT, MAY 8, 1771.

Dedicated to the Livery of London, the Constituents of Honiton, and all true Lovers of their King and Country.

Holman Del.   *Bland Sculp.*

Published 15th June 1771.

Engraving, with verses printed beneath. The title (above the design) is also printed. Britannia (l) with her shield and spear, followed by aldermen in civic gowns, advances with outstretched arms to meet Crosby and Oliver, who are coming out of the gate of the Tower (r.) Crosby, wearing his mayoral robe and chain, holds out the *City Charter* Oliver, in his gown, holds out *Magna Charta*. There is a sentry on each side of the gate, and a beefeater stands behind Crosby. Crosby was M.P for Honiton.

For the civic procession from the Tower to the Mansion House, see *Ann Reg*, 1771, 104–5; Walpole's *Letters*, viii 31, 32 It was escorted by members of the Artillery Company, who let off twenty-four pieces of cannon at the Tower Gates For the close of the dispute by the early rising

of Parliament, see *Letters of Hume*, ed Greig, 1932, ii. 241 For the imprisonment of Crosby and Oliver see Nos 4850, 4852, 4854, 4860
Beneath the design are verses (36 ll.). They begin,

Joy to my sons and Patriots!—high in fame.

My colonies shall toast you in their songs,
And hiss the men who glory'd in their wrongs.
Ye Foxes, Onslows, Ellis,¹ Luttrell, hear!
All Honourable Men!—to North most dear!
Doth not some vengeance on those Villains wait,
Who owe their greatness to a ruined State?

and end,

So shall ye live belov'd, lamented die,
Then rise two glorious Stars above the Sky.

Sold by S. Hooper 25, Ludgate-Hill. Price One Shilling
3¾×7¼ in Broadside 15×10½ in

4865 LA DECOUVERTE OU LA FEMME FRANC MAÇON
THE DISCOVERY OR FEMALE FREE-MASON.

Printed for S. Hooper, Nᵒ 25 Ludgate hill 25ᵗʰ June 1771, as the Act Directs.

Mezzotint. Portrait (W L) of the Chevalier d'Eon, as a woman. He is fashionably dressed, and resembles a good-looking woman of fashion, his head turned slightly to the l showing an elongated pearl ear-ring He wears a cap over high-dressed hair, a low-cut bodice with ruffled elbow-sleeves. His r. hand, on his hip, holds a sword With his l hand, which holds a cane attached to his wrist by strings, he points l towards a military coat which is spread over a chair. He wears the order of St Louis and a free-mason's apron Behind him on the r. is a table covered with a cloth hanging in heavy folds; on it is a document, *A Policy 25 P Cᵗ On the Chʳ D'Eon Man, or Woman*, and two uniformly-bound books, *Lettres du Chʳ D'Eon, L'Hist. du Chʳ D'eon* On the wall behind a military hat and sword hang directly over d'Eon's head. On each side of him is a picture: one (l.) represents Mrs Tofts producing rabbits (see Nos 1778–86); the other depicts the bottle-imp, seated in a large funnel which is in the neck of a bottle (see Nos. 3022–7). The implication is that by the changes in his sex d'Eon is carrying on a fraud comparable to the two most notorious hoaxes of the century. Beneath each picture is the bust of a man; that on the l is Wilkes, an associate of d'Eon, who was accused of trafficking in the insurances on his sex (see No. 4870).

Beneath the title is engraved in French and English *Lady Charles, Louis, Cezar, Augustus Alexander, Timotheus, D'Eon of Beaumont—Advocate of the Parliament of Paris, Secretary to the Ambassy at the Court of Russia, Aid de Camp of the Duke de Broglio, Captain of Dragoons, Royal Censor, Secretary of Ambassy under the Duke de Nivernois, Knᵗ of yᵉ Military order of Sᵗ Louis, Minister Plempotentiary to his Britanic Majesty, & accepᵗᵈ free Mason at the Lodge of immortality at the Crown & Anchor in the Strand.*

For d'Eon see Nos. 4308, 4862, 4870–3, 4881, 5108, 5427, 5512.
12¼×9⅞ in.

¹ For Welbore Ellis as Guy Vaux see No. 4384 (1770).

Chaloner Smith (iv, p. 1725) describes a print called

A FRENCH CAPT OF DRAGOONS BROUGHT TO BED OF TWINS, AND THE CAUSE OF THE CHEVALIERS DISAPPEARANCE EXPLAIN'D, ADDRESSED TO THE UNDER WRITERS OF HE, AND SHE POLICIES

Publish'd as the Act directs, by S Hooper No 25 Ludgate Hill 1 Septr 1771.

Mezzotint. D'Eon lying on a bed attended by Wilkes with a bowl of gruel. Parson Horne reads a baptismal service for children held before him by a nurse. Paoli is present in armour, also Mrs. Macaulay with a book under her arm. An officer's uniform hangs on the wall.

$9\frac{3}{8} \times 13\frac{7}{8}$ in.

4866 A PRIVATE ORDINATION. [1 July 1771]

Engraving. From the *London Museum*, iii. 375. The interior of a church. A bishop (l.) stands behind a semicircular balustrade, his l. hand outstretched over the head of a kneeling clergyman in gown and bands. Behind the clergyman stands a demon saying: *Fugiunt pudor, verumque fidesque. In quorum subeunt locum fraudes, dolique, insidiaeque, &c. &c.* The pavement is of black and white squares. In a window of Gothic design are armorial bearings. Below the design is engraved, *It is true, I have suffered the infectious hand of a Bishop to be waved over me: whose imposition, like the sop given to Judas, is only a signal for the Devil to enter. It is true that usually at that touch—fugiunt . . . [ut supra].*

A satire on Parson Horne, whose unfortunate reference to his ordination in a letter to Wilkes, which is here quoted, was repeatedly used against him. See Nos. 4863, 4948, &c.

$6\frac{1}{4} \times 4\frac{3}{8}$ in.

4867 [CARLTON HOUSE JUNTO IN FEAR & TREMBLING.]

[1771]

Original design in pen and wash for the engraving (reversed) with this title in the *Oxford Magazine*, vi. 200, June 1771, No. 4427, and for No. 4874. The Princess Dowager of Wales sits under a canopy of tartan (indicative of the alleged influence of Bute), with a face of dismay. Seven members of her supposed 'Junto' approach her. The words which the figures are supposed to be saying are written, without labels, and seem to indicate the beginning only of the sentences, each terminating in 'and', apparently a symbol for &c. The engraver has however copied them literally.

$3\frac{3}{4} \times 5\frac{7}{8}$ in.

CARLTON HOUSE JUNTO IN FEAR & TREMBLING.

See No. 4427 [1 July 1771]

Engraving. From the *Oxford Magazine*, vi. 200.
The Princess Dowager of Wales and her supposed advisers in dismay.

4868 ACTED FOR THE BENEFIT OF THE MINISTRY.

[1 July 1771]

Design'd & Engrav'd for the Political Register.

Engraving. From the *Political Register*, viii. 319. Parson Horne (l.) in gown and bands and Wilkes (r.) in an alderman's gown, face each other threateningly. Horne holds in his r. hand a rolled document, in the l a book inscribed *Composition of your Debts.* Wilkes has a rolled document in his l hand, in his raised r hand is a book inscribed *Subscriptions to your Pamphlets* They are in the act of hurling books and papers at each other· *Horne's Speeches at Mile End*, thrown by Wilkes, has just missed Horne's head Three documents inscribed *Wilkes's; Adresses to the*, and *Free-holders of Middlesex* are just behind Wilkes's shoulder, having been hurled by Horne. Each has one foot on a volume inscribed *Political Connections.* Wilkes's other foot is on a paper inscribed *Horne's Letter*

For the payment of Wilkes's debts see Stephens, *Memoirs of Horne Tooke*, i. 270 ff. The accusation that Horne was acting in the interest of the ministry was made by Junius in his letter to Grafton of 9 July 1771. For the quarrel between Horne and Wilkes see No 4861, &c.

The plate was also used in the *Royal Magazine*, xxv. 654, Oct. 1771.
$5\frac{3}{4} \times 3\frac{7}{8}$ in.

4869 THE TRUE PORTRAITS OF THE MAJORITY OF THE PAR—L—T OF PANDEMONIUM.

[1 July 1771]

Engraving. From the *Oxford Magazine*, vi 219
At each side of a table are seated figures with the heads and forms of grotesque monsters or animals The bull-faced Sir Fletcher Norton (the Speaker) presides; in one hand is a scourge, in the other a staff to which are attached bags of money and a coronet. He says: *He that dares be Virtuous shall be punish'd, but Ye my Friends shall be rewarded.* Bute and Grafton are hovering above as imps. The table is emerging from flames and is decorated with *The Coffin of Liberty.* Two demons act as clerks at the head of the table in front of the Speaker.

As usual in the series the explanatory text is in the form of a letter to the Editor, showing that the design represents 'the extraordinary appearance the present ministerial wretches will make in the next world. . . . I have erred on the favourable side; for it is impossible for many of them to assume any shape or character that is not less horrible than their own '

The only two who can be identified are North, on the Speaker's r , as a dog wearing a ribbon and star, and Lord Holland as a fox clasping a number of money-bags For the unpopularity of the House of Commons cf. also Nos 4850, 4889, 4893, 4944, 4970
$3\frac{3}{8} \times 5\frac{3}{10}$ in.

4870 NO. 1. THE RAPE OF MISS DEON FROM FRANCE TO ENGLAND.

[? July 1771]

Engraving No 1 of a series by the same artist,[1] see Nos. 4871–3. D'Eon

[1] Calabi attributes this plate to Bartolozzi, he describes another impression, with the date July 23, 1771, the words engraved beneath being an English version of the description on the r margin of this print: *Time, always noted for a Babbler of Secrets* . . . . *Bartolozzi*, 1928, No. 2229.

(r) dressed as a man and wearing jack boots, astride on the back of Time holding his scythe and hour-glass, flies across the Channel towards four satyrs who hold out a British flag to receive him   The figures have numbers which refer to notes engraved beneath the print. 1, a nude satyr holding aloft the cap of liberty, 2, a nude satyr with legal wig and bands, 4, a satyr wearing a short coat; and 5, a satyr wearing a woman's low-cut bodice. No. 3, in back view, is a wine-merchant with wine bottles slung round his shoulders, he watches d'Eon through a telescope.

The background is a view of the Channel, with two vessels, and Calais (r.) in the distance.

Beneath the design is engraved:

The Wind S W. from Mr Dessin at the English Hotel at Calais
No 1 Miss D'n Arriving at the Standard of Liberty the Madness of the Time.
No. 2. F——e at the Bloodsucker's publick office
No. 3 L——m at the Magazine of Sophisticated Wine.
No. 4 Ll——d's Coffee House or office of Policies.
No. 5. Mother Cole's near the Lock-Hospital

A printed description is on the r. margin of the print:

Enlevement de Mlle Deon. Le Tems dont le pouvoir devoile les secrets les plus cachès, s'etant mis en tête d'Eclaircir si Mr Deon est chevalier ou chevaliere rencontre ce heros problematique sous le portique de L'hôtel D'Angleterre á Calais; le vieillard le saisit, & a la faveur d'un coup de vent S.E. il transporte son nouveau Ganimede sur les Rives d'albion, on voit le groupe dans les airs se presser d'arriver, l'ún [sic] portant l'autre, tandis que les amis du beau cavalier se preparent a le recevoir au rivage sur une converture, L'homme au telescope est un fidel marchand de vin composé en Angleterre, le satire a sa gauche est un honete Procureur, Enemi des affaires embrouilléés; le faune qui tient le baton surmonté d'un bonnet,, signifie la liberté, et son in lustre [sic] Defenceur Wilks; les deux femelles a pieds de biche, sont renomées pour pretandre que m^{lle}. Deon ne l'ést point.

During 1771 the sex of d'Eon was the subject of a number of bets and gambling insurances. Wilkes, who was an associate of d'Eon, was accused of trafficking in these policies Cf. *Controversial Letters of Wilkes, Horne, &c.*, 1771, p. 72 See Nos. 4865, 4871, 4881. D'Eon was suspected of encouraging the bets in order to share in the spoil, and his mysterious disappearances heightened the suspicion. The question of d'Eon's sex as it affected these bets was decided in 1777, see No. 5427 See also No 4308 (1769)

$7\frac{3}{10} \times 10\frac{1}{2}$ in.

4871 NO 2 A DEPUTATION FROM JONATHAN'S AND THE FREE-MASONS

Pub^d as the Act directs July 17, 1771.

Etching. No. 2 of a series, see No. 4870, &c D'Eon, dressed half as a woman, half as a man, reclines on a couch (r.), he turns to speak to the wine-merchant (see No 4873) who leans on the head of the couch A small satyr or demon holds a cord which appears to be attached to D'Eon's head. The deputation stand round the foot of the couch: one man holds out a

Petition from the Bulls & Bears in Change Alley. Another wears the insignia of a Free Mason, behind him the head of Wilkes is partly visible.

Two satyrs advance from the l. holding a chair supported on poles. It has arm- and leg-rests and appears to be intended for operations or medical examinations. On the ground (l) is a pile of books, one inscribed *On the use of the Night Chair invented by D* *A. after twenty years study* A paper beside it is inscribed, *Vinegar of Saturn by D* *A. at the sign of the two Parrots*.

Behind D'Eon's couch is a chest of drawers on which stands a bust of Wilkes (cf. No. 4865). A heavy curtain drapes the r. side of the design.

Beneath the title is engraved,

Miss Epicœne D'Eon is discover'd in close consultation with its Wine Merchant & Privy Counsellor. The Free-Masons beg the Secret of its Sex may be kept inviolable; the Committee of Under-writers on the other hand Petition for the Discovery, & propose that Mons: A shall explore the sexual Signature manually after the manner used on the election of a new Pope, for which purpose the Doctor is seen introducing his new invented Night Chair.

Another satire on the gambling insurances on the sex of d'Eon, see No. 4870, &c. For d'Eon as a Free Mason see No. 4865.

$7\frac{3}{16} \times 10\frac{1}{8}$ in.

4872 NO 3. THE NUPTIALS OF MISS EPICÆNE D'EON.

Pub^d *as the Act directs July 17: 1771.*

Etching. No 3 of a series, see No 4870, &c D'Eon (r) dressed as a woman, is led by the hand by Wilkes towards an altar (l.), behind which stands a Jewish priest with two attendants. Wilkes holds the cap of liberty on a staff in his r. hand. Don Quixote, in armour, holds out his arms to prevent their approach to the altar. Behind d'Eon walks the wine-merchant holding aloft a trophy consisting of d'Eon's hat, sword, order of St Louis, jack boots, and (?) breast-plate. He turns round to look with anxiety at Sancho Panza who is threatening with his fists a nude satyr in clerical wig and bands who carries an infant in his arms The temple is indicated by large pillars (l) and a heavily-draped curtain Beneath the title is engraved,

The sex of Miss Epicœne being incontestibly determined by the Birth of a Male Child without the intervention of a husband, she is elected Queen of the Amazons, & chuses for her Royal Consort the Guardian & Protector of Liberty; but as they are proceeding to celebrate the Nuptial Rites in the Temple of the Amazons, Don Quixotte appears, defies the future husband to single combat, disputes his Right to her Person & declares that Miss Epicœne is a Virgin, though Sancho Panzais [sic] all the time in dispute with F—— & the trusty Wine Merchant (now her Amazonian Majesty's Standard-bearer) about the honour of being Foster-father to the Young Prince her Son.

'When the first policy was opened concerning D'Eons gender it was said with some mirth that the Chevalier was with child by Wilkes. Since the discovery of the fraud it is now said in sober sadness that Mr Wilkes has miscarried by M^{rs} D'Eon.' *Midx Journal* [1]

$7\frac{5}{8} \times 10\frac{1}{2}$ in. See No. 4873, a sequel.

---

[1] Transcript (n.d) by Mr. Hawkins.

4873 DON QUIXOTE'S PROCESSION TO THE INSTALLATION
JULY 25th, 1771.

Publish'd according to act of Parliament, 25 July, 1771.

Etching. One of a series relating to d'Eon, probably No 4, see No.
4870, &c., and a sequel to No. 4872. A procession, l. to r., conducting
d'Eon dressed as a woman in a two-wheeled chair through the window of
which his head appears 'The chair is drawn by the wine-merchant, his
bottles slung round his shoulders, and is pushed behind by a satyr on
whose back is a large cylindrical package. Behind the chair and on the
extreme l of the design, walks Don Quixote, in triumph, carrying his
sword and spear. Beside the chair walks Sancho Panza blowing a trumpet
and carrying on his head a cradle in which sits an infant, the order of St.
Louis round its neck. On the top of the cradle are d'Eon's hat, sword, and
breast-plate. In front of the procession (r.) march two satyrs. The foremost blows pan-pipes, and flourishes a knotted whip; to his back are slung
a pair of kettle-drums; he wears the jack boots of a French postilion
Behind him, the other satyr is performing, with a flourish, on the kettle-
drums; he wears a cap, a long gown, and a pair of legal bands.

The (printed) title continues ·

*The Champion of liberty, is worsted by the Knight La Mancha, who with the
Knights of St George were to Assemble at Windsor, resolves there to publish
the peerless Beauty and rare Virtue of Miss D'Eon, Queen of Amazons,
and dare to single Combat any Knight who should be hardy enough to gainsay
it His Entry was Marshal'd in the following Manner, first came her Majesty's
Sage of the Law beating kettle Drums, types of his Profession, next followed
the Queen drawn by her Wine-Merchant in a Vehicle known at Paris by the
Name of Brouette,[1] by the side Marched Sancho bearing the Infant Prince
in his Cradle, and last advanced the renowned & valourous Don Quixote.*

On 25 July there was an installation of Knights of St George at Windsor
at which the king's three eldest sons (among others) were installed
Ann. Reg. 1771, 216–18

$7\frac{5}{8} \times 10$ in

4874 A CONFAB ON THE EVENT OF A LATE ELECTION.

[*c.* July 1771]

Engraving. A copy of No 4427, *Carlton House Junto in fear and trembling*,
differing in several details, see No 4867 The Princess and her supposed
'Junto' are in dismay at the election of Wilkes as sheriff at midsummer 1771
in spite of the efforts of the king The Princess says *To have all power in
ye one hand, & all profit in ye other, & yet not to be obeyed, is Oh, Grief
of Griefs* North says: *I depended on Horne & the Lottery.* From his pocket
hangs a paper, *To B. Smith Liveryman* The next man says *Half a dozen
would not have been Sufficient.* Lord Holland (l.) says· *Damn ye Blockheads,
they know not their own Interest,* and is answered by the man next him:
They have not half your Wisdom The other three (r.) say: *I would rather
engage with ye whole House of l——s* [Lords]; *I cannot call it Virtue, but
a stubborn Brutality, to refuse such offers; Something must be done, lest they
should be another Mordecai, & gall ye pride of a ——*
The king had written to North hoping that no pains would be spared to

---

[1] The Paris equivalent of a Sedan chair. See No. 4932

secure the election of Plumbe and Kirkman, the two senior aldermen, next in succession for the office. *Corr. of George III*, ed. Fortescue, II. 255–7. Robinson, Secretary to the Treasury, wrote to Benjamin Smith urging him to 'push the poll' against Wilkes; the letter was taken by mistake to another Smith (Wilkite) who published it with great effect, and 'set the mob a flame'. Sharpe, *London and the Kingdom*, III. 121, *Letters of Hume*, ed. G. B. Hill, 212 Wilkes and Bull were elected by a large majority, the poll being declared on 3 July, see No. 4937 For the allusion to Horne, see No. 4861, &c For 'the lottery', see an attack on North, 23 Apr 1771, for using lottery tickets as bribes, *Parl. Hist* xvii. 173–4. The allusion to the House of Lords is to the quarrel between the two Houses in December 1770, see Walpole, *Memoirs of the Reign of George III*, 1845, IV. 218 f., *Parl. Hist.* xvi 814 ff Accusations against the Princess of Wales were revived by Alderman Townsend's speech on 25 March 1771, on 'the ambitious views of one aspiring woman . . . well known to direct the operations of our despicable Ministers'. Ibid xvii 135 See No 4852 For the election see No. 4937.

4875 L^D S——K AND HIS SECRETARY LEARNING FRENCH.

[1 Aug. 1771]

Engraving. From the *Oxford Magazine*, vii. 12. Suffolk seated at a small round table with an open book scratches his head saying *D—n the French and the Language too.* His instructor (r.) replies: *Oh Mondieu my Lor you no Improve at all . .* A man (l.) with the *Secretar[y's] Book* under his arm stands behind Suffolk's chair saying. *If I have a Secretary's Salary I am satisfied* On the table is a large book, *Fre[nch] Dict[ionary]*.

Suffolk was appointed Secretary of State for the Northern Department 12 June, 1771, he had previously been Lord Privy Seal. For his ignorance of French see *Corr. of George III*, ed Fortescue, II 205, Walpole's *Reign of George III*, 1894, IV 173, 217; *The Town and Country Magazine*, III 345–8. See also Nos 4652 (1772), 4876, 4908.

$3\frac{8}{8} \times 5\frac{7}{8}$ in.

4876 THE DISTREST EARL OF THE SOUTHERN FOLK PRATING FRENCH TO HIS FRENCH SERVANTS IS BY THEM MIS-UNDERSTOOD.

[1 Aug. 1771]

Engraving. From *Every Man's Magazine*, I 29 Probably an improved and corrected version of No 4876 A. Lord Suffolk sits in a high-backed chair, repelling with a gesture of despair the ministrations of his French servants He says: *Zounds! how I am Plagued with these Blockheads. I can speak French well enough, but they will not understand me.* His l elbow rests on a table on which are writing materials and documents; one, a letter signed *S——k*, falls to the ground. At his feet is a book, *The Grammar* Behind him (r.) stands a valet-de-chambre playing the violin and singing,

> *Ah! Mon Cœur-plein d'Amour*
> *Soupire pour un bon-Place a Cour fal al*

A cook, black all over but wearing a bag-wig, enters from the r. with a long spit on which are two birds. Behind him is a servant with a wine bottle in one hand, he holds out to Suffolk a glass of wine on a salver A valet or hairdresser approaches Suffolk from the l holding out in one hand a phial of medicine, in the other a chamber pot; he says· *Oh begar, my Lor parle Anglois & me entendez vous beacoup [sic] mieux*; a comb is stuck in his hair, which hangs loose down his back and is decorated with curl papers. Behind him enters a groom wearing top-boots and carrying a saddle on his shoulders. He is saying. *begar de Spanish Cow Speak better Franch, me no understand him.* Behind him, and on the extreme l , a maidservant says: *What! will he learn French before he can Speak plain English!*

In the foreground (l) an ape sits on the floor writing on a paper inscribed *The Modern History* A large cauldron and two pans lie on the ground, apparently the result of orders which have been misunderstood. See No 4875, &c

$3\frac{1}{4} \times 5\frac{7}{8}$ in.

4876A THE DISTREST EARL OF THE SOUTHERN FOLK, PRATING FRENCH TO HIS FRENCH SERVANTS, IS BY THEM MISUNDERSTOOD

Engraving Another version, reversed, of No 4876 The maidservant and the pots and pans are omitted. The words which the ape has written are turned so that they face the spectator not the writer. The words spoken are different: Suffolk says: *They have not the least Idea, of the Paris Idion [sic]—oh! mon Dieu!* The violin-player says: *Ah! Mon Cœur-plein d'Amour, pour un bon Place a Cour* The hairdresser says: *Ici, Je vous entends.* The groom says: *Begar de Spanish Cow is more intelligable [sic].* The book on the ground is *The Grammer.*

$3\frac{1}{4} \times 5\frac{7}{8}$ in.

4877 VICE TRIUMPHANT OVER VIRTUE OR BRITANNIA HARD RODE.   [1 Aug. 1771]

Engraving From the *Oxford Magazine*, vii 29. Britannia crawls on hands and knees over her shield. Her broken spear is on the ground The Princess of Wales sits on her back holding reins and a whip, and supported by Bute. Lord Mansfield and the duke of Grafton (l) pull her along by a hook through the nose. Lord North standing behind them, says. *Pull her right to North* Lord Sandwich (Jemmy Twitcher) aims a blow at her with his cricket bat, saying: *Hook her fast & I'll give her a twitcher.*[1] Hercules (r.) exclaims: *Oh Britannia, thou hast Cast all Virtue aside or Virtue should now assist you* Hibernia (r) reclines upon her harp, saying. *They have Rob'ed me of every thing but my Harp and are now tearing my Poor Sister to pieces.* In the background (r.) a volcano is in violent eruption.

The explanatory text begins 'Alas! poor Britannia!—To what a shocking situation art thou now reduced! Thy s——n [sovereign] is ridiculed, thy M——rs [Ministers] deservedly despised, detested and abominated! Thy people murmur and complain. Thy constitution is almost destroyed. Thou who was wont to be the envy of all Europe are now become the laughing-stock of the whole world.' It ends with an appeal for the removal of evil counsellors.

One of many satires on the supposed influence of Bute, Mansfield, and the Princess of Wales. See Nos. 4385, 4874, 4885, &c

Grafton had declined responsibility by refusing a seat in the cabinet on

[1] See No. 4859 n.

his appointment as Lord Privy Seal, 12 June 1771, and had little influence.
Autobiography, ed Anson 1898, pp. xxxv, 264 Cf No 4859
$3\frac{7}{8} \times 6\frac{3}{8}$ in.

4878 THE PAGEANT. [1 Aug. 1771]

Design'd & Engrav'd for the London Museum.

Engraving *London Museum*, iv. 1 George III driving (r. to l.) in an
ornate glass coach; facing him sits a courtier or minister wearing a ribbon.
At the back of the coach in place of a footman sits a small demon holding
over his shoulder a curiously shaped trident with barbed prongs which
may represent one of the recently invented electrical appliances such as
were used by Dr. Graham. A crowd of pedestrians run beside the coach,
they are addressed by one of their number, who says: *You Blackguards,
why don't you halloo' Don't you know you are to be paid for it*

A line of trees and a curiously-drawn view of Westminster Abbey in the
background indicate that the scene is the Mall

A satire on the king's unpopularity, see also Nos. 4373, 4374
$4\frac{5}{16} \times 6\frac{5}{8}$ in.   B.M.L., P.P. 5435 c.

4879 THE VICAR PURIFI'D BY THE SHADOW OF JUNIUS.

Pub^d accord^g to Act of Parl^t Augt 7th. 1771 by M. Darly 39 Strand

Engraving. Parson Horne (l.) starts in terror at the silhouette of a man (r)
whose face is blank who appears from clouds and threatens him with a
fulmen formed of a pen and darts of lightning Horne (dressed as a layman) has overturned his chair and table; his pens, ink, paper, and sand
are on the floor. The Devil escapes from the window (l).

Horne, having quarrelled with Wilkes, see No 4861, &c., supported the
ministerial candidates at the Sheriff's election, 24 June, see No. 4874. Junius
thereupon attacked Horne in his *Letter to the Duke of Grafton* (9 July) ironically recommending him for preferment and accusing him of 'the solitary
vindictive malice of a monk'. Horne replied vigorously (13 July) and
evoked a letter from Junius to himself (24 July), sent to him through the
printer of the *Public Advertiser*, ending, 'this letter you see is not intended
for the public, but if you think it will do you any good you are at liberty
to publish it'. Horne had it printed and retorted in a *Letter to Junus*
(31 July). Another letter from Junius (15 Aug.) and one from Horne
(17 Aug) closed the controversy, in which Horne held his own *Letters of
Junius*, ed C W. Everett, 1927, 217 ff.; A. Stephens, *Memoirs of Horne
Tooke*, 1813, 1. 352 ff.
$7\frac{3}{8} \times 5\frac{1}{2}$ in.

4880 WATKIN LEWES ESQ^R PRESENTING THE ADDRESSES FROM THE COUNTIES OF PEMBROKE, CARMARTHEN, & CARDIGAN, TO THE LORD MAYOR, ALDERMAN WILKES, & ALDERMAN OLIVER IN THE TOWER [1 Sept. 1771]

Engraving. From the *Oxford Magazine*, vii 70. In a room with stone walls
and barred window Lewes (r) presents the *Cardigan* Address to the Lord
Mayor, Oliver reads that of *Carmarthen*, Wilkes holds that of *Pembroke*,

CATALOGUE OF POLITICAL AND PERSONAL SATIRES

the place-names being engraved on the respective documents. The three prisoners wear furred civic gowns.

Beneath the design is engraved

Thus Ancient Britons, gen'rous, bold & free,
Untaught at Court to bend the supple Knee,
Corruption's Shrine with honest Pride disdain
And only bow to Freedom's Patriot Train.

During April the Lord Mayor received addresses from the three counties named and from the towns of Newcastle, Stratford, and Honiton, besides the freedom of the city of Worcester and of the town of Bedford. *Ann. Reg*, 1771, 100. Wilkes of course was not in the Tower; he had refused to obey the summons of the House of Commons and they had been afraid to enforce it. Lewes, a Welshman, a City attorney and prominent City Whig, became an Alderman in 1772, and was knighted in Feb. 1773, when sheriff Beaven, *Aldermen of the City of London*, 1913, ii 135, 200, &c. For the imprisonment of Crosby and Oliver see No. 4853, &c

$5\frac{7}{16} \times 4\frac{1}{16}$ in.

4881 CHEVALIER D—E—N [D'EON] RETURND OR THE STOCK-BROKERS OUTWITTED. [1 Sept. 1771]

Etching. From the *Oxford Magazine*, vii 56 Scene in a stockbroker's office, or perhaps in Jonathan's or Lloyd's, a room with a small writing-desk (r) and on the wall a *Table of Interest*. D'Eon, dressed as a man, enters from the l. and is greeted by a stockbroker who takes his l. hand and points with his r. to other brokers on the r. who watch the entry, some with dismay, others with pleasure. D'Eon says: *Well Broker, how have you Manag'd our Scheme* The broker answers· *Glad to see you return'd Chevalier, we have took the Knowing ones in Swingingly* One broker says to another: *Oh Ch——st I've lost my all;* the other answers: *Let us Waddle off Quietly* (a defaulter on the Stock Exchange was then called a lame-duck). A bearded Jew stooping over the desk with a pen in his hand, says: *Ay and 'tis time for me to be going* Two men standing behind him say: *I told you he would come back,* and *Ha! ha! ha! let them laugh that wins say I*

Another satire on the gambling policies taken out on D'Eon's sex, in which he was suspected of trafficking; his disappearances added to the mystery and suspicion which surrounded him In May 1771 a caveat was entered at Doctors' Commons against his goods, as he had been advertised and no account could be had of him *Gent Mag*, 1771, 236. A comprehensive appeal to the Lord Mayor (in the *Oxford Magazine*, June 1771, vi 193 ff) to put down abuses in his jurisdiction attacks gambling insurances and expecially 'the late scandalous transaction of the policies on D'Eon's sex', '*He* or *she* D'Eon absconds . . and the premiums are irretrievably lost . .' See Nos 4862, 4865, 4870-3

$3\frac{7}{16} \times 5\frac{7}{8}$ in

4882 LORD CHIEF JUSTICE MANSFIELD [1 Sept. 1771]

Design'd & Engrav'd for the Political Register.

Engraving From the *Political Register*, ix 57 Bust portrait (not caricatured) in an oval frame of Mansfield in wig and gown in profile to the l.

26

A smaller version of this, in a circle, appears in No 4439 (1770). It illustrates an article on *Thoughts, Reflections, and Considerations, on the abject Condition of the Great, especially Courtiers, and the folly of those, who seek Connections with them* Cf No 4884 For satires on Mansfield see No. 4440, &c. and index

Oval, $3\frac{5}{8} \times 3\frac{1}{8}$ in.

4883 FARMER G——E, STUDYING THE WIND & WEATHER.

[1 Oct 1771]

Etching. From the *Oxford Magazine*, vii. 88. The king in profile to the r. looks from a window (r) through a reversed telescope at a weather-cock. He wears a night-cap and a dressing-gown of chequered (or tartan) material intended to indicate Scottish influence A monkey (r) on a chair beside him imitates him A cat plays with a book lying open on the floor inscribed *The Art of Government by Mechanick Rules*. A dog sits on a torn document *To . . . Remonstrances* Five children are playing with a rocking-horse, which the eldest boy, the Prince of Wales, is riding. On the wall is a W. L. portrait of Bute, his r. hand resting on a table on which is a crown, implying that he is the actual ruler of the country.

Like others of the series this print illustrates a supposed letter to the editor: 'T. S' complains that 'a certain young farmer' neglects his farm and his flock 'while he is observing the fickleness of the wind or making a curious button, and a twopenny snuff-box', cf. Nos. 4380, 4417 (1771), 5573, and p 494. For the king's attitude to Remonstrances presented by the City see Nos. 4386, 4387 Reproduced, M. D George, *England in Transition*, 1931, p. 114.

$6\frac{3}{8} \times 4\frac{1}{8}$ in.

4884 CAMDEN
CHATHAM

[1 Oct 1771]

Design'd & Engrav'd for the Political Register.

Engraving From the *Political Register*, ix 105 Two bust portraits in ovals on one plate This faces an article on 'The Patriot's Vision' It is intended to contrast with No 4882. For Camden see Nos 4144, 4151.

Ovals, $2\frac{1}{4} \times 2$ in.

THE BLIND JUSTICE, & THE SECRETARIES ONE EYE & NO HEAD EXAMINING THE OLD WOMAN AND LITTLE GIRL, ABOUT THE FIREING PORTSMOUTH DOCK-YARD.

See No. 4405 [1 Oct. 1771]

Engraving From the *Oxford Magazine*, vii 96 A satire on the examination of suspects accused of firing Portsmouth Dock-yard on 27 July, 1770. These examinations took place in the summer and autumn of 1771, see *Cal. H. O Papers, 1770-1772*, pp. lv, 312-20.

4885 THE EXCURSION TO CAIN WOOD.

[1 Nov 1771]

Engraving. From the *Oxford Magazine*, vii. 128 Mansfield and the Princess of Wales fly through the air r to l astride a broom-stick towards Caen Wood or Ken Wood (Mansfield's country house). This is indicated by a thick grove of trees on the top of which Bute and Sir Fletcher Norton wait their arrival attended by a fiddling demon. Bute beckons to them; Mansfield says. *Liberty is to me a Joke but our Friends Madam at C——n Wood will advise us what to do.* The Princess sits behind him saying: *My Lord is my sure Councellour, what he dictates shall be a Law.* A demon as a running footman carries a document inscribed· *A Plan for turning Guildhall into a stable for the K——s Horses*; tied to his legs are papers, *Plan for a Coalition* and *Proceedings at Guildhall* A Scottish demon (r.) urges on the broom-stick with a pair of bellows In the corner (r) Wilkes says to the Lord Mayor. *These birds of Ill-omen forbode no good to Liberty.* The Mayor replies: *We'll be firm to the last and fear them not!* Only their heads and shoulders appear above the lower margin. Behind their heads London is in flames, indicating the supposed designs of the Court on the liberties of the City

One of many satires on the supposed influence of Bute, the Princess Dowager of Wales, and Mansfield. See No 4877, &c.

$6\frac{3}{8} \times 4\frac{1}{8}$ in

4886 N° XXX. Vol. III. THE CITY RACE. [1 Nov. 1771]

Engraving. From the *Town and Country Magazine*, iii 529 Illustration to 'The City Race; or, a peripatetic Dialogue amongst the late Candidates for the Mayoralty, and the Sheriffs'. The five candidates race from r. to l. across an open space towards their goal, the Mansion House, part of the façade of which is in the background The foremost is supported on crutches, inscribed *Treasury*, he is William Nash elected through the support of the Ministry. He and the next three, Sawbridge, Townsend, and Hallifax are hurrying with outstretched arms The last walks with folded arms, he is Sir Henry Bankes who was at the bottom of the poll with 36 votes. A sixth alderman has fallen to the ground, and lies face downwards, he is Brass Crosby the late Lord Mayor. Two dogs fight in the foreground (l), one with his collar inscribed *Court* hast he other by the throat In the background (r) a mob is being harangued by Parson Horne (see No. 4861, &c.), who leans from an open window. The two sheriffs, Wilkes and Bull, are near with their staves Bull attempts to restrain the mob; Wilkes turns his back on the disturbance holding the cap of liberty on his staff

The mayoral election, polling for which lasted from 28 Sept. to 3 Oct., was a victory for the Court, achieved in spite of an impassioned address from *Junius* to the Livery, urging them to elect Crosby and Sawbridge. Sharpe, *London and the Kingdom*, iii. 127–8; Walpole, *Memoirs of the Reign of George III*, 1894, iv. 229–30; Beaven, *Aldermen of London*, ii, p. xxvi. Cf. No. 4887.

$3\frac{3}{4} \times 6\frac{1}{2}$ in.

4887 PATRIOTICK METEORS [1 Nov. 1771]

Engraving. From the *London Magazine*, xl 520 Three heads, their necks decorated by civic chains, are being drawn swiftly through the air into the gaping jaws of a hippopotamus (l) inscribed *The Gulf of Oblivion.* The foremost is Wilkes, after him comes Brass Crosby, the outgoing Lord Mayor, and last a bull, representing Frederick Bull, who had recently been elected sheriff with Wilkes. On the ground is a furred livery gown on which rest the city arms and two sheriff's staves. Beneath the design is engraved *Exitus acta probat*.

One of the few anti-Wilkite satires, cf No 5245; it seems to represent correctly the actual state of opinion,[1] which had been much influenced by the quarrel of Wilkes with Parson Horne, Sawbridge, Townsend, and Oliver. See Walpole, *Memoirs of the Reign of George III*, 1894, iv 200, 202. Cf No. 4886 Wilkes's popularity with the mob continued, though Walpole wrote 15 Dec. 1771, *Letters*, viii. 122, 'Wilkes is almost as dead as Sacheverell, though sheriff' Nevertheless he was voted a cup by the Common Council, Jan. 1772, see No. 5237.

This plate was used in the *Hibernian Magazine*, i. 577 [1 Jan. 1772].
$4\frac{3}{4} \times 7$ in. (pl).

4888 THE GREAT LUMINARY OF THE LAW.   [1 Dec 1771]

Etching. From the *Political Register*, ix 233. The head of Bathurst, full-face, in a judge's wig, transfixed on the very elongated wick which projects from a candle in a candlestick. Beneath is engraved a parody of Pope's epigram on Newton:

> *England & England's Laws lay hid in Night,*
> *Bute said let Bathurst be — and all was Light*

Henry Bathurst was made Lord Chancellor and Baron Apsley on 23 Jan 1771, and is generally agreed to have been the least efficient Lord Chancellor of the eighteenth century.
$6\frac{3}{4} \times 4\frac{1}{2}$ in. (pl.)

4889 ROCKINGHAM   [1 Dec. 1771]
           TEMPLE

Design'd & Engrav'd for the Political Register.

Engraving. From the *Political Register*, ix. 169 Two bust portraits in ovals on one plate (the print has been cut into two).

This faces an article called 'Idea of a well-policed State', in which the House of Lords is to be 'the bust and trunk' of the constitution of the British Commonwealth, and is 'to direct the operations of liberty . . .' Indicative of the unpopularity of the House of Commons, cf. Nos. 4850, 4869, 4893, 4970.
Ovals, $2\frac{1}{4} \times 1\frac{15}{16}$ in

4890 [MARRIAGE OF THE DUKE OF CUMBERLAND.]

                                                    [1 Dec. 1771]

Woodcut From the *Town and Country Magazine*, iii. 581. Three figures: in the centre Colonel Luttrell stands threatening the Duke of Cumberland (l.) with a whip, while he points with his l. hand to a lady (r.) seated primly in profile to the l, her r. hand raised Luttrell says. *The Honour of my*

---

[1] At this time there was a lull in political violence: cf Burke, 31 July, 1771 'As to news we have little. After a noted fermentation in the nation, as remarkable a deadness and vapidity has succeeded it.' *Corr.* i. 256. Cf. *Ann. Reg.*, 1772. 1. 82.

Family; Cumberland answers with a propitiatory gesture: *I'll marry her indeed.* The lady, Mrs Horton, says: *I shall be a Royal Duchess*

The woodcut illustrates 'A Trio; or a Dialogue amongst three very respectable Personages, a P——e [Prince] without Brains, a Member without Suffrages, and a Duchess without a Title' Cumberland's illiterate love-letters had been satirized in Nos. 4400, 4401, 4402; on his affair with Lady Grosvenor, see No 4845. For Luttrell, notorious as Wilkes's opponent at the Middlesex election, see No 4284, &c

The marriage between the Duke and Anne Luttrell, daughter of Lord Irnham and widow of Christopher Horton, took place on 2 Oct. 1771. See Walpole, *Memoirs of the Reign of George III*, 1894, iv. 236 ff.

$3\frac{1}{2} \times 4\frac{3}{8}$ in.

4891 A CITIZEN OF THE WORLD SEARCHING FOR A WISE PRINCE.

Engraving Frontispiece to *The New Foundling Hospital for Wit*, Part IV, 1771. A blindfolded man walking in an empty street carrying a lantern He wears a long furred civic gown On a sign-board projecting from the corner of an adjacent house is a bust portrait of the Princess Dowager of Wales in profile to the r., inscribed *O thou Head of the Wrong Heads!* From the end of the bar supporting the board hangs a jack-boot, the emblem of Bute, in allusion to the supposed liaison between Bute and the Princess, see No 3848 (1762), &c From the toe of the boot hangs a bunch of grapes, the sign of wine for sale. On a distant house is a sign-board on which is a royal crown Beneath the design is engraved,

> *Alack, there lies more Peril in thine Eye,*
> *Than twenty of their Swords.*
> > *Shakespeare*

For the supposed influence of the Princess Dowager of Wales, see Nos. 4427, 4867, 4874, 4885.

$4\frac{9}{16} \times 2\frac{3}{4}$ in.   B. M. L. 992. a. 4

4892 THE YOUNG POLITICIAN   [? 1771]

Publish'd accorg to Act by H. Bryer London

Engraving. A young man, slim and elegant, with the head and tail of a fox seated between two hairdressers. He tears fragments from *Magna Charta* to be used as curl-papers. He is draped in a sheet, below which appear flowered breeches. A valet with a *Last dying Speech* hanging from his pocket holds a mirror. On a chair are a flowered coat and sword with a paper *Inquiries into the late Riots* (cf. No. 4850). On the floor are *A petition to the Commission[ers] of the Customs*, a book entitled *A New Essay on Politick By C — F — Esqr* and a bag of *Poudre à la Maréchale* On a table are jars inscribed *Bergamot, essence, rouge.* A bust [?Wilkes] is on a pedestal inscribed *Cato bewailing the loss of Liberty.* On brackets on the wall are statuettes of Venus and the three Graces and a clock whose hands indicate that the time is 12.30 (or 6)

For other satires of Fox as *petit-maître* and enemy of liberty see Nos 4810 (1773) and 4811 (1771)

$8\frac{1}{2} \times 7\frac{3}{8}$ in

4893 LORD CHIEF JUSTICE HOLT, THREATENING TO COM-
MIT THE SPEAKER &C. OF THE HOUSE OF COMMONS

[?1771][1]

Engraving. Holt (l.) sits above and between two other judges in Westminster Hall He addresses a man in the Speaker's robes (r.) who covers
his face with his hand and walks away abashed. A crowd stands round
This illustrates a mythical story current in the eighteenth century that
during the famous case of Ashby v. White, 1701, in which Holt upheld
the rights of voters against the corrupt assertion of privilege by the Commons, the Speaker in full state with a train of attendants entered the Court
and threatened to commit the judge. On this Holt ordered him to begone
or he would commit him, had he all the House of Commons in his belly
The application to the hated Speaker, Fletcher Norton, who had signed
the warrant for the arrest of the Lord Mayor and Oliver (see No 4853, &c.)
was obvious   See Junius's *Letter* of 22 Apr. 1771 on parliamentary
privilege   For the unpopularity of the House of Commons cf. Nos 4850,
4860, 4869, 4889, 4970.

$5\frac{5}{8} \times 3\frac{7}{16}$ in

4894 THE CHILD; OR A LEGACY FOR THE HOUSE OF
COMMONS.   [n d. 1771]

Etching   From the stage of a theatre, two figures address the audience:
Charles Fox (l.) with a fox's head, holds under his l. arm a tray in which
are two doll-like infants in swaddling bands; in his r. hand is a paper
inscribed, *Norton & Fox Sponsors.* He is saying· *Discovered by the Secret
Committee*   In the centre is another man with a wide open mouth, whose
head is perhaps intended for that of a dolphin. He holds a paper inscribed
The Child of the People. On the r. of the stage is part of a fountain supported by a satyr   On each side of the stage are two tiers of boxes; in the
lower box on the r. Punch is talking to a lady

On 10 April 1771 an infant was found near the House of Commons, by
a fruit woman, who collected money for its maintenance from members
of the House. It was reported (*Oxford Magazine*, 1771, p 157) that the
child was to be baptized Fletcher Norton after the Speaker, and that he
and Charles Fox were to be god-parents. An interesting indication of the
impression already made by Fox, cf. No. 4892.

$3\frac{7}{8} \times 7\frac{7}{8}$ in. (pl).

4895–4902

A series of engravings by Grignion after Wale of historical inci-
dents; they illustrate articles in the *Oxford Magazine*, applying
the subject of the print to the politics of the day, see also Nos.
4445–55 (1770).

4895 CONFERENCE BETWEEN THE EARL OF PORTLAND AND
MARSHALL BOUFLERS   [1 Feb 1771]

S. Wale del   *C. Grignion sculp*

Engraving. From the *Oxford Magazine*, vi 31. Two officers on horseback

[1] This should be dated 1 May 1774, it is from the *Sentimental Magazine*, ii. 148

conferring; tents and horsemen in the distance. The design is in an oval with a frame composed of oakleaves and architectural ornament

A representation of the conference before the Peace of Ryswick (1697). Bentinck is compared with his descendant the 3rd duke of Portland (1738–1809), especially in connexion with the attempt to dispossess the Duke of Inglewood Forest, giving rise to the Act to limit the principle of *Nullum Tempus occurrit Regi*, see No. 4851 Junius attacked Lowther for this in his Letter to the Duke of Grafton, 22 June 1771.

$3\frac{7}{8} \times 4\frac{1}{4}$ in. (pl.).

4896 SCOTCH PRIDE HUMBLED OR THE REBELLION CRUSHED MDCCXLV. [1 Mar. 1771]

S. Wale del   *C. Grignion sculp.*

Engraving From the *Oxford Magazine*, vi 70 Three highlanders (l) in tartan, their weapons on the ground, kneel bonnet in hand before three mounted English officers (r); a standing soldier directs their submission. In the distance are English soldiers and a castle (l) The design is surrounded by a frame headed by a trophy composed of a crown, laurel wreath, and weapons.

The plate illustrates an article contrasting the present Duke of Cumberland, who is attacked for his affair with Lady Grosvenor (see Nos 4440, 4441, 4844), and the previous holder of the title Scotland and the Scots are also attacked.

$4\frac{1}{8} \times 4\frac{3}{8}$ in (pl)

4897 THE GIFT OF NEPTUNE, OR BRITAINS BULWARK. [1 Apr. 1771]

S. Wale del.   *C. Grignion sculp.*

Engraving From the *Oxford Magazine*, vi 110. Neptune, his trident in his r. hand, points with his l. hand to Britannia seated (r.), with her sword and spear. He is showing her to a minister (l) wearing the ribbon of an order. Behind is Neptune's car, the horses emerging from the water held by a triton who is blowing his horn. On the l appears the stern of a man of war, flying the Union flag. The design is in a frame decorated by nautical emblems. The plate illustrates 'a vision' which ends ' . . . how came Britannia to loose [*sic*] Falkland Islands?' See No. 4849, &c.

$4\frac{1}{2} \times 5\frac{5}{8}$ in. (pl).

4898 THE AUSPICES, OR THE BIRTH OF THE PRESENT PRINCE OF WALES. [1 May 1771]

S. Wale del.   *C Grignion sculp.*

Engraving. From the *Oxford Magazine*, vi. 149. George III and Queen Charlotte direct the presentation by Diana of the infant prince to Jupiter, who is seated on clouds, across his eagle lies a scroll inscribed *Nascenti Puero*. A female figure reclining on clouds points to emblems of Justice and Liberty, and to a rampant British lion On a colonnade are medallion portraits: *Georgius*, *Fredericus*, and *Georgius II*. Through an archway is a street, apparently the Strand, where a wagon decorated by the Union flag and the Royal Standard is being cheered by the passers-by. This is the procession to the Tower of the treasure taken from Spain during the Seven Years' War. The design is in a frame decorated by a crown, garlands of flowers, cherubs' heads, and architectural ornament.

The accompanying text reminds readers of the auspices of the Prince's birth on 12 Aug. 1762: 12 Aug. (n s.) was the day of the accession of the Brunswick family to the English Crown. 12 Aug. 1762 was the day of the arrival of the Spanish treasure. But, 'If an increase of liberty were really pognosticated [sic] by this prince's nativity, How comes it, that the freedom of election has been infringed, the decision by juries has been abridged, murderers have been screened, pardoned, rewarded' (an allusion to the reprieve of Kennedy, see No. 4844, &c , and the so-called Massacre of St. George's Fields, see No 4196, &c) . .'and the greatest civil magistrate in the kingdom confined in the English *Bastile* for not acting contrary to his oath, and the charter of his corporation, and after refused his right to a *habeas corpus*, and release, which is the birth-right of every Englishman founded on MAGNA CHARTA . . .' See No. 4853, &c.

5×6⅛ in (pl).

4899 MARY QUEEN OF SCOTS SENDING HER RING TO LORD JOHN HAMILTON [1 June 1771]

S. Wale del.   *C. Grignion sculp.*

Engraving. From the *Oxford Magazine*, vi. 185 Queen Mary (l.), standing on a dais in a pillared room, gives a ring to a man who stands facing her, cap in hand. The royal arms of Scotland are over a partly-opened door through which Gothic arches are partly visible. The design is surrounded by a frame of conventional ornament.

This illustrates 'Memoirs of John Marquis Hamilton' [1532–1604], a panegyric on his loyal services to Mary and James VI; his descendants are urged to 'Go and do likewise'. The political intention is obscure since personal loyalty to the Crown by Scotsmen was regarded with high disfavour. The actual Duke of Hamilton (Douglas, 8th duke) was a minor.

4×4¼ in. (pl.).

4900 THE MARQUIS OF DORCHESTER ADDRESSING THE MILITIA OF NOTTINGHAMSHIRE AT NEWARK.

[1 July 1771]

S. Wale del.   *C. Grignion sculp.*

Engraving. From the *Oxford Magazine*, vi. 222. From a platform under an arcade, a man (r) in a long gown addresses a crowd in a market-place, surrounded by buildings. Below the platform (l.) are six men sitting at a table. The design is in a rectangular frame, decorated with garlands of oakleaves, a mace, &c. This illustrates 'Memoirs of the Marquis of Dorchester [1606–80], one of the Ancestors of the duke of Kingston', the episode illustrated being a speech 'to the trained band of Nottinghamshire at Newark, July 13, 1641' [sic 1.e 1642]. A panegyric on the virtue, political moderation, and learning of Dorchester, with an implied contrast to the character of modern peers.

3³⁄₁₀×3¹¹⁄₁₆ in. (pl).

4901 THE ALARM; OR EXECUTION OF LADY JANE GREY.

[1 Aug 1771]

S. Wale del.   *C. Grignion sculp.*

Engraving. From the *Oxford Magazine*, vii 24 Lady Jane (centre) stands on the scaffold, pointing to the block with her l hand; she hands a book to a man on her r. The headsman stands behind the block; five other persons are on the scaffold In the foreground appear the heads of spectators In the background is the Tower of London The design is in an octagonal frame, surmounted by drapery and a pediment beneath which are two skulls and an axe. The accompanying text describes the execution as 'one among the many instances where innocence has been punished while infamy has been rewarded'.

$3\frac{9}{16} \times 4\frac{5}{16}$ in. (pl.)

4902 THE DUKE OF LEEDS RELATING TO CHARLES 2^D A REMARKABLE CIRCUMSTANCE OF HIS ANCESTOR.

[1 Sept 1771]

S. Wale del.   *C. Grignion sc.*

Engraving From the *Oxford Magazine*, vii 49. Charles (l), seated and wearing a hat, in conversation with two men, one standing and gesticulating, the other seated. The background is the wall of a room or gallery, hung with pictures; to the r. is a door The design is in a rectangular frame decorated with garlands of leaves, &c.

Sir Thomas Osborne or Lord Danby, afterwards duke of Leeds, is narrating the well-known story of his grandfather Sir Edward Osborne, Lord Mayor of London, who as an apprentice is reputed to have saved from drowning the infant daughter of his master, whom he afterwards married The text remarks, 'it were to be wished, that some of our new made nobility had any thing that reflected so much honour upon their family.'

$3\frac{11}{16} \times 4\frac{5}{16}$ in. (pl.).

1771
PERSONAL AND SOCIAL SATIRES.

4470, 4903–4912

Series of Tête-à-Tête portraits.

N° XXXVII. THE SUBTLE SINNER   [1 Jan. 1771]
N° XXXVIII. SIR SIMONY SCRUPLE.   See No. 4470

An account of the Rev. Martin Madan.

4903 N° II. THE STABLE-YARD MESSALINA   Vol. III
N° III. THE HOSTILE SCRIBE   [1 Feb. 1771]

Engraving *Town and Country Magazine*, iii 9. Two bust portraits in
oval frames They illustrate 'Histories of the Tête-à-Tête annexed; or,
Memoirs of Lord B——n [Barrington] and L——y H' [Harrington],
between whom a 'permanent connexion' is alleged An account of the
political career and amours of Viscount Barrington (1717–93), styled
'Hostile Scribe' on account of the letters written by him as Secretary at
War approving the conduct of the soldiers at the riot of 10 May 1768, see
Nos. 4196–4202. The amours of Lady Harrington and her husband, both
of notoriously bad reputation, are recounted. Their town house was known
as the Stable Yard (St. James's Palace), see No 5033 She is said to have
damaged her reputation by association with Miss A——h and other 'demi-
reps of the same class', that is Miss Ashe, the 'Pollard Ashe' of Walpole's
Letters, who was reputed to be the daughter of the Princess Amelia and
Rodney. Wraxall, *Memoirs*, 1884, i. 224 and n.
    For the intimacy between Miss Ashe and Lady Caroline Petersham,
afterwards Lady Harrington, see Walpole, *Letters*, ii. 452–6, &c. Walpole
alludes in 1759 to a liaison between Lady Harrington and Barrington,
Letters, iv. 332.

Ovals, $2\frac{5}{8} \times 2\frac{1}{4}$ in.   B.M.L., P.P. 5442 b.

4904 N° IV. MISS H—— L——BE   Vol. III
N° V. THE DISGUSTED SECRETARY.   [1 Mar. 1771]

Engraving *Town and Country Magazine*, iii 65. Two bust portraits in
oval frames illustrate 'Histories of the Tête-à-Tête annexed; or Memoirs
of L——d W—— and Miss Harriot L—mbe'. Weymouth's resignation
of the Secretaryship in December 1770 is mentioned with approval, but
the 'Memoirs' are chiefly concerned with his career 'as a gentleman, a *bon
vivant*, and a man of gallantry'.
    Harriot Lambe is a well-known courtesan who is said to have borrowed
her name from 'Sir P—nn—g—n L—mbe (now Lord M——ne)' [Mel-
bourne].

Ovals, $2\frac{5}{8} \times 2\frac{1}{4}$ in.   B.M.L., P.P. 5442 b.

4905 N° VII. [*sic*] Mʳˢ D—V—S.   Vol. III
      N° VIII LORD C——GH.   [1 Apr. 1771]

Engraving. *Town and Country Magazine*, III. 113. Two bust portraits in oval frames, 'Histories of the Téte-à-Téte annexed ' An account of the career and amours of Lord Catherlough, son of Robert Knight, Cashier to the South Sea Company. Miss Davis is the daughter of a farmer, and has lived with him 'near seven years', at his house in Golden Square.

Ovals, $2\frac{5}{8} \times 2\frac{1}{4}$ in.   B M L , P P 5442 b

4906 N° X MISS EV—NS.   Vol. III
      N° XI. THE SORRY MOTION MAKER.   [1 May 1771]

Engraving. *Town and Country Magazine*, III. 177 Two bust portraits in oval frames They illustrate 'Histories of the Téte-à-Téte annexed; or, Memoirs of the Sorry Motion Maker and Miss Ev—ns'. An account of George Onslow (1731–1814) afterwards first Earl of Onslow, not to be confused with his cousin George Onslow (1731–92), 'little Cocking George', see No 4855. The name is an allusion to his motions in the Commons on 14 and 15 Apr. 1769, that Wilkes's election for Middlesex was null and void, and that Luttrell ought to have been returned

Ovals, $2\frac{5}{8} \times 2\frac{1}{4}$ in.   B.M.L., P.P. 8442 b.

4907 N° XIII Mʳˢ M—RSH—L   Vol. III
      N° XIV. LORD VAINLOVE.   [1 June 1771]

Engraving. *Town and Country Magazine*, III. 233 Two bust portraits in oval frames illustrate 'Histories of the Téte-à-Téte annexed . . .' An account of Viscount Vane (1714–89) who married in 1735 the widow of Lord William Hamilton, notorious for paying Smollett to insert her *Memoirs of a Lady of Quality* in *Peregrine Pickle*.

Ovals, $2\frac{5}{8} \times 2\frac{1}{4}$ in.   B.M L., P.P. 5442 b.

     N° XVI. MISS P——TT.¹   Vol. III
     N° XVII MUNGO   [1 July 1771]

Engraving. *Town and Country Magazine*, III 289 Two bust portraits in oval frames illustrate 'Histories of the Téte-à-Téte annexed, or, Memoirs of Miss Pr——tt and Mungo'. The lady holds in her hand a miniature, which is that of 'Mungo'. A hostile account of Jeremiah Dyson. After ending his association with Mrs. Brown, a courtesan in Pall Mall, he met Miss Pratt, the daughter of a deceased half-pay officer. After being seduced she was forced by a so-called mantua-maker to become a prostitute. Mungo is now infatuated with her. Lord Percy is also attached.

Ovals, $2\frac{5}{8} \times 2\frac{1}{4}$ in.

---

¹ The June number is missing from the B M copy of the magazine, its place being supplied by the number for June 1772. This is taken from a copy in the London Library.

4908 Nº XIX. Mʀˢ M——LLS. Vol. III

Nº XX LORD S——K. [1 Aug 1771]

Engraving *Town and Country Magazine*, iii. 345. Two bust portraits in oval frames illustrate 'Histories of the Tête-à-Tête annexed. . . . .' An account of Lord Suffolk, his ignorance of French, and his alleged amours. For Suffolk, see Nos. 4652, 4875, 4876.

Ovals, $2\frac{5}{8} \times 2\frac{1}{4}$ in. B M L., P P. 5442 b.

4909 Nº XXII. Mʀˢ D——KE Vol. III

Nº XXIII. JOHN OF THE HILL [1 Sept. 1771]

Engraving. *Town and Country Magazine*, iii. 401. Two bust portraits in oval frames. They illustrate 'Histories of the Tête-à-Tête annexed; or, Memoirs of the Duke of R—— and Mrs. D——ke.' An account of John, third duke of Rutland, 1696–1779, described as living like a patriarch at Belvoir Castle with his mistress, Mrs. Drake, his wife's lady's maid at her death in 1734, since when she has presided at his table, where her brother stands as valet-de-chambre behind his master's chair. His son by her, Mr. M——rs [Manners], was a captain in the foot-guards, his daughter, Miss M——rs, married Thomas Thornton, M P for Bramber A plan is given showing the arrangement of a dinner at Belvoir Castle, at which the Duke and Mrs. Drake sit side by side, and the guests include the duke's grandchildren by his mistress, and his son's mistress 'commonly called Little Infamy D——vis'.

Ovals, $2\frac{5}{8} \times 2\frac{1}{4}$ in. B.M L , P.P. 5442 b.

4910 Nº XXV. Mʀˢ W——LLS. Vol. III

Nº XXVI. ADMIRAL K——L [1 Oct. 1771]

Engraving. *Town and Country Magazine*, iii. 457. Two bust portraits in oval frames illustrate 'Histories of the Tête-à-Tête annexed . .' An account of the naval career and amours of Admiral Keppel. For Mrs. Sarah W——lls he is alleged to have furnished a house in Park Lane, settling on her £500 a year, with 'a genteel equipage' and the finest hunters, since she is a noted horsewoman.

Ovals, $2\frac{5}{8} \times 2\frac{1}{4}$ in. B M.L., P.P 5442 b

4911 Nº XXVIII. Mʀˢ S——MS. Vol III

Nº XXIX. THE SAVING STEWARD [1 Nov. 1771]

Engraving. *Town and Country Magazine*, iii. 513. Two bust portraits in oval frames illustrate 'Histories of the Tête-à-Tête annexed; or, Memoirs of Lord T—— and Mrs. S——ms'. An account of William, Earl Talbot (1710–82), Steward of the Household, alleged to be penurious. For attacks on his economies in the royal kitchen see Nos. 3914, 3989, &c. (1762)

Ovals, $2\frac{5}{8} \times 2\frac{1}{4}$ in. B.M.L., P P 5442 b

4912 Nº XXXI. MISS J—NS—N [1 Dec. 1771]

Nº XXXII. L— T—W—Y

Engraving. *Town and Country Magazine*, iii. 569. Two bust portraits in oval frames illustrate 'Histories of the Tête-à-Tête annexed .' An

account of the military career and amours of James O'Hara, second Lord
Tyrawley (1690–1773)

Ovals, 2¾ × 2¼ in   B.M.L., P P 5442 b.

DARLY, P. O. A. G. B.   See No. 4632—1 Jan. 1771

Portrait of Darly the artist and publisher of prints. Pub. Darly.

4913–4918

and related numbers catalogued in vol. iv

Darly's Series of Caricatures

Between 1771 and 1773 Matthew Darly issued six sets of twenty-four
'Caricatures', 'Macaronies', and 'Characters', which he reissued in six
volumes, each with an etched title-page Simultaneously, he was issuing at
least two other similar series of larger prints, one approximately 9 × 13, the
other 6 × 9 in. A number of the plates in these three series were described in
volume iv of this catalogue Since its publication a complete set of the series
in six volumes has been acquired. The order in the volume is not always that
of publication. These volumes deal particularly with the macaroni, a word
for an extravagantly dressed and usually effeminate fop, which came into
general use from about 1770, and apparently derived from the Macaroni
Club 'composed of all the travelled young men who wear long curls and
spying glasses'. Walpole, 6 Feb 1764. The macaroni superseded the
beau and anticipated the dandy; he was démodé by 1776. Cf. F. Burney,
Diary, ii 105 (1775) the 'present *ton* is not Macaronyism'.

Darly was the publisher *par excellence* of prints of macaronies which
were much in vogue from 1771 to 1773, his print shop being 'The Macaroni
Printshop', see No. 4701. Many of the prints in these three series were
reissued with others in a volume with a title-page dated 1 Jan. 1776, see
No 5369

VOLUME I.

24 CARICATURES BY · SEVERAL   LADIES · GENTLEMEN·
ARTISTS &C. PUBᴰ BY. M DARLY. STRAND.

See No. 4710—1 Nov. 1771

    1. THE DOG BARBER¹   See No. 4668—25 Apr. 1771
After Bunbury.

    V. 1. 2. MONᴿ LE MEDECIN.   See No. 4670—13 June 1771
[?After Bunbury.]

    V. 1. 3. A MACARONI   See No. 4671—4 May 1771
After E. Topham.

    4. THE CITY TONSOR.   See No. 4672—1 July 1771
    5. MONᴿ LE FRIZUER.   See No. 4673—2 May 1771

¹ Coloured impressions are in the B M Bunbury Collection.

38

4913 [6] FRENCH PEASANT.¹

[After Bunbury.]

Pubᵈ accordˢ to Act of Parllᵗ June 7th 1771 by M. Darly, 39 Strand.

Engraving A woman standing in profile to the l. She is neatly dressed and wears a cap with a frilled border, and a striped apron. Her hands are in a large fur muff; she wears shoes or small neat sabots and a cross hangs from her neck.

$5\frac{1}{2} \times 3\frac{13}{16}$ in.

Another impression (coloured), having the same publication line and the number 6, with the title *Peasant of the Alps*, see No. 4674.

V. 1. 7. PEASANT OF THE ALPS.¹   See No. 4675—2 Apr. 1771

After Bunbury.

An original etching by Bunbury of this subject in reverse is in B.M It differs from this plate. the background and foreground indicate undulating grass; fur tails protrude from the man's pocket *Paysan des Alpes* is etched on the plate which is signed *H. Bunbury fec.*

8. FRENCH · PEASANT.   See No. 4677—1 Apr. 1771

After Bunbury.

An original etching by Bunbury of this subject is No. 4751

V. 1. 9. FRENCH · LEMONADE MERCHANT.¹
See No. 4782—[18 June 1771]

[After Bunbury.] pubᵈ *T. Scratchley.*²

10. THE PARIS SHOE CLEANER¹ See No. 4679—[1 July 1771]

[After Bunbury.]

4914 11. AMINADAB.

Pubᵈ accordˢ to Act by M. Darly Novʳ 2ᵈ 1771 Nᵒ 39 Strand.

Engraving. A man standing in profile to l., his mouth wide open as if declaiming. Lank hair falls on his shoulders. He wears a low broad-brimmed hat, and is plainly dressed. His hands (gloved) appear to be clasped upon his stomach. Perhaps the portrait of a dissenting preacher.

$5\frac{3}{4} \times 3\frac{3}{4}$ in.

V. 1. 12. THE TURF-MACARONI   See No. 4634—2 Jan. 1771

The Duke of Grafton.

V 1. 13 ΜΑΣΤΙΓΕΥΣ   See No. 4680—1 July 1771

[ᵖAfter Bunbury] Probably Dr. Samuel Smith, see No. 4921.

V. 1. 14 HAPPY PEASANT¹   See No. 4681—2 Aug. 1771

[After Bunbury.]

¹ Coloured impressions are in the B M Bunbury Collection.
² Cf No 4919

39

4915 V. 1. 15. GANYMEDE.

[M. Darly *fec.*]

Pub^d according to Act of Parl^t March 1st 1771 by M Darly 39 Strand.

Engraving. A man standing in profile to the r., a cane in his r hand; his l is inside his waistcoat His shoulders are round, almost to deformity He wears a looped hat and ruffled shirt.

A portrait of Samuel Drybutter, bookseller in Westminster Hall, convicted of an unnatural offence in 1771. *B.M. Cat. Engr. Br. Portraits.* See No 4305 (Drybutter not Vaughan).

$5\frac{5}{8} \times 3\frac{15}{16}$ in.

4916 16. THE FRENCH MAROW-BONE SINGER.

Pub^d as the Act Directs Oct. 1st 1771, by M Darly 39 Strand.

Engraving A man (W.L.) stands in profile to the r., his mouth wide open as if singing. In his r. hand he holds blank sheets of paper evidently intended for music. His l hand holds the r side of his coat His hair is in an enormously long queue bound with ribbon. His hat is under his r. arm He wears a large cravat, his shirt sleeves are frilled but his stockings are conspicuously patched Probably the portrait of a French singer at Marylebone (then often called 'Marrowbone') Gardens depicted in the stock character of the beggarly Frenchman dressed in shabby finery.

$5\frac{1}{2} \times 3\frac{7}{8}$ in

17. DOCTOR GRUEL.   See No. 4682—3 Oct. 1771

Identified in an old hand as Lord L——n [Lansdowne?]. On another impression he has been identified as Sir Nash Grose. He strongly resembles No. 4917 He appears to be wearing a legal wig and gown which would make the identification with Sir Nash Grose more probable. The wig resembles that worn by serjeants at law, see No 5900; Grose (1740–1814) did not become a serjeant till 1774. *D N.B.*)

4917 V. 1. 18. THE ENGLISH JESUIT.

Pub^d according to Act of Parl^t by M Darly Oct 7th 1771.

Engraving. Man standing stiffly in profile to the r., head thrown back with a contemptuous scowl. His l. hand resting on a cane. He wears a low broad-brimmed hat, a tightly-curled wig, buttoned coat, and gloves The etching appears to be a copy of *Humihty*, No. 4795. The same figure appears conspicuously (attending a quaker's meeting) in No 4794. He strongly resembles No. 4682, and is probably intended either for Nash Grose or Lord Lansdowne (then Shelburne) to whom the title would apply, from the well-known name of Malagrida, the notorious Portuguese Jesuit, given to him in the *Public Advertiser* of 16 Sept. 1767. It is not unlike some portraits of Lansdowne, but is very different from the later caricatures, see No. 6022, &c Also a coloured impression without 'V. 1.'

$5\frac{3}{4} \times 3\frac{15}{16}$ in.

V. 1. 19. A CONNOISEUR ADMIRING A DARK NIGHT-PEICE

See No. 4683—12 Nov. 1771

Caricature portrait of Captain Grose

V. 1. 20. A HALF-PAY OFFICER, WHO HAS BEEN AT DINNER
WITH CAP^N BROAD   See No. 4684—26 Oct. 1771

21. MON^{SR} LE. VIRTU'   See No. 4685—3 Nov. 1771
Caricature portrait of Dr. Bragge.

V. 1. 22. MY LORD TIP-TOE. JUST ARRIVED FROM MONKEY
LAND.   See No. 4686—5 Nov. 1771

V. 1. 23. THE LILLY MACARONI.   See No. 4687—13 Nov. 1771
The Earl of Ancrum.

V. 1. 24. THE MARTIAL MACARONI. See No 4711—6 Nov. 1771
Ensign Horneck.

Four prints in Darly's second volume, see Nos 4986–9, are dated 1771.

Five prints from another series by Darly, see p. 38.

4918 13. VIEW ON THE PONT NEUF AT PARIS.

H. W. Bunbury Inv^r

*Pub^d accord^g to Act of Parl^t by M Darly 39 Strand Oct 1st 1771.
Where may be had all the Works of Mr. Bunbury, &c.*

Engraving. A smaller version reversed of No 4763 of the same date published by John Harris. Some of the same characters appear in No. 4919
$8\frac{7}{8} \times 13\frac{1}{2}$ in.

15. THE MASQUERADE DANCE See No. 4635—8 Dec. 1771

16 THE LONDON-JOCKIES, GOING TO NEWMARKET.
See No. 4636—14 Dec. 1771

21. BOARDING SCHOOL EDUCATION.
See No. 4639—Oct 19, 1771

31. THE WELL FED ENGLISH CONSTABLE.
See No. 4641—Oct. 1, 1771

Reproduced, Manchée, *Westminster City Fathers*, 1924, p. 28.

4919 A VIEW OF THE PLACE DES VICTORIES [*sic*] AT PARIS.

T. Scratchley [M. Darly] *Sc.*   [*c.* 1771]

B——[Bunbury] *Inv^t*

Engraving. Publication line cut off. Perhaps belongs to the same series as
No 4918, which it closely resembles. A street scene, the curving line of
the houses of the *Place des Victoires* with the monument to Louis XIV
forming the background. The central figure is a coachman, dressed as in
No. 4763, his hands in a large muff; he stands talking to a peasant woman
A lawyer, an umbrella under his arm, is having his shoes cleaned by a
décrotieur on the extreme l., the sign, resembling that in No 4679, is
inscribed, *A La Dauphine St Lovis Décroteve* [*sic*], from it a shoe-brush
dangles. The lawyer ignores a one-legged beggar holding out his hat. The
dog-barber is not present, but a newly-shaved dog sits behind the coachman. On the extreme r. walks a hairdresser, his hands in a large muff;

he looks over his shoulder at a girl carrying a basket. In the background are coaches, a mounted soldier, a gendarme, pedestrians, another *décrotteur* plying his trade.

$8\frac{11}{16} \times 11\frac{1}{4}$ in.

THE · KITCHEN · OF · A · FRENCH · POST · HOUSE

See No. 4764—1 Feb. 1771

After Bunbury, pub. John Harris.

A smaller version was published by Darly with the same date and was included in the volume with the title-page dated 1 Jan. 1776, see No. 5369.

LE CABRIOLET   See under No. 4633—17 Mar. 1771

Bunbury, pub. Darly.

This plate was reissued with the date 17 Apr. 1772 as No. 8 in a series by Darly, see No. 5056, etc.

4920 THE JUDGMENT OF PARIS

H. W. Bunbury fecit et a cere incidit 1766.

Pub. accor to Act by [name erased] . . . 1st 1771

Engraving. Another version, reversed and differing in many details, of No. 4752; etched by Bunbury (1750–1811) when a Westminster schoolboy. Outside a thatched cottage, partly visible on the l., Paris, a loutish peasant, hands the apple to an old harridan holding a fan and wearing a very wide hoop. Cupid, a hideous boy, holding a bow, is partly concealed by her petticoat. Juno (?), a hideous hag, strides towards them, brandishing a bottle. Minerva (?) in a soldier's coat and grenadier's cap, inscribed *J.R.* [?Juno Regina], walks away to the r. looking over her shoulder; one fist is clenched, she carries a bottle and is smoking a pipe. One sheep (l.) stands behind Paris who is holding a crook. A basket and his hat are on the ground. In the foreground his dog chases the peacock and the owl. Two doves fly over the head of Venus. Two broadsides are pasted on the cottage wall: one headed *Gods . . .* the other, *Thos the Wood Lous* (?). Mountains are indicated in the background.

 Above the design is etched,

   Jun: but to bestow it on that Trapes
   It mads me—Min: hang him Jackanapes.

Printed on the same sheet is an impression of No. 4633.

$6\frac{3}{8} \times 7\frac{5}{16}$ in.

4921 ΜΑΣΤΙΓΕΥΣ   [n.d. *c.* 1766]

[?Bunbury]

Engraving. Bust portrait in an oval of a clergyman in profile to the l. It is the same head as that of ΜΑΣΤΙΓΕΥΣ, No. 4680, who is probably Dr. Samuel Smith, Master of Westminster School. The oval is decorated by two emblems which appear to be birch rods. Probably an original etching by Bunbury when at Westminster School, included here from its connexion with No. 4680; see also No. 5021.

$3\frac{5}{16} \times 2\frac{3}{8}$ in. (oval $2\frac{11}{16} \times 2\frac{1}{4}$ in.).

A FRENCH HAIR DRESSER ...   See No. 4767—1 Mar. 1771

[?Bunbury] Pub. W. Darling.

GANYMEDE & JACK-CATCH   See No. 4305 [1771]

Pub. Darly.

Ganymede is Samuel Drybutter, not Samuel Vaughan, see No 4915.

Five prints from a series published by R. Sayer and J. Smith.

4922 A MODERN DEMIREP ON THE LOOK-OUT.

Brandoin pinx   *Grignion sculp*

London. Printed for Jn° Smith. N° 35, Cheapside & Rob Sayer,
N° 53 Fleet Street. Published as the Act directs 25 Sep* 1771.*

Engraving. A girl walking with mincing steps; her hands are crossed
below her waist and she looks over her shoulder. She wears a hat, a low-cut
bodice, over which is a little open coat, and a slightly hooped skirt. Cf.
Connoisseur, No. 4, 21 Feb. 1754, *Account of a New Order of Females called
Demi-Reps.* (By Colman and Thornton.)

$7\frac{7}{8} \times 5\frac{1}{2}$ in. (Pl.)

A MACARONY AT A SALE OF PICTURES.

        See No. 4601—25 Sept. 1771

Grignion after Brandoin.

4923 THE CHARMING MILLENER OF —— STREET.

Brandoin pinx   *Caldwall sculp*

London, printed for J. Smith N° 35 Cheapside, & Rob Sayer N° 53
Fleet Street, as the Act directs 1st. Dec* 1771.*

Engraving. A girl in dress and manner similar to No 4922. She wears
gloves and carries in her r. hand an arched-top coffer, in the l. a rectangular
box. Cf. Gay, *Trivia*, on the courtesan,

> With empty band box she delights to range
> And feigns a distant errand from the 'Change.
>   Reproduced, Paston, Pl cxcv.

$7\frac{7}{8} \times 5\frac{1}{2}$ in. (Pl.)

4924 AN OPERA GIRL OF PARIS IN THE CHARACTER OF FLORA.

Brandoin pinx   *Grignion sculp.*

London. Printed for Rob Sayer, N° 53 Fleet Street, & J. Smith
N° 35 Cheapside, as y* Act directs 1st Dec* 1771.*

Engraving A girl dancing holding out in both hands a garland of roses.
Her looped up skirt has a short train. From her head-dress of flowers and
feathers hangs a piece of striped drapery which is worn over one shoulder,
tied with tassels at the waist and falling in heavy folds down her back.

$7\frac{7}{8} \times 5\frac{1}{2}$ in (Pl)

4925 THE PRETTY SAVOYARD GIRL.

Brandoin pinx[t]   *Caldwall sculp.*

*London. Printed for R. Sayer, N[o] 53 Fleet Street, & J. Smith N[o] 35
     Cheapside as the Act directs, 1st Dec[r] 1771.*

Engraving. A girl in peasant dress carrying a hurdy-gurdy or vielle suspended round her neck. She wears a nosegay.

$7\frac{7}{8} \times 5\frac{1}{2}$ in. (Pl.)

CHARLES-JAMES CUB ESQ[R].   See No. 4811—[1 June 1771]

London Museum. Charles Fox, slim and elegant, dressed in the height of
French fashion.

4926 LE CHERCHEUR DE 20 P[R] CENT   [? *c.* 1771]

E. N. Sculp[t] [Sir Edward Newenham]

Engraving. Portrait: an elderly man walking or standing in profile to the
l. resting both hands on the head of his stick. He has a long nose and
pendulous under-lip, and wears a small hat and long coat with wide sleeves.
He is probably a Jew. In manner this resembles the caricature portraits
published by Darly in his Macaroni series from 1771. The collector,
Richard Bull, has written beneath it 'Etch'd by Sir Edward Nuneham of
Ireland'. Cf. Nos. 5012, 5578.

$5\frac{3}{16} \times 3\frac{7}{8}$ in. (clipped).   In book of 'Honorary Engravers', i. 164.

4927 THE GREATEST LAWYER IN PARIS   [? 1771]

A Smith sculp.

Engraving. Caricature portrait, W.L., of a man standing. In his r. hand
he holds out a book inscribed *Palace Almanac*. A note explains this as
Book of the French Laws. In his l. hand he holds gloves, hat, and tasselled
cane. Beneath is engraved *This strange Object has such (a) penetrating
Judgment in Law that he never undertakes a cause either for Plantiff or
Defendant but he proves successfull. He soon perceives if it's Equity or Fraud
the latter he never maintains & with ease baffles the falacious Attemps [sic]
of his opponent. 'Tis evident that all Act not in this manner for right or
wrong we often find*

> ——*the grave Knight that nods upon the Laws
> Wak'd by a Fee, hems, and approves the Cause. Dryden.*

In a contemporary hand is written, 'A Caracature of Matt: Duane Esq. of
Lincoln's Inn Barrister-at-Law, 1771. Nov.' His dress, with long coat,
wide cuffs, and high-quartered shoes, belongs to an earlier period.

   Duane (1707–85) was an eminent conveyancer, antiquary, and numis-
matist, F.R.S., F.S.A., and a trustee of the British Museum. See No. 4768.

$6\frac{7}{8} \times 5\frac{7}{8}$ in.

[PORTRAIT OF SIR W. BROWNE, M.D.]   See No. 4833. 1771

Another impression has been acquired on which the collector, Richard
Bull, has written 'Portrait of Sir Wm Brown, very like him'. The etched

quotation is from the Latin verses in defence of Browne's conduct as President of the College of Physicians believed to have been written by himself.

This portrait was copied for a *tête-à-tête*, see No. 4979.

4928 REMARKABLE CHARACTERS AT M^{RS} CORNELY'S MASQUERADE. [1 Mar. 1771]

Engrav'd for the Oxford Magazine.

Engraving From the *Oxford Magazine*, vi 64. A number of figures in masquerade dress without masks, in a panelled room lit with candles in wall brackets. They represent the characters at the public masquerade on 6 Feb (l. to r.)—a coffin, a monk, a nun, a harlequin, a madman with straw in his hair, a Savoyard playing a hurdy-gurdy and leading a dancing bear. The bear-leader and bear were a Mr. Hooke and a Mr. Hodges. The coffin was at first supposed to be Col. Luttrell, then his brother, *Town and Country Magazine*, iii. 81–4. See also Wright, *Caricature History of the Georges*, 1867, p 551. A plate with the same title, but a political satire, is No. 4376. See also No 4375.

$3\frac{3}{4} \times 6\frac{1}{8}$ in.

4929 TRIAL OF THE SOVEREIGN EMPRESS OF THE VAST REGIONS OF TASTE. [1 Apr. 1771]

Engraving From the *Oxford Magazine*, vi. 98 Sir John Fielding (r.) with his eyes bandaged, is seated on the bench holding the sword and the scales of Justice. His clerk sits below him on his r. hand. Mme Cornelys appears before him supported on the shoulders of a lawyer and of a duchess wearing a coronet and ermine-trimmed robes. Fielding says: *Not so blind but I can hit the right place for Intrigue.* Mme Cornelys holding up her l. hand, the other being round the duchess's neck, says: *You shall pay dearly for your Insolence* The duchess (of Northumberland) says, *Money shall not be wanting Councellor, You & I must defend her against the blind Boy's Insolence.* She hands the lawyer a bag of money; he takes it, saying· *Your Grace need not fear, you have a noble Spirit, & delight to encourage real Merit.*

Behind these three is a page or attendant in fancy dress or livery with feathers in his cap, he holds a flag inscribed *Empress of the Vast Regions of Taste and Magnificence.* Behind (l.) stands the singer Guadagni, holding up both hands and saying: *Pray Madame la Duchesse do make him repent taking Guadagni's L50—den you will Piercy* [a pun on Percy, the duchess's family name] *mine Art with your Goodness.*

Mme Cornelys was fined at Bow Street for performing an opera at Carlisle House without a licence under 10 George II, c 28. Guadagni was also fined, for singing. For Mme Cornelys, Guadagni, and the Duchess of Northumberland see Walpole to Mann, 22 Feb. 1771, *Letters*, viii. 12–13. For the proceedings at Bow Street see *Public Advertiser*, 22 Feb. 1771, from which it appears that Mme Cornelys' counsel was Kenyon, afterwards Lord Kenyon. For the consequences of these proceedings see No. 5066.

$3\frac{5}{8} \times 5\frac{15}{16}$ in

4930 HOSPITALITY ABUSED; OR GENERAL S——T [SCOTT];
CAPTAIN SUTH——D [SUTHERLAND] AND LADY MARY
S——T. [*c.* 1771]

Engraving. Probably from a book or magazine. Three people are seated
at a round dinner table, a young woman between a young man and an older
man While the older man turns towards a servant who is pouring out
wine the lady takes a note from the young man. On the wall is a picture
of a woman kissing a man while she stabs him to the heart. See the *Town
and Country Magazine*, iii. 516–18, Oct. 1771, for an account of the
elopement of Lady Mary Scott with her husband's young relative and
protégé. For Lady Mary Scott see No. 4352. See also *London Magazine* xl.
478–82 (pl.).

$3\frac{15}{16} \times 6\frac{3}{8}$ in.

JANUARY AND MAY. See No. 4606—16 Apr. 1771.

Grignion *sc* after Collet. Pub. Sayer and Smith.

THE LADIES DISASTER See No 4595—2 Apr. 1771

Caldwall *sc.* after Collet. Pub. Smith and Sayer.

Reproduced, Paston, Pl. cxiii.

THE COTILLION DANCE. See No 4599—10 Mar. 1771

Caldwall *sc.* after Collet. Pub. Sayer and Smith.

THE COUNTRY-MAN IN LONDON See No. 4600—1 Sept 1771

Bannerman *sc.* after Collet. Pub. Smith and Sayer.

RIDICULOUS TASTE OR THE LADIES ABSURDITY
See No 4628—15 July 1771

Pub. M. Darly and R. Sayer.

This plate, inscribed *Darly inv*, was issued with Darly's publication line
on 25 Mar. 1768 (in the collection of Mr. W. T Spencer, New Oxford
Street, 1932), and included in a volume dated 1 Jan. 1776; see No. 5369.

A French copy, with both French (*Coiffure du grand gout pour la presente
Année*) and English titles, attributed to the year 1780, is reproduced in
Fuchs und Kraemer, *Karikatur der Europaischen Volker*, 1901, p. 116

THE FEMALE PYRAMID. See No. 4630 [1 May 1771]

Oxford Magazine Reproduced *Social England*, ed. Traill, v, p. 482.

THE AUCTION; OR MODERN CONNOISSEURS.
See No. 4770—1 Dec. 1771

Oxford Magazine.

[A GENTLEMAN'S TOILETTE] See No. 4789—17 Dec 1771

1. Goldar after Pugh. Pub. I. Wesson.

THE CHELSEA GUARD   See No. 4791—21 Dec. 1771
Pub. S. Hooper.

THE FRENCH LADY IN LONDON....   See No. 4784—2 Apr. 1771
After S. H. Grimm. Pub. S. Sledge.
Reproduced, Paston, Pl. cciii.

4931 *L'Angloise a Paris.* THE ENGLISH LADY IN PARIS. *from an Original Drawing by Brandoin.*

J. B. Godfrey fecit.

Publish'd as the Act directs 18th Octr. 1771, for S. Hooper No 25 Ludgate Hill London.

Engraving. A stout middle-aged lady stands, facing T.Q. to the l., at her toilet table the draped mirror of which reflects her complacent expression. A maid puts the finishing touches to her coiffure She is elaborately dressed and wears a large nosegay on her l shoulder. A servant enters from the r. holding a circular tray on which are two cups, and a paper inscribed *To her Grace.* Another maid is adjusting her dress. Seated on a chair (l.) in profile to the r. is a gentleman holding his hat in his hand and looking towards the lady with an expression of deferential admiration.

Over the chimney piece is a large mirror, a cloak and hat hang on the wall. Over the chimney is a H L. portrait attached to the wall by a bow of ribbon The wall above the mirror is decorated by a classical medallion profile. Reproduced Paston, Pl. cci.

$11\frac{3}{8} \times 9$ in.

THE ENGLISH LADY AT PARIS.   See No. 4785. [5 Nov. 1771]
After S. H. Grimm. Pub. S. Sledge.

4932 A FRENCH PHYSICIAN WITH HIS RETINUE GOING TO VISIT HIS PATIENTS.

Brandoin Pinxt   *Caldwell sculp.*
London, Printed for Jno Smith, No 35 Cheapside & Robt Sayer, No 53 Fleet Street Published as the Act directs 20 Octr 1771.

Engraving. Street scene, evidently in Paris The physician, holding a large cane, sits in a two-wheeled chair or brouette which is being drawn from l to r. by a thin and ragged man, while another pushes the back of the chair. In front (r) runs a footman holding an enormous syringe over his r. shoulder. At the back of the procession (l) walks another doctor, short and stout, in a tie-wig and holding a large-headed cane, his hat under his r. arm; a bottle labelled *Anodyne* protrudes from his pocket Behind him walks a small shaggy poodle.

Behind the chair in the centre of the design a street or *place* recedes in perspective, with a church spire in the distance No. 4831 (n d) is a similar design. Cf. No. 4670

$7 \times 9\frac{1}{2}$ in.

4933 A FRENCH PETIT MAITRE AND HIS VALET.

Brandoin Pinx^t   *C. Grignion sculp.*

London, Printed for Robt Sayer, N° 53, in Fleet Street & J. Smith
N° 35 Cheapside, as the Act directs 1st Novr 1771.

Engraving. Street scene, showing houses irregularly placed, foliage and
rough stones on the ground, a stone tablet high on the side of a stone
building is inscribed *Rue d'Enfer* (then a well-known street in Paris). The
petit-maître (l) is walking from r. to l. but looks over his l. shoulder towards
his valet who advances from the r. holding out a paper inscribed *Au petit
Marquis*. The marquis wears an enormous black bag with a solitaire ribbon
loosely round his neck; a very large nosegay on his l. shoulder, a sword
whose hilt is decorated with ribbons; his coat is covered with heart-shaped
spots The valet though wearing a ruffled shirt and laced waistcoat has
his hair in curl-papers with a comb thrust into it.

The grass-grown street probably satirizes the solitude of Paris streets
compared with those of London.

Reproduced, Paston, Pl. ccii.

11⅞×9¾ in.

THE CITY CHANTERS   See No 4433—1771

Mezzotint by S. Okey after Collet.

A street scene with an allusion to the election for sheriffs at midsummer
1771, see Nos. 4874, 4937.

Series of mezzotints published by Carington Bowles.

HE! HO!—HEAVY, DULL AND INSIPID . . . (238)

                                       See No. 4514 [c. 1771]

HI! HO!—THESE LATE HOURS WILL SOON DESTROY ME (239)
In Carington Bowles's smaller series.   See No. 4515 [c. 1771]

POLITICAL SATIRES

4934 SPANISH TREATMENT AT CARTHAGENA. [1 Jan 1772]

Engraving *London Magazine*, xl. 610. A fortified sea port, with the Spanish flag flying from a circular fort (r) In the foreground five English sailors are in chains, being compelled by two Spaniards to do forced labour on the fortifications—a castellated sea-wall Two are prostrate on the ground, one stands protesting, one carries a hod, the last (l.) holds a spade Three ships are approaching the harbour. The nearest (l.) is being boarded by men from a boat and its flag is being hauled down; another boat rows to (or from) the ship.

The affair of the Falkland Islands had roused a storm of protest that the Government was acting in corrupt subservience to Spain, see Nos 4849, 4857. This satire reflects the impression made by a dispatch from Rodney which reached the Admiralty in October 1771, see No 4940.

This plate, showing the imaginary humiliation of England by Spain, was copied by Paul Revere for the *Royal American Magazine*, Vol. 1, July 1774 Stauffer, No. 2686.

4 × 6⁷⁄₁₆ in.   B M L , 159 n. 3.

4935 LORD NORTH AT THE SPANISH AMBASSADOR'S.
[1 Jan. 1722]

Design'd & Engrav'd for the Political Register

Engraving. From the *Political Register*, ix. 297. The Spanish Ambassador (Prince Masserano) seated on a throne-like chair under looped-up curtains. Lord North bows obsequiously before him, holding the Union flag which falls on the ground, the ambassador's feet resting upon it. In his r. hand is a paper inscribed *Falklands Islands.* Beneath is engraved,

> *Thus we would buy your Friendship;*
> *and treat you with gentle loving kindness.*
> *Shakespeare.*

One of many satires on the supposed subservience of the Ministry to Spain over the Falkland Islands, see No 4849, &c.

5⁹⁄₁₆ × 3¹³⁄₁₆ in

ADVICE TO A GREAT K——G   See No. 4424—1 Jan. 1772

Engraving. *Oxford Magazine.* George III reading Johnson's *False Alarm*, and receiving conflicting advice from an angel and a demon

4936 ALAS. POOR MUNGO   [1 Jan. 1772]

Woodcut From the *London Magazine*, xl. 610. A man with his hand raised to his head looks with horror at a paper on a table, inscribed *Resolved That . . £1000. . . .* A woman seated by the table holding a handkerchief to her eyes looks at him reproachfully An illustration to 'The Lamentations of Jeremiah, being a dialogue between Mungo and his Mistress'

A satire on the debate in the Irish House of Commons, 25 Nov. 1771, on the grant to Dyson of a pension on the Irish establishment, which was condemned by a majority of one and afterwards struck off the list. See Walpole, *Memoirs of the Reign of George III*, 1894, iv. 49; *Corr of George III*, iii 125, and No. 4942 For the name of 'Mungo' see Walpole, op cit., iii. 211, and No. 4267, &c.

$3\frac{3}{8} \times 3\frac{15}{16}$ in.

4937 QUIDNUNC, OR THE UPHOLSTERER SHAVING.

[1 Jan. 1772]

Engraving. From *Every Man's Magazine*, i 263 The interior of a barber's shop. A barber holds the [head of a seated man wrapped in a sheet, but negligently allows the bowl of shaving water he holds in his l. hand to pour over his customer. By the customer's side is a dog with a collar engraved *King*. A barber's assistant, raggedly dressed, is combing a wig on a block supported on a tall stand. Another holds up a looking-glass to a customer who is arranging his cravat. Another man brushes a hat In the background a spectacled man wearing a hat reads *The London Evening Post*, on which is inscribed

> *Wilkes* 2315
> *Bull* 2194
> *Kirkm^n* 1949
> *Plumb* 1875
> *Oliver* 119.

On a shelf are wigs of different kinds on barber's blocks on which faces are represented which are perhaps caricatures. Among them are two ladies' wigs, and a judge's wig. Two other wigs hang from the wall, and in the foreground two cats are playing with a wig which they have pulled out of a box

The figures are those of the votes recorded at the election for sheriffs at midsummer 1771, see No. 4874.

The subject of the satire is from Murphy's popular farce (first played, 1757), "The Upholsterer or What News?", in which meddling tradesmen neglect their business to discuss politics, one being *Quidnunc*, an upholsterer, another *Razor*, a barber. Cf. No. 5074, &c.

$6\frac{5}{8} \times 4$ in.

4938 CHARACTERESTICKS.

[1 Jan. 1772]

Engraving From the *Oxford Magazine*, vii 229. Three half-length figures in circles of laurel leaves Lord Mayor Crosby (centre) in his gown wearing a civic mural crown holds a scourge inscribed *For Monopoly* in one hand, in the other a scroll · *Thanks and Prayers of the Poor* Behind him is a figure of Justice with her scales and a view of the Tower of London in which he had been imprisoned, see No. 4850, &c. Wilkes (l.), as Hercules, with a sheriff's staff holds a club *For undue Influence* and a scroll inscribed *Herculas's Labours overcome Genl Warrants maintain'd Lib. of Press— Freedom of Election, &c. &c. &c.* A bull (r.) wearing an alderman's chain, holding a sheriff's staff and with one hoof on a column inscribed *Fortitude* denotes Alderman Bull who was elected sheriff with Wilkes in 1771, see No. 4874. In the centre, between the circles, are the City arms and motto, *Domine dirige nos*, and the cap of liberty inscribed *Libertas*.

Crosby as Lord Mayor was associated in the City with active measures against engrossers of wheat supplies, see *Ann. Reg* 1771, p. 66.

$4\frac{1}{8} \times 6\frac{3}{16}$ in. Diam of circles $2\frac{1}{8}$ in.

4939 THE CITY APPRENTICE AT ST JAMES'S   [1 Feb 1772]

Engraving From *Every Man's Magazine*, i. 310. A man stands in a panelled room or corridor wearing a toupet wig, a court suit with an elaborately embroidered and fringed waistcoat. He is taking a pinch of snuff from a box in his r. hand. Behind (l) stands a beefeater holding a halberd. In the distance (r) two men talking together are watching 'the City Apprentice'; one points at him, the other appears to be Lord North wearing his Garter ribbon

Probably intended to represent Thomas Harley, third son of the third Earl of Oxford, who was the leader of the Court party in the City. See Nos. 4069, 4190, 4202, 4213, 4235, 4269, 4852, 4953, 4966. No explanation accompanies the plate.

$5\frac{7}{8} \times 3\frac{7}{8}$ in.

4940 ADMIRAL RODNEY BEFORE CARTAGENA   [1 Feb 1772]

Design'd & Engrav'd for the Political Register

Engraving From the *Political Register*, x. 1. Rodney in back view stands on the shore watching thirteen ships at anchor. His hands are tied behind him by a strip of paper inscribed *Orders*. In the distance across the water is a town defended by a long castellated mole. Beneath the design is engraved,

> *I with thirteen Sail attended,*
> *Can this Spanish town affright;*
> *Nothing has its wealth defended,*
> *But my Orders—Not to Fight.*
>   *Hosier's Ghost.*

Rodney had accepted the command of Jamaica early in 1771 on the prospect of war with Spain over the Falkland Islands, see No. 4849, &c. In October 1771 a dispatch from him reached the Admiralty reporting an incident at Cartagena: a British schooner had been induced by threats to accompany two Spanish *Guarda costa* ships into the port without resistance, on a pretext of smuggling Rodney had made protests to the Governor of Cartagena, and the lieutenant in command had been court martialled and dismissed the service. Nothing more was heard of the incident beyond official protests to the Spanish Ambassador, &c., but it gave rise to a rumour that war was imminent. See *Calendar of Home Office Papers* 1770–2, pp. 310–11, 312, 324, 326 No. 4934 is a satire on the supposed humiliation of England involved in this incident. Glover's famous ballad, *Hosier's Ghost*, had been used in 1740 (as in 1772) to attack the Government for inaction against Spain, see No. 2422

$5\frac{1}{4} \times 3\frac{15}{16}$ in.

Frontispiece

4941 THE GENIUS OF THE LONDON MAGAZINE UNMASKING
     THE TIMES.   [1 Feb 1772]

T. Bonnor del et sculp.

Engraving. Frontispiece to the *London Magazine*, xli. A female winged figure (r) in classical draperies stands upon clouds surrounded by rays of light. Over her head fly two cherubs, one holding a shield with the arms of the City of London, the other a civic mace and chains Her r. hand rests on the head of a seated figure dressed as a harlequin round whose forehead is a placard inscribed *The Times*. In her l hand she holds a mask which she has just removed from his face, revealing an evil countenance; he turns away from 'the Genius of the London Magazine', and attempts to hide his scowling face with his hand. On his head is a weathercock inscribed *The Fashions*. In his r. hand he holds open a box from which are hanging narrow strips of paper inscribed. *Continental Histor[y]; State Sharping, Freewill; Bigotry, 200,000£; Dearness of Provisions, Prerogative; Pension; Patriotism; The Drama.* Similar labels decorate his person: *Bon Ton; Popularity; Corruption, Nabobships, Bankruptcies; Crim. Con., Fraud, Folly.* Beneath the titles is engraved,

> *Blest Genius! still be thine the arduous task;*
> *From motley Times to draw the Iron mask.*
> *On Errors eye to pour thy splendid ray,*
> *And give the glories of eternal Day.*

$6\frac{1}{8} \times 4\frac{1}{4}$ in.

4942 [HIBERNIA IN DISTRESS.][1]   [1 Feb. 1772]

Engraving. From the *London Magazine*, xli. 3. Hibernia lies on the ground with her harp broken. On a table (l.) are two money bags, one full and labelled *Exchequer*, the other decorated with the Irish harp and almost empty. Into this Lord North is plunging his hand while a negro with outstretched hand says: *Don't forget poor Mungo my good L^d N——h.* A man in hat and laced coat is trampling on Hibernia, saying to a bystander: *Sr George we must keep her down.* Sir George [Macartney] answers: *Ay my L^d T——d.* [Townshend] *and exert ourselves or she will be too Strong for us.*

This illustrates an article, 'The History of the last Parliament of Ireland,' pp 3–12 North is dipping deep into Irish revenue while the English Exchequer is full. The negro is Jeremiah Dyson whose pension on the Irish list has been rejected, see No 4936.

$3\frac{15}{16} \times 6\frac{1}{4}$ in.

4943 THE YOUNG CUB ATTENDED BY YE CLERKS OF YE AD—L—TY, AT AR——RS IN THE KITCHEN, WHILST THE FRENCH COOK AND SCULLION BOY LAUGH AT HIM
                                                     [1 Feb. 1772]

Engraving. From the *Oxford Magazine*, viii 28 A kitchen, Fox stands at a table about to sign a document. In his l. hand he holds four playing cards. From his pocket protrudes a book, *Hoyles Free Gamester.* He looks towards a slim young man (l), who addresses him, holding a document addressed *To James Fox Sq* They are watched with amusement by a cook (r.) who is holding two trussed birds on a spit and by a scullion boy Two Admiralty clerks (l.) stand behind their spokesman A fox hangs by its neck from the roof The accompanying letter runs, 'Sir, it is very remarkable, that none but the most abandoned of mankind stand any tolerable chance to receive the favours of the present M——y [Ministry]. The young cub, who is in possession of a very lucrative and honourable post, [Lord of the Admiralty, resigned Feb. 20, 1772] keeps his office chiefly at Arthur's,

---

[1] The title is taken from the index to the magazine.

and when any material business is transacted, that requires his signature, he is obliged to leave his Game and retire into the Kitchen for that purpose....'

$6\frac{5}{8} \times 4\frac{1}{16}$ in.

4944 A CORPORATION WITH THEIR CHAPLAIN IN EMBRIO TAKEN BY SURPRISE. [n d. Feb 1772]

[?After Viscount Townshend.]

Engraving. On a platform, behind a low parapet, eleven men stand, ten dressed in furred livery gowns as if members of a corporation The eleventh is dressed as a clergyman in gown and bands. Above them flies a large devil with a bull's head holding chains attached to two of the figures Below them is a table on which are writing materials, books, papers, and a large bag. A clerk writes at it; two figures stand behind it. In front of the table are standing figures. Engraved labels issue from the heads of the characters.

The devil says: *You have exceeded my most fervent wishes and shall have capital employments in my Infernal Empire.* The figures on the platform (1 to r) says: *Nor I Brother F——t, upon my credit; Consume ye all, are these your tricks I never cribb'd a Shilling; This is worse than the Ribb'd Stocking Patent; Or a Walpole Administration, O Cromwell thy active Spirit alone can save us* (a chain links this speaker with the devil); *I have discover'd your Villanys, and shall quit my Office with pleasure* (this speaker wears a hat) The clergyman says: *Make Restitution and give up your Trusts.* The remaining speakers on the platform say: *What shall we do I cannot face Justice! that is not our way* (this man is chained to the devil); *How could you think this wretch capable of succeeding my worthy Master, I have often told you what the animal would do for you; I have not shared in the Plunder nor will I join in the defence; Nor I Brother John*

A man stands on the table with a large bag under his arm, he holds out a paper: *Subpoenys in Chancery for defrauding the Burgesses, &c.* towards a man standing behind the table who exclaims: *But my dam'd Accounts will undo us.* The man next him, who wears a furred livery gown, says: *Defend I say defend ah Ben Ha Ha Ha.*

In the foreground (l.) a man wearing clerical bands, but with striped stockings, looks through a lorgnette made of a dice-box. Papers protruding from his pocket are inscribed: *Minuets and Country Dances 1770; Hoyle on Whis[t]* He is standing on a paper inscribed *XXXIX Articles* and says: *If this be the case the Devil may be your Chaplain for me.* A man with a maccaroni queue says to him: *Gad so Brother Charles You'l get no Credo here.* On the r stands a bellman with a long badged coat and staff saying *O yes, Gentlemen hear me, methinks the spirit of Cato inspires me, Petition his Grace and yᵉ Lords, that noble House allways supports their Friends tho' their Crimes be Murder & Treason Vid the Cases of L——n & B——* [? Bigby]. His bell is on the ground beside him Behind him stands a man wearing a gown and holding a mace, he puts his l. hand on the bell-man's shoulder, saying *Ah Mʳ Cato your Oratory is in vain that power alass is no more* On his extreme r is a tall man wearing a bag-wig and court suit, his r foot rests on a bale inscribed *China Silk Smuggled* He says: *Cato thou reasons well by such an expedient I escaped the Exchequer.*

This appears to be a general attack on the House of Commons who are pilloried as members of a corrupt corporation. Many of the allusions are obscure. The 'embrio chaplain' standing on the Thirty-nine Articles ; evidently C J Fox, who spoke (6 Feb. 1772) against the petition for relief from subscription to the articles (see *Ann. Reg.* 1772, pp. 171–2), and who prepared himself for his defence of the Church 'by passing twenty-two hours in the pious exercise of Hazard', Gibbon, *Misc. Works*, ii 74. See also Walpole, *Last Journals*, 1910, i 12. He resigned his office of Lord of the Admiralty on 20 Feb. 1772, which gives an approximate date to this print.[1] The man speaking to Fox is probably his brother Stephen. The man who deplores his 'dam'd Accounts' is perhaps Lord Holland, known as 'the public defaulter of unaccounted millions', see No 4066, &c., against whom proceedings had been taken in the Exchequer, and whose accounts were not cleared for many years, see Wraxall, *Memoirs*, 1884, ii 344–5 The 'ribb'd stocking patent' appears to be intended for the two famous patents taken out in 1758 and 1759 by Jedediah Strutt, for the 'Derby rib machine', of great economic importance, but not associated with any charge of political corruption. See Felkin, *Hist. of Machine-Wrought Hosiery*, 1867, ch vi.

For other attacks on the House of Commons see No 4869, &c.

The design is in the manner of caricatures by Lord Townshend.

$7\frac{3}{4} \times 12\frac{3}{4}$ in.

4945 THE Q——N OF D—N—RK CONVEYING TO PRISON.
[1 Mar. 1772]

Engraving. From *Every Man's Magazine*, i. 353. Queen Caroline Matilda, sister of George III, and wife of Christian VII of Denmark, richly dressed and wearing jewels, is being hurried down the palace steps by two soldiers. A man wearing a laced hat and the ribbon of an order, probably the King, stands by pointing at her; she holds out her l. hand towards him, in the r. she holds a handkerchief towards her eyes Behind him stands a woman with upraised hand, evidently the Queen Dowager, the King's step-mother, who was the instigator of the palace revolution against Struensee, the Queen's favourite, and the Queen. A soldier (r.) holding a musket with a fixed bayonet stands by. At the bottom of the steps is a coach, its door held open by a soldier; behind it are soldiers headed by a mounted officer with a drawn sword

This revolution took place on 17 Jan. 1772, Rantzau carried out the deportation of the Queen to Kronborg See *Cambridge Modern History*, vi, chap. xxi, and Nos 4946, 4950, 4956.

$4\frac{1}{4} \times 6\frac{1}{2}$ in.

4946 THE D—G—R [DOWAGER] QUEEN RIDING POOR D—M—K.
[1 Mar. 1772]

Engraving From the *Oxford Magazine*, viii. 56. A skimmington procession on a sorry-looking horse a man and woman sit astride, back to back; the woman, richly dressed, sits in front, her skirts pushed back to show breeches In her r. hand is a pistol, in her l. a sword The man holds a distaff. The procession is headed by a man (r.) holding aloft on a pole a petticoat and a pair of horns Behind him walks a man beating a drum.

---

[1] When the question was reconsidered (23 Feb 1773), Fox spoke against sub-scription to the Articles at the universities *Parl Hist* xvii. 749 f.

Behind the horse is a woman carrying a broom over her shoulder and a woman blowing a horn. A spectator points and jeers, another walks with folded arms.

The title, the design, and the explanatory text are contradictory: the design shows a faithless wife with a henpecked and acquiescent husband, punished in the barbarous and traditional way, by 'a skimmington', accompanied by rude music and jeers; the print is described as 'a representation of that amiable Queen conducting to prison by the merciless wretches employed by the wicked Dowager'.

Whether the woman is Queen Caroline Matilda being taken to prison or the Queen Dowager is doubtful. *Prima facie*, she appears to be the Queen, pilloried as the mistress of Struensee and his supporter in a virtual dictatorship. The Queen of Denmark was dressed as a man, wearing buckskin breeches, when she met her mother, the Princess Dowager of Wales, in 1770 Walpole, *Memoirs of the Reign of George III*, 1845, iv. 281. The man is evidently the feeble-minded and vicious Christian VII of Denmark, see *English Hist. Rev.*, Jan. 1916. For the palace revolution in Denmark see Nos 4945, 4950, 4956, and for a skimmington No. 1703

$3\frac{5}{8} \times 6\frac{1}{8}$ in.

4947 A VIEW OF THE ORIGIN OF SCOTCH MINISTERS, & MANAGERS.[1]   [1 Apr. 1772]

Engraving. *Political Register*, x. 137 A number of men fall to the ground from a sack or basket held up by two demons One demon (l.) says· *There's a plentifull stock of Scotch Caterpillars for poor England.* A third demon standing below says· *I think I and my Brother Fiends could not spit our Spight more Effectually.* The apex of an inverted pyramid of eight falling figures is a man seated on the ground saying: *Au my Saul Man, I have had a muckle dash, but hope we Shall rise again.* In the background a man in a laced suit is seated at a table blowing soap-bubbles Beneath the design is engraved,

> They go from the Devil to Court,
> And from Court to the Devil again.
> *Swift.*

This version of the favourite theme of abuse of the Scots is evidently directed against the speculation mania in Scotland (indicated by the bubbles) which had disastrous consequences in England, see Nos 4961, 5016, 5109.

$5\frac{7}{8} \times 4\frac{7}{8}$ in.   B.M L , P P. 3557 t a.

4948 THE APOSTATE PARSON

Publish'd as the Act directs April 14. 1772. by W. Darling, Engraver, Great Newport Street.

Engraving. A bishop (r.) standing behind an altar-rail, holds out both hands over the head of a kneeling clergyman. A demon kneels on the ground beside the latter, another has crept under his cassock, from which the tips of two wings project Over the door is a picture of the Last Supper with Judas as a prominent figure The lid of a large chest (l.) is slightly raised, from it hangs a paper inscribed· *I Suit of Scarlet & Gold,*

[1] This was catalogued as No. 4023, and dated April 8, 1763.

1 Suit White & Silver, 1 Suit Blue & Silver, 1 Suit Flower'd Silk, 1 Suit Black Silk, 1 Black Velv^t Surtout   On the Chest is pasted a label: *Left to Messrs Panchauld & Fo . . . Paris.* On the ground is a book, *A Course of Humanity on Miss S——rs*

Beneath the design is engraved: *It is true I have Suffer'd the infectious hand of a Bishop to be wav'd over me, whose Imposition like the Sop given to Judas is only a Signal for the Devil to enter &c.* The scene represents the 'infectious hand of a bishop' ordaining Horne, see Nos. 4863, 4866 The inscription is a quotation from a letter of his to Wilkes in 1766. The list in the trunk is identical with that sent by Horne to Wilkes in Paris, 25 May 1767, together with the clothes which he left in Wilkes's care (as unsuited to his clerical calling and to the English taste), writing 'If you have any fellow feeling, you cannot but be kind to them; since they too, as well as yourself, are outlawed in England; and on the same account—their superior worth'. In the course of their quarrel Horne accused Wilkes of having pawned these clothes. See Stephens, *Memoirs of Horne Tooke,* i. 76 ff. For the quarrel between Wilkes and Horne, see No. 4861, &c

$6\frac{7}{8} \times 9\frac{7}{16}$ in.

4949 THE JOINT STOOL. [1 May 1772]

Engraving. From the *Political Register,* x. 201. A large roughly constructed three-legged stool made of rock. In the background is a mountainous landscape, inscribed *Highlands,* from which a wide road descends passing under the legs of the stool. The top of the stool, in which are fissures, is inscribed *150 Millions.* The three legs, each showing signs of readiness to break, are respectively inscribed *Commons* (l), *Kings* (centre), and *Lords* (r.). A small figure, Bute, in highland dress, is kicking violently at the centre leg of the stool. Beneath the design is engraved, *It is easily overturn'd. Shakespeare.*

Intended to show that Bute's pernicious influence with the King will overthrow and has already shaken the constitution of King, Lords, and Commons, on which the National Debt depends The clamour against Bute had been revived by Chatham's speech on 2 March 1770, see No. 4841 &c.

$3\frac{5}{8} \times 6$ in.

4950 STRUENSEE'S GHOST, OR LORD B——TE & M—N—D IN THE HORRORS. [1 May 1772]

Engraving From the *Oxford Magazine,* viii. 145 Bute (l) seated at a table and wearing the ribbon and star of the Garter, starts in horror at a headless figure (r.), which floats towards him, holding in his hands his head dripping with blood Behind Bute stands Mansfield (l), also horror-struck A demon with a barbed tongue squats on the floor below the ghost, beckoning to Bute. On the table are a book, *Prerogative,* and a document inscribed, *A Plan to Establish Arbitrary Power.* On the floor are two papers: *A Plan for limiting all Court favours to the Worst men we can find,* and *Bill to Limit the Descendants of George y^e . . .* (an allusion to the Royal Marriage Bill, see No. 4970).

Struensee, the favourite of the Queen of Denmark, executed on 28 April (see No. 4956), actually experienced the fate with which the political satirists had long been threatening Bute, who was openly accused of being the lover of the Princess Dowager of Wales, and the power behind the throne and the ministry, and had been threatened with the fate of Mortimer, see No. 4150, &c. For Struensee see W. F. Reddaway, 'Struensee and the Fall of Berndorff', *Eng. Hist. Rev.*, xxvii, 1912, pp. 274–86, *Camb. Mod. Hist.* vi. ch xxi. See also Nos 4945, 4946, 4956

$5 \times 3\frac{5}{8}$ in.

4951 THE FAT PLURALIST AND HIS LEAN CURATES.[1]

[1 May 1772]

Engraving From *Every Man's Magazine*, i 459. An extremely fat bishop sits in an ornate two-wheeled chariot which is drawn (r. to l) by six curates wearing bands and long ragged gowns. In his r. hand he holds out a gothic church, two more churches are under his l arm. Behind his back, in place of a cushion, is a book, *Self Denial a Virtue*. Two pigs stand behind him, their front hoofs supported on the back of the chariot At his feet are two sucking pigs, a hen and a goose, representing tithes. The near chariot wheel passes over a book, *The 39 Articles*. The bishop says: *The Church was made for Me, not I for the Church.* One of the curates says · *Lord be mercifull to us poor Curates*, another says *And send us more Comfortable Living.*

The contrast between the higher and lower clergy was a constant subject of satire, see No 4236 At this time attention was particularly directed to the clergy by the Bill for relief from subscription to the thirty-nine articles, see No. 4944, and by the motion on 17 Feb. 1772 opposed by the Ministry for a *Nullum Tempus* Bill to protect the owner of real property against dormant claims of the Church. It was urged that danger to the poor parochial clergy was used as a screen for the rich 'to guard and defend luxury and superfluity', *Ann. Reg.* 1772, p. 89 f.; *Parl Hist*, xvii, pp 301 ff.

$5\frac{5}{8} \times 5\frac{5}{8}$ in.

4952 HE RULES AS ABSOLUTELY & WITH AS MUCH IN-DIGNITY TO EVERY DEPARTMENT OF ADMINISTRATION, AS WHEN HE OPENLY HELD THE REINS OF GOVERNMENT. *Anon.*

[1 June 1772]

Design'd & Engrav'd for the Political Register.

Engraving. From the *Political Register*, x. 265. The gateway of St. James's Palace. On its flagstaff is a standard bearing Bute's arms with the motto *Avito viret honore* (cf. No. 4423) Under the archway a Scotsman in kilt and plaid holds a prancing horse by the tail Another Scot stands by flourishing a whip and holding in his l. hand a saddle with stirrups.

The death of the Princess Dowager of Wales (8 Feb. 1772) had made the persistent accusations of the Opposition less credible The title appears to be an echo of Chatham's speech on secret influence, see Nos. 4841, 4949

$6\frac{3}{4} \times 4\frac{1}{8}$ in.

4953 THE DIFFERENCE OF WEIGHT BETWEEN COURT & CITY ALDERMEN

[1 June 1772]

Engraving. From the *Oxford Magazine*, viii. 189. On a large pair of scales a slim man standing in the l. scale completely outweighs two men in the

[1] This was incorrectly dated *c* 1733, and catalogued as No. 2003.

other All three wear furred livery gowns On the scales, at the feet of
the Court alderman (Harley), are a money-bag, and notes marked *10,000.*
He says: *Where are their Remonstrances now? Oh rare London Tavern!*
Behind him stand Mansfield and Bute, who points at him, saying· *Deel
down wi ye all ye loons, here is my Mon con give ye all a Drubbing.* The l.
scale rests on the ground, the r is high in the air, on it a very stout man,
probably Brass Crosby the ex-Lord Mayor, is sitting He is exclaiming
in alarm: *Oh Lord Oh Lord! I shall be down.* Wilkes stands behind him
saying *S' death that damd Scot has put false weight in the Scale!* A man
kneeling on one knee holds the r. scale with both hands saying: *Zounds!
shall this little Wine Merchant out-weigh us all?* In the foreground the cap
of liberty on a stick is supported in a chamber-pot On the wall is a picture
of Britannia hanging from a gallows The accompanying text runs, 'We
are now convinced that the weight of a city Alderman is not by any means
equal to that of a court Alderman, especially if they are weighed in the
scales of administration The Patriotic Citizens seem to have lost all their
influence, and Lord North has had very little difficulty in supporting a
majority upon all occasions.' The reference is to the Court of Aldermen
where Harley was the leader of the Court party in opposition to the Patriots.
The Court of Aldermen, in constrast with the Common Council and the
Common Hall, had in general a majority for the Court For Harley see
Nos. 4852, 4939, &c For the London Tavern, a meeting-place of the Bill
of Rights Society, see No 5104.

$5\frac{1}{8} \times 3\frac{3}{4}$ in.

4954 BRITANIA INTOXICATED, OR THE GREAT ONES IN A
BAGNIO   [1 June 1772]

Engraving From the *Oxford Magazine*, viii. 185. A drunken orgy in a
room with mirrors on the wall Britannia, dressed as a courtesan (r), leans
back in a chair, dead drunk, in her r hand is a wine-bottle. One foot rests
on her shield A man standing behind pours over her the contents of a
wine-bottle, in his r hand he holds out a wine-glass. In the centre is a
staggering figure wearing the ribbon and order of the Bath. His pocket
is being picked by a plainly dressed man, while another holds his shoulder.
Two men aimlessly flourish drawn swords. Another aims a blow with a
long pole at a mirror A courtesan has broken a mirror with a wine-bottle
which she is waving in the air In the background a woman, seated on a
man's knee, is picking his pocket On the floor in the foreground are
broken wine-glasses, and a broken punch-bowl inscribed *the Constitution.*
The explanatory text asks 'Who are the greatest drunkards?—Those at
the helm—Who set the most glaring examples of adultery, fornication,
&c.— . . .'.

$3\frac{1}{2} \times 5\frac{3}{4}$ in

4955 THE PREMIER DISTRIBUTING THE LOAVES AND FISHES
TO THE LABOURERS IN HIS VINEYARD MAY 9, 1772.
[1 July 1772]

Vol. IV. No. XVIII.

Engraving. From the *Town and Country Magazine*, iv. 304. The design
illustrates 'The Outs and the Ins, a Dialogue upon the Premier distributing
. . . [*ut supra*]' A scene in Palace Yard; part of the end of Westminster

Hall visible in the background (r.). North stands on stilts which are strapped to his legs and held up by Mansfield (l.) and Bute (r.), who are seated on the ground. From his pocket hang papers inscribed *Titles, Pensions*. In the foreground (r.) a disappointed patriot hurries away covering his face with his hand: Wilkes 'retiring in rage and despair'. Behind on the l. is a group of three smiling ministerialists, one holding up a bag of money. These are 'Mungo.' [Dyson], 'Geo. O.' [Onslow], and the 'duke of G' [Grafton]. In the background (r.) is a group of clergy, who are presbyterian parsons, returning to Scotland. (The dissenters had petitioned to be exempt from the penal laws, which were never executed against them; the Bill was rejected in the House of Lords. Walpole, *Last Journals*, 1910, i. 89–92.)

This satire attacks both ministerialists and patriots; Lord North says that 'the glorious stand against mock patriotism has placed it in such just disrepute that they are even ashamed of associating with each other'. He appeals for exertion and unanimity against 'the common foe . . the loaves and fishes will be all our own'.

$6\frac{3}{8} \times 3\frac{7}{8}$ in.

4955A Pen and wash drawing for this reversed
$6\frac{7}{8} \times 4\frac{1}{8}$ in.

4956 THE FATE OF FAVOURITES.　　　　　　　　[1 July 1772]

Design'd & Engrav'd for the Political Register.

Engraving. From the *Political Register*, x. 329. A man kneels with his head on the block, his hat and wig are on the ground, the executioner's axe is raised in both hands. Behind (r.) at a table a man sharpens a knife. Two men (l.) stand in conversation, one holds in his l. hand a paper inscribed *Struensee*. Below the steps of the scaffold are mounted soldiers holding drawn swords. Behind them are the faces of the crowd.

The parallel between the story of Struensee and Queen Matilda Caroline of Denmark (see No. 4945, &c.) and the allegations which Wilkes and the patriots had been making for years against Bute and the Princess Dowager of Wales (Queen Matilda's mother) was too obvious to be missed. Here the threat to Bute of Struensee's fate (he was executed on 28 Apr. 1772), though implicit, is clear. See also Nos 4945, 4946, 4950

$3\frac{5}{8} \times 5\frac{7}{8}$ in

4957 PICTURE OF EUROPE FOR JULY 1772.

Engraving. Probably from a magazine. A group of seven monarchs wearing crowns and ermine-trimmed robes. At a table sit three who are studying a large map inscribed *Map of the Kingdom of Poland*. They are evidently Catharine II of Russia, Frederick of Prussia, and the Emperor. Facing them (l.) sits a king whose crown is broken, his head is bowed, his hands are tied behind his back, evidently Stanislaus II of Poland. Behind the three studying the map, two standing monarchs (r.) look on with expressions of concern, they are Louis XV (indicated by *fleur-de-lys*) and Charles III of Spain. In a chair on the extreme r. George III lies back fast asleep, his chair is inscribed *Brit. . . .* Behind Stanislaus (l.) sits a bearded man with an elaborate triple turban, his wrists and ankles are chained; he probably represents the Grand Signor of Turkey with whom Catharine was at war. Above the map of Poland hang scales inscribed *The Ballance of Power*; on the lighter scale is a label inscribed *Great Britain*

A satire on the first Partition of Poland, the Russo-Prussian treaty for which was signed 17 Feb 1772, the partition taking place 5 May 1772, and on the first Russo-Turkish War (1768–74). Evidently by the same artist as No. 5222; both depict George III as regardless of England's interests and blind to events in Europe. For the attitude of the Government to the situation, see a Cabinet Minute of Nov 1772 in *The Sandwich Papers*, ed. G R. Barnes and J. H. Owen, 1932, pp. 30–2 George III was by no means blind to the Polish question, see a remarkable paper in his handwriting in *Corr. of George III*, ed. Fortescue, ii. 428–9. See Nos. 4958, 5110, 5124, 5222, 5229

$3\frac{3}{4} \times 6\frac{5}{16}$ in.

4958 THE TROELFTH CAKE   LE GATEAU DES ROIS
[*c.* 1772; perhaps later]

London Printed for Rob.t Sayer ar tthe [sic] Golden Buck facing Fetter Lane End of Fleet Steet

Engraving Four monarchs inspecting a large map of Poland inscribed *Pologne en 1772*, spread out on a table. Catharine II of Russia is seated (l.) and points with both hands to the part of South Poland nearest the Russian frontier. She looks up towards Stanislaus II of Poland who stands with his l. hand on the map, his r. clutching his crown which is slipping from his head; he looks at Catharine with a distraught expression. Opposite Catharine at the other side of the table (r.) stands Frederick of Prussia, in riding dress, his sword resting on the map near *Dantzik* and between *Brandebour* and *Pomeranie*. George III stands in profile to the r. between Stanislaus, to whom his back is turned, and Frederick, his l. hand rests on the map, from which, however, he looks away. France blowing two trumpets flies above and away from the four monarchs. Clouds and trees form a background Laurel branches are growing (r.) behind Frederick, two laurel wreaths lie at Catharine's feet. She wears an ermine-lined robe, and sits in an ornate chair, the arm of which is a carved eagle.

Probably a French print the engraving is in a French manner, and the publication line is evidently adapted (incorrectly) from an English print of an earlier date (before the numbering of the houses in Fleet Street *c.* 1766). 'Troelfth' is probably a French engraver's rendering of Twelfth, cf No. 5229. In 1772 France was powerless to prevent the partition of Poland, especially in view of the latent hostility of England, *Camb. Mod Hist*, vi 357. This print may be an effort of propaganda to suggest the joint action of France and England to prevent the partition (there were rumours in England in 1773 that such action was contemplated, see Nos. 5110, 5124), or at least, to secure the benevolent neutrality of England. George III is represented as indolently acquiescing in the Partition as in No. 4957. See also Nos. 5222, 5229.

$8\frac{13}{16} \times 6\frac{1}{2}$ in.

4959 BLACK HARRY.
[1 Aug. 1772]

Design'd & Engrav'd for the Political Register.

Engraving From the *Political Register*, xi 1. The knave of a pack of cards facing l. with the head of the Duke of Grafton In his r hand he holds an arrow. An anchor inscribed *Bradshaw* lies diagonally across his person.

This is an allusion to the appointment of Thomas Bradshaw, a Treasury Clerk, as a Lord of the Admiralty in succession to Charles Fox on 6 May 1772. An anonymous letter in the *Public Advertiser*, 8 May 1772, addressed to the Lords of the Admiralty and transcribed by Walpole, explains the intention of this satire '. . by means of his uncommon address in administering to the *pleasures of the great*, he was appointed one of the Secretaries of the Treasury, which office he held during the Duke of Grafton's administration, and by exerting his happy talents between his Grace and the celebrated Nancy Parsons, he so far ingratiated himself with the Duke that he became his chief confidant, . and of course became his Grace's *bosom friend*; for which service he first received a pension of *fifteen hundred pounds a year for three lives*, and that not being sufficient is now made *one of you* . .' Walpole's comment is, "The Duke of Grafton's ambition was to be at the head of the Admiralty, and he had insisted on Bradshaw being placed at the Board as a spy on Lord Sandwich, and to learn the business, that he might be his Grace's Secretary there, if he could obtain the command'. *Last Journals*, 1920, i 109–10. Cf. Grafton, *Autobiography*, ed. Anson, 1898, pp. 258–63.

Bradshaw, like Dyson, was one of the official M.P.'s who were singled out for distrust and abuse Cf Mason, *Heroic Epistle*, 'The R*g*ys, ——s, Mungos, B*——ds*s there' [Rigbys, Calcrafts. . .], and *Letters of Junius*, ed. Everett, 1927, pp. 153, 269. See Walpole, *Memoirs of the Reign of George III*, 1894, iv. 45–6 and n. See also Nos. 4962, 5018.

$5\frac{5}{8} \times 3\frac{7}{8}$ in.

4960 THE RED RIBBAND BESTOWED INSTEAD OF A HALTER.
[1 Aug 1772]

Engraved for the Oxford Magazine.

Engraving. From the *Oxford Magazine*, ix 24. The devil, as a man with horns, bat's wings, and goat's legs, stands surrounded by flames In his r. hand he holds out a ribbon from which hangs the badge of the order of the Bath. His l. hand is round the neck of a man who kneels on one knee, and stretches out his hand towards the ribbon This man wears a star and resembles caricatures of Lord North, but the allusion to the red ribbon suggests that he may be intended for Sir George Macartney, made K B. on 29 May, and unpopular as a son-in-law of Bute and leader of the ministerial side in the Irish House of Commons (see No. 5134) Facing him on the l and seated among four money-bags is a demon From a gallows on the l. hangs a coronet. The devil says: *Do as I command thee & I will heap favours & Honours on thee.* The kneeling man says: *I will sell my whole Country for a Ribband & a Coronet.* From his pocket hangs a paper, *Plan for paying off the National Debt* (an explicit allusion to Lord North, see Nos. 4961, 4969). The seated demon says: *How Happy is that Man who glories in the ruin of Millions*, he holds a paper inscribed *Plan of the best ways & means of Conciliating the Affections of the People by ruining them all* The money-bags are inscribed. *Purloined from the India Company, For bribing Juries; Pensions on Ireland; For Pensioning Parli—m—t.*

In spite of the allusion to Lord North, who got his Garter on 25 Mar. 1772, the red ribbon suggests Macartney, as does the accompanying text.

'. . . these honours are seldom conferred on any but those who will submit to the peremptory dictates of the minister. . . .' The ambiguity was perhaps a measure of precaution.

$6\frac{3}{8} \times 4\frac{1}{16}$ in

4961 A VIEW OF THE DELUGE OF SCOTCH PAPER CURRENCY FOR ENGLISH GOLD. [1 Aug. 1772]

Engraving. From the *Oxford Magazine*, ix. 1. A Scotsman in the air astride a broom is carrying off six large money-bags, three being inscribed *£2,000*, *£10,000*, and *£50,000*. He scatters banknotes or bills; men on the ground, some sinking into a bog, exclaim in horror at his action. In the centre Britannia is seated, she says: *This Scotch paper diet has brought me to a consumption*. In the foreground (r.) Lord North seated, his back to the other figures, writes on a paper inscribed: *Scheme for paying off the National Debt*, he says *I will not at present promise to pay 17 Millions in ten Years*. The scene is the sea-shore; three Scotsmen (l.) row out to sea in a boat loaded with money-bags, saying: *We'll over the Water to Charly*. The Scotsman on the broom, who resembles caricatures of Bute, says: *The deel away wi ye all ye English Pudding-bags ken ye nae that Paper is lighter of digestion than Gold*. A man sinking in a bog-hole says: *Oh I am Sunk for ever*. Another, covering his face, says: *Let me hide my Face, how can I now shew my self to my Creditors*.

A financial crisis in 1772, following the collapse of a speculative mania in Scotland, largely due to the Ayr Bank (see *Letters of Hume*, 1932, ii 263-4) was precipitated by the failure of Alexander Fordyce, a Scot, and the leading partner in an important London bank, see No 5016. There was a panic in the City, and the clamour against the Scots was revived. Walpole, *Last Journals*, 1920, i. 117 f. See No. 4947. North in his budget speech of 1 May 1772 estimated that if peace continued for ten years, the National Debt would be reduced by £17,000,000. *Parl. Hist.*, xvii 489. See also No. 4969.

$4 \times 6\frac{3}{8}$ in.

4962 [SIX REMARKABLE HEADS][1] [1 Sept 1772]

Engraving. From the *London Magazine*, xli. 360. Six caricature portraits in circles illustrating 'The Sale by Auction, A Dream', pp. 360-4, in which members or adherents of the Ministry are put up to auction at Christie's.

Nº 1. The head of an ass, 'a prime minister' (Lord North), Minister and an ass being synonymous terms.

Nº 2. The bust-portrait of a man in riding-dress, wearing a jockey cap, a riding whip under his l. arm 'A duke, a gambler, a privy-counsellor and a skeleton!' The Duke of Grafton, see No. 4959. Having refused a post in the Cabinet, he took little part in the Government, and attacks on him by caricatures were probably stimulated by the *Letters of Junius*, e.g. that of 27 Nov. 1771. *Letters*, ed Everett, 1927, 269 ff.

Nº 3 Bust-portrait of a man in laced coat looking to l., scarcely a caricature. He is described as 'the miraculous Br——w himself *alias* Cream-coloured *Tommy*', and pilloried as a procurer. Thomas Bradshaw, a Lord of the Admiralty and secretary to Grafton. Junius, *op. et loc. cit.*, attacks him, using and perhaps bestowing the epithet cream-coloured. He was

[1] Title taken from 'Directions to the Book-binder'.

surnamed 'the cream-coloured parasite'. Wraxall, *Memoirs*, 1884, 1 351 Walpole calls him 'Pimp to Lord Barrington'. Notes on *Mason's Satires*, ed. Toynbee, p. 64. See Nos. 4959, 5018.

N° 4. H.L. portrait of a negro in a striped suit. 'Mungo' or Jeremiah Dyson, here described as bought by the Irish patriots to be hanged in effigy, an allusion to the miscarriage of his Irish pension, see Nos. 4936, 4942.

N° 5. Bust-portrait of a macaroni, wearing a small hat, a club or queue of hair, and holding a tasselled cane. He is described as 'the Cub', and was to be thrown away not sold, 'for all people seem to be of opinion, "That a Macaroni is worth nothing"'. He is C J. Fox, who was the macaroni *par excellence*, as the term was used by Walpole, for the extravagant young gamblers who were leaders of fashion. Cf Walpole's comment on Mason's lines:

> The Jews and Macaroni's are at war:
> The Jews prevail, and thund'ring from the stocks
> They seize, they bind, they circumcise C——s F——.

Heroic Epistles. Written Summer 1772. 'The Chiefs of the Maccaronis became known beyond the limits of their fantastic Dominion by their excessive Gaming' Mason's *Satirical Poems*, ed. P. Toynbee, 1926, p. 70. See also No. 5010

N° 6. Bust-portrait of an elderly man He is 'Sir Gibby', one of the Scots who 'preside in our cabinets and lead kings as they list'. Sir Gilbert Elliot (1722–77), Treasurer of the Navy 1770, and reputed a special confidant of George III. Cf. *Corr. of George III*, ed. Fortescue, 1. 316.

$6\frac{13}{16} \times 4\frac{1}{4}$ in. (pl.); circles *c.* $1\frac{13}{16}$ in diam.

4963 THE WICKED STATESMAN, OR THE TRAITOR TO HIS COUNTRY, AT THE HOUR OF DEATH [1 Sept 1772]

Engraving From the *Oxford Magazine*, ix 69. A companion print to No 4965. A man (l.) wearing a ribbon and star is seated in a high-backed chair at a small round table; he shrinks back in horror at the sight of three monsters advancing towards him surrounded by flames. In the centre a horned demon with animal's legs, holds up in his l. claw a table resembling tables of the Commandments in churches of the period. Its double columns are headed, *Catalogue of the different Sins, Committed by the Earl of —— against God, his King & his Country*. With the other claw he points at what is written below. On the r a naked and emaciated figure with the head of a skull runs towards the statesman threatening him with a spear and outstretched talons. A crocodile (r.) advances with open jaws. A serpent coiling round the statesman's leg, opens its jaws to strike On the table are three money-bags and two documents, one headed *Scheme for selling England to the French*. On the floor are two books: *Art of Bribery* and *Machiavel*. The portrait is probably a generalized one, it has a certain resemblance to Grafton, none to Bute as suggested by the inscription 'Earl of ——'. Probably copied from No. 4964.

$6\frac{3}{8} \times 3\frac{15}{16}$ in

4964 THE MINISTER IN SURPRIZE. [n.d., see No 4963]

Engraving Another and probably earlier version of No 4960 reversed The words on the tablet held by the demon are *The American Resolves are a Devil of a Dose*   The papers on the table are inscribed *New Members* and *Civil List in Arrears*   The books on the floor are *American Constitution* and *List of Pensioners*   The crocodile and the figure with the head of a skull are absent. The minister is the same except that he has no ribbon and star. The 'American Resolves' may be the opposition to the Stamp Act which led to its repeal in 1766. For the succession of resolutions (1765–74) in the Colonies against trade with England see Schlesinger, *The Colonial Merchants and the American Revolution, 1763–76.*

$6\frac{13}{16} \times 3\frac{7}{8}$ in.

4965 THE CONTRAST; OR THE VIRTUOUS PATRIOT AT THE HOUR OF DEATH.   [1 Oct. 1772]

Engraving. From the *Oxford Magazine*, ix. 108.   A companion print to No. 4963.   In a large curtained bed a man lies surrounded by his weeping family. A clergyman kneels at the bedside in prayer   An angel radiating rays of light on the bed, points to the sky.

$6\frac{3}{8} \times 3\frac{15}{16}$ in.

4966 THE CITY JUNTO OR THE MIN—ST—L [MINISTERIAL] ALDERMEN OF GOTHAM IN CONSULTATION.   [1 Nov. 1772]

Engraving. From the *Oxford Magazine*, ix 128.   Six men in furred aldermen's gowns sit round a table on which is a punch-bowl. The most prominent alderman (r) holds a paper inscribed *A Treatise on good Eating and drinking*.   A seventh alderman stands, holding up a paper inscribed, *behold our Brethren* which serves as a title to a large picture on the wall, in which a bull, an ass, and a hog (H.L. figures) stand on their hind legs in conference   The presiding alderman appears to be Harley, see No. 4939, &c. The figures are caricatured, and in general of gross appearance.

$6\frac{1}{2} \times 3\frac{15}{16}$ in.

4967 THE PATRIOTS DECEIVED, OR TOWNSEND TRIUMPHANT.   [1 Dec. 1772]
Vol. IV.   No. XXXIII.

Engraving. From the *Town and Country Magazine*, iv. 585.   Wilkes, holding the cap of liberty on a staff and wearing a furred alderman's gown, is stepping into a state coach. He is being pulled back by another alderman. A third alderman (r) is clasping his hands in distress   On the l. one alderman takes, though with an air of reluctance, money-bags and notes from another. All wear furred gowns. Behind (l) a parson watches with a face of satisfaction, with him is a very obese man. In the foreground a small boy (l) appears to be clapping his hands while a dog barks, on the r a little chimney sweep with brush and bag of soot points derisively at Wilkes. Behind (r) a man wearing a laced hat weeps into a handkerchief.

Wilkes had been returned at the head of the poll for the mayoralty in 1772 but was rejected by the Court of Aldermen in favour of Alderman Townsend, one of the City patriots who had quarrelled with Wilkes. Sharpe, *London and the Kingdom*, iii 132–4. The clergyman in the background appears to be Parson Horne. The transaction with money-bags is probably intended to represent Harley distributing bribes from the ministry to secure the rejection of Wilkes, for which the King was extremely anxious. *Corr of George III*, ed Fortescue, ii 401. The accompanying dialogue consists of an altercation between Wilkes and Townsend without reference to the bystanders. For Townsend see *Notes and Queries*, 11th S v, pp. 2–4 (1912). For the quarrel between Wilkes and Horne (which involved Townsend and others) see No 4861, &c, and Nos. 5129–31; for Harley, No. 4939, &c

$3\frac{5}{8} \times 5\frac{7}{8}$ in.

4968 THE BALANCE OF CREDIT.

Publish'd according to act of parliament Decʳ 28. 1772 by J. Almon in Piccadilly. price one Shilling.

Engraving. An eagle holds in his beak the beam of a pair of scales; Lord North, in profile to the l., and looking through his spy-glass, stands below, adding a document to the l. and lighter scale; the r. scale rests on the ground (or ocean) within an area inscribed *The South Sea*. The l. beam of the scale is inscribed *1772*, the r beam *1720*. On Lord North's l. scale, that of 1772, are documents inscribed *Reduct. of Navy, Secret Com ; Select Com.*; North is adding one inscribed *Suspension of Supervision.* The r scale (empty) is inscribed *India Stock 00001* This is to show that the national credit in 1772 is even lower than at the time of the South Sea Bubble in 1720. Seated facing North is Britannia with her shield and spear; she holds out her hand saying to him *An Able Minister would Balance it* Her foot is on a *Map of England*, on which *Hayes* and *Stowe* are written in the south-west corner, to imply that able ministers might be found in those places, the seats of Chatham and Lord Temple. In the upper l. corner of the design is a view of the Tower of London, the bridge inscribed *Traitors Bridge*. The pendant to this in the upper r. corner is a view (on a larger scale) of the gateway of St. James's Palace. George III wearing a crown leans out of a window over the archway holding a fishing-rod, at the end of his line is a large begging-box inscribed *Date Obolum Belisario*. In his l. hand he holds out a paper inscribed *Arrears of Civil List* Beneath the title is etched,

> *Jove lifts the golden Balances that Show*
> *The fates of mortal men & things below*

The documents on Lord North's scale refer to the appointment of a Select Committee on East India Affairs voted 13 Apr 1772 and the further appointment of a Secret Committee in December. On 18 Dec 1772 a Bill was passed to restrain the East India Company from appointing supervisors in spite of the protests of the Company, see No 5102 On 23 Apr. 1771 orders had been issued for reducing the Navy to peace strength *Cal H O. Papers*, 1770–2, p 247 See also corr. of Sept 1772 between North and Sandwich on the reduction of the Navy, *Sandwich Papers*, i. 1932, pp. 19–26. For the Civil List see also Nos. 5105, 5124

$9\frac{1}{16} \times 13\frac{1}{2}$ in

4969 BOREAS.

Engraving From the *New Foundling Hospital for Wit*. Part V, 1772 (frontispiece). A portrait of Lord North (T.Q L) speaking in the House of Commons. He is in profile to the r. looking through an eye-glass held in his l hand, and reading from a paper held in his r hand. Beneath the design is engraved, *I Promise to pay seventeen millions in ten Years—if I am Minister (Parliamentary Register)*, an allusion to North's budget speech, 1 May 1772, *Parl Hist* xvii. 484, see Nos. 4961, 5099

A similar portrait, with the same title, probably copied from this one, was used in the *Oxford Magazine*, 1774, see No. 5231.

$5\frac{1}{2} \times 3\frac{3}{8}$ in (pl.).

4970 [THE SENATORS]

London: Printed for G. Kearsly in Ludgate Street.　　　MDCCLXXII.

Engraving. An oval design which decorates the title-page of the *Senators: or a candid examination into the Merits of the Principal Performers of S^t. Stephens Chapel. The Fourth Edition with Alterations and Additions* The Speaker, in the Speaker's chair, sits behind the table on which is the mace and a document inscribed *Royal Marriage Bill*. An axe is suspended above his head. His feet rest on two rolled documents beneath the table: *Magna Charta* and the *Bill of Rights* A standing figure (r) in armour, apparently intended for Cromwell, is pointing at the Marriage Bill. Members of the Ministry sit on the Treasury Bench. Other members are seen standing and sitting behind. Beneath is engraved·

> *Thus our Senators cheat the deluded People with a shew*
> *Of LIBERTY, which yet they ne'er must taste of;*
> *Drive us like Wrecks down the rough Tide of Power,*
> *Whilst no hold's left to save us from destruction.*
> 　　　　　　　　　　　　　*Otway.*

This illustrates a poem which appears to have reached a fourth edition in a year. It is a violent attack on members of the ministerial party by name —members of the Opposition are correspondingly praised.

For the opposition to the Marriage Act, see Walpole, *Last Journals*, 1910, i. 23-4, 27-31, 33-71. The Bill was introduced into the Lords on 20 Feb. 1772. *Parl. Hist.* xvii. 383 ff. It occasioned the resignation of Charles Fox, cf Nos. 4944, 5113.

Oval, $2\frac{7}{8} \times 4\frac{7}{8}$ in.; pl. $3\frac{3}{4} \times 5\frac{3}{8}$ in.

PERSONAL SATIRES

4971–4984

Series of Tête-à-tête portraits.

4971 N° XXXIV. MISS J——S.   [1 Jan. 1772]
N° XXXV. THE MIDDLESEX CHAMPION.

Engraving *Town and Country Magazine*, iii. 625. Two bust portraits in oval frames, illustrate 'Histories of the Tête-à-Tête annexed; or, Memoirs of the Middlesex Champion and Miss J——nes' An account of Luttrell, who opposed Wilkes at the Middlesex election, and of his amours. The seduction of Arabella Bolton, see Nos. 4285, 4852, is alluded to, though the story is qualified as 'greatly exaggerated to serve the purposes of party', in order to render the colonel obnoxious at the time of his election. Allusions are made to the marriage of his sister to the Duke of Cumberland, in which he is said to have played 'a capital part', see No. 4890. Miss J is identified by H. Bleackley as Polly Jones

Ovals, $2\frac{3}{4} \times 2\frac{1}{4}$ in.   B.M.L., P.P. 5442 b.

4972 Vol III. N° XXXVII. THE FEMALE POLITICIAN. [Jan.1772]
N° XXXVIII THE REVEREND JOINER

Engraving. *Town and Country Magazine*, iii 681 (Supplement). Two bust portraits in oval frames illustrate 'Histories of the Tête-à-Tête annexed; or, Memoirs of the Reverend Joiner and Mrs. L——n'. An account of Dr Wilson, Master of the Joiners' Company, and Rector of St. Stephen Walbrook, a member of the Bill of Rights Society He is said to have 'routed Horne', and to be a doughty advocate of Wilkes. His past mistresses include 'Lady G—nst—n', see No. 4979, alleged to have since served him as a procuress. Being anxious to find a lady who was 'a female patriot' he was informed that there was only one, Mrs. Macaulay, in default of her, he discovered Mrs. L——n, a widow of about forty, a 'public writer', proficient in history and politics.

The Doctor's later intimacy with Mrs. Macaulay became notorious, see Nos. 5410, 5441.

Ovals, $2\frac{3}{4} \times 2\frac{1}{4}$ in.   B.M.L., P P. 5542 b.

4973 N° II. M^{RS} L——SLE.   *Vol. 4*
N° III. LORD H——N.   [1 Feb 1772]

Engraving. *Town and Country Magazine*. iv. 9. Two bust portraits in oval frames illustrate 'Histories of the Tête-à-Tête annexed; . . . .' An account of the political and military career and amours of William, 2nd Earl of Harrington, 1719–79, see No. 5033. His wife is spoken of as 'a professed Messalina' who yet 'preserves some decency in her manners', see No 4903 Mrs. L—— is the daughter of an officer (P——ker) killed at the siege of Havannah and the widow of an attorney.

Ovals, $2\frac{3}{4} \times 2\frac{5}{16}$ in   B.M.L., P.P. 5442 b.

4974 Nº IV Mⁿˢ K——DAL. *Vol. 4*

Nº V. THE EQUESTRIAN HERO. [1 March 1772]

Engraving. *Town and Country Magazine*, IV 65 Two bust portraits in oval frames illustrate 'Histories of the Tête-à-Tête annexed; . . .'. An account of Henry, 10th Earl of Pembroke (1734–94), author of a 'treatise on horsemanship' (*Method of Breaking Horses*, 1st ed. 1762) His elopement with Miss H——r [Hunter] is recounted, the pair going to the Hotel d'Angleterre, Brussels, kept by 'madam Bougie' (de Bouget), mother to 'Mrs. Kn——les', wife of Admiral Knowles, then alleged to be divorced on account of an affair with Captain Gamb——r (James Gambier, 1723–89, afterwards vice-admiral) After his reconciliation with his wife he was reputed the lover of 'first rate toasts', who were supplanted by Mrs. K——dal [Kendal]. She is the reputed daughter of the late Lord P——t by 'the celebrated Peg Ham——n. After she eloped from school with her dancing master, K——, she became financially embarrassed, and established a successful boarding school at Brompton Here she met Lord Pembroke, who induced her to give up her school by giving her an annuity of double the annual profits.

Ovals, $2\frac{3}{4} \times 2\frac{1}{4}$ in. B M.L , P.P. 5442 b.

4975 Nº VII. Mⁿˢ V——T *Vol. 4*

Nº VIII. THE BATTERSEA BARON. [1 April 1772]

Engraving. *Town and Country Magazine*, IV. 121. Two bust portraits in oval frames illustrate 'Histories of the Tête-à-Tête annexed, . . .' An account of the amours of a descendant of 'St J', that is, Frederick, 3rd Viscount St. John and 2nd Viscount Bolingbroke, 1734–87. Mrs. (or Miss) V——nt is a clergyman's daughter and milliner's apprentice who was drugged by a procuress on behalf of Lord B.

Ovals, $2\frac{11}{16} \times 2\frac{1}{4}$ in. B.M.L., P.P. 5442 b.

4976 Nº X. Mⁿˢ G——N. *Vol. 4*

Nº XI. L——D IRON——HAM [1 May 1772]

Engraving. *Town and Country Magazine*, IV. 177. Two bust portraits in oval frames illustrate 'Histories of the Tête-à-Tête annexed, . . .' An account of the amours of Simon Luttrell, Baron Irnham, subsequently Viscount Carhampton and Earl Carhampton in the Irish peerage—then conspicuous as the father of Col. Luttrell and of Mrs. Horton who had recently married the Duke of Cumberland.

Mrs G., passing as an officer's widow, was married by arrangement to an oilman with a portion from Lord I.

Ovals, $2\frac{11}{16} \times 2\frac{1}{4}$ in. B.M.L., P.P. 5442 b.

4977 Nº XIII. THE CELEBRATED Mⁿˢ B—DL—Y.

Nº XIV. CAPTAIN H——R. [1 June 1772]

Engraving. *Town and Country Magazine*, VI. 233. Two bust portraits in oval frames on one plate illustrate 'Histories of the Tête-à-Tête annexed; . . .'. An account of George Hanger (1751?–1824), son of Baron Coleraine and of Mrs. Baddeley (1745–86). Captain H—— is said to have insisted on her admission to the Pantheon, on the second night, in spite of the decision to exclude women of doubtful character, see No. 4998.

Ovals, $2\frac{5}{8} \times 2\frac{1}{4}$ in.   B M L., P.P. 5442 b

4978 N° XVI. M^RS W——T.   [1 July 1772]
     N° XVII. THE MINDEN HERO.

Engraving. *Town and Country Magazine*, iv. 289 Two bust portraits in oval frames illustrate 'Histories of the Tête-à-Tête annexed, . . ' An account of Lord George Germain and of Mrs. W——st, widow of a Captain W—— who had served under Germain in Germany For Germain at Minden see Nos. 3680–7, &c.

Ovals, $2\frac{5}{8} \times 2\frac{1}{4}$ in   B.M.L , P.P 5442 b.

4979 LADY G——STON.   [July 1772]
     THE MODERN ESCULAPIUS.

Engraving From the *Town and Country Magazine*, iv 283* (Occasional Appendix) Two bust portraits in oval frames illustrate 'Histories of the Tête-à-Tête annexed, or, Memoirs of Sir William B——e and Lady G——ston'. An account of Sir William Browne, M D. (1692–1774) see *D N B*. Lady Gunston, a widow, is a demi-rep who forced a baronet to sign a paper promising marriage or a payment of £10,000 by threatening him with a pistol. She is 'celebrated for her amours, intrigues and procuring' and feigned illness to secure the doctor, said to be an easy conquest.

No Gunston baronetage is included in G E C. *Complete Baronetage*. The doctor's portrait appears to be copied from the W.L. caricature by Thomas Orde; see No. 4833.

Ovals, $2\frac{5}{8} \times 2\frac{1}{2}$ in.

4980 N° XIX MADAME P——LLE.   [1 Aug 1772]
     N° XX THE HEROIC MINISTER.

Engraving. *Town and Country Magazine*, iv. 345. Two bust portraits in oval frames illustrate 'Histories of the Tête-à-Tête annexed; . . ' The bravery of Sir Robert Murray Keith in protecting the Queen of Denmark at and after the palace revolution of January 17, 1772, see No. 4945, &c., is related with some accuracy Mme P. is a French milliner in London.

Ovals, $2\frac{5}{8} \times 2\frac{1}{4}$ in.   B.M L., P P. 5442 b

4981 N° XXII MISS BETSY WIL——X   [1 Sept. 1772]
     N° XXIII THE INFLEXIBLE PATRIOT

Engraving. *Town and Country Magazine*, iv 401. Two bust portraits in oval frames illustrate 'Histories of the Tête-à-Tête annexed, . . .' An account of Sir George Savile, 1726–84, identified by his refusal to accept nomination as a member of the Committee on East India affairs, see *Parl. Hist.* xvii. 464 From 'a pretty numerous list of his dulcineas', 'Nancy P——rsons' alone is named, besides Betsy Wil——x, a courtesan who 'passes for a relation' when she visits him. See No. 4851

Ovals, $2\frac{5}{8} \times 2\frac{1}{4}$ in.   B.M.L , P.P 5442 b.

4982 Nº XXV. Mᴿˢ O—SB—N.   *Vol. IV*
     Nº XXVI. LORD G——R   [1 Oct 1772]

Engraving. *Town and Country Magazine*, iv. 457. Two bust portraits in oval frames illustrate the 'Histories of the Tête-à-Tête annexed; . . .'. An account of the political career and amours of Granville Leveson-Gower (1721–1803), afterwards first Marquis of Stafford, alluding to the Westminster Election of 1749 Mrs Osbern was a foundling apprenticed to a milk-woman, who has had a succession of wealthy lovers and is still 'scarce twenty'.

Ovals, $2\frac{5}{8} \times 2\frac{5}{16}$ in.   B.M L., P.P. 5442 b.

4983 Nº XXVIII MISS L—B—T   *Vol. IV*
     Nº XXIX LORD P——Y   [1 Nov. 1772]

Engraving. *Town and Country Magazine*, iv 513. Two bust portraits in oval frames illustrate 'Histories of the Tête-à-Tête annexed; . . .'. An account of Lord Percy (1742–1817), afterwards second Duke of Northumberland, and of his relations with his first wife, Lady Anne Stuart, daughter of Lord Bute, from whom he was divorced, and of his amours. Miss L—— is a courtesan to whom his purse is entirely devoted.

Ovals, $2\frac{3}{4} \times 2\frac{5}{16}$ in.   B.M.L., P.P. 5442 b

4984 Nº XXXI. THE TEMPLE TOAST   *Vol. IV*
     Nº XXXII. THE AMOROUS ADVOCATE   [1 Dec. 1772]

Engraving. *Town and Country Magazine*, iv. 569 Two bust portraits in oval frames illustrate 'Histories of the Tête-à-Tête annexed; . . .'. An account of the amours of a distinguished Law Officer of the Crown and of a young woman who presided at the bar of a coffee-house near the Temple. He is Thurlow, then attorney-general, who was an habitué of Nando's coffee-house.

Ovals, $2\frac{11}{16} \times 2\frac{1}{4}$ in.   B.M.L., P.P. 5442 b.

4985–5055 and related numbers catalogued in Volume IV.

Darly's series of caricatures, continued from p. 41.

VOLUME II

4985 [TITLE PAGE.][1]

Engraving. In conventional garlands of laurel leaves with architectural ornament: VOL II. | OF | CARICATURES · | MACARONIES · | & | CHARACTERS · BY | SUNDRY · LADIES · GENTLEMᴺ | ARTISTS · &C | PUBᴰ | BY · MDARLY · Nº 39 · | STRAND · | 1772 · | 7×5 in. (pl.).

4986 V. 2. 1. CAPTᴺ CUTLASS.

Pubᵈ by MDarly Nº 39 Strand Novʳ 18ᵗʰ 1771 Accorᵗ to Act

Engraving A man (W.L) walking to l. and looking to his l. with a smile

[1] There is also a coloured impression

He wears an enormous cutlass. In his r. hand is a cane which rests on his r shoulder, his left hand is on his hip. Dress: military coat and hat with a cockade, knee-breeches, low buckled shoes. His hair is in a large looped club.

$5\frac{3}{16} \times 3\frac{3}{4}$ in.

4987 V. 2. 2. THE TIGER MACARONI, OR TWENTY MORE, KILL'EM.[1]

Pub^d by M. Darly accor^s to Act Decr 1st. 1771 (39 Strand)

Engraving. A W.L. profile figure of a man in a hat and military coat with facings. His hair stands out in a long, thin, stiffened queue His r. hand holds a tasselled cane which rests on his shoulder; his l is on the hilt of his sword. Possibly intended for Lieut. Alexander Murray, the officer in command of the Guards at the so-called Massacre of St George's Fields, 10 May 1768. (See No. 4196 and references there given) This was still a live issue, see No. 4852 and *Ann. Reg.* 1771, pp. 196–200

$5\frac{9}{16} \times 3\frac{13}{16}$ in.

4988 3. BILLY-BUTTON, MASTER OF · THE · CEREMONIES TO AN EIGHTEEN PENNY ROUT & ASSEMBLY.

Pub^d by MDarly accor^s to Act Decr 1st 1771 (39 Strand)

Engraving. A man standing (W L) in profile to r. He appears to be bowing, his r hand is held out, his l. fingers touch his breast. His profile is grotesque, with a bulbous nose and double chin. His hair is in a club He wears a laced coat and waistcoat, frilled shirt-sleeves, low buckled shoes, and a sword. Billy Button is a character in Foote's play of *The Maid of Bath*, first played 26 June 1771, the part being taken by Weston.

$5\frac{13}{16} \times 3\frac{13}{16}$ in.

4989 V. 2. 4. THE FEMALE TURF MACARONI [1]

Pub^d by M.Darly Decem^r 24th 1771 accor^s to Act.

Etching. W.L figure in profile of a lady in a riding-habit holding a riding-whip in her right hand. Her hair, without powder, is tied up in a club. She wears a cravat and a cap with an erect plume of feathers.

Probably the Duchess of Grafton, the Duke being the Turf Macaroni in this series, see No. 4634; see also No. 5324.

$5\frac{5}{8} \times 3\frac{7}{8}$ in.

4990 V. 2. 5. THE OXFORD · MACARONI.

Pub by MDarly accor to Act Jany 11th 1772

Engraving. W L. portrait of a man in profile to r. walking with mincing steps, both hands on his hips. He is slim except for a protruding stomach. He wears a tasselled mortar-board, a pair of bands, a long gown open and showing coat, waistcoat, and knee-breeches. His hair is curled on his forehead and is in a long looped club

$6\frac{1}{16} \times 4\frac{7}{16}$ in.

[1] There is also a coloured impression.

4991 V. 2. 6. THE PRETTY MANTUA MAKER[1]

Pub according to Act Jany 1 1772 by M Darly Strand

Engraving A young woman, W.L., walking to the r , she looks downwards over her r. shoulder. Her hands are crossed in front over a bundle wrapped in check material which she is carrying She is elegantly dressed in a hat with ribbons, a cloak, a trained skirt. In manner and dress she resembles, though with a more demure air and a longer petticoat, *A Modern Demi-rep* No 4922. Cf. No. 4923.

6 × 4⅜ in.

7. THE FEMALE CONOISEUR

See No 4692—1 Feb. 1772

A portrait of Mary Darly, by Matthew Darly. *B M Cat Engr. Br Portraits*

8. THE GRUB STREET MACARONI.

See No. 4693—3 Feb. 1772

4992 V. 2 9 THE UNFORTUNATE MACARONI

Pub accor to Act Feby 5 1772 by M Darly Strand

Engraving. A W L. standing figure, full-face, of a man dressed in the height of fashion. He stamps with rage, his r. leg being raised high; his r. arm is also raised, his fist clenched His face (adorned with two patches) is distorted with anger His hair is curled. He wears a small hat, a fringed cravat, a sprigged and laced waistcoat, sprigged stockings with clocks. A cane hangs from his l wrist and he wears a sword. Probably the portrait of an unlucky gambler, see No. 4697. For the gaming at this time see *Last Journals* of H Walpole under date Feb. 1772.

6⁷⁄₁₆ × 4½ in.

4993 10. THE NOVICIATE OF A MACARONI. RANELAGH. 1772.

Pub according to Act by M Darly Feby 10th 1771 [sic].

Engraving. Portrait of a man, middle-aged or elderly, W L walking in profile to the r He wears a macaroni wig with ringlets and a large club tightly bound with black ribbon A small three-cornered hat is in his l. hand, his r is on his hip. He wears a sword, a nosegay, a ruffled shirt, and low buckled shoes.

6 × 4½ in.

4994 V. 2. 11. A TEMPLE MACARONI.

Pub by M Darly accor^g to Act Feby 14th 1772

Engraving. Full-face portrait of a man walking to r. and looking to his r. His r hand is in his coat pocket, his l. thrust in his waistcoat He wears a looped hat, his hair or wig is in a long queue bound with black ribbon He wears a sword, laced coat, ruffled shirt and cravat, low buckled shoes. A dog of greyhound type walks in front.

He resembles portraits of Richard Grenville-Temple, 1st Earl Temple (1711–79)

6¼ × 5⁹⁄₁₆ in.

[1] There is also a coloured impression

4995 12. MISS LOVEJOY.

Pub accor to Act Feby 9th 1772 by MDarly Strand.

Engraving. A woman (W L) walking to the l. full face. Her hair is dressed high with tight curls at the side. She wears a fur-bordered cloak with a hood over a frilled and flounced petticoat with a looped-up train. Her hands are in a muff trimmed with frills of ribbon. A double row of pearls or beads is round her neck. A well-known house of ill-fame in the Piazza, Covent Garden, was known as Lovejoy's. H. Bleackley, *Ladies Fair and Frail*, p 154. Cf. Nos. 4786, 5057.

$6\frac{1}{8} \times 4\frac{3}{8}$ in.

4996 V. 2. 13. A LAW MACARONI.

Pub by M Darly Strand Feby 16th 1772 accor to Act.

Engraving. Portrait of a man, W L , walking in profile to l. He wears a macaroni wig with a looped and bound club, and a cravat over a pair of bands. His long gown reaches to the ground. His r. hand holds a rolled document, his l. is on his hip.

$6\frac{1}{8} \times 4\frac{3}{8}$ in.

4997 V. 2. 14. THE CLERICAL MACARONI.

R.St G.M. [St. George Mansergh] pinx^t   *I.W. sculp*

Pub accor^g to Act by M Darly Strand March 4 1772

Engraving. A man, W.L., grotesquely caricatured standing in profile to the r. He is in the height of fashion (burlesqued) and there is nothing clerical about his dress. His r. hand holds a large tasselled cane. His wig has enormous rolls of hair. He wears a nosegay, a flowered waistcoat over a protruding stomach, a large cravat, striped breeches, clocked stockings.

$6\frac{7}{8} \times 4\frac{7}{8}$ in. (pl)

15 THE PARADE MACARONI [Ensign Fitzpatrick]

See No 4704—25 Feb 1772

4998 V. 2. 16. A PANTHEON NO REP.

Pub by M Darly Strand March 3^d 1772 according to Act.

Engraving W.L portrait of a lady, standing in profile to the l In her r. hand she holds a ticket inscribed *PANTHEON admit Lady No. Rep.* She resembles portraits of Mrs. Baddeley and appears to be regarding her Pantheon ticket with a complacent smile. She wears a low bodice and a necklace; a train from her shoulders falls over a frilled and flounced petticoat. Her elbow sleeves have wide lace frills, and she wears long gloves. Her hair is dressed high and ornamented with lace.

Rep means a person of loose character. (O.E.D) It was rumoured that 'women of slight character' would not be admitted to the masquerade for the opening of the Pantheon in February 1772. This was supposed to be directed against Mrs. Baddeley, but a story that she was escorted into the building by fifty gentlemen with drawn swords appears to be an exaggerated version of action taken by George Hanger, see No. 4977.

Mrs. Harris comments on the mixed company, which included Mrs. Baddeley 'and most of the gay ladies in town and ladies of the first rank and character; and by appearance some very low people'. *Letters of the First Earl of Malmesbury*, i 247. The Pantheon was opened on 27 Jan 1772, 'the company were an olio of all sorts, peers, peeresses, honourables and right honourables, jew brokers, demi reps, lottery insurers, and quack doctors.' *Ann. Reg.* 1772, 69.

$6\frac{3}{8} \times 4\frac{5}{8}$ in.

17. THE SURRY MACARONI.
See No. 4694—12 Mar. 1772

18. THE FORTUNATE MACARONI.
See No. 4697—16 Mar. 1772

4999 19. THE CAMBRIDGE MACARONI.
Pub accor to Act March 17ᵗʰ 1772 by M Darly Strand

Engraving. W.L. portrait (caricature) of a stout man walking in profile to l. His l. hand is outspread on his protruding waistcoat. He wears a tasselled mortar-board, a very long and voluminous gown which rests on the ground. Except for his hair, which is in a doubled-up macaroni club, and ruffled shirt-sleeves, he is plainly dressed.

$6\frac{1}{16} \times 4\frac{3}{8}$ in.

5000 V. 2 20 A MACARONI LIVERYMAN [1]
Pub accor to Act March 25 1772 by M Darly Strand

Engraving A very stout man of plebeian appearance standing in profile to the r. He wears a furred livery gown, and his hair is in a long doubled-up macaroni club. In his r. hand is a knife combined with a spoon by a folding device; in his l is a two-pronged fork.

$6\frac{3}{16} \times 4\frac{5}{8}$ in

5001 V 2 21. THE MACARONI AUCTIONEER.[1]
Pub accor to Act March 24ᵗʰ 1772 by M Darly Strand

Engraving. A man standing, W.L., in profile to l., with an auctioneer's hammer in his r. hand, a taper or candle in a stand in his l. He is elegantly dressed in a laced coat, cravat, and ruffled shirt. Except for the exaggerated macaroni wig and an accentuated nose the portrait is hardly a caricature. It evidently represents Abraham Langford (1711–74) of the Covent Garden Auction Rooms, the leading auctioneer at this time. He is probably the auctioneer styled 'the Macaroni' by Junius in his Letter to Grafton of 22 June 1771. *Letters*, ed. Everett, 1927, p. 213. See No. 5171.

$6\frac{3}{16} \times 4\frac{11}{16}$ in.

5002 V. 2. 22 VENISON & CLARET OR Sᴿ HUMPʸ HAUNCH BARᵀ OF GLUTTON HALL [1]
Pub by M Darly Strand April 1ˢᵗ 1772 according to Act.

Engraving. A W L. figure standing towards the l. looking over his l.

[1] There is also a coloured impression.

shoulder. He is stout with an enormously protruding stomach. His r. hand is thrust inside his coat, his l is in his coat-pocket. His hat is under his l. arm. He wears a laced coat, a shirt with lace ruffles and a sword.
$6\frac{1}{4} \times 4\frac{5}{8}$ in.

5003 V. 2. 23. A PILLAR OF THE CHURCH. WITH IT'S PROPER CAPITAL.[1]

Pub. by M Darly Strand April 1st 1772 accor to Act

Engraving. A man, stout and elderly, dressed as a bishop stands facing T Q to l. His r. hand holds a tasselled mortar-board. He wears a silk gown, lawn sleeves, a pair of bands and an enormous wig. At the top of the plate is engraved, *Bishop of Eider Down*. Probably a portrait of the Bishop of Down, Dr. James Trail. Reproduced, A. E. Richardson, *Georgian England*, 1931, p. 57.
$6\frac{3}{16} \times 4\frac{0}{16}$ in.

5004 24. ROAST BEEF AND PORT · OR BULLY BRAMBLE ESQ^R JUSTICE OF PEACE IN WASP TOWN.[1]

Pub. by M Darly accor to Act April 1st 1772 Strand

Engraving. Portrait, W L., of a stout man facing T.Q. to r, looking to l. over his r. shoulder. His l. hand is thrust under his buttoned coat; his r. (gloved) rests on a cane. He wears a looped hat, a tightly curled wig and is plainly dressed
$6\frac{1}{8} \times 4\frac{1}{2}$ in.

VOLUME III

5005 [TITLE PAGE.]

Pub^d accor^g to Act by M Darly Inventor   1772

Engraving. Lettering in a frame ornamented with a garland of roses.

1772 | VOL. III. | OF | MACARONIES. | CHARACTERS | CARI-CATURES. | &C | DESIGN'D. BY. THE | GREATEST . PERSON-AGES | ARTISTS. &C. GRAVED. & | PUB^D. BY. M DARLY 39 | STRAND.
$7\frac{3}{8} \times 5\frac{1}{4}$ in. (pl).

1. THE SLEEPY MACARONI STE'—ALING A NAP.[1]

See No. 4649—1 June 1772

This appears to have been wrongly included in the series. It is published by Bretherton, not Darly. The same subject (a satirical portrait of Stephen Fox ('Ste') asleep) is No. 14 of this volume.

No. 1 in this volume should be *The Shuffling Macaroni*, 2 April, 1772.[2]

---

[1] There is also a coloured impression
[2] Volume exhibited by Mr Dyson Perrins at the Burlington Fine Arts Club, 1932

5006 V. 3 2 THE PORTER MACARONI.

Pub⁴ by M Darly Apˡ 3ᵈ 1772, accor to Act (39) Strand

Engraving. Standing figure, W L , of a tall slim man in profile to r. The profile and the enormous looped queue are caricatured. In his l hand he holds a long tasselled cane He wears a three-cornered hat and ruffled shirt Perhaps a portrait of some one named Porter

7¼×4⅞ in. (pl.).

3 A MACARONI IN A MORNING DRESS IN THE PARK   See No 4690—23 Apr. 1772

4 LADY DRUDGER GOING TO RANELAGH.
                              See No. 4647—25 Apr. 1772
See No. 5533.

5007 V. 3 . 5. THE MACARONI HABERDASHER

Pub by M Darly accor to Act (39) Strand May 7ᵗʰ 1772

Engraving A man, W L., dressed macaroni-fashion with a small hat, looped club, and cravat. In his l arm he holds an open arched-top coffer full of caps and laces In his r. hand he holds by a ribbon a woman's flat hat trimmed with ribbons.

7×4⅞ in. (pl)

5008 V. 3 6. THE RIDICULE.

Pub by M Darly accor to Act May 17ᵗʰ 1772 (39) Strand

Engraving. Two men, W.L , walk to the r in profile. One (r) is tall and slim, dressed in the extreme of fashion, with laced hat, lace-trimmed cravat, and shirt frills He wears a sword and looks through a lorgnette held in his l hand. In the r. is a tasselled cane. His looped club of hair is so enormous that it is supported on the head and shoulders of the short stout man (apparently a porter), who walks behind him, holding his coat-tails and grinning. Cf *The Ladies Ridicule*, No. 4653 (1772), also caricaturing the enormous wigs of the period.

7×4⅞ in (pl.)

5009 7. A CHARACTER

Eliz. B. fec [?Elizabeth B. Gulston.]

Pub⁴ by MDarly at 39 Strand accor to Act May 19ᵗʰ 1772.

Engraving. A man standing in profile to r , apparently caricatured for his old-fashioned dress and straight lank figure. His l. hand is outstretched, his r holds a sword of which only the hilt is visible. He wears a wide flat hat and bag-wig. His long narrow coat hangs well below his knees. Beneath the title is etched:

An Ugly Face & Staring Hat,
A Carcase which has lost its Fat.
An ill shap'd Coat, too bad for shew
Yet Hides the Aukward Legs below

The Sword a Thing not meant for Harm
And Therefore Hug'd betwixt the Arm.
Whene'er at Court he shews his Face
The Breeding Ladies Quit the Place
Take him in short from Top to Toe
And set him down the Queer Old Beau.

$7 \times 4\frac{7}{8}$ in. (pl).

5010 V. 3 8 THE ORIGINAL MACARONI.

Pub accor to Act by M Darly Strand May 20th 1772.

Engraving. Caricature portrait, W L , of a man in profile walking to the r. grotesquely dressed, probably for a masquerade. In his r hand he holds a rod to each end of which is slung a fox's tail A large fox's tail hangs from the back of his neck. A bell hangs outwards from the back of his waist. A ribbon flutters from his r arm He wears a small cap with a tuft of feathers at the top. Rows of feathers (quills) or ribbons hang from his cap, his waist, and from the tops of his stockings which leave his knees bare. Above is inscribed *Tom Fool the First*

At the masquerades (*c.* 1772) groups of young men from the universities, some dressed as 'Tom fools with cap and bells', were conspicuous. Walpole, *Last Journals*, 1910, 1. 85 n.

Evidently intended for C J. Fox, a leader of fashion and already a favourite subject of caricature See 'The senatorial Macaroni or Memoirs of a Young Cub' in *The Macaroni and Theatrical Mag* Jan 1773, with a plate, No 4810, and for Fox as the leader of the macaronies, see No. 4962 Cf *The Senators*, 1772, p. 13 (see No. 4970):

> By turns solicited by different plans,
> Yet fix'd to none, Fox dresses, games, harangues:
> Where varying fashion leads the sportive band,
> And whim and folly bound it hand in hand,
> Behold him ambling through these flow'ry ways
> A model macaroni, *A l'Angloise.*

$7 \times 4\frac{7}{8}$ in (pl.).

9 THE ISIS MACARONI

See No. 4705—27 May 1772

Reproduced, Paston, Pl cxix

5011 V 3 10. THE BALD FAC'D DOE[1]

E.T. [Topham] *Invt*   *Epping* [M Darly] *sc.*

Pub by M Darly Strand May 29th 1772, accor to Act.

Engraving Portrait, W.L., of a very stout woman standing in profile to r. Her r. hand is thrust beneath her apron, a bunch of keys hangs from her waist She wears a cap, elbow sleeves, a figured handkerchief or scarf, a straight full skirt over a quilted petticoat.

A portrait of Mrs. Owen, keeper of an inn at Epping, *B M Cat. Engr Br. Portraits* This was the Bald-Faced Stag in Epping Forest, a

---

[1] There is also a coloured impression.

well-known inn and a resort of Londoners for venison feasts and City hunts. Cf. *Public Advertiser*, Aug 20, 1754; *Life of Peter von Shaack*, p 158.
$7\frac{1}{16} \times 4\frac{7}{8}$ in. (pl).

5012 V. 3. 11. MODERATE INTEREST. 20 P^{R} CENT.

E.T. [Topham] *Inv^t*   *M.K. Sc.*

Pub by M Darly Strand June 1st 1772, accor to Act

Engraving. Three W.L. standing figures. On l. a man with a Jewish profile and a small beard is in profile to the r. In his l. hand is a long cane, in his r. a rolled document. Bundles of papers protrude from his pocket He wears a wide-brimmed hat. The centre figure is full-face, his hat is in his hand A paper, *Annuities 20 p^r cent*, hangs from his pocket. The third figure is in profile to the l. He smiles and holds the arm of the centre figure; in his l. hand is a cane. The two men in profile are dressed in an old-fashioned way with wide-brimmed hats and long coats. Cf No. 4926.
$7 \times 4\frac{15}{16}$ in. (pl.).

5013 V. 3. 12. THE BATH MACARONI.

Pub by M Darly Strand June 1st 1772 accor to Act.

Engraving. Portrait. A W.L. standing figure in profile to the r. His r. hand is in his breeches pocket, his l. is thrust under his waistcoat. He wears a small hat, a bag-wig, a sword, a ruffled shirt.
$6\frac{15}{16} \times 4\frac{7}{8}$ in. (pl.).

5014 13. A DANCING MASTER MACARONI.

Pub according to Act of Parl^t June 7th by M Darly 39 Strand

Engraving. A man, W.L., playing a violin He faces r. but looks over his r. shoulder, his mouth open as if speaking He is doing dancing steps. He wears a rather short coat, and a ruffled shirt. His hair is in an exaggerated macaroni club.
$7 \times 4\frac{7}{8}$ in. (pl.).

14. THE SLEEPY MACARONI. [Stephen Fox, afterwards 2nd Lord Holland.] [Bunbury]   See No. 4648—4 June 1772

5015 V. 3. 15. THE CATGUT MACARONI.

Pub by M Darly Strand, July 2^d 1772 accor to Act.

Engraving Portrait, W L., of a man playing the violin His figure faces the spectator, his head turned in profile to l. He is dressed macaroni-fashion with a large looped club.
$7 \times 4\frac{7}{8}$ in (pl.)

5016 V. 3. 16. A (four dice depicted) MACARONI. GAMBLER.

Pub accor to Act by M Darly Strand July 2^d 1772.

Engraving. W.L Portrait of a man, with his head turned in profile to l., with a dejected expression. In his r. hand is a money bag, in his l. a paper:

Scotch Bill for 10,000l The four dice of the title indicate that this is Alexander Fordyce, the most active partner in the firm of London bankers, Neale, James, Fordyce, and Down. He absconded in 1772, after which, 10 June 1772, the bank stopped payment. See Walpole, *Letters*, viii. 178–80, 1 July 1772 He was famous for speculations in 'Change Alley, at first very successful, and for his extravagant way of living. See *Every Man's Magazine*, July 1772, pp 11–12. He was a Scot, and the failure rekindled the outcry against the Scots The speculative mania which caused the crisis had begun in Scotland, see No 4961.

$6\frac{7}{8} \times 4\frac{7}{8}$ in. (pl).

17. THE FLY CATCHING MACARONI. [Sir Joseph Banks]
See No. 4695—12 July 1772

18. THE SIMPLING MACARONI. [Dr. Solander]
See No. 4696—13 July 1772

19. THE SCAVOIR VIVRE   See No 4698—12 July 1772

20. THE ILLITERATE MACARONI   [Lord Suffolk?]
See No. 4652—1 July 1772

5017 21 THE MADRAS TYRANT OR THE DIRECTOR · OF · DIRECTORS.

J.S. [monogram]

Pub according to Act of Parlt March 16 1772 by M Darly 39 Strand.

Engraving. A man in military dress riding in profile to the r on a horse with a long tail and a trimmed saddle cloth. His thin stiffened queue projects from his head. Beneath is etched, *Jos or the Father of Murder Rapine &c.* Probably Lord Clive: there is a certain resemblance to his portraits, he was a large holder of East India stock, and had considerable influence with the Company; the parliamentary enquiry into his conduct was going on at this time. See Nos 5101, 5102.

5×7 in.

22. THE LADIES RIDICULE.   See No. 4653—17 July 1772

5018 V 3. 23. THE MACARONI PROVIDER

Pubd according to Act July 21st 1772. by M Darly 39 Strand.

Engraving. A man W L. in profile to r. carries on his back a doll-like woman who takes the place of the macaroni club. She is swathed round in black ribbon and so attached to his shoulders in the manner of a club of hair. He leers, and carries a tasselled cane with a sharp handle set with what appears to be a snuff-box He wears a large frilled cravat and a very short coat. She wears a ribbon-trimmed hat, frilled elbow-sleeves, her body is covered with the black swathing, her clocked stockings are visible to the knees Probably a portrait of some (alleged) notorious procurer; perhaps Thomas Bradshaw whose portrait he somewhat resembles. See No. 4962.

$7\frac{1}{8} \times 4\frac{7}{8}$ in. (pl.).

24. A FEMALE MACORONI.

See No 4700—14 July 1772

She resembles the lady (? Mrs Baddeley) in No 4998 Reproduced, *Social England*, ed Traill, 1904, v, p. 482

VOLUME IV

5019 [TITLE PAGE.]

Engraving. In an oval frame· VOL | IV | OF | MACARONIES | CHARACTERS | CARICATURES | &C | BY · M DARLY.
$6 \times 4\frac{1}{2}$ in.

5020 V. 4 1. THE FARMER-MACARONI.

Pub^d accord^g to Act July 24th 1772 by M Darly 39 Strand.

Engraving A man W.L. standing in profile to l. He wears the macaroni looped club, coat, waistcoat, and frilled shirt With this he wears a round hat, loose gloves, and spurred riding boots In his r. hand he holds a rough stick cut from the hedge, in the shape of the cane carried by the Macaroni Provider, see No 5018 Beneath is engraved·

E'en Farmers dress & mount their Ponies,
And all alike, are Macaronies.

$7 \times 4\frac{7}{8}$ in. (pl.).

5021 V. 4. 2. THE LITTLE DEANS YARD MACARONI.

Pub by M Darly Strand July 30th 1772 accor to Act,

Engraving. A man W.L. seated in a chair, his r leg crossed over his l knee. He looks in profile to the r. and points with his l. hand, the other hangs over the arm of the chair holding a glove. He wears a flat three-cornered hat, a short tightly curled wig, a pair of bands, and a voluminous gown Beneath is inscribed:

Sanguineos oculos volvit, virgamque requirit.

Probably a portrait of the head master of Westminster School, Dr. Samuel Smith, see Nos. 4680, 4921.
$6\frac{7}{8} \times 4\frac{3}{4}$ (pl)

3. THE SOUTHWARK MACARONI. [Thrale M.P.]

See No. 4691—24 Aug. 1772

5022 V 4. 4 THE FUMIGATING MACARONI

Pub^d according to Act Augt 12th 1772 by M Darly 39 Strand

Engraving Man, W L , seated full face In his r hand he holds out a drawing of a curiously-shaped chair inscribed *Stool for the Piles*. In his l

he holds a drawing of a piece of furniture resembling a wardrobe inscribed *Fume*. From his pocket protrudes a paper, *To [h]is Excel[lency] The . . . an Emb[as]sador*. On the ground are broken medicine phials Bundles of dried herbs hang from a cord. He is dressed in a three-cornered hat, tightly curled short wig, coat and laced waistcoat with a ruffled shirt.
$6 \times 4\frac{1}{2}$ in.

5023 V. 4. 5. A COURTESAN AND FRIZEUR

Pub⁴ accord⁸ to Act August 9ᵗʰ by M Darly 39 Strand

Engraving. Two W.L. figures. A woman (l.) walks away from the man but looks round over her l. shoulder She wears a high conical cap trimmed with lace and ribbons, a hooded cloak over a voluminous skirt ornately embroidered at the hem. The man in profile to the l. walks after her His l. hand holds a tasselled cane which rests on his shoulder, his r. is thrust under his waistcoat. He is fashionably dressed with a laced hat, and his coat appears to have epaulettes.
$7 \times 4\frac{15}{16}$ in. (pl).

5024 V. 4 6. THE Sᵀ JAMES'S MACARONI.

Pub accord⁸ to Act Aug⁴ 12ᵗʰ 1772 by M Darly 39 Strand

Engraving. W.L. back view of a man wearing a bag-wig and solitaire. In his r. hand he holds a tasselled cane which rests on the ground. He wears a sword.

An etching by Bretherton after Bunbury with the same title is No 4712.
$7 \times 4\frac{15}{16}$ in. (pl.).

5025 V. 4. 7. THE NEWMARKET MACARONI.

Publish'd according to Act Aug⁴ 18. 1772. by M Darly, 39 Strand.

Engraving Portrait of a man standing full face in riding dress. His r. hand is in his breeches pocket, his l (gloved) holds the r. glove and a walking stick. He wears a small round hat with a knot of ribbon, a plain coat and waistcoat with a cravat and spurred top-boots. Beneath is engraved: *Return'd from the Black Legg'd Club.*
$7 \times 4\frac{15}{16}$ in. (pl).

5026 V. 4. 8. THE PICCADILLY MACARONI.

Pub⁴ accord⁸ to Act Aug⁴ 12ᵗʰ 1772 by M Darly 39 Strand

Engraving. Portrait (caricature) of a very stout man with short legs standing in profile to the l. He wears a three-cornered hat; his club is looped at the back of his very thick neck He wears a plain coat, ruffled shirt, spurred riding-boots.
$7 \times 4\frac{15}{16}$ in (pl.).

5027 V. 4 9 THE VAUX HALL DEMI-REP.

Publish'd according to Act Aug⁴ 20. 1772, by M Darly, Nº 39, Strand.

Engraving. A woman walking to the r. and looking over her r. shoulder.

Her wrists are crossed, she holds between them a large sprigged handkerchief. She wears an elaborate ribbon-trimmed hat over a lace cap, a low
bodice with a large nosegay and a cloak. A looped-up train shows a fairly
short quilted petticoat. Her face is patched.

$7 \times 4\frac{15}{16}$ in (pl.)

10. THE ELECTED COBLER.

See No. 4709—27 Aug. 1772

11. THE WESTMINSTER MACARONI

See No. 4654—1 Sept 1772

5028 V. 4 12. THE BUTCHER MACARONI

Publish'd as the Act directs, Sept' 7 1772. by M Darly, 39 Strand.

Engraving. W.L. portrait of a man standing, he sharpens a knife on a steel.
On the r is a butcher's block on which is a large calf's head He is
dressed as a man of fashion and wears a macaroni club, ruffled shirt and
cravat. Beneath the title is engraved: '*Watts* it you want *Watts* it you buy.
A portrait of a butcher named Watts, see H. Angelo, *Reminiscences*, 1904,
ii. 267.

$5\frac{15}{16} \times 4\frac{3}{8}$ in.

5029 13 BUCK & DOE MACARONIES

Publish'd according to Act, Sept' 7 1772. by M Darly, 39, Strand.

Engraving A man and woman (W.L.) who appear to be quarrelling. A
young woman (l.) runs l holding up in her r hand a glass whose contents
are being spilled. In her l. hand she holds a sword hilt downwards. She
wears a flat ribbon-trimmed hat, low ribbon-trimmed bodice. The man
(r.) dressed as a macaroni holds a cane above his head in his r. hand; his
l. hand is on the hilt of his sword. The mouths of both are open as if
shouting Beneath the title is engraved, *Keeping it up*

$4\frac{5}{8} \times 6\frac{15}{16}$ in (pl)

5030 V. 4 14 A MUNGO MACARONI

Publish'd according to Act, by M Darly, 39 Strand, Sept' 10. 1772.

Engraving. A negro, dressed as a macaroni except for his tightly curled
natural wool, walks in profile to the r. His r hand holds a cane, his l is on
the hilt of a short curved sword or sabre with an ornamental hilt affected
by macaronis. Perhaps a caricature of Jeremiah Dyson, always called
Mungo after the name had been given him in a debate by Col Barré,
29 Jan. 1769. Mungo was a negro slave in the comic opera *The Padlock* by
Bickerstaffe, and the name implied that Dyson was kept at dirty jobs for
the Government. He was a butt of the caricaturists, see No. 4267, &c,
and index. Perhaps Soubise, see No. 5120, a caricature of whom was drawn
by Angelo, *Reminiscences*, 1904, ii 268

$6\frac{15}{16} \times 5$ in. (pl.).

5031 V. 4. 15. THE MINIATURE MACARONI.

Pub^d accor^g to Act, Sepr 24, 1772 by M Darly (39) Strand

Engraving. W L. portrait of a man standing in profile to the r In his l. hand he holds up a handkerchief, in his r. is a cane with a large tassel. The figure is about half the size of others of this series; this, and the length of his sword, suggests that he is very small. He is dressed macaroni-fashion, though his looped club is small. Evidently Cosway, the miniature painter, who was very small, see No 6102, and whose portraits this resembles.
$6\frac{15}{16} \times 4\frac{7}{8}$ in. (pl.).

5032 V. 4. 16. THE EMACIATED BATH MACARONI

Publish'd according to Act Septr 7, 1772 by M Darly, 39 Strand.

Engraving. Portrait of a man walking to r. supported by crutches. He has a grotesque queue, wears a hat, cravat, and frilled shirt sleeves. His gouty legs are swathed beneath the knee.
$6\frac{7}{8} \times 4\frac{11}{16}$ in.

5033 V. 4. 17. THE STABLE Y——D MACARONI

Pub^d accor^g to Act Septr 29, 1772 by M Darly 39 Strand

Engraving. W L. portrait of a man standing full face. His r. hand rests on a tasselled cane. His l. is thrust inside his waistcoat. He wears a laced hat, embroidered waistcoat, ruffled shirt, a solitaire, and a sword He is knock-kneed. Probably a portrait of Lord Harrington whose house was called the Stable Yard (St James's), Lady Harrington was called the Stable Yard Messalina, see No 4903. See also No. 5322. Reproduced, *Social England*, ed Traill, 1904, v, p 229
$7 \times 4\frac{7}{8}$ in. (pl.).

18. THE MACARONI BRICKLAYER, PRIOR TO ANY OTHER MACARONI.   See No. 4656—17 Sept. 1772

Not George III, but a builder named Prior. Angelo, *Reminiscences*, 1904, ii 267

5034 V. 4. 19. THE WOOLWICH · MACARONI

Publish'd as the Act directs, Septr 21 1772 by M Darly, 39, Strand.

Engraving. A man in military dress walking or running in profile to the r. His r hand holds a cane, his l the hilt of a sabre. His queue, twisted like a rope, is looped up with narrow ribbon. He wears a hat with a feather, a coat with facings and epaulettes, a ruffled shirt, and half-boots.
$6\frac{7}{8} \times 4\frac{15}{16}$ in. (pl.).

5035 V 4. 20. THE MERIONETHSHIRE MACARONI

Pub^d accor^g to Act, Octr 1st, 1772. by M Darly (39) Strand.

Engraving. Caricature portrait, W.L, of a man walking to the r His profile is grotesque. He has a long, thin, tightly-bound queue. Under his r. arm is a knotted stick. His sword has a large old-fashioned hilt. He wears a hat trimmed with a leek, his coat is long; round his neck is knotted a striped neck-cloth.

$7 \times 4\frac{7}{8}$ in. (pl).

21. A MACARONI RETURN'D FROM RIDING.

See No. 4657—6 Oct. 1772

5036 V. 4. 22. THE JAMES^s SQUARE MACARONI

Pub^d accord^g to Act, Octr 6. 1772, by M Darly 39 Strand.

Engraving Portrait, W L., of a man in macaroni dress. In his l. hand he holds out a peer's black velvet hat trimmed with ermine; his r. is thrust inside his waistcoat. He wears a three-cornered hat, and a solitaire.

$7 \times 4\frac{15}{16}$ in (pl.)

5037 V. 4. 23. THE OXFORD ADONIS MACARONI

Pub^d accord^g to Act Octr 9. 1772 by M Darly (39) Strand.

Engraving. A man standing (W.L.) in profile to the r. whose face is grotesquely emaciated. He is high-shouldered almost to deformity, and hollow-chested His hair is in ringlets with a double club. He wears a three-cornered hat, coat, ruffled shirt, and riding-boots. In his r. hand is a long tasselled cane.

$7 \times 4\frac{5}{8}$ in.

5038 V. 4. 24. THE PROTECTING MACARONI

Pub^d accord^g to Act Octr 9. 1772, by M Darly (39) Strand.

Engraving. A man (r.) in shirt and breeches is being laced into stays by a shorter man who stands behind him. The taller man is knock-kneed and has some resemblance to the Duke of Grafton. On the ground is a chased goblet to which a label is attached, *Duplicate 5. 5. 0.* The valet or stay-maker is dressed in the prevailing macaroni manner.

$6\frac{1}{2} \times 4\frac{1}{2}$ in.

VOLUME V

5039 [TITLE PAGE.]

Engraving. In an oval frame VOL 5 | OF | CARICATURES | MACARONIES. | & |CHARACTERS | PUB^D BY | M DARLY. | 39 | STRAND

$6\frac{15}{16} \times 4\frac{15}{16}$ in (pl).

V 5. 1. THE CHELSEA MACARONI.

See No. 4658—10 Oct. 1772

V. 5. 2. THE BUN. MACARONI. [Portrait of one of the Bunbury family?]

See No. 4660—9 Oct. 1772

The little flags with the crest and the legend: 'Has the honour to sarve the Royal Family' in pencil and pen on the impressions there described has not been added. The figure is in profile to the r.

5040 V. 5. 3. THE CAMBLET MACARONI.

Pub. accord. to Act Dec' 2. 1772. by M Darly 39 Strand.

Engraving. Portrait, W.L., full-face, of a young man standing with hands
on hips, legs astride. He is not dressed in the macaroni manner, but wears
a round cap, beneath which his own hair appears, a plain coat and neckcloth, with a striped waistcoat.
$6\frac{15}{16} \times 4\frac{7}{8}$ in. (pl.).

5041 V. 5. 4 LIGHT INFANTRY.

Pub Dec' 18 1772 by M Darly 39 Strand

Engraving. An obese man in military dress marching in profile to the r. In
his l. hand he carries a musket with bayonet. His hat has a feather plume
and he wears spatterdashes.
$7\frac{1}{16} \times 5$ in.

V. 5. 5. A MACARONI WAITER. See No. 4661—11 Dec 1772

5042 6.[1] SOOTY DUN THE DEVIL'S MEALMAN.

Pubᵈ accord to Act Oct 30 1772 by M Darly 39 Strand

Engraving. A W.L. figure running forwards. He is grinning; in his r.
hand he holds up a short shovel, in his l is a brush His clothes are ragged;
his toes appear through remnants of buckled shoes. He wears a laced hat,
a cravat, and a ruffled shirt. In place of a wig is what appears to be a
tightly-curled lamb's fleece resting on his shoulders; two pieces of crossed
wood imitate a sword. A miniature figure in ragged clothes and a long
thin queue faces him astride a tasselled cane.

He is a chimney sweeper dressed for the first of May celebrations which
were usual in London. The small figure may represent a child-apprentice
or climbing boy, though there is nothing juvenile in its appearance.
$6\frac{15}{16} \times 5$ in. (pl).

5043 V. 5. 7. THE MACARONI MERCER

Publish'd according to Act Oct' 29. 1772, by M Darly, 39, Strand.

Engraving. A W.L. figure looking to l. carrying under his l. arm a roll of
material; in his r. hand is what appears to be a yard measure. He is dressed
macaroni-fashion with a large looped club, looped hat, and ruffled shirt.
$6\frac{15}{16} \times 4\frac{15}{16}$ in. (pl).

5044 V 5. 8. THE KNIGHTSBRIDGE MACARONI.

Publish'd according to Act Oct' 22, 1772. by M Darly, 39, Strand.

Engraving. W.L. portrait of a man walking in profile to the r. Under his r.
arm is a tasselled cane. His l. hand rests on the end of the scabbard of his
sword. His hair is in a macaroni club. His hat is low with a curved brim.
He wears a ruffled shirt and cravat, striped breeches, and spurred riding-
boots
$6\frac{15}{16} \times 5$ in. (pl.).

[1] The figure has been added in ink

5045 V 5 9 THE WHALE BONE MACARONI.

Publish'd according to Act, Oct 22 1772. by M Darly, 39, Strand.

Engraving W.L. portrait of a man standing with his feet crossed. In his r. hand is a tasselled cane and under his r. arm are sections of a pair of stays in course of construction. He wears a macaroni club, a laced hat, short coat and laced waistcoat, cravat, and ruffled shirt Probably a stay-maker
$7 \times 4\frac{15}{16}$ in. (pl.).

10. THE . BUILDER . MACARONI

See No. 4662—1 Nov. 1772

5046 V. 5. 11. THE BOTANIC MACARONI

Publish'd as the Act directs Novr 14th 1772 by M Darly, 39 Strand.

Engraving. W.L. portrait of a man walking in profile to the r. In his r. hand he holds a botanic drawing, in his l. a magnifying glass or lorgnette. His gouty r. leg is swathed; from his r. wrist hangs a knotted walking stick. A portrait of Joseph (afterwards Sir Joseph) Banks, see Nos. 4695, 5146, who at this time had recently returned from his expedition with Solander, see No 4696, to Iceland.
$6\frac{15}{16} \times 4\frac{15}{16}$ in. (pl.).

12. THE COURSING MACARONI

See No. 4663—19 Nov. 1772

13 THE FIRE-WORK MACARONI. [Leoni.]

See No. 4664—26 Oct. 1772

5047 V. 5. 14. THE ACCOUCHEUR MACARONI

Publish'd according to Act, Novr 14. 1772, by M Darly, 39, Strand.

Engraving. W L portrait of a man in profile to the r In his l. hand he holds out some obstetric instrument; a pair of forceps protrudes from his coat pocket He wears a bag-wig, three-cornered hat, laced waistcoat, shirt with lace ruffles, and a sword.
$7\frac{1}{16} \times 4\frac{15}{16}$ in. (pl.).

5048 V. 5. 15.¹ THE CLERICAL . BUTCHER . MACARONI

St. James. fec

Pub^d accord^t to Act by M Darly 39 Strand Nov 6, 1772

Engraving W L. portrait of a man with his head turned in profile to the l. In his r. hand he holds a butcher's cleaver, his l. is in his breeches pocket. He is plainly dressed in dark clothes, with a small wig, plain neckcloth, buttoned waistcoat concealing his shirt Probably some one called Butcher.
$7 \times 4\frac{7}{8}$ in (pl).

¹ '15' is written over or under an engraved '2'.

5049 V. 5 16. THE MARGATE . MACARONI.

Pub Nov' 30 1772 by M Darly 39 Strand accor to Act.

Engraving. W L. caricature portrait of a man in profile to the l He is obese, with very short fat legs. In his r. hand he holds an enormous cane which rests on the ground, in his l is a lorgnette He wears a looped macaroni club, a laced hat and coat and a sword.

Margate already had the reputation of a plebeian watering place: Gray writes, August 1766, 'one would suppose it was Bartholomew Fair flown down from Smithfield in the London machine . . .' Cf Cowper, 1779, ' . . Margate though full of company, was generally filled with such company, as people who were nice in the choice of their company, were rather fearful of keeping company with.' *Corr.* Ed. T. Wright, i. 155

$7 \times 4\frac{5}{8}$ in (pl).

17. THE TOWER MACARONI.

See No 4659—22 Oct. 1772

5050 V. 5. 18. THE HUNTING MACARONI.

Publish'd according to Act Dec' 17. 1772 by M Darly, 39, Strand.

Engraving. W L portrait of a man in profile to the r His hair is in an enormous twisted and looped club He wears a laced coat and waistcoat, a frilled cravat and shirt, riding-boots, and a short sword. A riding-whip is under his r. arm.

$7 \times 4\frac{7}{8}$ in. (pl.).

5051 V. 5 19. THE MACARONI SCHOOLMASTER

Publish'd as the Act directs Dec' 7. 1772 by M Darly 39 Strand.

Engraving. W.L portrait of a man standing in profile to the r. He holds a book in his r. hand, a strap in his l. He wears a short, tightly curled wig, and a light flowered dressing-gown over dark clerical clothes.

$6\frac{15}{16} \times 4\frac{15}{16}$ in. (pl.).

5052 20. A PATTERN ADJUTANT.

Pub^d accor^s to Act, Dec' 24th 1772, by M Darly (39) Strand.

Engraving Portrait of a stout man in military dress in profile to the r. He appears to be marching, his r. leg raised, his body thrown stiffly back In his l hand he flourishes a sabre. His hair is in a long thin stiffened queue and he wears high boots with spurs.

$7 \times 4\frac{15}{16}$ in. (pl).

5053 V. 5. 21. THE ORIENTAL MACARONI.

Pub^d accor^s to Act Jany 16th 1773, by M Darly (39) Strand

Engraving. W L portrait of a man standing. He looks towards the r. through a single eye-glass held in his l. hand; his r. is on his hip He wears a hat, sprigged waistcoat, shirt with lace ruffles and cravat, striped breeches

$7\frac{1}{8} \times 4\frac{5}{8}$ in. (pl).

5054 V. 5. 22. THE TIMOROUS SPORTING MACARONI.

Pub⁴ accor⁵ to Act Jany 16, 1773, by M Darly (39) Strand.

Engraving. A man stands in profile to the l. in a rural setting. He looks along the barrel of a gun with a raised trigger. He wears a large looped-up club, low hat, a coat with facings, half-boots and striped stockings

$7 \times 4\frac{15}{16}$ in. (pl.).

23 CAPTAIN BUN QUIXOTE ATTACKING THE OVEN.   See No. 4665—4 Jan 1773

5055 V. 5. 24. PINCHEE, OR THE BAUBLE MACARONI.

Pub⁴ accor⁵ to Act. Decr 29th 1772, by M Darly 39 Strand.

Engraving. Portrait of a man standing in profile to the r., holding in his r hand a conical vessel. He wears a tie-wig, three-cornered hat and frilled shirt.

The title, and the resemblance to his engraved portrait, show that he is Christopher Pinchbeck the younger (*c.* 1710–83), the inventor, holding one of his inventions, perhaps his celebrated candlesnuffers. He is described in his patents as 'toyman and mechanician'. As an anti-Wilkite he was a subject of raillery: *The London Evening Post*, 19–21 Nov. 1772, forecast the possible election as president of the Royal Society of 'no less a person than the noted Pinchbeck, buckle and knickknack maker to the King.' Cf. Mason's *Ode to Mr. Pinchbeck*, 1776

$6\frac{7}{8} \times 5$ in. (pl.).

Twelve prints from a series issued by Darly in three volumes 1772–5 [1]

5056 COURIER FRANCOIS.   [1 Jan. 1772]

W. H. Bunbury Inv.   T. Scratchley f. [Darly]

Printed for Robert Sayer, Fleet Street.

Engraving. A reissue with an altered publication line of a print issued by Darly with the above date. Darly also issued a larger version dated 1 July, 1771, published by 'T. Scratchley'. Both are in the collection of Mr. W. T. Spencer, New Oxford Street (1933).

The same design was etched on a larger scale by J. Bretherton, see No 4737, who also etched a smaller version in reverse.

$5\frac{3}{4} \times 9$ in.   In Sayer's book of 'Drolls'.

THE OPTICAL . CONTRAST.   See No. 4703—16 Jan. 1772

5057 2. THE COVENT GARDEN MACARONIES.

Pub by M Darly Strand Feby 24th 1772 accor⁵ to Act.

Engraving. Two men stand on the pavement outside a door-way under the pediment of which are the royal arms Beneath them and over the doorway

[1] Some were reissued, two on a page, in the volume whose title-page is No 5369

is inscribed, *Lovejoy, Kings arms Tavern*, cf No 4995 This appears to be a representation of the entrance to Covent Garden Theatre. The taller of the two men (l.) has snatched off the other's wig, and holds it up in his r. hand. In his l. hand is his sword, broken off below the hilt, his hat is on the ground. Behind and to the r. stands a short stout man with bare shaved head; his hat is in his r. hand. The taller man is dressed in the prevailing macaroni fashion and has a certain resemblance to Colman, then part-proprietor and manager of Covent Garden Theatre, see No. 5064. The wig of the other is of the type worn by 'cits', see No. 5463.

$8\frac{7}{8} \times 6\frac{3}{8}$ in.

5058 AN OLD MACARONI MISS-LED

[Pub accor to Act by M. Darly April 26ᵗʰ 1772][1]

Engraving. An elderly man, dressed in the macaroni manner with an enormous club of hair, walks, supported by a stick held in his l. hand. His r. hand is firmly grasped by a young woman who points with her other (l) hand in the direction to which she is leading him. She is tall and fashionably dressed and is evidently a courtesan.

$9\frac{1}{16} \times 5\frac{1}{4}$ in.

24. THE MACARONI PRINT SHOP

See No. 4701—14 July 1772

E. Topham. Invᵗ et del. (Darly's shop)

Reproduced, Paston, pl cv; A E. Richardson, *Georgian England*, 1931, p. 73.

5059 A MACARONI FRENCH COOK.

[Pubᵈ according to Act Augᵗ 9ᵗʰ [?1772] by M. Darly Strand][1]

Engraving. A man dressed macaroni-fashion with an enormous looped club but wearing an apron and a conical cap approaches a cooking-stove holding a saucepan in his r. hand; with his l. he appears to be taking snuff. His sword and an elaborately laced hat hang on the wall. The interior of the kitchen is neat, with cooking utensils arranged in an orderly way. A looking-glass is on the wall. A bunch of carrots is on a table, a ham hangs on the wall.

$8\frac{7}{8} \times 6\frac{1}{2}$ in.

5060 N. WOOD GAME-KEEPER TO THE Rᵗ HONᵇᴸᴱ Lᴰ MULGRAVE, AT HIS LORDSHIP'S SEAT IN YORKSHIRE.

[11 Aug 1772][2]

I. A. Fecit

Printed for Robert Sayer, Nᵒ 53 Fleet Street.

Engraving. A reissue with an altered publication line of a plate published

[1] The publication line has been cut off, but is supplied from an impression belonging (1932) to Mr W T. Spencer of New Oxford Street

[2] The original date is supplied from a print in the collection of Mr W. T. Spencer, New Oxford Street.

by Darly with the above date belonging to the series issued 1772–4. Wood is seated on horseback in profile to the r, his gun in his l hand. He has a grotesquely large nose, and has a somewhat clerical appearance. In the background (r.) beyond a piece of water is the façade of a large house with a pediment, evidently Mulgrave Castle, and a church.

$8\frac{9}{16} \times 6\frac{3}{8}$ in   In Sayer's book of 'Drolls'.

5061 THE MACARONI CAPTAINS

[Pub. Darly. 17 Sept. 1772][1]

Engraving. Two men in coats with military facings are having a violent fight with some geese. A goose (l.) is biting the end of the long pigtail queue of one, who holds another goose by the neck in his r hand and is about to strike it with his sword which is in his l hand The other (r) is threatening a goose with his sword and also with his tasselled cane Three geese hiss angrily with outstretched necks, one lies dead on the ground.

$5\frac{1}{4} \times 9\frac{1}{8}$ in.

20. THE MACARONI SHOE MAKER, TAKING HIS MUNDY'S RIDE.   See No. 4637—12 Oct. 1772

THE FLUTTERING MACARONI See No. 4706—7 Nov 1772

(Miss Catley and the Earl of Ancrum)

This plate was altered and reissued *circa* 1786 by Robert Sayer with the title *A Fashionable Shittlecock.*

22. AN OLD MACARONI CRITIC AT A NEW PLAY.
                                              See No. 4699—16 Nov. 1772

R. S[t]. G. M[ansergh]

Two prints from a larger series of Darly's Caricatures
continued from p. 41.

17. THE MACARONI CAULDRON.
                                          See No 4829—9 Mar. 1772

27. TIMOTHY TALLOW, AND HIS WIFE ..
                                          See No. 4640—10 Aug. 1772

5062 THE CUB'S FROLIC AT HOLLAND-HOUSE OR THE PIG BASTED.   [1 Jan 1772]

Engraving. From the *Oxford Magazine*, vii. 276. The interior of a kitchen. A pig is roasting on a spit (l) in front of a large open fire Lord Holland, obese, with a fox's head, stands watching a dispute between a cook-maid holding a wooden spoon, and one of his sons, who is young and slim with a fox's head and tail and appears to be intended for Henry Edward (1755–1811). The cook says: *Lord Sir he'll spoil the Pig, and my Lady will blame me*

---

[1] The publication line has been cut off, the date is supplied from an impression belonging (1932) to Mr. W. T. Spencer of New Oxford Street.

for it. Holland answers: *Pish! you fool he won't hurt it, let him baste it.* A maid-servant behind Holland (r.), clasping her hands, says: *Lack a day! Such a fool as you make of him!* In the foreground (r.) a young scullion with a basket of vegetables looks on in surprise.

The explanatory text alludes to 'the celebrated story of the roasted pig at Holland House'. For Henry Fox see No 5112.

$6\frac{3}{16} \times 4\frac{1}{8}$ in.

5063 BEHOLD THE MUSES ROSCIUS SUE IN VAIN, TAYLORS & CARPENTERS USURP THEIR REIGN.

MD[arly.]   [1772]

Engraving. Title-page to *The Theatres*, a poem, see No. 5064. Garrick between Tragedy and Comedy (l.) and two artisans or theatre carpenters (r.). On the r. a man with a Jewish profile smiling, holds out a paper inscribed *Processions for Ever*, from his pocket hangs a paper, *To Mr Messiah, Drury Lane Mechanist.* Garrick holds in his r. hand a paper inscribed *Arthur's Round Table*, his l. hand points to *Processions for Ever.* He is trampling on papers inscribed, *S . . pear, B. John . . [sic], Rowe,* and *. . . pear.* A note by Mr. Hawkins says that the poem (the first part of which is on Garrick and Drury Lane) attacks Garrick for his jealousy and ill-treatment of actors, illiberal conduct to authors, and neglect of the higher drama for spectacles and processions. This neglect had long been a stock subject of complaint. See No. 1838 ('Shakespear, Rowe, Johnson, now are quite undone .'), an illustration to *Cibber's Dissertation on Theatres*, 1759. Garrick had altered Dryden's *King Arthur or the British Worthy*, and produced it at Drury Lane as a splendid spectacle.

$4\frac{5}{16} \times 5\frac{5}{16}$ in.

5064 VIEW COLMAN IN THE LAP OF MOTHER SHIPTON A BETTER SUBJECT SATIRE NEVER WHIPT ON [1772]

MD[arly.]

Engraving From the first page of the second part of *The Theatres*, see No. 5063, which is an attack on Colman and Covent Garden. Colman sits on the lap of Mother Shipton, in his r hand is a harlequin's sword, in his l., a paper inscribed

> *For wooden Sword I've chang'd my useless Pen*
> *I ne'er could Write & Hate all writing Men*

A ribbon sash with long ends is round his waist from which hangs a child's coral and bells. At his feet lies a bundle of pens He looks towards Harlequin (l.) who is trampling on three books inscribed *Shak .., Johns ..* [Jonson], and *Shaksp .* Mother Shipton, in conical hat and ruff, has a walking-stick in her l. hand, her r. is over Colman's shoulder; she says ˙ *Oh my Coly my Coly oh my Coly my Deary* Across the engraving is printed, *Bad has begun and worse remains behind.* On the back is part of the poem

> *See curious Colman negligent of merit,*
> *Of Tragic energy and comic spirit*
> *Palm on his servile partners, and the town,*
> *Abject and vile dependents of his own;*
> . .

Colman is attacked for producing the pantomime of Mother Shipton at Covent Garden. This was played for the first time on 26 Dec 1770 and for the fifty-seventh on 30 May 1771, *Genest*, v. 307, 311

$4\frac{5}{16} \times 5\frac{5}{16}$ in.

5065 THE FIRST MEETING OF THE COTERIE FOR 1772

1 Nov. 1772.

Engraving. *The Macaroni and Theatrical Magazine*, i. 5. A number of ladies, richly dressed, conversing in a room Their dresses show the fashions of the day: hair dressed high, often ornamented with lace, trains over frilled and flounced petticoats, elbow sleeves with wide lace ruffles. These ladies are in a central group, to the r. and l. of which are single figures. On a chair (l.) a lady in a hat holds a dog. Two others converse by a mirror in the background The room has a striped wall-paper above panelling. On the wall are oval mirrors with candles in sconces, and a picture in an ornate frame Looped up curtains surround a small sash-window. On the floor is a fringed and patterned carpet. This illustrates a dialogue, 'Extraordinary Meeting of the Female Members of the Coterie on the Case of Captain J——s', which is a series of insinuations against the fashionable world and the character of certain leaders of note, in particular · 'D——ss of A——', 'C——ss of Upp——r O——sy' [*sic*]. For the coterie see Nos. 4472, 4847, 5095, 5425.

B.M.L., P P. 5201

$4\frac{1}{4} \times 7\frac{3}{8}$ in

5066 [CUPID TURN'D AUCTIONEER, OR, CORNELYS' SALE AT CARLISLE HOUSE]

S. Wale del.   *J. Taylor sculp.*

Publish'd Dec' 24. 1772.

Engraving. From the *Westminster Magazine*, i. 9. Illustration to an article with the above title. An auction-room. Cupid (centre) on a high rostrum holds up a hammer, pointing with his l. hand at the lot for sale, a tall macaroni standing on a stool in profile to the l, holding a cane, his hat under his arm. Behind the macaroni (r.) stands Mercury, who appears to have placed him on the stool. Other lots are on a high shelf behind Cupid's head, against which rests a ladder. Above them are numbered placards: [*Lo*]*t 1* and *Lot 2* have gone, their places are vacant. *Lot 3* is a fashionably dressed lady; *Lot 4* is a macaroni taking snuff, *Lot 5* is a plainly dressed lady wearing an apron Standing in front of the auctioneer (l) is a crowd of spectators, fashionably dressed men and women, who are elderly and ugly, a lady with a fan in profile to the r. being the most prominent. Beneath the design is engraved,

> *Cupid's soft Dart the softer Sex compels,*
> *And here the urchin knocks down Beaux & Belles.*

The text shows that the first three lots sold were a captain, Lady Bridget Lane, and the Duchess of Northumberland.

Mrs Cornelys was gazetted bankrupt in November 1772 and Carlisle House was advertised for sale in December This was due to the proceedings against her, see No. 4929, and to the opening of the Pantheon, see No. 4998. See also No. 5194, a sequel to this print.

Reproduced, E. Sherson, *The Lively Lady Townshend*, 1926, p. 266

$6\frac{1}{8} \times 3\frac{5}{8}$ in.

THE ANTIQUARIANS. See No 4771—1 Feb. 1772

From the *Oxford Magazine.*

5067 A GREAT MAN IN DISTRESS

Publish'd as the act directs, 20th July 1772. By J. Wood, on Ludgate Hill.

Stipple engraving. W.L. full-face portrait of an elderly man, wearing his own hair, a wide three-cornered hat, and a long old-fashioned coat. In his r. hand are a sword, a stick, &c , his l. is thrust under his coat into his breeches pocket. Beneath is engraved,

> *Il n'y a au monde que deux Heros*
> *Le Roi de Prusse et le Chevalier Descassau.*
> *In all the World, but Hero's two I know*
> *Prussia's fam'd King & Marquis Descassau.*
> *Vide the Chevrs own Poetry.*

In another impression the face and hand are printed in red. To this has been added *Born 10 Augt 1710. Died 16 Feby 1775.*

A portrait of the Chevalier Michel Descazeaux du Halley, for many years a debtor in the Fleet and a well-known London character, his vanity, his poverty, his (so-called) poetry, and his eccentricities being a standing subject of jest for many years. See Grosley, *Londres*, 1770, i. 173 ff ; R. Malcolm, *Curiosities of Biography*, 1855. Three earlier portraits have been described in this catalogue. No. 2852 (1736), No. 3092 (1750), No 3800 (1760) The 'Chevr Descarceaux' [sic] is one of an etched group of caricature portraits including Long Sir Thomas Robinson, by General Sir Archibald Campbell (1739-91) in book of 'Honorary Engravers', i fo 162 (Print Department), which must be of an earlier date than 1772 He is drawn exactly as in this engraving, but in reverse. See also *B M. Catalogue of Engr. Br. Portraits.* $8\frac{3}{4} \times 5\frac{1}{2}$ in (pl)

A reduced copy in line for a book illustration has a building with an outside staircase and in the distance Pegasus on Mount Helicon It is surrounded by a border decorated with a trophy of crossed swords and armour.

5068 THE MACARONI VICAR OF BRAY CONVERSING WITH PLATO

Pubd by J. Roberts Engraver St Martins Lane, accorg to Act, Octr 7th 1772.[1]

Engraving. A tall lean man in profile to the l. faces a shorter man in profile to the r. He wears plain dark clothes, a plain hat, short wig, plain shirt and neckcloth, no clerical bands. He looks perturbed and bites his r. thumb.

[1] This was also published by Darly and re-issued in a composite volume of which the title-page is No 5369

His l hand holds a long walking stick. From his pocket protrudes a book, *Mead on Poison* and a paper, *Wanted a Curate*. Behind him is a church inscribed *Hayes*, near it is a small detached house, probably the rectory, placarded *To Lett* The shorter man is smiling; he takes snuff out of a Scottish mull. From his pocket protrudes a book, *Farquhar's Works*. He is plainly dressed Underneath is written in Mr. Hawkins's hand, 'Dav. Wilson. Bookseller Strand at Plato's Head'. His companion is Farquhar, rector of Hayes at this time. The parish records bear witness to his turbulent and quarrelsome disposition.[1] For Wilson, see Nichols, *Literary Anecdotes*, iii. 625, 671.

$6 \times 4\frac{1}{2}$ in

CAPT^N H——. [Horneck], OR THE MILITARY MACARONI.

See No. 4813—1 Nov 1772

From the *Macaroni Magazine*.

5069 THE CHYMICAL MACARONI, CAP^N LUDGATE

Terry Fecit.

Publ^d as y^e Act directs Novr 25th 1772 by G Terry Pater Noster Row.

Engraving A man wearing quasi-military dress, a sash over his l. shoulder, holds a mortar inscribed *Cantharides* and a pestle. He has a very long narrow stiffened queue which sticks out, making an acute angle with his neck. On this is inscribed *Family Medicine Chests neatly fitted up*. From a building whose wall just appears on the r. hangs a sign *The Old Hog in Armour New Revived*. In the background (l.) a monkey holds up a cat by the tail and administers a *Purge*, the label of the bottle being so inscribed. Beneath the title is engraved,

> *With what sweet Chymic Airs, he leads ye City Band,*
> *Or deals his penny Wares from his important Hand.*

Apparently the caricature of an apothecary who was an officer in the City militia or Trained Bands.

7×5 in.

THE NOBLE GAMBLER [Lord Barrymore].

See No. 4828—1 Dec. 1772

From the *Macaroni Magazine*.

5070 A VERY DIVINE MACARONI OF WELBECK STREET

George Crosland delin   [c 1772]

Engraving. Portrait of a man walking in profile to the r. In his l hand is a tasselled cane, in his r is a pair of bands. He wears a three-cornered hat, short hair, dark coat and waistcoat, a bow cravat and frilled shirt sleeves. On the print is written in pencil, 'Revd Mr Langford son of the Auctioneer' (see No. 5001).

$6\frac{3}{8} \times 3\frac{15}{16}$ in.

---

[1] Information (1931) from Canon Thompson, Rector of Hayes.

5071 LE HÉROS DE FERNEY AU THEATRE DE CHATELAINE.

T. O. f¹ 1772. [Thomas Orde]

Engraving. Voltaire, in profile to the l, striding with much vigour and with theatrical gestures, r. arm bent, fingers touching his waistcoat, l. arm thrown out. He wears a plumed helmet, and a sword, and is lean and wrinkled   Beneath the etched title is etched,

> "*Ne pretens pas à trop, tu ne scaurais qu'ecrire*
> "*Tes Vers forcent mes pleurs, mais tes gestes me font rire*

The collector, Richard Bull, has written beneath the print, 'Mr Orde was at Turin in 1772, when Voltaire having Le Cain, and Mad¹¹ᵉ Clairon with him, wished to have one of his own Pieces represented, and got some Strollers to fill the under parts, but at the Rehearsal, being out of all patience at the performance of one of them, dashed the book on the floor, started up, and threw himself into the above attitude, to show the Fellow what Acting was.'

$6\frac{1}{4} \times 5\frac{3}{8}$ in   In book of 'Honorary Engravers', i, No. 53.

5072 THE BRISTOL DUEL   [Jan 1772]

Woodcut. From the *Town and Country Magazine*, iii. 700 (Supplement) A military officer (l.) holds his sword towards a man (r) kneeling on one knee, his hands held up, his sword with its hilt on the ground, who says: *What the D—l— had I to do with a Sword.* An illustration to an account of 'A Bristol Oddity' who, when acting as petty constable, had provoked a duel with a captain by arresting one of his men.

3×4 in.

5073 THE COFFEE-HOUSE POLITICIANS¹   [1 April 1772]

Engraving. *Every Man's Magazine*, i 409. The interior of a London coffee-house. The guests are absorbed in the newspapers and in conversation. A man (r.) in dressing-gown and night-cap sits behind a table on which are newspapers and a tray with coffee pot, &c   The coffee pours unnoticed from the cup in his hand as he looks round in consternation at two men who hold between them *The London Gazette* and appear to be reading it aloud. A boy, wearing an apron, who listens while he runs, spills the contents of his tray. At another table two men sit in deep consultation over a paper which they hold between them   Two men stand behind in consultation   The room is panelled, with an ornately framed mirror on the wall. A smiling and fashionably dressed young woman stands in the bar (r.), behind her are shelves with glasses, punch-bowls, &c.

$5\frac{15}{16} \times 3\frac{7}{8}$ in.   B.M.L , P P 5541.

5074 THE BLACKSMITH LETS HIS IRON GROW COLD ATTENDING TO THE TAYLOR'S NEWS   [1 July 1772]

Engraving. From the *Oxford Magazine*, viii 229   An illustration of the passage from *King John* from which the title is taken   The interior of a

¹ Catalogued with the incorrect date c 1733 as No 2010, and reproduced with this date in *Social England*, ed Traill, V, p. 196.

blacksmith's forge. Two men in leather aprons and rolled up shirt-sleeves stand at the anvil; one has a hammer in his r. hand, the iron in his l. Both gape in consternation towards a tailor, who stands on the r He holds in his hand a newspaper, *The Morning . . Monday July* and reads from it. Under his arm is a large pair of scissors, a yard measure hangs from his pocket. The other smith, behind and to the l., is similarly dressed; by him stands a man also wearing an apron but with a coat and a short wig. In the background is a woman holding a baby. On the l. is a large forge with a cone-shaped chimney and an enormous pair of bellows. The roof is raftered Four horse-shoes, a bent strip of iron, and the portrait of a man (possibly Wilkes) hang on the wall. A dog is asleep in the foreground.

A satire on the favourite theme of tradesmen and artisans who neglect their business to settle the affairs of the nation. See Nos. 4937, 5086, 5614, &c. There is a mezzotint of the same subject by J. Finlayson after J. Donaldson, published 1 May 1769

6×4⅛ in.

5075 THE ENGLISH FARMER'S WIFE CONVERTED TO A FINE LADY DURING HIS ABSENCE IN LONDON.   1 Sept. 1772

Engraving. *Every Man's Magazine*, ii 41. A plainly furnished but panelled room; into which a door (l) opens showing trees, &c. An extravagantly dressed woman sits on a high-backed seat with a clergyman in gown and bands, whose arm is round her waist. Their backs are to the door through which enters a farmer in riding boots followed by his waggoner. A mastiff regards the couple on the seat with hostility or surprise Her hair is dressed in an enormous pyramid decorated with lace and ringlets. She wears a low bodice and ruffled elbow-sleeves, in her r. hand is a closed fan, held in an affected manner. The clergyman gazes at her amorously and shows her an open book, *Ovid's Art of Love*. On a round table in front of them are two books: *Acting* and *Art of Dressing*. The husband is starting back in surprise, saying: *Blessing on us! can that be my Dame.* The waggoner, wearing a smock and carrying a long whip, says: *Woundy Maester her head is grown as high as our Barley-mow!*

4¼×6⁷⁄₁₆ in.   B.M L., P.P 5451

5076 THE MODERN EPHESIAN MATRON.   [1 Oct. 1772]

Engraving From the *Covent Garden Magazine*, a cutting from which is with the print. 'The Story of the Ephesian Matron given us by Petronius, is so universally known, that we shall not repeat it here, but attempt a parallel in the character of a modern widow, whose history the world is but little acquainted with.' On a sofa (l.) a woman in widow's weeds sits beside a barrister in gown and bands; he is embracing her They sit behind a table on which are documents, writing materials, and a wine bottle. Behind, an elderly man with a pen is making advances to a maid (r.), who holds a tray with two wine-glasses. On the wall is a picture of a crocodile shedding tears.

6⁵⁄₁₆×4⅛ in.

CERTAIN CITY MACARONIES DRINKING ASSES MILK.
See No. 4814—1 Dec. 1772

Oxford Magazine.

5077 A CERTAIN LITTLE FAT JEW MACARONI & HIS SPOUSE
GOING TO Y^E PANTHEON   [n d. *c* 1772]

Engraving. Probably from a magazine. A family group in the hall of a
house. A stout short man walks in profile to the l. In his r hand is a large
cane, in his l. a laced hat. A maidservant lifts up his enormous club of
hair while she brushes his coat. His wife, on his r, looks at him ad-
miringly, her l. hand under his chin; under her r. arm is a dog Her hair
is in an enormous pyramid decorated with jewels and lace At her side is
a little black boy wearing a feathered turban.
6 × 4 in.

OUT OF FASHION. IN FASHION   See No. 4817—1 Feb 1772
Pub. T. Bowen.

THE CONTRAST OR THE DIFFERENT DRESSES FOR 1745 AND
1772   See No. 4818—1 May 1772
From the *Oxford Magazine*

THE CONTRAST, OR A LADY IN Y^E DRESS OF 1745 & ANOTHER
IN Y^E DRESS OF 1772.   See No. 4820—1 July 1772
From the *Oxford Magazine*.

[A MACARONI]   See No. 4816—1 May 1772
London Magazine.

5078 THE POLITE MACARONI,   [1 June 1772]

Woodcut. *Town and Country Magazine*, iv **242** Illustration to 'Character
of a Macaroni'. A man in a macaroni dress standing in profile to the r.
In his r hand is a long cane He wears a looped club of hair, small hat,
ruffled shirt, a nosegay and a short, curved sword attached to his waist by
a chain so that it hangs horizontally. The text describes 'the origin and
present state of macaronies'
3⅞ × 3 in.   B M L , P P. 5442 b.

5079 A HIEROGLYPHIC EPISTLE FROM A (MACARONI) TO A
MODERN FINE (LADY)

*Invented & Publish'd by Wm Tringham, May 25th 1772, as the Act
directs under St Dunstans Church, Fleet Street, London.*

Engraved letter in rebuses and in rhyme The words and letters represented
by objects are here within brackets The figures of a macaroni (l) and a
lady (r.) facing each other form part of the title.

My (Lady)
(Eye) (Hope) (yew)'*ll* (knot) *frown* *w*(hen) (eye) *tell*
The (miss)*fortune* (witch) (ewer) *humble Servant* (bee)*fell*
My Wa(eye)*ting on* (yew) *this Mis*(Fortune) *prevented*
And (eye) (Eve)*r Since have* (bean) *quite discon*(tent)*ed*
The th(eye)*ng t*(hen) *w*(ass) (bee)*y cu*(rye)*os*(eye)*ty led*
The (pan)*theon* (awl)*ways ran* (eye)*n my* (head)
A Ticket (eye) s(pea)*dily got of her Gr*(ace)

T(hen) *re*(pear)'*d in my* (chair) (toe) *see the D*(ear) (plaice)
(Butt) *my* (chair)(men) *fell down and* (eye) *fell in the dirt.*
S(ewer) *no Maccaroni w*(ass) (Eve)*r so hurt*
And the (miss)*fortune d*(eye)*d* (butt) *the Ra*(bee)(bee)*le divert*
My (queue) *w*(ass) *Stol'n from me, my* (head) *w*(ass) *disgrac'd*
My (coat) *was* (awl) *d*(eye)*rt and my Waist*(coat) *De*(face)
My (sabre) (eye) *lost* (witch) *adorned my s*(eye)*de*
The (wig?) *of the* (ladies) *which w*(ass) *my* (heart)'*s Pride*
And my new f(ass)*hiond* (hat) *with a Brim ve*(rye) *narrow*
Shot away (eye)*n the* (crow)'*d and went of l*(eye)*ke an arrow*
Since the whole t(hat) (bee)*fell me Ive fairly d*(eye)*splay'd*
Let the S(tête) *of* (Yew)*r Health by* (ewer) (pen) (bee) *por*(tray)
　　　　(Eye) *am with* (grate) *respect*
　　　　　　(Ewer) *Lady* (ships)
　　　　　　　O(bee)*dient Serv*(ant)
　　　　　　　　　　Maccaroni.

See the answer, No 5080 For earlier examples of hieroglyphic letters
see Nos. 1551, 1552, 1553, ascribed to the year 1710. See also Catalogue IV,
p lxx.

13⅞×9 in (pl).

5080 THE ANSWER. AN HIEROGLYPHIC EPISTLE FROM A
MODERN FINE (LADY) TO A MACCARONI

*Invented & Publish'd by Wm Tringham, June 20th 1772, as the Act
directs under St Dunstans Church, Fleet Street.*

Engraved hieroglyphic letter An answer to No. 5079. The same etched
figures, reversed, ornament the title.

　D(ear) *delec*(table) *S*(eye)*r*
　　　　(Ewer) (letter) (eye) (saw)
And the (heart) *of a Rock* (ewer) *mis*(Fortune)*s wou'd thaw*
(Eye) *Pitied* (ass) *soon* (ass) *your* (lines) *met my* (eyes)
And (Yew) *may at* (pea)*resent w*(eye)*th me Sym*(pea)*athize*
For (eye) *in a* (tree)*aty of Marr*(eye)*age of Late*
Had come (toe) *Conclus*(eye)*on with Lord Awkward* (Gate)
The L(eye)*cence* (pea)*rocur'd and the Marr*(eye)*age gone thro*
(Toe) *re*(pear) (toe) *h*(eye)*s* (house) *w*(ass) *the next th*(eye)*ng* (toe) *do*
(Butt) *my* (head) *w*(ass) *so h*(eye)*gh and his door w*(ass) *so low*
T(hat) *in*(toe) *the* (house) *I was* (knot) *a*(bell) (toe) *go*
My Lord (eye)*n a* (pea)*et h*(eye)*s Instr*(yew)*ct*(eye)*ons X*(pea)*rest*
T(hat) *my* (head) (shoe)*ld in f*(yew)*t*(yew)*re* (bee) *otherw*(eye)*se Drest*
(Butt) *before* (eye) *wo*(yew)*ld my* (pie)*ramid Lower*
(Eye)*d lose* (coach) *and 6 and hus*(band) *and Dower*
For (eye)*ll tell* (Eve)*ry Mod*(urn) *drest* (Maid)*en or w*(eye)*fe*
The h(eye)*gher her* (head) *the* (grate)*r* (eye)*n l*(eye)*fe*
T(hen) (ladies) (toe) *Sh*(eye)*ne* (yew) *Must learn* (toe) (bee) *Vain*
Of the Mount on (ewer) (head) *and the length of* (ewer) *Train*
S(eye)*nce Equal Mis*(Fortune)*s on* (bee)*oth have at*(10)*ded*
Our (4)*ces let's Jo*(eye)*n* (ass) *our Troubles are* (bee)*lended*
　　　　　(Eye) *am* (grate)*ly Agreea*(bell)
　　　　　　　S^r (ewer)*s Awkward* (Gate)

13⅞×9 in (pl).

THE MACARONY DRESSING ROOM   See No 4781—9 Nov. 1772

C. White after Capt. Minshull.   Pub. T. Bowen.

Reproduced, Paston, Pl. XV

Another print (not in B.M), with this title was published by Darly, 26 June 1772, and was one of the large plates reissued in the volume whose title-page is No. 5369

A FRENCH MACARONY EATING OF MACAROONS

See No 4830—22 July 1772

THE FRENCH MAN IN LONDON.   See No. 4787—12 Oct. 1772

After Martin.   Pub. Turner.

5081 FRANCE.

ENGLAND.

Brandoine delin.

Publish'd by S. Hooper, Nᵒ 25, Ludgate Hill, 25ᵗʰ June 1772.

Engraving   A design in two compartments:

France (l) is represented by a lean French cook putting a cat on a long spit which he holds between his knees. On a table are fish (skate or dog-fish) and a small piece of meat in which the bone is conspicuous The border of the design is ornamented by a bunch of frogs (l.), a string of onions, (r.) and by *fleur-de-lys*.

England (r.) is a fat and jolly cook standing by a large butt of beer, beside which is a foaming tankard. A large sirloin is on a low table (r.). The border of the design is ornamented by a large ham (l), a fat capon (r), and by the English leopards.

One of many satires on the contrast between the beggarly Frenchman and the well-fed Englishman of which Hogarth's *Gate of Calais*, see No 3050, is the classic example.

Each subject $7\frac{1}{16} \times 4\frac{5}{8}$ in. (pl $8\frac{1}{8} \times 10\frac{7}{8}$ in)

4602–4604

From the same series as Nos. 4922–4925.

A LADIES MAID PURCHASING A LEEK

See No. 4603—1 Mar. 1772

Caldwall *sc.* after Brandoin.

CAPᵀᴺ CONQUEST AND HIS BAGGAGE WAGGON.

See No 4604—15 June 1772

J. Goldar *sc.* after S. H Grimm.

A MACARONY ALDERMAN AND HIS RIB.

See No. 4602—20 June 1772

Caldwall *sc.* after S. H Grimm.

5082 THE ALLEMANDE DANCE.

Brandoin Pinx^t   *Caldwall Sculp.*

London, Printed for J. Smith, N° 35, Cheapside, & Robt Sayer N° 53 Fleet Street. Published as the Act directs 20 March 1772.

Engraving. A panelled ballroom with a small musician's gallery on the r. in which are a fiddler and a flute-player In the centre a couple dance together, th eman standing behind his partner and holding her outstretched hands by the finger-tips. She looks serious, he leers towards her. On each side of the room seated spectators are in conversation pointing to, or looking at, the dancers. Lighted candles are in carved sconces on the wall.

Appears to belong to the same series as Nos. 4595, 4605, 4608, 4609, 4611, 4612.

$9\frac{1}{4} \times 13\frac{1}{16}$ in.

TROOPS FORDING A BROOK.   See No. 4608—25 Jan. 1772

After Collet. Pub. Smith and Sayer.

A MACARONY TAKING HIS MORNING RIDE IN ROTTEN ROW
   HYDE PARK.   See No. 4612—12 June 1772

Caldwall after Collet. Pub. Smith and Sayer.

THE UNWELCOME CUSTOMER.   See No 4605—17 Aug. 1772

Caldwall after Collet. Pub. Smith and Sayer.

5083 A MASQUERADE SCENE KENSINGTON GARDENS

Sam · Sharp-Eye del^t ad vivum [?Bunbury].   *J. Bretherton fec^t*

Publish'd as the Act directs 2^d July 1772, by J. Bretherton N° 134 New Bond Street.

Engraving. Two persons walking away from the spectator down a rectangular piece of grass, bounded by shrubs, and also on the l. by a symmetrical line of trees. Under the shrubs on the r is a garden seat The nearer figure wears a hood and cloak over very voluminous skirts, but a sailor's trousers are indicated through the petticoat. At this figure a dog (r.) is barking. He walks behind, and in pursuit of, a young woman. On a scroll in the upper part of the plate is inscribed, *JACK ON A CRUISE A MISSEY IN Y^E OFFING.* For another version of this design see No. 5313.

$7\frac{7}{8} \times 7\frac{1}{8}$ in.

4757–5086

Prints after Bunbury etched and published by J Bretherton.

THE VILLAGE BARBER L. M...   See No. 4757—1 Mar. 1772

JOHN JEHU   L'INGHILTERRA   See No 4738—6 Mar. 1772

MONSIEUR LE FOUET .   See No. 4753—6 Mar. 1772

THE DOG BARBER LA FRANCIA.   See No. 4669—29 Mar. 1772

THE S⸢T⸣ JAMES'S MACARONI   See No. 4712—29 Mar. 1772

THE FISH STREET MACARONI   See No. 4713—29 Mar. 1772

CANTAB.   See No. 4725—2 May 1772

EQUES CANTAB   See No 4723—May 1772

Another version, not in B M , was published by Darly, 12 Oct 1772, and was one of the plates in the book with the title-page dated 1 Jan. 1776, see No 5369.

STREPHON & CHLOE   See No 4755—28 Nov. 1772

THE FULL BLOWN MACARONI   See No 4714—6 Dec. 1772

5084 A SUNDAY EVENING.

M⸢r⸣ Bunbury delin.   *J. Bretherton f. New Bond Street N⸢o⸣ 134.*

Publish'd 7⸢th⸣ December 1772.

Engraving. A family scene of barren discomfort. An elderly man (l.) in profile to the r sits in a high-backed wooden arm-chair asleep. Next him his wife sits asleep, her hands clasped, her l elbow supported on a table. At the table sits a boy asleep over a book. On the r., very upright on the edge of her chair, sits a middle-aged woman, wearing a low bodice, her hair dressed high. In the foreground a dog and cat are fighting. The room is lit by one guttering candle which stands on the table. A window and a door are indicated.

Described (incorrectly) by F. de la Rochefoucauld, *A Frenchman in England* [1784]. 1933, pp. 81–2; reproduction.
$9\frac{3}{16} \times 11\frac{1}{8}$ in.

5085 I WILL PAY NO MORE DEBTS OF HER CONTRACTING.

M⸢r⸣ Bunbury delin.   *J. Bretherton f.*

Publish'd 7⸢th⸣ December 1772 by J. Bretherton New Bond Street.

Engraving. On the l. stands a thin man holding out his r hand as if for money. In his l hand is a long bill headed   . *Mercer* .. His hat is under his r arm. He faces a stout man standing in profile to the l. whose r. hand points at the bill. He is frowning and appears to be shouting His l hand is behind his back. An open door is indicated in the background.
$8\frac{3}{4} \times 6\frac{1}{4}$ in.

5086 THE MORNING NEWS

Bretherton f [after Bunbury]

Publish'd as the Act directs 10⸢th⸣ December 1772 by J. Bretherton N⸢o⸣ 134 New Bond Street

Engraving. A group of men standing outside a dilapidated building, part of which is visible on the r. One, wearing a broad-brimmed hat, holds in his l. hand a torn paper on which parts of words are visible [Pet]*itio*[n] .. [Fr]*eehold*[rs] ... *Minist*[ry] ... His r. forefinger is extended as if laying down the law to his companions. On his r. stands a man holding his chin with an expression of deep thought. In his r. hand is (?) a turncock. Next him (l.) is an artisan, listening intently, his breeches unfastened at the knee, his stockings ungartered; he holds a short hammer and is probably a shoemaker. Behind (r) a man wearing a waistcoat over a ruffled shirt, but no coat, lounges against the stump of a tree and listens open-mouthed. On the top of the stump is an open dish of food which a dog is eating, his head twisted backwards in a peculiar manner.

Beneath the design is engraved,

> *The Rabble gather round the Man of News*
> *And listen with their mouths.*
> *Some tell, some hear, some judge of news, some make it,*
> *And he that lyes most, is most beleiv'd—*

One of many satires on the absorption of the common people in politics to the neglect of their own business. See No. 5074, &c.

$8\frac{1}{4} \times 9\frac{3}{4}$ in.

THE HOUNDSDITCH MACARONI   See No. 4715—20 Dec 1772

Four prints after Bunbury etched C. Bretherton, Jun.,
published J. Bretherton.

POSTIGLIONE INGLESE   See No. 4739—Apr. 1772

POSTIGLIONE GERMANICO   See No. 4740—Apr. 1772

THE SHAVER AND THE SHAVEE.   See No. 4756—Apr 1772

THE DELIGHTS OF ISLINGTON.   See No. 4722—30 Apr. 1772

Three prints after Bunbury etched C. L. S. or Charles Smith.

THE JUDGMENT OF PARIS.   See No. 4752—4 July 1772
Cf. No 4920.

[A FRENCH POSTILLION]. Pub. J. Bretherton.

     See No 4742—30 July 1772

THE MUCKLE SAWNEY RIDING POST.

     See No. 4734—20 Aug. 1772

5087 THE SAILOR'S RETURN FROM PORTSMOUTH TO LONDON.

Charles Bretherton Jun[r] fecit. [? after Bunbury.]
*Publish'd as the Act directs March 2 1772 by J. Bretherton N[o] 134,
New Bond Street.*

Engraving A sailor seated on a sorry-looking horse rides from l. to r. along a country road In his r. hand he holds the horse's tail, in his l. a long horn

which he is blowing The harness is of rope with pulleys; a rope attached
to the horse's head is round the rider's waist. Round the horse's neck is
wound a coil of rope attached to an anchor; its head is decorated with
a Union flag, another flag is on the sailor's cap. The rider's r. foot is in
a rope-ladder which takes the place of a stirrup. The heads and fore-legs
of a pair of horses, on one of which a postilion is riding, advance into the
picture from the r.

$7\frac{7}{8} \times 12\frac{1}{2}$ in.

5088 A MASQUERADE SCENE AT THE PANTHEON, 1772.

Wale delin^t   *Grignion sculp^t*

Engraving Probably from a magazine The rotunda of the Pantheon,
with a number of figures in masquerade dress, not caricatured. An ornate
chandelier hangs from the centre of the roof. In recesses in the wall there
are statues of draped figures

$4\frac{1}{4} \times 5\frac{5}{8}$ in.

MONACHUM NON FACIT CUCULLUS [Grose and Forrest] N. Hone
Mezzotint.   See No 4474—30 Jan. 1772.

5089 THE EXHIBITION OF THE ROYAL ACADEMY OF PAINT-ING, IN THE YEAR 1771.

From an original Drawing in the Possession of Robt Sayer.

Charles Brandoin inv^t et delin. R. Sayer Excudit Richd Earlom fecit

*London Printed for Robt Sayer N° 53 in Fleet Street Published as the
Act directs 20 May 1772.*

Mezzotint. The exhibition room of the Royal Academy in Pall Mall
The back wall and walls to l. and r. covered with pictures up to the
cornice, which supports a top light. The room is crowded with visitors
looking at the pictures and conversing; some hold catalogues. In the
centre of the room is a bench on which sit a dejected boy and an old lady
reading a catalogue. A connoisseur with sword, chapeau bras, and
pigtail queue, stoops to peer into a picture on the r. On the l a man
wearing a hat and bag-wig, his profile caricatured, points out a picture to
his companion

For other states of this print in the Print Department see Chaloner
Smith, i. 259 Reproduced, A. E. Richardson, *Georgian England*, 1931,
p. 164

$16\frac{3}{4} \times 21\frac{7}{8}$ in.

5090 BAGNIGGE WELLS

I. Sanders pinxit   I. R. Smith fecit

published 15th june 1772

Mezzotint Letters scraped on work The interior of the long room at
Bagnigge Wells, filled with a crowd of tea-drinkers, fashionably dressed in
the macaroni manner The central group consists of a courtesan who
stands arm-in-arm with a macaroni, while with her l hand she beckons
to another macaroni (r) who bows, hat in hand On the r are groups

seated and standing at tea-tables; a serving-boy walks (l to r) holding a tea-tray in one hand, a large kettle in the other. In the foreground (r.) a couple in deep shadow sit at a table. Two chandeliers with lighted candles hang from the ceiling.

For Bagnigge Wells see Wroth, *London Tea-gardens of the Eighteenth Century*. Though a family resort for London citizens on Sunday afternoons, it was also reputed to be a place where apprentices were lured to disaster by courtesans; a later print of the gardens is called *The Road to Ruin*

J Frankau, *J. R. Smith*, 1902, No 20. Reproduced, E. B. Chancellor, *Eighteenth Century London*, 1920, p. 110

14 × 19¾ in.   Crowle's Pennant, xiv, No 42.

5091 THE INSIDE OF THE PANTHEON IN OXFORD ROAD. L'INTERIEUR DU PANTHEON DE LONDRES

Chas. Brandoin inv^t et delin   R. Sayer Excudit.   Rich^d. Earlom fecit

London, Printed for Robt Sayer N° 53 in Fleet Street as the Act directs 30 August 1772.

Mezzotint. A view of the interior of the Pantheon. Ladies and gentlemen in the full dress of the day sit and stand in conversation. In the background (l.) is the organ, with a musician's gallery beneath it, and on the ground below a crowd of figures in rapid movement On the r. are standing figures on the ground and in the gallery above; the wall being decorated with statues in niches. In the foreground on the extreme l is a short stout man, caricatured, turning his head to the spectators to look through an eye-glass; behind him and on his l. stands a tall lady   Chaloner Smith, i. 259.   Reproduced, M. C. Salaman, *Londoners then and now* (Studio), 1920, p 64.

17½ × 21⅞ in.

5092–5095 and numbers from Volumes III and IV

Series of mezzotints published by Carington Bowles.[1]

5092 MISS PRATTLE, CONSULTING DOCTOR DOUBLE FEE ABOUT HER PANTHEON HEAD DRESS.

240 *Printed for Carington Bowles, Map & Printseller, N° 69 in St Pauls Church Yard, London. Publish'd as the Act directs* [date erased, 1772].

Mezzotint (a coloured impression). The counsellor (l) and his client (r.) sit facing one another across a small round table, beneath which their knees touch Each has a tea-cup The lady wears a grotesquely-high pyramid of hair, decorated with pearls or beads, and a high lace cap with ribbons and lace lappets. She looks intently at the Counsellor, her elbows on the table. His foot is pressed against hers He is in profile to the l, wearing a legal tie-wig, gown, and bands On the wall is a framed picture of two monkeys sitting on each side of a round table, each with a tea-cup. One of many satires on the enormous pyramids of hair worn by ladies.

12¹³⁄₁₆ × 9⅞ in.   'Caricatures', ii p 30.   B M.L., Tab. 524

[1] Nos 4516, 4519, 4520, have the imprint of Bowles and Carver.

5093 MISS RATTLE DRESSING FOR THE PANTHEON.

246 *Printed for Carington Bowles, Map & Printseller, N° 69 in S¹ Pauls Church Yard, London, Publish'd as the Act directs* [date erased, 1772].

Mezzotint (coloured impression) A lady sitting at her toilet table adds the finishing touches to her pyramid of hair. Her head is in profile to the r., the mirror reflects a profile to the l. Her chair has a carved back of curious pattern. The draped muslin toilet-table, with trinkets, powder-puff, &c, is a good illustration of a toilet-table of the period On a stool (l.) is an open box filled with ribbons and lace. Behind the toilet table (l.) is a sash-window surrounded with drapery

One of many satires on the elaborate hair-dressing of the period.

$13\frac{1}{8} \times 9\frac{15}{16}$ in   'Caricatures', ii 118   B M.L, Tab. 524

THE ENGLISH GENTLEMAN AT PARIS (248).

See No 4516—17 Apr. 1772

5094 LADY BETTY BUSTLE AND HER MAID LUCY PREPARING FOR THE MASQUERADE AT THE PANTHEON

251 *Printed for Carington Bowles, Map & Printseller, N° 69 in S¹ Pauls Church Yard, London. Publish'd as the Act directs . . .* [date erased, 1772].

Mezzotint (coloured impression). A lady stands holding a black mask in her r. hand; she looks over her l shoulder towards a mirror on a dressing-table (r.) Her maid stoops over an open arched-top coffer on a stool Her dress is of the general character of the period, but its long gathered sleeves suggest that it is intended to be Elizabethan In her high-dressed hair is a jewelled crescent. The maid wears a frilled muslin cap over her high-dressed hair. On the dressing-table is a card inscribed, *Two Tickets for the Pantheon*. The circular mirror is draped with embroidered muslin On the wall are two mirrors in carved frames with candle-sconces. An arm-chair stands on the l A carpet with an arabesque pattern covers the floor.

13×10 in.   A coloured impression is in 'Caricatures', ii, p 119 B.M.L., Tab 524

5095 LADY FASHION'S SECRETARY'S OFFICE, OR PETTICOAT RECOMMENDATION THE BEST

Printed for Carington Bowles Map & Printseller, N° 69 in S¹ Pauls Church Yard, London. Published as the Act directs [date erased, c. 1772].

Mezzotint (coloured impression) A fashionably dressed young woman sits in an arm-chair (r) looking towards an elegantly dressed young man, in bag-wig and solitaire, who has entered from the l He hands her a card, inscribed, *Miss Kenedy recommended for 6 Pantheon Tickets*; she holds out her r. hand to take it In his l. hand is a sheaf of cards, one inscribed *Coterie*. She rests her l. arm on a small table on which is a card inscribed *Pantheon*, and an open book inscribed *Whist Quadrille*. In her l. hand is a ticket inscribed *Cornely's*. The luxury of the room is indicated by a marble column and a door surmounted by a pediment in which is a bust. A cockatoo on a perch screams at the visitor.

She is the well-known courtesan Kitty or Polly Kennedy who has been confused with Polly Jones and perhaps with another Polly Kennedy, see Bleackley, *Ladies Fair and Frail*, 1909, p. 147 ff. The allusion in the title is to the very unpopular reprieve granted through her influence to her brother who had been sentenced to death for the murder of a watchman in a drunken brawl, see Nos 4399, 4463, 4844. The (unsuccessful) attempt to keep ladies of bad reputation out of the Pantheon is also satirized, see No. 4998. The Coterie was a very fashionable and exclusive ladies' club which met at Almack's, see Nos 4472, 4847, 5065, 5425. The assemblies of Mrs. Cornelys' came temporarily to an end with her bankruptcy and the sale of Carlisle House in December 1772, see No. 5066. For portraits of Polly Kennedy (who may however not be identical with the subject of this print, see Bleackley, *op. cit*), see B M. *Cat. Engr. Br. Portraits*; see also No. 5204.

$12\frac{7}{8} \times 9\frac{7}{8}$ in.   'Caricatures', ii. 22. B.M L, Tab. 524.

THE PAINTRESS OF MACCARONI'S   See No. 4582—c. 1772

Mezzotint (coloured impression). Probably a portrait of Maria Cosway, see J. T. Smith, *Nollekens and his Times*, ed. W. Whitten, 1920, ii. 321, where an impression from the collection of Francis Wellesley, Esq is reproduced as of Mrs. Cosway. The portrait resembles portraits of Mrs. Cosway and shows little resemblance to Angelica Kauffmann, suggested by Mr. Stephens as the subject. It is, moreover, a companion print to No 4520, *The Macaroni Painter* [1772], a portrait of Cosway. See also No 6102. Reproduced, Paston, Pl. xcviii.

THE ENTERPRIZING MACCARONI . . . (254)
       See No. 4517—1772

THE POLITE MACCARONI PRESENTING A NOSEGAY TO MISS BLOSSOM. (255)   See No. 4518—1772

THE CITIZEN RETIRED, OR BUSINESS AT AN END TILL MONDAY. (256)   See No 4519—1772

THE MACARONI PAINTER .. (257) [Cosway]
Earlom after Dighton.
       See No. 4520—1772

Reproduced, Paston, Pl. xcvii, and *Nollekens and his Times*, ed W. Whitten, ii 320.

TWO BLOODS OF HUMOUR, RETURNING FROM THE BAGNIO, AFTER HAVING KEPT IT UP. (258)   See No 4521—1772

THE PARSON AND CAPTAIN (259)   See No. 3789—1772

HOW D'YE LIKE ME. (260)   See No 4522—19 Nov 1772

THE UNLUCKY VISIT . . . (261)   See No 4523—1772

LOVE AND WINE. (263)   See No. 4524—1772

LOVE AND OPPORTUNITY   See No 4591—c. 1772

THE OLD FREE METHOD OF ROUZING A BROTHER SPORTS-
    MAN (266)   See No. 3769—c 1772
A reduced version is No. 3770.

THE DOUBLE ATTACK, OR FRENCH POLITENESS . . .
                                                 See No 4573—c 1772
The costume appears to be c. 1772-3. The background suggests the
Pantheon, opened 1772.

THE APPOINTMENT OVERHEARD AND PREVENTED.
                                                 See No. 4576—c. 1772

From Carington Bowles's smaller series:

THE VICTORIOUS RETURN OF THE CITY MILITIA . . . (218)
                                                 See No. 4578—1 May 1772

4583, 5096, 4775, 5097

Similar mezzotints issued by other publishers.

THE MACARONI COURTSHIP REJECTED.
                                                 See No. 4583—20 Mar. 1772
P. Dawe.   Pub. John Bowles.

5096 THE FRENCH GENTLEMAN IN LONDON.

[P. Dawe?]

Publish'd May 15ᵗʰ 1772 by W. Humphrey, Sᵗ Martins Lane.

Mezzotint. Street scene, a lean and foppish Frenchman (r), clasping his
hands in distress, is being roughly handled by a stout, plainly-dressed
Englishman (l.). The Englishman holds the Frenchman's coat-collar, and
threatens him with his r. fist. A sluttish woman standing behind holding
a mop, holds her l fist over the Frenchman's head The Frenchman wears
a toupet-wig with a black bag and solitaire which has been broken in the
fray His sword-belt is twisted so that his sword hangs hilt downwards.
He is wearing a laced coat and waistcoat with lace ruffles The Englishman
wears his own unkempt hair, a broad-brimmed hat, long plain coat,
striped waistcoat and top-boots. A wall in which is a window (r) forms the
background A notice is pasted on the wall, the only legible words being
At the Royal . . .
    Cf. No. 4477.
    $12\frac{3}{4} \times 9\frac{11}{16}$ in.

A MILLENER'S SHOP.   See No 4775—9 Apr. 1772

Pub. W. Humphrey.

Reproduced, Paston, Pl cxcviii.

5097 THE PANTHEON MACARONI

London. Printed for Robt Sayer N° 53 Fleet Street. [c. 1772.]

Mezzotint. A group of three H.L. figures. Two ladies of meretricious appearance seated at a tea-table, a man with a large Macaroni club of hair is handing one of them a cup of tea. One holds a fan and looks coyly towards the man, the other leans over her shoulder.

A scene at the Spa Fields Pantheon which was open from 1770 till March 1774 when the buildings were announced for sale owing to the proprietor's bankruptcy. In the *Macaroni Magazine* for January 1773, p 162, is the notice, 'Pantheons The Nobility's, Oxford Road; the Mobility's, Spa Fields'. A writer in the *St James's Chronicle*, May 1772, professed to have been shocked at the request from more than one lady, 'Pray, Sir, will you treat me with a dish of tea'. Wroth, *London Pleasure Gardens of the Eighteenth Century*, 1896, pp 25-8.

$5\frac{1}{2} \times 4\frac{1}{2}$ in.

POLITICAL SATIRES

5098 THE STATE HACKNEY-COACH   [1 Jan. 1773]

Engraving. From the *London Magazine*, xli. 589. It illustrates 'A Dialogue between a Politician and a Chinese'. A richly carved glass-coach, surmounted by cupids holding a crown is being driven (r. to l.) on a road which leads past buildings to the Tower of London Inside is the king leaning back fast asleep. At the back stands a devil holding reins attached to a bit in the mouth of the coachman, in his other hand is a whip with a long lash. His feet rest on the heads of two carved figures, one being Neptune with his trident Above is engraved, *They go fast whom the Devil drives*. The place of the horses is taken by eight running men, reins being attached to bits in their mouths.

The coachman is Lord North, the man-horses being the ministers or 'king's friends'. They are poorly characterized, and the only two who can be identified are Lord Holland (or perhaps Charles Fox, see Nos 4859, 4892) with a fox's head, the near leader, and Dyson or 'Mungo' as a negro in a striped suit, see No 4962, &c, the near wheeler. In front of him is a man holding a thistle, indicative of Scottish influence The text explains that the harnessed men, since they 'submit their necks to the yoke of slavery, bridled, harnessed and obeying the lash', are on a level with 'beasts of burden or hackney horses'. The occupant of the coach being 'fond of his ease and careless of his interest and power, his servants drive him where they list'. Cf. No. 5132, &c.

$3\frac{11}{16} \times 6\frac{1}{4}$ in

5099 THE POLITICAL RAT CATCHER.   [1 Jan. 1773]

Engraving. From the *Oxford Magazine*, ix. 225. A W.L. caricature of Lord North as a rat-catcher. He stands holding in his l hand a rectangular cage which he supports on his hip, in it are a number of rats. In his r. hand is a staff headed by a *fleur-de-lys* to which are attached a money bag, a key, and a pennant inscribed *in Hoc Signo Vinces*. A document is displayed inscribed *A Calculation of how many Millions of Rats may be destroy'd if Ten Years of Peace is continued*. Five rats hang by their noses from his Garter ribbon, two others run on his shoulder. Round his r leg is a garter inscribed *no shame*. His legs are astride and on the ground between his feet is a large book, *Description of what quantities of Powder will Catch Ratts of different Species*. An open book shows a page inscribed, *A List of all the great Offices of State haunted by Rats of all Qualities*.

The text explains that by means of bribes, pensions, offices, ribbons and peerages North 'has constantly in his trap upwards of five hundred of different species. . . . Every seven years he lets loose all the Rats in his trap to range the country and create confusion', that is, at each general election For the allusion to "Ten Years of Peace', see Nos 4961, 4969 For the fleur-de-lys cf. No. 4935, for North's alleged corrupt support of the Bourbons over the Falkland Islands.

This anticipates Rowlandson's well-known satire, *The Apostate Jack R——* [Robinson] *The Political Ratcatcher* (1784)

$6\frac{1}{2} \times 4$ in.

5100 SHAH ALLUM IN DISTRESS. [Jan 1773][1]

Engraving. From the *Westminster Magazine*, i. 41. A design in two compartments illustrating an article in Biblical phraseology, 'The First Chapter of the Book of Kings' and 'The Lamentations'. In the upper part is depicted a meeting of the General Court of the East India Company; the directors seated at a table on which are writing materials, a book, and a hammer. In the foreground a large man, Governor Johnstone, is holding up by the seat of his breeches 'Shah Allum' or Sir George Colebrook for the derision of the other directors. In the background, behind a barrier, a crowd of men, apparently the proprietors of East India Stock, watch the proceedings with amusement.

This illustrates a meeting of the General Court of the Company on 1 Dec. 1772,[2] at which Governor Johnstone threw the blame of all the Company's miscarriages on their Directors who were 'buoying up the spirits of the Proprietary with a pompous account of their affairs. . . .' Colebrook, a banker and M.P. for Arundel, was a leading director of the East India Company, and had been chairman in 1769 and 1771. At this time his affairs were in great disorder as a result of over-speculation: he had contracted for 'all the alum in Bohemia, all the chip hats in Italy, . . .' *Letters of the Earl of Malmesbury*, i. 271, Ap. 6, 1773. See also Hume, *Letters*, 1932, ii. 263. The crisis was that in which Fordyce was ruined, see Nos 4961, 5016 The name Shah Allum is here given because he had become rich by monopolizing alum. *Westminster Magazine*, i 40.

Over the lower design is inscribed *The India-man wrecked L 12* (probably a reference to 'The Lamentations' on the opposite page).

A ship with broken masts in heavy seas is driving on to rocks (r.), on which is a flag-staff with a flag inscribed *Treasury Cape*. On the r. margin is inscribed *L. 40,00,00*. This symbolizes the ruinous state of the Company's finances, on the verge of bankruptcy and burdened with an annual tribute of £400,000 to the Treasury. See *Ann. Reg.* 1773, pp. 62 ff., and *Camb. Hist. of the British Empire*, iv, pp. 181 ff. See also No. 5101, &c

6½×4 in.

5101 THE GHOST OF OMICHUND [Jan 1773]

Engraving From the *Westminster Magazine*, i 67. It illustrates a dialogue in verse (a parody of *Hamlet*) between 'Nabob' (Clive) and Omichund Omichund, wearing a feathered turban, appears from clouds addressing Clive with a minatory gesture. Clive, who is supported on each side by a military officer, starts back in horror. Omichund stands under a high palm-tree, from whose branches a man, stripped to the waist, is hanging by the wrists. A note explains that he is 'the man under *Breeches* punishment' The scene is a walled enclosure or compound, on the r. behind Clive part of a high tent is visible.

Beneath the title is engraved the beginning of the dialogue, spoken by the ghost of Omichund·

> *What Woes, he cried, hath lust of Gold*
> *O'er my poor Country widely roll'd,*
> *Plunderers proceed!*

[1] The first (January) number of the *Westminster Magazine* appeared in January, contrary to the custom In 1774 each number appeared at the beginning of the following month
[2] Four Courts a year were held, the qualification for a vote being raised by North's Regulating Act of 1773 from £500 to £1,000 Stock

Clive's trick on Omichund who had threatened to divulge the negotiations with Mir Jaffier before the Battle of Plassey unless he was given 30 lakhs of rupees is said to have led to Omichund's loss of reason and death and is the chief stain on Clive's reputation See also Nos. 5017, 5100, 5102, 5111.

$5\frac{1}{2} \times 3\frac{1}{2}$ in.

5102 N°XXXIX Vol. IV. THE INDIA DIRECTORS IN THE SUDS
[Jan. 1773]

Engraving. From the *Town and Country Magazine*, iv. 705 (Supplement). It illustrates a dialogue, 'The Directors in the Suds or the Jaghire Factor dismayed at the Ghosts of the Black Merchants'. The scene is a room in the London Tavern at a meeting of Directors to consider opposition to the Bill for restraining the East India Company from sending out supervisors to India, see No 4968. They sit at a long table, the chairman (Sir George Colebrook) in the centre, and are astonished at the entry (l.) of a procession of Indians wearing turbans and surrounded by smoke which obscures the directors seated on the chairman's r. Three 'black merchants' in single file head the procession and threaten Lord Clive, who stands (r.) facing them, his hands outstretched in horror, his chair overturned. In the dialogue the merchants accuse him of crimes and demand justice, one addresses him as 'Thou maker and destroyer of nabobs, princes, and traders! . . .' Clive retreats, saying, 'truth and justice are too powerful for hypocrisy and guilt'. This is typical of the attacks made upon Clive in the Press at this time See Walpole, *Last Journals*, 1910, i. 162–4. See also Nos 5017, 5100, 5111.

$3\frac{1}{2} \times 6\frac{3}{4}$ in.

5103 WORTHIES.
[c Jan. 1773]

Engraving Frontispiece from *The Life of John Wilkes Esq ; in the Manner of Plutarch*, 1773. Four bust portraits in ovals arranged in two pairs: *Wat Tyler*, with *Ald^n Beckford*; *John Cade Esqr*, *John Wilkes Esqr*. Between the ovals are four clasped hands forming a cross Cade faces three-quarters to the r , Wilkes three-quarters to the l , each squints violently. Beneath is inscribed *These are thy Gods O Britain*. This illustrates the pamphlet ascribed to Horne, see No. 5104. One of the few attacks on 'the patriots', see No. 5334, &c , and for attacks on Wilkes Nos. 4326, 4887, 5130, 5131, 5245.

Ovals, $2\frac{1}{4} \times 1\frac{15}{16}$ in.

5104 THE BRENTFORD GUY FAUX SETTING FIRE TO THE PILLARS OF THE LONDON TAVERN, TO BLOW UP LIBERTY AND THE BILL OF RIGHTS
[Jan 1773]

Woodcut. *Westminster Magazine*, i. 71. Parson Horne, in profile to the l , wearing clerical dress, holds a piece of burning tow to a pillared doorway inscribed *London Tavern*. In his l. hand is a lantern From his pocket hangs a paper inscribed *Life of John Wilkes Esq*. The design shows part of the façade of the London Tavern, the meeting-place of the 'Society for supporting the Bill of Rights'. Beneath is inscribed:

> He has profan'd the sacred name of Friend,
> And worn it into vileness
> With how secure a brow, and specious form,
> He gilds the secret villain.   Dryden.

This illustrates a violent attack on Horne called 'Patriotism blown up . . .'. Horne is denounced as a rank apostate and Judas, a hypocritical parson and debauchee, who by his attacks on Wilkes has destroyed the cause of liberty. The occasion of the attack was a pamphlet just published, *The life of John Wilkes Esq attempted in the manner of Plutarch* (see No. 5103), of which Horne was the reputed author. For Horne's quarrel with Wilkes (which shattered the Bill of Rights Society, see *Ann. Reg.* 1771, p. 94) see No 4861, &c.

$6\frac{13}{16} \times 4\frac{1}{16}$ in.   B.M.L., P.P. 5443.

5105 THE MOTHER AND THE CHILD.   [1 Feb 1773]

Engraving. From the *London Magazine*, xlii. 33   Britannia seated, her spear and shield beside her, suckling an infant, George III She is thin, with a melancholy expression and her breasts are shrivelled. The child wears a star, a coral and bells are attached to his Garter ribbon, his hands are stretched towards his mother's breasts and he is saying, *more Supplies*. Above (l.) is a tasselled sack, quite full, inscribed *GR II*; a similar sack on the r., open and quite empty, is inscribed *GR III* Above one is engraved *Privy Purse in 1753*, above the other, *Privy Purse in 1773*. This illustrates 'Fragment of a Speech'· 'Supplies . . . were never greater, and occasion was never less. Our mother BRITAIN, has been drained of her nourishment till she is ready to expire   yet her SON, her best beloved, her eldest-born, still hangs upon her breasts, still suckles, and (barbarous!) still shrieks out for "More Supplies! More Supplies!" Unnatural boy!'

A satire on the arrears of the Civil List, see also Nos. 4968, 5124.

$7 \times 4\frac{1}{2}$ in. (pl.).

THE YOUNG CUB.   See No. 4810—1 Feb. 1773

Macaroni and Theatrical Magazine, i. 145. An illustration to 'The Senatorial Macaroni; or, Memoirs of the Young Cub'. (C. J. Fox)

5106 THE STATE COTILLON 1773.   [Feb. 1773]

Engraving. From the *Westminster Magazine*, i. 149. The interior of a panelled room. ten men holding hands dance in a circle to the tune of a bag-pipe played by Bute (l) wearing a kilt and appearing from behind a curtain. The king watches with pleased amusement from behind a door (r.) The dancers are trampling on papers and state documents.

Lord North, trampling on papers inscribed *National Debt* and *Grievances*, is between Lord Bathurst in his Chancellor's robes but wearing a hat, and Lord Barrington in a military coat under whose feet are *Dispatches from War Office*, under Bathurst's foot is a paper, *Appeals, Decrees* Next him (r) is a youthful-looking minister stepping on a paper inscribed *French Grammar* to show that he is Suffolk, Secretary of State, pilloried for his ignorance of French, see Nos 4875, 4876 His neighbour is only partly visible Next comes a military officer trampling on a paper inscribed *Middlesex Election* to show that he is Colonel Luttrell. On Luttrell's r , and the central figure of the design, is Lord Mansfield wearing tartan stockings to show that he is a Scot and dancing upon *Magna Charta*. On his r is an unidentified figure, then a minister treading on papers inscribed *Whitfield Hymns* to show (not very consistently) that he is Lord Dartmouth, whose strong attachment to the Methodists earned the nickname of the Psalm-singer. He had succeeded Hillsborough as Secretary of State for the Colonies on 14 Aug 1772. Between him and Barrington stands Sandwich, wearing a sailor's trousers and standing on *The Petition of the Navy Captains*. Bute stands on a paper *To Miss Vansittar[t]* Other papers on the ground are *The Remonstr[ance of the City]* and *Petition of the East India Comp.* The captains of the Navy had petitioned to the House of Commons for an addition to their half pay 9 Feb. 1773. *Parl Hist.* xvii 705-22 The request was approved by parliament, but opposed by North and the King *Corr. of George III*, ed. Fortescue, ii. 447, 451. At this time the latest City Remonstrance was that of 24 June 1771, that of 1773 was not decided on till 11 March 1773, nor presented to the King till 26 March Sharpe, *London and the Kingdom*, iii. 135-6. The petition of the East India Company appears to be that of 14 Dec 1772, against the Bill to restrain the Company from appointing supervisors for India, see *Parl Hist.* xvii 646 ff ; see also Nos. 4968, 5102.

The plate illustrates 'A vision' of a full Council of the Ministry in the Cockpit (the Treasury) at which, on the sound of bagpipes, the ministers seized the papers on the table, scattered them on the floor, and 'danced upon them with a furious glee.' It appears that the two unidentified dancers are Viscount Townshend (appointed Master General of the Ordnance, 17 Oct. 1772) and Jeremiah Dyson or 'Mungo'

Reproduced, Chase, *The Beginnings of the American Revolution*, 1911, I, p 350.

$3\frac{15}{16} \times 6\frac{1}{8}$ in

5107 THE ZEALOTS FOR, & AGAINST THE TRUE RELIGION.
[1 Mar. 1773]

Engraving. From the *Oxford Magazine*, x. 63 It illustrates 'A Modern Dialogue, amongst the Benchers and Anti-Benchers, Beelzebub, and his Imp'. A tall column, on the top of which is a book on which stands a lamb bearing a cross to which is attached a pennon with a St. George's Cross, the whole representing Religion. Two opposing bodies of clergy strain at it with ropes the bishops in lawn sleeves on the l , ministers in gowns on the r. Over the ministers (r) hovers Beelzebub, pointing to the column and saying: *My Children that is not your God, but I am.*

The bishops, whose aim is to prevent the opposing party from pulling down the column, say *Let us keep it for our own Benefit* and *If Religion falls Adieu to our Stalls.*

The ministers say. *We starve by Religion; Down with the 39 Articles*, and *Let them that live by the Gosple* [sic] *Support it* They are assisted by a ragamuffin who attacks the column with a pick-axe.

The dialogue concludes with the victory of the Benchers who say: 'Ha! Ha! Ha! How easily we can frustrate all their endeavours with a well-timed diversion.

> Ye Gods! What havock doth corruption
> Make amongst your works '

I

This plate is indexed as *The Zealots for and against the 39 Articles* On 23 February 1773 Sir W. Meredith moved without success for a committee to reconsider the subscription to the Articles at the universities *Parl. Hist* XVII. 742–59. A Bill for the relief of Protestant Dissenters was rejected by the House of Lords on 2 April 1773. *Ibid.* p. 759. Letter No. 1218 in *Corr. of George III* ed Fortescue, II. 468 refers to this rejection and shows the attitude of the King and Ministry. See Nos. 4944, 5188.

$5\frac{3}{4} \times 3\frac{3}{4}$ in

5108 CAROLA GENOVESA, LOUISA, AUGUSTA, ANDREA, TIMOTHEA, D'EON DE BEAUMONT.

Publish'd March 20 1773 by S. Hooper on Ludgate-Hill

Mezzotint. D'Eon, as a woman dressed as Minerva, stands outside a tent. In her r. hand is a spear, in her l the shield with the Medusa head inscribed *At nunc dura dedit vobis discrimina Pallas.* She is directed to the l. and looks over her shoulder to the r. She wears the cross of St Louis.

In the foreground (r.) are muskets, a drum, flags, &c , one flag inscribed *Impavidum Ferient Ruinæ* In the background (l.) is a camp, with a row of tents, a sentry and three mounted dragoons. Beneath the title is engraved *Knight of the Royal & military order of St Louis Captain of Dragoons Aide-de-Camp to the Marechal Duke de Broglio; Minister Plenipotentiary from France to the King of Great Britain.* Beneath, on a separate plate, is engraved an account of d'Eon; it concludes '. . . the secret of her sex was discover'd in London in feb^ry 1771 through many accidents and Particulary [*sic*] through the declaration of the Princess Askoft . . .'. See No 4865, &c C. E Russell, *English Mezzotint Portraits*, II. 457.

$13\frac{1}{8} \times 10\frac{13}{16}$ in.

5109 THE STATE JUGGLERS 1773   [1 May 1773]

Engraving. From the *Westminster Magazine*, I. 272. Lord North as a juggler squats on a table which is on a raised platform. He wears a harlequin's suit with his ribbon and star and holds a mask in his r. hand, in his l. a conjuror's box. On the table are three large money-bags, a pack of cards, balls, and cones. Behind him are ministers and ministerialists (l. to r): Dyson as Mungo the negro slave holds up a round box, Sandwich holds his cricket-bat over his shoulder, on his head rests the model of a man-of-war. Behind North on his r is Mansfield in judge's wig and robes; on North's l. is Bute, holding a coronet over North's head; in front of Bute is Charles Fox or Lord Holland with a fox's head. On the r. are three other ministers all wearing ribbons, one with a military coat being Barrington, Secretary-at-War. In front of the table is a serpent on a pedestal Below the platform is a crowd of people, some watching the juggler, others turning aside with gestures of despair. The principal figures are: a seated man holding a pole on the top of which is a pair of breeches with the pockets inside out to show his poverty; a standing man with a ragged coat holds his head in despair, an emaciated Asiatic lies on the ground.

The text explains the scene as a vision, a juggler's booth in St. James's Street, the serpent being a 'symbol of the Practitioner's address, cunning and deceit'. The figures round the juggler seeming to applaud were aiding his cheats. 'Handfulls of gold being thrown up in the air . . scattered mischief and destruction all round ' The exasperated crowd at last demolished the booth and the scaffold.

The commercial crisis of 1772, see No. 4961 &c , continued during 1773, see *Corr of George III*, ed. Fortescue, ii 436. The Secret Committee had made charges of rapacity and oppression against servants of the East India Company. *Parl. Hist.* xvii. 535, 829.

6 × 3⅝ in.

5110 THE POLITICAL DANCING BEAR. [1 May 1773]

Engraving. From the *London Magazine*, xlii. 160 Two men symbolizing France and Spain are in charge of a dancing bear which represents England. France (l), dressed as a French fop, plays the violin; Spain, in cloak and slashed doublet, holds the rope attached to the animal's head The bear has a shield on its forehead ornamented with the combined crosses of St. George and St. Andrew as in the Union flag. Round its body are scrolls inscribed *Evil be to him that Evil thinks*, and *Quisque me impune lacessit*. In the background (r.) are two sovereigns in crowns and ermine-trimmed robes, one leaning on the shoulder of the other; they watch the scene with amusement. Above the head of the bear-leader and in the centre of the design are two circles representing the reverse and obverse of a coin. On one (l) are three heads, two resembling those of the fiddler and the bear-leader, the central one that of George III; the first two have expressions of cunning satisfaction Above it is engraved *The triple alliance*. On the other are three clasped hands meeting in the centre of the circle; above it is engraved *Tria juncta in uno* Beneath the design is engraved *Music hath charms to soothe a savage Beast*.

The print is explained in 'A Dialogue between a Politician and a Chinese', pp 160–2. The Great Bear or G.B. is Great Britain, the fiddler is the French Ambassador [Comte de Guines], and the bear, 'clumsy, credulous, unsuspecting', dances to a French tune The three heads and the three hands symbolize a triple alliance between England, France, and Spain ('an honest fat open face [George III] between two scarecrows'). The two sovereigns in the background are the king of Prussia and 'his scholar the Emperor' who laugh at 'the folly of a triple alliance so motley and so unnatural'. The alliance is 'not yet' concluded.

At this time there were rumours that England proposed to make an alliance with France to oppose the invasion and partition of Poland. Walpole, *Last Journals*, 1910, i. 186. See an interesting paper in George III's handwriting of 1772 on a possible alliance of England, France, and Holland to protect Poland against Austria, Russia, and Prussia, if jealousies should arise between the three partitioning powers *Corr of George III*, ed. Fortescue, ii 428–9 See also Nos. 4957, 4958, 5124, 5222, 5229.

There was actually a crisis in March and April 1773 arising out of the Russo-Turkish war, which attracted little public notice, a threat of France and Spain to attack Russia which was checked by naval preparations in England (cf. No 5124), and the diplomatic action of Stormont, British ambassador in Paris Adolphus, *Hist. of England*, ii. 4–9; *Corr. of George III*, ed Fortescue, ii 470, 474 This shows how unfounded were the rumours of a triple alliance between England, France, and Spain in April 1773, although in the following year Vergennes, alarmed at the Treaty of Kutchuk-Kainardji (July 1774), contemplated the possibility of persuading England to join in an effort to check Russia. Corwin, *French Policy and the American Alliance*, 1916, p. 61.

3¾ × 6⁷⁄₁₆ in.

5111 THE PRESENT TIMES, OR THE NABOBS CL——VE AND

C—L—KE BROUGHT TO ACCOUNT. [1 May 1773]

Engraving. From the *Oxford Magazine*, x 144 Two men (r.) kneeling in supplication before Lord North (l.) who stands with a pistol in his r. hand, about to take the large money-bags which the two 'nabobs', Clive and Colebrooke, hold out to him Colebrooke, a very small man, is saying: *Save us my Lord or we Perish*, from his pocket hangs a paper inscribed *Job in the Alley 30,000£* On Colebrooke's r. is Clive saying: *You shall have the tenth of my Jaghire* (this was the quit-rent given to Clive by Mir Jaffier amounting to nearly £30,000 a year which the Directors had limited to ten years). Each has an iron band round his neck to which a chain is attached which is held in the mouth of a demon in the foreground Another chain from its mouth is attached to North's wrist. North stands on a paper inscribed *India Stock no Price*. He is saying· *I know the vileness of your deeds! But I must have more hush Money*. From his pocket hangs a paper inscribed *Report of the Secret Committee*. Justice, a blindfolded woman holding scales with her sword raised to strike, hovers in the air behind this group. Bute, holding out a highlander's target and with a sword in his l. hand, stands to protect the three men from the sword of justice; he wears a kilt and the Garter ribbon, and his face is covered with a mask to show that his influence is secret Above the design is engraved *A new Scene for the Proprietors of India Stock*. Below the title is engraved· *Deel awa wi em Au R——gues all alike, Bribers and Bribed*

The plate anticipates the great debates in which Clive defended himself from the accusations in the Secret Committee on the East India Company, see *Parl. Hist* xvii. 850 ff. He said 'Jaghires were as commonly given [by Indian princes] as pensions, lottery tickets and other douceurs by the minister in this' Clive is called the Jaghire Factor in No 5102, Baron Jaghire in No 5144 [1] See also Nos. 5100, 5102.

$5\frac{7}{8} \times 3\frac{5}{8}$ in.

5112–5123

A set of twelve prints by William Austin, some of which are not political. The title and price of the series are engraved on the first only.

5112 A MACARONI ASS MATCH BETWEEN THE [CUBS][2]

NB. ST——E [State] GAMBLERS. 1

[1] Cf 'Protestation' in *London Magazine*, 1773, p 44, beginning, 'You I love my dearest wife', has the line, 'More than Clive his black Jagheer' Quoted, G E C. *Complete Peerage*, i 1910 Appendix H

Also,

> Secure from Wars and dangerous Seas
> Colonel Jaghire enjoys his Ease
> Buys Land, and Beeves, with Indian Gold,
> Which some poor English 'Squire has sold.
> C. Anstey, *Election Ball* 1776, p. 7.

[2] 'Cubs' is written in ink, perhaps after having been first erased In another impression it is engraved

NATURE DISPLAY'D BOTH SERIOUS AND COMIC IN 12 DE-
SIGNS DEDICATED TO S FOOT ESQ^R *by L'eauforte & Burein
Pr^s a Guinea* [1]   1

Pub^d as ye Act Directs May 1st 1773.

Engraving. Two men riding (r. to l.) on asses, between them is a small
stream. The foremost ass is galloping, its rider sits facing its tail in order
to jeer at his rival. The other ass, braying with outstretched neck, refuses
to cross the stream in spite of the efforts of its rider who stands on the
saddle, vigorously using a long-lashed whip

The title shows that the riders are sons of Lord Holland. The standing
rider is short and stout and has a certain resemblance to caricatures of both
Charles and Stephen, but is probably intended for Charles. The other is
tall and lean, and is probably intended for Henry Fox (1755–1811), who
at the age of nine lived only for horses, see No. 5062 In 1773 he was with
his regiment at Boston

Beneath the dedication is engraved,

> *I'll no Man call an Ape or Ass*
> *Tis his own Conscience holds the Glass*
> *Thus Void of all Offence I draw*
> *Who Claims y^e Subject knows his Flaw.*

$10\frac{1}{2} \times 14\frac{5}{8}$ in (pl)

5113 A PEEP IN THE GARDEN AT HAYES   2

Pub^d as the Act Directs May 1st 1773   [W. Austin]

Engraving. An interview between Chatham and Charles Fox. Chatham (l)
in profile to the r has just left a wheeled chair, similar in principle, though
of ornate design, to the modern bath-chair. A pair of crutches is supported
in loops on the outside of the chair. Chatham is much caricatured and
very thin, his gouty l. leg and foot in a bulky woollen covering, probably
one of the 'bootikins' described by Walpole He wears a large night-cap
and a pair of clumsy woollen gloves. He holds out both hands and faces
his visitor with an expression of wary friendliness Fox faces him with a
somewhat truculent expression. His r. forefinger is extended as if making
terms; his l. hand is in his waistcoat pocket, and his hat is under his l. arm.

An indication of the political importance which Fox had already acquired,
and of his vacillating policy at this time Having 'commenced patriot'
(Gibbon to Holroyd, 21 Feb 1772) over the Marriage Act, see No. 4970,
he again took office as a lord of the Treasury in December 1772, and after
opposing the Ministry was dismissed on 24 Feb 1774 Chatham was then
living in retirement, but was actually at Burton Pynsent not Hayes.
Chatham Correspondence, vol. iv.

$10\frac{5}{8} \times 14\frac{3}{4}$ in. (pl.).

5114 THE VOLUPTUOS · LUXURIOUS   SPENDTHRIFT ·
MACARONI FROM HOLLAND IN A · BREATHING SWEAT
     3

Pub^d as y^e Act Directs May 1 1773   [W. Austin]

Engraving One of the sons of Lord Holland asleep, half-sitting, half-lying

---

[1] On another impression '12/6' has been substituted.

on a garden seat, his breath issuing visibly from his mouth His l foot is on the ground, his r. on the seat. He has a toupet wig with a large macaroni club, his hat has fallen to the ground. He is obese and is dressed as a macaroni, with a large nosegay. His curved sword or sabre hangs from his waist.

A caricature of Stephen Fox afterwards 2nd Lord Holland who was constitutionally lethargic, and is usually depicted asleep, see Nos 4648, 4649, 5223 In the *Covent Garden Magazine*, July 1773, he is 'a celebrated sleeping, gambling Macaroni'.

$10\frac{3}{4} \times 14\frac{3}{4}$ in. (pl)

5115 MAJOR G * * * * N & LADY LANDING AT SOUTHAMP-TON IN CRIPPLES WALK   4

Pub^d as the Act Directs May 1st 1773   [W. Austin]

Engraving. The scene is the sea-shore, with the Isle of Wight faintly visible in the background. A man followed by a woman walk in profile from r to l., both much caricatured. He is using crutches, his gouty l leg is swathed or in a bootikin, and suspended in a sling which goes over his r shoulder. He has an impossibly protruding waistcoat, and a large club of hair. A dog (l) is barking at him His wife holds in her r. hand a bottle labelled *Hartshorn*, in her l. a very long cane. Her profile is witch-like with hooked nose and protruding bearded chin. A large hood almost conceals her hair, and she wears a long cloak A cross hangs from a necklace round her neck. In the distance grotesque figures walk on the shore, most of them in various stages of decrepitude. One is labelled *The Rabbit Doctor, St. A——*, under his arm is a large rabbit. This is St. André (1680–1776), an unqualified but fashionable surgeon who investigated the case of Mary Tofts in 1726, who professed to be delivered of rabbits, see Nos. 1778–81. He vouched for her story in all its impossible details. In spite of the scandal caused by its exposure he eloped with, and afterwards married, Lady Elizabeth Molyneux on the night of the death of her husband whom he had been professionally attending. They settled in Southampton about 1750.

$10\frac{1}{8} \times 15\frac{3}{4}$ in. (pl).

5116 [LONG] T[HOMAS] & MAD^{LE} G——D GOING TO THE PAN-THEON IN THEIR NATURAL MASKS[1]   5

Pub^d as y^e Act Directs May 1st 1773   [W. Austin]

Engraving. A caricature of 'Long Sir Thomas' Robinson (1700?–77) walk-ing arm in arm with a short, fat and elderly woman, both in profile to the l. He is very thin and wears the large hat, tie-wig, wide-cuffed coat and high-quartered shoes which were then old-fashioned. His l. hand is on the hilt of his sword, his r. holds up a glass through which he looks. The lady is also much caricatured, a pair of spectacles is perched on her bulbous nose, she wears a calash hood, and a large nosegay. In her r hand is a closed fan, a microscopic dog is carried under her l arm. She takes Sir Thomas's l. arm She is perhaps identical with Mrs. G——s, a mistress of Sir Thomas who is described as short and stout and 'past her bloom'. See *Town and Country Magazine*, April 1774, and No. 5253.

[1] The letters in brackets are in ink.

Behind the couple walks a small lean foot-boy, in laced livery, his hair in a long pigtail queue He points jeeringly at the couple, and holds up a large key, looking through its handle as if through a glass in imitation of his master.

There is an earlier caricature of Sir Thomas in a group by General Sir A. Campbell, which includes a portrait of the Chevalier Descassau (see No 5067), 'Honorary Engravers', i. 161, and he has been identified with the figure standing in a side box in Hogarth's picture of the *Beggar's Opera*, D.N.B.

Reproduced, Fuchs, *Die Frau in der Karikatur*, 1906, p 352

$11\frac{3}{4} \times 14\frac{3}{4}$ in. (pl.).

5117 [HANS TURBOT][1] QUARRELLING WITH A FISHWOMAN · AT SOUTHAMPTON IN PRESENCE OF COUNT CORK SKREW

6

Pub[d] as the Act Directs May 1st 1773   [W. Austin]

Engraving An irate fishwife stands behind her trestle-table on which are fish. Her l. hand is on her hip, in her r. she holds a coin towards 'Hans Turbot' (l), whom she is scolding. He faces her, in profile to the l, holding a large turbot by the tail She is a gaunt woman with a hideous profile, wearing a flat hat and a short apron. Her r wrist is tattooed, *WL 45*, perhaps a memento of Wilkes and No. 45 of the *North Briton*. Hans, who is ugly and corpulent, is scowling at the woman. In his r. hand is a cane on the head of which is engraved *H. S* On the r., and in front of the trestle-table, stands Count Cork Skrew, dressed in an old-fashioned manner in large three-cornered hat and tie-wig, and coat with wide cuffs.

Perhaps a caricature of Hans Stanley of Paulton's near Romsey, M.P. for Southampton, the grandson of Sir Hans Sloane, who was awkward and eccentric He never married and shot himself in 1780 See Walpole, *Letters*, xi 105–6 His companion is perhaps the Earl of Cork (Edmund Boyle, 8th earl, 1742–98).

$10\frac{3}{4} \times 14\frac{3}{4}$ in (pl).

5118—RETURN[G] FROM READING MARKET IN A FULL BREEZE

7

Pub[d] as y[e] Act Directs May 1st 1773   [W. Austin]

Engraving Two men walk from r to l. one behind the other; a following wind blows their hair and clothes. Both are uncouth and wear cockaded hats and are perhaps intended for half-pay officers. The hands of the man in front are in a muff. His pigtail queue is blown in front of him The second man walks with crutches, his r. hand is replaced by a hook, in which he carries a nest suspended from strings on which are a hen and young chickens Tied to his back is a child. He is smoking a short clay pipe

$10\frac{5}{8} \times 14\frac{5}{8}$ in (clipped)

---

[1] The name is written in ink perhaps after the engraved words had been erased

5119 THE ANATOMIST OVERTAKEN BY THE WATCH IN CARRYING OFF MISS W——TS[1] IN A HAMPER   8

Pub^d as the Act Directs May 1 1773   [W. Austin]

Engraving A lean man (r) wearing a doctor's tie-wig, is running from l to r to escape from a watchman who stands (l.) springing his rattle On the ground is a basket or hamper, the lid of which has fallen open to show the body of a young woman in a shroud. A short irate man (centre) points at the escaping figure, turning towards the lean aged watchman, who holds in his l. hand a large lantern, and a tall stick, whose head is carved to represent a head In the watchman's hat, which is tied on with a scarf, is a tobacco pipe in full blast The fleeing Anatomist holds a tall cane in his l. hand, under his l arm is a dilapidated skull He has dropped a paper inscribed *Hunter's Lectur[es]*, showing that he is Dr. William Hunter (1718–83), the great anatomist. He built a house (1770) in Great Windmill Street to which were attached a dissecting room, lecture room, and a large museum, see No 6128. The caricature deals with the body-snatching for the sale of corpses to surgeons, which went on to a considerable extent in this period Reproduced, *Social England*, ed. Traill, 1904, v, p. 573.

10⅝ × 15⅝ in. (pl.).

5120 [THE DUCHESS OF QUEENSBERRY AND SOUBISE]

Pub^d as the Act Directs May 1st 1773   [W Austin]

Engraving. One of the series *Nature Display'd . .* but without title or number A fencing match between a negro (l.) and a lady (r) whose face is concealed by a fencing mask. The button of his foil touches her breast and he says: *Mungo here Mungo dere, Mungo Ev'ry where, above, & below Hah! Vat your Gracy tink of me Now.* He is fashionably dressed, a large nosegay lies on the ground beside him together with his laced hat, tasselled cane, and an open book *Les École des Armes Avec Les Attudes* [sic] *est Positions Par Angelo* [sic]. Two books lie on the ground by the lady, the uppermost being *Vol 5th Mungo Bill* The duchess (Prior's 'Kitty', 1700–77) is thin and tall, and dressed in the manner of many years ago, as was her custom, in laced stomacher, and short lace-trimmed apron.

'Mungo' generally connotes Jeremiah Dyson (see 4267, &c.), the quotation here given from Bickerstaffe's comic opera, *The Padlock*, having been applied to him by Barré. Here Mungo is Soubise, the black page and protégé of the Duchess of Queensberry. The young man having become very boastful and extravagant, she articled him to Angelo, to be trained as an assistant in his fencing-school He became 'one of the most conspicuous fops of the town', never seen 'without a bouquet of the choicest flowers in his bosom'. Angelo, *Reminiscences*, 1904, 1 348–51 The print is also a burlesque of Angelo's great illustrated folio on fencing, *L'École d'Armes avec l'Explication des Principales Attitudes et Positions concernant l'Escrime*, 1763, &c. Reproduced, Angelo, *Reminiscences*, i p 350, Paston, Pl cxxxiv.

10¾ × 14⅝ in (pl).

---

[1] The 'ts' has been added in ink, but is engraved in another impression

5121 THE LUCKY MISTAKE OR THE BUCK & BLOOD FLOURISHING MACARONI —— PLAYING A SOLO ON THE JELLY GLASSES   10[1]

Pub^d as the Act Directs May 1st 1773   [W. Austin]

Engraving. A military officer on a heavy cavalry horse, rides unconcernedly past a man whom he has knocked down. He wears a hat with a cockade, a sabre, cavalry boots, and a large nosegay. His hair is in a large macaroni club, tied with ribbons In his r hand he flourishes a short-handled whip with a long lash. His horse has a flowing mane and tail.

Behind the horse the prostrate man (r) looks round with a face of fury. He has a wooden leg which has been broken in his fall Both hands are outstretched on the tray which he has been carrying, on which are a number of overturned and broken jelly-glasses.

In the upper r. corner of the plate is a club of hair under which is engraved. *Club the First Both Natural & Artificial Flowing from Simple Nature The Size, about two thirds of his Carcase Weighs . Upwards of five pounds when full Dress'd & truss'd up with Powder Lambs Wool Horse & Asses hair Eau de Mille fleurs &c. &c. &c. &c. &c. &c.*

$10\frac{5}{8} \times 14\frac{5}{8}$ in. (pl).

5122 THE MERITS AND DEFECTS OF THE DEAD BY THEIR INGENIOUS SECRETARY   11

Pub^d as the Act Directs May 1st 1773   [W. Austin]

Engraving. A grave-digger (l) resting on his spade holds out in his l hand a decayed skull towards a skeleton-like man wearing an old-fashioned tie-wig, who is sitting on a rectangular tomb while he leans his r. elbow on another tomb at right angles to his seat. This man holds a scythe in his l. hand, a pen in his r. He uses the second tomb as a writing table; an ink-pot stands upon it His hand rests on two papers inscribed *Marcus Aurelius Servius Tullius* . . . and *Addison—Dr Swift* From the jaws of the skull held by the grave-digger issue the words,

Life is a jest & all things shew it
I thought so once but now I know it

In the foreground are bones and a skull; in the background (l) a rat scampers away.

Evidently a caricature of Lord Lyttelton (1709–73), author of *Dialogues of the Dead.* He was noted for his thin, lanky figure and awkward bearing, see 'The Motion', No. 2479. He died in August 1773.

$11\frac{5}{8} \times 14\frac{15}{16}$ in. (pl).

5123 A FLAW IN THE ICE OR STEPHENS DREAM OF THE MACARONI BUCKS & DOES TURN'D TOPSY TURVY   12

Pub^d as the Act Directs May 1st 1773.   [W. Austin]

Engraving. The heads and feet of persons suddenly submerged by the breaking of ice appear above the surface The central figure is Stephen Fox, whose shoulders and arms are above the water, his face expresses rage and alarm There are also the heads and shoulders of three other men, two in back view, one in profile to the l. clutching the shoulder of

---

[1] The number 10 appears to have been engraved over a partly obliterated 9

his neighbour, his pigtail queue flying wildly in the air. Three pairs of legs emerge from splashing water: one wearing spurred jack boots, another wearing low shoes with skates, and a third wearing the high-heeled shoes and clocked stockings of a lady. See also No. 5114.

$11\frac{5}{8} \times 14\frac{5}{8}$ in. (pl).

5124 A RETROSPECTIVE VIEW OF A CERTAIN CABINET JUNTO [1 June 1773]

Engraving. From the *Oxford Magazine*, x. 182. It illustrates a dialogue, called 'The Party Quare [*Carré*] in Council with their private but Grand Dictator hearkening to their resolves'. George III (r.) sits at a table in a high-backed chair or throne under a canopy, in conference with three Ministers. Round the door appear the head and shoulders of Bute (l) in Scot's cap and Garter ribbon, behind him is a demon. The King points out to North, who sits opposite to him, a paper on the table inscribed *The Civil List in Arrears* North holds up his hands deprecatingly; from his pocket hangs a paper, *Treaty of Alli[ance] with France & Spa[in]*; the demon's claws clutch at the back of his head. On the king's r. stands Sandwich holding a paper inscribed *20 Sail of the Line*. The third minister appears from the text to be 'J——n.', Charles Jenkinson, afterwards Earl of Liverpool, who according to Walpole, at this time 'began to assume the airs of a minister . .' *Last Journals*, 1910, 1 177 n. On the ground are papers inscribed, *Rights of the People of England*, which is being worried by a small dog, and *East India Affairs*.

The Junto agree that money must be had, and can be got by shamming war with France while taking a subsidy from France to preserve peace At this time there was a rumour of an alliance with France while actually there had been naval preparations against France in defence of Russia, see No 5110 The print may also be an echo from the reign of Charles II owing to the sensation caused by Sir John Dalrymple's *Memoirs of Great Britain and Ireland*, 1771; the Appendix with its documents incriminating Algernon Sidney the Whig hero was published in February 1773, see Walpole, *op. cit.* 1. 177, 179 f. For the arrears of the Civil List, see No 5105.

$5\frac{3}{4} \times 3\frac{1}{2}$ in.

5125 THE MORNING VISIT   42

Publish'd as the Act Directs June 1773

Engraving. Apparently No 42 in some series It illustrates a dialogue in verse engraved below the design between 'Lord' and 'Dean'. The 'lord', writing at a table, receives the visit of a dean, who bows, hat in hand, and proffers a money-bag, asking for a bishopric. On the wall hang a mirror (l) with a pair of candle-sconces and a framed landscape On the floor in the foreground are documents partly cut and destroyed: 'CHARTER COMMUNIUM *Johannes dei Gratia* and LIBERTATUM give [?sive] MAGNA CHARTA From a nearly closed box hang other documents also in bad repair: HABE . . CORPUS *Rex Magna B* , Bill of Rights; *nilla* [sic] *Ransom* In an open chest are neatly rolled documents, evidently recent patent rolls, or grants, one of which shows the words *and Grant beloved* The document on which the Minister is writing is inscribed:

List of persons proper for Pensions Rever[si]ons and Places for life &c
for his M——y's private inspection.
Sign'd *J E of B——e* [John Earl of Bute]
M——d [Mansfield]

Lord N——n [Northington] *a Pension—*   4000
L——d Bingley on the I——h E. [Irish Exchequer]   3500
S'. G— B——n. first Com. C——m   3000
Sinora B——a for Sr G——t   250
Mungo Cam——r. and a Pension [Dyson, Cofferer of the Household]   1500
D——n of G——r [Dean of Gloucester] *Vicar of Bray first B——k*
[Bishoprick]
insouable [*sic*] *C. J. F . . .* [Fox].

Beneath the design is engraved in two columns,

DEAN. *My Lord I hope your goodness will excuse*
This early Visit, since my only views
Are center'd in the glory of your House,
And now have brought a trifle—for your Spouse
Of which I beg her kind acceptance — — then
Rank me my Lord, amongst the happiest men

LORD. *My rev'rend Dean, I'm glad to see you now,*
Early or late; or any time, I vow:
What news abroad, my rev'rend Dean, what news?
Somethings behind—have you no trifling views
In which my Int'rest can the least avail — —?

DEAN. *Indeed, my Lord, there is a flying tale*
That my good Lord of B——h [Bath] *declines so fast*
With Age, and Gout, this fit will be his last.

LORD. *I know he's old and cannot long be here:*
But, rev^d Dean, you know—what 'tis a Year:
'Twill gain me Friends — — —

DEAN. *— — My Lord I know that's true,*
And all the Int'rest in my pow'rs your due
In future times the same shall me controul
My Friends — Estate — — my Body, and my — [soul].

LORD. *'Tis well my rev'rend Dean — all's very right;*
On these conditions you're put down to night,
You shall succeed — —

DEAN. *— — All grateful thanks are due,*
My gratitude shall shine, my Lord —: my Lord adieu

Dr Edward Willes, bishop of Bath and Wells, died 24 Nov. 1773, aged 80. Dr. Charles Moss, Bishop of St. Davids, succeeded him. (*Congé élire*, 23 April, 1774. *Cal H O. Papers* 1773–5, p. 272).

The Dean here depicted who is promised the 'first bishoprick', is Josiah Tucker, dean of Gloucester He was reputed a ministerial propagandist. See Mason, *Satirical Odes*, ed Toynbee, pp. 33, 91, 99, &c. The peer resembles portraits of Lord Rochford, one of the Secretaries of State. 8⅞ × 8¼ in

5126 SAMSON PULLING DOWN THE PILLARS.[1]   [1 July 1773]
Engraving. *Oxford Magazine*, x. 217. A print from the same plate, altered, as No 4179, an illustration to the *Political Register* for August

[1] Indexed as *Samson pulling down Magna Charta.*

1767. Bute has been altered to Lord North by the re-drawing of the head and the elimination of the tartan check on his drapery North, as Samson, pulls down four pillars which support the temple of the Constitution, one falls in pieces, the others, about to fall, are inscribed · *Accession of the House of Brunswick*; *Revolution 1688*; and *Magna Charta*. The cornice falls in fragments, from it fall a figure of Liberty, with her staff and cap, West-minster Hall, a number of judges, a dome resembling that of St Paul's, the cross on the summit of which is held by a bishop Other figures are falling headlong ('Lords, Counsellors, or Priests') Lord Chatham with his crutches, the king, his crown having fallen from his head, the queen (?), two other crowns are falling as well as a mitre The lowest objects, those which were the first to be hurled down, are Britannia, the Irish harp, and a broken anchor. Clouds and lightning form a background. Beneath the design are engraved the eighteen lines from *Samson Agonistes* ending,

> *Samson with these immixed, inevitably*
> *Pull'd down the same destruction on himself.*

Cf No. 5127, also an altered plate.

$5\frac{15}{16} \times 4\frac{5}{16}$ in.   B M L , P.P 6115

5127 THE OPERATION.   [1 Aug. 1773]

Engraving. From the *Oxford Magazine*, x. 254. An adaptation of No 4198 from the *Political Register* June 1768, the same plate being used. Britannia sinks to the ground, one knee on her shield, her broken spear beside her, while blood gushes from wounds in her breast. Above her, with a dagger raised to strike, stands a minister wearing a ribbon and star. Two others hold basins to catch the gushing blood, while two stand behind drinking from bowls of blood; another stoops to look at Britannia, a lawyer hands a bowl to Bute, seated (r) in a high-backed chair In the foreground (r), seated on steps, is Lord Talbot, a stout man drinking from a bowl; he wears a spit instead of a sword to show that he is Lord Steward of the Household.

In the original version, Chatham was seated in the chair taking a bowl, he has been altered to Bute, by the redrawing of the head and the removal of his crutch The judge offering him the bowl, identified by Mr. Stephens as Lord Mansfield, has been altered into a poorly characterized lawyer This suggests, as do the features of the judge, that the original was intended for Lord Camden, as Lord Mansfield would certainly not have been removed from obloquy. The head of Bute in the original has been altered by the removal of the Scots cap and some change in the features, as other-wise there would have been two Butes There is a slight change in the features of the minister identified by Mr. Stephens as Weymouth, and he is now probably intended for Lord Sandwich The other figures have not been altered. It remains an attack on the Ministry in general, and on Lord Bute, but the temporary unpopularity of Chatham had long been forgotten. Beneath the design is engraved, as before,

> *The Blood & Vitals from her Wounds he drew,*
> *And Fed the Hounds that help'd him to pursue. Dryden*

Cf. No. 5126, also an altered plate.

$5\frac{7}{16} \times 4\frac{1}{8}$ in.

5128 A RETROSPECTIVE VIEW OF THE DIFFICULTIES & EMBARASSMENTS OCCASION'D BY THE COIN ACT, OR BRITANIA & HER CHILDREN IN DISTRESS   [1 Sept 1773]

Engraving From the *Oxford Magazine*, x 195. Lord North sits complacently at a table weighing guineas in a pair of scales. Before him on the table are a bag of guineas and a pair of shears Behind him, among clouds, stands Justice (r), blindfolded, holding up her scales and threatening him with her sword At the table sit three men, owners of the coin, watching North with gestures of horror. At a side-table (l.) another man weighs guineas, holding a pair of shears to deface those which are defective. A countryman, hat in hand, protests in alarm; a mastiff snarls at him A doctor (l) threatens a patient with a raised syringe A judge (r.) fights with a man on the ground, whom he is about to strike with a rolled document. In the foreground Britannia reclines, clasping her hands in despair, three ragged children weep beside her.

The Coin Act (13 George III. c. 71 supplemented by 14 Geo. III. c. 70) provided that any person to whom gold coins were tendered might cut or break them if found of light weight or counterfeit, the tenderer to bear the loss of defacement if found of good weight. See *Ann. Reg.* 1773, pp. 195–6, *Corr. of George III*, ed. Fortescue, iii 5. 'Retrospective' in the title probably indicates that the Act was retrospective in falling on those who had accepted coin before it was passed. A guide book, Decremps, *Parisien à Londres*, 1789, informs visitors to England that the first thing to be done is to provide themselves with scales to weigh guineas and half-guineas, as none are taken without being weighed Mr. Hawkins notes 'as late as 1799, I saw light guineas offered to the Collector of taxes cut in two'. One of several satires on the Coin Act and on the use of scales which it involved, see Nos. 3759, 4534 (1774), 5158, 5234.

$4\frac{13}{16} \times 6\frac{5}{8}$ in.

5129 [BULL'S TRIUMPH]   [1 Nov. 1773]

Woodcut. From the *Town and Country Magazine*, v 524. Alderman Bull, wearing his furred gown and chain, is entering the Lord Mayor's coach. He treads on the back of Wilkes and his r. hand rests on the cap of Liberty which is on a long staff held by Wilkes Two men (r) lie prostrate and despairing on the ground, and two others, one a clergyman, stand behind, wringing their hands in consternation A little boy (l.) claps his hands with amusement, behind him a fat butcher laughs at the scene. A dog barks at the prostrate figures.

The accompanying dialogue shows that the prostrate figures are Sawbridge and Oliver who have been knocked down by 'bawling liverymen'. The two standing figures are Parson Horne, '*défroqué*', and an aspirant to the office of chaplain to the Lord Mayor if Sawbridge had been elected

At Michaelmas 1773 there was a heated contest for the Mayoralty between Wilkes and Bull on one side and Sawbridge and Oliver on the other. Wilkes and Bull were elected, Wilkes at the head of the poll. Their names were submitted to the Court of Aldermen which chose Bull, it was said by the casting vote of Townsend the outgoing Mayor Bull was Wilkes's creature and the election was a complete discomfiture for Wilkes's enemies while the rejection of Wilkes in spite of his majority only increased his popularity Walpole, *Last Journals*, 1910, i. 250 For Bull, see *City Biography*, 1800, p 84. For the quarrel between Wilkes and

Horne, the origin of the split among the City patriots, see No. 4861, &c.
See also Nos 5130, 5131, 5235
6¼×4 in.

5130 THE CITY PATRIOTS, OR A PICTURE OF THE TIMES
[1 Nov. 1773]

Engraving. From the *Macaroni . . . Magazine*, ii 1. A bull in an alderman's furred gown stands on his hind legs, leaning forwards His horns are held by Wilkes who wears an alderman's gown, while another alderman twists his tail. A dog in alderman's gown, his collar inscribed *Oliver*, barks at the bull, two men (l) point derisively, one dressed as an alderman, the other in parson's gown and bands. In the background (l.) a young man threatens with his cane a stout man who runs away weeping, his handkerchief to his eye. An alderman (r) is whipping a girl who has fallen to the ground, her bundle of sticks beside her

The accompanying text explains this satire on the squabbles among the City patriots, Wilkes, Townsend, Bull, Sawbridge, &c. Alderman Bull is standing quietly while Wilkes holds him by the horns, and the 'Macaroni Alderman Sir W[atkin] L[ewes] twists his tail' The 'Oliverian cur' [Alderman Oliver] tries to seize his nose; Parson Horne, 'the associate of Judas', and Alderman Sawbridge, M P , 'that austere tribune', look on and encourage the cur. Wilkes had pilloried his friends and former friends in the newspapers· he discovered that the Lord Mayor, James Townsend, had whipped a girl whom he found gathering sticks in his plantations, while the man of all the world who had served him most essentially was 'M——l L——l', but he had been caned and had wept and Wilkes had gibbeted him 'to divert the spleen of his countrymen'. See also Nos. 4861, &c , 5129, 5131.
4×6¼ in.

5131 THE BULL OF GOTHAM. [1 Dec. 1773]

Woodcut. From the *Westminster Magazine*, i 669. Wilkes in his alderman's gown approaches the Mansion House riding upon a bull, in his l. hand is a whip The bull has a human face and its forelegs are those of a man. It wears a long furred robe and mayoral chain. Behind walks a man in a furred gown, playing a Welsh harp decorated with a stag's head. This represents the election of Bull, Wilkes's protégé, as Lord Mayor, see No 5129. The man playing the harp is Watkin Lewes, Sheriff 1772-3 and knighted Feb. 1773. See Nos. 4880, 5155, &c., and *City Biography*, 1800, p. 16 For his attitude in the quarrels among the city patriots see *Oxford Magazine*, x 227-31.

The text 'A Canonical Fragment', which accompanies the woodcut, is an attack on Wilkes: 'He was of the tribe of the Wilkites of the race of the Jews and his father's name was Israel. Now this man was a hypocrite, a dissembler of the truth, and great was his cunning: and he laid false snares and gained the hearts of the People, insomuch that they despised their Rulers, and him only did they obey.' He determined to humble those of the City who had remonstrated with him by causing a Bull-calf to rule over them· '*Behold ye people of Gotham, I bring you a* CHIEF RULER *and a Head of the Elders!*' For other anti-Wilkite satires, see Nos. 4326, 4887, 5103, 5130, 5245.
2½×3¹¹⁄₁₆ in

5132 THE ASSEMBLY OF THE GRINDERS

Published Decem^r the 22, 1773.

Engraving. Round a circular table sit members of the Ministry and others. Standing on the l., his l. hand on the back of a chair, is Lord Bute. Behind him is a folding screen inscribed *This is a Horrid screen for Villany*. To his r. in profile is the Duke of Grafton On Bute's l. and arranged round the table from l to r. are Lord Suffolk (?), Jeremiah Dyson, as Mungo the negro slave with a metal collar round his neck, and wearing a harlequin's dress. Next is Lord Rochford [1] Next sits Lord Sandwich, wearing a cricketing cap and holding a cricket bat. Next, the central and dominating figure, is Lord Mansfield in judge's cap, wig, and robes Next come Lord North and the King, so posed as to stress their likeness to each other, each is wearing his ribbon and star, a bandage is over the king's eyes They are squeezed in between Mansfield and Sir Fletcher Norton, the Speaker, in his robes, with bull's horns projecting from his wig, to indicate his nickname of Sir Bull-Face-Doublefee. The outside figure on the r., facing Grafton, is Lord Holland, with a fox's head His r hand, fist clenched, is on the table, on which lie three documents, the most prominent being *The humble Address, Remonstrance and Petition of the Lord Mayor* It lies across the *Bill of Rights*; *Magna Charta* is the third. The room is panelled, and in each of three panels is a picture: on the l. faggots piled round a stake are burning in a mountainous landscape Next is an axe suspended over a block, with an adjacent thistle plant This is immediately behind Mansfield and North, the axe appearing to be suspended over their heads. Behind Fletcher Norton and Lord Holland (r) are spears, crossed muskets, a sword, and a pyramid of cannon-balls inscribed *Provision for the Poor* Beneath the design is engraved:

The Application of this subject is taken from Æsops Fables by Dr Croxall (Fab 18 page 33) The Moral of this Fable is that no body looks after a mans Affairs so well as he himself Servants being but hirelings seldom have the true Interest of their Masters at Heart but let Things run on in a Negligent constant Disorder and this generally not so much for want of Capacity as honesty their Heads are taken up with the Cultivation of their own private Interest for the Service and promotion of which that of their Master is postpon'd and often intirely Neglected. If this be the case as it certainly is among ordinary Masters and Servants and it is of so ill consequence to a Man not to Inspect the Œconomy of his own Household how deplorable must be the State of that People who have a King or Governor so Ignorant that he knows not or so Indolent that he Cares not what becomes of their Welfare & happiness Who leaves the Administration of every thing to the management of Servants and those Wicked self Interested ones perhaps some may fancy him a mild and good Prince because he does not like a Barbarian actually Butcher his people with his own hands But he is passively a sad Creature and the ultimate Author of all the Woe that his Subjects feel when by his neglect a Villanous Set of Ministers Triumph in the Ruin of the Nation or by his protection are screen'd from the just Resentment & Indignation of an injur'd People.

For the latest City Remonstrance to the King on 11 March 1773, see Sharpe, *London and the Kingdom*, 1895, iii 135–7, Walpole, *Last Journals*, 1910, pp 180 f., 182–5 The chief interest of this satire lies in its

---

[1] Identified by Mr Hawkins as Halifax, but Halifax died in 1771; he resembles portraits of Rochford, see No 5125

misrepresentation of the political situation, in treating George III as the puppet of his ministers and in giving so prominent a place not only to Bute, but to Holland, Grafton, Fletcher Norton, and Dyson. This attitude towards the King was common among satirists at this time. Compare the 'Invocation' to the first number of the *Westminster Magazine*, 1773: 'When, in the Cabinet, six grey-headed Statesmen sit round a green-headed King, now amusing him with rattles, now feeding him with Court-pap, while they follow the heady current of their own humours——' See also Nos 4883, 5098, 5288. For threats of the scaffold to North see also No. 5135, &c
$5\frac{3}{8} \times 9\frac{1}{8}$ in.

5133 [VISCOUNT TOWNSHEND]   [1773]

Engraving. Frontispiece to *Baratariana*, 2nd ed. 1773. A bust portrait in an oval frame of George, fourth Viscount, afterwards first Marquis Townshend 1704–1807. Lord Lieutenant of Ireland 1767–72. Outside the frame (l) is a hand inscribed *North*; it holds a string which passes through the mouth and is held on the opposite side by a hand inscribed *Bute*
Beneath the portrait is engraved,

> *In Cœlum jusseris ibit*
> *And bid him go to Hell, to Hell he goes.*

These are quotations from Juvenal's *Third Satire* and Johnson's translation, *London*, 1737
    In *Baratariana*, a reprint of letters from the *Freeman's Journal* by Langrishe, Flood, and Grattan, Townshend is ridiculed as Sancho Panza, Governor of Barataria, Ireland Hume wrote, 13 Aug. 1767, 'I am told that Lord Townshend openly ascribes his own promotion entirely to the friendship of Lord Bute', Hume, *Letters*, 1932, ii. 160. Townshend himself produced a number of caricatures directed against Bute See *Catalogue*, iv, pp. xix. 56. See No 5134 Copy in Print Department.
Oval, $3\frac{1}{4} \times 2\frac{9}{16}$ in.

5134 [THE PRIVY COUNCIL OF BARATARIA]

Baratariana P. 203.   [1773]

Engraving. Illustration for the 2nd ed. of *Baratariana*, Dublin, 1773, representing 'The Privy Council of Barataria' (p 20) at the meeting at which the summoning of parliament after repeated prorogations was decided on. (*Ibid.*, pp. 203–5.) The figures seated and standing round the table have been identified by Edmund Malone in a note with the print as. (l. to r.) Philip Tisdall, Francis Andrews, Godfrey Lill, John Hely Hutchinson, Anthony Malone. Townshend, the Lord Lieutenant, sits at the head of the table, behind him stands Sir George (afterwards Lord) Macartney and on his left sits Lord Annaly, from whose pocket hangs a fox's tail inscribed *tallho*. Walking into the room on the left is a figure leading two dogs *Prorogat[ion]* and *Protest*; from his pocket hangs a paper, *His Excellency to A. Cun To 1000 Vis[its] ... Castle £113710*. He is Alexander Cunningham, a Scottish surgeon On the table is a proclamation: *Townshend ... Given at the Council Chamb'* Jan 8th 1771, and also a *Mem. To sink ye Acc: of the Motions upon them* Malone (at this time at the Irish bar) ends his note: 'All these portraits were drawn from memory and are all somewhat caricatured except Mr. Malone [the writer's uncle] whose profile is extremely like and not at all caricatured. Of Mr. Tisdall, Mr. Andrews, Mr. Lill, and Lord Annaly there are I believe no engraved portraits. Edm. Malone scripsit.'

Baratariana is a reprint of letters in the manner of Junius published in the *Freeman's Journal*, April–May 1771, by Sir H. Langrishe, Flood, and Grattan attacking the administration of Townshend, see No. 5133. The occasion of the abuse was the prorogation of parliament by Townshend because the Commons had rejected the customary Privy Council money bill on the ground that it did not take its rise in that house. Townshend protested against this as an infringement of Poyning's Law, ordered his protest to be entered in the Journals of both houses and prorogued parliament from three months to three months The two dogs ('the beagles of Catalonia and Barataria', *op. cit*, pp. 203–4) are an allusion to the famous prorogation and protest. The proclamation of 8 Jan. was reported by Townshend to Lord Rochford in a letter of 9 Jan. 1771. (*Calendar of Home Office Papers*, 1770–2, p 184.)

A copy of *Baratariana*, 1773, is in the Print Department. The impression described can never have been bound in the book, where it is a folding plate.

$5\frac{5}{8} \times 8\frac{3}{8}$ in.

5135 TIME & TRUTH BRING STRANGER THINGS TO PASS.

[*c*. 1773?]

Engraving. Probably from a magazine, similar in manner to prints in the *Oxford Magazine*. Lord North on stilts carries Bute on his shoulders. He looks through his eye glass at a block and axe, in the foreground, against which lies a book inscribed *The Book of Fate* The stilts, which replace North's legs from the knees downwards, are inscribed (l.) *Lust of Pow'r, Fraud, Hypocrisy*, and (r.) *Arbitrary Power, Tyranny*, they are breaking in pieces, under the blows of Time (l) who raises his scythe to smite Truth (r.) raises her mirror in her r. hand, pointing with her l. at the block and axe. Bute, who holds North's eye-glass ribbon as if driving him by a rein, holds up his hands in horror at the sight, and has dropped from his l hand a sword inscribed *Military Law*. From his pocket hangs a label, *Plan to Enslave K——g L——ds, & C——ns*. In the upper r. corner of the print the head (in profile to the l.) and shoulders of the king appear from behind dark clouds and are surrounded by a glory of rays.

The king, Bute, and North wear Garter ribbons, showing that the print must be later than 18 June 1772, the date of North's Garter. Cf. No 5132, where North and Mansfield are threatened with the block, and Nos. 5238, 5660, 5661, 5964, 5969, 5986, 6046, 6179, 6282.

$6\frac{1}{8} \times 4$ in.

PERSONAL SATIRES

5136–5148

Series of Tête-à-tête portraits.

5136 N° XXIV. MISS L—W—S.   [1 Jan 1773]
    N° XXXV. THE CUMBERLAND BARONET.

Engraving. *Town and Country Magazine*, iv. 625. Two bust portraits in oval frames, illustrate 'Histories of the Tête-à-Tête annexed, . .' An account of Sir James Lowther, afterwards Lord Londsale (1736–1802), his miserliness, his litigation with the Duke of Portland, and the Cumberland election contest. Miss L. is the barmaid of an inn on the road from Cumberland to London, whom he has established in lodgings in London.
Ovals, $2\frac{13}{16} \times 2\frac{1}{2}$ in.   B.M.L., P.P. 5442 b.

5137 N° XXXVII. THE AMIABLE MISS P——N   [Jan 1773]
    N° XXXVIII. THE POACHING PREACHER

Engraving *Town and Country Magazine*, iv. 681 (Supplement). Two bust portraits in oval frames illustrate 'Histories of the Tête-à-Tête annexed; . . .' An account of the infatuation of a rich clergyman, Mr C——n, who is a great sportsman, with Miss Pl——n, his wife's companion and a farmer's daughter.
Ovals, $2\frac{3}{4} \times 2\frac{1}{2}$ in.   B.M.L., P.P. 5442 b.

5138 N° II. M^RS H——N.   *Vol. V.*
    N° III. LORD JOHN. [i e. Jehu]   [1 Feb. 1773]

Engraving *Town and Country Magazine*, v. 9. Two bust portraits in oval frames illustrate 'Histories of the Tête-à-Tête annexed, or Memoirs of Lord Jehu and Mrs. G——s.' The man is dressed as a coachman and holds a whip. An account of James, 6th Earl of Salisbury (1713–80), whose prevailing passion is 'driving a set of horses in the dress of a coachman'. His wife (*née* Keet) is said to have been the niece of his land steward whom he has sent out of his house with her children Before this he had formed a permanent alliance with Mrs H——n who changed her name to G——s, their son has now taken orders. Salisbury is said to have appeared only once (in 1745) in the House of Lords and to live now as a complete recluse Cf. W. Coombe, *Royal Register*, iv. 1779, pp. 80 ff.
Ovals, $2\frac{13}{16} \times 2\frac{7}{16}$ in.   B.M.L., P.P. 5442 b.

5139 N° IV. MADAME LA M——N.   *Vol. V.*
    N° V. L——D C——E   [1 Mar. 1773]

Engraving. *Town and Country Magazine*, v. 65 Two bust portraits in oval frames illustrate 'Histories of the Tête-à-Tête annexed, . . .' An account of Frederick, 5th Earl of Carlisle (1748–1825) and his amours, notably his liaison in Paris with a Madame la M——n, a widow who has now come to England.

Ovals $2\frac{3}{4} \times 2\frac{7}{16}$ in.   B.M.L. PP. 5442 b

5140 Nº VII. THE FAMOUS Mʀˢ B—Y—Y.   [1 Apr. 1773]
       Nº VIII. E. OF B—K—Y.

Engraving. *Town and Country Magazine*, v. 121. Two bust portraits in oval frames. They illustrate 'Histories of the Tête-à-Tête annexed, . . .' An account of Frederick Augustus 5th Earl of Berkeley (1745–1810). Mrs. Bayley was the mistress of the Duke of Cumberland between his affair with Lady Grosvenor and his marriage to Mrs Horton.

Ovals, $2\frac{13}{16} \times 2\frac{7}{16}$ in.   B M.L., P P 5442 b.

5141 Nº X. SIGNORA B——TINI.¹   [1 May 1773]
       Nº XI. E. OF EG——T.

Engraving. *Town and Country Magazine*, v. 177. Two bust portraits in oval frames illustrate 'Histories of the Tête-à-Tête annexed; or, Memoirs of the Earl of E—— and Madame du T——e'. An account of the 3rd earl of Egremont (1751–1837) and of his amours, especially with Mademoiselle du T——é who came under his protection on quitting her French convent to marry a rich financier, she accompanied him to England and lives under his protection.

She is Rosalie Duthé, a French courtesan, the first mistress of the Duc de Chartres; her liaison with Egremont, whom she is said to have ruined, was notorious. Britsch, *La Jeunesse de Philippe Egalité*, 1926, p. 77 and n.

Ovals, $2\frac{3}{4} \times 2\frac{7}{16}$ in.   B.M L., P.P. 5442 b.

5142 Nº XIII. MISS P——M   [1 June 1773]
       Nº XIV. THE HIBERNIAN HERO.

Engraving. *Town and Country Magazine*, v. 233. Two bust portraits in oval frames illustrate 'Histories of the Tête-à-Tête annexed; . . .' An account of an Irish peer, who had quarrelled with and challenged the Duke of Bedford when Lord Lieutenant of Ireland, and of Miss P. an actress, now his mistress, whom he first met at Bath in 1757. He is John Smith de Burgh, 11th Earl of Clanricarde (1720–82), G.E.C, *Complete Peerage*.

Ovals, $2\frac{3}{4} \times 2\frac{3}{8}$ in.   B.M.L , P.P. 5442 b.

5143 Nº XVI MISS GR—SL—Y.   [1 July 1773]
       Nº XVII. THE COMMISSARY.

Engraving. *Town and Country Magazine*, v. 289. Two bust portraits in oval frames. They illustrate 'Histories of the Tête-à-Tête annexed, ...' An account of Peter —— one of the Commissaries 'who in the last war in

¹ An 'unaccountable error' of the engraver. *Town and Country Magazine*, v. 177 n.

Germany increased the national debt many millions, to fill their coffers'.
He was the son of a glazier born in Wells, after being bankrupt made
a fortune during the war Miss G. was his cook-maid.
Ovals, $2\frac{13}{16} \times 2\frac{7}{16}$ in   B.M.L , P.P. 5442 b.

5144 Nº XIX. MISS CH——N.   [1 Aug. 1773]
    Nº XX BARON JAGHIRE

Engraving *Town and Country Magazine*, v. 345. Two bust portraits in
oval frames illustrate 'Histories of the Tête-à-Tête annexed, . . .' An
account of Lord Clive and a Miss Fanny C , a clergyman's daughter and
milliner's apprentice, who having been seduced and deserted accepted
a settlement of £100 a year from him. See No 5111, &c.
Ovals, $2\frac{3}{4} \times 2\frac{7}{16}$ in.   B M.L , P.P. 5442 b.

5145 Nº XXII. MADAME H—N—L   [1 Sept. 1773]
    Nº XXIII THE YOUNG CUB

Engraving *Town and Country Magazine*, v 401. Two bust portraits in
oval frames illustrate 'Histories of the Tête-à-Tête annexed; . . .' An
account of Charles Fox, in 'his political, his senatorial, and his gambling
character' and of his amours. He was infatuated by Madame Heinel,
then dancing at the opera, and approached her by buying and distributing
two hundred tickets for her benefit. In the *Westminster Magazine*, 1 561,
Sept. 1773, there are verses 'To the Young Cub on his keeping Madam
H—n—l'. The Macaroni Club complimented her 'with a regalo' of
£600. Burney, *Hist. of Music*, iv 498 n
Ovals, $2\frac{3}{4} \times 2\frac{7}{16}$ in.   B.M L , P P 5442 b.

5146 Nº XXV MISS B——N.   *Vol. V.*
    Nº XXVI. THE CIRCUMNAVIGATOR.   [1 Oct. 1773]

Engraving. *Town and Country Magazine*, v. 457. Two bust portraits in
oval frames illustrate 'Histories of the Tête-à-Tête annexed; . .' An
account of Joseph Banks, see No. 5046, &c. Miss B., the daughter of
a gentleman of fortune who died insolvent, lives with great decorum as
Banks's mistress.
Ovals, $2\frac{3}{4} \times 2\frac{3}{8}$ in.   B.M.L , P.P. 5442 b.

5147 Nº XXVIII. Mᴿˢ R——   *Vol. V.*
    Nº XXIX. THE LIBERTINE MACARONI   [1 Nov. 1773]

Engraving *Town and Country Magazine*, v. 513 Two bust portraits in
oval frames illustrate 'Histories of the Tête-à-Tête annexed; or, Memoirs
of the Libertine Macaroni and Mrs. R——n.' An account of Thomas,
2nd Baron Lyttelton (1744–79), and of his amours. See No. 5198, &c.
Ovals, $2\frac{3}{4} \times 2\frac{7}{16}$ in.   B.M L , P.P. 5442 b

5148 Nº XXXI. MADEMOISELLE LA P——E.   *Vol V.*
    Nº XXXII. THE D. OF S. A   [1 Dec. 1773]

Engraving. *Town and Country Magazine*, v 569 Two bust portraits in
oval frames illustrate 'Histories of the Tête-à-Tête annexed, . . .' An

account of the amours of George, 3rd duke of St Albans (1730–86) Mademoiselle la P warned him in Brussels that he was being fleeced by sharpers at the house of a pretended marchioness there, he brought her to England where she resides under his protection.

Ovals, $2\frac{3}{4} \times 2\frac{3}{8}$ in.   B.M L, P.P. 5442 b.

5149–5168 and numbers from Volume IV

Darly's series, continued from No. 5055.

VOLUME VI [1]

TITLE PAGE (Characters, Macaronies, and Caricatures by M Darly)

See No 4666—Nov. 1773

1. THE BANK MACARONI

See No. 4707—17 Apr. 1773

5149 V. 6. 2. WHO'S AFRAID

Pub accor^g to Act March 18th 1773 by M Darly 39 Strand

Engraving. W.L. portrait of an elderly man running forward, grinning, shouting with outstretched arms In his l. hand is a walking-stick A wide looped hat on the back of his head shows straggling locks of his own hair. He wears a long coat with wide cuffs, a plain neckcloth, ruffled shirt-sleeves, and high-quartered shoes.

$6\frac{13}{16} \times 5$ in (pl.).

5150 3. THE EQUESTRIAN MACARONI

Pub^d by M Darly (39) Strand Feby 13 1773.

Engraving. W.L. portrait of a man standing in profile to the r. In his r. hand he holds a bridle, a stick is under his l. arm. He wears a small looped club, a low hat, plain coat, striped waistcoat, and spurred riding boots.

7×5 in. (pl)

5151 4 [2] THE MILITARY MACARONI

Pub accor to Act by M Darly 39 Strand Feby 9th 1773.

Engraving. W.L. caricature portrait of a thin man with a large head walking or running in profile to the r. His wig is a high toupet with a queue in a black bag. In his l. hand he holds out a small three-cornered hat, in his r. is a sword whose point rests on the ground. He wears a short coat with facings and epaulettes, and a ruffled shirt. Beneath the title is engraved:

> O——[Wilkes?] *beware of this tremendous Hat and Arm,*
> *For should we by chance to meet it would me Harm.*
> *For tho I to the World a poli——n now Appear*
> *Yet d——n me but to my Angelic Wh——e am sincere.*

---

[1] Three prints issued in January 1773 are included in Volume v. See Nos. 4665, 5053–4
[2] Number added in ink.

Perhaps intended for Colonel Luttrell, Wilkes's opponent at the Middle-sex election 13 April 1769. When attacked by the mob at Brentford he was said to have lost nothing but his hat. See Nos 4285, 4852, 4971.

7 × 5 in (pl).

5152 5[1]. A HIBERNIAN ANTIQUE, TURN'D MODERN MACARONI.

Pub[d] by M Darly (39) Strand Feb[y] 5 1773.

Engraving W L. portrait of a man in profile to the r. He appears to have a scar on his cheek. He wears a bulky coat with a wide collar, a large neckcloth In his l hand is a curiously shaped walking-stick Except for his small looped hat there is nothing of the macaroni about his dress

7 × 5 in. (pl).

5153 V. 6. 6. THE UPPER CLAPTON MACARONI

Pub accord[g] to Act by M Darly 39 Strand April 2[d] 1772 [sic]

Engraving. Portrait of a man walking fast to the l. and looking round to his l. In his r hand he holds out a striped and spotted handkerchief, in his l. is a cane. Pens protrude from his coat pocket. His hair is in a twisted and looped club; he wears a three-cornered hat, frilled shirt, short coat, striped breeches, and a sword.

7$\frac{1}{16}$ × 5 in. (pl.)

V. 6. 7. THE WINDSOR. MACARONI.

See No. 4667—1 Apr. 1773

5154 [8] THE MACARONI WAITER OF DRURY L——E

Pub Feb. 28. 1773 by M Darly 39 Strand.

Engraving. Portrait, W.L., of a short man standing full face In his r. hand are a number of wine glasses, his l thumb is thrust under his apron-string. He wears a wide hat, a striped handkerchief knotted round his neck, a rough irregularly shaped apron over his coat and waistcoat.

7 × 4$\frac{5}{8}$ in (pl).

5155 V. 6. 9. CHEVALIER VATKENS LOUIS

[No publication line.]

Engraving W.L. portrait of a man wearing a furred livery gown and a double-peaked fool's cap with bells. His head is turned slightly to the r In his l. hand is a watchman's rattle

He is Sir Watkin Lewes, a recently knighted alderman and city patriot, Sheriff of London 1772–3. See No 5131, &c.

7$\frac{1}{8}$ × 4$\frac{7}{8}$ in. (pl.).

5156 V. 6. 10. THE AURELIAN MACARONI.

Pub accord. to Act by M Darly (39) Strand July 5th 1773

Engraving. A young man leaning against a bank under a tree holds out in his

¹ Number added in ink

r. hand a square frame in which are displayed dead butterflies and moths. In his l. hand is a butterfly net. His hat is a large butterfly, writhing caterpillars represent his curled hair. A butterfly rests on his l. coat cuff. His coat is adorned with symmetrical snails to represent trimming.

This is evidently Moses Harris, entomologist and engraver, secretary to the Aurelian Society, who published *The Aurelian, or Natural History of English Insects, Snails, Moths, and Butterflies, together with the Plants on which they feed*, 1766, with forty-five plates all drawn and engraved by Harris from life and brilliantly coloured (B M L 459 f. 11) The frontispiece, which is burlesqued in this print, is a self-portrait of the author with a large butterfly-net leaning against a bank with a box of butterflies in his hand

$6\frac{1}{4} \times 4\frac{1}{2}$ in.

5157 [11.] CHEVALIER DE L'ETOIL POLAIRE,

Juen-Ming del. Li Tsong Sculpt

Pubd by M Darly March 7 1773 39 Strand

Engraving. The standing figure of a man whose head is that of a double-headed animal, to the l. an ass, to the r. a bear. With his l. hand (which also holds a whip) he leads an elephant whose head and trunk appear from the r. His r. hand rests on the pinnacle of a Chinese pagoda ornamented with dragons. Suspended round his neck is the figure of a bear showing that he has the Swedish order of the Polar Star. He wears tartan trousers. Beneath is etched:

> *From North to the South, I came forth right,*
> *By favor in duplici modo a Knight,*
> *In primis an Ass, secundus a Bear,*
> *The one is a Fact, the other is Fair.*

A satire on Sir William Chambers, illustrating in detail Mason's *Heroic Epistle to Sir William Chambers, Knight,* . . . which had just appeared, and opens 'Knight of the Polar Star'; it is both a political satire and an attack on Chambers' *Dissertation on Oriental Gardening* and on the Chinese pagoda which he had built at Kew for the Princess Dowager of Wales. Chambers is said to have been of Scottish descent, he was born in Sweden and was made Knight of the Polar Star by the king of Sweden. The elephant and ass illustrate the lines,

> In some fair island will we turn to grass
> (With the Queen's leave) her elephant and ass.

They refer to Queen Charlotte's wild animals, including an elephant and a zebra known as the Queen's Ass (see No. 3870), which grazed in St. James' Park near Buckingham House. See *Satirical Poems by William Mason with Notes by Horace Walpole*, ed Toynbee, 1926

$5\frac{5}{8} \times 4\frac{3}{8}$ in.

5158 V. 6 12 AN EXCHEQUER CLERK, DREST AS THE ACT DIRECTS.

P[ub as] the Act directs July 22d 1773 by M Darly (39) Strand.

Engraving. W L portrait of a man walking fast in profile to the r In his l hand and resting on his l. shoulder is a long pair of scales: a small pair is in his r hand. An instrument resembling a pair of shears is attached to the r. side of his coat His hat is ornamented with the feather of a pen

'The Act' is evidently the Coin Act, see No 5128, &c., which had made scales necessary for all to whom payments were made in gold.

$6\frac{15}{16} \times 4\frac{13}{16}$ in. (pl).

13. THEODOSIUS HOMUNCULUS ESQ. [Theodosius Forrest]

See No. 4688—20 July 1779

5159 V 6 14. DR LOLL TONGUE, THE FILCHING CONOSIEUR

Pub accor^g to Act by M Darly (39) Strand Augt 1st 1773.

Engraving. Portrait of a man standing in profile to the l. He wears a bag wig, a long coat with large cuffs, and a frilled shirt His tongue protrudes. His hat is under his l. arm. He holds a walking-stick in his l. hand, and in his r. a print which appears to represent a fight between boxers in a room On another impression is written in pencil, 'Dr. Channing'.

$7 \times 4\frac{7}{8}$ in. (pl).

5160 V. 6. 15. THE ANTIQUARIAN.

Pub^d as the Act directs Sepr 9, 1773 by M Darly. 39 Strand.

Engraving. Caricature portrait of a man in profile to the r. He is smiling and holds up in his l hand a coin with a head inscribed *OTHO EMP.* In his r. hand is a cane with a chased handle He wears spectacles, a large flowing curled wig, an oddly-shaped cap decorated with a pair of horns like those worn on medieval women's head-dresses, an old-fashioned heavily-trimmed coat, a long brocade waistcoat and boots (which appear to date from the 17th century) with large spurs. His sword has a crescent-shaped hilt

Perhaps intended for Jeremiah Milles (1714–84), Dean of Exeter and president of the Society of Antiquaries 1768–84. Antiquarians were ridiculed in Foote's *Nabob*, Haymarket, 1772.

$7 \times 4\frac{7}{8}$ in. (pl.)

5161 V. 6. 16. A REV^D MACARONI.

Pub^d Accor^g to Act Octr 1st 1773 by M Darly 39 Strand.

Engraving. W L. portrait of a man standing in profile to the l. He wears his own hair, a plain coat, riding breeches, and spurred boots. His l. hand is in his breeches-pocket and under his arm is a riding-whip

$6\frac{3}{8} \times 4\frac{5}{8}$ in.

5162 V. 6. 14. [*sic*] JEHU THE TRUE ENGLISH COACHMAN

Pub accor to Act by M Darly (39) Strand Augt 10th 1773

Engraving. Portrait of a man standing in profile to r. He has a bulbous nose, a stubbly chin, a protruding waistcoat. In his r hand is a tankard with an open lid, in his l. a whip with a long lash. He wears a low wide three-cornered hat, a plain neckcloth, coat, long waistcoat, knee-breeches, buckled shoes.

$6\frac{1}{8} \times 4\frac{1}{4}$ in

5163 V. 6. 18. SEIGNOR CATGUTANEO.

Pub^d Accor^s to Act Octr 21. 1773 by M Darly Strand.

Engraving A man seated and playing a viol da gamba, the upper end of which is decorated by a carved head with a smiling face, wearing a laurel wreath, which is probably a portrait of the musician. He wears a small wig, a coat with large old-fashioned cuffs, and ruffled shirt-sleeves.

Probably Abel, well known in London concert rooms at this time. There is a certain resemblance to an etching of Abel published in 1787 called 'a Solo on the Viol di Gamba', Burney Collection of Theatrical Portraits, vol. i. fo. 4.

$6\frac{1}{8} \times 4\frac{7}{16}$ in.

5164 V. 6. 19 DOCTOR FORCEPS

Pub accor^s to Act Octr 21 1773 by M Darly Strand.

Engraving. Portrait of an elderly man walking in profile to the r. He wears spectacles and walks with a tall cane. He wears a sword and is dressed in an old-fashioned way with a low wide hat, large tie-wig and long coat

Evidently a well-known accoucheur, dressed in the manner of the old-fashioned physician, see McMichael, *The Gold-headed Cane*, 1827.

$6 \times 4\frac{7}{8}$ in.

V. 6 20. THE COUNTRY SINGING CLERK ON A SUNDAY.

See No. 4689—21 Oct. 1773

5165 V 6. 21. COUNSELLOR · HUBBLE · BUBBLE.

Pub^d Accor^s to Act Octr 24th 1773 by M Darly 39 Strand.

Engraving W.L caricature portrait of a lawyer walking in profile to the l. He is obese with several chins; his head is shaved and he carries a large wig. In his l hand is a rolled document. He wears a voluminous gown which rests on the ground.

$6\frac{1}{4} \times 4\frac{1}{2}$ in

5166 V. 6. 22. THE ANTIQUE ARCHITECT

Pub^d Accor^s to Act Oct 11. 1773 by M Darly Strand

Engraving Portrait of a man facing T.Q to l Under his l arm is a large book, in his l hand a drawing instrument His r hand is thrust under his waistcoat and under his r. arm is a macaroni cane. He wears a low three-cornered hat, frilled shirt and cravat, striped breeches and a sword. On the ground is a fragment of carved classical frieze, a paper and a pair of compasses.

Probably a portrait of Robert Adam, the most celebrated of the Adam brothers. The book is perhaps intended for *Works in Architecture* by Robert and James Adam, whose publication in folio parts began in 1773. Reproduced by A E. Richardson, *Georgian England*, 1931, p. 200.

$6 \times 4\frac{3}{8}$ in.

5167 V. 6 23. AN ODDITY IN CHANGE ALLEY.

Pub by Darly   39 Strand Oc^r 1. 1773.

Engraving Caricature portrait of a man standing or walking in profile to the l. He wears a long cape-like coat with a wide collar which reaches to his ankles, a low looped hat and a small curled wig. He holds a stick in a hand which is concealed under his coat.

$6\frac{1}{8} \times 4\frac{5}{16}$ in.

5168 V 6 24. A · POLITE · ARTIST · ON S^T LUKE'S DAY, UNDER THE PATRONAGE OF DR BARDANA, &c , &c.

Pub by M Darly 39 Strand Oct 18. 1773

Engraving. Portrait of a man standing in profile to the l. Under his arm is a large book, *Vegetab[le] Syste[m] by D* . . . He wears patched old-fashioned clothes and torn stockings, a short wig which fails to conceal his own hair. His hat is under his r. arm, a cane under the l.

A portrait of 'Sir' John Hill, a quack or charlatan with a diploma of medicine from the University of St Andrews, but a botanist of some repute. He began the publication of his *Vegetable System* in 1759, the last of twenty-six folio volumes coming out in 1775. He was said to be 'in a chariot one month, in jail the next for debt'. *D N.B.* One of his remedies was advertised as Elixir of Bardana or Essence of Water Dock, see No. 4040, &c.

$5\frac{7}{8} \times 4\frac{3}{8}$ in.

5169, 5170

Prints from a series published by Darly, continued from p. 90.

5169 29. HATS.

Pub^d Accor^g to Act Octr 1. 1773 by M Darly, 39 Strand.

Engraving. A companion print to No 5170 Twelve caricature heads showing the different types of hat then worn by men.

Four of the heads were copied in a Dutch print to represent 'English lords', see No. 5839.

$8\frac{3}{4} \times 13\frac{3}{8}$ in

5170 28. WIGS.

Pub^d Accor^g to Act Octr 12. 1773 by M Darly 39 Strand

Engraving. A companion print to No 5169 Fourteen caricature heads showing the different types of wig then worn. Most appear to be portraits: one is evidently a caricature of Lord Chancellor Bathurst, see No. 4888.

Three of the heads were copied (one twice) in a Dutch print to represent 'English lords', see No. 5839.

$8\frac{7}{8} \times 13\frac{3}{8}$ in.

Eleven prints

from a series published by Darly, continued from No. 4699, p. 90.

V. 2. 3 THE HOLY ORDER OF S^T ALMAC

See No 4642—20 Feb. 1773

5171 [V. 2. 5.]¹ TO BE SOLD TO THE BEST BIDDER

E. T. inv¹ [E. Topham].

Pub accor⁸ to Act by M Darly 39 Strand March 15ᵗʰ 1773.

Engraving. An auctioneer holding up his hammer in his l hand, stands in his rostrum, a box supported on four legs, and reached by a ladder (l.). He wears a toupet wig with a large black bag, wide cuffs, ruffled shirt-sleeves. His three-cornered hat is under his arm. He is in profile to the r., his mouth open as if shouting. Evidently a portrait of Langford, see No. 5001. Beneath the design is etched:

All the valuable goods and effects of a Scavoir-Vivre Bankrupt consisting of a collection of very scarce Books, (not to be met with in any of the Public Libraries) containing the most approved list of Cosmetics, Paints, washes, &c., &c., for beautifying the Skin: together with an unique set of Antiques after the present mode and an excessive fine Statue of a Venus taken from Himself, when abroad; with a number of suits of Cloaths, Hats, &c., &c., &c., all au dernier goût & very fit for any one who has an intention of entering on the Business, together with the right of Patronage to the best Productions of the Age, from a late resolution of that Society. NB.: the Subscription unpaid — Likewise to be sold a Quantity of Articles in Mrs. Phillip's way, not the least worse for Wear.²

Cf. a similar portrait of Christie, No. 6101.

6⅛ × 6½ in. (clipped).

5172 THE LAST DROP. [11 May 1773]³

Pubᵈ by Sayer, Print-seller, Fleet Street, London.

Engraving. A reissue (n.d.) with a different publication line of a print published by Darly dated as above, which was No. 1, Vol. 2 of the series published 1772–4. A short stout man stands on tip-toe by a table to drink from a large punch-bowl which he tilts forwards. Behind him stands a skeleton (r.), its l. hand on his shoulder, its r. holding up a dart which it is about to plunge into the head of the drinker. An hour-glass where sands have run out is on the ground at his feet. The table (l.) is a small round one, on it are a wine glass and pipe. Cf. No. 5513.

8⅛ × 6⅝ in. Book of Sayer's 'Drolls'.

5173 REFIN'D TASTE. [c. May 1773]

R.S¹G.M. [Mansergh] *Inv¹*

Printed for Rob¹ Sayer, Fleet Street.

Engraving. A reissue of a plate published by Darly (n d) which was No 6 of Vol. 2¹ in the series published 1772–4. A civilian (r) standing in profile to the l. gazes through a glass at a tall and bulky soldier in uniform (l)

---

¹ Number supplied from the impression in the volume belonging to Mr. Dyson Perrin, exhibited at the Burlington Fine Arts, 1931–2
² At a Pantheon masquerade of 12 May 1773 one of the characters was 'Mother Phillips, with a parcel of advertisements, denoting her *modest* commodities, and the place of their sale'. *Town and Country Magazine*, v, p. 265. She kept a shop, see Archenholtz, *Tableau de l'Angleterre*, Bruxelles, 1788, ii, 172
³ Date supplied from an impression in a volume belonging (1933) to Mr. W T. Spencer, New Oxford Street

who stands in back view, turning his head in profile to the r. towards the civilian The civilian is fashionably dressed wearing a bag-wig and sword, a cane under his arm. The soldier wears jack-boots and holds a long sword under his arm

Beneath the title is etched,

> *Eternal Infamy, that Wretch Confound,*
> *Who Planted first this Vice on English Ground*
> *A Crime that spite of Sense & Nature reigns,*
> *And Poisons Genial Love & Manhood stains*
>
> Vide *Rod. Random.*

$6 \times 9\frac{3}{8}$ in.   Book of Sayer's 'Drolls'.

2 9. THE ECLIPSE MACARONY   See No. 4643—12 May 1773

O'Kelly and his horse Eclipse

5174 V 2 18 THE BENGALL MINUET

Pub^d Accor^8 to Act Novr 3 1773 by M Darly Strand

Engraving. In a panelled room without furniture, two figures in profile face each other in a minuet On the l is an elderly man with a rather stiff manner, dressed in the fashion of the day, and wearing a toupet-wig with a black bag, he holds his hat in his r hand On the r. is a sharp-featured woman with her hair dressed high and ornamented with lace. She wears a low dress with elbow sleeves, long gloves, and a train over a flounced petticoat On the alternate panels of the room are square pictures and oval mirrors in carved frames.

The figures are perhaps satirical portraits of some 'nabob' and his wife preparing themselves for a London season or a Bath Assembly. Foote's *Nabob* was first played at the Haymarket in 1772.

$5\frac{7}{8} \times 9\frac{1}{8}$ in.

5175 V. 2. 19. SHYLOCK TURND MACBETH

Young Vanity inv^t   *Old Envy sculp.*

Pub by M Darly Nov 5. 1773 39. Strand . where any sketch that is fair game will have due Honor shewn.

Engraving Macklin as Macbeth, his dagger held up in his l. hand, his head in profile to the r. He wears a feathered hat, long hair, and Scottish dress . a large plaid, kilt, bare knees, and tartan stockings, a thistle badge hangs from his neck on a ribbon, a claymore (so-called) hangs at his waist. Beneath the title is etched,

> *I see thee yet, in form as palpable*
> *As that which now I draw——*

Macklin appeared, 3 October 1773, as Macbeth, the part being played for the first time in Scottish dress, before a very hostile audience, who expected to be 'spectators of his downfall', thinking his age would not allow him to go through the part to the end. 'Lady Macbeth's modern robes by no means accorded with the habits of the other personages, and Mr Macklin's flowing curls, like the locks of an Adonis, were unpardonably out of character.' *Macaroni and Theatrical Magazine*, ii. 8, Oct. 1773

Before this time Macbeth was dressed as a modern military officer Genest, v. 414. The public treated him with great injustice, and accustomed to see him in comedy, and regarding his Shylock as above criticism, refused to accept him in a heroic part. Finally, on Nov. 18, he was refused a hearing and the mob could not be pacified till Colman reluctantly agreed to his dismissal. Macklin's assumption of the part roused many personal jealousies, see No. 5203 For Macklin see also Nos 2599 (1743), 4846. There is an engraving of Macklin as Macbeth in the *London Magazine*, 1773, p 524, not in Scottish costume
$8\frac{1}{16} \times 6\frac{1}{4}$ in.

V. 2 21 S^R BIBO BULKY   See No. 4644—1 Dec 1773

V. 2. 22. MACARONIES DRAWN AFTER THE LIFE
                                    See No. 4645—1 Dec 1773

V 2 23. ARTILLERY DUTY   See No. 4646—1 Dec 1773
A satire on military effeminacy.

5176 A WELL-FED CITIZEN GOING TO HIS COUNTRY SEAT
AT HORN-SEY.   [*c.* 1773.]

[? After R. St. G. Mansergh.]

Publish'd by R. Sayer, 53 Fleet Street.

Engraving. Similar in manner to No. 5173 and probably also a re-issue of a print published by Darly An obese citizen sits in a small heavily-built phaeton, drawn (l to r.) by a clumsy pony ridden by an elderly postilion with a wooden leg, ambling slowly along. He takes his pipe from his mouth to say *Don't hurry me John* Behind the carriage stands a footman in macaroni dress; his master is dressed in a more old-fashioned manner The title derives from the old gibe that 'cits' were all cuckolds. No. 4640 (1772) is a similar subject by Mansergh.

$5\frac{7}{8} \times 9\frac{3}{8}$ in.   Book of Sayer's 'Drolls'.

5177-5186

A series of portraits of courtesans, &c [1]

5177 6. A NUN OF THE 3^d CLASS

Pub^d Jany 1, 1773, by M Darly 39 Strand.

Engraving. No. 6 in a series of bust profile portraits of women all styled either Nun, a common term for a courtesan living in a house of ill fame, or Abbess, the keeper of such a house. The sequence of the series is not that of date of publication. In all, the design is in an oval, enclosed in an oblong of the same dimensions, the oval and the rectangle being differentiated by engraved lines of different patterns.

A young woman in profile to the r., her hair neatly dressed over a high

[1] Six of these, with titles erased or stopped out, are included in a volume whose title-page is No. 5369, exhibited by Mr Dyson Perrins, at the Burlington Fine Arts Club, 1931–2.

cushion and decorated with loops of lace or ribbon She is of demure appearance and wears an ear-ring; a black ribbon is tied round her neck She appears distinctly the social superior of No. 5178.

$5 \times 3\frac{3}{4}$ in.   Fairholt's 'Collection for Costume', i. fo. 114 b.

5178 7. A NUN OF THE 2d CLASS.

Pubd by M Darly (39) Strand, Feby 10th 1773

Engraving. One of a series, see No. 5177. A young woman in profile to the r. She wears a muslin cap over straggling hair which falls on her forehead and neck. Suspended from her neck on a cord is a locket, on which is partly visibly the profile of a man.

$4\frac{15}{16} \times 3\frac{3}{4}$ in.   Fairholt's 'Collection for Costume', i. fo. 113 b.

5179 2 A NUN OF THE 4th CLASS.

Pubd by M Darly (39) Strand Feby 19. 1773

Engraving. One of a series, see No. 5177. Profile portrait of a young woman in profile to the l. She wears a large mob-cap, beneath which her hair appears on her forehead and below the ear Her dress is high to the neck and defines her breasts.

$5 \times 3\frac{3}{4}$ in.   Fairholt's 'Collection for Costume', i fo. 115

5180 3. A NUN OF THE 6th CLASS

Pubd by M Darly 39 Strand March 1. 1773.

Engraving No. 3 in a series, see No 5177 A young woman in profile to the r. wearing an elaborate cap, the frill of which conceals her eye. Her chin is patched. Her hair is fashionably dressed, her dress cut low; she wears a black ribbon round her neck.

$4\frac{15}{16} \times 3\frac{3}{4}$ in.   Fairholt's 'Collection for Costume', i. fo. 115 b.

5181 4. A MOTHER ABBESS OF THE LAST CLASS.

Pubd by MDarly 39. Strand March 1st 1773.

Engraving. One of a series, see No 5177, the title showing that she is the keeper of a brothel. A stout truculent-looking woman in profile to the l Her face is heavily patched. She wears a mob-cap, beneath which her hair appears on her forehead and below her ear; over her shoulders is a handkerchief, and round her neck a string of beads

$5\frac{15}{16} \times 3\frac{3}{4}$ in   Fairholt's 'Collection for Costume', i. fo. 116 b.

5182 8. A NUN OF THE 1st CLASS.

Pubd accor. to Act by MDarly (39) Strand March 22d 1773

Engraving. One of a series, see No. 5177. A young woman in profile to the l. wearing a cap. Round her neck is a black ribbon. Her cheek is patched.

$5 \times 3\frac{3}{4}$ in   Fairholt's 'Collection for Costume', i. fo 112

5183 9. A NUN OF THE FIRST CLASS

Pub^d by MDarly 39. Strand 24th March. 1773.

Engraving. One of a series, see No. 5177. Portrait of a fashionably dressed and dignified woman in profile to the r. She wears a necklace and in the front of her low-cut dress is a nosegay.

Possibly intended for Mrs. Baddeley, to whose portraits it has a certain resemblance, as also to the portrait called *A Pantheon No Rep*, No. 4998

$4\frac{15}{16} \times 3\frac{3}{4}$ in.   Fairholt's 'Collection for Costume', i. fo. 111 b.

5184 5 A LADY ABBESS OF THE 1st CLASS.

Pub accor to Act by MDarly March 30 1773 (39) Strand

Engraving. No. 5 in a series, see No. 5177, the title here implying that the subject is the keeper of a brothel. A woman in profile to the r. of dignified and refined appearance. Her hair is fashionably dressed over a high cushion and ornamented with lace. A black ribbon is tied round her neck. Her dress appears to be loose négligé.

$4\frac{15}{16} \times 3\frac{3}{4}$ in.   Fairholt's 'Collection for Costume', i. fo. 114.

5185 10. A NUN OF THE II^D CLASS.

Pub Accord. to Act April, 26, 1773, by M Darly, 39 Strand

Engraving. No. 10 in a series, see No. 5177 A woman in profile to the l. wearing a ribbon-trimmed hat whose brim conceals the upper part of her face. Her shoulders are covered with a flowered sacque trimmed with ruchings of ribbon.

$4\frac{15}{16} \times 3\frac{3}{4}$ in.   Fairholt's 'Collection for Costume', i. fo. 113.

5186 A NUN OF THE 2d CLASS   [n.d. *c.* 1773]

Pub by M Darly 39 Strand

Engraving One of a series, see No. 5177. A woman in profile to the r. wearing a cap whose frill conceals her eye and much of her cheek

$4\frac{15}{16} \times 3\frac{3}{4}$ in.   Fairholt's 'Collection for Costume', i. fo. 112 b.

<h2 style="text-align:center">5187-5189</h2>

Three Cambridge satires, by the same artist, probably an amateur.

5187 THE JUSTICE IN THE SUDS.

Publish'd accord^s to Act of Parliament Jany 14th 1773 by Mrs Sledge Henrietta Street Covent Garden London

Engraving. The interior of a panelled room; a young man wearing a three-cornered hat and the gown of a fellow commoner of Trinity College, with his hands behind his back and without any indication of passion, spits in the face of a man in a closely curled wig. A cat, with arched back, stands on a chair watching the encounter. On the wall behind are ranged objects to show that it is the room of an active justice of peace a picture (l.) of a man (T Q L.) with bare back standing at a whipping-post, a pair of jack boots hanging from nails on the lower edge of the frame gives an illusion of a W.L.

figure On the next two panels are hung a halter of rope and a chain. On the r. panel is a picture of Justice (H.L.) with ass's ears and wearing a fool's cap. One eye is blindfolded, in her r. hand is a wooden sword, in her l a pair of scales, one end of which she is holding down with her r forefinger. (The J.P. was often styled a justass, see No 6120) Below this hangs an academic gown surmounted by a hat, beneath which stands a pair of shoes. Beneath the design is etched,

Ah! Poor Justice,	*Oh fie —— [Stanley]*
Dud a cry,	*To treat him so scornfully,*
Ah! welladay,	*Shamefully, mournfully*
Wipe an Eye	*—— Fie.*

An impression of this print was one of a number sent by Cole the antiquary to Horace Walpole. He afterwards sent him the following explanation of it, April 18, 1775:

'The Hon Mr Stanley, Brother to Lord Stanley & Fellow Commoner of Trinity College, is spitting in Dr Ewen's face. The *Likenesses* are tolerably *well preserved*. Dr Ewen [Ewin] does not squint enough. He cast Mr Stanley on a Trial in *Westminster Hall*, made him *pay* & ask *Pardon*.' Add MSS. 5824, fo. 84 b.

A note by Cole on the occasion of a letter (n d.) from Ewin to himself announcing that Mr. Stanley had not got his degree ('Mr Stanley offered again and was stopped on the caput'), explains 'This refers to Mr Stanley's spiting in Dr Ewins Face about Christmas Eve on some offence or conceived offence from Dr Ewin of which a Print is now made & sold: He is grandson to the Earl of Derby ' *Ibid* , 5844, fo. 42 b.

He was the Hon. Thomas Stanley (1753–79), afterwards a major in the army W. H. Ewin (1731?–80), St John's College, a wealthy Cambridge brewer and usurer, was expelled from the university and suspended from his degrees in 1778 for lending money usuriously to an undergraduate, subsequently restored on a *mandamus* but severely censured by Lord Mansfield, and struck out of the Commission of the Peace. The subject of many lampoons by undergraduates. See *D.N.B.*

The print appears in No. 5189.

$5 \times 7\frac{1}{2}$ in.

There is a W.L portrait of 'Dr Ewing' walking in profile to the r. called *The Man of Accomodation*, etched by Anna Maria Dean after a drawing by 'Mr Porteus of Trin Coll.' in book of 'Honorary Engravers', ii, fo 157

5188 THE BEAR, THE LOUSE, AND RELIGION A FABLE

Athanasius Credo fecit   [1773]

Publish'd accordg to Act of Parliament on the 1st day of Trinity Term by Mrs Sledge Henrietta Street Covent Garden, London.

Engraving. Religion, a veiled woman holding a cross, is being roughly handled by two men wearing academic cap and gown with clerical bands. In the background is a half-ruined church (l.) 'The Louse', who is small and slight, has seized Religion by the hair, his r. hand grasps an upright post, his foot is on her gown and he is preventing her from being dragged away by her assailant. The other, 'the Bear', a large burly man, has seized her hood with his r. hand, with his l. he pulls at her draperies, leaving her shoulders and breast partly bare; his r foot is on an open book. A small dog barks at them. Beneath the title is etched,

A surly Bear in College bred,
Determin'd to attack Religion;
A Louse who crawl'd from Head to Head
Defended Her—as Hawk does Pigeon
Bruin, Subscription discommended,
The Louse determin'd to support it,
But . . . Desunt multa . . .

A satire on the petition to Parliament for relief from subscription to the Thirty-nine Articles rejected in 1772 and again in 1773, see Nos. 4944, 5107 The print is described by Cole in a letter to H. Walpole 'Dr Hallifax the present Law Professor, commonly called Louse Hallifax from his affectation of getting among the *Heads of Colleges* and consorting with them He *wrote* and preached excellently in defence of *Subscription to Articles* and against the *Clerical Petitioners*, than whom none was more violent and vehement than *Mr Barker*, a fat fellow of *Queens' College*, and warm *Republican*. The figures represent them very well: Barker particularly The insignificant mean figure of Dr Hallifax is *very well hit off.*' Add. MSS. 5824, fo. 84b. Samuel Hallifax, afterwards Bishop of Gloucester, was Regius Professor of Civil Law at Cambridge from 1770 to 1782. Some letters signed 'Erasmus' in 1772 in favour of subscription to Articles were generally attributed to him. See *D N B* John Barker, D D , became Master of Queens' College in 1780 *Royal Kalendar*, 1781, p. 236.

The print appears in No 5189.

5×7½ in.

5189 VENUS TURN'D PROCTOR [c 1773]

London publish'd by Mrs Sledge Henrietta Street Covent Garden. Price 1s 6d

Engraving. A man in academic gown and bands, with a small wig, stands with a complacent expression, 'in the attitude of the Venus de Medici'. A boy (l.) has just taken a dead cat from a hamper and holds it out towards him by the tail. A halberd stands against the wall, its spike transfixing a woman's ribboned hat, representing the spoils of a Cambridge proctor. On the wall are three framed pictures; three unframed prints are also pinned up: these are this print (Venus turn'd Proctor) in the centre; No. 5188 (l), and No. 5187 (r). The pictures are: (l.) *The Gentleman and Scholar United*, two T.Q.L. figures whose arms are tied together, one, in academic dress and wearing an old-fashioned coat with huge cuffs, is holding out a book in his r. hand; the other, dressed as a macaroni wearing an enormous bag-wig; he is holding up a sword in his l. hand Above their heads is a device of four crossed hands, inscribed *The Union* The centre picture, its frame inscribed *Dead Game*, is of two books. *Bible* and *University Statutes* (out of this projects a pair of clerical bands inscribed 6s 8d). On them lies an open pamphlet inscribed *A Sermon preached at Wisbech assizes before* . . . The third picture (r) is *Miss Boreas*, the portrait (H.L.) of a woman whose face is made out of a pair of bellows She was probably a Miss North. Beneath the print is etched,

O Venus Beauty of the Skies,
To whom a thousand Temples rise,
Gayly false in gentle Smiles,—

In Mathematicks he was greater
Than Tycho Brahe, or Erra Pater:
For he, by Geometrick Scale,
Cou'd take the Size of Pots of Ale;
Resolve by Sines & Tangents, straight;
If Bread or Butter wanted weight,
He knew What's What, & that's as high
As Metaphysick Wit can fly;
All lov'd him well, who knew his Fame,
And sent him Cats, instead of Game.

Cole sent an explanation of the print to H Walpole, 18 April 1775:

'Mr Purkes [William Purkis, M A] of Magdalen College, Proctor in 1773 to whom some *wag* advertised him by letter that a *Basket of Game* was coming to him by the *Cambridge Coach*, which turned out to be dead cats & dogs &c It is an *handsome likeness* of him. He stands in the Attitude of the *Venus de Medici* in which *Posture* he would frequently *place himself*, before his *Friends*. Indeed, he is a most *consummate vain coxcomb* Always talking of uniting the *Gentleman* & the *Scholar* which gained him the Name of Mr *Union*. Tho' People thought it *wrong* thus to *expose a worthy man*, for he was *no ways* vicious but a *good Tutor* & no bad *Scholar*, yet *others* thought his *Vanity deserved it*.' Add MSS 5824, fo 84 b.

$5 \times 7\frac{3}{8}$ in.

5190 PATRIOTIC MISFORTUNES, OR, SIR JOSEPH IN THE SUDS. [1 Mar. 1773]

T H. (monogram)

Woodcut *Westminster Magazine*, i. 157 It illustrates an 'Authentic Relation of the Quarrel between Sir J Mawbey and Rich. Wyatt Esq' quoting from Mawbey's letters to the newspapers in vindication of himself. Mawbey lies on the floor, warding off a blow from Wyatt, who stands over him, his nose bleeding. A waiter in the doorway starts back in alarm.

This was a fracas in the Ordnance Arms Tavern arising out of reports that Mawbey had not defended his honour by challenging Wyatt, followed by an attempted justification of himself by Mawbey in the newspapers, which revived the quarrel 'This transaction, ridiculous as it is, may have its use, in convincing the Patriotic Mob, what frail materials their firmest champions are made of; and how little those men have it in their power to be *patriotic* on extraordinary occasions, who cannot on common occasions behave in a *manly* manner' *Ibid.*, p 158

Mawbey (1730–98), a rich distiller, M.P. for Southwark, and Chairman of the Surrey Quarter Sessions, had been a supporter of Wilkes, but prided himself on being above party, so that he was a butt of the wits on both sides. See Nos. 5191, 5192.

$2\frac{9}{16} \times 3\frac{1}{4}$ in.   B.M L , P.P. 5443.

5191 THE DISTILLER IN THE SUDS, OR, A REAL REPRESENTATION OF THE SURRY BRUISING BOUT. [1 Mar 1773]

Woodcut From the *Town & Country Magazine*, v. 92. One of two combatants lies on the floor, one eye closed from a blow; the other stands over him with clenched fists Three men appear in the doorway. An overturned table, wine-bottle, &c , are on the floor. A representation of the quarrel between Sir Joseph Mawbey and Richard Wyatt. See Nos. 5190, 5192.

$5\frac{5}{8} \times 3\frac{9}{16}$ in.

5192 THE PISSING CONFLICT. [1 Mar. 1773]

Woodcut From the *Covent Garden Magazine* A coarse satire on the quarrel between Sir Joseph Mawbey and Richard Wyatt See Nos 5190, 5191.

$3\frac{7}{8} \times 3\frac{7}{8}$ in

5193 THE MACARONIES INTERCEDING WITH GRACE & RIGHT REVERENCE IN BEHALF OF THE POOR & PANTHEON.

[1 Feb 1773]

Engraving From the *Oxford Magazine*, x 17. It illustrates a dialogue, 'The Pantheon Petition; or the B——ps melted by the Tears of the Ladies'. Two bishops (r.), one seated on an episcopal chair, the other standing by his side, receive a deputation which enters through a door on the l. A fashionably dressed lady points to two kneeling beggars in rags, an emaciated man on crutches, his head bandaged, stands behind. Four fashionably dressed men, one wearing a ribbon, stand behind the lady.

The dialogue shows that the deputation is petitioning against a proposed suppression of masquerades on the ground that they are good for trade; the bishops are the Archbishop of Canterbury (Cornwallis) and the Bishop of London (Terrick); both make unctuous gestures of emotion and compassion. The deputation includes the Duchess of Northumberland, who speaks on behalf of the poor weavers, Lord and Lady Harrington, the Bishop of London's lady, the Lord Mayor (Townsend), and a 'Jew Macaroni', who are not all represented in the engraving.

There was a grand masquerade at the Pantheon on 18 Feb. 1773, *Oxford Magazine*, x. 60-1.

$5\frac{13}{16} \times 3\frac{3}{4}$ in.   B.M.L., P.P. 6115.

5194 CUPID BEATING UP FOR VOLUNTEERS [1 May 1773]

Engraving. *Westminster Magazine*, i. 237. A sequel to No. 5066 A recruiting party of ladies outside the gateway of St James's Palace Mrs Cornelys, in macaroni dress, holds a large flag inscribed *Folly* She wears a cap with bells on her high-dressed hair. Behind her walks another lady similarly dressed, her hair ornamented with pearls; slung from her shoulders is a pair of kettledrums which Cupid is beating They are watched by a crowd of fashionably dressed men and women. Beneath is inscribed,

> *Ye Maids, Dames, Courtesans, now lend your ears,*
> *FOLLY and LOVE beat up for volunteers.*

The text shows that Cupid is following Mrs Cornelys' flag of Folly, and beating up for volunteers to be sold and to buy at his auction His new quarters are 'at the French Ambassador's in Great George Street'. De Guignes was renowned for his lavish entertaining.

$5\frac{1}{2} \times 3\frac{1}{2}$ in.   B.M.L., P.P. 5443.

5195 HO HE, THE BLACKGUARD MACARONI

Van Grog fecit

Publish'd as the Act Directs June y^e 22 1773 by T Pether Berwick St Soho

Engraving. A companion print to No. 5196. W.L. full face standing portrait of a man. He wears a heavy overcoat open in front, a wide-brimmed hat on the back of his head, buckled shoes, a thick neckcloth round his neck. His r. hand is in his waistcoat pocket, his left holds a switch. Beneath the title is etched

This Animal tho Not so well known as many Among the polite Circle Nevertheless can claim as Much folly to his Share as those of higher Rank, but so peculiar to himself, that it can cause Emulation in none, but such as Jack Catch [Ketch] and the Devil hath reservd for their Own private purposes Sing I wonder we ant better company upon Tyburn tree.

$6\frac{3}{4} \times 4\frac{3}{16}$ in.

5196 STEPHEN STRUT Y^E TALLOW MACARONI

Van Grog fecit

Engraving. A companion print to No. 5195, publication line apparently cut off. A corpulent man walks in profile from l. to r., his l. leg stiffly raised. He looks through an eye-glass held in his l hand; in the r is a walking-stick. He is dressed elaborately, though not quite in the prevailing fashion: his bushy wig has a club, he wears a three-cornered lace-trimmed hat, laced waistcoat and a short coat Over the lower part of his sleeve is tied what appears to be a sleeve-protector of some thin material. Beneath the title is etched,

Ask me not what I was, See what I am, those who take me for a fool, Shew their Own Want, tis Money makes the Mare to go, & Sing tol lol de riddle lol fal lal de riddle lal fal lal de ra.

Probably the portrait of some rich tallow-chandler.

$6 \times 4\frac{1}{8}$ in.

5197 *This Day is publish'd*

THE RAT-TRAP, OR VILLAINY IN FULL BLOOM

[1773]

Woodcut. It illustrates an advertisement, clipped, printed on both sides, probably a hand-bill, for a book with the above title. A man stands, his r. leg in the teeth of a steel rat-trap, holding out in his r hand a paper on which is printed, *He means my Worship. Have I escaped the Gallows and pillory to come to* THIS His l. hand is clenched and his head turned in profile to the l Above his head is printed,

> *If in this vicious Age some Monster shou'd,*
> *With more than mortal infamy endue'd,*
> *Count o'er the Crimes that gave him Power and Wealth,*
> *To Gorge on Rapines, Murders, Frauds, and Stealth;*
> *To Life's last stage this miscreant I'll pursue,*
> *And greet the Villain with a Villain's Due.*

This is continued in a contemporary hand,

'Little villians must submit to fate
Whilst great ones do enjoy yᵉ world in State'
'Bishop

'to be heard of at the Rotation Office Litchfield Street, St. Ann's Soho London.'

The title is printed below the woodcut and continues: *containing a Portrait, or family piece of that Worshipful Banditti, emphatically called Trading Justices.*

The book, with a dedication to Lord Mansfield dated 30 July 1773, is a scurrilous attack upon the justices of the Litchfield Street Rotation Office, see No 5273, presided over by Saunders Welch, the friend of Dr. Johnson. It is directed more especially against Thomas Bishop, the subject of the woodcut, one of the magistrates at that office, against whom Robert Holloway, the writer, had personal grievances On the reverse of the sheet is a further advertisement of the book of a libellous character in which Bishop, though not named, is described as ' a worshipful Scoundrel, well known in the *polite* world; who from a Shoeless Vagabond is become the most corpulent Butcher in the *Litchfield Street* Slaughter-house.'

Holloway was prosecuted and convicted for the publication (B M.L. 12330. cc. 37). The case, Rex v. Holloway, is cited in *Barnewall and Alderson*, v, p. 595.

8 × 4¼ in.

5198 THE MACCARONI SACRIFICE

Engraving. Frontispiece (folding plate) to *An Appendix to the Vauxhall Affray or Macaronies Defeated . . .* 1773. Three macaronies chained together stand on the top of an altar from which rise flames and smoke, the result of a fire lit within the altar, which is being stoked by a nude man The altar stands outside a temple with Ionic pilasters whose pediment, partly visible on the r., is inscribed *Temp. of Virtue.* The 'sacrifice' is being directed by Parson Bate (afterwards Sir Henry Bate Dudley) who stands on the r., in profile to the l., pointing to the macaronies with an outstretched pen. His l. hand rests on a club of Hercules. He is saying· *This incense shall revive degraded Manhood.* The stoker asks him· *Master! is it hot enough now?* The three macaronies, who are small and effeminate, say: *I owe this infamy to you two, If I had been advised by Mother D——n I had not got in this damned Scrape*; and, touching a locket which he wears, *Oh! Save my Miniature Picture.*

They are the hon. Thomas Lyttelton, commonly known as the wicked Lord Lyttelton, see No. 5147, George Robert Fitzgerald, commonly called Fighting Fitzgerald, executed for murder in Ireland 1786, and Captain Crofts. The quarrel between these men and Bate began with the affair called the Vauxhall Affray, when Bate resented their impolite attentions to Mrs. Hartley, the beautiful actress, in July. This was followed by a 'bruising match' between Bate and a supposed Captain Miles, really a servant of Fitzgerald, see Nos 5199, 5200. The dispute continued in the newspapers during August 1773, particularly in letters from Bate to the *Morning Post*, reprinted in *An Appendix to the Vauxhall Affray.* See *The Vauxhall Affray*, 1773; *The Rape of Pomona*, 1773; Angelo, *Reminiscences*,

1904, i. 117 ff. Bate was a frequent subject of caricature. He is said to have acquired the name of the *Fighting Parson* from this affair. Angelo, *op. et loc cit.*

$7\frac{1}{8} \times 7\frac{3}{4}$ in

5199 THE BRUISING SCENE BETWEEN PARSON BATE AND MᴿFITZGERAL'S FOOTMAN IN THE CHARACTER OF A SUPPOSED CAPᵀ MILES [1 Aug. 1773]

Engraving. *Macaroni and Theatrical Magazine*, i. 489. The interior of a panelled room. Two men fighting with fists: Bate (r.) wears a shirt with clerical bands, Miles (r.) is stripped to the waist, one eye is closed from the effect of a blow. Two seconds stand behind each of the combatants two dignified-looking gentlemen behind Bate, two macaronies behind Miles, the foremost of whom wears a miniature round his neck. See Nos. 5198, 5200.

$4\frac{1}{8} \times 6\frac{7}{8}$ in. B.M.L , P.P. 5201.

5200 CAPᵀ MILES'S REVENGE, OR THE MACARONIES DIS-COMFITED BY THEIR CHAMPION. [1 Nov 1773]

Engraving *Macaroni and Theatrical Magazine*, ii 7 An illustration to 'Anec-dote of the Rev. Mr. H——y B——e' [Henry Bate] Interior of an ale-house. A footman (l.), his hair in a pigtail queue and tags on his shoulder, strikes with his fists a man dressed as a macaroni, another macaroni, a miniature round his neck, see No 5198, lies on the ground, a broken cane in his hand. On the wall are two prints each representing a *Morning Post* newsboy with his horn In the cap of one (l) is the letter B, he has a sheaf of papers inscribed *M Post*. The other's cap has the letter T. The text explains that Fitzgerald's servant, Miles, when at Epsom revenged himself on his master for the drubbing received from Bate, see No. 5199

A note explains that 'The Morning-Post was originally sold by boys habited in a particular manner, and blowing a horn. The whim struck Mr B——e, and he and Dr. T——r [Trusler] went to the Pantheon masquerade in that dress. This frolick appears to us so unworthy of a clergyman and a physician, that we have exhibited these two gentlemen so habited in the background of *Capt. Miles's Revenge*'. For the *Morning Post* newsboys see H Walpole, *Letters*, ix, 439–40. See No. 5550, &c.

$3\frac{15}{16} \times 6\frac{11}{16}$ in. B M L , P.P. 5201.

5201 FOOTE, THE DEVIL AND POLLY PATTENS. [1 Mar 1773]

Engraving. From the *Macaroni and Theatrical Magazine*, i. 211. This illustrates 'The Puppet Shew, . or, A dialogue between Foote, Geo. Alexander Stevens, Harlequin and Polly Pattens', the scene being the Green Room just after the audience had left the theatre. Two of the figures are puppets, with strings attached to their hands and legs, a man full-face, holding his hat, stands stiffly on the extreme l and Polly Pattens, the housemaid, in mob-cap and long skirts in profile to the r Between them stands Harlequin, club in hand, hat in the other, showing off the puppets.

The Devil in the form of a satyr, holding a trident, points at Foote (r), who stands in profile to the l facing his puppets; behind him is Punch. A curtain is festooned above the figures

A satire on Foote's puppet-play the 'Handsome House-maid or Piety in Pattens', produced in February 1773. The dialogue suggests that Stevens, famous for his lecture on Heads, had a share in the production.

$3\frac{5}{8} \times 6\frac{5}{16}$ in.

5202 THE WHIMSICAL DUET OR MISS C—TL—Y TEACHING HER FAT DANE BITCH TO RIVAL MISS Y——G.

[1 Apr. 1773]

Engraving. *Oxford Magazine*, x. 105. On a high-backed sofa sit Miss Catley (r.) and a man wearing regimentals with a cockaded hat. She holds a book of music open on her lap, her l. hand is raised as if teaching a spotted Dalmatian dog, which stands on its hind legs, to sing. A man in a long overcoat, holding a coachman's whip, his hat under his arm, stands behind the dog A cockatoo on a perch behind the sofa is screeching, a spaniel is barking, and a cat miaou-ing at the musical efforts of the dog. The room is panelled, a large oval mirror hangs on the wall The accompanying text (p 104) says that 'the celebrated Miss C—t—ly on her return home from Drury Lane Theatre, ordered her servant to bring up the fat kitchen bitch and set her on her hind legs, as she was positive she could learn her to sing as well as a certain lady ..'

For Ann Catley in 1773 see Walpole, *Letters*, viii. 360, 19 Nov. 1773. See also Nos. 4468, 4706. She was not playing at Drury Lane at this time; she sang at Vauxhall, Marylebone Gardens, &c, appearing in 1770 and 1773 at Covent Garden. Miss Younge (1744?-97) was a leading actress at Drury Lane, and one of the foremost of English actresses

$5\frac{3}{4} \times 3\frac{5}{8}$ in.   B M L , P.P 6115

5203 ROSCIUS IN TRIUMPH, OR THE DOWNFALL OF SHY-LOCK ALIAS MACKBETH.

[1 Dec. 1773]

Engraving. From the *Macaroni Magazine*, ii 41. Macklin dressed as Shy-lock in a furred gown, lies on his back on a platform or stage. In his r. hand is a knife, in his l a pair of scales. Behind him stand Tragedy with a dagger and Comedy holding out a mask; astride on their shoulders sits Garrick in triumph, smiling, his hands on his hips. He wears a slashed doublet and is surrounded by a glory of light sending out rays Beneath the platform are two demons, one has seized Macklin by the arm and is pulling him down into an abyss from which flames are rising, the other (l) uses a pitchfork for the same purpose.

The plate illustrates a detailed account of the repeated disturbances which led to Macklin's dismissal on 18 November, 1773. The public regarded Macklin's performance as Shylock as above criticism, but would not tolerate him as Macbeth. A plate of Macklin as Shylock, by J. Lodge, inscribed *This is the Jew, that Shakespeare drew*, illustrates the *London Museum* for April 1770, see No 4846

Garrick is said to have been jealous of Macklin's performance as Macbeth Though this is hardly credible, it is not improbable that he felt mortified that the change in the dressing of the characters should come from Macklin and not from himself. Genest. v. 414 Macklin's assumption of a part usually played by Smith at Covent Garden was also a cause of offence. See No. 5175.

$6 \times 4\frac{5}{16}$ in

5204 A WELL-KNOWN MACARONI MAKING LOVE TO THE FAMOUS POLL KENNEDY. [*c.* 1773]

Engraving. Probably from a magazine. A woman elaborately dressed in the fashion of the day sits on a high-backed sofa of an ornate French design On his knees before her, his hands clasped in supplication, is a man wearing the ribbon of an order. He is elaborately dressed in the French fashion with high toupet wig, exaggerated black bag, fringed waistcoat, feathered hat. His hat is on the ground. On the back of the sofa sits a monkey, his hair in a high toupet in imitation of that of the man and the woman. He regards the suitor through an eye-glass The room is panelled, and furnished in the contemporary French fashion. On the wall are a picture of a nymph and satyr, and a clock on a carved bracket.

Polly Kennedy, a well-known courtesan, described in *Harris's List of Covent Garden Ladies* for 1773, has been confused with Kitty Kennedy, see No. 5095. H Bleackley, *Ladies Fair and Frail*, 316–18.

$5\frac{3}{4} \times 3\frac{3}{4}$ in.

THE MACARONI PARSON [Horne]. See No. 4827—1 Jan. 1773

From the *Macaroni Magazine*. (Dr. Dodd was also known as the Macaroni Parson, see No. 5249.)

THE STABLE ADVENTURE . . . [Lady Ligonier]
See No. 4801—1 Feb. 1773

Macaroni Magazine.

LORD —— OR THE NOSEGAY MACARONI. [Viscount Villiers.]
See No 4825—1 Mar. 1773

From *Macaroni Magazine*. Reproduced, Paston, *Sidelights on the Georgian Period*, p. 72, and *Social England*, ed Traill, v. p. 229.

MY LORD —— OR THE CHAPEAU MACCARONI [Viscount Petersham].
See No. 4812—1 Apr. 1773

Macaroni Magazine.

5205 A SCENE IN ISLINGTON FIELDS [1 Apr. 1773]

Engraving. From the *Macaroni and Theatrical Magazine*, i. 265 It illustrates 'A Duelling scene in Islington Fields by Two Macaronies', between 'a young woollen-draper' and 'a military gentleman', the theme being the citizen's reluctance to fight. The duellists in macaroni dress face each other Their seconds are partly visible on the l. and r. margins of the design. The citizen (l) holding a pistol in his r hand raises his l to protect himself, dropping his other pistol. The other (r.) holds a pistol in his r. hand and fires another with his l

The antagonists are identified in an old hand as 'Fitzgerald' (r.) and 'Walker' (l.). This appears from the date to be incorrect. a duel between Thomas Walker Esq., well known on the turf, and Fighting Fitzgerald, see Nos. 5198–5200, caused a sensation in 1775, and was the occasion of a series of pamphlets addressed to the Jockey Club by the two combatants. $3\frac{13}{16} \times 6\frac{5}{16}$ in.

THE OLD POLITICAL MACARONI WITH HIS WISE FAMILY AT
    BREAKFAST.   See No. 4821—1 May 1773

LADY C——N DISCOVERED IN A CRITICAL SITUATION WITH
    A CERTAIN FOREIGN AMBASSADOR [de Guignes].
                    See No. 4835—1 July 1773
Macaroni Magazine.

A MACARONI FAMILY RETURNING FROM CHURCH.
                   See No. 4822—1 July 1773
From the *Macaroni Magazine.*

THE DEATH HUNTER MACARONI   See No 4823—1 Aug. 1773
From the *Macaroni Magazine*

A CERTAIN FAMOUS OLD FORNICATING FOREIGN M—N—TR .
[Count Haslang] *Macaroni Magazine.*
                   See No 4834—1 Aug. 1773

THE MIDDLE TEMPLE MACARONI   See No 4826—1 Sept. 1773
From the *Macaroni Magazine.*

5206 THE MACARONY BEAUS & BELLES IN AN UPROAR, OR
    THE LAST EVENING AT VAUX HALL GARDENS. [1 Oct. 1773]

Engraving. *Macaroni and Theatrical Magazine*, i. 529. A free fight in the gardens at Vauxhall, the weapons being swords, canes, and bottles The background shows trees (one with broken lamps) and part of one of the pavilions (l.). Women are escaping in alarm. The men are dressed as macaronies, but are of plebeian appearance
    It was customary (from *c.* 1772) on the last night of the Vauxhall season for the 'bucks' to break lamps, benches, bottles, &c. See F. Burney's *Evelina* (Letter XV), ed. Sir F. D. Mackinnon, 1930, pp. 244, 559.
$3\frac{7}{8} \times 5\frac{7}{8}$ in.   B M L., P.P 5021.

THE MACARONI CARD PLAYERS.   See No. 4824 [1 Dec. 1773]
Macaroni Magazine.

THE MACARONIES.   See No 4806—1 Feb. 1773
From *The Lady's Magazine*

THE FIRST OF APRIL   See No 2002—1 Apr. 1773
From the *Sentimental Magazine*, i 33 A satire on macaronies and others

THE GAMBLER DETECTED.   See No. 4836—1 Apr. 1773

From *The Covent Garden Magazine*.

5207 THE LONDON BEAU IN THE COUNTRY, OR THE DAIRY-HOUSE GALLANT.   [1 June 1773]

Engraving From the *Covent Garden Magazine*.[1] An illustration to a scurrilous story of 'Sir William L——' and a farmer's wife in Hertfordshire. The interior of a dairy with churn, milk-pans, &c. A man and woman embracing fall on the floor, a cat upsets a bowl of cream; the farmer with a hay-rake, and his man Hodge enter at the door.

$5\frac{1}{4} \times 3\frac{1}{2}$ in.

5208 STEPHEN CUB IN THE SUDS.   [1 Aug. 1773]

Engraving From the *Covent Garden Magazine*.[1] Stephen Fox in the bedroom of a tailor (indicated by the scissors and garments hanging on the wall) is being seized by his club of hair by the tailor, who is getting out of bed. He is also being attacked by a sweep and his two little 'climbing boys' who have entered by the door The text relates an alleged drunken escapade of Stephen Fox, 'a celebrated, sleeping, gambling Macaroni', who had mistaken the room for that of a woman.

$5\frac{1}{8} \times 3\frac{1}{2}$ in.

5209 THE DOUBLE DISCOVERY, OR THE DOCTOR BAULK'D OF HIS SUPPER.   [1 Sept. 1773]

Engraving. From the *Covent Garden Magazine*[1] An illustration to 'A whimsical Bagnio Adventure'. An overturned supper-table at which a man and woman have been sitting; he has fallen to the floor, she stands covering her face with a hand A military officer enters the room and threatens the man with a drawn sword, pointing to the woman. Behind him is another woman, equally horror-struck. The text relates the accidental meeting, at a 'house of rendezvous', of Doctor L—— and Captain D, each with the other's wife.

$4\frac{5}{16} \times 3\frac{5}{8}$ in.

5210 LORD G—— IN THE PORRIDGE POT, OR THE RAKES DISAPPOINTMENT.   [1 Oct. 1773]

Engraving. From the *Covent Garden Magazine*. An illustration to 'A curious Anecdote of Lord G——, . . .' Lord G——, in riding-dress, is seated in a cauldron, a kettle hung over one leg, and surrounded by other kitchen utensils. The scene is an inn kitchen, servants stand round and others are entering the room The text relates the misadventure of Lord G. in an inn on the Bath road. The cook-maid had defeated his amorous overtures by making him drunk, the ostler then decorated him with pots and pans.

$6\frac{1}{16} \times 3\frac{7}{8}$ in.

[1] The magazine is not in the B M L but cuttings from the book accompany the prints.

5211 SIR CHARLY DETECTED OR THE EXCISEMAN
CORNUTED. [1 Nov 1773]

Engraving From the *Covent Garden Magazine*. A fat man lies on the
ground, pointing angrily at a man and woman who hold up their hands
deprecatingly. Three men wearing hats threaten the couple with clubs
and clenched fists.

$5\frac{5}{16} \times 3\frac{3}{4}$ in.

5212 THE CITY 'PRENTICE AT HIS MASTER'S DOOR.

[1 Jan 1773]

Engraving From *Every Man's Magazine*, 1. 257 A young man stands on
the pavement outside an arched doorway through which can be seen
a short elderly man behind a counter. Over the door is inscribed, *Young &
Wife Mercers*. Rolls of material are piled up on shelves The apprentice
stands with his legs apart, his r. hand in his waistcoat, his l in his breeches
pocket. He is dressed like a macaroni and wears a nosegay On the r
a woman who has just passed by looks round at him; she carries on her
head a basket of vegetables. Just behind her walks a little chimney-sweeper
with his brush and bag of soot. On the l. two young women have just passed,
one looks round at the apprentice. Reproduced, M. D. George, *England
in Transition*, p. 172.

$6\frac{3}{8} \times 4$ in.

THE SPIRIT IS WILLING BUT THE FLESH IS WEAK

See No. 4609—1 Jan. 1773

Goldar *sc.* after Collet. Pub. Sayer and Smith.

THE BOLD ATTEMPT. See No 4607—1 Jan. 1773

Caldwell *sc.* after Collet. Pub. Smith and Sayer.

THE COUNTRY CHORISTERS See No. 4611—22 Mar 1773

Goldar *sc.* after Collet Pub. Smith and Sayer.

5213–5218 and numbers from Volume IV

Prints after Bunbury etched and published by J Bretherton.

5213 THE SIEGE OF NAMUR BY CAPT^N SHANDY & CORPORAL
TRIM *Tris· Shan.*

H. W. Bunbury del. 1772. *J. Bretherton f*

*Publish'd as the Act directs 26 Jany 1773. By J. Bretherton N° 134,
New Bond Street.*

Engraving. One of a series of illustrations to Sterne's *Tristram Shandy*, see
Nos 5214–16. Uncle Toby (r) marches from r to l., a crutch under his
l arm, pointing with his r. crutch towards the fortifications (l) built on
the bowling green, where the *Gate of St Nicolas* is flanked on each side

by a jack-boot. In his l. hand he holds the *London Gazette*. Trim, holding up a pickaxe, marches in front of his master. He has a long pig-tail, and a pad is tied over his l. knee. On the ground behind is a grenadier's cap Behind Uncle Toby is the sentry-box, in it is pasted up the plan of a fortification. The background is a rough paling behind which are trees. Shandy Hall appears behind the Gate of St. Nicolas.

Beneath the design is engraved,

"*What an honest triumph in my Uncle Toby's Eyes as he march'd to the Ramparts with the Gazette in his hand & Trim with a pickaxe ready to execute the Contents; what intense pleasure in his Eyes as he stood over the Corporal! Heaven! Earth! Sea!*"

$9\frac{3}{8} \times 15$ in.

5214 THE DAMNATION OF OBADIAH

Vide Trs. Shandy Vol. 2ᵈ

H. W. Bunbury delin. 1772   *J. Bretherton f*

Publish'd as the Act directs 30ᵗʰ Janʸ 1773. by J. Bretherton Nᵒ 134. New Bond Street.

Engraving One of a series of illustrations to *Tristram Shandy*, see Nos. 5213–16. Dr. Slop, short and fat, seated in an arm-chair (c.) holding in his l hand the book containing the form of excommunication, points with his r. at Obadiah who is disappearing (l), one leg and his back alone being visible. A handkerchief hangs over the doctor's cut r. thumb. Behind him on the l. stands Mr. Shandy, in dressing-gown and night-cap, smoking a long pipe, he is frowning and holds out his l hand in protest at the doctor's curses Uncle Toby, his crutch under his l. arm, stands on the r. pointing with his l. hand at a map of *Flanders* which hangs on the wall over Dr. Slop's head. He turns to speak to Corporal Trim, who stands (r) at attention in profile to the l. holding a long broom.

Beneath the design is engraved,

"*May all the Angels & Archangels, Principalities and Powers, & all the Heavenly Armies, curse & damn him—him—Obadiah. (Our Armies swore terribly in Flanders, quoth my Uncle Toby, but nothing to this*").

$9\frac{3}{8} \times 14\frac{7}{8}$ in.

5215 THE OVERTHROW OF Dᴿ SLOP

H. W. Bunbury delin.   *J. Bretherton f.*

Publish'd as the Act directs 3ᵈ February 1773. By J. Bretherton Nᵒ 134 New Bond Street.

Engraving One of a series of illustrations to *Tristram Shandy*, see Nos 5213–16. Obadiah (l.) mounted on the coach-horse at full gallop attempts to pull up his horse, leaning back in the saddle, his cap in his r. hand. On the ground is Dr. Slop's pony Behind the pony on the r Dr. Slop lies on his back; a spotted dog prances over him The doctor lies under a sign-post terminating in a hand pointing *To Shandy Hall*. Behind the coach-horse, which is wearing blinkers, is the angle of a high garden wall; in the distance (r) is a church spire among trees.

Beneath the design is engraved,

"*When Obadiah & his Coach Horse turn'd the Corner rapid, furious, pop, full upon him—nothing I think in Nature can be supposed more terrible than such a rencounter—Obadiah pull'd of [sic] his Cap twice to Dr Slop, once when he was falling & again when he saw him seated.*"—*Vide Vol 1st Tristram Shandy.*

9½ × 14⅞ in.

5216 THE BATTLE OF THE CATAPLASM.

H W. Bunbury delin.   *J Bretherton f.*

Publish'd as the Act directs 3^d February 1773. By J. Bretherton N°. 134 New Bond Street

Engraving   One of a series of illustrations to *Tristram Shandy*, see Nos. 5213-15   Dr. Slop and Susannah exchanging abuse. Susannah (r) stands behind the cradle in which lies the infant Tristram, a plaster across his nose   A lighted candle is in her l. hand, with her r. she holds the bridge of her nose, looking at the doctor with a face of fury, her mouth wide open. Dr. Slop stands scowling, his legs wide apart, the cataplasm in a ladle in his r. hand; he threatens Susannah with his fist. His wig is blazing, his hat lies on the floor. A chair has been overturned and lies by the cradle. Obadiah is hurrying into the room from the l, a basin in his r. hand, a bottle under his r arm, a chamber-pot in his l. hand. Behind is a screen, nine leaves of which are visible. A large grandfather clock pointing to 6.15 stands by the wall (r.); a table with two medicine bottles appears from behind the screen. On the wall are two portraits.

   Beneath the design is engraved,

"*Susannah, rowing one way & looking another, set fire to Dr. Slop's Wig, which being somewhat bushy & unctuous withal was as soon burnt as kindled— You impudent Whore cried Slop (for what is passion but a wild Beast) You impudent Whore cried Slop getting upright with the Cataplasm in his hand—I never was at the destruction of any body's nose said Susannah, which is more than you can say;—Is it? cried Slop, throwing the Cataplasm in her face—Yes it is cried Susannah returning the Complement with what was left in the pan*"—*Vide Tris. Shandy vol 4.*

9⅛ × 14⅞ in.

5217 CONCERTO SPIRITUALE.

Bretherton f.

Publish'd 23^d March 1773.

Engraving after Bunbury. Three men playing musical instruments. A fat man (l) sitting in a chair plays a viol da gamba, perhaps a portrait of Abel, see No. 5163   A thin man in profile to the l. plays a flute   He wears a bag-wig, laced coat, ruffled shirt and sword. A piece of music protrudes from his coat pocket. Behind, a stout man plays a horn

9 × 7¼ in.

5218 THE SLUMBERS OF RAGOTIN INTERRUPTED.

Mr Bunbury del.

Scarron B. 2^d   *J^s Bretherton f*

Publish'd May 29th 1773.

Engraving. An illustration to Scarron's *Roman Comique* (1651), Book II, ch xx. The scene is the room of an inn Ragotin, almost bald, sits in an upright chair wearing a long sword and jack boots; his legs do not reach the ground. The ram (l.), on its hind-legs, is about to butt him. The encounter is watched by a man who leans on the back of his chair, by another seated behind the ram, and by a third standing between Ragotin and a group of two ladies and a man on the r , one being Inezilla, who had just been reading her novel. Behind this group are the curtains of a bed. $7\frac{3}{4} \times 12\frac{3}{8}$ in.

LE FAMEUX BLAISE LACOSTE, LIMOSIN F.R:S.

                                  See No 4758—1 Jan 1773

A MILITIA MEETING.   See No. 4759—2 Jan 1773

THE X.MAS ACADEMICS .   See No 4728—20 Jan. 1773

JOLLUX   See No 4726—6 Feb. 1773

THE SALUTATION TAVERN.   See No 4716—20 Mar. 1773

.. PORTRAIT OF THE INIMITABLE MR JAMES MOSS ..

                                  See No 4721—15 May 1773

SNIP ANGLOIS.   See No. 4748—20 Dec. 1773

SNIP FRANCOIS.   See No. 4749—20 Dec. 1773

[UNIDENTIFIED SATIRICAL PORTRAIT]

                                  See No 4762—23 Dec. 1773

5219 and numbers from Volume IV

Series of mezzotints published by Carington Bowles.[1]

5219 AN EVENINGS INVITATION; WITH A WINK FROM THE BAGNIO.

269 Printed for Carington Bowles, Map & Printseller, N° 69 in St Pauls Church Yard, London Published as the Act directs [date erased, *c.* Jan 1773]

Mezzotint (coloured impression) Street scene. A fashionably dressed man walks (r. to l.) between two prostitutes, who have seized him by the

---

[1] No 4533 (but not the reduced version) has the imprint of Bowles and Carver.

shoulders and arm One (r.) hands to a man who lurks behind her a handkerchief she has taken from his pocket. A link-boy walks in front of the party holding his torch downwards. Through the glass panes which fill the upper part of the door of the bagnio (l.) a woman smiles and beckons Over the door is inscribed WINES The scene is probably under the piazza in Covent Garden. The women are fashionably dressed $12\frac{3}{4} \times 9\frac{3}{4}$ in.　　　　'Caricatures', 1, p. 186. B.M.L., Tab. 526.

BEAU MORDECAI INSPIR'D　　(270)　　　　See No 4525—c 1773

THE BLOOMING PEACH AND SHRIVELL'D APPLE . . . (271)
　　　　　　　　　　　　　　　　See No 4526—c 1773

DOCKING THE MACARONI (273)　　　See No 4527—19 Jan 1773

P'SHA YOU FLATTER ME　(274)　　　　See No 4528—1773

A DECOY FOR THE OLD AS WELL AS THE YOUNG. (278)
　　　　　　　　　　　　　　　　See No 4529—1773

THE BARGAIN STRUCK, OR VIRTUE CONQUER'D BY TEMP-
　　TATION　(281)　　　　　　　See No. 4530—1773

IRISH PEG IN A RAGE . . . (283)　　　See No. 4531—29 May 1773

THE OLD BEAU IN AN EXTASY. (286)
　　　　　　　　　　　　　　　　See No. 4532—13 July 1773

THE MODERN BEAU IN DISTRESS
　　　　　　　　　　　　　　　　See No 4590—c. 1773

THE CHURCH CHORISTERS. (289)　　　See No 4533—1773
After Grimm.

　Also a reduced version, No. 206 in the smaller series, pub. 2 Sept 1773.

5220, 5221 and numbers from Volume IV

Similar mezzotints issued by other publishers.

5220 MISS MACARONI AND HER GALLANT AT A PRINT-SHOP.

J Smith pinx^t [J. R. Smith].　　　　　　　*J. Smith fecit.*

Publish'd April 2nd 1773. Printed for John Bowles, at N° 13 in Cornhill.

Mezzotint. Four persons gazing at the prints displayed in a print-shop closely resembling though not identical with that in No. 3758 (1774) which is evidently by the same artist. A man and woman (l) in macaroni dress stand together, he holds her l. hand smiling, and pointing at one of the prints with his r hand. She turns aside smiling behind her fan. Two men (r) stand in conversation; one (r.) points out to the other, who is in back view, both hands held up in astonishment, one of the prints in the top row, apparently that of Wesley. A dog befouls the foot of the man facing the shop-window.

Beneath the title is engraved,

While Macaroni and his Mistress here,
At other Characters, in Picture, sneer,
To the vain Couple is but little known,
How much deserving Ridicule their own.

Some of the prints displayed are identical with those in No. 3758, the shop of Carington Bowles. In this design, however, the prints are displayed without margins In both shops the highest row consists of portraits which extend into the row below (r.) All are of leaders of religion, among whom Bunyan, John Wesley, and Whitefield are conspicuous. That of Whitefield is the much reproduced mezzotint by Greenwood after Hone, published by Carington Bowles, 1769. The others are humorous mezzotints including *The Paintress of Macaroni's*, No. 4582, *The Macaroni Painter*, No 4520, *Lady Betty Bustle*, No. 5094.

The print illustrates the close relationship between the two firms of Bowles who were partners in many prints. In spite of the close resemblance with the shop-window of Carington Bowles, as depicted in Nos. 3758 and 6352, it appears to represent 13 Cornhill. The panes are smaller and do not display the margins of the prints, the architectural detail above the window is different and the prints appear to be on a large frame fixed outside the actual window, part of which appears on the extreme r. Reproduced, R. T. Halsey, *Boston Port Bill*, Grolier Club, 1904, p. xvi.

$12\frac{3}{4} \times 9\frac{3}{4}$ in. Cheylesmore Collection.

THE SCRAMBLE, OR OLD GRIPUS PLUNDER'D BY HIS YOUNG WIFE.

See No. 4584—2 April 1773

P. Dawe. Pub. John Bowles.

5221 [THE MACARONI. A REAL CHARACTER AT THE LATE MASQUERADE]

[*Philip Dawe fecit*

Publish'd as the Act directs July 3ᵈ 1773. Printed for John Bowles at Nᵒ 13 in Cornhill.]

Mezzotint Proof before letters on which is written 'Pantheon Macaroni'. The title and publication line are supplied from an impression belonging to Mr. W. T. Spencer of New Oxford Street. A macaroni dressed in a grotesque exaggeration of the prevailing fashion. His hair is in a high pyramid with side curls, an enormous club hangs down his back. A small three-cornered hat is perched on the top of his hair. He wears a large nosegay. He stands in a mincing attitude by a toilet-table, draped with muslin on which are boxes and toilet jars, the latter inscribed *essence* and *Rose* The wall is panelled and ornamented with mouldings; the floor is carpeted and there are two cane-seated chairs of an unusual pattern [1] Reproduced, Paston, Pl. xx, J. T. Smith, *A Book for a Rainy Day*, ed. W. Whitten, 1905, p. 265. $12\frac{7}{8} \times 9\frac{7}{8}$ in.

THE ANTIQUARIAN PUZZLED . . .

See No. 4772—15 May 1773

P. Dawe. Pub. W. Humphrey.

COUNSELLOR COZEN CONSULTING CASES.

See No. 4788—1 Sept. 1773

Pub. H. Bryer.

[1] This probably represents the dress of 'Lord P——' as a macaroni buck at the Pantheon masquerade of 12 May 1773. See *Oxford Magazine*, x. p. 179, where his dress is described.

POLITICAL SATIRES

5222 MERLIN.[1] [1 Jan. 1774]

Engraving From the *Westminster Magazine*, 1. 684. A sequel to No. 4957.
Merlin (l) points with his wand to a procession of the sovereigns of Europe
which circles round him, moving from l. to r He stands within a circle
bordered with cabalistic signs, a globe stands beside him; he wears long
robes and his high cap is decorated with a skull and cross-bones. First walks
a sovereign with three heads, the centre head wearing a crown, between a
woman's head with ass's ears and a man's head with stag's horns This
appears to represent the king of Denmark, deceived by his wife and Struensee, an episode which belongs to 1772, see Nos. 4945, 4946, 4950, 4956. Next
walks a crowned personage carrying a halter in his r hand, and in the l. a
Book of Prayer which he is reading. Perhaps Frederick, called the Hereditary Prince, son of the Dowager Queen of Denmark, who had conspired
against Struensee and had shown great vindictiveness towards him.

Next walks Catharine of Russia in a furred robe. Her r. hand is on the
neck of an oriental who kneels beside her, whom she appears to be strang-
ling; another oriental wearing a jewelled turban stands beside her clasping
his hands in despair. With her l. hand she holds a monkey by the arm.
The two orientals probably represent the Grand Signior of Turkey (in
allusion to the Russo-Turkish War, 1768–74, and Pugachoff, the Cossack
who led a rising against Catharine (1773–5).

Next is a sovereign whose crown is breaking, evidently Stanislaus II of
Poland Behind him walk two sovereigns in consultation, one holding
a wolf or dog on a leash, and in his l. hand a mask; the other holds an open
map inscribed *Map [of Po]land*. probably the Emperor Joseph II and
Frederick II of Prussia discussing the Partition of Poland. Behind them
walks a prince wearing a feathered hat who appears absorbed in his snuff-
box (perhaps the king of Spain) Then comes a sovereign wearing a crown
and a long dressing-gown rubbing his eyes as if sleepy. He is perhaps
William V, Stadholder of Holland, who became sleepy after the slightest
exertion; he was not, however, a sovereign prince.[2] After him walks the
king of France, indicated by the fleur-de-lys which decorates his crown and
his robes; he holds an oval miniature, the portrait of a woman, probably
intended for Mme du Barry After him walks George III, carrying an
infant, whom he is feeding (Prince Augustus Frederick, born Jan. 1773).
Last in the procession is a countryman with a hay-rake, smoking a pipe, and
wearing the hat shaped like an inverted flower-pot which indicates Holland
in caricature.

In the background on a hill sits the Pope wearing his triple crown; his
papal chair is tottering and from his hand, raised as if in alarm, falls a paper
inscribed *Jesuits & treac[hery]*. In 1773 Clement XIV (d. 1774) suppressed
the Jesuits, a shock to the prestige of the Papacy, and the cause of calumnies
which probably hastened his death, which was ascribed, possibly with

[1] Indexed as *Merlin. A Picture of Europe for 1773*.
[2] Gustavus III of Sweden appears to be absent from the procession, though in
view of his recent *coup d'état* he might be expected to figure prominently.

truth, to poison See Walpole, *Last Journals*, 1910, i. 401–3; *Cambridge Mod Hist.*, vi. 594–6. For the Partition of Poland see *ibid.*, Nos. 4957, 4958, 5110, 5229.

$3\frac{1}{2} \times 6\frac{1}{16}$ in.

5223 ROBBED BETWEEN SUN AND SUN   [1 Jan. 1774]

Engraving From the *Oxford Magazine*, x. 502 (folding plate). Lord Holland with his two sons Charles and Stephen seated at a table. Each has the profile of a fox but wears a wig. Lord Holland (centre) in a high-back chair, looks towards Stephen (r.) holding up his hands with an expression of horror. Stephen is asleep, beside him on the table is a small phial or medicine-bottle. Charles (l.), very alert, picks his father's pocket, taking out a purse On the ground at his side are emblems of gambling: a dice box, dice, and a book inscribed *Hoyle*. Beneath the table crouches a demon: he is looking at Charles, and holds in each claw a chain which is round Charles's leg, his tail is wound round Stephen's ankle. Over Charles's head is engraved *Hic Niger est*. (With his black hair and eyebrows he was what was then called 'a black man', cf. Walpole, *Letters*, viii 359) Lord Holland wears an old-fashioned tie-wig. Both the sons are fashionably dressed, and wear bag-wigs, that of Charles being a very high toupet in the French fashion.

This appears to illustrate the last verse of a poem called 'To the Young Cub on his keeping Madame H——n—l' [Heinel] (see No. 5145) printed in the *Westminster Magazine*, Sept. 1773:

> From sons what Sire such blessing reaps!
> One never wakes—One never sleeps;
>   Yet both partake his bounty:
> The Law says, If a man's undone,
> And pillag'd thus 'tween *Sun and Sun*
>   He's free to sue the County.

In the winter of 1773–4 Lord Holland paid Charles's debts to the extent of £140,000. The print is described as representing 'a committee lately held on ways and means by a certain nest of F——s that infested the neighbourhood; whether the subject of debate was to find out some fresh method of satisfying the veracity [*sic*] of the old one; to preserve the plunder already got, or to repair the destruction made by the folly of the young Cubbs, is uncertain. . . .' Stephen Fox was called the Sleepy Macaroni, see Nos. 4648, 5114, &c.

E. Hawkins (MS. index) mentions another impression or version enclosed within a coiled snake

$6\frac{3}{4} \times 10\frac{1}{4}$ in.

5224 STRIKE—BUT HEAR.   [n d. Feb 1774]

Engraving. John Horne stands in the foreground, declaiming at the bar of the House of Commons. His r arm is raised, his l. hand is in his breeches pocket. From the r. of the design the mace appears On the other side of the bar the Speaker sits in his chair. On each side of him are three rows of members, many of them without heads; a number of heads with pendent bag-wigs are floating above the Speaker's head, showing that many of the members have lost their heads in excitement.

This depicts the appearance of John Horne at the bar of the House on 18 Feb. 1774 Horne's friend Tooke had appealed to him for help to prevent a pending enclosure Bill by de Grey which would pre-judge a case in litigation between himself and de Grey concerning the common-rights of Tooke's estate at Purley. The passing of the Bill was apparently inevitable, but Horne published in the *Public Advertiser* a nicely-timed letter to the Speaker, signed 'Strike but Hear', which was a deliberate and violent libel. He calculated that the House would be so exasperated at the breach of privilege that the business of the day would be neglected, that he would be summoned to the bar, and would have an opportunity of explaining his motives and the injustice of the Bill The event was according to plan: the members lost their heads and clamoured to the Speaker for the punishment of the libel. First Woodfall and then Horne were called to the bar. Horne made his speech; both were discharged; time was given for further consideration of the Bill and the clauses obnoxious to Tooke were dropped. See *Parl. Hist.*, xvii. 1005 ff.; Walpole, *Last Journals*, 1910, i 289 ff., *Corr. of George III*, ed Fortescue, iii 68–9, A Stephens, *Memoirs of John Horne Tooke*, 1813, i 422–30

7 × 4½ in.

5225 THE ORACLE REPRESENTING, BRITANNIA, HIBERNIA, SCOTIA, & AMERICA, AS ASSEMBLED TO CONSULT THE ORACLE, ON THE PRESENT SITUATION OF PUBLIC AFFAIRS, TIME ACTING AS PRIEST. DEDICATED TO CONCORD.
[30 Mar. 1774]

Inv *Drawn & Engrav'd by J. Dixon.*
Kempes Row Facing Ranelagh Walk Chelsea

Mezzotint Time, with a magic lantern, throws upon a curtain an allegorical vision of the triumph of Concord over Discord, which he is showing to figures representing Britannia, Hibernia, Scotia, and America Time (l), his scythe and two books on the ground beside him, supports his lantern on a globe on which he leans his elbow, he points at the vision on the curtain with his l hand, his mouth open as if declaiming On the globe is a paper inscribed, *Unite* Britannia, with her shield and spear, sits between Hibernia (l.) to whom she turns, and Scotia. Hibernia's l. arm is round Britannia's shoulder, her harp is beside her. Scotia stands looking at Time's vision All are dressed in pseudo-classical draperies in the manner of Reynolds, those of Scotia being of tartan Opposite them (r.) America sits on a bale of goods, another bale behind her, representing the commerce of the colonies She is in T.Q back view, gazing at the vision She has a feathered head-dress, is partly draped, like an Amazon, with bare arms and legs; in her l hand is a bow, a quiver of arrows is slung on her back.

In the circle of light thrown on the screen Concord is putting Discord to flight Concord, a crowned figure, a star on her breast holding out a bow, reversed and unstrung, advances (l to r) escorted by a winged figure wearing a medallion on her breast which resembles Britannia's shield Behind walk together Plenty (or Commerce) holding a cornucopia, and Liberty holding up her staff surmounted with the Phrygian cap of liberty. Last walk Truth holding up a mirror, and Justice holding out scales Cherubs fly above their heads; the foremost holds up a drapery on which is engraved *Publick Credit*, three are holding up an orrery. Before them flies Fame blowing her trumpet. Before this procession (r.) hag-like figures are being put to flight. One has two faces, the fangs of a serpent darting from one of the mouths Another holds up a serpent in his hand. A large coiled serpent hisses on the extreme r. The circle of light from the lantern falls on a heavily draped curtain.

This print indicates the renewed interest in America caused by news of the Boston Tea Party which first appeared in the *London Evening Post*, 20 Jan 1774 On 10 Mar. North read to the House of Commons the king's message on 'the outrageous proceedings at Boston .' *Parl Hist*, xvii 1159 The first print on American affairs since those on the 'Boston Massacre', 1770, see No 4839.

Exhibited at the exhibition of the Society of Arts in 1774 It is the basis of a well-known satire published in Paris, see No 5490

Chaloner Smith, i 218

20 × 23⅛ in.

5226 THE ABLE DOCTOR, OR AMERICA SWALLOWING THE BITTER DRAUGHT.   [1 May 1774]

Engraving From the *London Magazine*, xliii. 184. America, a partly-draped female figure, is being held down by Lord Mansfield (r) in judge's wig and robes, while North, holding her by the throat, pours the contents of a tea-pot down her mouth. America ejects the tea in a stream directed at North's face. From his pocket hangs a paper inscribed *Boston Port Bill* Sandwich (l) kneels, holding America down by an ankle, while he lifts the edge of her draperies and peers beneath them. Behind Mansfield (r) stands Bute in Scots cap and kilt, holding a drawn sword, its blade inscribed *Military Law*; pistols are thrust through his belt Behind America stands Britannia resting one hand on her shield; she averts her face and covers her eyes with her hand Behind Sandwich (l) stand two men dressed in the French and Spanish fashions and representing France and Spain or the monarchs of France and Spain; the order of the Golden Fleece hangs from the neck of Spain They stand close together, pointing towards America with expressions of interest and concern.

In the foreground is a torn document inscribed *Boston petition* In the background is the sea; on the horizon and on a minute scale are the spires of a town surrounded by ships, above is engraved, *Boston cannonaded*

The print illustrates a report of the debates on the Boston Port Bill. the text of the Bill is given in full because it is 'of vast importance to the mercantile part of the nation and indeed to the whole British Empire', pp 165–85 The Boston Port Bill became law on 31 Mar. (one of the 'five intolerable acts') passed as a punishment for the 'Boston tea-party' (16 Dec 1773) the port of Boston was closed and its rights transferred to Salem till compensation should be made for the destruction of the tea. Boston, of course, was not cannonaded, Gage was its military and civil governor and he closed the harbour in accordance with the Act on 1 June, see Nos. 5227, 5228, 5230, 5236 The 'Boston petition' is presumably the petition of Americans in London to the House of Commons against the Boston Port Bill, *Parl. Hist*, xvii 1189–92. For other references to the tax on tea see Nos. 5232, 5282, 5490, 5491, 6190 For the 'Tea Party' see Van Tyne, *Causes of the War of Independence*, 1921, ch xix.

Reproduced in Bernard Fay's *Franklin*, 1929, p. 362, but incorrectly dated 1770.

A copy signed *P. Revere Sculp* was published in the *Royal American Magazine*, vol 1 (June 1774), Stauffer, No 2673. Reproduced, *Propylaen-Weltgeschichte*, ed. W. Goetz, vi. 1931, p. 461, J. T. Adams, *Hist of the American People*, 1933, p. 93.

$3\frac{5}{8} \times 5\frac{15}{16}$

5227 THE WHITEHALL PUMP. [1 May 1774]

Engraving. From the *Westminster Magazine*, ii 168. Lord North pumps water upon the prostrate figure of Britannia while he looks at her through his spy-glass. On the top of the tall pump is a head of George III in profile to the l. adorned with a laurel wreath. Britannia holds her spear in her r. hand, beneath her is her shield; she lies across a Red Indian brave, also prostrate, and holding a knife, who represents America Beneath them on the ground are a number of documents Behind North (l.) is a group of ministerialists who are approving spectators. Two judges, each holding a document, appear to be Apsley, the Lord Chancellor, and Mansfield. Behind Mansfield stands Sandwich. Three others are less prominent and cannot be identified. Above their heads is an open window from which look Lord Holland, with a fox's head, and a companion wearing a ribbon who may be intended for Bute On the r two men hold out their hands in protest. One is Wilkes; his companion, who wears a long gown and bands, may be intended for Lord Camden.

The accompanying text explains the 'Vision'. North, under Scottish influence, is pumping upon 'that daft unruly body Mistress Britannia . . with her child America, and all her boasted rattles and gew-gaws such as Magna Charta, Coronation Oaths, Bill of Rights, Charters of Companies and Corporations, Remonstrances, Petitions . . .'. 'All the miscreants and tools of State' rejoice at the sight Round the head on the pump, though surrounded with fogs, could be read the words,

> His brows thick fogs instead of glories grace,
> And lambent dulness plays around his face.

The vision was inspired by 'the Dissentions of our Colonies and the Fever of the Mother Country' It is an attack on the Bills against Massachusetts on account of the Boston Tea Party, see No 5226, which were discussed between 1 Mar. and 25 Apr. *Parl. Hist.*, xvii 1163 ff ; see *Corr. of George III*, ed. Fortescue, iii. 80 ff. See also Nos. 5228, &c
$3\frac{15}{16} \times 5\frac{3}{4}$ in.

5228 THE MITRED MINUET [1 May 1774]

Engraving From the *London Magazine*, xliii 312 Four bishops wearing mitres dance together, each holding the hand of the one opposite him so that four hands cross in the middle. They dance round the *Quebec Bill* which lies on the floor Other bishops, not wearing mitres, are seated in a semicircle behind them, watching with approval. On the l are three figures who appear to be directing the dance: Lord Bute in highland dress plays the bagpipes, next him is Lord North pointing to the dancers, and on North's l. is a minister wearing a ribbon Above their heads flies the Devil pointing to North with his r. hand, his l forefinger laid against his nose. The scene is a panelled room.

The explanatory text is a violent attack on the Quebec Act, passed 22 June 1774, from the No-Popery standpoint: the bishops' 'crossing of hands was to show their approbation and countenance of the Roman religion'

The Quebec Act, though not a punitive measure, was classed with the three acts passed against Massachusetts, the Boston Port Act, the Massachusetts Government Act, the Administration of Justice Act, and with the Quartering Act as the five intolerable Acts, rousing far the most opposition though it was 'dictated by an enlightened liberalism . . . to secure the loyalty of the French Canadians. To these it granted complete religious liberty and the restitution of their peculiar legal and political institutions'. S. E. Morison and H. S. Commager, *The Growth of the American Republic*, New York, 1930, p 21 See also R. Coupland, *The Quebec Act*, 1928; Cavendish, *Debates on the Bill for the Government of Quebec*, 1889. Chatham on 18 June denounced it in the House of Lords as 'a most cruel, oppressive and odious measure, tearing up justice and every good principle by the roots'. *Parl Hist*, xviii 1402 See also the King's Speech, ibid., 1407. For the Act see also Nos. 5233, 5236, 5282, 5285, 5286 No 5681 perhaps relates to this Act

This plate was used in the *Hibernian Magazine*, iv. 451, Aug. 1774. It was copied by Paul Revere for the *Royal American Magazine*, October 1774, Stauffer, No 2688.

$3\frac{11}{16} \times 6\frac{3}{8}$ in.

5229 THE POLISH PLUMB-CAKE. [1 Sept. 1774]

J. Lodge sculp.

Engraving From the *Westminster Magazine*, ii. 416. Four monarchs sit round a table on which is a round 'cake' divided into four sections marked *Russia*, *Germany*, *Prussia*, and (smaller than the others) *France* In the centre sits the Emperor, crowned, a drawn sword in his hand On his r. is Catharine of Russia in profile to the r. holding a cleaver On his l is Frederick of Prussia, wearing a hat with a cockade; he also holds a drawn sword. In the foreground (l.) sits the French king (who in age more resembles Louis XV than his grandson who succeeded him in May 1774), he holds a knife, and his portion is much smaller than those of the other three. Behind (l.) is the king of Poland weeping, his crown about to fall from his head. On the r. stands a man in a jewelled turban flourishing his sword, probably the Grand Signior. From under the table-cloth appears a demon who points at the king of Prussia Beneath the design is engraved,

> *Thy Kingdom Stanisl'us, is now at stake,*
> *To four such stomachs, 'tis a mere plumb-cake.*

The accompanying text explains that Frederick 'a King more savage than an Indian', 'lets the Emperor of Germany [sic] and the Empress of Russia go snacks; while he offers the King of France a share to keep him from attacking Germany'. The demon says 'though they have executed his design they shall not long enjoy the plunder!' For the partition of Poland see also Nos 4957, 4958, 5110, 5124, 5222.

$6\frac{1}{4} \times 4\frac{3}{16}$ in.

5230 A POLITICAL LESSON.

J. Dixon invenit et fecit
Published 7. Sep͏ᵗ 1774. Printed for John Bowles, at N° 13 in Cornhill.
   Pr. 1ˢ 6ᵈ

Mezzotint. A black horse, rearing violently, has just thrown its rider, whose head has struck a mile-stone and broken it across The part still standing is inscribed *To Boston VI Miles* Behind it (r) is a sign-post inscribed *To Salem*. The rider lies on his back, clutching his head with his r hand, his legs are in the air He wears a laced coat and waistcoat and gloves, his hat and wig are on the ground The horse is looking wildly down at its rider The scene is a narrow country road, with bushes in the foreground and low mountains in the distance

General Gage, who succeeded Hutchinson as Governor of Massachusetts, removed the legislative assembly from Boston to Salem (May–June 1774), the Port of Boston having been closed under the Boston Port Act All shipping for Boston was forced to enter by Salem or Marblehead and thence through Cambridge by wagons The result was to inflame the opposition of the colony to England. Five representatives to a General Congress were elected and the subscribers to a Solemn League and Covenant pledged themselves to suspend all commercial intercourse with Great Britain until the Boston Port Act was repealed; and in a number of ways Gage was defied and insulted. The rider may represent either Gage or Great Britain overcome by the resistance of Massachusetts to the penal measures against the colony, cf No 5549.

The manner of this mezzotint is that of the history painter, not of political satire. Reproduced, R. T. Halsey, *Boston Port Bill*, p. 157.

12¹⁶⁄₁₆×9⅞ in

5231 BOREAS. [1 Oct 1774]

Engraving From the *Oxford Magazine*,[1] xi 276 A freely-drawn caricature of Lord North H L. in profile to the r He looks through an eye-glass held in two fingers. In the lower l. corner of the print is a small head inscribed *Æolus*, its inflated cheeks direct a blast of air against North's back. Beneath is engraved, *I Promise to reduce the Americans*. The figure of North appears to be copied from No. 4969.

5⅝×3¾ in.

5232 A NEW METHOD OF MACARONY MAKING, AS PRAC-
   TISED AT BOSTON IN NORTH AMERICA.

*Printed for Carington Bowles, N° 69 in Sᵗ Pauls Church Yard,
   London. Published 12 Octʳ 1774.*

Mezzotint No. 217 in Bowles's smaller series Two Bostonians tarring and feathering a customs officer. The victim, completely covered with feathers, kneels on one knee, his hands clasped. A rope is round his neck, its frayed end held by the American on the r. He looks round with a face of anguish to the other American (l.) who holds a large teapot, the spout of which is against the feathered man's r. shoulder. Behind is a gallows with

---

[1] The only political satire in the *Oxford Magazine*, vol. xi (1774)

a broken rope, suggesting that the victim has already endured a partial hanging The man with the teapot wears a large plain hat, the figure *45* written large both on the crown and the upturned brim The other Bostonian holds a club over his l shoulder, he wears a large favour in his hat showing that he is one of the Sons of Liberty. Both men look grinning at their victim, both wear striped breeches Trees form a background

A satire on the treatment given to John Malcom or Malcomb, an unpopular Commissioner of Customs, at Boston, as recorded in the English newspapers shortly before its publication. On 27 Jan 1774 he had been tarred and feathered, led to the gallows with a rope round his neck, on the way there being forced as a torture to drink enormous quantities of tea. His offence was in attempting to collect Customs duties; it was not connected with the Boston Tea Party R. T. Halsey, *The Boston Port Bill*, 1904, pp. 77–82 For his memorial to the Government of Massachusetts begging for relief and redress and his petition to the King for compensation and employment see *Hist. MSS. Comm., Dartmouth MSS.*, 1, p. 348, 11, pp. 192, 263.

Wilkes was a national hero in the colonies and '45' a patriotic symbol. 'Liberty Tree' at Boston was reported to be decorated with 'Number 45, Wilkes and liberty'. *London Chronicle*, 13–16 Aug. 1768.

Reproduced, *Social England*, ed Traill, 1904, v, p. 447.

$5\frac{1}{2} \times 4\frac{1}{2}$ in.

A larger version with the same date, not in the British Museum, was published by Bowles as No 306 in his series of folio mezzotints. The title ends at the word 'Boston', and beneath are the lines,

> *For the Custom House Officers landing the Tea,*
> *They Tarr'd him, and Feather'd him just as you see,*
> *And they drench'd him so well both behind and before,*
> *That he begg'd for God's sake they would drench him no more.*

Reproduced R. T. Halsey, *op cit*, p. 92

Another print, a folio line engraving, was issued by Carington Bowles on 2 June 1775 with the same title as No 5232 and the verses quoted above. Malcomb is being lowered by ropes from the window of his house into a cart, before receiving his 'American suit'. R. T. Halsey, op cit, 121 n.

Another mezzotint depicting the same incident as No 5232 probably by P. Dawe, was published by Sayer and Bennett, 31 Oct 1774 with the title, *Plate I The Bostonians Paying the Excise-man, or Tarring & Feathering.* Reproduced R. T. Halsey, op cit, p 83 and J. T. Adams, *Revolutionary New England*, p. 39. Malcomb, on his knees, tarred and feathered, his head pressed backwards, is being forced by five men to drink from a teapot, one of them holds a rope which is round his neck They are under *Liberty Tree* (r.) from a branch of which dangles a rope On its trunk is a placard inscribed *Stamp Act*, upside down Behind (l.) is a ship with furled sails from which masked men are emptying tea-chests into the water (the Boston tea-party) Nos 5241, 5284 belong to the same series

The treatment of Malcomb is also the subject of a French engraving, *John Malcom*, by Godefroy in *Recueil d'Estampes représentant . la Guerre qui a procuré l'Indépendance aux États unis .* (Print Department) Malcom, 'ce fier maltôtier', is being lowered by ropes from his house into a cart. *Collection de Vinck*, No 1164.

5233 [FAME'S REWARDS.][1]

Terry del. et sculp.

Engrav'd for the Whimsical Repository. According to Act, October 1ˢᵗ 1774. Pater Noster Row.

Engraving In a rotunda whose walls are decorated with Ionic columns and garlands, Fame stands on a high cylindrical pedestal, blowing her trumpet She is a winged figure, partly draped, in her l. hand is a second trumpet. Beside her stands a boy with butterfly wings, wearing a bow and quiver, in his r. hand he holds a flower. Four other winged boys fly down from the pedestal with gifts for a crowd of suppliants who kneel below. One of them offers to a naval officer a pair of crutches, a wooden leg, and a paper inscribed *Half Pay*; the officer holds a print of a man-of-war decorated with flags, his ankle is in a sling. A parson is about to receive a bishop's mitre and a paper inscribed *Living*; his foot rests on a *Bible*, beneath which is a paper inscribed *Protestᵗ Religion*, probably a reference to the Quebec Act, see No. 5228, &c. Behind him a famished-looking man, holding a large volume inscribed *Philosophy*, is being offered a paper inscribed *No literary Property*. (In the case of Donaldson *v* Beckett, 1774, the House of Lords decided that the Act of 1709 had abolished the perpetual copyright of the common law. See *Parl. Hist* xvii, pp 953, 1077 ff., 1400 ff ; Hume, *Letters*, 1932, ii. 286–9) A fashionably-dressed man kneels on Britannia's shield beneath which lies *M Charta*, a torn document; across it lies the cap of Liberty on its staff and a paper inscribed *General Warrants*; he is being offered a fool's cap and a collar or circlet attached to a chain. A man in legal robes is being given a bag of money and an order in the form of a Maltese cross.

In the foreground stands a small blindfolded cupid, holding an arrow and a heart On the l stand two spectators: one is evidently Sir John Fielding the magistrate, wearing a gown, his eyes bandaged as he was accustomed to sit at Bow Street, he holds a cross-hilted sword, emblem of Justice; the other is a military officer with a wooden leg. Beneath the design is engraved,

> *Plaudits of Fame, tho' Mortals prize[1]*
> *Fancy's the God they Idolize*

Cf. No. 5275, also a satire on social injustice.

6⅜×4⅝ in.

5234 A TUB TO THE WHALE OR THE RETORT COURTEOUS TO CITY REMONSTRANCES [n.d. *c.* 1774]

Sold by Mʳˢ Sledge next Southampton Street Covent Garden & Mʳ Swan facing Norfolk Street Strand, price Six pence.

Engraving. A freely-drawn representation of the gateway to St. James's Palace. From a window over the gate lean three men who have just thrown out a barrel labelled *The Coin Act*: in the centre is the king saying *This Coin Act will fully employ them to take of their attention to my immaculate Ministry*. On his r. is Bute wearing a Scots cap; he says. *Hoot awa ye Scum of the Earth I'll teach ye doctrine of Subordination* On his l. is a judge, evidently Mansfield. A man who holds out a pair of scales is about to enter

[1] No title

the palace; he wears a long gown held up by the devil who points at him. Beneath the man with the scales is engraved· *twas kind to help little Pinchy to a new Trade*. Beneath the devil is engraved: *I am always sure of my Friends here* Behind the devil walks a man in a furred alderman's gown holding his hat, he says. *I hope my Lord you will secure me for the City again* He must be Thomas Harley, M.P. for the City of London, 1768–74, and the leader of the Court Party in the City. At the general election of 1774 he resigned his seat for the City and unsuccessfully contested the county of Hereford, see No. 4953, &c Behind (l.) stand three Scotsmen in kilts talking together; one says: *let them get a Bank in Air or muckle penny Notes*, an allusion to the insolvent position of the Ayr Bank (Douglas Heron and Co.), see Hume, *Letters*, ed. Greig, 1932, ii. 263, 265, and No. 4961. Another says. *this will plague the Loons & humble their pride*. In the foreground (l.) a man in macaroni dress is accosting a courtesan, she holds him at arm's length, holding out a pair of scales and saying: *You Maccaronys are light Chaps y^r Gold may be as light as yourself I'll weigh first*. On the r. is a sentry-box before which stands a grenadier at attention. Beside him (r.) is a bearded Jew with a satisfied expression holding money-bags. A dog barks at him.

One of several satires on the Coin Act, see Nos. 3759, 4534 (1774), 5128, 5158. Pinchy is Christopher Pinchbeck, satirically called the King's Friend, see index, the Coin Act will be profitable to him as a maker of scales For City Remonstrances see Nos 4380, 4386, &c. The latest was that of 13 Mar. 1773, Walpole, *Last Journals*, 1910, i 180–5; Sharpe, *London and the Kingdom*, iii. 135–7; *Corr. of George III*, ed. Fortescue, ii. 462–5

$4\frac{3}{16} \times 6\frac{5}{8}$ in.

5235 THE VERY WISE ALDERMEN OF GOTHAM, SCRATCHING FOR A MAYOR. [n.d. *c.* Oct. 1774]

Engraving Probably from a magazine.[1] A throng of figures in furred gowns, most of whom have animals' heads, surround a table, on which are open polling books, with triple columns of names At the further side of the table sits Alderman Bull, with a bull's head, writing with a pen in his cloven hoof. On his r. hand is Wilkes Behind stands a man with a goat's beard and horns probably intended for Watkin Lewes. Harley as an ape wearing spurred boots enters from the r.

At the election for the mayoralty in Oct 1774 Wilkes was head of the poll, next being Bull, the actual mayor. These two were therefore returned to the Court of Aldermen, eleven of them voted for Wilkes, while only two, Townsend and Oliver, voted for Bull Sharpe, *London and the Kingdom*, iii. 143–4 Cf. Nos. 5129, 5130, 5131.

$5\frac{3}{4} \times 3\frac{5}{8}$ in.

5236 THE DISSOLUTION OF P——T [Parliament]   [1 Nov. 1774]

Engraving. From the *London Magazine*, xliii. 464 A street scene, in which a stage coach drawn by six horses and laden with passengers inside and out is being driven at full speed from r. to l They drive past a posting-inn, with an open gateway over which, as a sign, is a head of Wilkes in an

---

[1] From the *Sentimental Magazine*, Oct [Nov.] 1773. It relates to the election of 1773 when Bull was chosen by the aldermen, see No 5129, &c

oval, beneath it are the words *John Wilkes Esq' Neat Post Chaises.* To the postilion on the near leader is attached a label inscribed *Galloping Liberty.* The coach-door is inscribed *For the Corrupted Boroughs* Five passengers (ministerialist candidates) sit inside the coach, fashionably dressed. On the roof sit four men, two flourish clubs; one says: *May the Patriots ride uppermost.* The large boot or basket attached to the back of the coach holds six passengers; it is inscribed · *We are honest though poor, or who would be golted [sic] thus for his Country!* The coachman turns round to the passengers saying *I will not overset Ye, if Ye dont overset Yourselves.* On the ground are papers inscribed: *General Warrants* (see No. 4065); *Boston Port Bill* (see No. 5226); *Quebec* (see No. 5228, &c); *Inclosures.* Bystanders (l to r) point and jeer at the coach. A ragged man (l.) sitting on the ground with two wooden legs, one of which is broken off, says *Ah, rot such Members, my Members are better!* A ragged woman with two children says. *You have Starved me, and my Children.* A seated man points at the papers on the ground saying *What a litter they have left behind them* A man (r.) says to his companion · *There they go, & the D——l go with them*

The explanation of this 'Vision' is appended to a sarcastic comment on election addresses of individual candidates The candidates on the roof and in the basket are patriots and the coach was to stop at 'the Wilkes's Head in Brentford'.

Parliament was dissolved suddenly on 30 Sept , about six months before the expiration of its seven years' term, then a very unusual event, see *Ann. Reg* 1774, p. 152, Walpole, *Last Journals,* 1910, 1. 375–9. The illegality of General Warrants issued by a Secretary of State had been established by the decisions of Camden (1763–5) arising out of the arrest of Wilkes, and others, for the publication of No. 45 of the *North Briton* Throughout the reign of George III, private Bills for the enclosure of common fields, commons, and wastes were exceedingly numerous and very unpopular with cottagers and small farmers, cf No. 5224. On 20 Oct 'a vast train of carriages and horses attend Wilkes to Brentford . . ' T. Hutchinson, *Diary,* 1. 267.

$4\frac{1}{16} \times 7\frac{1}{2}$ in.

5237 THE CUP PRESENTED TO MR. WILKES BY THE CITY OF LONDON IN 1772.   [1 Nov. 1774]

R Dighton del.   *J. June sculp^t*

Engraving From the *Gentleman's Magazine,* 1774, p 457. An ornate two-handled cup with a lid. It is decorated in relief with the City Arms and with a scene representing the assassination of Julius Caesar under which is inscribed

> *May every Tyrant feel*
> *The keen deep Searchings of a Patriots steel*
> *Churchill.*

The maker's name is round the base of the cup ·

> *Morson & Stephenson fec. Ludgate Hill.*

In the background are the arms used by Wilkes but without the motto (*Arcui meo non confido*), cf. No 5245.

One of the three cups which had been voted by the Common Council 24 Jan. 1772 to the three City patriots, Wilkes, Crosby, and Oliver for their opposition to the House of Commons over the printing of debates, see Nos. 4850, 4853, &c Cf. No 4887

The cup is described on p 457 The bas relief 'seems to indicate an idea of the meaning of the dagger or short sword in the City Arms very different from what the Antiquarians have hitherto suggested', namely, either the dagger with which Walworth slew Wat Tyler, or the short sword of St. Paul.

The print is perhaps intended as an election warning against the excesses of the patriots.

$6\frac{1}{16} \times 3\frac{3}{4}$ in.

5238 THE PARL^MT DISSOLVED OR THE DEVIL TURN'D FORTUNE TELLER. [n.d. 1774?]

Engraved for y^e Whimsical Repository.[1]

Design'd, & Engrav'd by G. Terry, Paternoster Row

Engraving The room of a fortune-teller. The devil seated and holding a wand has just called up the figure of a Red Indian who stands (l.) on the body of a prostrate soldier, on whose high cap are the letters *G R* The Indian, personifying America, holds up the model of a large square building in his r. hand, the floors of which have given way, so that its occupants, crowds of tiny figures, fall headlong to the floor. In his l. hand is a wand with which he points to the building which symbolizes the parliament Behind him are clouds. Two ministers (r.) who have come to consult the fortune-teller start back, with arms raised in horror at the sight of the Red Indian. One appears to be intended for Lord North, the other wears a peer's robe. A demon looks out from under a tablecloth, holding the end of a cord which is attached to the ankle of the peer On the wall is either a picture or a vision of Temple Bar, with three heads on poles, suggesting the fate which awaits the heads of the Government, cf. Nos. 5135, 5661, 5969, &c.

On the table under which the demon crouches is a celestial globe, a skull and bones The fortune-teller and his clients are within a circle of cabalistic signs. On a shelf above his head are large books, the skeleton of a bird, and four bottles, in one of which is a body hanging from a gallows, in another a serpent-like monster

The *Whimsical Repository* prints appear in no other year but 1774, so that this almost certainly relates to the dissolution of parliament on 30 Sept. 1774.

$6\frac{5}{16} \times 9\frac{11}{16}$ in

5239 AN EMBLEMATICAL PILE

Emblematist Inv. et Sculp.

Publish'd Novr 7th 1774 Price 6^d

Engraving A pile of rotten timber, supporting a centre staff which stands on a cube-shaped stone block These timber props are lashed together with rope, but are splintered, broken, and worm-eaten From the broken centre staff hangs a tattered flag inscribed *Liberty* on which is a damaged cap of liberty. On the stone is an hour-glass, the sands of which are nearly run out, surrounded by a serpent The cube is inscribed *Time Shewith all Things* The supports of the drooping standard of liberty are inscribed

---

[1] These words partly cut off.

Magna Charta; Patriotism; Law; Liberty of Conscience; Religion (broken in half); *Liberty of the Press; Common Hall; Bill of Rights* (these last two are in good repair and represent the most radical body of the London Corporation and probably the Bill of Rights Society); *Juries; Honesty* (hanging by a splinter). From one of the posts hangs a broken pair of scales, emblem of Justice.

On the ground in the foreground is a piece of timber from the pile inscribed *Elections*; across it lies an axe inscribed *Bribery & Corruption* On the ground are also Britannia's broken shield, through a hole in which grows a thistle, emblem of Scottish influence; a torn *Map of England*, and a fragment on which is engraved a Tudor rose.

In the upper r. corner are clouds from which comes a hand holding a pair of scales, beneath which is engraved *1st Sam¹ 2d Chap: 3d, Verse*. ['Talk no more so exceeding proudly; let not arrogancy come out of your mouth: for the Lord is a God of knowledge, and by him actions are weighed.'] From the hand and scales come rays of light.

Parliament was dissolved on 30 Sept. 1774, and the new parliament met on 29 Nov. Cf. No 5240

$7\frac{7}{8} \times 6\frac{1}{4}$ in.

5240 THE CONSTITUTION OF ENGLAND. [n d. ? 1774]

Engraving Three sturdy tree-trunks stand against one another in the form of a tripod, bound by a ribbon inscribed *Respublica*. The centre one is surmounted by a crown, the others, one by a mitre over which is placed a baron's coronet, the other by a smaller crown which appears to represent the top of a sceptre From the centre hangs a pair of equally balanced scales, in each scale are three scrolls, inscribed respectively (l') *Religion, Law, Authority* and (r) *Liberty, Right, Obedience*.

Similar in the character of the design to No. 5239 and possibly intended as a counterblast to it.

$5\frac{1}{4} \times 3\frac{3}{4}$ in.

5241 THE BOSTONIANS IN DISTRESS.

[Philip Dawe?]

Plate II. London, Printed for R. Sayer, & J. Bennett, Map & Print-sellers, Nº 53 Fleet Street, as the Act directs, 19 Novʳ 1774.

Mezzotint. One of a series, see pp 169, 196–7, No. 5284. A cage inscribed *Boston* hangs from a branch of *Libert[y] Tree*. In it are ten hungry Bostonians being fed with fish by three men standing in a boat, at the side of the peninsula on which the tree stands. The men in the cage are lean with lank hair and of puritanic appearance Those in the front who have secured fish are thrusting them into their mouths, others with wide open mouths and clasped hands beg to be fed. They crouch forward to take the fish which are thrust between the bars in open boxes at the end of poles. One of the Bostonians stands in the centre with uplifted r. hand, holding out in his l. hand a paper inscribed: *They cried unto the Lord in their Trouble & he saved them out of their Distress Psal[m] cvii. 13*. He wears a minister's bands, and his expression and open-wide mouth shows that he is making a loud lamentation On the l a man who is eating a fish held on the end of a pole has thrust his hand through the bars, holding a large bundle of neatly folded documents inscribed *Promises*. On the r two men are fighting for a fish, one holds it tight, the other has seized him by the hair and tries to take it from him.

In the open boat at the foot of the tree are two baskets of fish on one of which is a paper inscribed *To —— from the Committee of ——*. Of the three men who stand in the boat holding out the fish, one (l.) wears a round hat, jacket, and striped sailor's trousers, another (c.) wears a round hat, apron, and striped jacket; the third wears a broad hat, dark coat, and loose breeches.

In the distance, behind the tree, on the sea-shore are British soldiers; a file of men with muskets over their shoulders drive off a flock of goats, the regimental band (three drums and two fifes) is playing Cannons pointed at 'Liberty Tree' are in a semicircle on the r. On the sea are four British men-of-war.

When the Port of Boston was closed (see No. 5230, &c.) many were in distress owing to lack of employment and the expense of conveying merchandise by land from Salem. Gifts of food, &c , were sent from all places on the continent, including a contribution of 'two hundred and seven quintals of codfish' from Marblehead, noted in the English press.

In the summer of 1774 Gage ordered some regiments of foot with artillery to be sent to Boston; they were encamped on the ground between the town and the narrow neck of ground, then called Boston Neck, connecting it with the mainland, and a guard was placed there to prevent desertion This was magnified into an attempt to cut the communication between Boston and its hinterland and to reduce the town by famine. Stedman, *History of the American War*, 1794, i 98. 'Liberty Tree', a rallying point for patriots, was cut down for fuel while the British were blockaded in Boston in the winter of 1775–6

Knowledge of America is shown by the depiction of the Bostonians as undergoing the punishment given in the Colonies to slaves convicted of capital offences who were thus imprisoned and left to starve to death The artist's irony seems directed against both sides, the English soldiers who direct their cannon at 'Liberty Tree', while the cage, symbol of slavery and barbarity, hangs on Liberty Tree

Reproduced R. T. Halsey, *The Boston Port Bill*, p. 172.

13 × 10 in.

5242 THE COLOSSUS OF THE NORTH; OR THE STRIDING BOREAS   [1 Dec. 1774]

Engraving From the *London Magazine*, xliii. 520 (folding plate) Lord North strides across a stream which flows from the door of Westminster Hall; floating down the stream is a crowd of members of parliament. North's feet are supported on two blocks inscribed *Tyranny* and *Venality*. In his r hand are three papers inscribed *Places; Pensions; Lottery Tickets*; in his l is a flaming torch inscribed *America*. By the stream on the r. stand two figures· Britannia, with shield and spear, holding out a paper inscribed: *Those that Should have been my Preservers have been my Destroyers*; and Wilkes (recently elected Lord Mayor) in civic gown and chain. He holds a broom towards the foremost of the floating members and by his hand is a label *I'll stem the Stream*.

Beneath the design is engraved:

See our Colossus strides with Trophies crown'd,
And Monsters in Corruption's Stream abound.

The plate illustrates 'A vision', headed by a quotation from a letter of Marvell (1665) 'The Parliament was never so embarrassed, beyond recovery We are all venal cowards except a few '

The elections of 1774 did not reduce North's majority; the new parliament met on 29 Nov.; Wilkes, returned again for Middlesex, took his seat without opposition.

This plate and the accompanying text appeared in the *Hibernian Magazine* for Dec. 1774 (1 Jan. 1775). Reproduced, J. T. Adams, *Revolutionary New England*, 1923, p. 420.

$5\frac{1}{8} \times 6\frac{9}{16}$ in.

5243 THE STA * * * MAN [Statesman] ON STILTS, OR A PRIME M * * * * * * R [Minister], IN HIS UNDRESS

Terry del et sculp.

Engrav'd for y^e Whimsical Repository, according to y^e Act, Decr 1. 1774.

Engraving. A grotesque monster on stilts It has two heads, one of an ass, the other of a rat, its body and tail resemble those of a hog. A ribbon and star indicate Lord North. Attached to each stilt is half a lottery wheel on which is inscribed (l) *Museum Lott'ry G 17 .. ,* (r) *State Lottery R 74.* (The two halves together reading *G R 1774*) The stilts stand on the prostrate body of Britannia, lying across her shield, and the cap of liberty on its staff On the ground are also flotsam from a wreck: a barrel, a bale of goods, a wheel, a broken anchor On the r appears the gable end of a shored-up but tottering public-house, the broken sign of which is a king holding an orb and sceptre inscribed, *GR II.* Behind, dismantled ships lie close to the shore, brooms at their mast-head show that they are for sale. Beneath the title is engraved,

A Lyon for Paws, for a Noddle an Ass,
A Crocodile's Heart, and a duplicate Face;
Voracious as Death, he's docile as a Hog;
Ambitious, yet fawns with the Foot of a Dog.

The lottery wheel indicates that North's finance depends on lotteries. The 'Museum Lott'ry' is that of James Cox, who obtained a private Bill in 1773 to enable him to dispose of his collection of mechanical and jewelled toys by lottery. It was on show in Spring Gardens, 'Cox's Museum' being one of the sights of the town, cf No. 5275 This lottery had no relation to national finance.

$6\frac{5}{8} \times 4\frac{1}{16}$ in.

5244 THE COURT COTILLION, OR THE PREMIERS NEW PARL * * * * * T JIG.

Terry del. et sculp.

Engrav'd for the Whimsical Repository, According to y^e Act, Decr 1. 1774.

Engraving Lord North (l.), plays the fiddle smiling while three men circle round a sign-post surmounted by a crown; its three arms are inscribed *America, England*, and *Scotland*; the post is inscribed *Politicks for 75*. It is supported on the hub of a wheel which is held in the r. hands of the three men, who walk round it, stripped to the waist, each applying a cat-o'-nine-tails to the back of the man in front. They are respectively America, as a Red Indian, with a feathered head-dress and a girdle of feathers, England as a sailor in trousers, and Scotland in a kilt, and with a ferocious expression. Behind stands Britannia (r.) in tears, leaning on her shield and on the staff supporting the cap of liberty, while she points to the three men. Beneath the title is engraved,

> *Rouze, Britons, Rouze! behold thy staggering State,*
> *Discord destroys you, Concord makes you great;*
> *While thus at variance, Brother scourges Brother,*
> *Friends disunited must destroy each other.*

$6\frac{1}{2} \times 4\frac{1}{2}$ in.

5245 THE TWO JACKS

Pubᵈ as the Act Directs 1774.

Engraving. The two Jacks, one (l) emerging from a jack boot, the other (r) from a funnel in the neck of a bottle, face each other. The boot, the emblem of Bute, see No. 3860, &c., is decorated with a thistle and a scroll inscribed *Nemo me impune Lacessit*. The end of the scroll is forked and represents the tail of *Jack Major*, a winged demon with horns standing in the boot.

Jack Minor, Wilkes, wears his Lord Mayor's gown and chain. His bottle is decorated with the City arms, across his funnel is a scroll inscribed with his motto, *Arcui non meo confide* [*sic*]. As the bottle-imp, see Nos 3022–7, 5275, he is identified with impudent imposture. Bute says to Wilkes *A' Jocky are ye there Lad. Weel Weel Ye'll soon be flat in Y'er G'ued Auld Cause nu, sa i'll e'en bottle ye up, and keep ye till bresk anu 'tull froth & fume on oor side the Question; what says tull't Jock.* Wilkes answers: *Say, why if I crack there is 500£ pʳ Ann for Poor Jack (you know) if my bottle holds tight, if that fails me I'll apply to you—you Understand me—I'm sinking going—going farewell.*

In the centre between the two Jacks is engraved. *Biennial Nᵒˢ*

$$Anno \left\{ {1774 \atop 1775} \right\} \text{N}° 45$$

The year 1774–5 was that of Wilkes's mayoralty.

Beneath the boot and the bottle, on a minute scale, are three labouring men wearing aprons, they are huzzaing with uplifted arms, two wave their hats. They are inscribed *Wa . . . king Dreamers* and are numbered *1, 2,* and *3. 1* (r.) says. *Huzza our Jack for ever, every Pint pot is to hold a Gallon my boys, down with the free booters. 2* (l) says: *Ay and every Quartern loaf is to fill a Bushel, down with the Rents & Taxes my Boys. 3* (c.) says: *they shan't Rob & murder us again I warrant me, have at 'em.*

Beneath the design is engraved:

> *The Gold Chain's won, without the wooden leg:*
> *How long for this, have we been big with egg!*
> *Wise too the Choise pronounc'd & well approv'd*
> *And Jack, by Scotch, & English both, belov'd;*

Religious Railers (mongrels) still Rail on;
Our Jack on Record Stands, an upright John.
Britons the joyfull, happy Æra boast,
In which ye have two Jacks to Rule the Roast.
One Cooks the Cab. [Cabinet] & one the Sapient City
We're finely cook'd indeed! 'tis vastly pretty!
Firm to his int'rest each with Zeal Abides,
The Secret Motive gain on both their Sides.

'Gued Auld Cause', the watchword of the republicans under the Pro-
tectorate of Cromwell, is an allusion to the republican sympathies of the
patriots. The election of Wilkes as Mayor in 1774 after being rejected in
1772 and 1773 by the Court of Aldermen, and his return unopposed for
Middlesex in 1774, coincide with the virtual end of his political importance,
though his house in 1774–5 was a meeting-place for English, American, and
French supporters of the Colonies, see No. 5246. For other Wilkite satires
ct. Nos 4326, 4887, 5103, 5130, 5131.

$6\frac{7}{16} \times 8\frac{3}{4}$ in. (pl)

5246 THE FRENCH LAWYER IN LONDON.

Pub^d Dec^br 10 1774

Engraving in the manner of a chalk drawing probably by a French artist.
A companion print to No 5247 A man-monster of repulsive appearance,
wearing the bands of a lawyer, and a long cloak which trails on the ground.
A pair of pistols is stuck through his belt He has pointed animal's ears,
on his head are open pamphlets among which serpents writhe. His feet
and hands are the paws of a lion or tiger; he has a bushy tail. In his l. paw
he holds by the hair a woman's head and a pen; in his r. (appearing from
under his cloak) are scales loaded with coins, a dagger, the hilt of a sword,
to which is attached a seal (?). Beneath the design is engraved: *The Body
Soul & Mind of the Gazetier Cuirassé.*

A symbolical portrait of the swindler and blackmailer Charles Theveneau,
who called himself Chevalier de Morande. Having fled from France on
account of a libel he had written, he arrived in London destitute, and lived
on vice followed by blackmail. He published in 1771 an attack on the Court
of France called *Le Gazetier Cuirassé* and followed this up by other scurrilous but well-informed pamphlets on Court scandals in France. In 1774
he had ready for publication *Mémoires secrets d'une Femme Publique*, i e.
Mme du Barry, compared with which he said the *Gazetier Cuirassé* was
rose-water. The woman's head in the print appears to be that of the
du Barry. The French Court made repeated efforts to secure Morande,
but failed. In Mar. 1774, Beaumarchais came to London and negotiated
the destruction of the whole edition for 32,000 livres and a pension of
4,000 livres, evidently symbolized by the money in the scales. See P.
Robiquet, *Theveneau de Morande*, Paris, 1882. Beaumarchais and Morande
at this date used to meet supporters of the American Colonies at the house
of Wilkes. Kite, *Beaumarchais and American Independence*, 1918, ii. p. 56.

$8\frac{1}{8} \times 5\frac{1}{2}$ in.

5247 THE WICKED IN TRIUMPH

Pub^d Decr 20. 1774

Engraving in the manner of a chalk drawing. A companion print to

No 5246 by the same artist. Two women stand, one in each of two baskets which are fixed pannier-wise across an ass. Each is draped in a sheet and the nearer figure has a rope round her neck. Between their heads is a large open volume, one page inscribed *Le Gazetier Cuirassé*, the other, *Memoire dune Fille Publique*. In front of the book is the head of Medusa, writhing with serpents, two serpents coming from its mouth. On the back of the ass is a wheel probably signifying that Morande, the writer of the two books whose titles are given, deserved to be broken on the wheel. The ass is covered with a voluminous drapery under the saddle, and from its nose come barbed darts. Behind is a gallows, and in the background on the l. a windmill. Beneath the design is inscribed,

If you know the Gazitier, You will know the Ass

An attack on Theveneau de Morande. In 1774 his blackmailing of the French Court had been signally successful, see No 5246. The head of Medusa in the design is taken from the frontispiece to *Le Gazetier Cuirassé; ou Anecdotes Scandaleuses de la Cour de France.* (B.M.L 1195, d 6 (1))
$8\frac{1}{4} \times 5\frac{3}{16}$ in.

PERSONAL SATIRES

5248–5260

Series of Tête-à-Tête portraits.

5248 N° XXXIV. PRETTY BETSY G——N [1 Jan. 1774]
N° XXXV. THE NAUTICAL LOVER.

Engraving. *Town and Country Magazine*, v. 625. Two bust portraits in oval frames illustrate 'Histories of the Tête-à-Tête annexed . . .'. An account of Commodore John Byron (1723–86), afterwards Vice-admiral and grandfather of Lord Byron. 'Betsy' was a servant in his household, whom he now entertains in a genteel manner in lodgings.

Ovals 2¾ × 2⅜ in. B M.L , P.P. 5442 b.

5249 N° XXXVII. M^RS R——N. [Jan. 1774]
N° XXXVIII. THE MACARONI PARSON.

Engraving. *Town and Country Magazine*, v. 681. (Supplement.) Two bust portraits in oval frames illustrate 'Histories of the Tête-à-Tête annexed . . .'. An account of Mr. D——, a popular preacher, who having been imprisoned in the King's Bench for debt now preaches at C—— [Charlotte] Chapel. He is the notorious Dr William Dodd, executed for forgery, 27 June 1777. M^rs R——n is the young wife of a rich merchant, whom he visits without exciting the jealousy of his wife or her husband

Ovals, 2¾ × 2⅜ in. B.M.L., P.P. 5442 b

5250 N° II MISS B——Y [Vol VI]
N° III. LORD LE D——

Publish'd as the Act directs, by A. Hamilton Junr near St Johns Gate, Feb. 1. 1774.

Engraving. *Town and Country Magazine*, vi. 9. Two bust portraits in oval frames illustrate 'Histories of the Tête-à-Tête annexed . . .'. An account of Sir Francis Dashwood, notorious as the founder of 'The Franciscans' of Medmenham Abbey, and his mistress. The barony of le Despencer was granted to him on his removal from the Chancellorship of the Exchequer in 1763.

Ovals, 2¾ × 2½ in. B.M L., P.P. 5442 b.

5251 N° IV MISS S——R. [Vol. VI]
N° V. THE HIBERNIAN DEMOSTHENES.

Published as the Act directs by A. Hamilton Junr near St John's Gate Mar^h 1. 1774.

Engraving. *Town and Country Magazine*, vi. 65 Two bust portraits in oval frames illustrate 'Histories of the Tête-à-Tête annexed . . .'. This repeats, or invents, scandals about Burke, including his supposed education at St Omer, which after the Gordon Riots caused him to be termed a Jesuit, in which guise he was often caricatured by Gillray, see No. 6026 &c Miss S——, his alleged mistress, is 'the daughter of an American Merchant'.

Ovals, $2\frac{5}{8} \times 2\frac{5}{16}$ in.; $2\frac{3}{4} \times 2\frac{3}{8}$ in.　　　　　B.M L., P.P. 5442 b.

5252 N° VI. MISS H——TER.
N° VII SIR C—— B——P.

Published as the Act directs by A Hamilton Junr near St John's Gate April 1. 1774.

Engraving. *Town and Country Magazine*, vi. 121. Two bust portraits in oval frames illustrate 'Histories of the Tête-à-Tête annexed; or, Memoirs of Sir C—— B——, and Sophia H——r'. An account of the amours of Sir C., an elderly man who has not a seat in parliament 'tho' his rank and fortune entitle him to a representation for a county'.

He is Sir Cecil Bishopp of Parham, Sussex, 6th Bart , M P. for Penryn 1727–34, for Boroughbridge 1755–68, m. 1726, Anne, 2nd d. of Viscount Falmouth, d. 1775. G.E.C. *Complete Baronetage*, i. 156.

Ovals, $2\frac{5}{8} \times 2\frac{1}{4}$ in.　　　　　B.M.L., P.P. 5442 b.

5253 N^o X. M^{RS} G——S.
N° XI. SIR TIMOTHY TALLBOY

London. Published by A. Hamilton Junr near St John's Gate 1st May 1774.

Engraving. *Town and Country Magazine*, vi 177. Two bust portraits in oval frames, an elderly lady with a minute dog under her arm, in profile to the r., a thin elderly man in a tie-wig in profile to the l. This illustrates 'Histories of the Tête-à-Tête annexed . . .'. An account of 'Long' Sir Thomas Robinson of Rokeby (? 1700–77), who had been Governor of Barbados. M^{rs} G——s is said to be his present mistress, a short stout woman, 'past her bloom'; see No 5116. Sir Timothy Tallboy is a character in Foote's play *The Nabob* (first played 1772).

Ovals $2\frac{5}{8} \times 2\frac{1}{4}$ in.; $2\frac{11}{16} \times 2\frac{5}{16}$ in.　　　　　B.M.L., P.P. 5442 b.

5254 N° XIII. MISS G——　　　　　Vol. VI.
N° XIV. THE MARTIAL ORATOR.

Publish'd as the Act directs, by A. Hamilton Junr near St John's Gate May 1. 1774.

Engraving. *Town and Country Magazine*, vi. 233. Two bust portraits in oval frames illustrate 'Histories of the Tête-à-Tête annexed . . .'. A flattering account of Colonel Barré, M P. for W——b [Wycomb]. Miss G. is a Scottish girl whose parents were reduced to poverty by the '45. Barré is said to have found her contemplating suicide and to have made her his mistress.

Ovals, $2\frac{5}{8} \times 2\frac{5}{16}$ in ; $2\frac{5}{8} \times 2\frac{1}{4}$ in.　　　　　B.M L., P.P. 5442 b.

5255 Nᵒ XVI Mᴿˢ SW——N

Nᵒ XVII BLOOMSBURY DICK

Published as the Act directs by A. Hamilton Junʳ near Sᵗ John's Gate July 1, 1774.

Engraving *Town and Country Magazine*, vi. 289 Two bust portraits in oval frames illustrate 'Histories of the Tête-à-Tête annexed . . .' Richard Rigby (1722–88) and his alleged mistress. Rigby, as one of the Bedford Whigs and a particular adherent of the Duke of Bedford, is called Bloomsbury Dick, the duke having been called Bloomsbury Jack, see No. 4842

Ovals $2\frac{5}{8} \times 2\frac{3}{8}$ in ; $2\frac{5}{8} \times 2\frac{1}{4}$.   B M L., P.P. 5442 b.

5256 Nᵒ XIX Mᴿˢ H——K

Nᵒ XX THE SUBMISSIVE DUELLIST

Published as the Act directs by A Hamilton Junʳ near Sᵗ Johns Gate August 1ˢᵗ 1774

Engraving. *Town and Country Magazine*, vi. 345. Two bust portraits in oval frames illustrate 'Histories of the Tête-à-Tête annexed . . '. The 'submissive duellist' is 'Captain S.', so-called from an encounter in Flanders with the notorious fire-eater Fighting Fitzgerald, arising out of the Vauxhall Affray, see No. 5198, &c. He is Captain Scawen, who actually behaved with bravery, see *Memoirs of George Robert Fitzgerald Esq., 1786*. Mʳˢ Horneck, with whom Scawen is said to have eloped to Brussels, is the wife of Captain H   See Gibbon, *Private Letters*, 1896, i, p 207

Ovals, $2\frac{11}{16} \times 2\frac{5}{16}$ in.; $2\frac{5}{8} \times 2\frac{1}{4}$ in.   B.M.L., P.P. 5442 b

5257 Nᵒ XXV. Mᴿˢ E——

Nᵒ XXVI LORD V——

Published as the Act directs by A. Hamilton Junʳ near Sᵗ John's Gate Septʳ 1. 1774.

Engraving. *Town and Country Magazine*, vi. 401. Two bust portraits in oval frames illustrate 'Histories of the Tête-à-Tête annexed; or, Memoirs of L—— V—— and Mʳˢ E——t'. An account of Arthur Annesley, Viscount Valentia (1744–1816) and of Grace Dalrymple Eliot or Elliott, afterwards known as Dally the Tall, see *D.N.B.* Her husband, Dr Eliot, is collecting evidence for a suit of crim. con., but she and Lord V 'do not now live upon the most agreeable terms'. Early in 1775 there was a rupture and Grace began her career of fashionable demi-rep H. L. Bleackley, *Ladies Frail and Fair*, 1909, p 207. See No. 5321 and index.

Ovals, $2\frac{3}{4} \times 2\frac{1}{4}$ in   B.M.L., P.P. 5442 b.

5258 Nᵒ XXVIII Mᴿˢ P——

Nᵒ XXIX LORD A.——

Publish'd as the Act directs by A. Hamilton Junʳ near Sᵗ Johns Gate. Octʳ 1. 1774.

Engraving *Town and Country Magazine*, vi. 457 Two bust portraits in oval frames illustrate 'Histories of the Tête-à-Tête annexed . . .'. An account of George Neville, Lord Abergavenny, and his alleged mistress, the daughter of a City contractor, who became an established demi-rep on her liaison with Lord A.

Ovals, $2\frac{3}{4} \times 2\frac{1}{4}$ in.   B.M.L., P.P. 5442 b.

5259 Nᵒ XXXI. Mᴿˢ M——N
        Nᵒ XXXII. GENERAL H——

*Published as the Act directs by A. Hamilton Junʳ near Sᵗ Johns Gate
Novʳ 1. 1774*

Engraving. *Town and Country Magazine*, vi 513. Two bust portraits in oval frames illustrate 'Histories of the Tête-à-Tête annexed . . .'. He wears a military hat, sash, aiguilettes, and gorget. An account of Edward Harvey, M.P. for Harwich, Adjutant-General and Major-General. His mistress is said to be Mᴿˢ M——tin, a professed courtesan and adventuress, *née* P——tt, 'sister to the renowned baronet who presented the Flintshire petition'.

This *tête-à-tête* appears to be published in order to cast yet more mud at the Perrott family, see accounts of Sir Richard Perrott (d 1796) under Nos. 4364, 4365, 4399. See also the scandalous *Life, Adventures and Amours of Sir R. P.* 1770; *D.N.B.* under Robert Perrot (d. 1550) and Burke's *Peerage and Baronetage*. The anti-Ministerial Press attacked him violently in 1770 because he presented a loyal address from the County of Flint to the Prince of Wales.

Ovals, $2\frac{11}{16} \times 2\frac{1}{4}$ in.   B.M.L., P.P. 5442 b

5260 Nᵒ XXXIV Mᴿˢ F——R
        Nᵒ XXXV LORD C——M

*Published as the Act directs by A. Hamilton Junʳ near Sᵗ John's Gate
Decʳ 1. 1774*

Engraving. *Town and Country Magazine*, vi. 569. Two bust portraits in oval frames illustrate 'Histories of the Tête-à-Tête annexed; or, Memoirs of Lord C——gh——m and Mᴿˢ F——r'. An account of the amours of Henry, Viscount Conyngham, d. 1781.

Ovals, $2\frac{11}{16} \times 2\frac{5}{16}$ in.   B.M.L, P.P. 5442 b.

Nine prints from a series issued by Darly continued from No. 5176.

5261 V 3. 22. SIGNOR GRUNTINELLI · PLAYING ON A NEW
        INSTRUMENT (CALL'D A SWINETTA).

Pubᵈ Accorᵍ to Act Janʸ 1. 1774 by M Darly 39 Strand.

Engraving. W L caricature portrait of a man playing the musette or pastoral oboe with a double pipe and drone resembling bag-pipes. His attitude is that of a man seated on a high stool, but there is no stool and he is chiefly supported by a wooden leg formed of one of the two pipes of his instrument. The bag of the musette, held under his r. arm, is a pig; he holds the animal's hind leg, which forms the second pipe, as if playing on it; in his r. hand he holds its tail. He turns his head in profile to the r. towards an open book of music on a music-stand. He is elderly and wears a curious tie-wig terminating in two corkscrew ringlets.

'Swinetta' appears to be a name invented to suit the travesty of the musette as a pig; the name of the player has probably been similarly altered to 'Gruntinelli'.

5261 A

Reissued (n.d.) with an altered publication line: *Printed for Robert Sayer, Fleet Street* (in book of Sayer's 'Drolls').
$8\frac{1}{2} \times 6\frac{3}{8}$ in.

5262 V. 3. 20. A JOURNEY TO LONDON

Pub⁴ Jan⁽ 11ᵗʰ 1774 by M Darly 39 Strand

Engraving. A middle-aged lady (caricatured) riding (l. to r.) preceded by her servant who carries two trunks behind him on his saddle. She wears the riding-habit of the period and a round hat with a feather. She rides with a single rein in her r. hand, in her l. is a whip. The horses are ambling very slowly, both riders are using their whips. Similar in character to No. 5266.
$5\frac{7}{8} \times 9\frac{3}{16}$ in.

5263 V. 3. 18. A KNIGHT OF THE SPIT.

Pub⁴ by M Darly Jan 20 1774

Engraving. W.L. portrait of a naval officer standing in profile to the r. His hair is in a small pig-tail queue; his hat is under his r. arm. In his r. hand is a telescope; in his l. a long cane. He stands in front of a low gun-embrasure behind which is the sea, with ships at anchor; in the distance is the Isle of Wight.

Probably Admiral Thomas Pye, commander-in-chief at Portsmouth 1770–73, knighted during the review at Spithead, 24 June 1773. *D.N.B*
$8\frac{3}{4} \times 6\frac{1}{4}$ in.

5264 V. 3. 19 A WELCH K——T ON THE LOOK OUT FOR A WIFE.
(BATH) by an Officer of the Guards. [M. Darly?]

Pub⁴ Jan⁽ 21. 1774 by M Darly 39 Strand

Engraving W L. portrait of a stout man standing in profile to the r. His r. hand is in his breeches pocket, his l. is thrust into his waistcoat; his hat is under his r arm.

Identified by Mʳ Hawkins as Sir Watkin Lewes.
$8\frac{1}{8} \times 6\frac{3}{8}$ in.

V. 3. 17. BARON FORCHETTA, AFTER A BETT OF FIFTY.
See No. 4651—24 Jan. 1774

[M Darly, *fec.*] 'Baron' Neuman.

5265 MY-SELF
[1 Feb. 1774]

Printed for Robert Sayer, Nᵒ 53 Fleet Street.

Engraving. A reissue with a different publication line of a plate published by Darly and dated as above which was No 10, vol. 3 of the series issued

1772–4. A fashionably-dressed young man, smiling fatuously, walks towards the spectators down a straight grass ride cut through trees. Beneath the title four lines of verse are engraved, beginning,

As I walk'd by my-self, I talk'd to my-self; and thus my-self said to me·

For the same subject differently treated, see No. 4551 (1777).

$7\frac{1}{2} \times 6\frac{1}{2}$ in. Book of Sayer's 'Drolls'.

V. 3. 15. AN ENGLISH MACARONI AT PARIS CHANGEING ENGLISH GUINEAS FOR SILVER. See No 4650—17 Mar. 1774

5266 V. 3. 11. GEORGE'S DELIGHT OR NECK OR NOTHING.

Pub as the act directs by M Darly 39 Strand Ap¹ 1. 1774

Engraving Two men ride in profile to the r. The one in front is fashionably dressed with a cockaded hat, in his l. hand is a cane. The forelegs of the horse are raised as if galloping, but both hind legs are on the ground The man behind, who is partly cut off by the margin, wears a round cap and is perhaps the servant of the other His horse appears to be walking. A wall, above which are trees, is indicated behind the riders. Similar in character to No. 5262.

$5\frac{3}{4} \times 9\frac{1}{8}$ in.

5267 V. 3. 14. THE CONSULTATION

Pub⁴ April 27. 1774 by M Darly 39 Strand

Engraving. A man with the profile of an animal, perhaps a sheep, wearing gown and bands, holds a large tie-wig of the kind worn by judges in his l. hand, the fingers of his r. hand are held out as if in calculation, he looks at himself in an ornately framed oval mirror on the wall with an expression of singular imbecility An open door in the back wall shows rows of books in a book-case: on its lintel stands a bust. An oval (H.L.) portrait hangs on the l. of the door, it is of a man in wig and bands, probably the subject of the caricature. Two high-backed chairs are the only furniture of the room Beneath the title is engraved,

To Wig—or not to Wig
That is the Question.

$5\frac{7}{8} \times 8\frac{7}{8}$ in.

5268 A NUN OF THE SIXTH CLASS.

Pub⁴ Oct ͬ 24 1774 by M Darly Strand.

Engraving. Though without a number it belongs to a series of portraits of prostitutes, see No. 5177. A young woman (H.L.) in profile to the r., very slim and erect She wears a small flat hat on her elaborately-dressed hair and a cape over her shoulders, in the front of which is a large nosegay.

$5 \times 3\frac{3}{4}$ in. Fairholt's 'Collection for Costume', i. fo. 116.

5269 NOSEE

Pub⁴ by M Darly 39 Strand Jan 1. 1774.

Engraving. T Q L portrait slightly caricatured, of 'Cervetto', or Giacomo Bassevi the 'cellist (1680–1783), noted for his large nose, playing the 'cello

He sits looking downwards and to the r An open book of music, from which he is not reading, is on a stand behind his l arm

When he played in the orchestra at Drury Lane the occupants of the gallery used to call 'play up Nosey'. Grove, *Musical Dict.*

Perhaps adapted from Zoffany's portrait of which there is a mezzotint by Picot published 16 Apr. 1771 Chaloner Smith, iii 978.

This print was reissued in a book of Darly's caricatures dated 1 Jan. 1776, see No. 5369, but does not appear to belong to a series.

$5\frac{1}{16} \times 4\frac{3}{16}$ in.

5270 THE HARROGATE, MEEK-ARONY   [M Darly?][1]

Pub by M Darly as the Act directs May 14th 1774.

Engraving. Bust portrait (caricature) in an oval of a very corpulent man, his enormously heavy jowl sunk between broad high shoulders. He is almost full face, looking to the r. His wig and features are small by comparison with his chin, neck, and body.

Probably portrait of a man called Meek. It was reissued in a composite volume dated 1 Jan. 1776, see No. 5369, but does not appear to belong to a series.

$3\frac{7}{16} \times 3\frac{3}{4}$ in.

A MEEK-ARONI HORNPIPE—   See No 4708—24 May 1774

Pub. Darly. W.L. portrait of the subject of No. 5270.
      (Catalogued as 'Mack-aroni . . .'.)

THE WESTMINSTER MACARONI.   See No. 4655—3 Nov. 1774

Pub. Darly.

5271 OLD HAMAN THE NORTHAMPTON-LAMP-LIGHTER DRAWN FROM LIFE   [1 Jan. 1774][2]

I. Read pinxt   T. Roberts Sculpr Northton

Engraving. A clumsy figure holding a ladder across his l. shoulder, in his r. hand is a lighted candle-lantern. He wears a cloak with a hood drawn over his head, above which is a hat with a brim extending into a flap at the back, his stockings and coat are in holes. From his waist hangs a pair of scissors. On the ground are a broom and a can with a handle and spout, with a hole in its side. On the print is etched,

> *His Ability & Agility will make a Man Laugh*
> *As he lights 18 Lamps in an Hour and a half.*

$7\frac{5}{8} \times 10\frac{5}{8}$ in

5272 [MATTHEW WYLDBORE M P. FOR PETERBOROUGH.]
                              Plate 2 [Oct 1774]

Photographic reproduction of an engraving. A man (l) from whose hat sprout large stag's horns, leads a large wild boar, by a rope through a ring

---

[1] With etchings by Darly
[2] Written in a contemporary hand

in its nose. On the boar a woman is seated wearing a cloak and hood; she carries a spaniel in her l. arm   From each side of the branching horns hangs a money-bag, that on the l. inscribed *£500, 1768*, that on the r. *£1000 1774*. Beneath the design is engraved, *And he arose, and took Jesse, and her Lap-Dog by night and departed unto the Land of Forty-Acres*

Wyldbore was M.P for Peterborough   the money-bags imply that his election cost him £500 in 1768, and £1,000 in 1774   A note attached to the photograph states that 15 Mar is called Wyldbore day in Peterborough, as Wyldbore (d. 15 Mar. 1781) left a bequest to the bellringers of St. John's Church for a peal of bells on the anniversaries of his death   He bequeathed money to all who voted for him at his election in 1774 who should attend his body to the grave and who would accept it.

$3\frac{3}{4} \times 4\frac{3}{4}$ in.

5273 A ROTATION OFFICE

H.W. [Rowlandson.]

Pub June 8th 1774 by H. Humphry Bond Street

Acquatint. A London justice of peace seated behind a table in his office, his hands clasped. On his r. and l. are three men holding their hats and canes, who may be either justices or visitors. At the end of the table (l.), sits the justice's clerk writing with his l. hand. On the wall over the presiding justice's head is a placard, *Robbery, Murder .   Beware of Justice.*

The Middlesex Quarter Sessions, in order to reform the abuse of the private justice shop kept by trading justices, established Rotation Offices for the different districts of London in imitation of Bow Street, where certain magistrates (one or more at a time) sat in rotation. The best-known was that of Saunders Welch in Litchfield Street, which Dr Johnson attended all one winter (Boswell, *Life of Johnson*, iii. 216, iv. 184). The figure wearing glasses, on the justice's l., has a marked resemblance to Johnson. That the Litchfield Street office is depicted is probable. Angelo records a visit paid by himself and Rowlandson to 'an office then in Litchfield Street', to identify a man who had robbed Rowlandson. *Reminiscences*, ed 1904, ii. 246-7 The initials H.W. show that the subject was suggested by Henry Wigstead. Grego, *Rowlandson*, i. 96.

$4\frac{3}{4} \times 7$ in.

5274 THE VILLAGE DOCTOR.

H.W. [Rowlandson.]

Pubd June 8th by H. Humphry Bond Street

Engraving (coloured and aquatinted impressions). A village doctor's house indicated by the sign of a pestle and mortar over the door, and by the placard, *Probe Surgeo[n and] Man Midwife*. From a casement window above the door the doctor in night-cap and shirt leans out, shaking his fist at a man who has knocked him up and is standing below, gaping with astonishment at the doctor's anger. The doctor holds his breeches in his r. hand   A wall (l) with trees and a building behind it and low railings in front, complete the design.

The initials H W. show that the subject was suggested by Henry Wigstead. Grego, *Rowlandson*, i. 96-7 (reproduction)

$8\frac{7}{8} \times 7\frac{1}{4}$ in.

5275 MODERN MOONSHINE, OR THE WONDERS OF GREAT BRITAIN.

Design'd & Engrav'd by G. Terry, Paternoster Row. Engrav'd for the Whimsical Repository Septr 1st 1774. Publish'd According to Act of Parliament.

Engraving. A scene on the sea-shore. A hoven cow, that is, a cow dangerously distended by eating green food, is being operated upon by a man who stands on a raised platform and pierces her flank with a pole; in his r. hand is a curved pipe for the injection of smoke. Three country-people and a child gape in astonishment holding up their hands; a fat alderman in a furred gown does the same; from his pocket hangs a paper inscribed, *Nine Days he liv'd in Clover*. On the r. three doctors or apothecaries are attending an emaciated and seemingly-dead woman (r.), who lies on straw, dressed only in a shift: one puffs smoke from a tobacco-pipe up her nostrils, another applies a pair of bellows, the third listens through an ear-trumpet. It appears that while the cow suffers from a surfeit, the woman dies of starvation. On the ground lies the hat of one of the doctors, in which is a letter, *To Mr Blake Plymoth*. Three spectators (l.) watch the efforts of the doctors: one, an oriental, wearing a turban and draperies, holds out his hands in astonishment; he appears to represent the wisdom of the East (or the noble savage) confronted with the effects of English civilization. His two companions, fashionably dressed Englishmen, look on unmoved.

Behind the sick woman (r) is the wall of a building, probably a theatrical booth, along it runs a narrow gallery where Punch is strutting; he points to a placard on which is a representation of the bottle-imp emerging from his bottle, the great hoax of the century, see Nos. 3022-7, 5245. Beneath the bottle is a placard, *Subscriptions taken in her^e for reducing the price of provision^s*. Other placards on the booth are inscribed, *Marybone Gardens Fete Champetre*; *M^r R——s Letters from ye Dead*, this is behind the dead woman; *Hearing Trumpets on a new Construction*, behind the doctor with the ear-trumpet; *Cox's perpetual motion, or the Elephant & Nabob*, an allusion to Cox's Museum, see No. 5243, his jewelled clockwork toys had been destined for an Indian prince; they are described in what Walpole calls 'immortal lines' in Mason's *Epistle to Shelburne*, see Mason's *Satirical Poems*, ed. P. Toynbee, 1926, pp. 29, 112, 122, see No. 5243. At this placard an oafish countryman (r) is gaping while a boy picks his pocket. In the background is the sea; on the beach is a boat raised on stocks but already breaking up; this is inscribed *The New Adelphi*. The building of the Adelphi had been an unprofitable speculation, partly owing to the financial crisis of 1773, and the Adam brothers obtained a private Act in that year to enable them to dispose of the new buildings by a lottery, which took place in 1774. Across the water on the further side of a bay is a town inscribed *A View of Plymouth*. A rope extends from a church steeple on the extreme l , behind the spectators, to a distant spire in Plymouth, down this a man is gliding.

A satire on the distresses, high food-prices, and financial failures of 1773-4, with some special application to Plymouth, where possibly 'Mr Blake' and 'M^r R——s' are niggardly parish officers, who have allowed a poor woman to starve to death. Cf. No. 5233, also a satire on social injustice.

$6\frac{5}{16} \times 9\frac{7}{8}$ in.

5276 THE GALLANT OUTWITTED. [1 Jan. 1774]

Engraving. *Covent Garden Magazine*. The interior of a barn. A woman, on the top of piled-up corn, has just overthrown a ladder, from which a fashionably dressed man is falling. A pig runs from behind the ladder.
$5\frac{1}{2} \times 3\frac{5}{8}$ in.

THE PAINTER SUBMITTING HIS PICTURE TO THE EXAMINA-TION OF CONNOISSEURS AND ANTIQUARIANS

See No. 2008—Jan. 1774

From the *Sentimental Magazine*, i. 505.

5277 THE COLLEGE BUCK. [1 Nov. 1774]

Engraving. *Hibernian Magazine*, iv. 567. A young man, far from sober, supports himself by resting his r. hand on the top of a post; in his l hand he holds a handkerchief on which is slung a large key. He wears a hat, is plainly but fashionably dressed, wearing bands instead of a cravat In the background are (r.) buildings of Trinity College, Dublin, on the l. a tavern, with its signboard and dangling bunch of grapes, is partly visible. The plate illustrates 'The College-Buck A Character' in the form of a mono-logue, from which it appears that he has left his gown in some house of ill-fame, and that the key is 'a devilish good weapon on a dark night, in a street wrangle or a gutter fray'. For Dublin 'bucks' at this time, see Buck Whaley's *Memoirs*, 1906, p 13.

$6\frac{7}{8} \times 4\frac{7}{16}$ in. B.M.L., P.P. 6154 k.

5278 THE PANTHEON, A POEM.

London. Printed for J. Williams at No 39, Fleet Street. 1774. Price Half-a-Crown.

Engraving. Title-page to a set of scurrilous verses attacking well-known people by name. The interior of the Pantheon with a number of figures: a centaur (r), ladies fashionably dressed, two men (one with a ribbon and star) with goat's legs, a parson in gown and bands ogling a lady, a group of three men (l.), one with a goat's head, another with a fox's head The foot of the third rests on a paper inscribed *Irish Protest*. Among the persons attacked are Count Haslang (H——g), see No. 4834, Lady Grosvenor (G——s——r), and Lady Ligonier (L——g——r).

In the centre of the upper edge of the design is a trophy composed of a scourge and a birch tied with ribbon.

A copy of the book is in the Print Department.

$5\frac{1}{8} \times 5\frac{5}{8}$ in.

Six prints after Bunbury etched and published by J. Bretherton.

5279 MUTUAL ACCUSATION.

Mr Bunbury del. *Js Bretherton f*

Publish'd by Bretherton 3d January 1774.

Engraving. Two quack doctors (l) are having a heated altercation in a street or square outside their respective houses From the corner of a house on the l hangs a sign, *Dr Walker's veritable antiscorbutic Pills. Beware of*

Impostors. From the house on the r. a sign projects, *True antiscorbutic Pills.* The doctors wear large wigs and swords, and carry three-cornered hats. One (l.) holds in his hand a medicine-bottle, behind them are two dogs fighting Their wives (r.) are fighting violently, one (l) has seized the other by the hair and is kicking her. Behind them (r) two cats with arched backs are spitting at each other. In the upper part of the print (c.) is a shield with two ducks, and beneath is the motto· *Quack Quack Quack.* Beneath the design is etched:

> *When once you've told & cant recall a Lye*
> *Boldly persist in't or your Fame will die*
> *Learn this ye Wives, with unrelenting Claws*
> *Or right or wrong, Assert your husbands cause.*

$8\frac{7}{61} \times 11\frac{1}{2}$ in.

THE HOPES OF THE FAMILY . . .   See No 4727—3 Jan. 1774

Also a later version, reduced (coloured impression) etched by Rowlandson, n.d., signed *H. Bunbury del.*

$4\frac{3}{4} \times 6\frac{7}{8}$ in.

Another version was published by Darly, 10 June 1772, and reissued in a composite volume dated 1 Jan. 1776, see No. 5369. (In the possession of Mr. W. T. Spencer, New Oxford Street, 1933.)

[A POSTILLION]   See No. 4747—10 Jan 1774

[AN ITALIAN VETURINO]   See No 4735—10 Jan. 1774

No title: boots, long pigtail queue and a *fleur-de-lys* badge worn by the postillion show that this is a French post-chaise

[A FRENCH POSTILLION]   See No. 4741—20 Jan. 1774

EVERY SOUS BEGAD!   See No. 4720—10 June 1774

Four prints after Collet, published by Sayer and Bennet.

THE MUTUAL EMBRACE   See No 4613—10 Mar. 1774
Goldar *sc.*

THE UNLUCKY ATTEMPT.   See No. 4614—10 Mar 1774
Goldar *sc.*

THE DISCOVERY   See No. 4615—10 Mar. 1774
Goldar *sc.*

THE GUARDS OF THE NIGHT DEFEATED
                                See No. 4616—1 July 1774
Caldwall *sc.*

Ten prints from the series of mezzotints published by
Carington Bowles.[1]

THE LIGHT GUINEA, OR THE BLADE IN THE DUMPS (291)
See No. 4534 [1774]

A satire on the Coin Act, see Nos. 3759, 5128, 5231.

THE HUMOROUS THOUGHTS OF A SCHOOL BOY . . . (294)
See No. 4535 [1774]

FRIAR BALD-PATE'S ABSOLUTION TO HIS FAIR PENITENT
(297)
See No. 3779 [1774]

WELL A DAY! IS THIS MY SON TOM? (298)
See No. 4536 [1774]

After Grimm. Reproduced Paston, Pl. clxxxix.
A smaller version was published on 25 June 1773.

BE NOT AMAZ'D DEAR MOTHER—IT IS INDEED YOUR
DAUGHTER ANNE. (299)
See No 4537 [1774]

After Grimm. Reproduced Paston, Pl. cxc, and *Social England*,
ed. Traill, 1904, v. 484 (coloured). Cf Chaloner Smith, 1. p. 2.

A smaller version was published 14 June 1771, see No. 4538.

SPECTATORS AT A PRINT SHOP, IN ST. PAUL'S CHURCH
YARD. (300)
See No. 3758 [25 June 1774]

J. R. Smith, see No. 5220. Frankau, pp. 221–2.

DR. GALLIPOT, WITH HIS WIG OF KNOWLEDGE. (301)
See No. 3759 [1774]

A satire on the Coin Act, see Nos. 4534, 5128, etc.

PROVISION FOR THE CONVENT. (304)   See No. 3777 [1774]

THE SOLID ENJOYMENT OF BOTTLE AND FRIEND. (305)
See No. 4539 [1774]

THE EXHIBITION OF WILD BEASTS (number cut off)
See No. 4580 [20 Oct. 1774]

Seven similar mezzotints issued by other publishers.

5280 A CALL TO THE UNCONVERTED

Cole fecit

Publish'd April 15, 1774, by W. Humphry, St Martin's Lane

Mezzotint. Whitefield preaching to a group of country-people by the road-
side. A sign, a lion rampant on a post with the chequers which denote an
alehouse, shows that the scene is outside an inn. Whitefield, his squint
very pronounced, stands in gown and bands, both arms raised, in the
attitude familiar from the mezzotints in print-shop windows, see No. 5220

[1] Nos 4535, 3779, 3777, 4539, have the imprint of Bowles and Carver. A political
mezzotint, No. 306 in this series, is described on p 169

191

Some of his hearers, men and women, clasp their hands in prayer, some kneeling; others grin slyly or scowl. Immediately in front of him an elderly man seated on a mounting-block, is asleep, his head resting on the head of his stick. A woman with three infants is seated in the foreground (l.). A pot-man (l.), his sleeves rolled up, holds out a foaming tankard, either to the preacher or to one of the audience. Behind, in front of the signboard (l.) is a countryman on horseback. Behind Whitefield is the trunk of a large tree, under which the group is collected.

Whitefield left England for America in 1769 and died in 1770.

$12\frac{3}{4} \times 9\frac{3}{4}$ in.   Cheylesmore collection.

FAT AND LEAN . . .   See No. 4776—2 May 1774

Pub. W. Humphrey.

THE ADVENTUROUS MACARONI, OR THE THREE JOLLY
    BLADES . . .   See No 4618—29 Aug. 1774

Pub. Sayer and Bennet.

ENGLISH FUNN OR DOCKING THE MACARONI
                       See No. 4619—14 Sept. 1774

Pub. Sayer and Bennet.

AN EXHIBITION OF WILD BEASTS OR THE MACARONI IN
    DISTRESS.   See No. 4620—10 Oct. 1774

Pub. Sayer and Bennet.

THE TUILLERIE MACARONIES   See No. 4783—3 Mar. 1774

Pub. F. E. Adams (probably by himself, cf. Chaloner Smith, i. p. 2.)

IS THIS MY DAUGHTER ANN.   See No. 4786—27 June 1774

Pub. S. Sledge. Watson *sc.* after S. H. Grimm.

POLITICAL SATIRES

5281 THE COUNCIL OF THE RULERS, & THE ELDERS
AGAINST THE TRIBE OF Yᴱ AMERICANITES.   [1 Jan 1775]

Engraving. From the *Westminster Magazine*, ii. 640. It illustrates 'The
XLVth Chapter of the Convention of the Gothamites' The scene is intended for the House of Commons   A number of men sit round a table
covered with documents; one turns to point at a map on the wall behind (l)
inscribed *North America*, which is bursting into flames. At the far end of
the table the Speaker in his gown has risen from his high-backed chair and
calls the members to order. In the foreground (l.) Lord North is slipping
bank-notes into the l. hand of a man who stands bowing obsequiously
From North's pocket hangs a paper, *List of the King's Friends*. On the r.
stands Wilkes in his mayoral gown and chain pointing out North to a
lawyer in gown and bands who stands on his l , evidently Serjeant Glynn,
who with Wilkes had been elected for Middlesex at the general election,
see No. 5236. Wilkes holds a document, *A Remonstrance against the
Proceedings of the Minʳ of the Prince.* Four men are sitting in the gallery.

The text explains that 'Boreas' 'renewed the oppressions' of the Americans begun by Bute, 'with the lash, the sword and the fire and they were
sorely smitten'. He put a 'bloody speech' into the mouth of the king 'and
he bribed the Ministers and Nobles' and 'they did unanimously and shamefully vote against the peace and posterity of this new tribe'. For the king's
speech of 30 Nov 1774 see *Parl Hist* xviii. 33 ('you may depend on my
firm and steadfast resolution to withstand every attempt to weaken or impair
the supreme authority of this legislature over all the dominions of my
crown. . ') The Remonstrance is probably that agreed upon in Common
Hall 11 Mar. 1773, reputed to have been drawn up by Wilkes, so that
his enemy Townsend, the Mayor, 'would be undone at Sᵗ James's if he
presented it and stoned by the people if he did not' Walpole, *Last Journals*,
1910, i. 180 f., 182–5. For Bute, as the chief author of measures against the
Colonies, see No 5289, &c

$5\frac{15}{16} \times 3\frac{15}{16}$ in.

5282 AMERICA IN FLAMES   [1 Jan 1775]

Woodcut. From the *Town and Country Magazine*, vi. 659 America, as
'a venerable lady' sits on the topmost of three steps, surrounded by flames.
Above her head from among clouds two figures blow at the fire with
bellows Bute (l.), in Highland dress, plies bellows inscribed *Quebec Bill*;
and in the centre Mansfield, in wig and gown, plies bellows inscribed
Masachusets Bay. On his l. sits the Devil (r.), an imp with horns, claws,
and bat's wings Beside America (r) stands Lord North in profile looking
at her through a lorgnette; in his l hand he holds the *Boston Port Bill*
Below four patriots are attempting to put out the flames, one with a bucket
of water, two with syringes Down the steps in front rolls a tea-pot spilling
its contents

The text explains the patriots as 'well-known faces . . . often seen in and
near the Mansion House and among the members of the society of the

Bill of Rights'. Wilkes is indicated by his squint, the man with the bucket has some resemblance to Parson Horne, the others are too rudely drawn for identification. North is 'the ostensible agent of the trio' in the clouds

The tea-pot is a symbol of the Boston tea-party which had caused the measures here pilloried (except the Quebec Act): the withdrawal of the charter of Massachusetts and the Boston Port Bill, see Nos. 5226, 5227, 5228, 5236, 5285. For other references to the tax on tea and its consequences see Nos 5226, 5490, 5491, 6190 For Bute as the chief instigator of measures against the Colonies see No. 5289, &c. For the Quebec Act see No. 5228, &c.

This woodcut was used in the *Hibernian Magazine*, Jan. 1775 [1 Feb. 1775]

$5\frac{1}{4} \times 3\frac{5}{8}$ in.

5283 FRONTISPIECE [1 Feb 1775]

Lon. Mag. 1775.

Engraving. Allegorical figures representing Peace, America, and Britannia Peace, a diaped figure, stands in the centre poised on clouds, in her r. hand is an olive branch, raised up and pointing towards a small circular temple in the clouds (l.) inscribed *Temple of Commerce*. In her r hand she holds the r wrist of Britannia who stands (r.) with her shield and spear. America, as a Red Indian woman with a feathered head-dress, a sheaf of arrows at her back and holding an unstrung bow, looks towards Peace and Britannia. At her side is a basket from which fruit is pouring Beneath the design is engraved,

> *When fell Debate & civil Wars shall cease,*
> *Commerce shall spread her Sails o'er all the Seas;*
> *England unrivall'd in the liberal Arts,*
> *Shall bear her Genius to remotest Parts,*
> *Take to thy Breast, America again,*
> *Thou may'st defy imperious France & Spain*

$5\frac{13}{16} \times 4$ in. B.M.L., 159. n. 7.

5284 THE PATRIOTICK BARBER OF NEW YORK, OR THE CAPTAIN IN THE SUDS. [? Philip Dawe]

Pl. III. London, Printed for R. Sayer & J. Bennett, N° 53 Fleet Street, as the Act directs 14 Feb. 1775

Mezzotint. One of a series, see pp. 169, 196–7, and No. 5241. The interior of a barber's shop. A customer is in the barber's chair, draped in a sheet, without his wig, one half of his face covered with soap From the pocket of his coat hangs a paper inscribed *Orders of Government*. A man standing on the r. hands him a letter inscribed *To Cap" Crozer*; the letter-carrier is raising his hat and grinning. The barber frowns and pushes his customer by the shoulder as if to eject him from his shop; he holds a razor in his l hand and points to a broken barber's bowl on the ground, from which soapy water is pouring out On the l. is a door, the lower part closed by a gate; a man standing outside, points to the captain, with a grin. Over the door is the word *Barclay*, showing that the shop was in Barclay Street, New York.

On a shelf against the back wall at r. angles with the door are two wig-blocks with carved faces On one (l.) is an elaborately curled wig with a queue evidently belonging to the captain, since on it is a laced three-cornered hat with a cockade. At this shelf (r.) sits the barber's assistant dressing a wig, a comb is stuck in his unkempt hair; he looks over his shoulder grinning at the captain's plight, showing a lean and grotesque profile. On the wall above the shelf are pasted up (l. to r) *The Speech of Lord Chatham*, an engraved T Q L. portrait of Chatham seated at a table writing, inscribed *Pitt* (it resembles the engraving by Houston after Hoare of Pitt when Paymaster-General, but unlike the original Pitt holds a pen instead of a letter); an engraved H L. portrait of Chief Justice Camden in judge's wig and gown, surrounded by a wreath (None of the engraved portraits in the B.M. collection resembles this.) Camden was popular owing to his part in the repeal of the Stamp Act, and his statue was erected in New York (Van Tyne, *Causes of the War of Independence*, 1921, 195–6). Next are the *Articles of Association*; the Association was signed by all members of Congress on 20 Oct. 1774, binding themselves and their constituents to cut off all trade with Great Britain; committees were named to secure signatures and all who refused to sign or who infringed the Articles were declared 'enemies to liberty', ibid 441–8, cf. No. 5297. Above the portraits and 'Articles' is a row of four wigs of different patterns hanging on the wall Over these is a shelf on which are wig-boxes inscribed with the names of colonial patriots *Cornelius Low the big; Abraham Levingston; Alexander McDugell; John Lamb* On the floor in the foreground are other wig-boxes *Isaac Sears; Bleck Johnno; William Lugg; Antony Griffiths; Francis Van-Dyke,   el Broome Jacobus V^n Zent; Welle Franklin* Beneath the title is engraved,

Thou Patriot grand, maintain thy Stand,
And whilst thou sav'st Americ's Land,
Preserve the Golden Rule,
Forbid the Captains there to roam,
Half shave them first, then send 'em home,
Objects of ridicule.

This depicts an incident which was the subject of a 'Card' dated Oct 3rd [1774] circulated by the Sons of Liberty in New York praising the patriotic conduct of Mr Jacob Vredenburgh in refusing to complete the shaving of Captain John Crozer, Commander of the *Empress of Russia*, a British transport in the river, after he had been 'most *fortunately* and *providentially* informed of the identity of the gentleman's person when he had about half finished the job'. All 'Gentlemen of the Razor' were urged to follow this example. The 'card' was printed in English newspapers, e g. *Kentish Gazette*, 7 Jan 1775 The names on the wig-boxes show great knowledge of New York politics, some were well known at the date of the print. Alexander Mc Dougell, 'the American Wilkes', John Lamb, the leader of the New York Radicals, Isaac Sears, the ultra-radical leader of the mechanics (Van Tyne, *Causes of the American War of Independence*, 270) Antony Griffiths and Francis Van-Dyke were 'Sons of Liberty' who were especially active in the policy of intimidation; Cornelius Low the big is presumably Cornelius P Low, a member of the Committee of One Hundred appointed to administer local affairs after the battle of Lexington Abraham Livingston was subsequently a captain in Marinus Willett's 'Regiment of the Line'. Bleck Johnno is identified by Mr. Halsey as John Blagge an active patriot William Lugg is unknown, Van Zandt, Broome, and Welle or Walter Franklin were influential merchants, the first among the most radical of the Sons of Liberty, the second Captain of the 'Union' Independent Company who drilled on the Common The last had been active in enforcing Non-Importation after 1765. Halsey, *The Boston Port Bill, as pictured by a Contemporary London Cartoonist*, New York, Grolier Club, 1904, pp. 217-22. Reproduction, ibid , p. 215.

12¾ × 9¾ in

Two other prints in this series, not in the B M , are here described from photogravure reproductions in the *Boston Port Bill* by R. T. H. Halsey, pp 277-317.

THE ALTERNATIVE OF WILLIAMS-BURG.   [? Philip Dawe]

Plate IV. London. Printed for R. Sayer & J. Bennett, Nᵒ 53 Fleet Street as the Act directs 16 Feb. 1775.

Mezzotint. One of a series, see pp. 169, 197, and Nos. 5241, 5284 Virginian loyalists being forced to sign either the Association or the Resolutions drawn up by the Williamsburg Convention in Aug 1774. A number of Liberty Men with large clubs are grouped round two casks on the top of which is a plank serving as a table; on this is the paper which the reluctant loyalists are being forced to sign. A man in profile to the r. is in the act of signing, while a truculent-looking cook stands over him with a large knife; the cook has a cockade in his cook's cap and smokes a long pipe On the l another loyalist is being dragged towards the gallows by a group of Sons of Liberty with clubs, his hands are clasped in supplication; one points at the gallows, another, who holds the victim by the collar, is about to cut off his hair with a pair of scissors The gallows (r) with its swinging sack of feathers and barrel of dripping tar is inscribed *A cure for the Refractory*. Among the spectators is a scowling woman (r) in profile to the l., holding up an infant, a little boy clings to her skirts holding a flag inscribed *Liberty* and wearing a wooden sword and a hat with a cockade. There are also a negro, and a sour-looking minister with lank hair. One of the two barrels is inscribed *Tobacco A Present for John Wilkes Esqʳ Lord Mayor of London*. The papers on it are inscribed *The Resolves of the Congress* and *Non Importation*. (The Resolutions of Williamsburg included an undertaking to conform to every resolution of the Continental Congress which should (in future) be consented to by the delegates from Virginia, and one that every exporter of tobacco should be considered an enemy to the community They were printed in full in the *Middlesex Journal* of Sept 17-20, 1774 and reprinted by R. T. H Halsey, op. cit , pp. 260-9) Behind, (l.) on a high pedestal inscribed *Botetourt* is a statue of a man standing, in peer's robes, pointing towards the gallows The conciliatory policy of Lord Botetourt, the popular Governor of Virginia, 1768-70, was so successful that the Virginian House of Burgesses on his death voted 'by acclamation for a statue by "the best statuary in England" as a lasting and elegant Testimony that this Country will ever pay the most distinguished regard and veneration to governors of Worth and Merit'. It was erected in 1774, and is now standing in Williamsburg

This appears to illustrate a paragraph in the *London Chronicle* of 26 Jan. 1774: 'Many Virginians being reluctant to sign [the Association] a gibbet was erected in the capital, Williamsburg, from which was hung a barrel of tar and a barrel of feathers, each inscribed *A Cure for the Refractory*, which proved very effective in securing signatures.' Virginia and Maryland subscribed tobacco towards the fund for Wilkes initiated by the Bill of Rights Society. D. M. Clark, *British Opinion and the War of American Independence*, 1930, p. 154. For the Association see Nos. 5284, 5297.

B M.L. Ac. 4714/14 (p. 277)

A SOCIETY OF PATRIOTIC LADIES AT EDENTON IN NORTH CAROLINA. [? P. Dawe]

Plate V London, Printed for R Sayer & J Bennett, Nº 53 in Fleet Street as the Act directs 25 March 1775. 377.

Mezzotint. The chairwoman, an ugly, elderly woman, sits holding up a banner at the head of a table (r.) on which is a large document inscribed, *We the Ladys of Edenton do hereby Solemnly Engage not to Conform to that Pernicious Custom of Drinking Tea, or that we the aforesaid Ladys will not promote yᵉ wear of any Manufacture from England untill such time that all Acts which tend to Enslave this our Native Country shall be Repealed.* A young woman in a hat bends over the table to sign the paper. Another sits facing her, pen in hand, she is of meretricious appearance, and is being kissed by a young man. Behind stand two women wearing hats, plainly dressed, and of puritanic appearance, one drinks from a large punch-bowl, the other helps her to support the bowl. On the r. is an open door, two ruffianly-looking men stand outside it, one holds out his hat; a lady pours into the hat the contents of a tea-caddy, two other ladies stand by with tea-caddies. On the l. of the chairwoman sits a demure young woman holding a fan; beside her on the ground are tea-caddies which a dog is befouling. The dog licks the face of a doll-like child sitting under the table.

B M.L. Ac. 4714/14 (p 317)

5285 THE THISTLE REEL. [1 Mar 1775]

Engraving. From the *London Magazine*, xliv. 56. Three men dance round a tall thistle. The stem of the thistle is decorated with a Garter ribbon inscribed *Hom soit qui Mal y pense*, its flower is surrounded by a glory of light from which issue rays terminating in a circle of black clouds; over it are the words *Carduus benedictus* Among the clouds (r) is seated the Devil playing the bagpipes. The dancers are (l. to r.) Bute in court dress wearing the Garter ribbon, &c., and pointing with one hand to the thistle, with the other to a scroll on the ground inscribed *Noli me tangere.* North, smiling, looks at the thistle through a lorgnette Lord Mansfield in judge's wig and gown holds the *Quebec Bill*, while by his feet is a scroll inscribed *Nemo me impune lacessit* (the motto of the Order of the Thistle).

The text explains this as 'a vision' seen in the Court Yard of St James's Palace 'after a long argument at the Cocoa with the putrid Jacobites of that club'. The 'boreal triumvirate dance to the tune of "Over the water to Charley" but flee at the appearance of a ghastly bleeding figure . . the injured Ghost of poor America', who asserts 'that her country would ruin ours, and France and Spain would profit by the downfall of both'. The guard rush out yelling 'a civil war, a civil war!'

The Government's policy to America is generally attacked in these satires as inspired by Bute and Scottish influence, see No. 5289, &c., a favourite theme also in America Here the Quebec Bill is singled out for especial condemnation, see Nos. 5228, 5286, &c. For the Cocoa Tree, a Tory club whose origin was a chocolate house formerly a resort of Jacobites, see Gibbon, *Misc. Works*, 1814, 1. 154.

$6\frac{5}{16} \times 4\frac{1}{4}$ in

5286 VIRTUAL REPRESENTATION. 1775.

April 1 1775.   *Price 6ᵈ*

Engraving Seven figures on the sea-shore represent the situation in America. four (l) take the offensive, two (r.) are prepared to defend themselves, while Britannia on the extreme r., blindfolded, is about to rush into a pit inscribed *The Pit prepared for others*. Each has a number referring to an explanatory note beneath the design giving the words spoken by each character. The two principal antagonists are Bute (1), who aims a blunderbuss at (5), America, a plainly dressed and sturdy man holding a club. Bute, who wears his Garter ribbons, tartan breeches, and a tartan plaid, is *One String Jack*, saying, *Deliver your Property* (Rann, 'Sixteen String Jack', was a noted highwayman hanged in 1774) America answers, *I will not be Robbed*. Behind him and holding his l hand is (6), an English sailor wearing trousers, who says, *I shall be wounded with you*. Behind Britannia (7) rushes towards the pit saying, *I am blinded*. The Speaker of the House of Commons in his wig and robes, holding the mace, stands in the centre pointing at America and saying to Bute, *I give you that man's money for my use* Two figures on the l. encourage Bute and the Speaker A monk (3), kneels on the ground holding out towards Bute a cross and the model of a gibbet saying *Te Deum*. Behind him, and on the extreme l., stands (2), a figure representing France, wearing bag-wig, solitaire, and feathered hat; he is flourishing his sword and saying, *Begar Just so en France*. The words spoken by (2) and (3) are bracketed with the word *Accomplices*.

In the background, on the horizon, are two towns (8) Quebec (l) standing on a cliff, its spires and buildings surrounded by a wall, its castle flying the Union flag, (9) Boston, on the sea level, is in flames, (8) is described as *The French Roman Catholick Town of Quebeck*, (9) is *The English Protestant Town of Boston*.

This contrast is an attack on the Quebec Act and on the punitive measures taken against Massachusetts for the Boston tea-party. The attack on the Quebec Act as the establishment of Roman Catholicism in Canada is further stressed by the figures of the monk and of France, see No. 5228, &c. It is to be noted that the date of the print is before the opening of hostilities at Lexington, 19 Apr 1775, cf No. 5287. The words of Bute and the action of the Speaker indicate that America was being taxed for the benefit of England, while the title derides the theory that the colonists, like Englishmen without the franchise, were 'virtually represented' in the House of Commons. See *Cambridge Mod. Hist*, vii. 193 f. and M.C Tyler, *Literary History of the American Revolution*, i 103–5, 305 ff.

Similar in manner and intention to No 5287 and probably by the same artist

$6\frac{3}{4} \times 11\frac{1}{8}$ in.

5287 THE SCOTCH BUTCHERY, BOSTON. 1775

Pubᵈ According to Act of Parlᵐᵗ . . 1775.

Engraving. Numbers on the plate refer to explanatory notes engraved beneath the design. A symbolical representation of the situation in Massachusetts. Groups of figures stand outside Boston which is being bombarded by ships of war. The directors of the 'Butchery' stand in the r. centre; on the r is a group of Scottish soldiers, on the l. a group of English soldiers (1) and (2) are B——[Bute] and M—— [Mansfield] standing in consultation, and pointing with satisfaction to the bombarding ships. Bute, wearing his Garter ribbon and star, is dressed as a highland chief in feathered cap, kilt, and plaid, a drawn broadsword in his hand. Mansfield wears a coronet, a judge's wig and robes, he holds books in his l. hand. B—— and M—— are bracketed together as *Super Intendants of the Butchery from the two great Slaughter Houses*. Slightly behind these two stand (3) and (4), one wearing a kilt and plaid with the hat and coat of a military officer; he holds a spear in his r. hand, a paper inscribed *Pardon 1745* in his l. hand. The other wears a legal wig and gown, in his l. hand is a paper inscribed *Solicit[or General]*; he points towards the ships, looking anxiously towards Bute and Mansfield. They are *Col. F——r* and *W——n*, bracketed together as *Deputies to the above* [to Bute and Mansfield]. (3) is evidently Simon Fraser (1726–82), eldest son of Lord Lovat, who was pardoned in 1750 for his share in the '45. In 1756 he raised a Highland regiment which fought brilliantly in Canada and was disbanded at the peace. Many of its officers and men joined a regiment raised by Fraser at the outbreak of the American War, the 71st or Fraser Highlanders. Fraser was then a major-general but did not accompany his regiment to America. (4) is Wedderburn, the Solicitor-General, who came to London with Fraser when they were both young men. The soldiers on the r. are (5), described as *Scotch Butchers*; they are in Highland dress, with lank hair and ruffianly faces, they have muskets with fixed bayonets, one holds a drawn broadsword, their standard is patterned with thistles. They press forward eagerly to obey the orders of Bute. The English soldiers (l.) stand with expressions and gestures of horror, their muskets and a pike on the ground at their feet. They are (6), *English Soldiers struck with Horror, & dropping their Arms*. The ships, which are bombarding the town at close range, fly flags decorated with a thistle; one has a thistle for a figure-head. They are (7), *The English Fleet with Scotch Commanders*. In the background is (8), *Boston*; outside its walls a number of men on a minute scale are fleeing in disorder, many bodies lie on the ground.

From the title, and from the fact that the fugitives appear to be unarmed, they are probably intended for harmless Bostonians killed by the British fleet. If an actual incident is intended, it must be the retreat of the British troops to Boston after Lexington[1] (19 Apr. 1775), though the bombardment may represent that of Charlestown during Bunker Hill.

One of a number of satires ascribing the measures against the Colonies to Bute, see Nos. 5285, 5289, 5328, &c.

$7 \times 12 \frac{15}{16}$ in.

5288 THE POLITICAL CARTOON FOR THE YEAR 1775.

[1 May 1775]

Engraving. From the *Westminster Magazine*, iii 209. A two-wheeled open chaise is being driven rapidly towards a chasm (l.), into which the two

---

[1] Four plates of Lexington and Concord by Amos Doolittle after Earl were engraved in 1775; in these the figures are drawn with a stiff incompetence which resembles caricature. Reproductions in Jonas Clark's *Opening of the War of Independence . . .* Boston, 1875. B M L 1851, b 8

horses, inscribed *Pride* and *Obstinacy*, are about to plunge. The driver, Lord Mansfield, flourishes a whip, on his l sits the king, his eyes closed, holding a paper inscribed *I Glory in the Name of Englishman* Behind the chaise in the place of a footman, stands Bute, a drawn broadsword in his r. hand; he holds out papers inscribed *Places, Pensions,* and *Reversions* towards a crowd of spectators. A wheel passes over an open book, *Magna Charta,* the horses trample on another inscribed *Constitution* In the air (l) a demon flies off with a sack inscribed *National Credit.* A group of four bishops wearing mitres, and two laymen, one being North, hold out their hands obsequiously towards the chaise; the foremost bishop is eating. The text explains that they are 'feeding on garbage, or picking up white sticks [rods of office], blue or red Rags [ribbons of the Garter or the Bath], &c., &c' Behind the chaise are a running footman and two men who stretch out their arms as if to check its disastrous course, one is Chatham with crutches and a gouty leg, the other in judge's robes is probably Lord Camden. Beyond the chasm (l.) is a group of Scotsmen, two write at a table, three others stand The text explains them as 'Scotch clerks—Secretaries—Governors, &c' In the background (l) is the sea; on the horizon is a town in flames inscribed *America.* In the foreground (r) is a crowd of men and women of all conditions, including a bearded Jew, and a macaroni holding up a lorgnette who offers a purse to a young woman. A grimacing minister wearing a ribbon faces the crowd offering a money-bag. They represent 'the incorruptible virtue of Modern Electors as practised lately in the immaculate Boroughs of Hindon and Shaftesbury'. George III is described as 'a full grown young man in leading-strings', driven to destruction by his advisers. Cf. No. 5132.

For the gross corruption at Hindon in 1774 see Oldfield, *Representative History of Great Britain,* 1816, v. 126 ff. For the Shaftesbury election see No. 5341.

The word cartoon appears to be used ironically in its meaning of a design for a picture as it was used by Leech in 1843 for his caricatures of mural cartoons. The earliest instance in the *O.E.D.* of its use for a satire is 1863.

$4\frac{3}{16} \times 7\frac{1}{8}$ in.

5289 BUNKERS HILL, OR THE BLESSED EFFECTS OF FAMILY QUARRELS.   [*c.* 1775]

Engraving. Probably from a magazine America and Britannia are fighting. America (l), a Red Indian woman with feathered head-dress, has a tomahawk in one hand, a scalping-knife in the other. Britannia (r) seizes her by the shoulder, her spear raised to strike Behind America stands Spain, he pierces with his sword the shield of Britannia which lies on the ground, in his l hand he holds a rope which is round America's shoulders. Behind Britannia stands France, who pulls off her draperies leaving her breast bare, while he pierces her through the heart from the back with his sword. The scene is the sea-shore; in the sea are the masts of sunken ships Spain strides across two globes on the ground representing the two hemispheres. In the upper part of the design are three figures seated on clouds who point with satisfaction at the scene below: Bute, wearing a Scots cap and tartan waistcoat, puts his l. arm round North's shoulder, on his r sits Mansfield holding a large book, a demon (l) clutches at him.

News of the battle of Bunker Hill (17 June) reached London on 25 July

One of many satires ascribing the American dispute to the influence of Bute, see Nos 5226, 5228, 5285, 5287, 5328, 5573, 5580, &c, and p 217. For the attitude of France and Spain see Corwin, *French Policy and the American Alliance of 1778*, 1916, chapters i–vi.

$5\frac{5}{8} \times 3\frac{9}{16}$ in.

5290 GEORGE WASHINGTON, ESQ^R.

Done from an Original, Drawn from the life by Alex^r Campbell, of Williamsburgh in Virginia.

Published as the Act directs, 9 Septr 1775 by C. Shepherd

Mezzotint One of a series of portraits of officers in the American War, some at least being imaginary, and the publication lines perhaps fictitious. Washington in uniform and cocked hat on horseback, a sword in his hand, looking over his r. shoulder to the l In the background is a battle, infantry with a flag firing point-blank at cavalry. Beneath the title is engraved, *General and Commander in Chief of the Continental Army in America.*

Washington was appointed C.-in-C on 23 June. Campbell is unknown as an artist, and was unknown to Washington, who writes, 31 Jan 1776, 'Mr Campbell whom I never saw to my knowledge, has made a very formidable figure of the Commander-in-Chief, giving him a sufficient portion of terror in his countenance '

For others of the series, whose political intention is clear, the American officers being heroes, the British unsuccessful or barbarous, see Nos 5291, 5292–3, 5296, 5331, 5332, 5336–9, 5405, 5406, 5407–8, 5561, 5582, 6034. Copies of most if not all were issued by J. M. Will of Augsburg, see No 6034.

Chaloner Smith, iv, p. 1717. C. H. Hart, *Engraved Portraits of Washington*, Grolier Club, 1904, No. 721 and p viii. Andrews, pp. 55, 90.

$12\frac{3}{4} \times 9\frac{3}{4}$ in.

5291 GEORGE WASHINGTON, ESQ^R

Mezzotint Inscription and publication line as in No. 5290, with the addition of *London* after Shepherd, and of *Ioh. Martin Will excud Aug.* [Augsburg] *Vind.* T.Q.L. standing portrait of Washington in uniform facing l. with outstretched r. arm, looking over his l shoulder to the r. In the background is a battle, cavalry among clouds of smoke.

A copy, probably by Will, see No. 6034, of a plate apparently belonging to the same series as 5290.

C. II. Hart, No 730 a.

$12\frac{3}{4} \times 9\frac{3}{4}$ in.

5292 ISRAEL PUTNAM ESQ^R

J. Wilkinson[1] pinx^t [? 'C. Corbutt'.]

Published as the Act directs by C Shepherd 9 Sepr 1775.

Mezzotint. One of a series, see No 5290. T Q.L. standing in uniform his r. elbow leaning on the muzzle of a cannon. In the background (r)

---

[1] Perhaps a fictitious name According to Fussli, *Künstlerlexicon*, 1816, p. 5096, he is known only for this portrait, but see Nos. 5294, 5408.

clouds of smoke with a battery of cannon firing Beneath the title is engraved, *Major General of the Connecticut Forces, and Commander in Chief at the Engagement on Buncker's-Hill near Boston, 17 June 1775.* Cf. No. 5329
Chaloner Smith, iv. 1716. Andrews, p 91
$12\frac{1}{4} \times 9\frac{3}{4}$ in.

5292 A

A copy of No. 5292 published in Augsburg having the same inscription with the addition of *London* after the date and of *Ioh Martin Will excudit Aug. Vind.*

5292 B ISRAEL PUTTNAM.

*peint par Jean Wilckinson a Boston
se vend à Londres chez Thom. Hart.*

A copy of No 5292, bust only, oval in rectangle. Beneath the title is inscribed *Major Général dans les Forteresses de la Province Connecticut, et Commandant en Chef de l'Expedition a Bunckers-Hill pres de Boston le 17. Juin 1776*
$7\frac{3}{4} \times 6\frac{1}{8}$ in.

5293 THE HONBLE JOHN HANCOCK.
[? 'C. Corbutt'.]
London, Published as the Act directs 25 Octr 1775 by C. Shepherd.

Mezzotint. One of a series, see No. 5290 Bust portrait in an oval, looking to right, wearing a bag-wig and laced coat. Beneath the title is inscribed, *of Boston in New England; President of the American Congress Done from an Original Picture Painted by Littleford* The artist's name and publication line are perhaps fictitious, cf. Nos 5292, 5294.
Chaloner Smith, iv, p. 1715. Andrews, pp. 89–90
$12\frac{3}{8} \times 9\frac{7}{8}$ in.

5294 JEAN HANCOCK.
peint par Jean Wilckinson a Boston
Se vend a Londres chez Thom Hart.

Mezzotint Apparently a copy, though an incorrect one, of No. 5293. Beneath the title is inscribed, *President au Congres des XIII Provinces unies d'Amerique né a Boston.*
$7\frac{3}{4} \times 6\frac{1}{8}$ in.

5295 SIX-PENCE A DAY.
[? W. Humphrey]
Publish d 26. Octr 1775 by W. Humphrey, Gerrard Street, Soho.

Engraving. An anti-recruiting satire, showing the calamities to which a soldier is exposed, and contrasting his lot with that of the working man. A tall emaciated soldier stands in the centre, his fingers interlaced, his expression one of bewildered melancholy; he is knock-kneed, his toes project through his tattered shoes. His wife and children are appealing to him: the woman barefoot and ragged, in an advanced state of pregnancy, with two crying infants in a basket which is tied to her shoulders, holds out her hands towards him. A ragged emaciated boy holds up his hands in supplication The words *The Target* are inscribed beneath the soldier's feet. On the extreme r across a stream a skeleton-like figure dressed in rags is seated on a stone inscribed *Famine* He beckons to the soldier with a claw-like finger; at his feet are a skull and cross-bones, and a thistle, to indicate Scottish influence At his back is a flag-staff and above his head flies a flag inscribed,

COURAGE BOYS!

> *If you Gentn Soldiers should die & be damn'd*
> *Your Wives & yr Infants may live and be cramm'd*
> *Vid. subscriptn*

Two American soldiers (r.) are firing across the stream point-blank at the English soldier one fires a musket, the other, torch in hand, a cannon. Across the front of their caps is written *Death or Liberty*, cf. No. 5329. Behind them is a hill on which is a fort

On the l are the representatives of 'the lowest trades' A chairman on the extreme l, stout and well-clad, holds with one hand the pole of a sedan-chair, with the other he points at the soldier. Next him a coachman, even more stout and prosperous, stands holding a whip and a large foaming tankard, inscribed in reverse *WH 1775*, probably the initials of the artist. Between the coachman and the woman stands a little chimney-sweep, ragged but grinning. He points derisively at the soldier, in his l. hand is a paper inscribed *He would be a soldier*, cf. No 5783. On the ground is a paper inscribed,

> *England shall exalt her Glories*
> *From her present* PATRIOT *tories*
> *See what vast Subscriptions fly*
> *To make the unwilling Soldier die*

Above the design is engraved, *Exposed to the Horrors of War, Pestilence and Famine, for a Farthing an Hour*. Beneath the design (l.) is engraved *3 Shillings a Day, 2 Shillings a Day, 1 Shilling a Day*, indicating the wages respectively of the chairman, the coachman, and the sweep. On the r is engraved *Yankees. Fire and Water. Sword and Famine*. Below these inscriptions is engraved, *This Sketch displays the Hardship a Soldier and his Family endure on the bare Subsistance of Six-pence a Day, while the lowest Trades earn sufficient to enjoy the Comforts of Life.*

At this time subscriptions were being raised locally to provide comforts for soldiers and to increase the bounty paid to recruits, cf *Corr of George III*, iii. 257, 263. For the great difficulty of obtaining recruits see E. C. Curtis, *The Organization of the British Army in the American Revolution*, 1926, chap. iii; Fortescue, *Hist. of the British Army*, iii. 1902, p. 170 f For the actual pay of the soldiers, which was complicated by a system of allowances, see Fortescue, ibid , iii 512 f One of several anti-recruiting prints, see Nos. 5403, 5471, 5551, 5552.

$8\frac{3}{8} \times 13\frac{11}{16}$ in.

5296 CHARLES LEE, ESQᴿ

Thomlinson Pinxt [? 'Corbutt'.]

Publish'd as the Act directs, 31 Octr 1775, by C. Shepherd.

Mezzotint. One of a series, see No. 5290. A standing T Q L. portrait of a handsome and rather stout man in uniform, looking to the l., pointing with the r. hand to the r. Behind (r.) are two cannon and a large flag inscribed *An Appeal to Heaven* to which Lee is pointing. Beneath the title is inscribed *Major General of the Continental-Army in America*.

This can have little if any resemblance to Lee who was 'tall and remarkably thin with an ugly face and an aquiline nose of enormous size' (*D.N.B.*), and is probably, like others of the series, an imaginary portrait. Lee, a British officer, who appears as a colonel on half-pay in the Army List for 1774, was appointed second Major-General of the American army before Boston on 17 June 1775, the day of Bunker Hill. A 'restless, unstable untrustworthy adventurer' L. C. Hatch, *Administration of the American Revolutionary Army*, New York, 1904, p. 10. For the flag see No. 5336. See also No. 5404.

Chaloner Smith, iv, p. 1716. Cf. Andrews, p. 91.

$12\frac{3}{4} \times 9\frac{7}{8}$ in.

5296 A A copy, probably by Will, inscription as above, with the addition of *London* after *Shepherd* and of *Ioh. Martin Will excud. Aug.* [Augsburg] *vind. Thomlinson* is spelt *Thomlinsen*.

5297 THE CONGRESS OR THE NECESSARY POLITICIANS

Engraving. Two men seated in a 'necessary house'. One (l.) is tearing fragments from *Resolution[s] of the [C]ongress*, he turns in profile to the l. The other, wearing spectacles, is reading intently a book called *Answer to a P[amphlet en]titled Taxation. . . . Tir . . .* On the wall behind them two prints are stuck up, one a bust portrait of Wilkes as *Mayor* (partly cut off by the l. margin of the print), the other a caricature of a tarred and feathered man; above this is etched *Album vertor in Altem &c.*, and below, *[Por]trait of W—— P—— Tarr'd & Feather'd 1774*.

The Resolutions of Congress, 14 Oct. 1774 and the Association 20 Oct. 1774 were widely printed in the English Press, e.g. *London Chronicle*, 15-17 Dec. 1774. See S. E. Morison, *Sources and documents illustrating the American Revolution*, 1929, pp. 118-25. They include a non-importation, non-consumption, and non-exportation association, cf. No. 5284. The book which one of the politicians is reading is evidently 'An Answer to a Pamphlet entitled Taxation no Tyranny, addressed to the Author and to Persons in Power'. The sub-title of S. Johnson's pamphlet, 'Taxation no Tyranny', published in Feb. 1775, is 'An Answer to the Resolutions and Address of the American Congress'. The Congress sat from 5 Sept. to 29 Oct. 1774. For tarring and feathering cf. No. 5232, and p. 169.

$6\frac{9}{16} \times 8\frac{1}{8}$ in. (pl.)

5298 THE CONTRAST. [c. 1775[1]]

Engraving. A pastoral landscape divided by a stream, the sea with ships in the distance. On the l. side a cow, representing the Colonies, is held by four men, two at her head, while the other two hold the tail; a fifth man holds a basin for blood which is pouring from a wound in her neck. Another man lying on the ground holding a shepherd's crook stabs her hind-leg with a knife. On a decayed tree (l.) is perched a crow or raven. A blanket or cloth hung over one of its branches makes a shelter; under

[1] Mr Hawkins has dated the print 1775.

this sits a man drinking from a bowl, which another man has just brought from the cow Behind, a man with an axe is cutting down an apple-tree laden with fruit. On the cow's hindquarter is a large stamp, representing the stamp imposed by the Stamp Act, 1765 (repealed 1766).

On the other side of the stream (r.) is a contrasting scene: A cow garlanded with flowers, and trampling on a yoke, is being milked by a young woman, children drink milk from bowls. Other children feed the cow with flowers Brimming milk-pails stand on the ground; a woman whose lap is full of flowers, gives flowers and milk to a child Five little girls dance in a ring, holding hands A boy stands in an apple-tree throwing down the fruit to a girl who holds out her apron On the top branch of the tree two love-birds kiss. The scene is arcadian and in the distance two figures pursue a stag with bow and spear Beneath the design is engraved *Let us not Cut down the Tree to get at the Fruit Let us Stroke and not Stab the Cow, For her Milk, and not her Blood, can give us real Nourishment and Strength.*

An appeal for conciliatory measures towards the Colonies in the interests of trade and the mother country For other references to the Stamp Act see No. 5487, &c.

$8\frac{11}{16} \times 14\frac{13}{16}$ in.

PERSONAL SATIRES

5299–5311

Series of Tête-à-Tête portraits

5299 Nᵒ XXXIV MISS C——

Nᵒ XXXV THE POWERFULL PLEADER

Publish'd as the Act directs by A. Hamilton Junʳ near Sᵗ John's Gate, Janʸ 1775.

Engraving. *Town and Country Magazine*, vi 625 Two bust portraits, a lady facing T.Q. to the r , a barrister in wig and gown in profile to the l. holding an eye-glass in r. hand. They illustrate 'Histories of the Tête-à-Tête annexed; or Memoirs of the Powerful Pleader and Miss Lucy C——n'. An account of Dunning (1731–83) and his amours Unlike most portraits in this series, his is well characterized and resembles later caricatures. Miss C—— is identified by H. Bleackley as Charlton

Ovals, $2\frac{13}{16} \times 2\frac{1}{4}$ in   B.M.L., P.P. 5442.

5300 Nᵒ XXXVII MISS D——PLE

Nᵒ XXXVIII THE PIOUS PREACHER

Publish'd as the Act directs by A. Hamilton Junʳ near Sᵗ John's Gate Janʸ 20. 1775.

Engraving. *Town and Country Magazine*, vi. 681 (Supplement). Two bust portraits in oval frames, that on the r. being a profile to the l. of John Wesley. They illustrate 'Histories of the Tête-à-Tête annexed; or, Memoirs of the Pious Preacher and Miss D——mple'. An account of John Wesley and his supposed relations with Miss D——, his 'fair Proselyte'. Miss D—— is the daughter of an 'eminent attorney'.

Ovals, $2\frac{5}{8} \times 2\frac{1}{4}$ in.   B M L., P.P. 5442 b.

5301 Nᵒ II. Mᴿˢ N——B——T.

Nᵒ III THE HON. CAPTᴺ H——.

Publish'd as the Act directs by A. Hamilton Junʳ near Sᵗ John's Gate Feb 1. 1775.

Engraving. *Town and Country Magazine*, vii. 9. Two bust portraits in oval frames illustrate 'Histories of the Tête-à-Tête annexed, or Memoirs of the hon. Capt. H——y and Mʳˢ N——t'. An account of Augustus John Hervey (1724–79) afterwards third earl of Bristol, of Miss Chudleigh (then known as the Duchess of Kingston, see No. 5319, &c.) and of Mʳˢ Nesbit, to whom Hervey bequeathed almost all his unsettled property, *D.N.B.*

Ovals, $2\frac{11}{16}$ $2\frac{1}{4}$ in.   B M.L., P P. 5442 b.

5302 Nº IV MISS W——MS
Nº V PEEPING TOM OF COVENTRY

*Publish'd as the Act directs by A. Hamilton Junʳ near Sᵗ John's Gate
Marᵏ 1. 1775.*

Engraving. *Town and Country Magazine*, vii. 65 Two bust portraits in
oval frames illustrate 'Histories of the Tête-à-Tête annexed . ' An
account of George William, 6th Earl of Coventry (1722–1809) and his
marriage to Maria Gunning. Also of Miss Williams, the daughter of
a Welsh clergyman, who had been seduced and deserted, and had been
found destitute by Coventry.

Ovals, $2\frac{5}{8} \times 2\frac{1}{4}$ in. B.M.L., P.P. 5442 b.

5303 Nº VII MISS M—TH—WS
Nº VIII THE E. OF A——M

*Publish'd as the Act directs by A. Hamilton Junʳ near Sᵗ John's Gate
Aprˡ 1. 1775.*

Engraving. *Town and Country Magazine*, vii. 121. Two bust portraits in
oval frames illustrate 'Histories of the Tête-à-Tête annexed . . .'. An
account of John, 2nd Earl of Ashburnham (1724–1812),[1] and of Miss
Matthews, said to have been till recently the mistress of one of the Perreaus
whose trial for forgery was pending.

Ovals, $2\frac{5}{8} \times 2\frac{1}{4}$ in. B.M.L., P.P. 5442 b.

5304 Nº X MISS L——Y
Nº XI THEATRICUS

*Publish'd as the Act directs by A. Hamilton Junʳ near Sᵗ John's Gate
May 1. 1775.*

Engraving *Town and Country Magazine*, vii 177. Two bust portraits in
oval frames illustrate 'Histories of the Tête-à-Tête annexed . ' An
account of a member of a noble family with a great fondness for the stage,
who was considered at the Bedford as a dramatic critic whose judgements
constituted 'the town'. He is the Fitzpatrick who led an opposition to
Garrick at the Bedford and in the Press and is the Fizgig of Garrick's
Scribbleriad. D N.B , s v. 'Garrick'. His amours after the death of his
wife with Mrs. G—— and with Miss L——y, the daughter of a bankrupt
tradesman who had been seduced, are described. He appears to be the
Hon. Richard Fitzpatrick, brother of the Earl of Upper Ossory and uncle
of Fox's friend, Colonel Richard Fitzpatrick. See a family group, in B.M.
Catalogue of Engr. Br. Portraits.

Ovals, $2\frac{5}{8} \times 2\frac{1}{4}$ in. B.M.L., P P. 5442 b.

5305 Nº XIII MISS HARRIET P——L
Nº XIV LORD S——

*Published as the Act directs by A. Hamilton Junʳ near Sᵗ John's Gate,
June 1. 1775.*

Engraving. *Town and Country Magazine*, vii. 233 Two bust portraits

[1] H Bleackley identifies him with the Earl of Ancrum (1737–1815, succeeded as
Marquis of Lothian 12 Apr 1775) A place at Court and an alleged liaison with
Peg Woffington (1714?–60) make the older man the more likely subject He
seems also from the text to be a peer of Parliament, which Ancrum was not

in oval frames, she looks T Q to the r , he T Q to the l. They illustrate 'Histories of the Tête-à-Tête annexed; or Memoirs of Lord S——th and Miss Harriet P——ll'. An account of Lord Seaforth (1744–81) and Harriet Powell, a courtesan. She is said to have been the daughter of an apothecary in the Borough, left destitute at his death, and after a succession of protectors entered the establishment of Charlotte II. [Hayes]; but was much superior to her profession. Her liaison with Seaforth appears to have become permanent; they married (in or before 1779) and her death, Dec. 1779, is recorded in the *Annual Register* as that of Lady Seaforth. *Notes and Queries*, 10th s. xii, p. 241. See B M. *Catalogue of Engr. Br. Portraits.*

Ovals, $2\frac{5}{8} \times 2\frac{1}{4}$ in.   B M.L., P.P. 5442 b.

5306 Nº XVI SIGNIORA BALL—NT—NI
          Nº XVII E OF C——D

*Published as the Act directs by A. Hamilton Junr near St John's Gate
July 1. 1775.*

Engraving. *Town and Country Magazine*, vii. 289. Two bust portraits in oval frames. They illustrate 'Histories of the Tête-à-Tête annexed . . .'. An account of Philip Stanhope (1755–1815), fifth Earl of Chesterfield, who succeeded his godfather in 1773, and his amours while on the grand tour.

Ovals, $2\frac{5}{8} \times 2\frac{1}{7}$ in.   B.M.L., P.P. 5442 b.

5307 Nº XIX MADLLE LE B——N
          Nº XX L——D S——T

*Published as the Act directs by A. Hamilton Junr near St John's Gate.
Augt 1. 1775.*

Engraving. *Town and Country Magazine*, vii. 345. Two bust portraits in oval frames He wears the ribbon and star of the Thistle. They illustrate 'Histories of the Tête-à-Tête annexed . ' An account of Lord Stormont (1727–96) and his amours with Mlle. Le Brun and others.

Ovals, $2\frac{5}{8} \times 2\frac{1}{4}$ in   B M.L , P P 5442 b.

5308 Nº XXII. MISS V—GH—N
          Nº XXIII. THE AMERICAN HERO

*Published as the Act directs by A. Hamilton Junr near St John's Gate.
Sepr 1. 1775*

Engraving. *Town and Country Magazine*, vii 401. Two bust portraits in oval frames. They illustrate 'Histories of the Tête-à-Tête annexed; or, Memoirs of G——l H——e and Miss V——gh—n'. A laudatory account of Sir William Howe (1729–1814) and Miss Charlotte Vaughan, his supposed mistress, the daughter of a poor parson at Denbigh.
For Howe see No 5405, &c

Ovals, $2\frac{5}{8} \times 2\frac{1}{4}$ in.   B.M L., P.P. 5442 b .

5309 N° XXV MISS S——TH

N° XXVI M—— OF G——

Published as the Act directs by A. Hamilton Jun' near S' John's Gate.
Oct' 1. 1775.

Engraving. *Town and Country Magazine*, vii 457. Two bust portraits
in oval frames They illustrate 'Histories of the Tête-à-Tête annexed; or,
Memoirs of the M——s of G——y, and Miss S——th'. An account of
Charles Manners (1754–87), styled Marquess of Granby, 1770–9; M.P.
for Cambridge 1774–9, Duke of Rutland 1779. His liaison with Miss
Smith, the seduced daughter of a Windsor shopkeeper, whom he had known
when at Eton, is expected to be temporary should his talked-of marriage
take place See No. 5358.

Ovals, $2\frac{5}{8} \times 2\frac{1}{4}$ in.   B.M L., P P. 5442 b.

5310 N° XXVIII MISS LA——LY

N° XXIX D. OF B——

Published as the Act directs by A. Hamilton Jun' near S' John's Gate
Nov' 1. 1775.

Engraving. *Town and Country Magazine*, vii. 513. Two bust portraits in
oval frames illustrate 'Histories of the Tête-à-Tête annexed; or, Memoirs
of the D——e of B——r and Miss L—gl—y'. An account, apparently,
of Francis Egerton, third Duke of Bridgwater (1736–1803), which says
nothing of the commonly known events of his life. Miss L. is a farmer's
daughter who became stage-struck and joined a company of strolling
players. The Duke gave her the superintendence of a small farm where he
visits her incognito.

Ovals, $2\frac{5}{8} \times 2\frac{1}{4}$ in.   B.M.L., P.P. 5442 b.

5311 N° XXXI. MISS K——T.

N° XXXII R—— H—— O——

Published as the Act directs by A. Hamilton Jun' near S' John's Gate.
Dec' 1 1775.

Engraving *Town and Country Magazine*, vii. 569. Two bust portraits in
oval frames illustrate 'Histories of the Tête-à-Tête annexed; or, Memoirs
of R—— H—— O—— Esq, and Miss K——n' [*sic*]. An account of
Robert Henley Ongley, M.P. for Bedfordshire, of Old Warden, Bedfordshire, and his mistress, a chamber-milliner

Ovals, $2\frac{5}{8} \times 2\frac{1}{4}$ in   B.M.L., P.P. 5442 b.

5312–5318, and numbers from volume IV

Prints published by Darly, of which only 5312 and 4638 appear
to belong to series.

5312 A NUN OF THE LAST CLASS

Pub⁴ by M Darly March 14 1775 Strand

Engraving. One of a series of portraits of prostitutes, see No. 5177. Bust
portrait of a young girl in profile to the r. Her skin is patched. She wears

a cap over her hair which falls loosely on her forehead and neck; over her shoulders is a patterned scarf

$5 \times 3\frac{3}{4}$ in.   Fairholt's 'Collection for costume', i, fo. 117.

THE MACARONY SHOE MAKER   [See No. 4638—1 June 1775]

5313 JACK ON A CRUISE A MISSEY IN Yᴱ OFFING MASQUERADE SCENE KENSINGTON GARDENS.

[? After Bunbury]

Pub Janʸ 10 by M Darly 39 Strand 1775

Engraving Another version of No. 5083. Two figures in back view walk across a grass lawn The nearer is apparently a woman of vast proportions wearing a hood and cloak; the title indicates that she is a sailor in disguise walking after a young woman A spaniel barks at the sailor. On the r. are trees, on the l. a line of trees. This differs from No 5083 in the drawing and position of the figures and in the arrangement of the trees and garden-seat. See also No. 5797.

$8\frac{13}{16} \times 6\frac{1}{4}$ in.

5314 THE BREECHES IN THE FIERA MASCHERETA

Pub by M Darly 39 Strand 25 April 1775

Engraving. An enormous pair of breeches reaching from the head to the feet of the wearer, and forming his (or her) sole visible garment A face in profile to the r. appears through an unbuttoned aperture; on the wearer's head is a ducal coronet surmounted by large ostrich-feathers. The tiny high-heeled shoes suggest that the wearer is a woman.

A companion-print to No. 5315, where the wearer of a petticoat appears to be a man. They are perhaps caricatures of a ducal pair where the husband was dominated by an overbearing wife, in which case she would appear to be Jane Maxwell (1749?–1812), wife of the 4th Duke of Gordon. The profile makes this not unlikely.

$6\frac{7}{8} \times 4\frac{15}{16}$ in. (pl.)

5315 THE PETTICOAT,
AT THE FIERI MASCHARETA [*sic*]

Pubᵈ Apr. 25. 1775 by M Darly 39 Strand

Engraving. (Coloured impression.) A companion-print to No. 5314. A voluminous petticoat worn over the head as a hood and reaching to the feet of its wearer, whose face, in profile to the l., appears through an aperture. One large gloved hand appears through a slit in the garment. A ducal coronet is on the wearer's head, low-heeled shoes suggest that the wearer is a man. Perhaps a portrait of Alexander, 4th Duke of Gordon (1745-1827), portraits of the Duke show that this is not unlikely.

$6\frac{7}{8} \times 4\frac{7}{8}$ in (pl).

5316 CORPORAL PERPENDICULAR

Pubᵈ May 20 1775 by M Darly 39 Strand.

Engraving. A H L. portrait (caricature) in profile to the r. in an oval, of a man wearing a soldier's conical cap, much elongated, on which the letters

G.R. are partly visible His profile, hair, and figure are almost in vertical straight lines. He wears a coat with military facings and a ruffled shirt.

Reissued in book, dated 1 Jan 1776, see No. 5369.

$4\frac{5}{8} \times 3\frac{3}{4}$ in.

5317 THE ABYSSINIAN TRAVELLER.

E. Topham inv^t

Pub by M Darly Decr 9. 1775 (39 Strand)

Engraving. A W L standing portrait (caricatured) in profile to the r. of James Bruce (1730–94). In his l. hand he holds out an open book, *Travels into Abyssinia by* . . . . His hat is under his r. arm Beneath the title is etched:

> *O Thou whose active search has dar'd explore*
> *Far distant Realms and Climes unknown before;*
> *Thy toils now finishd and thy dangers past,*
> *Spite of Thy self we fix thee here at last.*

Bruce had recently returned to England, where he was at first received with great attention which soon gave way to scepticism and dislike; this led to the postponement of the publication of his travels till 1790

Reissued in book, dated 1 Jan. 1776, see No. 5369.

$7\frac{1}{16} \times 5\frac{15}{16}$ in.

5318 ECCE HOMO.

Published as the act Directs by Dan. Demoniae. Bethel. 1775. B—b—y^1

Engraving. The window of Matthew Darly's print-shop in the Strand is being violently attacked by a man (William Austin), with the appearance of a maniac. He is shouting *Damn your foollish Caricatures.* In his r. hand is a cane, on his l. arm is thrust a portfolio in the manner of a shield; it is ornamented by a broken anchor in an oval, round which is inscribed: *Life's a Jest and all things show it. I thought so once but now I know it.* Papers flutter from the portfolio to the ground: sketches; a paper inscribed *M^{rss} Townshend com^{ts} to M^r A and says he may Dine there*; a ground-plan inscribed *the Plan for my Museum* and (in reversed looking-glass writing) *No 103 Oxford Street*; a doctor's prescription, *Black Hellebore $\mathfrak{z}$ D^r. Monrow*; a paper inscribed *Proposals for Opening A Museum of Drawings . . at 2 Gn^s Each Subs^r 1000 would do* (?) *& I have got already* Across the window is *Mt Darly*, and in each of three lower rows of panes a print is displayed, the most conspicuous being this print, entitled *A Bethlemhite*; the print beneath it suggests a chained maniac in Bedlam.

In the street a broken-down coach is slightly sketched, with its wheels twisted or broken off; on it is an anchor like that on the portfolio. In the distance is an equestrian statue, evidently that of Charles II at Charing Cross. A dog watches the onslaught on the window.

Beneath the design is etched. *Be it known to all Men, that I —— upon Just cause before God and men do Declare & Pronounce War with and against all and every Printshop and Printseller within and without the City of London*

---

^{1} The manner is not that of Bunbury.

for reasons hereafter set forth and shall on all occasions act offensivly and defensivly as oportunity shall offer. Whereas I by the Extream necessity of my circumstances was forced to wreek [sic] my brains to finde out some Scheme thereby to suport myself in that prudent maner I first set of in and having been in the country in order to strengthen my Ideas and to get what was necessary I luckeyley projected one which beyond a doubt must have answered my porpose, which was to open a Museum of Drawings by the best Masters, had it not been for the most malicious wicked and Diabolical combinations consultations and insinuations of that most unfeeling set of Men cald print-sellers so being overwhelmed with disopointments and Poverty takes this despairate method to rebuke their insolence.

The suggestion that Austin is a lunatic is stressed by the prescription of 'Dr Munrow', Dr John Monro being physician of Bethlehem Hospital with a great reputation in the treatment of insanity.

On one impression of this print is written 'William Austen, drawing-master', on the other 'Austen the Drawing Master & print-seller' in contemporary hands. William Austin (1721–1820), like Darly, was an engraver and teacher of drawing, and at one time kept a print-shop in London and published caricatures, see index of artists.

Attributed to Bartolozzi by Calabi, *Bartolozzi*, 1928, No. 2231.

$7\frac{5}{8} \times 7\frac{1}{2}$ in.

5319 THE MARRIED MAID OF HONOUR, OR, THE WIDOW'D WIFE AND HER TWO HUSBANDS.

Publish'd as the Act directs 1 Feb. 1775 by W. Nicoll St Pauls Ch. Yard

Engraving. From *The Matrimonial Magazine*, i 9, illustrating 'Memoirs of the Married Maid of Honour . . .'. Three bust portraits in oval frames surrounded with elaborate ornament. Above, and slightly larger than the two others, is that of the *D——ss of K——*, the Duchess of Kingston, so-called. She looks T Q to the l , a drapery falling from her head suggests widowhood.

Below are two profile portraits, that on the l. is of a truculent-looking naval officer in profile to the r · *C—— H——*, he is Augustus John Hervey, then Captain Hervey, who secretly married Elizabeth Chudleigh in 1744; he became 3rd Earl of Bristol 20 Mar. 1775. The other, in profile to the l., wearing a ribbon and star, is *D—— of K——*, Duke of Kingston, who died in 1773, whom Elizabeth Chudleigh had married bigamously in 1769 (having been his mistress for about ten years), after procuring a verdict in the Consistory Court that she was a spinster.

Beneath the design is engraved,

> *—————— And in each hand*
> *A wanton Lover which by turns caress'd her,*
> *With all the freedom of unbounded passion. Otway*

At this time an indictment for bigamy was pending, and on 24 May 1775 she appeared in the King's Bench to answer it, the trial taking place in Westminster Hall, 15–22 Apr. 1776, see Nos. 5301, 5362, 5425. For satires on the notorious Miss Chudleigh in 1749 as Iphigenia, see Nos. 3030–3.

$6\frac{7}{8} \times 4\frac{3}{4}$ in. (pl.).

5320 A BATH ADONIS WORSHIPING THE IDOL OF HIS AFFEC-
TIONS. [1 Feb. 1775]

Engraved for the Matrimonial Magazine

Engraving. *Matrimonial Magazine*, i. 34, illustrating 'the History of
Captain S——: or, The Bath Adonis'. A man, richly dressed, leans his r
elbow on a console table, turning his head to look at his reflection in a
mirror (l) in a curved frame. He holds an open snuff-box in his r. hand,
his l is on his hip. He wears a laced coat, an epaulette on the r. shoulder,
a flowered waistcoat, and a sword. The legs of the table on which he leans
are elaborately carved, the floor is carpeted, the wall papered. An oval
picture of Cupid shooting at a reclining figure hangs on the wall. The
scene is the pump-room at Bath

Captain S. is said to have been successively a runaway apprentice, then
billiard-marker, actor, fortune hunter, whose wife's fortune enabled him
to buy a commission in the army, his deserted wife having died he has
gone to Bath to secure another rich wife.

$6\frac{3}{4} \times 4$ in. B M L , P.P. 5433 m

5321 THE INDISCRETIONS OF NOBLE BLOOD CURED MEDI-
CINALLY. *See pa 65.*

Publish'd according to the Act March 1st 1775.

Engraving *Matrimonial Magazine*, i. 65, illustrating 'The Loves and
Amours of Lord V—— and the gay Mrs E——' A man kneels on one
knee kissing the hand of a lady seated on a settee (r) Her husband, a
doctor in a tie-wig, enters through a door unnoticed The panelled wall,
a carved pediment to the door, an oval mirror in a carved frame, &c,
suggest a richly-furnished room

Grace Dalrymple Elliott or Eliot is surprised by her husband Dr. John
Elliott (knighted 1776, cr a baronet 1778), with Lord Valentia (with whom
she eloped in 1774). See No. 5257 and index.

$6\frac{3}{16} \times 3\frac{7}{8}$ in B M L., P P. 5433 m

5322 THE H—R—G—N [Harrington] HARAM

Publish'd as the Act directs by W Nicoll St Paul's Church Yard
1 April 1775

Engraving. From *The Matrimonial Magazine*, i. 113, illustrating 'The
Haram, or the Memoirs of the E—— of H——n', in which the seraglio of
Lord Harrington is described. A group of six women, with one man who
wears a hat. One is a negress, wearing a feathered turban, another is in
pseudo-classical dress, a third is dressed as a country girl, the others are
dressed in the fashion of the day One who is seated is playing a mandoline.
The room is ornately decorated, the walls are faced with Corinthian pilasters.
On the wall is a picture of an ape riding a goat.

For Harrington see G E C *Complete Peerage* and No 5033.

$5\frac{1}{16} \times 3\frac{3}{16}$ in.

5323 THE DUELLIST; OR, THE MODERN MAN OF HONOUR.
[1 May 1775]

Engraved for the Matrimonial Magazine

Engraving. *Matrimonial Magazine*, i 185 Portrait of a young man in a swaggering attitude in a park, indicated by trees and a wall. He stands legs apart, hands in his breeches-pockets, a tasselled cane thrust under his l. arm He wears a sword.

A portrait of Fitzgerald, known as Fighting Fitzgerald, illustrating an article with the same title as that of the print. See Nos. 5198–5200.

$5\frac{3}{8} \times 3\frac{3}{16}$ in. B M L , P.P 5433 m.

5324 THE JOCKEY STATESMAN AND HIS D——SS.

Engrav'd for the Matrimonial Magazine.

Publish'd as the Act directs by W. Nicoll, St Pauls Church Yard,
  1 June 1775.

Engraving. *Matrimonial Magazine,* i. 234, illustrating 'The History of the Jockey Statesman'. The Duke of Grafton (r.) standing in open country in conversation, or altercation, with his wife (l.). Both are in riding dress, and both hold riding switches, the other hand being raised as if to enforce an argument. Grafton resigned his office of Lord Privy Seal Nov. 1775 His second wife (m. 1769) was Elizabeth, d. of Sir R Wrottesley, dean of Windsor, by whom he had twelve children; see Nos 4292, 4634, 4989.

$5\frac{3}{8} \times 3\frac{1}{4}$ in. B.M.L., P.P. 5433 m.

5325 SIR TRISTE SHADOW. [*c.* 1775]

[Lady Craven.]

Engraving. On the print is written in Miss Banks's hand, 'Lady Craven del.' and 'Edward Roe Yeo Esqr carrying up the Coventry Address'. A man, riding fast (r. to l.) in profile; behind him on the saddle is a large cylindrical package labelled *Coventry address.* From his mouth issues a label inscribed,

I'm very much frighted
but I shall be Knighted.

A street-scene is indicated by houses on the l From the window of a house in the foreground looks Peeping Tom.

At this time loyal addresses to the king on the American crisis were pouring in from counties, boroughs, &c. The address from 'the Gentlemen, Clergy, Traders and Principal Inhabitants of the City of Coventry' dated 25 Sept 1775 was presented to the king by the two members for Coventry, Walter Waring and Edward Roe Yeo. *London Gazette,* 26–30 Sept. 1775.

Lady Craven (1750–1828, afterwards Margravine of Anspach) in 1786 sent Horace Walpole a drawing of the Castle of Otranto *Letters,* xiii. 419–20.

$6\frac{1}{8} \times 8\frac{1}{4}$ in.

5326 AN EMBLEM OF A MODERN MARRIAGE

[Attributed to Gillray.]

Drawn by M H. from a sketch cut with a diamond on a pane of glass
  Publish'd according to act of Parliament June 15, 1775.

Engraving. Two figures stand side by side· a skeleton (l) wearing a feathered hat, a coat, and sword, a lady (r.) holding a cloak round her, and wearing feathers in her hair. She points with her l. hand to a rectangular tomb, on which is inscribed *Requiescas in pace* beneath a skull and cross-bones. They are standing on a road which leads to a large country house with a Palladian portico over which is a baron's coronet. In the air a cupid flies away, covering his face with his hand and holding his torch reversed. Beneath the design is etched :

—— *no smiles for us the God head wears!*
His torch inverted & his face in tears!

[From Lord Hervey's *Reply to Hammond's Verses to Miss Dashwood.*
Dodsley's *Collection of Poems*, iv. 73–8.]
Grego, *Gillray*, p. 27.
$7\frac{5}{8} \times 7\frac{7}{16}$ in.

Ten prints from the series of mezzotints published by Carrington Bowles, catalogued in Volumes III and IV.[1]

THE MISERIES OF A SINGLE LIFE. (310)
See No 4540—[c. 1775]

AN UNEXPECTED LEVEE FOR A NEW MARRIED COUPLE.
See No. 4581—2 Jan. 1775

THE WELCH CURATE (320)   See No. 3784—[1775]
A satire on the rich clergy.

EXTRA DUTY . . . (325)   See No. 3783—[1775]
A satire on monks.

THE CONSPIRATORS. (326)   See No. 3760—[1775]
A satire on the clergy, lawyers, and physicians.

BILLINGSGATE TRIUMPHANT . . . (327)   See No. 4541—[1775]

A PLEASING METHOD OF ROUZING THE DOCTOR—OR A TYTHE PIG NO BAD SIGHT. (328)   See No. 3785 [1775]
A satire on the clergy, Reproduced, Paston, Pl. clxxxvi.

A TRUE TOWN PICTURE: OR AN OLD HAG OF DRURY PRE-SENTING A CHICKEN TO HIS LORDSHIP. (329)
See No. 3788—[1775]

SEARCH THE WORLD YOU'LL SELDOM SEE—HANDSOMER FOLKS THAN WE THREE (332)
[P. Dawe]   See No. 4542—20 Oct 1775

CONFESSION. (333)   See No. 3775—[1775]
A satire on monks.

Similar mezzotint published by Sayer & Bennett.

THE BOTTLE COMPANIONS. (378)   See No. 4622—1 Aug. 1775

[1] Nos. 3784, 4542 have the imprint of Bowles and Carver.

POLITICAL SATIRES

Not in B.M., described from a photogravure reproduction, R. T. Halsey, *Boston Port Bill*, p. 42,

THE WISE MEN OF GOTHAM AND THEIR GOOSE

Pub⁴ 16ᵗʰ Febʸ 1776 by W Humphrey Gerrard Street Soho.

Mezzotint (coloured impression) Ministers and others grouped round a table on which lies a goose which Bute holds down by the neck as he raises his broadsword to kill the bird. Bute (r), in profile to the l., wears Highland dress and the Garter ribbon; the bird has a small chain round its neck. In the foreground (l.) a fat bishop leans back in an arm-chair watching intently: he is probably Markham, Archbishop of York, see No. 5958, &c Seven other spectators are poorly characterized· one wearing a ribbon and star leaning over the table may be intended for the king or North but resembles neither. A judge leaning on the bishop's chair may be Mansfield, but his profile is almost concave and has more resemblance to Bathurst. Two others wear legal robes, one is perhaps Wedderburn A profile head on the extreme l resembles Sandwich. Germain is probably one of the other two A tenth man (l) is walking to the l. holding up a large basket full of eggs. On the ground (l) is a map of *North America* which is being befouled by a dog; on the r are two bags, one inscribed *Taxes* is disgorging eggs. On the wall which forms a background is a picture of the British lion asleep, flanked by two framed inscriptions on which are verses (30 ll.) which explain the print, beginning,

> *In Gotham once the Story goes*
> *A lot of Wise-acres arose . .*

Their most prized possession was a goose (the colonies),

> *A Rara Avis to behold*
> *Who laid each Day an Egg of Gold¹*
> *This made them grow immensely rich*
> *Gave them an Avaritious Itch, . . .*

In order to make the bird lay two eggs instead of one.

> *About her Neck they put a chain,*
> *And more their Folly to compleat*
> *They Stampt upon her Wings & Feet*
> *But this had no Effect at all,*
> *Yet made her struggle, flutter, squall,*
> *And do what every Goose would do*
> *That had her liberty in view*
> *When one of more distinguish'd Note*
> *Cry'd D———n her, let us cut her Throat,*
> *They did, but not an Egg was found*
> *But Blood came pouring from yᵉ Wound*

¹ Walpole wrote to Mann, 16 June 1779, 'we killed the goose that laid a golden egg a day' referring to trade, not to taxes *Letters*, x. 427.

One of a number of satires attributing the measures against the Colonies to Bute, see No. 5289, &c For other references to the Stamp Act see No. 5487, &c. Cf No 5578.

B.M.L., Ac. 4714/14. (p. 43.)

5327 HOPKINS TRIUMPHANT, OR WILKES IN THE DUMPS
[c Feb. 1776]

Engraving Probably from a magazine. Street scene, the chairing of Alderman Hopkins elected City Chamberlain Feb. 1776. Hopkins, held aloft in a chair, holds a staff to which are tied three money-bags. The crowd waves hats and sticks; a man holds a flag inscribed *Hopkins for ever, down with Wilks & Liberty*. In the foreground (l.) Wilkes reclines on the ground supported by a woman holding the cap of Liberty on a staff and a large tankard decorated with the City arms. Wilkes holds a paper inscribed *Alass! how unstable the affections of a Mob*. A bull in alderman's robes, representing Alderman Bull, kneels at his side. From a window (l) a woman pours the contents of a jug over the cap of Liberty A ragged ballad-singer (r.) sings from a broadside.

When the Chamberlainship of the City fell vacant by the death of Sir Stephen Janssen, Wilkes stood for the post and was defeated by Alderman Hopkins He made a speech accusing the ministers and the Directors of the Bank of having corrupted the electors and announced his intention of standing again in Midsummer, although the post was normally held for life Wilkes was again defeated at Midsummer 1776, 1777, and 1778, but became Chamberlain in Nov. 1779 on Hopkins's death *Ann. Reg.* 1776, 121; Sharpe, *London and the Kingdom*, III. 163-4. For Hopkins see No 5398.

$5\frac{3}{4} \times 3\frac{11}{16}$ in.

5328 THE STATE BLACKSMITHS FORGING FETTERS FOR THE AMERICANS

Published according to Act of Parliament 1st March 1776.

Engraving. The interior of a blacksmith's forge. At the anvil stands Mansfield, in judge's robes, forging the links of a chain A number of ministers stand round: Lord North in the foreground (l.), holding up his lorgnette; in his r hand is *An Act for Prohibiting all Trade* Lord Sandwich stands by North, holding a hammer in one hand, an anchor in the other, apparently intending to break this emblem of the navy. Behind them stands Bute, working the bellows of the forge, looking over his shoulder at North while he works Through a window on the l. appears the head of the king who is smiling fatuously

Lord North brought in the Bill for prohibiting all intercourse with America and for the seizure of American shipping on 20 Nov. 1775 (16 George III. c 5). It met with great opposition. *Ann. Reg.* 1776, 109 ff ; Walpole, *Last Journals*, 1910, 1 495; *Parl. Hist.* xviii 992 ff., 1056-1106, *Autobiography of Grafton*, ed Anson, pp. 275 ff. One of many satires making Bute the instigator of measures against the Americans, see No. 5289, &c.

$6\frac{0}{16} \times 4$ in.

5329 THE YANKIE DOODLES INTRENCHMENTS NEAR BOSTON 1776

Publish'd as the Act Directs

Engraving. Behind a well-made trench, fronted with palisades, appear the heads of its defenders; words issue from their mouths in long labels. One man stands on the top of the trench, his cap is inscribed *Death or Liberty*, his coat and stockings are ragged, and he stands as if shivering with cold, his bayonetted musket tucked under his arm and pointing downwards; he says *I swear its plaguy Cold Jonathan; I don't think They'll Attack us, Now You* The other men, whose heads and shoulders only appear above the trench, say (l. to r.)· *I dont feel bold today* (the speaker is dressed as a minister, with flat hat, lank hair, and bands) His neighbour says, *I fear they'll Shoot Again*; a man wearing a *Death or Liberty* hat says,

> *How, Borgoine & Clinton*
> *let us keep a good Sqint on*
> *for if they come here*
> *they'll warm us I fear*

Another man wearing a *Death or Liberty* cap says

> *blast their Eyes*
> *We'll have no Excise*

Another minister of puritanic appearance says,

> *Tis Old Olivers Cause*
> *No Monarchy nor Laws*

He holds a flag on which is a tree, inscribed *Liberty*, surmounted by a fool's cap and flanked by two gibbets labelled *The Fruit*. Another man wearing a *Death or Liberty* cap, says, *I fear Our Gen[ll] is Still a Labourer in Vain.* The last man is in military uniform with epaulettes and a gorget; one hand is on a small cannon in an embrasure, the other holds a bottle which stands on a thick book, presumably a Bible; he says *The Spirit moves us in Sun—dry places &c. Yet I fear the Lord is not With us.*
Beneath the design is etched,

> *Behold the Yankies in there ditch's*
> *Whose Conscience gives such griping twitch's*
> *They'r ready to Be S—t their Brech's. Yankie Doodle do.*
> *Next see the Hypocritic parson*
> *Who thay all wish to turn an A—s on*
> *Altho' the Devil keps the farce on. Yankie &c.*
> *See Putnam that Commands in Chief Sir*
> *Who looks & Labours like a thief sir*
> *To get them daily Bread & Beef sir. Yankie &c.*
> *Their Congress now is quite disjoint'd*
> *Since Gibbits sis for them appointed*
> *For fighting gainst y[e] Lords Annointed. Yankie, doodle*

The artist appears to have been ignorant of Washington's appointment, 15 June 1775, as commander-in-chief. He took over the command of the troops round Boston on 3 July 1775, superseding not Israel Putnam (appointed fourth major-general June 1775) but Artemas Ward. Boston was evacuated by Howe on 17 Mar. 1776. Cf. No. 5292.

For the New England pine-tree flag, used before the stars and stripes, see No. 5336.

One of the few satires hostile to the Americans, cf. Nos. 5401, 6288.

8×9⅝ in.

5330 BUNKERS HILL OR AMERICA'S HEAD DRESS
[1 Mar. 1776[1]]

Engraving. A companion print to No. 5335. A lady (T.Q.L.) in profile to the r. with the enormous coiffure of 1776-7 grotesquely exaggerated Her hands are in a muff Her inverted pyramid of hair supports three quasi-circular redoubts surrounded by cannon on which troops are fighting On each is a flag large out of all proportion to the soldiers. There are also a train of artillery, and a number of tents. All the men in the redoubts are dressed as British soldiers but are firing point-blank at each other; their three flags are decorated respectively with an ape, with two women holding darts of lightning, and with a goose

Evidently intended to satirize the fighting at Bunker Hill, 17 June 1775. For similar satires on hair-dressing see No. 5378, apparently a parody of this print.

8³⁄₁₆×6¹¹⁄₁₆ in

5331 COLONEL ARNOLD.
[? 'Corbutt'.]
London, Published as the Act directs, 26 March 1776, by Thos Hart.

Mezzotint. One of a series, see No. 5290. T.Q L standing portrait of an officer in uniform, pointing to l. with his r. hand and looking over his l. shoulder to the r. A town with scattered buildings and several spires is in the background (l), perhaps intended for the outskirts of Quebec. Beneath the title is engraved, *Who Commanded the Provincial Troops sent against Quebec, through the Wilderness of Canada, and was wounded in Storming that City, under General Montgomery.*

Benedict Arnold (1741–1801) was wounded in the assault on Quebec, 31 Dec. 1775, when Montgomery was killed. He figures later in English caricature as an arch-traitor, see No 6173. See No. 5408, a copy, issued in connexion with Burgoyne's surrender at Saratoga.

Chaloner Smith, iv, pp. 1714–15. Andrews, p. 89.

12¹⁵⁄₁₆×9¹⁵⁄₁₆ in.

5331 A

A copy, probably by J. M. Will, see No. 6034, having the same inscription, except that *London* is after Hart and with the addition of *Ioh Martin Will excudit Aug* [Augsburg] *vind.*

12¾×9¼ in.

5332 DAVID WOOSTER, ESQ^R
[? 'Corbutt'.]
London, Published as the Act directs 26. March 1776, by Thos Hart

Mezzotint. One of a series, see No 5290. T.Q.L. portrait of a military officer between two cannon looking to the l ; his l. hand rests on the breech

¹ So dated in a contemporary hand

of a cannon, in his r is a long spear. In the background is a tent (l.) and a stone fortification (r.) with cannon. Beneath the title is engraved, *Commander in Chief of the Provincial Army against Quebec.*

After the assault on Quebec 31 Dec. 1775, by Montgomery and Arnold at which Montgomery was killed, the city was besieged with declining hopes of success, until 6 May 1776, when the Americans were routed by Carleton

Chaloner Smith, iv 1717. Andrews. p. 92.

$12\frac{5}{8} \times 9\frac{1}{4}$ in

5332 A

Copy, probably by J. M. Will, see No. 6034, having the same inscription, except that *London* is after *Hart*, with the addition of *Ioh. Martin Will excud Aug* [Augsburg] *Vind.*

$12\frac{5}{8} \times 9\frac{1}{4}$ in.

5333 THE BLESSED EFFECTS OF VENALITY.

Lon. Mag. Pub⁴ as yᵉ Act directs, May 1, 1776.

Engraving. From the *London Magazine*, xlv 171. A man half-seated on a three-legged stool which stands on the topmost of three steps, strikes with an axe at its legs; these are inscribed respectively *Commons* (from which a large piece has been chopped), *Lords*, and *Privy Council.* Behind him is a curtain decorated with the royal arms. In the foreground are four figures· Britannia, with her shield, seated and asleep, the staff on which is the cap of liberty about to drop from her hand, a Dutchman standing with his hands in his breeches pocket; a cloaked figure, representing Spain, points out the man with the axe to France, a man dressed as a French fop.

The man with the axe may be either North or George III, but the royal arms suggest the king. The axe stands for bribery. The plate illustrates an article 'On Venality and Corruption', whose thesis is that the contest with America is supported as an opportunity for bribery and corruption and leads to the aggrandizement of Spain, France, and Holland.

$4\frac{3}{16} \times 6\frac{3}{16}$ in.

5334 THE PARRICIDE. A SKETCH OF MODERN PATRIOTISM
[1 May 1776]

Engrav'd for the Westminster Magazine.

Engraving. From the *Westminster Magazine*, iv. 216. Britannia, held down by two men, is about to be stabbed by America, in the guise of a Red Indian woman with a head-dress of feathers, holding a tomahawk in one hand, a dagger in the other Britannia is also being clawed by a lion, which advances under the guidance of a judge who holds reins attached to the animal's jaws. Behind the judge (presumably Camden) stands Chatham supported on crutches. Wilkes in his civic gown stands between America and Britannia, directing the attack. Grafton, who had recently joined the Opposition, holds her by one arm, a man in a civic gown and chain holds her by the other; he is probably Alderman Hayley, Wilkes's brother-in-law, M.P. for the City, who was sheriff 1775-6 Among the other patriots is a fox, representing Charles Fox. Britannia's shield, trampled on by America, and her broken spear lie on the ground. In the centre of the foreground is an oval medallion on which is a pelican piercing her breast for her young A partly-draped man, probably representing Discord or Faction, stands (l.) brandishing a flaming torch in each hand; his hair is composed of serpents.

This illustrates 'Reflections on the Declarations of the General Congress' pp 216-19, and, more particularly, a quotation from a pamphlet, 'The Rights of Great Britain Asserted against the Claims of America', which is an attack on English 'patriots': 'With an effrontery without example in any other age or nation, these men assume the name of Patriots, yet lay the honour, dignity and reputation of their Country under the feet of her rebellious subjects. With a peculiar refinement on Parricide, they bind the hands of the *Mother*, while they plant a dagger in those of the *Daughter*, to stab her to the heart ...' This shows a complete reversal in the attitude of the *Westminster Magazine*, see No. 5288 The first appearance in this catalogue of Fox as a patriot, cf. No. 5113.

One of the few satires which attack the Opposition Cf. Nos. 5103, 5644, 5650, 5665, 5829, 5836 Cf. also Nos. 5832, 5833. $3\frac{3}{4} \times 6\frac{3}{16}$ in.

5335 NODDLE-ISLAND · OR HOW · ARE WE DECIEVED.

J. S. sc.

Pub⁴ May 12. 1776 by M Darly strand

Engraving (coloured impression) A companion design to No. 5330 A lady (T.Q.L.) on whose grotesquely extended coiffure military operations are proceeding She stands in profile to the l. holding a fan. At the top of her pyramid of hair soldiers fire cannon from a rectangular fort (l) which appears to be American at other soldiers firing cannon from an adjacent mound (r) composed of ringlets of hair. Two immense flags flying from the fort bear, one a crocodile, the other a cross-bow and arrows, the flags of their opponents, the English, are decorated one with an ass, the other with a fool's cap and bells Below this combat are tents and two men with a cannon On the lower rolls of hair are red-coats marching in single file, followed by a baggage waggon. Lower down again, red-coats in boats are rowing towards two ships in full sail.

This evidently satirizes the evacuation of Boston by Howe, 17 Mar. 1776. There were many protests against the misleading account given in the *Gazette*, see *London Chronicle*, 7-9 May 1776. Walpole wrote 'nobody was deceived', *Last Journals*, 1910, 1. 540 The 'How' in the title is a pun on the name of the commander-in-chief, see No. 5405, &c. $8\frac{1}{2} \times 6\frac{1}{4}$ in.

5336 COMMODORE HOPKINS,

[? J. M. Will, after a plate by 'Corbutt'.]

Publish'd as the Act directs 22. Aug⁴ 1776. by Tho⁵ Hart London. Joh. Martin Will excudit Aug. [Augsburg] Vind.

Mezzotint. Copy from one of a series, see No. 5290. T Q L. portrait of a naval officer standing apparently on the deck of a vessel; he holds a drawn sabre in his r. hand, looking to the l. and pointing with his l. hand to the r. where there is a ship in full sail displaying a large flag on which is the design of a conventional tree inscribed *Liberty Tree An appeal to God.*

Behind on the l. is another ship displaying an enormous striped flag with a rattlesnake coiled to strike and the words *Dont tread upon me.* Clouds of smoke suggest a naval engagement. Beneath the title is inscribed *Commander in Chief of the American Fleet.*

Esek Hopkins, an ex-sea captain and privateer in the war of 1756–63, was appointed by Congress, 22 Dec. 1775, commander-in-chief of the new navy, consisting of eight small ships hastily altered for war. In June 1776 he was censured by Congress for lack of success, in Dec. 1776 his fleet was blockaded in Narragansett Bay by the British fleet, in Mar. 1777 he was suspended and in Jan. 1778 dismissed the service. *Dict. Am. Biog.*

The two flags depicted were used for the American navy at the beginning of the war until superseded by that of the thirteen stripes resolved upon by Congress, 14 June 1777. The New England pine-tree flag, a flag with a white ground, a tree (Liberty Tree) in the middle with a coiled rattlesnake at its foot and the motto 'Appeal to Heaven', was used on the floating batteries about Boston in the autumn of 1775 and was six months later prescribed by the Provincial Congress for the Massachusetts navy. The other flag, that of the Continental Navy, was hoisted for the first time by Lieut. Paul Jones on Hopkins's flag-ship in the autumn of 1775. G. W. Allen, *Naval History of the American Revolution*, 1913, i. 64–5, 92–3. See No. 5973, &c. Similar in manner to Nos. 5405, 5406, signed Corbutt.

Plate from which this is a copy is described by Chaloner Smith, iv. 1715–16, Andrews, p. 90.

12¾ × 9¼ in.

5337 MAJOR GENERAL JOHN SULLIVAN,

Publish'd as the Act directs 22 Augt 1776 by Thos Hart London. Ioh. Martin Will excudit Aug. [Augsburg] *Vind.*

Mezzotint. Copy from one of a series, see No. 5290. T Q L. standing portrait of a military officer, looking to the r. In his r. hand is a long spear, his l is on his hip. The background is a tree-trunk (l) and foliage. Beneath the title is engraved, *A distinguish'd Officer in the Continental Army.*

Sullivan conducted the evacuation of Canada up the Richelieu River in the summer of 1776

An Augsburg copy of a plate which is listed by Chaloner Smith, iv, p. 1717. Andrews, p. 91

12¹¹⁄₁₆ × 9¼ in.

5338 JEAN SULIVAN   [*c.* 1776]

peint par Alexander Camphel [*sic*] *a Williambourg en Virginie. Se vend a Londres chez Thom. Hart.*

Mezzotint. H.L portrait in an oval within a rectangle apparently copied from the original of No. 5337. Probably a companion print to No. 5292 A.

7¹¹⁄₁₆ × 6⅜ in.

5339 MAJOR ROBERT ROGERS,

Publish'd as the Act directs Octr 1. 1776, by Thos Hart London. Joh. Martin Will excudit Aug [Augsburg] *vind.*   [*c.* 1776]

Mezzotint. Copy from one of a series, see No. 5290. Standing portrait, T.Q L of a fierce-looking military officer with fringed and beaded trappings to his uniform of Red Indian workmanship. He holds a musket against his l shoulder Behind, among foliage, are three Indian braves (r), one holding a tomahawk, another a knife Beneath the title is inscribed, *Commander in Chief of the Indians in the Back Settlements of America.*

Published at this date, the print was clearly intended to suggest that Rogers was leading scalping-parties against Americans, see No. 5470, &c. Rogers, an American frontiersman, had been a commander of Rangers against Indians and French in the Seven Years War, had taken part in the suppression of Pontiac's Rebellion, 1763, and from 1765-8 had been commander of troops at Mackinac, a frontier post. After being charged with mutiny and embezzlement (1769) he came to England, was restored to half-pay, went to America in 1775 hoping for employment which he eventually obtained from Howe in August 1776, with the rank of lieut-col. His sole service in America was as a recruiting officer of American loyalists; his only active service was in command of an outpost on Howe's east flank where he was surprised and crushingly defeated by Col Haslett on 21 Oct. 1776. Biography of Rogers by Allan Nevins, in his edition of *Ponteach*, Chicago, 1914. His association with Indians was well known in England from his published *Journals*, 1765, and his tragedy, *Ponteach; or the Savages of North America*, 1766, a sympathetic account of the Indian character. It is here evidently exploited for political purposes.

An Augsburg copy of a plate which is listed by Chaloner Smith, iv. 1717. Andrews, p. 91.

$12\frac{5}{8} \times 9\frac{1}{8}$ in.

5340 NEWS FROM AMERICA, OR THE PATRIOTS IN THE DUMPS [1 Dec 1776]

Lond. Mag. Nov. 1776.

Engraving From the *London Magazine*, xlv. 599. On a platform of three steps stand North and Mansfield; North, smiling, holds up a dispatch beginning *My Lord* and signed *How*, the intermediate text being illegible Behind them (r.), and on a lower step, stand Bute and George III. On the ground (l.) is a group of patriots who make gestures of distress, Wilkes being the most prominent. A seated and disreputable-looking woman holding the cap of Liberty is weeping On the r stand two ministers in conference, pointing with amusement and scorn at the patriots; one, Sandwich (r.), holds his finger to his nose, from his pocket hangs a paper inscribed *List of the Navy*; the other is probably intended for Germain. In the background is the sea, with ships of war, some in full sail, others sinking

This illustrates an article intended to counteract the effect of the news of the action on Long Island and the capture of New York, 'the friends of Ministry thinking every thing gained, the friends of America every thing lost', whereas it should be regarded as a fallacious and temporary success, 'the beginning of sorrows'. Howe's dispatch of 3 Sept. 1776, reporting the landing on Long Island, was published in the *Gazette* of 10 Oct. Fox wrote to Rockingham, 13 Oct. 1776, of 'the terrible news from Long Island'. *Memorials and Corr.* i. 145. Cf. No. 5923, a more realistic representation of patriots reading the news of a British success

$6\frac{1}{2} \times 4\frac{1}{4}$ in.

5341 THE SHAFTESBURY ELECTION OR THE HUMOURS OF PUNCH. [n.d. *c* 1776]

Mezzotint A design in compartments showing the malpractices at the Shaftesbury election of 1774 which became notorious owing to the petition of the defeated candidate, the subsequent proceedings in the House of Commons, and actions at law 1775-6 Three compartments in the upper part of the print show interiors labelled *Punch's Room* (l), *Secretaries Room*, and *Agents Room* (r), shown as three adjacent rooms, visible by the removal of the fourth wall. The interior of the rooms is revealed by Truth, a naked woman on the extreme r. who holds up an enormous curtain which would screen all the rooms if it fell Underneath these compartments are scenes taking place in the street outside and below these rooms. A broad gangway crowded with voters leads from the street-level to the central room

In *Punch's Room*, a man dressed as Punch with a large hump and wearing a peaked hat and jack-boots stands on a stool putting a packet through a small opening in the partition dividing this room from the centre or *Secretaries Room* Behind him a stout man stands by a round table, apparently making up the packets for Punch; he holds a paper in both hands, and says, *this Note for 68 will make 3 votes.* On the table are papers, a money-bag, and two piles of coins. At a rectangular table on the other side of the room (r) a man is seated, pouring out wine from a bottle, another man stands opposite him, holding a wine-glass and saying, *They swallow Pills well.* At the back of the room are two wheelbarrows filled with money-bags, other money-bags lie on the floor. The room is quite bare except for tables, stool, and chair. The ceiling is raftered, there is a window in the l wall, and two hats hang on the wall

In the next room, a man stands on a chair facing the l. wall and takes the packet which Punch is handing to him. Four birds, each with a coin (?) in its claws, appear to have just flown through the opening which is immediately above a padlocked door of communication Behind him stands another elector, his hat in both hands, looking up at the opening. Two other men stand by, one holding a long staff Two men sit at a round table; one with a large hump is writing; the other is in conversation with two men, one holding a paper, the other, holding his hat, appears to be making a request. Two hats hang on the wall. On the back wall hangs a large framed picture over which is inscribed *We'll purchase Europe* It represents an Indian scene: a corpulent man sits on a canopied howdah on an elephant, he is crowned and holds a sceptre, money-bags are piled on both sides of the howdah; a mahout sits on the animal's neck. The elephant appears to be picking up money-bags from the ground with its trunk; an Indian in a turban who lies across these bags is being beaten and kicked by a European.

In the third room, two men sit writing at a round table, one points to three supplicants, saying *Begone you Rogues you'll vote for Mort'* [Mortimer]. Of the three men whom he addresses, two stand hat in hand, the third hurries away putting on his hat and saying *Nothing for honest men.* Another disappointed voter stands between the two men at the table, his hands clasped.

The lower part of the print represents the street below the three rooms On the l is a procession (l. to r) escorting Punch; in front walks a man carrying a flag inscribed *Punch & Rupees for ever.* He is followed by six men with marrow-bones and cleavers, which they are striking together to produce the traditional election noise. All wear election favours in their hats, the men with the marrow-bones have aprons twisted round their waists and are probably butchers. Immediately behind them is Punch on horseback, with an immense hump on both back and chest, a conical hat and a frill round his neck. His face is covered by a net and he is saying *20 Guin[eas] for two Voices & one round Oath well swallowed* He is accompanied and followed by a number of electors who wave their hats. In the centre is a sloping platform leading up to the 'Secretaries Room'. A boy with a long staff stands on the r saying, *None but Voters come in.* A crowd of men stand upon it in conversation In the centre is a woman who says *My three tenants shall have more than 60.* A hunch-backed man on the l. says, *I shall discover their Schemes.*

On the r. are steps giving access to the r. side of the gangway. A balustrade divides the open front of the Agents' room from the street, and is continued down the r. side of the gangway and by the side of the steps. Two men are mounting the steps; in the road below two men, hat in hand, are in conversation with a third, who appears to be the candidate; he grasps one of them by the hand, placing his hand on his shoulder.

On the back of the print is pasted a press cutting from the *London Chronicle* (1776) 'A Card with the Figure of PUNCH holding a Paper with the under-written Lines, was lately sent to the present Mayor of S——y.

> With empty bags, and without noise or drum,
> In woful plight, behold, I'm once more come,
> Humbly to crave your Worship's kind protection,
> From threat'ning evils of the last Election.
> In justice guard me from your folly past,
> If 'tis your first, I trust, 'twill be your last:
> Though I was PUNCH, behind the Scene convey'd,
> You, and your Friends the magic wire play'd '
>
> Your's,
>
> PUNCH.

At the election of Sir Thomas Rumbold and Sir Francis Sykes, the two ministerial candidates for Shaftesbury in 1774, several thousand pounds were distributed to the voters at the rate of 20 guineas a man. The mayor and aldermen were entrusted with the distribution and they devised a scheme by which a man disguised as Punch delivered guineas in parcels to electors through a hole in the door. The electors were then taken to another room in the house where 'Punch's Secretary' required him to sign notes for the money received made payable to an imaginary character, 'Glenbucket' The defeated candidate, Hans Mortimer, petitioned against the return on the ground of gross and notorious bribery by the members and their agents. Two witnesses swore that they had seen Punch through the hole in the door, and knew him to be Matthews, an alderman of the town. Witnesses also proved that voters who had taken the 'bribery oath' at the poll had taken Punch's money.

The House of Commons resolved, 14 Feb 1776, that Sykes, Rumbold, and six members of the corporation of Shaftesbury should be prosecuted for subornation of perjury; a bill was brought in for disfranchizing Shaftesbury These proceedings were eventually shelved, but while they were pending Mortimer brought actions on 2 George III c 24 against Sykes for twenty-six acts of bribery, obtaining a verdict for twenty-two penalties amounting to £11,000. Oldfield, *Representative History of Great Britain*, 1816, iii. 396 ff

This case, like that of Hindon, see No. 5288, was notorious in 1776; see Walpole, *Last Journals*, 1920, i 545–6, 562 (May–June 1776) (though the places were not more corrupt than other rotten boroughs, Oldfield, iii. 405), partly because in both cases the candidates were nabobs. Sir Thomas Rumbold succeeded Pigot as Governor of Madras and was enormously wealthy. See Nos 5344, 6169.

$10\frac{11}{16} \times 18\frac{3}{8}$ in.

5342 THE CATCH SINGERS [n.d. 1776?]

Engraving. Four men singing and drinking at a small rectangular table. Each holds up a wine-glass in his r. hand, while he clutches a money-bag in his l At the head of the table (r) sits Lord North in profile to the l.; he sings, *They'l do no More then we Ha, Ha, He* His money-bag is inscribed *Treasury £100000*. On his r sits a man whose bag is labelled *000001 Minden* showing that he is Lord George Germain who became Secretary of State for the Colonies, 10 Nov. 1775 He sings, *With their Hearts so Strong and Bold*, and is clinking glasses with the neighbour on his r., who sings *When Merrily we Shall see*. The latter's bag is inscribed *100000 Navy* and he is identified by Mr. Hawkins as Lord Howe, then a vice-admiral, who was appointed commander-in-chief in North America in Feb. 1776. He has, however, a certain resemblance to Lord Sandwich, First Lord of the Admiralty, who was the 'soul' of the actual Catch Club. Charles Butler, *Reminiscences*, 1822, i 74, see No. 5668, &c. Standing in profile to the r is a man wearing military uniform, high boots, and a long pig-tail queue; his bag is *100000 Army*, and he sings *Ha, Ha, He, We have Fill'd our Bags with Gold*. He is Sir William Howe, Lord Howe's brother, who was then in command of the troops in America, having succeeded Gage in Oct. 1775. On the wall is a map of America, reversed, the *Atlantic Ocean* being on the west of the continent. Germain was repeatedly satirized for his conduct at Minden (see Nos 3680–7) in prints, as in the House of Commons. For the Howes, see No. 5399, &c.

$6\frac{3}{4} \times 6\frac{5}{16}$ in

5343 SPECTATUM ADMISSI, RISUM TENEATIS, AMICI?
[n d. 1776?]

Engraving. A man dressed half as a military officer, half as a bishop, stands with a drawn sword in his r hand, on his l. arm is a round shield inscribed *Thirty Nine Articles*, with a standard on which is a coat of arms. He wears half a cockaded hat, half a mitre. His r side is dressed in a military coat with epaulette, on his r. leg is a spurred top-boot. He wears a gorget round his neck ornamented with the head of Medusa or Discord, with snaky locks His l side is draped with a black gown and on his l leg is a dark stocking and buckled shoe. Two labels issue from his head, both on the military side, inscribed *In hoc signo vincimus* and *Woe to thee Boston Sword go through the Land.*

The escutcheon on the flag is a cross counter-imbattled; dexter chief, a crown and a mitre; dexter base, crossed swords; sinister chief, a mantle, sinister base, crossed keys. The supporters are, dexter, a seven-headed beast, traditionally representing the Church of Rome, cf Nos. 378, 5534;

sinister, a lady fashionably dressed and with her hair in an inverted pyramid surmounted by feathers, cf. No. 5370, &c. The motto is *Le Diable defend le tort*, and the crest is a mitre supporting a dragon holding a skull.

In the foreground (l.) is a drum inscribed *spirit stirring* with a fife and a pair of kettle-drums. On the r. a large organ is partly visible inscribed *soul inspiring*. Behind the soldier-bishop is a cannon inscribed *Alliance between Church and State*; from its muzzle issues a label inscribed, *Ecclesiastical Cannon*. Behind is the sea with ships of war and a coast-town probably intended for Boston. The title is from Horace, *Art of Poetry*, 5.

This indicates the opposition to episcopacy in the Colonies which was an important factor in the growing antagonism to England before the war (Van Tyne, *Causes of the War of Independence*, 1921, chap. xiii, see also No. 4227) and was also vocal in England especially in the City of London, the Quebec Act in particular being denounced as a popish measure, see No. 5228, &c. The bishops were attacked for their support of the American war. Like several others, this satire is perhaps directed against Archbishop Markham of York, see No 5400, &c. The date is probably before news reached England of the evacuation of Boston, see No 5335.

Cf. No 2635 (1745), a similar satire on Herring, Archbishop of York

$6\frac{5}{8} \times 4\frac{1}{8}$ in.

PERSONAL SATIRES

5344–5356

Series of Tête-à-tête portraits.

5344 Nº XXXIV. MISS K—GHL—Y.
Nº XXXV. THE SHAFTESBURY NABOB.

Published as the Act directs by A. Hamilton Junʳ near Sᵗ John's Gate Jan. I. 1775. [sic. i.e. 1776]

Engraving. *Town and Country Magazine.* vii 625 Two bust portraits in oval frames illustrate 'Histories of the Tête-à-Téte annexed, . . .' An account of one of the members for Shaftesbury, both nabobs, whose bribery was the subject of an inquiry by a Select Committee of the House of Commons in 1775 leading to an order for the prosecution of both members, see Nº 5341 This appears to be intended for Sir Thomas Rumbold, since the other member, Sykes, is the subject of another *Tête-à-Tête*, see Nº 5351 The canard that he began life as a shoe-black at White's is not mentioned: a merchant's counting-house led to a writership in the East India Company

Ovals, $2\frac{5}{8} \times 2\frac{1}{4}$ in.   B.M.L., P P 5442 b.

5345 Nº XXXVII THE IRRESISTIBLE Mᴿˢ S——NS
Nº XXXVIII THE CALEDONIAN ORATOR

Published as the Act directs by A Hamilton Junʳ near Sᵗ John's Gate Jan. 16. 1776.

Engraving. *Town and Country Magazine,* vii. 705 (Supplement). Two bust protraits in oval frames, one (r) of a man in clerical gown and bands, illustrate 'Histories of the Tête-à-Tête annexed, ...'. An account of a popular dissenting preacher in a London chapel, an alleged adventurer from Scotland, and of a young widow.

Ovals, $2\frac{11}{16} \times 2\frac{1}{4}$ in.   B M.L., P.P. 5442 b.

5346 Nº II THE ELOPED CLARA
Nº III THE COMBUSTIBLE LOVER

Published as the Act directs by A. Hamilton Junʳ near Sᵗ John's Gate Feb. I 1776

Engraving *Town and Country Magazine,* viii. 9 Two bust portraits in oval frames illustrate 'Histories of the Tête-à-Tête annexed; .   '. An account of the son of an 'eminent grocer' of London and of his amours, notably with Clara, a young actress at Drury Lane. Identified by H Bleackley as Miles Peter Andrews and Anne Brown, afterwards Mrs. Cargill *Notes and Queries* 10th series, iv. 343.

Ovals, $2\frac{11}{16} \cdot 2\frac{1}{4}$ in.   B.M L , P P. 5442 b.

5347 Nº IV CLARA H——D

Nº V P—— M—— ESQᴿ

*Published as the Act directs by A. Hamilton Junʳ near Sᵗ Johns Gate
Mar. 1. 1776.*

Engraving. *Town and Country Magazine*, viii. 65. Two bust portraits in
oval frames illustrate 'Histories of the Tête-â-Tête annexed . .'. An
account of Philip Medows (1708–81), deputy ranger of Richmond Park,
and of Clara Hayward (who had played Calista in the 'Fair Penitent' in
Foote's company) H Bleackley, *Ladies Fair and Frail*, pp 208, 210

Ovals, 2⅝ × 2¼ in. B M.L , P.P. 5442 b.

5348 Nº VII LADY PYEBALD

Nº VIII THE R—G—TE AMOROSO

*Publish'd as the Act directs by A. Hamilton Junʳ near Sᵗ John's Gate
Apr. 1. 1776.*

Engraving. *Town and Country Magazine*, viii. 121 Two bust portraits in
oval frames illustrate 'Histories of the Tête-à-Tête annexed . . ' An
account of Lady Weymouth, wife of Hugh Boscawen, 2nd Viscount (see
No 4460, where he is called Lord Pyebald from the colour of his horses).
She is here alleged to have been a milliner who induced Weymouth to
marry her by representing that she was on the point of death. Her supposed
lover is a young man from R—g—te in a counting-house in the City, with
social ambitions, whom she is said to pay for his attentions

Lady Weymouth (m. 1736) was Hannah Catherine Maria, widow of
Richard Russel and daughter of Thomas Smith of Worplesdon, Surrey;
she died 23 Nov. 1786 aged 79.

Ovals, 2⅝ × 2¼ in. B.M.L., P.P. 5442 b.

5349 Nº X. SIGNIORA G——

Nº XI LORD B——

*Published as the Act directs by A. Hamilton Junʳ near Sᵗ John's Gate
May 1. 1776.*

Engraving. *Town and Country Magazine*, viii. 177. Two bust portraits in
oval frames illustrate 'Histories of the Tête-à-Tête annexed, or, Memoirs
of Lord B——u, and Signiora G—b—lli' An account of the amours of
Sir Edward Hussey Montagu, cr. Baron Beaulieu 28 April 1762, Earl of
Beaulieu 8 July 1784, d 1802. See Walpole, *Memoirs of the Reign of
George III*, 1894, i 124 and note. The lady is the opera singer Gabrielli,
see Walpole, *Letters*, ix. 291-2.

Ovals, 2¹¹⁄₁₆ × 2¼ in B M L , P P 5446 b.

5350 Nº XIII ELFRIDA

Nº XIV KITELY.

*Published as the Act directs by A. Hamilton Junʳ near Sᵗ John's Gate
June 1 1776.*

Engraving *Town and Country Magazine*, viii. 233. Two bust portraits in
oval frames, the man in pseudo-seventeenth-century dress. They illustrate

CATALOGUE OF POLITICAL AND PERSONAL SATIRES

'Histories of the Tête-à-Tête annexed; . . .' An account of Mrs. Hartley, the original Elfrida in Mason's *Elfrida*, Covent Garden, Nov. 1772, and of the actor who played Edgar in the same performance. This was in fact Bensley, but 'Kitely' (in *Every Man in his Humour*) is William, known as Gentleman Smith (?1730–1819), who married the sister of Lord Sandwich. Mrs Hartley was the heroine of the Vauxhall Affray, see No. 5198, see also B.M. *Catalogue of Engr. Br Portraits*

Ovals, $2\frac{11}{16} \times 2\frac{1}{4}$ in   B.M.L., P.P. 5442 b.

5351 Nº XVI. MISS R——D
      Nº XVII THE DISAPPOINTED NABOB.

Published as the Act directs by A. Hamilton Junr near St John's Gate July 1. 1776.

Engraving. *Town and Country Magazine*, viii 289. Two bust portraits in oval frames illustrate 'Histories of the Tête-à-Tête annexed; . .'. An account of the amours of Francis Sykes, ex-M.P for Shaftesbury, see Nº 5341

Ovals, $2\frac{3}{4} \times 2\frac{1}{4}$ in.   B M L., P P. 5442 b.

5352 Nº XIX MRS A—ST—D
      Nº XX SIR MATTHEW MITE

Published as the Act directs by A. Hamilton Junr near St Johns Gate Augt 1. 1776.

Engraving. *Town and Country Magazine*, viii 345. Two bust portraits in oval frames They illustrate 'Histories of the Tête-à-Tête annexed .. ' An account of General Richard Smith, usually believed to be the Sir Matthew Mite of Foote's comedy *The Nabob*, though Foote denied it, and of Mrs. Armistead (afterwards the wife of C. J. Fox), here called 'that celebrated Thais . . . who for some time has been the reigning toast in that line upon the *haut ton*'.

Ovals, $2\frac{11}{16} \times 2\frac{1}{4}$ in   B.M L., P P. 5442 b.

5353 Nº XXII. THE VAUXHALL SYREN
      Nº XXIII COUNT DE B——

Published as the Act directs by A Hamilton Junr near St John's Gate Sep. 1. 1776.

Engraving. *Town and Country Magazine*, viii. 401. Two bust portraits in oval frames illustrate ' Histories of the Tête-à-Tête annexed . . . .'. De B., a foreign minister representing ' one of the greatest monarchs in Europe' at the Court of St James, appears from the *Royal Kalendar* to be Count de Belgioioso, Envoy Extraordinary and Minister Plenipotentiary of 'Germany and Hungary' [sic]. The lady is a singer, trained by a doctor in music [Dr. Arne], who has been singing nightly at Vauxhall during the season of 1776. She is identified by H. Bleackley as Charlotte Brent She married Thomas Pinto, 1766, see *D.N.B*

Ovals, $2\frac{5}{8} \times 2\frac{1}{4}$ in.   B M L , P.P 5442 b.

5354 Nº XXVIII MRS B——
Nº XXIX CAPTN BOBADIL

*Published as the Act directs by A. Hamilton Junr near St John's Gate.
Octr 1st 1776.*

Engraving. *Town and Country Magazine*, viii. 457. Two bust portraits on
one plate; the man dressed as Bobadil in pseudo-Elizabethan hat and cloak
They illustrate 'Histories of the Tête-à-Tête annexed or Memoirs of
Capt. Bobadil and Mrs. B—ll—my ' An account of the actor Henry
Woodward 1717–77, and of the actress George Anne Bellamy (1727?–88)

One of Woodward's best parts was Captain Bobadil, and it is said that
Garrick revived *Every Man in his Humour* in 1751 in order to employ
him to the best advantage. *Thespian Dict*

Ovals, $2\frac{11}{16} \times 2\frac{1}{4}$ in.   B M L , P P 5442 b.

5355 Nº XXVIII. MISS G——
Nº XXIX. THE NOBLE CRICKETER

*Published as the Act directs by A Hamilton Junr near St John's Gate
Novr 1. 1776.*

Engraving. *Town and Country Magazine*, viii 513. Two bust portraits in
oval frames illustrate 'Histories of the Tête-à-Tête annexed: . . .'. An
account of the third Duke of Dorset (1745–99) and his amours. Miss
G——m, the daughter of a Sussex farmer who had been seduced and
deserted, is said to be his mistress.

Ovals, $2\frac{3}{4} \times 2\frac{1}{2}$ in.   B M.L., P.P. 5442 b

5356 Nº XXXI MISS M—T—N
Nº XXXII THE HIBERNIAN PATRIOT.

*Published as the Act directs by A. Hamilton Junr near St John's Gate
Decr 1. 1776.*

Engraving. *Town and Country Magazine*, viii. 569 Two bust portraits
in oval frames illustrate 'Histories of the Tête-à-Tête annexed. . . .'.
An account of the amours of the son of one whose 'loyalty and patriotism'
had 'raised him to the first rank in Ireland', identified by H Bleackley as
Robert, 2nd Duke of Leinster (1749–1804), and of Miss M——, who told
him she was the illegitimate daughter of an Irish Lord Lieutenant. He
wears the conventional Elizabethan costume of the eighteenth century.

Ovals, $2\frac{5}{8} \times 2\frac{1}{4}$ in.   B.M.L , P.P 5442 b.

5357 A SALLY FROM TOMS.

Pub: 22 Feby 1776, by W. Humphrey, Gerrard Street Soho.

Engraving W.L. portrait of an obese and elderly man standing in profile
to the r. He is plainly dressed in an old-fashioned manner except for a
large nosegay in his coat and wears a wide broad-brimmed hat. His hands
are behind his back and he holds a roll of papers inscribed *Annuitys*
Beneath is etched *A real character*

He is identified by Mr. Hawkins as 'Mr. Thomas a Bank Director', and
is presumably Thomas of Hankey, Thomas and Co., 7 Fenchurch Street.

The title suggests that he is an *habitué* of Tom's Coffee House, that is, either Tom's in Birchin Lane, Cornhill, or the more fashionable Tom's in Russell Street, Covent Garden, see *Gent. Mag.*, 1841, ii. 265 ff

9¾×7 in.

5358 [THE WEDDING OF THE MARQUIS OF GRANBY]¹

[1 Apr. 1776]

Engraving From the *London Magazine*, xlv 96 Beneath the design is engraved, *To the most Noble the Marquis of Granby, and his fair Marchioness, this Plate is humbly inscribed by their most devoted Servant The Editor* An allegorical scene. A draped female is led to a circular altar (r.) by Cupid, her hand is taken by Hercules. Truth holds up her mirror; three other female figures accompany the lady. A priest and attendants stand behind the altar. Minerva (l.) attacks a prostrate figure who is holding up a torch and a serpent This is explained as 'Beauty and Modesty accompanied by the Goddess of Truth, Cupid and the Graces, invited by Virtue in the form of Hercules to sacrifice at the altar of Hymen, whilst Minerva, Goddess of Wisdom, destroys the evil Daemon of Envy and Discord'.

Charles, styled Marquis of Granby, 1770–9, afterwards 4th Duke of Rutland, married, 26 Dec 1775, Mary Isabella, daughter of the Duke of Beaufort. See Walpole, *Letters*, ix 226, 291, 313. Cf. No. 5309.

4⅜×7⅛ in.

5359 PRO BONO PUBLICO AND HIS LADY; REAL CHARACTERS.

[? J. Mortimer.]

Pubᵈ 27 Augᵗ 1776, by W. Humphrey, Gerrard Sᵗ Soho.

Engraving W L. portraits of a man and woman standing arm in arm, both in riding dress. He is tall and thin, with a black patch over his l eye; his r. sleeve hangs empty. She is very stout, wearing a feathered hat, a coat and waistcoat over a plain skirt; in her l hand is a whip

The manner resembles that of No. 5362

8⅛×6⅞ in.

5360 I. CALCULATOR ESQ:ᴿ ÆTAT 24, THE CELEBRATED CONJUROR.

This Plate is Humbly Inscribed to all Keepers of Lottery Offices By their Humᵇˡᵉ Servᵗ A.B.

Publish'd as the Act Directs, Augᵗ 30ᵗʰ 1776, by AB. London

Aquatint. Design in an oval Behind a table sits a conjuror, wearing a conical hat and a dressing-gown. He points with his wand at a lottery wheel, from which look two boys, wearing paper crowns He is saying, *Eo, Meo, and Areo, stick close my Boys, and let me have all the Capital Prizes, in my Calculation* One of the boys holds out a ticket to him. On the table in front of the conjuror, are books, one open, showing two pages of figures, *10,000, 20,000* . . . [&c. &c.], two volumes inscribed *Calculations*, and *Conjurations* and two other books, one being *The Life of Duncan Campbel*,

¹ No title

232

Deaf & Dumb Fortune Teller. A letter is addressed *To Mr. Williams, Conjuror, Old Bailey*. In the background is a second lottery wheel

A satirical portrait of John Molesworth who published calculations upon lottery numbers, the title probably suggested by that of a portrait of Molesworth standing by a lottery wheel, entitled, 'John Molesworth Esq': Ætat 24, the Celebrated Calculator', see B.M. *Cat. Engr Br Portraits*

In November 1775 a man bribed one of the Christ's Hospital boys who was to draw the lottery to secrete a ticket and draw it from the wheel. Ashton, *History of English Lotteries*, 1893, 81–5 Molesworth's calculations are here pilloried as equally fraudulent; in October 1776 the question whether his calculations were or were not an imposition on the public was decided in his favour at a debate of the Robin Hood Society (see No 4860, &c), *London Chronicle*, Oct 22–4, 1776 There is a trade card in the Banks collection (D 2 2762) representing the 'Curious Wheels . . used by Mr. Molesworth in proving his Calculations' Duncan Campbell (d 1730) was a Scottish fortune-teller and charlatan His life was written by Defoe.

$8\frac{1}{4} \times 6\frac{1}{2}$ in.

5361—FROM THE HAYMARKETT

P. L. de Loutherbourg Fecit.

London, Printed for R. Sayer & J. Bennett Nº 53 Fleet Street, as the Act directs 26 Decr 1776.

Engraving (coloured impression). W.L portrait (caricature) of a man in profile to the r. standing with his head and shoulders thrown back, his elbows crooked. He holds his hat in his l hand. He wears an exaggerated toupet-wig with a large club, a bulky cravat, short frogged coat, and a sword

Described by Angelo as the caricature of 'a *signor*, a celebrated performer at the Italian Opera House', one of four plates on the same sheet, the others being "From Warwick Lane", 'a well-known M D , the last remaining of the old school'; "From Oxford", 'a fat fellow of Brazen-nose College'; "From Soho", 'a certain well-known *lady abbess*' (cf. No. 5181). *Reminiscences* 1904, i. 334

He is probably Delpini, see *D.N.B.*, whose portrait he somewhat resembles and whose prominence in connexion with the Haymarket is attested by the *Probationary Odes*.

$5\frac{3}{8} \times 4\frac{1}{8}$ in.

5362 IPHIGENIA'S LATE PROCESSION FROM KINGSTON TO BRISTOL —BY CHUDLEIGH MEADOWS.   [n.d. 1776]

[J. Mortimer.]

Engraving Seven figures walk from l to r First is the (so-called) Duchess of Kingston, short and stout She is saying *By God and*, and holds out her hands with a gesture of affirmation. Behind her walk three young women, her 'maids of honour', who are tall and slim in contrast with their mistress. One carries a large square bottle inscribed cordial. All four ladies are dressed alike in the fashion of the day with low bodices and high coiffures decorated with feathers and flowers. Next comes a fat clergyman, his mouth open as of shouting He is followed by the physician wearing a big-wig and sword. Last walks the apothecary, lean and bent, also wearing a sword, and carrying an enormous and ornately decorated syringe which rests on his r shoulder. Beneath the design is engraved,

——*Then the Duchess was brought into Court attended by her Chaplain, Physician, Apothecary, and three Maids of Honor. Morning Post. May 16· 1776.*

Elizabeth Chudleigh, known as the Duchess of Kingston, was tried for bigamy before the peers in Westminster Hall from 15 to 22 Apr 1776 She was still remembered for her scanty dress as Iphigenia at a masked ball in 1749, see Nos. 3030–3. The words she is speaking represent her oath in the Ecclesiastical Court in 1769 that she was unmarried The title implies that the recent sentence in Westminster Hall transformed her from Duchess of Kingston to Countess of Bristol, by her secret marriage to Augustus Hervey, see Nos 5301, 5319, who had recently succeeded 'Meadows' in the title indicates the Medows, who, as nephews of the late Duke of Kingston, were concerned in the case as claimants of the Duke's estates. At the trial she was dressed as a widow followed by 'four virgins in white', see H. More, *Life and Corr*, by W. Roberts, 1 81–3. See also Walpole, *Letters*, ix 345–56; *Letters of the First Earl of Malmesbury*, 1. 343; *Hist MSS Comm.*, *Carlisle MSS.*, 1897, pp. 271, 310, 313. See also No. 5425.

$9\frac{13}{16} \times 13\frac{1}{2}$ in.

5363 [GEORGE COLMAN.]   [1776]

Engraving. Frontispiece from 'The Spleen or the Offspring of Folly . . . dedicated to George Colman Esq. author of The Spleen . . .'. Colman, dressed half as a lawyer, half as Harlequin, runs forward, holding out in his l. hand a newsboy's horn inscribed *London Packet*. In his r. hand is a book, *Viner Abrid[gem]ent.* Flying behind him is a figure wearing Folly's cap and bells on the top of which is perched Minerva's owl On the ground is an infant being suckled by a cat, while Spleen, an elderly hag, nude with dishevelled hair, stands behind Beneath her is inscribed (a misquotation from Canto II of 'The Spleen'),

> [Her] *favorite cat should wean her kitten*
> *And suckle little Master*
> > > *Canto 1st.*

Beneath Colman is etched another misquotation,

> *Mark but that look of his*
> *That half a smile, that half a grin,*
> *That speak the Eunuch-Soul within*
> *His feeble-featured Phiz!*
> > > *Canto 2ᵈ*

In the foreground (r.) a drum, a mask, a flag, half a broken lyre, and a broken trumpet inscribed *Flockton* lie grouped together.

'The Spleen' is an attack on Colman for his play 'The Spleen or Islington Spa', a farce produced 7 Mar. 1776 at Drury Lane by Garrick; it purports to be written by 'Rubrick' in revenge for the character of Rubrick in Colman's play Colman is supposed to be the offspring of Wit and Folly suckled by Spleen who consigned him to a cat. He is represented as half-lawyer, half-player because he had practised at the bar He was supposed to trumpet his fame in the *London Packet*

$8\frac{7}{8} \times 7$ in.

5364 THE THEATRICAL DISPUTE, OR THE PARSON BAITED

[n d *c* Oct 1776]

Engraving The stage of a theatre showing boxes l and r. On the l. a group of men fight with fists and sticks. A manager (centre), hat in hand, attempts to address the audience. On the r a man in clerical gown and bands holds up an open book inscribed *Blackamoor* [washed white] A dog tears at his gown; sticks and apples lie on the ground and are falling from above.

Parson Bate's comic opera, *The Blackamoor washed white*, was produced at Drury Lane in Oct 1776. It was greeted with uproar and after two nights of disturbance there was an organized riot on the third night. On the fourth Garrick had to promise that the play should be withdrawn. Baker, *Biog Dram* 1812. ii. 59–60. For Bate see index

$4\frac{5}{16} \times 6$ in

5365 LORD DIMPLE & HIS MAN, IN THE COAL PIT.

[1 Feb. 1776]

Engraving. From the *Oxford Magazine*, xiii. 418 The interior of a coal mine, supported by timber props. Two men, elaborately dressed and much alarmed, tied back to back, are being lowered by a rope down a shaft The miners, holding picks and shovels, watch the descent with amusement.

$6\frac{11}{16} \times 4$ in

5366 [TWO DESERTERS.]

[*Daniel Astle fecit, late Cap^n in the 46th Reg^t now not out of the Army.*][1]
Feb. 12, 1776.

Engraving on a printed handbill. Portrait heads of two deserters Beneath them is printed 'The above heads have a strong Resemblance of the underneath Deserters, the largest of which is Baker, and the other Sheenes.' The characterization is that of caricature, the larger figure in the centre of the plate has a villainous expression, both are in profile to the r. Behind the head of Baker is a pike (l.). A representation of a stolen watch hangs from a nail over the head of Sheenes (r.) In the background (l) is a gibbet from which a body dangles The handbill is headed *A Robbery and Desertion* The men are described and rewards offered. They had deserted from a recruiting party of the 46th Foot at Manchester. The bill is signed *Danl Astle*

The collector's note states, 'Immediately after the Robbery and Desertion, Captain Astle etch'd these two Portraits from memory, and had them distributed about as handbills, and the resemblance being so very striking they were taken up the next day, a great distance from the regiment '

$3\frac{7}{16} \times 4\frac{1}{8}$ in.   'Honorary Engravers', i. 214.

5367 [MATT DARLY][1]   [*c* 1776?]

Engraving. Matthew Darly the engraver and publisher of prints stands beside an ass He faces T Q to the r , his head in profile to the r He is elderly and corpulent, his gouty r. leg is swathed. He partly supports

[1] MS note on the print

himself by a short stick on which he rests his r. hand, his other stick is under his r. arm, it being his custom to use two walking sticks, see No. 4632. In his l. hand he holds a large scroll inscribed *The Political Designer of Pots Pans and Pipkins* The ass, which stands behind him, is urinating and braying, the words *we are Professors of Design* issuing from his mouth

Darly called himself P O A.G B or Painter of Ornaments to the Academy of Great Britain, see No 4632 He was noted both as caricaturist and as an engraver of architectural designs, ornament, and of plates for the great cabinet-makers, Chippendale and others. He published a medallion profile head of himself on 1 Jan 1775 inscribed *M Darly P.O A G B*. which shows that this print is a good portrait For Darly see Nos 3844, 4632, 4701, &c.

$4\frac{7}{8} \times 3\frac{15}{16}$ in. (pl).

5368 PARK—CHARACTER.

Pub Nov' 24 1776 by M Darly 39 Strand

Engraving Standing W.L. profile portrait of a man in an oval enclosed in a rectangle. He walks from l. to r. his head thrown back, his stomach projecting. He wears spectacles, a looped hat, a large tie-wig, and holds a tasselled cane. Probably a caricature of a doctor

$4\frac{15}{16} \times 3\frac{11}{16}$ in.

5369 DARLY'S . COMIC—PRINTS . OF CHARACTERS . CARICA-TURES MACARONIES &c. PRICE $\frac{4}{4}.\frac{3}{4}$ o
DEDICATED TO D GARRICK ESQ.

Pub^d by Mary Darly, Jany 1. 1776, according to Act of Parl^t (39 Strand)

Engraved title-page. The lettering of the title is in an oval, the dedication in a circle beneath the oval, both being enclosed by a continuous border of ornament. The border is surrounded by scrolls of conventional orna-ment; from the two lowest scrolls, on each side of the dedication, hang two medallion bust portraits of Garrick, one (l) in profile to the l., the other (r) in profile to the r. These resemble the decoration of the Society of the School of Garrick worn by Charles Bannister in a H.L. mezzotint portrait.

This title-page was used for composite volumes of caricatures bound in boards which include prints not only before but after 1776. It may have been originally issued in connexion with one or more of the series of folio prints issued by Darly, possibly to subscribers to the very numerous series which appeared in at least two volumes between 1776 and 1778 and perhaps in 1779, see Nos. 5370-6, 5429-51, 5513-22, 5599-5602. The contents of these volumes vary, some contain all six series of 'Maca-ronies' published 1771-3, see Nos 4913, 4986, 5149, &c , three plates being printed on one page.[1] They also include prints published between 1766 and 1779 belonging to a number of different series, and in three sizes, the plates being printed one, two, or three on a page.

The plates included in the composite volume appear to have Matthew

[1] As in the volume exhibited by Mr Dyson Perrins at the Burlington Fine Arts Club, 1932

Darly's imprint with two exceptions, No 5860, which has no publication line, and *The Repository or Tatter'd Sale*, a print of Tattersall's, published, perhaps etched, by Mary Darly, 1 Jan. 1777 [1] Mary Darly etched a portrait of Garrick as Abel Drugger (*B.M. Cat. of Engr. British Portraits*), and the dedication may indicate a personal compliment from her to Garrick She also published No 4752. For Mary Darly see her portrait, No. 4692.

$13\frac{13}{16} \times 9\frac{13}{16}$ in. (pl.).

5370–5376

Prints belonging to the very numerous series published by Darly apparently in two volumes 1776–8, see No 5369 There were several political satires in this series, see Nos. 5397, 5400, 5473–5, 5482, 5483.

5370 9 THE PREPOSTEROUS HEAD DRESS, OR THE FEATHERED LADY.

[M. Darly?]

Pub. by M Darly. 39 Strand March 20. 1776

Engraving (coloured and uncoloured impressions) [2] A lady seated at a dressing-table in profile to the l. A hairdresser, fashionably dressed, stands (r.) on a stool arranging the tall ostrich feathers in her hair, which is an enormous inverted pyramid decorated with feathers, lace, fruit, and carrots. A lady's maid, elaborately dressed, with her hair in the fashionable pyramid, stands by the table (l) facing her mistress and holding out a basket full of apples, carrots, &c Feathers and circular toilet-boxes for cosmetics lie on the dressing-table.

The looking-glass and dressing-table are draped The wall which forms a background is ornamented with mouldings. Two H.L. portraits hang on the wall. A carpet with a large arabesque pattern covers the floor.

The fashion for an inverted pyramid of hair, somewhat heart-shaped, and decorated with long ostrich feathers and other ornaments, was much caricatured in 1776. This use of ostrich feathers is said to have been introduced by the Duchess of Devonshire, to whom Lord Stormont presented a long feather on returning from Paris in 1774. (Fairholt, *Costume in England*, 1896, i 395 n) Lady Louisa Stuart wrote in her old age of 'the outrageous zeal manifested against the first introduction of ostrich feathers as a headdress. This fashion was not attacked as fantastic or unbecoming or inconvenient or expensive, but as seriously wrong or immoral The unfortunate feathers were insulted mobbed burned almost pelted . .' *Selections . . .*, ed. J A. Home, 1899, p. 187 They were the subject of a pamphlet, *A Letter to the Duchess of Devonshire*, 1777. See also H More, *Life and Corr.*, by W. Roberts, 1834, i 65

See also Nos 5330, 5335, 5371–81, 5383–8, 5393–5, 5396, 5427, 5429, 5430, 5436, 5439–42, 5444, 5447–51, 5452, 5454, 5456, 5459–62, 5466, 5467, 5515, 5517 Nos. 4546, 4547 also belong to 1776, and No. 4550 to 1777

[1] An impression from the collection of Mr Minto Wilson was exhibited at the Burlington Fine Arts Club, 1932 It is included in a volume belonging (1933) to Mr. W T Spencer, New Oxford Street.
[2] Only the uncoloured impression is numbered

The broad pyramid of 1776–7 differs from the erection of 1770–1 or 1772 which was elongated with a narrow apex, see Nos 4628 (p. 46), 4630.
Reproduced, Paston, Pl. xxi.
$12\frac{1}{2} \times 8\frac{7}{8}$ in.

5371 THE EXTRAVAGANZA OR THE MOUNTAIN HEAD DRESS OF 1776.

[M. Darly?]

Pub by M Darly April 10. 1776.

Engraving. An enormous triangular mass of hair, attached to the head of a lady (full face) whose head and shoulders appear at the bottom of the print The broad upper edge of the pyramid is decorated in the centre with a jewelled ornament from which spring ears of corn. The hair is adorned with long ostrich feathers, sprays of flowers, on one of which sits a bird, carrots, bunches of grapes, and other fruit. The central mound of hair is surrounded by symmetrical curls or ringlets.

One of many satires on extravagant hair dressing, see No. 5370, &c.

$12\frac{3}{8} \times 9$ in

5372 32 THE CITY ROUT.

Pub^d acco^g to Act by M Darly 39 Strand May 20 1776.

Engraving A satire on City manners Persons standing in conversation at a party The principal figures are two elaborately dressed ladies of plebeian, elderly, and unattractive appearance who face each other; one holds a card, the other a fan Their hair is awkwardly dressed in the enormous mounds then fashionable, see No 5370, &c. On the l a short, fat, and awkward footman brings in a tray on which is a triple stand of jelly-glasses, a foaming tankard of beer, &c. The other guests are men; one wears a furred alderman's gown. In the centre of the back wall is a picture of a man with a distraught expression dressed as a seaman or working man, who is being devoured by two lions, one on each side Above his head are the letters S P Q L On the back of the print a note in a contemporary hand explains this as '*Senatus populusque Londoniensis* the Aldermen and Commoners of London'. On the r. wall is visible the lower part of a W L. portrait of a man in a furred livery gown
In the manner of R. St. G Mansergh.

$8\frac{1}{2} \times 13\frac{7}{16}$ in.

5373 THE VIS . A .VIS . BISECTED OR THE LADIES COOP

[M Darly?]

Pub by M Darly May 25, 1776.

Engraving (coloured impression) The interior of a closed carriage made visible by being bisected longitudinally. In it two young ladies of pleasing appearance sit face to face in profile, apparently on the floor, or on very low seats, to make room for their monstrous mounds of hair These are decorated with feathers, flowers, vegetables, &c. as in No. 5370. One (r.) holds a paper inscribed *Pantheon 3^d Subscription*, the other holds a fan The roof of the carriage is ornamented with two ducal coronets.

A *vis-à-vis* was a narrow coach in which only two persons could sit facing each other, being 'seldom used by any other but persons of high character or fashion', and 'usually finished in a superior manner than what the generality of carriages are'. Felton, *Treatise on Carriages*, 1795, p 65. Cf. No. 5416.

One of many satires on monstrous hair-dressing, it is perhaps intended for the Duchess of Devonshire, cf. No 5370.

Reproduced, Fuchs, *Die Karikatur der Europäischen Volker*, p 278 C E. Jensen, *Karikatur-album*, 1906, 1 p 163.

$8\frac{9}{16} \times 12\frac{15}{16}$ in.

5374 5 A SCOTCH REEL
Pub. by M Darly. 39 Strand, July 11, 1776.

Engraving. Two couples dancing a reel The ladies wear the monstrous feathered coiffures then fashionable, see No 5370, &c The man on the l is short, ungainly, and very fat, he walks rather than dances. The other man dances with energy, one arm raised All wear gloves

$8\frac{1}{2} \times 12\frac{7}{8}$ in

5375 PHAETONA OR MODERN FEMALE TASTE
Pub. by M Darly 39 Strand Nov. 6 1776.

Engraving A lady driving (r. to l) in a high phaeton which is poised on very high springs. The two prancing ponies are very small relatively to the lady and the carriage. Her hair is extravagantly dressed in the manner of contemporary caricature. Perched on her mound of hair is a hat trimmed with ribbons and enormous ostrich feathers The phaeton has a folding hood, which if raised would be very far from covering the lady's coiffure. The side panel of the carriage is ornamented with a ducal coronet, and the motto SWIFT She is driving over turf, in the distance are trees.

Compare the prologue to Colman's comedy, *The Suicide* (Haymarket, 1778):

'Tis now the reigning taste with belle and beau
    Their art and skill in coachmanship to shew:
A female Phaeton all danger mocks,
Half-coat, half-petticoat she mounts the box. . . .'

Gent. Mag., 1778, 382.

Cf. No. 5936

The feathers and the coronet suggest the Duchess of Devonshire, see Nos. 5370, 5373 See also No 5394 Reproduced, Paston, Pl cxxii.

$8\frac{9}{16} \times 12\frac{3}{4}$ in.

5376 MISS . SHUTTLE-COCK.
R. S. [Monogram, i e 'Richard Sneer']¹

Pubᵈ by M Darly Decʳ 6 1776 (39) Strand

Engraving (coloured impression) A game of shuttlecock between two men who face each other, standing at opposite sides of the design, each with a raised battledore One (l.) is short, obese, and of clerical appearance;

¹ It is possible that R S , or 'Dicky Sneer', denotes R. B Sheridan A comparison with portraits of Sheridan shows that this is not unlikely. The signature may denote either the subject or the artist, or possibly both

the other is slim with a long pigtail queue   High in the air between them is their shuttlecock, a lady with the enormous head-dress decorated with the long ostrich feathers of contemporary caricature; her skirts fly up. Beneath the design is etched

> *Ladie[s] likes [sic] Shuttle-Cocks are now array'd,*
> *The tail is Cork'd and feather'd is the head.*

Cf. the lines in Garrick's prologue to Sheridan's *Trip to Scarborough* first played 24 Feb. 1777, perhaps suggested by this print.

> Ladies may smile—are they not in the plot?
> The bounds of nature have not they forgot?
> Were they design'd to be, when put together,
> Made up, like shuttlecocks, of cork and feather?

This print is shown in No. 5435, *Doleful Dicky Sneer in the Dumps,* from which it seems that the slim man is intended for 'Richard Sneer'. No. 5430 belongs to the same set, by the same artist.

One of a number of satires, 1776–7, on the prevailing fashion for 'cork-rumps', see No. 5381, &c., and for monstrous feathered head-dresses, see No. 5370, &c. See especially No. 5383   The cork rump was accompanied by excessive tightlacing, see No. 5444, &c.

$8\frac{3}{4} \times 13$ in.

5377 CUPID'S TOWER.

[M. Darly?]

Pub⁴ March 1. 1776 by M Darly 39 Strand.

Engraving. A lady (H.L.) in profile to the l with an enormous pyramid of hair in the fashion of the day. On the broad summit of the pyramid lies a miniature cupid fitting an arrow to his bow and about to aim in the direction in which the lady is looking   She wears the fashionable 'full-dress' of the period   Beneath is etched,

> *Fair tresses Man's imperial race ensnare,*
> *And beauty draws us with a single hair*

One of many satires on monstrous head-dresses, see No. 5370, &c. Others of a similar kind are Nos 5330, 5335, 5378–80, 5384, 5441, 5442, 5448, 5449.

$7\frac{5}{8} \times 5\frac{3}{8}$ in.

5378 BUNTERS HILL OR MAY DAY

Pub⁴ according to Act of Parl¹ May 1. 1776 by J. Lockington Shug Lane

Engraving   A companion print to No 5379   A woman (H.L.) in profile to the r. on whose enormous erection of hair are depicted a number of scenes illustrating low-life on May-day in London. On the summit is a galloping pig with two small pigs. Below are two pairs of street-sellers (?), one offers drink to a woman; the other, an old woman smoking a pipe, offers a tray of fruit or cakes to a woman and child   Below is a fruit or vegetable cart drawn by two asses or horses, tandem, their heads decorated with branches. In the lowest section of the coiffure is a jack-in-the-green surrounded by chimney-sweeps and bystanders. The woman's face is patched.

Bunter was 'a cant word for a woman who picks up rags about the street; and used by way of contempt for any low vulgar woman', *O E.D.* The pigs probably represent the animals which routed about the garbage-heaps where these women did their work.

Probably a parody of No. 5330 (Bunkers Hill). For similar designs see No 5377, &c.

$6\frac{7}{8} \times 4\frac{3}{4}$ in

5379 RURAL MASQUERADE DEDICATED TO THE REGATTA-ITES.

Pub^d accor^s to Act of Parl^t July 9 1776 by J. Lockington Shug Lane Golden Squ^e.

Engraving A companion print to No. 5378. On an enormous erection of hair are depicted a masquerade and regatta In the upper division of the coiffure a number of persons in masquerade dress are walking in a garden decorated by lanterns which surround the flower-beds and outline an archway, behind is a rotunda In the lower division are a number of boats and barges, the central boat flying the Union flag The hair is attached to the head of a H L. figure with the body of a woman, but with a grotesque face and beard, perhaps intended for Father Thames or Neptune.

This evidently represents the first regatta held in England, 23 June 1775, which took place partly on the Thames, partly at Ranelagh, where a temple of Neptune was erected See *Ann Reg* 1775, pp 132 and 216–18.

The chief regatta of 1776 was on 22 Aug, at Richmond, for the Prince of Wales's birthday. *London Chronicle*, 22–4 Aug

$5\frac{9}{16} \times 7\frac{5}{8}$ in.

5380 BETTY THE COOK MAIDS HEAD DREST.

London. Pub. 13th June 1776 by W. Humphrey Gerrard Street, Soho.

Price one Shill^s

Engraving An enormous heart-shaped pyramid of hair extends from the head (full-face) of a young woman. On the centre of the top rests a kitchen fireplace with a joint of meat roasting at a spit; on the chimney-piece sits a monkey in a fool's cap looking at itself in a hand-mirror Below the fireplace is a large circular cheese from which a wedge has been cut in which are three mice. Under the cheese, and draped across the hair, is a ribbon, decorated with household utensils· a mop, fire-irons, broom, gridiron, and ladle. A dog with puppies barks at a spitting cat with kittens. Round the cheese are vegetables: cauliflower, cabbage, asparagus, potatoes, &c Beneath the title is etched,

> *The Taste at present all may see,*
> *But none can tell what is to be,*
> *Who knows when Fashions whims are spread,*
> *But each may wear this Kitchen Head.*
> *The Noddle that so vastly swells,*
> *May wear a Fool's cap, hung with Bells*

One of many satires in 1776 on extravagant hair-dressing, see No. 5370, &c

$13 \times 9\frac{1}{8}$ in. (pl.).

5381 THE CORK RUMP OR CHLOE'S CUSHION.

Pub⁴ Nov' 19, 1776, by J. Walker Nᵒ 13, Parliament Sᵗ

Aquatint Perhaps a companion print to No. 5382 W L figure of a young woman standing in profile to r. and looking to the front Her hair is in the enormous pyramid of caricature, on its apex is pinned a frilled cap with long streamers of lace and ribbon The back of her skirt projects below the waist, and on the projection sits a poodle wearing a bow of ribbon. In her r hand she holds a spray of moss rose-buds. She wears an apron and a skirt which shows her ankles

The 'cork rump', a cork support which extended the dress at the back in the manner of the 'bustle' of the nineteenth century but also encircled the hips, was the subject of many caricatures, 1776-7, see Nos. 5376, 5383, 5403, 5429, 5430, 5439, 5458, 5460

A print with a similar title was published by Darly in 1777, see No. 5429

6⅜ × 4¹³⁄₁₆ in. (pl.)

5382 THE COLD RUMP OR TASTE ALAMODE

Pub⁴ Dec' 10. 1776.

Aquatint. Perhaps a companion print to No. 5381 A man warming his back at a fire, which is seen through his wide-apart legs; his heels are against the low fender. His hands are behind his back, holding out his coat-tails. His head is turned in profile to the l , looking over his r. shoulder. He wears a toupet wig with a plaited queue, an elaborate cravat, and a short waistcoat, a bunch of seals hangs from his fob, cf No 5443.

6⅜ × 4⅝ in

5383 THE CORK-RUMP THE SUPPORT OF LIFE.

[n.d *c.* 1776¹]

Engraving. A lake on which a boating accident has just occurred, the overturned boat partly visible on the extreme r. The central figure is that of a young lady seated serenely in the water supported by her voluminous petticoats and the concealed cork beneath them Her hair is dressed in an enormous inverted pyramid, its summit decorated with feathers, flowers, and lappets of lace, which dangle to her shoulders, on her lap she holds a small dog Two swans (l.) hiss at her.

In the foreground the head of a man and of an elderly woman, both shrieking, rise above the water, their arms extended; a tasselled cane hangs from the man's wrist. A pair of woman's feet in high-heeled shoes waves above the water These three, unsupported by cork, seem about to drown. Two men hang limply over the keel of the overturned boat. Beneath the title is engraved,

> *You smil'd when like a Shuttle-cock I flew,*
> *The scene is chang'd, and mine's the Triumph now—*
> *Despair ye Clods, behold the distant Shore,*
> *And for Cork-Rumps in vain the Gods implore!*

This is perhaps a comment on No. 5376, where the lady is used as a shuttle-cock. See also No. 5381, &c

7¼ × 11⅝ in.

¹ Publication line probably cut off.

5384 THE LADY'S MAID, OR TOILET HEAD-DRESS

[n d. *c* 1776[1]]

Engraving (coloured impression). A young woman (H.L) with her hair in a much exaggerated inverted pyramid which fills the greater part of the design and is the support for a dressing-table, draped with muslin festoons. On it are an oval mirror, a pair of tapers in candlesticks, two vases of flowers, a pincushion, toilet articles, a pair of buckles, rings, a necklace, &c , two books, a pen.

One of a number of similar satires, see Nos. 5330, 5335, 5371, 5377-80, 5442, 5448, 5449. For extravagant hairdressing see No. 5370, &c.
$8 \times 5\frac{13}{16}$ in

5385 [FRONTISPIECE TO ANSTEY'S ELECTION BALL, 1776]

C. W Bampfylde 28 March 1776.

Engraving From *The Election Ball*, 3rd ed , Bath, 1776 A bedroom A lady in stays and petticoat (Madge Inkle) seated at a dressing-table, decorating her hair with long cock's feathers. Her stout elderly husband (r.), leaning on a walking-stick, looks on in surprise. A maidservant (l.) is about to leave the room, holding a cock, from which all the tail-feathers have been plucked. A cat watches the cock, holding up one paw. A lady's dress hangs over a chair, shoes, cock's feathers, and a paper inscribed *Election Ball* lie on the floor In the background is the tester of a bed with curtains. A H.L. portrait on the wall is inscribed *Sr Sim · Blunderhead* Beneath the design is engraved:

> *Humano Capiti — &c., — — &c*
> *Jungere si velit, et varias inducere plumas—*
> *Spectatum admissi risum teneatis Amici?*
> *Horat. de Art: Poet:*

A note to the lines illustrated (p. 35):

'The Editor is sensible how very far Mr. INKLE's Description must fall short of the inimitable Design of the Frontispiece, which however he cannot value more as a masterly performance, than as a kind token of Approbation and Regard from his worthy and ingenious friend COPLESTONE WARRE BAMPFYLDE, Esq. of *Hestercombe* in *Somersetshire* '

See No. 5386 for another illustration of this subject. One of many satires on the monstrous hair-dressing of 1776, see No. 5370, &c.
$8 \times 6\frac{5}{16}$ in.

5386-5390

Five illustrations to Anstey's *Election Ball* designed by C. W. Bampfylde and etched by William Hassel, published at Bath in an *Epistola Poetica Familiaris*, addressed by Anstey to Bampfylde. (Copy in Print Department.)

5386 [MARGERY INKLE DRESSING HER HAIR]

C.W.B. del. W.H. sc. Pub by C. Anstey 30 Dec. 1776. as the Act directs.

Engraving. Margery in stays and petticoat seated before her dressing-table

[1] Miss Banks has written on the back, 'bought 1785', but it is clearly earlier

holds the monstrous erection on her head. Her father, Inkle, seated on a chair (r.), watches in astonishment. A maid stands by an open door (l.) holding the cock which has been robbed of its tail-feathers, some of which lie on the ground, others adorn Margery's head-dress A cat miaows at the cock. See also No. 5385.

$4\frac{5}{16} \times 4\frac{1}{8}$ in. (Inset on p. 27.)

5387 [MARGERY ENTERING THE SEDAN CHAIR]

C.W B. del. W.H sc. Pub. 30 Dec. 1776 by C. Anstey as the Act directs.

Engraving Margery crouches in the open sedan chair, (r.) one chairman raises the roof to accommodate the feathered head-dress, the other points to the chair, looking, hat in hand, to Inkle who stands (l.) supported on his stick.

$3\frac{3}{4} \times 4$ in. (Below the text, p. 28).

5388 [THE PROGRESS OF THE SEDAN.]

C.W.B. del. W.H sc. Pub. 30 Dec. 1776 by C. Anstey as the Act directs

Engraving. Two chairmen carry (r. to l) the sedan chair Margery in a crouching position is seen through the window Old Inkle hobbles beside her (r.) supported on two sticks

$3\frac{5}{16} \times 4\frac{3}{16}$ in. (Inset on p. 29.)

5389 [INKLE ASSURES LORD PERRIWINKLE OF HIS INTEREST AT THE NEXT ELECTION]

C.W.B. del. W H. sc. Pub. 30 Dec. 1776 by C. Anstey as the Act directs.

Engraving. Lord Perriwinkle stands, his r hand inserted in his waistcoat, listening with a calculating frown to Inkle who leans towards him, speaking into his l. ear

$3\frac{15}{16} \times 3\frac{1}{8}$ in. (Below the text, p. 31.)

5390 [INKLE AND LORD PERRIWINKLE TAKE LEAVE OF EACH OTHER.]

C W.B del W H. sc Pub. 30 Dec. 1776 by C. Anstey as the Act directs.

Engraving. Inkle (l) and Lord Perriwinkle (r.) take each other's hands, bowing very low; Inkle rests his l. hand on his stick, which supports him; the other, his hat under his arm, holds his l. hand to his breast.

$3\frac{1}{8} \times 4\frac{1}{2}$ in. (Below the text, p. 32.)

5391 THE COCK-PIT

Printed for R. Sayer & J. Bennett, N° 53 Fleet Street, as the Act directs, July 20, 1776

Engraving. Two cocks fighting in a cock-pit. Behind them eight specta-

tors, probably portraits, sit and stand. A man in riding-dress is having
an altercation with the well-dressed man on his r On their r is a working
man in an apron Behind the circular pit and the surrounding circle for
spectators is a straight brick wall with timber beams. On this is a burlesqued
version of the royal arms Probably suggested by Hogarth's print, see
No. 3706.
$5\frac{7}{8} \times 8\frac{1}{8}$ in.

Six prints from the series of mezzotints published by Carington
Bowles.

ALL SORTS. (337)   See No. 4543—[c 1776]
J R. Smith *del. et sc.*

THE YOUNG WANTON. (340)   See No 4544—[1776]
[? J. R. Smith[1]]

A BAGNIGGE WELLS SCENE, OR NO RESISTING TEMPTATION.
(341)   See No. 4545—[1776]

SLEIGHT OF HAND BY A MONKEY—OR THE LADY'S HEAD
UNLOADED. (344)   See No. 4546—25 Octr. 1776
A satire on hair-dressing, see No. 5370, &c.

BOB BLUNT IN AMAZE, OR FEMALE FASHIONABLE FOLLIES.
(345) A satire on hair-dressing   See No. 4547—[1776]

5392 346. DIOGENES LOOKING FOR AN HONEST MAN.

*Printed for Carington Bowles, at his Map & Print Warehouse, N° 69
in St Paul's Church Yard, London. Published as the Act directs* [date
erased, 1776.]

Mezzotint. Diogenes, a bearded elderly man wearing nondescript
draperies and carrying a lantern, walks (l. to r.) with a stick. He is followed
by a dog A young man and woman (l) point at him with derision;
a boy (r.), holding to a tree, looks round at him with amusement. In the
background is a piece of water with trees, and on its farther side, a house.
On the l a dove-cote is partly visible, one bird flies from it
$13 \times 9\frac{7}{8}$ in.

Ten similar mezzotints issued by other publishers

5393 397 AGE AND FOLLY, OR THE BEAUTIES.

[Philip Dawe.]

*London, Printed for R Sayer & J. Bennett, N° 53, Fleet Street; as the
Act directs, 1 Feb 1776*

Mezzotint. An aged and repulsively ugly couple walk under trees, both

---

[1] Similar in manner to other prints by Smith of courtesans illustrating verses
from *Proverbs*, see Frankau, pp 99, 125, and Nos. 5823, 5824

dressed in a grotesque exaggeration of the fashion of the day. The man (l.) ogles the lady, whose pointed chin he holds, she smiles at him. He has a wig with an enormous looped-up macaroni club; a comb stuck into the top of his head shows that he is a barber, and, except that Frenchmen in caricature are seldom fat, the three-cornered hat with a tuft of feathers at each corner suggests that he is French. He wears a sword and a large nosegay. From his fob hangs a chatelaine or group of chains ending in a heart, the model of a small animal, a thimble, &c.

The lady has a grotesque witch-like profile, her face is patched; she holds a fan, and wears a large earring, and a large nosegay. Her enormous pyramid of hair is decorated with ostrich feathers, ribbons, &c. In the feathers is a bird's nest with young birds gaping for food which is being brought them by a bird which flies towards them. She resembles the old woman in No. 5466 by the same artist.

Behind on the r. two simply-dressed young women wearing hats hold up their hands in amazement at the grotesque couple.

Beneath the title is engraved,

> *Search Court and City, Town and Country round,*
> *Two such Beauties scarce are to be found.*

For other satires on the monstrous hair-dressing of 1776–7 see No. 5370, &c.

13 × 9⅞ in.

5394 THE NEW FASHIONED PHAETON
SIC ITUR AD ASTRA.

[P. Dawe?]

London, Printed for R. Sayer & J. Bennett, Nᵒ 53 Fleet Street, as the Act directs, 22ᵈ Febʸ 1776.

Mezzotint. A phaeton and pair stands outside a town house. The body of the carriage, which is carved and decorated, has been raised above the wheels on an expanding trellis-work so that it is on the level of the first-floor windows. A gentleman who holds the reins in his l. hand leans forward to assist into the carriage a lady who is stepping through the window and over the low iron railing of the balcony. He wears a small hat, a looped macaroni club, laced coat, and top-boots. She is elaborately dressed in the height of the fashion with a vast pyramid of hair decorated with enormous ostrich feathers. On the ground below a man and woman (l.) stand gazing up at them; the woman holds a child in her arms, an older boy stands beside her, pointing up and waving his hat. In the doorway of the house (r.) a man and woman stand, looking up open-mouthed, the woman holding up a hand in astonishment.

The house has large sash-windows, those on the first floor have oval balconies with wrought-iron balustrades. The façade is ornamented by vertical strips of carving in low relief between the windows.

For phaetons see Nos. 5375, 5761, and for other satires on hair-dressing, No. 5370, &c. Reproduced, Paston, Pl. cxxiv.

13 × 9¹³⁄₁₆ in.

5395 A HINT TO THE LADIES TO TAKE CARE OF THEIR HEADS.

[P. Dawe?]

London, Printed for R. Sayer & J. Bennett N° 53 Fleet Street, as the Act directs 28ᵗʰ March 1776.

Mezzotint The interior of the rotunda at the Pantheon A lady stands in the centre, the feathers (taller than the wearer) in her grotesquely high coiffure of hair having caught fire from the hanging candelabra. A maid-servant directs a jet of water to the blaze from the nozzle of a large pencil-shaped fire extinguisher, which she holds in both hands. A man holds up in both hands a long narrow board marked in lengths of feet with which he appears to be measuring the height of the head-dress A lady and a gentleman sit on a sofa (r), each with a hand held up in surprise. On the l. are two ladies, seated, with a man standing behind them, bending forward as he looks through his lorgnette. The ladies are dressed in the fashion of the day, with long ear-rings, and large nosegays tucked into their low-cut bodices. On a scaffolding (r.) stand two workmen who are wielding mallets with great energy In a gallery high up under the dome, fronted by a balustrade, are musicians (l) partly obscured by the towering feathers, two violinists being visible.

For other satires on the monstrous hairdressing of 1776 see No. 5370, &c. Reproduced, Paston, Pl xxii; A. S. Turberville, *Men and Manners of the Eighteenth Century*, 1926, p. 100.

$12\frac{5}{8} \times 9\frac{15}{16}$ in

THE CONNOISSEUR AND TIRED BOY. See No. 4621—15 May 1776

[P. Dawe] Pub. Sayer and Bennett Cf. Chaloner Smith, i. p. 158.

Mezzotint

RIDICULOUS TASTE.   See No. 4629—10 June 1776

Pub. Sayer and Bennett

A satire on hair-dressing, a reduced version of No. 4628 (1771).

SAL DAB GIVING MONSIEUR A RECIEPT IN FULL (389)

See No. 4623¹—29 May 1776

Pub. Sayer and Bennett.

A reduced version was issued 1 Apr 1777.

5396 CAN YOU FORBEAR LAUGHING.

[P. Dawe?]

London Printed for R Sayer & J. Bennett N° 53 Fleet Street, as the Act directs 14 June 1776.

Mezzotint. A lady stands at her dressing-table (r.), her hair in an enormous pyramid decorated with feathers torn from a peacock, an ostrich and a cock. A young girl wearing a hat holds the peacock by a wing, another

¹ Incorrectly dated 1766

wearing a cap tugs hard at one of its tail feathers (which are very unlike peacock's feathers) An ostrich (l.), which has lost most of its tail feathers, is about to pluck out those which ornament the lady's hair A cock stands in the foreground (r.), having lost almost all its tail feathers, many of which lie on the floor. A black boy wearing a turban stands on his mistress's r , handing feathers from a number which he holds in his l hand. The lady, who faces T Q to the r., is elaborately dressed in the fashion of the day. Her pyramid of hair is decorated with lappets of lace and festoons of jewels as well as with feathers. She wears large ear-rings, a necklace with a cross, her bodice is cut very low, and her elbow sleeves have lace ruffles. A pannelled wall forms the background.

One of a number of satires on the hair-dressing of 1776-7, see No. 5370, &c.

$12\frac{7}{8} \times 10$ in.

THE CONTINENCE OF A METHODIST PARSON . .

See No. 4610—10 June 1776

After Collet.

Pub. Sayer and Bennett.

A smaller version (reversed) of No. 4609 (1773).

THE SPORTING LADY   See No. 4624—1 Oct. 1776

Pub. Sayer and Bennett. Reproduced, Paston, Pl cxvii.

A LOVELY YOUTH AND A CHARMING MAID, . . .

See No 4777—29 May 1776

Pub. W. Humphrey.

POLITICAL SATIRES

5397 19. V 2. POOR OLD ENGLAND ENDEAVOURING TO RECLAIM HER WICKED AMERICAN CHILDREN.

Pub Ap' 1 1777 by M Darly 39 Strand

Engraving England, as an elderly, emaciated man, with a wooden leg and crutch, stands on one side of water inscribed *The Atlantic Ocean* He wears a wide-brimmed hat; at his feet is Britannia's shield In his l. hand is a scourge with which he threatens five Americans on the other side. Four of them have hooks through their noses attached to cords which England is pulling Nevertheless, one turns his back and looks round jeering; another is firing a miniature cannon held in both hands. The fifth shouts and points, waving his hat Beneath the title is etched *And therefore is England maimed & forc'd to go with a Staff. shakespeare.* One of the few political satires in Darly's series, see Nos. 5369, 5370, &c.
$7\frac{15}{16} \times 12\frac{13}{16}$ in.

5397A An apparently earlier state without numbers and the words 'The Atlantic Ocean'. It is, however, dated *Sep' 1. 1777*

The American who turns his back bares his person indecently; this has been altered in No. 5397

5398 USURY BRIDLED OR HOPPY-KIKKI HALL, IN AN UPROAR.

Publish'd 1st April 1777.

Engraving. Hopkins, the City Chamberlain, seated in an armchair (r) outside a small one-storied building symbolizing the Chamberlain's office. He holds a document inscribed *16½ P' C'*, saying, *It's a fair price.* Beside him (l) is an open box inscribed *City Chest*, full of money-bags. The building behind him is decorated with the City Arms, and flies a flag inscribed *Honesty Rewarded* A small projection from the main building immediately above Hopkins's head is inscribed *Morgages Annuities Bonds in Judgement Colat'. Securities.*

He appears unconscious of a lawyer (l.) wearing a gown who advances towards him, holding by a chain a monster with the body of a dog and three human heads, two of which, and perhaps the third which is partly concealed, have bearded Jewish profiles The lawyer holds a rolled document inscribed *Bill to Pre*[?vent Usury]; he is saying, *If I can't extirpate ye, I'll bridle you.* Over his head flies Fame holding out a wreath and palm branch. The three heads of the monster are saying, *How cursedly the Lawyer pulls, Damn this Bill I can't keep my Horse and my Whore now,* and *May our holy Phrophet Moses Confound 'em.* In one paw is a rolled document inscribed *To the Clerk of the City Till,* in the other, *Morgage on the Green horn Estates.*

The Bill held by the lawyer appears to represent that 'for regulating the grants of life annuities and for the better protection of infants against such grants' (17 George III, c. 26). See abstract of the Act, *Ann. Reg.* 1777, p. 259 According to Walpole the Act was occasioned by a usurious bargain made by Hopkins for a loan to Sir John St Aubyn (see No 5414) in his minority, *Last Journals*, 1910, ii. 36–7 He was commonly called *Vulture Hopkins*, the noted usurer, *City Biography*, 1800, p 136 As Chamberlain, he was responsible for the City Chest, which contained funds deposited for annuities for City orphans Hopkins was Wilkes's rival, see No 5327 He was four times a Director of the Bank of England (1765–79); M.P. for Great Bedwin 1771–4. A. B. Beaven, *Aldermen of London*, ii. 135.

$7\frac{1}{2} \times 8\frac{7}{8}$ in. (pl.).

5399 THE CONFERENCE BETWEEN THE BROTHERS HOW TO GET RICH.

Publish'd by W. Williams Fleet Street as the Act directs Oct· 10, 1777

Engraving. Two men of identical appearance, one (l.) dressed as a military officer, the other (r.) as a naval officer, sit opposite each other, one on each side of a round table. Between them, behind the table, stands the devil, a hand pointing at each brother. He says *How How continue the War.* He addresses Admiral Lord Howe and General Sir William Howe, who were then making a joint attack on Philadelphia. Admiral Howe (r.) says, *Brother How poor we are How shall we get Rich*; the other answers, *I don't know How How we can.* In the background, seen through an open door, are four ships of war at anchor, they are lying off an encampment of tents In front of these is a plantation of cabbages, by which is a man with a cabbage cart, calling *Cabbages Ho . . . w.*

During September and most of October 1777 no news arrived from either of the Howes. According to Walpole 'the nation from impatience of news, grew much dissatisfied, and the Howes were infinitely abused and accused of thinking of nothing but their vast profits'. *Last Journals*, 1910, ii. 45 The cabbages probably indicate the alleged perquisites taken by the Howes, since cabbage was the name for pilfered pieces of stuff appropriated by tailors, the verb to cabbage meaning to pilfer. *O.E.D.*, cf. No. 5805.

The word How in the title and on the design is larger than the rest of the script to indicate the pun on the name of the brothers. This satire combines an attack on the Howes for dishonesty and inactivity with the suggestion that advice to continue the war comes from the devil.

See also Nos. 5405, 5406, 5472.

$8\frac{1}{2} \times 12\frac{1}{2}$ in.

5400 GENERAL SANGUINAIRE. MARK-HAM,[1]

Pub Oc· 28 177 [sic] by M Darly 120 New Bond street & 39 Strand

Engraving. Archbishop Markham, dressed partly as a bishop, partly as a soldier He wears a mitre decorated with a skull and cross-bones; his surplice is kilted up to show boots and breeches; his lawn sleeves appear through a sleeveless military tunic Round his neck, below his bands, is a gorget inscribed *Ectype*. On his r. arm is an oval shield, on which is a figure of the Devil holding a spear inscribed *Prototype*

---

[1] Margin cut off, but *38 v· 2* in a book of Darly's caricatures in the possession of Mr W. T Spencer (1933) See Nos 5369, 5370, &c

In his l. hand he holds up a sword, inscribed *York's Sermons*. Slung across his back is a cannon, inscribed *Cannon Law* His crozier lies on the ground and his r foot stands upon an open Bible inscribed *Biblia Sacra. John Cap. 10 V. 1* After the title is etched:

> *whom Patriarch Noah cursed,*
> *O Slave to Sem & Japheth*
> *O may on his Head vengeance burst,*
> *and push his Bones in Tophet,*
> *Pollutes the Lawn with human Gore*
> *What Devil can do more*

Markham was translated to York in June 1777 He was much attacked for his attitude to the war, notably in the House of Lords, 30 May 1777, by Grafton, Shelburne, and others for a sermon contrary to the spirit of the Revolution *Parl Hist.* xix, pp. 326–51 (sermon quoted, pp. 348–50 n); Walpole, *Last Journals*, ii. 29–30. Walpole calls him 'Archbishop Turpin', 10 June 1777, *Letters*, x. 59 See also Nos 5343, 5492, 5631.
11 × 8¹⁵⁄₁₆ in.

5401 THE FLIGHT OF THE CONGRESS.

Publish'd Novr 20 1777 by Wm Hitchcock, N° 5 Birchin Lane.

Engraving Animals in a wooded landscape with a mountainous background. Howe, as a lion, chasing (l to r) the American leaders in the shape of different animals. The scene is in front of a wooded mound in which is a cave inscribed *Cave of Rebellion. Resolv'd, nem: con never to run away.* On the mound grows 'Liberty Tree', a tree inscribed *Liberty*; a squirrel sits on a branch scattering papers, inscribed *Paper Currency*, '*30 dollers*', '*100 dollers*', &c An opossum is climbing up the trunk. A roaring lion advances into the picture, his breath inscribed *How*; one paw is on a squared sheet of paper, inscribed *Philadelphia, Delawar . . .* The animals he chases are: an ass with a lion's skin on its back, inscribed, *I Hancock Pres*; a tiger, *Laurens*, an armadillo, *Washington*, two foxes with collars round their necks, inscribed respectively *Adams* and *[A]dam[s]*, evidently intended for John and Samuel Adams, a pig or wild boar is *Putnam*; a wolf is *Lee*; a stag whose collar is inscribed *V . . . D.* ('Francis Van Dyke, a New York patriot); a puma and a badger (?) without names In the air (l.) an eagle clutches in beak and claws a rattlesnake inscribed *Independence*; and (r) an owl flies away holding a paper, inscribed *Louis Baboon a Paris.* In the background (l) is sketched a ship in full sail.

Beneath the design verses are engraved:

> *Impatient of Imperial sway,*
> *The Wild Beasts of America,*
> *In Congress met, disclaim'd allegiance.*
> *And to the Ass profess'd obedience,*
> *With such New Leader, feeling bold,*
> *No wonder they disdained the Old.*
>
> *Resolving roundly, one and all,*
> *In the good cause, to stand or fall,*
> *Then herding, underneath the Tree,*
> *Of Treason, alias Liberty;*
> *They boast the Baboon King's alliance,*
> *And at their own, hurl mad defiance.*

Their foul revolt, their Monarch hears,
And strait upon the plain appears,
Aloud the British Lion roars,
Aloft the German Eagle soars;
When, Lo! 'midst broken Oaths and curses,
The Rebel rout at once disperses.

This represents the occupation of Philadelphia by Howe in Sept. 1777 after the victory of Brandywine. In November there were reports in England of great successes over Washington which were not confirmed, Howe failing to bring him to a general action In the meantime the surrender of Burgoyne at Saratoga, 17 Oct (see No 5470), had disastrously altered the situation, but news of this did not reach London till 2 Dec (see No 5408) The owl flying to Louis XVI probably represents Benjamin Franklin's mission to France, where he arrived at the end of 1776 The 'baboon king' is the king of France, 'Lewis Baboon' of Arbuthnot's *Law is a Bottomless Pit*, 1712, but the alliance was not decided on until Dec 1777 and not signed until 6 Feb. 1778. Lafayette had sailed for America in Apr 1777 without the formal consent of the French Government. The rattlesnake was an emblem of the colonies and was on the earliest naval flag of the Americans, see Nos 5336, 5973, &c One of the few satires hostile to the Americans, cf. Nos. 5329, 5482, 5704, 5853, 6288

Reproduced, *Propylaen-Weltgeschichte*, ed. W. Goetz, vi 481, S. G. Fisher, *True History of the American Revolution*, 1902, p 346

$7\frac{15}{16} \times 13\frac{3}{16}$ in.

5401 A. An earlier impression in which a blank has been left for the day of the month in the publication line. The owl with its document inscribed *Louis Baboon a Paris* is omitted, as are the words *Lee, Putnam,* and *V ... D* on the wolf, boar, and stag. The background differs in several details, the plate having been reworked and strengthened for the later impression. In place of the ship is a group of trees.

5402 THE TAKEING OF MISS MUD I'LAND   [*c.* Dec. 1777]

Sold by W Humphrey 227 Strand London.

Engraving (coloured and uncoloured impressions) A rough plan of the Delaware river below the mouth of the Schuylkill which is shown as a quasi-rectangular piece of water In its centre is a pentagonal fort-shaped island, inscribed *Mud Islnd*. Across this straddles a woman astride a cannon which she is firing at the British ship *Isis*, while her l. hand fires a miniature cannon. Her hair is dressed over a broad cushion, cf. No. 5370, &c, on it are two cannon and two flags, one the striped American flag with a serpent, see No. 5336, &c, the other the Union flag On each side of the *Isis* are the *Roebuck* (l.) and the *Somerset* (r.), the latter in flames. In front of the *Isis* the topsails of the *Eagle* appear Above Mud Island is the *Vigilant*, firing a broadside *Chevaux de Frize* are marked in the river, above and below Mud Island

This appears to illustrate Lord Howe's dispatch of 25 Oct, published 2 Dec 1777 in an *Extraordinary Gazette*, see also *Ann. Reg.* 1777, p 134 ff ; Walpole, *Last Journals*, 1910, ii 79 In the attack on the strongly fortified Mud, or Fort, Island the *Isis* and the *Merlin* were destroyed. The *Eagle* was Howe's flagship, see No 5472. Mud Island was taken on 15 Nov., the news reaching London 19 Dec Its capture opened the navigation of the Delaware; Howe marched after Washington, but failing to draw him into an engagement, withdrew to winter quarters at Philadelphia, cf No. 5472.

$8\frac{15}{16} \times 7\frac{1}{4}$ in.

5403 HEAD QUARTER'S [*c* 1777]

Engraving Probably from a book. A recruiting soldier beats a kettle-drum which is placed on the projecting 'cork-rump' (see No 5381, &c) of a lady who stands in profile to the r, her hands in an enormous muff. Her head-dress is similar to that of *Bunker's Hill* and *Noddle Island*, see Nos. 5330, 5335. on the summit are battlements, from which project cannon surmounted by a British flag, round the erection are files of soldiers, cannon project from the loop of hair beside the face She stands by a signpost in the form of a gibbet. It points *To . Trenton*, from the hand of the signpost dangles a noose of rope. A small recruiting placard is pasted on the gibbet-post, headed by the figure of a soldier and *G R III*, and inscribed, *All gentlemen Volunteers that are able and willing to serve his M . . . y let them report to the 3 flying shit pots, &c* In the background is the gable-end of an inn (the recruiting headquarters) in the door of which stands a soldier beating a drum, another soldier stands by him with upraised cane Some one is pouring liquid from an upper window on to his head. The royal arms and the word *Head-quarters* are over the door, a British flag flies from a pole. In the distance (r) is a minute figure hanging from a gallows

The words *To Trenton* indicate that this is a gibe at Washington's capture of Trenton (27 Dec. 1776) with its garrison of Hessians One of several anti-recruiting prints, see No. 5295, &c

$5\frac{5}{8} \times 3\frac{3}{4}$ in.

5404 CHARLES LEE, ESQUIER [*c*. 1777]

peint par Thomlinsen a Novelle Yorck

Se vend a Londres chez Thom. Hart.

Mezzotint. H.L portrait in an oval copied from No 5296. The flag is very prominent and is inscribed, *An | une | Appeal | Appellation | To au | Heaven | Ciel* Beneath the title is engraved *Major Général d'Armee des XIII Provinces unies d'Amerique Prisonier de Guerre, fait par les Anglois* [1] Lee was taken prisoner by a scouting party on 13 Dec. 1776, he was then second-in-command to Washington. He was at length exchanged and rejoined Washington at Valley Forge in May 1778.

$7\frac{3}{4} \times 6\frac{3}{16}$ in

5405 THE HON^BLE S^R W^M HOWE.

Corbutt Delint^t et fecit. [? R. Purcell]

London: Publish'd as the Act directs, 10th Novr 1777 by John Morris, Rathbone Place.

Mezzotint One of a series, see No 5290; a companion print to No 5406.

[1] It is against the practice of this series to depict unsuccessful American generals Possibly the plate was engraved before news of the capture

T.Q L. portrait of a military officer facing front, looking to r. His r elbow resting on masonry; a stone fortification on r. with cannon   He wears a ribbon and star. Beneath the title is engraved, *Knight of the Bath, & Commander in Chief of his Majesty's Forces in America.*

At this time the Howes were much blamed both in England and by American Loyalists for forbearing to attack the enemy, it was alleged for political motives, both being strong Whigs, and also for desiring the prolongation of the war for financial reasons   See *Detail and Conduct of the American War*   , 3rd ed , 1780 (B.M L 1447, d 23)   See also Nos. 5399, 5406, 5472, 5548[2]   Sir W Howe sent home his resignation in Oct. 1777 and embarked for England in Sept 1778.

Chaloner Smith, iv, p 1716   Reproduced, R. Hughes, *Washington, 1762–1777, 1927,* p. 274

13×9½ in.

5405 A. A copy, probably by Will, dated *10. May, 1778* but inscribed as above except *delin* in place of *Delin¹ et fecit* and the addition of *Se vend chez J M. Will à Augsbourg*   Andrews, p. 90.

5406 THE RIGHT HONᴮᴸᴱ RICHARD LORD HOWE.

Corbutt delin¹ et fecit. [? R. Purcell.]

London: Publish'd as the Act directs, 10ᵗʰ Novʳ 1777, by John Morris, Rathbone Place.

Mezzotint. One of a series, see No. 5290; a companion print to No. 5405. T.Q L portrait of a naval officer standing in profile to the l. but looking to front, a sword in his r. hand, l hand pointing to l   He appears to be on the deck of a ship. In the background l. is a ship in action, with the sails of another ship. Beneath the title is engraved *Commander in Chief of his Majesty's Fleets in America*

For the attacks on the brothers Howe at this time for inactivity see No. 5405, &c.

For a reissue or copy of this plate, published 11 June 1794 by Laurie & Whittle, see Chaloner Smith, iv, p. 1733.

13¾×9⅞ in.

5406 A. A copy, probably by Will, dated *10 Nov 1778* but inscribed as above except for *Corbutt delin* in place of *delin¹ et fecit,* and the addition of *Se vend chez J. M Will à Augsbourg.*

5407 BENJAMIN FRANKLIN

Dessiné par C. N. Cochin Chevalier de l'Ordre du Roi, en 1777

Joh. Martin Will excudit Aug. Vind.

Mezzotint. Apparently belongs to a series, see No. 5290, though unlike some others in the series it is engraved from a portrait   Franklin, T Q L , stands at a table directed to the r , holding a letter in his r. hand   His l. rests on the table on which are writing materials. He wears his well-known fur cap, spectacles, a plain coat with fur cuffs   The table is of an ornate French design, with marble top. Behind his head is a curtain. Beneath the title is engraved *Né à Boston, dans la nouvelle Angleterre le 17 Janvier 1706*

It appears to be after a bust portrait by Cochin which was often engraved.

The three chief heroes of the American Revolution, especially in France, were Franklin, Washington, and Lafayette, their portraits being used as propaganda. Those of Franklin were especially numerous, cf. No. 5691.

13×9⅜ in.

5408 GENERAL ARNOLD [c. Dec 1777]

peint par Wilckenson a Boston

Se vend a Londres chez Thom. Hart

Mezzotint. H.L portrait in an oval copied from No. 5331. Beneath the title is engraved, *Qui avec le General Gates aidoit de environer le General Lieutenant Bourgoyne, que toute l'Armee se rendit Prisoniere, et l'obligea de mettre bas les Armes.*

At the two battles at Saratoga which caused the surrender of Burgoyne (Oct. 1777) Arnold took the most conspicuous part though nominally under Gates, see No 5469.

8×6¼ in.

PERSONAL SATIRES

5409-5421

Series of Tête-à-Tête Portraits

5409 N° XXXIV. MADAME GILB——T.
N° XXXV THE KIND KEEPER.

*Published as the Act directs by A. Hamilton Jun' near S' John's Gate,
Jan. I. 1777.*

Engraving *Town and Country Magazine*, viii 625 Two bust portraits
in oval frames. They illustrate 'Histories of the Tête-à-Tête annexed; . . .'.
An account of an Irish peer, who had been a Commissioner of the Treasury
and Postmaster-General. He is William, 2nd earl of Bessborough (1704–
93) See Walpole, *Memoirs of the Reign of George III*, 1894, ii. 138, 270–1,
280. His mistress is described as the widow of a French hairdresser.

Ovals, $2\frac{5}{8} \times 2\frac{1}{4}$ in.   B.M.L , P.P 5442 b.

5410 N° XXXVII / N° XXXVIII   THE POLITICAL PLATONIC LOVERS.

*Published as the Act directs by A. Hamilton. Jun' near S' John's Gate,
Jan 10. 1777*

Engraving *Town and Country Magazine*, viii. 681 Two bust portraits
in oval frames. They illustrate 'Histories of the Tête-à-Tête annexed; or,
Memoirs of the Political and Platonic Lovers'. An account of Mrs
Catherine Macaulay and of Dr Wilson, that of the latter being continued
from the point at which it was left in the *Tête-à-Tête* of Jan 1772, see No.
4972. The house at Bath with its bust of Alfred which he presented to
her is described, see No 5598

Ovals, $2\frac{11}{16} \times 2\frac{1}{4}$ in.   B.M.L., P.P. 5442 b.

5411 N° II THALIA
N° III. MALAGRIDA

*Published as the Act directs by A Hamilton Jun' near S' John's Gate
Feb' I. 1777.*

Engraving. *Town and Country Magazine*, ix. 9. Two bust portraits in
oval frames They illustrate 'Histories of the Tête-à-Tête annexed. .'.
The portrait of Lord Shelburne (*Malagrida*) is a link between satirical
portraits of *circa* 1771 (see No. 4917) in which he is represented with a thin
face and melancholy expression, and the caricatures of 1782 and later in
which his face is round and slyly jovial

Thalia is Mrs. Abington (1737–1815), to whom *Malagrida* is said to
allow £50 a week, a chariot and horses, with no interruption to her
profession or restrictions on her visitors of both sexes.

Ovals, $2\frac{3}{4} \times 2\frac{1}{4}$ in   B M.L., P.P 5442 b.

5412 N° IV. LADY T——

     N° V. C—— L—— S——H

Published as the Act directs by A. Hamilton Jun' near S' John's Gate
Mar 1. 1777.

Engraving *Town and Country Magazine*, ix. 65. Two bust portraits in oval frames. They illustrate 'Histories of the Tête-à-Tête annexed; . . '. An account of Charles Loraine Smith[1] and of Lady Tyrconnel, daughter of the Marquess of Granby, who is here said to have formed a liaison with S. after a rupture due to her husband's unjust suspicions

    She was divorced Oct 1777 for *crim con.* with C L. Smith, with whom she had eloped 13 July 1776, and married 28 Oct 1777 Philip Anstruther. G.E.C., *Complete Peerage.*

Ovals, $2\frac{7}{8} \times 2\frac{3}{8}$ in.   B.M.L., P.P. 5442 b.

5413 N° VII. MISS CHARLOTTE S——R

     N° VIII THE D—— OF D——

Published as the Act directs by A. Hamilton Jun' near S' John's Gate,
April 1. 1777.

Engraving. *Town and Country Magazine*, ix. 121. Two bust portraits in oval frames, the lady's hair elaborately dressed They illustrate 'Histories of the Tête-à-Tête annexed; . . .'. An account of William, 5th Duke of Devonshire (1748–1811), who is here said to have remained faithful to his mistress, Miss Sp——r, a milliner and the seduced daughter of a curate, who is no longer young, in spite of his marriage [1774] to 'an universal toast, still in her teens'. For Charlotte Spencer see H. Bleackley, *Ladies Fair and Frail*, 1909, pp 209–10.

Ovals, $2\frac{11}{16} \times 2\frac{1}{4}$ in.   B.M.L., P.P. 5442 b.

5414 N° X MADAME LE F——

     N° XI. THE COZENED MINOR.

Published as the Act directs by A. Hamilton Jun' near S' John's Gate
May 1. 1777.

Engraving. *Town and Country Magazine*, ix. 177. Two bust portraits in oval frames They illustrate 'Histories of the Tête-à-Tête annexed; or, Memoirs of the Cozened Minor and Madame Le F——re'. An account of a young Cornish baronet, who began a career of debauchery and extravagance while at Westminster School, and is now (aged 19) making the grand tour. He has formed a liaison at Geneva with the English wife of a Swiss watchmaker, whom he had known in London before her marriage.

    Sir John Saint Aubyn, 1758–1839, who succeeded his father in 1772 G.E C, *Complete Baronetage*, iv 53 A 'certain transaction' is mentioned 'that has lately made so much noise, and will probably be the cause of a still greater uproar upon Midsummer day'. This is a reference to a usurious loan by Hopkins, the City Chamberlain, see No 5398.

Ovals, $2\frac{5}{8} \times 2\frac{1}{4}$ in.   B.M.L., P.P. 5442 b.

---

[1] Described as the heir of a Northumberland baronet, evidently Sir W Loraine of Kirkharle, 4th Bart, a cousin of Smith, his son and heir was born in 1779 In the Act of divorce he appears as Charles Smith Esq of Enderby, Leicestershire. B M.L. 216 1 3/62 See index of artists

5415 N° XIII. MRS L——M
N° XIV. THE AMOROUS JUSTICE.

Published as the Act directs by A. Hamilton Jun' near S' John's Gate
June 1. 1777.

Engraving. *Town and Country Magazine*, ix. 233. Two bust portraits in
oval frames. They illustrate 'Histories of the Tête-à-Tête annexed: or,
Memoirs of the Amorous Justice and M^rs L——m'. The Justice was
'designed for divinity' and educated at Oxford but obtained a commission
in Burgoyne's regiment, retired on an inherited fortune, becoming a judge
'about four years ago'. He is Justice Addington of Bow Street; see *The
Farington Diary*, i. 173–4. She is Mrs. Lessingham, who had passed as
the wife of Derrick. John Taylor, *Records of my Life*, 1832, i, pp. 5–10.
For Addington see No. 6120.

Ovals, $2\frac{11}{16} \times 2\frac{1}{4}$ in. B M L, P.P. 5442 b.

5416 N° XVI. VIS À VIS T——D
N° XVII THE E—— OF C——

Published as the Act directs by A. Hamilton Jun' near S' John's Gate
July 1. 1777

Engraving *Town and Country Magazine*, ix 289 Two bust portraits in
oval frames. They illustrate 'Histories of the Tête-à-Tête annexed: or,
Memoirs of the E—— of C—— and vis-à-vis T——d'. An account of
the amours of Lord C., having no particulars by which he can be identified
with certainty Miss T——d is a young courtesan of humble origin whose
chief ambition is to own a fashionable carriage called a vis-à-vis. This
Lord C has satisfied

For Agnes Townshend see H Bleackley, *Ladies Frail and Fair*, 1909,
p. 282, and cf No. 5936. For the vis-à-vis see No. 5373.

Ovals, $2\frac{11}{16} \times 2\frac{1}{4}$ in. B M L, P P. 5442 b.

5417 N° XIX THE HIBERNIAN THAIS.
N° XX CAPT'N TOPER

Published as the Act directs by A. Hamilton Jun' near S' John's Gate
Aug' 1. 1777.

Engraving *Town and Country Magazine*, ix. 345. Two bust portraits in
oval frames. They illustrate 'Histories of the Tête-à-Tête annexed ...'.
An account of a man so notorious for his gallantry and dissipation 'that
his portrait will be immediately recognized'. It is of a good-looking man
facing T.Q. to the l. with an aquiline nose. He is in 'a constant state of
intoxication', with a 'natural disposition for riot and confusion'. Identified
by H. Bleackley as Captain Roper He is alluded to in vol xv, p. 122
(1783) as Captain R——r, who had died at Antwerp, after being continually drunk for the last six years of his life Thaïs is Miss F——m,
who, on the eve of her marriage in Ireland, eloped to England with a
captain who deserted her, after which, having nearly starved as a strolling
actress, she became a London courtesan.

Ovals, $2\frac{3}{4} \times 2\frac{1}{4}$ in. B.M.L, P.P. 5442 b.

5418 N° XXII. MISS D——N.
N° XXIII. LE COMTE DES LUNETTES

*Published as the Act directs by A. Hamilton Jun' near S' John's Gate
Sep' 1. 1777.*

Engraving *Town and Country Magazine*, ix 401. Two bust portraits in
oval frames They illustrate 'Histories of the Tête-à-Tête annexed: . . .'.
An account of the Earl of Peterborough (1710–79), the name in the title
given to him because he invariably wears spectacles. His mistress is a Miss
Dawson, whom he had persuaded to leave the house of an old lady to whom
she was acting as a companion.

Ovals, $2\frac{5}{8} \times 2\frac{1}{4}$ in.; $2\frac{3}{4} \times 2\frac{1}{4}$ in   B.M.L., P.P. 5442 b.

5419 N° XXV. MRS W—NT—R
N° XXVI. THE E. OF H——H

*Published as the Act directs by A Hamilton Jun' near S' John's Gate
Oct' 1. 1777.*

Engraving *Town and Country Magazine*, ix 457. Two bust portraits in
oval frames They illustrate 'Histories of the Tête-à-Tête annexed: . . .'.
An account of Lord Hillsborough (1718–93), afterwards Marquis of
Downshire, alluding to the Royal Society Club, the account of which
is in striking contrast to Sir A. Geikie's documented history of the Club.
He is said to have 'filled several high offices with dignity and general
applause'. Mrs. W is the widow of a lieutenant in the Marines.

Ovals, $2\frac{11}{16} \times 2\frac{1}{4}$ in.; $2\frac{5}{8} \times 2\frac{1}{4}$ in.   B.M.L , P.P. 5442 b.

5420 N° XXVIII. THE WANTON WIDOW.
N° XXIX. THE COMPLYING COLONEL

*Published as the Act directs by A. Hamilton Jun' near S' John's Gate,
Nov' 1. 1777.*

Engraving. *Town and Country Magazine*, ix. 513 Two bust portraits.
They illustrate 'Histories of the Tête-à-Tête annexed: . . ' An account
of the amours of a Colonel C. in the Guards and of the widow of 'Lord
A H ', once a great beauty but ravaged by small-pox.

Ovals, $2\frac{11}{16} \times 2\frac{1}{4}$ in   B M.L., P.P. 5442 b.

5421 N° XXXI MISS C—T—R.
N° XXXII THE SPORTING ROVER.

*Published as the Act directs by A Hamilton Jun' near S' John's Gate,
Dec' 1. 1777.*

Engraving *Town and Country Magazine*, ix. 569 Two bust portraits in
oval frames They illustrate 'Histories of the Tête-à-Tête annexed or
Memoirs of the Sporting Rover and Miss C—rt—r'. The man is son of
an old Mr. P——n, who was well known on the turf, said to have been
introduced to Charles Churchill by Lloyd. Identified by H. Bleackley
as Thomas Panton His amours and those of Miss Carter, a courtesan,
are described. For Panton see *Jockey Club*, 1792, pp 91–2.

Ovals, $2\frac{1}{4}$ '$2\frac{3}{8}$ in.   B.M.L., P P. 5442 b.

5422 THE SENATORIAL CONTRAST.

Pub⁴ 27ᵗʰ Janʸ 1777 by J. Jones Gerrard Street Soho.

Engraving A burly Roman senator and a small, thin, knock-kneed Englishman face each other. Over one is etched *The Roman Senator*; over the other, *The British Senator*. The Roman (l.) in profile to the r., wearing armour and a voluminous cloak, stands in front of a pillar with his l. foot on a raised step; he holds out his hands as if in surprise at the appearance of the Englishman. The Briton stands upon a square stool, his toes turned in; he looks at the Roman through a lorgnette, with an expression of dismay; his l. hand is raised in astonishment. His dishevelled hair is in a short queue and he is dressed in the fashion of the day. On the ground at his feet are cards, dice, a dice-box; another dice-box is on the stool He has just dropped the Knave of Clubs which falls to the ground. Behind him two game-cocks are fighting. In the distance the horizon is inscribed *Surry Hills*, indicating that he is M P. for Surrey.

He is James Scawen,[1] of Carshalton, Surrey, and Maidwell, Northamptonshire, whose gaming debts were notorious, see No 5423.

He was son of the nephew and heir of Sir William Scawen, a very rich merchant and great supporter of William III. Several estates in Surrey were sold by him (1774) or by his trustees (c 1781), including one to Robert Mackreth (1774), of White's (Bob), notorious as a money-lender (whose nomination for the borough of Castle Rising in 1774 so scandalized Walpole). Brayley, *History of Surrey*, iv. 66–7, 194, 226.

5⅞×7 1/16 in.

5423 THE PROFLIGATES LEVEE, OR THE KNIGHT'S INTERVIEW WITH ISRAEL THE JEW & TOMMY BLOODSUCKER.

[n.d. c Jan. 1777]

Engraving. A small thin man stands between two much larger men, who hold documents showing that they are money-lenders. He is James Scawen, M P. for Surrey, see No 5422 His thin legs are knock-kneed, his toes turn inwards. He looks towards the money-lender on his l and points with his l. hand at a paper held up by the latter, whose beard and hooked nose show that he is a Jew The Jew (r) wears a bag-wig, laced coat and waistcoat; the paper he holds out is inscribed, *Mortgage on the Surry Northamp*[ton] *Estates D⁰ on the Cornwal D⁰ on the . . . D⁰ . . .* Behind the Jew's back is an open window, within which sits a woman of forbidding appearance with a Jewish profile, who appears deeply interested in the interview.

A large obese man (l) stands in profile to the r., wearing a wide-brimmed looped hat, plain clothes, and a nosegay. In his l. hand is a larger document than that held by the Jew; in his r. hand is a large eyeglass. His document is inscribed, *Annuitys gⁱanᵈ to Tho: Bloodsucʳ. An. 100, D⁰ 20, D⁰ 150, D⁰ 75 D⁰ 100, D⁰ 120, D⁰ 25, D⁰ 100, D⁰ 150.* Behind him a cat stands on its hind legs, while behind the Jew a dog does the same. At Scawen's feet are dice-boxes, dice, and cards

7⅛×8¾ in.

[1] Miss Banks has written 'Mr. Scawen' on the print.

5424 THE DIABOLIAD.   [1 Apr. 1777]

Lond. Mag. March 1777

Engraving From the *London Magazine*, xlvi 152 Illustration to *The
Diaboliad*, a satirical poem by William Combe published anonymously in
1777. The Devil grown old is about to appoint a successor to reign in
Hell He rises from his throne (l) and is about to surrender his crown and
sceptre to an elderly man who mounts the steps on which the throne is
placed. Five disappointed competitors stand behind the successful
candidate, who is Lord Irnham The others are young men; two approach
together, one with a blank face on which is inscribed *Whitlow*; he holds
in his hand a book or MS. inscribed *Simiramis* and wears a military gorget
round his neck. Of the next couple, one holds a horseshoe in his l. hand,
a pen 'marked *A* in his r.; from his coat-pocket projects a letter to *Miss
Hunter*, under his l. arm is a riding-whip; he is in riding-dress. He is
described in the poem as a peer and rough rider, who assumed the authorship of a book 'by A[ngeloni][1] writ'. Last comes *Volpone*, Charles Fox,
with a fox's head, holding out dice. He is fashionably dressed, his coat
having very large buttons, see No. 5432. He is dismissed by the Devil,

to bait,
With mastiff zeal—a Minister of State.

One of the other competitors is a young peer who combines vice with
eloquence in the House of Lords [Lyttelton].

Behind, among clouds of smoke, stands a weeping man in chains
Demons and imps ('dragons and monsters') fly about. One, partly visible
on the l of the print, crouches by the Devil's throne, writing on a scroll;
he wears spectacles. In the distance on the r. angels escort a figure through
an opening in the roof of the cave; demons hold up a net between them
and the competitors. Beneath the print is engraved, *To reign is worth
ambition, tho' in Hell!* Milton.

According to Walpole (Jan. 1778) Combe was brutally virulent against
Lord Beauchamp and others, 'particularly Lord Irnham'. *Last Journals*,
1910, ii 95–6. Other persons attacked are Lord Hertford, Mr. Ayscough
(Lyttelton's cousin), Lord Pembroke, Fitzpatrick (but as one whom in
time the Devil will lose), and Selwyn for his supposed fondness for
attending executions; Selwyn to Lord Carlisle, Feb. 1777, *Carlisle MSS*,
Hist. MSS Comm, 1897, p. 320.

$3\frac{5}{8} \times 6\frac{5}{16}$ in

5424A THE DIABOLIAD.

Almost identical with No 5424 but in reverse and without *Lond. Mag. . . .*
imprint.

5425 THE DIABO-LADY   [1 May 1777]

Engraving From the *London Magazine*, xlvi. 208. Illustration to *The
Diabo-lady*, a satire by 'Belphegor', probably Combe, which rapidly followed *The Diaboliad*, see No 5424, to which this is a companion print
by the same artist. The new sovereign of Hell, Lord Irnham, decides to
choose a wife and sends his emissaries to 'Court, Cornelys' and the

---

[1] In the poem this is A——, but Angeloni is given in a quotation from it in the
London Magazine.

Coterie' (see No. 4847, &c.). He is depicted descending from his throne (r.) and leading up to it the successful candidate. Behind her (l.) are five disappointed aspirants. a fat and angry woman holds a paper inscribed *Road from Kingston to Bristol* showing that she is the so-called Duchess of Kingston, see No 5362. She is unsuccessful because she lacked the vice of hypocrisy. Next her (r.) is a lady dressed half soberly in black, and half more elaborately, one half being inscribed *Widow*, the other half *Bride*. Behind appear (l. to r.) a lady in riding-dress holding out a paper *Count[?ess] and the Stable Boy*, showing that she is Lady Ligonier, see No 4801; another holds out a paper inscribed *Bible Oath*, a lady who appears from the poem to have been acquitted for her first adultery on 'a Bible-Oath'. A woman holds up a paper on which is a gallows and the word *Pereau's*, showing that she is the notorious Mrs. Rudd, the mistress and instigator of one of the two Perreaus who were hanged for forgery, but who was herself acquitted

In the background is a crowd of disappointed candidates, dismissed because 'your Green-Room Dolls are kitchen Maids in Hell'. Imps fly about, some holding torches. Lord Irnham is fashionably dressed with horns, asses's ears, and cloven hoofs; the end of his queue is barbed. Beneath the design are five lines from *Paradise Lost* beginning,

> *O fairest of Creation, last and best*
> *Of all God's works . . .*

$3\frac{11}{16} \times 6\frac{1}{4}$ in.

5426 PHILOSOPHICAL JUDGMENT DEC^R 1. 1777

Engraving with roulette. A meeting of the Royal Society, the president in the chair and raised above the level of the other members. Members of the Council sit on his r and l behind a long table. Except for a clergyman on the president's r. all the Council appear to be asleep or yawning. The backs of the heads of members of the Society appear in the foreground; they seem to be lifting up their hands in astonishment at the proceedings of the Council. The president, who wears a hat, holds in his r. hand a MS., *Short on Grinding*; in his l the *Copley* medal. On the table is a mace, and papers inscribed, *Nat^l History*; *Anatomy*; *Nat. Philo*[sophy]. On the wall above the President's head is a bust of a man with the full wig of Queen Anne's reign. On each side of it is a picture: (l) Midas with long ass's ears judging between Apollo and Marsyas, above it is written *Aures Asininas habet Rex Midas*, and beneath *Veluti in Speculum*. On the r is a picture of the president with ass's ears, seated at the head of a table holding up a medal with sleeping members on each side of him; above it is written *Redivivus 1777 Dormiente Consilio*, and beneath, *Et in Arcadia Ego*. On the upper part of the design is etched in large letters *Nil Admirari*.

Sir John Pringle was president of the Society 1772–8, making six annual discourses on the value of the investigations rewarded by the Copley medal. James Short (1710–68), optician, a member of the Royal Society, deposited with the Society a sealed paper to be read publicly after his death, describing a method of working object-lenses to a truly spherical form. For the Royal Society see also No 2477 (1743).

$7 \times 7\frac{3}{8}$ in.

5427 MADEMOISELLE DE BEAUMONT OR THE CHEVALIER D'EON. [1 Oct. 1777]

*Lond. Mag. Sep*ʳ *1777*

Engraving From the *London Magazine*, xlvi. 443. D'Eon (W L) dressed half as a woman, half as a man On his r side he wears a lady's full dress, his hair in the fashionable inverted pyramid decorated by a feather; he holds a fan in his gloved hand. On his l. side he is dressed in a coat with military facings to which is appended the cross of St Louis. He wears a sword and his l. hand is on his hip, his hat under his arm. Beneath the title is engraved, *Female Minister Plenipo. Capt. of Dragoons, &c. &c.*

This illustrates 'Memoirs of Mademoiselle D'Eon de Beaumont . . .,' pp 443–6, occasioned by the recent decision (2 July 1777) in the King's Bench that one Hayes who had wagered that d'Eon was a woman, to be paid when he could prove it, had won his bet The jury thus settled (incorrectly) the long dispute and many wagers on D'Eon's sex, see No. 4865, &c.

7⅛ × 4⅞ in

5428 THE POACHER.

G. L. S (Monogram)

Engraving. W.L. caricature portrait of a man walking in profile to the l. His hair falls on his neck, but the top of his head is nearly bald He is roughly dressed, wearing a coat with a cape, and a neckcloth. In his r. hand is a walking-stick, in his l. a hat. Beneath the title is engraved

—————————*Mactat*
————————— *Sub rupe leones.*

On the print is written 'well known at Oxford' and in another hand, 'Sold by J. Seago, High Street Sᵗ Giles's London Pub. 1777'.

7¼ × 5⅝ in.

5429–5451

Prints from Darly's series continued from No. 5376 See No. 5369.

5429 1 CHLOE'S CUSHION OR THE CORK RUMP.¹

*Pub. Jan*ʸ *1. 1777 by M Darly 39 Strand*

Engraving (coloured and uncoloured impressions, the latter only being numbered). A lady dressed in a grotesque caricature of the prevailing fashion walking (l. to r) by the side of a lake. Her petticoats project behind her in an ascending curve, on which lies a King Charles spaniel. Her hair is dressed in a mountainous inverted pyramid, the apex represented by her head; it is flanked by side-curls and surmounted by interlaced ribbons from which hang streamers of ribbon and lace.

One of a number of satires, 1776–7, on monstrous hairdressing, see No. 5370, &c., and the 'cork rump', see No 5381, &c.

13 5/16 × 8¾ in

¹ Only the uncoloured impression is numbered This is the first plate in two of three volumes with the title-page of 1 Jan. 1776 (see No 5369) which have been examined, one belonging to Mr Dyson Perrins, the others to Mr. W. T. Spencer, New Oxford Street.

5430 THE BACK-SIDE OF A FRONT ROW.

R. S. (Monogram) ['Richard Sneer'[1]]
Pub⁴ by M Darly Janʸ 1. 1777

Engraving The back view of a number of persons seated on a low bench, caricaturing the dress of the period, especially the high-dressed hair, see No 5370, &c., and inflated appearance due to 'cork rumps', see No 5381, &c, which was combined with very tight lacing, see No. 5444, &c

The persons are (l. to r.)· a man with a clerical wig, his head turned in profile to the r ; a small child dressed like a woman with pinched waist, and cap trimmed with flowers and lace; a thin woman looking at her neighbour on the r., she has a monstrous erection of hair decorated with lace and flowers, pinched waist and inflated skirt; a fat woman, looking to the l , similarly but more plainly dressed; a man with a long pigtail queue, who is perhaps 'Richard Sneer', he turns to his neighbour on the r., his hand at the back of her waist; a woman with a rectangular variation of the prevailing head-dress and elaborately braided hair; she is rather smaller than the other women and appears to be intended for a young girl At the r. end of the bench sits a woman looking to the l whose head-dress is even more high and elaborate than that of the others.

These persons, as well as the print itself, appear in No. 5435. No. 5376 also belongs to the same set

$8\frac{1}{2} \times 12\frac{3}{4}$ in.

5431 [MODERN HONOUR][2]

Pub⁴ Febʸ 1. 1777 by M Darly. 39 Strand

Engraving (coloured impression). Two men face each other with pistols, their seconds stand behind them. The duellist on the l kneels on one knee, his r arm outstretched, his pistol in his l hand, the barrel pointing upwards as if to ward off his opponent's shot; his l elbow rests on his knee. His second stands with his arms folded The other has just fired his pistol which is aimed directly at his antagonist His second, with a pistol in his l hand, is shouting with his r arm raised They are in open country; hills are indicated in the distance.

$8\frac{1}{8} \times 12\frac{11}{16}$ in.

5432 BUCKLES AND BUTTONS
      I'M THE THING DEM—ME

Pub. by M Darly Feb. 7. 1777

Engraving (coloured impression). A man, wearing a large nosegay and holding in his l hand a thin tasselled cane, dressed to show the prevailing fashion for large metal buttons, and large shoe buckles The brim of his round hat is looped up at both sides by bands held by a large button on the crown; the buttons on his coat are enormous His waistcoat has also a double row of small buttons. His rectangular shoe-buckles curve across the instep, almost reaching the sole of the shoe.

---

[1] Possibly R B. Sheridan, see No. 5376 n
[2] The title has been cut off and is supplied from a book of Darly's caricatures in the possession (1932) of Mr. W. T. Spencer.

A cutting from the *Morning Post*, 14 Jan. 1777, is pasted on the print: 'The macaronies of a *certain class* are under peculiar circumstances of distress, occasioned by the fashion now so prevalent, of wearing enormous shoe-buckles, and we are well assured, that the manufactory of *plated ware* was never known to be in so flourishing a condition'

These buckles were called Artois buckles, it was the fashion to wear them of silver, and of a weight of from three to eleven ounces. *Morning Post*, 26 May, 1777. See also Nos 5437, 5443, 5446, 5452, 5454, 5462. Reproduced, Paston, Pl. xxv.

$12\frac{1}{8} \times 8\frac{3}{4}$ in.

5432A Another version in reverse, same size figure, smaller plate (clipped), same title, no publication line.

5433 THE BURTHENS OF PLENTY.

H. (or N.) R.   J. T. [?]

[Pub]^d *by M Darly Feby 24 1777 39 Strand.*

Engraving. An enormously fat man walks (l. to r) towards an eating-house followed by a lean and ragged man bent with the weight of a basket laden with food which he carries on his head and shoulders. The fat man is walking with a wheelbarrow, which he uses to support his enormously projecting stomach; the barrow is partly supported by straps which go over his shoulders and across his stomach. He mops his forehead with his l. hand. He wears a tie-wig, a laced coat and waistcoat, and is evidently intended for a rich and vulgar citizen His porter is dressed in rags, with bare legs and toes projecting through his shoes; he carries one wine-bottle in his r hand, two more under his r arm; his basket, supported on a large pad or cushion, contains a turtle, a hare, two snipe, a haunch of venison(?), and three bottles. The fat man is about to enter a door over which is a sign, *Good eating & cool rooms* This hangs from a projecting beam with pulleys; from it three barrels are also hung as a sign. Over the door is inscribed *Wines*. Behind the ragged man is a row of tenement houses, whose nature is indicated by the nearest one. A ladder leads down to its cellar over the door of which is written *Dinners & shirt wash'd for 2 pence.* Above the first-floor window is a large notice, *Shafe & Cut hear*; from it projects a barber's pole. Above the second-floor window is *I Nabbem Taylor*

The theme of a fat man supporting his own stomach on a wheelbarrow is an old one; it is that of a German caricature of a 'weinschlauch', a wood engraving of 1510, reproduced B Lynch, *A History of Caricature*, 1926, Pl vi, also of Luther (followed by Katarina von Bora), reproduced Ashbee, *Caricature*, 1928, p. 40; of a French caricature of General Galas, *c.* 1635, illustrated in Wright's *History of Caricature and Grotesque*, 1865, p. 356.

$8\frac{1}{4} \times 12\frac{1}{4}$ in.

5434 THE OLD MAIDS MORNING VISIT OR THE CALASH LADY'S [*sic*]

Pub^d M Darly 39 Strand Mar^h 11. 1777.

Engraving. A very fat and a very thin woman face one another, both wearing the hoods supported with hoops of cane or whalebone known as calashes, from their likeness to the folding hoods of carriages called by the same name (*O E D*) The fat woman (l) leans back in an armchair, one foot supported on a stool; her calash is like an almost spherical barrel. Her *vis-à-vis* sits upright, holding a fan, on a stool with folding legs; her calash is angular, showing its ribs, she wears a very skimpy skirt with a fullness at the back indicating a 'cork rump', see No 5381, &c. On the floor by the fat woman is a large trimmed bonnet, in which is a cat with kittens, one kitten prances at some distance. By the thin woman is a flat ribbon-trimmed hat, across which a dog is walking No other furniture is visible, except a hanging lamp with one beak, suspended from the wall. On the wall are four framed pictures, two of birds, one of some feline animal, one cut off by the l margin.

The calash is said to have been introduced by the Duchess of Bedford in 1765, Fairholt, *Costume*, 1896, ii 292. See also Nos 5450, 5527, 5532, 6100.

$8\frac{1}{8} \times 12\frac{1}{2}$ in.

5435 DOLEFULL DICKY SNEER IN THE DUMPS, OR THE LADY'S REVENGE.

R Sneer   *Sukey Spightfull fec^t*

Pub by M Darly Ap. 1. 1777

Engraving. A slim young man, fashionably dressed, sits at a table (r), a pencil in his l. hand, holding in his r. hand a print 'Miss Shuttle cock' (see No. 5376) reversed; the monogram *R.S.* is conspicuous, thus showing that he is 'Richard Sneer'.[1] On the wall above his head are two framed prints: one, *The Back-Side of a front Row* (see No 5430), reversed and showing five persons only; in the other, four ladies holding the four corners of a blanket toss a slim man, evidently 'Richard Sneer'; beneath it is inscribed *Lex Talio[n]s* Behind the artist, who is unconscious of their approach, three women and a man advance towards him dragging a blanket; they are characters from *The Back-Side of a front Row*: the elderly man advances into the picture from the l, then come the three elderly women, the one in the centre shakes her fist at the unconscious artist; all smile. They intend to punish him for his caricatures by tossing him in a blanket. Beneath the design is etched, *Heus bone, tu palles? pers* [*sic*]

$8\frac{1}{2} \times 12\frac{3}{4}$ in.

5436 i V. 2 THE OPTIC CURLS, OR THE OBLIGEING HEAD DRESS.

MD [Darly.]

Pub by M Darly 39 Strand April 1 1777

Engraving. The occupants of a box at a theatre A lady with an enormous inverted pyramid of hair decorated with the usual ringlets sits in front The ringlets have eye-pieces at the back and are completely cylindrical; two men who sit behind her look through the two lower ringlets as if they were the fashionable single eyeglass The lady herself looks through an eye-glass. On her pyramid of hair is an erection of rucked and interlaced ribbons, trimmed with sprays of flowers and surmounted by ostrich-feathers. Part of another box at right angles to this one is visible on the l; in it a

[1] Possibly R. B. Sheridan, see No. 5376.

man, in profile to the l , looks through an eye-glass. An ornamental chandelier with candles is suspended between the boxes.

One of a number of satires, 1776-7, on extravagant hairdressing, see No. 5370, &c. The same subject was treated by another artist, see No. 5462. Reproduced, Paston, Pl. xxiv.

$12\frac{1}{4} \times 8\frac{5}{8}$ in.

There is a chalk-drawing by James Roberts in the Print Department, 'Head Dress of Ladies 1777', of a lady's head in profile to the l. with an enormous pyramid of hair surmounted by ostrich-feathers from which fall lappets of lace and ribbon. The height is perhaps scarcely exaggerated.

5437 30 V. 2. Sᴿ WILLIAM WADDLE.

MD [Darly.]

Pubᵈ April 1. 1777 by M Darly 39 Strand.

Engraving. Portrait (caricature) of a very fat man, with short legs and a thick neck. Behind him is a lake or river He stands, legs apart, holding in his r. hand a tall cane. He wears the exaggerated buttons and shoe-buckles which became a subject of caricature in 1777, see No 5432, &c One button trims the front of his small hat, four decorate (and almost cover) the front of his coat, two are on his coat-sleeve. The collar of his coat appears to be black. Beneath the print is pasted a cutting from the *Morning Post*, 14 Apr. 1777: 'A correspondent remarks, the present *ton* of Gentlemen wearing black collars to all colour'd cloaths, looks as if *Taste* were dead, and all the fashionable part of mankind were in mourning for it.' Perhaps a caricature of Sir Watkin Lewes.

$8\frac{9}{16} \times 12\frac{1}{8}$ in.

5438 25. V. 2. A MARCH OF THE TRAIN BANDS.

E. Topham. del.   *MD* [Darly]

Pubᵈ April 10. 1777 by M Darly 39 Strand.

Engraving. Seven members of the City Militia, much caricatured, march (l. to r) in profile. First, the drummer, short and enormously stout, beating his drum, next a lean and stooping officer looking on the ground, his drawn sword in his l. hand. Then come two pairs of men carrying, at different angles, muskets with bayonets; they wear military uniform and gaiters, but are shambling along in a very unsoldierly manner Last comes a hunchback, holding a spear in his l. hand and marching with vigour. Two birds fly over their heads.

8×13 in.

5439 22. V. 2. LONG CORKS OR THE BOTTLE COMPANIONS

MD [Darly.]

Pub. by M Darly April 11 1777 Strand near York Buildings

Engraving. Two extravagantly dressed women face each other, each seated on, or rather supported by, an enormous cork which projects from the neck of a bottle Both are elderly, one (l) enormously fat, the other very thin Both wear the grotesque pyramids of hair, flanked by ringlets like large sausages and surmounted by ostrich-feathers, so much caricatured

267

since 1776, see No. 5370, &c. Their skirts are skimpy in front, showing the contour of their legs, but project in great panniers at the back
Both are gloved and hold fans The cork and bottle of the fat woman is
correspondingly broader than that of her thin *vis-à-vis*. This is a satire on
the fashions of the day, especially the 'cork-rumps' which appear to have
temporarily replaced hoops as a support to skirts and draperies, see No.
5381, &c.

$12\frac{3}{8} \times 8\frac{13}{16}$ in.

5440 THE LADIES CONTRIVANCE OR THE CAPITAL CONCEIT

MD [Darly.]

Miss Bath Inv[t]

Pub[d] April 30 1777 by M Darly. 39 Strand

Engraving (a coloured impression) Two sedan chairs pass one another,
going in opposite directions In the nearer, proceeding from l to r.,
sits a lady, whose enormous head-dress surmounted by feathers projects
far above the top of the chair, the roof has been made to slide up on rods
fixed at the corners, and is thus supported at a height above the top
of the sedan Through the window of the other sedan the head of a man
is seen; the roof of the chair is in its normal position, but rods at the
corners show that it can be raised if necessary. The chairs are private
ones, elegantly shaped and decorated, a tassel hanging from each corner
of the roof. The chairmen are in livery, wearing coats with coloured
facings.

For other satires on hairdressing see No. 5370, &c.

$8\frac{1}{4} \times 12\frac{3}{4}$ in.

5441 A SPEEDY & EFFECTUAL PREPARATION FOR THE NEXT WORLD.

Mathina [or *Mattina*] *Darly Sc.*

Pub May 1. 1777 by M Darly 39 Strand.

Engraving (coloured impression). A lady sits, in profile to the r., at a dressing-table; she is dipping a brush into a pot marked *Rouge*, other toilet
implements and a looking-glass are on the table. Her hair is in a grotesquely
caricatured erection, with side curls, intended to ridicule the fashions of
the day, cf No. 5370, &c.; on the top of it is a hearse drawn by six horses;
it is decorated with enormous ostrich-feathers. Similar feathers adorn
the heads of the horses. The lady is of commanding appearance with
an aquiline profile, she wears a morning gown.

Behind her back is a rectangular table at which (l) stands a skeleton,
both of whose hands are on an hour-glass standing on the table; its sands
have run into the lower glass, and have even been spilt on the table. On
the table is a knife The base of the skeleton's spine is transfixed by a
large arrow

On the wall behind the lady's dressing-table is a portrait bust of a
clergyman, in profile to the r

On the back of the print Miss Banks has written, 'M[rs] Macauley.
Dr. Wilson's picture'. Mrs. Catherine Macaulay (1731–91), the historian
and radical, was then living in the house of Dr Thomas Wilson (a non-

resident London rector) in Bath, where she had just received six odes from her admirers on her birthday, 2 Apr. 1777. Her practice of painting her face was well known, Dr. Johnson saying it was better she should 'redden her own cheeks' than 'blacken other people's characters' In 1778 she married as her second husband William Graham aged 21, and quarrelled with Dr. Wilson See Nos. 5410, 5598

For similar satires on hairdressing see No. 5370, &c.

$8\frac{3}{8} \times 12\frac{13}{16}$ in.

5442 15. V. 2. THE FLOWER GARDEN.

MD [Darly.]

Pub by M Darly May 1 1777 where may be had Bath Caricatures

Engraving A companion print to Nos. 5448, 5449. The H.L. figure of a woman in profile to the r. is the foundation of an enormous erection of hair on the top of which is a pear-shaped flower-garden, surrounded by a hedge, in which is a stile. At the lower edge (r.) a gardener stands raking the gravel which surrounds a number of formal flower-beds. At the upper end (l.) is a circular temple, surmounted by a figure of Mercury. The rest of the hair is decorated with sprays of flowers.

One of many similar satires on the fashionable pyramids of hair, see No. 5378, &c.

$12\frac{1}{4} \times 8\frac{3}{4}$ in.

5443 21. V. 2. A. NAMBIE-PAMBIE . IN THE TIP OF THE MODE.

Pub^d June 1. 1777 by M Darly 39 Strand. where may be had 500 comic subjects. &c &c.

Engraving. A man standing full face, r hand held out, his l on a thin tasselled cane. He wears a three-cornered hat trimmed with a button and tasselled cord; a coat tight at the waist and then cut away to show a short striped waistcoat from which hang two bunches of seals and trinkets. His coat has a black collar over a broad shawl-shaped collar, is decorated with large buttons and shows lace ruffles. His legs are thick, his shoes clumsy with the large rectangular 'Artois' buckles which, like large metal buttons, had recently become fashionable and a subject of satire, see no. 5432, &c. For black collars see No 5437. Beneath the title is etched in three columns:

> With Buckle large & buttons too,
> Behold the Puppy strutt
> With Irish legs, & collar black,
> Also a tight braced Gut,
> Besides the hat of Prussian form,
> With tossels dangling down,
> Of Monkies good Lord like to this,
> When shall we Rid the town.
> View follys picture as it stands,
> This present Seventy-seven;
> For so much folly never was,
> As now is under heaven

Although the large buckles and buttons were a very short-lived fashion, this satire appears to indicate the beginning of the fashion for tight coats and short waistcoats with bunches of seals hanging from the fobs which is associated with the Prince Regent. See also No. 5382

$8\frac{7}{8} \times 8\frac{13}{16}$ in.

5444 BATH STAYS OR THE LADY'S STEEL SHAPES.

MD [Darly.]

Pub by M Darly. June 4. 1777. Strand

Engraving. The interior of a blacksmith's smithy. On the anvil is a portion of a pair of stays, at which two smiths strike with hammers, one (l) holding the stays by pincers. A third man (r.) is measuring a lady round the chest with a tape; she stands very upright in profile to the right, and wears a deeply pointed bodice over an underskirt projecting at the back in the fashionable manner; the upper part of her dress hangs on the wall behind her. She holds a closed fan in both hands, her hair is in a monstrous inverted pyramid, flanked by great curls and surmounted by feathers, see No 5370, &c Sections of a pair of steel corsets and the tools of a smithy lie on the floor. Pincers and horse-shoes hang on the wall The forge with its fire is on the l. On a shelf on the wall are bottles and covered jars, one marked *alose*

A satire on the tight-lacing which was accentuated when 'cork rumps' became fashionable. See No. 5381, &c. See also Nos. 5452, 5464, 4552 (1777).

Walpole writes, 28 Mar. 1777, 'There has been a young gentlewoman overturned and terribly bruised by her *vulcanian stays* They now wear a steel busk down their middle and a rail of the same metal across their breasts.' *Letters*, x 31.

$8\frac{1}{2} \times 13$ in.

5445 42. V. 2 DEEP ONES

MD [Darly.]

Pub. by M Darly 39 Strand June 17. 1777.

Engraving. Seven profile heads (caricature) similar in character to *Hats* and *Wigs*, see Nos 5169, 5170 Three are enclosed in ovals.

All are evidently portraits: one of a very old man with closed eyes, one of a military officer, one of a bucolic-looking man wearing his own hair, possibly intended for Lord Surrey, afterwards Duke of Norfolk, one of a fat parson, one of a dissenting minister with lank hair and bands, one of a plebeian-looking man wearing the large buttons of the moment (see No. 5432, &c.), one of a military officer, his hair in a pigtail queue, and one of a man wearing a bag-wig.

$9\frac{1}{2} \times 13\frac{3}{4}$ in.

5446 31 MODERN SHEILDS OR THE VIRTUE OF STEEL BUTTONS

MD. [Darly.]

Pub. by M Darly 39 Strand June 26. 1777

Engraving. A burlesqued duelling scene. Two elderly men confront one another; one holds a sword in his l. hand; his r. arm is raised so that the enormous button on his sleeve acts as a shield, the buttons on his coat are about the size of dinner-plates; his coat has a black collar and his shoes have large buckles, called Artois buckles, see No. 5432, &c. His opponent (r) holds out a pistol in his r hand, his l is held up as if to protect his face. He is dressed in an old-fashioned manner, with broad-brimmed hat, tie-wig, a long laced coat and waistcoat with wide cuffs, high-quartered shoes with small buckles. They are in a grass field, with trees on the horizon.

$8\frac{13}{16} \times 12\frac{3}{4}$ in

5447 14. V. 2 DIVINE LOVE

[M Darly?]

Pub M Darly 39 Strand June 26 1777

Engraving A courtesan sits on the knee of a fat clergyman, probably a bishop, in a black gown She is dressed in the fashion of the day, her pyramid of hair is decorated with feathers, flowers and enormous curls; her waist is very constricted. The carpet and the decoration of the wall are important parts of the design and suggest wealth and luxury. The wall is decorated with lines of moulding. In the centre, above the woman's head, is a decoration composed of a mitre, a heart, an arrow, &c. On each side of it are two large framed landscapes, partly cut off by the margins of the print The carpet has an elaborate arabesque pattern. This is one of a number of satires on the clergy.

$12\frac{3}{8} \times 9\frac{1}{8}$ in.

5448 FRUIT STALL.[1]

MD [Darly] *Bath f.*

Pub by M Darly July 11 1777. Nº 39 Strand

Engraving. A companion print to Nos 5442, 5449 The head of a woman in profile to the r is the foundation of a monstrous inverted pyramid of hair, decorated with the wares of a fruiterer. On the top a basket of peaches and a large pineapple with its leaves Down the side of the pyramid, where curls were worn, are large gourds of different shapes. The hair is further ornamented by two tall pottles of strawberries, bunches of grapes, pears growing on branches, a basket of plums, a basket of raspberries (?), and other fruit For similar satires on the fashionable pyramids of hair see Nos. 5378, &c.

$12\frac{3}{4} \times 8\frac{1}{2}$ in.

5449 16. V. 2. THE GREEN STALL.

MD [Darly.] *Bath*

Pub by M Darly. 39 Strand July 11 1777

Engraving A companion print to Nos 5442, 5448. The head of a young woman in profile to the l is the foundation of a monstrous inverted pyramid of hair decorated with vegetables, carrots preponderating. On

---

[1] This impression is without a number, it is *V. 2, 17* in a book in the possession (1933) of Mr Spencer of New Oxford Street

CATALOGUE OF POLITICAL AND PERSONAL SATIRES

the top are heaped a large bundle of asparagus, a set of scales in one bowl of which are potatoes, a bunch of herbs (taking the place of the ostrich feathers of fashion), a cabbage, turnips, &c Large carrots take the place of the large curls then worn flanking the coiffure, three bunches of carrots are the main decoration of the surface of the hair, on which are also a cabbage and clusters of leaves (or lettuces). Trails of pea-pods hang from the top of the head-dress after the manner of the lace lappets and ribbons then worn.

$12\frac{1}{4}\times8\frac{3}{4}$ in.

5450 20 V 2. THE TON AT GREENWICH
A LA FESTOON DANS LE PARK A GREENWICH

Pub by M Darly N° 39 Strand Aug 11. 1777.

Engraving. A woman walking (l to r.) on a path in Greenwich Park followed by a man, probably a servant, carrying a huge umbrella under his arm. She wears one of the enormous hoods called calashes, from their resemblance to the folding hoods of carriages (see No. 5434, &c.) which the monstrous hair-dressing of the period had brought into fashion In her r hand she holds the strings of her hood, in the l. a tall stick with a crook. She has the compressed waist with a skirt projecting at the back then fashionable (see Nos 5381, 5444, &c.), a quilted apron, ankle-length petti-coat, her over-dress being looped-up for convenience in walking, and high-heeled shoes. Behind are grass and trees and Greenwich Observatory on its hill (r) Reproduced, Paston, Pl. xxviii.

$11\frac{3}{4}\times8\frac{1}{2}$ in.

5451 MISS HEDGEHOG.

Hen Ibb. fecit.

Pub⁴ Sep′ 9. 1777 by M Darly Strand.

Engraving A short fat woman stands full face. Her dress bristles with detail, and her pyramid of hair instead of being smooth, as was usual, is closely frizzed. Her wide hooped petticoat shows her ankles. She wears gloves with tight bracelets and holds a closed fan in her l. hand.

$11\frac{13}{16}\times8\frac{1}{2}$ in.

5452 TIGHT LACING.

R S   *J. H.*

Pub⁴ 5 Mar^h 1777 by W. Humphrey Gerrard Street Soho who has great variety of humorous Prints   *Price One Shilling.*

Engraving. Two elderly and ugly women in a bedroom One, who appears to be the mistress, clings with both hands to the post of a four-post bed, leaning backwards while her maid exerts all her strength to lace her stays The maid holds a poker in both hands, the stay-lace has been twisted round it, one foot is placed on the projecting skirt of her mistress, which is extended by a 'cork rump', see No 5381, &c ; she leans back in order to pull the harder. The lady's hair is dressed in the prevailing fashion of caricature, trimmed with feathers, lace, flowers, &c. She wears a large pocket over her under-petticoat On the wall are two H.L.

portraits which appear to be caricatures of costume: one (l.), contemporary, showing a woman with a compressed waist, a man with enormous buttons, see No 5432, &c.; the other (r.) perhaps Elizabethan. See also No. 5444, &c.

Similar in manner to Nos. 4778, 5453.

$7\frac{11}{16} \times 11$ in.

5453 OLD MAIDS AT QUADRILLE.

R S. [Monogram.]   *J. H.*

Pub⁴ 5 April 1777 by W. Humphrey, Gerrard Street, Soho. who has a great variety of humorous Prints.

Engraving. Four women seated at a square card-table The three whose faces are visible are old and ugly, the fourth, in back view, seated on a stool, appears to be a young woman. The woman on the l. has put down her cards on the table, to take a handful of snuff from a rectangular box. Two small dogs bark at each other. Two small pictures or prints hang on the wall. The room and the players have a poverty-stricken appearance. Above the design is engraved *Sans prendre vole.* Similar in manner to Nos. 4778, 5452.

$7\frac{5}{8} \times 11\frac{1}{2}$ in.

5454 STEEL BUTTONS COUP DE BOUTON

W. H. [Humphrey] *f.*

Pub⁴ 29 April, 1777, by W. Humphrey, Gerrard Street, Soho.

Engraving. A man (l.) and woman (r.), dressed in the height of the fashion, meet one another, walking in a park indicated by two trees. Rays of light spread from the large buttons on the man's coat and strike the face of the lady, who falls back dazzled, lifting her arms as if to ward off the blaze The buttons appear to be of cut-steel or silver with incised lines and a beaded edge, see No. 5432, &c. He wears a sword and carries a tasselled cane under his l. arm. His shoes have large Artois buckles. The lady wears the enormous pyramid of hair decorated with curls then fashionable, see No. 5370, &c.; on its summit is an erection of ribbons, feathers, &c., which appears to be a hat. She holds a fan and wears a nosegay. Her dress has the tight waist, and inflated draperies over a comparatively narrow petticoat supported by a 'cork rump', see Nos. 5381, 5444, &c Reproduced, Paston, Pl. xxvi.

$12\frac{5}{8} \times 9\frac{1}{4}$ in.

5455 A FOX-HUNTING BREAKFAST

J. H.   *R. S.*

Pub⁴ 5ᵗʰ May 1777, by W. Humphrey, Gerrard Street, Soho.

Engraving (coloured impression). Three men sit at a rectangular table, on which stand two lighted candles and a medley of breakfast things: a coffee-pot, tea-pot, wine-bottle, &c One stretches and yawns; one, drinking wine, is dressed as a huntsman; another, drinking coffee, is having his hair dressed by a servant who stands behind him. A fourth man stands by the table A very stout man (r.) sits back in a chair pulling on a top-boot, his other boot lies beside him   A clock against the wall points to 5.15. A dog lies asleep in the foreground. Beneath the design is engraved.

> *The Man that will not leave his bed*
> *For sport so blithe & bonny,*
> *We'll swear he hates fatigue & dirt,*
> *And call him Macaroni.*
>
> *We'll wonder at his want of Taste,*
> *Since nothing so bewitches,*
> *As living all the winter long*
> *in Boots & Leather Breeches.*

$8\frac{11}{16} \times 13\frac{3}{8}$ in.

[A SATIRE ON AMATEUR MUSICAL PERFORMANCES]

J H   R S   See No. 4778—9 May 1777.
Pub. W. Humphrey.

An illustration to Anstey's *Bath Guide*. Similar in manner to Nos. 5452, 5453.

5456 THE FARMER'S DAUGHTER'S RETURN FROM LONDON.

W H [Humphrey].

Published 14 June 1777 by W Humphry Gerrard Street Soho.

Engraving. The interior of a farm-house kitchen. A young woman, fashionably dressed, has just entered by a door (l.) through which trees are visible. Her enormous head-dress has caught in a rack above the door and its feathers, flowers and ribbons are about to be torn off as she runs with outstretched arms towards the farmer, who rises from his chair by the fire and starts back in amazement His wife, seated behind him, holds up her hands in astonishment, a child at her knee looks round in alarm. A boy, standing by the door, holds up his hands and gapes. A dog barks at her; a cat has jumped on to a bin which stands under the window and is miaowing at her. On the r. is a large fire in an open fireplace, above it a pot hangs from a chain, a spit projects from the fireplace. Hams and black puddings hang from the roof. See No. 5370, &c.
$8\frac{1}{2} \times 13\frac{1}{8}$ in

5457 DEATH AND THE DOCTOR.[1]

W. H. [Humphrey] *inv^t et fec^t.*

Pub Octr 29. 1777, by W. Humphrey

Engraving A fat doctor, wearing a large tie-wig, stands, his arms and legs wide-stretched, between a skeleton, representing Death, and his patient who is seen behind, unconscious of the conflict. Death (r), in a threatening attitude, holds up a sheaf of arrows, some of which he has already hurled; they are labelled *Consumption, Palsy, Gout, Dropsy; Scurvy; Venerial; Fever; Stone; Apoplexy; Suicide* (written in reverse). The doctor, with an

---

[1] The same subject differently treated was etched by Rowlandson (1782), coloured reproduction Fuchs, *Die Karikatur der europäischen Völker*, 1. 56.

expression of grim determination, holds outstretched a sheaf of remedies, some of which he has already hurled at Death. In his l. hand he holds out his cane. These remedies are papers inscribed *For the Dropsy* . . ; *For the Gout*; *Sovereign Remedy*; *Anodyne*; *Styptic*; *Solvent, Mercurials, Essence*; *Anti Venerial Drops*; *Tincture for* (in reverse); *Opeates*; *Balsams*; some of the words are followed by the signs used in prescriptions. Behind (l.), seen through an opening in the wall, is the patient, a woman, fully dressed and wearing a cap, seated at a round table, her head resting on her hand, in her l. hand she holds a cup. On the table are medicine-bottles. Behind her is a bed with curtains hanging from a tester.

After the title is engraved "*Touch my Patient if you dare*".

$8\frac{1}{2} \times 12\frac{3}{4}$ in.

5458 MONSIEUR LE QUE LADIES CORK CUTTER FROM PARIS WHOLESALE, RETAIL, & FOR EXPORTATION.

J. L.

Pub⁴ according to Act of Parl: March 7. 1777, by J. Lockington, Shug Lane, Golden Square.

Engraving. The interior of a shop where the dress-supports known as 'cork rumps', see No. 5381, &c., are made and sold. Two women (r.) sit at a counter, each finishing with a knife an almost complete cork rump. On the front of the counter is inscribed *Money for old Corks*. Cork rumps of different sizes are on shelves on the wall behind them.

A woman with a camel-shaped hump behind her waist stands on tip-toe to see the effect in a mirror behind her (l.) which reflects her figure (not a back view, but as seen by the spectator). She appears to be looking at a second mirror which is not shown in the design.

In the middle of the back wall, and in the centre of the print, an arched doorway is inscribed FITTING ROOM; the door, the upper part of glass, is wide open, showing a boy or very small man fitting a lady with a cork rump. He is dressed as a Frenchman with a toupet-wig with a very long queue and is evidently 'Monsieur Le Que'.

Very incorrectly drawn, apparently by an amateur.

$7\frac{1}{4} \times 10\frac{3}{8}$ in.

5459 PROPORTION

W. Smith inv. del. et sc.

Pub⁴ According to Act of Parl: Aug. 11 1777 by J Lockington, Shug Lane Golden Square London.

Engraving. A figure divided vertically from the top of the head to the feet, one half (l.) being dressed as a lady, the other as a man, to show how enormously a woman whose hair was fashionably dressed over-topped a man. The lady's head-dress is the inverted pyramid of the period; on its broad summit rests an arrangement of lace and flowers but no feathers. The masculine half of the figure is dressed without exaggeration. Cf. No. 5370, &c.

$7\frac{1}{2} \times 5\frac{1}{2}$ in.

5460 THIS IS SOMETHING NEW.

*Pub⁴ Accorˢ to Act of Parᵗ Septʳ 1 1777 by J. Lockington Shug Lane
Golden Square*

Engraving (coloured and uncoloured impressions). A lady walking in
profile to the l., her hair in a gigantic pyramid, protects the erection by an
enormous umbrella on a very long stick. Her draped over-skirt projects
at the back in mountainous folds On these is seated a foppishly dressed
man taking shelter under the projection of her hair; he leans forward,
holding his hat in his r. hand. He is in profile to the r., back to back with
the lady. A simple countryman (l.), whose hat has fallen to the ground,
gapes at the pair in amazement. A fashionably dressed man on the r
leers and points at them One of many satires on hairdressing, see
No 5370, &c., and the dress support called a 'cork rump', see No. 5381, &c.
$11\frac{1}{4} \times 8\frac{1}{16}$ in.

5461 PYRAMIDS, DISCOVER'D AT BATH, ANNO DOMINI 1777.

*Published According to Act Sept. 25, 1777 by I. Lockington Shug Lane
Golden Square.*

Engraving Figures (H L.) of three women, their hair dressed in caricature
versions of the enormous pyramids of hair then fashionable The centre
figure, full face, is the smallest but her pyramid of hair is the highest of
the three. The other two woman are in profile, facing towards the centre.
Poised on their heads are lace caps trimmed with flowers and dangling
lappets. Beneath the title is engraved:
   N.B. Fairer than the Egyptian, but not so lasting.
   For other satires on this fashion see No. 5370, &c. Apparently by the
same artist as Nos. 5378, 5379.
$8\frac{7}{8} \times 7\frac{3}{4}$ in.

462 A NEW OPERA GLASS FOR THE YEAR 1777.

Publish'd April 2ᵈ 1777. by S. Sledge Henrietta Street Covent Garden.

Engraving. Two seated figures (H.L.) apparently in an opera-box. A fat
lady (l) whose pyramid of hair is flanked with the enormous cylindrical
curls then fashionable and surmounted with flowers and feathers, looks
in profile to the l. smiling broadly. Her dress is cut low and she wears a
necklace of beads or pearls from which hangs a cross. Her companion (r)
sits on the lady's l, looking through one of her curls which he holds in his
r. hand; his l eye is closed. On his coat are visible two of the enormous
metal buttons then a subject of caricature, see No 5431, &c. Beneath the
title is engraved:

> *Behold how Jemmy treats the Fair,*
> *And makes a Telescope of Hair*
> *How will this suit high headed Lasses,*
> *If curls are turn'd to Optic Glasses.*

   See No 5436, for the same subject by Darly. For satires on this type
of hair-dressing see No 5370, &c.
$6\frac{5}{8} \times 6\frac{3}{16}$ in.

5463 ENGLISH BARBER, CARRYING HOME A COMMON COUNCILMAN'S WIG.

P. S. fecit

London, Printed for R. Sayer, and J. Bennett, N° 53 Fleet Street, as the Act directs June the 5ᵗʰ 1777

Engraving. A barber has just left his house, the open door of which is seen on the r He carries in his r. hand a large curled wig with a small queue tied with a ribbon bow. In his l. hand is an implement for curling hair, under his l. arm is a barber's basin; a pair of scissors projects from his coat pocket. He is neatly and plainly dressed, with a broad-brimmed hat A dog prances at his side. Round the corner of his house (l.) appears a thin foppishly dressed Frenchman, probably a hairdresser, wearing a bag-wig and solitaire; he points at the barber saying *Se de diffrence between de Aingleesh Barber & mineself, Ha! Ha! de Aingleesh Bougre.* From the barber's door projects a striped pole, from which hangs a board inscribed, *Shave for a Penny.* Above the door is inscribed, *Bleeding and Teeth drawn* and *Money for live hear.* Inside the door two wigs are suspended.

$7\frac{3}{16} \times 4\frac{15}{16}$ in.

5464 TIGHT LACING, OR THE COBLER'S WIFE IN THE FASHION.

Publish'd Nov' 4ᵗʰ 1777 by Wᵐ Hitchcock, N° 5 Birchin Lane Price 1ˢ

Engraving. The interior of a cobbler's work-room. The cobbler has seized his wife by the arm and is about to beat her with a strap. Her stays are partly laced, the end of the lace is twisted round a hammer. Her hair is dressed in the fashionable pyramid, surmounted by a meagre ostrich-feather, lace, &c. She wears a quilted petticoat and high-heeled shoes. On the r is a cobbler's bench with tools; lasts and tools are in a rack on the wall, a wicker cage in which is a bird hangs from a hook. A print of a leg of mutton and turnips is pinned to the wall Under the cracked casement window (l.) is a wooden chair. Beneath the title is engraved:

> *The Hoity head & Toighty waist,*
> *As now they're all the ton,*
> *Ma'am Nell the cobbler's wife, in taste*
> *By none will be outdone,*

> *But, ah! when set aloft her cap,*
> *Her Boddice while she's bracing,*
> *Jobson comes in, &, with his strap*
> *Gives her, a good tight lacing.*

For tight-lacing see No. 5444, &c., and for hairdressing No. 5370, &c

$7\frac{3}{8} \times 10\frac{7}{8}$ in.

5465 THE DEATH OF ROCHESTER.   [Oct. 1777]

W. H. fecᵗ [?William Humphrey.]

Engraving. This design has been attributed to Gillray. Rochester (1647-80) reclines in a large arm-chair, his legs outstretched, listening to the ministrations of an elderly clergyman, who sits by his side (l), a large open

Bible on his knee, his head is thrown back, his mouth open as if declaiming. The Bible is open at a page headed *XIX.C. Genesis* On the r. of the design are the draperies of a bed. At the head of the bed, on the extreme r. a large coat of arms is partly visible, with an earl's coronet, the supporter on the l being a very rampant lion Rochester wears a night-cap and a loose gown which falls back to show knee-breeches. The parson is in cassock, gown, and bands, his wig is of the kind worn by the clergy c. 1777. He is toothless except for two fang-like upper teeth

The edifying end of Rochester, wit and libertine, was made familiar by Burnet's *Some Passages of the Life and Death of Rochester*, 1680, often reprinted in the eighteenth century. The parson should be Burnet (1643–1715), though a much older man is depicted, perhaps a caricature of a living divine.

Grego, *Gillray*, p. 27.

$8\frac{7}{8} \times 13\frac{1}{4}$ in.

Five Prints after Bunbury etched by J. Bretherton.

NEWMARKET. A SHOT AT A PIGEON   See No. 4719—1 Mar. 1777

NEWMARKET. A SHOT AT A HAWK.   See No. 4717—n.d. *c.* 1777
A companion print to No. 4719

DAMN BUCHEPHALUS!   See No. 4730—n.d. *c.* 1777

DAMN MAMBRINO!   See No. 4731—n.d *c* 1777

POT FAIR. CAMBRIDGE.   See No 4729—25 June 1777

Nine prints from the series of mezzotints issued by Carington Bowles.[1]

THE HONEY-MOON (351)   See No. 4548—[1777]

SIX WEEKS AFTER MARRIAGE. (352)   See No. 4549—25 June 1777

THE FEATHER'D FAIR IN A FRIGHT. (357)   See No. 4550—[1777]

See also No. 5621.

Reproduced, Paston, Pl xxiii.

MY-SELF. (359)   See No. 4551—[1777]

TIGHT-LACING ... (362)   See No. 4552—[1777]
See also No. 5444, &c

[1] No 4552 has the imprint of Bowles and Carver.

BACHELOR'S FARE ... (365)   See No. 4553 [10 Nov 1777]

Reproduced with date, A. L. Simon, *Bottlescrew Days*, 1926, p. 20.[1]

THE AMOROUS THIEF ... (366)   See No. 4554—10 Nov 1777

Dated impression in the possession of Mr. W. T. Spencer, New Oxford Street, 1932.

FATHER PAUL IN HIS CUPS ... (367)   No. 3781—[1777]

An illustration to Sheridan's *Duenna*, first played Covent Garden, 1775.

A reduced version (273), published 10 Nov. 1777, see *Catalogue*, iv, p. 758.

FATHER PAUL DISTURBED .. (368)   No 3782—10 Nov. 1777

(Another impression, dated and not coloured)

Illustration to *The Duenna*.

Four similar mezzotints issued by other publishers.

5466 A NEW FASHION'D HEAD DRESS FOR YOUNG MISSES OF THREE SCORE AND TEN.

Philip Dawe invent et fecit.

Published as the Act directs. 8 May 1777. Printed for John Bowles, No 13 in Cornhill.

Mezzotint. The interior of a luxuriously furnished lady's dressing-room. An old woman sits before the dressing-table, smiling at her reflection in the mirror, while two hair-dressers lift on to her head a monstrous wig, decorated with a nosegay of flowers, ribbons, large ostrich-feathers, and flanked with curls. She has a grotesque and witch-like profile, frontal baldness, and short, lank hair. She is elaborately dressed in the fashion of the day, wearing large pendent ear-rings, voluminous lace ruffles to her elbow-sleeves and a lace-trimmed apron over a much-trimmed dress. She clasps to her breast a King Charles dog. The two hair-dressers are evidently French, both are grinning; one (l) wears a toupet-wig, with a large black bag and solitaire cravat, he is about to place the front of the wig on the lady's forehead. The other (r.) supports the back of the wig and is partly concealed by it; his toupet-wig has a very long pigtail queue.

The wall is hung with paper or brocade above a plain dado; a patterned carpet with a fringe covers the floor. A window on the l is festooned with a heavy fringed curtain. The dressing-table in front of the window, with an oval mirror, is elaborately draped with embroidered muslin; on it are toilet jars, &c. For satires on this type of hairdressing see No. 5370, &c. $12\frac{13}{16} \times 9\frac{7}{8}$ in.

[1] Another reproduction in C. N Robinson, *The British Tar in Fact and Fiction*, p. 280, is dated 1781, and appears to be from a line engraving of the same picture. Eight lines of verse show that it was issued in connexion with Rodney's victory of 1781.

5467 A HINT TO THE HUSBANDS, OR THE DRESSER, PRO-
PERLY DRESSED.

[? P. Dawe.]

*London Printed for R. Sayer & J. Bennett, N⁰ 53 Fleet Street, as
the Act directs 25 Janᵛ 1777.*

Mezzotint. A lady sits at her dressing-table, while a hair-dresser attends
to her elaborate coiffure. She turns round in astonishment towards her
husband (r.), who has entered from an open door and threatens the hairdresser with uplifted riding-whip and clenched fist He is in riding-dress
A maidservant enters behind him, smiling insolently, her l. hand on her
hip, her r. held up, the first two fingers extended. The lady's hair is
dressed in the elaborate fashion of the period, a pyramid with curls,
decorated with pearls, and an enormous head-dress of feathers She wears
a lace-trimmed wrapper over her low-cut dress. In her r. hand is a brush
or pencil for the complexion; the other is outstretched in alarm. The hairdresser, who wears an enormous toupet wig, with side-curls and large
looped club, is smoothing her hair with a comb. On the wall are two
family portraits a man with a beard (H L.) and a lady (T.Q.L.) wearing
a ruff. The floor is of boards without a carpet For satires on this type of
hairdressing see No. 5370, &c.

13 × 9⅞ in.

5468 JEWS RECEIVING STOLEN GOODS.

*London, Printed for R. Sayer & J. Bennett, Map & Printsellers,
N⁰ 53, Fleet Street; as the Act directs, 11ᵗʰ Octʳ 1777.*

Mezzotint. Two Jews seated at an oblong cloth-covered table, one of
whom is receiving coin, notes, watches, &c. from a highwayman who
stands on the opposite side of the table (r.). Two other Jews (l.) stand
behind the chair of the man receiving the booty. The highwayman, whose
features are Jewish, is in fashionable riding-dress; the butt of a pistol
protrudes from a coat-pocket, in his r. hand is a watch and seals, in his l.
a glove and riding-whip. In the foreground is a dog

Immediately behind the figures is a large screen, four leaves of which are
visible, elaborately decorated with birds and foliage. This, as well as the
dress of all but one of the men, suggests that the Jews are wealthy. The
print is in the manner of *genre* rather than of caricature.

12½ × 9⅞ in.

There is another issue having the same publication-line, with the title
A Scene in Duke's Place (not in B.M.). A reduced version was published
27 May 1778 (not in B M.).

THE RETURN FROM SCOTLAND, OR THREE WEEKS AFTER
MARRIAGE.   See No. 4625—5 Dec. 1777

Pub. Sayer and Bennett.

POLITICAL SATIRES

1778

5469 HORATIO GATES ESQ[R]

[? 'C. Corbutt'.]

London : Publish'd as the Act directs, 2nd Jan[y] 1778, by John Morris.

Mezzotint. One of a series, see No 5290. T.Q L portrait of a man in general's uniform standing under heavy drapery, probably that of a tent. He looks to the l., r. hand on hip, his l. resting on a document which lies on a small camp-table; it is inscribed *Arti*[cles] *of Convention between Gen[l] Gates & Gen[l] Burgoyne*. Beside it is a letter addressed *Gen. Gates*. Behind (l.) are two tents, one flying a large striped American flag, near them is a cannon.

News of Burgoyne's surrender reached London on 2 Dec. 1777. Walpole, *Last Journals*, 1910, ii. 80, 85. *Corr. of George III*, ed. Fortescue, iii. 501. The disaster was debated in the Commons on 3 Dec *Parl. Hist.* xix 532 ff. See also No 5408. For Saratoga see No. 5470, &c.

Chaloner Smith, iv. 1715.

12⅝×7¾ in.

5469A A copy having the same inscription, except that the date is 10 May 1778, with the addition of *Se vend chez J. M. Will à Augsbourg.*

5470 N° I. THE CLOSET. *Price. 1[s].*

Bute Inv[t]. Germaine Ex[t]. Mansfield Sculp.

Publish'd as the Act directs Jany 28th 1778. by I. Williams No. 39 Fleet Street.

Aquatint. A print in several compartments. In an inset rectangle in the r. upper corner is George III's 'Closet': the king seated at a table with his secret advisers around him. On his r. sits Bute, his l. hand on the king's shoulder. The Devil clutches the back of Bute's chair, and speaks into his ear through a trumpet; beneath the chair is a head, writhing with serpents, probably representing Discord Bute says, *Be Bloody, Bold, and Resolute, be Firm—fear nothing*. The king looks round him, his profile is malevolent, stupid and gross; he says, *Sic Volo—I am Firm. hem! who's afraid? eh!* On his left sits Lord Mansfield, in his hand is a scroll, inscribed, *A Code of Laws for America*; he is saying *Kill them or they will Kill you.* Next comes Lord George Germain holding out a paper, *Instructions to Generals Howe, Burgoyne, &c.* He says, *Tho Nature's Germins tumble all together, Ev[n] till Destruction Sicken.* On the table are two papers, one inscribed *I have closeted S[r] James the Cartouch Box Maker*; the other is addressed to *My Lord Mayor of London* Both appear directed against the Lord Mayor, Sir James Esdaile,[1] a strong supporter of the Court.

Below this rectangle are isolated figures: A man stands, blowing out his

[1] On Michaelmas Day 1778 Esdaile was censured by the Livery for refusing to put to the vote the thanks of the Livery to the members for the city for their consistent opposition to the ministry. *Ann Reg*, 1778, p 204

brains with a pistol; he says, *Amende Honorable for using General Warrants*;
at his feet lies dying a man in the wig and robes of the Lord Chancellor; he
says *I was Yorke-shire but honest, but curse the Closet*. He is Charles Yorke,
whose remorse at accepting the Chancellorship under pressure from the
king in his closet conduced to his sudden death in 1770, widely but
wrongly believed to be due to suicide. The standing figure appears also to
be intended for Yorke, who as Attorney General had advised that the committal of Wilkes for the libel in No. 45 of the *North Briton* was legal
On the l. is a man dressed as a fool in cap and bells; he is running
forward, in his r. hand are smoking firebrands, in his l., arrows   He says,
I am firm too, in Folly, and is not this precious Foolery, my masters.
Beneath him is engraved *The Fool casteth Firebrands, Arrows & Death,
and sayeth Am not I in Sport?* On the r. is a headless figure in long robes,
holding his head in his l. arm, and holding out *An h^{ble} Addr^{ess} from the Loyal
Town of Manchester to Cha*[erased] *Geo. the III with lives & Fort Murray
Sec.* The first of the loyal addresses of the autumn of 1775 came from
Manchester, see Nos 5325, 5471. It ended: '. . . We are ready to support,
with our Lives [and] Fortunes, such Measures as your Majesty shall think
necessary for the Punishment of Rebellion in any part of your dominions.
. . .' *London Gazette*, 12–16 Sept. The erasure implies a parallel with the
loyal addresses to Charles II on his dissolution of the Oxford Parliament in
1681. See *Eng. Hist. Rev.* 1930, xlv. p. 552 ff, and cf *Parl. Hist.* xix. 620
(22 Jan 1778).

In the centre of the print are a number of ships: at the top, three ships
in full sail are labelled *Quebec Hoy*, probably an allusion to the very unpopular Quebec Act, see No. 5228, &c, and cf. No 5286. Below, a small
ship labelled *Boston hoy* is followed by a larger ship in full sail, labelled
Weymouth Packet wth 20,000 in Doll^{rs} This probably indicates one of the
successes of the American privateers against British shipping Below is
a large ship at anchor, with furled sails, from which a boat rows to shore;
she is labelled *Chelsea Hoy* Below again, men are being helped ashore
from a boat, some have already landed; they are crippled, without arms,
with crutches, with a wooden leg, &c., indicating that the fate of the
English soldiers is to be maimed Chelsea pensioners Below again is a
small triangular gallows, from which hang three figures.

On the l side of the print, in four divisions, are episodes from the war
in America. In the uppermost section, Indians are using scalping knives
and tomahawks on prostrate and supplicating persons; in the centre,
a young woman *McRae*, kneeling and about to be killed by an Indian,
says *O horrid! is this the Marriage Ceremony*. She is Jane McCrea, whose
murder horrified both England and America. She was a loyalist and was
being escorted by two Indians to her betrothed who was serving with the
British forces, but she was killed by one of the escort.[1] For its effect on
opinion see Van Tyne, *The War of Independence*, 1929, pp. 398, 403.
Behind (r.) a church and some houses inscribed *Esopus* are in flames The
village of Esopus was burnt, after Clinton's successful campaign up the
North River in October 1777, by General Vaughan, who having been
fired on as he entered the place, burned it with its stores and provisions
See the comment on this in the *Ann. Reg.* 1777, p. 175*. See also No
5574.

Below in the next compartment more Indian atrocities are depicted.

[1] There is some uncertainty as to this, see Belcher, *First American Civil War*,
1911, ii. 295–6

A group of Indians sit round a naked man, bristling with darts, who is being roasted on a spit over a fire. An Indian, standing under a tree-trunk inscribed *The Cedars* (l), holds up a skull; on the r. an Indian with a tomahawk holds up a scalped and bleeding head, other figures sit round the fire, one gnaws a bone

The Cedars (on the Rapids of the St Lawrence) was the name given to an incident in the American expedition against Canada in 1776 A small American post was surprised by a party of regulars, Canadians and Mohawks, and captured without resistance. Arnold went out from Montreal to attack the captors, but to prevent the Indians from murdering the prisoners, he consented to a compromise for an exchange *Harper's Encyclopedia of United States History*. This satire is thus a gross calumny. It was perhaps suggested by Brackenridge's propagandist *Death of General Montgomery at the Siege of Quebec*, 1777, in which the writer apologizes in a note for some ferocious words put into the mouth of Carleton. 'I find my conscience pretty much at ease in this matter . . I have conversed with those who saw the scalps warm from the heads of our countrymen. I have had the relation from their mouths who beheld the fires lighted up, and heard . . the horrid shrieks and gloomy howlings of the savage tribes in the execution of the poor captives who, according to the threat of Carleton, were burned on an island in the river St. Lawrence after our unfortunate surrender at the Cedars.' Quoted by M. C. Tyler, *Literary History of the American Revolution*, ii 223. Carleton's humanity to the Americans in the Canadian campaign is well known.

Under this is Burgoyne marching at the head of his men who are without arms, their hands tied. He says, *I have led my Rag-o-muffians where they have been Peppered*. He is dressed not in military uniform, but in slashed doublet and cavalier's boots, in his hand is a broadsword whose blade is jagged and worn, inscribed *Physical Impossibility* His round shield is inscribed *Scale of Talents*, under each arm is a large book, *Maid of the Oaks and Bon Ton &c.*, and *the Devot^d Legions, a Poem*. At his feet is the word *Proclamations* On a hill in the distance is a serried rank of soldiers, on a minute scale, before them stands an officer holding a spear and a large striped American flag; they are Gates, see No 5469, and his Americans, to whom Burgoyne surrendered at Saratoga on 17 Oct. 1777.

Burgoyne's dress, &c , appears intended to represent him as a theatrical mountebank; his play 'Maid of the Oaks' was acted in 1774 ('Bon Ton', 1775, is by Garrick). He issued a bombastic proclamation before taking the field in May 1777 which was much ridiculed For contemporary opinion on the campaign see Van Tyne, *War of Independence*, 1929, 436–40. Many of the Opposition in England rejoiced at the catastrophe.

The lowest compartment shows Scottish soldiers and foreign mercenaries in flight, dying and dead. In the foreground (r) a Highland officer is dying, he says, *How hard O Frazer is thy Lot! Was it for this I sought the Court and Danced?* He is Simon Fraser (not to be confused with Simon Fraser of No. 5287); he was a brigadier under Burgoyne, and was mortally wounded on 7 Oct. 1777. A fleeing Scottish soldier looks round saying, *Hoot awa Lads, ken ye not that one Arnold is hard at our heels*. All the soldiers have thrown away their arms, one of three Hessians in jack-boots says, *De Devil vil ave mine Maitre, de Carcas Bucher*.

Down the l margin beside the two last designs is inscribed the word *Saratoga* The supposed artists' names are arranged so that *Bute inv^t* is under the fleeing Scottish soldiers, *Germaine ex^t* under the gallows.

Beside *Mansfield Sculp* (under the headless figure holding the Manchester Address) is an axe.

A satire which ascribes tyranny, failure, and savage atrocities to the influence of Bute, Mansfield, and Germain, and to the obstinacy of the king For Germain's responsibility for failure see Fortescue, *Hist. of the British Army*, iii. 242; G. H. Guttridge, 'Lord George Germain in office', *American Hist. Rev* Oct 1927 Chatham, on 2 Dec 1777, called the Americans 'Whigs in principle and heroes in conduct' whose affection had been lost 'by employing mercenary Germans to butcher them; by spiriting up savages in America to scalp them with a tomahawk' (*Parl. Hist* xix 477). For the employment of Indians see *Hist MSS. Comm. Dartmouth MSS.* ii. 1895, pp. xii, 344–5, 447.[1] For allegations of Indian atrocities see also Nos. 5339, 5473, 5631, 6024. For Saratoga see also Nos 5469, 5490, 5548[2], 5857. For 'the Closet' see No. 5638.
$8\frac{3}{4} \times 14$ in.

A French engraving (n.d.) by Godefroy, after Fauvel, *Sarratoga*, depicts the surrender of Burgoyne 'avec 6040 soldats bien disciplinés' to Gates with 'les milices Américaines nouvellement tirées de l'Agriculture . . .'.

Beneath is engraved a '*Précis*' of the campaign with a note on Indian soldiers in Burgoyne's army: 'Leurs affreux services refusés par les Américains, furent sollicités par le ministère britannique, qui convint de prix pour chaque chevelure d'infortunés colons qu'ils apporteraient, mais amis comme ennemis devenaient leurs [*sic*] proie. Le meurtre surtout de la jeune et belle Miss—Mac—Rea remplit tous les cœurs d'horreur . . . elle fut massacrée par ces sauvages le jour de son mariage avec un officier anglais de l'armée de Burgoine'.

No. 4 in *Recueil d'Estampes représentant . . . la Guerre qui a procuré l'Indépendance aux Etats unis de l'Amérique.* (Print Department.) *Collection de Vinck*, No 1167.

5471 AN EXACT REPRESENTATION OF THE MANCHESTER RECRUITS (ALIAS POOR DISTRESS'D WEAVERS) BEFORE THEIR EQUIPMENT À LA MILITAIRE.

Pub. feb 14; 1778. by a Non Subscriber.   *Price 6ᵈ.*

Engraving. Eight men stand in a row, holding muskets in a variety of ways. Their clothes are ragged, and they are thin and hungry-looking

At the beginning of 1778 places and individuals agreed to raise regiments at their own expense, Manchester began (Dec. 1777) by offering to raise a thousand men. Sergeants of the Guard were sent to Manchester to form the levies. Walpole, *Last Journals*, 1910, ii 85, 89–90 The legality of raising regiments without the previous consent of parliament soon became an issue between the Government and the Opposition Ibid. 93 ff. Fortescue, *History of the British Army*, iii. 245, 246. For the attitude of Manchester to the war cf. No. 5470.

One of a number of anti-recruiting satires, see No. 5295, &c.
$4\frac{1}{2} \times 8\frac{1}{4}$ in.

[1] Dartmouth wrote to Gage, 2 Aug 1775: 'The steps which you say the rebels have taken for calling in the assistance of the Indians leave no room to hesitate upon the propriety of your pursuing the same measure' Cf a letter of Col Ethan Allen, 24 May 1775, asking Indians for aid against the king's troops. Ibid , p. 310.

5472 A PICTURESQUE VIEW OF THE STATE OF THE NATION FOR FEBRUARY 1778.

1 Mar. 1778

Engraving. From the *Westminster Magazine*, vi. 66. A cow representing the commerce of Great Britain stands passively on the sea-shore while an American with a feathered cap saws off her horns; one horn lies on the ground. A Dutchman milks the cow, looking over his shoulder with a grin France, a foppishly-dressed Frenchman, and Spain, a don in slashed doublet and cloak, hold bowls of milk In the foreground (r.) lies the British lion asleep, unconscious of a pug-dog which stands on his back, befouling him. Behind the lion stands a plainly-dressed Englishman clasping his hands in despair.

In the background across the sea is a town inscribed *Philadelphia*; in front of it, on the shore, two men on a minute scale (General and Admiral Howe) are seated at a table. Both are asleep, a punch-bowl is on the table, on the ground beside them are wine-bottles and a barrel. Beside them, laid up on dry land, is a man-of-war inscribed *Eagle* (Howe's flag-ship).

The explanation (p. 64):

'I. The commerce of Great Britain, represented in the figure of a Milch-Cow.

II. The American Congress sawing off her horns, which are her natural strength and defence: one being already gone, the other just a-going.

III. The jolly, plump Dutchman milking the poor tame Cow with great glee.

IV and V. The Frenchman and Spaniard, each catching at their respective shares of the produce, and running away with bowls brimming full, laughing to one another at their success.

VI. The good ship *Eagle* laid up, and moved at some distance from Philadelphia, without sails or guns, . . . all the rest of the fleet invisible, nobody knows where.

VII. The two Brothers napping it, one against the other, in the City of Philadelphia, out of sight of fleet and army.

VIII. The British Lion lying on the ground fast asleep, so that a pug-dog tramples upon him, as on a lifeless log. he seems to see nothing, hear nothing, and feel nothing.

IX. A Free Englishman in mourning standing by him, wringing his hands, casting up his eyes in despondency and despair, but unable to rouse the Lion to correct all these invaders of his Royal Prerogative, and his subjects' property.'

These paragraphs are followed by an attack on the Conciliatory Propositions, see No. 5473, &c., as 'proof of the above'. There are no numbers on the plate.

This print was copied for circulation in America with the title *A Picturesque View of the State of Great Britain for 1778. Taken from an English Copy.* Beneath the plate in two columns is the explanation quoted textually from the *Westminster Magazine* but omitting the paragraph on the Conciliatory Propositions. Reproduced, S. G. Fisher, *True History of the American Revolution*, 1902, p. 358. This copy may have been the immediate origin of a series of Dutch and French copies (1780) which it closely resembles, see Nos. 5726, 5726 A, B, and C, 5727. It was also copied in America as *A Picturesque View of the State of Great Britain for 1780*, attributed to Paul Revere, in which the word *New York* has been substituted for *Philadelphia* (evacuated June 1778), see Stauffer, No. 2692.

These copies and No. 5859, a sequel to them, show how well the print illustrated the motives and hopes of France in the war, as also its value as enemy propaganda. Much was said in France of the capture of the trade of the colonies, but the real motive of Vergennes was rather the destruction of English trade (on Mercantilist principles) and so the enfeeblement of England, and the damaging of her prestige See E. S. Corwin, *French Policy and the American Alliance of 1778*, 1916, pp. 14 f., 49 f For Holland as a profiteering neutral see Nos. 5557, &c. For the Howe brothers see Nos. 5399, 5405, &c.

Part of the design resembles and is perhaps imitated from No. 2665, *The Benefit of Neutrality* (1745)

$3\frac{7}{8} \times 6\frac{3}{4}$ in.

A French satire on a similar theme is No. 1209, *Collection de Vinck*.

DÉDIÉ AUX MILORDS DE L'AMIRAUTÉ ANGLAISE PAR UN MEMBRE DU CONGRÈS AMÉRICAIN,

'*Dessiné d'apres nature à Boston par Corbut en 1778 et gravé a Philadelphie par Va de bon cœur*'

Numbers on the plate refer to an explanatory description in French. An English Admiral with wings and with the claws of a vulture for hands and feet is tied to a tree while the American Congress cuts the claws on his feet. A Spaniard holds one of the wings while a Frenchman cuts it off to prevent his flight Another Frenchman carries off packets of tobacco, while an Englishman in despair breaks his pipes A fat Dutchman collects feathers from the other wing of the eagle, while his companion trades under the nose of England. Beneath the explanation is inscribed:

> *Tel qu'un âpre Vautour dévorant l'Amérique*
> *Anglais, impunément tu crus la mettre à sac:*
> *Mais pour la bien venger d'un traitement inique*
> *Il ne l'y [sic] reste pas une once de Tabac.*

Probably a satire on the evacuation of Philadelphia, June 1778 For 'Corbut' cf Nos. 5405, 5406.

Van Stolk, No. 4289.

$6\frac{3}{8} \times 10\frac{1}{8}$ in.

5473 THE COMMISSIONERS.

M Darly

Pub⁴ April 1. 1778 by M Darly 39 Strand.

Engraving (coloured and uncoloured impressions). The five commissioners (r) recently nominated to negotiate peace with the colonies, kneel one behind the other at the feet of America, who sits (l.) on a pile of barrels and bales looking away from the Commissioners at a cap of liberty which she holds on a staff. She is a partly draped woman wearing a crown of feathers; her head is irradiated, and above it is suspended a laurel wreath. The bales and barrels on which she sits are inscribed *Tobacco for Germany; Rice for France, Tobacco for France; Tobacco for Holland; America 1778; Indico for Spain; Indico for the Mediterranean Ports, V.R.* (Monogram), cf. Nos. 5472, 5859, &c. The Commissioners are headed by Lord Howe in naval dress; he says, *We have block'd up your ports, obstructed your trade, with the hope of starving ye, & contrary to the Law of Nations compelld your sons to war against their Bretheren.* Behind him is General Sir William Howe, wearing the red ribbon of the Bath; he says *We have ravaged your Lands, burnt your Towns, and caus'd your captive Heroes to perish, by Cold, pestilence & famine* Next is Lord Carlisle wearing the green ribbon of the Thistle; he says *We have profaned your places of Divine worship, derided your virtue and piety, and scoff'd at that spirit which has brought us thus on our knees before ye.* He is foppishly dressed and appears deeply interested in his snuff-box, cf. No 5474 Behind him is William Eden (afterwards Lord Auckland) with a pen behind his ear, he says, *We have Ravish'd, Scalp'd, and murder'd your People, even from Tender infancy to decrepid age, altho Supplicating for Mercy,* cf. No 5470, &c. Last comes Commodore George Johnstone, known as Governor Johnstone, in naval dress; he is saying, *For all which material services, we the Commissioners from the most pious & best of sovereigns, doubt not your cordial duty & affection towards us, or willingness to submit yourselves again to recieve the same, whenever we have power to bestow it on ye.* The five swords of the Commissioners lie in a pile on the ground beside Carlisle.

The words of the speakers are in long labels, numbered, as are the five Commissioners, to show by whom they are spoken.

The Howes refused to act under Lord Carlisle; the other three Commissioners sailed for America on 21 Apr, arriving on 5 June. This satire anticipates even their Commission, which did not pass the Seal till 13 April. For the concessions offered and their reception see *Cambridge Hist. of the Br. Empire*, i. 765-7. The instructions to the Commissioners are printed in full in S. E. Morison, *Sources and Documents of the American Revolution*, 186-203. They yielded all the original points at issue, stipulating only for the maintenance of political union. *Ann Reg.* 1778, 315-32. The concessions would probably have been accepted if they had not been just anticipated by the French alliance. S E. Morison, *Growth of the American Republic*, 1930, p 96 For the dismay which the announcement of 'Lord North's Conciliatory Propositions' caused in Parliament see Walpole, *Last Journals*, 1910, ii. 110 ff. *Parl Hist.* xix. 762 ff, 19 and 23 Feb. See also Nos 5474, 5475, 5476, 5487, 6229.

Probably belongs to the same series as No. 5370, &c.

$8\frac{1}{4} \times 12\frac{7}{16}$ in.

5474 THE COMMISSIONER'S INTERVIEW WITH CONGRESS.

Pub⁴ by M Darly 39 Strand April 1 1778.

Engraving. Three members of Congress (r.) face the three Commissioners for the discussion of peace. Between the two parties and rather behind them stands a Scot in highland dress with an expression of alarm, probably intended for Lord Bute. The Congressmen wear long gowns with fur cuffs and caps similar to the 'death or liberty' caps worn by the Yankees in the trenches in No 5329 By their gestures and expressions they appear to be dictating terms to the Englishmen. Lord Carlisle, who is foppishly dressed, his hat under his arm, is taking a pinch of snuff and holding out his snuff-box to the foremost Congressman with an expression of alarm. Behind him Eden clasps his hands to his breast with a deprecatory gesture. Governor Johnstone, a reputed duellist, clenches his fists with a pugnacious expression The Congressmen stand under two palm-trees.

This appears to illustrate a speech of the Duke of Richmond on the American Conciliatory Bills on 9 Mar. 1778 After stating that one of the Governors in America had offended members of Congress by making exception to their wearing woollen caps in council: 'How inadequate therefore must this embassy be, where a noble lord [Carlisle] bred up in all the softness and polish that European manners make fashionable to rank— I say, how inadequate must such a meeting be amongst men in woollen night-caps!' *Parl. Hist* xix. 867. It should be noted that concessions to America, like severe measures, are attributed to Bute, cf 'An Ode addressed to the Scotch Junto and their American Commission . . .', 1778.

For the Commissioners see also Nos. 5473, 5475, 5476, 5487.

Probably belongs to the same series as No. 5370, &c.

$8\frac{1}{2} \times 12\frac{3}{4}$ in.

V. 2. [BRITANNIA TO AMERICA.][1]

Pub^d by M Daily May 6 1778 Strand

Engraving. 'Hieroglyphic letter' or rebus in which words are represented by small etched objects, those in the title being on a larger scale: Britannia (l) sits in profile to the r. holding out an olive branch.

(Britannia) (toe) *Amer*(eye)*ca*. My (deer) *Daughter I* (can) (knot) (bee)*hold w*(eye)*thout* (grate) *pa*(eye)*n* (ewer) (head)*strong* (*back*)(*ward*)*ness* (toe) *ret*(urn) (toe) (ewer) *duty in* (knot) *op*(posy)*ng* (awl) *the good* (eye) *long* (eye)*ntended for* (ewer) (sole) *Hap*(pin)*ness* & (bee)*ing told t*(hat) (yew) have *g*(eye)*v'n* ewer (toe) *a* (? circular object) *&* (doublefaced) (Frenchman) (eye) *have sent* (yew) 5 *over* (? over above wise) (men) *the* (grate)*est of all my* (*child*)*ren* (toe) *put* (yew) (toe) *r*(eye)*ghts &* (Hope) (yew) *w*(eye)*ll l*(eye)*s*(ten) (toe) *them &* m(eye)*nd w*(hat) *they say* (toe) (yew) *they have* (eye)*nstr*(yew)*ct*(eye)*ons* [instructions] (toe) *g*(eye)*ve* (yew) *t*(hose) *th*(eye)*ngs yew* (form)*erly required so* (bee) *a good* (girl) *d*(eye)*scharge* (ewer) (soldiers) *&* (ships) *of war &* (doe) (knot) *re*(bell) *ag*(eye)*nst* (ewer) (moth)*er rely upon me &* (doe) (knot) (? a carved bracket)*t toe t*(hat) *French R*(ass)*c*(awl) *sh*(awl) *tell* (yew) IC [I see] *he w*(ants) *toe b*(ring) *on an enm*(eye)*ty* (toe) (awl) (a snake with its tail in its mouth ? union) (bee)*tween* (yew) *&* (eye) (butt) *l*(eye)*s*(ten) (knot) (toe) *h*(eye)*m* (awl) *the* (world) *takes* (knot)*ice of h*(eye)*s* (doubleface) *I'll send h*(eye)*m such Messa*(g's) *from my* (grate) (gun)*s as s*([h]*awl*) *make* [sic] *h*(eye)*s* (heart) *repent & know t*(hat) (*I*) *good or* (eye)*ll t*(urn) *mer*(eye)*ts a*(knot)*her NB let* (knot) 8o [? hate] *take 2 much hold on* (ewer) (heart).

I am (ewer) *fr*(eye)*nd &* (Moth)*er*.

A satire on the mission of the Commissioners entrusted with North's Conciliatory Propositions, see No. 5473, &c. The Government had been attacked by Burke (16 Mar. 1778) for appointing commissioners after the Americans 'had been acknowledged an independent state by France' (*Parl. Hist.* xix 909). The treaty between France and the Americans was signed on 6 Feb. 1778; on 13 Mar. the French Ambassador informed Weymouth of the treaty. See No 5475, the answer to this letter.

$13\frac{3}{4} \times 9\frac{3}{4}$ in (pl.).

---

[1] Not in B.M., transcribed from a copy in the possession (1933) of Mr. W T Spencer, New Oxford Street, where it is the first plate in a volume of Darly's caricatures, the title-page being a dedication to Garrick, see No 5369 It belongs to the same series as Nos. 5370, 5429, &c.

5475 [AMERICA TO HER MISTAKEN MOTHER]

[Pub by M Darly May 11 1778 Strand][1]

Engraving. A 'hieroglyphic letter' or rebus in answer to the foregoing
America (l), as a Red Indian woman, seated and leaning to the l ; she holds
a flag with thirteen vertical stripes in her l. hand, in her r. she holds out
a fleur-de-lys Beside her is an oval shield on which are thirteen stars.

(America) (toe) *her* (Miss)*taken* (Moth)*er*. (Yew) *s*(eye)*lly* (old woman)
t(hat) (yew) *have sent a* (lure) (toe) *us is very* (plane) (toe) *draw our at*(ten)-
t(eye)*on from our re*(awl) (eye)*ntrests* (butt) *we are determ*(eye)*n'd* (toe)
ab(eye)*de by our own ways of th*(eye)*nk*(eye)*ng* (Ewer) [*your*] 5 (child)*ren*
(yew) *have sent* (toe) *us sh*(awl) (bee) *treated as V*(eye)*s*(eye)*tors, & safely
sent home aga*(eye)*n* (yew) *may* [? carved bracket]*t them & adm*(eye)*re
them,* (butt) (yew) *must* (knot) (X)*pect I of* (ewer) (puppet)*s w*(eye)*ll* (comb)
[*come*] *home* (toe) (yew) *as sweet as* (yew) *sent h*(eye)*m, twas cruel toe send
so pretty a* (man) *so many 1000* miles *&* (toe) *have the fat*(eye)*gue of
re*[t](urn)*ing back after* (spike?)(eye)*ng h*(eye)*s* (coat) *& d*(eye)*rt*(eye)*ng
[dirting] t[hose] *red* (heel) (shoes) (eye)*f* (yew) *are w*(eyes) *follow* (ewer) *own
ad*(vice) (yew) *gave* (toe) *me take home ewer* (ships) *sold*(eye)(ears) [*soldiers*]
guard (well) (ewer) *own tr*(eye)*fl*(eye)(ling?) [*a fish*]. *& leave me* (toe) *my
self as* (eye) *am at age* (toe) *know my own* (eye)*ntrests. w*(eye)*thout* (ewer)
(fool)(eye)*sh ad*(vice) *& know t*(hat) (eye) *sh*(awl) (awl)*ways regard* (yew)
& my Brothers as relat(eye)*ons* (butt) (knot) *as fr*(eye)*nds*

(Eye) (am) (ewer) (grate)*ly* (eye)*njured*

Daughter Amer(eye)*k.*

America turns away from 'her mistaken mother' holding a fleur-de-lys
symbolizing the French alliance. The 'pretty man' with the 'red heel
shoes' is Lord Carlisle, said by the Duke of Richmond to be unsuited to
treat with the homely Americans, see No 5474 A scurrilous poem, 'An
Ode addressed to the Scotch Junto and their American Commission . . .',
1778, has a line 'C—rl——le's *vermilion'd Heels*'. B.M L. 643, k 14/1
13¾×9¾ in pl.

Mr Hawkins describes a print, published by Darly, 177 *[sic]*

THE LION MUZZLED OR NORTH TRIUMPHANT

Lord North, holding a sword and olive-branch, is seated upon the back
of the British lion, which is lying down muzzled. This must be a satire on
the Conciliatory Propositions.

A French satire on the Conciliatory Propositions is No 1215, *Collection
de Vinck:*

THE OLIVE REJEC^TD OR THE YANKEES REVENGE

[After June 1778]

Pub^ds as the Act directs may 4 1778.

'Lord Burthe',[2] probably North, seated on an ass, which tries to cross the

---

[1] This publication line has been erased in the Museum impression and replaced
by *Published 12th May, 1794 by Laurie & Whittle, N 53, Fleet Street.* It is supplied
from an impression in a book of Darly's caricatures in the possession (1933) of
Mr. W T Spencer, New Oxford Street, see foregoing entry
[2] He is explained by F. L Bruel as 'Lord Burke   . l'un des principaux partisans

ocean in order to return to England. On his head is a crown and olive branch; from his pocket protrudes a paper inscribed *Conciatory* [Conciliatory] *Bill* Beneath the publication line is inscribed '*le Lord Burthe couronné sur un Ane Infortunez Anglois, à quoi vos Bills Conciliatoire [sic] ont-ils servis?* 1. *Le représentant de la Grande Bretagne pressé de fuir l'Amérique . . . ne pouvant regagner l'Angleterre qu'à la nage, sa Flotte étant dispersé ou deffaite. . . 2 plusieurs Américains faisant trève à leur modération naturelle que leurs ennemis ont gratuitement qualifiés de poltronerie, chassent honteusement l'agent qui sous un voile honete vouloit ébranler leur liberté en semant la division parmi eux. 3. Un Anglois faisant partie du petit nombre de ceux qu'on souffre encor en Amérique fait les plus [sic] pour y retenir l'Amiral 4. Un François représentant son Pays digne soutien et allié du plus beau de l'Univers s'empresse de couper le foible lien dont vainement l'Anglois vouloit se servir.*

The evident allusion (in 2) to Johnstone's attempt to open a private correspondence with members of Congress (June–July 1778), urging them to overthrow the French treaty, shows that the print is ante-dated in the fictitious publication line

$6\frac{13}{16} \times 11\frac{1}{2}$ in.

5476 A TETE A TETE BETWEEN THE PREMIER & J^{NO} HANCOCK ESQ^R [*c.* 1778]

Engraving. Publication line probably cut off North and John Hancock, the first president of the Congress, stand in a conventional American landscape. North (l) turns his head in profile to the r. towards Hancock, who faces him, holding out a handful of carrots while his r hand is on the hilt of his partly-drawn sword. North wearing the insignia of the Garter points to the ground, his l hand holding his sword by the scabbard. A spaniel licks his feet. Hancock wears a fur-trimmed belted tunic and fur-trimmed leggings showing bare knees, his hair falls loosely down his shoulders A puma (r.) paws the ground behind him. On North's r. is a sculptured head (? of George III) on a pedestal. There is a landscape background of trees and hills; on the r. are two palm trees. Beneath the design is inscribed:

> Hancock and N——th, Suppos'd to meet,
> And thus, the first, his thoughts repeat,
> Let some, like Spaniels, own thy plan,
> In me, behold a different Man
> Who ee'r he'd call thy House his Home,
> Wou'd with the mountain Tyger, roam,
> Live on the Roots, pluck'd from the Earth,
> From whence Himself, like Thee, had Birth.

This appears to represent the refusal of Congress to accept North's Conciliatory Propositions, see No 5473, &c. For the backwoods appearance of Hancock (a wealthy Boston merchant) cf. No. 5474.

$7\frac{11}{16} \times 10\frac{3}{16}$ in.

de conciliation, et l'adversaire de Pitt'. North seems more probable, though the artist has perhaps confused the two Burke's famous speech on Conciliation was on 6 Mar 1775; he spoke disparagingly of the mission of the Commissioners. *Parl. Hist* xix 778.

5477 THE ENGLISHMAN IN PARIS [c. 1777-8]

Sold by C. Sheppard, Lambeth Hill, Doctors Commons.

Engraving (coloured impression). Three people seated at a round dinner-table. A fourth, an Englishman wearing a hat, stands up gnawing a large bird which he has seized from a dish which a servant (l.) has just brought in. A Frenchman seated at the table wearing an enormous toupet wig from which hangs a grotesquely elaborate queue, holds up his hands in protest; a second Frenchman, sitting with his hands on his knees, looks on in amusement. A lady on the far side of the table, wearing an enormous cap on her pyramid of hair, is drinking wine as she watches the Englishman. On the wall are two pictures: two prize-fighters fighting (l), and a monk standing outside a church (r.). Beneath the design is engraved:

An American goose came hot from the spit
Egad says the Englishman I'll have a bit
His jaws he applies with wond'rous speed
To devour the viands on which others shou'd feed.
Fie, fie, Mons' La Anglois [sic] cries the frenchman;—forbear,
Why the limbs of your brother thus furiously tear?
Think you we'll tamely look on and starve?
No, no Mons' Anglois, we wait for to carve.

This appears intended to represent the attitude of France towards the American war before the signing of the Treaty on 6 Feb. 1778. See *Ann. Reg.* 1778, 37-8.

$8\frac{5}{8} \times 13\frac{1}{8}$ in.

5478 WILLIAMM PITT [sic] [c. 1778]

Engraving. A French print Chatham, supported on crutches, stands behind a balustrade, his r. hand held out in the manner of an orator. On each side of him is a seated figure, turning towards him, each wearing the ribbon of an order. Beneath the design is engraved *Il faut déclarer la guerre a la France.*

This appears to be a French artist's representation of Chatham's last speech in the House of Lords on 7 Apr 1778 to oppose the Duke of Richmond's advocacy of peace with America before war was declared with France: 'shall this great kingdom now fall prostrate before the House of Bourbon?' (*Parl. Hist.* xix. 1022 ff.; Von Ruville, *Chatham*, iii, p. 340 f) England and France were already virtually at war: Stormont had been recalled from Paris on the announcement (13 Mar) of the French Treaty with America. For the dread inspired by Chatham in France, c 1775-8, see Doniol, *Hist de la participation de la France à l'établissement des États-Unis*, i. 60-4; Corwin, *French Policy and the American Alliance*, 1916, p. 142

$6\frac{1}{4} \times 3\frac{15}{16}$ in.

5479 THE STATE OF THE NATION.

Pub^d June 24 1778 *price 1^s 6^d.*

Mezzotint. Fourteen single figures, in two rows one above the other, each seated in a little compartment representing a latrine. The upper row are all men, the lower all women All wear hats Almost all are in attitudes expressive of alarm, discomfort, or resignation. Names are written beneath each in an old hand, showing that all are in fact caricatures of men   They are (l. to r): upper row—'L^d B ' [Barrington ?] his face concealed by his hat; 'Ld M.' [Mansfield] with the face of an aged man; 'L N.' [Lord North] scarcely recognizable; 'L. G G.' [Lord George Germain]; 'Mr. Rigby'; 'Ld S.' [Sandwich?], his head concealed by his hat   'Ld Land', turning up his eyes sanctimoniously [Shelburne ?].

The lower row of women: 'Co^l Bare' [Barré], his head almost concealed by his hat; 'Mr Sawb ' [Sawbridge], the City patriot, his head leaning on his hand with a very melancholy expression; 'Ld Car ' [Carlisle?], a young woman of pleasing appearance, with an untroubled expression, 'S F. N ' [Sir Fletcher Norton]; 'Mr W.' [Wilkes], recognizable by his squint; 'D R ' [Duke of Richmond?]; 'Mr. Johnson', with a certain resemblance to Dr. Johnson

General attacks on the Government were made by moving for a committee on the State of the Nation; see motions by Fox and the Duke of Richmond (accepted by North) 2 Dec. 1777, followed by debates in committee, 2, 11, 16, 19 Feb 1778   Chatham's last speech 7 Apr 1778 was in a debate on the Duke of Richmond's motion for an address to the king upon the State of the Nation. *Parl Hist* xix, pp 472 ff., 513 ff., 672 ff., 718 ff , 745 ff., 1012 ff.

There are other versions of this design, see Nos. 5480, 5481; it appears on the wall in No. 5633 and also in a pen drawing by Rowlandson, *The School of Eloquence*, in the collection of Mr. Oppé, exhibited Burlington Fine Arts Club, 1931–2   It is mentioned in No 6199.

$7\frac{15}{16} \times 13$ in ; each compartment approximately $3\frac{1}{2} \times 1\frac{3}{4}$ in.

5480 THE STATE OF THE NATION. [2] [n.d. perhaps 1783]

Sold by W: Holland N° 50 Oxford St^r Price 1^s.

Engraving (partly mezzotinted). Another version (reversed), and drawn more freely, of No. 5479. Beneath each figure is engraved an exclamation. These are, upper row (l. to r): *O my back!* ['Ld Land'?], *Good Lack!* [Lord Sandwich]; *What a Stench!* [Rigby]; *Curse the French!* [Germain]; *I'm quite gone!* [Lord North]; *Damn the Don!* [Lord Mansfield]; *We're all aground!* [Lord Barrington]. Lower row (l. to r.): *How I'm bound!* [Dr Johnson]; *I'm quite sick!* [Duke of Richmond]; *It's a Spanish Trick!* [Wilkes]; *I'ts [sic] all in vain!* [Fletcher Norton]; *What a Strain!* [Lord Carlisle]; *Fine Fun!* [Sawbridge], *I've just done!* [Col. Barré]

Beneath the design is engraved·

> *In a certain Great House that there is in this Land,*
> *When a motion is made on your Feet you must stand,*
> *But in this little House it is quite the revarse,*
> *When a motion is made you must sit on your* . . .

$7\frac{11}{16} \times 13$; each compartment, upper row approximately $3\frac{5}{16} \times 1\frac{3}{4}$; lower row approximately $3\frac{7}{16} \times 1\frac{3}{4}$.

5480 A An earlier state, without the words beneath the figures and without publication line.

5481 THE STATE OF THE NATION [3]

Pub^d by H. Humphrey, St James's Street [n.d.]

Engraving. Another version of No. 5480 freely drawn in outline, with certain alterations in the hats, suggesting a publication some years later than 1778, perhaps 1784 or 1786. Words as in No 5480 The first figure, saying *O my Back!*, wears a high-crowned hat instead of a three-cornered hat, and top-boots instead of shoes The man saying *Damn the Don* wears a high-crowned hat instead of a low-crowned one.

Three of the women in the lower row wear hats with higher crowns, those of the third and fifth being Welsh in shape

The design and the words below the design are enclosed by a marginal line, this measurement being $9\frac{3}{8} \times 13\frac{1}{4}$ in

The size of the compartments is approximately the same as in No. 5480.

No 1220 in the *Collection de Vinck: Etat de la Nation Angloise* with the comic publication line, *A Londre à la taverne du vent*, is presumably a French copy of No. 5479, 5480, or 5481.

5482 V. 2. 69. A VIEW IN AMERICA IN 1778

M D [Darly] *sc.*

Pubᵈ by M Darly Augᵗ 1. 1778

Engraving A negro lies prone in the foreground (r); he has been wounded by a cannon-ball; cannon-balls of various sizes lie on the ground near him. A man wearing a military overcoat with a sash stands over him; he points with his three-cornered hat towards the negro, while he turns to a man standing on his r. whose dress resembles that of the members of Congress in No. 5474 with the addition of a large feathered hat and sword; the Congressman is smoking a short pipe with a large covered bowl. Behind the negro stands an American soldier, with a feathered hat, who smiles and points towards three *Death or Liberty* men, one of whom turns his back, the other two look down with closed eyes and expressions of deep misery. Their clothes are ragged, one, who is very short, wears a cap inscribed *Death or Liberty* and a powder-horn inscribed *Liberty or Death*. In the background behind a palisade is a rectangular enclosure, with a flag inscribed *U S*. Behind the enclosure is a ruined fortification, from which cannon are being fired by one man only. Four or five men are visible behind the palisade.

Perhaps a satire on the indifference of Congress to the sufferings of American soldiers, and on the attitude to negro slavery in America, illustrating Dr Johnson's familiar gibe.

One of the same series as No. 5370, &c. Probably from a sketch by an amateur, perhaps Mansergh

$8\frac{7}{8} \times 12\frac{9}{16}$ in.

5483 A HESSIAN GRENADEIR

M D sc

Pub by M Darly 39 Strand Aug 1. 1778.

Engraving (coloured impression). A soldier stands at attention in profile to the l holding his musket with fixed bayonet. A long pigtail hangs from short, shaggy hair. He wears a pointed cap tilted over his eyes, military coat, and jack-boots. On his back is a variety of objects, including a flask, a pouch, a leg of mutton, and (?) a turkey.

The Hessians were incorrigible plunderers of friend and foe in America Probably belongs to the same series as No 5482, but the numbered margin has been cut off.

$9\frac{3}{16} \times 6\frac{8}{16}$ in

5484 MONSIEUR SNEAKING GALLANTLY INTO BREST'S SCULKING-HOLE AFTER RECEIVING A PRELIMINARY SALUTATION OF BRITISH JACK TAR THE 27 OF JULY 1778

[n.d c Aug 1778]

Publ: as the Act directs by W. Richardson N° 68 High Holborn.

Engraving. An English sailor wielding a cat-o'-nine-tails chases a French sailor into the wide jaws of a dragon or sea-monster; they symbolize the British and French fleets. The French sailor, whose jacket is decorated with fleur-de-lys, carries a man-of-war on his head; he shrieks in alarm, his hands outstretched. His trousers are undone and he puffs a blast at his pursuer resembling the smoke which comes from the ships' guns Both men are running on the surface of the sea, within the jaws of the monster is a fleet; guns are firing towards a single British ship on the l which returns the fire. The jaws of the monster are inscribed *Grand Monarque.*

The battle of Ushant, the first naval engagement of the war with France, was indecisive, for though the advantage was with the British, the French made good their escape to Brest, see No. 5626. It resulted in the court-martials of Keppel and Palliser, see Nos. 5536–8, and gave rise to many satires, see Nos. 5486, 5570, 5992, &c.

$5\frac{3}{16} \times 7\frac{5}{8}$ in.

5485 AN EXTRAORDINARY GAZETTE OR THE DISAPPOINTED POLITICIANS

[? 1778]

P^r 6^d

Engraving, partly mezzotinted. A number of men sit and stand round a table in some coffee-house or club, smoking, reading, and drinking. A man in spectacles reads in the *Gazette* a dispatch signed *Clin[ton]*; another looks over his shoulder with an expression of satisfaction. A military officer tears a paper to pieces in disgust, on it is a row of ciphers On the edge of the table is a paper inscribed *Gazzette extro^y 1710. We have gain'd a battle & hav[e] the French General in my coach. Marlborough.* (Apparently an allusion to Blenheim 1704.)

On the wall (l.) is a large map· *Map of America belonging to the English in 1762 when Pitt was prime minister.* In the centre is *A Map of America belonging to the English in 1778*; only a fragment in the north is left, filled with writhing serpents On the r is a picture, *The Mountain in Labour,* from the bottom of a mound a mouse emerges, crowds of men throw up their arms making gestures of astonishment Under the map of America in 1778 is a play-bill: *At the Theatre Royal St James'es. A Play of All in the Wrong, Obstant by Mr King . which will be* [followed by] *a Farce of the sobject[ion] ... America.*

This appears to represent the *Gazette Extraordinary* of 24 Aug 1778 which contained Clinton's dispatch of 6 July, relating his encounter with

Washington and Lafayette on 28 June at Freehold or Monmouth on the retreat after his evacuation of Philadelphia. Both Clinton and the Americans represented the affair as a victory, see *Gazette*, loc. cit., and *Ann. Reg.* 1778, p. 225* *All in the Wrong* was a popular comedy by Murphy, first played in 1761; Thomas King the actor (1730–1805) was in 1778 at the height of his fame, though here George III is clearly indicated.
$4\frac{5}{8} \times 6$ in.

5486 [EMBLEMATICAL PRINT ADAPTED TO THE TIMES.¹]

[1 Sept. 1778]

Lond. Mag: August. 1778

Engraving From the *London Magazine*, xlvii. 339. In the foreground Neptune and Britannia (r) are seated on the sea-shore in conversation. Neptune points with his trident and Britannia with a finger at a young man with lank hair, seated on a rock (l), who holds a large striped American flag, a cock stands on his shoulder crowing. In the distance the British fleet is in line of battle among clouds of smoke; above flies Fame blowing her trumpet and holding a British flag. The design is surrounded by a conventional frame of garlands, palm-branches, &c. The accompanying text explains that this represents Neptune consoling Britannia and deriding America The Gallic cock crowing on the shoulder of an American represents the 'unnatural' alliance of America with France. The British fleet is represented as triumphant because 'the event of the action was more beneficial than many victories'

For the battle of Ushant, 27 July 1778, see Nos 5484, 5626. The *London Magazine* had been strongly pro-American, this print illustrates the change produced by the French alliance.
$3\frac{7}{8} \times 6\frac{3}{8}$ in.

5487 THE CURIOUS ZEBRA.

London. Printed for G. Johnson as the Act directs 3 Sepr 1778, and Sold at all the Printshops in London & Westminster.

Engraving A zebra, on whose stripes are engraved the names of the thirteen colonies, is being treated in various ways by four men. A man standing behind it is about to put on its back a saddle inscribed *Stamp Act.* This is George Grenville; he says, *I say, Saddle the Beast She will be able to bear great burdens for plac——n* [placemen] *& Pens——rs* [Pensioners]. Lord North (l.) holds the animal by a halter, saying *My name is Boreas the First I hold the Reins, and will never quit them till the Beast is Subdued* (cf. No 5231). Two men (r) hold the animal by the tail: one, whose coat, decorated with fleur-de-lys, shows that he represents France, is saying *You are doing un grand Sottise, and Begar I vill avail myself of it. Dis Zebra Vill look very pretty in my Menagerie* The other, dressed as an English military officer, says, *My name is Fabius the Second, & the Rudder is my Hand Pull Devil—Pull Baker, but She'll Stand upon her legs at last* This is evidently Washington (a second *Fabius Cunctator*), and he is so identified in a contemporary hand. Behind Lord North stand three men, who represent the three Commissioners sent to treat with the Americans, see No. 5473, &c. The central figure, probably Lord Carlisle, holds in his hands objects intended for a wisp of hay and a sieve of oats, he says,

¹ The title has been supplied from 'Directions to the Bookbinder'.

I imagined the Animal wou'd have accepted our Hay & Oates; the man on his *l*, probably Eden, says *Our Offers are Rejected no terms but Independence.* The third, Governor Johnstone, older and more burly than the other two, says, *I thought they wou'd have received us more Friendly, but now give over all hopes.* Behind the figures is the sea with a small town on the farther side of a bay. After the title is engraved, *alive from America! walk in Gem'men and Ladies, walk in.*

The bias of the print is clearly shown by the allusion to the Stamp Act, passed in 1765 and repealed in 1766, without having been put in execution, intended to raise money towards the expenses of the defence and administration of the colonies. For other references to the Stamp Act (usually attributed to Bute) see Nos. 4118, 4119, 4124, 4125, 4130, 4140, 4141, 4142, 4143, 4298, 4842, 5298, 5490, 5491, 6190, 6291, and p 216.

Collection de Vinck, No. 1216.

$6\frac{3}{4} \times 10\frac{1}{16}$ in

5488 THE CITY IN AN UPROAR—OR THE RE-TAKING OF UMBRAGE—BY SIR TONY CANDLESTICK KN^T

Price $6\frac{1}{2}d$

Published as the Act directs Septr 29th 1778

Engraving A satire on Irish Volunteers. A burlesque representation of volunteers from an Irish city, whose buildings are seen on the horizon (l); on the r. are hills. An allusion to 'the Poddle Hole' shows that it is Dublin Small companies of civic soldiers march from l. to r. The leading party, probably the Dublin Corporation, wear long civic gowns, their leader carries a long staff and a candlestick held upside down. Labels issue from the mouths of the three foremost. the man with the candlestick, probably the Mayor, says *What Billy is it Nothing*; the next man, who wears bands, and is perhaps the Recorder of the City, says *Thus I am lead about for 500 p. y^r*; the third carries a large key, and says, *I am <u>Done</u> wth the Keys of ye City.* These three are followed by twelve or thirteen obese men in gowns, probably the aldermen; they carry standards on which words are engraved evidently indicating their occupations · *Jallap; Adze; Titlepage; Teatub; Grape; Grogram, Starch; Figg; Taplash* In front of this party (r.), but looking away from it, stands a man in armour with an oval shield inscribed *The only Apprais^s Office*; he carries a flag on which are two castles.

The next party appears to be a company of beggars; they are nearly all maimed, with crutches, &c. Their leader is a well-dressed man carrying a spear, he says, *I Live & I'll die by my Beggars.* They carry a large ragged flag on which is a horse or ass drawing a two-wheeled cart, within which is a man (or woman), on it is inscribed *3400 to Support me.* With the party is a woman carrying an infant. The last beggar, waving his crutch, cries *Hey for Channell Row.*

The next party (six persons) appears to consist of surgeons and apothecaries. On their standard is a pestle and mortar. The last man carries an axe Their leader, holding a spear, looks over his shoulder towards his followers, saying *Tis we support the Gallows.*

The next (and last) party (l) appears to be a company of watchmen or police. Their leader carries a halberd and says *Ay Bro^r & ye Gallows Supports us.* This company of five carry halberds, and each has a lantern slung from his shoulders. Their standard is supported on a halberd to which is attached a watchman's lantern and is inscribed, *Col B . . . . n for ever Huzza.*

In the distance, between this party and the city, is a gallows on a minute scale, from it hangs a man inscribed *Rat*; spectators stand round. Near it walks a man with broadsides, shouting *The last speech of I do-no-who.*

In the foreground on the extreme r. is a tree. In front of it sits an ape, goat, or satyr playing a set of bagpipes, he says *A sure a Sett was never Seen so Justly formed to Guard our City.* Two men wearing hats and long gowns, each holding a sword, recline against the roots of the tree; one holds a paper inscribed *The House Scheme,* and is saying *I stop'd at Corke for w*[t] *I am now.* Between them and the Mayor's party runs a small boy on a minute scale, he carries a paper and cries, *The whole Order.* In the foreground, and extending to the roots of the tree, is a piece of water on which are two boats, full of men and rowed by two pair of oars, the rowers apparently facing the bows, where in each boat a man holds an anchor. One boat (r.) has a large flag inscribed *The Geography,* on the top of the flag-staff is a spinning-wheel. The man with the anchor says *Send D*[r] *G——d to the Adm*[l] *he's Seasick.* The other boat has a flag inscribed *The Salmon* The man with the anchor says, *Shall y*[e] *Pavers be Landed,* a passenger carries a pickaxe.

On the shore are various camp-followers, &c. Two men stand together, their backs to the parties of volunteers; one holds a staff surmounted by a ball and cross, saying, *Darby Smoke our S——ffs.*; the other says *I do so.*

Near them is a small tilt-wagon, drawn by two horses, a carter walking beside them, the wagon has a flag inscribed *Custard &c &c.* Behind it walks a woman with a child on her back holding up newspapers for sale; she is calling *High barny Jour*[l], and her paper is inscribed *Hiber*[nian] *Journal*; behind her walks a small boy who points at the marching watchmen

Beneath the design is engraved, *The Mayor of Bantam, hearing y*[t] *our perfidious Enemies the French, had taken Umbrage from his Majesty, calls in the aid of his Ally, Ben, King of the Beggars, who takes the Field with his Hussars, attended by Gen*[l] *Gallipot with the D——t S——t Militia, & Justice Bed-post at the head of S*[t] *A——s Watch, while Adm*[l] *Spinning Wheel, on board y*[e] *Geography, commands a fleet of Observation on the Poddle Hole* [1]

> *While grim S*[r] *Tony, that sagacious Blade,*
> *With Fury marches to attack a Shade;*
> *Behold him follow'd by a Num'rous Train,*
> *Coeval Some, in a sad Lack of —— Brain*
> *Oh! happy City, blest with such a Head,*
> *At once so Valorous and so well bred;*
> *That none, for parts & penetration quick,*
> *Can vie w*[th] *our well Polish'd Candlestick.*

This appears to be a satire on the Irish Volunteers of Dublin The volunteer movement began in Belfast in 1778, through fears of a French invasion, and spread rapidly, soon becoming political, see No. 5572.

6½ × 12¼ in.

[1] Cf. J. Isaacson, *The Choice,* . . in *Foundling Hospital for Wit,* 1772, p 137 A note explains that 'The Poddle (more properly perhaps the Puddle) is one of the great common-sewers of the city of Dublin, . . .'.

5489 GRACE BEFORE MEAT OR A PEEP AT LORD PETER'S.
[? Gillray[1].]

[n d. 1778]

Sold by W. Humphrey, N° 227 Strand.

Engraving Twelve persons seated round a circular table, their hands in various attitudes of prayer, their heads bent. In the centre, under a canopy, decorated with the royal arms, sit the king and queen. A man on the king's r. is intended for Lord Petre; a lady on the queen's l. for Lady Petre. A tall emaciated monk who stands on the l on a low stool is saying grace Two footmen stand behind On the wall (r) is a crucifix and (l) the picture of a saint with a halo. On the table are plates, knives, and various dishes including a sucking-pig and a pie. The guests, especially those facing the king and queen whose backs are turned to the spectators, are caricatured, the king and queen are not.

This represents the visit paid by the king and queen to Lord Petre at Thorndon, Essex, 19–21 Oct 1778, while visiting Warley Camp. This was a recognition of the Catholic Relief Act of 1778, which was unopposed and passed almost unnoticed, though it was to lead to the Gordon Riots It is the earliest in date of a number of anti-Catholic satires which heralded the Gordon Riots, see No. 5534, &c , and especially No 5670 The print does much less than justice to the magnificence of the entertainment provided by Lord Petre, see the extracts from his journal in M. D. Petre's *The Ninth Lord Petre*, 1928, pp 38 ff.

Grego, *Gillray*, p. 28. Wright and Evans, No. 368.

$9\frac{1}{8} \times 13\frac{1}{2}$ in.

5489A Another impression with the publication line

Publish'd Nov[r] 5. 1778. by Pat[k] Gahagan Oxford Road.

Date and name are probably intended to stress the no-Popery propaganda of the satire. 'Oxford Road' is probably an attack on the high-church sympathies of the Oxford clergy, see No. 5492, an attack on clergy who 'have learned their Exercises at the Loyal Schools at Oxford'.

5490 THE TEA-TAX-TEMPEST, OR THE ANGLO-AMERICAN REVOLUTION.

Angewitter entstanden durch die Auflage auf den Thee in Amerika. Orage causé par l'Impôt sur le Thé en Amerique. 1778.

[Carl Guttenberg of Nuremburg.]

Engraving An adaptation, in reverse, of *The Oracle* by John Dixon, see No 5225 Time, with a magic-lantern, throws upon a curtain an allegorical representation of revolution in America. He points this out to four female figures personifying the four quarters of the world.[2] Dixon's Britannia, Hibernia, and Scotia have been transformed into Europe, Asia,

---

[1] Attributed to Gillray, its manner has some resemblance to etchings after Mortimer, see No. 5362.
[2] See J H Hyde, 'L'Iconographie des quatre parties du monde dans les tapisseries'; *Gazette des Beaux-Arts*, Paris, 1924, pp. 253 ff.

and Africa Europe and Asia sit side by side, Asia's arm on Europe's shoulder. Asia, a fair woman, holds on her lap a censer, from which pour clouds of incense Europe wears a plumed helmet, and has a spear and a shield on which is a horse; both wear pseudo-classical draperies. Africa, a negress wearing a turban, stands behind Europe gazing in horror at the vision. This group is on the r. On the l. sits America exactly as in Dixon's mezzotint. On the bale of goods behind her are the letters *C G*, and beneath them *4 F.*; on the bale on which she sits is an inverted *M*. The letters C G. are the initials of the artist.[1]

Time also is copied from Dixon; his magic lantern throws a circle of light on a heavy curtain In the centre of the vision is a tea-pot (resembling a coffee-pot) placed over a fire in which stamped documents are blazing. A cock, the emblem of France, is blowing at the fire with bellows.[2] The contents of the tea-pot are exploding, and a serpent and the cap of liberty on its staff are being shot from it into the air, surrounded by rays of light and clouds of smoke This represents the consequences of the Stamp Act and the tax on tea. For the snake emblem on the American flag see No 5336, &c Beneath the clouds of smoke under the fire a prostrate lion is partly visible, and below, a flag with three leopards, representing the British royal standard, torn, its staff broken. By it lies part of a map, showing the English Channel, inscribed *Detroits* . and the head of a spiked club On the l. three beasts of prey are fighting They appear to be a lion, a bear, and a puma or lioness. Within the circle on the r American soldiers are advancing with a striped flag on which is a serpent Before them advances an allegorical figure of America resembling the woman watching the vision, her upstretched hand appears about to grasp the cap and staff of liberty which is shooting up from the exploding tea-pot. Behind her is a mounted officer with a drawn sword followed by soldiers with fixed bayonets. The muzzles of two cannon are also visible, with a man holding a cannon ball. On the l., British soldiers are fleeing in disorder, the heads of the rearmost men being under a yoke. A storm with darts of lightning rages over their heads.

The heavily festooned curtain shows pillars, and on the wall (r) is a picture or tapestry of two nude men fighting, one lies prostrate

In the centre of the lower margin are two medallions one (l) is inscribed *Auto da fe* and *Holland. 1560*; it represents a man tied to the stake, while a monk, holding up a crucifix, holds a torch to the pile. On the r. is *Wilhelm Tell, Switzerland. 1296*. Tell aims with a cross-bow at the apple on his son's head, while Gessler on horseback points at the child. Between the medallions is part of an oak-tree. The medallion representing Holland is supported (l) by the Dutch lion holding in his paw a sheaf of seven arrows representing the United Provinces. Hercules with his club (r.) supports the medallion of Switzerland.

The example of Holland and Switzerland in their contest with tyrants is depicted as emblematic of the revolt of the Colonies against England. See No 6190, an English adaptation of this design where the allusions are made explicit by words spoken by Time See also No 5491. For other references to the tax on tea see Nos. 5226, 5282, 5491, 5850, 5859 For the Stamp Act see No 5487, &c For Saratoga see No. 6470, &c.

13 × 17 in.

[1] Nagler, *Die Monogrammisten*, ii 27.
[2] Impressions with the cock are rare, as the engraver was compelled to remove this emblem. Portalis et Béraldi, *Graveurs du 18me Siècle*, 1881, ii 363.

5491 ORAGE CAUSÉ PAR L'IMPÔT SUR LE THÉ EN AMÉRIQUE.

[*n.d.*]

Engraving A reduced version in reverse of No. 5490. Beneath the title is engraved.

Le Temps fait voir avec sa Lanterne Magique, aux quatre parties du Monde, que cet Orage que les Anglois ont excité, les foudroye eux-mêmes, et va donner à l'Amérique les moyens de se saisir du bonnet de la Liberté.

$5\frac{1}{4} \times 6\frac{7}{8}$ in.

5492 REVIEW OF THE YORK REGIMENT.

[n.d , *c.* 1778, perhaps 1777]

*P. Canon del*ᵗ   *T. Parson Sc*ᵗ

Engraving. A bishop in lawn sleeves and mitre holds out his hands towards a troop of soldiers who advance through a gothic doorway (!), over which is inscribed *Gate to Preferment*. He turns round to speak to Britannia (r.), who leans against a pedestal inscribed *Constitution*; she holds her shield and a long staff, and wears a cap of liberty. The bishop, Markham, Archbishop of York, says to her, *Madam a noble Corps, True and Staunch Friends to the Cause, have learned their Exercises at the Loyal Schools at Oxford.* Britannia answers, *This Gate is not yᵉ Door to your Master's Sheepfold, he that entereth not by yᵉ Door is a thief & robber I will not trust you, you would ruin my Constitution & tear my Cap* Behind Britannia appear the head and shoulders of a man who appears to carry a musket on his back, perhaps an Irish Volunteer, he says to her, *Dear Madam Tory's & Jacobites were never Friends to the Brunswick Line remember ye Years 15 & 45.*

The soldiers wear clerical bands and low-brimmed hats and carry muskets with fixed bayonets, on their banner is a mitre; their leader holds a crozier; he is saying *Please you Madam, for Mitres, Deaneries and Prebendarys we will wade thro' an Ocean of Yanky Blood.* The heads and shoulders of a number of parsons, similarly dressed, who are rushing uphill towards the *Gate to Preferment* to join the 'York Regiment', appear between the troop and the archbishop.

In the foreground (r) two soldiers are talking together; one says, *Tom who the Devil will trust these Fellows who are neither true to God nor Man, for every one is a Deserter from the Prince of Life* The other answers, *Let them alone, they are but hirelings if I was King I would hang them all* On the horizon are churches or cathedrals falling into ruin

The names of the artists are probably a punning allusion to the supposed activities of the Church of England in support of the war Markham was attacked in the House of Lords by Grafton, Shelburne, and others, 30 May 1777, for a sermon contrary to the spirit of the Revolution (of 1689). *Parl Hist*. xix. 326–51. (Sermon quoted, pp. 348–50 n.) Walpole, *Last Journals*, 1910, ii 29–30, 86–8.

See also Nos. 5343, 5400

$6\frac{1}{4} \times 10\frac{7}{8}$ in.

5493 [A COAT OF ARMS FOR JOHN WESLEY.]   [1778]

Engraving Frontispiece from 'Perfection; a poetical Epistle, calmly addressed to the greatest Hypocrite in England', an attack on Wesley for his 'Calm Address to our American Colonies', 1775.

A fantastic escutcheon whose supporters are, dexter, a wolf wearing the fleece of a sheep, and sinister, a fox. Objects on the shield have letters referring to notes beneath the design giving references to the verses. Above a chevron are (dexter chief) *a*, an open book inscribed *Forms and Lies* and *Book of Common Prayer*, *b*, a key Middle chief, a money bag inscribed *40 Guis* Sinister chief, *d*, a mouse-trap and a crozier. Below the chevron. Middle base, the façade of a building with a pediment inscribed *I W* [John Wesley] surmounted by a cupola having a weathercock pointing to *N*, that is, to Lord North. It flies two flags, one inscribed *Calm Address*. p. 21, the other *Perfection*. At the centre base of an ornamental border to the escutcheon is the head of Wesley, wearing bands, his mouth open. Beneath it is a ribbon inscribed, *My . Son . get . Money*

The wolf, the dexter supporter (l.), wears a fleece inscribed *I W*, he excretes a blast inscribed *c*, *New Light 40 Articles* The reference is to:

> if Ministers but nod,
> Make earthly *Kings* co-equal with thy *God*
> To other rules of *Faith* add this of *thine*
> And tack one *Item* more to *Thirty-nine*.

He stands on three superimposed slabs, inscribed *Impostor Detected. Letters Contributions to the Stock Evans. I.W. detected.* The fox (r.) excretes *News from America*; he stands on three slabs inscribed *Subscriptions | to the Temple Rowland Hill*, p. 17.

The crest is a mitre inscribed *Erasmus*, with *e*, a dagger and the motto *Good Will towards Men.*

Since Wesley's 'Calm Address to our American Colonies', an unacknowledged abridgement of Johnson's 'Taxation No Tyranny' sold at a penny and achieving a great circulation, Wesley had been the target of virulent abuse which reached a climax of scurrility in 1778. See Tyerman, *Life and Times of Wesley*, iii 261 ff It was followed by 'A Calm Address to the Inhabitants of England', 1778 'A wolf in Sheep's clothing or an old Jesuit unmasked . . .' was published in 1775. The mitre is an allusion to the allegations of Toplady and Rowland Hill, that Wesley had asked Erasmus, bishop of Arcadia in Crete, to consecrate him bishop and had been refused. The dagger is supposed to indicate the effect of the Calm Address· 'And *massacre* Mankind with CALM ADDRESS.'

The slabs supporting the wolf and fox are inscribed with the names of attacks on Wesley· the chief attack on the 'Calm Address' had been by Caleb Evans, a Baptist minister and a 'patriot' in 'A Letter to the Rev. Mr John Wesley occasioned by his "Calm Address"' Rowland Hill's pamphlet of abuse was 'Imposture detected . ' 1777.

The weathercock pointing to the north indicates that Wesley has sold himself to the Ministry. Wesley's New Chapel in the City Road, opened in 1778, was built by subscriptions. The key on the escutcheon represents 'the Keys of Hell', because of Wesley's alleged fulminations against non-Methodists The mouse-trap is 'Priestcraft's Trap'

This print and Nos 5494–6, 5576, are all frontispieces to scurrilous pamphlets in verse by the same writer, all published by J Bew, Paternoster Row. 'Perfection' is attributed to W Combe by J. C. Hotten in his introduction to *Dr Syntax* [1868], p. xli.   •

$7\frac{7}{8} \times 7\frac{1}{4}$ in.

5494 TOOTHLESS, HE DRAWS THE TEETH OF ALL HIS FLOCKS. [1778]

Engraving. Frontispiece from 'Sketches for Tabernacle-Frames', another scurrilous attack on Wesley by the author of 'Perfection . . .', see Nos 5493, 5495, 5496, 5576. Wesley (l) as 'Reynard' with a fox's head, wearing an M A. gown with clerical bands, bends forward to extract the teeth of a working man (r.) with an ass's head, who kneels before him Wesley rests a cloven hoof on a pile of four books; inscribed *Locke, Sidney, Magna Charta,* and *Acherly's Constitut⁵*; he wears a collar inscribed *North.* Acherley's constitutional treatises ('The Britannic Constitution', 1727, &c) expressed an extreme form of the social contract theory of Locke and others. Beside him is a table (l.) on which are two open books transfixed by a dagger, across which is a scroll inscribed *Dispatch for America*; one book is *Impostor detected by R. Hill,* the other *Political Sophistry detected by Evans* For these pamphlets see No 5493

The working man, dressed like a blacksmith, opens his ass's jaws for Wesley's ministrations, in one hand is a bottle inscribed *Prim Phys ,* in the other a pamphlet, *A Calm Address* (see No. 5493); from his pocket protrudes a volume of *Hymns.*

Behind Wesley (l.) is a book-case, its pediment ornamented by a mitre, in allusion to Wesley's alleged desire for consecration, see No 5493. Its three shelves of books are inscribed *Primitive Physick*; *Political Pamphlets*; and *Prayers, Sermons, Hymns.* Wesley's 'Primitive Physick, or an easy and natural Method of curing most Diseases' went through many editions from 1747, it was first noticed and attacked by the medical profession in 1776 in a pamphlet by Dr. W. Hawes, an eminent physician, as 'calculated to do essential injury to the health of those persons who may place confidence in it'. On the back wall are two framed H L. portraits: *Jacobus II* and *Lucy Cooper,* the latter inscribed *Converted June 24 at 1 O'Clock in the Morning.* According to the *Explanation* which has been cut off the impression, the pictures show him to be a Jacobite and 'an old letcher' Lucy was 'a Lady still remembered in Covent Garden', 'Perfection', p. 14 n.

The allusions in this satire largely repeat those of No 5496, though their political animus is more pronounced. Wesley is depicted as 'a physical, a political and a Religious Quack', 'The Love Feast', p. 13 n See No 5496. His influence with the common people is alleged to have softened their animosity to the Government, an anticipation, though with a more limited application, of the conclusions of Lecky and Halévy.

$7\frac{5}{8}\times 7\frac{3}{16}$ in.

5495 WISE AS SERPENTS   1778

Engraving. Frontispiece from 'The Temple of Imposture', 1778, one of a number of scurrilous pamphlets in verse attacking John Wesley by the same author, see Nos. 5493, 5494, 5496, 5576. A large serpent, holding a bird in its mouth, encircles a number of objects indicating various phases of religious imposture (so called) The serpent, which represents Wesley, is inscribed *The subtlest beast of the field (a).* This is annotated below the design. *(a) NB some Hyper-Critics say it was not originally written Field but Moorfields.* Within the space enclosed by the serpent are (l.) a sealed letter inscribed *Aldeberts Letter,* and a Gridiron, inscribed *Mahomet's Gridiron*; beneath a scroll inscribed *Old Light at Mecca* is an open book,

Koran Above a scroll inscribed *New Light in Moorfields* are three books: *Bedlam Hymns; Druid Hymns; Ignat, Loyola Monita Secreta,* and a bottle inscribed *Gin* in whose neck is a lighted candle. Dividing the Koran from these objects is a short curved sword of the pattern worn by macaronies *c.* 1771–3 (see No 5030) inscribed, *Calm Address of Both.* Beneath the serpent is a scroll inscribed *Wise as Serpents* Below the design is engraved:

> *Thus modern Arts on Ancient Plans improve,*
> *A Bedlam-Serpent swallows Mecca's Dove.*

In the list (p. 31) Wesley is denounced as 'Of all *Impostors* since the Flood *the worst*'.

The Foundry, Moorfields, was from 1740 to 1778 Wesley's chief place of preaching and the head-quarters of Methodism in London. Its proximity to Bethlehem Hospital (Bedlam), combined with the hysteria which sometimes attacked his converts, was a common occasion of raillery.

For similar, though less scurrilous, attacks on Wesley see Nos. 1785, 2425, by Hogarth (1762).

$6\frac{3}{4} \times 4\frac{13}{16}$ in.

5496 REYNARDO'S CONSECRATION BY THE GODDESS MURCIA. [1778]

Engraving. Frontispiece to *The Love-Feast,* 1778; one of a number of scurrilous pamphlets in verse by the same writer against John Wesley, see Nos. 5493–5495, 5576 Wesley with a fox's head and a collar inscribed *North,* dressed as in No. 5494, kneels at the feet of Murcia or Venus (l), a half-nude woman seated on a throne under a curtained canopy, she is about to place a mitre on his head Her throne is decorated by a blind-folded cupid holding a cornucopia A cloven hoof projects from Wesley's gown. A disappointed candidate for the bishopric, dressed in gown and bands, holds up his hands, in one of which is his wig Another disappointed candidate slinks out of a door (r), though which a boy enters with his hat in his hand, holding out a paper inscribed *Wanted an Advowson.* The scene is the interior of a Georgian church or chapel, with a gallery supported on columns. On the r. is a double-decked pulpit. Two chandeliers hang from the roof, one inscribed *Gift of Miss Lucy Cooper* (see No. 5494), the other, *Gift of Alderman Gripus* Beneath the design is engraved.

> *Thine be the Diocese of all Moorfields*
> *Romano wav'd his Wig, & cry'd, Huzza!*
> *Simonio disappointed stalk'd away.*

Murcia has selected three competitors for the diocese of Moorfields, where the Foundry was the Methodist head-quarters until Nov 1778, see No. 5495. 'Romano' (William Romaine, 1714–95), 'Simonio' (Dr. Madan, 1726–90), and 'Reynardo', Wesley, all preach a sermon before her, she chooses Reynardo:

> Like other B . . . ps [Bishops] gorge the *golden Bait,*
> *Amphibious Expletives* of *Church* and *State*
> Strange, *Gothic, feudal, self-erected* things;
> Lord Priests, anointed *Ayes* and *Noes* for *k . . gs*
>
>   *The Love-Feast,* p. 44.

The intention of this satire, like others by the same writer, is largely political: Wesley wears North's collar:

He who on *Canting* lays so great a Stress,

Cou'd drink *hot* Blood, yet write a Calm Address, p. 33 (see No. 5493). Madan had been accused of simony in 1767–8 in connexion with the living of Aldwinckle, to which on his recommendation Thomas Haweis had been presented, see also No 4470. Romaine was a calvinist of the Church of England, and a great revivalist preacher. The attack on episcopacy should also be noted, cf. No. 5492, &c.

$7\frac{9}{16} \times 7\frac{3}{16}$ in

Mr. Hawkins describes another frontispiece to a similar satire on Wesley by the same writer:

INSPIRATION, ELECTION, PERFECTION

A frontispiece to 'Fanatic Saints; or Bedlamites inspired,' 1778.

(*a*) A bottle of gin, with a glass, labelled *Inspiration*.

(*b*) A pillory and a gallows, labelled *Election*.

(*c*) A satyr's head with clerical bands labelled *Perfection*.

Wesley and other Methodist preachers are charged in the poem with availing themselves of their character for sanctity to seduce their converts and turn their chapels into brothels.

PERSONAL SATIRES

5497–5509

Series of Tête-à-Tête portraits.

5497 Nᵒ XXXIV. MISS D——LE.
Nᵒ XXXV THE WHIMSICAL LOVER

*Published as the Act directs by A. Hamilton Junʳ near Sᵗ John's Gate
Janʸ 1. 1778.*

Engraving. *Town and Country Magazine*, ix. 625 Two bust portraits in
oval frames illustrate 'Histories of the Tête-à-Tête annexed, . . .'. An
account of the amours of 'a professed voluptuary'. He is George James,
Earl of Cholmondeley (1749–1827), see G. E C, *Complete Peerage*. See
No 5911. Miss D. is the seduced and deserted daughter of a Surrey
farmer.

Ovals, $2\frac{11}{16} \times 2\frac{3}{8}$, $2\frac{3}{4} \times 2\frac{3}{8}$ in. B M.L., P.P. 5442 b.

5498 Nᵒ XXXVII. THE PIOUS Mᴿˢ LEERWELL
Nᵒ XXXVIII. THE PREDESTINED PARSON.

*Published as the Act directs by A. Hamilton Junʳ near Sᵗ John's Gate
Jan. 17. 1778.*

Engraving. *Town and Country Magazine*, ix. 675 (Supplement). Two bust
portraits, the man in clerical gown and bands. They illustrate 'Histories
of the Tête-à-Tête annexed; . . .'. An account of T——y, a popular
calvinistic preacher, evidently Toplady (1740–78) Mrs. L. is the widow
of a rich tradesman.

Ovals, $2\frac{3}{4} \times 2\frac{5}{16}$ in. B.M.L., P.P. 5442 b.

5499 Nᵒ I. THE PERSUASIVE HOUSEKEEPER.
Nᵒ II. THE HEARTY ALDERMAN

*Published as the Act directs by A. Hamilton Junʳ near Sᵗ John's Gate
Feb. 1. 1778.*

Engraving. *Town and Country Magazine*, x 9 Two bust portraits in
oval frames. They illustrate 'Histories of the Tête-à-Tête Annexed; . .'.
Scandal about an alderman and his housekeeper They are identified by
H. Bleackley as Alderman John Hart, see *City Biography*, p 61, and Hannah
Hickman.

Ovals, $2\frac{11}{16} \times 2\frac{1}{4}$ in. B.M L , P P. 5442 b.

5500 Nᵒ IV. MISS C——LM——N.
Nᵒ V. THE ARTFUL LOVER.

*Published as the Act directs by A. Hamilton Junʳ near Sᵗ Johns Gate,
March 1. 1778*

Engraving *Town and Country Magazine*, x. 65. Two bust portraits in oval frames They illustrate 'Histories of the Tête-à-Tête annexed;...'. An account of Lord V—— and Miss C—m—n, the daughter of an officer killed in the Seven Years' War. He is conjecturally identified by H. Bleackley as Lord Villiers.

Ovals, $2\frac{3}{4}\times2\frac{5}{16}$; $2\frac{3}{4}\times2\frac{3}{8}$ in.   B.M.L., P.P. 5442 b.

5501 N° VII. MISS SP——C–R.
         N° VIII. THE PLIANT PREMIER.

Published as the Act directs by A Hamilton Jun' near S' John's Gate, April 1st 1778.

Engraving. *Town and Country Magazine*, x. 121. Two bust portraits in oval frames. One (r.) that of Lord North, facing T.Q. to the l. wearing his ribbon and star. They illustrate 'Histories of the Tête-à-Tête annexed; ...' The account of North as minister is favourable on the whole. He is said to visit Miss S , one of the most beautiful 'demi-reps' with a villa at Blackheath. For Charlotte Spencer see H. Bleackley, *Ladies Fair and Frail*, pp. 209-10

Ovals, $2\frac{3}{4}\times2\frac{3}{8}$ in.   B M.L., P.P. 5442 b.

5502 N° X. MISS L——N
         N° XI. THE MARTIAL LOVER

Published as the Act directs by A. Hamilton Jun' near S' John's Gate May 1. 1778

Engraving. *Town and Country Magazine*, x. 177. Two bust portraits in oval frames. They illustrate 'Histories of the Tête-à-Tête annexed; ....'. An account of Viscount Petersham, 1753–1829 (Earl of Harrington, 1779), Lieut.-Col. of the 3rd Foot Guards and A D C. to Burgoyne in 1777· G.E.C., *Complete Peerage*. He is said to have established Miss L——n, the destitute orphan of a doctor, as his mistress.

Ovals, $2\frac{3}{4}\times2\frac{3}{8}$ in.   B.M L , P P. 5442 b.

5503 N° XIII. M^{RS} P——T
         N° XIV. THE CAUTIOUS COMMANDER.

Published as the Act directs by A. Hamilton Jun' near S' John's Gate June 1. 1778.

Engraving. *Town and Country Magazine*, x. 233. Two bust portraits in oval frames The man wears armour with a ribbon and star. They illustrate 'Histories of the Tête-à-Tête annexed; or, Memoirs of the Cautious Commander and M^{rs} Pr—tt'. An account of Lord Amherst (1717–97) He is said to have relieved the necessities of Mrs P., the wife of a half-pay lieutenant, from charitable motives, to have fallen in love with her and to have procured the husband a captain's commission on condition that he gave up all claim to her

Ovals, $2\frac{3}{4}\times2\frac{5}{16}$ in.   B.M L , P P. 5442 b.

5504 Nᵒ XVI. MISS SP——KS
Nᵒ XVII. ADMIRAL STERNPOST.

*Published as the Act directs by A. Hamilton Junʳ near Sᵗ John's Gate
July 1. 1778.*

Engraving. *Town and Country Magazine*, x 289. Two bust portraits in oval frames illustrate 'Histories of the Tête-à-Tête annexed, ...'. Account of an admiral who distinguished himself in the war of the Austrian Succession and the Seven Years' War. Perhaps Lord Hawke (1705–81). His supposed mistress is a Miss Sparks.

Ovals, 2⅝ × 2¼ in.   B.M.L., P.P. 5442 b.

5505 Nᵒ XIX. THE PAPHIAN VOTARY.
Nᵒ XX THE SUCCESSFUL GALLANT.

*Published as the Act directs by A Hamilton Junʳ near Sᵗ John's Gate,
July [sic. i.e. Aug.] 1. 1778*

Engraving. *Town and Country Magazine*, x 345. Two bust portraits in oval frames illustrate 'Histories of the Tête-à-Tête annexed; . . . .'. An account of 'Mʳ B——d', William Bird, and of his amours with Harriet Lambe, Lady Archer, and Grace Dalrymple Elliott; and of Anne, daughter of Lord Bute, wife of Hugh Lord Percy Percy had begun a suit for divorce in May 1778 which was obtained in March 1779. H. Walpole, *Letters*, x. 232.

Ovals, 2¾ × 2⅜ in   B M L, P P 5442

5506 Nᵒ XXII MISS S——TT
Nᵒ XXIII THE BRILLIANT BARONET.

*Published as the Act directs by A. Hamilton Junʳ near Sᵗ John's Gate.
Sepʳ 1. 1778.*

Engraving. *Town and Country Magazine*, x. 401. Two bust portraits in oval frames They illustrate 'Histories of the Tête-à-Tête annexed; . . . .'. An account of Sir Michael le Fleming, of Rydal, Westmorland, who is said to 'give the *ton* in dress and equipage' and of his gallantries Miss (or Mrs) Scott is said to be the daughter of a clergyman, who had eloped with a recruiting officer, had been deserted, and had become a courtesan.

Ovals, 2¾ × 2¼, 2¾ × 2⁵⁄₁₆ in.   B M L, P P 5442 b

5507 Nᵒ XXV. LA FEMME SANS SOUCI.
Nᵒ XXVI. THE LICENTIOUS LOVER.

*Published as the Act directs by A. Hamilton Junʳ near Sᵗ John's Gate
Octʳ 1. 1778.*

Engraving. *Town and Country Magazine*, x. 457. Two bust portraits in oval frames. They illustrate 'Histories of the Tête-à-Tête annexed; . . . .'. An account of the amours of a man of fortune whose extravagance has compelled him to sell 'his choice collection of paintings at B.' The lady is the divorced Lady Grosvenor, 'sans souci' being an allusion to the villa of the Duke of Cumberland near Potsdam, cf No. 4844, &c.

Ovals, 2¾ × 2⅜ in.   B.M L., P.P. 5442 b.

5508 Nº XXVIII. MISS B——S

Nº XXIX. THE LIBERTINE LAD.

Published as the Act directs by A. Hamilton Junᵉ near Sᵗ John's Gate Novᵉ 1. 1778

Engraving. *Town and Country Magazine*, x. 513. Two bust portraits in oval frames. They illustrate 'Histories of the Tête-à-Tête annexed; . .'. An account of the extravagance and dissipation of Sir John Lade (1759–1838), nephew and ward of Thrale, now chiefly remembered for the prophetic verses written by Johnson on his coming of age. Boswell, *Life*, iv. 413 He married a woman of the town in 1789 and was a friend of the Prince of Wales See G.E C , *Complete Baronetage*, v 109-10; Hayward, *Life of Mrs Piozzi*, i 69 As the driver of a phaeton he is here said to rival Lord Molesworth. Miss B——s is a milliner's apprentice whose acquaintance Sir John made by the purchase of ruffles.

Ovals, 2¾ × 2⅛ in.   B.M.L., P.P. 5442 b.

5509 Nº XXXI MISS C——LE.

Nº XXXII. THE ADMIRABLE ADVOCATE.

Published as the Act directs by A. Hamilton Junᵉ near Sᵗ John's Gate Decᵉ 1 1778.

Engraving. *Town and Country Magazine*, x 569. Two bust portraits in oval frames illustrate 'Histories of the Tête-à-Tête annexed; . ' An account of Alexander Wedderburn (1733–1805), afterwards Lord Loughborough. Miss C. is the daughter of a rich citizen who had been drugged and seduced by a peer.

Ovals, 2⅝ × 2¼ in.   B M.L., P.P 5442 b.

5510 A SCHOOL OF ATHENS

T. O [Thomas Orde] invᵗ & delᵗ   Jˢ Bretherton f 3ᵈ Janᵉ 1778

Engraving. A satire on Cambridge. The interior of a large room showing two sash windows, through one of which (l.) is seen part of the south side of the Senate House, through the other, the tower of St Mary's Church, both drawn with topographical accuracy. Between the two windows is a niche in which is a statue of Athene holding her shield; in her outstretched l. hand is held out a laurel wreath towards some men beneath her who have entered from a door on the r. Her owl sits beside her on the stump of a tree. Beneath the title is etched, *dedicated to the illustrious Inheritress of her fame in Professors of Arts & Sciences. the University of Cambridge O Matre pulchra Filia pulchrior!* Immediately below Athene, and concealing the lower part of her draperies a man stands on a high rostrum covered with a cloth. He wears a furred academic gown and bands, and holds out a rolled document in his r. hand Immediately below the rostrum a man, not in academic dress, is seated at a table writing. He is in profile to the r. looking towards four men who have entered from the r. through an open door, apparently 'professors of Arts and Sciences', whose names he is recording The foremost of these is a dancing-master who stands holding a bow in his r. hand, a kit or small fiddle in his l. Next is a rough-looking elderly man wearing a round hat and long coat. The other two are middle-aged, one holding his hat and a cane and accompanied by a dog On the l, and behind the chair of the man writing, are two other 'professors': a fencing-master, wearing a fencing-jacket, stands in back view, turning his head in profile to the r., his l. arm raised, holding his foil horizontally. Behind him stands a thin man wearing a hat, one hand in his waistcoat pocket, the other thrust in his waistcoat.

All the figures are probably portraits. The man on the rostrum resembles the later portrait of William Cooke, D.D, Provost of King's College from 1772 The room is evidently in the old Provost's Lodge, probably that shown at the east end of the Chapel in fig. 55, Willis and Clark, *Architectural Hist. of Cambridge*, 1886, 1 548 Cf Bunbury's satire on Cambridge, No. 4729 (1777), where Athene's owl is flying away from the town

$18\frac{3}{8} \times 24\frac{1}{8}$ in. B M.L. K. 8 (100).

5511 A GROSS ADJUTANT.

Coxheath fecit [? Bunbury.]

Pub^d Nov 10. 1778 by M Darly Strand.

Engraving. (Coloured impression.) An enormously fat and short man dressed as a military officer rides a white horse in profile to the l His seat is grotesque Beneath the title is etched *Saddle White* SURR[Y] *for the Field to morrow. King Rich^d 3^d.*

The militia camp at Coxheath near Maidstone was formed in 1778 as part of the defences against France and as a centre for recruits.

Probably a caricature of Captain Grose (1731 ?–91), captain and adjutant of the Surrey militia from 1778 till his death. For Grose see No. 4577, &c; for Coxheath No. 5523, &c See also No 5787.

5511 A Re-issued (n d.) with an altered publication line: *Printed for Robert Sayer, N° 53, Fleet Street.* In book of Sayer's 'Drolls'.

$7\frac{1}{2} \times 5\frac{3}{4}$ in

5512 [CHEVALIÈRE D'EON.][1] [1778]

Engraving Frontispiece from 'An Epistle from Mademoiselle D'Eon to the Right Honourable L——d M——d [Mansfield] .. on his Determination in regard to her Sex. 1778' (B.M.L 11631. g 31/12) Two figures stand joined together back to back, each with one leg only: d'Eon as a man is in profile to the l, wearing a military hat, holding out a large sabre in his r. hand, his leg in a spurred jack-boot. D'Eon as a woman is in profile to the r dressed in the fashion of the day, wearing a large feathered hat, and holding a fan. Each face has a large circular patch on the cheek. Beneath the design is engraved:

> *Hail! Thou Production most uncommon,*
> *Woman half-man and man half-Woman!*
> > *vid. Epistle*

For Mansfield's decision in the King's Bench that D'Eon was a woman, see No 5427.

$7 \times 5\frac{3}{16}$ in (pl.).

[1] Written on the print in an old hand.

5513–5522

Prints from Darly's series, continued from No. 5451.

5513 43 V. 2 THE LAST DROP

Pub. by M Darly Jany 19. 1778 Strand.

Engraving. A lady seated in profile to the r. by a small rectangular table drinks from a wine-glass, on the table is a bottle labelled *Brandy* Her hair is in the grotesque pyramid then fashionable, decorated with ostrich feathers and large curls She appears unconscious of a skeleton which stands beside her, threatening her with an arrow held in its raised l. arm. On the wall behind the figures are two W L. portraits; one of a man, full-face, standing by a tree, holding a spear; he is dressed as a cavalier, wearing a feathered cap and short cloak; the other is of a stout man of plebeian appearance, in profile to the r., holding up a foaming pot of beer and a smoking pipe. Cf No. 5172.

$12\frac{3}{8} \times 8\frac{3}{4}$ in.

5514 45. V. 2. LADY PELLICE, AND MR MUFF.

II. J. (Monogram.)

. . . M Darly . . St rand Jany 20. 1778.[1]

Engraving. A man and woman in conversation. The lady (l.) stands in profile to the r., the man stands facing to the front, but turns his head towards her. The hands of both are in a muff, that of the man being the larger. She wears the high-dressed hair with large side curls then fashionable, but decorated only with a ribbon. She wears a hooded cloak with a border of fur, below which appears her dress The man's wig has side curls which resemble those worn by the lady.

$12 \times 8\frac{7}{8}$ in.

5515 V. 2. 60. SETTLING THE ODD TRICK.

M. M.

Pub. by M Darly N° 39 Strand Feb. 26. 1778

Engraving Four ladies sit at a square card-table; their cards have been thrown down face-upwards The two who sit in profile to l. and to r. are quarrelling violently; one (r.) points at her *vis-à-vis* in anger; the other (l.) has seized a candlestick and is about to hurl it at her partner, the lighted candle falls to the ground behind her shoulder; both are elderly harridans. Between them on the farther side of the table the player appears amused; of her partner only the back is visible The enormous pyramids of hair elaborately decorated in different ways play an important part in the design, as does the carpet, which is of an elaborate acanthus scroll design. The card-players sit in upright chairs with carved backs. On the wall is an oval mirror, on each side of which is a landscape. The dresses show the fashions of the day, the hair-dressing much caricatured, cf. No. 5370, &c.

Copy by F. W. Fairholt in Wright, *Caricature History of the Georges*, 1868, p 256.

$12\frac{5}{16} \times 9$ in.

[1] This line is scarcely legible; Miss Banks has written on the print '1777 or near that time'.

5516 V. 2. 62. THE IMPUDENT HAIR DRESSER DETECTED OR THE FRIZUER REWARDED

Pub by M Darly N° 39 Strand March 11. 1778.

Engraving. The interior of a well-furnished room. A plainly dressed man, wearing a hat, threatens a hairdresser with his fist and a shovel taken from the fireplace; he is being restrained by a neatly dressed maid-servant A lady (r) seated in an arm-chair watches the scene complacently. The hairdresser looks towards a dog (l) which is biting his leg. In his hand is a tress of long false hair, a pair of curling-tongs is pushed through the button-holes of his coat, in his hair or wig are stuck hairpins and a comb. The lady's hair is dressed in fashionable pyramid decorated with feathers, lace, and large curls. Over the chimney-piece, partly visible on the r, is a portrait of a lady in Elizabethan dress. The high, panelled door (l) has a carved lintel An elaborately patterned carpet covers the floor. Similar in manner to No. 5522. For satires on hair-dressing see No. 5370, &c
12¾×9¹⁄₁₆ in.

5517 THE VILLAGE BARBER.

H. J.

Pubᵈ M Darly 39 Strand. June 1 1778

Engraving. A barber is dressing the hair of a woman seated in profile to the r. An enormous heart-shaped cushion has been fixed on her head, and the barber, standing on tip-toe, is fixing to it a tress of false hair. The woman's own hair hangs loosely over her shoulders and forehead; in her hand is another piece of false hair. A woman wearing a cap and apron holds a mirror. On a round table are a number of curls and hair-pins. Wigs hanging on the wall and a barber's block indicate a barber's shop On a shelf is a book inscribed *Revᵈ Mʳ Spintext*, implying that the barber is also a minister or local preacher; he is neatly dressed and wears a check apron. In the wall is a small lattice-window; a vase of flowers stands on the sill For satires on hair-dressing see No. 5370, &c.
12¼×8⅝ in.

5518 V. 2. 68. MISSˢ DUMPLIN DUCKTAIL AND TITTUP RETURN'D FROM WATERING.

Pub by M Darly N° 33 Strand July 13. 1778.

Engraving Three women (caricatured) walking in profile to the r. beside the sea or a lake Their head-dresses are caricatures of the prevailing fashion. The foremost walks with a closed parasol on a long stick like a shepherdess's crook; in her r. hand is a small bag or basket. Her hair is in a pyramid, with curls, on it is a lace cap with lappets, and a flat hat trimmed with ribbons and feathers. She is followed by a very thin woman, whose pyramid is decorated with more curls but with a smaller cap and hat, she holds a closed fan, behind walks a short stout woman with a frizzed wig bound by a ribbon. The dresses show the prevailing fashion for skirts, straight in front, puffed out at the back and showing the ankles.

Miss Tittup, a character in Garrick's *Bon Ton*, was played by Eliza

Farren, 1777, *D N B*. The tall thin lady is perhaps intended for Miss Farren; there is a certain resemblance to later caricatures by Gillray. For hair-dressing see No. 5370, &c.

$8\frac{5}{16} \times 12\frac{3}{4}$ in.

5519 V. 2. 70. THE METHODIST TAYLOR CAUGHT IN ADULTERY   [? 1778]

Engraving. Another version in reverse of No. 4248, pub Sayer, 21 July 1768 It appears to belong to Darly's series, but is without publication line.

$8\frac{5}{16} \times 12\frac{13}{16}$ in.

5520 THE TALLE-HO PARSON GOING IN TO COVER

Pub by M Darly Octr 18. 1778. 39 Stra[nd.][1]

Engraving. A clergyman in hat, bands, and gown, under which appear spurred boots, walks between two watchmen, each with a lantern and staff. The three walk arm-in-arm in profile to the l., the watchmen supporting the parson, towards a door, the upper part of which is formed of open bars, through which appear the heads and shoulders of men and women, evidently the entrance to the parish 'cage' or lock-up. Outside it is a whipping-post and stocks, the post inscribed *Winning Post*

$8\frac{3}{8} \times 12$ in.

5521 V. 2 76 MISS. BUM—BARDINI.

H. J. fec.

Novr 5. 1778. M Darly 39 Strand

Engraving. The back view of a short stout woman who stands in front of an oval mirror in which her face is reflected. She wears a cap with lappets and a flowered dress. The mirror is hung above a marble-topped console; on each side of it hangs a portrait of a lady. A carpet with a bold design covers the floor.

$12\frac{3}{8} \times 8\frac{9}{16}$ in.

5522 JOSEPH AND HIS MISTRESS   [c 1778]

Engraving Margins have been cut off, but this appears to belong to the series published by Darly. A fashionably dressed woman seated on an upholstered settee attempts to pull towards her a footman who resists her with an expression of distress. The scene is one corner of a lofty room with panelled walls and a painted ceiling, probably domed. A decanter of wine and two glasses are on a circular table (l) A dog barks at the man. An elaborately patterned carpet covers the floor. The lady is fashionably dressed and of meretricious appearance.

'The salacious Lady Harrington' is written on the mount of the print. She was the subject of many lampoons and satires, see No. 4903. Apparently based on Fielding's *Joseph Andrews*. Similar in manner to No. 5516.

$12 \times 8\frac{7}{8}$ in.

[1] Margin cut off.

[A SATIRE ON SCOTCH MILITARY PERSONS.]

See No. 4779—1 Jan. 1778

Mʳ R. S. invᵗ W. H [Humphrey] *fec.* Pub. W Humphrey.

An illustration to Anstey's *Bath Guide* (Lady Pandora MacScurvy and General Sulphur).

5523 A TRIP TO COCKS HEATH.

I. M. Inv. [? J. Mortimer].   *W. H. Fe.* [? Humphrey]

Pub. Oct. 28. 1778 by W. Humphrey.

Engraving A crowd of visitors, chiefly women of disreputable appearance, making their way (r to l) towards the camp at Coxheath, near Maidstone. The foremost is a courtesan wearing a military hat and coat carried on the shoulders of an officer; she points to the camp with a spear; a dog barks at her. Next, a woman leads by the arm a fat, elderly and amorous officer, of very unmilitary appearance, who holds his sword in his hand Two elderly women, evidently brothel-keepers, are conspicuous; one holding crutches is being pushed in a wheel-barrow by a decrepit old man Facing the crowd (l.) are three cannon, inscribed *9 P.; 9 Pounder* and *G R 12 Pounder*, the last is being inspected by three women. In the background (l.) a cannon is being fired, and men are being drilled beside a group of tents Behind the walkers (r.) three women are driving rapidly in a two-wheeled chair drawn by two horses towards the camp.

The first of many satires on the militia-camps formed in 1778 in connexion with recruiting and as part of the defences of the country. Coxheath was visited by the king on 3 Nov, great crowds assembling. *London Chronicle*, 3–5 Nov 1778. 'Camp News' was a considerable item in the newspapers and 'the Camp' by Tickell, an entertainment, was produced at Drury Lane, 15 Oct. 1778, and was very popular for two seasons, its chief feature being a realistic representation of Coxheath Camp by Loutherbourg. For camps see Nos. 3752, 4563, 4760, 5525, 5600–2, 5620, 5773, 5775, 5778, 5794, 5950, 5953, 6156.

Attributed to Gillray (Grego, *Gillray*, p. 27), but perhaps after a drawing by Mortimer. Similar in manner to Nos. 5524, 5609.

9¼ × 13⁷⁄₁₆ in.

5524 SQUIRE THOMAS JUST ARRIV'D.

Publish'd Novʳ 18ᵗʰ 1778 by W. Humphrey.

Engraving. Street scene; a fat man, plainly dressed and wearing riding-boots, is being dragged into a brothel by three fashionably dressed courtesans. One kisses him, one pulls, the third pushes him towards an open door (l) over which is a projecting sign, a calf's head in a dish inscribed *The Old Calfs Head, Lodgings for Single Men by Sᵇ Fleecem* The door lintel is inscribed *Kind & Tender Usage.* The man holds out his hands in protest with an expression of dismay. A dwarfish ragged girl (r) appears to be picking his pocket A fat old procuress (l.) looks on laughing. A small dog (l) and the overturned equipment of a shoe-black (r.) add to the confusion In the background two men are in conversation, one smoking. After the title is engraved, *Touch me not! I'm still a Maid.*

Attributed to Gillray (Grego, *Gillray*, p. 27); evidently by the same artist as No. 5523.

12⅝ × 9¹¹⁄₁₆ in.

5525 THE WARLEY HEROES OR THE LIGHT INFANTRY ON
FULL MARCH [*c.* 1778]

London, Publish'd & Sold by W. Humphrey.

Engraving. Two couples of very obese soldiers march in profile to the r.
behind their equally obese leader. All carry muskets without bayonets and
are dressed alike in plumed hats, coats with military facings and epaulettes,
ruffled shirts and half-boots; their leader wears a sash

The two camps on Warley Common, Essex, and Coxheath, Kent, were
much visited by the civilian population, and these visits and the militia
were a popular subject of satire, see No 5523, &c George III stayed with
Lord Petre, see No. 5489, when visiting Warley Camp in Oct. 1778 The
camp is described, with an engraving of 'General Parker exercising the
Army', in the *Westminster Magazine*, 1779, p. 377

$8\frac{1}{16} \times 13$ in

5526 A NEW ACADEMY FOR ACCOMPLISHMENTS

*Published as the Act directs May 7th 1778, by Mrs Humphrey, St
Martins Lane.*

Engraving. A lady, seated (l.), watches through a lorgnette two small dogs
dancing on their hind legs, while a foppishly dressed man, evidently a
French dancing-master (r.), plays the fiddle One dog is a grotesquely
clipped poodle, the other appears to be a King Charles A cockatoo
watches from a perch. The lady is fashionably dressed and wears a hat
trimmed with feathers. The room is indicated by a looped-up curtain and
an ornate mirror with candle sconces hung on the wall by a bow of ribbon.
$12\frac{1}{2} \times 9\frac{1}{4}$ in.

5527 DRAWN BY MISS CALASH 1778.

Pub: as the Act directs. Octr 14 by W. Richardson No 68 High Holborn

Engraving Lady, standing in profile to the l., has drawn up, by a cord
attached to a pulley, an enormous calash hood extending from above her
high-dressed hair to her waist. She is fashionably dressed. For the calash
see No. 5434, &c.

Reproduced, Paston, Pl xxvii.

$12\frac{3}{4} \times 7\frac{13}{16}$ in. (pl.).

5528 LAUGH & GROW FAT.

[W. Austin.]

Published as ye act Directs November. 1778

Engraving. One well-dressed man is being thrashed by another to the
amusement of the bystanders. The victim is running away with clasped
hands and an expression of rage, his hat and cane are on the ground;
his enemy (r) raises his cane to strike. A woman (r.) of grotesque appearance, probably a fish-wife, grins and points at the fray; on her head is a
large basket in which are a dog and a child who waves his hat in delight.
Behind her appears the profile of an elderly man wearing spectacles. On
the l. is another group of spectators: a milk-girl, carrying pails attached to
a yoke on her shoulders; a fat man stands behind her, his hands on her

shoulders. A third man is faintly indicated behind them. In front is a little chimney-sweep's boy, holding up his brush and shovel, with him is a ragged boy wearing the large tie-wig which was worn by sweeps on May Day A dog is barking. In a scroll on the upper part of the design is etched: *Ha Ha Ha I Can't help Laughing, No No nor You For Every Body Laughs at Worstead Stockings Mi   .¹, yᵉ Acknowledged Coward What! retreat at Noon Day & Suffer him Self to be Caneᵈ thus in yᵉ heart of yᵉ City of London O Terrible! a Merchant too & a Patriot A disgrace to yᵉ Names ha ha ha he he he keep it Up My Dear Boy keep it up* [word erased] *Dedicatᵈ to Every Soul that has a Spark of Fire in him in College or Out by their Humble Servant Brother Bamboo P.S. If this Modest Patriot return yᵉ Complement yᵉ Public will be favoᵈ with a Companion to this Print A coward O dreadfull buy & stick it up for yᵉ joke sake. Price only 1 shilling.*

9¾₆ × 15½ in.

5529 BLANK THE TAYLOR

E. Martin iuvᵗ   *J. F. Martin Sculp*

publishᵈ Decemʳ the 8 1778

Engraving (stipple). The interior of a squalid room. A tailor seated cross-legged on a table, scissors and iron beside him, threading a needle, a garment on his lap Under the table, on a low plank bed a burly infant, too large for its bed, is asleep. A flight of stairs (r) leads directly from the room, showing that it is a garret Two women of low type leer into the room through an open doorway, one of whom, seated on the stairs, holds a glass, indicating gin. The tailor, though ragged, is of a more refined type. Garments hang on a line across the room. A fire burns in the grate, tea-things and half a loaf are on a stool.

7¾₆ × 6⅛ in.

5530 [COURT OF EQUITY OR A CONVIVIAL CITY MEETING   ⌐

Robᵗ Dighton Pinxit   Robᵗ Laurie Fecit

*Publish'd Novr 1ˢᵗ 1778 by John Smith Cheapside London.]*¹

Mezzotint. Proof before letters The interior of a club room at the Globe in Fleet Street, showing the l. and back walls. Along the walls are oblong tables, behind which most of fifteen guests are seated. The chairman (l) is seated in an ornate chair between two windows, the chair ornamented with a coat of arms which is repeated in a frame above his head: above a chevron is a punch-bowl with bottle and glass, below, a pair of scales. The motto, which enlaces two cornucopias, is *Mirth with Justice*. Five other framed coats of arms, probably those of similar clubs, and an ornate candle sconce decorate the back wall

The persons are well-characterized portraits. The chairman is 'Hurford, the Guildhall orator' (William Hurford, Deputy of Castlebaynard Ward) On his r., and on the extreme l are Wright, distiller in Fleet Street, and Hamilton, clerk to William Woodfall, printer, holding the *Morning Chronicle* Opposite the latter sits Smith the printseller. On the chairman's l. are (l to

¹ The inscription is taken, as are the names, from Chaloner Smith On the B M impression is written in a contemporary hand, 'Court of Equity or Convivial City Meeting Published as the Act directs by J Smith Cheapside 1779 '

r.), Lamb, silversmith in Fetter Lane; Clark, sausage maker; Stephenson, an attorney; Clark, a bricklayer in Shoe Lane; Russell, a broker of Harp-Alley; Good, the auctioneer; Thorn; Dighton, the artist, on the extreme r In the foreground (r.) by a small table sits Dighton's father; between the two Dightons is a man reading the *Morning Post*. In front of him and facing the chairman stands Towse of Vauxhall, speaking, pipe in his l hand, r hand thrust in his waistcoat. Pipes, glasses, pots, papers of tobacco, and a punch-bowl are on the tables. Tom Thorpe, of the Globe Tavern, advances in the middle of the room, carrying a punch-bowl.

For the convivial tavern-clubs of the period see Brasbridge, *Fruits of Experience*, 1824, pp. 33 ff He enumerates habitués of the Globe Tavern in Fleet Street who include Archibald Hamilton the printer 'with a mind fit for a Lord Chancellor', and William Woodfall Thorpe, a Deputy Alderman, keeper of the Globe, was 'too convivial and too liberal to make it anything but a losing concern'. Reproduced, A E. Richardson, *Georgian England*, 1931, p. 22.

Chaloner Smith, ii, p. 803.

$12\frac{1}{16} \times 15\frac{7}{8}$ in.

A TOUR TO FOREIGN PARTS.   See No. 4732—11 Mar. 1778

J Bretherton after Bunbury

5531 THE BLACK AND WHITE SCUFFLE, OR BARBER AND CHIMNEY-SWEEPER AT FISTY-CUFFS. 221

Printed for & Sold by Carington Bowles, at his Map and Print Ware-house, N° 69 in St Pauls Church Yard London. Published as the Act directs, 1 Jan. 1778.

Engraving Street scene. A barber (l.) and a chimney-sweep are fighting; the barber's dress is spotted with black from the sweep's blows, that of the sweep is marked with white spots caused by hair powder. A girl with a basket of lemons slung round her neck stands behind the barber holding out half a lemon; a dog is biting his leg Two of the sweep's climbing boys are enjoying the scene; one, seated on the ground (l), is putting on a large wig which has been taken from an open box inscribed *Alderman Sapscull* A baker (r) with a large basket of loaves on his shoulders looks on in amusement A man and woman from a neighbouring tavern also watch the fight with amusement, the man holds a wine bottle, and holds out a glass to the combatants On the tavern wall is inscribed *Punch in Large Quantities* and *Hollands Gin and Roman Purl* Its sign is a bull's head, beneath which is the name *Ben Boniface*. A chequered board by the door indicated that ale is sold. No. 221 of a series.

$7\frac{1}{4} \times 10\frac{7}{8}$ in.

Nine prints from the series of mezzotints published by Carington Bowles.[1]

MISS WICKET AND MISS TRIGGER. (370)

After Collet.   See No. 4555—1 Jan. 1778

Reproduced Paston, Pl. cviii.

A reduced copy (276) 1 Jan 1778

[1] Nos. 4557, 4561 have the imprint of Bowles and Carver.

5532 A MORNING VISIT——OR THE FASHIONABLE DRESSES
FOR THE YEAR 1777. (373)

*Printed for & Sold by Carington Bowles, at his Map & Print Ware-
house, Nᵒ 69 in Sᵗ Pauls Church Yard, London. Publish'd as the
Act directs, 1 Jan. 1778.*

Mezzotint A lady advances into a breakfast parlour wearing an enormous
calash or hood drawn over her pyramid of hair, on which is a cap of muslin
and lace She wears a short cloak over her dress, and carries a cylindrical
reticule ornamented with bows in her l. hand She holds out her hand
towards her hostess (l.), who runs forward to meet her holding out both
hands. Behind and between them is a young man seated on a settee,
holding a gun and wearing a three-cornered hat and top-boots; he looks
at the visitor's head-dress. Behind (r.), a maid-servant carrying a round
tray with tea-things follows the visitor into the room. The hostess wears
a hat tilted forwards over her high-dressed hair, showing clusters of large
curls At the back of the hat is a large bunch of feathers. She stands
between a small rectangular table, on her r , and the fireplace, where a
kettle is boiling. The room is panelled; a candle-sconce and mirror hangs
on the wall. For the calash hood see No 5434, &c
    Reproduced, M. C. Salaman, *The Old Engravers of England*, 1906,
p. 174, with the title, *The Spruce Sportsman: or Beauty the best shot* (1780).
13×9⅞ in.

THE MANCHESTER HERO . . . (381)   See No. 4556—[1778]
After Collet.

A satire on the battalion raised voluntarily by Manchester on the news of
Saratoga, see No. 5470.

ABELARD AND ELOISA. (382)   See No. 4557—[1778]

THE PRETTY BAR MAID (384)   See No. 4558—[1778]
After Collet.
Reproduced, A. L Simon, *Bottlescrew Days*, 1926, p. 38.

THE SAILOR'S PRESENT—OR, THE JEALOUS CLOWN (385)
                                             See No. 4559—[1778]
After Collet.

THE PROVERB REVERS'D . . . (386)   See No. 4560 [1778]
After Collet.

THE FEMALE FOX HUNTER. (387)   See No. 4561—[1778]
After Collet.

AN OFFICER IN THE LIGHT INFANTRY, DRIVEN BY HIS LADY
    TO COX-HEATH (391)   See No. 4562—[1778]
After Collet. A reduced version (284) is No. 4563.
A satire on the militia, see No. 5523, &c.

Four similar mezzotints issued by other publishers.

5533 THE LOVELY SACARISSA, DRESSING FOR THE PANTHEON.

[P. Dawe?]

Publish'd Febʸ 24, 1778

Mezzotint. A stout, ugly, and elderly woman holds in her l hand a barber's block, with a carved head in profile, on which is an elaborate pyramidal wig with ringlets. This she is covering with powder or flour from a dredger Her hair is short and scanty; on her head is a very large black patch, two smaller ones are on her temple She is dressed in under-garments, showing stays, and frilled petticoat over which is worn a pocket. Her dress, the bodice of which is almost cylindrical from its stiffening whalebone, is on a stool behind her. Her back is turned to the casement window (r) through which look two grinning old women, wearing frilled muslin caps. Over the window, and over the wall on its l, is a heavily festooned curtain. Sacarissa stands facing a low rectangular table (l), on which are a bottle and wine-glass, a candle (?) in a triangular shade, which is falling over, having apparently been knocked by the wig, patches, a comb, a paper, &c. Behind on the wall, in deep shadow, is a picture of a dome inscribed *The Pantheon* Beneath the title is engraved, *She Blooms in the Winter of her Days, like the Glastonbury Thorn.*

The design appears to be based on that of No. 4647, *Lady Drudger going to Ranelagh*, 1772.

12 ¹¹⁄₁₆ × 10 ¾ in.

FATHER PAUL IN HIS CUPS, OR THE PRIVATE DEVOTION OF A CONVENT.
See No. 4626—25 Apr. 1778

Pub. Sayer and Bennett.

A satire on monks. Eight lines from Sheridan's *Duenna* (first played 1775) engraved beneath the design.

A mezzotint of the same subject was issued by Carington Bowles 10 Nov. 1777, see No. 3782. Also a reduced version with the same date, see under No. 4626

THE SLIP, OR MISS, WILLING TO BE IN THE TON.
See No. 4631—[c. 1778]

No publication line; a reduced version was published by Sayer and Bennett, 10 Aug. 1778. It appears to have been re-issued by Laurie and Whittle, who include it in their Catalogue, 1795, with the word 'fashion' substituted for *ton*.

THE UNWILLING BRIDEGROOM ...
See No. 4780—15 May 1778

Pub. W. Humphrey.

POLITICAL SATIRES

5534 SAWNEY'S DEFENCE AGAINST THE BEAST, WHORE, POPE, AND DEVIL &c. &c.

Pub. as the Act directs 1 Ap. 1779

Engraving. An attack on the Catholic Relief Act of 1778. Symbolical figures are divided by the River *Tweed*. On the l. stands a Scottish soldier in Highland dress, in his cap is a thistle His drawn sword is in his r hand, he holds a shield inscribed *Begone Judas*, and a spear to which is attached a Union flag, inscribed, *See Articles Union Claim of Rights Protestant Succession.* He is saying, *A Protestant Church & King I'll defend* and *For shame Brother John arise.* Above his head is a symbolical figure inscribed *The Church as in Rev. XII*: a winged woman appearing from behind a sun sending out rays, beneath her feet is a crescent moon in which is a profile head. Two other figures stand on the Scottish side of the river: a man wearing a long gown and bands holds out a document inscribed *Popesh Bill*, he says, *It's quite harmless now Sawney* A 'popish' bishop wearing a mitre surmounted by a cross stands behind him, slipping into his hand a money-bag inscribed *140,000*, and saying *No Faith keep' with Heritiek.* A mountainous horizon indicates Scotland.

On the other side of the Tweed (r.) the forces of Rome are triumphant. *J^n Bull* lies prostrate on his back, his hands shackled; a seven-headed monster on which rides a woman holding out a chalice tramples on him. John Bull is saying, *Take care brother Sawney he took the advantage of me.* The seven heads of the 'Beast of Rome' are saying, *Fetter Sawney; Fire & Faggot; Burn your Bibles; We sit in the Place of God; To give pardon for broken Oaths; Monks Friar^s Jesuits fill the land*, and (this head turning towards the woman on the monster's back), *Madam Sawney has taken the Alarm.* The woman, who is the 'Whore of Babylon', is dressed in the fashion of the day to represent a courtesan, she says, *Lead on my Lord*; by her chalice is engraved, *Purgatory; works of Supererogation; Transubstantiation; Indulgencies* A man wearing a ribbon and star holds the beast by a scarf round its neck; in his r. hand he holds out towards Sawney a pair of shackles like those worn by John Bull. He tramples on a tattered flag inscribed *Union* which lies on the ground, its staff beneath John. He is saying, *That hot headed Scot will spoil my Plot*

Behind kneels the Pope, in profile to the r., wearing his triple crown, keys and a cross hang from his girdle He says *I absolve The [sic] from the breach of thy Oath*, showing that the man holding the Beast is the king, the words being an allusion to his coronation oath, of which so much was to be heard in relation to Catholic Relief [1] A flying demon points down at the king, over whose head he holds a crown, saying *Haman was but a Fool to Him.*

---

[1] Cf *An Heroic Epistle to an Unfortunate Monarch*, 1779 (an imitation of Mason), ll. 195–8.

> Proceed, great Sir! and, breaking all restraint,
> Embrace the *scarlet whore*, and be a *Saint.*
> *Sworn* to maintain th' *establish'd Church* advance
> The cross of Rome, the miracles of France . .

The proposal to pass a Bill to extend the provisions of the Catholic Relief Act of May 1778 to Scotland led to organized and violent rioting in Edinburgh, 1 Feb., and in Glasgow on 3 Feb. 1779, see Nos 5548[9], 5643. The rioters were pacified by a proclamation from the Provost and magistrates that the obnoxious Bill was 'totally laid aside' *London Chronicle*, 6–9 Feb. 1779.

One of a number of satires, directed against the Catholic Relief Act, which accompanied the active propagandist efforts of the Protestant Association in pamphlets and in the newspapers, see Nos. 5489, 5548, 5643, 5669, 5670, 5671, 5672, 5679, 5680, 5681, 5694, 5702, 5840, 5841 Cf. also Nos 5633, 5638, 5649, 5667 John Bull is invited to imitate Sawney and obtain the withdrawal of Catholic Relief by direct action, cf. also No 5540. The 'Beast' and the 'Whore' are in the tradition of a long series of No-Popery satires founded on the curious interpretation of *Revelation*, xvii. 1–6, see, e g, No 378 (1643), 5702, 5712, and cf Blake's water-colour of the Whore of Babylon, 1809, in the Print Department (reproduced, Figgis).
$6\frac{1}{4} \times 12\frac{1}{4}$ in.

5535 THE SINKING FUND.

London. Publish'd as the Act directs 9th April 1779 by Robert Wilkinson, at No 58 in Cornhill.

Engraving The interior of a pawnbroker's shop. Behind a counter (l.) an old man wearing a cap and spectacles is bargaining with a customer over a watch On the wall above his head is inscribed *Money lent by Judas Gripe.* The customer, a well-dressed man, leans on the counter. Next him is a young woman holding a garment which she intends to pawn Behind her a man standing on tip-toe reaches over her head to offer the pawnbroker a wig An elderly and ragged woman is counting the coins she has received. A man (r.) in profile to the r. has just taken the buckles off his shoes, his l. foot raised on a stool. Behind the figures and against the wall at r. angles to the counter is a large cupboard, the upper part fronted with panes of glass; behind this are many pawned articles including a number of watches, books, a violin, a sword, jugs, bowls, a barber's bowl, a hat. Inside the counter, which is hollow, are rolls of material.

A satire on the poverty and distress caused by the war and taxation, cf. No. 5548 [12].
$8\frac{1}{2} \times 11\frac{1}{2}$ in.

5536 A FRONTISPEICE TO ADMIRAL KEPPELS TRYAL

Drawn by Capn Bailly of the Porcupine Engraved by Christian Vincent.

Portsmouth Publish'd April 12 1779 & Sold at the Printing Office N. 3 Walker Court Berwick Street Soho London.

Engraving Six medallions arranged in three pairs

[1] (l.) The figure of Fame blowing her trumpet and holding out a laurel wreath; she flies over a number of ships in full sail. Round the medallion is inscribed *Great is the Truth and it shall prevail* Beneath the design, *Admiral Keppel Honorably Aquited From A False and Malicious Accusation By A Court Martial And His Claim To Victory Established Feby 11th MDCCCIX* [sic].

[2.] (r.) A winged female figure holds a wreath over a bust portrait of

Keppel. An Ensign flag inscribed *Vice of the Blue* is held downwards concealing her feet. Round the medallion is inscribed *Hon. Augustus Keppel* Beneath the design is etched

> *See Victory is Not Compleat*
> *The Vice has Crippled Both her Feet.*

[3] (l) A thin man in the dress of a naval officer holds out his hand as if confirming an assertion, round his neck is slung a large book inscribed *Log*. Round the medallion is *Sir H——s [Hugh's] Privy Councillor*, beneath the design is '*Be So Good To Explain What you Mean By A Rumour You Never Heard Off*'. *P 47*

Beneath this medallion is etched, within a border.

> *Pox On This Log Tis Such a Clog*
> *On A Free Swearer's Conscience*
> *Twill Make him Stare Swear and Forswear*
> *And Spout Ridiculous Nonsense*

[4.] (r) Another thin naval officer holding out a broken sword (?) in his r hand; in his l are pages of a book, inscribed *Log Book* Behind him the buildings of a town are faintly indicated, inscribed *Coventry*. Round the medallion is *Sir H—— Himself* Under the design is, '*We Only Waited Sir Hugh Pallisers Coming-Down to Re-Attack The French*' *p. 142*

Beneath the medallion is etched, within a border

> *With Marling Spike I Knot and Splice*
> *With Log Book Vampt Up Wondrous Nice*
> *With H——ds [Hoods] Orations And Advice*
> *Keppel Die And Triumph Vice*

[5] (l.) A naval officer is violently kicking a book inscribed *Log Book Formidable*; three leaves have fallen from it. Round the medallion is *I Hold A Ships Log Book Sacred* and *They Kick Them About the Orlop* Beneath the design is inscribed '*How Came Those Three Leaves Cut Out of This Book From the xxv To The xxviii*'. *Page. 70.*

[6] (r) A naval officer standing between two chairs He leans on the back of one (l) inscribed *Formidable*; his l hand is on his forehead as if perplexed The other chair (r) is inscribed *Fox*. Round the medallion is *Fox Cheerd The Formidable First* Beneath the design is '*Being On The Forecastle Can You Say There Was No Cheer From The Poop or Quarter Deck of The Formidable*' *p. 78.*

This illustrates the proceedings at the court martial (7 Jan –11 Feb 1779) on Keppel for the action off Ushant, 27 July 1778, on the application of Sir Hugh Palliser, his Vice-Admiral, here accused of preventing Keppel from achieving a complete victory. The quotations (not always textually accurate) are taken from the folio *Proceedings at Large of the Court-Martial . . .* published by Almon. In No 3 Palliser's 'Privy Councillor' is Captain Alexander Hood, captain of the *Robuste*, in whose Log Book alterations had been made after it was known that it would be produced at the court martial 'The Rumour' in question was that Keppel was to be tried. No. 4 relates to Rear-admiral Campbell's evidence on the failure of Palliser to obey the signal, so preventing any further attack on the French No. 5 relates to the evidence that three leaves for the days between 25 and 28 July were cut out of the Log Book of the *Formidable*, Palliser's ship, Bazely, the captain on the *Formidable*, being asked to explain, answered 'I do not know, so help me God— I hold a ship's log book sacred', adding that 'they kick them [a ship's rough log book] about the orlop'. No. 6 relates to evidence on communications between the *Fox* frigate and the *Formidable*.

The result of the court martial was a triumph for Keppel, the charge against him being pronounced 'malicious and ill-founded', and in popular opinion was a virtual conviction of Palliser, whose conduct was believed to be due to the influence of Sandwich The London mob attacked the Admiralty, burnt Palliser in effigy and gutted his house.

The artist's name is perhaps an allusion to Captain Baillie of Greenwich Hospital and his exposure of Sandwich, see No 5548 [4], [5]. He can hardly be Captain William Baillie, the well-known amateur engraver. The *Porcupine* appears in the Navy List of 1779 as a 16-gun sloop commanded by Captain Finch; in 1780 as a 6th rate (24 guns) commanded by the Hon. H S Conway.

The size of the plate and the page-references suggest that it was designed for Almon's *Trial* (B M L , 1890, d 13). For the battle see Nos 5484, 5486, 5626; for the court martial see T. Hutchinson, *Diary and Letters*, ii, 1886, pp. 242-3, 299; Walpole, *Letters*, x, pp 350, 352, 359, 360, 362, 366, 377–83, 385–7, and Nos 5537, 5538, 5548 [3], and for the blame incurred by Keppel Nos 5570, 5626, 5650, 5658, 5992, &c. See also Mason's *Ode to the Naval Officers of Great Britain*, 1779. For the use of the log-book incident for electioneering see No 5998 Cf also No 5999

14×8 in , medallions, 3⅝ in. diam

5537 [THE FATE OF PALLISER AND SANDWICH]   [1779]

Engraving Title apparently cut off A ship's-boat (c.) rowed by three sailors, they look exultingly at a gallows (r) from which hang Sir Hugh Palliser and Sandwich. The coxswain and the man in the bows wave their hats The boat flies a flag inscribed *Keppel for Ever*, surrounded by the words, *mergas profundo pulchrior evenit* From the sea rises a Triton (l) wearing a wreath, blowing his horn, and pointing to the gallows This is in the form of a cross, from the l end of the cross-piece, inscribed *S^r H Kn^t*, Palliser hangs by a chain; from his shackled ankles hangs his *Log Book*; from his neck hang labels inscribed, *5 Lies* (an allusion to his five charges against Keppel) and *Formidable* (the name of his ship). An arrow pierces him inscribed, *Honours tendrest part* From the r. arm of the cross, inscribed *Twitcher*, hangs Sandwich, his shackled ankles are weighted by a book or block inscribed £400,000 *Sunk* A label inscribed *Essay on Woman* is attached to his shoulders, a wine-glass appears to be stuck into the lapel of his coat, a cross hangs from a girdle round his waist, probably an allusion to the orgies of the brotherhood of Medmenham Abbey. A cross-piece on the top of the gallows is inscribed, *Exitus acta probat*, at the bottom is the date *1779*. At its foot, under Sandwich, sits a courtesan holding a handkerchief to her eyes, above her is written *Alass poor Kitty*.

Above the boat, Lord North sits on a pile of clouds, holding in one hand his eye-glass, in the other a large book, *the Art of Financing*. The devil behind him, pointing to the gallows, says in his ear *The Gibbet has got their Bodies my Boy their Hearts & Souls are mine*.

Beneath the design is engraved:

> *They reign'd a while but 'twas not long*
> *Before from world to world they swung*

As they had turn'd from side to side
And as the Villains liv'd they dy'd
Hudibras

Keppel's court martial, see No 5536, showed that in the action off Ushant, 27 July 1778, Palliser, his Vice-Admiral, had not obeyed Keppel's signal and that the log-book of his ship, the *Formidable*, had been altered. It was supposed that the political antagonism of Sandwich to Keppel was responsible for Palliser's inactivity. Palliser was tried by court martial, 12 Apr.–5 May 1779, and acquitted, though found 'reprehensible in not having acquainted the Admiral . . of his distress . . .'. Sandwich's great unpopularity dated from the part taken by him in producing a copy of the *Essay on Woman* to furnish ground for action against Wilkes in the House of Lords; see No. 4066, &c. It was given fresh impetus by the court martial on Keppel For Palliser see also No. 5705. For North's financial difficulties and expedients see Nos. 5243, 5541, 5542, 5543, 5548 [1], 5578, 5703, 5964, &c.

$4\frac{7}{8} \times 3\frac{1}{4}$ in.

5538 SAUNDERS' GHOST   [c. 1779]

Engraving, beneath which verses are printed in two columns Sir Hugh Palliser (r) sits at a round table; a horned demon with its arm round his neck holds up a large scroll inscribed *Five Charges against Keppel* On each side of him sits a man or demon paying out money on to the table · one is clothed in drapery covered with *fleur-de-lys* to imply that Palliser was in the pay of France at the Battle of Ushant On the l Britannia points out the scene to a companion who holds up his hands in horror He wears a ribbon on which is inscribed, *Sir Cha. Saund* She says to him, *Was it for this you gave 5000£*, alluding to a legacy of £5,000 left by Saunders (d. 1775) to Keppel The verses *Saunders Ghost, A Song to the Tune of "Welcome, Welcome, brother Debtor"* are an imitation of Glover's 'Admiral Hosier's Ghost'. They begin,

> "Haste thee! Saunders, England calls thee,
> "Awhile these blest abodes resign,
> "Treach'rous friends and foes conspiring
> "Threat my darling son and thine.

That is, threaten Keppel, at this time very popular owing to the court martial on charges made by Palliser who was regarded as the tool of Sandwich. See Nos 5536, 5537.

$4\frac{5}{8} \times 7\frac{3}{4}$ in. (pl) Broadside, $12\frac{1}{2} \times 8$ in.

5539 SAWNEY IN THE BOG-HOUSE

Publish'd 4th June 1779 by Mrs Holt No 111 Oxford Street London.

Engraving. (Coloured and uncoloured impressions) A satire on the Scots; an imitation but not a copy of the satire with the same title, No. 2678, c. 1745, repeated in 1762, see No 3988, which according to Angelo was by George Bickham. A Scot in Highland dress and wearing a feathered cap is seated in a latrine, his legs thrust down two holes in the board. He grasps in his l hand a rolled document inscribed *Act for [esta]blishing Popery*. Behind him a stone wall is indicated on which is etched (l) a thistle growing out of a reversed crown, inscribed *Nemo me impune lacessit* On the r and over Sawney's head is engraved

> *'Tis a bra' bonny seat, o' my saul, Sawney cries,*
> *I never beheld sic before with me Eyes,*
> *Such a place in aw' Scotland I never could meet,*
> *For the High and the Low ease themselves in the Street.*

The thistle and the crown express the common accusation that the Scots were Jacobites. The 'Act for establishing Popery' is the Catholic Relief Act, against which there were deliberately instigated and serious riots in Edinburgh and Glasgow in Feb. 1779, see Nos. 5534, 5548, 5678.

$12\frac{1}{2} \times 9$ in

5540 THE BIRTH-DAY ODE *   [c June 1779]

As it was performed before his M——, on the 4ᵗʰ of June, By the Royal Band.

Engraving on a printed broadside. Three musicians and four vocalists perform the 'Birth-Day Ode'. The musicians read from a large book open on a table on the r., the score on the r. page; on the l., *the Distresses of the Nation an Ode performd in honour of his Majesty's Birth Day* The centre figure, seated, plays with great vigour on a pair of kettle-drums; at his feet is a paper, inscribed *To the Blessed Memory of Miss Ray*. On his r. stands a violinist, Lord North; behind Sandwich is a flute-player, Lord George Germain, Secretary of State for the Colonies. Behind (l.) four men sing from a book which they hold open, the most prominent are a bishop (l.) holding a crozier, wearing on a medallion the arms of the City of London; and the singer on his r who wears a furred civic gown, bands, and tie-wig Beneath the design is etched *First Viol: by Lᵈ N[orth] Hautboy Lᵈ. G. G[ermain] Kettle Drum Lᵈ S[andwich] the Vocal parts by the Bᵖ of L[ondon] & Lᵈ M[ayor] &c. &c.*

Beneath the plate is printed the *Birth Day Ode* in two columns

I STROPHE

Now Caesar sits on Throne sublime
To snuff the Laureat's drousy Rhime
And take his annual Sleep in state,
To please the Slaves that round him wait;
Swift from the starry Courts above,
Descend some Dream, (for Dreams descend from Jove)
And to the Monarch's mental Ear
The wonders of his Reign declare
While a grateful People's Voice,
Shall in choral Peals rejoice,
And to the Nations round proclaim,
Caesar, Virtue, and Wisdom are the same

.   .   .   .   .

---

* 'As several spurious copies of the Birth-Day Ode have made their appearance in the News-papers, that the Public may be no longer deceived, they are here presented with the genuine Ode, as it was actually performed on the 4ᵗʰ of June' [Original note]

A bitterly ironical account of the achievements of the reign follows:

I. ANTISTROPHE

And hark, the spectre speaks! — G——e
Attend, and N——h, and all your pliant Train,

        .   .   .   .

To YOU *her Blessings Britain owes*
And yours the high Applause approving Heaven bestows

I EPODE

Hark, he sings the Caribb-War!
Brightest ray of Britain's Fame!

        .   .   .   .

II. STROPHE

'*Beyond the vast Atlantic Main*
'*What Myriads bless thy gracious Reign;*
'*To Jove their Prayers ascend, for thee,*
'*The Father of their Liberty!*
'*For thee their Prayers .   Ah! why that Groan?*
'*Why trembles mighty* CAESAR *on his throne?*'

        .   .   .   .

III ANTISTROPHE

'*Hibernia, Britain's Sister-Isle,*
'*With equal Freedom soon shall smile;*
'*Taught by thy prudent Sway to know*
'*No Blessing rivals thee below.—*
'*And lo! (their worth in Luxury drown'd)*
'*While Caledonia's Chieftains kiss the Ground,*
'*Her humble Sons, an untam'd Race,*
'*Instinctive feel the Fire of Grace,*

        .   .   .   .

II EPODE

'*Gallia, hide thy recreant Head,*
'*Vain thy Arms, thy Craft as vain,*
'*Spight of the Snares, by treachery spread,*
'*Britain preseves [sic] her Empire o'er the Main!*
'*But ah how long!—in aweful Gloom*
'*The Fates involve Britannia's Doom—*
'*Yet, ye who Courted* CAESAR, *hear!*
'*Perchance the Hour is nigh——Pursue*
'*Your Schemes, perchance 'tis fix'd that you*
'*The glorious wreath shall wear.*
'*His worth's the same in Jove's impartial Eyes,*
'*Who saves a sinking Empire or destroys* '

FULL CHORUS

Yes——we will our Schemes pursue,
We will the Wreath of Glory wear;
His Worth's the same in Jove's impartial Eyes,
Who saves a sinking Empire, or destroys

The date is probably that of the king's birthday (4 June 1779). it is evidently after the assassination of Martha Ray, Lord Sandwich's mistress, on 7 Apr 1779, and probably before the rupture of relations with Spain on 16 June 1779 Lord Sandwich appears to have been a performer on the kettle-drums, *Town and Country Magazine*, xv 9 The Lord Mayor, 1778–9, was Samuel Plumbe, very unpopular in the City as a Ministerialist, and reputed a miser, see No 5617 Lowth, the Bishop of London, though a Privy Councillor, was not an active politician, but the bench of bishops was unpopular for its attitude to America, cf Nos 5492, 5553 The 'Caribb War' was an expedition against the Caribs of St Vincent in 1772 which was denounced by the Opposition on 10, 12, and 15 Feb 1773 as 'the extravagance of despatching 2,500 against 700 poor savages' (Walpole, *Last Journals*, 1910, i 173–5). See also *Parl Hist* xviii. 722 ff B Edwards, *History of the West Indies*, 1793, i 402–3 Cf No 5675 The No-Popery riots in Scotland, Feb 1779, by Caledonia's 'humbler sons' are approved, as in No. 5534, &c The drawing is good, and resembles that of Nos. 5573, 5577.

$5\frac{15}{16} \times 7\frac{7}{8}$ in. Broadside, $17\frac{1}{2} \times 10\frac{5}{8}$ in.

5541 BRITAIN'S STATE PILOT FOUNDERING ON TAXATION ROCK.

Stuart pinx^t Yanky fec^t

Published according to act of Parliament. June 23^d 1779, for J. Almon, in Piccadilly, London.

Engraving. A bear, with the face, ribbon, and star of Lord North, negligently holds the tiller of a boat which is foundering and driving upon rocks (r). On the stern is a picture of Britannia seated with her spear and shield. On the top of the mast is a large thistle which is the centre of a broad streak of lightning and a black cloud, the sail is being blown from the boat From the shore (l) two figures point with scorn at the wreck Spain wearing a cloak and ruff, and with the face of some bird, and France, dressed in the French fashion with feathered hat and bag-wig, and with the legs and feet of an ape On the edge of the water squats a large frog smoking a long pipe.

Beneath the design is engraved, in continuation of the title, *To the great Amusement of Lewis Baboon, Don Strut, & Nic Frog*

These names for France, Spain, and Holland are taken from Arbuthnot's celebrated pamphlet, *Law is a Bottomless Pit, or the History of John Bull*, 1712. A printed sheet pasted on the back of the print explains 'The hint of this print was borrowed from Gay's Fable of the Bear in a Boat' The fable is printed at length North is thus 'the self-deemed Machiavel at large' whose conceit and folly bring disaster. The names of the artists and the thistle indicate that disaster was planned by Bute and effected by Americans For attacks on North's budgets see No. 5537, &c One of many representations of the United Provinces as an unfriendly and complacent neutral, see No 5557, &c.

$9\frac{1}{16} \times 12\frac{1}{2}$ in.

5542 AN HIROGLYPHIC [*sic*] EPISTLE FROM THE (DEVIL) TO LORD N . . TH. [23 June 1779]

Dublin printed for Willm Allen N° 88 Dame Street

A rebus, an engraved text in which words are represented by small etched objects The letter is headed by etchings of the devil (1), one of whose legs is a three-pronged fork, addressing an oval bust portrait of Lord North, headed *Lord N . . . . TH* The words enclosed in brackets are those which are represented by objects

My D(ear) *Ld*

(Ewer) *Pol——cal Con*(duck)*t h*(ass) (knot) *only made a* (grate) *Noise upon* (ear)*th* (butt) *has set* (awl) *Hell in an upr*(oar). *T*(hare)*s hardly a S*(tête)(man) *in the* (plaice), *and we have a good* (man)*y of them, but* (looks) *upon it* (ass) *uni*(form) *The o*(pen)*ing of* (ewer) (last) *Budget w*(ass) *in m*(eye) *o*(pinion) *a* (mast)*erstroke indeed* (witch) (yew) *may easily* (mask) *over with the Old Phrase Pro Bono Publico No* (body) (can) *stig*(mat)*ize* (ewer) *L——d*(ship) *as a griping* (minister) *nor* (can) *any* (1) *say* (yew)*ve in this Point laid a t*(axe) *on the Bowels of the Poor T*(hare) *are sever*(awl) *Articles m*(eye) *L—d in the Way of Eating* (witch) *might illustrate* (ewer) *Good Will* (toe) *the public, the quant*(eye)*ty of Meat* (witch) *is Consumed by the Common* (people) *Is the Occasion of t*(hat) *scorbutic or Scurvy Di*(sword)*er* (witch) *affects the English Constitution T*(hare)(4) *an Xcise laid upon flesh of* (awl) *sorts would* (bee) *the best* (ant)*iscorbutic in the Whole Materia Medica and* (ass) (ewer) *L—d*(ship) *is* (knot) *very* (car)*nally Inclined* (Eye) (don)*t doubt* (butt) (yew) *will shortly b*(ring) *such a* (bill) *in*(toe) *Parlia*(men)*t* (Fish) *and F*(owl) (2) *my L—d are of a very viscid Nat*(ewer) *and are apt to enrich the Blood of such* (ass) *ought* (toe) (bee) *kept low, a T*(axe) *on these Sorts of Food Would in* (Time) *p*(rope)*rly dilute & thin the Corpore*(awl) (deuce)*s* [juices] *and the Common* (people) *would* (knot) *t*(hen) (bee) (awl) (toe) (gate) (hare) [altogether] *so* (saw)*cy* (ass) (toe) *oppose the Measures of t*(hare) (ministers) *and per*(suns) *in power* (awl)*so a Smart dut*(eye) *on Bread* (mill)*k Sm*(awl) *Beer,* (Water) *&c. For wh*(eye) *should the Vulgar have any Thing* (toe) *Eat* (butt) *Grass Without paying Tri*(boot).

(Ewer) *Constant Friend & Ally*

BELZEBUB.

Pandemonim [*sic*] *June 23th 1779.*

This is interesting as a direct appeal to the poorer classes in Dublin, cf No 5572. It has no relation to facts · in making a surcharge of 5 per cent. on the excise North exempted beer, soap, candles, and leather, in the interests of the poorer consumers. *Parl. Hist.* xx 166, 1 Mar 1779. Attacks on budgets in English prints, however exaggerated, have always some foundation

See the answer, No 5543.

14 ¹⁄₁₆ × 10 ⅝ in (pl).

5543 AN HIEROGLYPHIC EPISTLE FROM L——D N——H TO (THE DEVIL) IN ANSWER TO THAT FROM PANDEMONIUM. [9 July 1779]

Dublin printed by W Allen Dame Street

A rebus, an engraved text in which words are represented by small etched objects The letter is headed by etchings of Lord North and the Devil as in No 5542, to which this is the answer, but reversed The Devil holds a letter.

(Grate), *Po*(tent) *and Respec*(table) (Monarch),

(Ewer) *H*(eye)*nesis's* [*sic*] *E*(pistol) *came Safe* (toe) (hand), (eye) *Have S*(hew)*n it* (toe) (awl) *m*(eye) *Friends on* (ear)*th, w*(hoe) (R) *glad* (toe) (hare) *t*(hat) *T*(hare) *Is so good an Under*(stand)*ing* (bee)*tween us, & t*(hat) (eye) *am* (lick)*ely* (toe) (bee) (ass) (grate) *a* (favour)*ite* (bee)*low* (ass) (eye) *am* (hare), *you* (C), (grate) *Mon*(ark), (Eye) *am so* (well) *v*(ears)d [versed] *in the* (R)*ts of In*(C)n(yew)*a*(tie)*on* [insinuation] *and* (diss?)*im*(yew)*la*(tie)*on*. *t*(hat) (eye) (can) *De*(sieve) *any* (man) (eye) (hope) (eye) *may* (bee) *a*(bell) (toe) *p*(rock)(ewer) [procure] (posts) *and* (plaices) *in* (ewer) (inn)*fern*(awl) (cow)*it for my faithfull F*(rein)*ds w*(hoe) *have So* (M)(eye)*nently Distin-quish t*(hare)*selves b*(eye) *t*(hare) *attach*(men)*t* (toe) *t*(hare) (King), *witness My d*(eye)*abo*(lick)(awl) *F*(rein)*d, S*ʳ *H*(yew) [Palliser], *w*(hoe) *has act*(yew) (awl)*ly* (sole)(lick)*cited* [solicited] *me* (awl) *Ready for t*(hat) *purpose, and* (eye) (can) (ass)(ewer) [assure] (yew) *t*(hat) *he h*(ass) (talons) [talents] (toe) *XEQ*ᵗᵉ *any Of* (ewer) *H*(eye)*ness Most Hellish* (Comma)*nds, He h*(ass) *gulld the Malcon*(tents) *by a pre*(ten)*ded Try*(awl), (Eye) *am proud* (yew) *apiove of my T*(axe)*s,* (Witch) (eye) (hope) *will shortly re*(deuce) *the* (people) *in 2* (toe)*t*(awl) [total] *Subjec*(tie)*on, & we Sh*(awl) (C) *the Day w*(hen) *the Freeborn English*(men) *sh*(awl) (knot) *dare* (toe) *rep*(eye)ne, *butt Groan in Secret* (bee)*neath the G*(awl)*ing halter*

(Eye) *have the Honour* (toe) (bee), (ewer) *most Devoted Serv*(ant)

London July 9 1779.

A reduced copy of the bust portrait of North in the heading follows the signature

For Palliser see Nos. 5536-8.

14¼ × 10⅞ in. (pl.).

5544 THE PATRIOT.   [? before 10 July 1779]

Mezzotint. Bust portrait of George III looking in profile to the r He wears a turban decorated with a jewelled crescent and aigrette, a furred robe over an embroidered tunic The dress and the ironical title are intended to show that the king is acting the part of an oriental tyrant The sign of the Turk's Head in No 5645 is taken from this design Compare also the allusion in No 5574, to 'Sultan ——' who is bringing ruin on the nation, and see also Nos. 5549, 5635. Perhaps a copy of No. 5545 or No. 5546.

5½ × 4½ in

5545 ECCE HOMO.

Mezzotint. Copy (?) of No. 5544

5½ × 4½ in.

5546 BEHOLD THE MAN

London *Printed & Publish'd as the Act directs, 10 Nov*ʳ *1779*

Mezzotint. (Coloured impression.) Copy (?) of No. 5544 See *B M Cat. Br. Engraved Portraits*

Chaloner Smith, iv, p 1757, mentions an impression of this or No. 5547 in the catalogue of Laurie and Whittle.

5⅞ × 4 in

5547 BEHOLD THE MAN [2]

Pub^d as the Act directs July 10th 1779. by I. Hawkins Strand, London.
Mezzotint   Copy (in reverse) of No. 5544 or 5545. An etching copied
from this was published in 1784 in the *Intrepid Magazine*
$5\frac{5}{8} \times 3\frac{11}{16}$ in.

5548 THE POLITICAL RAREE-SHOW: OR A PICTURE OF
   PARTIES AND POLITICS, DURING AND AT THE CLOSE OF
   THE LAST SESSION OF PARLIAMENT. JUNE 1779.

For the Westminster Magazine. June 1779

Published 1st of July 1779 by Fielding & Walker, Pater-Noster-Row
Engraving   From the *Westminster Magazine*, vii. 282 (folding plate)
Twelve views seen in a peep-show, the views being arranged in four rows;
the outside of the box or booth is seen on the l , a boy looks through a
round hole, the showman points, saying to him, *There you shall see*   His
words are given at length in the accompanying text.

[1] *The Distressed Financier.*

   Lord North, seated at a round table, on which are books, papers, and
money-bags, turns to look through his glass at three men (l.), whose
beards, noses, and long coats show that they are Jews. One holds an
empty money-bag, another, whose coat is ragged, holds out a document.
A clerk or secretary at North's elbow tries to draw his attention to a
figure (r) offering a money-bag, who is bearded like a Jew, but has a long
snout and the legs and horns of a goat or satyr. Papers on the table are
inscribed *Spanish Manifesto* and *Ways and Means 1780*   The Raree-Show-
man (in the accompanying text) says '. . . Vat is most curious, is, dat my
Lord Slumber is broad awake, and dat he is already contriving an excuse
for borrowing de moneys at ten per cent'   Cf Walpole, *Last Journals*,
1910, ii. 244, who says that 8 per cent was demanded. For the Spanish
Manifesto, presented by the Spanish Ambassador 16 June 1779, declaring
that Spain had taken the part of France, see *Ann Reg* 1779, pp 162-4,
359   This was followed by a declaration of the king of Spain, published
at Madrid, on 28 June, ibid , 367-86

[2] *The Generals in America doing nothing, or worse than nothing*

   A man asleep in a chair in front of an open tent (r), one foot is on a table
on which are playing-cards and a punch-bowl. On the ground are wine
bottles and a paper *To Sir Wm Howe.* Behind (l.), English soldiers, their
arms thrown down, are kneeling to American soldiers in close rank, whose
commander holds the striped American flag. Burgoyne, the English
general, kneels, holding down the British flag. On the horizon is a line
of huts or tents, inscribed *Saratoga Camp*   See for Howe, No 5405, &c ,
for Saratoga, Nos 5469, 5470, 5857.

[3] *Proving that they have done every thing.*

   The interior of the House of Commons; the Speaker in his chair,
behind a table; members on either side of it, some rising to speak   Lord
North (r.) with his arms folded, appears asleep   Behind him a member
says *The Southern Expedition is*   \member holds out a paper inscribed

Admir^ls Trials at Portsmouth. Sir Hugh Palliser having demanded a court martial on Keppel, see No. 5536, &c., on Keppel's acquittal, resigned his offices and his seat in Parliament, and demanded to be tried himself, his court martial taking place at Portsmouth on 12 Apr. and following days. A member in a military coat and pigtail queue holds out a paper *I move an Enquiry into* This is evidently Sir William Howe, who demanded and obtained a committee of the whole House to inquire into the conduct of the war, undertaking to prove (22 Apr.) that 'he had not been deficient in consultation or execution . . .' *London Chronicle*, 22–4 Apr. 1779 *Parl. Hist* xx. 675 ff. A member wearing a plumed helmet is saying, *Justice! Justice Ld. G. G——e* [Germain] *is* ——. Burgoyne defended himself in Parliament against the attacks made on him, accusing Germain of failing to support him. See *London Chronicle*, 20–2 May 1779, and *Detail and Conduct of the American War* . . 1780. B M.L , 1447. d 23. The plumed helmet appears to be intended to indicate Burgoyne's theatrical character and pompous proclamations, see No. 5470.

[4] *Jemmy Twitcher Overseer of ye Poor of Greenwich.*

Lord Sandwich (l), holding up a cane in one hand, faces a deputation of Greenwich pensioners, most of whom are maimed, some being supported on crutches. Their leader, hat in hand, offers Sandwich a paper inscribed *To restore Capt Bailley*; another says, *My Shirts are too Short*; a third, wearing his hat, says *D——n your Beef and Beer* Behind them is the river, on its farther bank Greenwich Hospital is in flames. A man-of-war without sails is seen behind Sandwich

The showman explains that Jemmy Twitcher is 'beating dem for complaining', while a ship is in the river instead of at sea *Westminster Mag*, loc. cit. Captain Thomas Baillie, Lieutenant-Governor of Greenwich Hospital, was dismissed by Sandwich for publishing in March 1778 *The Case of the Royal Hospital for Seamen at Greenwich*, showing great abuses in its administration and management, and implicating Sandwich directly and indirectly. Part of the Hospital was destroyed by fire on 2 Jan 1779.

[5] *The Duke of Richmond turned Linen-Draper*

The duke, a yard-measure in his hand, is measuring a sheet or cloth, held out for him by an assistant. Two men, one wearing the ribbon of an order, watch him, seated on a bench (l) A man (r) holds up a shirt, looking at Sandwich, who clasps his hands in dismay

This represents the attempts of Richmond in the House of Lords (16 Feb –7 June) to secure redress for Captain Baillie, maintaining that his allegations had been established (Baillie, at the instigation of Sandwich, had been sued for libel by officers of the Hospital, but had won his case) It had been established (*inter alia*) that 'the pensioners had been exceedingly defrauded in the length of their shirts' and in 'the quantity of their sheets'. (Richmond in the House of Lords, 7 June 1779) *London Chronicle*, 5–9 June 1779 See also *Ann Reg* 1779, pp. 159–61. *Parl Hist*. xx. 475 ff.

[6] *The Opposition Pudding-makers.*

A number of men are engaged in stirring the contents of a large dish on a table One empties into it the contents of a keg, two stand over it, each holding a spoon, another (r) advances with a large sack on his shoulders, another (l) brings a basket of flowers. Two others, one with a ribbon and star, watch the proceedings. There, says the showman, are 'Mr Burke wid the flowers of oratory, and de Millers Rockingham, Shelburne, &c wid de flour to make de pudding'.

[7] *Cha Ja Tod abusing yᵉ national Gamblers.*

Four men seated at a gaming-table. The most prominent is Fox (l.) with a fox's head; he holds a dice-box in his r. hand, under his arm is a paper inscribed *Resolves agaiˢᵗ Ld North*, from his pocket protrude papers inscribed, *Speech agaᵗ Sʳ H Palliser* and *Motions agˢᵗ Lord Sandwich*. The showman says 'Dere you see Cha Ja Tod abusing de national Gamblers, and dere you see him all night at de gaming-table'. *Westminster Mag*, loc cit. On 19 Feb 1779 Fox moved the dismissal of Palliser from the Navy and on 19 Apr. the removal of Lord Sandwich from the Admiralty. *Parl Hist.* xx, pp. 144 ff., 372 ff

[8] *The Jerseymen treating yᵉ French with Gunpowder tea.*

Three ships flying the French flag are sailing away from a fort (l.), flying the Union flag, from which guns are being fired. A number of ship's boats are attempting to regain the ships, some are foundering. On the horizon are five ships in full sail.

Jersey was attacked on 1 May 1779 by a small French expedition; an attempted landing was beaten off by the troops on the island and the Jersey militia. *London Gazette*, 4–8 May; Walpole, *Letters*, x. 407–8, 412.

[9] *The Scotch Presbyterians pulling down the Papists Houses.*

Three men, wearing flat Scots caps, attack a house (r.) with pick-axe, fire-brand, &c. On the l. is a bonfire by which are a book, a crucifix, medals; men and women crowd round it to throw their booty on the flames; one man holds a cloth or curtain, another a figure of the Virgin.

This represents with considerable accuracy the No-Popery riots in Scotland in Feb. 1779. See No 5534

[10] *The English Papists laughing at yᵉ Protestants.*

Four priests and two monks seated and standing round a circular table. A priest holds a document, *Plan for a Cathedral Sch. at Wolverhampton*; another says *We will make them good Catholics.*

The Catholic Relief Act of May 1778 had been passed without opposition and almost without notice, but a proposal to extend its provisions to Scotland provoked riots and was followed by a progressively increasing No-Popery propaganda which led to the Gordon Riots, see No. 5534, &c

[11] *A Picture of Irish Resolution.*

Hibernia lies on the ground (l.), as if fainting, her harp beside her; she is supported by two men. Two others stand behind, one of whom, wearing the ribbon of an order, says, *No Manufacture will I wear, but those of Ireland.* Beside Hibernia is a low table on which is spread out a large document: *Resolution of Citizens of Dublin not to wear English Manufacture.* Two men stand over it holding pens, one says, *Tho' we differ in religion, we will unite for our Country.* The other answers, *In that we all Solemnly agree.* On the farther side of a river (r.) is *Dublin*, church towers and buildings surrounded by trees. The showman says, 'de Irish resolving not to trade wid de English, while de English have resolved not to let de Irish have any trade at all'. *West. Mag*, loc. cit.

A great meeting at Dublin in April 1779 adopted a non-importation resolution, pledging all present to abstain from buying British goods which could be made in Ireland; all Ireland followed Dublin Cf Walpole, *Letters*, x. 408, 9 May 1779 The measures for removing the restrictions on Irish trade proposed in Parliament were defeated by pressure from English and Scottish industrial and commercial districts. *Ann. Reg.* 1779, pp 123-8 See No 5572

[12] *Inside View of the Long Room at ye Custom House*

Clerks seated at desks in a long room under a row of large sash windows, through which are seen the masts of ships. A woman (r.) lies in a fainting condition against a bale of goods. A man stands behind her clasping his hands in distress and saying *Alas, poor Commerce, she's almost dead* A man standing by, says *Let her die and be d——d, since she can't fill our bellies* One of the clerks, leaning on his desk says *A good Stomach with nothing to eat is very bad.*

The famous 'Long Room' instead of being filled with people doing business is almost empty. Cf the print of the Long Room by Rowlandson and Pugin, in the *Microcosm of London*, 1808, i. 218 Cf. also Nos. 5535, 5574

8 × 13 in.

5549 THE HORSE AMERICA, THROWING HIS MASTER.

[*Pub^d as the Act directs, Aug. 1, 1779 by Wm White, Angel Court, Westminster*].[1]

Engraving A horse snorting violently, its head down and hind legs in the air; his rider, George III, has lost his seat and is about to fall head downwards. In his hand is a scourge to each lash of which is attached either a sword, sabre, bayonet, scalping-knife, or axe; he wears the ribbon and star of the Garter Behind (r), a French officer walks (r to l.) towards the horse, carrying a large *fleur-de-lys* flag over his r. shoulder. Cf. No. 5230, and see Nos 5544-7, 5574

$6\frac{3}{4} \times 10\frac{13}{16}$ in

5550 A BAITE. FOR THE DEVIL

[Macnally?[2]]

Plate 3 of every thing Humorous (Tria Juncta in Uno) Ridiculous, & Satyrical

Pub^d Augt 12th by W Richardson N° 68 High Holborn.

Engraving Three figures, whose necks are tied together by a rope, represent three aspects of Parson Bate, afterwards Bate Dudley He stands full face, in clerical gown and bands, but with the wig of a man of fashion. His r foot stands on a *Holy Bible* which the devil is placing for him, his l is on a box, with a slit for letters inscribed *Morning Post Letter-Box.* On his r leg is a spurred top-boot in the latest fashion, on his l. foot a buckled shoe. He wears a sword and in his belt are two pistols Bate, who stands in profile to the l , wears a legal wig and bands and holds a bundle of papers

---

[1] Written on the print, the margin with the publication line having been cut off.
[2] A pencil note on the print attributes design and verses to Macnally (1752–1820), whose career curiously resembled that of the allegations here made against Bate He was barrister, duellist, editor of the *Public Ledger*, writer of comedies and farces; a professed Irish patriot, but actually in Government pay.

inscribed *Brief*, while in his l. hand is a dice-box On the dice-box are the letters *J* and *H*, perhaps the artist's signature The Bate in profile to the l. wears a feathered cap inscribed *Mor[ning] Pos[t]*, he is blowing a trumpet and holding out a sheaf of the *Morning Pos[t]* for sale.

On the ground at his feet are cards, dice, and papers inscribed, *Rival Candidates, A Comic Opera; Flitch of Bacon, Black a moor wash'd w[hite]* The rope round Bate's three necks appears to be held by the devil who is stooping down to adjust the Bible Beneath the design is engraved ·

> *A Various Compound is this Rev'rend Divine.*
> *In Speaking a Pedant, with Satire Malign*
> *A Canonical Buck, Vociferous Bully.*
> *A Duellist, Boxer, Gambler, & Cully.*
> *A Student at Law, Collector of News.*
> *A Preacher in Churches, an Actor in Stews*
> *If Vices like these, Recommend to the Great.*
> *Then who is so fit for a Bishop as B——e.*
> *A Government Runner, of Falsehood a Vender*
> *Staunch Friend, to the Devil, the Pope, & Pretender*
> *A Managers parasite, Opera Writer*
> *News paper Editor, Pamphlet Indicter.*
> *An Olla Padrina [sic] foul Mixture of Parts*
> *Is this Harlequin Parson Master of Arts.*
> *If many Vocations can make a Man great*
> *Then who is so fit for a Bishop as B——e.*

The central Bate is the parson and duellist, see No 5198, &c ; the Bate facing l is Bate as a barrister, the letters LL D are sometimes given after his name The Bate facing r is dressed as one of the body of men sent out with caps and trumpets to advertise the *Morning Post* (of which he was editor) to Walpole's indignation, see *Letters*, ix 439-40, 13 Nov 1776, a dress which he had worn at a masquerade, see No. 5200; 'The Rival Candidates' was a popular comic opera by Bate, played at Drury Lane, 1775; 'The Flitch of Bacon' was a ballad opera played at the Haymarket in 1778 'The Blackamoor Wash'd White' was hooted off the stage in 1776, see No. 5364 His position as 'Government runner' is confirmed by North's statement of expenditure made to the king in April 1782 For a pension of £200 and 'hopes of preferment' an arrangement was made through Garrick that 'he should keep a Newspaper [the *Morning Post*] open for all writings in favour of Government'; he proved 'a very constant, diligent, zealous and able, though perhaps too warm a writer on the part of Government' The pension ceased and in 1781 he was paid £3,250 towards the purchase of a living *Corr of George III*, v. 471 This sum 'to that worthless man Mr Bate' the king disallowed, since he had been ignorant of the transaction, 5 May 1782, ibid , vi 7 (By this time Bate in the *Morning Herald* was supporting the party of the Prince of Wales) See also Nos 5666, 5676.

10 ⅚ × 7⅞ in.

5551 THE MASTER OF THE ASSES, OR THE WESTMINSTER LOYAL VOLUNTEERS A MEWS——ING THEMSELVES

Pub Augt 24. 1779 by Darly

Engraving (coloured impression) A party of six recruits in civilian dress, except for their cockaded hats, march (l. to r.) carrying muskets, they are nearly all elderly. An officer in uniform, carrying a cane, walks beside them The rear is brought up by an old soldier with swathed gouty legs, walking with a crutch and a stick

The background, a long low building of one story, with attic windows, represents part of the King's Mews near Charing Cross.

An anti-recruiting satire. The Westminster Volunteers was the name given derisively to the 85th Regiment raised by Lord Harrington and Lord Chesterfield in London in 1778-9, Curtis, *British Army in the American Revolution*, 1926, pp 68, 74. Cf. Walpole, *Letters*, x 451. The regiments raised by individuals and by towns (e g Manchester, see No. 5471) were known as 'Loyalty Regiments', see No 5552. For the danger of invasion see No 5554. For other anti-recruiting prints see No. 5295, &c

$7\frac{3}{4} \times 13\frac{1}{4}$ in

5552 THE TERROR OF FRANCE, OR THE WESTMINSTER VOLUNTEERS. 1779

Published According to Act of Parliament, August 26 1779.

Engraving. Four couples of men of unsoldierly appearance, carrying muskets with fixed bayonets, march from r. to l. Some are dwarfish; their leader marches in front A beadle (l) with a raised stick is driving back a crowd of amused spectators who seem to be obstructing the line of march, he more particularly threatens two men who have fallen down. The foremost of the crowd are a little chimney-sweep and a badged fireman holding a pick-axe Beneath the design is etched:

> *Can we Invasions dread, when Volunteers*
> *Like these, propose to Fight the Gay Monsieurs?*
> *Certainly No! such Taylors, Cobblers, Bakers,*
> *Always must Conquer, led by Engine Makers.*

An anti-recruiting satire, the 'Westminster Volunteers' being the 85th Regiment, see No. 5551 The regiment was sent to Jamaica, and the greater part of it was lost in the wreck of Rodney's prizes, homeward bound in 1783. H. M Chichester, *Records of the British Army*, 1902, p 647.

When this print was published England was seriously threatened with invasion, the combined French and Spanish Fleet being in the Channel, see No 5554. For the indifference with which this 'imminent danger' was regarded see T. Hutchinson, *Diary and Letters*, ii, 1886, pp 279, 291.

$6\frac{7}{8} \times 12\frac{1}{8}$ in.

5553 THE CHURCH MILITANT

[Gillray]

Publish'd 5th Septr 1779, by W. Humphrey.

Engraving. A procession of bishops and clergy march from l. to r headed by a prelate, evidently Archbishop Markham, on a prancing horse, holding a drawn sword. After him walk two boy choristers chanting from an open music book held between them. One sings *O Lord our God, Arise*, the other, *Scatter our Enemies*. Next come three bishops a lean ascetic who carries their standard, between two who are stout and gross. On the standard, which is attached to a crozier, is *To Arms O Israel*, and a mitre between two crossed croziers The prelate on the standard-bearer's l. sings, *Give us good Beef in Store*, the other, who carries a musket on his shoulder, sings *When that 's gone, send us more* Behind them a fat bishop sings *And the Key of the Cellar Door*, while the cleric next him, who wears an academic gown and cap, sings *That we may drink*. Behind, the mitres of more bishops are visible, and a man in academic cap and gown, who sings, *From Labour & Industry—Good Lord deliver us*

One of many satires on the 'higher clergy'; cf. Nos 4236, 5492. Their attitude to the war had been much attacked by the Opposition. See Walpole, *Last Journals*, 1910, ii. 29, and Markham was especially denounced for his belligerency, see Nos 5343, 5400, 5492. Two of the bishops are identified by Wright and Evans as probably Cornwallis, Archbishop of Canterbury, and Butler of Oxford.

Another impression, aquatinted, and also an impression without date. Grego, *Gillray*, p. 29. Wright and Evans, No 5.

$8\frac{5}{8} \times 13$ in.

5554 A DANCE BY THE VIRTUE OF BRITISH OAK

Publish'd as the act directs Sept' the   1779 [sic]

Engraving. A British sailor (r) is threatening a Frenchman with an oak club; a Spaniard (l), a dagger in his hand, has been thrown to the ground. The sailor wears a cockaded hat, a coat with facings, striped trousers, and a cutlass; he tramples on the Frenchman's hat. The Frenchman, a *petit maître*, is shouting in alarm; his broken sword is on the ground; he wears a high toupet wig with a large black bag, his parasol has fallen to the ground. The Spaniard wears a feathered hat and slashed breeches Behind the English sailor appears (l.) the muzzle of a cannon; in front of it is a pyramid of cannon-balls, beneath which is etched *The most radical Cure for French Perfidy & Spanish Arrogance*. Beneath the design is inscribed:

> *Let others barter Servile Faith for Gold*
> *My Courage is not to be bought or Sold*
> *The French & Spaniards I unmov'd shall face*
> *Their Steps like a Briton bravely trace.*

From August to September 1779 the allied French and Spanish fleets were in the Channel, and England was in serious danger of invasion, 30,000 French troops having been collected between Havre and St Malo Admiral Hardy was in command of the fleet; he managed to slip past the allied fleet and reach Spithead, whereupon the French and some of the Spaniards retired to Brest, the other Spaniards returning to blockade Gibraltar, see Nos 5551, 5552, 5614.

The first in the Catalogue of the patriotic prints which were the result of the war with France and Spain; it is to be noted that America is not mentioned. See also Nos 5555, 5556

$8 \times 11\frac{5}{8}$ in.

5555 LES HEROS FRANCOISES.

MONSEIG^R LE DUC DE CHARTRES, & LE COMTE D'ORVILLIERS.

Publish'd, as the Act directs Sep' 28 1779 P^s 6^d del ad Vitam

Engraving. Caricature portraits with large heads of d'Orvilliers the

admiral, and the duc de Chartres, nominally in supreme command, of the
French fleet which, combined with the Spanish fleet under Cordova, was
in the Channel from 14 Aug. to 14 Sept. 1779, threatening England with
invasion. Beneath the title is engraved ·

> *The King of France with Twenty Thousand Men,*
> *Came down the Hill—and then went up Again.*

The combined fleet did nothing but sail in the Channel, retiring to
Brest when Sir Charles Hardy reached Spithead; see No. 5554 For the
Duc de Chartres and the engagement, see Britsch, *La Jeunesse de Philippe-
Egalité*, 1926, pp 282 ff

$10 \times 7\frac{1}{4}$ in (pl)

Another impression, coloured and undated (27 July 1778 has been incorrectly added by Mr Hawkins) A publisher's inscription has been
erased, but *68 High Holborn*, the address of W. Richardson, remains
legible. Over this has been engraved *Sold by W. Humphrey, No 227
Strand.*

5556 [ENGLAND FRANCE AND SPAIN]   [n d ? September 1779]

Engraving. A British soldier (l) threatens with his bayonet two men
personifying France and Spain who kneel in supplication before him. The
soldier says *Damn your Lanthorn Jaw'd Frog Faces! What Business have
you here.* France, whose foppish clothes are in holes, says *Ah Monsieur
Anglois Pardoner Moi Me Renounce de Americans to the Devil* His
feathered hat and musket lie on the ground Behind him kneels Spain,
wearing a cloak, his high-crowned feathered hat is on the ground. He holds
out a money-bag inscribed *Dollars* saying, *Pecavi Signior Inghteio!
Pecavi! I Renounce de France for ever.* The British soldier is about twice
the size of the other two. In the background British soldiers in close rank
are firing from the shore at ship's boats flying the fleur-de-lys flag, the
boats are foundering

Apparently a patriotic rendering of the doings of the combined French
and Spanish fleets in the Channel Aug –Sept. 1779 See Nos. 5554, 5555.

$4\frac{3}{4} \times 8\frac{5}{8}$ in

5557 THE EUROPEAN DILIGENCE

Pubd according to Act of Parliament Octr 5 1779

Engraving. A Dutchman (r) wheels a wheelbarrow over the prostrate
body of Britannia. In the barrow are (l to r.): a Frenchman, who leans out
to pierce Britannia to the heart with a sword; she is saying *Ah Cruil
Neighbours thus to assist Rebellious Children*, he says *O Madame 'tis de fine
Politique*; America, a woman with a feathered head-dress, sits on the
Frenchman's l., she says, *My Good & Great Ally Strike Home.* Next comes
a man partly concealed by his cloak and hat, to whom his neighbour, Spain,
says *Now Brother of Portugal join the Confedaracy and Agrandize our
Family.* The Dutchman, a boorish fellow smoking a pipe, is saying *What's
Treaties to Gelt*; he is treading on a paper inscribed *A Memorial presented
by Sr J Yorke to their High Mightenesses* On the side of his barrow is a
placard, *De Jonge Johana Petronella Cornelius Dirk Vander Meulen for Eustatia* On the l of the print a tall Russian soldier with a fur-trimmed hat,

336

standing behind Britannia, threatens the Dutchman with his bayoneted musket, saying, *My Mistress is determin'd to Chastise Y^r Hogen Mogen for y^r Ingratitude & Duplicity & Oblidge You to Assist that Power that first Assisted You*

In spite of three treaties of alliance between England and the United Provinces, Dutch merchants were carrying on an immense trade with her enemies, and the Dutch island of St. Eustatius was the centre of a vast traffic in military and other stores for the Americans. Dutch papers were freely given to American privateers. Fortescue, *Hist. of the Br. Army*, iii. 260; *Hist. MSS. Comm*, *Stopford-Sackville MSS.*, ii. 1910, pp. 196, 202 f., 279, 293-5 Sir Joseph Yorke, British Minister at The Hague, presented a series of memorials protesting against the views of the strong pro-French party, to 'their High Mightinesses' (*Hogen Mogen*) the States General. See *Ann Reg.* 1779, pp. 422, 425, 428; F P. Renaut, *Les Provinces-Unies et la Guerre d'Amérique*, i, 1924, chap. vii; J. F Jameson, 'St Eustatius in the American Revolution', *Am Hist. Review*, viii, pp 683 ff

At this time there were hopes of an alliance with Russia, see Malmesbury, *Diaries and Correspondence*, 1844, i. 237 ff, *Corr. of George III*, ed Fortescue, iv 470-1. French and Prussian influence, however, prevailed and Catharine issued the Declaration of Armed Neutrality, Mar 1780 See Nos. 5713-16, 5718-19, 5724, 5730, &c. For Holland as an unfriendly neutral, see Nos. 5472, 5541, 5568, 5571, 5579, 5624, 5636, 5654, 5663, 5664, 5667, 5726, 5727, 5728. For Dutch prints referring to profitable trade in contraband see Nos. 5712, 5716, 5724 For St Eustatius see Nos 5837, 5838, 5839, 5842, 5923, 6051 For the attitude to Dutch neutrality in other wars cf. Nos 2416 (1739), 3697, 3698, 3704 (1759).
$6\frac{1}{8} \times 9\frac{1}{8}$ in

5558 POLITICAL WHISPER.

Old Sly pinx^t   *Young Edger sc.*

London, Printed & Published as the Act directs, Octr 20. 1779 by W. Hinton Copper plate Printer, N° 12. Corner of Bell Yard, Grace Church Street, Books, Maps, Prints & Stationary; Engraving and Printing in general.

Two men, much caricatured, with large heads, in consultation Both are fashionably dressed, and wear hats, one (l.), standing full face, wears spurred boots, the other, standing in profile to the l, wears buckled shoes.

Perhaps an allusion to the incessant negotiations and intrigues which were going on for Cabinet reconstruction, see *Corr. of George III*, iv. 475-9, 7-8 Nov. 1779, &c
$7\frac{1}{4} \times 7$ in.

5559 CAPT PAUL JONES,

London. Pub^d Oct 22, 1779, by Thos Macklin, N° 1. Lincolns Inn Fields.

Engraving Design in an oval Jones, W L, standing on the deck of a ship in action, looking to r., a large sword in his r. hand, l. hand on hip. He is dressed as a sailor in short wide trousers, and wearing a round hat with an erect feather; a pistol is in his belt Beneath the title is engraved, *From an Original Drawing taken from the Life, on board the Scrapis.*

For the action between Jones, in the *Bonhomme Richard*, and Pearson in the *Serapis*, Sept 1779, see G. W Allen, *Naval History of the American Revolution*, 1913, ii 456 ff.

Probably the earliest of a number of portraits of Jones, published in England, France, and Germany, see Nos. 5560–5. For the great importance attached to Jones's exploit as a blow to English prestige, see No 5715. Cf. also Nos 5568, 5582.

$8\frac{1}{4} \times 6\frac{3}{4}$ in

5560 CAP PAUL JONES

Engraving Oval bust portrait, copied from No 5559, hand on a staff instead of a sword The oval is in a frame inset in a conventional border with a ship, anchor, &c. Beneath the title is engraved, *From an original Drawing taken from the Lise [sic] on Board the Serapis* Probably French.

$5\frac{1}{2} \times 3\frac{1}{2}$ in ; oval, $2\frac{7}{8} \times 2\frac{1}{4}$ in.

5561 IOHN PAUL IONES,   1779

[?R Brookshaw sc [1]]

Mezzotint Apparently one of a series, see No 5290. Standing portrait T Q L of a man in naval officer's uniform looking to r. holding a telescope; his l hand on the fluke of an anchor In the background are rocks (l.) and the sea (r.). Beneath the title is engraved *Commander of a Squadron in the Service of the Thirteen United States of North America*, 1779 This style is tendencious as the Articles of Confederation did not go into effect until they were ratified by all the states in 1781 The squadron consisted of five vessels, one being American, the others French, all under the American flag but sailing under French orders, Aug 1779. Probably published after the encounter of the *Serapis* with the *Bonhomme Richard* and the *Alliance* under Jones, 23 Sept 1779. See No. 5559, &c

Chaloner Smith, iv. 1735. C. E. Russell, ii, p. 464.

$12\frac{3}{8} \times 10$ in.

5561A A copy having the same inscription with the addition

Joh. Lorenz Rugendas Sculpsit et excudit Aug. [Augsburg] Vind.

5562 CAPT. PAUL JONES

London, Printed for R. Sayer & J Bennett N° 53 Fleet Street, as the Act directs 28 Oct' 1779.

Mezzotint. Similar to No. 5561 but holding out a pistol with raised trigger Beneath the title is inscribed, *Commander of a Squadron of Ships in the American & French Service.*

$5\frac{3}{4} \times 4\frac{1}{16}$ in

5563 IOHN PAUL IONES,   [c. 1779]

Dessiné par C. F. Notté se vende chez F. M. Will. à Augsbourg

Mezzotint. Perhaps one of a series, see No. 5290. T.Q.L. standing on

---

[1] From about 1773, Brookshaw was working in Paris, and from 1779 in Brussels and Amsterdam.

board a ship in action behind a splintered bulwark, sword in r. hand; l hand on one of five pistols in his belt Not in naval uniform, but dressed as a sailor. Background of smoke and rigging. Beneath the title is engraved, *Commodore au Service des Etats-Unis de l'Amérique, tel qu'il etait dans le combat du 22 7bre 1779, contre le Capt Pearson, son vaisseau le bon home Richard montait 40 canons, la frégate Anglaise le Serapis 32, avait l'avantage du calibre et de la légerté; le Comodore saisit l'instant ou le Beaupré de l'ennemi passa pres de son Artimon, il attache ces 2 mats, et combattant bord à bord s'empara du Serapis. L'action dura 2 h. et ½ le bon home Richard coula 36 h. aprés.* See No 5559, &c

$12\frac{3}{4} \times 9\frac{3}{4}$ in.

5564 PAUL JONES. [c. 1779]

O. I. Notte pinxt

Printed for R. Wilkinson at No 58 Cornhill.

Mezzotint. Reduced copy of No. 5563.

$5\frac{1}{2} \times 4\frac{1}{2}$ in

5565 JOHN PAUL JONES

Dessiné par C. J. Notté Gravé par Carl Guttenberg. a Paris chez Guttenberg rue St Hyacinthe .

Engraving. Another version of No. 5563 within a border. Inscription as No 5563

Guttenberg was apparently not domiciled in Paris until 1780, Thieme Becker

$7\frac{3}{8} \times 6$ in.; border, $10\frac{3}{4} \times 9\frac{1}{4}$ in

5566 PAUL JONES SHOOTING A SAILOR WHO HAD ATTEMPTED TO STRIKE HIS COLOURS IN AN ENGAGEMENT.

[c. 1779]

[411] *From the Original Picture by John Collet, in the possession of Carington Bowles.*

[*Printed for & Sold by Carington Bowles, at his Map & Print Warehouse, No 69 in St Pauls Church Yard, London. Published as the Act directs* [date erased]]

Mezzotint The deck of a ship in action Jones fires a pistol point-blank at a sailor (l.) who stands under the striped American flag, one hand raised towards a rope. Other sailors stand round, two wounded men lie on the deck Jones rests one foot on the body of a dead man, a cutlass is under his l arm, four pistols are stuck in his belt. Probably the incident during the encounter of the *Bon Homme Richard* with the *Serapis*, when a gunner shouted for quarter till Jones knocked him down with the butt of a pistol

In the manner of history rather than satire, and tending to the glorification of Jones, see No. 5559, &c

One of Bowles's series of mezzotints.

$12\frac{3}{4} \times 9\frac{7}{8}$ in

Also a coloured impression in 'Caricatures', B.M.L., Tab. 524, i, p 7, from which the publication line has been supplied.

5567 THE FAMILY . COMPACT

Publish'd Nov' 1. 1779 whether by Act or Order is not Material Provided it Sells

Engraving The kings of France and Spain clasp hands; between them, and holding them together, a hand on each, is the Devil Spain (l) stands in profile to the r., wearing a feathered hat, cape, and slashed doublet. Round his neck is a Maltese cross, perhaps intended for the order of the *St Esprit* France, in profile to the l, is dressed as French *petit-maître*, and wears a ribbon and star The Devil has widespread bat's wings, a quasi-human head and body, a barbed tail, and cloven feet. He wears the triple crown of the papacy, and clerical bands, round his neck are hung the same order as that worn by Spain and the order of the Golden Fleece The three stand on a map or bird's-eye view of the Northern American colonies, inscribed (l. to r.) *Pensylvania; Virginia;* [Conne]*cticut; Philadelphia;* [New] *Jer*[s]*ey; N. York;* [Can]*ada; Massic* [*sic*]

Spain had joined France against England owing to the Bourbon Family Compact and her desire to regain Gibraltar See *Camb Hist. of Foreign Policy,* 1922, p. 134 Corwin, *French Policy and the American Alliance,* 1916, Chaps viii and ix. F. P. Renaut, *Le Pacte de Famille et l'Amerique,* Paris, 1922, p. 255 ff.

$6\frac{13}{16} \times 9$ in.

5568 THE POLITICAL SEE-SAW OR MINHIR NIC FROG TURN'D BALANCE MASTER

Tim Tear foul fecit

Publishd as y Act Direts for y Proprietor —— by W. Wells N° 132 Fleet Street Nov' y 6 1779 Price one Shilling

Engraving Holland, a fat Dutchman, stands upon the centre of a see-saw, straddling across a heap of money-bags. In his r. hand he holds a torn and ragged document, inscribed *That y Dutch Deliver into y Hands of English Paul Jones.* [signed] *York* His l. hand, the palm curved as if to receive money, is held out towards a lean and foppish Frenchman kneeling on one knee on the see-saw. The Frenchman holds in his r hand a purse, in his l he holds up an oval portrait-head or medallion inscribed *P. Jones,* his hat is under his arm, his hair is in an enormous pig-tail queue, and his fur muff lies beside him The Dutchman is saying.

> *I never was in Such a Scrpe* [*sic*] *before in all my Life*
> *I must be for neither & Yet for both—*
> *For they do but Ask and I may Chuse*
> *Whether to Grant them or Refuse*
> *For 'tis their beter Parts their Riches*
> *That my enamoured Heart bewitches*
> *Let me yor Fortunes but possess*
> *Then Settle Your matters how your Please*
> > *Hudibrass.*

The money-bags at his feet are inscribed *Guineas, Dublons, Dollars, Luidors* The Frenchman is saying ·

> *Assit* [*sic*] *me but this once I now implore*
> *And I shall Trouble Thee no more.*
> > *—Hudibrass—*

Behind the Frenchman stands Spain as a Spanish don in feathered hat, cloak, and slashed breeches; in his r hand is a scourge; in his l a *Manefesto To y Court of London.* He says.

> *Ah me, What Perils do Environ*
> *The Man that Meddles with could Iron.*
> *Hudibrass*

Behind him, and at the extreme r and upper end of the see-saw, sits America as an American Indian, wearing a head-dress of feathers, his hands clasped round his knees. He holds a large scroll on which is inscribed :

> *Tho we with black & blues are fudgeld*
> *Or as y Vulgar Say—are Cudgeld*
> *He thats valhant and Dares Fight*
> *Tho Drubd can loose no Honour by t*

This is continued on a flag which he holds.

> *Yet am I loath my days to Curtail*
> *If I thought my Wounds not mortal*
> *Or that we had time enough as Yet*
> *To make an Honourable retreat—*
> *Hudibrass*

On the l and lower end of the see-saw sits England, wearing a feathered hat, pseudo-classical drapery with an ornamental breastplate or gorget, decorated with a head writhing with serpents, probably symbolizing discord or faction In his r. hand is a scroll, *Magna Charta*, under his arm is an oval shield bearing the royal arms He holds a cap inscribed *libertas* on a staff, the upper end of which broadens into a gnarled club, inscribed *Hart of Oak.* He is saying:

> *Perpend my Words O Mmheer Nic*
> *That if thou wilt not Give a categorical Answer—I shall*
> *Teach you to Feel y weight of my Displeasure—*
> *For Danger from his Life Accrew*
> *Or Honour from his Death to You*
> *Twere Policy and Honour too*
> *To say as You Resolve to do.*

By his side is a paper inscribed *To ye*
> *Immortal Memory of Capt Falmer—*
> *An Heroic Epistle*

The see-saw and the figures on it recede in perspective, the lower and l. end being nearer the spectator so that the figures diminish progressively in size from England to America who is on a quite small scale.

Beneath the design is etched:

This Plate representing our Critical Situation with y Dutch is Humbly Inscribed to every True Briton who has y Wellfare of his Country at Heart.

Twenty-six lines of Hudibrastic verse follow, beginning

> *For Now y Field is not far off*
> *Where we must give y World a Proof*
> *Of Deeds not Words & such as Sute*
> *Another manner of Dispute*
> *A Controversy that affords*
> *Actions for Arguments, not Words.*

The plate represents in general the diplomatic situation in which England was endeavouring through Sir Joseph Yorke, the British Minister at The Hague, to counter the pro-French party in the States General. The Dutch had infringed their treaties with England by allowing Paul Jones to remain in the Texel with his prizes after his encounter with the *Serapis*, see Nos 5559-66 He was received in Holland as a hero. Yorke presented a memorial to the States General requesting the delivering up of the prizes, 29 Oct. 1779. After being allowed to refit his ships Jones was at last ordered to depart with the first favourable wind and sailed 29 Dec 1779 *Ann. Reg.* 1779, 429 ff.; G. W. Allen, *Naval History of the American Revolution*, 1913, ii. 481 ff.; F. Edler, *Dutch Republic and American Revolution*, 1911, pp 62 ff. For the Spanish Manifesto, of 28 June 1779, 'declaring the motives which have induced his Catholic Majesty to act hostilely against England' see *Ann. Reg.* 1779, pp. 567-86. For the attitude of Holland before the declaration of war in Dec. 1780 see No. 5557, &c., and the Dutch prints, Nos 5712-31. Apparently by the same artist as Nos 5648, 5709.

$5\frac{1}{2} \times 11\frac{1}{2}$ in.

5569 A PRIVY COUNCIL

Published Nov' 24 1779 by M. S. Dareny Opposite to the Kings Head Strand.

Engraving. A number of animals sit or stand round a small rectangular table. At one end (r.) sits an ass, one foreleg on the table, the other extended, its mouth open as if braying; it wears an ermine cloak to show that it is intended for George III. Behind the ass, and whispering into his ear is a figure wearing a flat Scots cap and tartan plaid, with the wings and claws of a bird of prey. He evidently represents Bute, or Scottish influence, supposed to be embodied in Mansfield, Wedderburn and Dundas. On the ass's r. hand a bear, wearing a ribbon, is asleep, his head bent down, his fore-paws crossed on the table. This is Lord North, also depicted as a bear in No. 5541. On his r. are a boar, a bull, and a goat, the last probably intended for Lord Sandwich. Behind the bear are a blood-hound, an ape wearing bands, and some feline animal whose head only is visible. In the foreground (l.) a muzzled mastiff lies asleep, his collar inscribed *Jo^n Bull*. On the wall hangs a map: a deep ravine or river divides *America* from *England*; the *Channel* is also marked.

$7\frac{1}{4} \times 9\frac{5}{8}$ in

5570 WHO'S IN FAULT? (NOBODY) A VIEW OFF USHANT

Pub^d Dec' 1st 1779 by Wm Humphreys N° 227 Strand.

Engraving. A portrait of Admiral Keppel without a body He stands on the sea-shore pointing to a naval engagement (r) indicated by ships' masts seen through clouds of smoke In his r hand is a cutlass. His legs are joined to his shoulders, so that he has no body.[1] He wears the hat of a naval officer. Beneath the title is engraved *The Anatomists will have it that it can have no Heart having no Body—but the Naturalists think if it has a H̄eart, it must lay in its Breeches*

[1] This idea appears to date from a caricature of 1600, see Buss, *English Graphic Satire*, 1874, pp. 46-7

Keppel became a popular hero after the Court Martial, see No. 5536, found, 11 Feb 1779, that he had behaved as 'a judicious brave and experienced officer' Palliser, too (see No. 5537), was acquitted on 5 May, so that the failure to pursue the French and bring them to decisive action after the engagement of 27 July 1778 off Ushant, see No. 5484, &c., was the fault of 'Nobody'. He became unpopular after he was brought into rivalry with Rodney, see No. 5992, &c. The nickname of Admiral Lee Shore was used because he had given the proximity of a lee-shore as a reason for caution in the action off Ushant, see No. 5658.

Also a coloured impression in 'Caricatures', iv, p. 93. B.M.L., Tab. 524. 8½ × 12¾ in.

5571 THE LAST STAKE.

Design'd by Stuart. Murray Delin¹ Junto fec¹

Publsh'd according to act. Dec⁶ 6. 1779 for J. Almon in Piccadilly London.

Engraving On the further side of a stream, inscribed *Rubicon—Flu—*, a bull representing John Bull is being baited On his back sits Lord North in profile to the l., very obese and asleep; at his back is a large square pack, inscribed *Taxes*. The bull is held by a rope which is twisted round a post inscribed *The Last Stake*, the end being held by a Scotsman in Highland dress intended for Bute, and by a man in judge's wig and robes, evidently Mansfield Two other members of 'the Junto' are goading the bull on, one with a pole, the other with a club The bull is being attacked by France with a sword, and Spain with a spear. France wears a coat, hat and bag-wig of French fashion, Spain wears a slashed doublet, ruff and cloak. In front of an inn-door (l) behind them stands George III, watching the struggle complacently, his hands in his pockets. Above the door the signboard, on which is a crown, is falling off, and hangs from one hook only From a window a woman's arm empties a chamber-pot on to the king's head. In the foreground, on the nearer side of the 'Rubicon' a Dutchman (r) stands facing the wall of a building, urinating on a paper inscribed *British Memorial*

The names of the artists indicate that the plight of the country is due to the designs of Bute (*Stuart*), carried on by Mansfield (*Murray*) and executed by the *Junto*. For the various memorials presented to the States General by the British Minister at The Hague see No. 5568, &c., and *Ann Reg* 1779, 1780. See also No. 5557, &c 8¾ × 12¼ in.

5572 INISH NA GEBRAUGH.¹

Owen Roe Oneele sculp¹

Publsh'd as the Act directs Dec⁶ 21ˢᵗ 1779, by Owen Roe Oneele.

Engraving An Irishman, wearing a hat, short coat, and breeches, a shillelagh in his r hand, points with his l. to a pile of munitions of war on his r. Behind him are ships at anchor against a quay, their sails furled, in front (r) are bales, a barrel, rolls of material, &c, labelled *For Exportation* and *Success to the Trade of Ireland*. He is saying *Arrah, sure they Wont*

¹ *Anois nó gó brách*, Now or Never

gives us a Free Trade, Nabocklesh [never mind it] A cannon on a gun-carriage, to which he points, is inscribed *O Lord open thou our Lips and our Mouth shall shew forth thy Praise*, round its mouth is inscribed, *A short Money Bill, a free Trade, or else*. With the gun-carriage are bayoneted muskets, a drum and cannon-balls Above it floats a large flag, bearing a crowned Irish harp inscribed, *Crom a Boo*, the motto of several Irish families including the Fitzgeralds. Behind are fortifications

This represents the Irish Volunteer movement and the demand for a removal of the restrictions on Irish trade See Nos 5548 [11], 5653, and *Ann Reg* 1779, pp 123–8. On William III's birthday, 4 Nov. 1779, the Dublin Volunteers paraded round his monument on College Green which was hung with significant inscriptions; two cannon bore the labels 'Free Trade—or this'. Lecky, *Hist. of England*, iv 1890, p 598

The attribution to Owen Roe O'Neill (*d* 1649) is significant, and at variance with the character of the Volunteer movement, since he typifies the trained soldier who fights for the independence of his country, and for the resistance of Celtic Ireland to England S R Gardiner in *D N B Letters* [on Irish politics] were issued as a pamphlet in 1779 by one Pollock under the pseudonym of Owen Roe O'Nial, Lecky, op cit. Cf. Nos. 5542, 5543 for propaganda apparently intended to rouse the Dublin populace against the English Government. Cf. also Nos. 5548 [11], 5573, 5653, 5659, 5667. For the Dublin Volunteers see also No. 5488.

$10\frac{1}{8} \times 8\frac{1}{4}$ in.

5573 THE BOTCHING TAYLOR CUTTING HIS CLOTH TO COVER A BUTTON.

John Simpson Aqua forti

Publish'd by James Tomlinson Oxford Street Dec' 27ᵗʰ 1779

Engraving. The interior of a tailor's workroom George III sits cross-legged on the table or tailor's shop-board, a strip of material across his knees, which he is about to cut with his shears Part of the cloth is inscribed *Ireland*, part *Great Britain*, a very small piece is *Hanover* Beside the king (r) sits Bute in Highland dress, his r arm is round the king's shoulders, and he points to the cloth, directing the king, who looks towards him with an expression of distress, to cut it between *Ireland* and *Great Britain*; on the table between them is a button Lord North (l.) stands on the king's r.; in his r hand is a length of cloth which has already been cut off, inscribed *North America*; pieces inscribed *West Indies* and *Africa* lie on the ground at his feet. In his l. hand he clutches the piece inscribed *Ireland* which the king is about to cut off Behind and between North and the king stands Mansfield, wearing judge's robes, with a dismayed expression. His r. hand is on North's r. shoulder, his l. clasps the hand which Bute has placed on the king's r shoulder Behind North (l.) stand two men. One (Sandwich) holds a document inscribed, *A Scheme for ruining the Navy*; the other is probably Germain.

Behind the table (r.) the Pope, wearing his triple crown, embraces a Scotsman, wearing a kilt and a bonnet with a white cockade, a powder horn and flask hanging from his waist, who is evidently Charles Edward the Pretender, they watch the king with intense interest. Beneath the table lie strips of cloth inscribed, *Bill of Rights* (torn), *Magna Charta* (frayed), *Memorials*, *Pe[ti]tions*, *Intelligence*, *Expresses*, *Memorials*, *Remonstrances*,

Dispatches, Petition from Jamaica, Account of the distress'd situation of Ireland. The shadow under the table over the pieces of cloth is inscribed *Taylors Hell.*

On the wall are hung broadsides, a tailor's goose, a picture, and, spiked on a file, a large bunch of papers labelled *Addresses.* The broadsides (l to r) are [1] *The Highland Laddie, a favourite Court Air, proper to be Sung in all Churches.* At the bottom is a jack-boot in a circle, the familiar emblem for Bute, see No. 3860 (1762), &c. [2] *D'r Cromwell's effectual and only remedy for the Kings-evil* This is headed by two crossed axes in a circle, a gibe which verges on treason. [3] *The Button-Maker's Downfall or Ruin to Old England to the tune of Britons strike Home.* George III was much ridiculed *c.* 1770 for indulging in the hobby of button-making, see Nos. 4380 (1770), 4417 (1771), 4883, 5711, and p 494 [4] *Taxation No Tyranny A New Song as Sung at the Theatre Royal the Words by Jocky Stewart,* an allusion in general to the supposed arbitrary policy instigated by Bute, and in particular to Dr. Johnson's famous pamphlet The picture is entitled *Flight into Egypt* The king, astride an ass, holds before him an infant (round whose head is a halo); the Queen sits behind him. Behind walks a procession of the royal children, little girls and youths. A sign-post points *to Hanover* This satire illustrates the persistent belief in the influence of Bute.[1] For Ireland see No. 5572, &c

The drawing is skilful and expressive and resembles in manner that of Nos. 5540, 5577 The signature and publisher's name are probably fictitious.

$9\frac{15}{16} \times 11\frac{5}{8}$ in.

5574 MR TRADE & FAMILY OR THE STATE OF Y^E NATION

St——t, B——n—d, & Co Orig^t G—rm—e, N——h & Co Exec^t

Publish'd by Virtue of Parliament not this day in particular—Dec. 1779

Engraving A family of beggars standing in a row, the man (l.), his clothes in rags, holds out his hat; on his coat pocket, turned inside out and in holes, is the word *useless*, he says, *I was once a Capital Dealer but thro' ye Obstinacy of* ONE MAN *& ye Villainy of many More—am reduced to Beggary.* His wife, an infant in her arms, is a ballad singer; she holds a broadside and sings, *Oh I wish that ye Wars were all over.* The little girl next her sings, *were all over*, her arm is round her younger brother's neck, he sings, *all over*, while an infant on his l. clad only in a ragged shirt, echoes *over.* This last child holds by a string a toy-horse on wheels, on which sits a figure of the king wearing his crown and Garter ribbon. On the r is the side of a building on which is a rectangular sun-dial, inscribed *Dum spectes Fugio.* In front of it is a tree-stump with bare branches on which sit two owls They say *Long live* SULTAN—*as long as He lives, We shall never want Ruin'd Towns & Villages—Vid* SPEC From a branch hangs a kite by its tail, inscribed *in ye Reign of ye best of Princes.* On the l is a row of three houses

---

[1] In 1778 there had been a recrudescence of the attacks on Bute, owing to an attempt by Sir James Wright and Dr Addington, Chatham's physician, to bring about an alliance between Bute and Chatham. Bute re-asserted his determination to take no part in political affairs He wrote to his son, Nov 1778, 'The policy of Sir James Wright has, as you will see in the Papers, opened the mouth of Hydra malice and venom against me afresh. ' *A Prime Minister and his Son,* ed. the Hon. Mrs Stuart Wortley, 1925, pp 122, 141 See also von Ruville, *Chatham,* III, p 333

of diminishing size, all *To Let*. (There were in 1779 'no less than 1,104 empty houses within the City of London' Macpherson, *Annals of Commerce*, iii 649.)

In the middle distance is a hunting scene: the king wearing his crown followed by another rider holding a club, chases a stag with three dogs. On the horizon, on the farther side of a stretch of water, two towns are seen in flames; one, l., is inscribed *Norfolk*, the other, r., is *Æsopus*. Norfolk, Virginia, was bombarded 1 Jan. 1776 by Lord Dunmore the Governor and afterwards burnt by the Americans to prevent Dunmore's establishing himself there. Æsopus was burnt by General Vaughan, Oct. 1777, see No. 5470.

Beneath the design is engraved *To his Excel^y Genl Washington. Pat. Pat^a This Plate is humbly Address'd by His Obedient Servt Thos Tradeless*

> Oh Wash'gton is there not some Chosen Curse
> Some Hidden Thunder; in the stores of Heav'n,
> Red with uncommon Wrath, to BLAST those MEN,
> Who owe their Greatness to their Country's RUIN
> *Addis^s Cato*

Above the design are the words *Veluti in Speculum* (which then ornamented the proscenium of the theatre). The supposed artists' names indicate that the war and the distresses of the country are due to the designs of 'Stuart' (Bute), which have been carried out by Germain, North and Co., and (presumably) to Sir Francis Bernard, Governor of Massachusetts (1760–9), who gave great offence to the colonists. For the phrase 'State of the Nation' cf. No. 5479. For distress caused by the war cf. Nos. 5535, 5548 [12], 5667. The king is now regarded as a tyrant—'Sultan', through whose obstinacy the country is in distress, cf. Nos. 5544–7.

$7\frac{5}{8} \times 12\frac{3}{4}$ in

5575 A NEW MODE OF SETTLING THE AFFAIRS OF THE NATION, OR TRYING THE FORCE OF GOVERNMENT POWDER.

Pub^d Decr 11th 1779 [1]

Engraving (coloured impression). A representation of the duel in Hyde Park, 29 Nov. 1779, between William Adam, M P for Gatton, and Charles Fox. Adam (l.), in Highland dress but wearing spurred boots, takes deliberate aim, his pistol supported on his l. arm. Fox (r.) holds his pistol pointing upwards, his hat is in his l. hand. He says, *I have a breast that like an ample Shield can take in all & verge enough for more.* His second points at Adam. Adam's second stands behind him, in apparent unconcern, a number of pistols are stuck through his belt. At Adam's feet lie a broadside, *The Fox Hunter A New Song* and a letter addressed *For Mr Adam . from North.* On the letter has been added in faint water-colour, *Of the Fox bring me his Brush so doing . . . y^r W^t* [this shall be your Warrant]. Between Fox and his second lies a paper, inscribed *yours &c. Eden.* The background is an avenue of trees.

The duel arose out of a remark in Fox's speech on the address which was resented by Adam, who demanded a public disavowal in the newspapers. It caused great political heat since it was represented as an attempt by a Scot and Ministerialist to get rid of Fox. Adam's second was Major

---

[1] The rest of the publication line is cut off

Humberston, Col Richard Fitzpatrick acted for Fox. See *Ann. Reg.* 1779, p. 235, 1780, pp 56, 152. Walpole, *Letters*, xi. 67–8, 72–4. Fox said Adam would have killed him had he used any but Government powder. Wraxall, *Memoirs*, 1884, ii 221 n   See also No. 5625

$9\frac{1}{16} \times 12\frac{7}{8}$ in (clipped)

5576 AN ASS IN THE GREEK PALLIUM TEACHING[1] [1779]

Ja^s Green Sculp Oxon

Engraving. Frontispiece to 'Fanatical Conversion; or, 'Methodism Displayed', verses attacking John Wesley A design in an oval frame supported upon objects which rest on a carved bracket. Within the oval an ass on its hind legs (r) draped in a cloak, addresses two women, one seated on a bench of pseudo-classical pattern, the other standing They wear classical draperies and are in profile to the l The frame rests upon a birch rod and books, one inscribed *Priscian*, another *Lycophron* Beside them lie a flat clerical hat with a curved brim, bunches of poppies and a scroll. The title is engraved on a bow which decorates the top of the oval

The ass is Wesley addressing two converts. The verses, illustrated with citations from Wesley's 'Fanatical Journals', purport to unravel 'the delusive Craft of that well-inscribed System of pious Sorcery which turns Lions into Lambs, called, in Derision, Methodism'. A scurrilous pamphlet in verse, published by Bew, like Nos. 5493–6 by the same author.

$6\frac{13}{16} \times 5\frac{7}{8}$ in. (pl.).   B M.L , 840. l 33/2.

5577 DR ÆOLUS TROPE, [c. 1779]
PERFORMING A SIMILE, IN COACH-MAKERS HALL

Engraving An orator, bending forward and gesticulating, his r. arm raised, his l holding a cane. His audience, seated on benches to his r and l. or standing behind, listen with expressions varying from astonished admiration to amusement.

Beneath the title is etched, '*The Ministry Sir, is like a Thief in the Cellar eating his master's bowels.' See y^e Doctor's Speech Septr 16· 79*.

The speaker is possibly Dr. Richard Price, he has a certain resemblance to the later portrait of the doctor, but is not wearing clerical dress Many political meetings were held in Coachmakers' Hall. The manner resembles that of Nos. 5540, 5573

$7 \times 6\frac{1}{2}$ in.

5578 ANTICIPATION.
A NEW MODE OF RAISING SUPPLIES, BY S^R BOREAS BLUBBER, OR WAYS & MEANS, FOR 1780.

Engraving Lord North (r.), in profile to the l., points a pistol at two men who are squatting down, holding up their coat-tails He is trying to force them to evacuate supplies and says, *I'll drain both Jew & Gentile.* One is a fat Englishman, saying *We are quite exhausted my Lord.* The other, a bearded Jew wearing a hat, says, *Will you give Twenty p^r Cent.* Two coins and an empty purse inscribed *Vacuum* lie on the ground. Beside North is

[1] This plate was the frontispiece to *The Rod* by H Layng, 1754, B M L 11630. f 32, see No 3283

a sheet of paper inscribed *Annihilation of Empire by L^d N——h.* Behind North (r) hangs a map, *America*, the country indicated by a few lines. Behind the other two (l) hangs a picture, *The goose & Golden Eggs·* a man and woman have cut open a goose which lies on a table in front of a cottage, they hold up their hands in astonishment at finding it empty of eggs Cf p 216

One of many satires on North's budgets, cf No 5703 See also Nos. 4968, 5541, 5542, 5637, 5703, 5964, &c. For 20 per cent cf Nos. 4926, 5012

$8\frac{3}{8} \times 13$ in

5579 THE PRESENT STATE OF GREAT BRITAIN   [?1779]

J. Phillips Fecit

Pub^d by W. Humphrey, N° 227 Strand.

Engraving. Great Britain or John Bull (c) stands half-asleep, his arms folded, holding a staff on which is the cap of liberty (the word *Liberty* inscribed on it in large letters) America (r), a Red Indian with a head-dress of feathers, is about to take the cap from its staff A Scotsman, his arm behind John Bull's neck, holds the staff of liberty with his l. hand which rests on John's shoulder, while he looks ferociously towards a lean figure personifying France (l) whom he has seized by the cravat The Scot wears full Highland dress with a dirk and sporran, his cap is ornamented with a thistle and covered with ostrich-feathers. France threatens the Scot with his fists; he is lean with a cadaverous face, his hair in a high toupet with an enormously long, tightly-bound queue which is decorated with a fleur-de-lys John Bull is in quasi-military dress with cockaded hat, epaulettes and a sash. On the ground kneels a stout Dutchman wearing a steeple-crowned hat, his nose suggesting addiction to brandy. He draws a netted purse from John Bull's pocket

The apparently favourable representation of Scotland is exceptional, it may indicate the much greater activity of recruiting in Scotland than in England, and the number of Scottish regiments raised for the war For similar satires on Holland see No. 5557, &c.

$10\frac{3}{4} \times 15\frac{1}{4}$ in.

5580 BY HIS MAJESTYS ROYAL LETTERS PATENT.
THE NEW INVENTED METHOD OF PUNISHING STATE CRIMINALS   [? 1779]

Engraving. Britannia, her shield hanging from her shoulders, is about to be torn in pieces by three horses, who are being violently assailed by their riders with scourges and huge spurs. She lies at the centre of cross-roads, one (l.) inscribed *To America*, up this gallops a horse inscribed *Tyranny*, to which Britannia's r. ankle is bound Her wrists are tied by ropes to the horses *Venality* and *Ignorance*, which are galloping (r) on the roads *To Spain* and *To France* respectively. Her l ankle is attached to a post inscribed *Court Influence* which is grasped by a stout seated man wearing a riband, evidently Lord North, though his head is hidden by his arms. He sits on the fourth road, that of *Despotism*. The three horses are ridden by men ferociously using huge spurs; two flourish knotted scourges, the third a spiked club.

Behind Britannia is a large rectangular pedestal or altar decorated with a chain, and with the inscription *Great is our Lord, and Great is his Power: Yea, and his Wisdom is infinite* From this watches George III, smiling vacuously, with a watchman's rattle in one hand, a model of a cock, apparently standing on a pair of breeches, in the other This is perhaps an allusion to the king as a 'botching taylor', see No 5573 He lies supported on his elbows, across him strides a Scotsman in a kilt, evidently Bute, his arms outstretched, holding in each hand a whip with two long lashes, with which he urges on the horses below. He wears a large thistle. A long ladder leans against the side of the pedestal Above the road leading *To America* a winged figure is flying away, carrying the cap of *Liberty* on a staff.

The date is probably after the declaration of war by Spain in June 1779. Mason ended his *Epistle to Dr Shebbeare*, 1777, with the words:

> Till mock'd and jaded with the puppet-play,
> Old England's genius turns with scorn away,
> Ascends his sacred bark, the sails unfurl'd,
> And steers his state to the wide western world:
> High on the helm majestic Freedom stands,
> In act of cold contempt she waves her hands,
> Take, slaves, she cries, the realms that I disown,
> Renounce your birthright, and destroy my throne.

Cf. Wraxall, *Memoirs*, 1884, ii. 101–2.

$7\frac{5}{8} \times 10\frac{1}{2}$ in

5581 Ô QU'EL D'ESTAIN. [c. 1779]

Engraving A French satire. Design in a circle inset in an oblong Within the circle, on the border of which the title is inscribed, a tiger or puma is being attacked by a lion, a serpent and a cock The cock, which is about the same size as the lion, is taking the most active part, being on the tiger's back, and biting furiously. Beneath the fight is engraved, *Tu la* [sic] *voulu.* In the corners of the oblong are the heads of the four animals, in the upper r corner the cock, *La France*; in the upper r corner the lion, *L'Espagne*; in the lower l. corner the serpent, *L'Amerique*, in the lower r. corner the tiger, *L'Angleterre*, looking up with a despairing expression. Beneath the design is engraved *Du Sein de la tyrannie naquit l'Independence. M A Voltaire.*

The punning title indicates the one success (in an inglorious command) of d'Estaing (for Destin), the taking of Granada, 4 July 1779, of which there is a print in the Print Department called *La Valeur Récompensée* It is evidently after the rupture of relations with Spain 16 June 1779, and probably before news of the failure of d'Estaing before Savannah Oct 1779, after which he was superseded by de Grasse, see No. 5627. For a Dutch allusion to the capture see No 5719. See also B Edwards, *History of the West Indies*, 1793, i. 376 f., and cf Walpole, *Letters*, xi. 101. The print illustrates the importance attached by France to the destruction of Anglo-American commerce, as well as of English prestige and sea power See also Nos 5472, 5726, 5727, 5859, &c

Collection de Vinck, No. 1175 (For other French prints on this subject see ibid., Nos 1172, 1173, 1174–9. Of these, No. 1176, LE DESTIN MOLEST-ANT LES ANGLOIS is noteworthy D'Estaing presents a palm to America, as a Red Indian holding the staff and cap of Liberty. Fame publishes to the Universe the exploits of the French hero who leads a bear and two foxes chained and muzzled, representing the peoples of Great Britain America is enthroned on bales of goods and casks inscribed *Ris pour la France; Indigo pour le Repos de la Mer, Mediteranée, Tabac pour la Hollande; Tabac pour la Russie; Tabac pour la France 1780; Indigo pour la France, Tabac pour l'Allemagne.* Cf. No 5473)

$8\frac{6}{16} \times 12\frac{1}{8}$ in.

5582 GEORGE THE IIIᴰ KING OF GREAT BRITAIN & &.

[? 1779]

Se vend chez J M. Will a Augsbourg.

Mezzotint. Apparently one of a series, see No. 5290 George III T Q.L. leaning against a pillar (l.) looking to r. In his r. hand is a small telescope (?), he frowns, his l hand is extended as if in argument or protestation. In the background (r), behind a parapet, is an engagement between two ships at close range Beneath the title is engraved, not in Gothic script, *Geb 4 Jun 1738*   [&c , &c.].

Perhaps intended to represent the king's supposed dismay at the capture of the *Serapis* by Paul Jones, see Nos. 5559–5565 (the encounter was watched from the cliffs of Scarborough)

For the great importance given to this exploit as a blow to the prestige of England see No. 5715.

$13 \times 9\frac{7}{16}$ in.

PERSONAL SATIRES

5583–5595

Series of tête-à-tête portraits.

5583 N° XXXIV MADAME DE B——G
N° XXXV THE SKILFUL NEGOCIATOR

Published as the Act directs by A. Hamilton Jun' near S' Johns Gate Jan' I 1779.

Engraving. *Town and Country Magazine*, x. 625. Two bust portraits in oval frames illustrate 'Histories of the Tête-à-Tête annexed; . . ' An account of 'Count M——n', minister of the King of Prussia. He is the Comte de Maltzan, Minister Plenipotentiary of Prussia. Mme de B is the distressed widow of a French *marchand de drap*, who has come to England hoping to earn a living by teaching.

Ovals, $2\frac{5}{8} \times 2\frac{1}{4}$ in.   B M L., P P. 5442 b.

5584 N° XXXVII. THE ARTFUL MISTRESS.
N° XXXVIII. THE PRIEST OF NATURE

Published as the Act directs by A Hamilton Jun' near S' Johns Gate Jan' 20 1779.

Engraving *Town and Country Magazine*, x. 675 (Supplement). Two bust portraits in oval frames illustrate 'Histories of the Tête-à-Tête annexed, . . .'. The man, in profile to the l, is handsome with an aquiline nose and wears a fashionable wig with a clerical gown and bands. He is said to have been the son of a collier in Wales, educated by a benevolent clergyman He is a wit and an author, was a friend of Sterne, has visited Voltaire at Ferney, when he styled himself the Priest of Nature, and has a chapel in Marylebone, said to be lucrative. The lady is Mrs M , wife of a clergyman in Soho Square

Ovals, $2\frac{7}{8} \times 2\frac{1}{4}$ in.   B.M L., P P. 5442 b.

5585 N° II THE CAPRICIOUS MARCHIONESS.
N° III. THE BOISTEROUS LOVER

Published by A. Hamilton Jun' near S' John's Gate Feb. I. 1779.

Engraving. *Town and Country Magazine*, xi 9 Two bust portraits in oval frames They illustrate 'Histories of the Tête-à-Tête annexed; . . .'. An account of the daughter of the Earl of H. [Holdernesse] and of her lover She is Amelia, Baroness Darcy and Baroness Conyers, wife of the Marquis of Carmarthen, afterwards 5th Duke of Leeds. He is Captain John Byron, son of Admiral Byron. They married 9 June 1779 after her divorce in May 1779 by Carmarthen

Ovals, $2\frac{11}{16} \times 2\frac{1}{4}$ in.   B.M.L., P.P. 5442 b.

5586 N° IV. THE FAIR VIRGINIAN
      N° V. THE DEVOTED GENERAL

Published by A. Hamilton Jun' S' Johns Gate March 1. 1779

Engraving. *Town and Country Magazine*, xi 65 Two bust portraits in oval frames illustrate 'Histories of the Tête-à-Tête annexed; .'. An account of General Burgoyne The lady is the widow of a loyalist Virginian planter, who had been imprisoned in Ticonderoga by the Americans, released on the capture of Ticonderoga She is said to have accompanied him to England after Saratoga.

Ovals, $2\frac{11}{16} \times 2\frac{1}{4}$ in.   B M L., P P 5442.

5587 N° VII. M^RS A——ST——D
      N° VIII. LORD CHAMPÊTRE

Published by A. Hamilton Jun' near S' John's Gate April 1. 1779.

Engraving. *Town and Country Magazine*, xi. 121. Two bust portraits in oval frames They illustrate 'Histories of the Tête-à-Tête annexed; or, Memoirs of Lord Champêtre, and the celebrated M^rs A—mst—d'. An account of Edward, 12th Earl of Derby (1752–1834), so called from the fête given on his marriage 23 June 1774 with Elizabeth, d. of the Duke of Hamilton, and of Mrs Armstead who afterwards married C J. Fox. She is here said to be the daughter of a shoemaker, who turned methodist and became bankrupt, on which she became a courtesan She was Elizabeth Bridget Cane, 1750–1842.

Ovals, $2\frac{3}{4} \times 2\frac{5}{16}$ in   B M L , P P 5442 b.

5588 N° X THE LOVELY EMILY.
      N° XI THE MILITARY SECRETARY.

Published by A. Hamilton Jun' near S' John's Gate May 1. 1779.

Engraving *Town and Country Magazine*, x 177. Two bust portraits in oval frames illustrate 'Histories of the Tête-à-Tête annexed; . ' An account of Charles Jenkinson (1727–1808), afterwards Earl of Liverpool, recently appointed Secretary at War. The frequent inaccuracy of biographical detail in this series is illustrated by the statement that his father was 'in the mercantile line' but unfortunate in trade, and the son 'commenced stockbroker'. Jenkinson was third son of Sir Charles Jenkinson, Bart , colonel of the Royal Horse Guards Blue Emily Roberts is said to have been removed by him from a brothel to a private lodging

Ovals, $2\frac{3}{4} \times 2\frac{5}{16}$ in.   B.M.L , P P. 5442 b.

5589 N° XIII THE CAPTIVATING LAIS.
      N° XIV THE FAVOURITE OF THE FAIR

Published by A Hamilton Jun' near S' Johns Gate June 1. 1779.

Engraving. *Town and Country Magazine*, xi 233. Two bust portraits in oval frames illustrate 'Histories of the Tête-à-Tête annexed; . '. An account of the Duke of Ancaster, identified from the part he is said to have taken in the riots on the acquittal of Keppel He died in July of this year, of scarlet fever, and was to have married Lady Horatia Waldegrave (not mentioned here). Walpole, *Last Journals*, ii 248 and n. *Letters*, x, p. 542. The lady is a courtesan, Miss St——y, whom he is alleged to have met at a masquerade at the Pantheon.

Ovals, $2\frac{3}{4} \times 2\frac{3}{8}$ in   B M.L., P.P 5442 b

5590 Nᵒ XVI Mʀˢ S——L

Nᵒ XVII. THE NOBLE RETALIATER.

Published by A Hamilton Junʳ near Sᵗ John's Gate July 1. 1779.

Engraving *Town and Country Magazine*, xi. 289. Two bust portraits in one frame illustrate 'Histories of the Tête-à-Tête annexed; . .' An account of Lord Tyrconnel (1750–1805), who having divorced his wife, see No 5412, went to Ireland and the Continent. After returning he was sued by Mr S—— for *crim. con* with his wife, Lady Elizabeth B now Mrs. S. [*sic*] in Trin. Term, 1778.

Ovals, $2\frac{3}{4} \times 2\frac{5}{16}$ in.   B M.L., P.P. 5442 b.

5591 Nᵒ XIX. Mʀˢ P——T.

Nᵒ XX. THE MANILLA HERO

Published by A. Hamilton Junʳ near Sᵗ John's Gate August 1. 1779.

Engraving. *Town and Country Magazine*, xi 345. Two bust portraits in oval frames illustrate 'Histories of Tête-à-Tête annexed; or, Memoirs of the Manilla Hero, and Mʀˢ P—tts' An account of Sir William Draper (1721–87), praising his courage and ability in the controversy with Junius.

Ovals, $2\frac{3}{4} \times 2\frac{5}{16}$ in   B.M.L., P P. 5442 b.

5592 Nᵒ XXII THE AMIABLE LAURA

Nᵒ XXIII THE MODERN APELLES

Published by A Hamilton Junʳ near Sᵗ John's Gate Sep 1. 1779.

Engraving *Town and Country Magazine*, xi 401 Two bust portraits in oval frames illustrate 'Histories of the Tête-à-Tête annexed, . ' An account of Sir Joshua Reynolds Laura is Miss J——gs [Jennings], the mistress of Lord F., who commissioned a portrait of her from Reynolds, and left her on account of his jealousy of Reynolds, whose mistress she is thereupon alleged to have become.

Ovals, $2\frac{3}{4} \times 2\frac{3}{8}$ in   B M.L , P P 5442 b

5593 Nᵒ XXV MADAME VANB——N.

Nᵒ XXVI THE EXPERIENCED AMBASSADOR

Published by A Hamilton Junʳ near Sᵗ John's Gate Octʳ 1779 [sic].

Engraving. *Town and Country Magazine*, xi. 457 Two bust portraits in oval frames illustrate 'Histories of the Tête-à-Tête annexed, '. An account of Sir Joseph Yorke (1724–92), afterwards Baron Dover, see No 5568. Mme V. is the widow of a rich merchant of Amsterdam.

Ovals, $2\frac{3}{4} \times 2\frac{5}{16}$ in   B.M L , P.P. 5442 b.

5594 N° XXVIII. THE CYPRIAN VOTARY
     N° XXIX THE UNIVERSAL GALLANT

Published by A. Hamilton Jun' near S' John's Gate, Nov' 1. 1779

Engraving *Town and Country Magazine*, xi 513 Two bust portraits in oval frames. They illustrate 'Histories of the Tête-à-Tête annexed; . ' They illustrate an account of the amours of Mr Med——t, identified by H. Bleackley as Medlicott. Thomas Hutchins Medlycot was M.P. for Milbourne-Port, 1780–1, being part owner of the Borough See Oldfield, *Representative History*, iv 488. See also Bleackley, *Ladies Fair and Frail*, pp. 67–9. She is a courtesan who passes as Miss Sm—th.

Ovals, $2\frac{3}{4} \times 2\frac{5}{16}$ in.   B.M.L , P.P. 5442 b.

5595 N° XXXI. M^RS W——R.
     N° XXXII. LORD L——.

Published by A Hamilton Jun' near S' John's Gate Dec' 1. 1779.

Engraving. *Town and Country Magazine*, xi. 569. Two bust portraits in oval frames illustrate 'Histories of the Tête-à-Tête annexed; . . . .'. An account of Lord Loudoun (1705–82). Mrs. W——r is the widowed daughter of a curate, whom he is said to have engaged as housekeeper, 'to have the sole command of his house'. She is Kitty Walker. G E C , *Complete Peerage.*

Ovals, $2\frac{3}{4} \times 2\frac{5}{16}$ in.   B M.L , P.P. 5442 b.

5596 A TIP TOP—ADJUTANT.

Pub^d Feb. 11 1779 by H Humphrey N° 18 New Bond Street

Engraving (coloured impression). A man in riding-dress walking in profile from r. to l , a riding switch in his l hand A portrait of Edward Topham (1751–1820), captain and adjutant in the first regiment of horse-guards He brought his regiment to a high state of efficiency, for which he was thanked by the king and figured in print shops as a 'tip-Top-Adjutant' He was noted for his original style of dress and the care and elegance of his manners His dress with breeches and sleeves moulding the figure anticipates the fashions generally associated with a considerably later date. He was much caricatured later by Gillray and Rowlandson Topham was an amateur caricaturist, see index of artists

$8\frac{1}{4} \times 6\frac{1}{16}$ in.

5597 [EMANUEL HENDRICKS]

R. Dighton Pinx^t   R Laurie Sculp^t

Printed for Jn° Smith Cheapside June 25, 1779.

Mezzotint. Design in an oval frame H L portrait of a man seated behind a table wearing a hat He holds in his r. hand a large frothing pot of porter which rests on the table, looking at the spectator, his l. hand extended. On the table is a newspaper, *Daily A*[dvertiser], pipes, and a paper of tobacco. On the wall above his head the lower part of a framed picture of an ass is visible.

Portrait of a tailor in Cursitor Street, died *c.* 1787, celebrated for being able to empty a pot of porter at a draught

Chaloner Smith, II. 806

$7\frac{5}{8} \times 6\frac{3}{16}$ in.

5598 THE AUSPICIOUS MARRIAGE[1] [1 Jan. 1779]

TH (Monogram)

Woodcut From the *Town and Country Magazine*, x 623. A woman, fashionably dressed, is being led to the altar of Hymen by a youth The altar is decorated with a mask and chains. Hymen, who stands on the altar, draws a veil over her face, holding her torch downwards. On the ground is a sleeping cupid Behind the bride is a house, inscribed *Alfred House*; on the ground at her feet are books, the cap and staff of Liberty (which she is treading under foot), an inkpot and pen.

This symbolizes the marriage of Mrs. Catherine Macaulay, aged 57, with William Graham, aged 21, the younger brother of James Graham the quack doctor. Alfred House (2 Alfred Street, Bath) had been presented to her by Dr. Thomas Wilson; on her marriage he wished to eject her from it. She is here represented as throwing aside her historical writings and her patriotic zeal for an unnatural marriage For Mrs. Macaulay and Dr Wilson see Nos. 5410, 5441. See also the *Westminster Magazine*, VI. 59, Feb. 1778, for an article on her *History* illustrated by a W.L. portrait.

$4\frac{1}{4} \times 4\frac{1}{16}$ in.

5599–5602, though without numbers, appear to continue the series published by Darly 1776–8, see No. 5369

5599 A BOND AND JUDGEMENT.

Pub^d acc^g to Act Feby 20, 1779 by M Darly 39 Strand.

Engraving. Sir John Fielding conducting an examination at Bow Street On the l. sits Fielding on the bench, which is raised and divided from the room by a low partition He wears a hat and, according to his custom, has a bandage across his eyes. Over his head hangs a pair of equally balanced scales, emblem of Justice. Behind Sir John and standing on his r. is a man wearing a medallion inscribed *G.R.* On Fielding's l. sits an interested spectator, holding his hat and cane On the opposite side of the room (r.), behind the bar and standing on a raised platform, are two wretched-looking prisoners, their legs shackled Behind them (r) a constable, or perhaps a third prisoner, is partly visible. In front of Fielding sits a clerk writing at a small table; either he or the man standing behind Sir John must be Bond. A man stands beside him, holding up in his r hand two pistols, with his l he points to the prisoners. On the floor are house-breaking tools a pick or hammer, a club, and a bunch of keys. Behind him stands a woman with a ragged apron, holding a handkerchief to her face, which is concealed by her hat. Next her stands a man with a patch over one eye; a third man reads a book, perhaps administering an oath to one of the other two who are probably witnesses Behind them, at right angles to the bench, is a crowd of spectators divided from the room by a barrier.

Fielding's examinations at Bow Street were one of the sights of the town. Cf Somerville, *My Own Life and Times* For Bond see No 6120.

$8\frac{3}{8} \times 13\frac{1}{4}$ in.

[1] The title has been cut off, it is supplied from the magazine.

5600 THE THREE GRACES OF COX-HEATH [1]

Pub^d acc^t to act Mar 4th 1779 by Darly 39 Strand.

Engraving. Three ladies, wearing military coats with epaulettes, cravats, and frilled waistcoats Their hats are looped and cockaded, with tassels hanging from them; each carries a long riding switch The one in the centre is very stout, the other two who stand in profile looking towards her are slim. Circular tents fill the background.

They are probably the duchesses of Gordon, Devonshire and Grafton, who with other wives of commanding officers were presented to the king when he visited Coxheath Camp on 3 Nov 1778 *London Chronicle*, 3–5 Nov 1778, see also No. 5601 One of many satires on the camp at Coxheath, see No. 5523, &c.

In a volume in the Banks Collection ('English Costume 1760–1817', fo 24) there is an engraving with the title, *The Military Dutchess with a distant view of the Camp*, it is a tall and elegant lady wearing a quasi-military dress resembling that of the satire, except for the hat which is large and feathered as in No. 5601.

$8\frac{3}{8} \times 12\frac{1}{2}$ in.

5601 THE COXHEATH RACE FOR £100, NO CROSSING NOR JOSTLING, WON BY MISS TITTUP AG^T TUMBLING JENNY

Pub· by Darly 39 Strand, 29 of Octr 1779.

Engraving (coloured impression). Three ladies ride from r to l.; all are dressed in large cockaded hats with ostrich feathers, and military coats The foremost, holding up a large riding switch, turns round to look at the two behind her The next horse is falling on his knees, his somewhat stout rider has lost her seat and her stirrups and is about to fall head-first, her hat and riding switch are on the ground. The last rider appears to be holding back her horse. Two dogs run beside the horses.

They are perhaps intended for the 'Three Graces of Coxheath', see No. 5600, in which case 'Tumbling Jenny' would be Jane Maxwell, Duchess of Gordon ('Jenny of Monteith') For satires on Coxheath Camp see No. 5523, &c. 'Miss Tittup' is a character in Garrick's *Bon Ton* (1775), cf. No. 5518.

$8\frac{3}{4} \times 13\frac{5}{8}$ in.

5602 A VISIT TO THE CAMP.

Pub^d by M Darly 39 Strand Novr 25 1779

Engraving (a coloured impression) Three elderly couples, much caricatured, walk arm in arm, one after the other from l. to r. through one of the camps (Coxheath or Warley) which were then so much visited. A smartly dressed soldier, wearing epaulettes, points out the way. The women are dressed in the fashion of the day, one wearing a large calash-hood, see No. 5434, &c. The foremost man affects a military bearing and walks as if marching. In the background are tents, beside them stands a woman with a military air.

One of many satires on militia camps, see No 5523, &c

$8\frac{1}{2} \times 13\frac{1}{16}$ in

[1] There is a plate, v 2 78 in Darly's series, dated 5 Nov 1778, called 'The Graces of Coxheath', depicting an ungainly officer executing a goose-step In the collection of Mr W. T. Spencer, New Oxford Street (1933).

5602A Another impression, from which Darly's etched publication line has been erased, and an engraved imprint added·

Pub^d Novr 23^d [sic] 1779 by H Humphrey N° 18 New Bond Street.

5603 PRATTLE THE POLITICAL APOTECARY.

[? Gillray.]

Pub by M Darly 39 Strand Augt 12. 1779

Engraving Caricature portrait of a man standing in profile to the r. He holds his hat awkwardly in his r. hand, his l is thrust into his waistcoat, his toes are much turned out. He wears a thin pigtail queue From his pocket hangs some object resembling a syringe Beneath the title is etched, *Beg your pardon my Dear Sir—had it from my Lud Fiddle faddle, nothing to do but cut 'em off pass the Susquhanna and proceed to Boston possess himself of Crown point then—Philadelphia, and South Carolina woud have fallen of course—& a communication opend with the Northern Army—as easyly as I'd open a Vein.*

On the back of another impression has been written 'Mr Atkinson, Apothecary, Pall Mall'. This figure (reversed) appears in No 5614. In the manner of Gillray's *Bombardinian*, see Nos. 5606-8.

6 14/16 × 5 3/8 in.

5603A Another impression (coloured) from which Darly's imprint has been stopped out, with the publication line,

Pub^d by H Humphrey N° 18 New Bond Street.

5604 THE WHORE'S LAST SHIFT.[1]

[Gillray.]

Publish'd Feby 9th 1779. by W. Humphrey.

Engraving (coloured impression). A woman stands in a sordid and poverty-stricken room. She is naked except for her shoes and ragged stockings, and is washing a garment, her 'last shift', in a broken chamber-pot supported on a broken chair. Another garment is in a broken basin on the floor; her hat and outer-garments also lie on the floor. Beside them are two pill-boxes and a paper inscribed *Leakes famous Pills* Her hair is elaborately dressed in a pyramid, decorated with feathers, flowers, and ribbons. The low bed has tattered coverings A casement window (l) is open, showing the roof of a neighbouring house; on the sill a cat miaows A broadside ballad is pinned to the window recess. *The comforts of Single Life. An Old Song* On the wall is a torn print, *Ariadne Forsaken*. The plaster has peeled off the wall in patches, showing bricks.

Grego, *Gillray*, p 28

13 × 9 1/2 in

5605 PADDY ON HORSE-BACK

[Gillray.]

Publish'd March 4th 1779. by W Humphrey.

Engraving. An Irishman seated on a bull which is galloping across open

[1] On the plate is written (not in a contemporary hand) portrait of Lady Worsley Cf Nos 6105-12

country towards London, seen in the distance on the r , St. Paul's being visible He wears a short jacket and ragged knee-breeches, his legs and feet are bare. His hair is dishevelled and he is urging on the bull with his hat, which is raised in his r hand. He sits facing the animal's tail, which he holds in his l hand From his saddle-bag appear books: *St Pat* . . and *New System of Fortune Hunting*; a paper hangs out of it inscribed with a list of ladies with fortunes, beginning *Lady Mary Rotten Rump St James Square 30,000£* A sack inscribed *Potatoes* is tied to the bull in front of the saddle A milestone shows that it is *IIII Miles from* [London].

It was an old gibe that Irishmen came to London to make their fortunes by marriage. This attack on the Irish may be connected with the proposals for removing restrictions from Irish trade which were so much opposed by English merchants, cf. Nos. 5548, 5572.

Grego, *Gillray*, pp 28–9, Wright and Evans, p 1

$8\frac{7}{8} \times 13\frac{3}{8}$ in.

5606 BUMBARDINIAN [1]

    CONFERING UPON STATE AFFAIRS WITH ONE IN
       OFFICE.   [? 1779]

[Gillray.]

Pub^d by Darly 39 Strand

Engraving (a coloured impression). A tall thin man, much caricatured, in general's uniform, his hat held stiffly under his l arm, his head and shoulders thrown back with a self-important air, his toes turned out grotesquely. He wears the order of the Thistle A short stout man (l) looks up at him, his l thumb held to his nose, his r. hand on his hip, his legs and feet in a curiously contorted position They are Sir R Hamilton, Bart., Lt -General 1777, died 10 Aug. 1786, and Sir Grey Cooper, Secretary to the Treasury Two dogs, one with a bone, are near them. Behind (r.) the end of a small house appears, the door inscribed *Bombardinium 40*. A man and woman are about to enter it, he carries a cradle, she has bundles inscribed *Childbed Linen*

On a mound in the background is a small circular temple, its dome surmounted by a star on which a figure of Fame holding a wreath and a trumpet is grotesquely poised. Under the dome is a circular altar, on which stands a partly naked figure, visible from the waist downwards. Before this two figures on a minute scale, one representing Hamilton, the other Cooper, are kneeling. Near the temple a man is tipping on to the grass the contents of a small cart led by a horse. Beneath the title is engraved,

Important blanks in Nature's Mighty roll Churchill

A satire on the self-importance of General Hamilton (who had not the order of the Thistle), and on some scandal Apparently an earlier version of *Bombardinian*, see No 5608 See also No 5607

$11\frac{7}{8} \times 8\frac{1}{2}$ in.

[1] The *O E D* gives Bumbard, bumble bee, drone, and, fig , a droning person, a driveller

5607 BOMBARDINIAN.

IMPORTANT BLANKS IN NATURES MIGHTY ROLL;

[Gillray]

Pub by M Darly 39 Strand Sep' 19. 1779

Engraving (a coloured impression). Sir R Hamilton stands as in No. 5606 but reversed. Behind him a path leads across grass to the temple, which is larger; the two kneeling figures are reversed The figure of Fame is absent. Probably an earlier version of No 5606. See also No. 5608

$10\frac{3}{4} \times 8\frac{1}{2}$ in

5608 BOMBARDINIAN

CONFERRING UPON STATE AFFAIRS WITH ONE IN OFFICE. [? 1779]

[Gillray.]

Sold at N° 227 Strand [W Humphrey]

Engraving Another and probably later version of No 5606; the two men have labels coming from their mouths containing words, and are more correctly drawn The house on the r. is a more important building and its door has a plate inscribed *Lieut Gen' Bombardi . . N° 40*. Grey Cooper stands at a different angle, showing more than his profile, his forefinger is laid against his cheek. He is saying *Then—My Led and I—his Ledship introduced the Affair you and I know of.* Sir R. Hamilton (Bombardinian) answers *Hum—Aye—Mum* The same quotation from Churchill is engraved under the title. An inscription etched in the lower r. corner has been obliterated, the last words seem to resemble *J. Sayers.*

Grego, *Gillray*, p. 43, ascribes the print, and the contemporary scandal which led to it, to 'the early part of 1782', but since No. 5607 was published in 1779 this print probably belongs to the same year. See also No. 5606.

$12\frac{1}{4} \times 9\frac{5}{8}$ in.

5609 THE LIBERTY OF THE SUBJECT.

[Gillray]

Publish'd Oct' 15th 1779, by W. Humphrey, N° 227 Strand.

Engraving A press-gang at work in a London street, at the end of which appears the dome of St Paul's A sailor (c) strides towards the spectator, a club in his r. hand, dragging along a lean tailor, who holds up his hands in dismay An infuriated woman (l) has seized the sailor by his hair and the r. ear while she pummels him with her knee Another sailor behind has seized her wrist and raises a club to strike her. A third sailor (r) holds the tailor by the l arm. A naval officer (r) walks beside the party with a drawn cutlass. Behind are other sailors A woman (l.) wearing stays or 'jumps' raises a mop in both hands to smite a sailor; an infant clutches her petticoats. A group of spectators (l) includes a woman carrying a baby. A dog barks at the fray

Resembles the manner of Nos. 5523, 5524, and is possibly after Mortimer

Grego, *Gillray*, p 29

$9\frac{5}{8} \times 13\frac{1}{2}$ in

5610 IMPLEMENTS FOR SADDLING AN ESTATE—A PEICE OF STILL LIFE—ADDRESS'D TO THE JOCKY CLUB

[Gillray.]

Pub⁴ by W. Humphrey 6 Dec' 1779 N° 227 Strand

Engraving. A saddle (l), a jockey-cap, a riding-whip, and a covered vase or cup, fluted, with a square base (r) It is encircled with a plain band on which is drawn a horse-race, one horse and the hind-quarters of the one in front being visible. On the wall behind is *The Gamblers Coat of arms*: on an escutcheon are dice, a pair of legs from the knee downwards, playing cards, a pair of crossed pistols, and three billiard-balls. Behind the shield are crossed billiard-cues. A dice box serves as crest. On the wall on each side of the coat of arms is a placard · (l) *A Sweepstakes 3000 G^{ns} each* . and (r.) *Eclipse 30 Mares 50 g^{ns} a Mare* Beneath the title is engraved, *The Painter has drawn these implements with some degree of Success, but they are very seldom Successful to any body but a Painter, the Cap is made of so happy a size as to fit any Blockhead, it is Turfically call'd a Cap of Knowledge, but Œconomically, a fool's Cap*

Grego, *Gillray*, p. 29.

7 $\frac{13}{16}$ × 13 in.

5611 POLITENESS.

J N fecit et Inv⁴ 1779. [? Gillray]

Publish'd 8th Dec' 1779.

Engraving, partly mezzotinted John Bull (l.) and a Frenchman (r.) sit on two chairs, each scowls over his shoulder at the other. The Englishman is stout and plainly dressed, his hair is short and without powder, he wears top-boots. In his r. hand he holds a foaming tankard which rests on his knee, in his l is a gnarled stick. The Frenchman is thin, wears a pigtail queue, ruffled shirt and laced waistcoat. He clutches in both hands a bowl in which is a spoon, evidently the soup-meagre of English caricature. Each man has a dog under his chair, and the beasts snarl at each other. The English dog is some sort of mastiff, his collar is inscribed *T Crus*[ty]; the French dog is of greyhound type. Over John Bull's head is engraved *You be D——m'd*, over the Frenchman's, *Vous etes une Bete*

An early representation, the first in the collection, of the typical John Bull, cf. No 5860 See also No 5790.

Apparently an earlier version of No. 5612 Cf the signature of No. 5616, in which Gillray may have been using J Nixon's initials, as he afterwards did those of James Sayers.

6¼ × 8¼ in.

5612 POLITENESS

[Gillray.]

Pub⁴ by H. Humphrey, St James Street¹　　　　　　　　　　　[n.d.]

Engraving A more elaborate version of No 5611 drawn with more freedom A joint of beef hangs on the wall behind John Bull; a bundle of

¹ Another publication line has been obliterated *Pub⁴ by J. A . . N° . . . Castle Street London . is just legible*

frogs behind the Frenchman The Frenchman holds an open snuff-box
instead of a bowl of soup; a laced hat is under his arm; he wears a bag-wig.
John Bull's tankard is inscribed *John Bull the Buttock of Beef* . . .
Beneath the design is etched:

> *With Porter Roast Beef & Plumb Pudding well cram'd,*
> *Jack English declares that Mons.' may be D——d.*
> *The Soup Meagre Frenchman such Language dont suit,*
> *So he Grins Indignation & calls him a Brute.*

Cf. No 5790. Reprinted, *G W G.*, 1830.
$6\frac{5}{8} \times 9\frac{7}{8}$ in.

5613 A MEETING OF CITY POLITICIAN'S.

*Plate 2 of every thing humorous, ridiculous, and satyrical Published
July 30.th 1779 by W. Richardson N.o 68 High Holborn.*

Engraving Men seated round a table, drinking, smoking, and reading
newspapers On the r an artisan, wearing a flat cap and apron, drinks
from a tankard while he reads *The Morning Post*. Next him a man in
back view reads *The Daily Adver[tiser]*, a monkey sitting on his shoulder,
pulls the string-like queue of his ill-made wig Next (l.), an elderly man
in an arm-chair, wearing spectacles and a cap, holds up his hand as if to
demand attention; he reads *The London Chronicle*, on which is inscribed
*It is reputed that next [sic] sessions of Parliament, there will be a tax laid upon
horn'd Cattle*, his neighbours listen to the news with expressions of consternation The farther side of the table is crowded; one man reads *The
Evening Post*, another the *London Gazette*, on which is inscribed *Extract
of a Letter from America*. Beneath the design is engraved:

> *With staring Eye, & Open Ear,*
> *Each Cobling, Horned, City seer,*
> *Swallow's down Politics with Beer.*
> *Neglects his Family & Calling*
> *To enter into Party Brawling*
> *Gets Drunk & Swears—the Nation's falling.*

The absorption of tradesmen and artisans in politics to the neglect of
their business was a common eighteenth-century theme, see No. 5074, &c.
$7\frac{1}{8} \times 11\frac{3}{4}$ in.

5614 APOTHECARIES—TAYLORS, &c. CONQUERING FRANCE AND SPAIN.

[? Gillray.]

Publish'd Sep.t 29.th 1779. by W. Humphrey N.o 227 Strand

Engraving. A scene of disorder; men sitting and standing round a circular
table, they are smoking, gesticulating and drinking A very fat man,
seated on the farther side of the table, wearing a hat and smoking, his hands
folded, says, *we want men of Activity* His neighbour, also smoking, adds
To destroy all their Looms The next man (l.), clenching his fists, says,
*Blood & Guts, what are we all about—our Armys are grazing in Idleness, like
a Flock of Sheep till they die of the Rot - I'd send them to Slaughter all the*

Cattle on the Enemy's Coast & make the Papist Scoundrells keep a long Lent of it A man (r.) holding up a foaming tankard, says *Old England will never be conquer'd while we can Brew such Drink as this.* A barber, a comb stuck in his hair, an implement for curling hair protruding from his pocket, leans back in his chair, saying, *We're all in the Suds—I could shew them a way to lower their French Toupees* On his r stands the figure of 'Prattle' (Atkinson of Pall Mall), as in No 5603 but in reverse. He is saying, *Beg your Pardon my Dr Sir, meant no Offence my Dr Mr Tallow—too much Love & Respect—your Perfectly in the Right—of the same Opinion of my Led & I—they'll never Invade us as you say & my Lud Chatter observed to me the other Night at Lady Carbuncles.* He is addressing a stout man standing on the l of the table, who flourishes a stick in his l. hand while with a blow from his fist he overturns a punch-bowl, having upset a tankard, a lemon, and a number of wineglasses which are falling to the ground He says *Dont Talk to me of your Dukes & your Lords, I'm a True Born Englishman, & dont care for Nobody not I—they dare not invade us—Damme they dare not—you Glister Pipe, you pitiful Plaister Spreader You——.* A dog barks at him A thin and rather ragged-looking man on his r., his hands in his breeches pockets, says *Invade us—Damme, what can Soup Meager do against Beef & Plumb Pudding*; a pair of scissors projecting from his coat-pocket shows that he is a tailor; his stockings are ungartered and his shoes are unbuckled. On the extreme l an elderly man with a tie-wig and wearing a hat and pince-nez, sits in a chair reading a newspaper; he holds up a hand in dismay saying, *All's lost* Behind stands a waiter, his napkin under his arm, saying *Dr Prattle says right—I'll go over to the Opposition and never drink another Pot with my Lords Footman* Hats are hung up on the wall, and a bracket-clock shows that it is one o'clock.

At this time the French and Spanish fleet in the Channel had recently threatened invasion, see No 5554, &c Cf Nos. 5074, 5086, &c.

Resembles the manner of Gillray in Nos. 5606-8

$9\frac{3}{8} \times 13\frac{1}{4}$ in.

5615 CITY BLOCKHEADS. [1 Oct. 1779]

Woodcut From the *Town and Country Magazine*, xi 453. Illustration to a dialogue called *The Battle of the Old Bailey.* Aldermen are guzzling round a dinner-table, at the head of which is the Lord Mayor. The City arms are on the wall behind him. One of the aldermen (Plomer) has risen and aims a blow at the Lord Mayor (Plumbe), but is himself seized by another alderman

This represents an affray which took place at the Old Bailey after dinner, when the glass was going round and the judges were present, see *Public Advertiser*, 18 Sept 1779, and No. 5616

$3\frac{1}{2} \times 4$ in.

5616 THE MAGISTERIAL BRUISERS

J. N. fecit 1779. [? Gillray.]

Publish'd Octr 5th 1779 by W. Humphrey

Engraving. A more elaborate representation of the affray depicted in No. 5615. The scene is a room in the Old Bailey after a dinner during the

Sessions Two combatants, wearing civic gowns, one the Lord Mayor,
on the ground in front of a long dinner-table are being pulled apart. One
(r.) has seized his opponent's wig and is kicking him under the chin, the
other (l.), the Mayor, has seized his neck-cloth. A judge in wig and gown
(r.) holds the arm of the combatant on the r. and attempts to separate them.
Behind them stands an alderman resembling Wilkes, holding up his hands
in horror. On the far side of the table sit two judges, one drinking wine
quite unconcerned, and a third man An alderman with a gouty leg
supported on sticks stands on the r. The Lord Mayor's chair at the head
of the table is empty
    On each side of two deeply-recessed windows is an arched alcove, one
(l.) with a statue of Justice, blindfolded, with a hood and scales; the other
(r.) is Liberty, holding the cap of liberty on a staff The cloth has been
removed from the table, and on it are dishes of fruit, wine-bottles and wine-
glasses. A chair (l.) has been overturned, fruit and broken china lie on the
floor Several ranks of wine-bottles stand in clusters behind the head of
the table.
    Beneath the design is etched·

> Two Wealthy Dons, at an Old Bailey Feast,
> In City Pride and Honors, not the Least,
> Some time ago, so rumour spread about
> Differing in thoughts, Pell Mell, they both fell out,
> DROSS the Lord Mayor, was first to raise the Flame,
> And thus addresses MANGO, by his Name,
> "If sixpence is to be had in any Place,
> We're sure to see your Crabbed Sower Face,
> For Gold has so wrap'd up thy Flinty Soul,
> To get a Guinea you would reach the Pole,"
> MANGO at this with Indignation burns,
> And at My Lord the Compliment returns,
> "Thy Years (Old Gouty Dross) and shallow Sense,
> Shields from my wrath thy matchless Impudence,
> Yet, for thy Equal, search the City round,
> So Base, so mean a Wretch, there can't be found "
> Words brought on Words, when each with Passion glows,
> And now from Fool and Knave, they fall to Blows
> The Attack was fierce, till Friends did Intervene,
> And put a Stop to this alarming Scene.

MORAL.

> The Men who Fight in Broughton's Way
> May live to Fight another Day
> But he who is in a Duel slain
> He'll never rise to fight again.

    The affray, said to be 'occasioned by a dispute about a few pence on   .
a pot-house reckoning', and (presumably) this print are mentioned in
City Biography, 1800, p 24 The Lord Mayor was Samuel Plumbe, his
antagonist William Plomer. Plumbe was a reputed miser, see No. 5617.
In the manner of Gillray, for the signature J.N. cf. No. 5611.

$7\frac{5}{8} \times 12\frac{3}{4}$ in

5617 MAGISTERIAL ŒCONOMY. [*c.* 1779]

[? J. Nixon.][1]

Engraving. A reception at the Mansion House; a clock on the wall shows that it is twelve, the guests are hurrying away because the servants are extinguishing the candles. In the foreground (l.) two elderly bedizened women and two men are playing cards; they are unconscious that a stout man with a chain round his neck, apparently the Mayor himself, is directing a footman to blow out the candles on the table with a pair of bellows The bellows are marked *P* , probably indicating Samuel Plumbe. Two other footmen are extinguishing candles, one with a pair of bellows, another with an extinguisher on a long rod A group of three departing guests (r), look over their shoulders in annoyance Through a wide doorway is seen an inner room in which there is a procession of departing guests, led by the musicians carrying their instruments From a gallery at the back of this room two other footmen are putting out candles The large wall clock is over this gallery. On the wall behind the card-players are two H.L. portraits, one of *S*ʳ *Richard Whittington* wearing an eighteenth-century wig, and resting his hand on a cat which stands on a table; the other of a lady wearing a ruff, probably intended for Dame Whittington. Beneath verses are engraved, beginning,

> *A frugal Lord Mayor siez'd with Kindness one Day,*
> *Gave a Rout to the Town in a general way,*

and ending,

> *All Joy now extinguish'd they betook to their Coaches,*
> *Each loading his Lordship with bitter Reproaches,*
> *If ye knew his kind meaning ye Maidens & Wives,*
> *His Friendship you'd pray for, the rest of your Lives,*
> *He consider'd Late Hours destructive of Health,*
> *A blessing to Mortals superior to Wealth,*
> *As this was his Motive, Pray Railers be Dumb*
> *For this Generous Good Soul is at least worth a Plumb.*

The last word indicates Plumbe (Mayor, 1778–9), brother-in-law of Johnson's friend Thrale This story is related in *City Biography*, 1800, p. 135, as an instance of his avarice. He used 'the long-tubed fumigating bellows of his gardener to blow out the candles in the ball-room at the Mansion-house' See also Nos. 5615, 5616.

$8\frac{1}{8} \times 12\frac{1}{2}$ in.

5618 [THE MIDNIGHT MAGISTRATE[2]]

*Publish'd by Fielding & Walker, Dec*ʳ *1. 1779.*

Engraving. From the *Westminster Magazine*, vii 593 (folding plate). An adaptation, reversed and altered, of No 3275, *The Midnight Magistrate, or the Humours of a Watch House*, after E Heemskirke A satire on 'hireling

---

[1] On the print is written in a contemporary hand 'Nixon fecit', it has some resemblance to his manner
[2] The title has been cut off, but is supplied from the *Westminster Magazine* The design is said to be 'taken from a slight painting of Hemskirk Junior, but here altered, adapted, and highly finished by that promising young artist, M. Moreland junior', the print being engraved from his painting.

constables', that is, on constables who were paid as substitutes for parish-ioners who were bound to serve annually without pay The interior of a watch-house, where the constable of the night sits in an armchair, wearing a hat and holding a long staff Watchmen are bringing in persons arrested during the night, others sit or stand about; some are smoking All the figures have the heads of apes. A watchman bringing in a young woman shows the constable his broken lantern He is followed by a watchman bringing in a well-dressed young man Other watchmen, with a woman wearing an apron, are seen through a large open doorway, behind them are buildings and the tower of Westminster Abbey. On the top of the door, which opens inwards, sits a large owl A large fire blazes The room is lit by a lantern hung from the roof and two large candles. Large flagons of drink are in evidence. Verses (eighteen lines) are engraved beneath the design, whose tenor is that the young woman is used by the constable as a decoy, the man is charged (falsely) with having assaulted the watch and broken the lantern. The constable acts as if he were a magistrate: *At Night Mr Constable, great as Sir John* (that is, Sir John Fielding, see No 5599), and discharges the young man, ordering him to

Give the Man half a Crown for a Lanthorn & Plaister,
And somewhat for Drinking & then good Night Master.
Thus one Cull aquited, Confederate Whore
Is Dispatch'd with a Charge to Decoy in some more.

5619 STILL LIFE A' L'HOLLANDOIS.

Publish'd as the Act directs Feby 1. 1779

Engraving (coloured impression) On the floor of a room are six pieces of blue Delft china in the shape of men and women. Descriptions are etched beneath the design, headed *Scene Delft Dramatis Personae,* the first (1) being, *Mynheer Van Vase of an Ancient Etruscan Family long since broken to pieces by ye vile Visigoths in deep love with Miss Cruet but discarded by her.* On the walls are pictures in the Dutch manner, two portraits, a still life and a landscape, and in the back wall is a casement window. Across the ceiling is etched, *Collateral branch of the Heidelbergh Family.*
$7\frac{5}{8} \times 14\frac{3}{8}$ in.

Five prints after Bunbury.

| COURIER ANGLOIS | No 4736—3 May 1779 |
| J Bretherton *fec.* | |

| COURIER FRANCOIS[1] | No 4737 [n d] |
| J. Bretherton *fec.* | |

| COXHEATH HO[1] | No. 4760—3 July 1779 |
| J. Bretherton *fec.* | |

One of many satires on Coxheath and other militia camps, see No 5523, &c.

| A VISIT TO THE CAMP | No 4765—1 Dec. 1779 |
| Watson and Dickinson (stipple). | |

See No. 5523, &c.

[1] Another version was published by Darly, 1 July 1771, and re-issued in his book dated 1 Jan. 1776, see No. 5369.

5620 A VISIT TO THE CAMP.   [? 1779]

H Bunbury Esq. Del.

Engraving (coloured impression) Another version, in reverse, of No. 4765.
It is a narrower design, with less sky and slightly less ground Part of the
dog (l.) has been cut off.

$8\frac{8}{16} \times 12\frac{7}{16}$ in

5621 THE FEATHER'D FAIR IN A FRIGHT.
     RESTORE THE BORROWED PLUMES.

*From the Original Picture by John Collet, in the possession of Carington
   Bowles. Printed for & Sold by Carington Bowles at Nº 69 in St
   Pauls Church Yard, London. Publish'd as the Act directs, 24 June
   1779.*

Engraving. For a mezzotint from the same picture see No. 4550 (1777).
It satirizes the fashion of wearing long erect ostrich feathers on the summit
of a grotesquely high and elaborately-dressed coiffure. See No 5370, &c.
   Beneath the print are twelve lines of verse, beginning

   Two Lasses who wou'd like their Mistresses shine,
   On their Heads clap'd some Feathers, to make them look fine:

$18\frac{1}{4} \times 14$ in.

Nine prints from the series of mezzotints published by Carington
Bowles.

SPRING. (392)   See No. 4564—[? 1 Jan. 1779]

After Collet.

SUMMER. (393)   See No 4565—1 Jan. 1779

After Collet.

Another impression in *The Sunday Ramble*, B M L., 578, i 10.

AUTUMN (394)   See No 4566—1 Jan. 1779

After Collet.

WINTER. (395)   See No. 4567—1 Jan. 1779

After Collet.

Also another impression, uncoloured

DISCIPLINE OF A NUNNERY (396)   See No 3776 [1779]

PAULO PURGANTI AND HIS WIFE . . . (399)   See No 4568 [1779]

KITTY COAXER DRIVING LORD DUPE, TOWARDS ROTTEN
   ROW. (400)   See No. 4569 [1779]

After Collet.

5622 AN ACTRESS AT HER TOILET, OR MISS BRAZEN JUST BREECHT. (403)

From the Original Picture by John Collet, in the possession of Carington Bowles.

Printed for & Sold by Carington Bowles, at his Map & Print Warehouse N° 69 in St Pauls Church Yard, London. Published as the Act directs [date erased, 1779].

Mezzotint (coloured impression) The interior of a well-furnished dressing-room. A young woman stands in the centre, arms akimbo, putting on a pair of breeches and looking towards the mirror which stands on a dressing-table (r.) in which a small monkey is also looking. A maid-servant (l.) stoops to fasten the buttons at the r knee. A poodle, partly shaved, barks at the actress; it stands on a play bill inscribed *and the Part of Capt Macheath by Miss* . A pair of top-boots lies on the floor. On a stool (r.) is a sword, a pair of stays, and a paper inscribed *To be seen a most surprising Hermaphrodite.*

Perhaps Mrs. Farrel who played Macheath in the *Beggar's Opera* at Covent Garden, Oct. 1777, Genest, vi. 15.

12⅞×9 in.   B.M.L, Tab. 524, 'Caricatures', i, p. 207.

THE CHURCH MILITANT. (408)   See No. 3752 [15 Sept 1779]

After Collet.

Camp scene—the chaplain conducting a service, see No. 5523, &c.

POLITICAL SATIRES

5623 THE BRITISH TAR AT OMOA

Pub^d Jany 1. 1780 by W. H Strand.

Engraving The storming of the fort of Omoa in the Bay of Honduras by British sea and land forces on 16 Oct 1779. A British sailor has just entered the fortifications from a ladder (l) up which two soldiers with fixed bayonets are climbing He holds a cutlass in each hand, offering one to a Spanish officer who is unarmed and incompletely dressed, wearing a night-cap, one leg being bare, and his stocking ungartered The sailor says *Damn your Eyes, Don, take your Choice!*; the Spaniard answers *Ah Misericordia Segnor Inglese! me beg to be excused.* In the foreground British troops with fixed bayonets advance towards Spaniards who flee in disorder, holding up their hands in alarm The Spanish flag has been hauled down, and is under the feet of the British sailor, above it flies the Union Jack. A British ship (l.) is firing at the fort

This incident attracted great attention at the beginning of 1780 An English sailor, having scrambled over the wall, a cutlass in each hand, met a Spanish officer just roused from sleep who had forgotten his sword; the sailor therefore gave him one of his cutlasses, saying 'he scorned any advantage, you are now upon a footing with me'. *Ann. Reg.* 1780, p. 214. See also Walpole, *Letters*, xi. 79–80, and No. 5624.

Has some resemblance to the manner of Gillray.

$9 \times 13\frac{1}{8}$ in

5624 JOHN BULL TRIUMPHANT.

[Gillray]

Publish'd Jany 4th 1780. by W Humphrey N° 227 Strand

Engraving (coloured and uncoloured impressions). A bull, snorting ferociously, has tossed a Spaniard high in the air, a shower of coins falls from his pockets The bull is attempting to charge a Frenchman and an American (r), the latter being an Indian brave, holding a spear and wearing a girdle and head-dress of feathers, they shrink back in alarm, the American sheltering behind the Frenchman But the bull is checked by a Scot in Highland dress, who holds its tail saying, *Luton, a—Ho* (Luton being one of the estates of Bute). Bute's waist is held by North, who says *Bushey Park, a Ho* (North lived at Bushey Park, Lady North being the Ranger of the Park), and North's by Lord Mansfield saying *Caen Wood a Ho* (Caen (or Ken) wood being the estate bought by Mansfield from Bute. Cf. No 4885). In the foreground (l) a Dutchman sits grinning on a cask inscribed *Hollands Gin*, he is about to light his pipe with a burning paper on which is inscribed *? TM*, presumably representing the memorials of Yorke, see No 5568 Beneath the design is engraved

The Bull see enrag'd has the Spaniard engag'd,
  And gave him a Terrible Toss,
As he mounts up on high, the Dollars see fly,
  To make the bold Britton rejoice,

The Yankee & Monsieur, at this look quite queer,
For they see that his Strength will prevail,
If they'd give him his way, and not with foul play,
Still tug the poor Beast by the Tail.

The 'terrible toss' is the capture of Omoa, see No 5623, when the value of the prizes in the harbour was estimated at 3,000,000 dollars Stedman, *American War*, 1794, ii 173. Rodney's more important successes in the Mediterranean were on 8 and 16 Jan.; his first dispatches did not reach London till 11 Feb

Bute and Mansfield are usually represented as inflaming England against America, cf. No 5287. One of many satires in which Holland appears as a neutral profiting by the war, regardless of treaties, see No 5557, &c.

Grego, *Gillray*, pp. 29–30.
Van Stolk, No. 4303.

$8\frac{3}{4} \times 13\frac{3}{8}$ in

5625 "AND ADAM HAD POWER OVER ALL THE BEASTS OF
THE EARTH" *Gen[s]*

[Gillray?]

Publish'd Jan[y] 9th 1780. by W. Humphrey N[o] 227 Strand.

Engraving A burlesque representation of the duel between William Adam and C J Fox on 29 Nov 1779. Adam (r) dressed as a Highland chieftain, in tartan, with a very short kilt, a target on his l arm, fires a pistol at Fox, who holds out both his arms and leans back as if wounded, his pistol falling to the ground. Fox has a fox's head and a brush. Adam's second, a fat man (Humberston), stands full face with clasped hands, not watching the contest. That of Fox (l.), who is thin (Fitzgerald), holds up his hands in alarm and appears about to intervene

For this duel see No 5575 and cf. a lampoon by 'A B' · *Paradise Regain'd; or the Battle of Adam and the Fox An heroick Poem.* (B.M.L. 163, m. 21.)

The duel between Lord Shelburne and Fullarton, on 22 Mar. 1780, was attributed to the same motive and increased the unpopularity of the Government, see No. 5659.

$6 \times 9\frac{1}{16}$ in.

5626 THE ENGAGEMENT BETWEEN D'ORVILLIERS & K—P—L

Pub[d] Jan[y] 12th 1780. *by T. Low.*

Engraving. D'Orvilliers (l) and Keppel (r.) bending down, their backs turned to each others, bombard each other with excrement, that of D'Orvilliers going over Keppel's head The French admiral's sword and the English admiral's cutlass lie on the ground. Behind is the sea, with men-of-war firing, one flying the British flag Beneath the design is engraved:

Don't you think my good Friends this a comical Farce is,
To see two Great Admirals fight with their A———,
Mons[r] Squirts Soup-meagre across K—p—ls back,
But he in return gives a far harder Smack.
What a Smoak & a Stink! & yet neither prevails
For how can it be? when they both turn their Tails.
Price 6d.

This represents the engagement off Ushant, 27 July 1778, when the two fleets passed on opposite tacks; the British, firing at the hulls, inflicted heavy damages, the French firing at the masts crippled their enemy's power of movement, but having the power to attack, they did not use it Mahan, *Influence of Sea Power*, p. 351. Keppel failed to close with the French and the French fleet regained Brest. See Nos. 5484, 5486 for the engagement and Nos. 5536, 5537, 5570 for the resulting court martials on Keppel and Palliser Keppel, after being a national hero at the time of his court martial, became unpopular after Rodney's victory and recall in 1782, see No 5992, &c.

5 ⅛ × 10¾ in.

5627 THE FRENCH SEIZURE ON THE COAST OF SUSSEX.

[T Colley?]

Pub⁴ by Thoˢ Colley Clare Market London Janʸ 18. 1780.

Engraving Six French sailors attempt to drag a bull towards the sea-shore off which lies a ship flying the French flag Four of them tug at the animal's tail, the other two at a rope round its neck A French officer in the attitude of a fencer holds his sword to the bull's nose In the foreground a sailor drags a stoutly-resisting sheep by a rope held over his shoulder while an officer pierces frogs with his sword. All have long pigtail queues, and the officers are foppishly dressed in the French manner.

5⅝×8⅞ in

Another impression (Colley's publication line partly erased):

Pub Jan 18 1780 E. Hedges Nᵒ 92 Under the Royal Exchange Cornhill

5628 DON BARCELLO, VAN TRUMP, & MONSIEUR DE CRICKEY, COMBIN'D TOGETHER

[T Colley?]

Pub· Janʸ 23 1780 by E. Hedges.

Engraving. Figures, much burlesqued, representing Spain, Holland, and France, stand back to back, their necks surrounded by a rope, one end of which is being pulled by a British sailor in trousers (l), the other by a British sailor wearing the petticoat then worn by sailors One sailor (l) says *D—n me Jack how the Dutchman Grins.* The other says *Ah Monsieu You have got your Neck in a halter.* The Spaniard, in profile to the l, and the Frenchman in profile to the r, are crying for mercy, their hands raised in supplication The stout Dutchman, full face (centre), has an expression of intense melancholy and holds up his hands deprecatingly; a pipe is thrust in his cap.

Holland was not yet at war with England but a number of Dutch ships laden with naval stores for the French were brought by Captain Fielding to Spithead on 2 Jan 1780 The Dutch admiral, van Bylandt, who was giving them protection, refused to allow a search for contraband, shots were exchanged, and some of the ships brought to Portsmouth, Bylandt accompanying them Other ships escaped to French ports This roused great indignation in Holland, see Nos. 5712, 5719. Don Barcelo was a

Spanish admiral whose capture of two Dutch ships in Nov. 1779 led to the Armed Neutrality F. P. Renaut, *Les Provinces-Unies et la Guerre ..*, 1924, pp. 294 ff.

$5\frac{13}{16} \times 9\frac{1}{8}$ in.

5629 BRITANNIA PROTECTED FROM THE TERRORS OF AN INVASION

Published Jany 26 1780 by Ja^s Dareny opposite the King's-head in the Strand

Engraving. Britannia (l.) sits on a raised seat with her shield and spear. At her feet stand two women, one, a stout fish-wife with her arms akimbo, wearing a cloak, hat, and apron, a knife at her waist, her fish beside her; the other, lean and elderly with a face of fury, her fists clenched, a pair of scissors and a pin-cushion hang from her waist. Both are shouting defiance at three figures (r.) representing Spain, France, and America who, on the other side of a narrow stream inscribed *English Channel*, are fleeing in alarm America (r), with a feathered head-dress, carries the striped American flag France and Spain hold each a drawn sword Darts of lightning reach the fugitives from the mouth of the lean virago. Beneath the design is etched, "*A loud-crying Woman & a Scold shall be sought out to drive away the Enemies.*" Cf. No. 5552.

$8 \times 12\frac{3}{4}$ in.

5630 GOLDEN RULES . OF FREDERICK K . OF PRUSSIA.

Publish'd as the Act Directs For the Proprietor by W Humphrey Jany 29 1780 N° 227 Strand or N° 18 New Bond S^t

Engraving The double-headed Hohenzollern eagle clutches in its claws a ribbon on which is inscribed *The Glorious Discharge of Arnold the Miller*. In the centre of the body is a circle, containing the initials *F R* [Frederick Rex], surmounted by a crown. Framing this design is a garland of oak-leaves, olive-leaves, &c , intertwined with a ribbon on which is inscribed, *Take away the Wicked from ye Presence of ye King and his Throne shall be exalted; No respect of Persons, May the name of Justice never be violated by Acts of injustice or Oppression, in the Presence of Justice all should be equal wither [sic] Prince or Peasant; To bring all Law Suits to a speedy conclusion* To the garland are attached medallions which hang in the two lower corners of the print containing miniature figures: r , Perseus in Roman armour holding a spear and a shield with Medusa's head, (l.) Justice holding scales and uplifted sword The design has a background of horizontal lines.

An implied censure on political and social conditions in England, cf. No 4388 (1771).

$5 \times 5\frac{3}{4}$ in.

5631 THE ALLIES —PAR NOBILE FRATRÛM[1]

Indignatio fecit

Pub^d as the Act directs Feb^ry 3, 1780 by I. Almon, Piccadilly.

Engraving. George III sharing a cannibal feast with an Indian chief

---

[1] Cf 'A Merry Song about Murder' (on George III), quoted from the *London Courant*, 25 Mar 1780, by Walpole as an instance of the horrid length to which 'party will carry men' *Last Journals*, 1910, ii. 264.

Under a palm-tree (l) are three American Indians; one, standing, holds the dismembered body of an infant, so that its blood pours into a cup formed of a skull held by a kneeling Indian (l). The third (r), whose feathers and bracelets show that he is a chief, sits on the ground holding a tomahawk in one hand, a long bone which he is gnawing in the other On his l, and in the centre of the design, sits George III on the ground, gnawing the other end of the Indian's bone, while he holds a smoking bowl made of a skull He is wearing the ribbon and star of the Garter. On the ground in front are the head and limbs of an infant, and a dog vomiting. On the king's l is a flag-staff, surmounted by a cross, from it hangs a ragged flag on which is inscribed *GEO . . . E the T[hird] by the Grace of . of . . . King* [Def]*ender of the Faith &c* Beneath it, a *Holy Bible* stands upside down.

Two figures hasten towards the feast from the r A very fat bishop wearing a mitre holds in his r. hand a crozier, in the l a paper inscribed *Form of Prayer 4ᵗʰ Febʳʸ General Fast* He is saying *That thy Ways may be known upon Earth, thy saving Health among all Nations.* Behind him is a sailor carrying on his head a packing-case inscribed *Scalping Knives, Crucifixes, Tomahawks, Presents to Indians 96,000*; he says, *D——n my dear Eyes, but we are hellish good Christians.* Beneath the design is engraved, *Qui facit per alium, facit per se. Princ. Leg Ang* In the upper r corner of the print is engraved on a scroll, *The Party of Savages¹ went out with Orders not to spare Man, Woman, or Child. To this cruel Mandate even some of the Savages made an Objection, respecting the butchering the Women & Children; but they were told the Children would make Soldiers, & the Women would keep up the Stock Remembrancer, Vol. 8. p. 77.* This is a quotation from 'A Narrative of the capture and treatment of John Dodge, by the English at Detroit', printed in Almon's propagandist annual publication, 1779 (It is an extract from 'The Narrative . . .' written by Dodge and published at Philadelphia in 1779. M. C. Tyler, *The Literary History of the American Revolution*.)

The print appears to derive also from Burke's speech on 6 Feb 1778 when Barré said 'with many invectives against the Bishops, that it ought to be posted up in every church under *their* proclamation for the fast . . .'. Walpole, *Last Journals*, ii 105. *Ann. Reg* 1778, p. 110 *Parl Hist.* xix. 594 ff.

In the Declaration of Independence the king was accused of having 'endeavoured to bring on the inhabitants of our frontiers the merciless Indian savages. . . .' Franklin's faked *Supplement to the Boston Independent Chronicle* printed at his private press at Passy (1782) published letters purporting to be from Indians and British officers, which accompanied bundles of scalps of men, women, and children to be sent to George III in expectation of reward. In the same paper was a letter by Franklin purporting to be from Paul Jones (1781) to Sir Joseph Yorke in which the king is accused (*inter alia*) of engaging 'savages to murder their [his people's] defenceless farmers, women and children'. L. S Livingston, *Franklin and his Press at Passy*, New York, Grolier Club, 1914, pp 58 ff For Indian atrocities see also No 5470, &c. The bishop is probably Markham, archbishop of York, see No. 5400, &c.

Reproduced, S G. Fisher, *True History of the American Revolution*, 1902, p 380

8⅝ × 14 in

¹ The original here adds 'under Le Mote'.

5632 MINISTERIAL PURGATIONS, OR STATE GRIPINGS.

Publishd Feby 9th 1780 & Sold at N° 132 Fleet Street.

Engraving. A design in six approximately equal compartments (numbered) in two rows, in each of which is a figure seated in a latrine, words issuing from his mouth in a label:

1. (The central compartment of the upper row.) Lord North, his hand to his forehead, with an expression of alarm, says,

The People I've Tax'd till with rage now they burn
And they've Curst my poor guts, now I find in return

He wears his Garter ribbon and star and resembles the king.

2. (l.) Lord Mansfield in judge's wig and gown, says,
I wish Doctor Stewart was here once again,
His Pills I am Sure would relieve all my Pain

'Dr. Stewart' is Bute. On the ground is an open book, one page inscribed *Millar*, the other *Mansfeild*

3. (r.) Lord Sandwich (Jemmy Twitcher), his hands clasped, is saying,

O! my Guts! what a Twitcher!—in life I've no Ray
For my Soul to Old-nick is now Fleeting away.

An allusion to the murder of Sandwich's mistress, Martha Ray, by Hickman in 1779, see No 5540, &c For 'twitcher' cf No 4877. By his side is an open book inscribed *Pleasures of Love*

4 (Lower row, l) Lord George Germain, his arms folded, his sword broken, the hilt hanging on the wall, the blade on the ground, is saying,

My Purging at Minden I'd almost forgot,
But this Griping—has tied all my Gutts in a knot.

For Minden see Nos. 3680-7, &c.

5. (Centre) The Devil, smiling, and turning to the r. to address 6, says,

Come Parson for thou! art my best Child of all,
Assist, or your Brothers, will purge till they fall

6. (r.) Parson Bate in clerical gown and bands, the *Morning Post* on the ground beside him, says,

I'm Grip'd 'till I'm ready to give up the Ghost,
Yet I'll Strain! all I can in the fam'd Morning Post.

For Bate as ministerial journalist see No. 5550, &c.

Beneath the design is engraved:

To see such Great Men! their faces thus screw,
Is a terrible Sight —if the Picture is true;
For it wants, you'll allow, but a small penetration,
To find out that these, are the Heads of the Nation,
But we guess who has Serv'd them this D—m'd stinking trick
When amongst them you see their adviser Old-nick,
O! who but must Pitty the case of Great Britain
When its Ministers purge thus,—that must be beshitten.

Cf Nos 5479-81.

$8\frac{1}{2} \times 12\frac{1}{4}$ in

5633 THE COUNCIL

Publishd as y^e Act Directs for y^e Proprietor by W Humphrey Feby 9 1780 N 227 Strand or N° 18 Bond Street.

Engraving. Three men seated in a latrine: North (centre), Mansfield (l) in judge's wig and gown, and Sandwich (r), *Boreas, Caen Wood* (Mansfield's house near Hampstead), and *Jemmy Twitcher* being inscribed over their respective heads. North looks with an expression of satisfaction at Mansfield; in his r. hand is a large torn paper inscribed *National Debt 206,000 000 00 60 000£ for Razors, Jews Harps* (probably implying that the Jews were making large profits in taking up loans and were shaving their beards on becoming wealthy). In his r. hand is a fragment of paper inscribed *Improvements in Bushy 1780*, implying that he is drawing on the Exchequer for improvements to his own house Under his feet is a large torn paper inscribed *Protestant Association Lord G   Gordon President.* North refused (5 Jan 1780) a request from Lord George Gordon that he (North) should present the petition of the Protestant Association for repeal of the Catholic Relief Act (presented 2 June by Gordon with disastrous consequences) de Castro, *Gordon Riots*, p 15

Mansfield turns round to tear fragments from *Magna Chart[a]* which is pasted on the wall behind him. Sandwich, with an expression of exultation, is tearing an ensign flag, implying that he is playing havoc with the Navy. Under his foot is a torn paper, *Petition . . . County of Huntingdon* (Walpole writes, 'Sussex, Hertfordshire, Cheshire, Devonshire, and even Lord Sandwich's favoured Huntingdonshire voted to hold meetings in the manner of Yorkshire,' *Last Journals*, 1910, ii. 265)

Pasted on the wall are three prints· *The State of the Nation*, a free but fairly correct version of No. 5479, in ten compartments instead of fourteen , *Poor Old England*, the single figure of a man standing full face, not identical with No. 6200 or with a print of the same title published in 1784. *The Family of ye Wrong Heads*, a stout man stands full face, his r. arm round a cupid, his l. round (?) a man. This is over the head of Sandwich There is also on the wall a paper inscribed :

> *Neglecting faithful Worth for Fawning Slaves;*
> *Whose Councels weak & Wicked, easy rous'd*
> *To Paltry Scheems of Absolute Command,*
> *To seek their Splendour in their sure Disgrace,*
> *And in a broken ruin'd Peoples Wealth.*
> *When such o'ercast the State, no Bond of Love,*
> *No Heart, no Soul, no Unity, no Nerve,*
> *Combines the loose disjointed Publick, lost*
> *To Fame abroad, to Happiness at Home*
> > *Vide Thompson, Liberty Book y 4.*

For the Association movement see No 5638, &c. For a similar association of the Protestant Petition with County Petitions see Nos. 5638, 5649, 5680, 5687.

$8\frac{3}{8} \times 13\frac{1}{16}$ in.

Another impression, n d., with the title

5633A THE PRIVY COUNCIL.

Pub^d by H . Humphrey N° 227 Strand.

5634 THE POLITICAL MOON

OR THE PRESENT STATE OF THE MAJORITY AS THEY
APPEAR EVERY WHERE

[? Gillray.]

Publish'd as the Act directs Feby 10. 1780.

Engraving A design in three circles within a larger circle which is covered
with a shading of zigzag lines In each inset circle is the figure of a man
Above, a man walks rapidly from l to r , a large stick under his arm, his
face half-concealed in a blanket or covering worn as a cloak. His dishevelled hair is full of straw and he looks suspiciously over his r. shoulder
Beneath the circle is engraved the word *Mad.*

In the lower (r) circle a man in profile to the r. leans back in a chair
asleep, his head sunk on his breast Beneath the circle is engraved *Asleep.*

On the r. of this is a circle in which a man walks staggering and bent,
his head a featureless blank. Beneath is engraved *Drunk.*

Diameter, $9\frac{1}{2}$ in ; inset circles, 4 in.

5635 THE STATE TINKERS.

[Gillray.]

Publish'd Feby 10th 1780. by W. Humphrey N° 227 Strand

Engraving. Three men with mallet, hammer, and chisel are breaking an
enormous bowl which is already much damaged, cracked, and patched.
The bowl is supported on its end by a block (l.) on which stand two of the
tinkers On the ground (r) kneels Lord North, working on the interior
of the bowl with a hammer and chisel On the ground beside him is
a paper inscribed *Ld North* Behind the bowl (l), and about to strike
it with a large mallet, a man dressed as an artisan stands on a block;
a paper in his pocket is inscribed *Ld Sandwich* and pasted on the
wall behind his head is a *List of the Navy.* Next him, wielding
a hammer and chisel, is a man dressed as a military officer; the *Plan
of Minden* on the wall behind his head shows that he is Lord George
Germain Behind North, his hands raised in pleased surprise, stands
George III, wearing a feathered turban surmounted by a crown, probably
intended to indicate that he is behaving like an oriental despot, see Nos.
5544-7 Over his shoulder looks Bute in tartan, also smiling, his r. hand
raised, as if admonishing the king Beneath the title is engraved:

*The National Kettle, which once was a good one,
For boiling of Mutton, of Beef, & of Pudding,
By the fault of the Cook, was quite out of repair,
When the Tinkers were sent for,—Behold them & Stare.
The Master he thinks, they are wonderful Clever,
And cries out in raptures, 'tis done! now or never!
Yet sneering the Tinkers their old Trade pursue,
In stopping of one Hole—they're sure to make Two.*

$10\frac{7}{8} \times 9\frac{1}{4}$ in.

5636 THE BULL ROASTED, OR THE POLITICAL COOKS SERVING THEIR CUSTOMERS.

Publish'd as the Act directs Feby 12, 1780, by I. Harris, Sweetings Alley, Cornhill, London.

Engraving A companion print to No 5640. A large bull transfixed on a spit roasts before a fire (l) over which hangs a large covered pot Beside the animal sits George III (l.) wearing a ribbon, in his r. hand he holds the end of the spit, in the l a handkerchief, saying *Turning the Spit, has made me Sweat; by George.* Sandwich holds a large spoon to baste it, saying, *Not quite so fat as he was formerly.* Bute, in tartan, stands behind the bull, saying, *Twas a Noble Beast, Jemmy Twitcher.* On the r is a dinner table, behind which sit figures representing France, America, and Spain France is saying *A bit of the Brown for Louis* America, a Red Indian woman, with a feathered head-dress, her knife raised to her mouth, her l. hand in her plate clutching a fork, is saying, *A Dish of Buttock for Congress* Spain, in cloak and feathered hat, says *Some of the Flank for Don Diego* On the ground in front of the table sits a Dutchman eating with a spoon out of a bowl; he says *I've got a Dish of Memorial Broth*, an allusion to the succession of memorials presented by Sir Joseph Yorke to the States General on breaches of their treaties with England, see Nos. 5568, 5571, &c. Lord North is bringing a dish from the fire to the table, saying *I'll serve you all my good Friends as fast as possible.* Beneath the design is engraved:

> Behold the poor Bull! once Britania's chief boast,
> Is kill'd by State Cooks, and laid down for a Roast!
> While his Master, who should all his Honours maintain,
> Turns the Spit tho' he should such an Office disdain
>
> Monsieur licks his gills at a bit of the Brown,
> And the other two wish for to gobble him down,
> But may ill digestion attend on the treat,
> And the Cooks every one soon be roasted, & Eat.

$7\frac{3}{4} \times 12\frac{7}{8}$ in.

5637 THE CONTRAST OR SACK & BUDGET.

Publish'd as the Act directs, Feby 12. 1780 by J. Harris, Sweetings Alley, Cornhill

Engraving. Two standing figures: Lord North (l.) and Jeffery Dunstan (r). North, a substantial sack over his l. shoulder, inscribed *Budget*, his r. hand in his breeches pocket, is calling *Tory rory Gold* The other, copied from a print published by I. Whitehead, 15 Nov. 1779, holds an empty sack over his shoulder, inscribed *Sack*, and is calling *Whigs Whigs Brass*, he wears a coat over a torn shirt and his ungartered stockings are falling down his legs. Beneath the design is engraved:

> How different the Figures which here you behold!
> The one asks for BRASS and the other for GOLD
> Each are droll Fellows, 'tis known in their Station,
> And each of Some Service 'tis hoped—to the Nation.

Dunstan's chief occupation was buying old wigs, his droll way of crying 'old wigs' always attracted a crowd in the London streets. He was elected Mayor of Garratt in 1785, *D N.B.*

One of many satires on North's budgets, see Nos. 5578, 5703, &c $7\frac{3}{8} \times 8\frac{1}{4}$ in (pl.).

5638 ASSOCIATION, OR PUBLIC VIRTUE DISPLAYED IN A CONTRASTED VIEW.

J.S. inv:

Published as the Act directs 15 Feby 1780 London Printed for Danl Wilson at N° 20 Portugal Street Lincolns Inn   Price 1^s

Engraving   Several scenes combined in one design.   The Associations of various counties to present petitions and form committees to demand reforms are represented in the upper r portion of the plate: A procession of men walks (r to l), their leader holding a standard with the arms of the county inscribed *County of York 30 Decr 1779* (the date of the meeting at which it was agreed to present a petition and prepare a plan for an Association to secure reform)   He holds a paper inscribed *Petition* and says, *Virtue & Fortitude shall Guide us.*   Representatives of the other petitioning and associating counties follow, with the appropriate dates on labels issuing from their mouths. *Middlesex 7 Jan; Chester 13 Jan; Hertford Jan 17; Cumberland 20 Jan, Huntingdon, Surrey Sussex Dorset 21 Jan* ('Huntingdon' being in large letters, cf No. 5633), *Essex & Bedford 24 Jan; Gloucester, Somerset & Wilts 26 Jan, Norfolk 29 Jan, Brecon Feb 9.*   The last man carries an ensign flag on which is inscribed *London Newcastle upon Tyne Bristol Westminster &c. &c &c*   Beneath the procession is engraved *Immortal Gods! What Honor waits the men who save their Country from impending Ruin*   The leader is probably intended for Sir George Savile.

On the l George III is seated in his closet; a young man stands before him addressing, not the king, but an imaginary audience, saying, *The only Patriot His Power is too Confined*   This is perhaps intended for Lord George Gordon's private interview with the king on 27 Jan 1780; several satires associate the Protestant Petition with the county petitions, see Nos 5633, 5649, 5680   Outside the door of the royal closet and facing the petitioners is a monster with wings and three heads, breathing fire.

In the lower r part of the print Britannia sits on a ruinous stone pedestal which is being further undermined by a female figure with a forked tail and the legs of a satyr; she is applying a lever to its base saying, *And shall not I, Corruption is my name, Undermine the British Constitution.*   Lord North attacks the pedestal with a pickaxe, saying, *I will assist you Sister in the same Design*   Bute, in Highland dress with the Garter ribbon and star, flourishes a broadsword, while he takes from Britannia the staff and cap of Liberty; he says, *Away wi ye to the Deel Where is your Liberty now.*   Britannia, holding her shield and *Magna Carta*, says to the marching petitioners above her head, *Tis you alone my Friends who can revive my Drooping Hopes & save me from Distruction.*   Behind Britannia (l) and in a glory of rays stands a man inscribed *Chatham* with outstretched arms, saying *O Cleanse Yon Augean Stable.*   He points towards the design beneath the king's closet   This represents the House of Commons (l.); the Speaker in his chair, members seated on each side of a table. It is seen through two pillars, up one (r) climbs an alligator, round the other is a serpent with a branch of apples in its mouth   Above is inscribed *Ruled by*

Powerful Influence A procession of members walks (l to r) from the House up a path leading to the door of the king's closet above. They carry scrolls inscribed *25 000, 5000; £40,000, 15,000 £10,000, £50 000* One says, *Secure in the Enjoyment of Places Pensions & Emoluments of Office we fear not the Clamour of Yorkshire Clodpoles*; another says, *God help the Rich the Poor can beg.* Their leader carries an *Address of Thanks.* Beneath this gang of ministerialists a mythological figure leaning against an anchor and a gushing water-conduit (? Neptune) says,

> *Is there not some Chosen Curses,*
> *Some Hidden Thunder in the Stores of Heaven*
> *Red with Uncommon Wrath to Blast the Men*
> *Who build their Greatness on their Country's Ruin*

A man stands in the foreground holding out a scroll inscribed,

List of Grievances
Public Credit—Weakened Nation
Debt Increasing Fresh Taxes
Accumulating Trade & Commer[ce]
Expireing Independance cast down & the
Public Treasure Wasted in Corrupting the Morals of the
People He is saying, *No New Taxes but a Retrenchment of Public Expences.*

The county associations and petitions began with a great meeting at York on 30 Dec. 1779 See C Wyvill, *Political Papers*, 6v , 1794-1802. Smelt, L., *Account of the Meeting at York* 1780. Walpole, *Last Journals*, 1910, ii. 260-1, 263 ff. Adolphus, *Hist. of England*, 1841, iii. 93 ff. Fitzmaurice, *Shelburne*, 1912, ii 46 ff Veitch, *Genesis of Parliamentary Reform*, 1913, chap. III. On 8 Feb. Shelburne's motion for a committee of both Houses, excluding all pensioners and place-men, to inquire into the expenditure of public money, was rejected, and Sir George Savile presented the Yorkshire petition in the House of Commons. Cf. also the debate of 8 May 1781, *Parl. Hist* xxii. 138 ff. and Wraxall, *Memoirs*, 1884, ii. 442 f. For Gordon in the closet see Walpole, *Letters*, xi 135 For the county petitions and the Association movement see also Nos. 5633, 5640, 5645, 5649, 5657, 5665, 5668, 5675, 5693, 5829, 5958. For the evil influence of the king's closet see No. 5470.

$8\frac{1}{8} \times 13\frac{11}{16}$ in.

5639 WHELPS TAUGHT TO READ BY AN ORATOR FROM THE NORTH

Pub^d acco^s to act Feby 17 1780 by D Long

Engraving. A dog with a human face intended for that of George III, wearing a crown and the ribbon and star of the Garter, sits on a bench; on his collar is inscribed *Hon so . qui* [*Honi soit qui mal y pense*]. Lord North stands by, patting him and holding by its handle a horn-book on which is the alphabet He is looking round at a bystander on the r On the l. stands Charles Fox, obese, with a fox's head, pointing at the dog. Behind the dog's bench are Bute in tartan and a man dressed as a military officer (? Lord George Germain) who points at the dog, grins and looks at Fox

This appears to be a reversion to the idea prevalent before 1778 that the king was his ministers' tool, cf. No. 5288.

7⅜ × 10 ¹³⁄₁₆ in.

5640 THE BULL OVER-DROVE OR THE DRIVERS IN DANGER.

London Publish'd as the Act directs Feby 21, 1780, by I. Harris, Sweetings Alley Cornhill.

Engraving A companion print to No. 5636 A bull (c) tramples on the prostrate body of a drover holding a long spiked staff, whose words, *O! I'm as dead as Miss Ray* (cf Nos. 5540, 5632), show that he is intended for Sandwich The bull is kicking violently towards the other drovers, the foremost of whom, Lord North, leaning back, with a large rent in his waist-coat, says, *He has Kick'd the Treasury of my Guts out.* Behind him is another minister, Lord George Germain, wearing a ribbon (incorrectly), he says *This is worse than the Battle of Minden* (see No 3680, &c). Behind (l), spectators, a sailor and three other men, wave their hats, shouting *Huzza*

In front of the bull (r) are figures representing France, America (as a Red Indian), and Spain France says *By Gar, my friend America I must leave you, dis Bull vil play le Diable* America says, *I fear Monsieur I shall get little by your Friendship* Spain says, *I wish I was safe out of his way, he beats the Bulls of Spain* For British naval successes, 1779–80, see Nos 5623, 5624, 5642, 5646, 5647, 5648, 5658. Beneath the design is engraved:

The State Drovers to madness, had drove the poor Bull,
Their Goads and their Tethers no longer can rule,
He Snorts Kicks and Tramples among the curst rout,
Who fall by his Jury or Stagger about

O! may all such Drovers thus meet with their Fate,
Who Hamper, and Gall so, the Bull of the State,
May his Terror, thus fill them with fear, and dismay,
While the People all Chearfully Cry out, Huzza!

The activities of the associated counties, see No 5638, &c, were so hostile to the Government that Walpole considered that civil war was imminent unless the king dismissed the Ministry and called upon the Opposition. *Last Journals*, 1910, ii. 275 (24 Feb 1780) See No 5644, perhaps intended as an answer to this print, and No 5645

Reissued, 21 Feb. 1782.

7⅞ × 12⅞ in

5641 GEORGE WASHINGTON, COMMANDER IN CHIEF OF Yᴱ ARMIES OF Yᴱ UNITED STATES OF AMERICA.

Engrav'd by W Sharp from an Original Picture

London. Publish'd according to Act of Parliament Feby 22d 1780

Engraving Frontispiece to *A Poetical Epistle to his excellency George Washington Esq* [as in title] *from an Inhabitant of the State of Maryland Annapolis Printed 1779 London Reprinted for C. Dilly . J Almon,* [&c] Bust portrait directed to l. of Washington in uniform, in an oval frame, within a rectangle The frame is surmounted by the rattlesnake emblem with the cap of Liberty, on which rays are directed Below it are a striped flag on l , a flag with stars on r , cannons and cannon-balls, with branches of palm and olive. Above is inscribed *Dont tread on me*, the motto on the flag of the continental navy until superseded by the stars and stripes.

The verses are a violent attack on 'proud Britain', e.g.,

> What tho' to glut her unrelenting ire,
> Of German tyrants German slaves she hire (p 8)

The pamphlet was sold to raise money for 'American prisoners now suffering confinement in the gaols of England', cf No 5853

The many portraits of Washington[1] published in London during the war emphasize the fact that he was regarded by the Whigs as a national leader, Washington's army being called 'our army' in the House of Commons, see Onslow's speech, 15 Mar. 1782 and No. 6065, and cf Chatham, 2 Dec 1777 'our bretheren in America, Whigs in principle and heroes in conduct' *Parl Hist* xix 477 Cf also No 5340 The term 'United States' had as yet no legal significance even in America, as the Articles of Confederation were not ratified by all the states until 1781. For the snake emblem see No. 5336, &c. C. H. Hart, *Catalogue of Engraved Portraits of Washington*, No. 92

$6\frac{1}{4} \times 4\frac{7}{16}$ in.   B.M L 11630. b. 1/12.

This plate was used, date and publication line as above,[2] as a frontispiece to 'The Constitutions of the Several Independent States of America . . . Rev. William Jackson', 1783, with a dedication to the Duke of Portland.

B M L. 1197. f. 22

A copy by Brunton was used as a frontispiece to another London reprint of the 'Poetical Epistle' published by Bennett Wheeler, 1781. C. H. Hart, No 93 Not in B.M L

5642 THE 3 KINGS.
    WHO PAYS THE RECKONING, OR DON DIEGO IN THE DUMPS

Published as the Act directs Feby 26. 1780 by W Richardson, Nᵒ 68 High Holborn.

Engraving. The kings of England, France, and Spain stand or sit by a table on which is a punch-bowl, wine-bottles, and glasses. Behind the table is a four-leaved screen A waiter with the bill in his hand, a napkin under his arm, says to George III, who is standing beside the table (l), *Who pays the Reckoning*. He answers, *O! the French king Pays for me* France, wearing a coat patterned with fleur-de-lys, points to the king of Spain on his l. saying, *The King of Spain Pays for all* Spain, seated, in cloak and feathered hat, says *D——n the Family Compact*. Cf No 5567. For the recent victories of England over Spain see Nos. 5623, 5624, 5646, &c. Cf Walpole to Mann, 3 Mar. 1780, on Rodney's success, 'It secures Gibraltar, eases your Mediterranean a little, and must vex the Spaniards and their Monarch, not

---

[1] e g the mezzotint by Valentine Green after Trumbull published in 1781.
[2] C H Hart lists a copy No 92 a, where the publication line is altered to *Feby 22ᵈ 1783 by J. Stockdale.*

satisfied before with his cousin of Bourbon'. *Letters*, xi 134 See also F. P. Renaut, *La Pacte de Famille et l'Amérique*, 1922, pp 305 ff Cf. No. 5664.

$6\frac{7}{8} \times 7\frac{3}{8}$ in

5643 THE TIMES

Publish'd as the Act directs by T M C. Feby 26 1780

Engraving The Pope enthroned on a raised circular dais of three steps inscribed respectively *Superstition, Ignorance,* and *Absolute Power*, he wears his triple crown, holds a crosier and a document inscribed *no faith to be keep with Heritick[s]* Two keys hang from his waist, and serpents writhe under his feet Two sceptres lie across one another at his feet. Three sovereigns wearing crowns and ermine robes sit by him, their seats on the ground besides his dais· On his l. the King of Spain holding a circular shield on which is a globe representing the world; his crown terminates in a fool's cap, very inapplicable to Charles III,[1] but see the libel on the king of Spain quoted in Walpole, *Memoirs of the Reign of George III,* 1845, iv. 169, 372–5 On the Pope's r. sits the king of France, his fleur-de-lys shield at his feet, holding a paper inscribed *Grande Alliance.* Behind him is the Emperor, his sceptre ornamented with the Hapsburg eagle. Between these two appears the monster with seven heads (six visible) which denotes the 'Beast', its fore-paws resting on a large book, *Bible.* On the ground in front of the Pope are documents inscribed, *Articles of the Catholic Faith* and a list of *Pardons murder .. 10, Adultry 9, Robbery 8 Beating a Priest 12.* Behind (r.), a martyr is being burned at the stake, a pikeman and monks standing by, one holding a cross in front of the victim; beneath is inscribed *Popish cruelty.*

In the foreground (r), George III, a drawn sword, point upwards, against his shoulder, receives a deputation of Protestant petitioners: two ministers in gowns and clerical wigs kneel at his feet, one holding a paper inscribed *Address,* the other saying *These Persecutions must be always remembered by Protestants,* he points to a Scotsman, partly visible on the extreme r., with a drawn broadsword, who is saying *The Deel a ane o' that Popish Crew shall come this way.* He wears Highland dress and a large thistle decorates his cap. Above his head appear the ends of three bayoneted muskets inscribed *150,000.* He represents either Lord George Gordon, or Scotland, where the riots had prevented the passing of a Catholic Relief Act, see No 5534, &c Behind these figures is a sign-post inscribed *the Way to Scotland,* on it is a sign-board. the Pope mounted on a beast, the Devil seated by him, confronted by a prancing unicorn Next the sign-post (r.) is an obelisk inscribed *Gun Powder Plot; Massacre of the Protestants in Ireland; Fire of London 1666; Burning of Cranmer, Bradford &c &c* Behind the king stand two courtiers, one wearing a star At their feet lies *Magna Charta* torn, and the cap of Liberty which a dog is befouling.

In the foreground on the l a Dutchman sits on two boxes, he is smoking a pipe and reading a paper inscribed *Instructions Mynheer van. . . .* The upper box is inscribed *For the use of ye Catholics in Ireland,* the lower one *A T* and a mark **+** Beside him is another box, inscribed, *For ye Pro-pegating ye Holy Catholic Faith in Great Britain AD 40* Behind are three monks, one of whom holds up the Host, three people kneel before it.

[1] Cf No 5717

The scene is a market-place or public square; on the l is a row of houses in which the nearest and largest building is inscribed *Monastery* Behind the burning martyr, and forming the centre of the background, is a public building with a pillared portico, surmounted by a pediment on which are the royal arms It has a tower with a hexagonal belfry and cupola, surmounted by a cross

A manifestation of the very active propaganda of the Protestant Association which was going on under Lord George Gordon against the Catholic Relief Act. Wesley had written to the Press in support of the Protestant Association, see No 5685 See No. 5534, &c.

$8\frac{5}{8} \times 11\frac{7}{8}$ in

5644 OPPOSITION DEFEATED

published as the act directs 27 Feb^ry 1780 by W. Macintosh

Engraving Perhaps intended as an answer to No 5640 North rides on a bull which has been damaging prominent members of the Opposition. In front of the bull stands Charles Fox, with a fox's head, a large rent in his l sleeve, saying, *Here end the hopes of me and the Jews*. He is supporting on his shoulders a young man, probably the Prince of Wales, who holds up both hands, saying *Borias thou hast blasted all my attemps at the Crown* From North's mouth a blast of air is directed towards a signboard, on which is a royal crown, blowing it sideways so that it is out of reach of the young man on Fox's shoulders Astride the pole on which the board hangs sits a sailor, waving his hat and saying *D——n my eyes Huza Boreas and John Bull have don for them* The bull is kicking violently; under him lie three prostrate figures, representing France, his coat decorated with fleur-de-lys, Spain, in slashed doublet, and America, holding in his hand a flag on which is the number *13*, for the thirteen colonies. A man with a bow from which he has just shot an arrow, falls backwards, having first received a fatal kick from the bull's hind leg, he is saying *I die d[amnatio]n stares me in the face* He sinks back into the arms of two men in clerical gowns; one says, *Dam——n is a Jest, the soul is not immortal*, the other says, *natural moral religeous and civil liberty authorizes the murder of a minister thou hast nought to fear* The devil standing beside them says, *Trusty servants support my faithful Malagrida*, showing that the wounded man is Lord Shelburne His two supporters are evidently Dr. Richard Price and Dr Priestley, friends of Shelburne and of each other Price's 'Observations on Civil Liberty . . .', 1776 had encouraged the American Declaration of Independence. Both men were Unitarians, and Priestley called himself a materialist A one-eyed dog, his collar inscribed *Poliph*[emus] stands by, saying *then my Jewel its all over I should have worried him if you had got him down.* On the l. is a group walking or running from l to r · the foremost, looking through a lorgnette, says *Arrah make haste or we shall not be in at the Death*; from his pocket projects a paper inscribed *Junius*; evidently Burke, believed by many of his contemporaries to be the author of the *Letters of Junius* He holds a rope attached to the nose of the man behind him, probably Lord Rockingham, who is saying *Teague and ambition will be my downfall*, he is about to stumble across a block inscribed *Stumbling Blo[ck] of Ambition.* Behind is partly visible an aged and emaciated woman, partly naked, perhaps representing Famine, she appears to be urging on Burke with a stick, probably an allusion to his 'Plan of Economical Reform', see No. 5657 A man running forward and blowing a horn inscribed *Horn of Rebellion* is faintly sketched.

At this time the activities of County Associations and Committees for reform and a change of the Government were giving rise to fears of civil war, see Nos 5638, 5640, &c

The first allusion in the Catalogue to the association of the Prince of Wales with Fox and the Opposition, cf No 5700

One of the few satires attacking the Opposition, cf Nos 5334, 5650, 5665, 5829

$7\frac{1}{4} \times 12\frac{1}{4}$ in.

5645 THE BULL BROKE LOOSE

[? After Viscount Townshend]

Pub^d 1st of March 1780 by J Kearly Stafford St Old Bond S^t &
E Hedg under the Roy^l Exchange,

Engraving A bull, snorting violently, has broken the rope by which he was attached to a post and is charging Lord North who flees before him, throwing towards the bull a paper inscribed *A Committee of Accounts*, in his other hand is a paper inscribed *Pro[te]st*. The bull has trampled over torn papers inscribed *Hertfordshire Pr[o]test, Hunt[ingdon Prot]est, Prot[est]*; his collar is inscribed *Grievances* North's flight is impeded by a heap of cylindrical rolled documents, inscribed *Taxes, Unfunded Debt, National Debt, Extraordinaries, Pension List, Civil List, Indian Paents* [? Patents], *Exch[equer] Bills, Treasury Contracts, Navy Debt, Private Contracts, Sinecure Places* Facing North on the r are France, holding out his sword in the attitude of a fencer, America as a Red Indian holding a scalping knife, Spain holding out a spear Behind them a Dutchman (Holland) watches with an expression of satisfaction The bull is being urged on by four leaders of the Opposition (l) who run (l to r) holding documents inscribed *Petition*. One says *Extraordinaries*; another, who resembles the Duke of Richmond, says *K——s Civil List*, a third (Burke?), *Extravagant Emoluments, Places & Pensions*, the last, *Huzza the Majority of two*

In the background on the r is a view of the southern part of Buckingham House; outside its palisade stands the signboard of an inn on which is a head of George III (taken from the mezzotint published as *Ecce Homo* or *The Patriot*, see Nos 5544-7), beneath the head is etched *Turks Head*. In front of the house George III confers with Mansfield, who holds a paper inscribed, *The good ship Obstinacy bound for Hanover*. Behind the king, and stooping so that his head is concealed, is a Scotsman (Bute) in a kilt Between this group and the bull stands a man holding a *Circular Letter to the Irish Association*. He is saying *Factious Libellous & unconstitutional* From his pocket hangs a paper inscribed *Speech on the Address*. He is Lord Hillsborough, see his speech on the Address 25 Nov. 1779 *Parl Hist* xx 1045, &c (appointed Secretary of State for the Northern Department on that day) During the debate the Duke of Richmond ridiculed Hillsborough and reminded the House of his 'celebrated circular letter written in 1768 wherein he pledged not only his own word, but that of his sovereign and the British legislature, that no more taxes would be laid on the people of America for the purpose of raising a revenue', ibid , p. 1077.

Beneath the design is etched:

> *Here, as in a glass you see*
> *The Scene that is, or soon, will be·*
> *The BULL, long prick'd in back & side,*
> *Breaks from the stake, to which he's tied*
> *He plunges, darts, and springs around,*
> *Now tears PROTESTS, and now the ground,*
> *You see him rage, you hear him roar,*
> *And rush on BOREAS just before·*
>
> *Dismal and horrid is HIS plight,*
> *While GRIEVANCES oppose his flight·*
> *Piled are the Bills with which he racks us*
> *And see—he stumbles over taxes:*
> *As Dogs are hushed to peace with sops,*
> *A COMMITTEE of ACCOUNTS he drops:*
>
> *Anxious, since vain is all protest,*
> *To grant a part to save the rest:*
> *But even this cannot give breath*
> *To one within TWO VOTES of death:*
> *In vain LORD CIRCULAR scolds and squalls,*
> *And 'factious, libellous, illegal' bawls:*
> *While in his famous Speech we trace*
> *The terms on which he took his place*
> *And by his Letter, see him Cherish*
> *The Associations of the Irish.*
> *The TURKS-HEAD Tavern stands behind*
> *Where grouped in harmony we find,*
> *The guilty two, and tutored one*
> *By whom this bustle &c &c &c.*

A comment on the important debates of Feb 1780 On 8 Feb Sir George Savile presented the Yorkshire petition, see No 5638, making a speech which Walpole feared portended civil war. (*Letters*, xi, p. 130) On 11 Feb. Burke made his great speech on Economical Reform, and on 21 Feb Savile's motion for a list of all places and pensions paid by the Crown was defeated by two votes only On 14 Feb North received favourably Burke's proposal for a Committee of Accounts. The protests trampled on by the bull are those made by certain counties against the petitions of Yorkshire and the other associated counties. See *Parl. Hist.* xx. 1318 ff., xxi 1 ff *Ann Reg.* 1780, pp 85 ff Walpole, *Last Journals*, 1910, ii 270 ff. For the county petitions see No 5638, &c Here George III, though depicted as an obstinate despot is yet the tool of Bute and Mansfield. Perhaps intended as an answer to No. 5643. Resembles the manner of Viscount Townshend.

9 × 12⅞ in

5646 THE TRIUMPHANT BRITONS.

[Gillray.]

Pubᵈ March 8ᵗʰ 1780 by H. Humphrey New Bond Street

Aquatint. A bayonet charge of British soldiers (r.) against Spaniards and

Frenchmen (1). The Spaniards, wearing feathered hats, are fleeing un-armed A thin Frenchman dressed as a *petit-maitre* staggers back in alarm, his arms outstretched, one hand on the shoulder of an equally terrified Spaniard A Spaniard in cloak and slashed doublet has fallen to the ground and tries to shelter behind the Frenchman; coins apparently from his pockets lie on the ground beside him The British advancing with bayonets are led by an officer who holds a sword raised to strike; a soldier holds a British flag For English successes over France and Spain, 1779–80, see Nos 5623, 5624, 5647, 5648, 5652, 5658, 5710.

Reprinted, *G.W G*, 1830.

Grego, *Gillray*, p 30

$8\frac{7}{8} \times 13\frac{1}{4}$ in.

5647 BRITANIA AND HER DAUGHTER.

Publish'd as the Act directs March 8th 1780, by I Mills No 1. Ratcliff Row near the French Hospital Old Street.

Engraving, a song engraved beneath it in two columns. Britannia, dressed as a Roman soldier, advances with shield and raised spear towards figures representing Spain, America, and France. She says, *Daughter return to your duty, and let me punish those empty Boasters; those base Villains, who keep you from your Alegiance, and desturb our Quiet* America, wearing a feathered head-dress and pseudo-classical draperies, holds a knife in her r hand, a tomahawk in her l. She says, *Mother if you would punish those Villains, who forced me from my Alegiance, and desturb our quiet, you must find them at home: those Gentlemen are my Allies, we are now Arm'd and seek your Life* Spain, on America's r., holds a shield and a raised sword; he says, *Signora Britania, I'll take care your Daughter shall be true to me, I'll make her wear a Spanish Padlock.* France, on America's l., with a drawn sword and shield with fleur-de-lys, says, *Sacra Dieu! I vill have your Daughter vether you vill let me or no; and vat you tink besides, By Gar, I vill make you my Servant, to vait upon us, you shall Roast your own Bull for our Wedding Dinner.*

Beneath is engraved:

A Song

Miss America North, so News-paper records,
With her Mother Britania, one day had some words,
When behold Monsieur Louis, advanc'd a new whim,
That she should leave her Mother for to live with him.
                    Derry Down,

The Damsel consented but quickly found out
That her Paramour was not sufficiently stout;
Besides he was poor, and she wanted fine things,
So he sent to Don Carlos for Cash and Gold-rings
                    Derry Down,

Says Monsieur to the Don, if you take my advice,
Then you of young Miss may come in for a slice;
The Don being am'rous was easy brought o're,
And he Cuddled, and Kiss'd, as Monsieur did before.
                    Derry Down,

Britania beheld her with tears in her eyes,
O! Daughter retuin to your duty she cries,
But she replies no I'm a Woman full grown,
And long for to keep a good house of my own;
Derry Down,

If you'd used me kind when I was in your power,
I then had lived with you at this very hour,
But now on my Lovers so much do I doat,
That we're Arm'd and I'll help 'em to cut your old throat.
Derry Down,

Then with Hatchet, and Scalping-knife Miss did advance,
On one side of her Spain, on the other side France,
Britania thus threatned, does all three oppose,
And how it will end the Lord above knows;
Derry Down,

Britania of late sent out one of her* sons,
Who has given Don Carlos, a thump o' the Munns,
Knock'd out Five of his Teeth, all double ones too,
And keeps 'em to help Old Britania to chew.
Derry Down.

Now for the Old Lady let all of us pray,
May Monsieur, and the Don, for their perfidy pay,
May young Miss, return to her duty agen,
And may Britons be true in despight of Base Men.
Derry Down.

Rodney, after capturing a Spanish squadron on 8 Jan. and relieving Gibraltar, defeated and captured another Spanish squadron off Cape St. Vincent on 16 Jan, Rodney's second dispatch was published in a Gazette Extraordinary of 29 Feb. 1780. Spain was never an ally of America, being unwilling to recognize a revolt of colonies.

A naively conceived and drawn satire apparently by the same artist as Nos. 5636, 5640. For Rodney's victories see Nos 5648, 5658, 5780.

$6\frac{7}{16} \times 9$ in., pl. $13\frac{3}{4} \times 9\frac{3}{4}$ in.

5648 RODNEYˢ TRIUMPH

Published for y Proprietor by W Humphrey as y Act directs March 10 1780 Nº 227 Strand or Nº 18 New Bond Sᵗ

Engraving. Rodney (l.) prancing over the emblems of France and Spain (fleur-de-lys and cross), a cudgel inscribed *Oak* in his r hand He resembles the Dutchman of contemporary satire more than an English admiral, and is obese, being dressed as a sailor in a plain coat or waistcoat and a short petticoat [1] He says,

My Name is Sʳ G. Rodney
Bibbaty Bobody Binn O
Did I not Drub you well at Sea
With my little Club of Oak. O.

* *Rodney* [Original note].
[1] He is grotesquely unlike Rodney's portraits and his description as elegant, with 'something that approached to delicacy and effeminacy in his figure'. Wraxall, *Memoirs*, 1884, i. 223.

Facing him, in profile to the l., stands Spain, in cloak and slashed doublet, being violently sick, one hand held to his head, he says, *O I am very Sick This Damd Rodney will doo for me*. Behind him stands France, wearing a cloak trimmed with fleur-de-lys His knees are knocking together, and with a face of consternation he says, *Begar me never feel a my knees go so Nicky Naky Nicky Nacky in a . . . la my Life before as a me do at present*. Behind the figures is a small tree. Beneath the design is etched:

> *To fight against Britons y*^e *task is in vain,*
> *For Triumphant we ride still Lord of y*^e *Main,*
> *Success to Brave Rodney whose Valor renown*
> *Now Frightens y*^e *French & Sicken the Don*

See Nos. 5645, 5647, 5658. Apparently by the same artist as Nos. 5568, 5709.

$4\frac{7}{8} \times 6\frac{3}{4}$ in.

5649 THE ENGLISH LION DISMEMBER'D
OR THE VOICE OF THE PUBLIC FOR AN ENQUIRY INTO THE PUBLIC EXPENDITURE.

[? T. Colley]

Pub. by E. Hedges No 2, under the Royal Exchange Cornhill March 12th, 1780.

Engraving Lord North (l), with a sack over his shoulder inscribed *Budget*, drags by a chain a large lion. The lion's r. fore-paw, inscribed *America*, has been cut off, and his leg is bleeding. With the lion walk America, France, and Spain. America, a Red Indian with a head-dress and kilt of feathers, holds out a tomahawk in his l. hand; in his other hand is the staff supporting the cap of liberty; he says, *This Limb belongs to me in Spite of Fate* France holds out a sword in his l hand, his r. is on the lion's head; he says, *Either by Policy or Force I must Obtain some limb or Other* Spain, standing by France, says *I am afraid I shall lose all my Dollers & get Nothing*. Behind the lion (r.) three men advance with a flag inscribed *Associations*, two of them with drawn swords; they point towards North; one says, *Let our Associations Stop that lump of Iniquity from Ruining our Country*, the next says, *One limb is lost Already by his Infernal tricks*. The third says, *Give us an Account how you Spend our money*. North is saying, *D——n these Associations they will put a Stop to my Proceedings at last*. He is walking over documents inscribed *York, Middlesex; Petitions*, and *Protestant Petition* (the monster petition for the repeal of the Catholic Relief Act to which Lord George Gordon was then collecting signatures) In the foreground a large thistle is growing, emblematic of the evil influence of Scotland; near it appears part of some striped material, perhaps the American flag, but with many more than thirteen stripes.

For the Associations and Petitions see No 5638, &c For the Protestant Petition see No 5534, &c , and Nos. 5633, 5680.

An imitation of No. 3547 (1756), *The English Lion dismembered or the Voice of the Public for an enquiry into the loss of Minorca* . .

$7\frac{1}{2} \times 12\frac{1}{2}$ in.

5650 PATRIOTIC SOUP FOR POOR OLD ENGLAND

Pub^d March 16th 1780 by T. Cornell Printseller Bruton Street.

Engraving. A large pot stands over a fire on the ground, a number of men stand round it, some throwing ingredients for the soup into it. A man (r.) holds a torch to the bottom of the pot saying *I'll sett the whole in a blaze*; another (l.) feeds the fire with folded documents inscribed . *esq. Bonds*, saying *A new way to pay old Debts* His squint and Mephistophelian wig indicate Wilkes Behind him an obese man looks on with his arms folded and his breeches' pockets hanging out empty; he says, *I cannot do that but I'll vote to burn the Owners*. He is probably Charles Fox. A sailor wearing striped trousers hurries away from the pot, into which he is excreting, saying *Heavens a Lee Shore I'd rather face*. He is evidently intended for Keppel, known as Admiral Lee Shore (see No 5992, &c) after the action off Ushant of 27 July 1778 (cf. No. 5626, &c), who after his court martial (see No. 5536) had protested against serving under Sandwich as First Lord and had been ordered to strike his flag Next him a man holding a large basket puts a potato into the pot, saying, *G——d fire me now if I've a Potatoe left* He may be Burke (or Barré) Next sits Louis XVI facing the pot; he wears a crown and a coat covered with fleur-de-lys; with one hand he points to the sailor, with the other he holds up a frog, saying, *Dis an dat make ver good Soup*. On his l stands a man with turnips (?) under his arm saying, *A very good strengthener—but will it cure. . . .* The next man holds a cow's heel over the pot saying *by Jasus nothing makes better Mutton Broth than a good Cow heel* He is perhaps Barré (or Burke) The Duke of Richmond with a ribbon and star comes up with a coal-scuttle saying *and I'll find Coals* He was the grantee of a duty on coals (granted by Charles II to his grandfather, son of the Duchess of Portsmouth). This was the notorious 'Richmond Shilling' denounced in Paine's *Rights of Man*. A woman runs forward from the r, her sleeves turned up and wearing an apron and ragged petticoat; she says, *Stop Thief the son of a W——e has stole my Coals*. On the extreme l. is a grotesque monster or devil, with horns and a barbed tail, at his feet, in profile to the l. kneels a bishop, his hands raised in prayer, saying, *We are gathered together in thy name* On the extreme r. a spectator looks from a doorway, pointing at the scene and saying *Sing tantarara a Rogues all Rogues all.*

Probably an attack on the County Associations and Petitions, see No. 5638, &c., and the adoption of Fox, 2 Feb. 1780, as candidate for Westminster, to counteract which the Court party is said to have distributed bills on the dearness of coals, due to the 'Richmond Shilling'. Fitzmaurice, *Shelburne*, 1912, ii. 47. Richmond was the advocate of manhood suffrage and annual parliaments, see *Parl Hist* xxi. 686 ff. One of the few satires on the Opposition, see No. 5334, &c.

8 16/16 × 14 in

5651 [LORD NORTH AS AN AUCTIONEER]

London. Published March 17th 1780 by E. Hedges No 2 under the Piaza's Royal Exchange Cornhill.

Engraving Lord North as an auctioneer stands on a rostrum holding up a hammer in his r. hand, in his l. is a sheaf of papers inscribed: *Crown Lands*, *A Plan of Œconomy for striking off Unmerited Pensions*; *York Patition [sic] &c; Bill*. Round his forehead is a bandage inscribed *Taxes*; he is saying *Just a going Just a going* He is irradiated with light A crowd of men stand below looking up at him, their heads and shoulders being visible. A bishop in mitre and lawn sleeves, cf. No 5553, &c., holds up his r. hand, his arm round the shoulder of a man wearing a three-corned hat and his own hair, perhaps intended for Wesley, see No 5493, &c, to whom he says, *from the Prayers of the upright we alone hope for Prosperity.* The other answers, *Verily verily it doth not become Us to Meddle with your Church or State affairs* A man of fashion wearing a bag-wig looks up at North through an eye-glass. Next him is Lord Sandwich, holding the model of a ship under his arm. On the extreme r is a judge, a book inscribed *Law* under his arm Behind these is a crowd of faces; labels coming from some of their mouths are inscribed: *This is an alarming Crisis that must be decided by one fatal Blow to the Redress of one or Ruin to the other, If these Plans are not Prevented from taken [sic] Place we shall lose both Places & Pensions; This is not a Consumation devoutly to be Wished; Is a Public Service to be knock'd down att the Price of accomodating a few Individuals?; If this Lot is knock'd down the People will sweat under the load of Taxes they must bear.*

Beneath the design is etched:

> He with Hammer in hand
> can opposing withstand
> And knock down Patitions [sic] at nought
> tho they rail & they bawl
> He can answer them all
> And put them & their Plans to the Route
> For of those Ther's enough
> Who are Ready to puff
> When ever he needs their Support
> If he dont tip the wink
> they know well where ther's chink
> Or the dream of some Place Sir at Court
>
> He gives Places tis sure
> And perhaps to procure
> Him intrest to carry the Day
> then how vain the attempt
> of Patriots to exempt
> Us from Taxes whilst he has the Sway

A satire in support of the County Petitions and Burke's plan of economical reform, see Nos 5638, 5645, &c.
5½ × 5⅛ in.

5652 THE GAME AT FOOT-BALL.

Pub by M Darly Mar^h 17. [' 1780] by M Darly [sic] 39 Strand

Engraving A sailor (l.) has just kicked a Spanish don whom he holds by the hair, he looks towards another sailor, who faces him on the r, and says, *Damme Jack lets have a game of football* The Spaniard wears a cloak, slashed doublet, and spurred boots, his feet are higher than his head, from his pockets drop coins His broken sword falls to the ground The other sailor (r.) stands with his arms folded, saying, *With all my heart, kick him up Tom* Probably a representation of Rodney's important naval victories of 8 Jan. and 16 Jan 1780, leading to the relief of Gibraltar, when valuable prizes were taken. See Nos. 5646–8, &c.

$6\frac{5}{16} \times 9\frac{3}{16}$ in.

5653 SUITERS TO HIBERNIA ON HER HAVING A FREE TRADE.

Publish'd March 18, 1780 by I. Mills, N° 1. Ratcliff Row London.

Engraving Hibernia (l.) seated under a tree receives advances from four men representing France, Spain, Holland, and Portugal. She holds a spear, and a shield on which is the Irish harp. At her side is a large roll inscribed *Irish Linnen* and a corded bale or packing case The tree is inscribed *Shelaley*[1] and a branch over Hibernia's head is encircled with a wreath inscribed *Shamroke*. She says, *I was once the Wife of John Bull, but now Ive a License to trade for myself, my Ports are free for all Mankind to enter*. Lord North looks from behind the trunk of the tree, saying, *Had it not been for the Disturbance in America you should never have had a free trade I'm as far North as any of you* France approaches, hat in hand, his r. hand outstretched, saying *I have no vear de Shirt since Fielding take de Holland vich Mynheer sent me, I'm forced to make shift vith de Ruffle, if you vill let me into your Port for to get a bit of Linnen, I vill give you de French P—x, vich is all I shall have left ven de var is over.* (It was a common gibe among the English populace that Frenchmen wore ruffles without shirts) Spain, wearing a feathered hat, cloak, and slashed doublet, says *Let me enter your Port I'll give you plenty of Spanish Gold for your Linnen, tho' if Rodney comes to see me often I shall have none left* Holland, wearing a high-crowned hat and smoking a pipe, says *I want a piece of Linnen to send to America, she wants a new Shift but can't come for it least she should catch cold, if you'll let me enter your Port I'll give you a Dutch Herring and a glass of Hollands after it to keep it from rising in your Stomach.* Portugal, dressed like Spain, except that his doublet is not slashed, says *I keep a Vineyard in Portugall, if you'll let me into your Port, I'll supply you with Wine at a cheap rate for your Linnen, if you'll drink none from France or Spain.*

Bills for removing the restrictions on Irish trade were passed in Dec. 1779, see No. 5572. The trade between Holland and France which was impeded by the British Navy was that in naval stores, sail-cloth being an important item, cf. Nos. 5628, 5724, &c

$5\frac{3}{4} \times 7\frac{8}{16}$ in.

5654 FOR OR AGAINST IS EQUALLY ALIKE.

Pub by M Darly Mar 27ᵗʰ 1780 39 Strand

Engraving A Dutchman stands full-face, his r. hand on his bulging breeches pocket, his l. forefinger to his lips. He says *Let them fight I'll sack the chink.* He stands on the sea-shore; at his feet are a box inscribed *Dollors* and a bale of goods. On the horizon an English and a French man-of-war are blowing each other to pieces, both ships appear to be sinking in clouds of smoke.

---

[1] An obsolete form of shillelagh, the term for a cudgel deriving from 'a wood of that name [in County Wicklow] famous for its oaks'. Grose, *Dict Vulg Tongue*, 1785, cited *O E D*

Holland was using her neutrality to make large profits out of the war, especially in carrying naval stores, see No. 5557, &c. She is usually represented as anti-British, cf No. 5628, &c.

$4\frac{5}{8} \times 3\frac{1}{2}$ in.

5655 A SCENE IN LEADENHALL STREET,
HUMBLY INSCRIBED TO SIR GEORGE WOMBWELL BARONET, BY THE ENGRAVER

Publish'd as the Act directs this 29ᵗʰ March 1780.

Engraving   Two men stand on a large rectangular pedestal: Sir G. Wombwell (l) is urinating and is supported by his companion (r.) and by a pillar, almost broken through, on which he rests his r arm; in his r. hand is a label inscribed *My situation begins to alarm me*   He is saying *on this Ground I stand*, the other says *I was afraid your Insolence would bring you to this.* Under their feet, and hanging over the front of the pedestal, are papers; on one is a design of four ships, their sails lowered and flying British flags. Wombwell is befouling them. Over the ships is inscribed *An Avowed Opposition.* Wombwell's supporter stands on a paper inscribed *Admiralty*, showing that he is Sandwich. The pillar supporting Wombwell is composed of three blocks inscribed respectively, *Twice Chairman*, *Zeal*, and *Integrity*, the last nearly broken away.   On the ground stands a square pillar composed of five blocks of stone which is breaking into three pieces. The stones are inscribed *For Bye-laws*; *For Project of Building Ships in India*; *For Supporting the Propositions of the Court of Directors*, *For Rudeness & insolence in Office*; *For the Injured Lord Pigot.*

Sir George Wombwell (d. Nov. 1780) was twice Chairman of the East India Company   He had opposed in the House of Commons (16 Apr. 1779) a resolution of Admiral Pigot for inquiring into the deposition and imprisonment of his brother, Lord Pigot, Governor of Madras in 1776, who had died in captivity May 1777   Pigot's resolutions were adopted and led to the trial of those responsible for the imprisonment, Stratton, Brooke, Floyer, and Mackay, members of the Madras Council   This print appears to be a comment on the trial (Dec 1779) and sentence (10 Feb 1780), and on the commanding influence of Sandwich over the East India Company (see Wraxall, *Memoirs*, 1884, i. 403–5). Wombwell, M.P. for Huntingdon, a borough dependent on Lord Sandwich, was a supporter of the Ministry. The East India House was in Leadenhall Street, cf No 6276, &c.

10×8 in. (pl.).

5656 VAMP IN TRIUMPH.   [1 Apr. 1780.]

Engraving. *Town and Country Magazine*, xii. 128. A man standing in the pillory; from his coat pocket hangs a newspaper with the caption *A Courant.* It illustrates a dialogue 'Vamp in triumph; or the Pillory properly filled Being the Sequel of a Dialogue between Vamp and Squib, his news-collector.' The man stands on a raised circular platform, his head and hands in the pillory. A circle of grinning men surrounds him, some of them with the decorated staves which show that they are constables. The illustration is described as 'an emblematical etching, and a striking likeness, suitable to the Subject'. The dialogue is strongly hostile to the Opposition journalists Vamp's 'daring pamphlets' have been highly profitable to him; he says,

'Why, if I thought I could raise the sale of my paper five hundred, I would abuse Charles Fox as much as I now do Lord North'. For the libellous character of the *London Courant* see No. 5631 n.

5 $\frac{1}{16}$ × 3 $\frac{3}{8}$ in. B.M.L., P.P. 5442 b.

5657 [ASSOCIATION MEETING AT YORK][1]

London. Publish'd as the Act directs, April 6th 1780 by Robt Laurie.
No 17. Rosomonds Row Clerkenwell. Price 2s

Mezzotint. A representation, partly allegorical, of the meeting of the Association at York on 30 Dec. 1779 when the petition of the county was agreed to and a committee of sixty-one appointed. Men sit and stand in ranks on each side of a large table strewn with documents, though on a small scale, many appear to be portraits. On a raised dais at the back of the room three women sit behind a smaller table, each with a document, one holds an olive branch They are identified by Mr. Hawkins, evidently from a contemporary key to the print, as Civil Union, Moderation, and Harmony influencing the conduct of the meeting. Athene, with her spear, an owl on her helmet, holds out to them a scroll inscribed *Constitution Liberty Peace Œconomy*, the primary objects of the meeting The chairman [Christopher Wyvill] holds in his hand a paper inscribed *York Decr 30th 1779* On the table are books *Ct Kal 1779, Ct Kal 1780*, i e the Court or 'Royal Kalendar' giving lists of office-holders and place-holders, *Hist of England*,[2] *Bacon, Lydney* [sic. i.e. Sydney], *Newton, Lock.* Documents are inscribed *Partiat Cont3 M.S. & A* ; *Unmeri[ted] Pentio[ns]*, *Sinecures*; *Magna Charter*; *Bill of Rights*; *Navy Extra[ordinaries]*, *Army Extr.*; *Board of Trade*; *Board of Works*; *Customs Qrs N.B x*; *Ordnance Qys N.B. xx*

Four female figures approach the table on the l : Hope, with rope and anchor, points to *Magna Charter* Election holds out a paper inscribed *Short Par[liaments]*, *Equal Rep[resentation] Ballot*; Public Virtue, with a spear, holds a paper *Chat[ham] Cam[den]*, Liberty, with the cap of liberty on a staff, holds out *Hab. Cor. Attachm Inform. ex officio*, i e Habeas Corpus, Attachment, Information ex Officio (criminal proceedings by Information without the intervention of a grand jury being regarded as infringements of liberty). At their feet is a satyr chained to the ground, representing Corruption vainly struggling to regain his ascendancy A man holds a large book and a paper inscribed *£10,000,000*; at his feet is a pelican Behind, on the extreme l., is a female figure in a dress patterned with fleur-de-lys; she is the demon of discord and is fleeing away. On the r other allegorical figures approach the table: Commerce, a man with a stork standing on his arm, holds out a paper, *Exports Protection Dispatch* Manufacture, a woman holding out an implement for carding wool; the Landed Interest, a woman with a sheaf of corn, holding out a paper inscribed *Taxes* Public Credit is an old woman crowned with a wreath holding a paper inscribed *Nekar*. (The reforms of Necker in France had been extravagantly extolled by the Opposition in Parliament) In front of these figures are a stag lying down, a cock running to the r. signifying 'the just disappointment of french perfidy', and the tail feathers of a peacock, expressing the humiliated condition of Spain In the foreground is the British Lion, he is being unchained by a sailor and a soldier.

---

[1] The title has probably been cut off
[2] Probably that of Mrs Macaulay
[3] Presumably 'partial contracts'.

The design is surrounded by a garland, the lower part of oak leaves, the upper part of olive. In the centre below the design is a trophy of the royal arms, flags, drums, cannon, an anchor and other munitions of war In the centre above the design are the arms of the city of York supported by two cornucopias. Below this is a picture of Britannia and America embracing On the l are the arms of Edwin Lascelles,[1] on the r. those of Sir George Savile, the two members for Yorkshire, the latter having presented the Yorkshire petition to the House of Commons, see No. 5638

The print is also an approving comment on Burke's great speech of 11 Feb. 1780 on his 'Plan of Economical Reform' in which he made a panegyric on the finance of Necker and urged the abolition of (*inter alia*) the Board of Works, Board of Trade, and Board of Ordnance *Parl. Hist.* xxi 1–74. See also Nos. 5644, 5645, 5662.

For the Yorkshire Association see No. 5638, &c

$8\frac{5}{8} \times 11\frac{1}{2}$ in

5658 AN HERIOGLYPHYCAL EPISTLE FROM (BRITANNIA) (TOE) ADMIRAL (RODNEY)

Pub^d April 4th 1780 by W Richardson N° 68 High Holborn.

A rebus. An engraved text in which the words in brackets are represented by small objects. It is headed by a figure of Britannia and a portrait head of Rodney which form part of the title.

To (yew) my Darling Child (eye) Deign (toe) Wr(eye)te
Who Dar'd the Haughty Span(eye)sh Dons (toe) Fight
The Cause l(eye)ke others (yew) did (knot) (bee)tray
Who faintly Fought (hand) (awl)most Ran away
L(eye)ke a Bold (man) U us'd (Britannia's) Power
(Hand) Scorn'd t(hat) Dreaded C(eye)rcumstance—LEE SHORE
Close on their Coast (yew) d(eye)d Attack the Foe.
(Hand) Gave their (ships) a (toe)tal Overthrow.
Aga(eye)n the (flag) of (Hen)gland was un(fur)l'd.
My Thunders roar'd (toe) Awe the Subject (world)
The Prince (bee)held with Rapture (hand) Surpi(eye)se.
Wh(eye)le the true Hero, Sp(ark)l'd (eye)n his (eyes)
To (yew) the (wreath) of vic(toe)ry (eye) Send
Thy Countrys Guard(eye)an (hand) m(eye) trusty Fr(eye)end
Go on Brave (Rod)NEY in th(eye) Bold (car)eer
(Hand) let th(eye) Vengeance, Burst on False (Mounseer)
Then lost Ameri(k) no m(oar) shall Roam
(Butt) find w(eye)th me true (Grate)ness is (hat) Home
Pe(ace) shall aga(eye)n her Olive (branch) expand
(Hand) Smiling (plenty) (crown) the Happy L(hand)
          Brittania.

For Rodney's victories see Nos 5646, 5647, 5648, 5710. 'Lee Shore' is an allusion to Keppel nicknamed Admiral Lee Shore, who defended his conduct at the Battle of Ushant by the plea (*inter alia*) that he was off a lee shore, cf Nos. 5673, 5992, &c. The line is literally true of Rodney's action

[1] Lascelles was a supporter of the Court, and through the efforts of Wyvill and Mason, the chief organizers of the Yorkshire Association, a large sum was raised in Sept 1780 to oppose his re-election Walpole, *Letters*, xi 280.

on 16 Jan. 1780 'regardless of a blowy night, lee shore and dangerous shoals', Mahan, *Influence of Sea Power*, 1890, p 404.

The letter illustrates the habitual misuse of the aspirate by the humbler classes, 'and' being represented by a hand, 'at' by a hat; see No. 5677, a very similar letter.

11 × 5⅜ in.

5659 PREROGATIVES DEFEAT OR LIBERTIES TRIUMPH

Publlsd [sic] Aprill 20 1780 by E. Darchery S^t Js' Street.

Engraving. Bute (l.) and Lord North (r.) lie on the ground, their heads close together, and are trampled on by Dunning who steps from the shoulders of North to those of Bute, assisted by Fox who takes his hand and rests one knee on Bute's back Bute is in Highland dress and wears his Garter ribbon. Dunning is saying, *I'll trample on Corruptions favolite Minions*, Fox says, *Influence of the Masked Battery of Tyranny* Dunning is being attacked from behind by another Scot in Highland dress, who has a ferocious aspect and raises his sword to strike, his l hand resting on his enemy's shoulder. He says, *Dom his Phiz I'll cut his Weezen.*

The scene is watched by America and Ireland who stand together on the l. America, wearing a feathered head-dress and a belt of feathers, says, *Now we will treat with them* Ireland is a young man dressed as an Irish volunteer and holding a bayoneted musket whose butt rests on the ground. His hat is decorated with a harp. He says, *We are Loyal but we will be Free.*

A representation of Dunning's famous resolution on the influence of the Crown, moved 6 Apr. 1780; it also illustrates the first defeat of the Government in the House of Commons 13–14 Feb., when the clause for abolishing the Board of Trade, see No. 5657, was carried by 207 to 199. It anticipates (by almost two years) a change of ministry and subsequent peace with America.

The Scot who attacks Dunning is probably William Fullarton, who had attacked Shelburne in the House of Commons for the latter's denunciation of his appointment to the command of a regiment raised by himself. Fullarton challenged Shelburne, and the duel, 22 Mar. 1780, was compared with that of Fox and Adam, see Nos. 5575, 5625, as an attempt by the Ministry to get rid of an Opposition leader. *Ann. Reg* , 1780, pp. 148–53, 202–4 Fitzmaurice, *Shelburne*, 1912, ii. 52 ff. For Ireland see No. 5572, &c.

9¼ × 11¾ in.

5660 THE HUMBLE PETITION OF (TEMPLE BAR) TO SOME OF THE (HEADS) OF THE NATION.

Published April 16th 1780, by W. Wells N° 132 opposite Salisbury Court, Fleet Street.

A rebus; an engraved text in which the words in brackets are represented by small objects Etchings of Temple Bar and portrait heads of Lord George Germain, Lord Sandwich, and Lord North form part of the title. On Temple Bar are three spikes, ready for the heads of the three ministers.

May it Please ye,
  'Tis very (well) (key)*nown* [known] (bee)*y Some People al*(hive)
  Some Honors (eye) *had from the* (ear) *Forty f*(hive),
  When (oar) *my* (bee)*road* (gate) *Re*(bell) (heads) *did ap*(pear)
  (Yew) *sure cant forget Fletch*(ear) (Town)*ley* (hand) *L*(ear),
  (Butt) (Time) *has A*(lass) (awl) *my Honors de*(key)*'d.*
  My (spikes) (hare) (awl) (bear) (toe) *the* (world) *now d*(eye)*splay'd,*
  (Knot) *a* (tray)*tor is* (hang)*'d my sad loss to re*(pear)
  Tho' enough now (die)*serve it* (eye) *vow* (hand) (die) *clare:*
  (Toe) (yew) *who preside* (hat) *the* (head) *of the Nat*(eye)*on*
  (Eye) *send this* (pea)*tition for some Consolat*(eye)*on,*
  Let my (ornament)*s once again r*(eye)*se* (toe) *the Sight*
  T'will fill (awl) *the* (people) *with Joy* (hand) *del*(eye)*ght;*
  Lord (Boar)*as* [Boreas], *Tw*(eye)*tcher* (hand) *Min*(den) (will) *do,*
  (Eye)*f once they were placed* (inn) *a* (capitol) (view)[1]
  (Eye)*f this yew* (comb)*ply w*(eye)*th no more I*(hive) (toe) *say*
  (Butt) *t*(hat) *eye* (inn) *duty Bound ever* (will) *Pray*
                      (Temple Bar)

One of several appeals for the execution of members of the Ministry, based doubtless on attacks made in the House of Commons by Fox and others See No. 5661, and cf Nos. 5964, 5969, 6046. The Jacobites Towneley and Fletcher were executed at Kennington 30 July 1746, see No. 2799; theirs were the last heads exposed on Temple Bar. 'Lear' is perhaps Alexander Leith, a Jacobite executed on 28 Nov. 1746.
$12\frac{5}{8} \times 8\frac{3}{4}$ in.

5661 THE HEADS OF THE NATION IN A RIGHT SITUATION
Pub. by M Darly (39) *Strand, May, 1. 1780.*

Engraving. A view of Temple Bar, with three heads on spikes. The heads are being pelted with stones, dead dogs, &c , by a crowd of men, women, and children. A market-woman smoking a pipe kneels before her basket, and is about to use its contents as missiles Another woman says *This is a sight I have long wish*[ed] *to see.* A boy holds a stone in one hand, a dead dog or cat in the other A man waves his hat, crying, *Steer to the North,* indicating that one of the victims is Lord North; another says, *There goes for Germany* (Lord George Germain). The third is evidently Lord Sandwich. Another man says *This is a happy day for England.* A man waves his wig in delight. Small figures hurling missiles are seen through the centre arch; passers-by appear through the two side arches. On the upper part of the masonry of the arch is sketched a figure of Justice, seated on clouds, her scales in one hand, a spear in the other. The statues of two kings in the alcoves show that this is the west side of Temple Bar. On Temple Bar are placards: *Lecture upon Heads,* a punning allusion to the popular 'Lecture' of George Alexander Stevens, *A Cure for a Distress*[ed] *nation* and *1745,* in allusion to the heads on Temple Bar after the Jacobite rebellion. See No. 5660, &c.
$8\frac{5}{16} \times 12\frac{7}{8}$ in.

5662 A VIEU OF PLYMOUTH
Pub^d by M Darly (39) *Strand, May 4th 1780, acc^g to Act.*

Engraving (coloured and uncoloured impressions). A raree-show man (r) is exhibiting his peep-show, in a box inscribed *A View of Plymouth*, to Lord Amherst, in profile to the r., who stoops down, his hands on his knees, to look through one of the two round holes. The showman says, *There you see Cannons without Carriages and Carriages without Cannons. There you see Generals without Orders there you see &c. &c.* The show-box is supported on trestles. Amherst is in general's uniform, wearing the ribbon of the Bath. Behind him, partly cut off by the l. margin of the print, stands a Grenadier at attention, holding a musket; he watches the general with a grin. Beneath the design is engraved:

Col Mushrooms Comp^ts to Lord Am——t recommends this cheap but Satisfactory mode of viewing distant Garrisons hopes his Lordship has received the Golden Pippins a few of them are for his Secretary.

Amherst was Lieutenant-General of the Ordnance, and acted as Commander-in-Chief, being adviser to the Government on the American War. The print probably echoes Burke's attack on the Board of Ordnance in his speech on Economical Reform, *Parl. Hist.* xxi. 38–9, as well as the recriminations after Saratoga, ibid., xv. 675 ff. In the debate of 25 Nov. 1779 the defenceless state of Plymouth was denounced by the Opposition, and Fox asked if, except for 'an invisible cabinet influence', there could have been 'in one place cannon without balls, and in another balls without cannon'. Ibid., xx. 1120, see also pp. 1150–1 ff. Cf. No 5657. Perhaps one of a series, see No. 5682, &c.

$5\frac{1}{2} \times 6\frac{1}{2}$ in.

5662 A Another impression with the imprint,

Pub^d by H Humphrey N° 18 New Bond Street.

5663 DUTCH GRATITUDE DISPLAY'D.

Pub^d accor^s to Act 4 May 1780.

Engraving. A design in two groups, one (l) representing the past, the other (r.) the present A Dutchman personifying the Dutch Republic, threatened by Spain (l) kneels, hat in hand, before a military officer representing England, imploring help. He says, *the poor distracted States of Holland* The Englishman answers, *I am your Friend Mynheer I'll help you up & beat your foes.* A Spaniard stands (l) behind the Dutchman's back, his sword raised to strike, his l fist clenched, saying, *I am determined Mynheer you shall never rise more* On the r. is another group of figures representing Holland, England, America, France, and Spain. A Dutchman on the extreme r, smoking a pipe, his hands in his breeches pocket, scowls at an English officer, saying, *I am now ye high & Mighty.* (The States General of the United Provinces were addressed as Hogen Mogen, 'High Mightinesses'.) The Englishman, a drawn sword in his hand, says to him *Now is ye time to pay ye debt of Gratitude* America, an Indian holding a tomahawk, says to France, pointing to England, *It shall never have my Colonies again* France, a French military officer with a drawn sword, wearing spurred jack-boots, points to England, saying, *begar me will have half his Possessions.* Spain, in cloak and feathered hat, also with a drawn sword, stands behind France saying *Don Diego has vow'd the downfall of England.* Beneath the design verses are engraved:

See Holland oppress'd by his old Spanish Foe,
To England with cap in hand kneels very low,

The Free-hearted Britton, dispels all its care,
And raises it up from the brink of Dispair.

But when three spitefull foes old England beset,
The Dutchman refuses to pay a Just debt;
With his hands in his pockets he says he'll stand Neuter,
And England his Friend may be D——d for the Future.

An allusion to the treaties of alliance to which Sir Joseph Yorke at the Hague so unsuccessfully appealed The first scene (l) represents the United Provinces at the time of the wars of William III and Anne, or? temp. Elizabeth, the other (r.) the situation in 1780

One of many satires on the attitude of the Dutch Republic before the declaration of war, see No 5557, &c For opinion in Holland, see No. 5712, &c.

$4\frac{1}{2} \times 10$ in.

5664 LEWIS BABOON ABOUT TO TEACH NIC FROG THE LOUVRE   [n d. 1780]

Sold by W. Humphrey N° 227 Strand.

Engraving (coloured impression). A stout man with seven heads, representing 'Nic Frog' or Holland (r.), each head symbolizing one of the seven United Provinces, receiving overtures from 'Lewis Baboon' (France), a slim foppish man with a simian profile, who clasps Nic's r hand in both of his, saying, *Come Mynheer, and I will teach you to dance the Louvre, and my Brother Don Pedro, the Findango* One of the seven heads (smoking a pipe) answers *Yaw, Yaw Mynheer Lewis, but who pays the Piper, I'm afraid of the Ducaten*; while another head (with a Jewish profile), facing in the opposite direction, says *Quick Quick Mynheer, Yonder comes John Bull, who with his Hornpipe will spoil your Ball I'm afraid* Spain (l) turns his back on the couple, saying *Not I Brother Lewis I am wearied to Death with dancing to your cursed French Music* Behind, the Devil in the form of a satyr is playing a pipe as he walks from r. to l The central and largest of Holland's seven heads has a tub on it in place of a hat; round his shoulder is slung a chain of small fish, head to tail; from this hangs a small cask. In his l hand is a stick inscribed *Russia*. Behind is the sea, with a vessel at anchor, flying the British flag, a ship's boat is pulling to the shore Beneath the design is engraved:

Ornamented with Butter Fish Cheese does appear
The Monster seven headed whose name is Mynheer
Tho' he's heavy in bottom the Baboon of France
Invites him along with Don Pedro to Dance
The Don turns his back for some Reasons of State
Which tis thought he receiv'd from the English of late
Old Nic he keeps piping in hopes to please all,
Yet all are afraid least John Bull spoil their Ball

The cudgel marked Russia is an emblem of the Declaration of Armed Neutrality by Russia, 26 Feb /9 Mar. 1780, which was a surprise to England, cf No 5557 The 'reasons of state' are an allusion to Rodney's victories over the Spaniards in Jan 1780, see No. 5646, &c. The names are taken from Arbuthnot's famous pamphlet, 'Law is a bottomless Pit, or the History of John Bull', 1712 For other satires on the attitude of Holland before the declaration of war in Dec 1780, see No. 5557, &c. Cf. also No. 5712, a pro-English Dutch print, in which France is trying 'to bring Holland gradually to the dance with England', and No. 5825. For the attitude of Spain cf. No 5642.

8 × 12½ in.

5665 A PETITIONING, REMONSTRATING, REFORMING, RE-PUBLICAN.

R. S. (Monogram).

Pub⁴ acc⁵ to Act May 8, 1780 by M Darly (39) Strand.

Engraving. The 'Republican', out at elbows, his stockings in holes, squats over an inverted crown, an inverted mitre in front of him, using these as chamber-pots. He supports himself by the staff of liberty, on which is a cap inscribed *Liberty* (deleted), *Rebellion*. Its drooping peak terminates in the bell of a fool's cap. Beneath the design is engraved:

> YOUR PETITIONER SHEWETH,
> *That he Humbly wishes to*
> *Reduce yᵉ Church to Gospel Order*
> *By Rapine Sacrilige & Murther*
> *To make Presbyty [sic] supream*
> *& Kings themselves submit to him*
> *& not content all this to do*
> *He must have Wealth & Honor too*
> *Or else with Blood & desolation*
> *He'll tear it out of the Heart of the nation*

A satire on the methods and aims of the Associations which had made petitions for reform, and formed committees of correspondence, see No. 5638, &c. These were regarded by many Whigs as going too far, both in their demands and their methods, which followed those adopted in America where delegates from Committees of Correspondence had constituted the Continental Congress Cf. Walpole, *Letters*, xi, p 130. *Ann. Reg*, 1780, pp. 87-8 Wraxall, *Memoirs*, 1884, ii, pp. 442-8. For the Association movement see No. 5638, &c. One of the few satires attacking the Opposition, cf. No. 5334, &c.

6 ⅜ × 7 ⅛ in

5666 THE BALANCE OF POWER.

Publish'd 8 May 1780 by W. Renigald.

Engraving. The beam of a pair of scales supported on a post, from each end of which, instead of a scale, dangles a man as if from a gibbet On the centre of the beam is perched an owl wearing a ribbon and star, inscribed *Center of Gravity* On the lighter side (l) hangs a man over whose eyes a fool's cap has been drawn, through which protrude ass's ears. In his r hand is a *Plan for enlarging Newgate*, in his l. a copy of the *General Advertiser*. On the r. hangs a man in parson's gown and bands, his eyes covered by a turban-shaped cap; in his l. hand is a copy of the *Morning Post*, in his r. a newsboy's horn, from which issues a blast inscribed *Blast ye*, directed against the other body hanging from the gibbet. On his breast is a playing-card, the knave of clubs Over his head are falling a castle, two

churches, and two mitres He is Bate, editor of the *Morning Post*, noted as
a bruiser, see No. 5550, &c On the ground stand two figures pointing to
the gibbet: Justice (l.) leans on her sword, holding her scales, above her
head is engraved.

> *Grave wisdom takes the centre of the Beam,*
> *And leaves to Knave & Fool, the wide extream.*

The owl perhaps represents North, often accused of unseemly levity, and
his attitude towards Ministerial journalists. The Devil (r.) stands holding
a coffin on which is a skull and cross-bones surmounting a freely sketched
inscription suggesting the words *Here lies P*[arson] *B*[ate] and two reversed
mitres. He points grinning to Bate; above his head is inscribed, *Here I
wait; To take my B——.*

Bate's companion is perhaps William Cooke, who started the *General
Advertiser* in Nov. 1776. Bourne, *English Newspapers*, i 233, 249 The Duke
of Richmond had recently instituted proceedings against Bate for offensive
'Queries' published in the *Morning Post* of 25 Feb. 1780, virtually accusing
him of treason, *Gent. Mag.*, 1780, pp. 247-8; *Ann Reg.*, 1780, p. 216, for
which Bate was afterwards imprisoned. See Nos 5550, 5676, 6162, &c.
$6 \times 13\frac{1}{4}$ in.

5667 ARGUS

[Gillray.]

Pub^d May 15th 1780 by W Renegal

Engraving (coloured and uncoloured impressions). George III, wearing
a crown and ermine-trimmed robe is seated in an arm-chair asleep. The
tassels of his girdle are thistles, indicative of Scottish influence Round
his neck is a chain from which hangs a cross, indicating the Romanizing
tendencies of which he was accused at this time, see No 5534, &c. His
crown is being taken from his head by a judge in wig and ermine-trimmed
robes, evidently Mansfield. Over the king's shoulder looks a Scot in Highland dress, evidently Bute, holding the sceptre which he has taken from
the king's hand. He leans towards Mansfield saying *What shall be done
with it?* Mansfield answers, *Wear it Your sel my Leard.* On the king's l.
a man stands who holds in both hands the other side of the crown, he says,
No troth I'se carry it to Charly & hel not part with it again Mon! He is
dressed an an English gentleman, though his language indicates that he is a
Scottish Jacobite, he is perhaps intended for some unpopular Scot, perhaps
Wedderburn, then attorney-general Behind the king's chair America,
wearing a feathered head-dress, watches the scene; he says *We in America
have no Crown to Fight for or Loose.*

In the foreground (r.) sits Britannia asleep, her head resting on her hand;
by her side lies the British lion, also asleep and chained to the ground. At
her feet are two maps, one of *Great Britain* (torn) lies on one of *America*.
On the l. stands a man in rags with bare legs and dishevelled hair, clasping
his hands together and saying *I have let them quietly strip me of every Thing*;
he appears to represent the British commercial community. An Irishman
next him, a harp under his arm, walks away saying *I'le take Care of Myself
& Family* The background to these figures is a hedge, behind it on the r
is a Dutchman (the United Provinces) helping himself to the contents of
two hives.

For Ireland see No 5572, &c. For Holland as a profiteering neutral see No. 5557, &c. For commercial distress see No. 5574, &c.
Grego, *Gillray*, p. 30. Van Stolk, No. 4304.
$9\frac{3}{8} \times 13\frac{1}{4}$ in.

5668 CHATHAM'S GHOST, OR A PEEP INTO FUTURITY.
CHE SARA, SARA,

Published as the Act directs May 16, 1780 by W. Wells Nᵒ 132 opposite Salisbury Court Fleet Street. London.

Engraving. George III (l), seated in a chair, is being shown by the ghost of Chatham a procession of figures walking towards a pit (r.) inscribed *Chaos*. Chatham wears pseudo-classical draperies, a tie-wig crowned with a laurel wreath, and is surrounded by a glory of rays. He holds up a circular glass to the king, who looks through it with an expression of alarm. On the back of the king's chair is a crown surmounted by a weathercock which points to the South, probably to indicate that North's power is over, cf No 5659 Under his feet are torn county petitions, and an open book, *Lock on Government*. The petitions are those of *York, Westminster, Middlesex, Hampshire, Surrey*. There is also the design of the façade of a building inscribed, *The Elevation of [a] Baby House* The leaders of the procession, who are on the brink of the pit, are the kings of France and Spain. A devil (r.) with wings, horns, and a long barbed tail, points into the pit Behind the two kings come North and Sandwich. North holds a rolled document inscribed *Taxes* Under his arm is a large money-bag with a gaping hole in it, by which is an open book or paper inscribed *New Way to pay old Debts, A Farce by Boreas* (Massinger's comedy had recently been revived at Drury Lane). On his r. Sandwich walks with his arms folded, a paper under his arm is inscribed *Catches & Glees Mr Arne* (Arne (1710-78), the musical composer, is generally styled Dr, Sandwich was 'the soul of the Catch Club', see No. 5342) From his pocket protrude papers, one inscribed *Greenwich Hospital*, in allusion to the scandal caused by Captain Baillie's exposure of abuses there, see No. 5548 The other is inscribed *Love & Madness*; this is the title of a series of fictitious letters recently published purporting to be the correspondence of Hackman and Martha Ray, Sandwich's mistress, see No. 5540, &c, but really by Herbert Croft See Walpole, *Letters*, xi. 139-40, 13 Mar. 1780. Behind come Mansfield, in judge's wig and robes, and Bute in Highland dress, both with expressions of despair; they are being hurried along by a man with the face of a fiend who has seized Mansfield by the arm and Bute by the shoulders. Beside them walks a Dutchman, his hands in his breeches pockets, being propelled from behind by a devil, significant of the unpopularity of the Dutch Republic, see No. 5557, &c. For the Association Movement see Nos. 5638, 5665, &c.
$13\frac{3}{8} \times 8\frac{11}{16}$ in.

5669 THE ROYAL ASS

York Sculpsit.   *Stewart del*

Pub accs to act May 20. 1780. by M Darly (39) Strand.

Engraving. An ass, wearing a crown, is being led by a man who has the legs and tail of a devil, towards a dome and two steeples intended for St. Peter's and inscribed *Rome*. The man, evidently Bute, is dressed partly in tartan, and is saying *This is my Ass & I'll lead it where I please*. Behind, a bishop wearing a mitre and a long gown, flourishes a birch-rod and points at the animal's hind-quarters, saying, *Lead on my Lord I'll drive the beast along* This is Markham, the unpopular Archbishop of York (see No. 5553, &c) His birch-rod indicates that he had been head master of Westminster School; he was also (1771–6) preceptor to the Prince of Wales and his brother. Two little boys, one wearing the ribbon of an order, stand by Markham and point at the ass; one says to the other *Where are they driving Papa too* [sic].

This is evidently inspired by the propaganda of Lord George Gordon and the Protestant Association, it being one of their tenets that in giving his assent to the Catholic Relief Act of 1778 the king had broken his coronation oath; see No. 5534, &c. The artists' names imply that the 'popish' policy of the king was inspired by Bute and furthered by Markham. For Bute and Rome cf. No. 4841.

Similar in character and design to No. 5670. Cf. the crowned ass in No. 6007.

$5\frac{5}{8} \times 8\frac{3}{16}$ in.

5670 FATHER PETERS LEADING HIS MANGY WHELP TO BE TOUCHED FOR THE EVIL. [n.d *c*. May 1780]

Pub by M Darly No 159 Fleet Street.

Engraving. A monk walks through a ford leading a dog with a crown on its head: 'Father Peters' leading George III to Rome. The monk says *He cocks his Tail yet.* He is going towards a wayside cross (r.), above which are rocks, on which is seated the Pope, holding out a cross towards the travellers and saying *Hold out my Sons to the End & I'll give you a Crown of Glory.* Behind him is a dome surmounted by a cross indicating St. Peter's. On the other side of the pool (l) there are also rocks, on them stands a sheep (?) and in the distance, by the sea-shore, are two small churches of rural appearance, off the shore are three dismantled ships with brooms at their mast-heads to show that they are for sale, the scene being inscribed *Little Britain.*

Edmund Petre or 'Father Peters', the confessor of James II (see Nos. 1156, 1177, 1235, 1236, &c.), was the subject of abiding hatred by the London mob, and had been regularly burnt in effigy until the end of Anne's reign. But the allusion is probably intended in part at least for Lord Petre, regarded as the head of the Catholic community in England, see No. 5489. One of many satires reflecting the aims and propaganda of the Protestant Association, see No. 5534, &c.

Similar in character and design to No 5669.

$5\frac{11}{16} \times 9\frac{1}{4}$ in

5671 THE INVISIBLE JUNTO,
DEDICATED TO THE TRULY HONORABLE LORD G. GORDON, [n d *c*. May 1780]

Pub. by M Darly No 159 Fleet Street.

Engraving. A hand coming from a cloud holds a pair of scales The r scale, which appears to rest on the ground, contains two books, *H. Bible* and *Sidney on G* [*overnment*], surmounted by the *Cap of Liberty* On the l scale stands George III, his hands on his hips, his crown beside him, his ears project at r. angles, and he is called *K. Menassah*; on a rock (l.) is inscribed *II Kings Ch xxi, Dan¹ Chap. iv* (the former an account of King Manasseh's reign, his wickedness and idolatry, the latter of Nebuchadnezzar's dream). A label over the scale, which issues from the hand in the clouds, is inscribed *Mene Mene Tekel Uphasin.* The four ropes which support this scale are continued below it and disappear into the ground, the points of contact are inscribed *pull North, pull Bute, pull Mansfield, pull Devil,* indicating that these four have secret influence over the king, but that their combined powers are easily outweighed by the *H. Bible,* &c. Behind the centre of the scales is an irregular stone pinnacle, from the l of which a hand emerges pointing towards the king, the pinnacle is inscribed, *And he filled the Land with Blood* In the upper r corner of the print is an eye looking from a cloud, inscribed *He that formed the Eye shall he not see us* Below it is a large two-storied palace on a raised terrace, supported by a stone wall, over which is inscribed, *And Sodomites were in the Land.* Beneath the title is engraved:

> *Though Knaves & Fools combine how light the Scale,*
> *But Truth & Liberty shall still prevail.*

The dedication shows that this is the propaganda of the Protestant Association, not of the Opposition which (individuals excepted) regarded Lord George Gordon and his No Popery campaign with contempt. See No. 5534, &c.

$4\frac{5}{8} \times 8\frac{7}{8}$ in.

5672 THE PROTESTANT ASSOCIATION, OR THE SCOTCH Sᵀ GEORGE AND THE DRAGON.

[n d *c.* May 1780]

Engraving. A Scot on horseback in Highland dress fights a dragon in the mouth of a cave The Scot (l), on a prancing horse, holds a round shield on his l. arm and threatens the dragon with his drawn broadsword. The dragon wears the triple crown of the Papacy, his fore-paws are on an open book, *Holy Bible,* he breathes out flames saying *et Tu Brute,* probably in allusion to the fact that Lord George Gordon, 'the Scotch Sᵗ George' and President of the Protestant Association, belonged to a family which until the death of his grandfather in 1728 had been Catholic. On the horizon, seen through the mouth of the cave, is the sea, in front of it a town is indicated with a castle on a rocky hill, perhaps intended for Edinburgh, and signifying the riots in Edinburgh against a Catholic Relief Act in 1779.

One of a number of satires published in the interests of the Protestant Association and Lord George Gordon, see No. 5534, &c For Gordon as the Protestant Hero, see also Nos. 5694, 5840, 5841.

$7\frac{1}{8} \times 10\frac{7}{8}$ in.

5673 THE APPOINTMENT OF Yᴱ BRAVE ADMᴸ RODNEY & JEMMY TWITCHER IN Yᴱ DUMPS.

Baldrey fecᵗ

Publish'd as yᵉ Act directs May 25ᵗʰ 1780 by P. Mitchell North Audley Sᵗ Grosʳ Sqʳ & Sold by J. Harris, Sweetings Alley Cornhill.

Engraving. George III stands in profile to the l., Rodney (l) kneeling, kisses his hand; in the king's l. hand is a rolled document inscribed *Instructions*, he says, *Rodney do all in Your Power for the honour of my Crown & the Good of ye Nation.* Rodney answers *May it please your Majesty I will never fear a Lee Shore but Conquer or Die*

Behind the king on the r stands Sandwich, full-face, looking down with an expression of disgust, saying, *I would recommend Sr Hugh P . . . r* [Palliser] Two walls of the room are visible; in the back wall is a door, on its l. a picture of ships. A window (l) is partly visible on the other wall, next it is a W.L. portrait of Queen Charlotte, the frame surmounted by a crown.

Rodney and Sandwich were on very bad terms, and though the former had been promoted admiral in Jan. 1779, it was not till the end of 1779 that he was given a command, when no other officer of repute would accept office under the Government. Even then it was believed that it was given only at the direct desire of the king. For Palliser, Sandwich's protégé, see index. For the allusion to Lee Shore see Nos 5658, 5992, &c.

$7\frac{3}{8} \times 10\frac{1}{4}$ in.

5674 THE CONTRAST.

[T. Colley?]

Pub^d Accor^g to Act May 27th 1780 by T. Colley, N° 88 Strand.

Engraving. An enormously fat English naval officer (l.) and a very lean French one, face one another. Beneath the former is inscribed *England*, beneath the latter, *France*. England wears a laced hat, the cockade at the back, a coat with facings and epaulettes, buckled shoes. France wears a feathered hat, a long pigtail queue, ruffled shirt, a cross hanging from his shirt-front, a fleur-de-lys on his shoulder; his spindle legs are in spurred jack-boots. He says, *We beat you every battle.* England answers, *you Lie.*

Perhaps an allusion to the indecisive action between Rodney and de Guichen on 17 Apr. 1780 in the West Indies. Cf. No. 5695

A note by Mr. Hawkins states that this was reissued by Holland

$9 \times 12\frac{11}{16}$ in.

5675 THE R—Y—L HUNT OR THE PETITIONERS ANSWER'D

Pub acc^g to act June 4. 1780 by M Darly 39 Strand

Engraving. George III riding Britannia, who is on hands and knees, and accompanied by ministerial dogs with human faces, their names on their collars, proceeding from the *House of Venality* (l), towards a phalanx of petitioners (r.) standing behind the cylindrical rolls of the county petitions; these surround the *Temple of Patriotism* The king holds Britannia by the hair and pierces her breast with a spear; he says, *Cease Mortals, Cease your prayers I'll have my will. Tho' half my Empire lost I am Sovr'g'n still.* Britannia says, *Thare [sic] thus he gores me to the heart Himself unconscious of the Smart* The dogs are barking menacingly at Liberty who sits on a mound holding her cap on a staff; she says, holding out her l. arm towards the petitioners, *O Save me Save me.* A dog (North) wearing a ribbon and star, with *Boreas* (in reversed looking-glass script) on his collar, says, *I'll gnaw the Strumpets liver.* Mansfield, a dog whose collar is inscribed *Caen Wood* (cf. No. 4885), says *I'll be round upon her with as much speed as if it were to take a fee, but I am afraid these dam'd Petitions will save her.*

Germain, a dog with *Minden* on his collar, turns his back on Liberty and is addressed by *Woolsack* (lord Thurlow) who says, *Hey day Minden dont be ashamed dont give up the Chase by turning tail* 'Minden' answers, *No No I am not asham'd its only a way that I have got always to turn my tail when I fight* (an allusion to the battle of Minden (see Nos. 3680–7) *Caribb* says *Bow vow vow vow. This Phrenzy of Public virtue must be* [word erased] *down.* This is probably Lord Hillsborough, regarded as responsible for the expedition against the Caribs of the Island of St. Vincent which had been the subject of bitter complaint in parliament, see No. 5540 The last dog *Twitcher* or Sandwich, is very lean and walks on three legs. He wears a ribbon and star (though actually he had no order), an ensign flag is thrust through his ribbon, and by his side is a broken anchor, indicating his bad management of the Navy. He says,

> *Condemn me not for being last*
> *The Dog unskill'd and lame cannot go so fast*

The petition-rolls (r.) are inscribed (l to r) *Herts, Bucks, Hants, Der*[by], *Wilts, Kent, Deven* [sic], *Essex, Cambrid^e, Nottingh^m, Middlesex, Sussex, Surry, York, Westmin^r, Petition of City of London* The petitioners are massed in front of and beside the *Temple of Patriotism*, they say *The Constitution will aid us in our Protection.* To the l of the petitioners is a tree in full leaf, its trunk inscribed *The sound will florish* The roof of the temple is decorated by statues or figures, comic in effect and perhaps in intention, of *Wisdom* (Athene with a spear), *Hope, Perseverance, Fortitude, Faith* Above it, in clouds, is a coat of arms held up by an angel who says, *Behold their arms* On the escutcheon is Justice holding scales, the supporters are cylindrical documents: *Bill of Rights* (script reversed) and *Magna Charta.* The crest is a dove, or possibly a hawk. The motto, *our cause is just.*

On the other side (l) is another circular building, *House of Venality*, similar in construction to the Temple of Patriotism Over the centre doorway is written *Placemen*, over the l door *Contraitors* [sic], over the r. *Pensioners* The figures on the roof are *Folly, Cruelty, Despair, Ignorance, Oppression.* By it is the decayed stump of a tree inscribed *The Saps corrupted.*

On a hill behind stands Bute, in Highland dress, with his arm round the shoulders of the devil, they both point to the dogs who are baiting Liberty. The devil says *Dear Sawney I am indeted to you for this sport* Bute answers *Ay Belzy you may say that our nation has been very active for you.*

For county petitions, associations, and committees of correspondence see No. 5638, &c. It is to be noted that the date of the print is the king's birthday

$8\frac{5}{8} \times 12\frac{1}{2}$ in.

5676 POLITICAL STAG HUNT OR THE M——L [MINISTERIAL] HOUNDS IN FULL CRY. [n d c. 1780]

J. Slapbang fec.

Pub^d by W. Humphrey, N° 227 Strand

Engraving A huntsman (l.), mounted on a horse snorting flames which are inscribed *Faction*, preceded by the 'ministerial hounds', chases a stag, inscribed *Constitution.* The huntsman is Bate, afterwards Bate Dudley, representing the Ministerial Press. He is dressed like the body of newsvendors with drums and trumpets to advertise the *Morning Post* seen by Walpole in Nov. 1776 (see No 5550), and is blowing a trumpet. His cap is inscribed *Post*, round his shoulders is slung a bundle inscribed *Materials for Post*, made up of *Satire, Malice, Scandal, Falsehood*. From his pocket hangs a paper, *The Art of Lying made Easy by B*. He leaps a fence inscribed *Bounds of Discretion*. The hounds are taking a circular course as the stag has doubled back and is advancing towards a ravine, a signpost pointing *To the Vale of Oblivion*. The stag says *I shall fall like Lucifer never to Hope again*. The two foremost hounds have human faces; the first (North) says *We shall soon be in at the Death—She can go no further. N . . . h*. The next, inscribed *Twitcher* (Lord Sandwich), says *I have long had her Destruction at Heart & the sooner the better*. The third (Lord G Germain) says, *I run almost as fast now as I did at Minden* (cf No 5675) Next is a dog with a judge's wig (Mansfield) saying, *She will find no Covert near Caen Wood* (cf No 4885) A dog inscribed *L S* says *I am the sort to go Thro Thick & Thin*; perhaps intended for Lord Stormont, Secretary of State, and Mansfield's nephew, or possibly for Lovel Stanhope, who was appointed Comptroller of the Board of Green Cloth in September 1780. A dog with the face of a demon,[1] probably representing the Devil as in No 5675, says, *I allways was firm to the cause*. The next dog is inscribed *Log* and is saying *I stick at Nothing*. This is evidently Sir Hugh Palliser, whose log-book was found at his court martial to have been altered, see Nos. 5536, 5537. The last dog says *I am Adam'd Good Dog but y*e* last Fox Hunt Had like to be Death of me* He is William Adam, whose duel with Fox on 29 Nov. 1779 roused much bitterness against the ministry, see Nos. 5575, 5625. The scene is a wooded hill and the going is rough. Behind Bate on the l is the partly ruined *Templum Libertatis* overgrown with shrubs and shored up by timbers inscribed *Richmond, Barre, Camden, Burke & Fox, Wilks*.

Beneath the design is etched:

> *Hungry Dogs the old Proverbs say*
> *Eat dirty Pudding, when in their way*
> *So Will these Dogs as oft we are told*
> *Catch at any thing which looks like Gold.*
> *Or bears the least Aspect of doing*
> *Good for themselves tho their Country ruin.*
> *Tis little Rogues submit to fate*
> *Whilst y*e* Great enjoy y*e* World in State.*

Bate was prosecuted by the Duke of Richmond for some libellous *Queries* published in the *Morning Post* of 25 Feb 1780, on 1 Nov. 1780 he started the *Morning Herald*, an anti-ministerialist paper, supporting the party of the Prince of Wales Lord North admitted that his advocacy of the ministry in the *Morning Post* was 'perhaps too warm', see Nos 5550, 5666. 8 × 13¼ in.

5677 AN HERIOGLYPHYCAL [*sic*] ADDRESS FROM (NEPTUNE) (TOE) PRINCE (WILLIAM).

*Pub*d* as the Act directs June 10*th* 1780 by W Richardson, N*o* 68 High Holborn.*

A rebus, an engraved letter in which the words in brackets are represented by small objects. Neptune (l) with his trident and a bust portrait of Prince

---

[1] Mr. Hawkins has written 'Jer. Dyson' on this dog, but he died in 1776.

William (afterwards William IV) in a circle draped with a flag (r) form part of the title.

From my (coral) (crown) (throne) *deck'd with Spars* (awl) *around.*
The God of Old Ocean now r(eye)*ses Profound*
Yes (Neptune) *rejoices* (thigh) *Tr*(eye)*um*(pea)*h* (toe) *See.*
My (child) (eye) *ado*(pea)*t thee m*(eye) *Darl*(eye)*ng thou shall't* (bee)
(Britannia) *La*(men)*t*(head) *the Loss of her* (sons)
Her Court's st(eye)*ll* (eye)*nsult*(head) *by* (Frenchmen) (hand) *Dons*
Till (Rodney) *w*(eye)*th thee Launch'd* (yew)*r hearts on the Main.*
T(hen) *t*(hen) *rev*(eye)*vd* (hand) *app*(ear)*'d once again*
(Eye) (saw) *a fair Stem, from the true Roy*(awl) (bee)*lood.*
(Bee)*id Danger def*(eye)*ance* (hand) *r*(eye)*de on the Flood*
(Eye) *C*(awl)*'d out my* (Tritons) (toe) *s*(hound) [sound] *out Success*
The Ne(rye)(adze) [Nereids] (hand) *Sea Gods* (awl) *jo*(eye)*n'd me to Bless.*
(Toe) *st*(eye)*ll my* (grate) *Em*(pea)*re* (hand) *this tell* (toe) *thee*
Young Will(eye)(ham) *sh*(awl) (bee) *my* (vice)*Roy of the Sea*
Go on No(bee)*le* (yew)*th* (hand) *on* (Neptune) *De*(pen)*d*
(Toe) (thigh) *Count*(rye) (thigh) *Father,* (hand) *thee,* (eye)*'m a Friend*
The (sons) *of Old Engl*(hand) *sh*(awl) *never* (bee) (slaves)
Wh(eye)*le* (Neptune) (bee)*ids W*(eye)*ll*(eye)(ham) (pea)*res*(eye)*de on the*
                                                                    Waves
                                                         Neptune.

Prince William, the king's third son, aged 14, was serving as a midshipman with Rodney. On 8 Mar. 1780 he appeared at Court having brought with him Spanish colours taken in Rodney's naval victories in Jan. 1780. *Letters of the First Earl of Malmesbury,* i. 453. *London Chronicle,* 9–11 Mar. 1780 For Rodney's victories see Nos 5646–8, 5658, 5710.

$11\frac{3}{4} \times 6\frac{1}{8}$ in.

5678 ECCLESIASTICAL, AND, POLITICAL, STATE OF THE NATION.

[? Gillray.]

Published June 2ᵈ 1780 by W. Humphrey Printseller Strand London.

Engraving George III guides (l to r) a plough which is drawn by a snorting bull; he is blindfolded and wears a crown and the garter ribbon; from his pocket hangs a fragment of *Magna Charta.* Lord North rides on the bull, urging him forward with a whip, attached to his shoulders is a knapsack or bundle inscribed *Ways & Means.* Another man goads the bull with a spear. A Scot in highland dress, probably Gordon, tugs violently at the bull's harness, trying to pull it back; two other men who have been tugging at the bull have fallen to the ground and the wig of one has fallen off. The bull is advancing towards the *River Tweed* (r.), on the farther side of which are a large thistle and some fir trees on a hill This shows that Scotland has not as yet been ploughed up for the emissaries of the Pope, see No 5534. In the foreground (l) lies a sleeping bishop, his head on his hand, holding a crozier, and leaning on a book and a *Map of Bishoprick* Behind him and the king a Jesuit, a Catholic priest, and a monk are sowing in the ground which has been already ploughed. Above their heads the Pope is seated on clouds which are supported by a swarm of demons and imps. He wears his triple crown, a royal crown is suspended over his head; in his r. hand is a crozier to which are attached keys, in his l. hand is a sheaf of thunderbolts. At his side is an inverted cornucopia, pouring out documents inscribed *Absolutions, Persecutions, Releases from Purgatory, Pardons for Money, Excommunications, Curses on Heriticks, Indulgences, Bulls, Confessions.* Truth, an almost nude female figure, stands upon clouds (r.) surrounded by a glory of rays; on her breast is a face surrounded by rays. She holds up a large scroll inscribed *40000 English Protestants massacred in Ireland 1641 Protestants burnt at Smithfield in the reign of Queen Mary. Gunpowder Plot or an attempt to blow up the Parliament House Protestants massacred at Paris, in the Vallies of Piedmont Tortures of the Inquisition.* Beneath the design are the dedication and explanation:

To the Respectable Association of Protestants & to every Worthy supporter of both Church & State this Plate is Dedicated by their Humble Serᵛᵗ the Publisher.

Explanation.

The State Husbandmen Plowing up the glebe of the Constitution, whilst the Popish Emissaries take the Advantage of the supineness of the Established Church who is fast asleep in the Vineyard where its grand Adversary the Pope, and all his host of Devils, are permitted to Sow the Seeds of their Pernicious Doctrine: Opposition attempts to stop their Progress, but the band of Unanimity is broke, & they have fallen off. Truth descends, showing a Scroll of Melancholy proofs of popish cruelty, Soliciting the Aid of her Friends, to vanquish the Inveterate Enemy, who threatens the Ruin of thair Religion, thair Posterity & thair much injured Country.

This suggestion that the Opposition was in any way concerned in Lord George Gordon's attempt to obtain the repeal of the Catholic Relief Act is of course unfounded, although the Protestant Petition was associated with the County petitions (see No 5638, &c.) in several satires (see No 5633, &c.), and the propaganda of the Protestant Association was combined with attacks on the Government, see No. 5671, but after the riots the equally unfounded accusation was made that the Government had fostered the agitation in order to discredit the Opposition and petitioners in general, see No 5687.

This print appears to have been prepared to coincide with the great meeting of the Protestant Association in St. George's Fields and the march to Westminster (2 June) which gave rise to the Gordon Riots It resembles the early manner of Gillray Reproduced, De Castro, *Gordon Riots*, 1926, p 12.

8⅝ × 12¹³⁄₁₆ in.

5679 NO POPERY OR NEWGATE REFORMER.

[Gillray.]

Publish'd as the Act Directs, June 9ᵗʰ 1780 by I. Catch of Sᵗ Giles's.

Engraving. The H.L. figure of a ruffianly man, shouting *Down with the Bank* and raising in both hands a stick or bar In his hat is a ribbon favour inscribed *No Popery.* On the r. and behind is the façade of Newgate in flames. Beneath the title is engraved:

> *Tho' He says he's a Protestant, look at the Print,*
> *The Face and the Bludgeon will give you a hint,*

Religion he cries, in hopes to deceive,
While his practice is only to burn and to thieve.

'I. Catch' probably means Jack Ketch or the hangman; and, oddly enough, Dennis, the official hangman, was tried as a rioter and convicted, but afterwards reprieved, cf. No. 5734.

For the anxiety of the Protestant Association to escape responsibility for the riots cf. No. 5841. For the riots see Nos. 5682-90, 5722, 5723, 5725, 5728, 5734, 5841, 5844.

Grego, *Gillray*, p. 31. Reproduced, De Castro, *Gordon Riots*, p. 104.

9 × 7¾ in

A print entitled REAL CHARACTER *Pub. Accord to Act June 18th 80*, in the possession of Henry Carrington Esq , is reproduced, De Castro, *Gordon Riots*, p. 138. A ruffian, flourishing a bludgeon, and a ragged hat with a favour in it, shouts, *No Pope No K— No Ministry [sic] Dam my Eyes*. In the background is a building, probably Newgate, in flames and attacked by a group of rioters.

5680 A PRIEST AT HIS PRIVATE DEVOTION.

Protestant Sculpt

Published as the Act directs June 10th 1780 for the Proprietor, & Sold at Nº 132 1 Fleet Street.[1]

Engraving. George III in monk's robes and with a large tonsure kneels, in profile to the r., before an altar in an attitude of prayer. His r. leg emerges from his robe showing knee-breeches and clocked stocking. On the altar is a crucifix; on the wall behind it, within a circle surrounded by rays, is *Ecce Homo*. On the end of the altar-cloth *The Holy Catholic Faith* is inscribed in a similar circle. On the wall on each side of the crucifix is a bust portrait; one of Sandwich inscribed *Twitcher* (l), and the other of North inscribed *Boreas* (r) Two walls of the room or closet are visible; in the back wall is an open door leading to a latrine; on its floor are papers inscribed: *Protestant Petitions for necessary uses, Middles[ex] Petitio[n], Surrey Petition*. For a similar association of the Protestant Petition with the County petitions see Nos. 5633, 5638, 5649 Over the latrine door is a bust-portrait of a pope wearing his triple crown. On the wall beside the door is a large print, torn and unframed, of *Martin Luther* It is interesting to note the date of publication: immediately after the riots which had raged 2-7 June, the first day on which the shops ventured to open, and the day of Lord George Gordon's arrest For similar attacks on George III see Nos. 5534, 5669, 5670

12⁵⁄₁₆ × 9 in.

Another impression from which the publication line has been cut off; 'Priest' has been erased and 'Great Man' written in its place, in ink.

5681 EVERY MAN IN HIS OWN HUMOUR

[n d. 1779, 1780, or perhaps 1774][2]

Engraving. The Pope seated on a chair raised on three semicircular steps. In his r. hand is a tall triple cross, on his head, in place of his triple crown,

[1] 132 Fleet Street was the address of W Wells
[2] Publication line perhaps cut off

is a head-dress resembling three inverted flower-pots, one inside the other. His l. hand is stretched out to bless a man (l.) who kneels at his feet to kiss his toe. Another man (r.) kneels behind the Pope and is about to kiss him. A large looped curtain over the Pope is an important part of the design. On the l. part of the façade of a building decorated with Ionic pilasters is visible. Beneath the design is engraved:

> A certain Knight brimfull of hope,
> Knight of the Shire also;
> To gain the Papists pleas'd the Pope,
> And humbly kiss'd his Toe.
>
> Poh, cried his Colleague in a pother,
> That's but a simple Farce;
> And that he may outdo his Brother
> He's gon to kiss his A—se.

This piece of No-Popery propaganda probably relates to the Catholic Relief Act (18 Geo. III, c 60) and is one of many propagandist prints, see No. 5534, &c., in which case 'a certain knight' is Sir George Savile, Bart, M.P. for Yorkshire. Alternatively it may relate to the Quebec Act of 1774 which was violently opposed by the Opposition and especially by the City of London as 'the establishment of Popery', see No. 5228, &c. The Bill was introduced from the Lords into the Commons, where it was advocated by North; 'Nobody', Walpole writes, 'would venture to own himself the parent,' *Last Journals*, 1910, i. 353. Archibald Edmonstone, with Bamber Gascoyne, was teller for the Bill on its second reading, 18 May 1774, and two days later was made a baronet.

$8\frac{3}{4} \times 7\frac{5}{8}$ in.

5682 L——D AM——T [AMHERST] ON DUTY, 10

Pub accˢ to act June 12 1780 by M Darly 39 Strand.

Engraving (coloured and uncoloured impressions). Lord Amherst in profile to the r. in general's uniform rides a prancing horse, holding up a large sword, dripping with the blood of two geese, one of which lies dead beside him, the other staggers, with its neck slashed. Beneath the design is engraved:

> If I had Power,
> Id kill 20 in an Hour.

Behind, red-coats on horses with drawn swords are indicated among clouds of smoke. Behind and on the l. a large square house is on fire, flames coming from the windows.

Lord Amherst was in command of the troops acting against the rioters. There were attempts to raise fears that the use of the military and the camps formed in London were part of a design by the Court to establish a military despotism, see No. 5687, &c. For the Gordon Riots see No. 5679, &c.

The number 10 on all three impressions suggests that it belongs to a series; it is similar in character to Nos. 5662, 5683, 5690.

$7\frac{7}{8} \times 5\frac{7}{8}$ in.

5682A Another impression (not coloured) with no title.

5682ʙ Another impression (coloured) with the publication line, *Pubᵈ by H Humphrey, Nᵒ 18 New Bond Street.* [n.d.], Darly's imprint having been erased or stopped out.

5683 ASS UPON ASS.   [n.d. June 1780]

Pub by H Humphrey Nᵒ 18 New Bond Strᵗ

Engraving. Lord Amherst in uniform in profile to the l. riding an ass from whose head a large crown has just fallen. The animal (representing the king) wears a large collar inscribed *Honi Soi[t]*, its fore-feet are planted on a large *Protestant Petition*; its side is being gashed by its rider's spur, so that a stream of blood pours on to the petition. Round its near fore-leg writhes a fanged serpent inscribed *Gordon.* Amherst's hat is falling off, in his r. hand he holds a sword with an irregular blade inscribed *Rebellion.* A mitre is suspended (or falling) above the ass's head.

The suggestion seems to be that the riots are being used as a pretext to damage Protestantism and establish military power, see No. 5687, &c For no-popery satires see No. 5534, &c. For the riots see No. 5679, &c.
7⅝ × 5¹³⁄₁₆ in

5684 THE BURNING & PLUNDERING OF NEWGATE & SETTING THE FELONS AT LIBERTY BY THE MOB.

Published 1ˢᵗ July 1780 by Fielding & Walker, Pater-Noster-Row.

Engraving. The mob outside Newgate. Among the most prominent figures are those of a ragged young woman of dissolute appearance, who holds up her plunder, a picture in one hand, a purse in the other, a man waving a scroll inscribed *No Popery*, a young man in irons doing the same. Men in irons, released from the prison, are being welcomed by friends or bystanders. Flames pour from the central windows of the prison and the bonfire of the governor's furniture is seen behind the mob There are many bludgeons and one *No Popery* banner. For the burning of Newgate (on 6 June) see also Nos 5686, 5844. See also No. 5679, &c.
6¾ × 8 in.   *Crace Collection*, xxvii. 55.

5685 FANATACISM REVIVED   [n d c June 1780]

P. Carey Invᵗ & Sculpᵗ

Engraving An imaginary scene during the Gordon riots. On the r a partly-destroyed building is in flames. In the foreground (c) a man in the gown and bands of a minister, evidently intended for John Wesley, holds out his arms as if preaching Two men wearing 'No Popery' cockades are drinking, apparently from the chalices of a plundered chapel. On the r. a working man holds up a large paper inscribed, *June 7 The Protestant Association. The Rᵗ Honbˡᵉ Lord George Gordon Presᵗ in the Cha[ir] Res*
A woman holding a baby sits on the ground Behind, a man holds a torch to the burning building

On the l. a man kneeling, fires point-blank with a pistol at a dog which has been tied to a post and sits on its hind-legs with a cross in its fore-paws. A large open book, its pages torn, is on the ground. Behind, men are carrying off plunder, one has a dish or tray, another a candle-stick. On the wall behind them is a placard inscribed *Now publishing and to be had*

at M* Thomsons a new Pamp* entitled *England in Blood* This was the title
of an inflammatory pamphlet advertised to appear during the riots, for
which one W. Moore[1] was arrested and committed to prison by Wilkes.
See De Castro, *Gordon Riots*, pp. 77–8, 191, and Nos. 5829, 5844. Beneath
the design is engraved:

> *Religious strife is rais'd to Life,*
> *By canting whining John,*
> *No Popery he loud doth cry,*
> *To the deluded throng.*

John Wesley wrote to the *Public Advertiser* a letter dated 21 Jan. 1780,
approving of the Protestant Association and denouncing all concessions to
the Church of Rome, which had great effect, see Tyer, *Life and Times of
Wesley*, iii, pp. 318 ff. This was reprinted in other papers, see *London
Chronicle*, 5–8 Feb., and Walpole, *Last Journals*, 1910, ii. 269

The only print in the Catalogue directed against the Protestant Association and its propaganda, for which see No. 5534, &c. But cf. the gibe at
Gordon in No. 6256 For the riots see No. 5679, &c.

$7\frac{3}{8} \times 12\frac{1}{8}$ in.

5686 THE DEVASTATIONS OCCASIONED BY THE RIOTERS OF
LONDON FIRING THE NEW GOAL OF NEWGATE, AND BURN-
ING MR AKERMAN'S FURNITURE, &c JUNE 6. 1780.

[c June 1780][2]

Hamilton delin.   *Thornton sculp.*

London, Published by Alex Hogg at the Kings Arms N° 16 Paternoster
Row*

Engraving. Rioters in front of Newgate, the southern part of its façade in
flames In the foreground is a large bonfire on which a table and other
pieces of furniture are being thrust and flung. Men wave hats, bludgeons,
hatchets, and pick-axes A man capers, holding up a stick in one hand, the
keys of Newgate in the other. On the r. is a flag inscribed *No-Popery*.
Dense clouds of smoke and the flames of the bonfire obscure the southern
part of the building, the rest is brilliantly lit. The design is surrounded by
a border representing a carved frame, with medallions, garlands, &c On
it is inscribed *All the Prisoners to the amount of 300 were released this Night*.

For the burning of Newgate see also Nos 5684, 5844

Reproduced, S G Fisher, *Struggle for American Independence*, 1908, ii 276.

$7\frac{3}{8} \times 11\frac{5}{8}$ in.   *Crace Collection*, xxvii. 54.

5687 READ, MARK, LEARN & INWARDLY DIGEST.

*Publish'd according to Act July 13, 1780 for J. Almon in Piccadilly,
London.*

Engraving. George III speaking to Lord Amherst, who wears general's
uniform and holds a bull (John Bull) by one horn. They are T Q L figures,

---

[1] Probably the W. Moore of 22 Fleet Street who published *The Whisperer*,
17 Feb. 1770–7 Dec. 1771, a violent attack on North's Government W. Plomer,
Dict of Printers and Booksellers, 1726–1775, 1932

[2] A plate from E Barnard's *History of England*, published in parts and completed
c. 1791.

411

the legs of the men and the bull being cut off by the margin of the design. Amherst, in profile to the r., very thin, holds out in his l. hand to the king a paper on which are crossed sabres inscribed *A plan for taming A Bull*. The king says, *I hear You made a fine Disposition You You You soon tame'd the Bull* (a burlesque of George III's manner of conversation). Amherst answers, *Yes Sir and now is Your time to make this Bull so tame as to bend like a Camel to recieve his Burden*. The bull says, *Dont Reckon without Your Host*. George III is holding a document, *[Pe]titions the Groom of the Stool* (cf. No. 5680, &c.). A minister or courtier standing behind him (r.) holds *petitions from the Scum of the Earth*.[1] His profile suggests Lord Sandwich. An outstretched arm, the hand holding a spying-glass, appears, its owner cut off by the r. edge of the print, on the sleeve is a large fleur-de-lys On the l., behind the bull, a citizen is in conversation with a soldier holding a musket, with its bayonet thrust through *The Humble petition*. In the background burning houses and a crowd are indicated. Beneath the design is etched:

A Dialogue

Citizen—Now Soldier if I & my Neighbours were all of us to get Guns we should have no Occasion for you Red Coats Among us should we?
Soldier—No to be sure you would not.
Cit—Then we could from our Windows shoot Rioters or defend our Liberties and the British Constitution if need were?
Sol—You Fool, have you found that out at last. A Word to the Wise.

The attempts (after the suppression of the riots) of the citizens of London to arm themselves, as well as their resentment at the presence of troops in the city, caused considerable trouble, but were dealt with tactfully and successfully by the Government, by Amherst, and by Colonel Twisleton who was in command of the Guards in the city, see *Ann. Reg.*, 1780, pp. 266–71

This attitude towards the troops was supported by Lord Shelburne and some others of the Opposition, see *Parl History*, xvi. 671, 691, 726 ff. It was the opinion of some of the Opposition that the riots had been encouraged by the Government for political ends: 'the deepest schemers for absolute power long for insurrection'. Walpole, *Letters*, xi 281, 24 Sept. 1780. See also Nos. 5682, 5683, 5689, 5690, 6006. For the riots see No. 5679, &c.

$6\frac{7}{8} \times 12\frac{5}{8}$ in

5688 THE MAYOR OF L——N ON THE THRONE OF EASE

Pub by M Darly (39) Strand acc^s to act July 14. 1780.

Engraving. Lord Mayor Kennett seated in a latrine. A footman, in a laced coat with tags on his shoulder, enters from the l, holding his hat and saying *My Lord the Guards are now arriv'd*. The mayor clutches papers in each hand, those in his l hand are inscribed *Riot Act* He is saying, *The Mob has frighten'd me so, that they've give me the Gripes*. His hat, inscribed *Kennett*, is on the seat beside him. On the wall behind are papers covered with meaningless scratches, one inscribed *Maps of London*, implying that

---

[1] Burke had called the Middlesex magistrates the 'scum of the earth', 8 May 1780, in a debate on calling out the military to suppress riots. *Parl Hist.* xxi 592.

London is reduced to ruins Two prints, one of a cottage, the other of a tree, are on the r and l. walls. Beneath the design is engraved:

> The Riots so frighten'd the Mayor,
> And where's the Wonder when it,
> Was so critical an affair,
> His lordship could not—Kennett.

When Catholic chapels, &c. were being destroyed in Moorfields on Sunday, 4 June, the Lord Mayor refused to give orders (as Justice of the Peace) to the Guards to act, showed manifest signs of fear, and in other ways behaved scandalously. For this he was reprimanded by the Privy Council, see No. 5689. See also Nos. 5690, 5692, 5866.
$6\frac{7}{8} \times 6\frac{5}{16}$ in.

5689 A VIEW OF THE COCKPIT,
WITH THE REPRIMANDED MAGISTRATE IN DISGRACE.

Thos Tagg Sculp^t

Published according to Act of Parliament, July 14, 1780.

Engraving, beneath which two songs are printed in three columns. The Lord Mayor, Brackley Kennett, wearing his gown, hurries along Whitehall covering his face with his hands. His head is surrounded with a cloud of smoke, a winged imp above his head blows at him, another puffs at him with a pair of bellows. The Recorder (James Adair), wearing a grotesque mask (l), squirts at him with a large syringe; a satyr (l.) rushes towards him with a scourge raised to strike. Behind the Recorder (l) stands a group of four aldermen in their furred gowns, one holds a paper inscribed *had he exerted his Authority he would have saved much Bloodshed*, another holds a paper inscribed *and would prevented* [sic] *the Army from being our Masters.* On the r. is a group of spectators: a little boy, holding out *History of the Riot in Moorfields & who were the calm Spectators*, points at the Mayor; the others are a chimney-sweep and his boy, a woman, and a man wearing the favour of the Protestant Association in his hat. Behind is the Whitehall front of the Treasury building known as the Cock Pit with a sentry-box; a sentry on duty is walking from l. to r. Beneath is printed:

Song I. The Words by R. Rusted. Tune—The Vicar and Moses [cf No. 6130]; *Song II the Words by O——— N———. To the Scots Tune of,*

> Ye took your Packs upon your Backs;
> You would na stay, you ran away.

One verse of Song I:

> At length forc'd to wait on a Council of State,
> For his Wisdom display'd in Moorfields,
> Where the strange city tool, well known for a F———,
> Got kick'd out of doors, neck and heels.
> Fol de rol &c.

The Lord Mayor was summoned before the Privy Council on 9 June. Evidence was given of his refusal to order the Guards to interfere with the rioters in Moorfields on 4 June and other delinquencies He was reprimanded and the Attorney-General was ordered to report on what proceedings should be taken against him. *Privy Council Register*, P R O. On

10 Mar 1781 he was tried before Lord Mansfield, found guilty of neglect of duty and fined

For the cowardice of the Lord Mayor see Nos 5688, 5866 For the contention that the Government was attempting to establish a military despotism, see No. 5687, &c. For the riots see No. 5679, &c.

$6\frac{11}{16} \times 10\frac{1}{16}$ in. Broadsheet, $17\frac{7}{16} \times 10\frac{3}{4}$ in.

5690 THE MAYOR RETURNING THANKS TO L^D AM——T, AT THE SAME TIME HAD THE HONOUR TO KISS AN ASS.

[c. July 1780]

Pub: by H Humphrey, N° 18 New Bond Street.

Engraving. Lord Amherst (l), in uniform, stands in profile to the l., his r. hand on a post inscribed *10,,000 £*. His breeches are lowered, and he holds up his coat-tails in his l. hand. The Lord Mayor (Kennett, see Nos. 5688, 5689) kneels behind him, he holds his hat in his hand, and wears a large bag-wig and sword. Behind him stands an obese alderman in a furred gown; he holds his hat in his r. hand, a long staff in his l.

While the troops remained on duty in the city after the riots Amherst, in spite of a dispute with the Corporation over the arming of civilians as a defensive force (see No. 5687), managed to remain on good terms with the city. He wrote on 29 July to the Secretary of State's office to say that to continue the troops in the city for another week would endanger 'the harmony that has subsisted to this moment' *State Papers Domestic*, George III, 21. On 24 July a Common Council resolved 'That the Thanks of this Court be given to the Officers and Privates who have done duty in this City, for their exemplary Conduct and strict Attention to Military Discipline during the late alarming Riots'. On 28 July the Lord Mayor, Aldermen, and Common Council went to St. James's with an address of thanks to the king for his care in restoring order by the use of armed force. *London Gazette*, 25–9 July.

Perhaps the £10,000 indicates the cost to the city of feeding the troops. This was said to be £100 a day, and on 18 July a Court of Aldermen decided that the allowance should cease from 22 July. *Ann. Reg*, 1780, p. 224. See also No 5687, &c Similar in character to Nos. 5662, 5682, 5683, and perhaps belongs to a series which was issued both by Darly and Humphrey.

$4\frac{1}{2} \times 6\frac{5}{8}$ in.

5691 BENJAMIN FRANKLIN

N.L.G D.L.C.A.D.L. del. et Sculp.

A Paris chez Bligny Lancier du Roi, M^d dEstampes, Peintre, Doreur et Vitrier, Cour du Manege aux Thuilleries [July 1780]

Engraving Emblematical portrait of Franklin. Diogenes (l) supports a bust portrait of Franklin in a carved oval frame, the portrait being that by Van Loo, wearing a fur-trimmed robe over a loose shirt. Diogenes holds out his lantern, he supports the portrait on a stone block inscribed *Stupete gentes! Reperit vivum Diogenes* Behind him is a spear on whose point is a Phrygian cap of liberty In front of Diogenes and the portrait are carrots and a cabbage, symbols of frugality, a staff, a broken yoke, emblem of the power of England in America, an eagle from whose claws spring thunder-bolts over a map of *Ameriq Septent.* A bird which has been tethered by a cord flies away, symbolizing liberty. Beneath the title is engraved *Ministre plenipotentiaire a la cour de France pour la Republique des Provinces unies de l'Amerique Septentrionale,* and *Né a Boston le 17 Janvier 1706.*

For the influence and popularity of Franklin in France as philosopher, sage, and minister, see B Fay, *The Revolutionary Spirit in France and America,* 1928, pp. 83 ff. See also Nos. 5407, 5704. Reproduced Fay, *Franklin,* 1912, p. 512.

10½×8 in.

5692 THE FEAST OF THE GODS.

An explanatory Key may be had with this Print.

Published according to Act of Parliament, by G. Kearsly, at N⁰ 46, in Fleet Street, London July 18ᵗʰ 1780.

Engraving. All the figures are numbered, but the key being missing interpretation is impossible. A feast, the tables supported on clouds, below which is the sea with ships and a coast-line. At a high table raised above two others at right angles to it, sit a man smoking a pipe, and a woman fast asleep. He resembles the Lord Mayor, Brackley Kennett. At one table (l) sit seven men, three having the appearance of mechanics. One is Wilkes, holding a key, a military officer with a wooden leg sits with his arm round the shoulders of a young woman. A ruffianly-looking man holding irons or fetters appears to be picking the pocket of his neighbour. On the table are punch-bowls, wine-bottles, glasses, and a tankard. At the other table (r.) sit three women singing from two musical scores inscribed *Once the Gods.* An elderly man seated opposite to them plays the violin, his score inscribed *Violino primo.* Two men are asleep. The man at the head of the table listens with pleased attention. A fourth woman (r) caresses a dog. Punch-bowls, &c., are on the table. Two servants (l) lift a barrel; wine-bottles stand on the ground. In the foreground (l) a man lies asleep, an overturned tankard beside him. He is perhaps dreaming of the scene above the clouds

Perhaps a satire on some civic entertainment, possibly to the troops quartered in the city, given by Brackley Kennett, who had become notorious by his conduct during the Gordon Riots, see Nos. 5688, 5689, 5690.

9¾×15¼ in.

5693 POLITICAL REFORMATION. [1 Aug. 1780]

Engraving. From the *Universal Magazine,* July 1780 (frontispiece). A man raises his hands to beat off a swarm of hornets from his head. He stands near a tree by which is a covered shelf on which are three bee-hives. His cane projects from a hollow in the tree showing how the hornet's nest has been stirred up. From his pocket hangs a paper, *Reduction of Placemen and Pensioners.* A dog lies on the ground. Beneath the design is engraved:

> As in the hollow of a rotten Oak,
> So in the rotten hollows of the State;
> A nest of plund'ring hornets to provoke,
> Calls thousands forth to urge their venom'd hate,
> Tis hard the honey of industrious Bees,
> Should fatten drones, in pensions and in fees!

A reference to the County Associations and petitions and to Burke's plan of economical reform, see Nos. 5638, 5657, &c.

$5\frac{1}{4} \times 3\frac{1}{4}$ in.

5694 LORD GEORGE GORDON,

Drawn from the Life by R. Bran.

London. Published as the Act directs, Augt 4, 1780; by John Harris, Sweetings Alley, Cornhill—

Engraving   Gordon stands full face, pointing with his cane to a roll inscribed *Protestant Petition*, which shows signatures in two columns, another roll lies beside it   His r foot rests on a book inscribed *Popery*. He is plainly dressed, lank hair falling on his neck, in his l hand, which is gloved, he holds out his hat and his other glove   Behind him is the point of intersection of the five roads which crossed in St. George's Fields, beside which are drawn up in close order members of the Protestant Association as they are supposed to have met before marching to Westminster on 2 June, but with a complete and military regularity which is very different from fact. Letters refer to explanations below the print. A circle (1) inscribed *B* is the *London Division*; two concentric circles, *D*, are the *Scotch Division* (r). Behind (1) is a large tent, and a semicircle of petitioners *A* which represents the *Southwark Division*. Opposite them (r.) and drawn up facing two roads is *C*, the *Westminster Division*. Beneath the title is engraved, *President of the Protestant Association.*

For Gordon as the Protestant Hero see also Nos 5672, 5840, 5841. Cf. also the Dutch prints on the Gordon Riots, 5722, 5723 (an English copy of 5722), 5725, 5728, 5734

$12\frac{3}{8} \times 8\frac{7}{8}$ in.

5695 NATIONAL DISCOURSE.

M. M. fecit. [Gillray?]

Publish'd Augt 9th 1780 by W. Humphrey N° 227 Strand.

Engraving   A British and a French sailor addressing one another   The British sailor stands full-face, a club in his r. hand, his l. hand on his hip. He wears a crowned hat, a handkerchief knotted round his neck, and wide, knee-length trousers. He scowls threateningly. The Frenchman, very thin, stands facing him, in profile to the l., he grins, saying *Ha! Ha! we beata You* the Englishman answers *you Lie.* The Frenchman wears a feathered hat, ruffled shirt, long trousers, and a cutlass. His hair is in a very long pigtail queue, tied with a bow of ribbon. In the background a naval battle is indicated by ships and clouds of smoke slightly sketched. Cf. No. 5674.

$7\frac{5}{8} \times 9$ in.

5696 [SAMUEL HOUSE[1]]

T R. [Rowlandson.]   *J. J.*

[*Pub^d According to Act Sept 1 1780 by J Jones at N° 103 Wardour Street Soho*][1]

Engraving. A stout publican with a completely bald head stands outside

---

[1] Written on the print in a contemporary hand.

his house, legs astride, a tankard with an open lid in the r hand, a long pipe in the other He faces T.Q. to the r. On the tankard is a monogram, *S. H* Behind him is a large barrel, on which is scrawled *No Pope*, a relic or reminder of the Gordon Riots Two windows of the house are visible; in one (r.) two men are sitting, one smoking a long pipe From the other (l) a man leans to vomit On a seat under the window (r.) a man sits smoking a pipe and holding a tankard A bird-cage hangs on the wall.

A portrait of Sam House, the Wardour Street publican and politician. He was a well-known character and always dressed in the same way, as he is here depicted no wig, no coat, a black waistcoat with sleeves, clean linen never buttoned at the collar, breeches always open at the knee, fine silk stockings or bare legs, and neat black slippers. *Life & Political opinions of the late Sam House* [1785], the frontispiece to which is an etched portrait of House by Rowlandson. (B M.L. 1419 b. 13) See also *Gent. Mag.*, 1785, p 326

On the print is written in a contemporary hand 'the first man who jumped off Westminster Bridge. He was a wellknown partisan of Mr Charles Fox in Westminster'.

House was much caricatured in prints of the Westminster election of 1784 He kept open house for Fox during elections. He is said to have 'commenced politician' in 1763 in support of Wilkes and liberty, and to have been much distressed at the coalition between North and Fox He was a bird-fancier, op. cit. See No. 5697 and index

Grego, *Rowlandson*, 1 98–9

$8\frac{1}{16} \times 7\frac{1}{16}$ in.

5697 Sᴿ SAMUEL HOUSE.

Pubᵈ According to Act Septᵗ yᵉ 18ᵗʰ 1780 by T Rowlandson & J Jones at Nᵒ 103 Wardour Street

Engraving A copy of No 5696 in which the curiously ill-drawn leg of the man sitting with a pipe and tankard has been corrected. On the barrel, instead of *No Pope* is inscribed *Fox for Ever Huzza*. It seems to have been issued as an election print, see No. 5699, &c

Grego, *Rowlandson*, 1 98–9

$8\frac{9}{16} \times 7\frac{1}{2}$ in

5698 THE F—X [FOX] AND H——D [HOUND] OR RIVAL CANDIDATES HUMBLY ADDRESS'D TO THE WORTHY ELECTORS OF W——R.

Pubᵈ as the Act directs Septʳ 18 1780.

Engraving. Fox (l), obese, with a fox's head, stands holding out a paper inscribed *On the Freedom of Elections* Lord Lincoln, the court-candidate for Westminster, stands facing him with the head of a dog, holding out a paper, *Services done in America* He is very thin and wears top-boots.

An electioneering print, see No. 5699, &c.

$6\frac{5}{8} \times 9\frac{1}{2}$ in.

5699 WESTMINSTER ELECTION, 1780.

E——g inv.

Publish'd as the Act directs Sept' 25, 1780. by P. Mitchell North Audley St' Gros' Sq' & J. Harris, Sweathing Alley, Cornhill.

Engraving The three candidates stand under the portico of St Paul's, Covent Garden. Immediately below them is a long table behind which the poll-clerks are sitting with their books; in front is the mob. The clock in the pediment shows that it is 2 30. Fox stands in the centre holding out an open book inscribed *Magna Charta*. Britannia sits beside him, holding a fox on her knee, while with her l. hand she holds up a paper inscribed, *Let Britania's Friends be Britons Choice* On the l. stands Neptune with his trident and Admiral Rodney, a sword in one hand, in the other a scroll inscribed *5298 The Spanish Fleet totally defeated off Gibraltar Jan'y 16 1780* On the r stands Lord Lincoln (son of the Duke of Newcastle), a sword in his r hand, in his l a scroll inscribed, *4257 Votes purchas'd. I brought the news from America of the taking of Charles Town.* (Lincoln, A.D C to Sir Henry Clinton, arrived in London 15 June 1780 with a dispatch on the capture of Charlestown *Extraordinary Gazette*, 15 June 1780) Over Lincoln's head flies the devil inscribed *A*, referring to a note below the title: *A Devil looking over Lin——n.* A voter stands by the polling table, taking the oath against bribery, his hand on a book which one of the clerks holds out to him Another clerk holds up a paper, *We must guard against bribary.*

In the foreground is a band of Fox's supporters, among whom are butchers in their aprons playing on marrow-bones and cleavers, a man with a fiddle, another with a horn They wear fox's tails in their hats and carry papers on one of which is inscribed *200 Plumpers . Liberty & Freedom.* The hat of the man who carries it is decorated with a fox's head and a large brush and a notice, *Volunteers Fox.* On the l. is a man with a placard . *The Honble M^r F's Friends presents comp^s to Lord L—— & his modest abettors and desires to know why Justice H—— should interfere* (probably Justice Hyde, reputed a trading-justice). A man holds up a long pole on which is a stuffed fox placarded, *4878 Reynard for ever* Beside it on the r. is a barrel, a kneeling man drinks from a spigot, a small boy catches beer in his hat, others stand round with pots. A man stands on the top of a barrel singing a song, he holds the ballad: *Ye free born Electors of Westminster City Derry Down.*   On the r. a woman is selling fox's tails, a purchaser fixes one in his hat. On the l. are two men with *Lincoln* on their hats, baskets of apples are being overturned, a woman lies on the ground A dead dog or cat flies through the air A Jew is conspicuous; a man stands on a box beating a gong.

Behind the foreground figures is a dense crowd; hats are being waved in the air, a man on horseback (r.) and a coach (l) try to make their way through the mob. On each side of the church is a large house at the windows of which are spectators. One doorway (l.) is inscribed *Procter*, probably an allusion to the Middlesex election of Dec 1768 when bludgeon men were said to have been hired by Sir William Beauchamp Proctor, the Court candidate and opponent of Wilkes, see Nos. 4223, 4224.

Parliament was dissolved on 1 Sept The Westminster poll lasted from 7 to 22 Sept. Admiral Young was proxy for Rodney, who was at sea, the votes being 4,878 for Fox, 5,298 for Rodney, 4,257 for Lincoln. On the 23rd Fox was chaired and 'carried to St. James's Gate to insult the Court',

Walpole, *Last Journals*, 1910, ii 330 See also Nos. 5697, 5698. Lincoln demanded a scrutiny and the poll-book was published in Nov. (B M L 100, k. 45)

An earlier state is in the Crace collection

$10\frac{1}{2} \times 15\frac{13}{16}$ in.

5700 THE STABLE VOTERS OF BEER LANE WINDSOR,[1]

Pub acc^s to act, Oct. 9 1780 by M Darly 39 Strand.

Engraving. Three stalls in a stable; in one (l) is a pony, in the other two are horses, the names of the animals are inscribed over the mangers: PONEY, LIBERTY, and MONTAGU They are the three candidates for the borough of Windsor. Penniston Powney, Admiral Keppel, and John Montagu, son of Lord Beaulieu, the two last being the members in the last parliament In the rack over 'Poney's' head (l) lies a thin man saying *I'll serve Poney, Lord North bed me* In Keppel's stall (c.) a man in military dress lies face downwards in front of the animal saying *I'm hearty in the cause I'll stick at nothing*; in front of this stall a riding-whip and a hat with a cockade lie on the ground. These two are identified by Miss Banks as Colonel Conway (l) and Colonel Egerton, supporters of Powney against Keppel A man in a long robe and wearing a tie-wig enters the stable from the r.; he holds up a forefinger, saying, *Come Colonels damn Liberty lets go poll for the poney's started*. He is perhaps one of the Windsor Corporation. Beneath the design is engraved:

> *Poll C——way & Eger——n twice if youre able,*
> *No votes are so Valid as those that are stable.*
> *When ye S——n's [Sovereign's] a mule & the Premier an Ass,*
> *A Poney for Senator surely may pass,*
> *And Stables are Houses & Dwellings of course,*
> *When two of the Voters are two of the Horse.*

The Windsor election attracted great attention from the personal canvassing of the king against Keppel, which began in Apr. 1780, before a general election had been decided on *Hist MSS. Comm*, *Abergavenny Papers*, 1887, pp 29, 30 Porritt, *The Unreformed House of Commons*, 1. 415. For Conway's support of Powney see *Life and Letters of Lady Sarah Lennox*, 1901, i. 303–4. The 'Prince of Wales took great part for Keppel, and would not speak to Colonel Egerton who voted against him', Walpole, *Last Journals*, cf No 5644. Conway was M.P. for Orford, Egerton, l.t.-Governor of the Scilly Is. See Nos 5701, 5708.

$7\frac{1}{8} \times 12\frac{7}{8}$ in

5701 HARRY THE FATHER TO S^R HARRY THE SON OR THE WINSOR BREWER.

Pub acc^s to act Octr 15 . 1780 by M Darly 39 Strand.

Engraving. A man holds up his hands in horror at the sight of the ghost of his father, a slightly draped figure (r.) standing on a cloud and surrounded by rays of light. They are standing outside a house the centre of which has a plain pediment; probably the Windsor brewer's house. The ghost

---

[1] No 5723, dated 29 Sept. 1780, is catalogued next 5722, a Dutch print, one being a copy of the other.

says *Remember your promises on my death bed and be true to Keppel.* The son drops from his outstretched hand labels inscribed, *Promises of Preferment, Patents of Knighthood, Brewer to his Majesty, Poney's engagement.* Beneath the title is engraved:

> *O O my Son Harry since on my death bed,*
> *And all that when dying unto thee I said,*
> *Could not have the power to keep the [sic] true blue,*
> *To Hell thou may'st go & give Satan his due.*

For the Windsor election see Nos. 5700, 5708.

$7 \times 6\frac{9}{16}$ in.

5702 THE WHORE OF BABYLON'S CARAVAN WITH A CARGO OF POPISH BLESSINGS

Pub^d as the Act directs Octr 17th 1780, by W Richardson, N° 68 High Holborn.

Engraving Two monks, tandem, drag (r to l) a small wooden cart, driven by a woman, who sits on a cask inscribed *Holy Water,* her legs hanging down in front of the cart. She holds reins in one hand, whip in the other, and wears on her high-dressed hair a conical triple head-dress, surmounted by a cross, representing the triple crown of the Papacy. Her dress is cut low She says *I will make the Hereticks repent calling me Whore of Babylon* The monks say, *I perceive our Holy Flame break out Already,* and, *Brother, we seem to Move pretty Fast* On the side of the cart are crossed keys inscribed *St Peter's Keys.* Inside it are a gibbet, a wheel (for purposes of torture), a barrel of *Combustibles,* a chest of *Indulgences,* a cask of *Holy Water,* an axe, and birch rods Chains hang from the back of the cart.

On the l. is a group of three a bishop, a soldier holding a bayoneted musket (his uniform resembles that of the Irish Volunteers), and a citizen holding a tasselled cane The bishop says, *The Purity of the Protestant Religion, will Confound the Arts and Errors, of the Church of Rome.* The soldier says, *We must upon them, with Spirit* The citizen says, *They have got too much Footing Already* In the foreground (l) is the British lion, asleep. Beneath the design is engraved:

> *With a load of Destruction, here Babylon's Queen,*
> *Triumphant, a driving to England, is Seen.*
> *Chains, Combustibles, Rods, with Gibbets & Racks*
> *Declare her Religion, besides Whips, & Axe.*
>
> *Yet I hope, tho' the Lion appears fast Asleep,*
> *An Eye o'er our Church some good People will keep*
> *That the Bald pated, Bare footed Bigots may see,*
> *Our Worship is pure, & our Country is Free.*

Perhaps an attempt to throw the responsibility for the Gordon Riots on 'emissaries of the Papists', see No. 5841 For 'the Whore' see No 5534.

The cart of the 'Whore' is copied, in reverse, from No. 5712, the fleur-de-lys being replaced by crossed keys, or, possibly, this print was the earlier design. A similar cargo is drawn in a sledge (as in No. 5713) in Hogarth's *The Invasion, Plate I,* see No. 3446

$5\frac{3}{8} \times 10\frac{1}{2}$ in.

5703 THE OLD PACKHORSE BRITAIN, LOADED . OR WAYS & MEANS FOR 1781.

Pub⁴ as the Act directs Oct⁰ 24ᵗʰ 1780 by C. Jones Brewer street Golden square.

Engraving A heavily-laden pack-horse is being driven (r. to l) by Lord North who walks behind it, holding a whip, with an expression of anxiety. In his l. hand is a rolled document inscribed *Extra[ordi]naries*, from his pocket protrude papers inscribed, *Ways & Means for 1781, Sinking Fund.* A large pack on the horse's back is inscribed *Budget*, a smaller one, *Taxes.* The horse is in blinkers. A signpost (r.) points *To London* (l), and to *Bushey Park* (r), North's country house.

One of many satires on North's budgets, see No 5578, &c.

$5\frac{1}{2} \times 10\frac{7}{16}$ in.

5704 B. FRANKLIN, L.L.D F R.S.   [1 Nov. 1780]

Pollard sculp.

Engraving *Political Magazine,* 1 631 A head of Franklin in profile to the r , drawn to simulate low relief against a dark background within an oval. Beneath the oval is a rectangular view of the American war· a body of American soldiers (r), in close order with two flags, faces, and appears to be parleying with, a smaller force of British soldiers also with a flag. All carry muskets with fixed bayonets In the foreground (r.), reclining under trees is a nude woman, with two infants, who watches the encounter. In the background is the sea, with two ships. The design is engraved with delicacy on a minute scale. The portrait and the view of America are set in a rectangle decorated with engraved lines

The plate illustrates a very hostile account of Franklin as 'the author and encourager of American rebellion'. See Nos 5407, 5691 One of the few prints hostile to the Americans, see No 5401, &c

$5\frac{7}{8} \times 3\frac{3}{4}$ in.   B M L , P.P. 3557 v.

5705 NAVAL TRIUMPH OR FAVORS CONFER'D

[Rowlandson]

London   Printed for J Harris, N⁰ 3, Sweetings Alley, Cornhill, Nov⁰ 13 1780.

Engraving (coloured and uncoloured impressions). A naval officer wearing a ribbon and star is mounted on the back of an old naval pensioner, with a wooden leg and a blind eye who is supported on crutches. He gives his r. hand to another officer who is dancing along by his side, his r. hand on his hip The old pensioner says,

> *To what a Condition alas! am I brought,*
> *Who so many Battles so bravely have fought*

The scene is outside the gates of Greenwich Hospital. A pensioner lies in the road, in front of the triumphant pair, leaning against a post or mile-stone (r) He says,

> *Alas! what a Scene to each Son of the wave,*
> *Who in Thunder & Fire have always been brave*

CATALOGUE OF POLITICAL AND PERSONAL SATIRES

Immediately behind the old pensioner who is being used as a beast of burden walks a man with a surly expression, beating a drum Behind him (l.) three pensioners supported on crutches and sticks, walk away turning their backs on the procession. One looks over his shoulder, saying,

> *Is this the reward for services past,*
> *While —— with Honor & profits are grac'd.*

In the background buildings of the Hospital are freely sketched. Beneath the design is engraved

> *The shake of the hand, with such Goodness & grace,*
> *Shews who is in Favour & who is in place,*
> *At Greenwich the poor Invalids will proclaim*
> *What at present we do not think proper to name*

This appears to be a satire on the extremely unpopular appointment by Sandwich of Sir Hugh Palliser as Governor of Greenwich Hospital in July 1780: abuses in Greenwich Hospital had been brought home to Sandwich, see No. 5548, and Palliser was regarded as the instrument by which the Ministry had attacked Keppel, see Nos. 5536, 5537. Fox made a violent speech on 1 Nov on the appointment: 'There could', he said, 'be only one of the King's servants [Sandwich], so abandoned, and so lost to all sensibility and honour, as to have dared to advise any such measure as the giving the governorship of Greenwich Hospital to that object of universal detestation, Sir Hugh Palliser . . .' C. J. Fox, *Speeches*, 1815, i. 287. *Ann. Reg*, 1781, p 156 Wraxall, *Memoirs*, 1884, i. 261–3; cf. also ibid, ii. 65. See also Nos. 5707, 5999.

Grego, *Rowlandson*, i. 99 [1]

8¾×13 in.

5706 COUNT DE ROCHAMBEAU
FRENCH GENERAL OF THE LAND FORCES IN AMERICA
REVIEWING THE FRENCH TROOPS

[T. Colley.]

Pub by T. Colley Nov. 25. 1780 Strand

Engraving A burlesque of Rochambeau's army. The French general stands on the r holding a tall spear in his r hand, the head of which is a fleur-de-lys; his l. hand is on his hip He wears a feathered hat and an enormously long pigtail queue. He and all his men wear extravagantly large shirt frills Facing him is a rank of three soldiers standing at attention with bayoneted muskets, then an officer holding a fleur-de-lys flag; then another rank of three privates. The privates' knapsacks have the appearance of enormous muffs.

For Rochambeau's army, intended to be 8,000, but actually only 5,500, which arrived off Rhode Island 11 July 1780, see J. B. Perkins, *France in the American Revolution*, pp. 400 ff., J. J. Jusserand, *With Americans of past and present days*, 1916, pp 1 ff. Reproduced Drepperd, *Early American Prints*, p. 204.

8¼×13 in.

[1] His explanation of the print as the triumphal procession of Keppel seems quite erroneous.

5707 THE STATE DUNCES

[W. P. Carey?]

Pub^d for the Proprietor by W Humphrey N° 227 Strand Dec 2 1780 Price 1^s

Engraving. Britannia (r.) seated, with her shield and spear, on a raised dais; she is addressing George III, who supports on his back Lord North, who is being flogged by Charles Fox Britannia, holding up her r. hand, says, *My Dominion diminish'd my Blood spilt my Treasure exhausted my People burdend with Taxes my Colonies Revolted Deserted by my Allies my Flag insulted and now no longer Mistress of the Ocean and shall the abettors go Unpunished? forbid it Justice.* The king, who wears long robes, bends forward, holding North by the wrists. He says, *For supporting them in their Design's thus am I obliged to carry them through condign Punishment.* Under his feet is a document, *Petition of the People* Fox, raising his knotted scourge above his head, says, *Was I to give as many lashes as he has made blunders in the State I should not be done these three hours by G——d.* North says, *D——n Patriotism for its stripes I dont like to bear* Four onlookers (members of the Opposition) stand behind North and Fox; one (l.) somewhat resembling the Duke of Richmond says, *When you are tired F——x let me have a spell*; another says, *This is all Pro bono Publicoo therefore its hoped our Labour will not be in vain* On the l. is a group of five men. Sandwich (c.) stands full-face biting his thumbs, his knees knocking together, a member of the Opposition holds him by the arm and shoulder, saying *Thou shalt not fly from the Wrath to come for it will be your turn Next* Sandwich is saying, *D—— the Minority for they are always taking me to task to drub me for Something or Other.* From his coat pocket extends a label inscribed *Merit Rewarded or S^r H——h [Hugh] at Greenwich a New Song the Burden*

> *"Tis my Maxim still I say,*
> *To favour him that Runs away."*

Under Sandwich's feet is a paper inscribed *Britannia Rules the Waves.* On the l stands Lord George Germain biting his nails and saying *At Minden my Exploits will will [sic] be handed down to Posterity as will my feats ever since.* Under his arm is a paper *The Hum Gazett[e] or Extraordinary bad News from America.* A man standing by him says, *My L——d you may take the Dutchmans Comfort "Tis well its no worse"*

In the foreground (l.) is a cock looking at itself in a looking-glass; beneath it is etched:

> *The Cock who can see and not feel for the Elf* } *British*
> *Who at home and abroad is fighting itself.* } *Breed*

In the back ground is Westminster Hall

Beneath the design is inscribed:

> *Let Britons behold, and glory to See,*
> *The Min——y flogg'd as they ought well to be*
> *For those evils Britannia is heard to relate,*
> *Is the cause of their numerous blunders in State,*
> *For which those behind who stand biting their nails*
> *Will shortly be hoisted and get the nine Tails*

On 13 Nov. 1780 Fox had pledged himself to move for the dismissal of Sandwich and for 'bringing him to condign punishment' for the appointment of Palliser to Greenwich Hospital and for shameful neglect of the Navy *Ann. Reg*, 1781, p. 156. See No. 5705.

Resembles the manner of W. P. Carey.

$8\frac{3}{16} \times 13$ in.

5708 OLD ENGLAND, OR AN ELECTION IN THE YEAR 1580
GREAT BRITAIN, OR AN ELECTION IN THE YEAR 1780

Surrey Sculpsit   *Windsor delin[t]*

Published as the Act directs Dec[r] 12 1780 for J Stockdale N[o] 181 Piccadilly. G Kearsley, N[o] 46, Fleet Street, and E Hedges. Royal Exchange.

Engraving A design in two compartments: The l (1580) depicts *The Freeholders of a County requesting an Old Englishman to become their Representative*. A man stands (l), with his hat under his arm, holding out a deprecating hand towards a deputation advancing towards him all bowing, hat in hand; it consists of three men, with the head of a fourth appearing from the r. All are dressed in quasi-Elizabethan dress; the 'Old Englishman', as appears from his profile, is intended for Keppel, who on being defeated at Windsor had been offered election by Surrey and Sussex, and had chosen, and been returned by, the former (Walpole, *Last Journals*, ii 330) in spite of a contribution of £4,000 from the Treasury to the support of his opponent, Onslow *Corr of George III*, v. 466. This is indicated by the names of the supposed artists.

On the r. (1780) is depicted *A modern fine Gentleman bribing the Electors of a Borough to make him their Representative*. The electors (l) are represented as tradesmen, receiving the offers of the candidate (r.), who advances towards them with a mincing gait, holding a purse in his l hand, and coins in the r He is dressed in the extreme of foppishness and smiles ingratiatingly. Behind him stands the king, partly cut off by the r edge of the print His l hand is on the candidate's shoulder and he holds up towards the electors notes inscribed *50£; 50*. Of the five electors, one is a butcher (l) with a steel hanging from his belt, another is a tailor, with scissors and a yard-measure A third holds what appears to be the beam of a pair of scales; he is being addressed by a bearded Jew. All are of repulsive appearance. The candidate is Powney

George III canvassed actively against Keppel from Apr. 1780. On learning of Powney's intended candidature he wrote 'I shall in consequence get my tradesmen to appear for him' Porritt, *The Unreformed House of Commons*, i 415. For the Windsor election see Nos 5700, 5701.

An advertisement of this print, 'in a few days will be published', from the *General Advertiser*, 2 Dec. 1780, is pasted on the back.

$8\frac{7}{16} \times 12\frac{1}{8}$ in.

5709 THE THING IN A NASTY SITUATION.   [? *c*. 1780]

Publish[d] by Some Body in y[e] Caracter of No Body one of y[e] Minority[1]

Engraving Six figures stand in an extended circle playing a game of handball with Lord North, who is in the air, his round body and globe-shaped

---

[1] Etched within the design, as if in a shadow cast by Fox.

head representing a ball. He is wearing his garter ribbon and star and says *I am in a Nasty Situation. I almost wish I was no-Thing*. Strips inscribed *Bribery* and *Taxes* decorate his stockings; the *privy purse* is falling from him, as is a paper inscribed *How to Diminish Public Money by Private Contract*. The players wear large muff-shaped gloves with which to strike the ball Three stand in the foreground: Wilkes (l), with a violent squint, is saying *I will have 46 Strokes at him*, a man in gown and bands (possibly Parson Horne, afterwards Horne Tooke) is saying *O he will be a Nice Bone for ye Divil to pick*, Charles Fox (r), in the form of a fox, is saying *Keep it up my Boys*. In the middle distance are two small figures: one (l.) says *There he goes Neck or Nothing*, the other [Burke] says *This is sublime & Beautiful*. The sixth player in the distance is very small and not character-ized Beneath the design is etched:

> *I Hope you're Pleas'd with this Game at Hand Ball*
> *Which seems to Prognosticate* SOMEBODYS *fall*
> *Ah may it be Bandied about—— and so forth*
> *To shew we Can beat all the Games of the* NORTH.

Fox had on some occasion called Lord North 'that thing'. (Note by Mr Hawkins) Perhaps an allusion to the loan of 1781, see Nos 5834, 5835. Hand Ball was played especially in the south of Scotland. *O E D*
  Apparently by the same artist as Nos. 5568, 5648.
5¼×7 in.

5710 THE GENEROUS JACK TARS, OR FEASTING AFTER FIGHTING. [? *c* 1780]

Engraving Figures seated and standing round an oval table covered with a cloth, on which is a sirloin, a plum pudding, and a foaming tankard of beer Four sailors act as hosts to Spain and France; Holland sits aloof in the foreground (l) clutching a bottle and saying *I have got a bottle of Hollands but I will keep to my self*. A sailor sits at the centre of the farther side of the table, holding a large money-bag and saying *I dont care a Fig now for here is a bag of spanish dollars*. On his l sits a woman who says, *I am glad of it honest Jack for thou art a jovial fellow*. On his r. sits Spain, in feathered hat and slashed doublet, saying to another sailor who offers him a slice of beef, *Signior English, I like your beef better than your bullets* This sailor stands in front of the table, holding out a slice of meat on a fork and saying, *Here Don Diego is a taste of our English roast Beef*
  France stands at the r end of the table, between two sailors, who invite him to partake of a large round spotted pudding He says, *By gar I dont like it tho it be* [sic] *better then de frogs & soup Meager* One of the sailors (r.) holds his arm saying, *Take it take it Monsieur you may not have another offer*. The other (l) beckons to him, saying, *Here Monsieur is fine plumb pudding of the best spanish plumbs*.
  On the wall is a framed picture of a naval battle, inscribed *View of Admiral Rodney beating ye Spanish fleet* Beneath the design is engraved:

> *The Don & Monsieur our Jack Tars having beat,*
> *And taking them Prisoners yet give them a treat,*
> *Of the best Fruit of Spain a plumb Pudding is made,*
> *And a Sirloin of English Roast Beef is display'd*
> *Monsieur does not like it, because not his own,*
> *But the Don licks his gills at a bit of the Brown.*

Probably after Rodney's defeat of the Spanish squadron under Langara, 16 Jan 1780, when Langara's flagship was taken and Gibraltar relieved. See No. 5648, &c.

6 × 10 in

5711 LE PROCÈS DES TROIS ROIS. [1780]

John Phileps Pinx   *William Jones. Sculp.* [sic]

Engraving Frontispiece (folding plate) to 'Le Procès des Trois Rois Louis XVI de France-Bourbon, Charles III. d'Espagne-Bourbon et George III. d'Hanovre, fabricant de Boutons [see No 5573, &c], Plaidé au Tribunal des Puissances-Européennes'. This has the imprint of 'George Carenaught', London, but was published in Paris [1] The names of the artists are evidently fictitious.

The sovereigns of Europe are ranged in three tiers on each side of the President, the Sultan of Turkey, Abdul Hamid, who sits cross-legged on a raised dais under a canopy, at the foot of which is a long table at each end of which a man is writing. The three kings stand before the table looking up at the president. Each stands between his two 'avocats' and each wears a long ermine-trimmed robe, his crown and sceptre on the ground at his feet. George III (1) stands between Bute and North, there is little or no attempt at characterization except that North is stout The 'avocats' of Louis XVI are Maurepas and Choiseul, of Charles III, d'Aranda and Florida Blanca. On the r. of the president on the highest tier sit seven sovereigns, including 'Mhemet Empereur de Maroc'. On his l sit Maria Theresa, Catharine of Russia, and Maria of Portugal. Below sit nine sovereigns to the r. of the president and eight on his l. They include five Electors Below, on the level of the floor sit eight 'Représentans des Républiques', and the Pope with two cardinals on the extreme l. Corsica is represented by Paoli and America by Benjamin Franklin.

The names are supplied from the text, which is an elaborate satire on the political situation and on the monarchs of Europe The sentence of the court is (*inter alia*) that George III be placed on an ass facing its tail, and that America has gained independence, provided the English be driven from the New World. A notice from the fictitious publisher attributes delay in publication to the Gordon Riots.

8⅞ × 15 in   Copy in Print Department.

5712-5734

A set of Dutch prints (with some French and English copies), reflecting opinion and propaganda of various parties in the United Provinces between the seizure of Van Bylandt's convoy, 1 Jan 1780,[2] and the English declaration of war on 20 Dec. 1780. Those with an asterisk are bound together in a book lettered *Caricatures on American History*, which includes explanatory pamphlets issued with the prints. Without the explanations printed beneath the plates, or accompanying them, the prints would be unintelligible. Other Dutch prints are Nos. 5839, 5959, 6292. See also No. 5825, &c.

[1] A Dutch translation (n.d) was published at Ostend. It has no plate
[2] Nos 5721, 5726 would appear to be earlier, but are included in No 5728 as prints of 1780

5712 DEN DOOR LIST EN GEWELD AANGEVALLEN LEEUW.*
[THE LION ATTACKED BY CUNNING AND FORCE]

[1780]

Engraving. Similar in arrangement to No 5714, figures isolated and in groups are arranged over a sketch-map, or bird's-eye view, showing, very incorrectly, the coast from *Brest* (l) to *Amster*[dam] (r), with the Channel and *Portsmouth* in the upper part of the design The towns are indicated by buildings, the figures have numbers referring to an Explanation printed beneath the plate (which is here translated). 'showing what each person is supposed to say' and serving as a continuation to the 'Letter of Cato-Batavus' Off Portsmouth the names *Byland* and *Fielding* are engraved, indicating the encounter of 1 Jan 1780, see No. 5628, &c Opposite Brest is engraved *Hollandsche Schepen met Scheeps materialen*, indicating 'the arrival of Dutch naval stores'.

On the extreme r., near Amsterdam, are two men, one gesticulating, the other, behind him, is smiling They are (1) 'some well-known merchants calling out with great passion "Restitution, Satisfaction, unlimited convoy". Yet one of these, turning round, says smiling, "We have meanwhile already won some little capital, but however it is good to complain, in order to embitter people's minds, although the English pay for what falls into their hands, and a war with England, the greatest of our allies, would probably harm us, and our possessions in the East would be endangered".' The Stadtholder (2), wearing a sword and holding his hat and a cane, turns his head in profile to the r towards the merchants, he is 'His Highness pointing out to the merchants the lion . . ."See Sirs what is happening, this have I long foreseen, and for that reason although without success, have I tried to put the Republic in a state of defence. We are lost if we let ourselves be deluded by passion and cunning! Yet I shall at last be obliged to let the ship drift".'

Between (1) and (2) stands (3), Sir Joseph Yorke, wearing a ribbon and star, and holding out his l hand towards the merchants 'The English Ambassador, shrugging his shoulders, says, "I am sorry about the incident, but I tried to avoid it and warned you resolutely It is hard on an ally to see the enemy supplied with everything by force of arms while the help due to us is refused. Yet the die is cast, and things will probably not remain as they are" '

Immediately under the Stadtholder's feet is the Dutch lion, holding in his r. fore-paw the sheaf of seven arrows symbolizing the seven United Provinces which are bound by a ribbon symbolizing the bond of union The French Ambassador (4), his coat dotted with fleur-de-lys, holds his hat before the animal's eyes, while (5) a well-dressed man stoops forward to take one of the arrows 'The French Ambassador full of compliments, strokes the lion with one hand, and with the other holds a hat before his eyes, saying, "All will go well if I can only keep the Lion blind and bring the Dutch gradually to the dance with England [cf. No. 5664] Oh what a fine part shall we play, when we have added to our land-power the dominion of the sea".' (5), an 'ex-Jesuit, following the Society's grand rule, *divida & impera*, loosens the bond of union, and has already pulled out one of the seven arrows, saying, "That goes well, when, disguised as a Patriot, I shall succeed in taking unnoticed some arrows from the Lion, and then might the Pope indeed restore our order, if the Dutch, who are less easy to beguile than our good Spaniards, do not smell a rat before our work is completed!"' Near (4) is a small serpent with a forked tongue. Near (5) are some papers inscribed *III. Art. Goed Patri* . . and *Certificat.*

Behind the lion (6), a Spaniard (r) in slashed doublet threatens him with a spear, saying 'Who knows if once again now we shall bring our old Beggars to their knees? Yet first must Neighbour France have accomplished his crafty business for we are now of one family, though this has not been exactly to our advantage [cf. No. 5642]. But when we have once got Gibraltar back, then shall we be able to dictate the law finely to the other Powers Meanwhile we have made a beginning and have given the Dutch some pinches.' He is perhaps La Herreria, the Spanish Minister at the Hague

A plainly-dressed man wearing a hat holds a pen in his r hand, his l arm is outstretched He is (7) 'A Minister of State looking with pain on the blinded lion' He says, 'Oh Heavens, where will all this end for the beloved Fatherland! Yet I cannot do more than truly make known my discoveries.' A man stands in back-view, r arm outstretched, looking towards the Channel. He is (8) another Minister of State, looking at the convoy being taken to Portsmouth and saying 'That's bad Although we have given the English some grounds for complaint Is it possible to remain friends with two contending parties? What is to be done now? For by force of black-magic and to the joy of some of our windy poets, all our light frigates are turned into three-deckers, where shall we find sailors to man them! The Northern Powers themselves are in want of sailors. Meanwhile we are on the hook and must pay the reckoning, at which France will laugh heartily!'

A monk (9) drags (l to r) a little cart containing emblems of 'Popery', probably the original of the cart in No 5702, but decorated with fleur-de-lys; the monk, dragging a sledge in place of a cart, appears in No 5713. Its contents are a gallows, a wheel, an axe, faggots, tar-barrels, an iron-bound chest, and shackles In front sits a courtesan holding in her hand a high-feathered head-dress; she represents the 'Whore of Babylon' or the Church of Rome, cf No 5534 The monk is 'joyfully journeying to Holland on the rumour of a breach between England and the Republic'. He says, 'our object is reached thanks to our pretended tolerance now that we have set the Dutch at variance with their old ally, and the heretics have been brought into a scramble, a game in which we should indeed again become masters, and to which purpose I bring good provisions!'

In the upper r corner, close to 'Amsterdam', two men stand in conversation They are *A*, a naval commissary from 'Fr——k [France] in Amst[erdam] looking for certificates to help the sailor' He is fashionably dressed and holds out a paper to *B*, a Dutch skipper in bulky trousers, who is dancing with rage, saying, 'if this piece of paper should be found on me by the English, then they will make a prize of my ship and cargo, in place of paying for the one and giving me back the other as they have done till now'.

On the paper is a watermark with a portrait of the Stadtholder, William V, on horseback, with the words, *P. W de Vyfde*

Propaganda of the pro-English party of the Stadtholder which was opposed by the 'Patriots' of the Dutch cities and especially of Amsterdam, where French influence was potent It is answered by No 5719, where its 'author' is said to be 'Cato-Batavus', who is alleged to be influenced by his investments in British securities, cf. also No. 5718. The prophecy voiced by one of the (pro-English) Dutch merchants proved well-founded, see

No. 6292 and cf Nos. 5827, 5830 'Unlimited convoy', of which much is said in this series, was the revival by the Republic of a claim put forward by Sweden in the middle of the seventeenth century that ships under convoy could not be searched without insult to the national flag. Lecky, *Hist of England*, IV, 1890, p 160 f. See also No. 5724. For the activities of the French Ambassador, La Vauguyon, see F. P Renaut, *Les Provinces-Unies et La Guerre d'Amérique*, Paris, 1924, pp 154 ff

A reduced copy is No. 1 in No. 5728. Van Stolk, No 4313, where it is described as a copy of a similar plate without the two figures *A* and *B*, the explanation being in French. Muller, No. 4362 c.

$6\frac{1}{8} \times 14\frac{3}{4}$ in

5713 DE ONTWAAKTE LEEUW*   [1780]
[THE LION AWAKENED.]

Engraving A sequel to No 5712. The print is elucidated by numbers referring to a printed explanation pasted on the print A number of figures stand on the sea-shore. The central figure is that of Catharine of Russia (2), her crown poised on her high-dressed hair. She holds in her outstretched hands a ribbon, the r. end of which is in the l. fore-paw of (1) the Dutch lion, who snarls angrily towards the French ambassador, who is posturing, hat in hand, on the extreme r of the design In the lion's r fore-paw is the sheaf of seven arrows symbolizing the United Provinces. Two figures on Catharine's r hold the l. end of the ribbon they are (3) and (4), and represent the kings of Sweden and Denmark A man has just fallen to the ground in front of the Empress and the lion, he is (5) de Pylen, ex-Jesuit. On the r. behind the lion, the Stadtholder (8) and the English ambassador, Sir Joseph Yorke (7), are having an interview Yorke (r), contorted with rage, stamps and clenches his fist; the Stadtholder, hand on hip, points disapprovingly towards him. Behind and to the r. of the empress stands a Spaniard (9) pointing at the French ambassador.

On the extreme l a ragged, bare-footed monk (10) drags off rapidly a wheeled sledge on which sits the 'Whore of Babylon' as in No 5712, but her cart is reduced to a sledge, piled with the same contents

In the foreground, in front of this group, are piled emblems of sea-power and commerce. a trident, a gushing culvert, a caduceus, &c. Along the horizon are ships in full sail: on the l. is inscribed *Calis*, on the r. *Dolver* [Dover].

The explanation translated:

1. Depicts the Dutch lion, showing his teeth at all who by trick or force attack him. Neither trick nor force shall break the bond of unity [binding together the United Provinces].

2 A Russian lady wearing an imperial crown, unable any longer to endure the injustice inflicted on the lion, invites him to a bond of friendship, for that purpose bringing with her two Northern Princes [Nos. 3 and 4] who likewise hold fast to the bond of friendship. Thus is the Lion again given courage to oppose the proud tyrant

5 The ex-Jesuit, de Pylen, seeing the lion's awakened countenance, falls to the ground in terror—'Ignatius! Ignatius! what have I done! The lion is awake, my dismay is very great! Oh, we have now no more hope that the good Pope will restore our Order'.

6. The French Ambassador, having succeeded in dazzling the Lion by his flattery and compliments, is ashamed that his cajolery is now being

discovered, and as the lion is looking at him with an angry countenance, he withdraws shamefacedly: 'It is best that I make off and rouse the Lion no further, otherwise things might go badly.'

7 The English Ambassador, in a fury of rage at the refusal to help in the concluding of an alliance, says, 'Is that the reward of friendship, an alliance concluded to our hurt, and to leave us, who are your allies, in misery and without help'

8 His Highness, in a stately attitude, says to the English Ambassador: 'Who is the cause of the whole misfortune' had you not acted thus arbitrarily and masterfully, things would not have come to this extremity, you are yourself the cause of your misfortune, therefore do not venture any more to the verge of ruin, or you will be threatened with complete disaster'

9. A Spaniard turns sadly away, calling to his friend, the French ambassador, 'It is all over Brother, the Lion has too many friends, we cannot get to Holland so easily.' [He is perhaps La Herreria, the Spanish Minister]

10 Shows a monk, seeing the lion awakened, and fearing that the baggage he brings with him will be ill received, draws it away, calling on all saints and holy things to come to his help, and cursing the burden with which he is laden. 'What shall I do now, all my labour is lost I thought I should be allowed to sell my small wares in Holland, but the cursed Protestants saw on my arrival that my little lady was painted and my money was stamped with [French] lilies I see clearly that if I and my wares are not out of harm's way in good time, my freight will prevent my return.'

'Finally, in the distance, is a combined fleet which protects the commerce of the Lion, who keeps a watchful eye on all who try to hinder it Henceforth the convoys will not be so easily taken'

A print on the Armed Neutrality, one of several much over-rating the assistance which Holland might expect to derive from it It assumes that resistance to England's claim to seize enemy goods in neutral ships, and her interpretation of contraband as including naval stores, could be combined with an independent or even hostile attitude to France and Spain See Mahan, *Influence of Sea Power*, 1890, p 405 f See also No 5714, &c. For the suppression of the Jesuits see No. 5222.

A reduced copy is No 2 in No 5728 With the print is a pamphlet, 'Nadere Verklaring van de   ontwaakte Leeuw', which amplifies the explanation printed beneath the plate.

Van Stolk, No. 4314 Muller, No. 4363.

$6\frac{1}{2} \times 11\frac{13}{16}$ in.

5714 DE MOEDIGE EN WAAKZAME LEEUW*
[THE BRAVE AND WATCHFUL LION]   *1780.*

Engraving, with a printed explanation below it in two columns. Similar in arrangement to No. 5712. A number of figures, stiff and ill-drawn and poorly grouped, their identity is indicated by numbers. The upper part of the print depicts topographically the English Channel; on the south side, on the extreme r. is *Amsterdam*, represented by a harbour in which are ships at anchor, and a town conventionally indicated by buildings surrounding a church The Hague, *Haage*, is similarly indicated some way to the l , and on the extreme l is Brest, with ships at anchor off the coast. At the top of the print in the centre is Portsmouth, a fleet of ships within and outside the harbour is inscribed *Fielding*; following it, and on the l. is another fleet, inscribed *Byland*.

The Russian ambassador (1) gives a paper inscribed *Memorial Declaratie* to (9) a Dutch minister of state. To the r of this couple (3) the Stadtholder, his head turned in profile to the r, his hat in his hand, holds out his l. hand towards three men (2) who face him, hat in hand He is receiving 'some well-known Dutch merchants' 'in a very friendly way'

In the foreground (l.) is the Dutch lion (4) very rampant, trampling under foot two documents, *Tractaaten van Commercie*, and *Traktaaten van Alliantie* In front of him and on the extreme l stands (5) Sir Joseph Yorke, British Ambassador at The Hague, holding out a chain with a padlock at one end. Beside the lion, his r hand resting on the animal's back, is (6) the French ambassador, his coat decorated with fleur-de-lys. Behind the lion's outstretched tail stands (7) a Spaniard, holding open a large pair of shears, he is perhaps Herreria, the Spanish Minister

Behind the Spaniard and to the r. stands (8) a Dutch minister of state, wearing a hat, a pen behind his ear, his hands clasped, watching the lion.

The explanation translated

1. Prince Galitzin, Envoy Extraordinary of Her Majesty of all the Russias, handing over a Memorial to the First Minister of State of the Republic, wherein her Majesty makes known her declaration made at the Courts of Versailles, Madrid, and London, and the Republic is invited to make common cause with Russia for the protection of Commerce· 'Your high mightinesses will easily understand the necessity for hastening this resolution, concerning matters so important and advantageous for all mankind, wherefore the signatory requests that a speedy answer may be given '

2. Some well-known merchants speaking to His Highness. 'Our ships have long been exposed to the attacks and plunder of war-making powers, to the great disadvantage of the trade of the inhabitants, while we are not in a position to resist it by force of arms Now is our opportunity to be respected by England, Spain, and France, if we do not refuse the invitation of the illustrious Empress of all the Russias. We therefore beg very humbly and earnestly that your Excellency will be pleased to support by your authority and wise counsel the just and beneficent proposal of her Imperial Majesty, so that henceforth our commerce may be carried on safely and unhindered.'

3. H.H saying to the merchants in a very friendly manner· 'Your request is very just, I have always made the greatest efforts to maintain the Republic and make her commerce secure Therefore I have already urged that we should increase our sea and land forces and put ourselves in a state of defence against our too-powerful neighbours, before we declare ourselves. Still, since the illustrious Empress of all the Russias will now take the same course as ourselves, I shall use all my powers to support her proposal in the States, to restrain by strong measures the wanton presumption of our seeming friends.'

4. The Dutch lion, standing with his hind-paws on the Treaties of Alliance and Commerce between the Republic and England, Spain, and France, and one of his fore-paws lifted, says: 'I have always supported treaties as inviolate and thought that each Power must consider them as sacred, I trusted that I was perfectly safe. Still I perceive it to be clear that there is neither trust nor uprightness among the nations, I shall therefore make use of all my powers to punish those who by trickery or force insult or injure '

5   The English Ambassador holds shackles in his hands, to throw over the lion and prevent his being in a position to defend himself, yet he notices that the lion has raised one of his fore-paws to punish him for his audacity, whereupon he retreats, saying, 'I thought I had already made the lion so tame that he would put up with anything from me, but I am mistaken, I see that he begins to be angry. For we have more than once found to our shame that the Dutch lion can revenge himself, when he is too much teased, I shall therefore try to respect him and avoid him '

6   The French Ambassador, his hat in his r hand, and pushing the lion gently with the other, says, 'How brave is the Lion, I fear however that he relies too much on his security and trusts too much to his treaties with England and will allow himself to be ensnared by this Power. This however does not please me now, although at other times I am accustomed to break my word very lightly, and to violate treaties I shall therefore disturb him in his tranquillity for this touches my own advantage; nevertheless I shall pose as friendly, lest suspicion is raised and it is taken amiss '

7.   A Spaniard with a great pair of shears in his hand intends to cut short the lion's mane, yet hearing the lion begin to roar, he springs back 'I thought I could at least make myself master of some of his mane, so that the loss I suffer through England might be somewhat made good, but I see that this is not the case The lion is vigilant, and is angry I shall therefore try to keep him as a friend so as not to have any more enemies, for alas' one alone can do me harm enough.'

8   A minister of state, his pen behind his ear and rubbing his hands, says: 'What a fortunate change in affairs I thought that the beloved Fatherland was in a dangerous situation through the superiority of our neighbours and because we were not sufficiently armed, but now the Russian Empress will join her power to ours, and Sweden and Denmark will probably enter the alliance, my fear vanishes and gives place to pleasant sensations, also I shall now at last receive some more rest '

9.   Another minister of State, taking the memorial from the Russian Ambassador, with a delighted expression and bowing in a friendly manner· 'I have supported the English party with all my might, so long as it was at all possible I thought that the safest way to protect the Republic from danger, but I see now that England is a faithless ally, who under the appearance of friendship tries to destroy our trade, and further demanded more help from us than we were pledged to give, and embroiled us in war. This necessitates my leaving my own party, but I knew not how best to behave in that matter But thank the Empress of Russia, who saves me from this difficulty, through her friendly offer to uphold neutrality with us Now I shall easily explain myself to the Convoys, so far as the treaties allow, and I shall not again permit myself to be frightened by the threats of England.'

A print on the Armed Neutrality similar in its attitude to No 5713. Though such high hopes were entertained in Holland of the Neutrality (which Catharine told Harris ought to be considered an Armed Nullity, Malmesbury, *Diaries*, i 355, 431, see also i 385), the United Provinces did not decide to adhere to it until November, the Stadtholder's party holding out for a guarantee by Russia of Dutch possessions in the East and West Indies. Fitzmaurice, *Life of Shelburne*, 1912, ii. 78 Prince Galitzin, the pro-French Russian Minister at The Hague, urged the Dutch to act against England, Malmesbury, op. cit , i 295 See also Nos 5664, 5713, 5715, 5716, 5718, 5719, 5724, 5730, 5732, 5733, 5850, and for the attitude of England to the United Provinces, No 5557, &c.

On the paper is a watermark of the Stadtholder on horseback with the letters P. W. de V (not identical with that on No. 5712).

A reduced copy is No 3 in No 5728.

Van Stolk, No. 4315. Muller, No. 4364.

$6\frac{5}{8} \times 14\frac{7}{16}$ in

5715 LOON NA. WERK 1780*
[A DUE REWARD 1780]

1780.

de puis is 8 stuijoen [pence].

Mezzotint. The figures have numbers which refer to an explanation engraved beneath the design. A large dog muzzled and chained to a low round post is being maltreated by figures representing England's enemies He is (1) 'an English dog chained to a round neutral stake'. A Dutchman (2) holds his tail and pinches it with a pair of pincers, he is giving him 'a pinch in the tail before being bitten by him in the leg'. Behind him is a crowned woman (Catharine of Russia) holding up a caduceus (as the protectress of commerce) in her l hand, a sword in her r., behind her stand two men, representing Sweden and Denmark They are (3) 'The Neutrality at the head of which is a crowned Princess nobly protecting free trade', and assisting Holland A lean Frenchman (4) in back view, wearing a bag-wig, raises a parasol to beat the dog, looking towards the Dutchman, he is 'beating the dog to encourage the Dutchman and showing him his friends'. A Spaniard (5) raises a large tasselled cane to beat the dog, his l. hand is on the shoulder of (6) an American, in quasi-military uniform, holding a knotted scourge in each hand 'The Spaniard deftly strikes the cur with his cane and the American joins heartily in beating this pest of humanity on his impudent muzzle'

In the background (I) a crowned woman stripped to the waist is tied by her wrists to a gallows, she is being flogged by a man dressed as a naval officer who holds a birch in each hand She is 'the proud Queen of the Sea being lashed by Paul Jones' Jones, when he took refuge in the Texel after his fight with Pearson (see Nos. 5559–66, 5582), was treated as a hero by the Dutch. Van Loon, *Fall of the Dutch Republic*, p 237

The misunderstanding of the international situation common in these Dutch prints appears in the association of Spain and America, since Spain, though an ally of France, was not an ally of America and had no desire to help rebellious colonies. For the Armed Neutrality see No 5714, &c.

A reduced copy is No. 4 in No 5728

Van Stolk, No 4316 Muller, No. 4365.

$5\frac{3}{4} \times 9\frac{5}{8}$ in.

5716 DE MAN IN 'T HEMBD, OF DE GEFNUIKTE HOOGMOED *
[THE MAN IN THE SHIRT OR PRIDE BROUGHT LOW]

Engraving The figures are numbered, referring to a short printed explanation beneath the plate. A man (1), England, dressed only in a shirt, with an expression of horrified rage, is being held by two men, (4) and (5), representing Denmark and Sweden. France (7) stands behind him about to place a fool's cap on his head. Russia (r) (3), a stalwart man wearing a fur cap and long gown, is about to strike him with a large club. A plainly dressed man (2), America, runs off to the l with his clothes, looking back with a smile Holland, as a Dutchman (6), kneels on the ground fixing shackles to the ankles of the Man in the Shirt.

The scene is the sea-shore Small vessels (l.) (8) have boards on the top of their bare masts, behind them are ships in full sail (9) A man (10) clenches his fist at the sight of the vessels In the foreground lie torn documents (11)

The explanation, translated·

(1). 'A man in a shirt in a great rage; (2), an American, who carries away his money and clothes laughing; (3), a Russian threatening to strike him; (4) and (5) hold each an arm; (6), a Dutchman who puts chains on him; (8), some dismantled privateers; (9), a fleet of merchant ships sailing undisturbed, (10), a man who sees this, stamping his feet, (11), some torn-up treaties.'

With this print is an *Uitlegging* (interpretation), in verse, which is confused and contradictory. 'Each explains it in his own way and I in mine.' Holland (6) is 'The trade spoiler, the most cunning of all' Russia is 'The strongest of the six who passes for arbiter'

One of a number of prints on the Armed Neutrality, see No 5714, &c It also shows how potent was the idea that England was to be despoiled of her commerce, see Nos 5726, 5727

A reduced copy is No. 7 in No. 5728.

Van Stolk, No. 4317. Muller, No 4366 a

6⅜×7¾ in.

5716A An earlier state in outline, but having numbers and the printed *Verklaring*.

5717 [VI DE EERSTE ŒCONOMISCHE PLAAT *]
[EEN JONGEN RYKEN HOLLANDER]   [1780]
[THE FIRST ECONOMIC PRINT. A RICH YOUNG
DUTCHMAN]

Engraving A companion print to No 5720. The 'rich young Dutchman', who is the subject of the print, appears in it in two different situations. He sits (r.) on his open money-chest, which is supported on four low wooden wheels, and filled with money-bags, holding a paper in his hand and pointing contemptuously to the r , where another Dutchman stands by a booth of Dutch wares He pays no attention to an Englishman (r), 'Meester John altyd op en te kort' (Master John always short of cash), who takes one of his money-bags and points with his l. hand towards a temple falling to ruin in the distance The Dutchman carelessly allows the money-chest to be dragged to the l by Folly in cap and bells, by a Frenchman, and by two richly dressed women, one of meretricious appearance with loose hair, the other with a haughty expression and hair dressed in an enormous pyramid. A third man, wearing a high toupet-wig, turns his back on the money-chest as he drinks from a large bottle

On the l. of this group the 'rich young Dutchman' appears again standing passively with a pleased expression while he is decked out in French garments. a little boy wearing a bag-wig hands him a high toupet-wig with a long queue, a man helps him to put on a coat, and on the l a Frenchman bows low before him holding a feathered hat Another Frenchman standing behind holds out a sword.

Behind this group is a booth of English goods with a placard: *Engelsche kraam*, in front of it is a draped platform on which stand the English salesman (l.) and his assistant (r.), the latter dressed like the zany who accompanied mountebanks and quack-doctors. The salesman holds out a roll of figured material and points to the r., he appears to be addressing the spectators. His assistant hands a pile of crockery to a man (r.) who holds out his hands to receive it The shelves of the booth are stacked with crockery, &c., while textiles hang from projecting poles

On the extreme l is a solid and lofty stone gateway or triumphal arch Over the arch is carved a fool's head, with cap and bells; festoons of bells from the cap decorate the façade. Four men, partly visible, blow trumpets and horns from the summit of the arch.

In the foreground (l.) a stall or booth of French wares is partly visible in front of the arch. Its penthouse roof has a placard inscribed *Modes de Paris*. Elaborately trimmed hats and ribbons hang from a cord Beneath it, beside a chest, stands a man dressed in the French manner holding out his hands persuasively towards the 'rich young Dutchman' as if to recommend his wares. He appears from the explanation to be Charles III of Spain (allied to France by the Family Compact). At his feet is a pile of feathered hats, &c., and a monkey who holds out a feathered hat towards the Dutchman Through the archway is seen a formal garden with clipped hedges and a fountain in the distance. In alcoves in the hedges two couples are making love Two men are fighting with swords At two tables parties of men and women dressed in the French fashion are feasting. A couple advance towards the tables through the archway. These figures are on a minute scale.

In the foreground on the extreme r., a pendant to the 'Modes de Paris', is a Dutch booth with a placard inscribed *Hollandsche Waaren* By it stands the plainly dressed Dutch salesman at whom the 'rich young Dutchman' with the money-chest is pointing disdainfully. His wares are all solid and plain corded bales, rolls of textiles, a pile of plain round hats. Under the roof of the booth stands an enormous chest; stockings, gloves, and garments hang from a line.

In the distance (r.) is the sea, two ships in full sail are fighting On the shore is a circular temple (the temple of the state), its roof supported by tottering pillars which a crowd of men on a minute scale are pulling down (? or shoring up)

The print, though clearly a plea for economic self-sufficiency, would be unintelligible without the printed explanation here translated:

'This print depicts a rich young Dutchman, sitting on his well-stocked money-chest, pointing contemptuously to the products of industry and craftsmanship of his nation, while he allows a large part of his treasure to be taken by Master John, always short of cash, and lets himself be dragged by Luxury, Delight, Wantonness, Drunkenness, and Folly. Further, he stands in front of an English booth, where they were working busily at the delivery of yellow and green pottery, knives, combs, &c. He was greeted in a very friendly way by *Jean Poli* [the Frenchman]; meanwhile he was being busily decked out in a laced coat and a wig with red powder, feathered hat, and sword, all offered *à la Henri Quatre*. Thus fitted out, he is called to and winked at by Charles 'always foolish' [Charles III of Spain],[1] who will show him through the open gate the manners of the great world, such as banquets, card-playing, duelling, and make him thoroughly acquainted

[1] For this inapt description of Charles III cf No 5643

435

with these things. From above the gate trumpets sound and other sounds of music are heard On the right in the distance is seen a building, falling to ruin through carelessness, on the open sea is a ship taken by a hostile friend '

This ship probably represents the Dutch convoy of naval stores taken by Captain Fielding, see No 5628, &c

The money-bag stolen by 'Master John' probably represents the Dutch investments in British funds which checked the war fever in Holland among the investors, see Nos 5718, 5719, 5720, 5724 280,000,000 florins were said to be invested in England in 1780 Blok, *Geschiedenis van het Nederlandsche volk*, vi. 439

A reduced copy is No. 6 in No. 5728, the first title is taken from the pamphlet which accompanies No. 5728.

Van Stolk, No 4318. Muller, No. 4367.

$8\frac{7}{8} \times 14$ in

5718 DE TYD GEEFT VERANDERING *
[TIME BRINGS CHANGES]

Engraving. Figures on the sea-shore, on ships, and in the clouds symbolize the relations between Holland, England, France, and Russia They have numbers referring to a printed explanation in two columns beneath the print which gives the words spoken, here translated In the foreground (1) the Dutch lion (1) is about to rise. An Englishman (2) stoops over him with a bit and bridle The lion holds in his paw a sheaf of seven arrows representing the provinces of the United Netherlands The lion says, 'What will they do to me, shall I keep quiet thus, under every sort of pressure, where are my old sea-heroes, my Witts, Brakels, Ruyters, and Tromps?' The Englishman says, 'Keep still my beast, then everything will go well, we can no longer dictate the law to America, our work there was bungled, we shall now make the Netherlands dance to our piping Should we not force them? Oh yes, they will help us, we demand it, in a masterful tone. We, the English, speak and our word is law.'

A second Englishman (3) stands by, holding open a chest full of money-bags, and addressing (4) 'a covetous Dutch capitalist', who stands in a 'despairing attitude', that is, scratching his forehead in perplexity (3) says, 'Will you refuse to help us? No, you are pledged to give us aid, we are masters on the sea, we are monarchs! and we possess your gold, take care, take care to please us, we are cock of the walk. Will you contradict a Briton? His pride would not endure that!' The disconsolate Dutchman says, 'Ah if our valuable treasure were not in England. What shall I do if we become involved in war with England? My gold will go! Then I must sell my goods and dismiss my servants Oh, how unfortunate I am High interest and good security have allured me, I see it now, but alas too late!'

Next him stands (5) an 'old Dutch hero', in seventeenth-century armour, holding 'the hat of liberty on the spear of freedom'; he puts his r. hand on the shoulder of (4), and with the l points up to the clouds (r.) where sit (9) Tromp and de Ruyter. He says, 'Where is the courage of old, money-grubbing Dutchman? Is that faithful dealing with our Fatherland, that you for big profits give our money to that nation which had the law dictated to them by those laurelled heroes who show themselves there; had you used our gold for our Fatherland, and for the production of praiseworthy manufactures, arts, and armaments, then you would see our Fatherland flourish in spite of foreigners! Then you would see the Cromwellian yoke lifted from our necks by men of worth'

Next (r) stands (6), a Frenchman 'in an Henri IV costume', with a large box slung from his shoulders inscribed *Mode de Paris* and *slaapkruit voor der Hollanders* (dope for Dutchmen) In his r hand he holds up a fashionable French wig, or head-dress, in the other a placard inscribed, *Amsterdam en ome Haag se vrinden* (Friends at Amsterdam and The Hague) He says, 'To show my compliments and friendship, mixed with soft but sharp threats, and then my letter of safe-conduct! I shall shine in these fashion-loving Netherlands who are now echoing my opinion that however much one may flatter Dame Economy, she yet lacks that charm and attractiveness possessed by our Madame La Mode'

On the extreme (l), behind the Englishman bridling the lion, is the prow of a small vessel in which stands (7) an Englishman, holding up a British flag Immediately behind the three Netherlanders (3), (4), and (5) is the poop of a war-ship. On it are two men, one (8) dressed as a naval officer is hauling down a flag with three stripes The Englishman with the British flag says to him, 'Strike I say! Will you defend yourselves against us? You must see every thing in the proper light Have you shot at the sloop, and that to defend the honour of your flag? That you shall indeed smart for, you shall fear our complaints! We will break our treaties with you, merely from pride, however much we also groan under the burdens of the war, we are Britons' The naval officer answers, 'I will strike the flag, in spite of my own courage and all noble Dutchmen My orders, my orders I have followed, and I shall in time show that Holland still has heroes'

Two men in seventeenth-century dress, sitting among clouds in the upper r. corner of the print, are (9) Tromp and de Ruyter They say, 'Alas, dear Fatherland! Where is your old heroism? Where is the glory of your free flag which we, with our wealth and blood, defended? You still have friends, show that no Dutchman will let himself be wronged, famous Fatherland, consider the State'

The two admirals are being addressed by (10), who stands, hat in hand, on the poop of the ship, partly concealed by a flag with three stripes, which was that of the Stadtholder (F P Renaut, *Les Provinces-Unis et la Guerre d'Amérique*, 1924, p 144) He is 'a famous member of the Fatherland', evidently the Stadtholder, cf. No. 5714, and says, 'We deal with the affair, according to our abilities at this time in which we live, oh true heroes of our Fatherland! Changes will occur, and something will happen in spite of those who hate us. We will no longer allow ourselves to be bullied, but will show ourselves not afraid of brutal demands or windy threats' William V, hereditary head of the Navy, was completely ineffective He was pro-English by family tradition and as a grandson of George II

In the background (r) are three ships (11), 'an English ship bringing in some Dutch merchant-ships Look, it goes well, it is altogether ours, who will hinder us? We act in an arbitrary manner, and care for nothing'

In the upper l corner of the print, immediately over the Englishman holding the British flag, a crowned woman leans out from clouds, holding a paper in her r. hand, a sheaf of thunderbolts in the other She is Catharine II, saying 'Long enough, presumptuous B . [Britain] and *complaisant* F . [France] A great law-giver will change your opinions by the lightning of her face and statesmanship Come, free Netherlands, see a protector in the greatest lady of Europe'

One of a number of Dutch satires on English arrogance shown by the capture of Dutch shipping, see Nos 5628, 5712, &c, and on the Armed Neutrality, see No 5714, &c For the 'Cromwellian yoke', cf. Nos. 5719, 5729, &c. For this curious combination of hostility to England and to her enemy France, see No 5717, also a plea for economic self-sufficiency. For Dutch investments in English Government and other securities, see Nos 5717, 5719, 5720, 5724 Higher interest in England was a great attraction to Dutch capital, the Republic could raise loans at 2½ per cent. Van Loon, *Fall of the Dutch Republic*, p. 269

A reduced copy is No 7 in No. 5728

Van Stolk, No 4319 Muller, No. 4368.

13⅜ × 8½ in

5719 DEN BRITSEN LEOPARD TOT REDEN GEBRACHT.*
[THE BRITISH LEOPARD BROUGHT TO REASON]

Engraving An answer to No. 5712. The figures have numbers which refer to a printed explanation pasted below the print, giving the words supposed to be spoken. In the lower half of the design a 'pro-English Dutchman' (1) stands (l.) facing and addressing (2) the British leopard, and (3) the Dutch lion, behind whom stand a row of persons representing the powers of Europe, &c. In the upper part of the design are (1) *Portsm* [*outh*], represented by a coast-line and group of buildings. Off the coast is the word *Byland*, representing the convoy taken to Portsmouth by Fielding, see No. 5628, &c. *Lisbon* is represented by a similar group of buildings. situated east (on r) of Portsmouth. Two crowned columns represent Dutch overseas possessions (the same symbol was used in English satires, cf No 5961), with the words *Berbic*, *Curac.*, *St Eust*, *K Bon Esp*. Three isolated figures (13–15) fill the remaining upper part of the print (r.).

The pro-English Dutchman (1) is '*Cato Batavus*', author of the print, 'The lion attacked by cunning and force' (No. 5712). He stands (l.) in profile to the r, arms outstretched, papers protruding from his coat pocket: 'English bank notes to show that the money which he draws from that Court, and the capital that he has in the bank of London is to induce him to sacrifice his country to a foreign power which is injuring her.' He points to the Dutch 'établissements' [the two columns] and seems to say 'the English have been, are, and will be our best allies, we are in their debt; the trade with which they furnish us makes us prosperous, it is even for our good that they capture our ships, which are destined for France, they know better than we, that we harm ourselves by trading with France. Do you not see, that should we be headstrong enough to neglect our interests which they understand better than our blind rulers, they will take away the Cape of Good Hope, Surinam, St Eustatius, Curaçoa, de Molukken &c, and all our merchant ships? They suppose that we have reason to complain of the English, but the English might rightly complain of us, who have the audacity to desire the independence of our colonies' He faces two snarling beasts. the British leopard (2), looking round at the Dutch lion, whom he strikes with his paw 'He sees with fury that the Dutch lion is getting up after he had thrown him down, yet he sees in the distance a crowned woman [Catharine II] and this holds him in awe'

The Dutch lion (3) is a heraldic-looking beast holding in his l. fore-paw a trident. 'He is not yet recovered from his fall, yet he is in a fit state to defend himself, whenever the leopard attacks him again'

438

Behind the leopard and the lion stands (4) an Englishman, one hand
on the lion's head, the other on his trident, from which a chain ascends to
Lisbon. (Portugal, England's ally, at first refused to join the Armed
Neutrality but eventually did so.) He 'takes Neptune's trident from the
Dutch lion, yet flatters him, in order to bind him to the same fetters with
which he holds Portugal in chains'. It is as if he were saying 'to give
the Dutch the illusion that our interests are the same, we have cleverly
managed that they have invested a great part of their money in our funds
Although we cannot withhold payment from them, without losing our
credit, which is our only support, yet nevertheless we shall continually
make them fear our bankruptcy in order to hold them to our interests. In
order the better to show them that their interests are ours, we have taken
from them their sceptre of the seas, New York, Pouleron, Sillebar,[1] &c
and our Navigation Act has transferred into our hands much of their trade
To bring them the better under our yoke we shall, by our persistency, make
them afraid of the Papacy and the tyranny of the House of Bourbon, thus
we shall gradually make them believe that we are the sovereign of the seas,
that we keep them all blockaded, and at the same time are in all corners of
the world, on land as well as at sea, that nothing is so much to be feared as
a universal monarchy.' Between him and the next figure (5) is a placard
inscribed *Nieuw Jork Pouleron Acte Navig* [Navigation Act] *Sillebar.*

Next stands (5) a Dutch merchant holding up a paper inscribed with
a list of names *Falst., Duyn., Chat., Dov., Nieuwp., Van Gal., Rutt.,
Trom , Everts,* and pointing to the figures in the upper part of the print
(France, Spain, and America); these are 'the names that are so terrible to
the English' *Chat.* indicates the burning of the ships at Chatham in 1667,
Jan van Galen, de Ruyter, Tromp, and Everts are Dutch admirals The
significance of the other words is obscure; the English beat the Dutch off
Nieuwport, June 1653. He seems to say to the pro-Dutch Englishman,
'you contend that France and Spain are decadent and that intolerance and
tyranny and the Universal Monarchy will rise up anew How is it that they
have been able to take Grenada, St Vincent, Domingo, Florida, &c. from
the English? How is it that they have the reckless policy, for tyrants, of
supporting the independence of America? You say that the English will
soon take away our over-seas possessions, how comes it that they let all
theirs be taken from them? . '

Next stands (6) Catharine II, in profile to the l., a sceptre in her r hand,
her l. resting on an anchor She stands just within a circle or hoop in which
stand four other persons (7–10). In the centre is an imperial crown, resting
on an escutcheon inscribed *Hanzee,* showing that the Hanse towns had
adhered to the Armed Neutrality The Empress, 'disturbed at the arrogance (*despotismus*) of the English, wishes to restore the freedom of the
seas by an alliance between the neutral powers'. At sight of her the Dutch
lion has raised his head On her alliance he already counts.

(7) and (8) are insignificant-looking men representing the kings of
Sweden and Denmark. (9) is the king of Prussia in military uniform and
jack-boots (10) is a woman holding up the hat of Liberty on a staff, in her

[1] New York (New Amsterdam) was captured by the English in 1669, 'Pouleron',
i e. Polaron or Pulo Run, one of the Banda Islands, is an indication of the Dutch
preoccupation with Cromwell, see No 5732, &c Run was disputed between the
English and Dutch between 1620 and 1667. At the peace of 1654 Cromwell forced
the Dutch to restore it, it was taken again in 1664 and kept at the peace of Breda. It
changed hands, 1796–1814, being finally restored to the Dutch in 1814 'Sillebar'
is obscure.

l hand are the seven arrows symbolizing the United Provinces. She is 'the United Provinces depicted as the Dutch Maid'.

The English Ambassador [Sir Joseph Yorke] (11) stands just outside the circle, holding it with his l. hand, in his r is a knife with which he is about 'to cut to pieces the bond which joins the allied powers' Next him stands (11) the French ambassador, his coat patterned with fleur-de-lys, restraining him from cutting the bond. This 'shows the absurd stupidity of the author of the *Awakened Lion* and of those who have not realized that this alliance is to the great advantage of France and was perhaps the fruit of her statecraft'.

In the upper part of the design, next the two pillars representing the Dutch colonial possessions, stands (13) the king of Spain, holding a sword pointing to the word *Florida* 'which he has captured from the English'. Next him is (14) the king of France, his sword pointing to the words *Granada, St Vincent, Dominique*, 'the places won from England'; in his l hand he holds a hat, 'the hat of freedom', over the head of (15) *N. America*. America is a young woman seated on a bale of goods, beside which the muzzle of a cannon is visible In her r hand is a sheaf of thirteen arrows (like the seven of the United Provinces), in her l a cross-hilted sword, the point of which rests on a yoke which lies beneath her feet, symbolizing the yoke of England.

War propaganda directed against the contentions that war with England would mean loss of Dutch colonial possessions, see No 5712, and of Dutch investments in English securities, see Nos 5717, 5718, 5720, 5724 One of a number of prints greatly over-estimating the benefits to Holland of the Armed Neutrality, see Nos 5713–16, 5718, 5720, 5724, &c It is unlike Nos. 5713–18, also anti-British, in being pro-French. For other prints showing the rancour left by the Dutch wars of the seventeenth century see Nos. 5718, 5729, 5730, 5731, 5732, 5733

The Dutch colonial possession of Berbice (in Guiana) was taken in 1781 by English privateers, but was retaken by the French in 1782 Curaçao, a Dutch trading-post in the West Indies, escaped capture. The Cape of Good Hope was saved from Commodore Johnstone by Suffren, see Nos 5960, 6048.

For St. Eustatius see No 5557, &c For the capture of Granada by the French see No. 5581.

A reduced copy is No 8 in No. 5728

Van Stolk, No. 4321. Muller, No. 4369.

$8\frac{15}{16} \times 13\frac{5}{16}$ in.

5720 [EERWARDIGEN NEDERLANDER WORTHY DUTCH-MAN]*
[IX DE TWEEDE OECONOMISCHE PLAAT]

Engraving. A sequel to No. 5717. A scene on the sea-shore, similar to that of No. 5717, but without booths or archway; the temple on the r. is somewhat nearer, larger, and in better repair. The central figure is again a Dutchman with a money chest, but he is 'a worthy Dutchman' and an older man, standing over his chest, which is not on wheels. On the r. is a group of Dutch working-men, on the l a group of obsequious foreigners. The Dutchman empties a money-bag into the outstretched apron of an artisan; two others walk off towards the r, satisfied, carrying money, one a peasant with a spade, the other a man with a mallet. He looks contemptuously towards the group on the l, his r arm outstretched in a gesture of negation. A Frenchman bows low before him holding his feathered hat, an Englishman holds a paper inscribed *obligatie* while he points to himself, in allusion to the treaties between England and Holland. Between the Englishman and the Frenchman, a plainly-dressed man with outstretched hands bows towards the Dutchman, he probably represents America Behind them a Spaniard in feathered hat, cloak, and ruff holds up a paper inscribed *Murcia.*

A group on the l stands by a large chest inscribed *Oeconomische Brillen* [economic glasses], on it is a stand on which are displayed many pairs of spectacles or rather *pince-nez* Here a man, clasping his hands in a fervour of gratitude, is being fitted by the same 'worthy Dutchman' with glasses, a third man wearing glasses stands behind him. Between this group and the group of obsequious foreigners stands a man turning to the l and clasping his hands in a gesture of despair.

In the middle distance (r) a figure, with helmet, spear, and sword, resembling Britannia, but probably an allegorical figure, perhaps of Victory, is leading a number of men, the foremost of whom, whose hand she holds, wears a feathered hat and bag-wig. The others are more plainly dressed; they walk from l to r

On the extreme r is a circular temple supported on pillars, as in No 5717, all the pillars but one are now upright, and that one is being moved into position by a number of tiny figures, a crowd in the distance watches their efforts In the temple is a figure holding a hat upon a staff as an emblem of liberty

Immediately above the temple are clouds, on which sit and stand six allegorical figures from whom rays of light radiate They hold various emblems one has a book, *Biblia*, another a lamp They appear to represent Piety, Truth, Love, Faith, and Steadfastness.

In the foreground (r.) a lion (Holland) advances towards a lean and cringing dog (England) on whose back stands a cock (France) (cf. No. 5581).

In the background is a fleet of ships in full sail, each flying a flag with three stripes, that of the Stadtholder. Over them flies Mercury, representing commerce.

The explanation, here translated, is printed on a separate slip ·

'This picture shows a worthy Dutchman who pours out his treasure into the lap of a diligent labourer, peasant, and artisan, while he is deaf to the humble prayers of foreigners that he should entrust his gold to them, they seem to compete with each other to promise the highest interest And as his treatment of the former cannot lessen their evident diligence, gratitude, and satisfaction, so his behaviour to the latter must cause visible dejection and vacillation.

'The same Dutchman and two other gentlemen are busy making a trial of home-made spectacles, which are beheld with the greatest attention and rapture.

'There is also a crowd of persons   hurrying towards the State Building in order to join with those who are already there, not only to support it, but to restore it to its former bloom and lustre, and to Piety, Truth, Love, Trust, and Steadfastness, which previously were ready to sink down In the foreground is a proud lion, making a motion to rise, whereat an emaciated dog crawls in fear, and a cock, who is biting the dog's back, springs aside. Finally, in the distance, there is a prodigious fleet on the open sea, safe and sailing to port under the direction of Mercury.

'Dedicated to all the people of the praiseworthy patriotic company of Hoorn and to the economic branch of the Dutch Company at Haarlem.'

A warning against investments by Dutchmen in British securities, both on economic and political grounds, see Nos 5717–19, 5724, and a plea for economic self-sufficiency; see also No 5724

The title is taken from the printed explanation, the second title from the printed pamphlet which accompanies No 5728. A reduced copy is No 9 in No 5728.

Van Stolk, No. 4322. Muller, No 4370.

$8\frac{7}{8} \times 13\frac{7}{8}$ in.

5721 [HET TEGENWOORDIG VERWARD EUROPA.]*   [' 1780]

[EUROPE IN HER PRESENT DISORDERED STATE]

Engraving A printed explanation accompanies the print A curiously carved chest, or seat, representing 'The English Bank of Exchange' (Wisselbank) is suspended like a pair of scales by chains from the horn of a unicorn whose head emerges from clouds. It tilts down on the r., where a stout Englishman, 'an English lord', sits precariously, exclaiming in alarm as a Frenchman (r.), standing on the ground beneath, pulls him by the leg. The Frenchman's r. hand is on the hilt of his sword. The balance is further depressed by America, a naked child crowned with feathers, who is seated on the 'Bank' beside the Englishman and holding his arm, admonishing him with an upraised finger. A Spaniard holding a crutch crouches on the ground beside the Frenchman

A 'Dutch skipper' (l.) holds one leg of the 'Bank' to prevent its being dragged down by France. He turns to speak to a 'merchant of Amsterdam' seated on a chest and writing in a ledger. Round the chest are 'sacks of gold', bales of goods, cheeses (one stamped with crossed keys), and rolls of textiles In the background (c) is a Dutch landscape; a group of six windmills flying a flag with three stripes, and four cows, two of which are being milked.

Beneath the design, verses are engraved in two columns, English (l.) and Dutch (r.).

Bold Jack! pray, what's the business to-day!
Phoo—! pox—! a plot, mistaken for a play.
This hurly-burly spoils your sport—: you'll find,
There's humour to your face—, and more behind
Amazing Fool—! yet tottering on thy bench,
Tho' scorn'd by Spain, and cozen'd by the French — —
Only the Dutch, not laughing at your nose,
Good-natur'd helps, to snatch what-e'er you lose.

Hoezee! tienduizendmal! van dikhout zaagt men deelen.
't Gaat wel. by kris en kras! dat heet een hoofdiol speelen
Puf Spaansch en Fransch Messieurs! die poen heeft maakt figuur.
Maar lieve Jack! zie toe: dat stoolen staat je duur.
O Boston! Delaware! ó Washington! ó Franschen!
Zo mogt Mylord welhaast een hangman's hoornpyp dansen.
De Batavier houdt noch uw Bankspel in den haak
Vermeetle! Loon die trouw, of vrees geregte wraak

442

A translation of the last three lines:

> So might Mylord soon dance a hangman's hornpipe.
> The Batavian still holds your bank on the square
> Do you dare! Reward this faithfully or fear revenge.

From this and from a printed explanation which accompanies No. 5728, it appears that the Englishman is in danger of falling because his 'Bank of Exchange' begins to fall aslant America (though an infant), France, and Spain combine to humiliate him, only the Dutch skipper saves him from further disaster. The merchant of Amsterdam is 'in a dispassionate and quiet posture giving to each his due'. In Holland in the distance, 'no corn comes from the mills and the cows are being milked', probably an allusion to the toll of Dutch commerce taken by the English Navy and privateers, see No. 5628, &c. The Batavian holding 'your bank on the square' is probably an allusion to Dutch investments in England, which were attracted there by the higher rate of interest than in Holland, see Nos. 5717–20, 5724, here supposed to be maintaining British credit. England is warned that Holland is her sole protection against France, Spain, and America Evidently designed before the capture of Bylandt's convoy (cf. No. 5712), see No. 5721 A

The title is taken from the pamphlet which accompanies No. 5728.

No. 10 in No 5728. Van Stolk, No. 4323 Muller, No. 4371

$6\frac{1}{8} \times 8\frac{5}{8}$ in.

5721 A*

Another state in which the design is surrounded by a heavy border of masonry with plants growing from the crevices between the stones, representing a wall through an opening in which the figures and the Dutch landscape are seen The verses are engraved on the masonry.

Van Stolk, No 4323. The drawing for one of these two states was advertised for sale at 'f 40' in the *Leydse Vrydagse Courant* of 29 Oct. 1779 Ibid.

$9\frac{3}{4} \times 11$ in.

5721 B*

A water-colour drawing, the original (or possibly a copy) of No. 5721. It differs in the arrangement of the bales of goods, &c , across a sack lie two long-stemmed pipes. Perhaps the drawing advertised in 1779.

$11\frac{1}{2} \times 14\frac{3}{4}$ in.

5722 ENGELSCH NIEUWS.*
[ENGLISH NEWS.]

Engraving Men grouped on the sea-shore with allegorical figures in the clouds above They have numbers referring to a printed text in two columns beneath the print giving the words they are supposed to speak There is no relation between a Dutch group, an English group (l), and the solitary figure of Lord George Gordon (r) The central group is that of a Dutch sailor (i), wearing striped trousers, who holds a paper inscribed *Nieuwe Klaghten* [Complaints] He stands between (2) a man wearing a gown and bands, who admonishes him with upraised forefinger, and (3) Mercury with his caduceus, symbolizing Commerce, who is also addressing him

Beside (2), 'Staatkunde' (Policy or Politics), is an iron-bound padlocked chest inscribed *in hande*, on which are money-bags, inscribed *600, 275*. Beside it lie a scroll inscribed *credit* and a yoke. In the foreground is a paper inscribed *Plan van verbetering [Plan of Reformation]*

The Dutchman says "The English must get to know us better, we ourselves know best what we should do Trade and politics are always our business I do not doubt but that the daily oppressions will turn out to the disadvantage of their perpetrators.' Policy advises him, 'Complain unceasingly, forget not to recite the violations of our coasts and ships in the strongest terms, hold fast to your friend Mercury, through him will you be welcome everywhere, and so long as he stays with you you will be necessary to, and respected by, all your neighbours, for since everyone would gladly be under his protection, so will each one always keep an eye on him. It would be a disgrace for a lion not to roar once if his tail is unjustly pulled, it is imprudent to provoke him, because he grants everything in reason, and it is known that he is generous by nature.' (For the Dutch lion see Nos 5712-14, &c)

Mercury says, 'So long as you remain a true Dutchman, I will not leave you I am in my right place with you, for my disposition is rather to take care of myself than another. Your continual industry, your enterprise and reasoned though slow ingenuity, can make me flourish although the present times are very dangerous for me, but where can I now enjoy permanent rest, without being one day obliged to rise out of my little cell from my book of reckoning, in order to extend my thoughts and vision over more spacious fields '

On the l is a group of five Englishmen· (4), 'a very eminent Englishman', wearing a long cloak, evidently George III, stands with outstretched arm facing (5) 'Lord N****' [North]. He says, 'Ah my dear Lord, what is wrong now, let your eyes feast once on this still unfinished picture, troubles within and without consume us.' He is pointing to a picture inscribed *Het verwar de Eiland* (the distracted Island), which a kneeling man holds up. It depicts the Gordon riots, incendiaries are burning a building. North, with a downcast expression, answers 'Let us treat this hot fever with which the entrails of the state tremble, even if it should become worse, on the old lines, like the Scottish affair, firmly but according to their wish It is well, since we can now grant it as masters, but above all things do not leave out the words "since we now find it of service to us". A reward has been offered for the discovery of the Delinquent of Delinquents, but as regards foreign troubles, shall we begin with the Dutch? Their complaints, I fear, are not without reason, it would be fortunate if there were one among us who could discover the suitable remedy, we expect much from Lord Shelburne—but unfortunately a duke is indisposed, and thus an important matter intended to be settled as soon as possible, was held back. Our navy also ought one day to be overhauled Rodney writes a great deal, but what avails a victory which decides nothing; daily we risk a frigate with officers whose conduct demands an enquiry—soon it will be as hard to get captains as sailors, yet this task Sandwich and the others can bungle. I hope Heaven may bless us all.'

Lord Shelburne (6), his back towards North and the king, puts a finger to his forehead as if in deep thought. He says, 'What a heavy burden it is to carry a weight which the whole nation might lighten, each new event encroaches on my schemes The Dutch make ever stronger complaints, and now begin to threaten a little. The French have now a strong influence

444

in that country, they do not obstruct their trade, or capture their ships, yet it is we who pass for friends and what is more, for allies.' With this group, but without a number, is a man seated on the ground in back view, writing

On the r Lord George Gordon (7) stands alone on a hillock, supporting his head on his hand. He says, 'Well begun, but not yet completed. Should the resentment of the passionate public not subside, what will happen to Gordon? It does not become a nobleman not to adhere to his purpose. People might say, "What is that hot-headed fanatic beginning to do? If he meant well, why is his country in such straits, filled with domestic disturbances and disasters? This is the conduct of a fool, and if he is not that, he must surely be a rogue, since he lays in wait in order to overthrow by violence and mishandling, when he was engaged on other business, suited to a proud nobleman, which never gave occasion for unrest and entanglement" But those who say this, may be pleased to know that our religion lies close to my heart, although many moral precepts, such as, love your enemies, . . meekness of spirit, &c , I find rather difficult to practise —To oppose the great influence of the Catholic doctrine, I would even support with my presence a question, a petition, but who knew that passion would go so far? . even to violence and arson—truly, I have nothing to do with it. Do not believe that I who humbly embrace the pure doctrine in my heart, can so far degrade my reason in order to trumpet forth my name everywhere, even if it should cost me . my life . No, all my desire is for the salvation, alleviation and comfort of my fellow citizens, could my bonds only heal the wounds which the imprudence of zealots have inflicted on my worthy fellow citizens. Ah if only we were all like lambs and not like wolves in the sheepfold!'

In the clouds a helmeted figure (? Victory) holds out a picture of a small single-masted vessel with a crew of four men, on whose mainsail is an eye, it flies a pennant with three stripes On the l. is the Dutch lion holding up a spear supporting the hat of freedom and a striped pennant. On the r. is a winged female figure (? Fame) with a globe on her head, holding out a laurel wreath towards the picture. She holds a cornucopia from which fall flowers and a hat.

At sea, between the Dutch and English groups, is a naval engagement between ships flying the British and (?) French flags Behind Gordon (r) are two parties of men firing at each other, a dead body lies between them. Black clouds extend over the heads of the English group (l) and over Gordon (r.), above whom is a large flash of lightning

The violation of Dutch coasts refers probably to the case of a French privateer which was beached off the port of Helvoetsluis in 1779, boarded and captured by English ships. It was the occasion of a protest to London from the States General as 'an insult to the Republic's sovereignty'. Van Loon, *Fall of the Dutch Republic*, pp 248-9. See also three Memorials from the Dutch Merchants to the States General, 12 Sept 1778, against search and seizure of Dutch ships bound for French ports. *Ann Reg*, 1779, pp 412 ff For the incessant complaints of Dutch merchants see Edler, *The Dutch Republic and the American Revolution*, 1911, pp. 101, 105, &c

North and George III discuss the situation after the Gordon Riots They propose to repeal the Catholic Relief Act as it had been withdrawn in Scotland, see No. 5534. In July 1780 there were renewed proposals for a coalition ministry The obstructive Duke is probably Richmond, who was unacceptable to the king *Corr. of George III*, ed Fortescue, v 99 ff. *Hist MSS. Comm., Abergavenny MSS.* 1887, pp. 31-2. No overtures were made at this time to Shelburne, who is not mentioned in the correspondence, and who expressed indignation at the negotiation with Rockingham and retired into the country. Fitzmaurice, *Life of Shelburne*, 1912, ii. 62-3. Shelburne had, however, made an important speech on 1 June 1780 denouncing the English policy with regard to Dutch shipping as 'a most bullying and oppressive conduct', and interpreting the Anglo-Dutch treaties of 1674 and 1716 in a manner favourable to Holland. *Parl. Hist.* xxi. 629 ff The 'Delinquent of Delinquents' appears to refer to the suspicion that the riots had been engineered by one of England's foreign enemies For Rodney's victory, 16 Jan. 1680, see No. 5646, &c.

One of several prints showing the great impression made in Holland by the Gordon Riots, see Nos 5725, 5728(13), 5734

A reduced copy is No. 11 in No 5728.

See No. 5723, an English copy.

Van Stolk, No. 4324. Muller, No. 4372.

$8\frac{1}{16} \times 12\frac{1}{16}$ in

5723 THAT & THIS SIDE OF THE WATER OR DUTCH & ENGLISH POLITICKS.

Publish'd as the Act directs Septr 29th 1780 by Wm Richardson

Engraving An ill-drawn copy of No 5722 The figures are numbered as in the original, but the explanation is missing. The thin Dutch sailor (1) is altered into a stout Dutchman wearing baggy breeches His paper is inscribed, *Fresh Complaint Whereas*. The other inscriptions are translated. The picture of London in flames is inscribed *Confus'd Island*. George III and Lord North (4) and (5) have been altered to make them less grotesquely unlike their subjects At Gordon's feet lies a document inscribed *Protestant Petition*

$8\frac{3}{16} \times 12\frac{7}{8}$ in.

5724 DE WANHOOPIGE BRITTEN, EN DE VERNOEGDE AMERI-CANEN, OP DE TYDING VAN DIFFENSIVE ALLIANTIE, ON-BEPAALT CONVOY, EN GEWAPENDE NEUTRALITEIT[*]

[THE DESPAIRING BRITON, AND THE CONTENTED AMERICAN, AT THE NEWS OF DEFENSIVE ALLIANCE, UNLIMITED CONVOY, AND ARMED NEUTRALITY]

Engraving. Plate between two pages of printed explanation, to which numbers on the print refer. On the r 'George Garther' (1), George III, sits on a pile of papers leaning his head on his hand, his elbow resting on a block on which is a document with pendent seals. At his feet are playing-cards, broken china, and papers Behind him, North (2), his hands clasped in dismay, stands in front of a circular tent. 'George Garther' looks with a melancholy expression at empty money-bags and at the sealed papers of the recently concluded negotiations. He exclaims, 'Ah had we only dealt more tolerantly with our brothers the Americans, we should not have squandered such countless treasure in a useless war, and the English nation would not have such countless debts, but alas! Now we are in desperate straits and I am at my wit's end.'

(2) 'North, A well-known English Lord in a despairing posture . . exclaims, "This neutrality, this defensive alliance, of Russia, Sweden, Denmark, Portugal,[1] the United Provinces, and all the Hanse Towns! . Oh Garther, Garther! [Garter] only now do I begin to become rightly anxious I now see clearly that one cannot let the ship drift, as was foretold by No 2 in the plate of *The lion attacked by cunning and force*".' (See No 5712)

Four Dutchmen in the middle distance are Nos. 3–6. (3) 'A master of a Dutch merchant ship sitting on a bale of sail-cloth and recounting with a joyful face to the Merchant (5), and the Manufacturer (4), various smuggling expeditions, which were carried out by himself and others in former times, and are still performed in these troubled times, he also tells of rough and unfair treatment inflicted on him by the English privateers, . . giving the Manufacturer (4) a printed book called *The Mirror of Youth or British Tyranny* . . saying, "read, read, my friend, what fine allies and friends of our country are the English, see here in this book what fine encounters the Dutch have had with their friends, and alas! allies".

(4) 'A Dutch manufacturer showing a Dutch cloth to Nos. 3 and 5, pointing out the good quality of the Dutch in contrast to the English, and lamenting over the decline of manufactures in our fatherland, and the trifling trade in Dutch manufactures; at the same time, telling not much good of the English, with regard to the displacing of our manufactures and the adroit collecting of our ready cash by alluring trade propositions and prompt payment of high interest

(5) 'A Dutch merchant in a dejected posture informing (3) and (4) that in these troubled times he has not yet made so good a bargain as many of his *confrères*, and that it is good to fish in troubled waters, this he further learnt from an account of the Dutch merchant shipping which recently arrived in the port of Brest, and the Dutch convoy of Byland, thus escaping the attention of the English commodore Fielding at the right time, when the others were captured, at which he and other ship-owners, insurers, agents, skippers, &c. have recently made great complaints by memorials, because others who sail free and unhindered, rejoice greatly and make great profits.

(6) 'A Dutch distiller of gin and brandy pushes (3) on the arm with a full bottle of Hollands gin, asking him if he will offer George Garther and Lord North a Dutch drink since they both seem so anxious and downcast never ceasing to cry out "Oh this Neutrality, oh these 6000 Northmen on the sea, and then alas, twenty Russian war-ships and perhaps another twenty standing by "'

In front of the Dutchmen, two Spaniards sit on the ground in conversation, they are '(7), a Spanish Don and (8), a Spanish Duke . seeming to be in earnest conversation over the fate of Spain, as well at the present as in former times, they complain of the conduct of the Spaniards at all times, and at the seizures suffered by them during all the last wars as well as in the recent war . (7) now complains no more about the past, but rather at recent events, of the encounter between Rodney and Don Langara, and the sea-battle near Gibraltar (that great apple of discord) between Spain and England. .'

In the foreground (l.) (9) a French project-maker ('Project maaker') holds up a canvas on which are various animals to (10), a seated man wearing a

---

[1] Portugal did not join the league till 1782, the allusion to Rodney's encounter with Langara as recent suggests an earlier date for the print

gown who is 'a pious and demure Dutch philosopher'. He is showing 'some of the fables of the French De la Fontaine, as that of the Ape and the Cat, the Fox and the Ape, the Lion and the Bear, &c whereat the Philosopher appears to marvel, . pressing his heart to demonstrate his anxiety at these fables with double meanings'.

In the background is the sea with ships, on the coast (l) a cannon is being fired from a castle Near the shore stands a man on a minute scale dressed as an American Indian holding a spear. He is (11) 'Massina Ramby [*sic*] an American, at a safe distance watching the turbulent English, French, Spaniards, &c and himself speaking about the prudence, and the dispassionate and wise conduct of H H.M [their high Mightinesses the States General] and praising also the punctilious and praiseworthy neutrality so far maintained by the Fathers of the Fatherland   . '

Behind him two tiny figures manipulate a barrel on the sea-shore They are (12) and (13), 'Balsepf and Jersey [*sic*], both well pleased and zealously continuing carefully to collect and pack the produce of their country to deliver it to the ships; at present they are not anxious about their Mother Country which has gone astray, but full of peace over their forthcoming independence and free trade, which they hope for under the protection of France —I hope that they will not see themselves cheated of it, it would make my heart very sad for those good men '

It was a burning question whether naval stores were contraband, as England contended, involving the principle of Limited Convoy, or whether they could be freely carried in neutral ships and covered by convoy, as France contended, the principle of Unlimited Convoy. F. P. Renaut, *Les Provinces-Unies et la Guerre d'Amérique*, 1924, pp. 217 ff Edler, *The Dutch Republic and the American Revolution*, Baltimore, 1911, chap v. See No. 5712

One of a number of prints on Van Bylandt's convoy, see No 5628, &c.; on the situation caused by Dutch investments in English securities, see Nos. 5717–20; on the Armed Neutrality, see Nos 5713–16, &c , and on relations in general between Holland and England, see Nos. 5712–22.

A reduced copy is No 12 in No 5728

Van Stolk, No. 4325. Muller, No 4373.

$6\frac{1}{16} \times 4\frac{1}{8}$ in.

5725 DAN ONDER DAN BOOVEN *
[UNDER AND OVER]

Engraving The figures have numbers referring to an explanation printed in two columns below the print The naked figure of Time stands (1) beside a large wheel whose hub is supported by a stand, he turns a handle attached to the hub with his l hand In his r hand is his scythe, on his head is his hour-glass He is 'keeping the wavering wheel of war in a continued motion' On the top of the outer rim of the wheel are four figures England (r), holding a firebrand or torch, fights with France and America: a lean Frenchman seizes him by the cravat; America, wearing a feathered Indian head-dress, strikes him in the eye with her fist These three are kneeling. Lower down the wheel (l) Spain lies behind France watching the combat 'Now the Englishman is shifting a little, the reason being that the Frenchman, American, and Spaniard have had abundant dealings with him and to profit by some good blows from the Englishman [who says] "would you fight against an Englishman? Then you deceive yourself, we might yet rule over the whole world, therefore it is the same thing if we have friends or foes" '

Beside the wheel (1) stand two Dutchmen One (2), a 'young, lusty Dutchman' dressed as a sailor in a short petticoat, holds out his arms imploringly. The other (3), 'a prudent statesman', wearing a long cloak, puts a restraining hand on his shoulder. (2) is asking for restitution for the damages he has suffered. He says, 'If you my lord consider me as not damaged in my honour and property, I shall one day see if I am always to be opposed by you. Be sure that my patience is coming to an end, and however haughty you may be, you should know that no-one can hold out against superior numbers, and you will certainly repent of it in the end. I put it to you once more ..' The 'prudent statesman' answers, 'Calmly, calmly, Brother, and cease to ask vainly for restitution or to deliver memorials; will you secure restitution, then arm yourself and make good preparations I have left no stone unturned to get their High Mightinesses [the States General] to face the danger but in vain They may be English, but let us show that we are Dutchmen '

A monk (4) stands behind Time, his arms outstretched towards a burning city (r.) in the background. Another spectator (5) also points to the conflagration. They are watching London, during the Gordon Riots; the monk says, 'See those mad heretics making havoc, it is intolerable! Oh Roman Powers! Is that doing your duty? Punish such sacrilegious persons, or what will be the end?' (5) is a 'Protestant calming the monk', he says, 'Do not make so much noise my friend. I feel ashamed myself over the shamefulness of these doings But these fellows did not respect their own king, but cut off his head, shall they then respect their fellow-citizens and not do violence to them. They are only fanatical and rebellious persons and for such scum one cannot venture, moreover we shall soon see what a glorious reward they will receive '

A plea for war with England which differs from others of the collection in making no reference to the Armed Neutrality The allusion to the Gordon Riots illustrates the preoccupation of the Dutch with the affair, see Nos. 5722, 5728 (13), 5734 A reduced copy is No 14 in No 5728.

Van Stolk, No. 4328. Muller, No 4376.

5726 [TOESTAND DER ENGELSCHE NATIE]*   [? 1780]
[STATE OF THE ENGLISH NATION]

Engraving A copy on a larger scale of No. 5472. The ship is inscribed *Eagle* and the town *Philadelphia* as in No. 5472. With the plate is a printed explanation (*verklaring*) which is a translation of the original explanation in the *Westminster Magazine*, the allusion to the appointment of commissioners to negotiate with the Americans being omitted. The artist was ignorant of the evacuation of Philadelphia (June 1778) and the return of the Howes to England. The multiplication of copies of this print, see Nos. 5726 A, B, and C, and No. 5727, shows its propaganda-value as damaging to British prestige, and illustrates both the hopes which were entertained in Holland and France of securing the commerce with the colonies which England had monopolized, and also the belief in the efficacy of commerce-destroying in war, especially against a commercial country like Great Britain. See Mahan, *Influence of Sea Power upon History*, 1890, p. 539. It was also copied for American circulation in 1778 and (apparently) again in 1780, by Paul Revere, see No 5472. See also No. 5859, a sequel to this print.

A reduced copy is No 15 in No 5728 The title is taken from the explanatory pamphlet which accompanies No. 5728. In the *Verklaring* it is *den Staat der Engelsche Natie in 1778.*

Van Stolk, No 4287 (1) Muller, No 4337 (1).

$6\frac{3}{4} \times 10\frac{1}{2}$ in

5726 A [No title.] [? 1780]

Engraving A copy (?) of No. 5726 with the same inscriptions but without numbers on the plate.

$6\frac{3}{4} \times 10$ in

5726 B [No title] [? 1780]

Engraving (partly coloured) A copy (?) of No 5726 with the same (English) inscriptions. Beneath the plate is a printed explanation which is a French translation of (probably) the Dutch version of the English original It differs in Nos 4 and 5. *Derriere la vache sont un* François *& un* Espagnol; *le premier, d'un air très-content, emporte une jatte pleine de lait; & le second, tenant toute prête une moindre jatte, semble en attendre sa part.*

$6\frac{5}{8} \times 10\frac{3}{8}$ in

5726 C [No title]* [? 1780]

Engraving. A copy (?) of No. 5726 or of No 5726 B, the ship inscribed *Aigle*, the town *Philadelphia*, and with numbers on the print which refer to the French explanation printed beneath it which is the same as in No 5726 B With it is a copy of the printed explanation to No 5726

$6\frac{5}{8} \times 10\frac{1}{4}$ in.

5727 MAL LUI VEUT MAL LUI TOURNE[1] DIT LE BON HOMME RICHARD. [? 1780]

Engraving. A copy of No 5472 or No. 5726, or No. 5726 A, B, or C It differs from all in having no name on the ship's stern, the town is *Philadelphie* Below the title is engraved *Sujet Mémorable des Révolutions de l'Univers.* Numbers are engraved on the plate which refer to the engraved explanation beneath the plate, which appears to be a free translation either of the original English or the Dutch version (1) *Le Commerce de la Grande Bretagne sous la forme d'une Vache.* (2) *Le Congrès representés* [sic] *par l'Amériquain occupé a lui enlever ses armes deffensive en lui sciant les Cornes* (3) *Le Hollandois d'un air content tire la Vache.* (4) *Un François s'avance avec politesse pour avoir du lait.* (5) *Un Espagnol d'un air grave se presente aussi pour le même objet* (6) *Un seul Vaisseaux* [sic] *de la formidable Flotte Anglaise paroit seul et est embourbé pres Philadelphie* (7) *Les Généraux dans l'inaction dans cette Ville.* (8) *Le Lion Britannique profondement endormie pendant qu'un petit dogue simbole de la vigilance lui marche sur le corps.* (9) *L'Anglais en deuil, consternés et abatue n'a pas la force de réveillé* [sic] *de Lion pour deffendre ses prerogatives*

'Le bon homme Richard' is a reference to Benjamin Franklin, then American envoy in France, it was the name given to the French ship (previously *Duc de Duras*) in which Paul Jones attacked the *Scrapis*, see

---

[1] A translation of one of Poor Richard's maxims

Nos. 5559–64 For the immense vogue in France of Franklin's *Poor Richard's Almanack* see B. Fay, *The Revolutionary Spirit in France and America*, 1928, p 154 f

Collection de Vinck, No. 1212.

$6\frac{1}{2} \times 10\frac{1}{8}$ in.

Another version is No 1211 in the *Collection de Vinck*. The Frenchman, carrying off his bowl of milk, is walking on a peacock. The French text is identical with that of No 5726 B and C, with the addition of the words, after 'le Francois . emporte une jatte, pleine de lait', *et marche sur le paon, Symbole de l'orgeuil* [sic] *Britannique qui malgré la perte de sa plus belle plume fait encore entendre l'aigre son de sa Voix* It is without numbers on the plate

$6\frac{1}{4} \times 10\frac{1}{16}$ in.

5728 ALGEMEENE STAATKUNDIGE KONSTPLAAT VAN 'T JAAR 1780 * TAILLE DOUCE POLITIQUE ET GENÉRALE DE L'ANNÉE 1780.

Engraving Reduced copies of political satires arranged in five rows, divided only by lines, and numbered (1) to (13). In the topmost row are Nos. (1) to (4), copies of Nos 5712–15. In the second row are Nos (5) to (7), copies of Nos 5716–18 In the third row are Nos. (8) to (10), copies of Nos 5719–21. In the fourth row are Nos (11) to (13), copies of Nos. 5722, 5724 (13) is not copied from a published print but was designed on a small scale to fill a gap in the plate. In the lowest row are Nos (14) and (15), copies of Nos. 5725, 5726; they are divided by a rectangular space decorated with a conventional scroll of ribbons and bows, ornamented with the seven arrows representing the United Netherlands, in the centre is a group of a trumpet, horn, and palm-branch with an open book inscribed *Staatkundige Fabel Rol*. [Sheet of political fables.]

The printed explanations which accompany the original plates are reprinted in a pamphlet of 60 pages It begins with *Bericht aan der Leezer* (title-page perhaps missing)

No 13 is also described in this pamphlet:

[ENGELAND VAN BINNEN EN BUITEN BEROERD.]
[ENGLAND MISERABLE WITHIN AND WITHOUT.]   [1780]

Engraving (part of No. 5728). A small coach (l.), in which a man is seated, is drawn by a number of men in place of horses Behind (l) are buildings on fire. In a river or harbour (r) are ships Above them are clouds from which looks out the sun with a face in it, sending out rays. From the cloud issues a scroll and a pair of scales, unevenly balanced, on each of which is a large book. In the foreground (l.) are buildings, probably intended for the Tower of London, a great crowd of people, and, at the water-side, a gallows from which three bodies hang. Isolated figures stand in the foreground. The figures have numbers referring to the explanation.

(1) is Lord George Gordon's coach, his lordship inside, drawn in triumph by the people of London. Beside the coach stands (2) the coachman, saying, ' . you my lord have henceforth no need of horses, still less of a coachman Therefore I take my leave.' (3) 'Lord Gordon' says, 'You must stay you comical fellow, . . . it will not be for ever that I shall be

treated like Wilkes' (2) answers, 'So much the worse for me, good Sir, for if you lose the people's esteem, you run the risk of going to a place where you will not need a coach or even shoes ' (4) A magnificent English lord (Heer) calls out in astonishment, 'What an honour! .. I would rather be you than any king. . .' (5) An elderly, intelligent, and experienced London citizen says to (4), 'You have not had much experience, . . if Gordon only looks at the building before which we are standing, . . . so must he tremble with fear. Experience has taught me that the homage of rebels leads to rigorous imprisonment, yes, even to worse and more shameful things.'

(6) A dissolute English sailor says, 'Ha, it goes well, I see what I have long wished for God bless Lord Gordon that he gives us this chance to satisfy the lust for plunder innate in the British nation on the pretext of challenging Popish liberties.'

(7) A virtuous, reasonable, and freedom-loving Englishman in a dejected posture says, 'Go ahead you scum, through you and your like, the honour of the English Nation is stained All these tumultmakers, now leaping with joy, will surely wish to be called Protestants. But no, they are rather barbarians. . . . But it seems that Englishmen must always be astir. Why do they not look at our neighbour Holland? Balance and scales whereon lie the books of war and peace should teach us what is most beneficial for us. One might well liken the Blessed Netherlands to the great sun . . which through her light lets it be seen that peace is better than war. No wonder that one sees in this picture, a letter flung from the sky, by the clamours and sighs of the Dutch, couched in these terms and written in letters of gold. "Nowhere is there any more freedom except in the Netherlands, God bless our high and mighty and beloved Prince " Yet there is nothing here for the British nation. Heavens, what a blow. The mighty power of gunpowder does the work and our ships are blown to pieces. This thundering voice will, I hope, sober the people. Ah, but no! for look at the conflagration made by the plunderers, on all sides rise up horsemen and soldiers, servants of the crown to oppose the Prince's own subjects, and what will their consequences be? Before long the gallows, which are there in the distance, will be covered with rioters. I am frightened and turn back, methinks the Heavens forbear to lighten on the building since Parliament is assembled Ah I can no longer look. Heavens! to you I entrust our country. Give vision to the Prince, to the Ministry, to see that they give such consideration to affairs as do the States and Stadtholder of the Netherlands '

For other Dutch prints showing the great impression made in Holland by the Gordon Riots, see Nos. 5722, 5725, 5734. The intention here seems to be to identify English sailors with the plundering London mob.

Muller, No. 4375.

3 × 5⅞ in.

The whole design, Van Stolk, No. 4329 Muller, No. 4361

15½ × 15½ in.

5729 [A DUTCH VIEW OF GEORGE III, LORD NORTH AND OLIVER CROMWELL]* [? 1780]

Engraving. Beneath the plate is a printed *verklaring* (explanation), to which refer numbers engraved on the design. (1) George III (r) seated on a throne in profile to the l., two young men wearing trousers and feathered caps have seized each a leg and are pulling off his stockings. *G R.* is engraved on the king's coat, he is calling for help. *O Nord Nord*

(2) A man on horseback, to whom the king is calling, slowly rides towards him, a placard on his breast inscribed *L. Nord King from London.*

(3) A large head on a pedestal (3) inscribed, *Uytvinder van Heersch en baatzugt* (Inventor of ambition and covetousness) (l), is intended to represent Oliver Cromwell. Three men (4) kneel obsequiously before it. Above their heads is (5) Justice, holding scales in her l. hand, and in her r. a sheaf of thunderbolts with which she is about to strike them down

The king, who is being stripped of his clothes by 'good-natured Americans', calls Lord North to his assistance. Cromwell, as representative of English 'insupportable ambition and covetousness' is adored by 'some English lords' who are about to be struck down by Justice. Cromwell, however, wears a flat Tudor cap, and is a portrait of Thomas Cromwell (executed 1540), ignorantly mistaken for Oliver For other prints showing the rancour with which Cromwell was regarded by the Dutch see Nos. 5718, 5719, 5730, 5731, 5732. Cf also the Dutch prints attacking Cromwell for the Dutch War of 1652–3 and the peace of 1654· Nos 741, 742, 754, 757, 784, 818, 844, 850, 857, 863, 866, 874.

$7\frac{1}{4} \times 11\frac{3}{8}$ in

5730 GEWAPENDE NEUTRALITEYT [1780]
[ARMED NEUTRALITY]

Engraving. A number of figures in pseudo-classical costume are grouped on the sea-shore. They have numbers referring to a printed explanation below the plate. On the extreme l sits Justice, (3), enthroned beneath a canopy holding her sword and scales Before her are two figures, both symbolizing the Netherlands (1) 'Vryheid' (Liberty), and (2), 'Voorzichtigheid' (Prudence) Liberty kneels holding up the hat of liberty on a staff, Prudence stands holding a caduceus and a book, at her feet are an hourglass and an owl. In the centre the Netherlands are again represented by (5) 'Lankmoedigheit' (Endurance), a woman on hands and knees beneath a yoke which (4) 'Heerschzucht' (Ambition), a feeble-looking woman personifying England, presses on her shoulders. A man in Roman armour (9), 'Dapperheid' (Valour), personifying Denmark, stoops forward to raise Endurance from the ground, (10) 'Wysheid' (Wisdom), and (11) 'Sterkte' (Strength), representing Sweden and Russia, stand by approvingly, Wisdom (or Minerva), a woman with a helmet and spear, holds out a directing hand, Strength holds a large club and a sheaf of arrows. Behind Strength stand (13) 'Hoop' (Hope), with an anchor, and (14) 'Standvastigheit' (Constancy), with a pillar. Behind Ambition (r) stand three other figures also personifying England: (8), 'Armoede' (Poverty), (6), 'Onbedachtzaamheid' (Thoughtlessness), and (7), 'Roofzucht' (Rapine) Poverty is a beggar woman with outstretched hand, a sack over her shoulder, a bird sits on her head. Thoughtlessness is a woman poised insecurely on one foot on a mound of sand. Rapine is a figure in Roman armour, a wolf by his (or her) side, a bird of prey perched on his helmet On the ground at their feet is a torn document inscribed *Traktaat Cromwell.* On the extreme r. stands (12), 'Dankbaarheid' (Gratitude), a woman wearing an imperial crown with the arms of Amsterdam on her breast; beside her stands a stork.

In the centre of the upper part of the design which it dominates, an arm holding a sword emerges from clouds. From it are suspended by a chain the arms of Russia in an oval, surrounded by three shields, bearing the arms of Denmark, Sweden, and the United Provinces. Across them all is the motto *Gewapende neutraliteyt*, these words forming the title of the print. From other clouds (l) a large eye directs rays upon Justice and the figures numbered 1, 2, 3, 14, 13, 11, 9, and 10

From the explanation printed below the design it appears that Liberty and Prudence (the Netherlands) complain to Justice of the rupture of their alliance, the infringement of maritime rights, and the capture of their vessels. 'Are we then to sigh for ever! To be for ever the toy of ambition! . .' Ambition says to Endurance (the oppressed Netherlands), 'This yoke is to gall her shoulders, whilst her commerce still ploughs the ocean, whilst her navy is still far distant or dispersed and her frontiers are devoid of troops and succour.' Thoughtlessness, Rapine, and Poverty, representing England, say, 'Whatsoever it may cost we must remain masters and whosoever does not act according to our wishes, we will rob him of his own, even though destitution should ensue.' Valour, Wisdom, and Strength, representing Denmark, Sweden, and Russia, say to Endurance 'Could we stint our courage, ability, and force whilst we see you attacked by the claws of ambition and love of plunder? No! We will save you and then will Thoughtlessness led by love of rapine probably bring about her own ruin. Gratitude (Amsterdam) says, 'To eternity we will not forget to offer unto you, O Valour, Wisdom, & Strength! our gratitude, if by your united forces we shall triumph over despotic and rapacious ambition' Hope and Constancy say 'We will hope and be content, convinced that Justice cannot behold our oppression, without also rescuing the oppressed.'

The explanation ends with an appeal to the Deity represented by the all-seeing eye: 'O thou Supreme Being so just, assist with thine awful power those firmly-knit forces of war, may our fortune thus soon attain its height, then shall we with joy waft up to thee frankincense from our altar of thanksgiving'

One of a number of prints which were part of the propaganda of the anti-British interests in the Dutch Republic (notably Amsterdam) which were eager for war. It expresses the exaggerated expectations formed of the Armed Neutrality; see Nos. 5713–16, &c.

For the rancour with which Cromwell was regarded see also Nos. 5718, 5719, 5729, 5731, 5732, the 'treaty of Cromwell' being that of 1654, which ended the first Anglo-Dutch war, see *Cambridge Hist. of the Br. Empire*, I. 224.

Van Stolk, No. 4331. Muller, No. 4378.

$6\frac{1}{2} \times 11\frac{3}{4}$ in.

5731 DEN ENGELSMAN OP ZYN UITERSTE * [c. 1780]
L'ANGLOIS A TOUTE EXTREMITEZ

A Lyon, chez Nicolas Ciseau, à l'Enseigne des Armes de Bourges.

Engraving. On the print are numbers referring to a printed explanation below the plate in two columns, Dutch (l), French (r.) The Englishman (1) lies on a low bed draped with curtains, he is vomiting into a chamberpot held by (7) a Dutch peasant Standing behind his patient is an apothecary (2), holding a syringe which he is about to use Behind the apothecary is an American (3), who wears trousers and a feathered cap. A crowd of

454

doctors and apothecaries (4), some holding syringes, appear through a wide doorway on the extreme l. Their desire to succour the patient is frustrated by (5) a Frenchman, sword in hand, and (6) a Spaniard Over the doorway is an oval medallion containing a head in profile to the r, perhaps intended for Cromwell. On the extreme r. through an open window two ships (8) are visible.

The French explanation:

1. *L'Anglois couché sur un Lit, demande un remede à ses maux*
2. *Un Apoticaire, la Seringue à la main, veut le secourir.*
3. *Un Américain l'en empeche, en le retirant.*
4. *Une Troupe de Medecins & d'Apoticaires viennent en foule, avec des Seringues dans les mains.*
5 *Un François L'épée à la main.*
6. *Et un Espagnol, leur en deffendent l'entrée*
7. *Un païsan Hollandois, tend le Pot de Chambre à ce Gourmand & regarde s'il ne vomira pas quelque Article du Traitez de Cromwel* [Traktaat van Cromwel].
8. *Etonnement de deux Batiments Anglois, qui viennent s'échouer sur les Côtes de la Hollande, & y apporter des richesses pour faire la Guerre à l'Angleterre.*

England declared war on Holland on 20 Dec. 1780. For other allusions (direct and indirect) to the Traktaat van Cromwell see Nos 5718, 5719, 5729, 5730, 5732

For other Dutch prints on the relations between England and Holland before the outbreak of war, see Nos 5712–30, 5732.

Van Stolk, No 4333 Muller, No. 4379

$6\frac{7}{16} \times 9\frac{15}{16}$ in.

5732 DE VERLOSTE HOLLANDER, OF DE GEDWONGEN DOG. [THE LIBERATED DUTCHMAN OR THE CONQUERED DOG] [1780 or 1781 ?]

Engraving. A flat landscape with the sea as background, into which a slightly raised causeway (l) extends. In the foreground (l) is a bridge (resembling rather an embankment) with a railing, over which leans a Dutch peasant pointing with satisfaction to what is going on beneath the bridge: on a wall supporting the bridge is a placard inscribed *traktaat van Cromwel*, this a woman is tearing down, while another woman looks from a doorway in the wall holding up her hands in delight. On each side of the door is placarded a portrait head in profile to the r On the bridge are three prostrate bodies, or corpses, lying face upwards, on one of them (r.) a second Dutch peasant is walking in profile to the r, his arms outstretched towards America, in the person of an Indian brave with a girdle of feathers, who advances to meet him also with outstretched arms.

Between the bridge and the sea, on an ornamental seat or throne with a high back, lies a lion, small and of strangely dog-like appearance Between his paws is a staff supporting the hat of liberty. A crowned woman (l.) advances towards the lion holding out a dish, in her l hand is a sceptre. Behind the lion's throne stands Justice, holding her sword and scales. On the r. a Frenchman wearing a hat and sword holds on a leash a dog, which he forces with a scourge to lap up the excrement which comes from the lion. Behind the Frenchman stands a Spaniard, in slashed doublet, cloak, ruff, and feathered hat, he puffs with a pair of bellows into the French-man's ear

On the causeway in the background an Englishman (l.) kneels in supplica-tion before a Dutchman, who offers him a piece of bread On the horizon (r.) is a town, some of its buildings are falling over and sinking below the sea From the clouds a glory of rays descends upon the group of the lion, Justice, and the crowned lady.

Beneath the plate is a printed explanation here translated 'A Dutch peasant standing on a bridge points with a satisfied smile at what is happen-ing beneath it. On the bridge some dead Englishmen are lying, over whom another Dutch peasant goes to meet an American to embrace him, at which the American (rejoiced at the overthrow of the English) appears very well pleased.

'The lion, holding between its paws a staff bearing the Hat of Freedom, is sustained, that is, offered help, by a Crowned Woman, while a dog laps up the excrements of the Lion, being constrained thereto by a Frenchman, through love of the Lion, who holds the Dog on a leash, thereby signifying that he has been victorious over him. A Spaniard blows into the French-man's ear instructions for his further behaviour as regards the Dog.

'In the distance is seen, among other things, a decrepit Briton, who kneels before a Dutchman and is offered by him a piece of bread, whereat the Briton snatches greedily There is also seen the English kingdom, already more than half submerged.'

As in other Dutch prints, the 'crowned lady' represents Catharine of Russia, giving aid to Holland by the Armed Neutrality. Holland is the lion, England is the dog. The 'treaty of Cromwell' is that of 5 Apr. 1654 ending the first Anglo-Dutch War. By it the Dutch had been forced (*inter alia*) to submit to the Navigation Act of 1651, embodying a policy which was renewed and extended after the Restoration, see Nos 5718, 5719, 5729, 5730, 5731. For other Dutch prints on the relations between England and Holland before the outbreak of war see Nos 5712–31, those on the Armed Neutrality being Nos. 5713–16, 5718–19, 5724, 5730, 5733.

This print may have been issued after the declaration of war by England on 20 Dec 1780.

Van Stolk, No. 4334. Muller, No. 4380.

$6\frac{3}{4} \times 10\frac{1}{8}$ in.

5733 [ECHTE UITLEGGING VAN EENE ENGELSCHE KUNST-
PRENT]   [1780 or 1781]
[TRUE INTERPRETATION OF AN ENGLISH PRINT]

Engraving. The title is taken from a printed explanation which accom-panies the print. The interior of a room in which a man sits on a chair (l.), legs crossed, in profile to the r , listening attentively to a man who stands opposite him at the other side of the room, gesticulating theatrically.

The only furniture, except the chair, is a draped table, somewhat resembling an altar, which stands against the centre of the back wall supporting a framed picture which is the 'English print' of the title It represents a sea-battle, with flags unattached to ships; in the water rolled documents are just visible. High up on each side wall is another picture of a sea-fight, that behind the seated man being inscribed *1665*.

The two men are an English 'lord' and his colleague, discussing the policy of war with Holland, as appears from the explanation here translated:

'This picture shows an interior A large drawing is seen, upon which, in the background, is portrayed the stopping and plundering of Dutch ships. In the foreground is seen the capture of the ship in which Laurens had been, and his papers being fished up. Under this is *hinc ill[e Lacrimae]* the remaining words being illegible Moreover, it is shown that the whole picture has been heavily varnished over, yet in such a way that the varnish seems to be a film of vapour or smoke But by some cracks at the side it is clear that the panel has been painted over, and that there was originally something else, under the place where the words are. It is also evident, from some tops of masts which can be seen appearing in places through the later painting—faintly, yet clearly enough for the flags of Russia, Sweden, Denmark, and Holland to be distinguished, showing that it was the Armed Neutrality which was first portrayed there, and therefore the cause of their [the English] action is not to be found in the present picture but was rather determined by their acting according to what was represented before, and that which is on it now was a handy way for them to give an appearance of legality to their actions.

'Before the picture sits a well-dressed gentleman. He seems to have wished to wash off the vapour or smoke, and is unhappy because he cannot manage it and is afraid that the secret will be discovered. A lord standing opposite him points at a picture which hangs on a side wall, and shows a sea-battle under which 1665 is written, and seems to say, "How now Sir! What do you fear? Collect yourself, consider what has happened, and believe that the courage of our heroes is not yet extinguished." But the other, instead of being relieved by this, seems to answer him, "Yes indeed, Sir, I remember what happened all too well. But remember what the outcome was, never forget their heroes, think of de Ruyter, Tromp, Brakel, and the others, and consider that they still have heroes who are fully their equals. Just look at this picture," pointing to a small painting hanging opposite him [r.], on which the Dutch expedition to Chatham is portrayed —"if they were to come again   .!"'

The first picture evidently depicts the English victory over the Dutch off Harwich on 3 June 1665, which was succeeded in 1667 by the Dutch entry into the Medway, and the burning of the ships at Chatham, cf No. 5719 The papers which Laurens threw overboard when the ship in which he was sailing was taken by the English were recovered and showed that a treaty with Congress had long been under negotiation by Pensionary Van Berckel, on behalf of Amsterdam, see No. 5845, and was on the point of being concluded. The discovery was the occasion of the Declaration of War on 20 Dec. 1780, see No. 5825, the cause being the way in which the Dutch flag had long been used to cover French and American goods, including naval stores and munitions.

For the Armed Neutrality see Nos. 5713-16, &c. For the rancour left by the Anglo-Dutch wars of the seventeenth century cf. Nos. 5719, 5729, &c.

$8\frac{1}{8} \times 12\frac{3}{8}$ in.

5734 WAARE AFBEELDING VAN LORD GEORGE GORDON, GEVOLGT NA HET ECHTE POURTRET.
[A TRUE LIKENESS OF LORD GEORGE GORDON, TAKEN FROM HIS REAL PORTRAIT.]   [n.d. 1780 or 1781]

Engraving A (supposed) room in the Tower of London. A man (very unlike Gordon) clasps his hands and exclaims in despair He wears a wig, laced coat, &c., has black bushy eyebrows. The back wall of the room consists of stone arches, the two behind the prisoner (r) being filled with a rectangular pattern of stout iron bars, through which appear buildings, a gallows, and the execution of rioters On the extreme r is the cart in which a man stands, another is suspended from the gallows Two men stand below, one a clergyman; behind are the faces of a crowd of spectators, the masts of ships appearing above their heads. The arch on the l. of these gratings is filled with a heavy door in which is a small aperture, through which can be seen the head of the 'Warden' who is watching his prisoner, one finger raised admonishingly.

The room, though of dungeon-like appearance, is furnished with chairs and tables of elaborate design. On the r is a round table with a festooned cloth, showing carved legs with claw-feet. On a round table on the l are elaborately bound and clasped books and writing materials. Beneath the title is an explanation, of which the following translation is pasted on the print· 'Representing his Lordship in a wild despairing situation; occasioned by the News told him by the Warden of the Tower, viz. several of the Rioters and particularly Jack Ketch [cf. No. 5679] were hanged (which is seen; through the Grate), which News his Lordship heard with great astonishment, but without emotion; standing at a Table covered with victuals and drink but as soon as left alone, he flew like a wild Creature, stamping with his Foot on the floor of the Prison (which is here represented to the Life); the noise which his lordship made, made the Warden return to look through the Wicket of the door to hear what was the matter, by which means he not only was an eye Witness, but who heard his Lordship exclaim with folded hands, O Heaven!—O God!—was I then to be the occasion to bring so many unfortunate People to this shameful Death! Commons of Britain, wherefore was I not understood. Never did I think of making a Riot (then he kept silence for some time—). After that with a frightfull loud Passion, he cried O God!—what shall be my Fate?'

One of several prints showing the impression made in Holland by the Gordon Riots, see Nos 5722, 5725, 5728. Reproduced in De Castro, *Gordon Riots*, p. 208.

Van Stolk, No. 4337. Muller, No. 4389

$7\frac{3}{4} \times 11\frac{1}{8}$ in.

PERSONAL SATIRES

5735-5747

Series of Tete-à-tete portraits.

5735 N° XXXIV. THE ABANDONED WIFE.
N° XXXV. THE SEDUCING CAPTAIN

Publish'd by A. Hamilton Jun' near S' Johns Gate, Jan' 1. 1780.

Engraving. *Town and Country Magazine*, xi 625 (Supplement) Two bust portraits in oval frames illustrate 'Histories of the Tête-à-Tête annexed; .' An account of a nephew of Lord Falmouth, evidently George Boscawen, and of the wife of a baronet with a large property in the W. Indies She is evidently Annabella, second d. of the Rev. C. W. Bunbury, who married (*c.* 1765) Sir Patrick Blake of Langham, Suffolk, and St Kitts. She was divorced by Act of Parliament in Apr 1778 and subsequently married George Boscawen (b 4 Sept. 1745), M.P. for St. Mawes 1768–74 and for Truro 1774–80. G E C , *Complete Baronetage.*

Ovals, $2\frac{11}{16} \times 2\frac{5}{16}$ in. B M.L , P.P. 5442 b.

5736 N° XXXVII. MISS LUCY LEERWELL.
N° XXXVIII. THE CONSCIENTIOUS PARSON.

Published by A. Hamilton Jun' near S' John's Gate Jan' 20. 1780.

Engraving. *Town and Country Magazine*, xi. 681 (Supplement) Two bust portraits in oval frames illustrate 'Histories of the Tête-à-Tête annexed; ..'. An account of the holder of a Yorkshire living who took part in the movement for relief of the clergy from subscription to the thirty-nine articles, subsequently resigned his living and officiated in a chapel opened in 1774. He is apparently Theophilus Lindsey, the Unitarian (1723–1808), rector of Catterick 1763–73, see *D.N.B.* Lucy is a wronged and unfortunate young woman who has attended his chapel, their relations being probably platonic.

Ovals, $2\frac{3}{4} \times 2\frac{5}{16}$ in. B M.L , P.P. 5442 b.

5737 N° II. THE LOVELY MISS L—WS—N.
N° III. THE HARDY COMMANDER.[1]

Published by A. Hamilton Jun' near S' John's Gate, Feb' 1. 1780.

Engraving. *Town and Country Magazine*, xii 9. Two bust portraits in oval frames illustrate 'Histories of the Tête-à-Tête annexed, . '. An account of Sir Charles Hardy (1716?–80), defending him from the sarcasms on his conduct in a late naval campaign· 'the caricatures in the shop-windows are the effects of insignificant poverty stimulated by calumny' He had been given command of the channel fleet in 1779 on the resignation

---

[1] H. Bleackley identifies him with Lord Howe, who is, however, also mentioned (though incorrectly) in the *Tête-à-tête.*

of Keppel, and did not attack the combined French and Spanish fleet, his cautious policy being probably correct. J. K. Laughton in *D N B*. He died of apoplexy in May 1780 Miss L (the seduced and deserted teacher in a boarding-school) claims to be the daughter of 'the *celebrated* Doctor L—ws—n' who became notorious because his absurdities were mimicked by Foote on the stage. A doctor John Lawson is mentioned by Munk (ii 264) as 'a native of Middlesex but not a graduate in Arts or Medicine' Admitted L.R.C.P. 1 Apr. 1765 In Foote's *Diversions of the Morning*, 1747, one of the characters was 'a certain physician who was much better known for the oddity and singularity of his appearance than from his eminence in his profession'. Baker, *Biog Dram*, 1812, i 246.

Ovals, $2\frac{3}{4} \times 2\frac{3}{8}$ in. B.M.L., P.P. 5442 b.

5738 Nᵒ IV. Mᴿˢ LOV—B—ND.
Nᵒ V. LORD M—T—T.

Published by A. Hamilton Junʳ near Sᵗ John's Gate March 1; 1780.

Engraving. *Town and Country Magazine*, xii 65. Two bust portraits in oval frames illustrate 'Histories of the Tête-à-tête annexed; . . .'. An account of Lord M , one of the smallest men in England, whose near relation Lord —— shot himself because he could not pay a gaming debt at Arthur's. He is Thomas Bromley, Lord Montfort (1733–99), his father shot himself on account of debts, 1 Jan 1755 H B. Boulton, *White's*, i 105. Mrs L is a widow, the daughter of an Irish father who traded for large amounts in America, became bankrupt owing to the political situation, on which she married her father's attorney L , whose death left her destitute.

Ovals, $2\frac{1}{4} \times 2\frac{5}{16}$ in. B.M.L., P.P. 5442 b.

5739 Nᵒ VII MISS C——E.
Nᵒ VIII. THE ADMIRABLE ADVOCATE.

Published by A. Hamilton Junʳ near Sᵗ John's Gate April 1; 1780.

Engraving. *Town and Country Magazine*, xii. 121. Two bust portraits in oval frames, one (r) that of a barrister in wig and gown. They illustrate 'Histories of the Tête-à-tête annexed; . . .'. An account of a barrister born in Herefordshire and of Miss Ch—d—le, daughter of an eminent cabinet-maker of St. Martin's Lane, evidently Chippendale, alleged to have been his mistress for two years He is conjecturally identified by H. Bleackley as Howarth.

Ovals, $2\frac{3}{4} \times 2\frac{5}{16}$ in. B M.L , P.P. 5442 b.

5740 Nᵒ X. Mᴿˢ B——TT
Nᵒ XI. ADMIRAL P——E.

Published by A. Hamilton Junʳ near Sᵗ John's Gate. May 1. 1780.

Engraving. *Town and Country Magazine*, xii. 177. Two bust portraits in oval frames, that of the man in profile to the l. having a very large nose. They illustrate 'Histories of the Tête-à-Tête annexed, . .' An account of the amours of Sir Thomas Pye (1713?–85), which were in fact notorious, see *D.N.B.* Mrs B. is the daughter and widow of a naval officer and is identified by H. Bleackley as Agnes Maria Bennett. They are said to have lived together for some years and to have several children.

Ovals, $2\frac{13}{16} \times 2\frac{3}{8}$ in. B M L , P P. 5442 b.

5741 Nº XIII. THE DRAMATIC ENCHANTRESS
Nº XIV. THE DOATING LOVER

Publish'd by A Hamilton Jun' near S' John's Gate June 1ˢᵗ 1780.

Engraving. *Town and Country Magazine*, xii. 233. Two bust portraits in oval frames, better characterized than is usual in this series. They illustrate 'Histories of the Tête-à-Tête annexed; . .' An account of Mrs. Robinson (Perdita) and of George Capel, Viscount Malden, 1757–1839, Earl of Essex, 1799. G.E.C., *Complete Peerage*. His lavish proposals, and a pair of diamond ear-rings at the first interview, are said to have overcome the scruples of Mrs Robinson, after she had rejected many other proposals.[1] Malden introduced her to the Prince of Wales, see *Corr of George III*, v. 269. See also Nos. 5767, 5858, &c.

Ovals, $2\frac{13}{16} \times 2\frac{5}{16}$ in. B.M L , P.P. 5442 b.

5742 Nº XVI. THE ADORABLE ALICIA.
Nº XVII THE MANAGER IN DISTRESS!

Published by A. Hamilton Jun', near S' John's Gate July 1ˢᵗ 1780.

Engraving. *Town and Country Magazine*, xii 289. Two bust portraits in oval frames illustrate 'Histories of the Tête-à-Tête annexed, . . .'. An account of George Colman (1732–94); the 'distress' alluded to appears to be his loss of the large fortune said to have been promised to him by General Pulteney if he would quit the stage and give up Miss Ford, his subsequent wife, here alluded to as secretly married to him. Alicia is a young woman of great beauty, the daughter of an impecunious army officer, who came to London to make her fortune by marriage and has now become Colman's 'ostensible and favourite sultana'.

Ovals, $2\frac{3}{4} \times 2\frac{3}{8}$ in. B M L , P.P. 5442 b.

5743 Nº XXII. THE FAITHFUL MISTRESS.
Nº XXIII COL. W——.

Publish'd by A. Hamilton Jun' near S' John's Gate Aug' 1; 1780.

Engraving. *Town and Country Magazine*, xii 345. Two bust portraits in oval frames illustrate 'Histories of the Tête-à-Tête annexed; . .' Col W. 'is descended from an ancient and illustrious family, who have for some centuries figured with great éclat in our history; having filled many important offices as well civil as military'. Of eight colonels and lt.-colonels in the *Royal Kalendar*, 1780, whose names begin with W., Sir John Wrottesley, Bart., Col in the 1st Foot Guards, appears the most likely. The lady is a Miss Lennox, daughter of a gentleman keeping a boarding-school at Hammersmith, said to have been decoyed by a procuress, and rescued by Col W.

Ovals, $2\frac{3}{4} \times 2\frac{3}{8}$ in B.M.L., P.P 5442 b.

[1] Mrs Robinson mentions in her *Memoirs* many persons who made proposals to her about this time which she rejected. they include the Duke of Rutland, Lord Lyttelton, the Earl of Pembroke, 'a royal Duke', a 'lofty Marquis'.

5744 Nº XXII. MʀˢC——XE.

Nº XXIII. LORD C——.

Publish'd by A Hamilton Junʳ near Sᵗ John's Gate Sepʳ 1; 1780

Engraving. *Town and Country Magazine*, xii 401 Two bust portraits in oval frames illustrate 'Histories of the Tête-à-Tête annexed,   .'. An account of Lord Craven (1738–91) His extravagances and that of his wife, Lady B—— are said to have induced him to go to the Continent. She was Lady Elizabeth Berkeley (better known as the Margravine of Anspach), they separated in 1780 G E C., *Complete Peerage*. Mrs. Coxe's story as told to Lord C. is that she was a parson's daughter who tried to support herself by novel-writing, married, was deserted and destitute and became a prostitute, until taken under the protection of Lord C.

Ovals, 2¾ × 2⅜ in.   B M L , P P. 5442 b.

5745 Nº XXV. MISS H——

Nº XXVI. THE VALIANT COMMANDER.

Publish'd by A. Hamilton Junʳ near Sᵗ John's Gate Octʳ 1; 1780.

Engraving *Town and Country Magazine*, xii 457 Two bust portraits in oval frames illustrate 'Histories of the Tête-à-Tête annexed; . . .'. An account of a naval commander, separated from his second wife, whom he had married for her fortune, and of Miss H., a relative of his first wife, who keeps house for him and looks after his children.

Ovals, 2¾ × 2⅜ in   B M.L., P P. 5442 b.

5746 Nº XXVIII MʀˢFL——D.

Nº XXIX. SIR J—— HOGSTIE.

Publish'd by A Hamilton Junʳ near Sᵗ John's Gate Novʳ 1ˢᵗ 1780

Engraving. *Town and Country Magazine*, xii 513. Two bust portraits in oval frames illustrate 'Histories of the Tête-à-Tête annexed, or, Memoirs of Sir J Hogstie and Mʳˢ Fl——yd' An account of Sir Joseph Mawbey, Sir Joseph of *The Rolliad*, the Southwark distiller, recently elected for Southwark. He is here the subject of ridicule, cf. Nos. 5190–2. Distillers kept large quantities of hogs, fed on the grains which had been used in distilling. An anonymous satire of 1773 beginning You I love my dearest life . . has the couplet,

> More than country squires their dogs
> More than Mawbey loves his hogs

quoted in G E C., *Complete Peerage*, i. 1910, Appendix H. Cf. No. 5829.

Miss Fl——d is a tricked, seduced, and deserted parson's daughter and milliner's apprentice whom Mawbey has established in 'an elegant villa near Vauxhall'.

Ovals, 2¾ × 2⅜ in.   B M L , P.P 5442 b.

5747 Nº XXXI. MISS B—DG—R.

Nº XXXII LORD L——N

Publish'd by A. Hamilton Junʳ near Sᵗ John's Gate. Decʳ 1; 1780.

Engraving *Town and Country Magazine*, xii. 577. Two bust portraits in oval frames illustrate 'Histories of the Tête-à-Tête annexed; . .'. An account of Lord Lincoln, recently defeated at the Westminster election, see Nos. 5698, 5699, it is here said, because he unduly despised his opponent's interest and influence. Miss Br—dg—r is the daughter of an eminent hosier, whose losses forced him to flee to Dunkirk; she therefore became waiting-maid and companion to a peevish spinster, at whose house Lord L met her.

Ovals, $2\frac{7}{8} \times 2\frac{7}{10}$ in ; $2\frac{7}{8} \times 2\frac{3}{8}$ in   B.M.L., P.P. 5442 b.

5748 [LADY CECILIA JOHNSTON]

[Gillray.]

Publish'd May 18ᵗʰ 1780 by H. Humphrey Nᵒ 18 New Bond Street.

Engraving. H L. sketch portrait of a thin and elderly lady in profile to the l. Her hair is dressed high and decorated with feathers and lace

She is Lady Cecilia Johnston (1727–1817), the daughter of Lord De La Warr, m. 1763, Lieut -General James Johnston, known as 'Irish Johnston'. She was much caricatured by Gillray.

Grego, *Gillray*, p 30

$2\frac{13}{16} \times 2\frac{1}{8}$ in.

5749 [LADY (MOUNT) EDGCUMBE]

[? Gillray.]

Publish'd May 18ᵗʰ 1780 by H. Humphrey Nᵒ 18 New Bond Street.

Engraving. Bust portrait in profile to the l. of an elderly woman, thin and of witch-like appearance. Her hair which recedes from her forehead is dressed high and ornamented with a lace cap.

A portrait of Lady Mount-Edgcumbe, who, like Lady Cecilia Johnston (see No. 5748), was a favourite subject of Gillray's satire, they both appear in *La Belle Assemblée*, 12 May 1787. She was Emma, d. of John Gilbert, Archbishop of York, m in 1761 George, 3rd Baron Edgcumbe, cr. Viscount Mount-Edgcumbe, 1781, Earl, 1789 She died in 1807. Identified by Miss Banks.

$3 \times 2\frac{3}{8}$ in

5750 [EARL OF HERTFORD]

[Gillray.]

Pub June 1ˢᵗ 1780

Engraving. Caricature bust portrait of Lord Hertford in profile to the r. His hair or wig receding from his forehead is in a black bag. He is wearing the ribbon and star of the Garter. He is Francis Seymour Conway (1719–94), then Lord Chamberlain, cr. Marquis of Hertford, 1793. See Nos. 5966, 6018.

Grego, *Gillray*, p 30 (Reproduction.)

$3\frac{3}{8} \times 2\frac{1}{16}$ pl.

5750 A [EARL OF HERTFORD]

[Gillray]

Publish'd 1ˢᵗ June 1780.

Engraving (coloured impression). Portrait of Hertford, similar to No. 5750 but reversed.

5751 I HAVE LOST MY STOMACH

[Gillray?]

Pub. June 1ˢᵗ 1780.

Engraving (coloured and uncoloured impressions). Caricature head of Lord Kelly in profile to the r. He is bending forward, his face bloated and pimpled, his lank and scanty hair in a black bag Lord Kelly or Kellie, the 6th Earl, b 1732, d. unmarried at Brussels in Oct. 1781. He had a considerable reputation as a musician. Cf No. 6128

$3\frac{3}{8} \times 2\frac{3}{16}$ in. (pl.).

5751 A [LORD KELLY.]

[Gillray?]

Publish'd 1ˢᵗ June 1780.

Engraving. Portrait of Lord Kelly, similar to No. 5741 but reversed On it is written in ink 'I have lost my stomach'

$3\frac{13}{16} \times 2\frac{7}{16}$ in (pl.)

5752 [LORD AMHERST]

[? Gillray.]

Publish'd 3ᵈ July 1780.

Engraving. Head of Lord Amherst in profile to the l. much caricatured. Amherst, as acting commander-in-chief, responsible for the suppressing of the Gordon Riots, was much caricatured.

$3\frac{5}{8} \times 2\frac{9}{16}$ in. (pl.)

5753 [COL. BODENS]

Pub by M Darly July 24, 1780, 39 Strand

Engraving (coloured impression). Portrait (H L) in profile to the r. of a fat man with a small head and very thick neck. His wig has a small looped queue; he wears a small hat with a cockade, a very bulky great-coat, with a nosegay under his chin. George Bodens (or Boden or Bowden) was commissioned in 1762. A member of Boodle's, 'the fattest, best-tempered and most popular man in London', and a protector of Mrs. Mahon. H. Bleackley, *Ladies Fair and Frail*, p 279 See No. 5868. A companion portrait to No. 5754.

$2\frac{3}{4} \times 2\frac{1}{8}$ in.

5754 [LORD CLERMONT.]

Pub by M Darly July 24, 1780 (39) Strand.

Engraving (coloured impression). A companion portrait to No. 5753.

Lord Clermont (H L.), wearing a hat, stands in profile to the l., his eyes screwed up, his mouth open as if shouting. He is very high-shouldered. He is William Henry Fortescue (1722–1806), cr. Baron Clermont of Clermont, Co Louth, 1770, Viscount, 1776; Earl, 1777. He was looked on as the father of the Turf, winning the Derby in 1785. He was a friend of C. J Fox and the Prince of Wales. G.E.C , *Complete Peerage*. Wraxall, *Memoirs*, 1884, v. 25–31.

$2\frac{13}{16} \times 2\frac{3}{16}$ in.

5755 A SPIRITED ATTACK [n d ? 1780]

Engraving. C. J Fox (W L), in the attitude of an orator, his head turned in profile to the l. His r. arm is raised and extended, the fist clenched, his mouth open as if shouting In his l. hand he holds his hat He stands with his feet apart. He is plainly dressed, except for a ruffled shirt.

Cf No. 5878 where his gesture is less violent.

$5\frac{1}{2} \times 3\frac{5}{8}$ in.

5756 BENJAMIN B. [? 1780]

[G. Humphrey]

Pub^d march 20 by H Humphrey Old Bond S^t.

Engraving (coloured and uncoloured impressions) H L portrait of an elderly clergyman in profile to the r with a long sharp nose and receding chin. He wears bands and an academic hood. One impression has been dated (by Mr. Hawkins) 1782, another has been identified as 'Dr Benjamin Buckler of All Souls Cambridge' [*sic*], i.e. Buckler (1718–80), fellow of All Souls, Oxford, where there is a portrait of him ascribed to Gainsborough. Below one impression is written 'My first Etching—G H. May 1813', G H being identified on the back as G. Humphrey.

$6 \times 3\frac{13}{16}$ in (pl)

5756A BENJAMIN B.

A close copy or perhaps an earlier version of No. 5756.

$7 \times 4\frac{1}{2}$ in (pl).

5757 THE ANTIQUARIAN MASTIFF [*c.* 1780 ?]

F Grose Del: et Sculp·

Engraving Caricature bust portrait full face of Michael Lort, D D (1725–90) He wears a bag-wig, squints, and his pug-nose and heavy jowl have something of the bulldog.

$3 \times 2\frac{1}{4}$ in.

5758 [PORTRAIT OF A VIOLINIST.] [n d. *c.* 1780 ?]

Engraving An elderly man seated in a chair in profile to the r playing a small violin or dancing-master's kit He wears pince-nez, has a large nose and small pointed chin. His high toupet wig and pigtail queue suggest that he is Italian or French He reads from music supported on a stand. The manner resembles that of the two Brethertons.

$7\frac{1}{2} \times 5\frac{13}{16}$ in.

5759 EX MUSEO NEAPOLITANO. [n.d. *c.* 1780?]

C. Bretherton fecet [*sic*]

Engraving Design in an irregular oval Bust portrait in profile to the r. of
Gaetano Pugnani (1727–1803), violinist and composer. He has a grotesquely
large nose, large arched eyebrow, and small slit-like eye. He wears a bag-
wig and ruffled shirt. Under his arm is a violin

$5\frac{1}{16} \times 3\frac{7}{8}$ in

5760 NOSCITUR EX NASO. [*c.* 1780?]
NOSEE NOSEE

J. Ironmonger inv.

Engraving W L caricature portrait of a man sitting on a four-legged stool
in profile to the r. He has a large sharp nose. In his l. hand he holds a
paper inscribed *Newgate Contract*. On the ground are two papers, one
inscribed *To M͗ Nic*, the other, *Speech ag͗ City Place Bill*. He is plainly
and neatly dressed, his wig in a tight pigtail queue. Mr. Hawkins has
written on the print *Sharp an Ironmonger in Leadenhall Street*. In the
London Directory for 1780 James Sharpe, Ironmonger, is at 15 Leadenhall
Street. The building of new Newgate Prison began in 1770 and was not
finished until after 1780.

$6\frac{1}{8} \times 4\frac{1}{4}$ in.

5761 THE DELIGHT OF PLY—(MOUTH[1])

Pub͟ by H Humphrey N° 18 New Bond Street Jan 1͟ 1780.

Engraving A fat man in profile to the l. climbing up a ladder to reach the
seat of a phaeton, perched on springs high above the wheels of the carriage.
He is identified by Mr Hawkins as the fifth Earl of Plymouth (1751–99)
Behind him (r) appear the heads and forelegs of two horses (whose relation
to the phaeton is obscure) held by a neat groom. To the head of each horse
is attached a small closed sunshade

This is in the manner of the series issued by Darly 1776–8, see Nos. 5369,
5370, &c.

$13 \times 9\frac{1}{4}$ in.

5762 A GARTER'D DILLY, OR MASTER OF A HORSE TURN'D
TRADER.

A Critical Observer pinx͟. *A Queer dog fecit.*

Published as the Act directs, Jan͟ 30 1780.

Mezzotint. The duke of Northumberland (caricatured), his arm round
the shoulder of a lightly-draped woman. She holds a scroll inscribed
300 per Ann for life He is wearing the ribbon of the Garter at his knee
and a star. A small dog stands on its hind-legs behind him. Beneath the
title is engraved, *Solving a Problem in the Rule of Barter—O tempora!
O Mores!* Northumberland (1715–86) was Master of the Horse from
1778–80

Oval, $6\frac{3}{4} \times 5\frac{1}{2}$ in.

[1] Depicted.

5763 AQUILA HAPSBURGHIENSIS

['*Lord de Ferrars delin*'.]¹   ['*Publish^d 27th May 1780*']²

Engraving   The Habsburg eagle with a single head, that of a man in profile to the l. wearing a bag-wig, with a huge aquiline nose. On the body of the eagle on a shield surmounted by a coronet are the arms of the earls of Denbigh, who claimed descent from the Habsburg family, the Fieldings (including Henry Fielding) using as a crest the double-headed Habsburg eagle. Over the head is suspended a conical-shaped cap with an ermine border. Beneath the title is inscribed,

> *Monstrum, Horrendum Informe, Ingens, cui Lumen Ademptum.*
>   *Quale Portentum neque militaris*
>   *Daunia in latis alit Esculetis,*
>   *nec Jubae etellus generat, &c &c*

Humbly dedicated to Garter King at Arms, and all other the Officers of the College of Arms, London.

A satire on Basil, 6th Earl of Denbigh (1719–1800), who was a Lord of the Bedchamber, Master of the Harriers and Foxhounds, and a strong supporter of the Ministry in the House of Lords. His features were given a political significance by Barré's description when denouncing Court Lords· '. . . with such a villainous aspect, squinting eyes and features so compressed that his hooked nose could scarce squeeze itself into its place, was so hideous that he had been persuaded it was not a human face but a mask' (13 Dec. 1770) Walpole, *Memoirs of the Reign of George III*, 1845, iv. 288 See also Walpole, *Last Journals*, 1910, ii. 102–3. See Nos. 5976, 6162.

11 × 8¼ in.

5763A [AQUILA HAPSBURGHIENSIS.]

Engraving   The head and neck surmounted by the cap, copied from No 5763, masked, in a lozenge.

3¼ × 2 in.

5764 ITALIAN AFFECTATION
REAL CHARACTERS

[Rowlandson.]

                                      P^e 6^d

Pub^d According to Act Sepr 1st 1780 by T. Rowlandson & J. Jones at N° 103 Wardour St Soho

Engraving (coloured and uncoloured impressions)   Two Italian opera-singers, much burlesqued, singing a duet. The man (l) is Pacchierotti, his three-cornered hat is clutched in both hands, and he sings with a love-sick expression. The lady with her arms outstretched to the r looks upwards over her r. shoulder. Both are fashionably dressed.

---

¹ Written on one of the impressions in a contemporary hand Walpole calls Ferrers 'a great herald'. *Letters*, x 381

² Contemporary note on the print. (On another impression is written 'Publish'd 28th Decr 1780'.

467

For Gasparo Pacchierotti (1744–1821) see Mme d'Arblay's *Diary*, i 155, 323, 324, &c. 'Mrs Sheridan declared [1779] she could not hear him without tears,' ibid , p. 187

Grego, *Rowlandson*, i. 98.

8⅝×7⅜ in

5765 A BARBERS SHOP

[Rowlandson.]

Pub^d Acc^d to Act Dec 13th 1780 by T Rowlandson & I. Jones N° 103 Wardour Street Soho

Engraving, partly mezzotinted. The interior of a barber's shop A very old and completely bald man reclines in an arm-chair (l), a cloth over his shoulders; a fat barber is about to place on his head a tie-wig On the ground at his side lies a wig with a long pigtail queue which is being befouled by a dog Behind, on a tall stand, is a barber's block fitted with a small wig. The barber's assistant, a lean man wearing spectacles and an apron, fits a small wig on the head of a stout man, who stands in profile to the r , his hand in his coat-pocket. On the r. is a lattice window in three divisions; a man sits in a chair facing the window. Wigs are hung up in the window On a high shelf (l.) are round wig-boxes. Next the shelf is nailed up a print of Absalom hanging from a tree, while his horse gallops away. Beneath this is written in ink, *Oh! Absalom my Son. If thoud'st worn a Perriwig This wou[ld] neever been done.* The ceiling is raftered.

9⁷⁄₁₆×13 in

5766 THE QUINTESSENCE OF QUACKISM, FOUNDED ON PRINCIPALS TRULY CHIMERICAL ÆTHERIAL MAGNETICAL, ELECTRICAL, & IMMATERIAL, & THE FOUR QUARTERS OF THE GLOBE RANSACK'D TO MAKE IT INGENIOUSLY REDI-CULOUS DEDICATED TO THE EMPEROR OF QUACKS, BY MYSELF

Publish'd as the Act directs Oct 30th 1780. P. Mitchel North Audley St^t Grosvenor Sq.

Engraving. Beneath the design is engraved a musical score with the words of a song. A burlesque representation of the quack doctor James Graham (1745–94), who opened his 'Temple of Health' in the Adelphi in the autumn of 1779 Graham stands full-face; he holds in his mouth the end of the tail of a monkey which sits on his head. The monkey holds out a duck by one leg, which is saying *Quack Quack* Graham holds out in his r. hand a circular box inscribed *Æthereal Pills* A medallion hangs round his neck, on which is a woman's head, inscribed *Female Historian* She is Mrs Catherine Macaulay (see index) whom he treated at Bath, so gaining his first start He stands between two gigantic men wearing large laced hats and long coats; one, *Gog* (l), in back view, the other, *Magog* (r.), stands full-face holding a paper inscribed *Sketch of the Plan of the Temple of Health* These represent the gigantic footmen or porters who were among the attractions of the 'Temple' and who distributed bills advertising the establishment, see No. 6346 and Angelo, *Reminiscences*, 1904, i 97.

Between them, and above Graham's head, the words *Hail Wonderous Combination!* are etched. By the l margin of the print, two men are gazing at the spectacle, one clasps his hands in admiration or supplication. On the opposite side is a man grinning with two small boys who laugh and point, one of them a little chimney-sweep with brushes and sack The song beneath the design begins,

See Sirs, see here a Doctor rare, who Travels much at home,
Here take my Bills, take my Bills I cure all ills past, present, and to come.

Graham was a lavish advertiser, now chiefly remembered for his 'celestial bed'. At this time Colman was producing at the Haymarket the *Genius of Nonsense*, an extravaganza which 'faithfully delineated The Bottle Conjuror of the Adelphi', Bannister playing the 'Emperor of the Quacks' (Graham). Baker, *Biog. Dram.*, 1782, ii. 134 For Graham see *D.N B.* and Nos. 6323–7, &c. As the 'Bottle Conjuror' he is compared with the great hoax of the century, see Nos. 3022–7

$7 \times 13\frac{1}{4}$ in.

5767 FLORIZEL AND PERDITA.

Publish'd as the act Directs November 10ᵗʰ 1780

Price Six Pence

Engraving (coloured impression), beneath which is a printed song. Perdita (Mary Robinson, 1758–1800) stands in profile to the r. in the centre of a circle holding a wand which rests on her shoulder. In her l. hand she holds out a book, *Essay on Man*, to 'Florizel', the Prince of Wales (1762–1830), who looks at her with admiration, both hands raised as if dazzled by her beauty. She wears a high-crowned Welsh hat on the top of a pyramid of hair with its head-dress of lace and ribbons He wears a loose tunic over Roman armour, a long furred cloak, and the insignia of the Garter. His coronet, decorated with two ostrich feathers and a leek, emblem of Wales, is falling from his head Behind Perdita stands a man who points at her with his r. hand. His head is decorated with stag's horns, and in his l. hand is a paper inscribed *Sʳ Peter Pimp.* he is Thomas Robinson, her husband. The scene is probably the Green Room at Drury Lane At Perdita's feet are rectangular and arched-top boxes inscribed *Whitewash*, *Carmine*, *Dentrifice*, *Perfume*, *Pomatum*, on the last is a paper inscribed *To Florizel*. Behind her is an elaborately carved sofa with satyr's legs, its head ornamented with a cupid and two birds The wall behind is draped with a large looped curtain Against it stand two ornate pedestals each surmounted by a tazza. On the wall are two medallions the larger represents a nymph and goat-herd with two goats (?) and is surmounted by a cupid with a bow and arrow who wears a high-crowned Welsh hat decorated with a leek The other is the profile-head of a satyr (?)

Mrs Robinson played Perdita in Garrick's adaptation of the *Winter's Tale* in her last season at Drury Lane, 1779–80, and attracted the admiration of the Prince of Wales who sent her a letter signed 'Florizel', thus beginning a correspondence between Florizel and Perdita which led to her short-lived establishment as the prince's mistress.

The first meeting in the Green Room at Drury Lane is said to have occurred on 3 Dec 1780, after the date of this print, Genest, vi. 136–7. For the liaison see also *Corr of George III*, vol v 269, Walpole, *Last Journals*, 1910, ii 350; Tom Taylor, *Life of Reynolds*, i 345–6.

The song, *Florizel and Perdita*, is to the tune of 'O Polly is a sad slut! &c'. The second of eight verses is:

> *A tender Prince, oh well-a-day!*
> *Of Years not yet a Score,*
> *Had late his poor Heart stol'n away,*
> *By one of 's many more,*

The first of many satires associating the Prince and Mrs Robinson. See Nos. 5865, 6115, 6116, 6117, 6221, 6263, 6266, 6318, 6319, 6320.
$5\frac{1}{4} \times 7\frac{1}{4}$ in.

5768 THE POLYGAMICAL DOCTOR [c 1780]

Engraving. Dr. Madan (pilloried as the author of *Thelyphthora a treatise on female ruin . .* which advocated polygamy) is seated on a chair against the wall (r) at the back of the room, he rests his chin on two books which he holds in each hand. He wears a bushy wig and a doctor's gown which is turned up to show his knees and under-garments. A dog sits by his side barking; a cat on a shelf above his head stretches a paw to clutch his wig In front (l.) one woman helps another to put on a pair of breeches, which Madan has apparently taken off. Both are fashionably dressed, and of meretricious appearance. Beneath the print is written *Rara Avis in Anglia tres in una conjunctae*; this appears to be copied from an inscription which has been cut off. *Thelyphthora* was reviewed in the *Gentleman's Magazine* for August 1780. It was the subject of two farces at Covent Garden, *Thelyphthora or More Wives than one*, by Pilon (8 Mar. 1781), and *Chit Chat or the Penance of Polygamy* by Welwyn (20 Apr. 1781). Genest, vi. 192–3, 194.
For Madan see Nos 4470, 5496.
$7\frac{3}{8} \times 8\frac{7}{8}$ in.

5769 [COLLA DI PARMA] [c. 1780]

[Ph. L. de Loutherbourg *del.*[1]] [F. Bartolozzi sculp.[2] *c.* 1780].

Engraving. A pretty young woman, elegantly dressed, stands, her petticoats lifted up, while a lean and elderly man (l) fits on false posteriors. She wears feathers in her hair, and a nosegay; she looks over her r shoulder. At his side is a large pot, inscribed *Colla di Parma* [glue of Parma], in which is a brush This is intended to indicate that he is the composer Colla born at Parma about 1730, who came to England about 1770, finally returning to Parma, where he died in 1806. From his coat-pocket papers protrude inscribed *Abel riceuta* and *Cantata del Principe Chigi in occasione del apertura del Pantheon*. On the floor is an oboe lying under a paper inscribed *Cantata per il Benefizzio* [*sic*]. By the pot are a lyre, a laurel wreath, and a paint-brush
Colla married (1780) Lucrezia Agujari, 1743–83, known as la Bastardina, the famous soprano, who was engaged at the Pantheon for a salary of £100 a night See Grove, *Dict. of Music*. She is the lady here depicted.[3]
Calabi, *Bartolozzi*, 1928, No. 2232.
$5\frac{1}{4} \times 3\frac{1}{2}$ in.

[1] Written on the margin in an old hand. [2] So attributed by Calabi.
[3] Note by Mr Hawkins See also Mount Edgcumbe, *Musical Reminiscences*, 1834, p 10

5770 IL MILANESE.

[G. T. Stubbs after Cosway]

Published as the Act Directs may^th [sic] 25 1780

Engraving. Portrait (T.Q L.) of a man seated in a chair in profile to the r., addressing a rat which he holds in his r. hand, his l fore-finger raised admonishingly, saying *God dammuck the devil a bit nothing at all Signify to me, you be one damm Rat you broil very well* He is thin and old and wears spectacles, but is neatly dressed. His bag-wig is well curled and his shirt is ruffled. His r elbow rests on an oval table on which is an open rat-trap; beside it lies the dead body of a rat, labelled *for Supper*. On the table (l.) are also a cracked chamber-pot and a wig-block. On the print is written in an old hand, 'Nobody Know wat sort a man I be'. On the back of one impression is 'Marini an Italian painter', but according to the *Catalogue* of Cosway by F. B. Daniell, this is Magnini a picture-dealer with whom Cosway probably quarrelled, as on the impression in the possession of Sir Philip Currie is written in a contemporary hand, 'Cosway had this print etched in ridicule of him'. Perhaps Gaetano Manini, painter, of Milan $9\frac{3}{8} \times 7\frac{7}{8}$ in. (pl).

5771 THE CATCH SINGERS.   [*c.* 1780?]
      REAL CHARACTERS

Mezzotint. Three catch singers (H.L.) seated round a small circular table on which is a punch-bowl. Two sit facing each other in profile, each has a punch-glass in his hand; the one on the r. who resembles Lord Sandwich points his forefinger at his *vis-à-vis*. The third singer (c) is on the farther side of the table, looking towards the singer on the r and pointing with his r. forefinger to the man on the l.

The scene is lit by one candle standing on the table, on which are also a piece of music (l.) and an overturned punch-glass spilling its contents. A violin hangs on the wall (r).

Beneath the design the words of the catch are engraved:

T'was you S^r T'was you Sir—
I tell you nothing new Sir,
T'was you that kiss'd the
Pretty Girl—T'was you S^r you.

$4\frac{1}{2} \times 6\frac{3}{8}$ in.   In book of Sayer's 'Drolls'.

5772–5776

A set of prints by William Austin.

5772 BRITISH INVALID DRIVING FOREIGN ANIMALS FROM PROCEEDING TO THE CAMP

Wm Austin inv^t et sculp^t

London Published as the Act directs Jany 1 1780.

Engraving. On the l is a troupe of men with performing bears and monkeys On a bear's back sits a monkey. The cavalcade is starting back in alarm at the sight of a countryman and his wife advancing towards them across a stream. The men with the animals, from their ragged foppishness and lean and vagabondish appearance, are evidently intended for French-men. The bear leader, wearing a bag-wig and ruffled shirt, plays a trumpet. Behind is a monkey dressed as a *petit-maître* with a sword and bag-wig. The countryman (r) threatens the troupe with a crutch, his hat has fallen into the stream The woman rides a donkey which is braying at the bears; she has let go the ducks and hens which she was carrying, a basket of eggs is being upset and the contents of a barrel are pouring out. A dog barks violently. In the distance are tents. Beneath the title is engraved *You vile pack of Vagabonds what do you mean.*

$9\frac{7}{8} \times 12\frac{5}{8}$ in.

5773 THE SPANISH DONS OVERTAKEN BY AN ANCIENT BRITON IN ATTEMPTING THEIR ESCAPE.   [1 Jan 1780][1]

Wm Austin inv^t et sculp^t

Engraving. A soldier on a great horse holds a rope attached to the legs of two prisoners who sit behind him facing the animal's tail; a drawn sword is in his r. hand. Behind (r.) is a haystack, on the top of which are two other Spaniards, much alarmed at the approach of a countryman who threatens them with his pitch-fork. A man and woman (l), both wearing coats with military facings, watch the scene, she points, he looks through a small telescope. In the foreground a sow and three young pigs are galloping In the background is the sea, with fishing-boats.

$9\frac{7}{8} \times 12\frac{5}{8}$ in.

5774 RECRUITING SERJEANT AND CONTENTED MATES.
[W Austin.]

London Published as the Act directs 1st Jany 1780.

Engraving. A thin man wearing a coat with military facings, draws after him (r. to l) a small four-wheeled carriage, similar to a bath-chair or perambulator, inscribed *Cox Heath* In it sits a child with a doll. A dog stands at her feet barking at the man who draws the carriage, who has a bundle strapped to his back, apparently containing hay. At the back of the carriage in the place of a footman stands a ragged dwarfish man On the farther side of the carriage is a recruiting sergeant playing a fife. In the foreground (r.) a fat woman, the wife of the man drawing the carriage, walks along carrying a basket containing bottles and a large umbrella in her r hand, a musket is tucked under her l arm. She and the three men all wear oak-leaves in their hats. In the distance the tents of the camp are indicated. An inscription beneath the title has been cut off.

One of a number of satires on the militia and the camp of Coxheath, see No. 5523, &c.

$10 \times 12\frac{1}{2}$ in.

5775 FRENCH SPIES ATTACKED BY BRITISH BEES ON THEIR FIRST LANDING 5.

Wm Austin inv^t et sculp^t

London Published as the Act directs 1st Jany 1780:

Engraving Two grotesquely caricatured Frenchmen attacked by a swarm

[1] Publication line cut off

of bees One (l.), who is very lean, wearing a bag-wig and the huge jack-boots worn by French postilions, fires a pistol at the bees. The other waves his hat, flourishing a cutlass, bees are in his hair, which stands on end, his long pigtail queue streams out in the wind On the extreme l. appear the head and arms of a Frenchman who appears to be lying on the ground, he has dropped his cane and is clasping his hands, A small poodle also appears to be in distress On the r. is the sea, with fishing-boats On the edge of the shore is a Frenchman on a horse whose head, like that of his rider, is being attacked by bees—the horse is kicking violently. In the distance on the r. are soldiers, with muskets, their officer on a horse. Beneath the title is engraved, *Mon Dieu they make my Hair all stand on end.*

$9\frac{3}{4} \times 12\frac{3}{8}$ in

5776 PUBLIC ORDINARY

[W. Austin.][1]

London. Published as the act directs 1ˢᵗ Jany 1780: by Robert Wilkinson at N° 58 in Cornhill.

Engraving Men and women eating in the open air, at a table, some sitting, others standing. In the background are the tents of a camp; in the middle distance (r.) eight men and women holding hands are dancing in a ring. A man of grotesque appearance, one eye covered with a circular patch, sits full-face, plying a knife and fork Behind him stands Wilkes, who is chucking a pretty maid-servant under the chin so that she spills the wine which she has just poured out This attracts the amused attention of a man standing behind Wilkes, and of one sitting at the table. The other figures are indicated only by their heads, which are perhaps portraits: there are two women of attractive appearance, one, whose high-dressed hair is decorated with feathers, the other with a hat trimmed with a cockade and feathers, a grotesque-looking old man with unkempt hair who is drinking wine, an old man with a grenadier's cap. A man seated on the bench shows only a wig and a broad back. On the bench is also a sucking-pig which a dog is seizing. On the ground are bottles, a pile of plates, and a brimming punch-bowl Two cocks (r.) are fighting.

Beneath the title is engraved *Oh what a charming Thing is eating.* One of many satires on militia camps, especially that at Coxheath, see No. 5523, &c

5777 THE MINOGOAT.[2] [c 1780?]

[W. Austin.]

Engraving The interior of a fruiterer's shop. Behind a counter sits a man (l.) with long goat's horns and a goat's beard He holds up his hand with an expression of dismay at a man who shows him a bust portrait of himself with horns and beard The man, who wears a cockaded hat, is laughing. His arm is held by a man who stands behind him smiling and pointing a cane at the horned man, or 'Minogoat'. The latter's hand rests upon the counter on a sheaf of newspapers. *Gazeter, London Spy, Morning Her[ald], London Chronicle, London Gaz[ette]* A dwarfish newsboy stands in front of

[1] On the print is written in ink 'Austin J fecit'
[2] Mino is an obsolete form of mina, myna, &c, the talking jackdaw of India It was used in combination, as mino-grackle (O E D) Perhaps used here to mean a chattering goat

the counter blowing his horn, and offering him the *Morning Post*. The boy is very bandy-legged; his cap is decorated with a leek, suggesting that it is St. David's day. On the ground (r.) is a basket containing pottles of fruit which a goat is befouling.

In what appears to be an inner room or recess (r.) a table is laid with dishes of fruit, glasses, and an urn, four people are seated at it: a man and woman laughing and talking together in an absorbed way, a man who points out this couple to a companion. Wilkes (unmistakable from his squint) stands behind holding out his hat.

Fruit hangs in the panes of the shop window which is immediately behind the Minogoat, who appears to be a Welsh shop-keeper. On the upper and lower margins of the print ten lines of verse are engraved, beginning,

> *Come & purchase poor Taff's dainty cakes & fine Fruit,*
> *Hur will give you Lies, Noise, News & Nonsense to boot.*

This print cannot be earlier than Nov. 1780, as the first issue of the *Morning Herald* was on 1 Nov. 1780.

$9 \times 13\frac{3}{8}$ in.

5778 FRONTISPIECE [to the *Town and Country Magazine*]

Dighton del.

Published as the Act directs 1st Feby 1780.

Engraving. *Town and Country Magazine*, vol. xii. A woman, fashionably dressed and of rather meretricious appearance, holds in her hand a number of the magazine, the open page showing a *Tête-à-tête* engraving, to which she points angrily, looking towards Mercury holding a caduceus, who sits (r.) one foot resting on three bound volumes; he points at the open page with a mocking smile. A grinning face looks over his shoulder with a hand pointing also at the open magazine. Behind the lady (l.) is a leering satyr, a bound volume under his l. arm, his r. finger laid against his nose. At the lady's feet are another number of the magazine open at a *Tête-à-tête*, and a closed number inscribed *Town and Country Magazine 1780*. The background is of pseudo-classical architecture with a heavily draped curtain.

The lady is angry at finding herself the subject of a *Tête-à-tête*, the chief feature of the *Town and Country Magazine*, see Nos. 4903–12, &c.

$5\frac{3}{4} \times 3\frac{5}{8}$ in.　　　　　　　　　　　B.M.L., P.P. 5442 b.

5779 THE RECRUITING CUCKOLD A SONG.

[? Gillray.]

Publish'd Feby 4th 1780 by W. Humphrey No 227 Strand.　　*Pr 6d*

Engraving. Three women are recruiting: a tall woman (l.) holds up her r. hand in an appeal for recruits, in her l. is a long staff surmounted by stag's horns, she wears a gorget and military coat, a looped hat with a feather is on her high-dressed hair; a short stout woman (c.) beats a drum. She wears a very low-cut dress with a grenadier's cap. A woman (r.) wearing a hat in the prevailing fashion blows a flute. Behind them (l.) march a company of recruits, their hats decorated with horns. On the r. is a group of spectators; a thin man looks at the women through his glasses, a woman puts her arm on his shoulder. Beneath the design a song of four verses is engraved in two columns: the first being,

> *Since the Foes of Old England so Saucy appear,*
> *And the land is in danger, from Spain & Monsieur,*
> *For each Subject to Arm, in the Nation's defence,*
> *Is the Language of Reason, the Language of Sense,*
> *Like bold Volunteers, let each Cuckold attend,*
> *For Cuckolds we know—have their Horns to defend!*
> > *Come Cuckolds, Come! Come!*
> > *At the Sound of the Drum!*
> *These boasting Invaders, we soon will drive Home.*

For satires on the militia and militia camps see No. 5523, &c.
$5\frac{3}{4} \times 7\frac{3}{4}$ in.

5780 [HEADS]

I. Mortimer del.[1]   *C. R. Ryley fecit.*
Publish'd as the Act directs, by C. R. Ryley March 1st 1780.

Engraving Heads arranged in three groups, almost all gazing intently with varying expressions. Two of the groups are theatrical in character; the lowest group appears to have been sketched from life. a row of four profile heads, caricatured, looking intently over a barrier protected with spikes; a woman's head, full-face, is at one end (l.) of the row; at the other a man looks over his shoulder. They are probably seated in the gallery of a theatre. The dresses suggest the period 1778–9
$10\frac{1}{2} \times 6\frac{1}{2}$ in. (clipped).

5781 [SKETCHES IN CARICATURE.]

J. Mortimer del.   *C. R. Ryley fecit.*
Publish'd as the Act directs, by C. R Ryley March 1st 1780.

Engraving. An arrangement of profile heads, with three W.L. figures, apparently taken from a sketch-book. Five of the heads, all in profile to the l., are of men wearing academic dress: mortar-board, gown, and bands. Of the W L. figures one, a seated man draped in robes, is not caricatured, and is perhaps an artist's model. The other two are on a smaller scale, one is in academic dress, the other is a doctor with an enormous syringe held over his l. shoulder; he wears a voluminous coat or gown A H L. sketch of a man similarly dressed with his hands in a muff is perhaps of the same person
$11\frac{1}{2} \times 9$ (clipped).

5782 SUNDAY EVENING.

J. N [Nixon?] *fecit.*
Pub.d March 29, 1780 by W. Wells, Printseller No 132 opposite Salisbury Court, Fleet Street.

Engraving (coloured impression) Two London citizens driving home from their Sunday outing, along a country road, by a milestone (r) *III Miles*

[1] Mortimer died 4 Feb 1779.

from London. They sit side by side in a small two-wheeled cart drawn by a diminutive horse or pony. Both are smoking long pipes. The one who holds the reins (l) is gazing reflectively at the scene on his r , he wears a hat, but has taken off his wig which is on his knee.

$6\frac{3}{8} \times 5\frac{1}{2}$ in.

5783 HE WOU'D BE A SOLDIER, &c.

R. Dighton delin[t]

London. Printed for J. Smith, N° 35 Cheapside, and R. Sayer and J Bennett, N° 53 Fleet Street, as the Act directs, August 1st 1780.

Engraving. W.L. portrait of a fat citizen-soldier walking or marching in profile from r. to l. He holds a bayoneted musket in his l hand against his shoulder. In his r is a nosegay which he holds to his face He wears a cockaded hat, a coat with military facings, a ruffled shirt, crossed bandolier, and spatterdashes His curled wig has a long pigtail queue

After the Gordon riots had been suppressed by the army, 'Military Associations' were formed in the City and in several other parishes, both to guard against further disturbances and to show that the use of troops was unnecessary, cf No 5687, &c. This soldier is, however, probably one of the London Trained Bands.

No. 5784 is a sequel to this print

$6\frac{7}{8} \times 5$ in. (pl).

5784 THE SOLDIER TIRED OF WARS ALARMS

[R. Dighton]

Published as the Act directs Sep[r] 6th 1780 & Sold at N° 132 Fleet Street.[1]

Engraving. The citizen-soldier of No 5783 stands at his bench, wearing an apron. He is looking intently at his own caricature, *He wou'd be a Soldier,* see No 5783, which he holds in his l. hand. In his r. is an implement for rolling or pressing, and on the bench are small disks, perhaps indicating that he is a button-maker On the ground at his feet lie his hat, musket, bayonet, bandolier, and cartouche box, the last decorated with the City Arms. His shoes are unbuckled, his stockings ungartered, his breeches unbuttoned at the knee

'The Soldier tired of War's Alarms' was sung by Ann Catley at Marylebone Gardens in 1771 Wroth, *London Pleasure Gardens of the Eighteenth Century,* 1896, p. 105.

$6\frac{7}{8} \times 5$ in.

5785 HE LEADS THE—VAN—AGAIN,

Pub by M Darly Aug[t] 26 1780 39 Strand.

Engraving (coloured and uncoloured impressions) A fat citizen-soldier marching in profile from l. to r A cartouche box attached to his bandolier flies out behind him. In his r. hand is a musket His hat has an oval ornament in place of the usual cockade On his bandolier he wears a flat brush indicating his trade He marches on a flag-stone pavement, behind is the dome of St. Paul's; two steeples and tall houses are freely sketched

[1] The address of W Wells

A caricature of Thomas Vanhagen, 'a famous fat pastry cook', who had a shop facing the north gate of St Paul's, and held a commission in the trained bands or city militia. E Hardcastle [W H. Pyne], *Wine and Walnuts*, 1823, ii 204 He was Common Councillor for the Ward of Farringdon Within in 1780.

$6\frac{3}{8} \times 4\frac{3}{4}$ in

Another impression with the publication line, *Pub by W Wells Augt 26 1780 N° 132 Fleet Street*, Darly's name, &c , having been obliterated.

5786 THE CHESELD¹ SOLDIER, RETURN'D TO BUISNESS, OR THE NEWGATE STR——T BUTCHER

[T. Colley ?]

Pub Accor · to Act Oct 5 1780 by T. Colley N° 288 Strand.

Engraving A fat butcher, full-face, stands beside his block In his l. hand is a calf's head, in the r he holds up a knife He wears a wig, an apron, and over-sleeves from wrist to elbow His musket leans against his block, on which is a joint of meat His cockaded hat, bandolier, and bayonet hang together on the wall behind him. A caricature of a member of the London Trained Bands or of the London Military Association which had sprung into activity after the Gordon Riots, as soon as the troops had secured the City from danger, see No. 5687, &c.

$8\frac{3}{4} \times 6\frac{1}{8}$ in.

5787 FEILD DAY, OR THE ADJUTANT IN A BUSTLE,

[? 1780]

Pub by W. Holland N° 50 Oxford Str^t

Engraving A short and fat military officer in uniform walking in profile from r to l. He is raising his hat in salutation of some passer-by. His hair is in a very small pigtail queue which sticks our rigidly. He wears a sash, sword, and spurred top-boots He resembles the caricature of Captain Grose, called 'a Gross Adjutant', see No 5511. Possibly, however, this is intended for some adjutant called Feild

$5\frac{1}{2} \times 4\frac{5}{8}$ in

5788 ALL JOY AND TRANQUILLITY HIGH LIFE AND FESTIVITY AS LONG AS WE LIVE

Publishd as the Act Directs Novr 1. 1780 by W. Phelps²

Engraving It decorates a printed list of lottery schemes for raising sums of from one to five millions, the prizes being annuities of from £20,000 to £2 a year, the tickets costing from £100 to £20 Two marginal columns of explanatory text headed 'Plate the Second. To the Public', show that the schemes are not ironical

¹ A rope-maker called Chesel appears in the London Directory for 1780 Chesel is an obsolete form of chisel or chesil, small pebble, gravel, or shingle.
² The sheet is *Published as the Act directs, November 1, 1780, and Sold by Messrs. Almon and Debrett, in Piccadilly, Messrs Bull, Ludgate Hill, Edward Hedges, at the Royal Exchange, and James Mathews, No 18 in the Strand, near Charing-Cross. Price one-shilling and sixpence Plain, and Two shillings colour'd*
[Entered at Stationers Hall]

A lottery wheel stands on the r surmounted by a crown, on two panels is an *A*, that on the r. being surmounted by a crown. The third panel (l) is concealed by Fortune, a woman in pseudo-classical draperies, who holds up a scroll inscribed *20·000£* which she has just drawn; she is blindfolded; her r. hand rests upon a coach-wheel. A coach drives off (l), a fortunate couple seated inside it clasp hands; the lady holds a scroll inscribed *10,000£ P' annum for our Lives* The footman behind the coach waves his hat, a scroll coming from his mouth is inscribed *50£ P' Annum* Between the coach and the lottery-wheel prize-winners are dancing in glee, scrolls coming from their hands or mouths showing what prizes they have won, a woman in a cap and apron waves *1000£ P. Annum*, a man waves his hat and a scroll inscribed *5000£ P' Annum*. Figures in the background have won *2000£ . . , 40£ . , 100£ . . ., 100£ . . ., 400£ . . ., 5£ P' Annum*.

According to the accompanying text, 'Had such Plans as these been adopted when I first offered them in the year 1773 when the Stocks bore a good Price . . . I am bold to say, this Nation would have been *Thirty Millions* less in debt at least; the War might have been carried on with Vigour, and not a single Tax laid on any Article whatsoever . . and by this Time that unnecessary word *Financier* erased out of the English Dictionary'.

One of a series, the first plate dated 1 May 1780, the third, 1 Mar. 1781. See No. 5834.

$3\frac{5}{8} \times 9\frac{1}{4}$ in.

5789 THE LOTTERY ADVENTURERS

London, pub⁴ as the Act directs Dec' 1ˢᵗ 1780, by Rob' Wilkinson at N° 58 Cornhill.

Engraving A design in two compartments, one (l) inscribed *Prize*, the other *Blank*. On the l. a man stands holding out in his r hand a ticket inscribed *20ᵐ000*, he smiles, saying,

> *I own I had enough before,*
> *Yet this is pleasing to be Sure.*

His l. hand is in his waistcoat pocket. Behind him (l.) is a lottery-wheel, surmounted by a crown, its panels inscribed *G R.*, beside it is another wheel in back-view.

On the r. the loser stands frowning, his chin resting on a stick held in his r hand; in his l. is a ticket inscribed *Blank* His waistcoat pockets are turned inside out. Behind him are two lottery wheels.

Beneath the winner is inscribed:

> *One Hand in his Pocket, in t'other a Prize,*
> *What Joy is exprest, in this lucky ones Eyes!*
> *O, Fortune; we know, thou art a frolicksome Jade,*
> *Tho; this you've raised high, you've the other, betrayd.*

Beneath the loser:

> *How gloomy alas; this poor Fellow is seen,*
> *His Luck is sufficient, to give him the Spleen,*
> *In chance Work he must deal, like those in high Rank,*
> *He's emptied his Pockets, to buy him a Blank.*

This print was published during the drawing of the lottery for 1780, which began on 16 Nov., the thirty-sixth day's drawing being on 28 Dec. *London Chronicle*, 16–18 Nov. and 28–30 Dec. For lotteries see also No. 4077, &c., and index.

6⅞ × 11 in.

5790 "AH, GRANT A ME VON LETEL BITE".

[Gillray]

London Publshd Decr 1st 1780 by W. Humphrey No 227 Strand

Engraving. Design in a circle. Two boys (T.Q.L.) stand against a stone wall. An English boy (r.) with tousled hair and wearing a shirt which is out at elbows, holds a large bone in both hands. Ribs of beef project from the pocket of his apron. He is perhaps intended for a butcher's boy. A French boy (l.) stands beside and slightly behind him, the tips of his fingers held together, begging for 'von letel Bite'. He wears a toupet-wig and bag, and is fashionably dressed. This is the familiar theme of the foppishly dressed but starving Frenchman. Cf. Nos. 5611, 5612.

Diam., 5½ × 5⅜ in.

5791 BRUTALITY DISPLAY'D, IN A LATE INSTANCE NEAR TRUMP STREET.

Pubd as the Act directs 26 Decr 1780 & Sold at No 132 Fleet Street.

Engraving. A man (l.) is pushing and kicking into the street from the door of a house a young woman with an infant in her arms; another woman is with her, clasping her hands in despair; both are clad only in shifts, and have bare feet. The man wears a nightcap, waistcoat (unbuttoned), shirt, and breeches which are unbuttoned at the knee. A building on the opposite side of the street (r.) is in flames, outside it a small detachment of soldiers stands at attention, beyond them a crowd is indicated. A fireman directs a stream of water at the blaze. Over the door in which the man stands is inscribed . . APMan, Stationer. A side street at r. angles to the house is *Lawrence Lane.* In the background a steeple appears, beyond or upon a high building.

Lawrence Lane is a turning off Cheapside. In 1780 William Chapman, stationer, lived at 36 King Street, Cheapside. *London Directory*, 1780.

7¾ × 7⅛ in

5792 AN ENGLISHMAN'S DELIGHT OR NEWS OF ALL SORTS.

Published as the Act directs 30 Decr 1780 by W. Richardson No 68 high Holborn

Engraving. A newsboy blowing his horn as he runs from l. to r. His sheaf of papers is supported by a band over his l. shoulder inscribed *Noon Gazett[e]*; the topmost paper has a list of the papers he sells. *Morning Herald* [1st issue, 1 Nov. 1780], *Morning Chronicle, Morning Post, Gazeteer, St. James Evening* [Post], *Lloyds Evening* [Post], *Public Ledger, Public Advertiser, Sunday Chronicle.* He holds a purse or wallet in his r. hand. A street is indicated by a freely sketched house. Beneath the design is engraved:

> *All Englishmen delight in News*
> *In London there's enough to chuse*

479

Of morning papers near a Ream
Fill'd with every kind of theme
At Noon there's such a duced Clatter
Strangers must wonder what's the matter
And E'en that day the Lord hath blest
Is now no more a day of rest
Forth from the Press the Papers fly
Each greedy reader to supply
Of battles fought, and numbers slain,
Of Towns besieg'd and prisoners ta'en,
Engagements both by Sea and Land
Eccho from Aldgate to the Strand
Hail! happy land, sure none's so blest
With News to comfort every breast.

All the newspapers whose titles are here given (in whole or in part) were current in 1780 except the *Sunday Chronicle*, which did not appear till 1831. The first Sunday newspaper was *F. Johnson's British Gazette and Sunday Monitor*, appearing in 1779, of which Crabbe wrote.

Then, lo! the sainted Monitor is born,
Whose pious face some sacred texts adorn.
The Newspaper, 1785

Bourne, *English Newspapers* and *Times Hand List of Newspapers.*
$6\frac{3}{8} \times 6\frac{1}{2}$ in

5793 A MUSHROOM FROGSTOOL AND PUFF.   [1780][1]

B E [or *E B*] *f.* (Monogram).

Engraving (coloured impression) A design satirizing the umbrella and the broad-brimmed hat. A man stands full-face wearing a hat with an enormous circular brim slightly turned up at the edges Wisps of hair project stiffly from each side of his head. His hands are thrust into his breeches-pockets Under his l. arm is a whip with a short handle and a thick plaited lash. He is wearing top-boots. A stone by his feet is inscribed *From a Dunghill.* Behind (r) a rough-looking obese man walks in profile to the l He wears a similar hat and jack-boots, he holds a knotted stick resting on his r. shoulder; his l. hand is on his hip. On the r. a man foppishly dressed with a wide three-cornered hat, coat with epaulettes, and sword is walking away from the spectator carrying an umbrella A shop window is indicated in the background in which broad-brimmed hats are displayed on blocks. There is faint or obliterated lettering on the print, partly illegible: *Modern Extinguishers* and *And A Broadb. . . .* Beneath the title is etched *Here to-day & gone to-morrow.*

The umbrella, in spite of the efforts of James Hanway (d. 1786), was still an object of derision in London when used by men. John Macdonald, a footman, used one from Jan 1778 and was at first greeted with the shout 'Frenchman, Frenchman! why dont you call a coach?' John Macdonald, *Travels*, ed. J. Beresford, 1927, pp xxiii. 236. See No. 6132

$5\frac{3}{16} \times 3\frac{7}{8}$ in

[1] Dated 1780 in Miss Banks's hand Such dates are usually those of purchase, not necessarily of publication.

5794 SHOOTING OF RUBBISH. [*c* 1780?]

I. Nixon del^t

London Pub^d by W. Holland. Oxford Str^t [1]

Engraving. An overturned cart on a country road leading to a camp (r.). The cart lies on its side as does the horse, its occupants, four men, two women and a boy, lie on the ground or fall on each other, one, the driver (r.) has fallen into a stream which is in the foreground of the design and runs beside the road. Another man with a wooden leg appears about to fall in The cart is two-wheeled, shaped like a box, with planks across it for seats The men appear to be citizens, the women are perhaps courtesans Two young pigs (l.) run away from the cart, the boy falls against one of them

A man and woman ride pillion away from the camp (r to l.), in the opposite direction from that in which the cart was driving. A signpost points (l.) to the camp, *To* . . . [word erased, the traces resemble *Coxheath*]

A party of soldiers are cooking over a camp-fire in the middle distance (r.), and behind them soldiers are being drilled The scene is a wooded landscape, with fields and hedges, resembling the scenery of Kent, and is possibly intended for the Maidstone district near Coxheath. In the foreground (r.), by the stream is an enormous thistle, so much out of scale with the figures that it is probably intended to express antipathy to Scottish influence.

Perhaps a reissue after visits to Coxheath had ceased to be of topical interest

For Coxheath see No. 5523, &c.

$8\frac{5}{8} \times 12\frac{3}{4}$ in

5795 BILLIARDS. [*c.* 1780?]

R Dighton delin

Publish'd by R. Sayer, 53 Fleet Street.

Engraving A group of eight men (caricatured) round a billiard table. One player is about to make a stroke, his opponent (r.) looks on with an expression of horror, biting his thumb. Bets are depending on the result, a pleased spectator (l.) holds a handful of coins, another puts his hand into his purse. A very obese man (l.) with a wooden leg watches through a glass. The score is shown by two clock-face dials, on one of which the marker puts his hand. Cues stand in racks against the wall For billiards see also Nos 5803, 5913

$6\frac{3}{4} \times 8\frac{15}{16}$ in. In book of Sayer's 'Drolls'.

5796 BEATING UP FOR RECRUITS. [*c.* 1780?]

R. Dighton delin.

Printed for Robert Sayer, N° 53 Fleet Street.

Engraving A recruiting officer stands holding a drawn sword against his shoulder and holding up a netted purse before the eyes of four yokels (caricatured) who stand in a row facing him· one stoops down, his hands on his knees, the next, a waggoner holding a whip, holds out his hand for

[1] Another publication line appears to have been burnished out.

the King's shilling, grinning sheepishly at the companion on his l , a very lean man, scratching his forehead The fourth, whose body is cut off by the r margin of the print, gazes with a fixed grin at the officer. Behind the officer is a smart drummer (l) beating his drum and looking with a cynical half-smile at the yokels The scene is outside a country ale-house (l) In the distance is a wagon drawn by three horses.

$6\frac{5}{8} \times 8\frac{11}{16}$ in   In book of Sayer's 'Drolls'.

5797 JACK ON A CRUISE.   [? 1780][1]

Printed for Robert Sayer, N° 53 Fleet Street.

Engraving. A sailor follows a young woman walking (r to l) in a park She (l.) holds a closed umbrella or sunshade in her r hand, and looks coyly to her l She wears a large hat tilted forwards, ankle-length skirt, projecting paniers at the back arranged over a petticoat which is ornamented in front with an apron. The sailor wears striped trousers and a cutlass, his arms are folded, and he carries a cane; he looks insinuatingly at the lady A small dog runs beside her On the r is an urn with serpents on a high rectangular pedestal under a large tree. In the background among trees is a pavilion in the form of a temple with a dome, pediment, and Corinthian columns. Beneath the title is engraved, *Avast there, back your Main-top-sail.*

A companion print to No. 5797. Cf also Nos 5083, 5313

A mezzotint of this design is reproduced in C. N Robinson's *British Tar in Fact and Fiction*, 1909, p 266 The subject is sometimes found on mugs and jugs; ibid

$8\frac{1}{8} \times 6\frac{11}{16}$ in.   In book of Sayer's 'Drolls'.

5798 JACK GOT SAFE INTO PORT WITH HIS PRIZE. [? 1780]

Printed for Robert Sayer, N° 53 Fleet Street

Engraving. A sequel to No 5797. Jack and his prize, the young woman of No. 5797, sit side by side on a settee, his l arm round her waist Beside the woman (r) is a circular table, on which is a wine-bottle and two glasses, one of which she holds The room is well furnished with a patterned carpet, on the wall which forms the background is a picture of a man seated at a table drinking punch, and a mirror in a carved frame with candle sconce.

$8\frac{1}{16} \times 6\frac{5}{8}$ in   In book of Sayer's 'Drolls'

5799 CHARITY BEGINS AT HOME.   [? c 1780]

R. Dighton delin.

Printed for R Sayer 53 Fleet Street.

Engraving A stout parson (l) riding a good horse towards the spectators on a country road is accosted by a ragged sailor with a wooden leg who holds out his hat to beg. The parson, who is putting a flask to his mouth, scowls at the sailor. A country-girl (r) holding a basket of chickens, apparently for tithe, is counting some money, and a small boy has put down

---

[1] A small mezzotint of this subject was published by Sayer and Bennett, 14 Nov. 1780. (In the collection of Mr. W T. Spencer, New Oxford Street, 1932)

the basket he was carrying to search in his pocket. Although burdened with tithe they are more charitable than the well-to-do parson. One of many satires on the clergy, see Nos. 6153, 6154, also by Dighton

$6\frac{3}{4} \times 8\frac{3}{8}$ in   In book of Sayer's 'Drolls'.

5800 THE CONTEMPTABLE PARSON, SLAUGHTERING HOGS FOR MARKET AT THE PARSONAGE HOUSE   [c 1780?]

Engraving. A yard in which a pig has just been killed. Behind a paling is a village church and other buildings among trees. The pig lies on its side on a bench, beside a tub The parson in his gown and bands throws a pail of water over its head. His man (r) pours the contents of a bowl over the animal. A maidservant stands behind the parson, saying, *Sir a man is come to know what you will sell your Pork a Pound*, he answers, *Five pence half-penny Dont you think I can afford to sell it at that Price John* John says, *You cant afford to sell it for less, they are full as good as those you Advertised last Year I am sure; consider how much Tythe Milk they have had*

The carcass of an enormous pig hangs head downwards (r) Three young pigs (l) feed from a trough One of a number of satires on the clergy and tithes.

$10\frac{3}{16} \times 9\frac{3}{4}$ in.

5801 TIGHT BASTING,

AS IT WAS PERFORM'D AT THE W——E B——R [WHITE BEAR] IN P—C—LLY   [c 1780?]

Engraving. A scene in the White Bear Inn, Piccadilly An elderly man stands between two young ones. He holds one (l.), who is kneeling, by the collar, while he threatens the other, whom he appears to have just kicked, with his stick. Both the young men have expressions of anger and alarm. On the ground (l.) is a bag (?) inscribed *From Oxford*, and a mortar-board cap, and (r) a hat, sword, pistol, and a paper inscribed *Hazar[d] & C° [St]ate Lott[ery]*

A waiter, his napkin under his arm, stands behind a chair. A coachman or carter looking like a countryman stands (r) holding out his hat as if asking to be paid. Through an open door (r.) is the head of a staircase. On a table are a punch-bowl and glass. It appears to represent the escapade of an undergraduate just arrived in London from Oxford, perhaps interrupted by an irate father

$7\frac{1}{8} \times 11\frac{5}{8}$ in.

RECRUITS   See No 4766—1. Jan. 1780

(Watson and Dickinson after Bunbury. No. 2 of a Series.)

There is a French copy in reverse, called *Recrues anglaises* (caricature), by J Juillet, 1780. *Collection de Vinck*, No. 1201.

5802 A RIDING-HOUSE

Mr Bunbury del.   *J^s Bretherton f*

Published by J^s Bretherton, 15 Feb^y, 1780.

Engraving The interior of a riding-school. A number of men riding round in a circle; those in the foreground ride from r to l, those in the background from l to r. The riding-master stands in the centre, pointing with hand and cane, and grinning at a short fat man in a clerical wig who is running across the room, alarmed at the horses A short obese man in back-view on the extreme r., who is about to mount his horse (r), is identified by a contemporary note as Captain Grose (see Nos. 4683, 5511, 5787, 6145) Next him is a man with a grotesque impression of alarm riding a plunging horse Among the riders are two with clerical wigs. One horse is galloping, out of control, the others are quietly ambling round

Two sides of a high rectangular room or hall are visible; in each wall are two high arch-topped windows

Two impressions, one aquatinted.

$14\frac{3}{8} \times 21\frac{3}{8}$ in.

5803 BILLIARDS.

H. Bunbury Esqʳ Delinᵗ   *Watson & Dickinson Excudⁱ.*
London Publish'd Novʳ 15ᵗʰ 1780 by Watson & Dickinson, Nᵒ 158, New Bond Street.

Stipple No 4 of a series A game of billiards is being played on a table, one corner of which only is visible, so curiously elongated that it gives the impression of a triangular table. The two players stand by the corner of the table, the one who is about to make a stroke appears from his leanness, frogged coat, and long pigtail queue to be a Frenchman, he leans over the table in profile to the l , wearing pince-nez. His opponent watches him, standing on top-toe, his cue held over his l shoulder, his face screwed up in anxiety; he wears a bag-wig A number of spectators look on with expressions of amusement or concern: on the r. two men stand together grinning, on the l a man watches open-mouthed, behind the table a man watches with an expression of alarm, another takes cover behind him with a grin; a small boy stands beside them. In the foreground are two dogs, one, a greyhound, stands between the player's legs.

On the wall behind the table is a rack of cues and two clock-faced scoring boards both pointing to the figure X On the r is a door, on the l. a small casement window. Pictures and prints decorate the wall (l. to r.)· a print of Wilkes (bust) with two caps of liberty, a print of a nymph and satyr, a print of a man seated, T Q.L , a print of a man and woman W.L ; two framed landscapes.

There is another version of this design, apparently etched by Rowlandson, impression (n.d.) in the Fitzwilliam Museum, Cambridge.

$10\frac{1}{16} \times 14\frac{5}{8}$ in

5804 A COLLEGE GATE,
DIVINES GOING UPON DUTY.

H. Bunbury Esqʳ Delinᵗ   *Watson & Dickinson Excudⁱ.*
London Publish'd Novʳ 15ᵗʰ 1780, by Watson & Dickinson Nᵒ 158, New Bond Street.

Stipple. No 5 of a series. Three men riding in different directions, having come through a large gateway of square brick pillars surmounted by stone vases. The rider in the centre on a clumsy horse wears a clerical wig, broad-brimmed hat, and gaiters. On the r , and riding in profile to the r., is a man on a stout cob, wearing boots and a bob-wig. Behind him is a fat old woman with outstretched arms shouting in alarm. On the l., riding in profile to the l., is a thin man riding a more spirited horse, and dressed like a layman Behind him walks a fat divine wearing an academic cap, bands, and a long gown.

Through the gateway in the distance a short fat man in a clerical wig stands on a mounting block, a groom beside him holding his horse. With him are two men wearing mortar-boards and long gowns. Behind a large rectangular building is indicated and behind it a church steeple. For other Cambridge caricatures by Bunbury see Nos. 4723–9

$10 \times 14\frac{3}{4}$ in.

5805 THE TAYLOR TURN'D JOCKEY, OR GOOSE UPON GOOSE.

[c. 1780?]

W.H.B. [Bunbury] *inv*[t]

Engraving. A tailor, in profile to the r, rides a goose, his legs thrust forward on each side of the bird's neck. He wears a small lace-trimmed hat perched on a high toupet-wig. In place of a bag, a cabbage is tied to his queue, emblem of the pieces of cloth called 'cabbage' which tailors were supposed to appropriate, cf. No. 5399 He holds a yard-stick for a whip, on the end of which is a gherkin-like cucumber A pair of shears protrudes from his coat-pocket. He wears spatterdashes and sharp spurs resembling those worn by game-cocks In the upper r corner of the plate is etched, *A Poor Taylor riding against time for a bushell of cucumbers N B   A Dung*[t]

In a perennial dispute between London master-tailors and their journeymen, those who belonged to clubs (embryo trade unions) and resisted the masters were called Flints, the others were stigmatized as Dungs See F. W Galton, *The Tailoring Trade*. In the summer there was much seasonal unemployment among tailors and there was a London saying, 'Tailors two a penny, cucumbers twice as many'.

$5\frac{5}{16} \times 4\frac{5}{8}$ in.   In book of Sayer's 'Drolls'.

5806 THE COMPLIMENTS OF THE SEASON
KIBE HEELS AND CHILBLAINS.   [c. 1780?]

W H B [Bunbury] *inv*[t]

Engraving. The interior of a poverty-stricken room. An old man (l.) seated in a chair is rubbing one foot which rests on a low stool with the contents of a bottle held in his r. hand. He wears a night-cap, his hat and wig hang on the back of his chair A witch-like woman, wearing large spectacles, is seated by the fire, she holds on her lap the bare leg of a young man, and is about to apply to it the contents of a pot which she is stirring on the fire He is yelling with pain. On the wall is a placard, *D*[r] *Steers Opodeldoc for Chilblains*

Poverty is indicated by the untidy bed, a broken casement window, and the character of the chimney-piece, on which is a lighted candle, a tea-pot, and a broken cup Over it is a print of a man, T Q L Probably a quack chiropodist's establishment of a very humble kind.

$6\frac{3}{8} \times 5\frac{11}{16}$ in.   In book of Sayer's 'Drolls'.

5807 [PEDLARS]   [n.d.]

Eliza B. Gulston[1] fecit.

Engraving. A freely drawn sketch of three figures. A Jew in profile to the r. holds a glass show-box which is supported by a strap round his shoulders. Facing him in profile to the l is a man with a large pack tied to his back, he is looking at the Jew's wares, one hand held up as in surprise Between them, and full-face, stands a Dutchman (?) wearing trousers and smoking a pipe, he is looking at the Jew's show-case [2]

Above the heads of the figures a devil is flying, he holds two strings, one of which is attached to the neck of each pedlar

Probably a satire on the dishonesty of pedlars and hawkers Cf Colquhoun, *Treatise on the Police of the Metropolis,* 1796, &c.

$7\frac{3}{8} \times 6$ in   'Honorary Engravers', ii, No. 70.

5808–5813

A series of six plates, numbered 1–6, all with the same publication line and date.

5808 BOOK 25 THE MODERN HARLOT'S PROGRESS, OR ADVENTURES OF HARRIET HEEDLESS

HARRIET HEEDLESS, APPLYING TO A STATUE [*sic*] HALL FOR A PLACE, IS SEEN BY A RAKE, AND DECOY'D BY A BAWD AN OLD FELLOW CHUCKS A GIRL'S CHIN, AND OTHER CHARACTERS ARE LOOKING FOR SERVANTS, OR SERVICES 97

Printed for & Sold by Carington Bowles, at his Map & Print Warehouse, No 69 in St Pauls Church Yard London.

Published as the Act directs, 15 May 1780.

Engraving (coloured impression) The first of a series of six plates, they appear to have formed 'Book 25' of a larger series, in which this is No 97. As the title shows it is a modernized imitation of Hogarth's *Harlot's Progress* (see Nos 2031, 2046, 2061, 2075, 2091, 2106) As in Hogarth's series, the first plate represents the arrival of a country girl in London to find a place as a servant The place of the inn-yard is taken by a 'Statute Hall', that is, a room where masters and mistresses went to inspect and engage servants, a few pence being paid for admission

The hall here depicted appears to be well built and clean The window is in three divisions, the centre one arched On each side of it hangs an elaborately framed oval mirror The door (r.) opens on a rod, to ensure its automatic closing Two sporting prints or pictures are on the wall (l.). The manager of the place stands at a high writing-desk writing, and in conversation with the 'Rake' who is looking at Harriet Heedless through an eye-glass. He is in riding-dress

The two centre figures are Harriet (r.) and the 'Bawd' who stands in profile to the r. handing the girl a card inscribed [*Pal*]*l Mall*. Harriet is neatly dressed like a country girl in a cap, a kerchief over her bodice, and an apron In her l. hand is a small box inscribed *H. H.* The 'Bawd' is dressed like a woman of fashion, with high-dressed hair. A man in riding

---

[1] d. 1780
[2] In 1765 Cole compared the Paris shop-windows to the show-cases carried about by Jews *Cole's Paris Journal,* 1931, p 50

dress seated on a stool watches their conversation with interest. A dog lies near him. A woman of similar appearance and dress to the bawd, holding a fan, stands against the wall (l) with a younger woman who is more plainly dressed. By the door (r) is a group of maid-servants and men who may be either servants, spectators, or employers. Behind, a man is chucking a demure-looking girl under the chin

Such statute-halls are described by R. King in *The Frauds of London detected* . . . [c. 1770] as a flagrant and bare-faced cheat, the proprietors often procurers. The name derives from the annual statute fairs or mops held in the country for the hiring of servants.

$6\frac{1}{8} \times 10\frac{1}{8}$ in.

5809 HARRIET INTRODUCED TO THE RAKE, IN THE CHARACTER OF A SERVANT, WHILE THE BAWD SKULKS BEHIND THE DOOR. 98

Engraving (coloured impression) See No. 5808 A well-furnished panelled room in which a large curtained bed (l.) is partly visible A man is seated beside a table on which is a white cloth: on it are a book and the *Morning Post* newspaper. He wears a flowered dressing-gown and his hair is in curl-papers Harriet advances into the room carrying a round tray, on it is a bowl and plate. She wears a cap, a kerchief round her bodice, and a looped-up apron over a quilted petticoat. 'The bawd' stands by the door (r.), which she appears to be opening for Harriet. Through the open door is seen the staircase with a tall sash window A maid-servant with a broom stands outside watching Harriet's entry

The room has a carpet with an arabesque pattern, two chairs stand against the back wall on which are two T.Q L. portraits. one of a lady in a domino holding a mask, the other of a man wearing a hat Between them is an oval picture of Cupid, blindfolded, with a bow and arrows On the r. of the door (r.), which is at r. angles to the back wall, is an oval mirror in an ornate frame, with candelabra.

$6\frac{1}{8} \times 10\frac{1}{8}$ in

5810 HARRIET IN HIGH KEEPING, EQUIP'D IN A RIDING HABIT, ATTENDED BY A BLACK; THE FOOTMAN PEEPING AT HER WITH INTENT TO DELIVER HER A LETTER PRIVATELY. 99

Engraving (coloured impression). See No 5808. Harriet and her protector sit side by side on a settee. He looks at her, holding her l. hand, his r hand rests on her shoulder. He is in riding-dress; she wears a riding habit: full skirt, coat and waistcoat of masculine cut, and a cravat, elaborately-dressed hair, and a feathered hat In her r hand is a riding switch She looks straight in front of her, not at her lover. A little black boy (l) offers her a glass of wine on a salver. A dog sits on the settee, his front paws on his master's knee On the r. is an open door round which a footman is furtively looking

They are in a panelled room, of which two walls are visible In the centre of the back wall is a window through which can be seen a lady driving in a high phaeton, a coachman on the box; behind are houses. On each side of the window is a framed landscape. In the l wall is another window, through which trees are visible. Next it (r.) is an oval mirror elaborately framed. In front of the window is a small oblong table covered with a cloth, on which are a bottle of wine, a glass, &c. To the r of the settee stands a dressing-table, with a muslin cover, its looking-glass draped with white muslin. Chairs with carved oval backs stand against the wall On the floor is a carpet with an arabesque pattern.

6×10 in.

5811 HARRIET BEING DISCOVERED BY HER KEEPER IN MAK-ING AN APPOINTMENT WITH HIS FOOTMAN, FAINTS AWAY, WHILE THE MAID LISTENS TO KNOW THE RESULT. 100

Engraving (coloured impression) See No 5808 Harriet sits as if asleep in a high-backed arm-chair by a round table, over which her protector leans, holding a large sheet of paper on which is engraved *Dear William meet me under the Piazza at 6 o'Clock.* An ink-stand and pens are on the table. Harriet is plainly dressed in a cap, a checked kerchief, a lace-trimmed apron, her dress is worn over a quilted petticoat Her lover is in riding dress Through an open door (l) a maidservant is looking Two walls of the room are visible. In the back wall is a window in three sections, the centre one having a semicircular top. Through the window trees and a lake or river are visible On each side of the wall are two pictures, one above the other; three are landscapes, the fourth (r) is of a lady (T Q L) at whom a cupid is aiming his bow. To the r. of the window is a semi-circular dressing-table. A flowered dressing-gown lies on a chair by the table. Against the wall to the l of the window is a tall curtained bed, whose curtains are almost completely drawn. The room has a carpet with an arabesque pattern

$6\frac{1}{16} \times 10\frac{1}{16}$ in.

5812 HARRIET BEING DISCARDED FOR HER INFIDELITY, TAKES LODGINGS, TURNS COMMON, IS ATTENDED BY RAKES AND GAMESTERS, AND FURNISHED BY THE MILLENER, WITH DRESSES TO CONTINUE HER PROSTITU-TION. 101

Engraving (coloured impression) See No. 5808 Harriet seated by a table; she holds a snuffbox and appears to be taking snuff. A negress stands by her (l) filling a wine-glass from a jug. They are being watched by a man who stands behind the table holding a cane or riding whip, his hands on his hips At the end of the table (r) sits a fashionably dressed milliner in profile to the l ; she holds a lace cap with lappets On the table are playing cards and an open book, *Hoyles Games* Behind the milliner and standing near the open door (r) is her apprentice, holding a box; she is being chucked under the chin by a soldier who sits in a chair against the wall. At a round table (l.) a soldier sits with a tankard, a pipe with a broken stem is on the table.

Only the back wall of the room is visible; in it are two open doors, one on the r., the other behind Harriet; a man looks from behind this door with a grin. Through it a window is visible, and through the window appear the masts of a ship, suggesting that Harriet has found lodgings in the doubtful neighbourhood of Wapping. Next the door (r) a ballad is pinned up, *Man of Fashion*, headed with a design of a ship Next this is a large framed picture of Roman architecture in ruins A plain mirror hangs next it. Over the door on the r is a framed picture of a naval battle. On the extreme l. is a curtained bed, the curtains hanging from a bent rod. The floor is of boards, but under and round the table is a carpet or large rug. Except for the bed the room has no appearance of squalor

6 × 10⅛ in.

5813 HARRIET TAINTED WITH DISEASE, GOES INTO A WORK-HOUSE; WHERE THE DOCTOR ATTENDED BY HIS FOOT-BOY, BRINGS HER A DRAUGHT, THE NURSE DESCRIBES HER ILLNESS, AND THE OTHER FIGURES ARE CURIOUSLY EM-PLOYED 102

Engraving (coloured impression) See No 5808 The interior of a large room Harriet reclines in an arm-chair, her head and shoulders wrapped in a shawl, looking very ill. The central figures of the design are the doctor and the nurse; she is a stout gaily-dressed woman, standing full-face, one hand on her hip The doctor is handing her a bottle, with a label inscribed *Going to rest.* He wears a hat, a large curled wig, and a cloak, and holds a long cane, behind him stands his foot-boy carrying a basket containing medicine bottles. On the r is a large open fire, by it sits a woman nursing an infant, an old woman smoking a pipe sits on a bench opposite the fire, two old women stand by it, one supported by crutches holds out a wine-glass to the other In the foreground (r) a heap of coal lies on the floor, a shovel lies beside it. A kneeling man fills a tankard from a large leather bottle, he has perhaps been shovelling the coal A small boy sits on the ground (r) by a large window, using the window seat as a table, he is eating with a spoon from a plate. Above the fireplace is a framed inscription. *Rules for the better Regulation of Workhouses.* On a shelf beneath this is a teapot, cups, and other pieces of crockery Two square posts support the ceiling, to each is hung a woman's hat and cloak. They serve as supports for a clothes' line on which hang a patched blanket or curtain, a pair of stockings, and other garments Along the back wall of the room are high curtained beds.

This series shows an interesting change of manners since Hogarth's *Harlot's Progress* (1734) The most striking change is in the substitution of the workhouse for punishment in Bridewell (see No. 2075). In this print the doctor and the nurse appear to be doing their best for the patient in marked contrast with the scene in Hogarth's fifth plate (No 2091)

6⅛ × 10⅛ in.

Thirteen prints from the series of mezzotints published by Caring-ton Bowles [1]

5814 A MAN-TRAP

[? J. R. Smith.]

412. *Printed for & Sold by Carington Bowles, at his Map & Print Warehouse, No 69 in St Pauls Church Yard, London. Publish'd as the Act directs* [date erased c. 1780].

Mezzotint (coloured impression). A young woman, fashionably dressed,

[1] No 3761 has the imprint of Bowles and Carver, the uncoloured impression that of Carington Bowles.

reclining on a garden seat, under trees, her dress cut very low. Behind the seat (r) is a notice board, *Spring Guns set here*.

Similar in manner to Nos 5820, 5823, 5824.

Reproduced, M. C. Salaman, *Old English Mezzotints*, 1910, Pl. lxxv.

12¾×9⅞ in   'Caricatures', ii, p 92. B M.L , Tab 524.

5815 THE CONTEMPLATIVE CHARMER.

413. *Printed for & Sold by Carington Bowles, at his Map & Print Warehouse, N° 69 in St Pauls Church Yard. Publish'd as the Act directs, 6th Jany 1780.*

Mezzotint (coloured impression). A young woman seated on a settee, directed to the l but looking coyly to the r Her legs are crossed and are well defined under her skirt, she wears an elaborate muslin cap Behind her (l) hangs on the wall a vertical letter-rack with divisions for each day of the week from *Sunday* to *Saturday*, in each of these are cards, the lowest being inscribed *Admit two to the Boxes Ca Bo. . . .* A candle sconce also hangs on the wall.

Another impression is in 'Caricatures', ii, p 93.

12¾×9⅞ in.

5816 A SOFT TUMBLE AFTER A HARD RIDE   [c. 1780]

John Collet, del.

414. *Printed for & Sold by Bowles & Carver, at their Map & Print Warehouse, N° 69 in St Pauls Church Yard, London Published as the Act directs*

Mezzotint (coloured impression). A hunting scene. A huntsman falls over the head of his horse, which has fallen in leaping a five-barred gate (l) He is about to fall on to a young lady who lies on her back, having been thrown from her horse, which is galloping away (r.). A second lady is leaping the gate, her whip raised high above her head. Four dogs add to the confusion

12¾×9⅞ in   'Caricatures', i, p 226. B.M.L., Tab. 524.

5817 THE LADIES SHOOTING PONEY.

415. From the Original Picture by John Collet, in the possession of Carington Bowles

Printed for & Sold by Carington Bowles, at his Map & Print Ware-house, N° 69 in St Pauls Church Yard London Published as the Act directs [date erased c. 1780].

Mezzotint (coloured impression). A lady, in profile to the r , is firing a gun which she supports on the neck of a pony which is quietly grazing She wears a feathered hat, a coat of masculine cut over a narrow skirt, with high-heeled shoes. A powder-horn is slung across her shoulder. A man dressed as groom or postilion crouches down behind her (r.). A second lady stands behind him putting a ramrod down the barrel of her gun. Trees and water form a background.

12⅞×9¾ in.   'Caricatures', ii, p 73. B M.L., Tab. 524.

5818 THE PLEASURES OF SKAITING—OR, A VIEW IN WINTER.

417. From the Original Picture by John Collet, in the possession of Carington Bowles

Printed for & Sold by Carington Bowles, at his Map & Print Ware-house, Nᵒ 69 in Sᵗ Pauls Church Yard, London. Published as the Act directs 12 Apr. 1780.

Mezzotint (coloured and uncoloured impressions). A skater lies on his back on the ice, his hat has fallen off, his muff and cane lie beside him From his pocket projects a paper, *The Art of Rolling made easy* Behind him a lady skates with ease and assurance, her arms folded. Behind her another man lies on the ground Behind (r) a skater looks at the prostrate man through an eye-glass In the middle distance two skaters, a man and a woman, face each other. In the background are bare shrubs and trees and a country house.

Another impression in 'Caricatures', B M L , Tab 524, 11, p 75.

$12\frac{3}{4} \times 9\frac{3}{4}$ in.

5819 THE PRETTY WATERWOMAN, OR ADMIRAL PURBLIND JUST RUN A-GROUND BY PEGGY PULLAWAY.

418 From the Original Picture by John Collet, in the possession of Carington Bowles.

Printed for & Sold by Carington Bowles, at his Map & Print Ware-house, Nᵒ 69 in Sᵗ Pauls Church Yard London Published as the Act directs, 12 April 1780.

Mezzotint (coloured impression). A gaily-dressed young woman sculling a naval officer who sits in the stern, holding his cane in the water and looking through a single eye-glass at a swan accompanied by a cygnet A King Charles dog puts its paws on the edge of the boat and looks at the swan. The admiral is in naval uniform with a pigtail queue. The lady wears a feathered hat tilted forward on her high-dressed hair and a low-cut bodice; on the stern of the boat is a design of a cupid riding on a dolphin. The water winds among lawns, trees, and bushes. In the middle distance two ladies are fishing; one holds a rod over the water, the other, seated beside her, holds up a fish.

Reproduced, C. N. Robinson, *The British Tar in Fact and Fiction*, 1909, p. 248

$12\frac{3}{4} \times 9\frac{7}{8}$ in.

5820 THE ANGELIC ANGLER. [1780]

[J R. Smith *del et sc*]

420. *Printed for & Sold by Carington Bowles, at his Map & Print Warehouse, Nᵒ 69 in Sᵗ Pauls Church Yard, London. Published as the Act directs* [date erased].

Mezzotint (coloured impression). A young woman stands full-face beside a stream, in her r. hand is a fishing-rod, in her l. she holds the line, pulling out of the water a fish she has hooked She is dressed in the fashion of the day, wearing a hat and a cloak over her dress with its muslin apron. Trees form a background.

Beneath the title is engraved,

To be decoy'd is Men and Fishes fate,—With Cupid's Line when Beauty is the Bait

$12\frac{7}{8} \times 9\frac{7}{8}$ in.   'Caricatures', ii, p. 80   B.M.L., Tab. 524.

A smaller version·

5820A THE ANGELIC ANGLER.

309. Printed for Carington Bowles, N° 69 in S¹ Paul's Church Yard, London. Published as the Act directs 12 Apr. 1780

$5\frac{1}{2} \times 4\frac{1}{2}$ in

This design (pl. 9×7 in.) was published by J R Smith, June 10, 1780. Frankau, p. 53·

5821 MISS CALASH IN CONTEMPLATION.

421 Printed for & Sold by Carington Bowles, at his Map & Print Warehouse, N° 69 in S¹ Pauls Church Yard, London. Published as the Act directs [date erased 1780].

Mezzotint (coloured impression) A young woman walking (r. to l), looking towards the spectator, her arms folded, holding a book She wears a barrel-shaped calash-hood (see No. 5433) She is framed in the mouth of a grotto, behind her is a piece of artificial water which surrounds a grass plot planted symmetrically with trees Beneath the title is engraved, *This Lady reads, then Tripping Thro' the Grove.—Turns all her thoughts to rural bliss and love.*

$12\frac{7}{8} \times 9\frac{7}{8}$ in   'Caricatures', ii, p 97. B M L , Tab 524

THE TRIPLE PLEA (422)   See No 3761—15 May 1780

After Collet

A satire on the Clergy, Lawyers, and Physicians. Also a dated impression, uncoloured.

5822 THE VICTIM

From the Original Picture by John Collet, in the possession of Carington Bowles.

426. Printed for & Sold by Carington Bowles, at his Map & Print Warehouse, N° 69 in S¹ Pauls Church Yard, London. Publish'd as the Act directs [date erased, 1780].

Mezzotint (coloured impression). An elderly man seated in an arm-chair, in night-cap and dressing-gown, a crutch by his side, holds by the wrist a young girl, who is being brought to him by a stout woman The girl holds a handkerchief to her eyes; she is gaily and meretriciously dressed.

A monkey (l) holds a cat, a dog sits on a chair (r.); a cat plays with a glove which hangs from the chair. On the wall (r) is a framed picture of a sheep about to be sacrificed before an altar. On the ground are books:

on the *Art of Love* (l) stands a bottle of *Viper Wine* A large volume (l)
is labelled *Rochester*, indicating that it contains the works of the rake,
Rochester (d 1680) On it is an open book inscribed,

> *This Bud of Beauty, other Years demands,*
> *Nor should be gather'd by such wither'd hands*

This is adapted from a picture by Collet, an engraving after which is
No. 4184 (1767), where the figures are T Q L Among other changes, the
costumes have been altered to adapt them to the prevailing fashion
$12\frac{7}{8} \times 9\frac{15}{16}$ in   'Caricatures', B M.L., Tab. 524, 1, p. 199.

Reproduced C. E. Jensen, *Karikatur-album*, 1906, 1, p. 152

5823 A LADY IN WAITING.

[J. R. Smith *del et sc*]

*427 Printed for & Sold by Carington Bowles, at his Map & Print
Warehouse, N° 69 in St Pauls Church Yard, London. Publish'd as
the Act directs* [date erased *c.* 1780]

Mezzotint (coloured impression). A lady seated on a grassy bank under
trees in the fields near London, the buildings of which with the dome of
St. Paul's are seen in the distance (r), across a piece of water She is
fashionably dressed, with a large hat and elbow-length gloves She looks
coyly expectant

Reproduced, M. C Salaman, *Old English Mezzotints*, 1910, Pl lxxiv.

This design (pl $9\frac{3}{4} \times 7$ in.) was published by J. R. Smith, June 10,
1780, see Frankau, pp. 156-7.
$12\frac{7}{8} \times 9\frac{7}{8}$ in.   'Caricatures', ii, p 95 B M L , Tab 524.

5824 A FOOLISH WOMAN.

[J. R. Smith *del et sc.*]

*428. Printed for & Sold by Carington Bowles, at his Map & Print
Warehouse, N° 69 in St Pauls Church Yard, London. Published as
the Acts directs 2 Sep 1780.*

Mezzotint (coloured impression) A courtesan seated on a curiously
shaped wooden seat placed against a wall at right angles to the door of a
house. She sits directed to the l , her legs crossed, one hand raised as if
beckoning She is similar in dress and appearance to No. 5823. The seat
is ornamented with a satyr's mask and a carved vine-branch with clusters
of grapes. Beneath the title is engraved, *For she sitteth at the door of her
house on a seat, in the high places of the city: To call passengers who go right
on their ways. Proverbs, Ch. IX vers 14 & 15*

Frankau, p. 125. Another impression is in 'Caricatures', ii, p. 99.
B M.L., Tab 524.
$12\frac{7}{8} \times 9\frac{7}{8}$ in.

A WIFE AT CONFESSION . . . (429)   No. 3778—[1780]

POLITICAL SATIRES

5825 THE DUTCH IN THE DUMPS

Pubᵈ Jan · 4 1781 by H Humphrey Nᵒ 18 New Bond Street.

Engraving (coloured and uncoloured impressions). Two English sailors (l) exulting together over Dutch prizes They clasp hands, one (r.) holds up a Dutchman's breeches, the pocket turned out, and shakes coins from it; he has a club under his l. arm. The other holds the end of his club in his r. coat-pocket saying, *Dam-me Jack who Pays the Reckoning now*, the other answers, *The Dutch my boy* A Dutch sailor (r.) stands with his hands held by his sides, his shoulders hunched despondently; he is saying, *Damn de French & Spaniards I vish ve had nothing to do vit dem for dis Jack English vil trim our ludes most damnably.* Three small Dutch single-masted vessels are lying by the shore, dismantled, the British flag flying above the (plain) Dutch flag On the ground in front of the figures are a square bottle inscribed *Hollands Gin*, another pair of breeches, with the pocket inside out, disgorging coins, and a bale of goods.

Beneath the design is etched:

> *Perfidious Dutchmen now beware*
> *When e'er you treat with France*
> *For as they all can caper well*
> *It's we will make you dance.*

On 20 Dec 1780 a manifesto was published giving reasons for the commencement of hostilities, letters of marque and reprisal were granted against the Dutch and within a few days many ships were taken. See *Ann. Reg*, 1781, pp 162 ff

The declaration of war was popular in general, though it was attacked by the Opposition. Cf Walpole, *Last Journals*, 1910, ii 342.

See also Nos. 5664, 5712-33, 5826, 5827, 5828, 5830, 5837.

Van Stolk, No. 4310.

$6\frac{1}{2} \times 9\frac{3}{16}$ in.

Van Stolk describes (No. 4338) a pseudo-English, Dutch print by P. Dutsman, BEDLAM OF THE WORLD, *Published according to Act of Parliament, 5 Jan 1781.* George III as the button-maker, see No 5573, &c., with a card of buttons in his hand, asleep, holding the manifesto to the Netherlands of 10 Dec 1780 [? 20 Dec.] A snake is inscribed *Sir J. York.* On a placard is the inscription *New Description of the whole of Great Britain except the estates of Richmond, Portland, Devonshire, Ferrers, Rockingham, Harcourt and Fitzwilliam.*

The names show that the print was published after 25 Jan. 1781, and is a comment on the important debate in the Lords on that day on the rupture with Holland, when a protest against the Address on the rupture was signed by Richmond, Portland, Fitzwilliam, Harcourt, Ferrers, Rockingham, Devonshire, Pembroke, and Coventry *Parl Hist.* xxi. 1075-7.

For other Dutch prints see Nos 5712-34, 5839, 5859, 6292

5826 TRIA JUNCTA IN UNO.

OR

THE THREE ENEMIES OF BRITTAIN.

I. Nixon, Fecit.

Pub^d as the Act directs, 17 Jany 1781, by W Wells N° 132, opposite Salisbury-Court, Fleet Street.

Engraving Caricatures of a Frenchman, a Dutchman, and a Spaniard, representing France, Holland, and Spain. All have large heads, and expressions of great alarm France (l.), in profile to the r , a foppish *petit-maître* with an enormously long pigtail queue and voluminous lace ruffles, holds out his hands, saying to Holland, *Ah¹ Myneer vat is de mater?* Holland (c) is a fat peasant or burgher wearing breeches reaching almost to the ankles, and a hat like an inverted flower-pot, a pipe thrust through the hat-band His hands are in his breeches-pockets and he says *Oh Yontle-mans, Yontlemans¹ da Unglish be playing de very diable mid us* Spain (r.) is a don with a feathered hat, ruff, slashed doublet and breeches, cloak, and spurred boots, he has a beard and long moustaches He holds out his hands in alarm and turns to Holland, saying *Vat News Myneer?* Beneath the design is engraved:

> *Three Bullys in three distant Countries born*
> *France, Spain & Holland, would adorn;*
> *The first in Craft & Cowardice, surpased*
> *The next in Haughtiness, in both the last.*
> *Old Satans power could no further go*
> *To make a Third he join'd the former Two.*

One of many satires on the Dutch in connexion with the declaration of war, 20 Dec. 1780. See No. 5825, &c.

$6\frac{3}{8} \times 9\frac{1}{8}$ in

5827 THE BALLANCE OF POWER

R S (Monogram)

London. Published as y^e Act directs, Jany 17. 1781. by R Wilkinson, at N° 58 in Cornhill.

Engraving A pair of scales whose beam is engraved *The Ballance of Power.* On the l. scale, which rests on the ground, stands Britannia holding her shield in her r hand, and in the left a short Roman sword inscribed *The Sword of Justice* She says, *No one injures me with impunity* On the other scale are the four enemies of England, in spite of the desperate efforts of Holland who clings to one of its ropes, his feet on its base, this scale is in the air, outweighed by Britannia America as an Indian woman with a head-dress of feathers sits on the scale, her head resting on her hand, her eyes closed in an attitude of despondency, she says *My Ingratitude is Justly punished.* France and Spain dressed in the conventional manner of carica-ture, one as a French fop, the other in the slashed doublet and cloak of a Spanish don, stand behind America. France says, *Myneer assist or we are ruin'd,* Spain says, *Rodney has ruined our Fleet.* Holland, as a Dutchman smoking a pipe, is saying *I'll do any thing for Money,* coins inscribed *Ill got wealth,* are pouring from his unbuttoned breeches-pocket, two papers are also falling from him, one inscribed *St Eustatia Saba St Martin*, the other *Demerary Issequibo*

Beneath the design is engraved:

> America, dup'd by a treacherous train,
> Now finds she's a Tool both to France and to Spain;
> Yet all three united can't weigh down the Scale:
> So the Dutchman jumps in with the hope to prevail.
> Yet Britain will boldly their efforts withstand,
> And bravely defy them by Sea and by Land:
> The Frenchman She'll Drub, and the Spaniard She'll Beat
> While the Dutchman She'll Run by Seizing his Fleet
> Th' Americans too will with Britons Unite,
> And each to the other be Mutual Delight.

This is an allusion to the 'ill got wealth' of Holland by contraband trade in which she used her islands in the West Indies and her possessions on the South American coast, see No 5557, &c It anticipates the capture of the Dutch colonies· the capture of St. Eustatius, 3 Feb. 1781, with its dependencies, St Martin and Saba, and the capitulation of Demerara and Essequibo to privateers, 14 Mar. 1781 Adolphus, *Hist of England*, 1841, iii. 259, 261. See No. 5825, &c. Cf No 5712

$8\frac{7}{8} \times 13$ in.

No 5827 appears to be the original of a German print altered by the addition of a background showing Gibraltar, published *A Augsbourg chez J Mart Will Fauxbourg S Jacques* Beneath the print is an explanation in German and bad French in two columns, the French being, (1) *La balance de la puissance.* (2) [England] *Ne persoñe m'offense sans puni* (3) *L'Epee de la Justice* (4) [Spain] *Rodney a ruiné notre Flotte* (4) [France] *Monsieur, aidez à nous ou nous soñes perdu* (6) [America] *Mon ingratitude est puni come tous raison.* (7) [Holland] *Je ferai quelque chose pour l'argent.* Probably issued after the defeat of the attack on Gibraltar, see No. 6035, &c. *Collection de Vinck*, No. 1181

5828 JACK ENGLAND FIGHTING THE FOUR CONFEDERATES.

Printed for Jno Smith N° 35 Cheapside, Robt Sayer & Jno Bennet N° 53 Fleet Street, Jany 20, 1781

Engraving (coloured impression). An English sailor (l.) with clenched fists faces Holland, France, Spain, and America, all but the first appearing *hors de combat* Numbers indicate the names of the 'Four Confederates' which are given below the design (1) America (r), *Yanky Doodle*, an Indian brave with a feathered head-dress and girdle, is prone on the ground, his spear beside him; he says *This fall has hurt my Back.* (2) France or *Monsieur Louis Baboon* dressed as a French fop with a bag-wig, is vomiting, his hand across his breast, his knees bent; he says, *Dem Jersey Pills have made a me Sick* (3) Spain or *Don Diego*, dressed as a Spanish don, is bleeding from one eye, he stands behind America, saying *by St Jago he has almost Blinded me.* These three are grouped together on the l, turning away from Jack England. No. 4 or *Mynheer Frog*, dressed as a Dutch peasant, is standing with his legs wide apart, his fists clenched, smoking a pipe, he faces Jack, saying *I have almost forgot how to fight.* In the background are ships.

Beneath the title is engraved:

> *To Arms you Brave Britons to Arms the*
> *Road to Renown Lyes before you.*

This represents the situation at the beginning of 1781 The taking of Charlestown on 12 May 1780 by Clinton, the victory of Cornwallis at Camden (16 Aug. 1780), and a temporary British naval supremacy on the American coast had reduced the Americans to serious straits. The declaration of war with Holland (20 Dec. 1780) was hailed as an opportunity for the British navy and privateers, since Holland was 'less troublesome as a declared enemy than as a very nominal neutral'. *Camb Hist of the Br: Empire*, 1 750 See No 5557, &c. At the beginning of 1781 the French made a second attempt on Jersey and surprised St. Helier on 6 Jan , but were immediately afterwards completely defeated by Major Pierson and forced to surrender *Ann Reg*, 1782, pp. 96-9 *London Gazette Extraordinary*, 9 Jan. 1781.

There is an aquatint of the fighting in St Helier on 6 Jan. in the Print Department, published on 24 Apr. 1781 by Colley and Hedges, 288 Strand $6\frac{5}{8} \times 8\frac{1}{16}$ in.

5829 ADMINISTRATION & OPPOSITION AS EXHIBITED APRIL 3RD 1780 AT THE PANTHEON MASQUERADE

O'Brien Inv[t] &c[t].
Publish'd as the act directs Jan'y 1781 price 1s. plain, Col[d] 1 s 6[d].[1]

Engraving (coloured impression) Two men dressed as if for a masquerade stand side by side The bodies of both are covered with grotesque masks, which are intended as caricatures of supporters of the Ministry and Opposition respectively Each wears a peaked cap almost covered by a pictorial placard *Administration* (l) is a stout rubicund man capering with an expression of convivial jollity, he holds a wine-bottle in his r hand, an embossed goblet in his l. On the placard on his cap is a fat pig guzzling grapes inscribed *Administration*. His person is almost covered by seven masks, all grinning with expressions of sly satisfaction. One beneath the wearer's chin appears to be intended for North, next it on the r. is probably Sandwich; all are grotesquely caricatured, with large mouths and a display of teeth

The figure on the r and the masks with which he is decorated have expressions of melancholy ferocity. The placard on his cap is inscribed *Opposition* and depicts a fox trying in vain to reach the grapes above his head The only mask which can be identified with any certainty is that of Wilkes, squinting violently *Opposition* holds out to *Administration* a paper inscribed *The Scourge N° 17 To the Ministry*. This was a libellous and scurrilous pamphlet against the Government issued by one W. Moore weekly from 1 Jan. to 8 June 1780, which was followed up during the Gordon Riots by inflammatory leaflets entitled 'The Thunderer' and 'England in Blood', see Nos 5685, 5844 No 17 (20 May 1780) contains inflammatory verses, 'The Cries of Liberty for a Redress of Grievances Vox Populi Vox Dei', ending with an appeal for 'another glorious Revolution', unless grievances are redressed. (B M L , P P. 5394 d)

---

[1] '1 s' and '1 s 6[d]' have been written in ink in space left by the engraver

In his l. hand *Opposition* holds out papers inscribed *Scheme of Oeconomy in the State* and *Count[y] Petit[ions]*

Beneath the design, in two columns, songs are etched:

Song by ADMINISTRATION.

Let hungry Patriots lick their lips at our rich-season'd dainties,
And snap & snarl, we mind them not, well knowing all in vain 'tis;
Inquiries & Impeachments, & State Reformation schemes Sir
To Us (when seated round good Wine) are but as mirthfull themes Sir,
For of our annual Thousands sure in Coffers we can store 'em,
To laugh & joke & sing & smoke & push about the Jorum

(Two more verses follow)

Song by OPPOSITION.

Tho' laughter now characterize our vile Administration,
The Curs will snivel when we've jostl'd each one from his Station.
For like Distiller's grain-fed Hogs they swill & gorge & sleep,
But soon for food they shall be forc'd a sharp look out to keep,
So Brother Patriots, one & all, let's steadfast be & warm O,
In carry'ng on our rustling, bustling tustling State Reform O.

(Two more verses follow)

Across the bottom of the sheet is etched:

Song, sung by the above Characters, after having form'd a Coalition

1ˢᵗ Since Opposition has at length put on her Wings & fled,
 And Coalition's taken place in party jingling's stead.
  A drinking we will go &cᵗ
2ⁿᵈ I say since we're all friends together let us sing & drink,
 And deem that Man an Ass who from his bumper first does shrink,
  And sneaking home does go &cᵗ
3ʳᵈ Now North Germaine & Sandwich Richmond Shelburne Fox & Barre,
 No longer need bark at each other till their jaws are weary,
  But a drinking may all go &c
4ᵗʰ And as for State reforming plans—why we shall let them drop,
 Since from the dripping pan each party now can take a sop
  Then a drinking may all go &cᵗ

This, of course, is far from representing the political situation in 1781. The overtures to the Rockingham Whigs in 1779 and 1780 had come to nothing and the coalition of Fox and North could not then have been anticipated. One of the few satires attacking the Opposition, see Nos. 5334, 5644, 5665, 5836, 5962. For County Petitions see No 5638, &c
$8\frac{3}{16} \times 11\frac{11}{16}$ in.

5830 MYNEER NIC FROGS LAMENTATION;
       OR DUTCH MILK A FINE RELISH TO ENGLISH SAILORS.

Wells del.

Pubᵈ as the Act directs by W. Wells (Febʸ 2ᵈ, 1781) Nᵒ 132 Fleet Street.

Engraving A Dutchman (1) stands in front of a cow, holding up his hands and turning up his eyes in lamentation; he is smoking a pipe and his

breeches pockets are unbuttoned. He says *Oh I have lost mine Milk &
I shall break mine heart* An English sailor (r.) walks off with a full milk-
pail, he turns towards the Dutchman, saying *You shall have no more Manifesto's Mynheer Bushel A—se,—but a little of your milk we will have by
Virtue of Mam-Fisto's* In the background is the sea, with two ships,
one of which is firing her guns

As a result of war the situation shown in Nos. 5472, 5726, 5727 has been
reversed, see No 5825, &c. 'Nic Frog' was the name given to Holland
in Arbuthnot's famous pamphlet, *Law is a bottomless Pit . . . 1712*, cf.
No. 5541.

$5\frac{3}{4} \times 8\frac{3}{8}$ in.

5831 THE JUNTO, IN A BOWL DISH.

*Pub^d as the Act directs Feby 11th 1781 by W Richardson, N° 68 High
Holborn.*

Engraving. A bowl or boat floats on the sea within the jaws of a monster
with a cat-like face. In it sit seven people, full face, all but one with cat's
whiskers. In the centre is a judge, probably Thurlow the Lord Chancellor,
on his l. is a Scot wearing a plaid, probably Bute, still regarded as potent,
or perhaps Lord Loughborough (Wedderburn), next, a figure whose
anchor shows that he is Sandwich, first Lord of the Admiralty. Then comes
North, wearing his ribbon and star and (incorrectly) a baron's coronet. On
the Chancellor's r is a man with a Grenadier's cap and a banner, perhaps
Jenkinson, the Secretary at War. Next him is a cat-faced man, and on the
outside (l) a judge whose head is framed in a gallows, probably Mansfield.

Four dogs are swimming towards the bowl, their collars inscribed respectively *America* (l), *France, Spain*, and *Holland* (r), the last smaller than
the others and smoking a pipe. In the foreground on the r is the shore;
on it is a decayed oak-tree, overgrown with fungus, in which is planted a
Union flag. Beneath it a skeleton-like greyhound (Scotland) is devouring
a heart and entrails (England's vitals) Beneath the design is engraved·

> *Behold the Ministerial foul Fish*
> *Float in Political Bowl Dish,*
> *Drove at the Pleasure of the Tide,*
> *Assail'd by Foes on ev'ry Side.*
>
> *Alas, Old England, must you Fail*
> *And for such Miscreants turn Tail*
> *America Insults the Nation*
> *And says a Fig for your Taxation.*
>
> *France, Spain & Holland, Join the Cry*
> *And Drive them to their Destiny,*
> *While Scotland pleas'd at all their Deeds*
> *Upon Old Englands Vitals Feeds.*

Van Stolk, No. 4339.

$7\frac{1}{8} \times 12$ in.

Another impression, n d *Pub^d by W Humphrey, N° 227 Strand*

5832 THE VIRTUOUS AND INSPIR'D STATE OF WHIGISM IN
BRISTOL 1781   [*c.* Feb. 1781]

Engraving. A companion print to No 5833 An electioneering procession
A candidate (Henry Cruger) seated in a chaise drawn (r to l) by two men;
behind them is the Devil   Cruger is saying *I come to Establish America's
Independance Listen to my Voice behold my People* In his l. hand he holds
a striped flag inscribed *The Voice of Rebellion is a supreme Law which
passeth all Understanding.* The men drawing the chaise are saying, *America
shall be independent* and *We'll have his Head if the Devil & You will help Us*
One tramples on the royal crown, the other on the scales of Justice The
Devil says, *I'll help You my Children Down with their Ch——h & K——g*

Behind the chaise walks a bull, decorated with rosettes, as if to represent
John Bull decked out for sacrifice, and ridden by an American sailor who
holds out a flag inscribed with thirteen stars. At his back is a bundle
inscribed *Secreted Copies* He is saying *You English Scoundrels hers the
American Flesh & Blood of a Bull.*

In front two men with favours in their hats are conversing· one (l) says
You have made Your Escape for Forgery robery & a Rape P——n [*Parson*]
Green The other (r.), who wears a parson's wig and bands, answers, *And
tis my Belief You'r a Pauper & Thief Mr Chairman.* A pregnant woman
holds up a broken pitcher saying *Croker shall have it*, a child standing
beside her asks *Is that Daddy Croker Mammy* Behind her a man waves his
hat saying *D——n your Eyes you Bch cry Croker* A chimney-sweep (r)
holds up his brush shouting *No blue* [word obliterated], *Obadiah & St
Abigal for ever*

Henry Cruger was member for Bristol from 1774 to 1780, when (like
Burke) he was defeated at the general election Sir Henry Lippincott, one
of the successful candidates, died shortly afterwards, and there was a close
contest between Cruger and George Daubeny. By 20 Feb 1781 both
candidates had obtained 2,474 votes. *Public Advertiser*, 20 Feb. 1781 His
election was financed by the Treasury, see *Parliamentary Papers of John
Robinson*, ed. Laprade, 1922, p. 37, *Corr of George III*, v. 466, 470. See
also Oldfield, *Representative History*, iv 415 Cruger was born and educated
in America, and his correspondence shows that he had in fact been eager
for the independence of America [1] Namier, *England in the Age of the
American Revolution*, p. 297 At the election of 1780 the American flag was
hoisted on many of the churches to suggest that he wished for the success
of America Einstein, *Divided Loyalties*, 1933, p 260 He became Mayor
of Bristol in 1781, and again M P. for Bristol in 1784

Evidently the work of an amateur.

$5\frac{5}{8} \times 7\frac{3}{4}$ in.

5833 LIBERTY ENLIGHTNED   [n d 1781]

Engraving A companion print to No 5832. An elderly man supports on
his head and shoulders a younger man wearing a bag-wig, who lies limply,

---

[1] He congratulates John Hancock (5 Mar. 1783) and his countrymen on 'the
accomplishment of our most sanguine wishes—the Liberty and Independency of
America', and informs him of the connexion he has formed with men 'whose attachment to the American Cause and whose open exertions in it, have at times brought
upon them the most furious persecutions of the Enemies of Liberty As we have
long been united in one political principle, which at length is happily Triumphant,
we are encourag... to form a Commercial Connexion ...'. *New-England Historical
and Genealogical Register*, xxviii 51

holding a striped American flag, and saying, *Go on the Voice of My People is the Voice of God, But Oh Im Sick I feel myself Falling*; CRUGER A ticket is tied to his leg addressed *To Peter Wick Philladelph[ia]* A little boy says to the man supporting Cruger, *Twig Father Peach* Cruger was the son-in-law of Samuel Peach, a prominent Bristol merchant and slave-trader America, as an American Indian with a head-dress and girdle of feathers, a tomahawk and scalping-knife in his belt, stands (l) looking at Cruger, saying *Is our Poor Doodle sick then Farewell, Independence*, his feet are the claws of a bird of prey (Cruger was known in Bristol as Doodle Doo. Einstein, *Divided Loyalties*, p. 247) On the l three men stand behind America one holds up his hands saying, *O we Poor Devils of Yankeys the English have Deceiv'd us*, another says, *and our Spy, is Surrounded by a Thousand Various Difficulties*. The third, who holds a staff and a lantern, says *Lighten our Darkness we beseech O Liberty*; these two wear election favours in their hats. At their feet is a large coil of rope inscribed, *I shall be of Service to Your Congress*, probably implying that Cruger had been exporting naval stores to America On the r a man with a wooden leg is playing a fiddle, from his mouth comes a label *In Old Oliver's Days &c.* Behind are two small figures with flags, one inscribed *Cruger and Wooden Loaf will gull the Mob*, the other, *Supporter of rebellion*, one waves his hat saying *Behold this Pious Dame*. At their feet is a fire on which is an open book inscribed *Fast Day Prayer* (Fast days were ordered from time to time, when there was a service with prayers and sermon for the successful issue of the war.)

Behind is a church, a flag flies from its tower inscribed *Everlasting Prosperity to our Church & King* DAUBENY Outside it are men holding up clubs and stones, saying *an excellent place for S' Abigals*. In the sky (r) is a figure of Fame with two trumpets, through one she announces, *A Broughtonian Bully a Slanderer of Virtue a Yankey Whoremonger.*

This illustrates the contest between Cruger and Daubeny at the by-election for Bristol in February 1781. Cruger was born and educated in America, and eager for the independence of America, see No. 5832 n , though his speeches in the House of Commons in 1775 had been moderate. Einstein, op. cit., Chap. vii, and *Dict Am Biog.*

6×9⅜ in (pl.)

5834 THE BUDGET

Published as the Act directs March 1, 1781 by W Phelps.[1]

Engraving between two columns of explanatory text attacking the finance of the Government Plate III in a set of three, see No 5788. A grotesque monster with four feet, two arms with claws, and a second head in place of its tail represents the National Debt. On its back sit three headless men. It carries a standard inscribed *I am the Kings Friend It's I that Builds his Ships, Mans his Navy, Recruits his Army & I am Grand Pay Master*. A label above its head is inscribed *I will support my friends I have head enough for them all* It devours a paper inscribed *20 millions more* Under

[1] The whole sheet is *Published as the Act Directs, March 1, 1781, and Sold by Messrs Almon and Debrett, in Piccadilly, M* Shepperson, No. 137 Oxford-Road; James Mathews, No 18, in the Strand, near Charing-Cross; Messrs Bull on Ludgate-Hill, and Edward Hedges, at the Royal Exchange; &c &c &c [Price One Shilling and Sixpence plain, & Two Shillings and Sixpence coloured]*

its feet are papers inscribed *30 Millions more* and *40 Millions more* With one of its claws it gashes the breast of Britannia (l.), who stands by its head, one of its fore-paws rests on her foot She puts her hand on a small British lion which frolics beside her, saying to it, *Oh Woe is me poor fellow thou canst not help me.* The monster is saying to Britannia, *I have you & will keep you fast.* On one of its arms hangs a watch and a bunch of seals. The headless rider in the centre (whose figure suggests Lord North) is saying *my heart will Burst through my skin for Joy we Carry every thing our own way*, the other two say. *& mine, and mine too.*

The head at the tail of the animal resembles that of a tiger, it is disgorging a quantity of empty bags and papers inscribed, *empty; empty, &c.,* and is saying, *there my Friends take all the Produce for you Richly Deserve it.* A well-dressed man (r.) stoops over the heap and picks up a bag, saying *heres nothing in it! what all Empty.* Another behind him says, *we are all undone.*

Behind the monster (r.) stands a man holding a flag, pointing to the beast and saying *Your Friends have no Heads* His flag is inscribed *I should be sorry he had no Better* [? head]. *It is you that Strips the Country of our finest Youths and Robs the Parents of their Children the Maidens of their Sweet hearts & Drain the land of its wealth for a Shadow.* Behind him stands a crowd of melancholy-looking citizens, the two foremost are saying *we are all undone what must we do*, and *Oh, oh, oh*

In the lower part of the print (l.) a basket and a sack are inscribed *Salt*, three casks inscribed respectively *Tobacco, Porter, Wine*, and two chests, one inscribed *120,000 guineas for America*. A cat-faced monster is nibbling at the barrel of Porter. In the centre is a low square table laid for a meal, the centre dish being an infant inscribed *a luscious Bit*, demons and almost-nude men with claws surround the table, one is about to devour the child. Behind the table two monsters, one semi-human, are devouring a ham, one saying *its Mine*. A basket of loaves and three fish are inscribed *Provisions for our Friends* Another group (r.) of casks, &c., is inscribed *Cider, Sugar, Rum, Brandy*, two monster-like animals are trying to devour their contents.

In the upper l corner of the print is engraved as if on a placard or poster.

Stock Exchange

3 pr Cent Reduced .	*Nil*
3 Do Consol	*58*
3 & ½ .	*Shut.*
4 pr Cent Consol .	*57*
4 pr Cent 1777 . .	*71*
Short Annuities .	*Shut*
South Seas .	*Shut*
Navy	*13 Dist.*
Omnium Nil	

The explanatory text suggests, though not explicitly, that these monsters are financiers fattening on the wealth of the nation, while the population is heavily taxed and impoverished

This (unless ante-dated) anticipates the attack by the Opposition on Government finance and the 1781 Loan. See *Parl Hist.* xxi. 1325 ff , 1379 (1, 7, and 21 Mar), and Wraxall, *Memoirs*, 1884, ii 90 f. See No. 5835. $8\frac{1}{8} \times 9\frac{1}{2}$ in.

5835 A FOLLOWER OF ST LUKE.

T P G

Pub by M Darly Nᵒ 159 Fleet Street, March 20. 1781.

Engraving. A market-woman sits on a low stool; beside her is a wicker cage containing ducks, one of which has escaped and walks across the pavement She says to a boy who stands watching, *Go my lad catch that duck for me its lame & cannot run far*. He answers *Tis a pity to spoil an old proverb—Birds of a feather flock together*. The duck is walking behind a man foppishly dressed, but out at elbows, and with holes in his coat and breeches. His beard and profile show that he is a Jew. He says, *Tis hard to be cut off with a 6ᵗʰ part when I sent up my name for £100,000. I had borrowed money to make up the first payment & I now find I am quite thrown out*. Behind is the wall of a building inscribed *Bank*; in it are two open arches Beneath the title is engraved, *St Luke Chap. 10 & 4 Verse, Carry neither purse nor Scrip*

A person who cannot keep his engagements on the Stock Exchange was called a lame duck, the Jew and the duck being 'birds of a feather'; cf. No. 6273 A satire on the then common practice of raising Government loans by which the loan was distributed among bankers and merchants, subdivided among their customers, and sold at a premium, the first contractors being seldom called on to pay more than a first instalment, after which they sold at a profit. The Government was violently attacked for using the 1781 Loan (twelve millions) as a means of corruption. See No. 5834

6⅛ × 9¼ in.

5835A Another impression, probably earlier, in which the publication line is without a date The Jew is saying, *Tis hard to be cut off with a Shilling* [ut supra].

5836 THE HONᴮᴸᴱ CHARLES JAMES FOX.   [1 Apr. 1781]

Engraving. *Political Magazine*, ii. 157 Bust portrait of Fox in an oval frame, beneath the oval is an 'Emblematical Representation of Opposition' (p. 159) illustrating a very hostile account of Fox and the Holland family, pp. 156–9. In front of Westminster Hall stands the headless statue of a king holding the orb; he stands on a rectangular pedestal inscribed MAGNA CHARTA. A satyr (l) is breaking the sceptre across his knee. The king's head lies on the ground beside him A man with ass's ears raises a pickaxe to strike the pedestal, he is '*Ignorance* with his mattock attacking Magna Charta'. A dishévelled woman holds the staff and cap of liberty, she is '*faction* disguised under the ensign and masque of liberty' A man with a raised club (r.) is about to strike the statue. He is '*popular rage* depicted under the figure of a clown' (p 159) This scene is bordered by a draped curtain, it and the portrait of Fox are set in a rectangle decorated with engraved lines.

For similar attacks on Fox cf Nos 5962, 5979, &c. One of the few prints attacking the Opposition, see No 5334, &c

5⅞ × 3¾ in.   B M L., P P 3557 v.

5837 THE DUTCHMAN IN THE DUMPS

[Gillray]

Pub⁴ April 9ᵗʰ 1781, by W Humphrey N° 227 Strand.

Engraving Figures representing the five countries who were at war. A tall Dutchman stands looking up with a face of despair, in his l. hand he holds out a paper inscribed, *Eustatia lost, Oh! Oh!* He says,

> *I shall Die, I'm undone!*
> *My best hope is now gone!*

A laughing English sailor (l) standing on his r holds a small bottle inscribed *Gin* to his nose, saying,

> *High & Mighty's¹ your Grief,*
> *Smell this for Relief.*

In his r hand he holds a netted purse taken from the Dutchman On the r stand the other enemy powers Spain, in slashed doublet, cloak, feathered hat, and top-boots, is reading a newspaper *Gaze,* [*London Gazette*] and saying,

> *If this News is true,*
> *It will make us all rue.*

Behind him are France (l) and America (r.) France holds up his hands with an expression of alarm, saying,

> *Sᵗ Eustatia by Gar,*
> *Vas de Storehouse of War.*

America, a slim youth, the most insignificant of the five, is saying,

> *America now,*
> *To Old England must bow.*

The Dutch island of St. Eustatius, a great depot under a neutral flag for provisioning the enemy since the beginning of hostilities, see No. 5557, &c , was seized by Rodney, with much shipping and valuable stores, on 3 Feb 1781. A convoy which had just left for Europe with a Dutch flag-ship was also taken. The news was published in an *Extraordinary Gazette* of 13 Mar 1781. See Nos 5838, 5839, 5842, 5923

$7\frac{13}{16} \times 7$ in.

5838 THE OVERJOY OF M DE. LA. MOTTE. PIQUET. AT THE BRINGING OF THE Sᵗ EUSTATIA FLEET INTO BREST

L. Sandwig Invᵗ

Pub May .11. 1781. by E. Hedges Cornhill London as the Act Directs

Engraving (coloured impression) The French admiral grotesquely caricatured is dancing with joy, trampling on a flag inscribed *Colour*[s of] *England.* He is lean and dressed like the French officer of caricature, with a very long pigtail queue, a laced and feathered hat, a tasselled cane under his l. arm, and tassels on his sword He wears top-boots, striped stockings, ruffled shirt, and large epaulettes. His r fist is clenched Over his head is engraved *Begar how we did make the English run.* In the distance is

¹ An allusion to *Hogen Mogen,* 'the high mightinesses', or the States General of the United Provinces

504

a fleet of ships in full sail making for a castle flying the French flag and inscribed *Brest*

Rodney sent captured merchandise from St Eustatius in thirty-four merchant ships convoyed by two ships of the line and three frigates under Commodore Hotham The British Grand Fleet was relieving Gibraltar, so La Motte Piquet was ordered to sea on 25 Apr. to intercept the convoy. He captured twenty ships whose cargoes were valued at nearly £5,000,000 and took them into Brest. The remainder managed to reach Berehaven W. M James, *The British Navy in Adversity*, 1926, pp. 305–6. The artist's name attributes the misfortune to Lord Sandwich See Nos 5837, 5839, 5842

$5\frac{3}{4}\times4\frac{5}{8}$ in

5839 ENGLISCH PRINTET [1781]
[ENGLISH PRINT]

Engraving. The figures have numbers referring to a printed explanation in Dutch below the print. In the foreground is a procession (l. to r) of men and animals. in front is a stout-looking man (4) being thrown by a donkey whose heels are in the air Next comes a unicorn on whose back sits a cock (5), reins going from the animal's mouth to the cock's feet. Next is a goat on which sits a man (6), his face to the animal's tail. Last comes a small two-wheeled cart drawn by a lion which is rather smaller than the goat. A man (7) sits in the cart driving the lion.

Behind, across two-thirds of the design, is a long table behind which sit eight men conversing with each other in pairs The four on the l wear wigs, without hats, the other four wear hats All wear clerical or legal bands. The first four heads have been copied from the heads in No 5170, *Wigs*, one (r) being that which is probably a portrait of Lord Chancellor Bathurst. All are in reverse except that two heads facing one another in profile are from the same original. The other four heads are copied, also in reverse, from No 5169, *Hats*, bands having been added in two instances. These eight persons are all numbered (1)

In the upper r corner of the design four sailors (2), wearing trousers, are dancing to a fiddle which is played by a man (3) with long feathers in his cap

The explanation is here translated:

Nº 1. *My lords and noblemen in the parliament assembly Lord North pointing to the atlas [not depicted] where he wishes to have a good part for himself, and the rest for his good friends.*

Nº 2. *Four French sailors dancing, delighted at the capture of the convoy from St Eustatius which has arrived safely at Brest*

Nº 3 *An American musician playing an English 'Contredans'*

Nº 4 *The Englishman on an American ass which flings him to the ground. Although the long-eared beast is accustomed to bear burdens He feels this one is too heavy, and will endure no British blows He flings down this big idiot, yet it seems that he calls out, I am, oh sick of roast beef, your living stink-ass no more*

Nº 5. *The French cock driving the British unicorn. One can well keep a snorting horse from running away, So shall I, your lordship, prevent it from running away;*

While this brisk cock with its spurs
Shall teach you your paces in the hot open sand

Nº 6   *The Englishman sitting backwards on a Spanish goat.*
How this goat smiles at the British appearance and tricks:
Let England's chief wear baby-clothes
Would the man then become a child? Wretched Parliament!
Do it all in a mad fit of passion' but look however to the conclusion.

Nº 7   *An Englishman sitting in a small cart driving a lion*
Already the Dutch lion begins to look round
Fear then faithless Ally, he shall not yield to you
Ancient Batoos, famous of old, known everywhere
Makes him see how this wheel turns round and round

Batoos is the legendary founder of Batavia. For the capture of the convoy from St. Eustatius see No. 5838 For other Dutch prints see Nos. 5712–34, 5859, 6292.
Van Stolk, No. 4336. Muller, No. 4383.

6 × 11⅝ in.

5840 A MEMORIAL CYPHER, PORTRAIT AND ARMS, OF LORD GEORGE GORDON, PRESIDENT OF THE PROTESTANT ASSOCIATION.

C Hall del et Sculp.

Published as the Act directs May 18. 1781. by Hall Nº 2. Grafton Street Soho London

Engraving. A miniature bust portrait in an oval, as if suspended from a cypher, *G G*, formed of garlands of ivy-leaves (the Gordon badge) and roses. From the base of the oval is suspended (incorrectly) a baron's coronet and arms, three boars' heads on a shield. Intertwined with the cypher is a ribbon on which is engraved *Called and Chosen and Faithful.* Above the cypher is a wreath, from which spring conventional palm-branches to suggest a martyr's crown Within the wreath is engraved *Feb'y 6ᵗʰ 1781*, above the wreath is *Patiens, Passus, Honorably Acquited.*

Gordon was tried for high treason in the King's Bench on 5 Feb., the court sitting from 8 a.m. till 5.15 a m. on the following day. He had at this time gained great popularity among the Methodists. Walpole, *Last Journals*, 1910, pp 348, 366, 373.

For Gordon as the Protestant Hero see also Nos. 5672, 5694, 5841. For other prints published in the interests of the Protestant Association see No 5534, &c. For the Riots see Nos 5679, 5684, 5685, 5686, 5841, 5844
6⅞ × 4⅜ in.

5841 THE MEMBERS OF THE PROTESTANT ASSOCIATION OF LONDON, WESTMINSTER, SOUTHWARK, &c. . .   [? 1781]
Engraved from an Original Drawing by Mr Wooding.

Published by Alexr Hogg at the Kings Arms Paternoster Row.

Engraving. Plate from *Fox's Book of Martyrs*, ed. Paul Wright, n.d. (after p 952) Palace Yard filled with an orderly procession of soberly-dressed and highly respectable men marching l to r. At their head, but preceded by a body of men with a banner, is a stout man carrying on his shoulders an enormous roll inscribed *Protestant Petition* Three banners are carried, two inscribed *Protestant Association*, the other *No Popery*. A few men wave their hats. In the background (l) are houses, the windows filled with spectators, and (r.) the House of Lords. In the foreground (l) sits an apple-woman beside her stall After the title is engraved, *peaceably proceeding to the House of Commons, on Friday June 2, 1780 (in consequence of which being previously advertised, upwards of 40,000 Persons had assembled in St George's Fields . . . with their Petition which was carried by Mr Hodgkinson, and presented to the House by their President, Lord George Gordon . on which occasion the mischievous Emissaries of the Papists, taking advantage of the opportunity, caused the subsequent Insurrections & Riots that the odium might be thrown on the Protestants . . & Lord George Gordon was committed close Prisoner to the Tower, as the principal Abettor of the Riots but was honourably Acquitted . . . Febry 6 1781, to the entire Satisfaction of all real Friends to Civil & Religious Liberty, and the Protestant cause Nor was there ever one single Person either convicted, tried or even apprehended, on suspicion . . . who was a member of that Respectable Body, the Protestant Association*

No-Popery propaganda, the procession having no resemblance to the disorderly scene in Palace Yard on 2 June 1780. For the Gordon Riots see Nos. 5679, 5684, 5685, 5686, 5844, and for Gordon as Protestant Hero Nos 5672, 5694, 5840 For other prints published in the interests of the Protestant Association see No. 5534, &c.

$7\frac{3}{16} \times 12\frac{1}{2}$ in. (subject), $8\frac{7}{8} \times 13\frac{7}{8}$ in. (pl.).

5842 THE LATE AUCTION AT ST EUSTATIA

[T Colley?]

1781. Pub: by E. Hedges N 92 Cornhill London June 11.

Engraving. The interior of an auction-room; through an open door (l.) is the sea, with ships flying the British flag. In the auctioneer's rostrum, on the extreme r , stands Admiral Rodney, in profile to the l., holding up a shoe-buckle in his r. hand, a hammer in his l. He is saying, *This fashionable Pair of Buckles going to be knock'd down to their Original Owner at one Guinea does nobody advance upon one Guinea 2 going going 22s is bid Gentlemen.* His clerk, in officer's uniform (General Vaughan), stands below him in the desk which forms the lower part of the rostrum; he is writing (with his l. hand) *The Last days sale. . .* A man stands obsequiously in front of him, hat in hand, a folded umbrella or parasol under his l. arm, saying *if I purchase the Provision & naval Stores that were formerly mine, may I Ship them to any Neutral Island.* Vaughan answers, *Ay Ay, if you give a good price for them you may Ship them to the Devil, & goe with them yourself as super-cargo if you like it* On the side of the rostrum papers are nailed up inscribed, *Inventories of Effects belonging to the Inhabits of St Eustatia* Below hangs a bunch of keys labelled *Keys of the Stores.* Behind the man speaking to Vaughan is a group of three men: a Spaniard in a cloak and feathered hat is seen in back-view; a man facing Rodney bids *a Guinea* for the buckles, his own shoes are without buckles and unfastened, behind him a Dutchman with a folded parasol under his arm says, *Twenty two Shillings*

On the l three men stand in conversation, one says, *When will Ad——l Rod——y & Genl: Vaun leave this Island* A Spanish don answers him

I shou'd imagine tomorrow, as the Sale will be closed to night. The third, who holds a closed umbrella, says, *if he had done his Duty, & had been with his fleet instead of keeping 3 ships of the line here while he was minding the sales we should have beat the french off Martinico.*

On the extreme l., looking out to sea through the open door are a Frenchman and a Dutchman. The Frenchman asks *What ship is that*; the Dutchman (in back view) answers *The Sandwich waiting till the sales are Close'd to take Adm——l Rod——y & Gen Vaun to the Fleet.* Outside the door a man is about to enter the auction-room. A man standing by the door offers him a paper, saying *walk in Sir heres a Catalogue.*

A satire on the conduct of Rodney and Vaughan at St. Eustatius. Rodney wrote, 4 Mar. 1781, to Germain, 'Except for supplies from the island and from British subjects there, who meanly condescended to become Dutch burghers (and as such they shall be treated) the American Revolution had long been at an end'. *Hist. MSS. Comm., Stopford Sackville MSS.,* ii, 1910, p. 202. The spoils were given by the king to the Army and Navy, consequently, it was alleged, Rodney and Vaughan remained there for three months, and were accused of plundering and deporting Englishmen. Rodney confiscated the whole of the merchandise, sold some by auction and sent the rest under convoy to England (see Nos. 5837–5839), and deported English, Dutch, Jews, French, and Americans. Charges and counter-charges filled the newspapers, and there was an important debate on 14 May 1781, on Burke's motion for an inquiry (cf. No. 5854). It was defeated, but was again brought forward on 4 Dec. 1781, when Rodney and Vaughan defended themselves, Rodney asserting that his seizure was for the sole benefit of the Crown, since he did not learn of the king's gift till long afterwards. *Parl. Hist.* xvii. 218 ff., 769 ff. *Ann. Reg.,* 1781, p. 195; 1782, pp. 137 ff. Wraxall, *Memoirs,* 1884, ii, pp. 115–17. W. M. James, *The British Navy in Adversity,* 1926, pp. 254 ff. The seizure of English goods involved Rodney in long and expensive lawsuits, claims being made against him exceeding the whole value of the captured property. Mundy, *Life of Rodney,* ii. 366–9. J. F. Jameson, 'St. Eustatius in *the American Revolution', Am. Hist. Review,* viii, p. 697 ff. To Rodney's prolonged stay at St. Eustatius has been attributed the loss of the command of the sea leading to the surrender at York Town. Mahan, *Influence of Sea Power,* 1890, pp. 382–400.

For St. Eustatius see No. 5557, &c., and p. 559.

For the dismay caused to the patriots by its capture see No. 5923.

$8\frac{3}{8} \times 12\frac{7}{8}$ in.

5843 A PHILLIPICK TO THE GEESE

Pub. by E. Hedges N° 92 Under the Royal Exchange Cornhill June 25 1781

Engraving. A fox (l.) on its hind-legs addresses four geese standing by the side of a pond who stretch out their necks towards him. In the pond five goslings are swimming. The fox, C. J. Fox, says, *I promise ye upon my Honour that I always was & will be a friend to the Geese.* The geese (l. to r.) say *pray accept of a Gosling; Fox is the guardian of the Geese; Fox for ever; O Noble Fox.* The scene is a field with a hedge in the background. Beneath the design is engraved:

> *As far as Geese could Judge they Reason'd Right*
> *But as to Fox mistook the matter Quite. Pope*

The first of many satires in which geese represent the electors of Westminster, or other persons beguiled by Fox, see Nos 6013, 6211, 6215, 6220, 6261, 6278, 6287 (2).

$6\frac{5}{8} \times 8\frac{1}{2}$ in.

5844 AN EXACT REPRESENTATION OF THE BURNING, PLUNDERING AND DESTRUCTION OF NEWGATE BY THE RIOTERS ON THE MEMORABLE 7ᵀᴴ OF JUNE 1780.

O Neil del.   *H. Roberts sc.*

London Publish'd as the Act directs, July 10ᵗʰ 1781 by P. Mitchell North Audley Street Grosvenor Square and J. Fielding Nº 23. Pater Noster Row

Engraving Gordon rioters in front of Newgate, which is in flames This is a more or less exact representation of the scene (with some details introduced which occurred elsewhere during the riots) as described in letters, &c , in the press, and by the witnesses at the subsequent trials—a combination of frenzy, drunkenness, and good humour Flames are pouring from the central façade of the prison, a man on a ladder holds up a torch and a hammer The foreground is crowded with figures There are three *No Popery* flags. A man on horseback (r) harangues the mob with a drawn sword saying *Courage my boys this is for the glory of the good old Cause* Released prisoners (r) still in irons are talking and drinking with young women. On the l. a smith removes the irons from a prisoner A black wields an axe, another carries off a large box. On the l. a man is delivering pamphlets inscribed *England in Blood, The Scourge,* and *The Thunderer* These were very inflammatory pamphlets directed against the Government, the King, Lord Mansfield, &c , published on the eve of the riots by W Moore, against whom Wilkes issued a warrant on 10 June De Castro, *Gordon Riots*, p. 191, see also No. 5829. A man stands on an improvised platform holding up a sword and a paper inscribed *Death or Liberty & No Popery* The keys of the prison are held up on a pitchfork. A man rings a hand-bell. A man (l.) sits on the box-seat of a coach waving his hat A woman wheels a drunken man in a wheelbarrow. A released prisoner in irons is carried on a man's shoulders, he waves his hat, calling *No Popery d—n my eyes.* Almost all the men wear ribbon favours in their hats, the blue ribbon of the Protestant Association.

For the Gordon Riots see Nos. 5679, 5684, 5685, 5686, 5841, &c.

11×17 in.

5845 PENSIONARY VAN BERKEL

J. Van Shroeter pinxᵗ—J. Kent fecit.   [Gillray.]

London. Pubᵈ July 4ᵗʰ 1781 by J Kent

Aquatint H L. portrait in an oval, facing T.Q to r , of Van Berckel He is stout, wears a conical cap, a furred robe over a waistcoat, a plain cravat is tied round his neck He was Pensionary of Amsterdam, very hostile to England, and the chief advocate in the United Provinces of war with England See F P. Renaut, *Les Provinces-Unies et la Guerre d'Amérique,* v, 1925, p 235, &c , and No 5733. The names of the artists may have some political or personal significance now obscure. A companion print to No. 5846. A coloured impression is in 'Caricatures', v, p. 17. B.M.L., Tab. 524.

Grego, *Gillray*, p. 32.

$8\frac{7}{16} \times 6\frac{3}{8}$ in.

5846 MARQUIS LA FAYETTE.

La Fevre pinx^t J. Kent fecit.   [Gillray.]

London Pub^d July 4th 1781 by J. Kent

Aquatint. Bust portrait in an oval of Lafayette looking to the l. Scarcely a caricature except that the face and figure are somewhat elongated. At this time Lafayette was at the head of the forces opposing Cornwallis in Virginia. A companion print to No. 5845.

Grego, *Gillray*, p. 31.

$8\frac{5}{16} \times 6\frac{3}{8}$ in.

5847 F H DE LA MOTTE

Pub: as the Act directs By J^{no} Smith Price Sixpence 27 July 1781

Engraving. Bust portrait (not caricature) in profile to the r. of the French spy de la Motte. His hair is in a short pigtail queue, he wears a plain coat and ruffled shirt. The portrait is in an oval which is tied by a ribbon (on which the title is engraved) to a nail. The oval is surrounded by foliage and by objects representing and symbolizing the sentence for high treason: a knife and broken column (l.), an axe, a rope, and a fire (r.).

De la Motte was sentenced at the Old Bailey, 14 July 1781 (*State Trials*, xxi. 687 ff.). He had systematically collected important naval and military information since Jan. 1780 and had sent it to France. On 27 July he was executed at Tyburn before an immense crowd. There seems to have been little hostility towards him, and newspaper comments on his death are sympathetic. Cf. *London Chronicle*, 26–8 July 1781.

$5\frac{1}{2} \times 4\frac{1}{4}$ in. (oval, $4\frac{1}{16} \times 3\frac{1}{2}$ in.).

5848 A SKETCH OF THE ENGAGEMENT UNDER THE COMMAND OF VICE ADMIRAL PARKER ON THE DOGGER BANK WITH THE DUTCH SQUADRON OF MUCH SUPERIOR FORCE AUG^T 5. 1781

Drawn by an officer on the Spot. [T. Colley?]

Pub Augt 9. 1681 by Thos Colley N° 288 Strand.

Engraving (coloured and uncoloured impressions). A plan of the naval engagement of 5 Aug. 1781, showing the English coast from the Wash to Ipswich and the Dutch coast west and east of the Texel. The English ships, the Dutch fleet in action, and the Dutch convoy are indicated by letters (*A* to *Q*). The English ships are named, and a flag above the surface of the sea shows *A 74 Dutch ship sunk in 22 fathoms of water*. The title and the key to the letters indicating the ships are engraved in a rectangle inset at the lower l. corner. This rectangle partly conceals an English sailor who strikes with his fist the head of a disconsolate Dutchman, who makes no resistance. The sailor says, *Bla——t my Eyes Get Back in the Texel*. The Dutchman says *I'm sinking*.

This engagement was claimed by the English and Dutch as a victory: the Dutch losses exceeded the British, the British homeward-bound convoy returned safely, the Dutch convoy, outward-bound, returned to the Texel in disorder. See W M James, *The British Navy in Adversity*, 1926, pp 310 ff It was the subject of many Dutch prints, see *Van Stolk*, Nos. 4365–84, 4387–9 (Nos 4385 and 4386 are English prints of the battle)

Parker's letter (not dispatch) of 6 Aug was published in an *Extraordinary Gazette* of 9 Aug , which suggests that the print may be ante-dated.

$9\frac{3}{8} \times 13\frac{1}{2}$ in.

5849 THE C——Y [CITY] CANDIDATES.

Publis⁴ as the Act Sept ͬ 11ᵗʰ 1781 [sic] Price 6ᵈ

Engraving. A race between three candidates for the by-election for the City of London, caused by the death of Alderman Hayley on 30 Aug In front is Sir Watkin Lewes, the Lord Mayor, riding a goat as an emblem of Wales; his civic chain is round his neck and he holds up the City mace in his l. hand He wears a gorget and the hat of a military officer. (He was colonel of the Sixth Regiment of the City Militia) He says, *Ye Quakers of Wors'ter Farwell*. Next comes Lord George Gordon riding on the back of a Scottish presbyterian minister, wearing a plaid and clerical bands, who proceeds on his hands and feet, spurred by his rider. Lord George holds up an open book, inscribed on one page *Scotlands Opposition*, on the other, *To the K——g* He had recently written to North, asking leave to present to the king in person a book, 'Scotland's Opposition to the Popish Bill'. *London Chronicle*, 4–6 Sept ; *Corr. of George III*, v. 277–82. He is saying *My Flaming Virtues will recommend me* (an allusion to the Gordon Riots) Lord G Gordon, amongst others, 'presented himself as a candidate' to succeed Hayley Walpole, *Last Journals*, 1910, ii. 372

The third candidate is riding astride on the stone of a grindstone which is inscribed, *knives to grind* He holds up a short staff inscribed *Law* and is saying *I hope I sha'nt be allways Last*

The only two candidates who ultimately presented themselves for election were Watkin Lewes and Alderman Clark Lewes, one of the City patriots (see index), was elected, in his speech to the Livery he said he had thrice been a candidate, had had 'an undoubted majority of the legal, uncorrupt voters' at Worcester [1774] but had been defeated on petition. He was elected (29 Sept 1781) by 2,685 to 2,387. *London Chronicle*, 22–5 Sept , 27–9 Sept For the king's anxiety for his defeat see *Hist. MSS Comm., Abergavenny MSS* , 1887, pp. 43, 44–5. See also No. 5852.

An undated print, *S ͬ Watty on full gallop to the election*, has been dated by Miss Banks Apr 1784, showing that it was used for the general election of that year, and it is catalogued under that date It may, however, have been first issued for the election of 1781.

$5\frac{9}{16} \times 10$ in

5850 THE STATE NURSES.

[? After Viscount Townshend]

Pub · by T. Colley Oct ͬ 1 1781. High Holborn

Engraving The British Lion in a cradle, surrounded by barking dogs, the two 'State Nurses' are Mansfield and Sandwich, one on each side of the cradle The lion is asleep, and tucked under a coverlet on which are laid a rose and a thistle, the thistle lying across the rose to indicate the supposed predominance of Scottish counsels. The head of the cradle is decorated by three crowns Two dogs stand together (r.), one inscribed *Spain*, the other, very lean, is *France* Spain says *I'll have Gibralter Minorca and Florida*; France says, *Barbadoes Jamaica Jersey &c. &c. for me* The two other dogs, *America* and *Holland*, stand in front of the cradle. America is befouling a paper inscribed *Tea Act* and is saying, *Independance & no Taxation* Holland says *Armed Neutrality & free Navigation*. Mansfield (l.) is seated on a chair by the head of the cradle, he is in judge's wig and robe which is thrown open to display knee breeches and bare legs with short tartan stockings indicating his Scottish nationality. He holds two broken poles against his shoulder, and is saying to the dogs, *Hoot awau ye bougers do ye no ken the bauns asleep* One foot rests on two documents, *Habeas Corpus* and *[Magn]a Charta*. Sandwich stands by the cradle on the other side, saying *Get away raw head & bloody bones here is a Child dont fear ye*. From his pocket hangs a musical score and a paper inscribed *Lets drink & lets sing together*, an allusion to his fondness for singing catches, see No. 5540, &c For other references to the tax on tea see No. 5490, &c , for the Armed Neutrality No. 5714, &c

In the background (l) is a rocky mound inscribed *Gibralter* round which is a semicircle of guns, lobbing cannon-balls over a line of fortifications. On the r., on rising ground, is a castle flying the Union flag inscribed *Windsor* At the base of the hill a stag-hunt is in progress, the stag, dogs, and three huntsmen being on a minute scale The third rider, who is partly cut off by the r margin of the print, appears to wear a Garter ribbon and is evidently the king, cf. No 5961

In the manner of Lord Townshend

$7\frac{5}{8} \times 10\frac{11}{16}$ in.

5851 ADDRESS

Capt Morse del   *Stephanoff Sculp, Oct 4 1781*

Publish'd as the Act Directs

Stipple. The king on the throne (r.) Behind him on the dais is a group of ladies, among whom Queen Charlotte, putting a smelling-bottle to her nose, is conspicuous. They watch the approach of the Lord Mayor followed by aldermen in furred livery-gowns, Wilkes being on the extreme l. The Mayor with a deprecatory expression is being dragged forward by Hertford, the Lord Chamberlain Officers holding halberds make a pathway for their approach to the throne Ministers and courtiers stand round the dais. Thurlow, in Chancellor's wig and gown, holds the bag of the Great Seal. North stands on the king's l The ladies have expressions signifying contempt or amusement After the title is written in a contemporary hand, 'or Approach of the Mayor and Corporation of London to the Throne' The Mayor, 1780-1, was Sir Watkin Lewes

An imaginary scene Unless ante-dated it cannot represent the 'Address, Remonstrance and Petition' from the Lord Mayor, Alderman, and Livery voted in Common Hall 6 Dec 1781. This was a protest against the war and a request that the king should dismiss all 'the Advisers both public and secret of the measures we lament'. As this was not the address of the

Corporation (the Common Council having abstained) the king refused to
receive it on the throne, offering to do so at the levée, to which the City
would not consent The Address was therefore not presented *London
Chronicle*, 6 Dec 1781; Walpole, *Last Journals*, 1910, ii 286; Sharpe,
London and the Kingdom, iii 193 ff ; *Corr. of George III*, v. 308–12.
Cf No. 5959

$8\frac{1}{2} \times 14\frac{1}{8}$ in.

5852 AN ELECTIONEERING [*sic*] PROCESSION FROM THE
M——N [MANSION] HOUSE TO G——D [GUILD] HALL.

J N. [Nixon]

Pub^d Octr 25,[1] *1781. by W. Wells N° 132 Fleet Street*

Engraving (coloured and uncoloured impressions) An election procession
of thirteen patriots walking from r to l. wearing the colours of Sir Watkin
Lewes, elected M P for the City, 29 Sept. 1781, see No 5849. Two flags
are carried, one *Lewes & Freedom*, the other, *No Ministerial Influence*, in
reference to Lewes' speech on his election on 29 Sept. Two of the men are
playing flutes, a third blows a horn. The figures are probably portraits;
two are butchers wearing aprons, their steels hanging from their waists;
beside one of them walks a muzzled dog with a collar inscribed *Liberty*;
this butcher is eating as he walks. One man drinks a glass of wine, holding
a lump of food in his l. hand. One with a swathed and gouty leg walks on
crutches. All have election favours in their hats, these are inscribed
respectively *Lewes for ever*; *Sr Watkin for ever*, *Freedom*, *Lewes*, *No
Bribery*; *Lewes*; *No Corruption* In the hat of the butcher with the dog is
Freedom's my plan Sr Watkin is the Man.

The background is formed by the lower part of the façade of two houses
in a street, the front of two shops being indicated. On the pavement (l)
four little chimney-sweeps are shouting and waving their hats and brushes.

Beneath the title is engraved ·

> *These stanch friends to freedom you here do behold,*
> *Will be bribe'd with good eating tho' they spurn at y^r gold*
> *For offer them money it's such a disgrace,*
> *'Tis a thousand to one they dont spit in your face.*
> *But give them pudding & beef with compliments civil,*
> *To serve you they'll go ay e'en to the devil.*

$9\frac{1}{2} \times 15\frac{5}{8}$ in

5853 VIEW OF THE GUARD-HOUSE AND SIMSBURY-MINES
NOW CALLED NEWGATE,

A Prison for the Confinement of Loyalists in Connecticut

Pub: by J Bew Pater Noster Row Nov 1st 1781. London.

Engraving *Political Magazine*, ii. 596 The elevation of a small building
and beneath it the section of a mine showing a vertical shaft or ladder
leading from under the building, or guard-room, to the gallery of a mine
which descends from it A pipe descending vertically from the surface
of the ground to the lower end of the mine, representing a shaft 70 feet in

[1] In the coloured impression '25' appears to have been altered to '26' or '28'

depth, and $1\frac{1}{2}$ inches in diameter, 'the only passage by which the prisoners are furnished with air' Letters on the plan give references to the explanation which has been quoted.

One of the few pieces of graphic propaganda hostile to America, since it appears to have been an accurate representation of the mines which were used as a prison

The explanation of the diagram concludes. 'The perusal of Capt. Hathaway's case, and glance at the sketch of the dungeon in which the Connecticut Rebels confine the loyalists, are recommended to the orators who harangued in Parliament in favour of the Rebel Prisoners ' A reference follows to the printed debates of 29 June 1781, in which the Opposition had complained that the food of American prisoners at Plymouth was insufficient. See *Parl. Hist.* xxii. 608 ff.

An account of the mines and of the escape of Hathaway was published in *Rivington's Gazette*, 9 June 1781, and is quoted by F Moore, *Diary of the American Revolution*, 1863, ii. 434–6. For other anti-American prints see No 5401, &c.

$6\frac{1}{16} \times 4\frac{3}{4}$ in.   B.M L , P.P 3557 v.

5854 DON VOLASEO. THE FAMOUS SPANISH PARTIZAN.

Pub by T. Colley Nov. 21. 1781. N° 257, high Holborn

Sold by Cornell Bruton Street Bond Street

Engraving. A man in the dress of a military officer seated on a horse in profile to the r He holds a drawn sabre in his r. hand. He wears spectacles and resembles caricature portraits of Burke. In the middle distance is a large military tent or marquee, like those in representations of the camps at Coxheath and Warley. In front of it, at a small round table, sits a lady drinking wine and gazing at the cavalier On the sky-line is the façade of a house, the pediment of which has been grotesquely elevated into a steeple, perhaps intended for Gregories, Burke's country house

Perhaps a satire on Burke's attitude to the war He had violently attacked the confiscation of property on the Dutch island of St Eustatius, see No. 5842, which included the property of Dutchmen, Americans, French, and Spaniards. *Parl. Hist* xxii 218 ff , 769 ff

$8\frac{1}{4} \times 12\frac{1}{8}$ in

5855 STATE COOKS, OR
THE DOWNFALL OF THE FISH KETTLE.

Pub⁴ Dec' 10. 1781, by W. Wells N° 132 Fleet Street

Engraving George III (l) and Lord North (r) stand disconsolately in a kitchen looking at a large open pan which has fallen to the floor from a hook over the fire, the fish, inscribed with the names of American colonies, have fallen out. There are thirteen, but *New England* is one and they include *Quebec, Nova Scotia, E Florida,* and *W. Florida* The king and North are wearing aprons, and the insignia of the Garter; their facial resemblance is stressed From North's coat-pocket hangs a paper inscribed *Plan of Taxes 1782* The king is saying *O Boreas, the Loss of these Fish will ruin us for ever.* North answers, *My Honored Liege never Fret. Minden* [Lord George Germain, Secretary of State for the Colonies] *& I will cook* *'em yet* On the wall behind North is a large *Plan of North America* in which *York Town* is conspicuous.

A satire on the effect of the surrender of Cornwallis at York Town on 19 Oct., news of which reached London on 25 Nov. See Walpole, *Last Journals*, ii. 378. Wraxall, *Historical Memoirs*, 1884, ii. 138 ff. See also Nos. 5856–61

10×8¼ in.

5856 THE STATE WATCHMAN DISCOVER'D BY THE GENIUS OF BRITAIN, STUDYING PLANS FOR THE REDUCTION OF AMERICA.

[Rowlandson.]

Pub^d by I Jones, 10 Dec. 1781.

Engraving. A circular design. George III (or Lord North) asleep on a sofa. He is in profile to the l., his head falling forwards, his r. arm resting on the back of the sofa, his r. leg extended on the sofa, his l. leg on the ground. Behind the sofa stand two figures: Britannia (l.) holding the cap of liberty on its staff, while her r. hand rests on the back of the sofa. An oval medallion ornamented with a St. George's cross hangs from her wrist, probably respresenting the arms of the City of London. She says *Am I thus Protected?* A small man leans on the back of the sofa saying *Hollo Neighbour! what are you asleep.* Published after news of the surrender at York Town, see No. 5855, &c.

Grego, *Rowlandson*, i. 105.

Diam. 5½ in

5857 LE GÉNÉRAL BURGOYNE A SARATOGA, LE 17 O^bre 1777. A ÉTÉ PRIS PRISONNIER DE GUERRE AVEC TOUTE SON ARMÉE   [n d 1781]

Engraving. A French satire. A soldier stands behind a turkey-cock holding both ends of a staff which has been put in the bird's beak. The turkey, which represents Burgoyne, wears top-boots and is shackled by his r leg, on which is a garter inscribed *Honi soit*, though he was not a knight of the Garter. Other soldiers of the Continental Army stand in a semicircle behind the bird. Beneath the title is etched·

Extrait d'une lettre du général burgoyne. Et quoi vieux Renard, toi qui avais promis a la patrie de venger ses malheurs et réparer le mien, te voila pris toi même! Cependant, Milord, ne nous decourageons pas; tant quil restera un anglais, les destinées de la grande bretagne ne seront pas désésperées.

This purports to be a letter to Cornwallis on his surrender at York Town, which is the subject of a companion print by the same artist, see No. 5858

Collection de Vinck, No. 1185.

4 5/16 × 4 15/16 in.

5858 LE GÉNÉRAL CORNWALLIS A YORCK LE 19 8bre 1781 A ÉTÉ PRIS PRISONNIER DE GUERRE AVEC TOUTE SON ARMÉE   [n d 1781]

Engraving A French satire on the surrender at York Town A companion print to No. 5857. A seated soldier (r.) holds a fox by its brush, while

another lifts an axe in order to chop off the animal's tail A third soldier
with a musket stands at the head of the fox, Lord Cornwallis The scene
is the sea-shore and the sails and figure-head of a ship appear on the r.
Beneath the title is etched:

*Extrait de la réponse du général cornwallis Oui, je suis pris, mais nompas
[sic] comme un dindon· je le suis sans que mon Etourderie ni ma jactance aient
contribué a l'exécution des sages projets de nos Ennemis, cependant le sort
maccable [sic] sans me décourager. J'espère tout de la fortune britannique et
de la valeur de nos braves anglais; ils ont juré comme nous ils tiendront leur
parole.*

An answer to Burgoyne's letter, see No. 5857. See also No 5855, &c.
For another French satire on Cornwallis see No. 6048. *Collection de
Vinck,* No 1185

$4\frac{15}{16} \times 4\frac{5}{16}$ in.

An engraving by Godefroy, *Reddition de l Armée du Lord Cornwallis,*
after le Barbier, shows English officers giving up their swords and British
soldiers piling their muskets.

No 10 in *Recueil d'Estampes représentant   la Guerre qui a procuré
l'Indépendance aux Etats unis de l'Amérique.* In Print Department.
Collection de Vinck, No 1184.

5859 YORK TOWN [1781]

Nᵒ 2.

Engraving. A Dutch print, a sequel to No 5726, which was copied from
No 5472 A symbolical representation of the surrender of Cornwallis at
York Town In the foreground (l) is the cow representing English commerce,
much emaciated, one horn cut off, the other broken, she tries to graze from
bare thorny branches which lie by the sea-shore. Behind her is a Spaniard
leaning on an altar inscribed *Mexico Peru Chili,* on which lies his sword;
he holds a bowl In front of him are a Frenchman and a Dutchman,
representing France and Holland, the former holding a bowl and pointing
towards buildings inscribed *York Town;* the latter walks off carrying a
heavy pail. In the foreground is a large thistle and bare thorn branches,
indicative of the Scottish advice which has brought English commerce to
this extremity.

In the foreground (r) is the grave Englishman of Nos. 5472, 5726, and
5727, kneeling on one knee, his hands clasped with an expression of
despair. Behind him (r.) is the British lion seated, howling with pain and
holding up a wounded paw. He has been hurt by the 'American Tea-pot',
which lies at his feet The dog looks at the Englishman. From an open
chest rats have dragged bank-notes and bills, which they are gnawing, one
is inscribed *600*

In the middle distance (r.) the surrender at York Town is taking place.
Under a canopy, America, as a Red Indian woman, is seated on a bale of
goods holding an unstrung bow, and stretching out her r. hand towards
a Scot in Highland dress and three Englishmen who approach her with
gestures of humility. At America's feet lie a yoke and shackles, both
broken Behind her stand a number of Americans with feathered head-
dresses and persons in classical draperies: Justice with sword and scales,
Perseus (?) with his Medusa shield, Hercules with his club, Truth with
her mirror Beside them (r.) another American is nailing up a cask

inscribed *Kadix*, two other casks are inscribed *Nantes* and *Marseille*, indicating the commerce between America and Europe in which England (by implication) will no longer share These figures are drawn with delicacy on a very small scale. Behind are towers and other buildings and a palm-tree Off the shore is the ship *Eagle*, of No 5472, &c., wrecked and half-submerged, but flying the British flag. Farther out is the French fleet with a ship's boat flying the French flag.

No title except the words etched over the buildings.

Another indication (cf No. 5726, &c) of the advantages which the Dutch expected to derive from commerce with America For York Town see No. 5855, &c. For the Boston tea-party see No. 5490, &c.

Van Stolk, No. 4287 (2). Muller, No. 4337 (2).

$6\frac{13}{16} \times 10\frac{7}{16}$ in.

5860 JOHN · BULLS · ALTERNATIVE

[Pub M. Darly. ? 1781]¹

Engraving. John Bull stands on a stone on tiptoe under a tree, a rope round his neck attached to a branch of the tree. He holds the rope with both hands, to prevent strangulation. On the r stands a Frenchman (France) holding out a leek to John Bull, between them is a stream or river. John Bull is a moderately stout man with a thick neck, wearing an ill-made bob-wig, not the characteristic John Bull of later satires, who had already appeared, see Nos. 5611, 5612. The Frenchman is very thin, wearing a night-cap, a long pigtail queue, a ruffled shirt, and sabots stuffed with grass

John Bull must either eat the leek or be hanged. Perhaps a comment on York Town, see No 5855, &c.

$6\frac{1}{8} \times 9$ in

5861 THE ANTIGALLICAN SPIRIT; HUMBLY INSCRIB'D TO CAPT: FORSTER & THE MANAGERS OF THE ANTIGALLICAN PRIVATE SHIP OF WAR.   [? 1781²]

Sold by T. Ewart the Corner of Hudsons Court near St Martin's Lane Strand.   *Pr. 6^d*

Engraving. Two sailors stand on a quay, a river with ships behind them. Each grasps the other's l. hand. One (r) waves his hat, saying, *May the French Fleet be put up to Auction & the French King not have a penny of money to bid for it.* A French flag flies from a building behind him. The other (l) holds a brimming punch-bowl, and says, *Here's to our noble Capt Forster and a safe Arrival of the Three Prizes in the River Thames* Beneath the design is engraved.

> *Would Statesmen but this Picture View*
> *Wear Hearts as honest and as True*
> *The Haughty Gauls with Purse proud Spain*
> *Would be our Vassals on the Main.*

$6\frac{3}{4} \times 6\frac{3}{8}$ in

¹ One of the prints included in the volume of Darly's caricatures with the title-page dated 1 Jan. 1776, see No 5369 It is, however, without date or publication line The latest print in the collection with Darly's imprint is No. 5835.
² Dated 1781 by Miss Banks, the date presumably of purchase

5862 RECRUIT FRANCOIS | RECRUIT ANGLOIS OR THE CON-
TRASTED RECRUITS   [? c 1781]

T. Colley Inv^t

Engraving A French recruit (l), an English recruit (r.) face each other
in profile, both are standing erect in a soldierly way, but are in civilian
clothes except for the favour in the Englishman's round hat, and except
for the bulky knapsack of fur or skin which each wears. They are described
in words engraved beneath the title *Monsieur all ruffles no Shirt Wooden
Pumps and Stockingless* and *Jack English with Ruddy face and belly full of
Beef*. The Frenchman holds a slim cane, the Englishman a stout cudgel.
Behind the former (l) are frogs and rats or mice, behind the latter cows and
sheep, to illustrate the supposed contrast between French and English fare.
$11\frac{7}{16} \times 8\frac{5}{8}$ in.

PERSONAL SATIRES

5863–5875

Series of Tête-à-tête portraits.

5863 Nº XXXIV MISS SP——R.
Nº XXXV. LORD S——.

Publish'd by A Hamilton Junʳ Fleet Street, Janʸ 1, 1781

Engraving *Town and Country Magazine*, xii. 633 Two bust portraits in oval frames They illustrate 'Histories of the Tête-à-Tête annexed; or, Memoirs of Lord S——, (the Proselyte Peer) and Miss S——r'. An account of the Earl of Surrey (1746–1815), afterwards 11th Duke of Norfolk He abjured the Roman Catholic Church in 1780 and became M.P. for Carlisle Miss S is the daughter of an attorney who did business for Lord S., but died insolvent.

Ovals, $2\frac{3}{4} \times 2\frac{3}{8}$ in. B.M L., P.P 5442 b.

5864 Nº XXXVI THE SUBTLE SEDUCER.
Nº XXXVII. THE AMERICAN FINANCIER

London, Published by A. Hamilton Junʳ Fleet Street Janʸ 20, 1781

Engraving *Town and Country Magazine*, xii. 689 Two bust portraits in oval frames They illustrate 'Histories of the Tête-à-Tête annexed; . . .'. A very hostile account of Dr. Richard Price, stressing his treatise on population, quoting his remarks on the increase of building in London, which he ascribes to an increase in luxury combined with a decrease in population Miss P. is the daughter of an underwriter who has lost a fortune during the American War. Their relations are thought to be platonic, on account of the man's age, though he is alleged to be an adherent of Dr. Madan's views on polygamy, see No. 5768

Ovals, $2\frac{3}{4} \times 2\frac{3}{8}$ in B.M L., P P 5442 b

5865 Nº II THE FAIR OPHELIA
Nº III THE ILLUSTRIOUS HEIR

Published by A. Hamilton Junʳ Fleet Street Febʸ 1.; 1781

Engraving. *Town and Country Magazine*, xiii. 9 Two bust portraits in oval frames illustrate 'Histories of the Tête-à-Tête annexed; . ' An account of the Prince of Wales, and of an actress who had married an attorney's clerk, whom the prince saw first in the part of Ophelia Evidently Mrs Robinson, but no allusion is made to the part of Perdita in which she impressed the Prince on 3 Dec 1780 [1] *Hamlet* was played at Drury Lane

---

[1] The rupture between the Prince and Mrs Robinson, and her threat to publish his letters, is referred to as 'chocolate house chat' in the *Town and Country Magazine*, Apr 1781, xiii 210.

on 21 Apr. 1780 Genest. vi 133 This *Tête-à-Tête* is written with a certain reticence and decorum, with no allusion to the earlier one on Mrs. Robinson, see No 5741. For the liaison see No. 5767, &c.

$2\frac{3}{4} \times 2\frac{5}{16}$ in.   B M.L , P.P. 5442 b.

5866 Nº IV MʳˢB——N.
            Nº V. THE DARING MAGISTRATE.

Publish'd by A. Hamilton Junʳ Fleet Street March 1; 1781.

Engraving. *Town and Country Magazine*, xiii. 65. Two bust portraits in oval frames illustrate 'Histories of the Tête-à-Tête annexed; or, Memoirs of the Daring Magistrate and Mʳˢ Br——n'. An account of Brackley Kennett, Lord Mayor, notorious for his cowardice during the Gordon Riots Beginning as an ostler in Yorkshire, he became a waiter in a Pall Mall house; he saved money and won a lottery prize, and 'commenced wine merchant'. Having acquired the good will and patronage of persons of quality by 'his former faithful services in many *particular cases* that required some address', he acquired a fortune, and his patrons, 'finding he made an excellent *Butt*', often admitted him into their company. He has admitted to 'a certain patriotic alderman' [Wilkes] that during the riots he was seized with a fit of *temerity*, and had not the power to move' See also Nos. 5688, 5689, 5690, and *City Biography*, 1800, p. 139 f. Mrs. Br——n is the daughter of a bankrupt soap-boiler and the young widow of an officer in the customs, forced by destitution to accept the disagreeable offer of the daring magistrate.

Ovals, $2\frac{3}{4} \times 2\frac{5}{16}$ in.   B.M.L., P.P. 5442 b.

5867 Nº VII. Mᴿˢ B——E.
            Nº VIII THE CEREMONIAL MASTER

Publish'd by A. Hamilton Junʳ in Fleet Street, April 1, 1781.

Engraving. *Town and Country Magazine*, xiii 121. Two bust portraits in oval frames illustrate 'Histories of the Tête-à-Tête annexed; . .' [*ut supra*] An account of a descendant of a noble family which has for a succession of years held a conspicuous post in the royal household He is Sir Clement Cotterell-Dormer, Master of the Ceremonies, a post held for several generations in the Cotterell family. Mrs. B. was Betty Williams, daughter of a labouring man in Cobham, who became a nursemaid, lived with a naval surgeon, passing as his wife, and was left destitute.

Ovals, $2\frac{3}{4} \times 2\frac{5}{16}$ in   B M.L., P.P. 5442 b.

5868 Nº XIII. THE BIRD OF PARADISE
            Nº XIV COL WITWOU'D

London. Publish'd by A. Hamilton Junʳ Fleet Street May 1ˢᵗ 1781.

Engraving. *Town and Country Magazine*, xiii 177 Two bust portraits in oval frames illustrate 'Histories of the Tête-à-Tête annexed;   ' From his portrait he appears to be Colonel Boden, a favourite subject of the caricaturist, see Nos 5753, 6064 He is here called Witwou'd because he is 'one of the greatest simile mongers in the three kingdoms' His father was an officer in the army, much esteemed by the late Prince of Wales, through whose interest 'our hero obtained a pair of colours at a very early age'. He has thus been 'so long a public character' He always paid great attention to 'the first-rate demi-reps, who took a pleasure in his company on account of the singularity of his conversation, accompanied by an extraordinary stammering'.

The lady, Mrs M. [Mahon], descended from a noble family, tried unsuccessfully to make a good match, married M., from whom she separated, being kept first, it is said, by Lord L——n [Lyttelton] On finding herself without a protector she obtained an engagement at Covent Garden, and 'has acted several times this season'. This was followed by a settlement from a nobleman, which enabled her to keep an elegant chariot with the arms of her family His marriage was followed by overtures from Colonel W. See No. 5948.

Ovals, $2\frac{3}{4} \times 2\frac{3}{8}$ in.   B.M L., P P. 5442 b.

5869 Nᵒ XIII. Mᴿˢ F——G.
     Nᵒ XIV. THE LENIENT COMMANDER.

Publish'd June 1ˢᵗ; 1781 by J. [sic] Hamilton Junʳ Fleet Street.

Engraving. *Town and Country Magazine*, xiii 233. Two bust portraits in oval frames illustrate 'Histories of the Tête-à-Tête annexed, . .' An account of Thomas Gage (1721–87), here called 'the Lenient Commander' because of his reluctance to engage in hostilities in America Mrs F——g was the daughter of one L——d, a poor parson, who became a fashionable milliner's apprentice, a 'high road to perdition'. After being seduced she passed as the wife of Mr. F——g, a naval lieutenant, whose prolonged absence at sea forced her to seek another supporter.

Ovals, $2\frac{3}{4} \times 2\frac{1}{4}$ in.   B M.L , P P. 5442 b.

5870 Nᵒ XVI. Mᴿˢ L—B—T
     Nᵒ XVII THE NAUTICAL SCRIBE.

London. Publish'd July 1; 1781, by A. Hamilton Junʳ Fleet Street

Engraving. *Town and Country Magazine*, xiii. 289. Two bust portraits in oval frames illustrate 'Histories of the Tête-à-Tête annexed; .   '. He is evidently Philip Stephens, Secretary (since 1763) of the Admiralty and M.P. for Sandwich, cr. a baronet in 1795 He is here said to have assisted Beau Nash at Bath and to have first introduced the Gunnings to public places in London. Mrs L is the wife of a penniless man, after acting at Brighton she became the mistress of a peer, and on being deserted by him accepted the arrangements offered by the Nautical Scribe.

Ovals, $2\frac{3}{4} \times 2\frac{1}{4}$ in   B M.L., P P. 5442 b.

5871 Nᵒ XIX. THE CAPTIVATING Mᴿˢ C—PB—LL
     Nᵒ XX. THE GENEROUS GALLANT.

London Publish'd by A Hamilton Junʳ Fleet Street 1 Augˢᵗ 1781.

Engraving. *Town and Country Magazine*, xiii. 345. Two bust portraits in oval frames illustrate 'Histories of the Tête-à-Tête annexed, . . .'. He is 'descended from an ancient and noble family who have made a conspicuous figure in the annals of this country'. He built himself 'an elegant house from a plan drawn by himself   now a very conspicuous building in the purlieus of Marylebone'. This would apply to Stratford Place, built *c* 1775, from the plans of Edward Stratford, second Earl of Aldborough, d 1801, on the site of the Old Banqueting House on the Tyburn Road (Oxford Street). But there is nothing by which the subject of this Tête-à-Tête can be identified with certainty. Mrs. Campbell is the widow of a lieutenant in the army killed in America, who is seeking for a place as housekeeper to a single gentleman, and is said to have agreed to a settlement of £300 a year.

Ovals, $2\frac{3}{4} \times 2\frac{5}{16}$ in.   B M L., P P 5442 b.

5872 Nº XXII. MRS W—TS—N.
          Nº XXIII THE CONNOISSEUR

Publish'd by A. Hamilton Jun' Fleet Street 1 Sep' 1781

Engraving. *Town and Country Magazine*, xiii 401 Two bust portraits in oval frames illustrate 'Histories of the Tête-à-Tête annexed; . ' He is descended from an ancient family, a near relation of his father being a Lord Chief Justice at the beginning of the century. He is thought the best whist-player in England, with expert knowledge of pictures. He married a dowager duchess, after which he was promoted to the rank of colonel, and has since obtained an office of profit under Government He is presumably Staats Long Morris who married in 1756 the widow of the 3rd Duke of Gordon, who died 1779 He was then (1756) of New York, in 1781 a Major General and M.P. (1774–89) for Elgin Burghs

Mrs W is the daughter of a poor parson and the widow of a lieutenant of marines, to whom he makes 'as ample an allowance as his circumstances will afford'

Ovals, $2\frac{3}{4} \times 2\frac{5}{16}$ in.   B.M L., P.P. 5442 b.

5873 Nº XXV. THE ENGAGING MRS F——Y.
          Nº XXVI THE CONSTANT ADMIRER.

London, Publish'd by A Hamilton Jun' Fleet Street Oct' 1ˢᵗ 1781.

Engraving. *Town and Country Magazine*, xiii. 457. Two bust portraits in oval frames illustrate 'Histories of the Tête-à-Tête annexed, . . . '. An account of George, third Earl of Orford, grandson of Sir Robert Walpole, the nephew whose attacks of insanity gave so much anxiety to Horace Walpole. Nothing of that appears in this account which is concerned with his travels, and his judicious avoidance of politics Mis. F——y is Patty, daughter of a Norfolk farmer, one of his tenants, who became his house-keeper and to whom he has been faithful for over twenty years She is the 'Patty' whom Walpole calls Orford's 'Dalilah' Ap. 9, 1779 *Letters*, x. 218.

Ovals, $2\frac{3}{4} \times 2\frac{5}{8}$ in   B.M.L , P.P. 5442 b.

5874 Nº XXIX MISS F——
          Nº XXX. THE INTREPID COMMODORE

London, Publish'd by A. Hamilton Jun' Fleet Street 1 Nov' 1781.

Engraving *Town and Country Magazine*, xiii. 513. Two bust portraits in oval frames illustrate 'Histories of the Tête-à-Tête annexed, . . . '. An account of the career of Commodore George Johnstone (1730–87), alluding in veiled words to his expedition against the Cape of Good Hope of 1781, see No. 5960

Ovals, $2\frac{11}{16} \times 2\frac{1}{4}$ in.   B M.L., P.P. 5442 b.

5875 N° XXXI. MRS J.——S
    N° XXXII. THE HUMANE J——E [JUDGE]

London, Publish'd by A Hamilton Jun' Fleet Street 1 Dec' 1781.

Engraving *Town and Country Magazine*, xiii. 569. Two bust portraits in oval frames, one that of a judge in wig and gown. They illustrate 'Histories of the Tête-à-Tête annexed; . . ' An account of Sir Henry Gould (1710–94), the clues being his Somersetshire origin, his appointment as K.C. in 1754, and an allusion to the Gordon Riots His early (supposed) amours are recounted Mrs. Jones is the daughter of a Welsh clergyman, and a milliner's apprentice, who became a courtesan, whom the judge is said to have established in a snug house in Marylebone

$2\frac{3}{4} \times 2\frac{5}{16}$ in   B M.L., P.P. 5442 b.

5876 SIR SAMUEL HOUSE.

[Gillray.]

London Published July 12. 1781, by C Knight, Berwick Street.

Aquatint Portrait (W L) of Sam House seated in an arm-chair, a wine-glass in his r hand, his l. hand on his hip. At his r side, on a small rectangular table, is a punch-bowl inscribed *Fox for eve*[r]. He is in his well-known dress, see No. 5696, &c, and wears ungartered stockings. Beneath the title is engraved ·

    Libertas et natula [sic] *Solum*

A companion print to No. 5877.
Grego, *Gillray*, p. 32.

$8 \times 6\frac{9}{16}$ in.

5877 SIR TOBY THATCH, CANDIDATE FOR GARRET.

[? Gillray.]

London Published July 12 1781 by C Knight Berwick Street.

Aquatint A companion print to No. 5876. Portrait (W.L) of a man leaning back in an arm-chair, his legs crossed His r hand hangs down-wards, holding a tankard whose contents are pouring on the floor In his l. hand he holds the stem of the pipe which he is smoking. He wears a small wig, and is neatly and plainly dressed, with buckled shoes. On the r is a rectangular table on which is a foaming tankard, inscribed *Sam House, Wardour Street, S' Ane* Beneath the title is engraved *Jocando Bibendo Vivimus. His utere.*

He is evidently a well-known frequenter of the public-house kept by Sam House, see Nos 5696, 5697, 5876 After a dissolution of Parliament a burlesque election was held at Garrett, Wandsworth, to elect a 'Mayor of Garrett', who was usually some well-known character in low-life. See

Malcolm, *Manners and Customs of London*, 1808, p 222. The successful candidate in 1785 was Jeffery Dunstan. Toby Thatch was a character in O'Keefe's *London Hermit*, 1793

$8 \times 6\frac{5}{8}$ in.

5878 THE HON^{BLE} CHA^S JA^S FOX

[After Bunbury]   *J. Baldrey Sculp^t*

London Publish'd April 12th 1781 by J Baldrey N° 37 Green St Gros^r Sq^r & E Hedges N° 92 Cornhill.

Stipple. Fox (H L.) in profile to the l. in the attitude of an orator, r arm outstretched, the hand and wrist cut off by the margin of the print. See No 6313, a later copy. Cf No. 5755.
Reproduced, W. Sichel, *Sheridan*, 1909, ii 2.

$4\frac{3}{4} \times 5\frac{3}{4}$ (oval).

5879 [LADY ARCHER]

Bretherton Junr f: Pub^d as the Act directs J^y 8th 1781.

Engraving (coloured and uncoloured impressions). Portrait (H.L.) of Lady Archer in profile to the r., her aquiline nose exaggerated, and she is frowning. She wears a hat tilted forward, her hair being dressed high with a club resting on her shoulders.
She was Sarah (1741–1801), d of James West, and widow of Andrew, 2nd Baron Archer. Her profile shows no trace of the 'perfect and lovely' features admired by Fanny Burney in 1783 *Diary*, ii 179. See No. 6114. She was a noted whip, and was also noted for painting her face, cf. 'A was an Archer and painted her face', Walpole, *Letters*, xiii 322, and 'Lacker faced A—ch—r', Lord Townshend, *Misc. Poetry*, p. 10.

$4\frac{7}{8} \times 3\frac{7}{8}$ in. (pl).

5880 [GENERAL OGLETHORPE.¹]

Publish'd as the Act Directs J^y 13th 1781   C. B [Bretherton] Junr

Engraving (coloured impression) Profile head, caricatured, of Oglethorpe the philanthropist (1696–1785) He has an enormous nose and a projecting jaw, giving the appearance of extreme old age. He wears a short bushy wig. At his death he was believed to be a centenarian L. F. Church, *Oglethorpe*, 1932, p. 1

$3\frac{7}{8} \times 3\frac{7}{8}$ in.

5881 [JOHN WILKES]

C B J^r [Bretherton.]

Publish'd according to Act of P^t J^y 16th 1781

Engraving (coloured impression) Caricature bust portrait of Wilkes in profile to the l., the r. eye just visible, showing his squint. He has the appearance of an old and toothless man, 'in corporeal ruin', as described by Wraxall, *Memoirs*, 1884, ii 49. See No. 6067.

$4 \times 3\frac{1}{8}$ in (pl.).

¹ Identified by Miss Banks

5882 [LORD THURLOW.]

Chs: Bretherton f.   [After James Sayers?][1]

Publish'd Augt 8th 1781

Engraving. Bust portrait in profile to r. A caricature of Thurlow, the Lord Chancellor, wearing a low-crowned hat and tie-wig

$4\frac{1}{4} \times 3\frac{1}{8}$ in. (pl.).

5883 [JAMES WALLACE.]

Ch^s Bretherton J^r   [After James Sayers?][1]

Publis^d Novr 23^d 1781

Engraving (coloured and uncoloured impressions). Bust portrait in profile to the l. of Wallace, Attorney General, Aug. 1780–Apr. 1782. He wears a legal wig and gown.

$4\frac{1}{4} \times 3\frac{1}{8}$ in.

5884 [VESTRIS JUNIOR OR VESTR' ALLARD.[2]]

C^s Bretherton f.

Publish'd Augt 18th 1781

Engraving (coloured and uncoloured impressions). Bust portrait in profile to the r. of the famous dancer. His head is thrown back with an arrogant expression and protruding under-lip. His hat is under his arm; his hair or wig is in a black bag. See Nos. 5903, 5905, 5906.

$5\frac{7}{8} \times 4\frac{15}{16}$ in. (pl.).

5885 [UNIDENTIFIED CARICATURE PORTRAIT]

Ch^s Bretherton Junr Published Novr 26th 1781.

Engraving. Bust portrait of a man in profile to the r., much caricatured. He is narrow-chested, wears a bag-wig and ruffled shirt.

$4\frac{1}{8} \times 3\frac{1}{16}$ in. (pl.)

5886 THE PAW-MINY.

THE COCK A TOE VULGURLY CALL'D COCKATOO.

Publsh'd as the act directs J^y 23^d 81. C.B.J: [C. Bretherton Junr?]

Engraving. A man in profile to the r. standing on tip-toe in the attitude of a dancing-master. His elbows are held out, he holds his hat. He is very thin and is dressed like the Frenchman of caricature, with a high toupet wig. Mr. Hawkins writes 'a MS note calls him "Mr. Fitzgerald"'. He has some resemblance to caricatures of the elder Vestris

$6\frac{1}{2} \times 4\frac{1}{8}$ in. (pl.).

5887 ['SIR' JOHN GALLINI[3]]

C^s Bretherton f.

Publis'd Augt 16th 1781.

Engraving. Bust portrait in profile to the r. of a man holding under his

[1] Impressions with the works of James Sayers
[2] Identified by Miss Banks
[3] Identified by Mr Hawkins.

arm a kit or small violin. A ballet dancer and dancing-master (1728–1805) who, having been given the knighthood of the Golden Spur by the Pope, assumed the style of Sir. He married Lady Elizabeth Bertie, daughter of the Earl of Abingdon

$7\frac{7}{8} \times 5$ in (pl.).

Another impression, coloured, with *T Cornell, Bruton S^t* in place of signature.

5888 [LOUIS WELTJE]

C. Bretherton Junr f.

Publish'd Novr 1st 1781.

Engraving. W.L. portrait in profile to the r. of a plainly dressed man standing, his r. hand in his breeches-pocket. A well-known German cook and confectioner who kept the Cocoa-nut in St James's Street, born 1745 Brunswick, died 1810 At this time there was 'a club at Weltje's' consisting of young men associated with the Ministry. *Hist. MSS. Comm., Carlisle MSS*, 1897, pp. 555, 573, 579, 580. He was afterwards associated with the politics of the Prince of Wales, and from 1785–9 was Controller of the kitchen and cellars of Carlton House, where he was a well-known character. See *Gent. Mag*, 1800, ii 1109, Angelo, *Reminiscences*, 1904, i. 330, ii. 35–8; Wraxall, *Memoirs*, 1884, v. 307. For Mrs. Weltje's shop see No 6317.

$10\frac{7}{8} \times 7\frac{3}{8}$ in.

5889 [THE DUCHESS OF NORFOLK?]   [n.d. *c.* 1781]

Publish'd as the Act Directs   *C^s Bretherton f^t*

Engraving (coloured and uncoloured impressions). Caricature portrait of a lady (T.Q L) seated at a table playing cards. She is in profile to the l., is stout, with a small nose and projecting underlip. She wears a cap over her high-dressed hair. She holds her cards in her r. hand; her l. hand is in her lap, under the table, holding an ace, another card lies beside it. A pile of coins is on the corner of the table to her l. On one impression is written in an old hand 'The Dutchess of N——k'.

She was Katharine, d of John Brockholes, m. Charles Howard, the 10th duke, 8 Nov 1729, and d 21 Nov. 1784.

$4\frac{3}{16} \times 3\frac{5}{16}$ in

5890 [UNIDENTIFIED CARICATURE PORTRAIT]

B. T. Smith F Publish'd Decr 30th 1781.

Engraving (coloured impression). Bust portrait, caricature, of a man in profile to the r His nose projects sharply, almost at a r angle with his forehead. He is deep-chested, and wears a shirt-frill. Similar in general character to the small portraits etched by Charles Bretherton.

$4\frac{1}{4} \times 3\frac{1}{8}$ in

5891 LORD R—B—H

Etch'd by a Lady   [*Aug. 1781?*[1]]

Engraving Bust portrait of a young man in profile to the r. much carica-

[1] Dated in Miss Banks's hand, presumably the date of purchase.

tured. He has a large aquiline nose, large eye, receding forehead and chin, long thin neck, and sloping shoulders

The letters suggest no peer except the Duke of Roxburghe (1740–1804), noted as a collector of rare books and broadside ballads. The portrait has no resemblance to that engraved after W. Hamilton in Doyle's *Official Baronage*, ii. 294.

$4\frac{1}{4} \times 3\frac{3}{8}$ in.

5892 SIGNOR PUPPY. FIRST CATGUT SCRAPER.

Pub^d Nov. 27. 81. by H. Humphrey N° 18 New Bond Street.

Engraving (coloured impression) Portrait (W.L.) of a man standing in profile to the r. holding a violin in his r. hand, a bow in his l.

He is Giuseppe Puppo (1749–1827), an eminent violinist who was in England for some years before 1784 Grove, *Dict. of Music*

The original water-colour is in the Print Department, No 12 in volume lettered 'Designs supplied by Amateurs to Gillray'.

$4\frac{3}{4} \times 3\frac{5}{8}$ in

5893 [HENRY GORDON. BUTLER TO TRIN. COLL· CAMBRIDGE 1781.][1]

J. H. fec^t.[1]]

Engraving. Bust portrait, looking to the r., of an elderly man with a large nose and a stern expression He wears a short curled wig, his staff of office rests against his r. shoulder Beneath it is etched·

> *Ecce minister ego Bacchi, custosq sacelli,*
> *Indicat officium candida virga meum.*
> *Multa equidem merin de praesule, multa decano*
> *Sedulitatae, Fide, relligione, mero.*

$4 \times 3\frac{1}{4}$ in. (pl).

5894 M^R C—M—L THE JOLLY PRESENTER OF THE CANNONGATE KIRK IN EDINBURGH,

Pub^d by H Humphrey N° 18 New Bond Street [c. 1781][2]

Engraving H.L. portrait in profile to the l of a man holding a music score. He is fat and smiling, and wears his own scanty hair After the title is engraved, *Singing Psalms of a Morning and over a Bowl of Punch Scotch Tunes at Night*

He is John Campbell, teacher of music and precentor of the Canongate Church from 1775 to his death in 1795 The subject of a portrait by Kay. See Paton, *Portraits and Etchings by John Kay*, 1887, ii, pp. 92–5.

$4\frac{1}{2} \times 2\frac{7}{8}$ in.

5895 [GEORGE III AND HIS FAMILY]   [1781]

Drawing in pen and wash, indented with a stylus and blackened on the reverse for transfer to a plate A procession walking in couples (r to l) across a quadrangle or court They go in order of age· the two youngest

---

[1] Written on the print in an old hand   [2] Dated 1781 by Miss Banks

infants, each in the arms of a lady, go first, the king and queen last Prince Frederick and the Prince of Wales walk together, the next couple, the Princess Royal and Prince William Henry, turn round to look at their elder brothers. Princess Augusta Sophia has her arm round the shoulders of her brother Edward, next, Princess Elizabeth walks with an arm across the shoulders of Ernest, two little boys, Augustus and Adolphus, are next. In front of them are two little girls, Princess Mary and Princess Sophia. The two infants in arms are Octavius and Alfred (born in 1779 and 1780). The figures, on a very small side, are drawn with much delicacy, and a certain humorous intention.

$4\frac{1}{4} \times 6\frac{5}{16}$ in.

5896 [A SATIRE ON ONE FLINT.]

Pub^d Augst 20th 1781 by I. Williams N° 34 Strand

Engraving, above engraved verses The head of a military officer, grossly caricatured, in profile to the r. within a circle formed by a snake. His unkempt hair is in a small pigtail queue The outside circle is engraved ·

> *He's Ugly, He's False, His Friends he'll betray*
> *In this, & in that, & in that kind of way*

On each side of the circle are military emblems: a flag, a tent, a pile of drums, a row of halberds

The verses are signed *Belzebub* and begin,

> *My best Friend,*
> *O thou despis'd of all Mankind*
> *Whose Soul to me has been consignd*

The lines,

> *To deck thy Lady's Room Dear Fl . . t*
> *I with my Love send thee this Print,*

leave no doubt as to the name of the subject

$2\frac{3}{8} \times 3\frac{13}{16}$ in. (pl 6×4 in).

5897 WINDSOR CASTLE IN A CONSUMPTION, OR THE LITTLE MAN'S MISTAKE

Pub^d acc^g to Act Feby 3 1781 by M Darly N° 159 Fleet Street.

Engraving in illustration of a dialogue printed below it. The figures have numbers referring to the dialogue Windsor Castle is falling into ruins, part of it shored up by beams; a stream of water pours through an archway In the foreground are groups of small figures discussing the repairs · 'The Little Man' appears to be 'No. 1', or 'M^r T—ds—y', evidently T. Tildesley, Clerk of the Board of Works at Windsor Castle and the Queen's Lodge He is in naval dress, and stands (r.) holding a handkerchief to his eyes, saying '1 would rather been [*sic*] buried in the ruins than thus treated'. A group of officers of the Board of Works is seated at a round table (l.) with books and plans. Among these are (11) 'Sir Wm. C—mb—rs [Chambers], see No 5157, the Comptroller, (12) 'M^r S—db—y' [Thomas Sandby, Architect]; (13) 'M^r C——se' [Kenton Couse, Secretary and Clerk Itinerant] On one of the towers stands the Devil with a trident, and on the top of the broken wall (6) 'Sl—gs—y', who says, 'Huzza, boys, this is a rare job for me'. Labourers are working at the walls It appears from the dialogue that Tildesley is to be dismissed because, owing to his alterations by stopping up drains or watercourses, the building has been endangered; moreover, he has acted without consulting the Board of Works, and is accused of a 'firey pitch, tow and tar temper'. The disasters, says the Clerk to the Board, are 'no wonder . . . when sailors are appointed surveyors' 'All the tradesmen' say 'If a worse come in his place it must be that gentleman [the devil] upon the adjacent tower'.

In the centre is (8) smoking a pipe and holding a cane who is 'Mr W—ds—r [? George III], he says, 'Well B——th, I understand that part of the Castle is tumbling down, if so I shall have more labourers to pay all the winter Let me have a fresh pipe and a pint upon the strength of it ' Surveying implements lie on the ground. See also No. 5898.

$7\frac{5}{16}$-$13\frac{1}{8}$ in.

5898 JOHN DOUBLE FACE OR THE DECEITFUL VULCAN OF WINDSOR

Pubd as the Act directs Augst 1st 1781 by I. Williams No 34 Strand London.

Mezzotint A tall thin man and his wife walking (r. to l.) in a street. He has two faces and the long ears of an animal; the face in the normal position has a regular profile, the one facing backwards, though resembling it, is sinister and more aquiline. He has a forked tail, his l. leg is that of an animal with a cloven hoof. The woman has a feathered hat, beneath her skirt appear a forked tail and a cloven hoof. She looks at him, holding a ball or medallion between her r. thumb and fore-finger, saying, *My dear Jacky as we have lost the Sun-fire Office let us pursue our plan* He answers, *I will my dear & ruin him that got it if we can* Attached to his coat is the sign of the Sun Fire Office, a sun with a face surrounded with rays Beneath it is the date (or number) *1777*. He holds in his hand a print headed *D**n Fall of the Little Man*. It represents part of Windsor Castle as in No. 5897 with a stream of water flowing through an archway as in that print. At their feet are papers inscribed *Mr Miller Printer of the Lonn Eveng* [Post] and *To Mr Say in Ave Maria Lane* [1]

Behind (r.) two men (father and son) are standing in conversation. One, stout and middle-aged, wearing an apron, the other, slim and fashionably dressed, has his r. hand on his father's shoulder, his l. fist is clenched The father, whose r hand holds his son's r. wrist, is saying *O Son O Son remember I am your Father and you had better not have drawn the plan*. The son answers, *Let me hear no more I was perswaded to it*

In the background (l.) is a shop-front; the door, whose upper part is of glass panes, is surmounted by the royal arms. On one of the panes is inscribed *Davis Smith* In the windows on each side of the door watches are suspended, and one pane (l.) is filled by the dial of a clock. A very slim passer-by, with papers under his arm and walking with a tasselled cane, is looking in at the window

This satire evidently relates to the same subject as No 5897, that is, to the dismissal of Tildesley, the Clerk of the Works at Windsor, whose alterations to the castle have endangered its stability.

$8\frac{5}{8} \times 12\frac{1}{2}$ in.

[1] Edward Say, in Ave Maria Lane, was Printer of the *General Evening Post* in 1763 T. Mortimer, *Universal Director*, 1763, p. 61

5899 THE CONTENDING LAWYERS OR WHO SHALL FIRST BOARD THE CATHARINE FRIGATE.

publishd as yᵉ Act Directs 10 Febʸ 1781.

No 4086 oposite Hungry Market in the Stand. [sic]

Engraving The interior of a grocer's shop. A lady wearing a hat and short cloak sits on a chair, her wrists crossed, she is saying *I'll Do any thing for money* On each shoulder leans an admirer. One (l) is labelled *Pady Swirk*, from his pocket protrudes a document *Rygate Assize*. He is saying, *Hara by my shoul if you'l Leave your Jerry Sneak you shall have your Law for nothing atll atall my Dear Kitt fig.* The other (r.) wears a cockaded hat; a document projecting from his pocket is inscribed *Spirituall Court*. He is saying, *My Dear Kitty Figg I are an Officer in the Malitia yet Bread to the Law & have a Damnd good Memory My Dear Mʳˢ Figg* Behind these three stands the husband holding a pair of stag's antlers on his head and saying *I think the[y] fit me what cant be cur'd must be endur'd* On the l stands a man whose r leg ends in a cloven hoof, he holds a label inscribed *Willegig Tea Dealer Bishop Street* and points to his l saying *Though I Dare not own my self a Partner I'll be your very good Friend for old acquaintance sake in the Bench* (implying that both have been prisoners for debt in the King's Bench) It is not clear whether he is addressing the husband or Pady Swirk. A little boy says to him *Pa Pa what shall I sware.*

On the r of the room, ranged on a shelf or in the window (r), are rows of sugar-loaves, below them are boxes and canisters inscribed *Bohea Tea Gree Tea.* At the back are more rows of canisters, and a festooned curtain probably dividing the shop from the parlour behind it.

This appears to record some personal scandal relating to a grocer's wife. It is the ill-drawn work of an amateur.

6¼ × 8¼ in.

5900 A PEEP INTO WESTMINSTER HALL ON A CALL OF SERJEANTS.

R. Dighton del.

London, printed for R. Sayer & J Bennett Nᵒ 53 Fleet Street, & J Smith Nᵒ 35 Cheapside, as the Act directs March 1. 1781.

Engraving. The interior of a panelled room Two judges (r) sit side by side on a settee, in profile to the l., in their wigs and furred robes. On the l. stand a number of barristers in wigs and gowns, one of whom (l) already wears the coif of the serjeant-at-law. Two barristers, one wearing the black patch of a serjeant,[1] appear to be acting as masters of the ceremonies, both hold papers On the ground before the judges are two flat mattress-cushions, on one kneels a serjeant-elect, the judge is putting the coif on his head. Behind the judge stands a barrister grinning and looking through a single eye-glass.

A note on an impression in the Ashmolean Museum identifies the judges as Mansfield and Loughborough.

[1] The serjeants-at-law were a superior order of barrister (distinguished by wearing a white coif or cap with a black patch) from whom the judges were chosen. They were abolished in 1880

On 8 February 1781 Cranley Thomas Kirby and Giles Rooke were admitted Serjeants Haydn, *Book of Dignities*, p. 249 Beneath the design is engraved,

Esto Perpetua.

$8\frac{1}{8} \times 6\frac{7}{8}$ in.

5901 [LORD DERBY FOLLOWING MISS FARREN]

[After Bunbury]

Publishd July 20ᵗʰ 1781 by J. R Smith No 83 Oxford Street nearly oposite the Pantheon.

Aquatint A short man riding (r. to l) after a coach, the back of which only appears in the print, with a footman standing behind it The rider's head is turned to his r concealing his profile. His legs are thrust forward on each side of the horse's neck On a building (r) is a placard, *Angel Fetter Lane Derby Diligence continues flying daily as usual Inside* [the poster is torn at this point] *Outsides & Children on the Lap half price perform'd (if God permit by Bull & Co.* Beneath the design is etched.

> *When I follow'd a lass that was froward & shy*
> *Oh l stuck to her stuff but she would not comply*

A portrait of Edward, 12th Earl of Derby, following the coach of Miss Farren (1759–1829) the actress. The attachment was the occasion of many squibs, and of other caricatures. Lord Derby married her in 1797 on the death of his wife, from whom he had long been separated

This must be the print of which Hare wrote to Lord Carlisle, 29 Dec. 1781, 'Derby is still in pursuit of Miss Farren. . . I really believe he has attained his object, which is, being stared at by the whole Play-house, and talked of by the whole Town The Caricatura has had the good effect of mending his seat on horseback which is totally changed and consequently improved.' *Hist. MSS Comm., Carlisle MSS* , 1897, pp. 555–6. See No 6263

7×9 in.

5902 A VISIT TO CAMP OR THE ROGUES MARCH, [1781]

[Imprint perhaps cut off]

Engraving. An elderly and obese man, wearing spectacles and a hat, a dark gown over his coat, is walking slowly (l to r), his hands behind him, in front of a crowd of soldiers (l), blowing fifes and beating drums, while others wave their hats, point and laugh On the r is a military marquee. Two small dogs bark at the man's heels. In the foreground (l) is a milestone, *Rye 1 Mile*

With the print are verses, cut from a newspaper, entitled, *To T Lamb Esq. Mayor of Rye, on being, what they call, Drumm'd out of Camp by the Sixth Regiment of Foot.* They do not explain the incident, but the press-cutting incidentally shows that their date is 1781

$7 \times 12\frac{3}{8}$ in.

531

5903 BASS RELIEF FOUND AT THE OPERA HOUSE.

[P. Sandby.][1]

Published 7 April 1781 as the Act directs by R Meadows.

Engraving, partly mezzotinted A design in several compartments purporting to represent five fragments of a stone bas-relief dug up 'at the
laying of the foundation of the Opera House', depicting the dancing of the
two Vestris. In the upper part of the print are two equal fragments of a
frieze · [1] An ape capers between Vestris *fils* (l) and Vestris *père* (r). The
two dancers are standing on one leg, their arms held out, in attitudes which
though caricatured are graceful. The son has a feathered hat, the father
a cap surmounted with a coronet of ostrich-feathers. The ape, dressed in
a coat and waistcoat, has a muff slung round its neck and a head-dress of
peacock's feathers. He mimics the pose of the dancers On the r is a
classical statue of a nude man, the l. hand broken off at the wrist Beneath
the ape are the words *In Fashione*, beneath the statue, *Out of Fashione*, across
the top of the fragment is inscribed *Son of this Father.*

[2] A similar design of an ape dancing between the two Vestris. The ape
is not dressed up, but has branches of oak leaves attached to its head in
imitation of the head-dress of the elder Vestris On the l. is a similar statue
inscribed, *Grace in olde Times.* Across the top of the fragment is *Vest . . s
father and son*; and below Vestris *père* (l.), *Moderne Gracefull Postures*

The lower part of the print is in three compartments. [3] Vestris *père* (l)
dances, above his head is inscribed *I am alone.* An ape dressed up in
feathered hat, coat, and sword, takes a pinch of snuff, above its head is
inscribed, *No Pardieu behold your tutor* Behind (centre) is the lower part
of a classical statue of a man from which the torso and head have fallen
and lie on the ground. It is inscribed *Simplicity adieu.*

[4] On the r is a companion design inscribed *Vestris en Roy.* Vestris,
in feathered hat, coat, and top-boots (l), capers in front of a dressed-up ape
who bows before him, doffing its hat, a large muff is slung across its
shoulders and hangs down its back.

[5] In the centre between [3] and [4] is the principal and central design,
within a shield whose supporters are, dexter, a zany in a striped suit, and
sinister (r), a fool in parti-coloured dress and high fool's cap. In the centre
of the shield is a man in pseudo-Elizabethan dress wearing a ribbon and
star, behind him are two ladies, one of whom wears a coronet. All three
hold out bags of money to a dancer who strikes an attitude on their l. In
one hand he holds out a ticket inscribed *Box*, in the other, a paper, *Vestris
Opera second benifit.* His tunic is decorated with fleurs-de-lys. On the
nobleman's r. a man kneels with a face of distress, holding out a paper
inscribed *Opera . . Sufferers . . . Barbadoe[s] . . . America* Behind him a
building has been shattered by a violent storm, clouds and lightning fill the
sky above it. The nobleman repels the suppliant with his hand, while he
tramples under his feet a paper inscribed *Barbados.* Beneath the shield
is a scroll, inscribed with words addressed to the suppliant from Barbados
(l.), *Away we have no time to attend to Trifles* and (r) addressed to Vestris,
Your owne price secure us but places. The shield is surmounted by a crest
of a fool's cap and bells with the motto *Wear me who will.*

Beneath the r. and l. compartments of this design is engraved: *To such
of the Nobilitie, Gentrie &c of G***t B***t**n whose hearts are so un-*

---

[1] So attributed by E. Hawkins Similar in manner to Sandby's aquatinted
balloon satires of 1784

natturallıe devoide of feelıng, as to prefer the squanderıng away of that Wealth, which God has put them in possessıone of (as Stewards of hıs bountıe) upon ımpertınent Coxcombs, the very scum of a rıval Natıon, and at best but the shadow of a Contemptable anımal, to nobly relıevıng the Dıstresses of their unfortunate Countrıe Men, thıs Sculpture ıs humbly Dedicated

Attached to the prınt ıs a printed 'Description of the curious ancient BASS RELIEF which was found upon layıng the Foundatıon of the present Opera-House, ın the Haymarket'. The 'frıendly Reader' ıs requested to 'compare the *Barbarity* of the old Tımes wıth the *Polıteness* of the present'. 'Could we . . believe that our Ancestors were so totally lost to true Taste and Judgment as to sıt wıth patience to behold the rıdıculous unmeanıng Attıtudes of a French *Posture-Master* especıally when the Artıst had so evidently produced the *orıgınal Brute,* from whence this wretched Plagıary borrowed hıs chıef Graces?' The supporters of the Arms are explained as 'Folly and Absurdıty'. The prınt 'ıs faıthfully copied from an old Drawıng ın Bıster . . '

Barbados was devastated by a hurrıcane ın October 1780. On 24 Jan. Lord North proposed a grant of £80,000 for the relıef of the island, which was unanimously agreed to. The prınt contrasts the support gıven to the performance on behalf of the Barbados sufferers wıth that gıven to the benefit of the younger Vestrıs, see Nos. 5905, 5906.

In the season of 1780–1 London society went mad over the dancıng of the two Vestrıs who had come from Parıs. Walpole, *Letters,* ̇\1. 340–1, 346, 368, 374, 381, 406, 422 For the sake of the benefit of Vestrıs *fıls,* on 23 Feb. 1781, the second reading of Burke's Bıll of Economic Reform was postponed, Burke saying, 'to a great part of that House, a dance was a much more ımportant object than a war, and the Opera House must be maıntaıned whatever became of the country' *Parl̷ Hıst.* xxı. 1243. Walpole, *Last Journals,* 1910, ıı. 348. Much resentment was roused by the popularity of the French dancers and the enormous sums made by them durıng a war wıth France See 'Memoirs of Signor Vestris, Senıor' ın the *London Magazıne,* Apr. 1781. The king ıncurred disapproval by not attendıng the Barbados benefit gıven by Sherıdan but going ınstead to Covent Garden. *Hıst̷ MSS. Comm., Carlısle MSS.,* 1897, p. 459. See also Nos. 5904–11. 7⅞ × 12⅛ ın. (pl.).

5904 THE MODERN MERCURY AND HIS TWO WINGS OR MONSIEUR V—STR—S IN TRIUMPH

Pub^d Acc^g to Act Apr^l 26th 1781 by J. Staton and J. Jones N° 13 Parlıament Street London.

Mezzotınt Design in an oval within a rectangle Vestrıs in the centre dancıng wıth two ladıes of the ballet, the three holdıng hands He wears a cap decorated wıth heavy plumes of ostrıch feathers; his hair falls in curls on hıs shoulders He wears a striped suıt cut low ın the neck wıth a sash round the waist, full sleeves to the elbow. The ladıes are perhaps dressed as shepherdesses They have feathered hats poısed on their hıgh-dressed hair, which falls on their shoulders. Their petticoats and the panıers of their dresses are trımmed with wide borders of flowers On each sıde of the stage a scene of trees ıs indicated.

For Vestrıs see Nos. 5903, 5907, 5908, 5909, 5910, 5911. 6⅛ × 8¾ ın.

5905 *TΩN MENTOI XIINΩN OUK EΣTIN OΣTIS OU*

[? N Dance *del*. Bartolozzi and Pastorini *sculp*]

Published 2ˢᵗ April 1781

Aquatint. Design in a circle inset in a square. A companion print to No. 5906 A young dancer, Vestris *fils* (Vestr' Allard) in the centre of the stage. He is poised on the r. toe, his l. leg extended horizontally, his arms held out, a wide-brimmed hat, trimmed with ribbon and flowers in his r hand, his head thrown back rests on his r shoulder and he is smiling Trees form the background, and on the r of the stage are flats, also of trees. In each of the lower angles of the square is a goose, standing on one leg Beneath the design is engraved:

A Stranger at Sparta standing long upon one Leg, said to a Lacedaemonian, I do not believe you can do as much, 'True (said he) but every Goose can'. See Plutarch's Laconic Apothegms Vol 1. Page 406.

In spite of the satiric intention the dancer has much grace and charm A satire on the benefit of the younger Vestris, see Nos. 5903, 5906. Attributed to Nathaniel Dance by Angelo, who says it was 'exhibited in all the print-shops and very much like'. *Reminiscences*, 1904, ii. 348 Calabi, *Bartolozzi*, 1928, No. 2235 (attributed to George Dance) Reproduced, Paston, Pl lxx

Also a later impression, *By Torre, No 44 Market Lane* engraved below the date.

Also an impression before aquatinting, without inscriptions but with date.

12⅝ × 12⅝ in.

5906 OH QUI GOOSE-TOE" [O CHE GUSTO']

[? N. Dance *del* Bartolozzi and Pastorini *sc*.]

Pubᵈ May 16ᵗʰ 1781 by W. Humphrey Nº 227 Strand.

Aquatint. A companion print to No. 5905. Vestris *fils*, as in No. 5905, on the same stage, is dancing in a similar pose, poised on his r toe, his back to the audience, looking over his l. shoulder smiling. In his r. hand is his hat, held out as before but full of notes or bills, inconspicuously inscribed *gui*, £1100, and £20,000. In his l. hand he holds out a netted purse to which is attached a label inscribed *English Guineas* In place of the goose of No. 5897 in each lower angle of the square is an ape dressed as a dancer and with his hat held out, cf No 5903; one (l) matches the pose of Vestris in No 5905, the other (r) his pose in this design Beneath the design is engraved.

He Danc'd like a Monkey, his Pockets well cram'd,
*Caper'd off with a Grin, "kiss my A*** & be D——d".*

Calabi, *Bartolozzi*, 1928, No. 2236

12⅝ × 12⅝ in.

¹ The prologue for the opening of the summer season at the Haymarket, 27 June 1781, referring to the (belated) end of the opera season:
No more from *Voice*, or *Ear*, her profits flow;
The Soul of Opera fixes in Goose-toe!

Public Advertiser, 27 June 1781

5907 A VESTRICIAN DISH, OR, CAPER SAUCE FOR A GOOSE PYE.

Pub⁴ Acc to Act June 16 1781 by F. Assen & J Jones Hayes's Court Soho

Mezzotint. A satire on Vestris. The stage at the Opera-House in the Haymarket. A dancer is posing gracefully on the r foot, his body thrown back, his arms extended; he has the head of a fox and a fox's brush The l. of the stage is seen from the r., with three tiers of boxes on the l and some of the seats in the pit immediately below the stage. In these seats and boxes are men and women with the heads of geese, their necks thrust eagerly forward. A scenery of trees is indicated on the l of the stage.

Beneath the design verses are printed, 'The Words by G S C.'. They express the strong feeling against the Frenchman's receiving so great an ovation and so much money while England and France were at war The first and last verses are:

I

If a Fox should appear from a pilfering band,
Who has rifl'd your Roots and have damag'd your Land
What Loons wou'd allow such a Thing still to fleece,
If they were not a meer Set of *Cackling Geese.*

6

I now have a Guess at the Reason, I vow;
So the longer we live, still the wiser we grow;
It is a French Fox, all Pomatum and Grease,
That so prettily tackles our *English Geese*

For Vestris see also Nos. 5903–4, 5908, 5909, 5910.
6¼×8⅛ in.

5908 SIX GUINEAS ENTRANCE AND A GUINEA A LESSON

[1781]

[P. Sandby.]

Aquatint. Design in a circle, the heading to engraved verses Gaetan Vestris stands stiffly, his elbows bent, his toes turned out, facing a goose to which he is giving a dancing lesson. He wears a high toupet wig. Behind (l.) and in shadow, a man seated on a chair plays the violin. The floor is of boards, a plain wall forms the background Shadows fall from the l. leaving Vestris and the goose in full light. The title is engraved on a scroll beneath the circle. Below the verses is a miniature tailpiece of a fool's cap, a cap and bells, and a dancing-master's kit or fiddle The ten verses are printed in full in W Sandby's *Thomas and Paul Sandby*, 1892, pp 41–3 No 8 runs:

The Soldier risks Health, Life and Limbs, his Fortune to advance,
While Pique and Vestris Fortune make, by one Night's single Dance
And a dancing we will go, will go, &c.

Sandby is said to have called at a house to give a drawing lesson, to have been obliged to wait until a dancing lesson by Vestris was finished, and to have made the sketch while waiting Ibid. For dancing lessons by Vestris cf. Walpole, *Letters*, xi. 368, 14 Jan. 1781, to Lady Ossory, 'shall not Lady Anne learn of Vestris, while you have a shilling left?' and No. 5911.

Apparently not intended for publication. An impression in R Bull's collection of 'Honorary Engravers', p 250, has the note 'Engraved by Paul Sanby [*sic*], sibi et Amicis; the song by J. Sanby'.

For the two Vestris see Nos. 5903-11.

3⅛ in. diam. Pl. 9⅛ × 6⅜ in.

5909 SIX GUINEAS ENTRANCE AND A GUINEA A LESSON

[P. Sandby.]

Publishd as the Act directs by P Sandby Sᵗ Georges Row. June 20 1781.

Aquatint. An enlarged version of No. 5908. (W. Sandby, *T. and P Sandby*, 1892, p. 43.) The circle is inset in a square. No verses.

12½ × 12½ in

5910 JASON ET MEDÉE   BALLET TRAGIQUE.

[? N. Dance *del* Bartolozzi *sc.*]

Publishd July 3ʳᵈ 1781 by John Boydell Engraver in Cheapside London.

Aquatint. Design in an oval. Gaetan Vestris as Jason between two ladies of the ballet. He staggers back, with an expression of horror facing Medea (r.), who clutches a dagger. Behind him (l.) the danseuse appears about to swoon The dresses are interesting examples of theatrical costume. Jason wears a toupet wig, a tunic with a jewelled star on the breast, a cloak, and elaborately puffed trunk-hose The ladies wear wide hooped and flounced petticoats, their hair dressed in a high pyramid with feathers. The background is architectural, at the back a high archway leads to a balcony backed by trees Below the level of the stage and in the foreground are the heads and shoulders of three members of the orchestra, one (centre) plays a flute, the others play oboes. Below the design a line of music is engraved.

A satire on the combination of tragic poses with the steps of the ballet. For Selwyn's opinion of the ballet see *Hist. MSS. Comm , Carlisle MSS.* 1897, pp. 502-3. Its performance, 19 June 1781, was expected to be the last appearance of Vestris in London, ibid. This was actually not until 26 June 1781. For the Vestris see Nos. 5903-11. Cf. No. 6322.

Similar in manner to Nos 5905, 5906.

Reproduced, Paston, Pl. lxxi.

14¹⁵⁄₁₆ × 18 in.

5911 REGARDEZ MOI   [1781]

[Gillray.]

Engraving, slightly aquatinted Gaetan Vestris (r) giving a dancing lesson to a gigantic goose with a human head and long pigtail queue They face each other in profile. Vestris stands with his legs together, chest thrown out, his arms curved 'Regardez-moi' was his characteristic admonition. On a stool behind the goose is an open book inscribed *Electrical E. E. L* ; on the ground at its feet is another inscribed *The Torpedo Dedicated to Lᵈ—— C—— My Lord, I take the Liberty —— The greatness of whose Parts are known* .. This indicates that the goose is Lord Cholmondeley (1749-1827), 'The Torpedo, a Poem to the Electrical Eel addressed to

Mr John Hunter Surgeon' and 'Dedicated to .   Lord Cholmondeley,' 4th ed. 1777, was a coarse and scurrilous poem, three lines of which are,

'What tho' Lord Ch—lm—d—ly may conceal
A most enormous length of Eel
Admir'd for Size and bone:'

In the wall which forms the background are two sash-windows and a door (l.) round which a grinning youth, probably a servant, is looking On the wall are H L. portraits: three in ovals of elderly ladies in profile, one of a clergyman, full-face, wearing a biretta, his l hand on a book. There is also a picture of Fox, with a fox's head, seated opposite Cholmondeley; they are throwing dice. Fox appears satisfied, the other clenches his fist and exclaims in anger. A devil is climbing on the top of the frame and holds out a claw to grab the head of Fox On the picture are the words *A Nick by God* Like Fox, see No 5972, Cholmondeley held a faro bank at Brooks's. G.E C , *Complete Peerage.*

Walpole alludes to prints on dancing lessons by Vestris, *Letters*, xii. 30, see also No. 5908. For the Vestris see Nos. 5903-11. For Cholmondeley, No. 5497

Reprinted, *G W.G.*, 1830.

Grego, *Gillray*, p. 44.

10$\frac{1}{4}$ × 14$\frac{1}{8}$ in.

5912 SKETCH'D BY HUMPHREY—SPOIL'D BY GILLRAY

Sold by R. Wilkinson, N° 58 Cornhill London   Nov. 1st 1781

Engraving T.Q.L portrait of a child wearing a hat. A satire by Gillray on his own work as an engraver A portrait of William Lamb, afterwards Lord Melbourne (b. 15 Mar 1779) The plate has been defaced by scratches Beneath the title is engraved, *Dedicated to all Lovers of your bold, Masterly Touches, & Publish'd Novr 1st 1781 by J. Gillray, to shew the bad effect of Cobbling & Altering.*

"*Fool that I was thus to Cobble my Shoe.*"

Oval, 7 × 5$\frac{1}{4}$ in. (pl. 10$\frac{5}{8}$ × 8 in.).

5913 BILLIARDS.

Mr Bunbury del.   *J^s Bretherton f.*

Publish'd 27th Jany 1781.

Engraving One corner of a billiard-table is visible, the rest being cut off by the r margin of the print A player, in profile to the r., holds up with exaggerated care a cue in front of a ball lying near the corner. He wears a long pigtail queue, on the back of his coat is a large ribbon bow or cockade to which a key is attached. A number of spectators stand round watching intently : of two behind the player, one resembles a footman. Two others stand behind the corner of the table, one wearing a hat like that of a coachman; two others stand on the r. behind the table. They are probably all men-servants.

The wall behind is papered or stencilled in a pattern of horizontal lines and spots. On it are a rack of cues, the [Rules of the Ga]*me* [of Billia]*rds*, three framed pictures. (a horse-race, a duel, and an oval portrait) and what appears to be a satirical print.

For billiards see also Nos. 5795, 5803.

10$\frac{5}{8}$ × 14 in.

5914 Nº 6. HINTS TO BAD HORSEMEN.
   Nº 1. SYMPTOMS OF RESTIVENESS.

H Bunbury Esqʳ delin   *Watson & Dickinson Excudᵗ*

*London, Publish'd May 10ᵗʰ 1781, by Watson & Dickinson Nº 158
New Bond Street*

Engraving No 6 of a series. A stout rider on a small horse or cob standing by a sign-post (l) on a country road The horse's head is held down and looks back along the road behind him. In the background on the r is a church spire surrounded by trees. The first of a series of four 'Hints ..'; beneath the title in this and the other prints in the series, Nos. 5914–17, is engraved.

*Ah me! what various Ills betide
The Looby who presumes to ride.*

Other prints after Bunbury on bad horsemanship are Nos. 6339–41. Cf. also No 5901.

$6\frac{7}{8} \times 8\frac{3}{4}$ in.

5915 Nº 7. HINTS TO BAD HORSEMEN.
   Nº 2 SYMPTOMS OF STARTING

H Bunbury Esqʳ delin.   *Watson & Dickinson Excudᵗ*

*London, Publish'd May 10ᵗʰ 1781, by Watson & Dickinson Nº 158
New Bond Street*

Engraving. No. 7 of a series. A man on horseback on a country road; the horse is shying violently at a man (l) crouching among some bushes by the roadside. The rider has lost his seat, and is clutching the reins; his hat is in the air behind him In the distance is a windmill (r.). One of a series of four 'Hints . ', see No 5914

$7\frac{1}{16} \times 9\frac{1}{4}$ in

5916 Nº 8. HINTS TO BAD HORSEMEN.
   Nº 3. SYMPTOMS OF KICKING.

H. Bunbury Esqʳ delinᵗ   *Watson & Dickinson Excudᵗ*

*London, Publish'd May 10ᵗʰ 1781, by Watson & Dickinson Nº 158
New Bond Street.*

Engraving. No. 8 of a series. A horse is kicking violently, its head down, the rider has lost his seat and his stirrups and is clutching the animal's mane. The scene is a country road, a village is indicated in the distance (r.). One of a series of four 'Hints . . .', see No. 5914

$6\frac{3}{4} \times 8\frac{7}{8}$ in.

5917 Nº 9 HINTS TO BAD HORSEMEN.
   Nº 4 SYMPTOMS OF TUMBLING.

H. Bunbury Esqʳ delin   *Watson & Dickinson Excudᵗ*

*London, Publish'd May 10ᵗʰ 1781, by Watson & Dickinson, Nº 158
New Bond Street.*

Engraving A horse has fallen on its knees, its rider is flying over its head, his hands clutching the animal's neck, his legs in the air. The scene is a farmyard, a goose (1) hisses at the falling man, ducks run away quacking In the background are trees, a barn, and a paling One of a series of four 'Hints . . .', see No. 5914.

$6\frac{5}{8} \times 8\frac{1}{2}$ in

5918 5 CORPORAL FEAR.

H Bunbury Esq del*   *J. Baldrey Sculp*:

London. Publish'd Nov 1st 1781, by R Wilkinson, N° 58 Cornhill.*

Stipple. Design in a circle. A highwayman has stopped a couple who have been driving in a two-wheeled gig. He stands behind the horse aiming a candlestick as if it were a pistol, in his l. hand is a netted purse. His victim stands up in the gig, his waistcoat-pockets turned out, his hands outstretched, with an expression of distress, his attitude implying that he has given up all his possessions His hat and whip lie on the ground, and with them a miniature violin, or dancing-master's kit, and bow A fat woman has just clambered out of the gig, her l foot is on the shaft, her r. on the ground, and she appears to be taking cover behind the vehicle. The horse stands quietly, the reins hang to the ground. The scene is a country road, on the l is a milestone inscribed *11 Miles*, and a group of trees, on the r is a signpost.

Putting 'in corporal fear' was part of the phraseology of an indictment for highway robbery, &c.

Diam. $11\frac{3}{4}$ in

5919 MORNING, OR THE MAN OF TASTE.

Design'd by W. H Bunbury Esq

London, Publish'd Oct the 10th 1781, by J R Smith, N° 83 opposite the Pantheon, Oxford Street*

Stipple Design in a circle A man and wife seated at a circular breakfast-table. The man, who is obese and a gourmand, sits in profile to the r. holding a bowl with a spoon in it in one hand, a bill of fare in the other inscribed *Soup   Turbot. Duck . . Lamb* He is wearing spectacles and a large piece of food projects from his mouth. The cook (r.) is showing his master a dead duck, which he holds up in his r. hand, in his l , and partly supported by his knee, is a tray on which are two lobsters and a turbot. The lady, who is also fat, holds up her hands in horror at the cook, who, from his leanness, his profile, and his bag-wig, solitaire, and ruffled shirt, is evidently a Frenchman He wears a white cap and an apron, a large knife is thrust under his belt On the l a footman enters carrying in each hand a plate piled with muffins. Tea-things are on the table. Under the table a small dog, befouling the floor, is partly visible. Behind is a screen of several leaves, on the top of which is a bird, resembling a large dove. A companion print to No. 5920.

Diam. $11\frac{3}{8}$ in.

5920 EVENING, OR THE MAN OF FEELING

Design'd by W. H. Bunbury Esqʳ

London, Publish'd Octʳ the 10ᵗʰ 1781, by J. R. Smith Nº 83 opposite the Pantheon, Oxford Street

Stipple Design in a circle. Three men sit by a rectangular supper-table, a grandfather-clock behind them points to XI. The man on the l is having his jack-boots pulled off by a small boy, the boy stands astride his r leg pulling hard, his back to the man, who is scowling and pushes his other booted foot against the boy's back, on the floor are a pair of spurs, a pair of slippers, and a boot-jack. A man (r) wearing a night-cap, but otherwise completely dressed and wearing spurred boots, leans one elbow on the table, his face contorted as if in pain, he holds his hand to his thigh. On the table beside him is a small packet inscribed *Diaculum*. In the centre, and on the farther side of the table, the third man leans both elbows on the table, his hair is tousled and his eyes are shut. A man-servant behind, yawning, is carrying off a square box, probably a wig-box, while a maid-servant stands on the r, a candle in one hand, a warming-pan in the other, watching with amusement the efforts of the boy to pull off the boot.

Three hats hang on the wall; a bottle, a plate, three wine-glasses, and a guttering candle, burnt down to the socket, stand on the table.

A companion print to No. 5919.

Diam. 11⅜ in.

5921 Nº 10 A FAMILY PIECE

H. Bunbury Esqʳ Delin. *W. Dickinson Excudᵗ*

London, Publish'd October 15ᵗʰ 1781, by W. Dickinson Nº 158 New Bond Street.

Stipple. No 10 of a series. A portrait-painter painting a family group of a man and wife and their little boy. The group (r.) is raised on a low semicircular platform, the couple sit on a high-backed settee without arms, the little boy on a stool in front of his mother. The child, though in his ordinary clothes, is holding a cupid's bow and a sheaf of arrows (reminiscent of the family portrait in the *Vicar of Wakefield*); a large quiver holding arrows is slung across his shoulders, a wreath is on his head; he yawns violently.

The man, in profile to the l., is obese and wears a short bushy wig, a dove sits on his l wrist; only the toes of his shoes reach the ground. His wife sits on his r. holding a dove on her r. hand, she turns towards her husband, looking straight forward with a fixed and painful smile; she wears ringlets and a cap of lace and ribbons on her high-dressed hair The artist (l.) stands at his easel which supports a large canvas and is placed close to his sitters. He wears spectacles, a bag-wig, and ruffled shirt, and holds a palette in his l. hand He looks towards his sitters with an insinuating smile, which, together with his attitude and the figure of the man sketched on the canvas, shows that he is intent on flattery High up on the wall behind him are two oval bust portraits, one (l) of a clergyman, the other of a lady. Behind the sitters is a tall screen of several leaves

Reproduced, S. Brinton, *The Eighteenth Century in Caricature*, 1904, p. 42.

9⅞ × 14½ in.

5922 N° 11. A CHOP-HOUSE.

H. Bunbury Esqr delin^t   *W Dickinson Excudit*

London, Publish'd Oct 15th 1781, by W Dickinson N° 158 New Bond Street

Stipple No. 11 of a series. The interior of a chop-house. At a small square table, a fat elderly man (r) with a bushy wig sits facing a younger man. The older man is identified in a contemporary hand as 'Dr Johnson', who is much caricatured. His *vis-à-vis* is evidently Boswell (cf a profile etched by S. Lysons). Johnson is intent on his plate, Boswell's elbows rest on the table, holding his knife and fork vertically erect he looks at Johnson, a cutlet-bone (?) protrudes from his mouth. He wears a three-cornered hat and spurred boots. Johnson's hat is supported on his massive stick, which is propped up beside him Two dogs look expectantly at the table A waiter (r.) with a napkin under his arm is bringing in a dish On the l. is a small round table, at which sits a man who is not yet served. He is reading a newspaper with a scowl of concentration Behind him a man in back-view stands looking at himself in an oval wall-mirror. Behind the waiter (r) is a tall screen of several leaves.

11⅝ × 13¾ in.

5923 N° 12. THE COFFEE-HOUSE PATRIOTS; OR NEWS, FROM S^T EUSTATIA

H. Bunbury Esqr Delin^t   *W. Dickinson Excud^t*

London. Publish'd Octr 15: 1781; by W. Dickinson N° 158 New Bond Street.

Stipple. No. 12 of a series The interior of a coffee-house, the customers, with one exception, deeply interested and dismayed at the news in a *Gazette Extraordinary*, which the title shows is that on the capture of the island of St. Eustatius by Rodney, see Nos. 5827, 5837, &c., the *Extraordinary Gazette* being that of 13 Feb. 1781.

On each side of the room is an oblong table flanked by wooden settles. Between the tables and in the centre of the design three men stand, one of whom reads from a *Gazette Extraordinary* His two companions look at him with scowling attention; one, his hat under his arm, has both hands thrust deep into the pockets of his coat; the other holds his forehead, from which his wig has been pushed back A dog gazes up at them

At the table on the l a man sits in full face gaping with dismay, his hands rest on the table grasping his knife and fork. Two men sit on opposite sides of the table on the r ; one holds a glass in his l. hand, while he looks up at the group with the newspaper His *vis-à-vis* has turned sideways, his hands on his knees, with an expression of melancholy alarm. Behind him, one hand on the back of the settle, stands John Wilkes, conspicuous by his squint and his characteristic wig; he holds a glass of wine and frowns. At his side is a man leaning back asleep.

A cockatoo's cage is hung from the roof, the bird head downwards, as if about to screech. Half of the dial of a large wall clock is visible on the extreme r. On the l. is a folding screen

A satire on the dismay with which the city patriots received news of English successes, cf No 5334 On the taking of St. Eustatius it was found that many British merchants had been using the island as a base for trading with the enemy. The news of the capture was 'a thunderbolt to the Opposition', Selwyn to Lady Rodney. Mundy, *Life and Corr of Rodney*, 11. 51. See Nos. 5557, 5837, 5839, 5842

$11\frac{3}{4} \times 14$ in.

5924 N⁰ ¹ THE RELIEF.

H. Bunbury Esqʳ delinᵗ   *W. Dickinson Excudᵗ*

London, Publish'd Octʳ 21ˢᵗ; 1781, by W. Dickinson, Engraver N⁰ 158 New Bond Street.

Stipple. One of a series, the number illegible. Three soldiers stand at attention outside a tent (r) holding bayoneted muskets. Two wear high plumed busbies, the third a laced three-cornered hat. The officer facing them (l.), holding a musket without a bayonet against his shoulder, gives the word of command. A stout man and a fat woman stand behind him. In the foreground (r) a drummer boy, sitting on the ground, one arm resting on his drum, puts a plumed busby on the head of a dog. Two rough-looking men wearing ribbon favours in their hats, probably intended for Gordon Rioters, point jeeringly at the three soldiers. In the background are trees.

Camps were established in London during the Gordon Riots in Hyde Park, St James's Park, and the garden of the British Museum, remaining there for several weeks. For the camp in Hyde Park see the series of prints by Paul Sandby.

$10\frac{1}{2} \times 13\frac{1}{4}$ in.

5925 HYDE PARK 1780   [1781?]

H Bunbury del.

Engraving. Riders in Hyde Park. A fat coachman (r) rides (l to r) a coach-horse in blinkers, his mistress is seated behind him, in back-view, wearing an enormous calash hood, see No. 5434, &c , and holding a fan. The horse has planted its forefeet on the ground, its rider is applying spurs and a coach-whip On the l. a lady and a slim and elegant young man are galloping from r. to l.; he turns towards her, she looks straight ahead Behind them rides a groom. In the background (l) is a group of trees, in the foreground grass and (l) three dogs.

The title and artist's name are etched conspicuously across the lower r corner of the design.

Nos 5926, 5927 are companion prints, all three probably etched by Bretherton.

$23 \times 21\frac{1}{2}$ in.

5926 [HYDE PARK?]

[After Bunbury]   *J Bretherton f. 23ʳᵈ Febʸ 1781*

Engraving Riders, probably in Hyde Park, with a pedestrian who is being worried by four dogs, apparently on account of his dress. He stands (l) on tiptoe, in profile to the r., holding up his arms, a stick in his r. hand. His coat is spotted like a leopard and it and his waistcoat are edged with fur. He is probably a Frenchman. Two dogs worry at his coat, a larger

¹ Blank or illegible

one standing on its hind-legs, puts one paw on his chest, a fourth is biting his long pigtail queue Three riders, riding from r. to l, look with interest at the man and dogs. The foremost is a military officer in uniform, with holsters and rolled cloak on his saddle. A fourth man rides stiffly from l. to r, looking straight in front of him. A companion print to Nos 5925, 5927.

$23\frac{1}{3} \times 20\frac{7}{8}$ in

5927 [HYDE PARK?]

[After Bunbury.]

Engraving Riders, probably in Hyde Park, looking with astonishment at an elderly lady (r.) walking from l. to r. followed by a little black boy carrying her umbrella She wears an enormous calash hood, see No. 5434, &c, and holds in her l hand a shepherdess's crook. Three men (l) ride side by side, from l. to r., the nearest pulls on his reins, leaning back, the next looks at the lady through his spy-glass, the third, staring open-mouthed, lashes his horse The horse of a stout man riding from r to l, immediately behind the lady, is rearing. In the foreground an old woman sits by the roadside with a sheaf of ballads or newspapers Behind (l.) are trees A companion print to Nos. 5925, 5926

$23\frac{3}{16} \times 20$ in.

5928 E, O, OR THE FASHIONABLE VOWELS.

[Rowlandson]

Pub^d Oct. 28 1781 as the Act directs

Engraving. Gamblers seated and standing round an E O. table. The table is octagon-shaped, the circular roulette mechanism being sunk in its centre, surrounded with the letters E O for even and odd. In the foreground (r.), in profile to the l, a man leans back in his chair asleep, an empty purse on the table beside him; he resembles Captain Topham [1] The others are probably also portraits, but are more caricatured, they watch the table with gestures and expressions of anxiety and despair. There are fourteen figures Rowlandson, a confirmed gambler, must have taken part in many such assemblies. See also Nos 6118–20.

Grego, *Rowlandson*, 1. 101–3 (Reproduction.)

$7\frac{1}{4} \times 9\frac{7}{8}$ in.

This print was reissued by Fores with the date *Jany 1st 1786* and the title *Private Amusement*

5929 BROTHERS OF THE WHIP

A. Grant del^t [Rowlandson][2]

Pub: as the Act Directs Nov: 27. 1781 by H Humphrey N° 18 New Bond Street

Engraving. A group of four men On the l, in profile to the r, stands a stout coachman, with short wig, three-cornered hat, and laced coat; he holds a tankard in his r. hand, a whip in his l, the butt resting on the

[1] See a caricature of Topham by Rowlandson called *Capt Epilogue*, published 7 Mar 1786   [2] Attributed by E Hawkins to Kingsbury

ground. Next him, full face, is a postilion wearing a livery coat with epaulettes, round hat, and top-boots; he holds a whip resting on his l. shoulder. The other two appear to be amateur whips· one stands in profile to the l. holding a large oval snuff-box, he wears a long coat, broad-brimmed hat, and buckled shoes In the centre is a man wearing a short striped jacket, broad-brimmed hat, and buckled shoes.

In the background (r) are elaborately built stables, with two pediments over semicircular windows. Outside them stands a coach and a groom with two carriage-horses For the signature A. Grant, cf. No. 6133.

Grego, *Rowlandson*, i. 103.

$7 \times 9\frac{3}{8}$ in

5930 CHARITY COVERETH A MULTITUDE OF SINS

[Rowlandson.]

[Published by H. Humphrey. Novr 27, 1781]

Engraving (coloured impression). A young military officer wearing a gorget stands at the door of a house, his l. hand on the knocker, looking up at two courtesans who lean out of a sash-window over the door He puts a coin into the hat of a disabled sailor who stands behind him, supported on crutches, his forehead bandaged Behind the sailor are two itinerant musicians: a man carrying a rectangular box, and a woman turning the handle of a hurdy-gurdy or vielle which is slung round her neck, her mouth is open as if singing.

The door of the house is ornamented with a carved wooden pediment, and bears a plate *Mrs Mitchel*. The knocker has a lion's head. Only the corner of the house appears, the street is *Cleveland Row*. A brick wall extends from the house to the l., over it appear trees, and a notice-board inscribed *Men Traps are laid here· every Night also . . .* On the wall a placard is pasted, *Dr Leaks Pills. . .* .

Mrs Mitchell was one of the chief keepers of fashionable houses of ill fame, a Mrs. Welch kept such a house in Cleveland Row. H. Bleackley, *Ladies Fair and Frail*, pp 143, 183.

Grego, *Rowlandson*, i. 105 (Reproduction.)

$12\frac{1}{4} \times 9\frac{13}{16}$ in

The publication line has been cut off

5931 AN ESSAY ON HATS.

I Nixon Fec^t

Pub^d: May, 16. 1781 by W. Wells, N° 132, Fleet Street, London

Engraving. Three men, two on horseback, wearing new-fashioned hats. The centre figure is seen in back view on horseback, he wears a large hat with a high cylindrical crown round which are spaced six hat-bands In the foreground (r.) is a man wearing a wide-brimmed hat whose crown is shaped like an inverted flower-pot. He is looking through a small telescope. These two both carry knotted sticks. The third man who is cantering (l. to r.) in the middle distance (l.) wears a similar hat. All three wear spurred top-boots in the fashion of the moment, with very long tops descending well below the calf of the leg.

This seems to be the first appearance of the embryo top-hat. See also Nos 5933, 5934, 5935.

$8\frac{3}{8} \times 8\frac{15}{16}$ in.

5932 [A CORNISH HUGG. SCENE BILLINGSGATE]¹

I. Nixon Del

Publish'd June 5ᵗʰ 1781 by Wᵐ Wells Nᵒ 132, (opposite Salisbury Court,) Fleet Street, London.

Engraving A tall, stout fish-wife has seized a fashionably dressed man round the waist and lifted him up, his hat and tasselled cane have fallen to the ground She is neatly dressed, with a flat hat tied over her cap, a checked apron, clocked stockings, and buckled shoes, but she wears a soldier's coat over her dress. There are three spectators. a woman (r.) in profile to the l, gapes with astonishment, a neatly dressed man wearing an apron standing behind a fish-stall looks on with quiet amusement; an apple-woman sits (l) grinning, arms akimbo. Beside her is a large basket heaped with a pyramid of fruit. A fish-stall and a basket have been over-turned (r) and the contents lie on the ground.

In the background is Billingsgate Dock, with masts and rigging, on the r. is one of the market buildings, inscribed BILLINGSGATE

$11\frac{5}{8} \times 8\frac{7}{8}$ in.   Crace Collection, xx, No 71.

5933 THE NEW GIG.

Colley Fecᵗ.

Pubᵈ Augᵗ 11. 1781. by E. Hedges, N. 92. Under the Royal Exchange. Cornhill.

Engraving Two people seated in the minute body of a gig which is poised on springs high above the spider-like wheels The two horses are tandem, a groom rides the leader (l.) as postilion. Both occupants wear the high-crowned hats and boots with deep tops which had just become fashionable, see No 5931. Beside the gig a man rides a small horse, looking up at the driver; he also wears one of the new hats, and carries a grotesquely knotted stick. On the panel of the gig is a coronet. Reproduced, Paston, Pl. cxxi.

$9 \times 13\frac{3}{8}$ in.

5934 GIGG DRIVER.

H. A——o del.

Publish'd 24ᵗʰ August 1781 by John Williams Nᵒ 34 Strand.

Engraving A man wearing the new-fashioned hat and boots for riding and driving, see Nos 5931, 5933, 5935 He stands in profile to the l., slightly stooping, a driving whip with a long lash under his r. arm. He is gaping with a vacant expression. Beneath the design is inscribed.

> *Thus view him gifted and accouter'd*
> *Not on the Inside but the Outward*
> *The Chapeau Blanc serves as a Token*
> *Of Puppies grown up into Fashion.*

$7\frac{13}{16} \times 5\frac{7}{8}$ in.

¹ Written in ink.

5935 BOOTS AND SPURS

Pubᵈ Octʳ 31ˢᵗ 1781 by J Williams N° 34 Strand.

Engraving (coloured impression). A young man standing in riding dress, holding a long riding whip, his l. hand is in his breeches pocket. The tops of his boots descend almost to his ankles, as do their dangling straps; one enormous spur is visible. His hat has a high crown like an inverted flower pot, and his hair without wig or powder hangs on his coat-collar. He wears a very long coat, a short check waistcoat, with a bunch of seals hanging from his fob. Behind him an ass is freely sketched. See also Nos 5931, 5933, 5934.

Reissued 1 Sept. 1791 by Fores, with the title *A Buck of 1781.*

12¼ × 8¾ in.

5936 [MODERN WOMAN, 1781.]

Agnes T——n

Pubᵈ 29ᵗʰ June 1781 by H Humphrey N° 18 New Bond Street

Engraving (coloured and uncoloured impressions). A phaeton, whose small body is raised on springs high above the wheels, drawn by four long-tailed horses, absurdly small in proportion to the carriage. It is driven by a lady standing up and wielding an enormously long whip, next her sits a man without a hat, his hands held up, his face contorted with terror The lady wears a hat of rather masculine fashion, with two erect ostrich feathers, a short coat, waistcoat, and ruffled skirt. On the side of the carriage is a crest—a stag's head in an oval, with the motto *Fashion.*

Beneath the design is engraved:

> *Talk not to me Sir of yʳ old Fashion'd rules,*
> *E'en laugh'd at by Children, the Joke of the Schools·*
> *They might do for yʳ meek minded Matrons of old,*
> *Who knew no use of Spirit but their Servants to scold*
> *But for me Z——ds & Blood am not I fit to command,*
> *I can swear Sir, & What's more drive four Horses in Hand.*

The signature suggests that the lady may be Agnes Townshend, a noted courtesan, known as *vis-à-vis* Townshend, see No. 5416, a noted whip, who drove her phaeton and four all over the country H. Bleackley, *Ladies Fair and Frail*, p 282 See also No 5375. For the signature cf. Nos. 5937, 5938.

6 × 9⅞ in.

5937 THE GREAT AND GLORIOUS DAYS OF QUEEN BESS.

Agnes T——n

Pubᵈ 30ᵗʰ June 1781 by H Humphrey, N° 18 New Bond Street.

Engraving. A procession (from l to r) of Queen Elizabeth and her maids of honour on horseback, the ladies all seated sideways, behind the rider of the horse, the cavalier always in profile, the lady in full face, except for one lady who is in back view. Two soldiers on foot carrying muskets, march in front, a mounted soldier rides behind The dresses are pseudo-Elizabethan. The ladies wear ruffs and stiff wide-patterned petticoats, with scarves or hoods over their caps. One lady holds her hood. The procession consists of the Queen and three of her ladies Beneath the design is inscribed.

> *Think of the great Days when void of all fears*
> *Of Wind & Rain sweet Queen Bess appears*
> *She taught her Maids of Honour their Caps to defend*
> *With oil skin hoods—when her Breakfast they attend.*
> *Behind her good Chancellor seated;*
> *And are with Beef Steaks & Onions all treated.*

Though drawn in a different manner, this appears to be a companion print to No 5936; it contrasts the Elizabethan woman with the woman of 1781.

$5\frac{7}{8} \times 9\frac{7}{8}$ in

5938 LES PLAISIR [*sic*] DU MÈNAGE.

Agnes T——n [Gillray.]
Pub^d Augt 1st 1781 by H. Humphrey New Bond S^t

Engraving (coloured impression). A domestic interior In the upper margin is engraved, *Give me the sweet delight of Love—a Catch,* and the design illustrates the lines of the catch:

> A smoky house, a failing trade,
> Six squalling brats, and a scolding jade

A man (full-face) stands disconsolately, his hands clasped while his virago of a wife (l.) threatens him with her fist. One small child pulls his coat and points to a little brother kicking on the floor, while a rather older girl weeps with her pinafore to her eyes, and another boy blows a trumpet. This group is on the r. On the l. one child clutches another by the hair.

The man's toes protrude through one of his shoes, he is without breeches, and these hang from a nail on the wall (r.) next his wife's hat A parroquet sits screeching on the outside of its cage. The plaster has fallen from the wall in patches, showing bricks. A smoky fire burns in the grate (l.); on the chimney-piece are tea-things.

Grego, *Gillray*, p. 32.
Reprinted, *G.W.G*, 1830.

$7\frac{1}{4} \times 10\frac{1}{2}$ in.

5939 TWO IMPURES OF THE TON DRIVING TO THE GIGG SHOP, HAMMERSMITH.

R. Dighton del.

London Printed for R. Sayer & J. Bennett N° 53 Fleet Street,
J. Smith N° 35 Cheapside, as the Act directs Feby 6; 1781.

Engraving. Two ladies driving in a gig, advancing diagonally towards the spectator from l. to r, on the road from Hyde Park Corner to Knightsbridge. The gig, which has a crest on its panel, is drawn by a pair of ponies with long tails and manes The lady driving is standing up, she wears the fashionable driving dress of the period, coat and waistcoat of masculine cut, full skirt without a hoop, large feathered hat; a bunch of seals hangs from her waistcoat. Her companion (r.) sits demurely with folded arms; her dress is more feminine. The faces of both are patched The background shows the front of St. George's Hospital (l), under the pediment is a large board inscribed *Saint Georges Hospital for Sick* Next it (r.) is a gate into Tattersall's, over the wall appears the top of a pedestal inscribed *Tattersal* which supports the statue of a horse.

$8\frac{3}{16} \times 6\frac{11}{16}$ in.   Crace Collection, IX. 61*

5940 DEFENDING NATIONAL HONO'R

A^{xr} Mc Pharson fec^t

Publish^d accor^d to the Act Feb^{ry} 14. 1781 by T^s Gundry. p^{ce} 6^d

Engraving A sow is rubbing herself against the base of a wooden lamp-post. A Highlander (r.), in tartan kilt and plaid with a feathered cap, raises his sword and is about to strike the animal, saying *No national reflection yea auld Bitch.* A coachman standing behind the Scot raises his whip, saying *Ill cool your Pride Sawney* The scene is the road at Hyde Park Corner, showing wall, buildings (l), pavement, and part of the road in the foreground On the l. of the lamp-post are spectators a woman in cloak and hat carrying a bundle, says *Well don Jehu* A fat woman beside her says *Heaven deliver us from Evel.* Two little boys stand together, one says to the other, a chimney-sweep, *Tom will crack his Lice.* A carter with a whip, wearing a smock, says *egad he has him* Another man (l.) says, *Well don Tom give him a cooler.*

Beneath the title is etched, *Once upon a time as the Historian relates Sr Andrew Mc Ire in his peregrination near Hydepark-Corner, where an old Sow was rubbing her scabby sides against a Lamppost: It so enraged the valiant Knigth [sic] that old Bess should partake, or cast reflections on his Country's pleasures; with great wrath drew his Andrewfararara to avenge that Affront; but the happy incident of Tom the hackney Coachmans Whip prevented the tremendious [sic] blow—so saved poor Bess*

6×11 in

NORTH AND SOUTH OF GREAT BRITAIN

See No. 3799—11 June 1781

Willm Hogarth delin. F. B.—— sculp. [? Bartolozzi]

Probably designed not by Hogarth but by Paul Sandby.

A satire on the Scots.

5941 THE FLOWERS OF EDINBURGH,

Pub^d Augt 1st 1781 by J Langham, St Brides Passage Fleet Street.

Engraving (coloured and uncoloured impressions). An Edinburgh wynd or close A man seated on a bucket is using it as a latrine. A man holding a bucket stands behind him, screening him with his cloak, and turning round to call *Haud your Hond Lossie* to a woman who is emptying a bucket of filth from a first-floor window A man is seated on the ground on the r. by a steaming cauldron, across which is a large spoon. He is calling *Twa dips & a wallop for a Baubee* The men are in Highland dress. Beneath the title is engraved:

Yi dunna ken what I can dee
For I can set ye doon & cure ye tee

For this well-known danger of the Edinburgh streets see Boswell's *Johnson*, 1 119, n. 1, and cf the Edinburgh word gardyloo (*gardez l'eau*).

A print with this title was advertised by Holland in a 'Catalogue' appended to Jordan's *Elixir of Life*, 1789, cf No. 6126.

$12\frac{13}{16} \times 9\frac{3}{8}$ in.

5942 SAINT GEORGE FOR ENGLAND. *1*

Published as the Act directs, 2 Jan 1781.

Seven Prints of the Tutelar Saints.

Printed for Carington Bowles, No 69 in St Pauls Church Yard, London.

Engraving No 1 of the series. A sailor riding (r. to l) the British lion; in his r. hand he holds out a foaming tankard, in his l. is a sword resting on his shoulder and thrust through a huge sirloin of beef. His hat is decorated with a St. George's cross in a medallion, and with sprays of oak-leaves and acorns On the lion's head is a spray of roses, his r. fore-paw rests on a plum-pudding in a dish. His tail is raised almost vertically. Behind, seen through the lion's legs, are ships in full sail, clouds of smoke showing that a naval battle is in progress.

This design is surrounded by a border: The two circles are of hops twining round a pole, with oak-leaves and ears of wheat at their summit. The upper edge is the title on a scroll, with oak-leaves. The lower is formed of oak-leaves, acorns, and roses centred by a punch-bowl. Below the border is engraved

> *Behold your Saint with Glorious English Fare,*
> *Noble Sirloin, Rich Pudding and strong Beer.*
> *For you my Heart's of Oak, for your Regale,*
> *Here's good old English Stingo Mild & Stale.*
>
> *This Porter is by Famous Calvert made,*
> *Justly Renowned of all the Brewing Trade*
> *Such cheer as this will make you Bold & Strong,*
> *Who'd not on such a Noble Saint, Rely on.*

See also Nos. 5943–5
Reproduced, M D. George, *England in Transition*, frontispiece.

$8\frac{3}{4} \times 9\frac{1}{4}$ in.

5943 SAINT DAVID FOR WALES. *2*

Publish'd as the Act directs, 2 Jan. 1781

Printed for Carington Bowles, No 69 in St Pauls Ch Yard, London.

Engraving. No. 2 of the series, see No. 5942. A man riding (l to r) a goat. In his r. hand he holds out a large leek, in his l. is a slice of cheese on a toasting-fork At his back is slung a Welsh harp ornamented with the head and torso of a winged woman His hat is decorated with a leek, he wears jack-boots with large spurs Fish are thrust through his belt, and a holster containing a bottle is inscribed *Welch Ale*

In the background are mountainous hills on which goats are prancing. The border at each side is formed of a leek garlanded with leaves and surmounted by a goat's head. At the top is the title on a scroll and some small leeks. The lower border is of foliage centred by a crown surmounted by the ostrich plume of the Prince of Wales. In the two lower corners are piles of cheeses at which rats are nibbling

Beneath the border is engraved.

> *The Glorious Ancient British Saint Behold,*
> *David the great in Fames Records Inroll'd,*
> *Loaded with Grand Repast his Sons to Treat*
> *And set's before them fine Welch Ale & Meat.*
>
> *Herrings, Leeks, Black Puddings mustard, toasted Cheese,*
> *With Goats Milk, Butter & such food as these.*
> *Then brings his Minstrells Harp of gracefull sound.*
> *Whose Musick cheers their Hearts & makes their Voice Rebound*

$8\frac{3}{4} \times 9\frac{1}{4}$ in.

5944 SAINT ANDREW FOR SCOTLAND *3*

Publish'd as the Act directs, 2 Jan. 1781.

Printed for Carington Bowles, N⁰ 69 in St Pauls Church Yard, London.

Engraving. No 3 of the series, see No. 5942. A Scotsman in kilt and plaid riding (l. to r.) a horse with a unicorn's horn and the tufted tail of a lion He holds across his l shoulder a long broadsword on which is spitted a sheep's head. In his r. hand he holds out an open snuff-box or mull. Between his teeth he holds the stem of a rose. His cap is decorated with feathers and a medallion of St Andrew on his cross, in his belt are pistols and a dirk The horse's bit is decorated with thistles From the front of the saddle hang a small sack and a fish, from the back a set of bagpipes Behind is the sea-shore, with two castles.

The border of the design at the two sides is of targets and broadswords, pistols, the Union Jack flag, roses and thistles, and of two bunches of leaves which are perhaps tobacco-leaves. The upper border is the title on a scroll Below are roses and thistles. Below the design is engraved.

> *View well St Andrew a saint of Muckle Pride,*
> *In Northern Robes Array'd and by his Side*
> *His trusty broad Sword, Dirk, & Pistols ride,*
> *Likewise his Oatmeal pouch, Snuff, mull & Ling fish dry'd.*
>
> *His roast Sheep's Head, Haggoss & Scotch Cale*
> *With Sparkling Viskey Barley Cakes & Ale.*
> *Then on the Bagpipe plays a pleasing Tune,*
> *To celebrate his Joyfull Month of June.*

$8\frac{3}{4} \times 9\frac{1}{4}$ in.

5945 SAINT PATRICK FOR IRELAND. *4*

Published as the Act directs, 2 Jan. 1781.

Printed for Carington Bowles, N⁰ 69 in St Pauls Church Yard, London.

Engraving. No. 4 of the series, see No. 5942. An Irishman riding (l. to r.) on a horse. He is dressed as a military officer, with epaulettes In his hat is a cross in a medallion In his r. hand, and resting on his shoulder, is a sword on which potatoes are spitted. In his l. hand he holds out a wine-glass Two fish are slung on his r. arm, under it is a sickle. Various objects are attached to his saddle or his person including a tankard, a small set of bagpipes, a candle-stick, a large fish; a small Irish harp decorates the hind-quarters of his horse. The background, seen between the horse's feet, is the sea-shore with ships

A border decorates the two sides of the print, surmounted (l) by a frowning mask, with a dagger through one eye, and (r) by a smiling mask. To a vertical line of conventional fruit and foliage are attached a number of objects, including a horn and goblet, a flute, a flail and rake, a wine-bottle and glass, a sheaf of corn and a sickle

Beneath the design is engraved·

So sweet St Patrick comes, Dear Joy to Day,
Smiles on his face with Merriment & Play.
With good store of Tattoes, Sweet Buttermilk, & Whisky,
Small Pipes, & Usquebaugh to make us Dance Frisky.

Then banish all care, and meagre sorrow,
We'll Celebrate this Day not trust to morrow.
Let's Rant & Roar & make the House Ring,
Drink to St Patrick's Day in the Morning

$8\frac{1}{2} \times 9$ in.

5946-5957
Series of mezzotints published by Carington Bowles.

5946 DECEITFUL KISSES, OR THE PRETTY PLUNDERERS.

From the Original Picture by John Collet, in the possession of Carington Bowles.

432 *Printed for & Sold by Carington Bowles, at his Map & Print Warehouse, No 69 in St Pauls Church Yard, London. Published as the Act directs* [date erased, 1781] [1]

Mezzotint (coloured impression) Interior of a bedroom A stout man is being kissed by three pretty young women who put their arms round his neck. One takes his watch and seals from his fob, another robs him of his pocket-book, the third pulls a ring from his finger. On a table (r) is a punch-bowl and a wine-bottle. A monkey seated on the top of a cupboard holds an open book inscribed, *Who's the Dupe*; this was a farce by Mrs. Cowley, first acted at Drury Lane, 1779.

$12\frac{15}{16} \times 9\frac{7}{8}$ in   'Caricatures', i. 228. B.M.L., Tab. 524

5947 FIELDING'S MYRMIDONS SPOILING BOB BOOTY'S MORNING DRAUGHT.

From the Original Picture by John Collet, in the possession of Carington Bowles.

433 *London: Published as the Act directs, 1 May 1781 by Carington Bowles No 69 in St Pauls Church Yard.*

Mezzotint. Three Bow Street officers burst open the door (r) of a room where three persons are sitting up in bed, much alarmed at their entry. The highwayman or burglar in the centre, wearing a night-cap, spills the

---

[1] Collet died in 1780.

contents of a punch-bowl held in his l. hand; over his arm is a netted purse containing coins. The two girls wear mob-caps, one (r) seizes the man's arm in terror, the other (l) takes up one of a pair of pistols lying by the bed (r) On the ground lie top-boots, a mask, &c., the man's coat lies across the foot of the bed, on it is a bank-note. The constables are forcing backwards furniture with which the door had been barricaded; a chair, placed on a table, is falling over. On the wall is a framed print of *Jack Sheppard*, shackled and sitting on the ground in prison. The foremost Bow Street officer, wearing a striped waistcoat, has a sword under his arm, behind him are two men with constable's staves Sir John Fielding died in Sept. 1780.

$9\frac{7}{8} \times 13\frac{7}{8}$ in.

5948 THE BIRD OF PARADISE.

435 *Printed for & Sold by Carington Bowles, at his Map & Print Warehouse, N° 69 in S¹ Paul's Church Yard, London. Publish'd as the Act directs* [date erased, 1781].

Mezzotint (coloured impression). A lady, seated on a settee smiling, her r. hand rests on the arm of the settee, in her l. is a black mask. On the cushion of the settee is a card *Admit M^{rs} M—— to the Mask'd Ball*. She is attractively dressed in the fashion of the period, with a muslin apron. Her coiffure is extravagantly large, with curls on her neck, and is covered by an elaborately frilled muslin cap. A rural landscape is seen through a window (r).

She is Gertrude Mahon, *née* Tilson, b. 1752, whose mother was the daughter of the Earl of Cavan and widow of the Earl of Kerry After eloping (1769) with Mahon, a musician and gamester, and being deserted by him, she became a courtesan She also attempted to go on the stage (Covent Garden, 1780-1). She was called the Bird of Paradise (c. 1776-) from her love of bright colours, and was the subject of many press paragraphs. H Bleackley, *Ladies Fair and Frail*, 1909, pp. 247 ff See No 5868

The subject of this portrait is incorrectly said to be Perdita Robinson by Wright, *Caricature Hist. of the Georges*, 1867, p 257, and by Grego, *Gillray*, p 38. Reproduced, Paston, Pl. clxiii. Bleackley, *op. cit*, p. 290.

$12\frac{3}{4} \times 9\frac{3}{4}$ in. (clipped).   'Caricatures', ii. 94. B.M.L , Tab. 524.

5948A A reduced version, No. 325 in Bowles's smaller series, published 2 Jan. 1781.

$5\frac{3}{8} \times 4\frac{3}{8}$ in.

5949 LIKE MISTRESS—LIKE MAID.

[J. R. Smith?]

438 *Printed for & Sold by Carington Bowles, at his Map & Print Warehouse, N° 69 in S¹ Pauls Church Yard, London. Published as the Act directs* [date erased, 1781].

Mezzotint (coloured impression) Two women meet on the pavement outside a public-house. The mistress (r.) totters with dangling hands and half-closed eyes, the maid (l) looks pertly at her with arms akimbo. The background is part of the front of the house, showing the lower part of a sash-window (l) and an open door (r) within which are seen a cask marked *B* and a shelf with glasses Between window and door is a board inscribed *Dealer in Spirituous Liquors . . . unds &c.*, the rest being obscured by the lady's large hat

Beneath the title is engraved

Wine is a mocker, strong drink is raging, and whosoever is deceived thereby is not wise Proverbs Ch xx verse 1st

Similar in manner to No. 5824; it appears to belong to the set of prints illustrating *Proverbs*, see Frankau, pp 125, 199.

$12\frac{15}{16} \times 9\frac{7}{8}$ in.   'Caricatures', ii. 40. B.M.L., Tab 524

5950 MASTER LAVENDER QUALIFYING HIMSELF FOR THE ARMY.

439 *Printed for & Sold by Carington Bowles, at his Map & Print Warehouse, N° 69 in St Pauls Church Yard, London. Publish'd as the Act directs* [date erased, 1781].

Mezzotint (coloured impression) A young man in profile to the r. (l.), elegantly dressed, lounges beside a lady on a settee He holds a coffee-cup She sits before a round table on which is a coffee-pot, &c , on a tray Her dress is of quasi-military cut and she wears a large feathered hat; they look towards each other. On the wall (l) is a framed picture of a camp scene. Through the large sash-window (r) are trees and (?) tents

One of many satires on the militia camps at Coxheath and Warley See No. 5523, &c Similar in character to Nos. 6156, 6157.

$12\frac{5}{8} \times 9\frac{13}{16}$ in.   'Caricatures', i. 105. B M L , Tab 524.

441. LOFTY RIDING, OR MISS FOLLY'S HEAD EXALTED

            See No 3786—[1781]

(After Collet)

320 LOFTY RIDING   (Reduced version.)   See No 3787—[1781]

5951 AN ENGLISH MAN OF WAR, TAKING A FRENCH PRIVATEER

454 *Printed for & Sold by Carington Bowles, at his Map & Print Warehouse, N° 69 in St Pauls Church Yard, London. Published as the Act directs* [date erased, 1781].

Mezzotint (coloured impression). A young sailor overtakes and takes by the r hand a young woman walking from l. to r., carrying one of the arched-top coffers which were used by milliners. She wears a hat, long gloves, and a cloak bordered with ermine. The sailor is dandified, in spite of his striped trousers, jacket, and round hat; a bunch of seals dangles from his waistcoat, and he carries a thin cane under his arm

The background is the wall of a bridge over the Thames, it is surmounted by balustrades, through which is seen the river, and buildings on the opposite bank. A bill is posted on the wall, *All Able Bodied Seamen. . . .*

Reproduced, C N Robinson, *The British Tar in Fact and Fiction*, 1909, p. 172.

$13\frac{1}{16} \times 10$ in.   'Caricatures', i. 66. B.M.L., Tab. 524.

5952 AN ENGLISH SLOOP ENGAGING A DUTCH MAN OF WAR

455 Printed for & Sold by Carington Bowles, at his Map & Print Warehouse, Nᵒ 69 in Sᵗ Pauls Church Yard, London. Published as the Act directs [date erased, 1781].

Mezzotint (coloured impression) A Dutchman (l), smoking a short pipe, hands in his pockets, is being chucked under the chin by a gaily dressed courtesan (r), her l. hand on her hip. He wears the round hat and baggy breeches of the Dutchman in caricature. Both stand full-face, each looks towards the other

The background is formed by the lower part of houses in Covent Garden showing the arcade of the Piazza, a sedan chair (r) stands under an arch Immediately behind the two figures are vegetables and baskets.

Reproduced, C. N. Robinson, *The British Tar in Fact and Fiction*, 1909, p 166

12¹⁵⁄₁₆×9⅞ in. 'Caricatures', i. 67. B M.L., Tab. 524.

5953 LADY GORGET RAISING RECRUITS FOR COX-HEATH.

456 Printed for & Sold by Carington Bowles, at his Map & Print Warehouse, Nᵒ 69 in Sᵗ Pauls Church Yard, London. Published as the Act directs [date erased, 1781]

Mezzotint (coloured impression). A lady seated on a settee (r.) looking towards three yokels who stand before her (l.). She is wearing riding-dress of a military cut, an officer's coat with epaulettes, and a gorget, the sign of an officer on active service. A bunch of seals hangs from her double-breasted waistcoat She wears a large feathered hat with a military cockade, and holds a tasselled cane under her l. arm. She is addressing a young man wearing spatterdashes and holding his hat, he smiles sheepishly. Another young man wearing a hat stands behind him (l), one hand on his shoulder. The third, wearing a smock frock, holds his hat to his mouth, grinning Outside the window (l) are the tents of the camp.

One of many satires on camp-life connected with the camps at Coxheath and Warley. See No. 5523, &c.

12⅞×9¾ in. 'Caricatures', i. 55 B.M L, Tab. 524

5954 A MAN OF WAR, TOWING A FRIGATE INTO HARBOUR

459 Printed for & Sold by Carington Bowles at his Map & Print Warehouse Nᵒ 69 in Sᵗ Paul's Church Yard London. Published as the Act directs [date erased, 1781].

Mezzotint (coloured impression). A sailor walking (r to l) arm in arm with a young woman, her r. arm in his l He wears striped trousers, and carries a cane She wears a ribbon-trimmed hat, short petticoat with an over-dress draped above it at the back, and an apron. Behind are steps leading to a sea-wall, with ships. On the l are trees

Reproduced, C. N. Robinson, *The British Tar in Fact and Fiction*, 1909, p 296.

12½×9⅞ in. 'Caricatures', i. 68 B M L, Tab 524.

5955 MR DEPUTY DUMPLING AND FAMILY ENJOYING A SUMMER AFTERNOON.

463 *Printed for & Sold by Carington Bowles, at his Map & Print Warehouse, N° 69 in St Pauls Church Yard London* [1781].

Mezzotint (coloured and uncoloured impressions). A family party walking past the entrance to Bagnigge Wells A fat citizen, his wig awry and dripping with perspiration, carries a little girl who holds a whip His stout wife walks behind (r) holding a fan in one hand, a tasselled cane in the other, she smiles complacently. In front, a small boy drags a small four-wheeled chair in which sits a doll-like child holding a doll. The background is the corner of a brick house (r.) showing part of a bow-window inscribed *Dealer in Coffee*, and a gate inscribed *Bagnigge Wells* with an ogive-shaped decoration surmounting the architrave Behind are trees The design evidently derives from Hogarth's *Evening*, see No. 2382 (1738)

$12\frac{5}{8} \times 9\frac{7}{8}$ in.

Coloured impression in 'Caricatures', ii. 43. B M.L , Tab. 524

5956 AN ENGAGEMENT IN BILLINGSGATE CHANNEL, BETWEEN THE TERRIBLE AND THE TIGER, TWO FIRST RATES.

464 *Printed for & Sold by Carington Bowles, at his Map & Print Warehouse, N° 69 in St Pauls Church Yard London. Published as the Act directs* [date erased, 1781]

Mezzotint (coloured impression) Two Billingsgate fish-women face each other with clenched fists, one (l.) is very stout, a small boy clasps her by the leg, in alarm The other wears a cloak, the hem of which is being tugged at by a small boy who stands behind her, attempting to stop the engagement Their baskets of fish are on the ground Two men (r) watch the fray, one, holding a sack over his shoulder, has a beard and appears to be a Jew; a boy puts his hand into the sack. The side of a vessel (r.) shows that the place is by the side of Billingsgate quay or dock. Behind is a public house, the sign displayed on a first-floor balcony: three barrels, and the name CHURCH

$12\frac{15}{16} \times 9\frac{13}{16}$ in   'Caricatures', i 73 B.M L , Tab 524.

5957 A FLEET OF TRANSPORTS UNDER CONVOY.

[After R. Dighton.]

465 *Printed for & Sold by Carington Bowles, at his Map & Print Warehouse, N° 69 in St Pauls Church Yard London Published as the Act directs* [9 Nov. 1781].[1]

Mezzotint (coloured impression) A man (l) leads by a rope the foremost of a crowd of prisoners sentenced to transportation who follow him from l. to r. The two foremost are bearded Jews Behind comes a knock-kneed

---

[1] The date has been erased but is supplied from an impression in the possession of Mr W T Spencer, New Oxford Street.

youth taking a pinch of snuff, a man behind him is gnawing a large bone. There are ten prisoners in all   The background is part of the façade of Newgate prison.

At this time the transportation of convicts had temporarily ceased, owing to the American war, and hulks in the Thames were used as a substitute.

$12\frac{3}{4} \times 9\frac{13}{16}$ in.   'Caricatures', ι 196. B M L , Tab 524

.

POLITICAL SATIRES

5958 A——B^p LAUD CHARGING HIS CLERGY,

Burnet Inv^t &c.

Pub^d as the Act directs Jany 1st 1782 Price 1^{sg} to be had at N° 14 Dover Street.

Engraving The interior of a church Archbishop Markham (l) delivering a charge to his clergy. He stands (l.) within the chancel rails; in his left hand he holds up a flaming torch; in his r. hand, which rests on a balustrade, he holds a birch-rod and a paper inscribed *Factious C—y—n. [Countrymen], A Lamentable Want of Sobriety, Foremost in mischief. This is no Gainfull Traffick—Nonresistance &c Explain'd. Vide my Sermon. Charity Thinketh no Evil &c A perfectly detestable Faction &c*

On the r , in the body of the church, sit clergymen dressed in gown and bands, they listen with varying expressions. Behind the archbishop is a table of the Ten Commandments, on which is inscribed, . . . *VI Thou shalt do no Murder* and *IX Thou shalt not bear false Witness &c.*

Below the design is etched, *Remarks upon a late charge delivered not 100 Miles from Y—k. Vide Remem^r p^t. 2nd 1781—page 239*

Beneath the title is etched, *"Hac itur ad astra" Anglicé—This is the Road to Lambeth*

The print illustrates a criticism in the *Remembrancer* on a charge of Markham to the York clergy in which he blamed them for having 'not only cast away the gravity of their character, but stood foremost in mischief'. This was directed against the part taken by some of the York clergy in the County Association (see Nos. 5638, 5657, &c.), the chief of whom were Christopher Wyvill and Mason See Walpole, *Last Journals*, 1910, ii, 302, 330, 339; Wyvill, *Political Papers*, 6 v. York, 1794–1802. Markham's openly expressed opinions on the American War and party politics had made him very unpopular with the Whigs, see No 5553, &c

The artist's name is perhaps an allusion to Gilbert Burnet (1643–1714) as both a bishop and a leading Revolution Whig

By the same artist, perhaps an amateur, as Nos 5975, 6045, 6181.

7$\frac{1}{8}$×9$\frac{3}{8}$ in

A design in two compartments,

5959 TIME PAST

Pub by E. Hedges Jany 20. 1782 Cornhill

Engraving A stout English soldier pursues with clenched fists two French soldiers, who are emaciated *petits-maîtres* They wear long pigtail queues, ruffled shirts, and large top-boots The Englishman says, *Lower your Topsails Monsieurs*; the Frenchmen say *We are bold Frenchmen*. The Englishman is trampling on a French flag which lies on the ground A British flag is partly visible on the l. behind the Englishman. In the distance (r) a party of French soldiers is seen in flight, over them is inscribed, *Run Frogs.*

Beneath the title is etched, *When we beat them ten to one*

8$\frac{3}{16}$×6$\frac{1}{2}$ in.

TIME PRESENT.
Pub. Jany 20. 1782 by E. Hedges Cornhill

Engraving A French soldier (l), with clenched fists, kicks the back of a fat English soldier. He says *Begar we will make you now lower your Topsails* The fleeing Englishman looks round to say *I'm an English man of War.* In the distance (r.) English soldiers with a flag, the words *Run Beef Heads* inscribed over their heads, are in flight The British flag, inscribed *Discolour'd,* lies on the ground. A French flag. inscribed *Lewis le Grand,* extends over the head of the victorious Frenchman

Beneath the title is etched, *The Case is alter'd.* This represents the resentment at the military and naval situation on 4 Dec the Livery of London voted a remonstrance to the king, using the words, 'Your armies are captured, the wonted superiority of your navies is annihilated; your dominions are lost.' Walpole, *Last Journals,* 1910, ii. 386.

$8\frac{3}{16} \times 6\frac{1}{2}$ in   Pl. $9\frac{3}{4} \times 13\frac{3}{4}$ in.

5960 COMMODORE ST. JAGO RETURNING VICTORIOUS

Ch^s Bretherton Junr

Publish'd Jany 22^d 1782.

Engraving Commodore Johnstone, in naval uniform, walking in profile to the r , two large bundles attached to his shoulders, on the top of which sits a small monkey with a label round its neck inscribed *Caught at St Jago by the people ashore.* The bundles are inscribed *Plunder, Plunder* and *A large Body of News digested by a very promising officer Lieu^t D—* Under his r arm are bundles of papers inscribed *List of Kill'd at St Jago; Romney none,* and *Charge against Capt Sutton.* In his r hand he holds documents inscribed · *Articles of Capitulation in Case I had taken the Cape—But alas! I was mistaken; Prize Lists* and *Blank Commission* Above the design is etched, *I took the charge of Pilotage on myself—turn'd by traverses into the Bay and made even the kings of the East bow to my victorious arms*

These words burlesque Johnstone's dispatch of 21 Aug 1781 published in an *Extraordinary Gazette* of 15 Oct 1781. The print is a satire on Johnstone's Expedition against the Cape of Good Hope. He put into Porto Praya in St. Jago, one of the Cape Verde Islands, on 11 Apr for supplies, where he was followed by de Suffren, whom he defeated in circumstances which showed his lack of seamanship. French reinforcements reached the Cape which made Johnstone relinquish his intended attack. As an alternative he attacked some Dutch East Indiamen in Saldanha Bay. His dispatch relates the pursuit of the East Indiamen; in it he says, 'I took the charge of pilotage upon myself and run in shore under cover of the night At this time also a Boat was seen rowing to our ship, filled with People in Eastern garb, making humble signs of submission They proved to be the Kings of Tamare and Tidore, with the Princes of their respective Families; whom the Dutch East-India Company had long confined on the Isle Robin, with different Malefactors, but had lately removed them from that island to Saldanha.' The monkey sitting on the bundle of 'plunder' appears to represent these kings and princes. Cf. *Ann. Reg* 1782, pp 110–12 The reference to the 'large body of News . ' is also to Johnstone's dispatch 'From Captain Pigot I received a Body of Intelligence [of the East Indiamen], digested by Lieutenant d'Auvergne, a very promising young officer . . .'. The *Romney* was Johnstone's flag-ship, a Fourth Rate of 50 guns.

In this expedition Johnstone lost important opportunities by lack of seamanship, see W. M James, *The British Navy in Adversity*, 1926, 381 ff. Mahan, *Influence of Sea Power upon History*, pp. 421 ff Cf. Wraxall, *Memoirs*, 1884, ii. 129 and n. Cf. also No 6048.

$10\frac{7}{8} \times 7\frac{1}{2}$ in. (pl).

An English satire on the capture of St. Eustatius, No 1202, *Collection de Vinck*,

BE NOT SURPRISED. NE SOYEZ PAS SURPRIS

Kobon [Cockburn] *pinxit. Marq de Bouillé fecit.*

London, Publish'd Feb 12. 1782. by H. Humphrey N⁰ 18 New Bond Street.

Engraving. A French officer (de Bouillé) with a drawn sabre, holding four British flags which trail on the ground, escorts two prisoners, one in night attire, the other (James Cockburn, commandant at St. Eustatius) in uniform. In the background are the fortifications of St. Eustatius, with other prisoners (l.) being led off. A French soldier stands in a sentry-box, his cap inscribed *d'Auxerrois*. On the wall is a placard inscribed:

$$667 \left\{ {Anglois \atop English} \right\} 68 \; peices \; of \; cannon$$

$$379 \left\{ {Francois \atop French} \right\}$$

Point de Retreat.
Retreat cut off
4 pair of colours.
4 Pavillons.

The garrison of St Eustatius, taken Feb. 1781 by Rodney, see No 5837, &c , was surprised at 6 a m on 26 Nov 1781 by a party of *Chasseurs d'Auxerrois* and of Dillon's Irish brigade The names of the artists indicate the defeat by de Bouillé of Colonel James Cockburn, for which he was tried by court-martial (1783) and cashiered The inscription on the print states accurately the relative strength of the garrison and of the French

$5\frac{15}{16} \times 10\frac{13}{16}$ in

5961 THE ROYAL HUNT, OR A PROSPECT OF THE YEAR 1782

South Briton fecit North Briton Inv^t   [? After

Viscount Townshend.]

Published according to Act of Parliament by R. Owen, in Fleet Street Feby 16th 1782.

Engraving beneath which are printed verses entitled *The Chase*. A companion to No. 5988 also ascribed to Townshend In the foreground (l) a party of ministers is carousing. Members of the Opposition watch them with indignation. In the distance (l.) behind them mounted men with hounds chase a stag. On the r. the Temple of Fame is being demolished by the enemies of Britain Many of the figures have numbers referring to notes engraved beneath the design

The central figure in the ministerial group is (4) Sandwich (S—h) seated on the ground playing a violin, between two courtesans, each of whom holds a goblet of wine. He turns to one of them, saying, *D—mn the Navy, Give me t'ther Glee*; she holds a torn paper inscribed *How merrily we live* An open book, *Catchs Glees*, in front of him, is supported by a wine-bottle In the l. corner of the print is (5) North (*N—h*) seated on a small sack inscribed *Budg[et]*, he is yawning, his arms stretched above his head Three men stand behind him a man in Elizabethan dress wearing a tall hat and ruff who is (9) *R—by* [Rigby] *in the Character of Bobadil* He says (apparently of Sandwich) *I would he were in the Bottomless Pit* Cf. Nos 5982, 6052 For the time-serving Rigby's attack on Germain and Sandwich, and flattery of Pitt (14 Dec. 1781) see Walpole, *Last Journals*, 1910, ii. 390, and *Parliamentary Hist* xxii. 847. Behind him and whispering into his ear, stands 8, Lord Amherst (*A—rst*), very thin, saying, *Dick Rugby* [*sic*] *Stand Close* Behind Amherst stands 7, Lord George Germain (*G—mn*) saying *Jeffry Barebones* [i.e. Amherst], *this is worse than Minden*.

Next on the r stands the group of patriots· (6) Pitt (*W—P—t*) looking towards North, says *Shake off this Indolence*. (3), Fox (*F—x*), pointing towards the Temple of Fame (r.) and frowning, says, *Wheres your Navy, wheres your Islands*. (2), Burke (*B—k*) is saying *Wont even Destruction move ye* (1), The Duke of Richmond (*R—d*) says *Curs'd be those men who owe their Greatness to their Countrys Ruin*.

In the foreground (r) Britannia, seated on the ground on her shield, weeps, a handkerchief held to her eyes Behind her is (10) *The Temple of Fame, formerly the Wonder of the World, but now in Ruins*, a building with a fluted dome on which the winged figure of Fame without her trumpet is poised on one foot, the other leg being broken off The building is supported on a colonnade of pillars, all but two of which have been broken away and lie on the ground The largest fallen column is inscribed *America*, it lies across another, *Rh . de Island*, suggesting that the artist believed Rhode Island to be one of the West India islands The other fallen columns are: *St. Kitts, Tobago, Eustatius, Nevis, Dominique, St. Vincents, Grenadoes, Minorca* St. Kitts and Nevis did not capitulate until 12 Feb 1782; the news did not reach London till 3 March. *Corr. of George III*, v, p 376. The two still remaining columns are *Gibraltar* and *Jamaica Barbadoes*. A chain of four men is tugging at a rope placed round the 'Gibraltar' pillar, the first is Spain, next Holland, next America, and last France

On the r , between Britannia and the temple, the kings of France and Spain stand looking on , France says, *Brother our Work is near Over*.

The upper part of the temple, though precariously poised, is still intact. In the centre of the façade is a pediment decorated with the head of *Geo Secundus*, wearing a laurel wreath in an oval, and with smaller ovals inscribed with the names of British admirals· *Hawke, Saunders, Boscawen, Pocock*. These surround a tablet inscribed with British victories: *Quebec, Portobello, Havannah, Belle-Isle, Martinique* On each side of the pediment is a window. Within one (r.) are minute figures in Highland dress, one says *Egad Sawney we'd better gang*. A Scotsman is getting out of the other window. This scene and the names of the supposed artists imply that disaster in the war has been due to the schemes of Bute and a Scottish faction, carried out by English ministers, but that this faction is now ready to depart, an allusion to the expected fall of the ministry.[1] See Nos. 5963, 6005.

---

[1] Cf *Morning Herald*, 30 Mar 1782: 'The Butean system is to be entirely abolished, and all Scotsmen to be wrested out of public offices, military as well as civil, in as quick manner as possible '

In the distance is a fleet of ships in full sail (r.) advancing towards four dismantled ships with brooms at their mast-heads showing that they are for sale (l.), a gibe at the (supposed) comparative positions of the British Navy and the allied fleet The Royal Hunt is taking place on the l. George III is on horseback, a label hanging from his pocket is inscribed *The mightiest Hunter I.* With him are four other riders and dogs; they chase the stag up a hill.

Much importance was ascribed to this print by the *Morning Herald*, Bate's newspaper, see No. 5550, &c. On 25 March a paragraph alleged that it had been shown by the Prince of Wales to the king and (a clearly baseless assertion) had induced him to dismiss the Ministry. On 28 March the paper attributed the print to 'a noble lord .   ' [Viscount Townshend]. On 30 March it called for the withdrawal of satirical prints, especially the *Royal Hunt*, a 'well-timed but most insolent exhibition', since 'His Majesty has at length returned to the voice of his people'. On 1 Apr. it records the publication of a 'new descriptive song' of eight stanzas, given with the print 'with which the people seem much captivated'.

This song appears to be the one printed beneath the plate, showing that it is a reissue at some date probably after 1 Apr. News of the loss of Minorca did not reach London till March The verses (*The Chase. To the tune of The Dusky Night*) are put into the mouth of George III, who expresses his disregard of national disaster, provided he can still go 'a hunting'. One verse, to which is added a note 'This song was written before the change of the Ministry', runs:

VI

If Fox and Burke and Barré still
   Should circumscribe our space.
Leave me but round sweet W—d—r's [Windsor's] hill,
   Sufficient for the chase
     That a hunting we may go, &c.

It ends.

VIII.

Half Nimrod's fame belongs to me,
   Ev'n patriots wont deny,
The mightiest of all warriors he,
   The mightiest hunter I.   ·
     Then a hunting . . . &c.

The exaggerated allegations of disaster to British arms resemble Burke's speech of 6 March, which, however, the print anticipates. See Wraxall, *Memoirs*, 1884, ii. 214 f, *Parl. Hist.* xxii 1110 f. The first appearance of Pitt in the Catalogue.

$8\frac{3}{4} \times 12\frac{15}{16}$ in.

THE BULL OVER-DROVE. OR THE DRIVER IN DANGER.

London Publish'd as the Act directs Feby 21. 1782, by I. Harris, Sweetings Alley Cornhill.

A reissue of No. 5640.

5962 THE KNAVE OF HEARTS.

Published as the Act directs Feby 1782. Price 6^d.

Engraving (coloured impression) The Knave of Hearts in a pack of cards, but with a fox's head and representing Charles Fox, standing within an oval border round the top of which is twined a vine branch with dangling bunches of grapes inscribed *Places and Pensions*. Fox looks up towards them, his tongue out, his mouth dripping saliva, saying, *They are Sour*. In his r hand he holds a staff on which is the cap of liberty, from inside the cap hangs a streamer inscribed *Liberty and Property*, to which are attached small bells, implying that the cap is a fool's cap, cf. No 5010.

The only example in the Catalogue of a satire directed against the Opposition shortly before the change of government. Cf. Nos. 5829, 5836, 5970, 5972, 5979, &c.

$5\frac{3}{8} \times 3\frac{3}{4}$ in. (pl. $6\frac{1}{4} \times 5$ in).

5963 ['AS IT WAS, OR']¹ THE STATE SAMPSON FIREING THE FOXES, OR BOREAN MAJORITY.

['*Pub^d March 15 1782 by H. Humphrey N° 18 New Bond Street*'¹]

Engraving. Lord North, in profile to the l, kneels on one knee holding a fire-brand to the tail of a fox. He blows a visible blast at the flame to kindle it. Other foxes with flaming tails run away from him. Above his head a number of cherubs seated on clouds are directing blasts of air at the burning foxes, some puff with distended cheeks, one plies a pair of bellows, another, labelled *Scotch Assistance*, and wearing a tartan plaid, puffs from a set of bagpipes. Above North a monkey collects in a funnel held in his mouth the blasts blown by three cherubs and discharges them at the foxes through his fundament.

By 15 March the 'Borean majority' had virtually disappeared. Conway's motion on 22 Feb to declare the subduing of the colonies impossible was defeated by one vote only, cf No 5985 On 13 March it was publicly given out that Lord North was to resign Walpole, *Last Journals*, 1910, ii. 406 ff. The situation, however, was still full of uncertainty, see Walpole, *Letters*, xii. 190–3, 197–8. On 8 Mar. Lord John Cavendish's Resolutions of Censure had been defeated by ten votes, the 'Scotch Assistance' may allude to the speeches in defence of the Government by Dundas, the Lord Advocate, and by Adam, who had taunted Fox with looking outside parliament for the wishes of the people, *Parl Hist* xxii. 1114 ff. North thereupon wrote to the king (at 3 a.m. 9 Mar.): 'After such division, Lord North is obliged to repeat his opinion that it is totally impossible for the present Ministry to conduct His Majesty's business any longer.' *Corr. of George III*, v. 381. Negotiations took place between the king and Rockingham through Thurlow but were broken off after eight days *Rockingham Memoirs*, ii 451–9 Cf. No. 5972, where Thurlow is the 'shuffler'. On 20 Mar. North announced in the House of Commons that his Majesty's ministers were no more. *Parl Hist.* xxii 1215.

A companion print to No 5981 by the same artist

$6\frac{3}{4} \times 9\frac{7}{8}$ in.

¹ The words in brackets have been added in a contemporary hand, evidently after the fall of the Ministry on 20 Mar.

5964 CHANGING PLACES,—ALIAS; FOX STINKING THE BADGER OUT OF HIS NEST.

[Gillray]

Pub⁴ March 22ⁿᵈ 1782 by W. Humphrey N⁰ 227, Strand

Engraving. North (l) in the guise of a badger, runs off leaving a little cave under a rock. Charles Fox as a fox (r) snarls at him, while he excretes a stream inscribed *Eloquence* The badger is identified as North by a ribbon tied round his body, and by the four points of the compass in a circle on his head, his snout being inscribed *North* The fox stands over a bag inscribed *Faro Bank* from which guineas are pouring, playing-cards are strewn on the ground at his feet In the foreground is a small bundle inscribed *Budget* within which are bars inscribed *Soap* and a small barrel inscribed *Small Beer* in allusion to the taxes proposed by North in his budget speech of 11 Mar. Behind the badger is a sign-post, the two arms of which terminate in well-drawn hands. The hand of the arm pointing l., in the direction to which North is running, holds the head of a halberd, the arm is inscribed *To Tower Hill*. The other arm points downwards at the cave which the badger has left, and is inscribed *To the Treasury*. Behind Fox is a terminal statue inscribed *Janus*, one head being that of a bearded old man, the other that of a fox, it is crowned by a cylindrical head-dress (?a dice-box) on which are two dice The scene is a wooded landscape with hills In the distance a hunt is in progress, a stag pursued by dogs; the foremost rider is the king, a minute figure who is falling from his horse after having leapt a gate His crown falls from his head, his saddle, with the stirrups flying, is falling to the ground

North resigned on 20 Mar , see No 5963, on the 25th Fox took office as foreign secretary under Rockingham For Fox's faro bank see No 5972 and for North's budget, Nos 5965, 5968, 5969, 5970, 5971, 5974, 5975, 5977, 5982, 5986, 5988

For threats to North of the scaffold see No 5969, &c No 6176 is a sequel to this print, see also Nos 6186, 6196, 6204.

9⅜ × 13⅞ in.

5965 L——D SAND——G DROVE FROM HIS MOORINGS OR TACK ABOUT IS FAIR PLAY.   [c 25 Mar. 1782]

Sold by W. Humphrey N⁰ 227 Strand

Engraving Three outgoing ministers are being knocked off their seats by their successors. The ministers are or have been seated on stones resembling mile-stones, engraved with the title of their office They are all in profile to the l., facing their successors Sandwich (centre), on a stone inscribed *First Lo—d of the Adm—ty*, is being knocked backwards by Admiral Keppel, his successor, who threatens him with clenched fists, saying, *Strike your false Colours*. Sandwich is saying *That broadside has broke my Bowsprit*. From his pocket falls a small paper, *List of the navy* Round his waist is a rope with a broken end, the other end of which is still attached to an anchor which lies on the ground beside him, inscribed *Rotten for want of care*

Lord North (r.), very short and fat, is being knocked backwards by Fox, who has a fox's head His stone is inscribed *Prime Minus-—r*, he says, *O Reynard if I fall I shall burst* Fox says to him, *Buss Constable* By this

563

stone lie two bars inscribed *Soap* and a cask inscribed *12 Shilling Small Beer*, to indicate the taxes recently proposed by North, see Nos 5964, &c To the l Lord Amherst, in general's uniform and wearing spurred top-boots, is seated on the stone inscribed *[Gen]eral of al[l] the Land Forces.* Conway stands opposite him, threatening him with his fists and saying, *That Staff shall be mine.* Amherst says, *Where's my reserved courage—oh—its in my breeches.*

In the foreground (l) sits Britannia, her shield beside her, holding her spear and stretching out an arm towards Keppel. She says *Britons strike home.*

This print was probably published after North's resignation on 20 Mar. and before the formation of the new ministry on 27 Mar The artist's anticipations are correct as regards Conway and Keppel; there had of course been no likelihood that Fox would succeed North as premier, although he was the leading spirit of the Opposition (cf Wraxall, *Memoirs*, 1884, ii. 25.), the possible alternatives to Rockingham being Shelburne and Gower. Walpole, *Last Journals*, ii 422 ff.; Fitzmaurice, *Shelburne*, 1912, ii. 87. Cf No 5963. The title of the print stresses the replacing of Sandwich by his old enemy Keppel, see No. 5537

$7\frac{7}{8} \times 12\frac{3}{16}$ in.

5966 DAME RAT, AND HER POOR LITTLE ONES.

[Gillray.]

Publish'd March 26th 1782 by J: Browning. Oxford Street

Engraving (coloured and uncoloured impressions) Lord Hertford, Lord Chamberlain since 1766, with his wife, five sons and two daughters, who are making obsequious overtures to Charles Fox, the central figure of the design. Hertford stands stiffly in profile to the l., his staff of office in his hand. His wife and children all have rat's heads Fox, with a fox's head, strolls past the family ignoring their advances, and turning his back on Lady Hertford. She, very stout, has her r hand in her husband's arm, and turns to her l. to address Fox, saying *Happy to see you on Monday Mr Reynard* The sons and daughters (r.) stand in a line behind their parents. on the r. is an elder daughter holding the hand of a little girl, who holds a young brother by the arm Next come four tall young men, all holding their hats and bowing obsequiously towards Fox. The scene is an open rectangular space with buildings on the r and at the back, perhaps a free rendering of one of the courts of St James's Palace.

This illustrates a paragraph in the *Morning Herald*: Lord Hertford gave a grand ball on 19 Mar ; Fox received an invitation on that morning in the presence of Selwyn, and smiled as he read it, 'Pray what have you got there says George. A petition, replied the other, from a poor woman with thirteen children.'[1] The origin of the story appears in a letter from Selwyn to Lord Carlisle of 18 Mar 'Charles called the card which he had from Lady Hertford, a letter from a poor woman with a large family of small children.' *Hist MSS Comm , Carlisle MSS* 1897, p 598; see also pp. 589, 590 Hertford was very reluctant to resign his office, and is said not to have surrendered his gold key until after the appointment of the Duke of Manchester on 10 April 1782 Cf *Carlisle MSS.*, pp. 606, 607, 621 Walpole, *Last Journals*, 1910, p. 428, and No. 5988. Hertford (1719-94),

[1] Transcript (n d) by E Hawkins.

afterwards 1st Marquess Hertford, had seven sons and six daughters, none of whom was so young as the youngest son and younger girl here depicted. The youngest child was the Hon. George Conway, b 1763, called by Walpole, 3 June 1780, 'the handsomest giant in the world' *Letters*, xii 5. Hertford closely resembles the small caricature head by Gillray, see No. 5750. His brother General Conway became Commander-in-Chief under the new ministry, see No 5965 For the Conways as rats see also No 6018. For Hertford's restoration to office see No. 6218.

$7\frac{5}{8} \times 10\frac{13}{16}$ in.

5967 THE NORTHERN PHIZ

[T Colley ?]

Pub^d by T. Colley March 27, 1782 Rolls Buildings fetter Lane

Engraving. Lord North, very short and fat, in profile to the r. conversing with a Jew He holds up in his l hand a mask, representing his own face, and says, *This countenance is always the Same let your deeds be ever so Black.* The Jew, in profile to the l, has a beard, and wears a wide-brimmed hat and long coat, he holds up his r. fore-finger, saying to North, *Its such Base Metal its only fit to make Halfpence on't* Fox, with a fox's head, stands behind North (against whom he is urinating) and says, *he'll come North about you if you don't mind Mordeca[i]* Beneath the design is engraved, *A Copper Countenance, Selling by Private Contract, the property of a Noble Lord out of office having no further use for it.*

A satire on the fall of North's ministry, 20 Mar. 1782.

$7\frac{7}{8} \times 6\frac{1}{4}$ in

5968 LORD NO——H IN THE SUDS

Pub. by T. Evans Oxford Street M^{ch} 27. 1782. London

[? T. Colley.]

Engraving. North seated in a circular wash-tub, which froths with lather, he is surrounded by angry women On the extreme l. the head and fore-paws of a fox (Charles Fox) appear, he is saying, *Give him Pearl ash ha ha ha.* A woman (l.) in profile to the r, looks towards him clenching her fists, she is smoking a short pipe and carries a large basket on her head, a knife hangs from her waist, she is probably a Billingsgate fish-wife. A short woman wearing a hat stands behind him, she applies a scrubbing-brush to his shoulder and says, *Salt the Scoundrel* Next her on the r another woman pours soap-suds on his head from a ladle or dipper, saying *Lather him he has taxt Soap.* A fourth woman (r.) holds out an open snuff-box towards him, saying, *Snuff his Eyes out.* On the extreme l. stands the devil, with horns, hoofs, and a tail, holding a trident; he says, *I'll Contract for him.* North is saying *Da—n that Fox.* Beneath the design is engraved:

> *For taxing of Salt Tobacco and Soap,*
> *Some say that Lord North is deserving a Rope.*
> *His Lordship you see he his now in a Tub,*
> *While the old woman lathers & give him a Scrub.*

North in 1782 proposed to increase the duty on soap, which, since 1714, had been 1½d. a lb by ¾d a lb. on hard cake soap and ¼d. a lb. on soft soap[1] (22 Geo. III c. 68) He also increased the salt duty (22 Geo. III. c. 39). The budget was actually passed after his fall He was accused of using Government contracts as bribes, cf *Parl Hist*. xxi, p 1391, and No 5835. For other references to North's budget see No 5964, &c. See also No 5988

5⅞×8½ in

5969 LORD SOPESUDS WASHING FOUL LINEN FOR THE GOOD OF THE NATION.

Publish'd April 1. 1782 by E. Dachery, N° 11 St James's Street.

Engraving Lord North at a wash-tub, washing clothes, with women standing round him He stands in profile to the l stooping over a tub resting on a square stool or table; he is in his shirt, with his sleeves tucked up, but wearing his garter ribbon His coat, with its star, lies on a stool behind him. He says, *Oh Lord I wish that Fox at the Devil* In the foreground (l.) a fox with playing-cards under its feet, is biting a sack inscribed *Budgett.* One woman, in profile to the r., holds up her hands, saying *Poor man he must want a drop of comfort* [i e gin]. A woman standing full face, behind the tub, says, *Look at him, see what he has got by his Taxation.* The third woman stands behind North holding a cloth, and saying *He deserves this Clout pin'd to his tail.* A small child with curly hair is looking over the edge of the wash-tub. Over North's head is suspended an axe, suggestive of the impeachment and capital punishment with which he had been threatened by the Opposition and Press, cf Nos. 5660, 5661, 5964, 6046, &c.[2] The room is poverty-stricken, with plaster coming off the walls. On the table (l) is bottle and glass. In the foreground (r) is a barrel lying on its side inscribed *Gin.* On the wall hangs a paper or broadside inscribed, *to praise Lord North i thirst it* (?) *no ten for he has* [?illegible *forborne*] *to tax our Dear Gin.*

North is not caricatured, but his profile shows little resemblance either to his portraits or to the conventions of pictorial satire.

For North's budget see No. 5964, &c.

8 5/16 × 11⅞ in.

5970 A WARM BIRTH FOR THE OLD ADMINISTRATION.

[Gillray.]

Pub^d April 2^d 1782 by W. Brown.

Engraving (coloured impression) George III on his throne asleep, while the new ministry, helped by devils, drive out the king's old advisers The king, his throne raised on a dais of three steps covered with a fringed carpet, leans back, his mouth open, his feet crossed His ermine-trimmed robe hangs open and shows a crown stuffed into the pocket of his coat.

---

[1] North justified this at some length, maintaining that it would not be burdensome to the poor, since their consumption of soap was very small, and since the price of soap had fallen considerably, owing to new processes, &c, and would probably continue to fall *Parl Hist* xxii 1153-4

[2] Threats of impeachment and the block had been made by Burke and Fox, e g. by Fox, 27 Nov 1781, *Parl Hist.* xxii 692 Ministers would be trusted expiate their measures 'on the public scaffold'.

From his r. hand his sceptre is falling, in his l he holds a book, inscribed *Pinchee on Snuffers*, an allusion to Pinchbeck, the supposed 'king's friend', see No. 5234, &c Cf W Mason's 'Ode to Mr. Pinchbeck upon his newly invented candle-snuffers', 1776 In the centre of the room, at the foot of the dais, stands Charles Fox with a fox's head, in back view, his l. hand on the shoulder of the Devil, his r. holding North by his neck-cloth. He looks at the Devil saying, *This is Boreas, he'll make an excellent pair of Bellows Old Boy*. Large bunches of grapes protrude from the pockets of Fox's coat, cf. No 5962 The Devil wears a toupet-wig and queue, coat, ruffled shirt and trousers, showing bare feet with talons. He has horns, tail, and claws, and holds in his r. hand a long pitchfork, ornamented with tassels North puffs from his mouth a visible blast, from his coat pocket project bars inscribed *Soap*, an allusion to the tax laid on soap. Cf. No. 5964, &c

Behind, demons are carrying off the king's late advisers through a wide doorway, over which is carved *Pandaemoniu[m]*, towards flames and smoke A demon (r), clad in a pair of breeches, runs towards the door holding on his shoulders Sandwich and Germain (created Viscount Sackville on 11 Feb 1782) tied back to back, Sackville underneath looking over the demon's back, he holds in his r. hand a broken sword, in his l. a *Pla[n] of Minden* in allusion to his supposed cowardice at Minden Sandwich's legs hang over Sackville's shoulders, he holds out his arms, crying *Wee'r sailing in a damn'd hot Latitude*. A small imp or winged serpent above their heads darts flames at them. Bute in Highland dress is being pushed towards the flames by a small demon who prods him with a pitchfork saying Gee up lazy *Boots* On Bute's l. is Mansfield,[1] in judge's wig and gown, a flying demon has clutched him by the wig and is dragging him towards the flames. A demon's head looks out of the fire at the advancing victims.

On the wall of the room, to the r of the king, is a picture, the *Wisdom of Solomon*, where the incident of the two mothers, the infant, and the executioner is freely sketched on a small scale

Beneath the title is engraved, *Take the Wicked from before the King and his Throne shall be establish'd in Righteousness*, a text hardly consistent with the representation of Fox, in league with the Devil, his pockets stuffed with the grapes which he has at last reached, cf. No. 5962 See also Nos. 5982, 5984. Grego, *Gillray*, p. 46, giving the date as 2 April 1783, when the plate was reissued. Reproduced, C. E Jensen, *Karikatur-album*, 1906, 1. 263.

$8\frac{7}{8} \times 13\frac{1}{2}$ in.

5971 SAILING TO THE HOUSE, WIND FULL NORTH

[? T. Colley.]

Pub⁴ April 10ᵗʰ 1782, by W. Humphrey Nᵒ 227 Strand.

Engraving North, very short and fat, walking in profile to the l., carrying a large sack on his shoulder. The Devil, with horns, hoofs, and forked tail, walks behind, supporting the sack North says, *Give us a Hoist Nick* The sack is inscribed *BUDGET Small beer Soap Tobacco Insurance Carriages Tea* The Devil says, *mind the Small Beer my old Boy*. They are walking towards a rectangular brick building partly visible on the l., out of a window or opening in which looks a fox (Charles Fox), saying *This North wind blows*

---

[1] Thurlow, according to Grego.

no good. The road on which North is walking is bordered by posts and chains which form a background.

One of many satires on North's budget of 1782, which was introduced on 11 March shortly before his resignation on 20 March, see Nos. 5964, &c. See *Parl Hist*. xxii. 1150 ff. The items are correct, except that while beer was taxed, small beer was favourably treated. He also proposed to tax salt, see Nos 5968, 5977, and entertainments, see No. 5974.

$4\frac{1}{16} \times 6\frac{1}{8}$ in.

5972 BANCO TO THE KNAVE.

[Gillray.]

Pubᵈ April 12ᵗʰ 1782 by H. Humphrey, Nᵒ 118 New Bond Street.

Engraving. Members of the old and new Ministry seated and standing round a large card-table. Coins, cards and bank-notes lie on the table, two rectangular wells sunk in the centre are full of coins. In the centre of the farther side of the table sits Lord North throwing his cards down on the table; he looks down dejectedly, saying *Its all over.*[1] On the r. sits Fox, with a fox's head, a pile of coins and bank-notes in front of him, on which lies a court-card with its corners turned up. He is saying *Gentlemen the Bank is mine, & I will open every Night at the same hour* Streamers issue from the mouths of the late Opposition and join a scroll which floats over their heads, inscribed *HUZZA, HUZZA HUZZA* The defeated Ministry is represented by four figures only, who sit at the centres of the farther and nearer sides of the table, and of its r. and l. sides. Facing Lord North, in back view, is a player whose chair is inscribed *John Shuffler Esq* He is saying *Alas! what a Deal*. This is Thurlow, the Lord Chancellor, who retained his office under the new Ministry, cf. No. 5963. At the extreme r of the table is a dejected player in profile to the l., saying, *I want a new Master*; his chair is inscribed, *Sir Grey Parolle*, that is Sir Grey Cooper, one of the Secretaries of the Treasury who commonly sat on North's l hand and supplied him with facts for points arising in debate, giving him 'the parole'. These two are without cards or coins; croupier's rakes lie on the table in front of them On the extreme l., at the opposite point of the table, sits a man holding a croupier's rake and saying, dejectedly, *Atkinson cut the cards*. (Richard Atkinson, of *The Rolliad*, had been a prominent contractor for loans issued by North (cf. No. 5835). Wraxall, *Memoirs*, 1884, iii. 433–5) He is perhaps Robinson, the other Secretary of the Treasury.

The other players (twenty-two) are all partisans of the new ministry and all, except Fox, are saying *Huzza* They are grouped chiefly on the farther side of the table, some looking over the shoulders of those who are seated. On Fox's r. sits a minister with a ribbon and star who appears to be Rockingham, the new prime minister; his guineas are very few compared with those of Fox. Standing behind Grey Cooper, his hand on the back of his chair in profile to the l., is the Duke of Richmond. Standing next him (l.) is Dunning, in a barrister's wig and gown. Two men standing together on the l. can be identified with some certainty from their resemblance to portraits as Barré and Lord John Cavendish Sitting behind Sandwich and on his l. is Wilkes, leaning eagerly forward. A man standing behind

[1] Temple wrote to Rockingham on 20 Mar to tell him 'that Lord North, after having been with the King for near three hours, said to several persons   . that the game is up ' *Rockingham*, ii. 462. *Memoirs*

Lord North, looking downwards with a broad smile, is perhaps intended for Burke. A complacent player on North's r resembles the Earl of Surrey The figure most resembling portraits of Shelburne stands immediately in front of Cavendish and Barré, leaning forward with both hands resting on the table.

While this is a satire on ministerial changes, Fox and North as usual being the chief protagonists, cf. No. 5964, &c, it is also a satire on the faro bank at Brooks's held by Fox and some of his friends, which had been very profitable, see *Hist. MSS. Comm*, *Carlisle MSS*, 1897, pp 476, 483, 484, 489–90, Walpole, *Letters*, xi 441, and Nos 5996, 5997. Fox gave it up while he was a minister, cf No. 6013. Grego, *Gillray*, pp 34–5; Wright and Evans, No 2 Reprinted, *G W G*, 1830

Another impression in which Rockingham (?) has no ribbon and star $9\frac{2}{8} \times 13$ in.

5973 THE AMERICAN RATTLE SNAKE.

[Gillray.]

Pub^d April 12th 1782, by W. Humphrey, N° 227 Strand.

Engraving An enormous snake, so coiled as to make three circles; from its mouth protrudes a forked fang and a label inscribed

> *Two British Armies I have thus Burgoyn'd,*
> *And room for more I've got behind.*

Inside two of the circles are solid squares of British soldiers, while British flags lie on the ground They represent the armies of Burgoyne and Cornwallis which had been forced to surrender. The last coil, nearest the tail, is empty, on the top of the tail which rears in the air a placard is hung, inscribed *An Apartment to lett for Military Gentlemen.*

Beneath the design is engraved

> *Britons within the Yankean Plains,*
> *[Mind?][1] how ye March & Trench,*
> *The Serpent in the Congress reigns,*
> *As well as in the French.*

In the foreground are stones and foliage, the background is a mountainous landscape

The snake emblem[2] had been chosen by the Americans and used as a device on their flag before the adoption of the stars and stripes, see Nos. 5336, 5401, 6004, 6039, &c. Reproduced, Drepperd, *Early American Prints*, p 209.
$8\frac{11}{16} \times 10\frac{3}{4}$ in.

5974 A CHILLING NORTH BLAST OR A TAX UPON LAUGHTER.

(Pub^d April 13th 1782 by H. Humphrey at N° 18 New Bond Street[3])

Engraving. A harlequinade scene on the stage. North, in profile to the r.,

---

[1] Mutilated

[2] A disjointed snake had been designed by Franklin in 1754 for the *Pennsylvania Gazette,* and was frequently used in other colonial newspapers from ten to twenty years later, with the legend 'unite or die' After the first Congress in 1774 this was superseded by a living snake encircling a tree or staff of Liberty which is supported by the arms of the twelve colonies represented at Philadelphia with the legend 'united now alive and free ' This headed the *New York Journal or the General Advertiser* of 15 Dec 1774. Reproduction, Halsey, *The Boston Port Bill,* p. 125; see also pp 3, 270

[3] Written in ink on the plate.

reclines on a settee, one foot on the seat, one on the floor; he points at one of several figures who are rising through openings in the floor, saying, *Hence Babbling Visions, you threaten here in Vain.* He has a cap on his head, and wears a ribbon and star Behind him (r.) stands Harlequin, masked, who has just risen through an opening in the floor, in which his feet are still hidden, he strikes North on the head with his club, saying, *Do you hear tax them not for they are the abstract and brief chronicles of the time after your death you were bett' have a bad Epitaph than their ill report while you live.*

In the foreground three figures visible from the waist upwards emerge from separate apertures looking at North: A man (l) in profile to the r., wearing a ruff, and holding a cross-hilted dagger in each hand says *Oh I have fed upon this woe already and now excess of it will make me surfeit doth Shakespear know that we are tax'd* A man in back view (centre) with a feathered cap, holding a round shield and short broad-sword says *Hang him a taxing salt butter Rogue I will awe him with my Cudgell It shall hang like a Meteor ov'r his Head.* A man in armour (r) wearing a helmet, holds a cock in his r. hand, a small lantern in his l., says *List O List tax us not.* This is the man at whom North is pointing.

Behind (r) the figures of three witches are emerging from one circular hole; they wear steeple-crowned hats and point at North. One, holding a torch says, *Boreas, Boreas, BO!* Another says, *For this be sure thou shalt have crampt side stiches that shall pen thy breath up.* The third, holding up a broom, says *Thou shalt be pinch'd as thick as honey-combs each pinch more stinging than bees that made them.* A stage curtain in festoons is indicated across the upper part of the design on which the title is engraved

A satire on North's proposed tax on places of public entertainment, which varied from 3d where the price of admission did not exceed 1s. to 5s. on each admission over 10s.6d. *Parl. Hist.* xxii 1158–9, 11 Mar 1782 It did not become law. One of many satires on North's budget proposals. See No. 5964, &c.

$8\frac{7}{16} \times 10\frac{3}{4}$ in

5975 THE M—N—S—R [MINISTER] REDUCED, OR SIR OLIVER BLUBBER IN HIS PROPER STATION.

B. K. inv[t] & [sic]

Publish'd as the Act directs April 16th 1782 at N° 14 Dover Street

Engraving. Lord North caricatured as a very fat old woman, stands washing linen at a shallow tub which is supported on a stool He is in profile to the r., a cloth tied over his head, a large handkerchief over his shoulders. The bag of his wig hangs over the handkerchief, and his Garter ribbon is worn under it The background shows the corner of a room, in the wall on the r., in the upper r corner of the print, is a window, through which two grinning old women are looking in at the washer-woman. On the wall (l) is inscribed, *Linen Wash'd 50 PC[t] Cheaper than at any oth[er] Place in London by Mary North. Author of the Treatise upon washing without Soap, and many other Ingenious Performances*

Another allusion to North's tax on soap; see No 5964, &c.

By the same artist as Nos. 5958, 6045.

$6\frac{5}{8} \times 5\frac{1}{8}$ in.

5976 THROWING UP HIS MAJESTY'S FOXHOUNDS.

Publish'd as the Act directs April the 16. 1782 by J. Langham. N⁰ 11 S¹ Bride's Passage.¹ & sold by T. Cornhill. Bruten [sic] Street.

Engraving (coloured and uncoloured impressions). Lord Denbigh (r.) stands in profile to the l. on a country road, his aquiline nose exaggerated. A procession of six foxhounds, the last of which has just left his mouth, runs down his body and along the road from r to l A fox runs across a field on the r. and Denbigh holds out his r arm as if directing the hounds towards it The road is edged by trees, a sign-post behind Denbigh has two arms, one (l.) points *To Coventry*, the other (r) *To Lutterworth.* On the r. is a milestone, *XI miles to Coventry* The background is an undulating landscape of grass and trees with a rectangular country house in the distance.

Basil Feilding (1719–1800), Earl of Denbigh, was Master of the Royal Harriers and Foxhounds from 1762 until the change of ministry in March 1782. The post disappeared as a result of Burke's Bill of Economical Reform Wraxall, *Memoirs,* 1884, ii. 287. The house probably represents Newnham Paddox, his estate in Warwickshire. Walpole called him in 1773 'the lowest and most officious of the Court-tools'. *Last Journals,* 1910, i. 175. See Nos. 5763, 6162.

$8\frac{9}{16} \times 10\frac{3}{4}$ in.

5977 L   N   [LORD NORTH] ON THE STOOL OF REPENTANCE OR THE ILL EFFECTS OF MEDDLING WITH SALTS

Published According to Act of Parliment   [? J. K. Sherwin²]

[n.d. c. April 1782]

Engraving North, fat and ungainly, seated on a close-stool, his chin supported on his hands, his face is contorted and he clutches *The London Courant,* one of the most bitter of the anti-ministerial newspapers On the design is etched, *The Primier's only Motion made to fill the Treasury and enrich the Country or a Dose before the Tax Given by the Op[position] by way of Experiment* An allusion to North's tax on salt. He raised the duty on common salt by 25 per cent. and put a duty of £1 per cwt on medicinal salts, which, he said, 'although they pay no duty, bear an extraordinary high price'. *Parl. Hist.* xxii. 1155. For other satires on his budget see No 5964, &c.

$7\frac{5}{8} \times 6\frac{3}{4}$ in. (pl.).

5978 THE MINISTER IN.
   THE MINISTER OUT.

[Gillray]

Pub⁴ April 22ᵈ 1782 by W Humphrey N⁰ 227 Strand.

Engraving (coloured and uncoloured impressions). A design in two compartments.

[1] (l) Fox, indicated by his fox's head, and the brush which replaces the queue of his wig, is squatting down, his hands clasped, three obsequious

---

¹ The address omitted on one (uncoloured) impression
² According to a pencil note on one impression this is 'Said to be the only caricature etched by J K. S '

men surround him. One (r) offers him a chamber-pot decorated with the royal arms. One standing behind holds in both hands a smoking receptacle. The third (l.) kneels supporting Fox by one hand, while he licks his r. forefinger. Beneath is etched

> *When the Ministers In, how subservient his Friends,*
> *They'll wipe his Backside, to obtain their own Ends*
> *Hold the Pot of Convenience, their Fingers will lick,*
> *And at no dirty Work, you will e'er find them stick.*

$7\frac{3}{4} \times 6\frac{3}{8}$ in

[2] Lord North, standing, his arms outstretched in dismay is being insulted by the three sycophants of the companion design. One (r.) holds him by his Garter ribbon, while he pours the contents of the chamber-pot over his head. Another empties his receptacle on North's head, the third holds a piece of paper to his face. Beneath is etched.

> *Yet change but the Scene; shew him once out of Place,*
> *And the Stink Pots they'll empty direct in his Face,*
> *'Tis the Post, not the Person, they worship you find,*
> *And when out of Office, they're soon out of Mind.*

In both designs the floor is flagged and the background is a panelled wall. Reprinted *G.W.G.*, 1830.

$7\frac{3}{4} \times 6\frac{1}{8}$ in (pl. $9\frac{1}{2} \times 13\frac{7}{16}$ in)

5979 THE CAPTIVE PRINCE—OR—LIBERTY RUN MAD.

Pub^d 23^d [April?] 1782. by Eliz D'Achery St James's Street.

Engraving George III stands passively in profile to the r. while members of the new ministry fix shackles to his wrists and ankles. He is saying, *Oh! my misguided People.* Rockingham is walking off (r) holding the crown in his r hand, saying *Dispose of these Jewels for the Publick Use* He wears trunk hose and cross-hilted sword, a long robe trails on the ground behind him The Duke of Richmond, in profile to the l, is fixing a shackle to the king's l. wrist; he says, *I Command the Ordnance.* (On 30 Mar he was appointed Master General of the Ordnance.) In front of him a thin man kneeling on one knee, in profile to the l, is adjusting a fetter on the king's l ankle, he is probably Lord John Cavendish On the king's l. Fox kneels attaching a fetter to his r leg; he has the head of a fox and is saying, *I Command the Mob.* Behind him, holding the chain which the king holds in his r. hand, is Admiral Keppel in naval uniform, saying, *I Command the Fleet.* He had been made a Lord Commissioner of the Admiralty on 30 Mar, the Admiralty being put in commission. On his r. stands General Conway in military uniform, clasping his hands, and looking to his r, he says *Which way shall I turn? How can I decide?* He had been made Commander-in-Chief on 30 Mar.; in spite of his famous resolution of 22 Feb. (see No. 5963) he was not a whole-hearted supporter of the new ministry. On the extreme l stands Burke, looking to the r. but taking no part in the proceedings He holds a paper inscribed *Pay Master*, and is saying *The best of Ministers The best of K* ... A reference to Burke's eulogy, on 15 April, of the king's message recommending the 'effectual Plan of Œconomy', his words being, 'It was the best of messages to the best of people from the

best of kings'. *Parl. Hist.* xxii. 1269. See also Walpole, *Last Journals,*
1910, ii. 440–1; *Camb Mod Hist* vi. 460.

For allegations of republicanism against the new Ministry cf. Walpole
to Mann, 2 Apr. 1782, *Letters,* xii. 216: 'Every devil is at work to divide
us, and half Styx at work to calumniate our party and represent us as worse
levellers than John of Leyden and his Anabaptists.' See also Nos 5964,
6006, 6007 For Fox's conversation (real or alleged) see Selwyn to Carlisle,
19 Mar. 1782, 'He talked of the king under the description of Satan . . .'
and 23 Mar 1782, [Charles said] 'That this Revolution which he brought
about was the greatest for England that ever was; that excepting in the
mere person of a King, it was a complete change of the constitution . '
Hist. MSS. Comm , Carlisle MSS , pp. 599, 604, see also p. 623. See Nos.
5962, 5970, 5987, and cf. Nos. 5665, &c , 5843, &c

According to a note by Mr. Hawkins the print was re-engraved [?re-
issued] on 29 May. The month is here omitted from the publication line.
$8\frac{1}{2} \times 12\frac{3}{4}$ in

5980 A GAME AT PUT FOR THE CHIEF JUSTICE SHIP.

Pub^d Ap^l 25. 1782 by E Darchery St James Street

Engraving (coloured and uncoloured impressions). Two birds with human
heads in profile stand opposite each other on a circular table playing a game
of cards One is a magpie (l.), with a short wig surmounted by a baron's
coronet; his cards are held up in his l claw. This is Dunning who, with Fox,
Burke and others, had been admitted to the Privy Council on 27 Mar. and
was created Baron Ashburton on 8 Apr. An owl (r.) with a judge's wig,
his cards held in his r claw, represents Lord Mansfield [1] Both portraits
are good. On the table are two wine-glasses, a decanter labelled *claret,*
a punch-bowl, three pipes, a book, and a paper of tobacco

The new ministry were anxious to provide for Dunning, and would have
liked to get rid of Mansfield, but he retained the Chief Justiceship of the
King's Bench till his resignation in 1788. Dunning became Chancellor of
the Duchy of Lancaster on 17 Apr Cf. a paragraph in the *Morning Herald*
22 Mar. 1782, 'The King's Bench will probably hold its present principal
durante vita. But the privy council is no longer to be benefited thereby '
On 27 Mar that paper announced, 'The terms which Mr. Dunning has
made for himself are the reversionary grant of the Chancellorship or Chief
Justiceship of the King's Bench according to the first vacancy in either, by
resignation or death, till when he accepts the Attorney Generalship.'
$7\frac{1}{2} \times 11\frac{5}{8}$ in.

5981 AS IT IS OR THE WIND CHANGED

Pub^d April 1782 by H Humphrey Bond Street

Engraving. A companion print to No. 5963. Lord North fleeing from l
to r. before a number of pursuing foxes, his hands held up in alarm He
looks over his shoulder at the foxes with an expression of terror saying,
Take it, take it, I resign I'm out I'm out. This is addressed to the foremost
fox (evidently Charles Fox), who has seized the end of North's garter ribbon
in his mouth and is pulling it off. Labels in the mouths of the three foxes who
come next after their leader are inscribed. *Where's your Puffing Majority*

---

[1] This has been written on one impression in an old hand, and is clearly correct.
On another impression, however, Miss Banks has written 'Lord Camden'.

now; You might have kept your breath to have cool'd your porridge, Let the boisterous Gentleman go for I have piss't his fire out & he cannot Longer do any Mischief; this animal is urinating on a smoking torch which lies on the ground. North resigned on 20 Mar. See *Parl. Hist.* xxii. 1214 ff and No 5963, &c.

$6\frac{7}{8} \times 9\frac{1}{2}$ in.

5982 THE POLITICAL MIRROR OR AN EXHIBITION OF MINISTERS FOR APRIL 1782 [1]

Razo Rezio inv.[2]   *Crunk Fogo sculp*

Engraving. Members of the old Ministry (r.) falling into a pit, clutched by demons, while supporters of the new Ministry (l.) watch the spectacle. Britannia with her shield and spear sits in the foreground (l.) saying *They would have ruined me if they had staid in power* In the air (r.) Bute, in Highland dress, is about to fall from the back of a witch on whom he has been riding. She is riding on a broom and is heading downwards towards the pit in which North and others are being engulfed. To her leg is tied a bag inscribed *Ill gotten pelf.* Bute wears a large jack-boot, and his Garter ribbon, his riding whip falls from his hand. Above this couple is inscribed on a label *England's Evil Genius unhorsed or the downfall of Witchcraft* Truth (l.), a winged and naked woman in the clouds, directs the rays from a circular disk inscribed *The Mirror of Truth* on to the ex-Ministers.

The figures, l to r, are Thurlow the Lord Chancellor in profile to the r., standing behind Britannia holding a book. He is saying, *England shall never be wronged whilst a Thurlow lives,* showing how little the artist knew of the political situation, since George III had insisted on retaining him as Chancellor from the old Administration, cf. No. 5987. Next stands General Conway, in military dress, saying, *Your War with America I allways condemned.* Behind him stands a judge saying, *Your whole proceedings were contrary to Equity & Justice,* he is Lord Camden, President of the Council in the new Ministry. Next stands Col. Barré, in military dress, holding a document inscribed *Bill for the Examination of Accounts,* and saying *Your Army expenditures have been enormous & Shameful;* an allusion to Barré's speech on 26 Apr on 'Army Extraordinaries', see *Parl Hist* xxii 1344-5 Burke, in the attitude of an orator, r. hand extended, l. pointing upwards, is saying *You have denied God deceived your King plundered you* [blank]. The Duke of Richmond, wearing a star, says, *Their duplicity as Ministers is beyond parallel* Rockingham turns towards Richmond saying *Honest Yorkshire will be true to the last* (He was Lord Lieutenant of the West Riding) Next, and the most prominent of the new Ministry, is Charles Fox, holding a document inscribed *Petition for redress of Grievances,* and saying *Your Crimes stink stronger than all the Foxes in England.* Two small figures stand behind: one (?Wilkes) says, *Your tax on Women Servants fills our Streets with Whores;* the other says, *Your partiality in the house has ruined you,* the words suggest George Byng, M.P. for Middlesex, see Wraxall, *Memoirs,* 1884, ii 90 ff

The remaining figures are those of the old Ministry· on the brink of the

---

[1] Perhaps the frontispiece to the April number of a periodical, in which case the date of publication would be 1 May. It seems to have been folded to fit a book

[2] Two satires against Bute (by Lord Townshend) are similarly signed No 3829 (1761) is *Siegnor Rhezio Invt*, No. 3847 (1762) is *D Rhezzio Inv* Bute is compared with another Scottish favourite, Rizzio

abyss and hurrying towards it is Sandwich holding a violin in his l. hand; a label inscribed *Catches & Glees* hangs from his pocket, and he is saying *Damn the Navy give me a Who˙? and a Bottle* (cf No. 5961) Inside the pit appear the head and shoulders of a demon, he holds up a bottle in one hand, a glass in the other, saying to Sandwich *Wellcome my dear Lord to your old Friend.* Next Sandwich, about to fall over and covering his face with his hands, is Rigby, saying *This is a damn'd Rigg by the Bye* North is falling backwards into the pit, he holds a paper inscribed *Taxes on Soap, Salt and Small Beer* and is saying *I died of an Apoplexy and made no Will* Behind him stands Mansfield, in a furred gown, stooping and covering his face, saying, *This Truth is a most cruel Label on us all* (an allusion to Mansfield's unpopular directions to the jury in libel trials (1770) arising out of the publication of Junius's 'Letter to the King'). In front of Mansfield the head and shoulders of another man are visible. Lord George Germain, falling backwards, is being clutched round the body by a demon who says *Ah Cousin Germain I have got you fast.* These unfortunates are in the full rays of 'The Mirror of Truth'. Black clouds (r.) are a background for Bute and the witch, the sun (l.) appearing from clouds directs its rays on the new Ministry. For North's unpopular budget proposals see No 5964, &c Cf Nos 5970, 5984

$5\frac{13}{16} \times 9$ in.

5983 THE GAME OF HAZARD

[? After Charles Loraine Smith]

Published as the Act Directs May 1ˢᵗ 1782 by Mʳ Rack London.

Aquatint Fox and North sitting at a small round table throwing dice, surrounded by spectators who watch the contest with intense interest Fox (l.) in profile to the r holds the dice-box, and has just thrown, his much-tilted chair rests on one leg, his r. hand is in his breeches pocket. He is plainly dressed North (r) in profile to the l watches with an expression of concern, he holds the front of his hair or wig with his r. hand, his l rests on the table Three divines in gowns and bands stand over Fox, one puts his arm across Fox's shoulder and leans over the table with an expression of satisfaction Another (l.) rests his hand on the shoulder of the former The third looks up stretching out both arms as if in thankfulness Behind North a parson walks away, looking over his l shoulder and holding up the back of his gown Two men wearing ribbons look on, one clasping his hands with an expression of distress All are probably portraits, caricatured except Fox, who has the appearance of having been observed from life Beneath the design is inscribed, *Here goes at the Treasury and all in the Ring, Seven's the Main & Seven's a Nick*

This satire was out of date at the time of publication since North resigned on 20 March, see No. 5963. For the episcopal preferments dependent on the change of ministry see Wraxall, *Memoirs*, 1884, iii 31 f, where it is assumed that the appointments of the Rockingham Ministry would be made by Fox, who was believed to have designed the Archbishopric of Canterbury for Shipley of St Asaph or Hinchcliffe of Peterborough. The manner resembles that of No 6125.

Attributed to Bartolozzi by Calabi, No. 2237, who describes another state without aquatint.

$10\frac{3}{8} \times 13\frac{1}{4}$ in.

5984 WAR OF POSTS

T. Colley Fec[t]

Pub[d] by W. Richardson N° 68 High Holborn London May 1, 1782.

Engraving (coloured impression). The new Ministry (l.), seated on 'posts' or small columns inscribed with their offices which they ride like hobby-horses, holding reins, attack the old Ministry (r.), who are being driven by the help of a devil into the jaws of Hell. Behind in the centre is the temple of the *Constitution*, a dome supported on five pillars and built on a rock. Its base is inscribed *Founded on a Rock*, and its three nearer pillars are inscribed *Habeas Corpus* (c.), *Representation* (r.), and *Free Press* (l.).

The identity of the combatants is shown by numbers which refer to names in the lower margin. (1) (*Pi—t*) stands (l.) holding a sheaf of thunderbolts, a black cloud is above his head, from which dart zigzags of lightning inscribed *Vox Populi Vox Dei*, and extending across the design to the ex-Ministers; he is saying, *The Lightining [sic] of my father.* (2) (*Kepp—l*), astride on a post inscribed *L[d] of the Adm*[iralty], in naval uniform with a drawn cutlass is saying *Encrease your navy.* (3) (*Conw—y*), in general's uniform with a drawn sword, on a post inscribed *of all the [land] Forces* is saying *The Cloven tongued crew.* (4) (*Burk—*), riding a post inscribed *Pay Master*, holds a paper inscribed *Œconomy* and says, *Pay the Taxes by Œconomy.* (5) (*Fox*), in the form of a fox, astride a post inscribed *Secretery [sic] of State*, says, *An infamous administration.* (6) (*Richm—n*), astride on a cannon or gun-carriage, inscribed [*Mas*]*ter of the Ordnance*, points, saying, *They have Sapped the Constitution.*

The *Treasury Bench*, a four-legged stool, lies upside down between the two parties. The Devil (7) (*Nick*) prods (8) (*Sand—ch*) with a fork, saying *Bid them go to Hell to Hell they go*,[1] Sandwich says *All hope is Over.* He stands by a broken anchor on which (9) (*Amher—t*) stands, saying, *I'd promote the Devil for money.* (10) (*No—th*) stands on papers inscribed *Taxes, Soap, Beer*, he says *beat in the War of Posts*; his arms are stretched out and his back is to the spectator. Behind him stands (11) (*Mansf—ld*), who says, *we have passed the Rubicon*; he is standing in the flames inscribed (12) (*Hel—*), which issue from the jaws of Hell, the open mouth of a monster, partly cut off by the r. margin of the print.

Behind (r.) three minute figures dangle from a triangular gallows inscribed respectively *An English Sec* . . . *An Irish Sec.* . . . *a Scotch Sec.* . . . The three Secretaries of State in the outgoing Ministry were Lord Stormont, a Scot and a nephew of Lord Mansfield, Lord Hillsborough, an Irish peer, and Lord George Germain (Colonies). As a pendant to this a stout man (l.) stripped to the waist stands in a pillory, while another man scourges him. This is inscribed *Thirteen Stripes* and probably represents John Bull beaten by America, see No. 6202.

The second appearance of Pitt in this Catalogue, an interesting indication of the part he already took in popular estimation, though he was not in the Ministry. Cf. Mason's *Ode to the Honourable William Pitt*, dated 11 May, 1782 (B.M.L. 840, l. 4/13). For North's unpopular taxes, see No. 5964, &c.

$8\frac{1}{4} \times 12\frac{1}{2}$ in.

---

[1] A quotation from Johnson's translation (*London*) of Juvenal's third satire, cf. 5133.

5985 THE LATE BOMBARDMENT OF GOVERNMENT CASTLE.

C. Goodnight Sculp.

Pub^d May 1st 1782 by J. Barrow. Sold by E. Rich at the little Print Shop faceing Anderton's Coffee House Fleet Street. And at Mr Turners Frame maker and Print Seller, N° 40. Snow hill.

Engraving. A companion print to No 5986 by the same artist. The late ministers and the new Ministry spitting cannon-balls at each other, the former from a partly ruined castle flying a flag with a St. George's Cross. The heads are poorly characterized and few can be identified with certainty. 'Government Castle' (r.) stands on the edge of a ravine into which part of it has disappeared, its door being cut vertically in half, only the r. half remaining Three heads look from the top of the tower, five emerge from lower apertures Immediately over the door the head of the king appears, he has not ejected a cannon-ball but is saying, *My Lords and Gentlemen remember Kingdoms fall by discord.* A man (r.) wearing the large wig of the Speaker (Cornwall) says *To order, to order* From the mouths of the others come blasts, each connected by a dotted line with a cannon-ball to which is attached a label or streamer on which the words of the speakers are inscribed. These say: *You plague us more than Congress* (?North); *You are enemies to both Church and Castle* (this is probably from Markham, Archbishop of York, he wears a clerical wig and bands); *You expose all our plans to the enemy; You want our heads to get into our places; Our plans were good tho' unsuccessful* (Germain); *Destruction to Patriots.*

The late Opposition stand below and on the r spitting out similar balls, some of which are about to descend on the heads of the defenders of the castle. A crowd of spectators stand behind them on the extreme r. in two groups three members of the group in the foreground say, *Success Boys to the Bombardment; Give them no Cessation* and *The Fox Bomb for ever.* The other group is better dressed and is inscribed *Expecting promotion,* the foremost of these is saying, *They will certainly soon surrender.*

The words attached to the balls bombarding the castle are *How much Specie have you got left?* (The speaker is probably Fox.) A man dressed as a military officer (Conway) is saying *Treat speedily with America* (a reference to Conway's famous resolutions of 22 Feb. for treating with America, and of 27 Feb declaring its subjugation impossible, see No 5963. *You have brought us to a State of Bankruptcy* (the speaker resembles Dunning). *No Landman ought to preside at the Admiralty* (the speaker appears to be Keppel) Burke (wearing spectacles) says *the war hath cost 100000000£; You have lost us America; You err both in law and policy.* A man turns aside, holding a handkerchief to his face, saying *This is hot work for both parties.*

This was out of date when published as North announced his resignation on 20 Mar and the new Ministry was formed by 30 Mar. See No. 5963. $9\frac{3}{4} \times 13\frac{7}{8}$ in.

5986 THE SURRENDER OF GOVERNMENT CASTLE, IN MARCH 1782, TO THE LATE BESIEGING MINORITY

Pub^d according to Act of Parliament by J Barrow, May y^e 10th 1782. Sold by E. Rich, at the little Print Shop opposite Anderton's Coffee House Fleet Street

Engraving. A companion print to No. 5985 by the same artist Government

Castle (r.) is in good repair, cannons instead of heads project from the embrasures The king in profile to the l leans over the battlements, his arms held out, saying to his defeated ministers,

> To lose you Sirs, concerns me more
> Than all I lost by you before

A foot-guard stands as sentry at the gate.

In the upper part of the design a procession of defeated ministers and their adherents (the garrison) walk r. to l. from the castle, headed by a tall thin man in general's uniform (Lord Amherst), he says, *We ought to have had the honours of war for we have stood a long Siege.* After him walks North, one hand on his breast, saying, *I leave the Castle as clean as Soap can wash,* one of many allusions to his unpopular tax on soap, see No 5964, &c. The next two say *There are stores in the Castle but the Specie is almost spent,* and *We have held out like veterans.* A stout man in clerical wig and bands, probably Markham, Archbishop of York, says *These hot Patriots deserve cooling in a Spanish Inquisition* (Cf No. 5958.) A man in a tie-wig says, *My Lord they are guilty of an Assault, or I do not understand Law* (he is probably Mansfield). The next three say: *It is better to surrender than hold out and lose our heads; Our fate is not the hardest, we have got something, and lost neither head nor limb; G Conway's attack carried all before it* Next comes Sandwich, saying, *Well I shall be no more plagu'd with combin'd fleets* The last two say *We were overpower'd by numbers,* and *Let us be resign'd to the fortune of war.*

After these leaders, and in front of a group of followers, walks the Devil, with horns, hoofs and forked tail, saying, *I am sorry we have lost Brimstone Hill.* (Brimstone Hill, a fortification on St Kitts, surrendered to de Bouillé on 12 Feb 1782) The followers, who represent the subordinate placemen, are immediately to the l of the castle, they say, *We shall have no more golden Eggs for Fox has got the goose*

The castle and the departing garrison fill the upper part of the print. Below is a procession of the new Ministry and their camp-followers marching from l. to r. to occupy the castle Facing them and immediately beneath the castle is a mob (r.) of men and boys shouting acclamations to the new garrison One shouts *General Conway for ever* A man with an apron bawls, *Fox for ever,* another shouts *Keppel for ever.* The new Ministry is headed by a man in military uniform holding up a drawn sword, saying *For our Country let us be vigilant.* As in No 5985 the figures are poorly characterized, appearance and words often appear out of character. The succeeding figures say· *Let us be vigilant and faithful, There must be much better œconomy;* Keppel in naval uniform says, *We must watch the Combin'd Fleet like a Hawke.*[1] The next say, *We shall silence the Dutch, Early Intelligence must be attain'd; I hope we shall reconcile America; We must shew the Monsieurs old English play; Placemen and salaries must be reduc'd.* The last, who is in riding dress, says *No contractor must sit in Parliament.* The Contractors' Bill was in committee before the fall of North, it was

---

[1] Hawke died in 1781 and his name had scarcely come before the public since his retirement from the Admiralty in 1771, except that he had signed in Dec 1778 the protest of the admirals against the court-martial on Keppel The remark, however, is singularly apt, as his views had been expressed in a memorandum 'Our enemies being peculiarly attentive to their marine, our fleet could only be termed considerable in the proportion it was to that of the House of Bourbon ' W. M James, *The British Navy in Adversity,* 1926, p 15

debated in the Commons 8 April, and became law 27 May. The placemen and followers say, *We shall do pretty well with half their Salary.*

Beneath the title is engraved N.B. *The old Garrison and Placemen are marching out, the new Garrison and new Placemen are marching in. Success to Old England.*

In the upper l. corner of the print is engraved, *Articles to be observed by the Garrison*

1 All the Privates to remain in the Garrison.

2. All the principal Officers to march out, not allowed the honours of war.

3 They shall lay down their Titles and Symbols of honour where they received them

4 They shall not enter any of his Majesty's Fortifications eccept it be the Tower.

5. They shall be accountable for the Specie expended in Government Castle.

6 Their parole shall be from Government Castle to Tower hill, and from Tower hill to Temple bar and no farther, till they shew satisfactory accounts.

Threats of impeachment were hanging over the heads of the ex-Ministers; for North's fears see R. Lucas, *Lord North*, 1913, ii. 209 ff Cf. Nos. 5660, 5661, 5969, 6046

$9\frac{3}{4} \times 12\frac{7}{8}$ in

5987 BRITANIA'S ASSASSINATION.
OR — THE REPUBLICANS AMUSEMENT

[Gillray.]

Pub[d] May 10th 1782 by E. D'Archery S[t] James Street

Engraving. The new Ministry attempting to pull from its base a headless stone statue of Britannia, who is seated on a globe, holding a broken spear; her r leg from the knee and her l arm have been broken off. A fox (Charles Fox) with its fore-paws on the square base bites her leg Two judges in their robes, Thurlow and Mansfield, on the extreme r. pull at ropes to keep her in position. Within the ropes stand a group of patriots threatening Britannia· Wilkes in the forefront, a book *No[rth] B[riton]* under his l. arm, his r hand, holding a rolled document inscribed *Libel*, is raised to strike Behind him Dunning holds over his head in both hands a book inscribed *Sydney on Government* Next is the Duke of Richmond, holding above his head in both hands a musket by its barrel, with which he is about to smite the statue. He is saying *Leave not a Wreck behind.* Behind him stands Burke (?) raising in his l hand a rolled document inscribed *Reformation Bill* The last is Keppel, who, turning his back on Britannia, holds a flagstaff from which he is hauling down the flag, saying

He that Fights & runs away,
May live to fight another day

This is an allusion to the battle of Ushant, 27 July 1778, see No 5992, &c.

Britannia's foreign enemies are running off with the spoil. On the extreme l. America, as a Red Indian in a feathered head-dress and girdle, runs holding Britannia's head in his l. hand while her arm, in which is an olive branch, is held over his r. shoulder. Next comes France running in pursuit with arms extended, saying *You dam Dog, you run way wit all de Branche,* prophetically implying America would forestall France by separate peace negotiations, cf No. 6051. Spain follows, carrying Britannia's leg over his l shoulder. Holland, a short cheerful-looking burgher, runs towards the spectator carrying Britannia's shield on his head and shoulders.

Britannia, assassinated by republicans at home and despoiled by enemies abroad, is defended by Mansfield and Thurlow. Cf. a letter of 8 Mar. in which North anticipates that Thurlow 'will oppose a firm barrier against any dangerous popular measures', *Corr. of George III*, v. 380.

This print was described in the *Morning Chronicle* of 15 May as 'a very extraordinary caricature. . . . Since the Newcastle administration there has not been seen a bolder satire in caricature stile against ministers than the above described. This is the second production in the print way that has ventured to arraign the conduct of the present gentlemen in office' The first was probably *The Captive Prince*, No. 5979 Cf also Nos. 5962, 5970. For other allegations of republicanism see Nos. 6006, 6007, in Nos. 6217, 6239 Fox is compared to Cromwell. Cf also Nos 5334, 5836.

Grego, *Gillray*, p 35.

$8\frac{1}{2} \times 13\frac{1}{2}$ in.

5988 ANTICIPATION, OR, THE CONTRAST TO THE ROYAL HUNT.

Publishd May. 16ᵗʰ 1782. by Wᵐ Wells Nᵒ 132 (opposite Salisbury Court) Fleet Street. London.

Britons facᵗ   [? *After Viscount Townshend.*]

Engraving. A sequel to No. 5961, probably by the same artist. The new Ministry in process of restoring the temple of Fame In the foreground on the extreme r Britannia sits on a globe, her shield and spear beside her, holding out an olive branch. Some of the figures are identified by numbers referring to names in the lower margin. *1*, C—n—y (Conway), standing (r) in front of the Temple of Fame, is holding erect the broken pillar inscribed *America*, a reference to his famous resolutions, see Nos 5963, 5985, 5986 A military officer and two sailors are lifting up fallen pillars inscribed *Charles Town* and *St. Vinc[en]ts* The only pillars remaining on the ground are *Eustatius* lying across *Rhode Island*. The Temple has still only two columns intact, *Gibraltar* and *Jamaica Barbadoes*, but these are stouter. One of the broken columns, *Tobago*, is in process of repair by two sailors, one of whom, standing on a ladder, is about to fit in a missing section The rope which was tied round Gibraltar trails on the ground and the figures which were pulling it in the earlier print are otherwise engaged: America holding a short or broken spear in the l. hand holds out in the r. an olive branch, while a naval officer standing next him with a cutlass in his r hand, holds out an olive branch towards America. Holland, a pipe stuck in his hat, kneels before the officer, his hands raised in supplication. Spain and France are in flight towards the l , their hands outstretched.

The upper part of the Temple has undergone a change The figure of Fame has regained her trumpet and her lost leg and is now intact. Three minute figures stand within the r. window *2*, Fox (F—x), with a fox's head, is saying *Manus haec inimica tyrannis*. *4*, Camden (C—md—n), in Judge's robes, says *Peace with America War with all the World*. Burke, standing behind the other two, says *Nummi¹ post virtutem*. From the l window, *9*, C—rlt—n (Sir Guy Carleton) is firing a musket to the l , and bringing down the Gallic cock, which is about to fall on the head of the fleeing

¹ The second 'm' has been added in ink.

figure of France (Carleton had been appointed Commander-in-Chief to succeed Clinton on 23 Feb., after the old Ministry had shown that their intention was merely to keep the posts they held in America and direct their efforts against France and Spain.) The centre of the temple façade is now decorated with the head of George III crowned with laurel in an oval and with four smaller ovals, in which are heads, all with laurel wreaths, inscribed *Howe, Ross, Parker, Barrington*, showing that much was hoped from the recent naval appointments of the new Ministry: Howe (2 April 1782), Commander-in-Chief in the Channel, Sir John Lockhart Ross, Bart., was with Howe as Rear-Admiral. Vice-Admiral Parker was appointed Commander-in-Chief in the East-Indies. Vice-Admiral Barrington was Howe's Second-in-Command.

In the background a naval engagement is in progress, ships flying the British flag are firing at the enemy, some of whose ships are sinking. This cannot represent the Battle of the Saints (12 April), news of which reached London only on 18 May, but an old hand has written over two of the ships 'Formidable S^r. George Rodney', and 'Ville de Paris', the French flagship which surrendered to Rodney.

In the centre foreground 5, *S—h* (Sandwich), in profile to the r., his cane under his r. arm, stands holding a sheaf of broadside ballads in his r. hand labelled *Catches and Glees*. On this is a print of a man hanging from a gallows. In his l. hand he holds a ballad from which he is singing, *A Sow'r Reformation crawls outthorough the Nation An Old Song new set*. From his pocket hangs a paper inscribed *24 Songs in a Book for a Halpenny*. He has been reduced to the position of a ballad-singer.

In the foreground on the l., in profile to the l., Lord North as a stout woman, his bag-wig showing under a cap, stands at a wash-tub. From his mouth comes a label inscribed *My *Northstrums had almost totally blinded him* [the king] *& ruin'd his constitution. The wash tub was a lucky Thought Welcome my Dernier resource Few even of my Friends will know me in the Suds *Erratum lege nostrums* (cf No 5968). Behind North are two packing-cases, one marked with a circle and anchor and inscribed *Untaxed Soap 2200 lb.*; a small case behind it is marked *119 lb.* For other satires on North's tax on soap see No. 5964, &c

In front of North, in the l. corner of the print, is a bundle inscribed *M—nd—n's* [Minden's, i.e. Lord Sackville's] *foul linnen* Next it is a bundle inside a basket inscribed *For Sr J. Delaval* On 8 Mar. 1782, during the debate on Lord John Cavendish's resolutions of censure on the Ministry, Sir John Delaval (M.P. for Berwick) 'rose as a country gentleman just to say that he had a high opinion of his Majesty's Ministers.' (*Parl. Hist* xxii 1134.)

Behind North and to the l. George III is seated in an arm-chair while an oculist applies an instrument to his eye. The oculist wears a ribbon and is Lord Rockingham; a label attached to his hand is inscribed:

—to nobler sights
——the film removd
which that false Gold that promisd
clearer sight had bred.

The king and Rockingham are in front of a small building from which curtains have been pulled back showing part of a window On the extreme l. part of another building is visible, with the royal arms over the door. Above the arms is inscribed *D^r R——M.* (Rockingham) *occulist to his* [Majesty].

In the middle distance are two small figures *6. H—d* (Hertford) with clasped hands saying *My L—d I have lost the key of the House of Office*, an allusion to the story that Lord Hertford was loath to surrender the gold key of his office as Lord Chamberlain (cf No. 5966) to the Duke of Manchester, who succeeded him *7, G—m—n* (Germain) runs with out-stretched arms towards Hertford, saying *Where, Where shall I fly*, an allusion to his supposed cowardice at Minden

In the background (l.) is a building, open in front to show an auction of horses and hounds. This is *TATERSHALLS* and on the roof is inscribed *All the Hunters & Hounds of a certain great personage now selling off by Auction* Although on a minute scale, four horses, dogs, the auctioneer in his box, and the spectators are visible. This shows that the king's 'Royal Hunt' depicted in the companion print is now over, with the curious implication that he no longer neglects matters of State for the chase Jamaica, &c were saved not by the new Ministry or the naval officers here mentioned, but by the victory of Rodney, whom they had determined to disgrace, see No 5991, &c.

Above the design is engraved 'The Prospect of the glorious restoration of the Temple of Fame'.

$8\frac{1}{2} \times 13\frac{1}{2}$ in.

5989 THE RECONCILIATION BETWEEN BRITANIA AND HER
DAUGHTER AMERICA.

[T. Colley.]   [*c* May 1782]

Pub^d by W. Humphrey. N° 227 Strand.[1]

Engraving Britannia and America embrace, while France and Spain try to pull America away, Holland (l.) watches their efforts and Fox (r.) points out the struggle to Keppel. Britannia, in profile to the l, with her shield beside her decorated with a St. George's Cross inscribed *George for Ever*, rushes into the arms of America, in profile to the r., a Red Indian wearing feathered head-dress and girdle, sandals and flowing hair confined by a ribbon. Britannia has her spear, America her flag, its staff surmounted by a Phrygian cap inscribed *Liberty* Britannia says, *Be a good Girl and give me a Buss* American answers, *Dear Mama say no more about it*. France holds both ends of a scarf passed round America's waist and tugs hard at it, Spain behind him pulls at a strap or ribbon which is passed over France's shoulder, over this tie between them is inscribed *Combin'd*. France, as a *petit-maître* with feathered hat and large bag-wig, is saying *Begar they will be friends again if you dont pull a little harder Cus . . .* Spain, pulling hard and looking over his r shoulder at France, says, *Monsieur Toad stool me do all I can to keep them asunder pull her hair, but take care she Dont kick you*. On the extreme l. Holland, a fat Dutchman smoking a pipe, leans against a barrel of *Dutch Herrings* By his side is a square bottle of *hollands Gin*. He is saying, *I'll Delliberate a little to see which is weakest, then I'll give you a direct answer Kate Rusia*

Russia had offered to mediate in 1781. Fox's first step on taking office was an unsuccessful attempt to negotiate separately with Holland through the medium of Russia *Corr of C J Fox*, 1 331; Wraxall, *Memoirs*, 1884,

---

[1] Another publication line has been etched within the design and almost obliterated by cross-hatching *Pub by T Colley N° 5 Acorn Court Rolls Buildings Fetter Lane Old England*

ii. 277–9; *Camb. Hist. of the British Empire*, i. 773; see No 6014 It is clear, however, that the simple-minded artist knows little of the realities of politics and diplomacy

Fox stands pointing to the l Under his feet are cards, dice, and a dice-box inscribed *Forgot* (While in office Fox suspended his systematic gaming at Brooks's, see No. 5972.) A fox's head appears from behind him, perhaps from his coat-pocket, saying *Sharp as a Sword.* A fox's brush hangs down below his coat. He is saying, *Da—n that Frenchman & his Cousin Don, how they strain to part them, make haste my boy Keppel & give them a Spank.* Keppel, in profile to the r, partly cut off by the margin of the print, is saying *That I will my Prince of bold Action they shall have fore and aft.*

Beneath the title is engraved

1

A curse upon all Artifice
May Briton never thrive

2

While Roguish Minis—rs they keep
to Eat them up alive

3

By Lots they sell oh Dam—em Well
Each place we put our trust in

4

Cut them of [sic] short twill make good sport
Whilst honest men are thrust in

The date of this print is probably after the formation of the new Ministry on 30 Mar, and before 18 May when news arrived of Rodney's victory, a favourite subject with this artist. Reproduced, Drepperd, *Early American Prints*, p. 203.

$8\frac{1}{16} \times 12\frac{7}{8}$ in

5990 EVACUATION BEFORE RESIGNATION.

[Gillray.]

Pub^d May 21st 1782 by H. Humphrey New Bond Street

Engraving Design in an oval Rockingham, in profile to the r., sitting over a circular close-stool inscribed *Publick Reservoir.* A document projecting from his pocket inscribed *Marquiss of R* . leaves no doubt of his identity Members of the new Ministry stand round him. He is vomiting into a hat held out to him by Burke (r), who kneels before him Rockingham is saying *All for the Public Good*; Burke says *We must save every thing*, an allusion to his 'Economical Reform' Behind stands a man holding in both hands a hat with steaming and unsavoury contents, saying *This is really for the landed Interest* Over his head is inscribed *P . S* He is Thomas Powys, M.P. for Northamptonshire, cr. Baron Lilford 1794, who was himself the mouthpiece of the country gentlemen or independent county members and who had played an important part in the defeat of North, see Wraxall, *Memoirs*, 1884, ii. 154–5, 200, 217–19 Fox stands on his r, and on Fox's r. is Lord John Cavendish holding up both hands, saying, *Oh how he strains every Nerve for the Publick Good He does my business, 'tis I who should cast up the Accounts.* Cavendish was Chancellor of the Exchequer.

Burke and Cavendish, neither of whom is recognizably drawn, are indicated by hands drawn like those on the end of the signpost in No 5964, inscribed *Bu—ke* and *Ld J. C—n—sh*. Apparently a satire on Burke's Bill of Economical Reform. Reprinted, *G.W G*, 1830.

7×9$\frac{11}{16}$ in.

5991 COUNT DE GRASSE DELIVERING HIS SWORD TO THE GALLANT ADMIRAL RODNEY.

[T. Colley.]

Pub. by P Mitchell May 27th 1782 as the Act directs North Audley S^t

Engraving. An imaginary picture of the quarter-deck of Rodney's ship the *Formidable* after the Battle of the Saints (12 Apr) De Grasse, the French admiral, a tall figure, on a larger scale than the English sailors, is exchanging compliments with Rodney. He stands, bowing, in profile to the r ; in his l. hand he holds out his sword, in his r he holds a cross which is suspended round his neck. He wears the bag-wig and top-boots characteristic of French officers in English caricature. He is saying *You have fought me handsomely*. Rodney, a much smaller figure in profile to the l., holds out both hands saying, *I was glad of the Opportunity* Two sailors stand in the rigging of the after-mast (l.), waving their hats and shouting *Huzza*, one wears a petticoat, the other striped trousers On the lower deck, part of which is visible on the l, a sailor holds up a bottle in his r. hand, a full wine-glass in his l., he is looking up and shouting. He stands by a midshipman who waves his hat, shouting *Huzza Rodney* An ensign flag riddled with holes hangs at the stern and is an important part of the design. Cannon-balls lie on the deck, and there are holes made by the cannon of the enemy in the sides of the ship. The poop is carved and decorated. The details of the rigging, port-holes, &c appear to be drawn with accuracy.

News of this important victory (which was the subject of great controversy) reached London on 18 May. The *Ville de Paris*, de Grasse's flagship, actually surrendered to the *Barfleur*, commanded by Sir Samuel Hood Lord Cranston went on board the *Ville de Paris* and received the sword of de Grasse, who was removed from the *Barfleur* to the *Formidable* after two days. The *Ville de Paris* was the great ship presented by Paris to Louis XV, 'the finest national trophy ever won at sea' (Rodney to Lord Dalrymple). Rodney wrote to his wife, 'I hope the good people of England will now be pleased, and Opposition hide her head.' Mundy, *Life of Rodney*, ii, 243, 263, &c Stanhope, *Hist of England*, vii, p 176. For the political aspect of the victory see No. 5992, &c. See also Nos. 5993, 5994, 6000, 6008, also by Colley, and No 6031. Cf. No 5988.

There is a plate of de Grasse delivering his sword to Rodney on the *Ville de Paris* in E. Barnard's *History of England* [n d. c 1791].

10$\frac{7}{8}$×16$\frac{1}{8}$ in.

5992 RODNEY TRIUMPHANT—OR—ADMIRAL LEE SHORE IN THE DUMPS.

Political Characters & Caracatures of 1782. N° 3 [Gillray]

Pub^d. May 31st 1 1782 by E'D'Achery St James Street London.

Engraving. A representation of Rodney's victory causing dismay to the

¹ Mrs D'Achery advertised on 30 May that the plate was worn out and would be

new Ministry. Rodney, standing on the sea-shore, receives the submission of de Grasse, who bows before him in profile to the l, holding down the French flag so that Rodney stands on it, while in his r. hand he holds out the hilt of his sword to Rodney De Grasse is excessively lean and elegant, frogs are jumping from his coat-pocket. Behind him stand ranks of emaciated French sailors with expressions of distress, their hands tied behind them; they wear bag-wigs, ruffled shirts, long trousers, with bare ankles and wooden shoes A baron's coronet is suspended above Rodney's head, inscribed *from Jove*, implying that the honour did not come from the Ministry. Behind him is a procession of cheering sailors, waving their hands and shouting *Huzza*. Two of them carry chests, one inscribed *Lewis d'or's*, the other *D° N° 26*, which they have just brought on shore Behind them are ships in full sail, the nearer ones with the British flag flying above the French flag, showing that they are prizes. A ship's boat rows towards the shore with the Ensign flying above the *fleur-de-lys*, in it a minute figure stands waving his hat.

In front of a dilapidated building (l) stand the politicians Fox, Keppel and the Duke of Richmond are in consultation in the foreground watching Rodney's triumph with expressions of displeasure Fox, with a fox's head in profile to the r., says *Dam the French for coming in his way say I*. Keppel (Admiral Lee Shore) stands with his hands folded, thumbs touching, saying, *This is more than we expected more than we wished* Richmond (Master-General of the Ordnance) says, *Tis the last Fleet he shall have the opportunity of beating however*. Behind them North and Sandwich walk together, North in profile to the l, his r hand holding Sandwich by the arm, points to Keppel saying, *Ha! Ha! Ha! behold Augustus ye 27th*, an allusion to Keppel's action off Ushant on 27 Apr. 1778 for which he was court-martialled Sandwich says, *Ha! Ha! Ha!—new measures—send a Pig to supercede a Lyon*. On the wall of the building behind them and above the heads of Richmond and Keppel is a representation of a ship, bottom upwards in a hatchment, with the motto *27th July, Gloria* Below the ship is an axe inscribed *Rusty*, implying that Keppel deserved execution for his conduct. Plaster is coming off the wall, showing bricks.

When the new Ministry came into office, Vice-Admiral Hugh Pigot was made a Lord of the Admiralty, soon afterwards promoted admiral, appointed Commander-in-Chief in the W Indies to supersede Rodney, whom the Ministry had determined to disgrace He actually sailed on 18 May, the day that news of Rodney's victory reached London An attempt to stop him as a concession to public opinion was too late and he took over the command at Jamaica on 13 July This was a political appointment of a quite inadequate officer. 'Public dissatisfaction' was 'loudly and generally expressed in every part of London'. Wraxall, *Memoirs*, 1884, iii. 127 [1]

The chests of Lewis d'ors represent the thirty-six money chests captured in the *Ville de Paris*, the French flag-ship. Stanhope, *Hist. of England*, 1858, vii. 177.

One of four satires by Gillray on Rodney's victory as a blow to the Ministry, see Nos. 5996, 5997, 6001. A special importance attaches to them republished next day with some alterations (Note by Mr. Hawkins) These probably include the coronet, Rodney having been created a baron on 28 May Cf. *Corr of George III*, vi. 36.

[1] Keppel told the king on 18 May 'He thought it absolutely necessary that some ostensible reward should be bestowed on Sir George Rodney, the more so as he did not wish this event should stop Admiral Pigot's being sent to relieve him . ' George III to Shelburne, *Corr. of George III*, vi, p. 33.

since it was actually argued in Parliament that 'popularity which, running against him [Rodney], had occasioned his recall, should, now that it flows in his favour, prevent it'. (Lord Nugent) 30 May, *Parl. Hist* xxiii. 79–80. The recall of Rodney, the grudging reward to him contrasted with Keppel's Viscountcy (24 Apr. 1782) and the commission to Pigot, were a blow to the popularity of the Ministry For Keppel as Admiral Lee Shore, see Nos 5570, 5626, 5650, 5658 For Rodney at St. Eustatius, the cause of his (alleged) unpopularity, see No 5842 Rodney, however, was a popular hero for his defeat and capture of the Spanish Admiral Langara, 16 Jan. 1780, followed by the relief of Gibraltar, see Nos 5646–8, 5710. Prints of this action had been published on 15 Apr. 1782 (after Luny) and on 6 May 1782 (after Paton) For the battle of the Saints see No. 5991, &c For the nature of the 'public exultation' in London at the victory see Wraxall, *Memoirs*, 1884, ii. 319 ff. Grego, *Gillray*, p. 36.

$9\frac{1}{16} \times 13\frac{3}{16}$ in.

5993 THE VILLE DE PARIS, SAILING FOR JAMAICA, OR RODNEY TRIUMPHANT

[T. Colley]

Pub. by T Colley, Acorn Court June 1. 1782.

Engraving (coloured impression) Rodney standing on the back of de Grasse, who is crawling on his hands and knees on the water, symbolizing his own flag-ship the *Ville de Paris*, and drawing after him at the end of a rope a small open boat. Rodney, in profile to the r., holds in his l. hand the end of the French admiral's long pigtail queue, in his r. hand is a drawn cutlass. Along the admiral's body is engraved *Count de Grasse*. A cross suspended from his neck touches the water From his head projects a torn French flag, on which is engraved *Discolour'd*, it hangs from a broken staff. Behind, flies erect, a British flag, inscribed *Displayed*. In front of de Grasse's grotesquely large nose is inscribed *o Bourbon*. In the distance (r) is a castle on a promontory, flying the British flag and inscribed *Jamaica*. In the bows of the open boat which is being towed by de Grasse a sailor stands, shouting *Down with the French; Georgey*, he waves his hat, while in his r. hand he holds a club Three French sailors in the boat kneel to him in supplication, saying *o Begar*.

A crude rendering of Rodney's victory on 12 Apr. in the battle of the Saints, when the French admiral surrendered, see No. 5991, &c, as a result of which the threat to the W. India islands (Antigua, Barbados, and Jamaica) was removed De Grasse was taken to Jamaica and afterwards brought to England, see No. 5997.

$4\frac{1}{4} \times 6\frac{1}{4}$ in.

5994 COUNT DE GRASSE TAKING A PEEP IN THE WEST INDIES

[c. May 1782]

[T. Colley]

Sold by W Humphrey, N° 227 Strand.

Engraving. A caricature of the French admiral in profile to the r., tall and thin, with an enormous nose, drawn much as in No 5991 He holds a telescope to his l. eye, while his drawn sword is held vertically, point upwards, the blade resting on his shoulder. The deck of his ship is indicated in the background, a smoking cannon shows that the ship is in action. The cannon is inscribed *Lewis*, beside it is a pile of cannon-balls.

This depicts the battle of the Saints on 12 Apr., at which de Grasse's flag-ship, the *Ville de Paris*, was captured. See No. 5991, &c.

$6\frac{1}{16} \times 4\frac{9}{16}$ in

5995 A CONSISTENT CHARACTER.

Publish'd June 4ᵗʰ 1782.

Engraving. A portrait of Lord Effingham standing on a terrace in profile to the l. pointing to a flight of steps (l.) leading upwards. The steps are flanked by a low wall on which is inscribed *I can now serve my country with honor*. Beneath this, and between two pointing hands, is inscribed, *The true road to prefirment* [sic]. On each step is inscribed a word, these are, reading upwards, *Sincerity*, *Plain-dealing*, *Honesty*, *Justice*, [Co]*untry*, [Reli]*gion*, . . .*y* [?*liberty*]. An open book lies at the foot of the steps, inscribed *Patriotism upon Principle*. Effingham holds a baton in his l. hand, in front of him, on the low wall, is his military hat, against which leans a long wand of office. He is plainly dressed, wears his own hair, but has a sword and ruffled shirt, which recall the *mot* of Burke, when Effingham changed his habitually plain manner of dress for the court-suit and sword worn by those in office, that he was wearing the coat in which he had been killed in the Gordon Riots; Wraxall, *Memoirs*, 1884, i. 250–1. In the distance, and below the terrace on which Effingham stands, a battle is in progress, indicated by men in close rank on a minute scale, with a British flag, and clouds of smoke. A large sun is rising above the horizon (r.) inscribed *Pro Patria non sibi*.

Thomas Howard, Earl of Effingham (1747–91), one of the Patriots, was very popular for having resigned his commission rather than fight in America. This resignation was perhaps not unconnected with his unsuccessful attempt to obtain promotion, see his letter of 1 June 1774 to the king complaining that he was only a captain of foot. *Corr. of George III*, iii. 107–8. Between 1770 and 1782 he had signed seventeen protests in the *Lords Journals* (G. E. C., *Complete Peerage*). On the formation of the Rockingham Ministry he was made Lord Treasurer of the Household and given a commission as Lieutenant-Colonel. As he carried his official wand as Treasurer with his Deputy Earl Marshal's baton (as he is here represented) he was called the 'Devil on two sticks'. Wraxall, *op. et loc. cit.* See No. 6061.

$7\frac{1}{16} \times 6\frac{3}{16}$ in.

5996 RODNEY INVESTED—OR—ADMIRAL PIG ON A CRUIZE.

Political Characters & Caracatures of 1782, Nᵒ IV.

[Gillray]

Pubᵈ June 4ᵗʰ 1782 by E. D'Achery Sᵗ James's Street London.

Engraving. A satire on the appointment of Pigot to supersede Rodney, one of a set of four, see Nos 5992, 5997, 6001. Rodney stands on the sea-shore, with a melancholy expression, his r. hand holding Britannia's spear, his l. Neptune's trident. Neptune rises from the sea on the r. and holds out to Rodney his trident, saying, *Accept my Son the Empire of the Main*.

Britannia (l.), seated on the globe, holds out her spear to Rodney, saying, *Go generous gallant Rodney, — go on, pursue, maintain your Country's noble cause.* In her r hand, which rests on her shield, she holds an olive branch. The French flag lies on the ground under the feet of Rodney and Britannia, the British lion, standing behind Rodney, tears at it with his claws

On the r. behind Neptune is a small open boat, sailing towards Rodney; it is composed of playing-cards, a knave of hearts acts as a sail From the mast flies a pennant on which are two dice; below it, on the mast, is a dice-box A small figure in naval uniform, with a pig's head, stands in the stern looking towards Rodney through a telescope This is 'Admiral Pig', Admiral Hugh Pigot, who had been appointed by the new Ministry to supersede Rodney, see No 5992 On a point of land in the distance on the r. stands Fox, a minute figure with a fox's head, he holds out a paper inscribed *I. O. U. 17000*, and is saying, *Does the Devonshire Member want Reasons—£17000 contains cogent ones.* This is an allusion to the questions asked in the House of Commons by Rolle, M P for Devon, on 22 May, on the superseding of Rodney in his command. Fox answered 'that for what appeared to him wise and prudent reasons he had advised his sovereign to adopt such a measure, and though he should have such reasons as all the world should approve he never would give any other answer . . . for though he was an enemy to the Crown, he would always stand forward to support its just and constitutional prerogative'. *Parl Hist.* xxiii 53, 54. See also Wraxall, *Memoirs*, 1884, ii. 328–30.

The implication of the satire is that Pigot, a great gambler, owed his appointment to his indebtedness to Fox. This is made explicit in No. 5997. See also No. 5992. Grego, *Gillray*, p. 36.

$8\frac{7}{16} \times 12\frac{7}{8}$ in.

5997 RODNEY INTRODUCING DE GRASSE.

[Gillray]

Pubᵈ June 7ᵗʰ 1782, by H. Humphrey New Bond Street

Engraving (coloured impression). One of four satires by Gillray on Rodney's victory as a blow to the Ministry, see Nos. 5992, 5996, 6001. Rodney, in profile to the r , kneels before George III (r.), seated on a throne, his sceptre in his r hand. Rodney's r. hand is held out towards de Grasse, who stands behind him and on his r.; in his l. hand he holds a sword, its hilt resting on the ground at the king's feet. He is saying, *Sire, I have done my Duty & at your Royal Feet, I lay the Scourge of these Destroyers.* De Grasse, grotesquely thin and tall, stands erect, his hands folded. Fox and Keppel stand one on each side of the king. Fox, on the king's r , both hands thrust into his waistcoat, is saying, *This Fellow must be recalled, he fights too well for us—& I have obligations to Pigot, for he has lost 17000 at my Faro Bank* (see No. 5972). Keppel looks at a paper held in his r. hand saying, *This is the very Ship I ought to have taken on the 27ᵗʰ of July* The word *Ville* is just legible on the paper, the allusion being to de Grasse's flag-ship the *Ville de Paris*, taken on 12 Apr. 1782. The king is seated on a small square dais, covered by a fringed carpet On the back of his throne is a crown to which is attached an ostrich feather, the feather which Rodney has added to the Crown by his victory.

The losses of Pigot in 1781 to the faro bank held at Brooks's by Fox and Fitzpatrick were notorious, see letters of Selwyn and others to Lord Carlisle,

Hist MSS. Comm., Carlisle Papers, 1897, pp. 489-90, 491, &c Pigot's appointment provoked the grossest allegations, cf. *Morning Herald*, 29 May 1782, 'It is the whisper at Brookes's that Admiral Pigot's sailing to take upon him the chief command in the West Indies could not be countermanded because it was deemed the only situation that could enable him to liquidate his debts contracted at St. James's Street Pharo Bank in a reasonable time, which he has pledged himself to do by handsome instalments.' For the faro bank see No. 5972, for de Grasse in London see No. 6019. Grego, *Gillray*, p. 36, Wright and Evans, No. 3. Reprinted, *G.W.G*, 1830

$8\frac{3}{8} \times 13$ in.

5998 A LOG-BOOK CANDIDATE IN FULL SAIL TO DEFEAT A WRAY OF HONESTY.

[? Hixon][1]

Pub^d June, 11, 1782, by J Langham, N° 11, St Brides Passage, Fleet Street.

Engraving. A naval officer in uniform stands on a large open book which serves as a boat, he holds a small mast to which three pages from the book are attached as sails The book is inscribed *LOG BOOK*, the sails (respectively) as *torn from, the Log,* and *Book* The officer says, *This vessel and Sails will never carry me into Westminster Port.* In the upper l. corner of the print North's head appears from clouds directing a blast at the sails of the log-book boat in order to send it to the shore (r.), where two men are waiting to receive it

A satire on Admiral Sir Samuel Hood, afterwards Baron Hood in the peerage of Ireland, who was a candidate for Westminster at a by-election caused by Rodney's peerage. Hood was then at sea with Rodney, and his candidature was managed by his son, Henry Hood. One of the two men on shore is Sandwich, who holds out both hands saying, *Save your Wind Boreas for the Admiral has founder'd in is* [sic] *Voyage.* Behind him stands a young man dressed as a naval officer, who says, *My Father was blown into this Harbour, but then the North Wind was in full Power.*

The other candidate for Westminster was Sir Cecil Wray, supported by Fox, who acted as chairman for his committee,[2] Hood being attacked as a friend of Sandwich[3] This support was so effective that Hood's candidature was withdrawn on 8 June. See addresses to the Electors of Westminster published as advertisements in the daily papers of 5-10 June 1782.

The allusion to the Log Book, however, is a confusion (perhaps intentional) of Sir Samuel Hood with his younger brother Alexander Hood, who admitted that the Log Book of his ship the *Robust* had been altered after the Court-Martial on Keppel had been ordered. Party faction at this time raged round the antagonism between Rodney, who belonged politically to the party of North and Sandwich, and had been supported by Sandwich, and Keppel. See Wraxall, *Memoirs*, 1884, ii. 324-8. But cf. No. 5673.

[1] So attributed by E Hawkins
[2] Pitt was expected by Shelburne to replace Rodney as M.P for Westminster. This had the king's approval, *Corr of George III*, vi 37, 39 20, 21 May
[3] 'Two candidates are proposed by their different friends Sir Cecil Wray by the Westminster Committee and Lord Hood by the friends of their Country unconnected with Party.' *Morning Herald*, 5 June, 1782

It was complained that the important part taken by Hood (and Drake) in the Battle of the Saints was scarcely mentioned 'in the Public Prints'. Cf letter in the *Public Advertiser*, 24 May 1782. The popularity which Hood ultimately gained by the victory secured his election at the head of the poll in the Westminster election of 1784, though Fox succeeded in defeating Sir Cecil Wray. For the log-book incident see Nos. 5536, 5537.

12 × 8 $\frac{1}{16}$ in.

5999 THE GOVERNORS FAREWELL

[? Hixon.]

Pub^d June, 11th, 1782. by I. Langham N° 11 St Bride's Passage, Fleet Street.

Engraving. Sir Hugh Palliser (l), Governor of Greenwich Hospital, walking with a stick, and supporting himself on the shoulder of a shorter man (r) who looks up at him. Palliser is saying, *My evil Genius still pursues me, & false Oaths & Jemmy Twitcher can no more avail me*. His companion, who has a wooden leg and supports himself on two short sticks, answers, *What can't Jemy give you no relief alas poor Twicher, then his Fiddle is out of Tune*. They are walking beside the Thames, across the river, and forming the background of the design, is Greenwich Hospital. By the river bank (l) part of a ship is visible, flying a flag with a St Andrew's cross. On the ground by Palliser (l.) is a large book inscribed *Log-Book*, an allusion to the evidence given at Keppel's court-martial, that three important pages of the log-book of Palliser's ship were missing, see Nos 5536, 5537, 5998 Two boats are being rowed on the river, one (l.) with two oarsmen, who look round to watch Palliser and his companion, the other (r) with a man sculling.

Palliser had been appointed by Sandwich as Governor of Greenwich Hospital, see No. 5705; his dismissal is here anticipated as a result of the fall of Sandwich He was, however, undisturbed in his Governorship, though the new ministry, especially Fox, who called it 'indispensable after what he had said in the House of Commons', were determined on his removal and the king did not intend 'to break with the Phalanx for such a business'. *Corr. of George III*, v. 503-4 (29 Apr 1782) There were many paragraphs in the newspapers asserting that he had resigned.

By the same artist as No 5998

8 $\frac{3}{8}$ × 10 $\frac{3}{4}$ in.

6000 THE GRUMBLING PRINCES OR THE DEV—L TAKE THE MONSIEURS

T. Colley In

Pub 12th June by T. Colley.

Engraving. George III (l.) stands on one side of a narrow channel, looking at three figures representing *France, Spain,* and *Holland* (these words being engraved on the ground at their feet. In the background are ships in action. The king stands solidly turning his head in profile to the r to look at his antagonists He is saying, *Da—n* [sic] *the Peace*. In his hand is a paper inscribed, *Rodney Victorious. de Grasse prisoner with 6 Sail of the Line. NB. if they had not run away we Shoul'd have taken the Whole fleet*. On the ground at his feet is engraved *Little Britain*, the channel is *Georges Channel*. France, dressed as a *petit-maître*, stands in profile to the l , one leg raised as if about to stamp, his hand clenched; he says to George, *O Da—n the War*. Spain, in cloak, ruff and feathered hat, stands behind France with an expression of distress, saying, *O Miserable War*. Holland (r), a very stout Dutch burgher, stands full face, looking sideways towards George III and biting his thumb with an expression of angry alarm. In his r hand is a dagger. Both his pockets are hanging out, one inscribed *Empty*, the other *Ditto*. He is saying *We 3 Logerheads be* [1]

In the background, and between George III and France, are two ships of war in close action, surrounded by smoke The British ship (l) is the *Formidable*, the French ship, with her flags hanging down from broken masts, is the *Vile* [sic] *de Paris*, de Grasse's flag-ship which surrendered to Hood at the Battle of the Saints, see No 5991, &c

Beneath the design is engraved:

> *I Swore (said Lewis) t'other day,*
> *My fleets should rule the Sea;*
> *Assur'd that Britain must give way*
> *To angry Spain and me.*

> *Says Neptune, I who heard the Boast,*
> *Vow'd George should rule the main*
> *You reckon'd, friend, without your host,*
> *So reckon o'er again* [1]

$8\frac{5}{8} \times 12\frac{1}{2}$ in.

6001 ST GEORGE & THE DRAGON.

[Gillray.]

Pub⁴ June 13ᵗʰ 1782. by H. Humphrey New Bond Street.

Engraving (coloured impression) One of a set of four satires on Rodney's victory as a blow to the Ministry, see Nos. 5992, 5996, 5997. Rodney, in naval uniform, strikes down an enormous dragon (r) which lies back wounded. He stands in profile to the r , with his r foot on the dragon's thigh, his l. hand holds the monster's jaw, his cutlass is raised to give the final blow. The dragon clutches his leg with its claws, and is breathing out fire and smoke as well as frogs. These frogs and the *fleur-de-lys* which decorate the dragon's wings show that it is the power of France which is being destroyed. Fox (l) runs towards Rodney holding up his l. hand, while with his r. he holds out a baron's coronet, he is saying *Hold my dear Rodney, you have done enough, I will now make a Lord of you, and you shall have the happiness of never being heard of again*

For Rodney's recall, and peerage, see *Parl. Hist* xxiii. 51 ff., 59 ff., 77 ff., debates of May 22, 27, 30, 31; June 3, 5, 7; Wraxall, *Memoirs*, 1884, ii. 324 ff.; *Corr of George III*, vol v, pp 33–6, 39, 42, 45

Grego, *Gillray*, pp 36–7; Wright and Evans, No 4. Reprinted *G.W.G.*, 1830.

$8\frac{7}{8} \times 12\frac{7}{8}$ in.

---

[1] The sign of the Three Loggerheads depicts the heads of two men, with the legend as above, indicating that the spectator was the third A signboard by Wilson is now preserved at an inn of this name in Wales

6002 THE RESCUE.

A VOLUNTEER DELIVERING HIBERNIA FROM THE CLAWS OF THE LION. [Probably after 27 May 1782]

Engraving. An Irish volunteer (l.) draws Hibernia from the British lion (r.), who holds between his fore-paws a book and a paper inscribed *Poyning's Law's*. The volunteer is in uniform and wears a large cockaded hat in which are two feathers Hibernia is dressed in pseudo-classical draperies, and holds her harp in her r. hand. Behind the lion is a square tower of dilapidated appearance, with a tree growing from (or behind) its battlements In the background is a river, and on its farther side another square tower, flying a flag.

The demand of the Irish volunteers for legislative independence could not be disregarded, a civil war seemed imminent. The Irish political demands were formulated and advocated by Grattan, see No. 6003. On 27 May the new Lord Lieutenant, the Duke of Portland, announced that the English parliament had resolved 'to remove the causes of your discontents and jealousies'; shortly afterwards Poynings' Law and the English Declaratory Act (6 Geo. I, c. 5) were repealed, giving Ireland legislative independence.

$10\frac{1}{2} \times 8\frac{3}{8}$ in

6003 IRISH GRATITUDE.

[Gillray.]

Pub^d June 13th 1782 by H. Humphrey New Bond Street

Engraving. Henry Grattan stands (c) in profile to the r facing a deputation of Irish notables who are making the presentation of the money voted to him in the Irish Parliament for his services in securing Irish independence. At the head of the deputation is a short man, the Irish Speaker, E. S. Pery, in his Speaker's wig and robes. He holds out a paper inscribed, *Grant of the Sum of £100000 to H. Grattan Esq'* and saying, *To you S^r as the deliverer of our Country & the establisher of our Peace, the Senate & People of Ireland dedicate this Small token of their Gratitude.* Behind the Speaker are two men, arm-in-arm, both wearing ribbons, others crowd behind them. A prominent figure in profile to the l., very lean, resembles caricatures of Flood.

Behind Grattan (l.) is a larger crowd of the Dublin populace, all kneeling, with hands held together as if in prayer. They are headed by a monk, behind him are a man in broad-trimmed hat and beard, probably a Jew, and a dissenting minister with lank hair and clerical bands. Other conspicuous figures are a little chimney-sweep in ragged clothes, his brush under his arm, a stout woman with a basket (? of oysters) on her head, a barber with his shaving-dish under his arm, a watchman with staff and lantern, a soldier, a tailor with scissors under his arm. Behind are buildings.

The sum first moved (on 30 May) was £100,000, but this was reduced to £50,000. Grego, *Gillray*, p 37; Wright and Evans, No 6 Reprinted, *G.W.G.* 1830. Reproduced, S. C. Roberts, *Picture Book of British History*, iii. 1932, p. 39.

$8\frac{5}{8} \times 12\frac{9}{16}$ in.

6004 THE BRITISH LION ENGAGING FOUR POWERS.

Pub^d by J. Barrow June 14th 1782. Sold by Richardson Print Seller, N° 68 High Holborn.

Engraving. A lion (r) stands facing four animals standing opposite to him in a row; his r. paw is held up, his tail is erect, and he says, *You shall all have an old English drubbing to make you quiet.* The head of a fox (C. J Fox) appears from the lower r corner of the print, saying, *I counsel Your Majesty to give Monsieur the first gripe.* The animals stand one behind the other, from the spectator's standpoint, all in profile to the r. facing the lion. In the foreground is a pug dog (Holland) its fore-paws raised from the ground, saying, *I will be Jack of all sides as I have always been.* Next him is a large snake, representing America, with a barbed fang, saying, *I will have America and be Independent* Next is a cock with the steel spurs of a fighting-cock saying, *I will have my Title from you and be call'd King of France* Next the Gallic cock is a spaniel, saying, *I will have Gibralter that I may be King of all Spain*

In the lower margin beneath the lion is engraved.

> *Behold the Dutch and Spanish Currs,*
> *Perfidious Gallus in his Spurs,*
> *And Rattlesnake with head upright,*
> *The British lion join to fight;*
> *He scorns the Bark, the Hiss, the Crow,*
> *That he's a Lion soon they'll know*

For the snake as the emblem of America see Nos. 5336, 5401, 5973, 6039. For Holland as a profiteering neutral see No 5557, &c. See also No 6229, a similar design by the same artist.

$7\frac{9}{16} \times 12\frac{9}{16}$ in.

6005 SAWNEY GANGING BACK AGAIN BEING TURNED OUT OF PLACE

['?Bartolozzi after Viscount Townshend.]

Pub^d 14th June 1782 by Kearsley Fleet Street

Engraving. Beneath it is a printed song. The *Morning Chronicle* ascribes the design to 'a well known Rt. Hon. artist' [Lord Townshend], the song to 'the Man of the people', that is C. J Fox A Scot in Highland dress is walking away from the 'Crown Inn', he looks round at a chained mastiff (l) which is barking savagely at him. He carries off his plunder: in his r hand is a purse, a sceptre appears over his r shoulder, a sack is slung on his back

In a ground-floor window of the Crown Inn George III is visible, his head thrown back as if asleep, a bandage across his eyes. From an upper window Fox, with a fox's head, leans out, holding a rope to pull back into position the sign of the Crown which is falling from its support. Two other men, one in a judge's wig (perhaps Lord Camden), stand behind him in the window. From the next window (l) a military officer, perhaps General Conway, leans out, pointing at the sign as if giving directions. Across the front of the house, below the upper windows, is inscribed *Mrs Bull late in Partnership with Sawney Mc Kenzie, with her Steward*

The house is shored up by two timber props inscribed *Paper Credit* and

Liberty of the Press. Two iron stanchions also support the house. A man in the street is putting a ladder against the beam from which the sign hangs. The end of the beam is decorated by a wide pair of horns, beneath which is suspended a small cask on which an infant Bacchus sits astride. To the r are larger and more imposing buildings than the Crown Inn. On the l a tree appearing above a wall forms an important part of the design, it conceals part of the inn.

Beneath the design is printed·

1.

John Bull had a sister, her name it was Peg,
From the North of the Tweed came to London to beg,
In a filthy condition, and not worth a souse,
Whom John, out of pity, took into his house
                    Derry Down, &c.

2.

She perverted John's wife, as I have been told,
Who from a good housewife, was grown a great scold,
And by drinking strong liquor, in Scotland call'd Whiskey,
Was grown beyond measure wrong-headed and friskey.
                    Derry Down.

3.

A lad from the North she took into keeping,
To do her odd jobs while poor John was a-sleeping;
But, lest he should wake, it plainly appears,
She bandaged his eyes, and she stopp'd up his ears.
                    Derry Down.

4

Sawney, John's servant, grew a braw bony chiel,
Who wish'd to send John and his wife to the de'el;
He eat up his victuals and purloin'd his treasure,
Then he left his good master, to repent at his leisure
                    Derry Down.

5.

His land being mortgaged in country and town,
Tho' he long kept with credit the Sign of the Crown,
His house in decay, and now wanting propping,
His Sign off the hinges, and down almost dropping.
                    Derry Down

6.

But John had some friends, who together agreed
To give him some help in the great time of need,
They turn'd out his sister, divorc'd his bad wife,
And got him a new one to comfort his life.
                    Derry Down

7

They kick'd Sawney out, unmuzzle'd John's dog,
They propp'd up the Sign, and took off the clog,
Then kindly they bad him, take leave of all cares,
Since they for the future wou'd guide his affairs.
                    Derry Down

8.

Ye Natives of England, pray mind what I sing,
Who wou'd save this poor country and preserve our good King,
Make a strong pull, a long pull, and pull all together,
Let it scoul in the North, ne'er regard the foul weather.
                                    Derry Down.

The *Morning Chronicle*, 28 June 1782, regards this print as 'much superior to any thing that has appeared since the change of the ministry, that called the Royal Hunt not excepted'.

For 'Sawney ganging' as the result of the new Ministry, see No 5961. John Bull, his sister Peg, and Sawney Mackenzie are the subject of No. 3904 (1762), a satire on Bute. In No. 3890 John Bull is George III, his house being St. James's Palace. Attributed to Bartolozzi by Calabi, No 2239

$11\frac{3}{8} \times 8\frac{1}{8}$ in.

6006 MALAGRIDA & CONSPIRATORS, CONSULTING THE GHOST OF OLIVER CROMWELL.

Political Characters & Caracatures [of 1782][1] *N⁰ 5.*

[Gillray.]

Pub^d June [?] 1782 by E. D'Achery St James [Street London][2]

Engraving (coloured and uncoloured impressions). The ghost of Cromwell (r) addresses Fox, Shelburne, and Richmond. He is in armour, his r. foot crushing a crown, his l foot on a broken sceptre In his r hand is a sword whose point rests on the ground, a long cloak is slung across his shoulders and falls to the ground behind him He turns his head in profile to the l, stretching out his r. arm and saying, *To obtain your end your Measures are right, You Arm the People—like me, you trample on Prerogative—Republicans favourite Plan—but all in vain—The Spirit of the Constitution never dies.* Fox stands disconsolately on the extreme l, holding his hat in both hands, his back to Cromwell, Shelburne's hand is in his r arm. Shelburne, holding his l hand to his chin, looks meditatively towards Cromwell. Richmond stands on Shelburne's l, his fists are clenched, and he looks at Cromwell over his l. shoulder He and Fox appear to be walking away from Cromwell, while Shelburne stands meditatively.

This relates to Shelburne's plan for 'arming the people'[3] in a circular letter of 7 May 1782, sent to Mayors, &c, and the subject of a debate on 10 May. *Parl. Hist* xxiii. 1 ff The scheme was defended by Fox as 'an association for the defence of their common rights and properties'; he approved of the example given by the Irish Volunteers as 'an example of public virtue, activity and perseverance'. The scheme, which appears to have resulted from the attitude of the Opposition towards the use of soldiers during the Gordon Riots, see No 5687, &c, was dropped.

For allegations of republicanism against the new Ministry see Nos. 5979, 5987, 6007.

$8\frac{7}{8} \times 12\frac{7}{8}$ in.

[1] Deleted with a stroke and partly erased.
[2] This publication line has been almost obscured by a line across it
[3] Cf a print (?by Colley) *L Shelburne's Plan Seconded*, pub 23 July 1782 by Turner, Snow Hill, reproduced Wheeler and Broadley, *Napoleon and the Invasion of England*, 1908, i. p 28.

6007 GUY VAUX   [c. June 1782]

Political Characters & Caracatures of 1782. No 6.

[Gillray]

Pub by W Humphry N° 227 Strand

Engraving. George III, with an ass's head, sits on a throne asleep, his wrists shackled. Through a wide doorway a crowd of conspirators is entering led by Fox with a fox's head, as Guy Vaux, holding a dark lantern The king, in profile to the r , is on a raised dais against the l wall He wears a fool's cap. Beneath his chair is a barrel inscribed *Gun Powder*. On the wall above his head as a decoration is an ass carrying on its back a huge crown (cf Nos 5669, 5683), this is enclosed in an oval formed of a buckled Garter-ribbon inscribed *Honi.soit qui.mal y pense*. On the floor by his side, leaning against the wall is a sack, from which protrude a crown and sceptre. He is perhaps contemplating departure for Hanover, cf. Walpole, *Last Journals*, 1910, ii. p 494, and the draft message of abdication in the king's hand of March 1782, *Corr. of George III*, v, p. 425.

On either side of Fox, and slightly behind him, are Shelburne (r.) smiling, with a cask under his l. arm inscribed *Gunpowder*, and Richmond (l.) holding a bundle of faggots. Behind Richmond is Wilkes.[1] Between Fox and Shelburne is the head of Keppel Behind Keppel is Burke, wearing spectacles; Dunning is in profile to the l , like Fox and Shelburne he wears a conspirator's cloak. On the wall behind the conspirators, seen through the doorway, is the lower part of the W.L. portrait, inscribed *Cataline*, of a man holding a sword.

For allegations of republicanism against the new Ministry see also Nos 5979, 5987, 6006.

Grego, *Gillray*, p 34; Wright and Evans, No. 7. Reproduced, Fuchs and Kraamer, *Die Karikatur der Europaischen Volker*, 1901, i. p. 258.

$8\frac{9}{16} \times 12\frac{9}{16}$ in

6008 RODNY'S NEW INVENTED TURN ABOUT.

[? T. Colley]

[*Pub by T Colley July 1 1782 Rolls building London.*][2]

Engraving. Men representing America, France, Holland, and Spain each tied to the end of a turn-about, or two bars crossing at a right angle where they are pivoted on a post. They are running stripped to the waist, their wrists tied to the four ends of the turn-about, while Rodney (l) holds up a scourge which he is applying to their backs, saying *Peace you Combin'd fools, I'll give it you Monsieur for your Presumption* France, his hair in a long pigtail queue, looks over his shoulder to the l saying, *O Rodny my back*. At his feet is engraved *French navy reduced*, an allusion to the battle of the Saints, 12 Apr. 1782.

Holland (r.) running in profile to the r. says, *these strokes are to[o] severe*. At his feet is engraved *Tranquin . . le* [Trincomalee] *lost &c*. This was captured by Admiral Hughes in Jan 1782, but the news did not reach London till 16 May (Walpole, *Letters*, xii. 250. *London Gazette*, 18 May.)

---

[1] Identified by Mr. Hawkins as Powys, he has some resemblance to Powys in No 5990, but his squint, and his striking resemblance to the Wilkes of No. 5987, leave little doubt.

[2] Written on the print in pencil

Spain, behind Holland, and running from r. to l, is saying *I'll be peace-able on any terms* He wears a feathered hat, ruff, slashed breeches, and top-boots America, a red Indian, with feather head-dress and girdle, running in the same direction says, *O the Deceitful French* The four ends of the turn-about are inscribed *France, Dutch, Spain, America.* A jack-tar (l.) looks on holding a club in his r. hand, waving his hat and saying, *Da—n [sic] the Frog give him another Dozen*

Beneath the design is engraved *The Little Admiral giving the Enemy's of Great Britain a Flagellation.* For Rodney's victory see No. 5991, also by Colley.

$4\frac{11}{16} \times 7\frac{3}{4}$ in.

6009 THE STATE COOKS MAKING PEACE——PORRIDGE

Pub^d July 6th 1782 by E. Hedges N° 92 Cornhill.

Engraving (coloured impression) English ministers standing over a large copper (l.) and offering the contents, or proposals for peace, to America, Holland, France, and Spain (r.). The drawing is crude and the Englishmen are poorly characterized Standing behind the copper (l), a man in naval uniform, probably Keppel, converses with a colleague: Keppel says, *We had better empty this & make another mess*; the other answers, *They like high season'd things, a few force meat Balls will make it go down.* A minister kneels before the copper, blowing the fire beneath it with bellows, and saying, *I must give it tother puff.* Behind him stands Fox, as the chief cook, with a fox's head, he holds a large spoon over the copper, while with his l hand he hands a bowl to a military officer, probably Conway. He wears an apron, with a knife at his waist, and is saying, *I have Cook'd speeches before now, Sure I know how to Cook Porridge* Conway answers, *They wont Swallow it they say it is not palatable.* A plainly dressed man, perhaps Shelburne (? or John Bull), standing behind and between them says, *Put in more peper of Rodney and salt of Wood* [1] Between the two groups stands the Duke of Richmond in profile to the r, dressed as a waiter with an apron, addressing Holland, to whom he has just handed a bowel of soup, saying, *Pray sup a little Mynheer* Holland, a stout burgher in baggy breeches, turning his head to look at Richmond over his r shoulder, empties his bowl saying, *I have thrown mine to the ground.* Behind Holland stands America as a Red Indian, with head-dress and girdle of feathers, he holds up a tomahawk in his l. hand, in his r. is a bow, a quiver is slung to his shoulders; he says, turning to Richmond, *I'll have none without my friends like it* On the extreme r stands Spain, in feathered hat, ruff, cloak, and top-boots, he looks over his r. shoulder towards his neighbour France, saying, *I'll not taste a drop till I have taken Giberalter* France, a lean fop, his hat under his arm, says to him, *By gar its not so good as soup Meagre.*

Beneath the design is engraved.

> *The State Cooks a making Peace-Porridge are found*
> *Which they hand to our different Enimies round*
> *But they all seem averse, and will not hear Reason*
> *And swear that it wants more Ingredients & Season,*

---

[1] Probably an error for Hood, James Athol Wood, afterwards rear-admiral, was in the battle of the Saints as Lieutenant of the *Anson*, but he was then unknown to the public

Ah! what can the Cooks do in such a hard case?
If such folks will not eat tho' F—x has said grace
Why give them what obstinate Children deserve
Beat them well, & if they won't eat it then let em Starve.

For the peace negotiations see Fitzmaurice, *Life of Shelburne*, 1912, ii,
p 111 ff.; *Cambridge History of British Foreign Policy*, i, p 137 ff ; E. S.
Corwin, *French Policy and the American Alliance*, 1916, Chap XV; S. E.
Morison, *Growth of the American Republic*, 1930, pp 102–6. See also
No 6168, &c.

$7\frac{3}{8} \times 12\frac{3}{4}$ in.

6010 FOX TURNING TAIL ON THE GRAPES FOR REASONS

Pub^d by J Barrow July 13: 1782. N° 11 St Brides Passage Fleet
Street.

Engraving A fox (C. J. Fox) standing on his hind-legs rests his r. fore-
paw on a large jar (r.), full of leaves (?or raisins). In his r. paw he holds a
small branch taken from the jar, saying, *For these Raisins I turn from the*
Grapes. On the l. of the design is a tall vine laden with grapes on which
the fox is turning its back.

On Rockingham's death (1 July) Lord Shelburne was appointed first
Lord of the Treasury, whereupon Fox and Lord John Cavendish resigned
(5 July), being followed by Burke and other members of the Ministry. On
9 July Fox gave his reasons for resigning, stating that he differed from the
cabinet on the independence of America, that is, on the peace negotiations.
Parl. Hist. xxiii. 159 ff. But the reasons were generally understood to be
resentment at the appointment of Shelburne, with whom Fox was on very
bad terms, and the claims of the Rockingham Whigs to a monopoly of
leadership. See Walpole, *Last Journals*, 1910, ii. 445 ff , Wraxall, *Memoirs*,
1884, ii 350 ff ; Fitzmaurice, *Life of Shelburne*, 1912, ii 151 ff.; *Journal and*
Corr. of Lord Auckland, 1861, i, p. 1 ff. See also Nos 6011, 6012, 6013,
6015, 6018, 6020, 6022, 6023, 6027, 6044, 6164, 6166, 6167, 6191, 6208.

$6\frac{1}{8} \times 7\frac{1}{8}$ in.

6011 PARADISE LOST.

J. S. f. [James Sayers.]

Published 17th July 1782 by Charles Bretherton New Bond Street

Engraving. The first of the series of political satires by Sayers, which were
directed chiefly against Fox. Fox and Burke stand arm-in-arm, looking
disconsolately to the ground, outside the gates of Paradise. Fox (l.)
holds a large handkerchief in his r hand: his l. is in Burke's arm.
Burke's r. hand is thrust in his waistcoat, his l hangs by his side, holding
a handkerchief Behind them is a high stone wall, in which is a closed gate
of high iron spikes surmounted by a stone arch. On the keystone of the
arch is a smiling head of Shelburne The other stones are decorated
alternately by heads and by crossed pistols or crossed swords. The lowest
stone on the r. bears the head of Dunning, the lowest on the l that of
Barré. The other two heads are those of satyrs Behind the wall and in
the upper r. corner of the design is a hand holding a sword pointing downwards, whose blade is inscribed, *Commission to the Lord of ye Treasury.*

Beneath the design are etched lines from *Paradise Lost.*

> *. . . . to the eastern Side*
> *Of Paradise so late their happy Seat*
> *Waved over by that flaming Brand, the Gate*
> *With dreadful faces throng'd and fiery Arms*
> *Some natural Tears they dropt, but wiped them soon*
> *The World was all before them where to chuse*
> *Their Place of Rest and Providence their Guide*
> *They Arm in Arm with wandring Steps and slow*
> *Thro' Eden took their solitary Way.*

This represents the resignation of Fox and Burke on Shelburne's appoin ment as First Lord of the Treasury after the death of Rockingham on 1 July, and their chagrin that their example was not followed by more members of the Ministry; other resignations were those of Lord John Cavendish, the Duke of Portland, Sheridan, and Townshend. Barré and Dunning accepted pensions for life obtained for them by Shelburne. See Walpole to Mason, 17 July, 1782 *Letters*, xii 298 See also p 307

Fox and Burke on their resignation became the objects of bitter satire and ridicule. 'The man of the people is snouted and fox'd in the window of every gin shop and in the tap-rooms of every porter house. Such is the ingratitude of public friendship that a man no sooner behaves wrong than he is immediately abused and vilefied ' *Morn. Herald*, 3 Aug. *The Morning Post*, 3 Aug , singled out for praise *The Exit from Paradise*, probably this print, and the *Devil's Address to the Sun*, see No. 6012. See also No. 6010, &c., and for Burke's retirement, No 6026; for Barré's pension, No. 6028. Reproduced, Fitzmaurice, *Life of Shelburne*, 1912, ii. 155 For other applications of *Paradise Lost* to Fox's exclusion from office see Nos. 6012, 6044.

$9\frac{5}{8} \times 8\frac{7}{8}$ in.

6012 GLORIA MUNDI, OR—THE DEVIL ADDRESSING THE SUN *Par* Lost. Book iv.

[Gillray.]

Pub^d July 22^d by W. Humphrey

Engraving Fox, with the legs and brush of a fox, and with horns like those of a cow, tipped to prevent mischief, projecting through the crown of his hat, stands on an E. O. table, which is placed on the summit of the globe (over the North Pole) Above, in the upper r corner of the design is a bust portrait of Shelburne, within a circle which represents the sun and is sending out rays. He smiles cynically, looking down at Fox. Fox stands full-face, his head slightly turned upwards and to the r. towards Shelburne, saying,

> *To thee I call,*
> *But with no friendly voice, & add thy name,*
> *Sh   ne! to tell thee how I hate thy beams,*
> *That bring to my remembrance from what state*
> *I fell. &c. &c &c*

His waistcoat pockets are turned inside out to show that he is penniless, and the E. O table, see No. 5928, &c., indicates that gambling is the cause of it. On the globe is sketched a map showing the British Isles, N Europe, &c. Clouds rise above the globe (l) and form a background.

For Fox's resignation see No. 6010, &c It was unusual for the resignation of office to give rise to unpopularity. For Shelburne's appointment see also No 6018, &c. Grego, *Gillray*, p. 40; Wright and Evans, No. 11.
$12\frac{1}{2} \times 8\frac{7}{8}$ in.

6012 A A reduced copy (coloured impression), n d , or date cut off.
$\frac{1}{8} \times 5$ in.   'Caricatures', xi, p. 2. B M.L., Tab. 5247.

6013 THE KETTLE HOOTING THE PORRIDGE-POT.

[Gillray.]
Pub⁴ July 23ᵈ 1782 by P. J. Leatherhead.

Engraving. Shelburne (l.), as the kettle, looks at Fox (r.), the porridge-pot, who is running away. Shelburne's body is in the form of a kettle, much blackened underneath; the handle, attached to his chest and shoulders, extends over his head. He has a complacent smile and holds out his hands, pointing towards Fox; his l. foot is on the neck of a goose, which lies on its back on the ground. He is saying, *Oh do but look how black his Arse is!* Fox (r.) with the head of a fox, his body a large circular pot, blackened underneath, is running away with an alarmed expression, his hands held up, his tongue hanging out In the centre of the design, between the two figures is a sign-post, its arm, pointing to the r., is terminated by a well-drawn hand holding a die in its fingers, but pointing with its fore-finger in the direction in which Fox is running. The arm of the post is inscribed *TO BROOKS'S*; from it hangs a rope with a noose at the end of it On the post is hung up a placard inscribed *To be Lett—either as a Gibbet or Direction Post.* A landscape with bushes forms the background.

Fox, destitute on leaving office, is running off to his gambling associates at Brooks's for his support, cf. No. 5972; while, politically speaking, Shelburne is depicted as equally black. See Walpole to Mann, 8 July, 1782. *Letters*, xii 292. Fox's geese, in caricature, usually represent the electors of Westminster, see No. 5843, &c.
$8\frac{7}{8} \times 12\frac{7}{8}$ in.

6014 THE HIGH AND MIGHTY PUG ANSWERING FOX'S PROPOSALS OF PEACE

Pub⁴ by J Barrow July yᵉ 25· 1782 Nᵒ 11 Sᵗ Bride Passage Fleet Street.

Engraving. A fox stands with a pen in its r paw looking up at a pug dog which sits on a raised platform (l) The pug (Holland) holds a tobacco-pipe in its r. paw, beneath its feet is a torn document inscribed *To their High Mig &c. . . .* (The States General at The Hague were styled their High Mightinesses, *Hogen Mogen*) He is saying to Fox, *The King Your Master proceeding so arbitrary, obliged me to join the powers at war with him; I cannot therefore treat of a separate peace.* The head and shoulders of George III appear just within the r margin of the print, he leans forward addressing Fox, whose back is turned towards him, *My Fox in this negotiation thou art a mistaken goose*

When Fox became Foreign Secretary he at once made overtures through the Russian Minister in London for a cessation of hostilities with Holland as a step to a separate peace. This was received by the States General with coldness and contempt. Fox had asserted before he came into office that he had the means of making a separate peace with the Dutch Wraxall, *Memoirs*, 1884, ii. 277-8, Malmesbury, *Diaries*, i 497 ff ; *Corr of George III*, vi, pp 10, 38-9, 62. Cf. No. 5989 For the actual peace with the United Provinces see No. 6292.

$4\frac{7}{8} \times 9\frac{1}{8}$ in.

6015 AHITOPHEL IN THE DUMPS.

[Gillray.]

Pub⁴ July 30ᵗʰ 1782 by E. D'Achery Sᵗ James's Street.

Engraving. Fox, with a fox's head, riding (r to l.) an ass, his hands are clasped in front of him, the reins hang on the animal's neck, he looks down with a dejected expression. The ass is looking up and braying at a gallows (l) which bestrides the road and through which he is about to pass; it is inscribed "*Let desert mount,*" and from it hangs a noose. In the centre of the road, and directly under the gallows, is a block against which leans a headsman's axe. Beneath the title is engraved ·

"*And when Ahitophel saw that his counsel was not followed, he saddled his Ass, and arose, and went & hanged himself, &c*"

A satire on Fox's resignation, and chagrin at the appointment of Shelburne to succeed Rockingham instead of the Duke of Portland, who, it was supposed, would have been a man of straw, leaving Fox virtual premier. Walpole, *Last Journals*, 1910, ii 448 ff. See also No 6010, &c Reissued in 1785 with the imprint, *Pub⁴ July 30ᵗʰ, 1785 W Humphrey, Strand.* Grego, *Gillray*, p. 71; Wright and Evans, No. 17.

$8\frac{1}{4} \times 12\frac{3}{4}$ in.

6016 SIR P. J. C   Eˢ HAMPSHIRE STORY.

taken from the Gazetteer & New Daily Advertiser, June 18ᵗʰ 1782
    Page 2ᵈ Colⁿ 3ᵈ

Jˢ Pollard del.   *John Roberts Aqua⁴*

Published as the Act directs Augˢᵗ 1ˢᵗ 1782, by W. Humphrey Nᵒ 227 Strand

Aquatint. The kitchen of a country inn, three women paying great attention to two customers in Highland dress, while the host walks off with an expression of anger This illustrates a press report of the debate on a motion by the Marquis of Graham to repeal the clauses of 19 Geo II, c. 39: 'For the more effectual disarming the Highlands of Scotland', passed after the rebellion of 1745, which forbade the wearing of Highland dress in the Highlands. Sir Philip Jennings Clerke proposed on 17 June, that this dress should not be permitted to be worn in England: 'He remembered that there were six highlanders once quartered in a house in Hampshire, who were really as well-behaved soldiers as any he had seen, but still the singularity of their dress had put the man of the house to very great inconvenience; for finding that his wife and daughter could not keep their eyes off the Highlanders, he was obliged to take a lodging for them both ' *Parl Hist.* xxiii. 114-15.

The two highlanders sit one on each side of a round table in the middle of the room, both paying attention to the landlady, who stands behind the table pouring wine on to the table instead of into the glass held out for it Two girls of coquettish appearance are much attracted, one negligently pours the contents of a frying-pan on to the floor, scalding a cat The host (l.), a bottle of wine in his r. hand, a napkin under his arm, walks with a clenched fist towards an open door on the extreme l. A little girl (r.) rides astride a broadsword. A set of bag-pipes lies on the floor, on which is perched a magpie.

The room is raftered with a large open fire-place (l) with a projecting chimney, on the front of which is the sign of the inn, a parti-coloured pig, inscribed *Hampshire Hog* Above the fire-place are also a stag's head with antlers, a shelf with jug and tankard. On its side is a placard, *J Clarke Breeches Maker* , in allusion to the speech of Jennings Clerke, and beneath it a salt-box. Over the door is a cuckoo clock. Two hams hang from the rafters Against the r. wall is a dresser, with plates and dishes. On the back wall is a bust portrait in an oval of *Gulielmus Rex* and a gun. Through a doorway two men are seen drinking and smoking at a table in another room. See also No. 6017.

$7\frac{3}{4} \times 9\frac{5}{16}$ in.

6017 THE SCOTCH MADE HAPPY BY A LATE ACT OF PARLIA-
MENT [1782]

J. Grot [mutilated][1] *pinxt.*   *Thistle Sculp.*

Publish'd as the Act directs.

Engraving. Sixteen men in various attitudes taking off breeches and putting on kilts One of them wears a peer's robe over his kilt Their hair falls lankly on their necks and they wear flat Scots caps. An old Jew (l) walks off towards a door carrying breeches on his back and in his hand, a sack on his back inscribed *They Have use for Monies But none for Breeches Now.* Behind a sixfold screen (r.) three young women are peeping. Another woman stretches out an arm from behind it to take possession of a pair of breeches which lies on the floor The screen is decorated with pictures or prints, oblong and oval. Some are portraits, faintly indicated. One is a W.L. figure of Justice with sword and scales. Beneath the design is engraved, *The Sixteen Elect robeing and Disrobeing.*

The sixteen representative peers of Scotland are supposed to be taking advantage of the Act removing the ban on the wearing of Highland dress, see No 6016. This ban applied only to the Highlands of Scotland, see *Parl. Hist.* xxiii. 115.

$8 \times 13\frac{1}{8}$ in.

6018 THE JUBILEE.

[Gillray.]

Pubd August 2d 1782 by E D'Achery St James's Street.

Engraving (coloured and uncoloured impressions). A sequel to No. 5966. A fox (C Fox) hangs from a gibbet, the Conway family, as rats, dance trium- phantly round him holding hands, the leader, General Conway, blindfolded

[1] Perhaps intended for John o' Groat's

POLITICAL SATIRES 1782

and led by the nose by Shelburne. Shelburne (r) has two faces, his own looks smiling towards Conway (not a rat), saying,

> *Huzza! my friends—huzza—the Monster's dead, and we*
> *Full-merrily will dance, around his fatal Tree*
> *Honours thick falling, shall our steps attend,*
> *Come where I lead—to Glory we'll ascend*

He waves his hat over his head. His other face, looking to the r. is that of a devil; it says,

> *Unthinking Fools!—who will as tenderly be led by the Nose, as Asses are—*
> *but if he (at whose overthrow they rejoice) scourged them with Whips! they shall*
> *find I will chastise them with Scorpions!*

General Conway, blindfolded, looks towards Shelburne. His sheathed sword is in his r. hand, with his l he points up to the fox on the gallows, saying, *What I'm—Political Innocence—to be sure—Ha! Ha! Ha! I'm the last to see what's obvious to all the World—am I? He! He! He!*

Behind Conway and holding to his coat-tail with his r. hand is his brother, Lord Hertford (not a rat), in profile to the r, saying,

> *All my prayr's are not in vain*
> *For I shall have my Place again.*

Hertford had been forced to resign his post as Lord Chamberlain on the appointment of the new Ministry, and the newspapers accused Lady Hertford of trying to curry favour with Fox. See No. 5966.

Hertford is in profile to the r. His l hand holds that of Lady Hertford, a stout lady with a rat's head, saying, *He! He! He!—well—I always said that Dismal would come to be Hang'd—Ha! Ha! Ha!* With her l hand she holds that of her youngest son, here depicted as a young boy, who holds the hand of his young sister, cf. No. 5966 The two children are on the extreme l of the circle of dancers; the little girl holds the hand of a grown-up sister wearing a hat, who says, *La Mama! he stinks like Poverty.* Next comes a brother in regimentals, saying, *Zounds! I'm almost afraid of this Gun-powder-Guy-Fox—'though he be dead—*He holds by the hand a brother dressed as a clergyman, evidently the Hon Edward Conway, Canon of Christchurch, who is saying,

> *The Year of Jubillee is come*
> *He's gone to his Eternal home.*

The next brother, looking up at the fox with upturned eyes, says, *Quite Chop-fallen by Heav'ns!—Ha! Ha! Ha!* The last brother, in cockaded hat, says, pointing up at the fox with his r hand, *A Nick by Jupiter!—He! He! He!* On the gallows is inscribed, *Sic transit gloria Mundi.* Below the design is engraved, '*Let me die the death of the Righteous—and let my latter end be like his.*' A cloud beside the cross-bar of the gibbet is drawn as a profile to the r, looking with an anxious expression towards Fox and the words *Sic transit.*

Conway, who was Commander-in-Chief with a seat in the Cabinet under Rockingham, not only failed to resign with Fox, but defended Shelburne's administration from the attacks of Fox on 9 July. For this he was compared by Burke to Little Red-Ridinghood, hence the allusion to 'Political Innocence'. *Parl. Hist* xxiii, pp. 165-8, 183, Walpole, *Last Journals*, 1910, ii. 451-2; Wraxall, *Memoirs*, 1884, ii. 367 ff. Lord Hertford was reappointed Chamberlain in April 1783 For Fox's resignation see No. 6010, &c. For Shelburne as a triumphant conspirator see Nos. 6011, 6012, 6013, 6028, 6032, 6044, 6046, 6166.

Grego, *Gillray*, i 41, where the rats are explained as members of the Ministry, No 5966 leaves no doubt that they are members of the Conway family. Wright and Evans, No 8

$9\frac{1}{4} \times 13\frac{3}{16}$ in.

6019 MONSIEUR LE COMTE DE GRASSE

Drawn from the life by M. Jones. [?Gillray]

Publish'd Augt 10th 1782 by John Harris Sweetings Alley Cornhill. Price 1^s 6^d.

Engraving. Bust portrait of de Grasse in an oval in profile to the l. His hair is plainly dressed, he wears a plain coat with epaulettes and the ribbon of an order over a laced waistcoat His appearance and dress are in marked contrast to the caricatures of de Grasse. Cf. No. 5997, &c.

De Grasse arrived in London as a prisoner of war on 3 Aug 1782, staying at the Royal Hotel, Pall Mall, and walking freely about London, and it is said being recognized by a jack tar in Pall Mall was given three cheers by the crowd which collected. *Lond. Chronicle*, Aug 1–3, and 6–8. Cf No 5997.

$6 \times 5\frac{1}{8}$ in.

6020 THE SOLILOQUY

S: B. [Gillray]

Pub^d Augt 12th 1782 by H: Humphrey New Bond Street.

Engraving Design in an oval Fox with a very melancholy expression, standing with folded arms facing T Q to l outside a closed and padlocked gate repeating Wolsey's soliloquy from *Henry the Eighth*. The gate fills an archway, its top being of iron spikes, the padlock is inscribed *Fast*. The stone arch over the gate is inscribed *Treasury*. On the stone wall of the Treasury building (l) are torn placards. One is a broadside, *Last Dying Speech* headed by a print of a man hanging from a gibbet; another is headed *Gamester*. Beneath the title is inscribed·

"*Farewell, a long Farewell to all my Greatness! this is the state of Man, to Day he puts forth the tender leaves of hopes, tomorrow Blossoms & bears all his blushing Honours thick upon him: the Third Day comes a Frost a killing Froast [sic], & when he thinks good easy Man full surely his Greatness is a Ripening, nips his Root & then he falls as I do!*"

Another satire on Fox's exclusion from office, by his resignation on the appointment of Lord Shelburne to succeed Rockingham See No 6010, &c.

$8\frac{1}{4} \times 6\frac{7}{8}$ in.

6021 THE V—— [VICTUALLING] COMMITTEE FRAMING A REPORT.

[Gillray]

Pub^d according to Act of Parliament Augt 12th 1782 by C. Atkinson and sold in Mark Lane!!!—"let the gall'd Jade wince!"

Engraving. Members of a parliamentary committee seated round an oblong table; two tiers of raised seats are on the farther side of the table, in the centre of the upper tier sits the chairman, immediately below him the clerk of the committee is 'framing' the Report

This is the Committee appointed to examine the conduct nominally of the Navy Victualling Board, actually that of Christopher Atkinson, a corn factor of Mark Lane, M.P. for Heydon, employed by the Board to purchase malt, &c on commission, who was accused of cheating by overcharges and false accounts He had been attacked by letters in the *General Advertiser*, at first anonymously, and then from Oct. 1780 by one Bennett. In Feb 1781 he was dismissed by the Board, in the same month he brought an action for libel against Bennett He did not produce his books to the Board as requested and in the winter of 1781-2 burned them. The Committee sat from 7 Mar 1782 to 25 June 1782 and examined members of the Victualling Board.

The persons in the print are portraits, and are indicated by numbers, but any explanatory notes there may have been are missing With the print was issued a *New Song* of which there is a MS copy [1]

The Chairman (l.) (Samuel Whitbread) is saying, *This is certainly the first instance of an accused Man sitting as Judge on his own Cause and requires particular attention* The clerk (2) is writing; he says, *The Man who ventured to hold forth such Malpractices, has rendered his Country service.* A man (3) standing on the r of the Chairman, who from the Song appears to be Montague Burgoyne of the Victualling Office, is saying, *His whole defence rests on the proof of his Partners & Clerk, & such Evidence should be cautiously trusted, they being interested* No 4, on the l of the Chairman, evidently one of the seven Commissioners of the Victualling Office, is saying, *He has behaved so well to us that we must endeavour to bring him through, but the burning his Books is the greatest preventative.* No 5, seated on the r. of the clerk, is saying, *Such infamous overcharges besides 3500£ a year, deserves the severest punishment.* No. 6, on the clerk's r., says, holding down his head, *We must be tender, we may be in the same situation at a future time, then this will appear as a precedent* No 7, on the r. of the middle tier, has two faces, one in profile to the l., the other to the r. One says, *He has much Money, that is what I deal in I must be tender*, the other says, *I must carry appearances against him to please the Public.* Probably Bamber Gascoyne, Junior, the two faces being an allusion to his house *Bifrons* at Barking, which had two fronts, see No. 6056, see *infra* the words spoken by No 14. The next four are seated on the farther side of the table, immediately under the two upper tiers of seats: No. 8 (l.) says, clasping his hands and raising his eyes, *Oh Heavens, what can we expect of the Man who burns his Books & denies his Affidavit?* (That is, in his libel action against Bennett, where he swore that he charged no more for his purchases for the Victualling Board than the prices he paid) His neighbour (9) is saying, *The great overcharge on the 250 l Malt at Plymouth, should not escape our notice* No 10 turns to his neighbour on the r. saying, *You must instruct me for his Interest, I have a refreshing Fee for You* No 11 answers him, *This damn'd Affidavit entirely oversets us!—But still we can't leave him*; he is pointing to a paper which he holds in front of him inscribed, *Kings Bench . . . C A.*, representing the affidavit in question.

No 12, evidently Atkinson himself, is standing up at the r end of the table, in profile to the l, his hand on his breast, looking towards the clerk; he says, *Upon my Honor & Reputation notwithstanding the Charges against*

[1] Printed in Wright & Evans, pp 11-13, 'from a unique impression in the possession of Mr. George Fores.'

me, I served them with Industry and Sometimes with Integrity. The next two are seated at the r end of the table, both in profile to the l. No. 13 (next Atkinson) says, pointing to No 11, *The getting him upon the Committee was a noble stroke, we can now leave out the Evidence that affects him, as we have a Majority* The man next him, without a number, sits with a book on the table in front of him inscribed *Letter, Scourge, W. Bennett, C. A*, evidently containing the Press attacks on Atkinson. He is saying, *Suppressing Evidence so material to the Enquiry & deliver'd by such unimpeachable Characters, must deserve Censure*

The next six sit, r. to l., on the nearer side of the table facing the chairman. No 14, with a pen in his hand and papers in front of him, is saying, *The Quibbles used by Bam* [Bamber Gascoyne] *are intended to tire out the Committee.* No. 15, evidently one of the Commissioners of the Victualling Office, says, *The letter we gave him was intended to do him honour, & should have contented him after detection* No. 16 says, *The overcharges did not affect us, & I wish the Fellow damn'd that first made them public, I feel the loss of presents.* No. 17 says to No. 16, *A very decent account of overcharge in which he bo* of one Person*; he is holding in his hand a paper inscribed *Flour 1300 at 1*s*, 826 at 2. 300(?) at 9, 10, 11* . No 18 says, turning to No. 19, *We did not dismiss or accuse him till an instance was clearly traced out & proved of his not having done Justice to the Crown.* No. 19 answers, *We thought him to be our confidential Servant* Nos 20 and 21 sit at the l. end of the table, 20 says, *This Burning Books seems to be a concerted plan between his Lighterman & himself, to prevent detection, as every other Person in the Trade preserve theirs*

In October 1782 Atkinson was indicted for perjury, as a result of the inquiries of the Victualling Committee. He was eventually tried and found guilty in the King's Bench before Mansfield on 15 July 1783 He was expelled from the House of Commons 4 Dec. 1784 and afterwards stood in the pillory, 25 Nov. 1785. This print appears to amalgamate the proceedings of the Commissioners of the Victualling Office with those of the Parliamentary Committee whose names are given in the *Commons' Journal*, vol 38, pp. 871–2, 895, 1000 Nos. 3, 14, 15, 16, 18 and 19 are evidently Commissioners of the Victualling Board; these were Jonas Hanway, A. Chorley, Joah Bates, James Kirke, John Slade, William Lance, and Montague Burgoyne The print is further explained by the song, 'The V—— Committee A new song of the year 1782': in this 'Bam' (Bamber Gascoyne), 'Air' (Anthony Eyre, M.P. for Borough Bridge, or Francis Eyre, M P for Great Grimsby), and K**ke (James Kirke) are accused of shielding Atkinson. 'Sir Philip' (Jennings Clerke) is praised for his honesty. The affair produced a considerable literature in the years 1784–5, see B M. L. Catalogue See also Walpole, *Last Journals*, 1910, ii. 259, 410. There are several prints of Atkinson in the pillory. Grego, *Gillray*, p. 41. Wright and Evans, No. 10.

$9\frac{1}{4} \times 13\frac{3}{8}$ in.

6022 "GUY-VAUX & JUDAS-ISCARIOT".

[Gillray.]   *Dialogues of the Dead: Page 1782*

[*Pub*d *Aug*t *14*th *1782 by E. D'Achery S*t *James's Street*][1]

Engraving Fox (l.), with a fox's head and brush, directs the rays from the

[1] Supplied from the reproduction in the *Life of Shelburne*

dark-lantern of a conspirator upon Shelburne (r), who is wrapped in a cloak, and carries a small sack inscribed *Treasury*. Fox, who is out at elbows, his breeches unbuttoned at the knee, his stockings ungartered, his shoes dilapidated with his bare toes protruding, is saying, *Ah! what I've found you out, have I? Who arm'd the high Priests & the People? Who betray'd his Mas——* Shelburne, with a smile of complacent triumph, is saying, *Ha! Ha!—poor Gunpowder's vexed!—He, He, He!—Shan't have the Bag I tell you, Old Goosetooth!* (Cf No. 5843, &c) The background is shaded to suggest night, Shelburne's head and shoulders being brilliantly lit by the rays of the dark lantern.

A satire on Fox's chagrin at the appointment of Shelburne to succeed Rockingham, Fox having demanded the appointment of Portland. See No. 6010, &c. For Shelburne as the triumphant conspirator, see also Nos 6012, 6013, 6019, 6032, 6044, 6162, 6166. Cf. also No 6007. Grego, *Gillray*, pp 41-2 Reproduced, Fitzmaurice, *Life of Shelburne*, 1912, ii. 164

$8\frac{9}{16} \times 12\frac{13}{16}$ in

6023 TIME WORKING OUT THE NEW M——Y [MINISTRY] IN PROPER CHARACTERS.

Pub^d by J. Barrow Augt 14. 1782 N° 84 Dorset Street, Salisbury Court, Fleet Street.

N. 8.

Engraving. Time (l), an old man with wings, wearing a loin-cloth, turns a handle which turns a mill, resembling a modern coffee-mill In the cone-shaped receptacle or hopper the heads of ministers appear: Dunning, cr. Lord Ashburton 30 Mar., (l.) in profile to the r. says, *We came in for Solomons, but I fear we shall turn out Simpletons.* The other heads (l. to r) are Burke, wearing spectacles, Lord Shelburne, Keppel, and the Duke of Richmond[1] who is in profile to the l., facing Dunning. Facing these are two heads in back view, and a boy's head turned in profile to the l, evidently Pitt, who became Chancellor of the Exchequer on 10 July. From a spout below the cone a goose, Charles Fox (r.) is emerging, its legs and tail still in the machine. It says, *I went in reputed a wise Fox, but Time now proves me a silly cackling goose.*

Fox had lost credit, not only by his resignation, see No 6010, &c, but by his unfulfilled boasts of being able to secure a separate peace with Holland, see No. 6014. Burke had also resigned, see No. 6026 Dunning was Chancellor of the Duchy, Keppel First Lord of the Admiralty, Richmond Master-General of the Ordnance in Shelburne's Ministry, whose progressive disintegration is here prophetically depicted Keppel resigned in December, Richmond ceased to attend the Cabinet, others were restive and threatened resignation, the result being the coalition between Fox and North See Fitzmaurice, *Life of Shelburne*, ii. 229 ff The speedy fall of the Ministry and the coalition of Fox and North was anticipated in July by Eden and Loughborough. *Journal and Corr of Lord Auckland*, 1861, pp. 5-7. See also No. 6165 Nos. 6029, 6039, by the same artist, belong to the same series.

$6\frac{11}{16} \times 6\frac{1}{2}$ in.

[1] Miss Banks has written 'Col Barré', but the resemblance to Richmond is unmistakable.

6024 THE HORRORS OF WAR A VISION OR A SCENE IN THE TRAGEDY OF K RICH^D 3d.

London, Published as the Act directs, Augt 20th 1782, by I: Sharpe.

Engraving Two ex-ministers see a vision of the horrors of war. Lord North (l) in profile to the r. stands with his hands behind his back, saying, *Perdition seize thee! Hadst thou finished the intended Purpose, the triumphs of the junto had been complete. But now disgrace and public detestation, mark the awful resignation of our Places* Behind him, in a landscape, is the vision Britannia (c.) sits, holding her spear and shield, saying *Oh I have drank of the deadly pois'ned cup administ'red by corruption.* Between her and North stands a figure (Corruption) with the head and breast of a woman, the legs and tail of a devil, holding a cup and looking towards North. She says, *My good lord I have nearly done the business*
On the r. is a room, from which the l. wall has been removed, revealing the vision to its occupant who lies back on a sofa, with hands held up in alarm. He is poorly characterized, but is evidently either Germain or Sandwich. He is looking at a Red Indian woman symbolizing America. She stands on a cloud on and under which are four naked children. They lie on a number of weapons. swords, bayonets, a pike, a scalping-knife. A sword is thrust through her breast up to the hilt, she points to it, addressing the reclining minister· *Canst thou behold this mangled breast—this dreadful carnage of my children & feel no keen remorse! Oh forego this bloody warfare, else can revolted nature 'eer forget her wrongs or close in amity the dire catastrophe of recent woes.* The minister says to her, *Hence bloody Phantom, Shake not thy gory locks at me. Approach thou like the rugg'd Rhinoceros, or fierce Hyrcanian beast take any shape but that, & my firm nerves shall never tremble.* Behind him in the background is a minister wearing a bag-wig and sword (Sandwich or Germain) looking at a map inscribed *Map of the British Empire in the Year 1775*, which is hung on the back wall of the room. It covers a great part of two hemispheres, but the details are obscure. He is saying, *O'er America's lofty summits And Africa's dusky plains; From Europe to the Ganges. And wher'eer the Atlantic bathes the western shores.*
For Indian atrocities see also No. 5470, &c.
8⅝ × 12⅜ in.

6025 THE CASTLE IN THE MOON

[Gillray.]

Pub^d Augt 22^d 1782. by H. Humphrey New Bond Street.

Engraving (coloured and uncoloured impressions). Don Quixote personifying Spain, mounted on a dejected Rozinante, sits erect on his saddle, addressing Sancho (Holland) astride on a small ass. They are on the edge of a cliff by the sea On the neck of the Don's horse stands a small monkey (France) dressed like a Frenchman with a long pigtail queue, he holds the slack reins with his l hand while he points with his sword towards a castle in the sky in a circle inset in a crescent moon which is inscribed *Gibraltar.* He says, *Sa—Sa—Ah—ha! dere I was have dem! & dere! Ah—ha!* Don Quixote, who wears Mambrino's helmet with a feather in it, a cloak, slashed doublet and breeches, and top-boots with large spurs, has an expression of melancholy dignity; he says, *Sancho! we'll sit down before the Castle & starve them out; Sancho* Sancho wears a hat like an inverted flower-pot with a short pipe stuck through its band, he says with an expression of dismay, *Starve them out. O Lord! O Lord! we're like to be starv'd Ourselves first! ther's not a mouthful left in the Wallet, & I'm grown as thin as a Shotten Herring.* He is far too large and heavy for the small ass which grazes the sparse plants at its feet Beneath the title is engraved *A New Adventure, not mentioned by Cervantes*

The final effort of the allies was a combined attack on Gibraltar by land and sea, the great preparations for which were well known in London. Cf *London Chronicle*, Aug 8–10, 1782 Its fall was confidently expected, France having pledged herself (12 Ap. 1779) not to lay down arms without securing its restitution to Spain. For the great attack on Gibraltar and its repulse, see Nos. 6034, 6037. Cf. also No. 6210. Grego, *Gillray*, p. 42. Reprinted, *G W G* , 1830

$9\frac{1}{4} \times 13\frac{1}{8}$ in

6026 CINCINNATUS IN RETIREMENT.

[Gillray.]

Pub^d Augt 23^d 1782 by E^h D'Achery St James's Street.

Engraving (coloured and uncoloured impressions). A satire on Burke's resignation after the death of Rockingham Burke, as an Irish jesuit, seated at a table eating potatoes While he wears a monkish robe, a rosary hanging from his rope and girdle, and bare feet with sandals, he wears a wig and under his robe, which is open at the neck, a cravat, shirt frill, and coat-collar are visible He wears spectacles, and is seated on a three-legged stool, facing l., and peeling with his long fingers a steaming potato taken from a chamber-pot on the table in front of him which is filled with potatoes, in which is stuck a two-pronged fork The pot is inscribed *Relick N° 1. used by St Peter.* On the table are also a wine-glass, a plate with a bare bone on it, a steaming saucepan, a birch-rod, two candles stuck in bottles, one of which hangs down broken and guttering At the opposite end of the table from Burke is a crucifix standing on a small cask inscribed *Whiskey* The figure on the cross is mutilated, the head and one leg from the knee are broken off. Beneath the table, which is oblong, plain and solid, three imps or demons dance, holding hands, naked quasi-human figures of revolting appearance

Two walls of the room are visible; on the r behind Burke is a large open fire-place, with wood burning on the hearth, a fender and firearms. Over the fire-place is an oval bust portrait (caricature) of a monk inscribed *Bonni-face.* On the back wall, over Burke's head, is a framed picture of a monk standing on the shore, preaching to fishes, among which a dolphin is conspicuous Bricks showing in irregular patches on the plastered wall heighten the impression of squalor.

Beneath the title is engraved, *falsely supposed to represent Jesuit-pad driven back to his native Potatoes See Romish Commonwealth.*

Burke, for his attitude to the Catholic Relief Act which provoked the Gordon Riots, was much abused in the virulent No-Popery pamphlets which multiplied in 1780 The *Romish Commonwealth* was perhaps one of these. The first of many satires by Gillray and others in which Burke is dressed as a jesuit. Cf No 5251. For the resignation of Burke see also Nos. 6011, 6027. Grego, *Gillray*, p 41.

$9 \times 12\frac{7}{8}$ in.

6027 "CRUMBS OF COMFORT"

OR—OLD-ORTHODOX, RESTORING CONSOLATION TO
HIS FALLEN CHILDREN. [c Aug. 1782]

[Gillray.]

Engraving (coloured and uncoloured impressions). The Devil stands (c.), his widespread wings stretching across the design, between Fox (l.) and Burke (r.), who kneel at his feet facing each other in profile. He is tall, stout, plainly dressed in the manner of the day, with a legal wig and bands. Horns project from his forehead, he has a small beard and moustache, and his toes, which are talons, project through his top-boots To Fox he hands a dice-box and dice, for which Fox, hat in hand, holds out his l. hand eagerly. Fox has a fox's head, and his hair is in a pigtail queue. Burke, wearing spectacles and kneeling on one knee, holds out his hat to receive the scourge and rosary which the Devil is handing to him, in this, as in other satires, he is depicted as a concealed Roman Catholic, see No. 6026. Behind the Devil's head is a shaded circle or dark halo, clouds form the background, suggesting that the figures are on a mountain top. One of many satires on the resignation of Fox, see No. 6010, &c., and Burke, see Nos. 6011, 6026. Grego, *Gillray*, p. 41.

$8\frac{15}{16} \times 12\frac{11}{16}$ in

6028 DATE OBOLUM BELISARIO.

J. S. f. [Sayers.]

Published 24th August 1782 by Charles Bretherton New Bond Street

Engraving. Colonel Barré stands outside a gate in a high brick wall. Shelburne (r) stands, half within, half outside the gate, his l foot on the outside; he has a cynically complacent smile and is putting into Barré's l. hand a paper inscribed *Pension 3000£ p' Ann.* Barré, who wears a coat with military facings and half-boots, holds out his cockaded hat in his r hand as if asking for alms Beneath the design is engraved:

> *Rome's Veteran fought her rebel Foes*
> *And thrice her Empire saved*
> *Yet thro' her Streets bow'd down with Woes*
> *An humble pittance craved.*
>
> *Our Soldier fought a better Fight*
> *   Political Contention*
> *And grateful Ministers requite*
> *   His service with a Pension.*

Shelburne had obtained for Barré a pension of £3,200 a year, which only became known when the death of Rockingham broke up the Ministry, when Barré himself obtained the lucrative post of paymaster-general. This was attacked in the House of Commons and defended by Barré in a speech which doubtless suggested the title of the print,[1] see *Parl Hist.* xxiii. 153 ff.; it was regarded as scandalous and contributed to the unpopularity of the new Ministry. Walpole, *Last Journals*, ii. 456–7; Wraxall, *Memoirs*, 1884, ii. 360 ff.; Fitzmaurice, *Shelburne*, 1912, ii, p. 156 f. See also Nos. 6011, 6032. For Shelburne as the successful conspirator see No 6018, &c.

$12\frac{1}{4} \times 9\frac{3}{16}$ in.

[1] The story that Belisarius was blinded and reduced to beggary is a medieval legend, appearing, perhaps for the first time, in the *Chiliads* of Tzetzes

6029 THE HABEAS CORPUS, OR THE WILD GEESE FLYING
AWAY WITH FOX TO AMERICA. [No. 9]

*Pub^d by J. Barrow August. 27. 1782. N° 84. Dorset Street, Salisbury
Court Fleet Street.*

Engraving A flight of wild geese flying diagonally upwards across the
print from r. to l ; a ribbon intertwined with the birds is tied to the hind-
legs of a fox, whose fore-paws are just leaving the ground, as he is borne
away by the geese in their flight. The fox (Charles Fox) whose head is in
the lower r corner of the print is saying, *I hope they will bear me safe to the
dear Independent Congress.* Above his head on the branch of a small tree
sits a magpie, saying *Farewell Brother Chatter*

From the beak of each goose issues an inscribed label The leader of the
flight says, *To America he shall go for his heart is there.* The others say:
*He is fitter to sit in Congress than in a British Parliament; My advice is to
drop him in the Atlantic, How jovial he will be with Congress; Let us pity
him, tho' he is a fox in form he is a great Goose in Policy, He bids fairer now
to be the man in the moon than The Man of the People; We should have done
this seven years ago.*

Behind a straight margin of grass is the sea, above which the birds are
flying; on it are two ships flying the British flag, one of which is firing her
guns, farther off (l) is a third ship.

Fox and Shelburne differed on the policy of peace negotiations: Fox
wished to acknowledge at once the independence of America, Shelburne
wished to defer this acknowledgement in order to use it in bargaining with
France. *Camb. Hist. of the Brit Empire*, 1. 772 ff. Fox's geese in satire are
generally electors of Westminster or other persons beguiled by him, see
No. 5843, &c. Belongs to the same series as Nos. 6023, 6039 by the
same artist.

8½ × 13¼ in.

6030 THE GHOST OF TYRIE [n d After Aug 24, 1782]

*Published as the Act Directs by C. Westenholt N°. 34 Church Street,
Soho.*

Engraving (coloured impression). The ghost of Tyrie (l.), holding up a
halter, appears to Fox (r.), who raises his hand in horror Tyrie, wearing
a shroud, stands among clouds, surrounded by rays of light; he says to
Fox, *Deceitful Wretch remember my End & Repent.* Fox says, *Why do you
shake your gory locks at me you cannot say I did it.*

On the wall which forms the background of the design is an oval mirror
with a candle sconce, beneath it is a marble shelf supported by a carved
bracket on which are an ink-pot, pen, and a paper inscribed *Insolvent Act.*
Behind Fox (r.) is a door Fox is plainly dressed, his hair hanging loose
except for a ribbon confining it at the neck.

Tyrie was tried at Winchester, 10 Aug. 1782, for sending naval intelligence to France and executed at Portsmouth on 24 Aug According to a
paragraph in the *Morning Chronicle*, 4 Sept. 1782, before his execution he
sent an offer to the Secretary of State 'to discover a person in an elevated
line of life who is caressed by the people of this country, whose connections and situation enable him to give our enemies the best information . . .'

Tyrie had become bankrupt before he procured a place in the Navy Office at Portsmouth.

Fox's supposed relations with Tyrie were one of the canards of the Westminster election, see 'Queries to the late Man of the People', a squib reprinted in *The History of the Westminster Election*, 1784, p 93.

$6\frac{1}{16} \times 9\frac{1}{16}$ in.

6031 SCENE LE VROG HOUSE.

[Gillray.]

Pubᵈ Sepʳ 3ᵈ 1782 by E D'Achery Sᵗ James's Street

Engraving. Rodney (r.) stands holding an ensign flag, looking towards three French Admirals in a state of humiliation. Their names are indicated by numbers referring to notes below the design. (1) Rodney (*Admiral Ro . . . y*) is taking a pinch of snuff with a fastidious air, saying, *Damn these stinking Dogs! brought him to Stool by G—d* (2) *De Grasse* is crouching down, his hands on his knees, saying, *Cest Matheureux* [*sic*], *but we do dese tings wit a good grace*. (3) *Vadruvil*, i e de Vaudreuil, de Grasse's second in command, who took command of the French fleet on the surrender of de Grasse, a fat man, kneels behind de Grasse, holds a chamber-pot which de Grasse is using, and saying, *Il faut Vassister* [*sic*] *dans ses Manœuvres*. (4) *Bougainville* (l) runs off in profile to the l., holding out a snuff-box and taking a pinch of snuff, saying, *Ma foi me only run way to avoid de Stink!* De Bougainville, one of Montcalm's generals in 1759, served as a rear-admiral in the American war, first under d'Estaing, then under de Grasse. The French flag lies on the ground at Rodney's feet, de Grasse and de Vaudreuil stand and kneel upon it For Rodney's victory on 12 Apr. 1782 see No 5991, &c.

$8\frac{7}{8} \times 12\frac{15}{16}$ in.

Also a coloured impression in 'Caricatures' IV, p. 22. B.M.L. Tab. 524.

6032 JOVE IN HIS CHAIR.

[Gillray.]

Pubᵈ Septʳ 11ᵗʰ 1782 by E. D'Achery Sᵗ James's Street

Engraving Shelburne, in a triumphal car, drawn (l to r) by two decrepit asses, with the heads of Dunning (Baron Ashburton) and General Conway He holds reins in his l. hand, which his two steeds hold in their mouths; in his r. he flourishes a whip. He is saying, with a subtly complacent smile,

> *In my presence, scoundrel Peasants*
> *Shall not call their Souls their own!*

Under his feet is Britannia's shield; a fleur-de-lys as a crest decorates the side of the car His head is irradiated. At the back of the car, as a footman, stands William Pitt, very young, and holding up in his l. hand a 'horn book' with the alphabet to indicate his extreme youth. Under his r. arm are two rolled documents inscribed [*Chan*]*cellor of Excheqʳ* and *Ways & Means* Pitt was Chancellor of the Exchequer in the new Ministry, see Nos 6023, 6044 In front of the asses, as a running footman, runs Col. Barré with a melancholy expression In his r. hand is a money-bag inscribed *3000£ pʳ Annᵐ*, indicating the pension which caused so great a scandal, see No 6028 The wings of Mercury are attached to his hat and shoes, in his r hand he holds the staff carried by running footmen, with the egg-shaped top which held the egg for the runner's sustenance

One of several satires on Shelburne as a triumphant conspirator, see No. 6018, &c., he is accompanied by his chief supporters against the attacks of the Portland or Foxite whigs See Fitzmaurice, *Shelburne*, 1912, ii, pp. 155 ff. Grego, *Gillray*, p. 42.

$9 \times 13\frac{1}{8}$ in.

6033 ECCE!

R F. inv^t   H Hyder sculp^t. [?Gillray].

Printed as the Act directs Octr 1st 1782 by S. Hooper corner of Arundel Street Strand.

Engraving. Frontispiece from *Beauties of Administration, a Poem* . . (B.M L 644 k. 21/17). A group of half-length figures in an oval George III (l.), looking to the l, and downwards, with a melancholy expression, supporting his head on his r. hand, in which is a handkerchief. Lord North, in profile to the l, with an expression of great distress, tries to comfort him, his r. arm is over the king's shoulders, handing him a paper, *Fresh Supplies*; his l hand holds that of the king. Over the king's head flies an evil spirit, a hag with serpents in her hair and bat's wings, she is 'Corruption', and is removing the crown from his head. Immediately behind the king, and looking upwards over the king's shoulder with an expression of malign pleasure, is a head wearing a Scots cap The verses show that this is Bute though it has no resemblance to him. Lord Amherst looks smiling over North's shoulder Behind North (r) is Lord George Germain (Sackville), who turns round frowning towards Sandwich, who leans on his shoulder with a smile. Above and behind Germain and Sandwich three men (r.) look down towards the king with sinister smiles, they are (l to r) Bathurst (in profile), the Duke of Grafton, and Rigby (in profile) Behind their heads is a curtain. Beneath the title is engraved, "*Mollia cum Duris, Sine pondere habentia pondus*"

The author (p ii, n.) explains that he gave directions to have the head of a satyr placed next that of Rigby, and next that, the head of an old woman: 'The Draughtsman in some measure defeated my scheme, introducing instead of them (by mistake) the Heads of L——d B—th—rst, and His *Grace* the D—— of Gr—ft—on ' See also No 6121 where the verses are quoted.

Resembles the manner of Gillray, cf. the signature of No. 6044.

$6\frac{3}{16} \times 7\frac{5}{8}$ in.

6034 GEORG AUGUST ELLIOT.

Corbutt [?R. Purcell] *delin.* [Will *sc.*]. *Se vend chez J. M. Will à Augsbourg.*

London: Publish'd as the Act directs, 1782 by Iohn Morris, Rathbone Place.

Mezzotint. One of a series, see No. 5290. T Q L. portrait of a military officer standing with his r. hand on the muzzle of a cannon, pointing with his l to the bombardment of Gibraltar, but looking in the opposite direction with a distressed expression. Ships are firing shells against the fortress (r), the trajectories showing that all reach the rock.

Probably a fictitious portrait of General Eliott, afterwards Lord Heathfield, prepared when the fall of Gibraltar was confidently anticipated: it was actually represented on the stage in Paris, while the ladies had Gibraltar fans which fell to pieces Grafton, *Autobiography*, 1898, p. 341. The print depicts the bombardment by the (supposed) gun-proof floating batteries and gunboats from which so much was expected, see No. 6025. For the actual attack see Nos. 6035–8

J M. Will or Wille, engraver as well as print-publisher, was a copyist of portraits, and this plate is attributed to him by Füssli, *Kunstler Lexicon*, 1816, p. 5098, so that he is probably the engraver of the other Augsburg copies of plates in this series. For 'Corbutt' cf. Nos 5405, 5406.

$13\frac{1}{8} \times 9\frac{5}{8}$ in.

A French print anticipating the fall of Gibraltar is No 1180 in the *Collection de Vinck: Siège mémorable de Gibraltar, par Terre et par Mer, par les Arrmées combinées de France et d'Espagne, sous les ordres de M le duc de Crillon.* . . . The Comte d'Artois, the Duc de Crillon, the Duc de Bourbon and two other personages are represented on horseback in the foreground. See No. 6036.

6035 GOV^R ELLIOT GIVING THE SPANIARDS A DOSE OF HOT BALLS FOR THEIR BETTER DIGESTION, OR PRINCE NASSAU IN A NASTY PREDICAMENT SHEERING OF IN A OPEN BOAT HAVING REC^D HIS BELLY FULL OF ENGLISH PILLS.

[T. Colley]

Pub. by T. Colley Oct. 15. 1782 London

Engraving. A rowing boat is being rowed from r. to l. under a rain of cannon-balls, inscribed *Red Hot, red,* and *hot,* which are descending from *Gibraltar,* a fort indicated in the distance and in the upper r. corner of the print, where a British flag is flying, and small figures are waving their arms, shouting *Huzza.* In the boat are figures representing commanders of the allied fleet which bombarded Gibraltar on 13 Sept. The officer seated at the stern is leaning forward, vomiting cannon-balls The title indicates that he is William V, the Prince of Orange and of Nassau, the Stadtholder of the United Provinces, who was in command of the battering ship *Talla Piedra,* see No. 6038. Facing him sits a French officer with an enormous bag-wig, he is holding up a cross and rosary in both hands in an attitude of prayer, saying, *mon petit D—u.* He is perhaps intended for the Comte d'Artois. Behind him sit three men rowing, with expressions of distress. All the figures are caricatured with an effective *naïveté.* In the water in front of the boat the heads of three drowning men appear. Between the boat and Gibraltar two vessels in flames inscribed *Gun Boats* are foundering and minute figures are indicated in the water.

A representation of the great French and Spanish bombardment of Gibraltar from land-batteries, floating batteries, and gunboats supported by the combined fleet on 13 Sept. 1782, which the allies believed irresistible, it was completely defeated by cannonades of red-hot shot from Gibraltar. Drinkwater, *History of the late Siege of Gibraltar,* 1785, pp. 288 ff. See also Nos. 6025, 6034, 6036, 6037, 6038.

There is a plate of Eliott directing the cannonade in E. Barnard's *History of England,* n.d., *c.* 1791. (B.M.L 9502, i. 6.)

$6\frac{3}{4} \times 12$ in.

6036 THE BUM-BARDMENT OF GIBRALTER, OR F—T—G AGAINST THUNDER.

T. Colley fect. [sic]

London Pub by W. Holland N 50 Oxford Street Sold by W. Humphrey 227 Strand London [c. Oct. 1782]

Engraving (coloured impression). From *Gibralter* (l), represented by a stone fort built on a rock, five cannon fire balls at four figures (r) crouching on hands and knees, who are ejecting blasts at the fort from their bare posteriors. These four figures are in a row and are dressed in the manner of French and Spanish officers in English caricature. The front figure, a Frenchman, is *C. Artois*, or the Comte d'Artois, the third is *D. Crillon*, or Duc de Crillon, the second and fourth are Spaniards They are on the sea-shore At sea (r) are two of the 'gun-boats' of the allied fleet, with furled sails. Beneath the design is engraved:

> 'Gainst Elliot the French, & the Spaniards, Combin'd
> Are Throwing their Stink Pots you see from behind
> That the Garrison's Safe you must own is no Wonder
> For all that they do is but F—t—g at Thunder.

The Bourbon royal princes and the Stadtholder of the United Provinces were present at the bombardment of Gibraltar, since its fall was confidently expected. See Nos. 6034, 6035, &c.

$5\frac{7}{16} \times 8\frac{3}{4}$ in.

6037 OH! LORD, HOWE—THEY RUN OR JACK ENGLISH CLEARING THE GANGWAY BEFORE GIBRALTER

[T. Colley.]

Pub: by T: Colley Nov. 2 1782 London.

Engraving (coloured impression). A stalwart English sailor (r.) in profile to the l. firing a blunderbuss at figures representing France and Spain. Strapped to his back is an enormous pack inscribed *Provisions for brave Elliot*. In his hat is an Ensign flag, he wears trousers and a cutlass His blunderbuss is emitting a cannon-ball as well as much fire and smoke. Spain, a Spanish flag in his hat, has fallen to the ground, and is holding a blunderbuss in his l. hand France, behind Spain, is running away, his blunderbuss, held over his l shoulder, is going off and ejecting a cannon-ball in the direction of 'Jack English'. His hat, in which is a French flag, flies into the air. In the distance a naval engagement is in progress; a ship flying the British flag, is sinking one of the enemy

This represents the breaking of the blockade of Gibraltar by Lord Howe after outmanœuvring the allied fleet under Cordova. The combined fleet, though greatly superior to that of Howe, did not accept his challenge on 20 Oct, and there was only a short cannonade from the enemy, who withdrew, making no attempt to come to close quarters. Gibraltar was now well provisioned and secure and opened its gates on 6 Feb. 1783 on news of the signing of the peace. For the failure of the allied bombardment see Nos. 6035, 6036.

$5\frac{5}{8} \times 9$ in.

6038 PRINCE STADHOLD—R RESUMING HIS DELIBERATION.

[T. Colley.]

Pub. by T. Colley Oct 24. 1782 London

Engraving. The figure of a man dressed partly as the Dutchman of English caricature, but wearing laced coat, ruffled shirt, and a star. He is holding a sheathed sword which rests against his shoulder, hilt upwards; with his l hand he is scratching his head, he puts out the tip of his tongue, with an expression of dismayed perplexity. His breeches pockets, marked *M T* (empty), are inside out

A crude representation of William V, Stadtholder of the United Provinces, see No 6035. Four labels project into the design from the r. and l. margins containing words as if spoken by persons outside the design *Your settlements in the East are taken by the English; your seamen will not fight with the french, Your fleet is now ready but dare not sail for the English; we have lost our Trade.* At his feet is a ring of papers inscribed: *America can't pay her Debts; French Politics Da—'d, Ville de Parris for that; English navy Encreas*[d]*; Gibralter not taken; Spain in the Dumps; Holland Sick.*

A satire on the irresolution and delay characteristic of William V and of Dutch policy. Cf Van Loon, *Fall of the Dutch Republic*, p 164 f. Trincomalee and Negatapatam had been taken from the Dutch. See also No 6292. For the *Ville de Paris* see No. 5991, &c.

$6\frac{3}{8} \times 4\frac{13}{16}$ in.

6039 THE AMERICAN RATTLESNAKE PRESENTING MONSIEUR HIS ALLY A DISH OF FROGS. *N° 10.*

Pub[d] *by J. Barrow, Nov*[r] *8. 1782. N° 84 Dorset Street, Salisbury Court, Fleet Street.*

Engraving. A large snake representing America, its head erect, addresses France (r), a man standing in profile to the l., dressed as French *petit-maître* with high toupet-wig, black bag and solitaire, laced suit, sword and *chapeau-bras*. Between the two stands a circular basket full of frogs; behind the snake (l) is a small pond in which frogs are swimming, inscribed, *A Fish pond for Frenchmen.* The snake is saying,

> *Monsieur be pleas'd to accept the frogs*
> *I just have killed them in the Bogs.*

Monsieur answers, holding out his r. hand,

> *I give you thanks my good Ally,*
> *Some will make Soup the rest a Fry.*

Beneath the design is engraved:

> *O Britons be wise*
> *And part these Allies,*
> *Or drive them both into the Bogs;*
> *I think it is fit*
> *They both should submit*
> *To Old England, or live upon Frogs.*

N.B. The Rattlesnake is a Character chosen by America.

Separate peace negotiations with America were going on at this time, and a preliminary treaty, not communicated to France, was signed on 30 Nov. See No. 6009. For the rattlesnake as the emblem of America see Nos. 5336, 5973, 6190. Belongs to the same series as Nos. 6023, 6029 $7\frac{11}{16} \times 13\frac{7}{8}$ in.

6040 LABOUR IN VAIN OR LET THEM TUG AND BE DA—ND
[T. Colley.]

Pub. by T. Colley Novr 27. 1782.   Pub. as the Act directs Nov. 27. 1782 by T Colley. London. [sic.]

Engraving. England, on one side of a channel of water, is being tugged at by her four enemies, who are pulling at ropes attached by grappling-hooks to the ground on the English side of the water England (l) is represented by Neptune, the British lion, Britannia, and a sailor The sailor (l.), in short jacket and striped trousers, stands with his l hand on Britannia's shoulder, saying with a grin, *avast heaving.* Britannia is seated with her shield and spear, she smiles, saying, *ha ha ha* Neptune with his trident, seated on a culvert from which water is gushing, smiles and points derisively across the water at the efforts of England's enemies Between him and Britannia sits the British lion, also grinning This piece of land, jutting into the sea is inscribed *England* England's enemies (r.) lean backwards hauling at taut ropes, all, except France, open-mouthed as if singing a chanty. In the foreground is Holland, a stout plainly-dressed Dutchman. Next is France, a lean fop, his knees bent, holding a rope. Spain, taller and stouter, stands behind him holding him round the waist and shouting Next is America, a scantily draped woman, with a feather head-dress and sandals holding a tomahawk as well as her rope. In the background is the sea.

Beneath the design is engraved:

Four Foes to old England have Wickedly Join'd
To run with old England Away
Old Neptune declares it is not to his mind
And Brittania cries Stay you fools Stay

You may tug, & may tug, & strive all that you can
And put your selves into great pain
While Freedom & Honour is fixt on our Plan
You will find it all Labour in Vain.

See also No. 6051. For the naval successes of 1782 see Nos 5991, 6034-8, &c.
$7\frac{7}{16} \times 13\frac{1}{4}$ in.

6041 A COURT MARTIAL,—OR—A SCENE AT THE HORSE GUARDS.
[Gillray.]

Pub^d Decr 5th 1782, by E D'Achery St James's S^t

Engraving The court-martial on Lieut.-General James Murray (Nov.-Jan 1782-3) on charges brought against him by his second-in-command, Lieut.-General Sir William Draper, for conduct in Minorca, before, during, and after the siege. A number of officers seated on both sides of a large table; at the head, and facing the spectators, is the Judge-Advocate-General who presided at the trial, Sir Charles Gould, above his head is drawn a pair of evenly balanced scales, inscribed *Sterling*. He looks towards a witness (r.) who is speaking On the r. behind a barrier and raised above the level of the Court are Murray, who clutches the barrier with an anxious expression, and two counsel (?), Draper and four witnesses or spectators; a partition divides Murray and his counsel from the others Above Murray's head is inscribed *Matrimony* Draper wearing his ribbon and star (he was made K B in 1764) stands with both hands on the barrier with a composed expression. On his r. is a lean and ugly man speaking and gesticulating. All the men seated at the table are in uniform except Gould. On Gould's r. is an officer wearing a ribbon, evidently General Sir George Howard, K.B., the senior officer there. On Howard's r. and on the l. side of the table sit two officers looking at a map, one wearing glasses is inscribed *Yankee Doodle*; he is probably Lieut.-General Thomas Gage, ex-Governor of Massachusetts. The two officers on the l. of the table lean against each other, asleep, and are inscribed *Capacity*. Six officers on the r. of the table are in attitudes varying from sound sleep, head and arms on table, to rapt attention. Over one sleeper is inscribed *Amen!!!*, over another is a hand with a pointing finger and the word *Attention*. On the l. of the Court, behind a barrier, two men write at a raised desk, one perhaps Gurney, the famous shorthand writer who transcribed the proceedings. Papers, pens, and inkstands are scattered on the table Beneath the title is engraved *Humbly dedicated to the Duc de Crillon*.

Murray was honourably acquitted of all but two (and these trivial) of the twenty-nine counts, the charges were recognized as the result of personal rancour on Draper's part. The surrender of Minorca (5 Feb. 1782) had been due to the ravages of scurvy in the small garrison The dedication is an allusion to a bribe of a million sterling secretly offered to Murray by de Crillon, who commanded the blockading force of 16,000 French and Spaniards, and to its rejection. The names of the court—two generals, thirteen lieutenant-generals, and two major-generals—are given in the shorthand report of the trial (B.M.L. 112 e. 2)

The design is freely drawn in the manner of a sketch from life. It is consistent with newspaper accounts of the trial which describe Murray as 'very much broke' while Draper looked 'exceedingly well and in the flower of his age, his star was very conspicuous and his arm always carefully disposed so as never to eclipse it' (*D.N.B.*). For a portrait of Murray probably sketched at the trial see No 6097.

$8\frac{7}{16} \times 12\frac{3}{4}$ in.

6042 RAISING THE ROYAL GEORGE.

Boreas designd it.   *twitcher. sculpt.*

Publishd as the act directs. Decembr 5. 1782. by J. Langham, print Coulourer N 84 Dorset Street &c Sold at the print and bookseller the Corner of the Piazzas Covent Garden

Engraving Four men stand in an open boat, each tugging at a rope attached to the king, whose hands and crowned head appear above the water. A *Diving Bell* with the head of a judge floats behind the king, attached to the boat by a slack rope. On the shore (r.) stand two men looking at the boat; one is Fox with a fox's head, the other Burke. The stern of the boat (l.) is inscribed *Victory's Boat*. Holding the tiller and looking over his l shoulder with a frown is Keppel, saying, *Yeo Oh*;[1] next him, one foot on the gunwale of the boat, and pulling his rope with both hands, is Shelburne, saying, *I Oh* Next him is Dunning (Ashburton) in legal gown and bands, he turns his head to Shelburne saying, *Hum Oh* (cf. Nos 6091, 6173) On the r. of the boat, and leaning over to the r., one foot on the gunwale, is the Duke of Richmond. He looks down at the judge in the diving-bell (probably Thurlow) saying, *Never fear to dive my Lord, that's Born to be hang'd will never be Drown'd.* The Judge says *I'll go down because I am a Judge.* Fox, who stands with his hands in his pockets, says,

> *As maligrida* [Shelburne] *now does reign,*
> *all their labour is in vain.*

Burke, pointing at the boat, says,

> *if Boreas was here he woul'd much Swell*
> *and prevent the efects of the Diving Bell*

The title of this rather confused satire on the political situation is an allusion to the loss of the *Royal George* with Kempenfeldt and about 1,000 persons on 29 Aug. 1782. The meaning appears to be that Shelburne and his Ministry are endeavouring to restore the royal influence which the Rockingham Ministry, and especially Fox, had aimed at destroying, thus reverting to the policy of North and Sandwich.

Reissued 21 Jan. 1783.

9 × 13⅝ in.

6043 TALEO, OR THE ROYAL SPORTSMAN, RUNNING DOWN THE ENEMIES OF GREAT BRITAIN.

[T. Colley.]

Pub. by T: Colley Dec* 9. 1782 London

Engraving. George III, on horseback, hunting with dogs whose names are those of admirals, the quarry being Spain, France, and Holland. The king (l) on a galloping horse in profile to the r. leans forward holding out his whip, and saying with a stern expression, *Taleo. Taleo. Taleo. o o.o.* Just in front of him Holland, a stout Dutchman, lies on his back, his feet in the air, his hands clasped shouting for mercy, coins are falling from his pocket He is being worried by a dog with a collar inscribed *Park[er]* an allusion to the battle of the Dogger Bank, 3 Aug. 1781, see No. 5848. On the king's r run two dogs *How* in front (Admiral Lord Howe who had recently relieved Gibraltar, see No. 6037); behind and partly cut off by the l margin of the print is *Pigot*, the admiral who was sent out to supersede Rodney, see No. 5996, &c. In front of Holland is a gate over which France (or the King of France) is leaping, his arms outstretched; his leg is gripped by a dog named *Rodney*, in allusion to the battle of the Saints, see No 5991, &c France wears a crown, a ribbon and star, large bag-wig and embroidered suit. On the farther side of the gate is Spain (or the King of Spain) wearing a crown and cloak, shouting, his hands held up in alarm He is being worried by a dog whose collar is inscribed *Elliot*, in allusion to the defence of

---

[1] On the print in an old hand is written 'Lord Sandwich' But he resembles Keppel, not Sandwich, who moreover could scarcely be associated with the other three in the boat, all members of Shelburne's Ministry.

Gibraltar, see No 6035, &c Across the top of the design is engraved *Lewis Baboon, taking a flying leap.*

The association of Pigot and Rodney illustrates the absence of political rancour characteristic of Colley's work.

$7 \times 12\frac{1}{4}$ in.

6044 "ASIDE HE TURN'D FOR ENVY, YET WITH JEALOUS LEER MALIGN, EYD THEM ASKANCE".

S. B. inv E· *Hyder sculp* [Gillray]

Pub Dec* 12* 1782, by H. Humphrey New Bond Street.*

Engraving Design in an oval A woodland scene; Shelburne and Pitt seated side by side at a rectangular table (l) draped with a cloth on which are coins and money bags Fox (r) stands aloof scowling towards them over his r. shoulder, his hands thrust in his breeches pockets Shelburne looks at Fox with a complacent smile, he holds Pitt's arm. Pitt holds a money-bag and looks at Shelburne with a sly smile.

Pitt was Chancellor of the Exchequer in Shelburne's ministry, see Nos 6023, 6032. The first satire in the collection pointing directly to the rivalry between Pitt and Fox, but cf No. 6023. For other applications of 'Paradise Lost' to Fox's exclusion from office, see Nos. 6011, 6012. For his resignation see No. 6010, &c. Reprinted, *G.W G*, 1830. Grego, *Gillray*, pp. 42–3.

$7 \times 9\frac{1}{2}$ in.

6045 [THE SHELL-BORN JES——T¹]

Ignatius Loyala Inv Pub* Dec* 18* 1782. K*

Engraving. Shelburne, dressed as a monk but wearing a wig, stands in profile to the l., his mouth open as if making a speech, one hand on his heart, he has an alert, propitiatory smile In his l hand is a rolled document, *The Speech.* Beneath his feet is etched (as is the publication line) *He wou'd & he wou'd not &c.* In the distance is the sea with the sun, inscribed *Poor Old England,* sinking below the horizon.

The old name of Malagrida the Jesuit, given in 1767, was used for Shelburne after he succeeded Rockingham as First Lord of the Treasury, see No. 4917 and cf No 6018, &c. 'The speech' is probably that of 13 Dec. 1782 when he refused to answer questions on the exact interpretation of the independence of America in the provisional Treaty. *Parl Hist.* xxiii. 305 ff. Cf. also the famous lines on Shelburne's evasive speeches in *The Rolliad,* quoted Rosebery, *Life of Pitt,* p. 51. By the same artist as Nos. 5958, 5975.

$7\frac{1}{2} \times 5\frac{1}{4}$ in (pl).

6046 [SANDWICH AND SACKVILLE AT THE BAR] [?1782]

Engraving. A slight sketch of two men standing at a spiked semicircular bar before a judge. Only the upper part of the figures is drawn. The culprits stand in profile to the r, the nearer resembles Sandwich, the musical score hanging from his pocket confirms the identification His companion is probably Lord George Germain (cr. Lord Sackville, 11 Feb 1782).

¹ Written on the back in Miss Banks's hand.

Behind and above the two men hovers Justice, threatening them with a drawn sword and holding up a pair of scales, one of which is weighed down by a label inscribed *Crimes* The judge, whose face is hidden by his wig, also holds up a pair of scales, one of which is weighed down by a label inscribed *30,000*. He is identified by Mr Hawkins as Lord Loughborough, but Thurlow would seem more probable. According to a pencil note this is a first state with only two figures at the bar, the third would almost certainly be North.

North, Sandwich, and Germain had frequently been threatened with impeachment, and the new Ministry were blamed, e g by Walpole, for failing to attempt to punish them. Walpole attributes their escape to Shelburne, 'who had devoted himself to the king', and to Thurlow, 'whom they had pardoned and adopted'. *Last Journals*, 1910, ii 430. Burke said in the House of Commons on 26 April 1786, that he had drawn up seven distinct articles of impeachment, but had been induced by Rockingham to give up the project Wraxall, *Memoirs*, 1884, iv. 311. Cf. Nos. 5660, 5661, 5964, 5969, &c

$5\frac{3}{4} \times 8\frac{1}{2}$ in.

6047 VELUTI IN SPECULUM. [?1782]

Engraving. The Devil (r) supports a large mirror which rests on the floor, and invites a number of military officers to look at the reflections of themselves. The foremost is Lord Amherst, who as commander-in-chief had been adviser to the Government on the American War. He advances with a gesture and smirk of satisfaction Behind is an officer who frowns, holding his chin; he resembles General Murray, see No 6041 Behind him Burgoyne's profile is recognizable. There are four other officers, a very small man with a riding-cane under his arm, looking with pleased satisfaction at the mirror, is perhaps Tarleton, see Nos. 6085, 6116 The other three cannot be identified, they are perhaps Cornwallis, Clinton, and Sir William Howe. On the wall are two maps one, the plan of a fort inscribed *Fort St. Philip*, points to the loss of Minorca in Feb 1782; the other, a map of *America* with *Montreal* in the south, implies that America has been turned upside down. The mirror is surmounted by a trophy of flags, a drum, a helmet, &c.

A satire on the military command during the American War. It is drawn with freedom and expressiveness

$4\frac{1}{4} \times 6$ in.

6048 LE LORD CORNWALIS SORTANT DES CAROLINES APRÉS
  Y AVOIR ÉTÉ LONGTEMS RESSÉRÉ [After February 1782]
LE LORD RAWDON ARRIVANT DES CAROLINES.

Engraving. Two caricature portraits on one plate They are numbers 9 and 10 in a series of twelve caricature portraits called *Collection des Grands Hommes qui se sont le plus distingués dans la Marine Anglaise*, with the imprint of *Esnauts et Rapilly* of Paris; Van Stolk, No. 4486 For 11 and 12 see No 6049. The first eight (not in the B.M. collection) are *Képpel au Conseil de Guerre*, *Hugues Paliser accusant Képpel* [see Nos. 5536, 5537], *Lamiral Graves cherchant Hoode*, *Jonsthone à San jago* [see No. 5960] *le Commodore Stewart hêlant la flotte Hollandaise*, *Le Lord Sandwick*

Premier Lord de L'amirauté, Le Gal Murray Voyant debarquer Les Espagnols à Mahon [see No. 6041], *Le Colonel Fergusson revenant de Tabago* [taken by de Bouillé 2 June 1781].

[9] H.L. in profile to the r. with no resemblance to Lord Cornwallis. See Nos. 5855–60.

4$\frac{1}{8}$ × 3$\frac{1}{8}$ in.

[10] A bust-portrait in profile to the l. with no resemblance to Lord Rawdon (1754–1826), afterwards Marquis of Hastings. Rawdon was obliged to leave America for reasons of health in the summer of 1781 and the vessel in which he sailed was captured by a French cruiser and taken to Brest. He shortly afterwards returned to England on an exchange of prisoners.

4$\frac{1}{8}$ × 3$\frac{3}{8}$ in. (pl. 5$\frac{5}{8}$ × 8$\frac{1}{4}$ in.).

6049 DARBY ALLANT SE COUCHER À PORTSMOUTH
LE LORD NORTH ATTENDANT DES NOUVELLES DE
L'AMÉRIQUE. [c 1782]

Engraving. Nos. 11 and 12 in a French series, see No 6048 Two caricature portraits on one plate.

[11] Head and shoulders of a man in profile to the r., wearing a nightcap and striped jacket, and resembling an old woman. It has no resemblance to Darby's engraved portrait (published 28 June 1781).

Darby was given command of the British fleet in Aug. 1780. He relieved Gibraltar Apr. 1781 and escorted convoys, but failed to take opportunities of attacking the combined French and Spanish fleet. On 6 Nov. 1781 he returned to Spithead, and never served again. He was 'a man of no distinction and very slender abilities', J. K. Laughton in *D N B*. See James, *The British Navy in Adversity*, pp. 246–7, 302 ff.

4 × 4$\frac{1}{8}$ in.

[12] 'Lord North' (H L.) seated, in profile to the l. wearing a round hat. He has a long pointed nose and is grotesquely unlike North.

4 × 3$\frac{3}{8}$ in. (pl. 5$\frac{5}{8}$ × 7$\frac{15}{16}$ in.).

6050 RETALIATION OR STATE OF NATIONS.

Pub^d 1782 by Humphrey Bond Str:

Engraving. Outside a small cottage or summer-house a bee-hive stands on a table. Two men are being attacked by bees: one lies on his back waving his arms and legs, the other is behind him, running away and beating off the insects which beset him. Behind (r.) a man with a broom is coming to the rescue, but is about to be attacked himself.

Beside the cottage (l.) a man (or woman), smoking a pipe, is squatting down and excreting. From a window just above him, a man leans out, vomiting on the head of the figure beneath. A figure seated on the roof is urinating on the head of the man at the window.

The application of this satire to the international situation is general rather than precise. The coarseness of the subject is mitigated by the small scale and a sketchy treatment.

3$\frac{1}{16}$ × 4$\frac{3}{4}$ in.

6051 THE BELLIGERENT PLENIPO'S

T: Colley Fec^t   [*c* Dec. 1782]

Sold by W Humphrey 227 Strand, London.

Engraving. A figure representing each of the five powers between whom peace negotiations were going on stands each on a little island or peninsula of turf behind which is the sea. On the extreme l George III stands holding the ensign flag He is wearing half a crown and turns his head in profile to the r., saying with an angry expression, *I give them Independence.* At his feet lie a purse, an arm, and a foot, representing spoil taken by England from the other belligerents Next him is France, wearing a crown, holding the French flag, with his l. arm (the arm which lies at the feet of George III) cut off above the elbow and dripping with blood. He is saying, *I must have Canada and Grenada for my Arm*

Next, and in the centre, is Holland, holding a flag with three horizontal stripes (that of the Stadtholder), the r. foot amputated above the ankle, a crutch under his r arm. He is weeping and holds a large spotted handkerchief to his eyes, his pockets being inside out, to show the impoverishment caused by the war to Holland He says, *I insist on Eustatia & Ceylon for my foot.* Next him is Spain, with the Spanish flag, holding up both arms, he waves a crutch held in his r hand, and stands on his r. leg, raising in the air a wooden leg He says, *By Saint Anthony I must have Gibralter for my Leg.* America, a scantily draped woman wearing a feather head-dress, holds in her r hand the striped American flag, the cap of liberty on the flag-staff. She clasps to her breast the other half of George III's crown, and says, *I have got all I wanted Empire!* She is smiling, in contrast with the melancholy expression of the other figures. The little island on which she stands is fringed by miniature pine-trees. On clouds in the centre of the design, above the flags held by France and Holland, reclines Hibernia wearing a spiky coronet, holding a harp. She is saying, *I deny all foreign Jurisdictions & will roast my own potatoes*

Peace negotiations had been going on actively since March On 30 Nov. 1782 Preliminary Articles were signed at Paris between England and America, with a reservation intended to obscure the breach of the Treaty of Alliance between France and America, that peace was not to be concluded till terms were agreed upon between France and Great Britain. The naval successes of 1782 are reflected in this print, which should be contrasted with No. 5959, see also No 6040. For Ireland see Nos. 6002, 6003 The French of course made no claim to Canada, and St. Eustatius and Trinkomali had been recaptured by the French, see p. 559, No 6292. $8\frac{1}{2} \times 12\frac{7}{8}$ in.

6052–6077

A series of W.L. portraits, slightly caricatured, by James Sayers, apparently begun in connexion with the ministerial changes of Mar 1782 The changes were accompanied by changes of costume on which these portraits are probably comments, see Wraxall, *Memoirs*, 1884, ii. 269–70. See also Nos. 5984–6, 6256

6052 [RICHARD RIGBY]

J S ff

Published 6th April 1782 by C Bretherton

Engraving. Rigby, standing in profile to the l. holding out his hat in his r.

hand, as if speaking in the House of Commons, his l hand on the hilt of his sword For Rigby's part in the political manœuvres of Dec. 1781 to get rid of Sandwich and Germain, and so lessen the unpopularity of the Ministry, see Walpole, *Last Journals*, 1910, ii 390, 393. Burke succeeded him in April as Paymaster-General. See No. 5961.

$6\frac{15}{16} \times 4\frac{7}{16}$ in. (pl)

6053 [LORD AMHERST]

J S Published 6 April 1782 by C Bretherton

Engraving. Amherst standing in profile to the l. He is in uniform and wears his ribbon of the Bath. He is smiling, his l hand rests on his sword. At the change of ministry General Conway succeeded him as Commander-in-Chief.

$6\frac{7}{8} \times 4\frac{3}{8}$ in. (pl.)

6054 VOX POPULI.

J S ff

Published 6th April 1782 C Bretherton

Engraving. Fox, standing, almost full-face, directed to l , in the attitude rather of a speaker on the hustings than in parliament, his fists clenched, r arm raised, l. arm akimbo, feet wide apart.

$6\frac{7}{8} \times 4\frac{3}{8}$ in. (pl.)

6055 [EDMUND BURKE]

J S f

published 6th April 1782 by C Bretherton

Engraving. Burke making a speech. He stands in profile to the l , wearing spectacles. His r. arm is extended, his hand grasping a paper on which is etched *Plan Œcon*, in allusion to his Bill for Economical Reform. His l. hand, holding his hat, is behind his back. Beneath is etched:

> *For Rhetoric he could not ope*
> *His Mouth but out there flew a Trope*

Reproduced, A S Turberville, *Men and Manners in the Eighteenth Century*, 1926, p 272.

$6\frac{15}{16} \times 4\frac{3}{8}$ in. (pl).

6056 [BAMBER GASCOYNE]

JS ff

published 6th April 1782 by C Bretherton

Engraving Portrait of Bamber Gascoyne A stout, plainly dressed man wearing a hat and a buttoned-up coat, he stands almost full-face, his hands in his coat pockets.

Gascoyne (1725–91), M.P for Truro, was a supporter of North, and lost his post as a Lord of the Admiralty on the fall of North's Ministry.

He was very wealthy, son of Sir Crisp Gascoyne, the Lord Mayor who is remembered for the part he took in the case of Elizabeth Canning in 1753 See No. 6021.

$6\frac{7}{8} \times 4\frac{1}{2}$ in (pl.).

6057 [HENRY DUNDAS]

JS ff

published 6ᵗʰ April 1782 by C. Bretherton

Engraving. Dundas, the Lord Advocate of Scotland, in profile to the l., stands in the attitude of an orator, his r. arm extended, his legs apart He wears a sword and holds his hat in his l hand. Dundas (1742–1811), afterwards first Viscount Melville, managed to keep his place under the new Ministry. For a hostile account of his part in the ministerial changes of March 1782 see Walpole, *Last Journals*, ii, pp 410, 417.

$7 \times 4\frac{3}{8}$ in. (pl.).

6058 7. [EARL OF SURREY.]

JS ff

Published 14ᵗʰ May 1782 by C Bretherton

Engraving. Charles Howard, 1746–1815, afterwards 11th Duke of Norfolk, styled Earl of Surrey 1777–86, known as the Jockey of Norfolk. He stands in profile to the l., holding a stick in his r. hand, his hat under his l. arm, his l hand in his breeches pocket He is plainly dressed and wears his own hair cut short He was noted for the slovenliness of his dress. He became a protestant and was M.P. for Carlisle, 1780–6, being a supporter of Fox.

$7 \times 4\frac{7}{16}$ in. (pl.).

6059 8 [EARL NUGENT.]

JS ff

Published 14ᵗʰ May 1782 by C Bretherton

Engraving. Portrait of Robert Craggs Nugent (1702–88), Irish peer and M.P. for St Mawes. He stands, bending forward from the waist, his head in profile to the l , his r. hand extended, his hat in his l. hand as if speaking in the House of Commons, where he was noted for speeches in a rich brogue and for his support of every Ministry in turn He was nicknamed 'Squire Gawkey' and was also called 'the old rat of the Constitution', see Nos. 6212, 6255, 6256. Walpole calles him a 'noisy vociferous and ridiculous Orator' *Satirical Poems by William Mason with Notes by H. Walpole*, ed. Toynbee, 1926, p. 121. See Wraxall, *Memoirs*, 1884, i. 91 ff.

$7 \times 4\frac{1}{2}$ in (pl).

6060 9 [DUKE OF GRAFTON.]

JS ff

Published 14ᵗʰ May 1782 by C Bretherton

Engraving. Grafton, standing in profile to the l., his hands thrust into his waistcoat. He wears a bag-wig, sword, and ruffles Grafton, who had been

Lord Privy Seal in North's Ministry from June 1771 to November 1775, again became Lord Privy Seal under Rockingham, retaining office under Shelburne, whose fall was made inevitable by his resignation, 20 Feb. 1783 *Autobiography of Grafton*, p 322. Fitzmaurice, *Life of Shelburne*, ii, pp. 245 ff. Reproduced, Turberville, *Men and Manners of the Eighteenth Century*, 1926, p 261

7 × 4⅜ in. (pl.)

6061 *10.* [EARL OF EFFINGHAM.]

JS ff

published 14ᵗʰ May 1782 by C Bretherton

Engraving, A portrait of Lord Effingham, standing in profile to the r., holding a long slender staff in his r. hand, a short staff in the l, the two staffs of office for which he was known as the Devil on two sticks See No. 5995. Though he is plainly dressed, wearing his own hair, he wears a sword.

7 × 4⅜ (pl.).

6062 *11.* [EARL OF SHELBURNE.]

JS ff

published 14ᵗʰ May 1782 by C Bretherton

Engraving. Portrait of Shelburne, standing, facing three-quarters l, his r. hand thrust under his Garter ribbon, with which (with the Dukes of Devonshire and Richmond) he had been invested on 17 Apr. His l. hand rests on his sword He wears a bag-wig and ruffles, and has the sly, complacent smile and half-closed eyes which are conspicuous in satires of Shelburne at this time. See Nos. 6018, &c

6⅞ × 4⅜ in. (pl.).

6063 *12.* [LORD NORTH]

JS ff

published 14ᵗʰ May 1782 by C Bretherton

Engraving. Portrait of North, standing in profile to the l. clutching a document in his r. hand, as if speaking in the House of Commons. Reproduced, A S Turberville, *Men and Manners of the Eighteenth Century*, 1926, p. 54, and *Propylaen-Weltgeschichte*, ed. W. Goetz, vi, 1931, p. 460.

7 × 4⅜ in. (pl.)

6064 [COLONEL BODEN.]

JS

Published 4ᵗʰ June 1782 by C Bretherton

Engraving. Portrait of a stout man in profile to the l. wearing a looped hat and buttoned overcoat, his hand thrust in his coat pocket. He was not an M P. See No. 5868.

6¹⁵⁄₁₆ × 4⅜ in. (pl.)

6065 GAME

Published 7ᵗʰ June 1782 by C. Bretherton

Engraving Portrait of George Onslow as a cock-fighter, walking from the spectator, but turning his head in profile to the l. He wears a plain hat and coat, top-boots with spurs like those attached to the legs of game-cocks, and holds a riding-whip in his r. hand. In the foreground stands a spurred game-cock, crowing.

Colonel Onslow (1731–92), M.P. for Guildford, called little Cocking George, see Nos 4852, 4855, was a firm supporter of North's Ministry. He made a notable speech on 15 Mar. 1782 denouncing Opposition leaders as the chief cause of the loss of America Wraxall, *Memoirs*, 1884, ii 229–30 *Parl Hist* xxii. 1175–7. Cf. Nos. 5641, 6029.

$5\frac{7}{16} \times 3\frac{9}{16}$ in. (pl.)

6066 XII. [COLONEL BARRÉ]

JS ff

Published 17ᵗʰ June 1782 by C Bretherton

Engraving Portrait of Barré full face, standing, his legs apart, his hat in his r. hand, his l hand thrust into his waistcoat.

Barré was the subject of Sayers's second important political satire, see No. 6028.

$6\frac{7}{8} \times 4\frac{3}{8}$ in. (pl.).

6067 XIV. [WILKES]

JS ff

Published 17ᵗʰ June 1782 by C Bretherton.

Engraving. Portrait of Wilkes standing looking to the r., his arms hanging at his side He wears a hat, bag-wig, ruffled shirt, and sword, with wrinkled riding-boots His squint is very pronounced, he looks toothless and much older than in the earlier caricatures, cf. No. 5881. Reproduced, Turberville, *Men and Manners of the Eighteenth Century*, 1926, p. 46

$6\frac{7}{8} \times 4\frac{3}{8}$ in. (pl).

6068 XV. [GENERAL BURGOYNE.]

JS ff

Published 17ᵗʰ June 1782 by C Bretherton

Engraving. Portrait of Burgoyne, M P. for Preston, standing legs apart, smiling, his head turned in profile to the l., and holding out a paper in his r. hand as if making a speech. He wears general's uniform and holds his hat in his l hand.

Burgoyne became a supporter of the Opposition after the attacks on him which followed his return from America, cf Wraxall, *Memoirs*, 1884, ii. 45–8. Under the Rockingham Ministry (on 7 June), he was made Commander-in-Chief in Ireland

$7 \times 4\frac{3}{8}$ in. (pl.).

6069 XVI. [MARQUIS OF ROCKINGHAM.]

JS

Published 17th June 1782 by C Bretherton

Engraving. Portrait of Rockingham standing in profile to the l. He wears a bag-wig, sword, Garter ribbon and star   Reproduced, Turberville, *Men and Manners of the Eighteenth Century*, 1926, p. 271.

$7 \times 4\frac{3}{8}$ in. (pl.).

6070 XVII. [EARL BATHURST.]

JS ff

Published 17th June 1782 by C Bretherton

Engraving. Bathurst standing almost full-face, but looking slightly to the r. His hands are thrust under his waistcoat; he wears a tie-wig and sword. He has a senile and almost imbecile expression.

Bathurst (1714–94), though he was removed from the Chancellorship in 1778, so that Lord Thurlow might strengthen North's Ministry, was Lord President of the Council from November 1779 till North's fall in March 1782   See No 4888.

$6\frac{7}{8} \times 4\frac{3}{8}$ in. (pl.).

6071 XVIII [LORD GRANTLEY.]

JS

Published 17th June 1782 by C Bretherton

Engraving. Grantley standing in profile to the l. His r. hand is thrust under his partly-buttoned coat, his l. is held under his coat-tail. He wears a tie-wig and a sword.

Sir Fletcher Norton (1716–89), Speaker from 1770 to 1780, had been created Baron Grantley on 9 Apr. 1782. He was called by satirists 'Sir Bull-face Double Face', see index. Mason in '1777 published an *Ode to Sir Fletcher Norton*; see *Mason's Satirical Poems with Horace Walpole's Notes*, ed. Toynbee, 1926, pp. 127 ff. See also Wraxall, *Memoirs*, 1884, i, pp 257 ff , ii, pp. 259 f   Reproduced, *Mason's Poems (op. cit.)*, p. 123.

$7 \times 4\frac{3}{8}$ in (pl)

6072 XIX. [LORD MAHON]

JS ff

Published 17 June 1782 by C Bretherton

Engraving. Portrait of Charles Stanhope (1753–1816), afterwards 3rd Earl Stanhope, styled Viscount Mahon 1763–86, M.P. for Wycombe, 1780–6. He is lean and tall, and stands in profile to the r. as if making a violent harangue, body bent forward, r. hand extended. He holds his hat and cane in his l. hand. He is plainly dressed, his lank and scanty hair tied at the neck.

Mahon, a Whig and an opponent of the American War, had come into prominence by his Bill for preventing bribery at elections. *Parl. Hist.*

xxiii, pp. 101 ff., 3 June, 1782; see Wraxall, *Memoirs*, ii, pp 341 ff For his revolutionary sympathies he was afterwards called 'Citizen Stanhope' and was much caricatured by Gillray, 1791–1808

$7 \times 4\frac{3}{8}$ in. (pl).

6073 XX [SIR CHARLES TURNER.]

JS ff

Published 17ᵗʰ June 1782 by C Bretherton

Engraving. Sir Charles Turner, Bart , standing in profile to the l. He is bent forward, his r. arm extended, holding his hat, as if making a speech. He is excessively thin, a cane is under his l arm, and his l hand is in a muff.

Turner of Kirkleatham, Yorkshire, was a Whig and a consistent opponent of the American War. He represented the City of York till his death in 1783. He was made a baronet on 20 Apr. 1782. See Wraxall, *Memoirs*, 1884, ii. 267–9. Selwyn (1 Mar. 1782) calls him 'that starved weasel'. *Hist MSS. Comm , Carlisle MSS.*, 1897, p 585. See No. 6256.

$6\frac{1}{8} \times 4\frac{1}{2}$ in. (pl.).

6074 [SIR FRANCIS MOLYNEUX AND Mᴿ QUARME.]

JS ff

Published 17ᵗʰ June 1782

Engraving. Sir Francis Molyneux, tall and broad, stands full-face, his hands behind his back, looking down at Robert Quarme, a very small man, standing in profile to the l Quarme's r. hand is thrust in his waistcoat, his l. rests on his sword, his hat is under his l arm Both wear bag-wigs, ruffles, and swords.

Molyneux was Gentleman Usher of the Black Rod, and Quarme was Yeoman Usher, both officers of the House of Lords. For Molyneux see Pigott, *The Jockey Club*,[1] 6th ed. 1792, pp 36–8

$7 \times 4\frac{3}{8}$ in. (pl.).

6075 [LORD JOHN CAVENDISH]

JS ff

Published 3ᵈ July 1782 by C Bretherton

Engraving. Cavendish standing in profile to the r., his r. leg advanced, holding his hat in his l hand as if making a speech in the House of Commons. He holds a document in his r hand

Cavendish, M P. for York and Chancellor of the Exchequer under Rockingham, by his absolute refusal to remain in office after Rockingham's death on 1 July, removed (it is said) all chance of Fox's remaining in office. Fitzmaurice, *Life of Lord Shelburne*, 1876, iii. 225–6 See No. 6167.

$6\frac{7}{8} \times 4\frac{3}{8}$ in. (pl.).

---

[1] According to Pigott. 'For him the word Bore was first brought into use. It was he who chiefly contributed to promote the currency of that word long has he been considered as the head of that numerous body of citizens . .' The *O E D*. has no instance of the word in the sense of a tiresome *person* earlier than 1812, but see No. 6144.

6076 [EARL OF SANDWICH.]

JS ff

Published by C Bretherton 3ᵈ July 1782

Engraving Sandwich, standing directed to the r., his head in profile, his r. hand thrust in his waistcoat, his l. in his waistcoat pocket

With the fall of North's Ministry in March 1782 Sandwich virtually retired from public life. As the accuser of Wilkes (Jemmy Twitcher), and afterwards as First Lord of the Admiralty under North, he was the subject of innumerable caricatures and lampoons.

7×4⅜ in. (pl.).

6077 [DUKE OF RICHMOND.]

JS ff

Published 3ᵈ July 1782 by C Bretherton

Engraving. Richmond standing in profile to the l. holding his cockaded hat in his r. hand. He wears the uniform of a general with epaulettes. His scanty hair is in a small pigtail queue

Richmond was Master-General of the Ordnance in Rockingham's Ministry At the date of this print the question of whether he should remain in office under Shelburne, or resign with his nephew Fox, was a burning one. See Walpole, *Last Journals*, ii. 449–51. Though he remained in office, in January 1783 he refused to attend the Cabinet meetings, disapproving of Shelburne's 'assumption of too much power' in the peace negotiations. *Ibid.* ii. 477. Fitzmaurice, *Life of Shelburne*, 1912, ii, pp. 208, 303 f. See No. 6023. Cf. also No. 6163.

7×4⅜ in. (pl.).

PERSONAL SATIRES
6078–6089
Series of *Tête-à-tête* portraits

6078 No. XXXIV. MISS R——DS
No XXXV. THE PATRIOTIC SENATOR

London, Publish'd by A Hamilton Jun', Fleet Street 1 Jan² 1782.

Engraving. *Town and Country Magazine*, xiii. 625 Two bust portraits in oval frames illustrate 'Histories of the Tête-à-tête annexed . . .' [*ut supra*]. He is the relative of a peer and the anti-ministerial member for a great county, having previously sat for a borough, the Government having attempted to frustrate his election for the county at a by-election by refusing him the Chiltern Hundreds. He is George Byng, elected for Middlesex at the General Election 1780, who had previously been M P. for Wigan. Cf. *Corr of George III*, v 23 See *Royal Register*, viii. 1783, p. 24; *Fox's Martyrs*, 1784, pp. 11–13.

Miss R. is a Miss Reynolds, reputed a near relation of Sir Joshua from her name and 'her masterly stile of painting in crayons'.

B.M.L., P.P. 5442 b.

Ovals, $2\frac{3}{4} \times 2\frac{5}{16}$ in.; $2\frac{3}{4} \times 2\frac{1}{4}$ in.

6079 No XXXVII THE PLIANT PENITENT.
No XXXVIII THE TITHE HUNTER

London, Publish'd by A. Hamilton Jun' Fleet Street, Jan² 20; 1782.

Engraving. *Town and Country Magazine*, xiii. 673. Two bust portraits in oval frames, both facing **T Q.** to the l., one that of a clergyman in gown and bands. They illustrate 'Histories of the Tête-a-tête annexed . . .' He was tutor of the son of Lord S—— on the grand tour, was given a valuable living near London, and also a good living in the City, and is in litigation with his parishioners over tithes He is probably James Waller, D.D, nephew of Terrick, bishop of London, Vicar of Kensington (1770–95), Rector of St Martin Ludgate, Prebendary of Mora and Archdeacon of Essex. E. H. Pearse, *Sons of the Clergy*, 1928, pp 202–3 n An attempt to collect tithes in kind on the choice fruit raised under glass by the Kensington market gardeners had caused much indignation. The case was decided in the vicar's favour. J. Middleton, *Agriculture of Middlesex*, 1798.

The lady has been one of the *haut ton* and a leader of fashion, and a distinguished *female phaeton* (cf. No 5936) until she became converted by a sermon of the Tithe Hunter, which was followed by a friendship between them. B.M L., PP. 5442 b.

Ovals, $2\frac{3}{4} \times 3\frac{3}{8}$ in.

6080 No. II. Mrs W——ST.
No. III. THE GALLANT ADMIRAL.

London, Publish'd Feb² 1ˢᵗ 1782 by A. Hamilton, Jun' Fleet Street.

Engraving *Town and Country Magazine*, xiv. 9 Two bust portraits in oval frames illustrate 'Histories of the Tête-à-Tête annexed...' Account of an admiral from whom a brother admiral obtained damages in a suit of *crim con*. Mrs. W is the daughter of a master and commander R.N , and the widow of a midshipman, who accepted the admiral's proposals and 'genteel present'.

Perhaps James Gambier (1723–89), vice-admiral 1780, who was tried for *crim. con.* with 'Admiral Knowles's lady', 11 June 1757. See No. 4974.

$2\frac{3}{4} \times 2\frac{5}{16}$ in. 　　　　　　　　　　　　　　B M L., P P 5442 b.

6081 No. IV. MRS P——LL.
No. V. THE BRITISH FABIUS.

London, Publish'd March 1, 1782, by A. Hamilton Jun' Fleet Street.

Engraving. *Town and Country Magazine*, xiv 65. Two bust portraits in oval frames illustrate 'History of the Tête-a-Tête annexed. or, Memoirs of the British Fabius and Mrs. P—w—ll.' An account of Sir Henry Clinton,[1] maintaining that accusations against his fondness of dress and parade while in America, 'so that New York has .. been another Capua', are exaggerated. The only lady with whom he was suspected of a connexion was Mrs. P——ll, daughter of an opulent planter and widow of Lieutenant P——ll who served in the British Army. She applied to the British Fabius for his protection. Clinton wears the ribbon and star of the Bath given in 1777. 　　　　　　　　　　　　　　　　　　　B.M.L., PP. 5442 b.

Ovals, $2\frac{3}{4} \times 2\frac{5}{16}$ in.

No VII. MRS C—N—Y.[2]
No. VIII. THE PERSUASIVE LOVER.

London, Publish'd April 1st 1782 by A Hamilton Jun' Fleet Street

Engraving. *Town and Country Magazine*, xiv 121. Two bust portraits in oval frames illustrate 'Histories of the Tête-à-Tête annexed . .' An account of Lord P——, a young peer who made a brilliant figure in Paris, introducing English fashions for riding dress. He returned to England on the outbreak of war (1778). Miss Connolly eloped from Ireland to be married in Scotland, where her lover died. Lord P—— used the mediation of Lady Ligonier, with whom he had been intimate, to induce her to become his mistress, but her character makes her friends suspect they may be married.

Of the peers whose names begin with P., Lord Plymouth seems best to fit this description, see No. 5761

Ovals, $2\frac{1}{4} \times 2\frac{1}{4}$ in. 　　　　　　　　　　　　　　B.M L., P.P. 5442 b.

6082 No. X. LADY MAGNET.
No. XI THE POLAR NAUTICUS.

London, Publish'd by A. Hamilton Jun' Fleet Street May 1st 1782.

Engraving. *Town and Country Magazine*, xiv. 177. Two bust portraits in oval frames illustrate 'Histories of the Tête-à-Tête annexed...' An account of Constantine John Phipps, 2nd Baron Mulgrave 1744–92. In 1773 he took

---

[1] He is identified by H Bleackley as Cornwallis, but the details, the accusation of supineness, and the ribbon and star of the portrait point to Clinton
[2] The plate is missing from the B M. copy of the magazine, the caption is taken from a copy in the London Library.

part in an expedition to discover a northern route to India, which returned without result from Spitzbergen. He published *A Voyage to the North Pole* in 1774.

Lady Magnet, widow of a baronet, has a son who 'though still a minor, gave the *haut ton* in the most *elevated manner*, drove one of the highest phaetons in Europe, and played as deep as any man upon the turf'. This points to Sir John Lade (see No. 5508). It was to Lady Lade, sister of Thrale, that Dr. Johnson said,

> With patches paint and jewels on
> Sure Phillis is not twenty-one!
> But if at night you Phillis see,
> The dame at least is forty-three!

Mme D'Arblay, *Diary*, i, pp. 141–2.

Ovals, $2\frac{3}{4} \times 2\frac{1}{4}$ in   B.M.L., P.P. 5442 b.

6083 No XIII. THE LOVELY M^{RS} ELL——S.
No. XIV. THE POPULAR GOVERNOR

London, Publish'd by A. Hamilton Junr Fleet Street, June 1st 1782.

Engraving *Town and Country Magazine*, xiv 233 Two bust portraits in oval frames illustrate 'Histories of the Tête-à-Tête annexed . . .' An account of the 3rd Duke of Portland 1738–1809, Lord-Lieutenant of Ireland 10 Apr –31 July 1782, with a reference to his quarrel with the Duke of Grafton in 1766 over the attempt of the Crown to dispossess him of Englewood Forest.

Mrs E. is Emily, daughter of a Cumberland farmer (a tenant of the duke's), and a widow, whom he met in London in distressed circumstances and provided with elegant apartments

Ovals, $2\frac{3}{4} \times 2\frac{5}{16}$ in.   B M.L., P.P. 5442 b.

6084 No XVI MISS C——Y [*sic*]
No XVII THE GALLANT COLONEL.

London, Published by A. Hamilton Junr Fleet Street 1 July 1782.

Engraving. *Town and Country Magazine*, xiv. 289. Two bust portraits in oval frames illustrate 'Histories of the Tête-à-Tête annexed: or, Memoirs of the Gallant Colonel, and the lovely Miss Claver—g'. The Colonel is a young gentleman of an ancient family, distinguished as a leader of fashion, has not seen active service, but has fought in duels. His recent promotion was due to the favour of 'a certain illustrious character' (evidently the Prince of Wales) at whose convivial parties and *petits-soupers* he attends He does not encroach upon his friend's territories, with 'Perdita, the Amst—ds, the Ell—ts, and the Birds of Paradise', i e Mrs Robinson, Mrs Armstead, Grace Dalrymple or Elliott, and Mrs. Mahon, see index

He is conjecturally identified by H Bleackley as Col St Leger
Miss C. is the daughter of an officer killed at York Town.

Ovals, $2\frac{3}{4} \times 2\frac{1}{4}$ in.   B.M.L., P.P 5442 b

6085 No XIX. THE AMIABLE MISS W——BB.
No XX THE INTREPID PARTIZAN

London, Publish'd by A. Hamilton Jun' Fleet Street. Aug¹ 1. 1782

Engraving. *Town and Country Magazine*, xiv 345 Two bust portraits in oval frames illustrate 'Histories of the Tête-à-Tête annexed . ' One is taken from Sir Joshua Reynolds's full-length portrait of Colonel Tarleton (1754–1833). It differs in certain details (the plume of the helmet, the ruffles at the neck, and the tilt of the shoulders) from the mezzotint by J R Smith published 11 Oct. 1782. An account of the career of Colonel Banastre Tarleton, mentioning the attentions he received from the Prince of Wales among others on his return to England after York Town, and his appearance in public with 'Perdita, the Bird of Paradise and the Arm—d'. See Nos. 6084, 6116.

Miss W is the daughter of a solicitor of eminence who died insolvent. She became companion to a lady of fortune, and eloped with the Colonel

Ovals, $2\frac{5}{8} \times 2\frac{1}{4}$ in. B M.L , P P. 5442 b.

6086 No XXII. M^{RS} P——PE
No. XXIII. THE FAVOURITE OF THE FAIR.

London. Publish'd by A. Hamilton. Jun' Fleet Street. 1 Sept' 1782.

Engraving *Town and Country Magazine*, xiv. 401. Two bust portraits in oval frames illustrate 'Histories of the Tête-à-Tête annexed. or, Memoirs of the Favourite of the Fair, and the beautiful Mrs. P——pe'. An account of the amours of the heir of a Scottish duke noted for being 'an accomplished gentleman', identified by H Bleackley as James, Marquis of Graham, b. 1755, succeeded as 4th Duke of Montrose 1790, d. 1837. See Wraxall, *Memoirs*, 1880, iii 385–7. Pigott, *Jockey Club*, 1792, Part ii, p. 27.

Mrs P is the daughter of a Cheapside hosier, married to an old and infirm merchant, who eloped with her husband's head clerk and was left destitute till she accepted her present lover's attentions.

Ovals, $2\frac{5}{8} \times 2\frac{3}{16}$ in. B.M.L , P P 5442 b.

6087 No. XXV. M^{RS} C——X.
No XXVI THE STEADY PATRIOT

London. Publish'd by A Hamilton Jun' Fleet Street Oct' 1. 1782.

Engraving *Town and Country Magazine*, xiv. 457. Two bust portraits in oval frames illustrate 'Histories of the Tête-à-Tête annexed ...' An account of Lord Effingham, referring to his throwing up his commission when his regiment was ordered for America.

During the late Ministry he lived in retirement and met in Yorkshire Mrs. Amelia C——x, deserted by her husband after six months' marriage. This is said to be the cause of his long absence from London (after the Gordon Riots). See Nos. 5995, 6061.

Ovals, $2\frac{9}{16} \times 2\frac{1}{8}$; $2\frac{5}{8} \times 2\frac{3}{16}$ in. B.M.L., P.P. 5442 b

6088 No. XXVIII. THE AMIABLE MISS D—S—T
No. XXIX. THE RECLAIMED ROVER.

London, Publish'd by A. Hamilton Jun' Fleet Street, Nov [1] 1782.

Engraving. *Town and Country Magazine*, xiv. 513. Two bust portraits in oval frames illustrate 'Histories of the Tête-à-Tête annexed; . . . or, Memories of the Reclaimed Rover, and the amiable Miss D—rs—t.' The descendant of a noble family, a 'very near relation' of his having been stabbed in the King's Arms, Pall Mall, by 'Mrs Philips',[1] as she records [sic] in her *Apology*. This was 'Sir H. P.' of Westwood Park, Worcester, i.e. Sir Herbert Pakington, d. 1748. The subject of the Tête-à-Tête is therefore probably Sir Herbert Pakington, who succeeded his brother in 1762 and died in 1795. His health was so much impaired by dissipation that he went for some months to Lisbon, where he recovered, and since his return has changed his manner of living

Miss D., the daughter of an eminent brewer in Kent, aimed at a coronet; at a fête-champêtre at Sevenoaks she yielded to a certain duke ['Dorset], became pregnant, and has now yielded to the Reclaimed Rover.

Ovals, $2\frac{3}{4} \times 2\frac{5}{16}$ in.   B M.L , P P. 5442 b.

6089 No XXXI MISS O'BR——N.
No. XXXII. THE HIBERNIAN ORATOR.

London, Publish'd by A. Hamilton Jun' Fleet Street, Dec' 1, 1782.

Engraving. *Town and Country Magazine*, xiv. 569. Two bust portraits in oval frames illustrate 'Histories of the Tête-à-Tête annexed . ' An account of Henry Grattan (1746–1820). As a student of the Middle Temple he is said to have been particularly distinguished by Kitty Fisher and others. His grant of £50,000 for his services to Ireland (see No. 6003) is referred to, and he is reputed to have refused an Irish peerage.

Miss O'Brien is the daughter of a rich merchant of Cork who has 'been distinguished in all the gay and elegant circles of Dublin'.

Ovals, $2\frac{6}{8} \times 2\frac{3}{10}$ in   B M.L , P P 5442 b.

6090 [MRS FRENCH]

Publish'd as the Act Directs Jy 23ᵈ 1782 C B. Jr [Bretherton]

Engraving (coloured impression). Sketch portrait (H L.) of an old lady in profile to the l. wearing a cap. She is seated in a chair holding a fan A rectangular frame is suggested, below is a small oval medallion containing a standing figure very freely drawn on a minute scale.

She is identified by Mr. Hawkins as Mrs. French and is presumably 'Old Madam French who lives close by the bridge at Hampton Court' Walpole, *Letters*, xiv. 11, 28 July 1787. She collected pictures, china, &c , dying 'at last' in Jan 1791. *Ibid* xiv. 359, 390.

$4\frac{1}{4} \times 3$ in (pl.).

6091 ORATOR HUM.

Chs Bretherton Jun' f. Publish'd Jany 30ᵗʰ 1782.

Engraving (coloured and uncoloured impressions) A bust portrait in profile to the r. of Dunning (cr. Baron Ashburton 30 Mar 1782), wearing a legal wig. For the title cf. Nos. 6042, 6173 It here anticipates both the acceptance of a pension in addition to a sinecure office which was so inconsistent with his former professions, and his becoming the confidential adviser of Shelburne after Rockingham's death. This and Nos. 6092, 6093 resemble similar sketch portraits by Gillray

$4\frac{1}{4} \times 3\frac{1}{10}$ in.

[1] Mrs Teresia Constantia Phillips

6092 [SIG^R PACCHEROTTI¹]

Ch⁵ Bretherton Jun' f Publish'd Jn^y 03th [sic] 1782

Engraving (coloured and uncoloured impressions). Bust portrait of Pacchierotti the singer, in profile to the r. See No 6125.

4¼×3⅛ in. (pl.).

6093 BŎRĔAS

[C. Bretherton]

Publish'd a[s the] Act Directs J^y 31st 82 C. B. f.

Engraving (coloured and uncoloured impressions). A very slight sketch (caricature) of Lord North, head and shoulders, full face, wearing his ribbon.

4×3⅛ in (pl)

6094 [C J FOX]

July 1782 J⁵ Bretherton f.

Engraving. A freely sketched portrait of Fox standing, full face, his hands under the flaps of his waistcoat in his breeches pockets. He wears a looped hat, and appears younger and less heavily jowled than in the caricatures of Gillray and Sayers at this time

7½×5⁷⁄₁₆ in. (pl.).

6095 [WILLIAM PARSONS]

[Gillray]

Pub^d May 4th 1782 by H Humphrey New Bond Street

Engraving (coloured impression) H L portrait of Parsons the actor, standing in profile to the l, taking a pinch of snuff from a box held at arm's-length. He wears a bag-wig and ruffles, his hat is under his l. arm. He is represented in the part of Sir Fretful Plagiary, he was the original Sir Fretful in the first production of Sheridan's *Critic* on 29 Oct. 1779 *D.N.B.* Grego, *Gillray*, p. 35. (Reproduction.)

2¾×2½ in (pl).

6096 THE GERMAN DANCING MASTER

H. I. H.² [Gillray]

Pub^d April 5th 1782 by H. Humphrey N° 18 New Bond Street

Engraving. A dancing-master, said to be Jansen, the German *maître de ballet*, in profile to the l., playing a kit or dancing-master's fiddle He stands on his r. toe, his l. leg held forwards. His lips protrude and he has a fierce expression. Facing him is his pupil, a boy, holding his hat in his l hand, his r arm raised: he imitates the pose and expression of his master. Behind him (l.) stands a younger boy, holding his hat in both hands. The back-

---

¹ Written on the back in an old hand.
² These letters are faintly etched in the l corner of the design.

ground is a panelled wall, on it is the lower part of an oval mirror in a carved frame, beneath which is a chair on which lies an open book.

Reprinted, *G.W.G.*, 1830. Grego, *Gillray*, p. 34, Wright and Evans, No. 369.

$6\frac{1}{8} \times 8\frac{1}{2}$ in.

6097 GENERAL MURRAY.

[? Gillray.][1]

London Pub^d Novr 15th 1782. by S. J. Neale, N° 352, near Exeter 'change, Strand.

Stipple. Bust portrait in an oval of Lieut.-General James Murray, probably drawn at his court-martial, see No. 6041. He is in profile to the r., wearing military uniform with epaulettes, has an expression of pained surprise, and looks old and worn.

$3\frac{7}{8} \times 3\frac{1}{8}$ in.

6098 A MODERN ANTIQUE,

Trumps Fecet [sic] 1782

[? Gillray.][2]

Pub^d Nov. 26th 1782 by H Humphrey N° 51 New Bond Street.

Engraving (coloured and uncoloured impressions) A very stout and short old lady seated at a card-table in profile to the l. frowning at the cards which she holds in her gloved l. hand. She wears a cap on her high-dressed hair, and from the back of her cap a spider is suspended on its thread. She wears a flowered dress, with lace-trimmed ruffles and apron. On the table in front of her are three coins and the ace of hearts

Probably one of the elderly leaders of fashion whom Gillray was so fond of caricaturing, cf. No. 6104.

$6\frac{1}{8} \times 4\frac{3}{8}$ in

6098 A A MODERN ANTIQUE;

Trumps Fecet, 1782.

A first state, without publication line On this has been drawn in pen a profile of the lady with a still more ferocious scowl, opposite this is written 'Losing Game'.

6099 THO^S WEST, D.D., FELLOW OF MAGDALEN COLLEGE OXFORD.

C. Knight Sculp.

Pub. Nov 1. 1782 by J. Thane[3] Printseller and Medalist Rupert Street Haymarket London

Engraving (coloured impression). W.L. profile portrait of a man in clerical wig, bands and gown, wearing a large mortar-board cap, walking to the r., his gown blowing stiffly behind him. He holds a glove in his

---

[1] Supposed to have been engraved by Gillray Note by Mr Hawkins
[2] Supposed to have been etched by Gillray Note by Mr Hawkins
[3] Almost illegible

gloved r. hand. Beneath the title is engraved *From an Original Drawing in the Possession of the Editor late in the Collection of Geo. Scott Esq* *F.R. & A S. S.*

West (1712(?)–81) was rector of Horsington, Lincs.

$8\frac{3}{8} \times 7$ in

6100 THE CALASH.

[?1782]

[Viscount Courtenay]

Engraving. Caricature of a thin lady, walking or standing in profile to the r., wearing one of the enormous hoods known as calashes from their resemblance to the hood of a gig This entirely obscures her face; the wearer holds the edge of it with a claw-like hand. A slight and amateurish sketch. Beneath it, the collector, R. Bull, has written, 'L^y Loughborough by y^e late Visc^t Courtney'

Charlotte, daughter of the first Viscount Courtenay (d. 1762), married Lord Loughborough in 1782 as his second wife, see *Corr. of Lord Auckland*, 1861, 1 33-4 Probably by her brother, the second Viscount, 1742-88. For the calash see Nos 5434, &c.

$4\frac{1}{4} \times 3$ in   'Honorary Engravers', i. No. 194.

6101 ELOQUENCE OR THE KING OF EPITHETS

Pub^d Jany 1st 1782 by H. Humphrey N° 18 New Bond Street

Engraving (coloured impression) A portrait of James Christie the elder (1730-1803) standing in his auctioneer's rostrum. His head is turned in profile to the l. He smiles insinuatingly, his hands held out, his hammer in his r. hand. The word 'eloquence' in the title is engraved at the bottom of the rostrum, and beneath the title is inscribed, *Let me entreat—Ladies—Gentlemen—permit me to put this inestimable piece of elegance under your protection,—only observe; — — — The inexhaustible Munificence of your superlitively* [sic] *candid Generosity must Harmonize with the refulgent Brilliancy of this little Jewel.!—!—.*

Cf a similar portrait of Langford, No 5171

Reproduced in colour, H. C. Marillier, *Christies 1766 to 1925*, p 18.

$10\frac{1}{4} \times 5\frac{11}{16}$ in.

6102 A SMUGGLING MACHINE OR
A CONVENIENT COS$_{\Lambda}$UWAY FOR A MAN IN MINIATURE.

Publish'd Jany 1782 by H. Humphry New Bond Street N° 18.

Engraving. A portrait of Richard Cosway, R.A., standing under the wide hooped petticoat of a tall lady, his wife, Maria, who puts her arms round him. His head and shoulders emerge from the petticoat slightly below the level of her waist; his face is in profile looking upwards. His r hand clutches her cloak, his l. is round her waist. She wears a flat ribbon-trimmed hat, and looks down at him saying, *Tis geting nothing—nay—tis geting worse than nothing*

In the background, on the wall (r.), is a picture of a little man wearing a bag-wig and sword, climbing up a ladder which rests on the breast of a woman. Beneath it is engraved

> *Lowliness is Young Ambitions Ladder,*
> *Whereto the climber upward turns his Face*
> *But when he once attains the upmost round*
> *He then unto the Ladder turns his back,*
> *Looks unto the clouds—scornin [sic] the base degrees*
> *By which he did assend.*
>
> Shak *Jul. Caesar.*

This represents Cosway climbing to fame, the woman being either Angelica Kauffmann or the Duchess of Devonshire. J. T. Smith, *Nollekens and his Times,* ed. W. Whitten, ii. 329, where the print is reproduced.
$9\frac{1}{2} \times 8\frac{3}{8}$ in.

6103 OLD WISDOM.

BLINKING AT THE STARS.

[Gillray]

Pub^d March 10th 1782 by W. Rennie.

Engraving (coloured and uncoloured impressions). Design in an oval. Dr Johnson, the head in profile to the r., with an owl's body and ass's ears, stands on two books, the lower his *Dictionary,* the upper his *Lives of the Poets.* The busts of poets stand on brackets (r.) above Johnson's head, each is irradiated with a star-shaped halo. They are *Pope, Milton,* a third head wearing a laurel wreath, the inscription concealed by Johnson's head; a fourth halo (l.) is visible. These are 'the stars' at which Johnson is blinking, but, though screwing up his eyes short-sightedly, he is not looking at them. The back wall, at right angles to the wall on which the busts are placed, is covered with bookshelves, in which folio volumes lean against one another. An open book lying beside the *Dictionary* is *Beauties of Johnson*

The *Prefaces Biographical and Critical to the Works of the most eminent English Poets,* which were the occasion of this satire, were published in 1779 and 1781. See also No 6328. Reprinted, *G.W G* 1830. Grego, *Gillray,* p. 33 Reproduced, Paston, Pl c.
$7\frac{7}{8} \times 6\frac{3}{4}$ in.

6104 ST. CECILIA.

[Gillray]

Pub^b April 24th 1782. by H. Humphrey. New Bond Street

Engraving (coloured and uncoloured impressions) Design in an oval A burlesque of Reynolds's painting of Mrs Sheridan as 'St. Cecilia'. Lady Cecilia Johnston sits at the organ in profile to the r , on a low stool, her face lit by rays which descend through clouds The place of the two angels in Reynolds's picture is taken by two squalling cats, who sit on the player's l , a book of music propped up in front of them

There is nothing to explain Gillray's animus against Lady Cecilia, whom, with Lady Archer, Lady Mount Edgcumbe, and Lady Buckinghamshire, he repeatedly satirized for gambling and other fashionable activities

Reprinted, *G W.G ,* 1830 Grego, *Gillray,* p 35
$6\frac{3}{4} \times 5\frac{3}{8}$ in.

6105 THE SHILLING OR THE VALUE OF A P . . Y C . . . R'S MATRIMONIAL HONOR

Publ: as the Act Dir · by H Humphrey New Bond S^t N° 18 Feb. 27, 1782[1]

Engraving. A stout man, seated (r.) with stag's horns growing from his forehead, turns away from a lawyer in wig and gown who approaches him from the l. One of a number of prints on an action brought by Sir Richard Worsley against one Bisset, a captain in the Hampshire Militia, for criminal conversation. The case was tried on 21 Feb. 1782 before Lord Mansfield, Worsley was awarded a shilling damages on the ground that he had countenanced and connived at his wife's adultery. The action was brought after Lady Worsley had eloped with Bisset.

The lawyer (his counsel were the Attorney-General (Wallace), Lee, Dunning, and Erskine) throws down a coin on the table beside Worsley, saying, *They would not believ you posses [sic] any your contrivance for his peeping has ruined your cause.* In his r. hand is a document, S^r R W . . .y Pl . . . f against Cap . . D . . D . . .t.

Worsley is exclaiming *O Lord O Lord no more than one shilling for my lost Honor* His horns are inscribed *W . m D . . st &c. G . . m &c P . . gh &c,* representing the names of those who gave evidence at the trial (Wyndham, Lord Deerhurst, Marquis of Graham, Lord Peterborough).

Above their heads, reclining on clouds, is Justice, blindfolded, her scales in the l hand, a sword in her r hand; she says, *Take away that badge of Distinction, Shame may transfer the colour to his face.* This refers to a coat of arms on the wall over Worsley's head in which the (red) hand of a baronet is conspicuous His hat and sword lie on the ground beside him A panelled wall forms the background; on the l. is a framed *Plan of the Isle of Wight.* Worsley (1751–1805) was Governor of the Isle of Wight, 1770–Apr. 1782, and published *The History of the Isle of Wight,* 1781.

For the scandal see H Walpole, *Letters,* xii. 134, 31 Dec. 1781, and xii. 179–80, 22 Feb. 1782. The trial, and several scurrilous pamphlets in verse on the subject, are in B M.L. 11631. g. 31, 1–5. See Nos. 6106–6112.

$9\frac{1}{8} \times 7\frac{3}{8}$ in.

6106 A BATH OF THE MODERNS.

Publish'd March 4 1782 by E. Darchery N° 11 St James's Street.

Engraving. The interior of a room in which a lady is dressing, an attendant standing beside her. The outside of the building is shown on the l.; a stout military officer supports on his shoulders a thin one, who is looking into the room through a window under the thatched roof. This is Sir Richard Worsley, Colonel of the Hampshire Militia, helping Captain Bissett to look into the room of a cold bath establishment at Maidstone. Worsley is saying, *Captain do you view the whole Garrison.* He answers *Only the Breast work & cover'd way.*

Lady Worsley is sitting on a chair in profile to the l. pulling on her stockings, fully dressed except that the front of her dress exposes her breast. She wears a military coat with epaulettes, and is saying, *Bliss —it he goes all lengths to pleasure me* The attendant, an elderly woman in cap and apron, holds up her hands saying, *Lord my lady I believe the Captain*

---

[1] The *Morning Herald,* 9 Mar. 1782, advertises this as published 'This day . . . price 1s. plain and 2s. coloured. . . .'

wants to be in the watering place. Beneath the title is engraved, *lately discovered at Maidstone, by Sr Cuckeldome Worse-Sly, Fellow of the Society of Antiqueereones.*

The evidence at the trial was that Lady Worsley was in the habit of going to the cold bath at Maidstone, where the Worsleys lived when Sir Richard was in camp at Coxheath, while her husband and his friend Bissett waited for her; that on one occasion, when she had almost finished dressing, Worsley tapped at the door, saying, 'Bissett is going to get up to look at you', and his face appeared at the window. This was the occasion of a number of pictorial satires. Worsley was F.R.S. and F.S.A. See Nos. 6105, 6107-12

$7\frac{1}{4} \times 10\frac{5}{8}$ in

6107 MAIDSTONE WHIM.

Pub Mar^th 8. [sic] 1782 by W Wells N° 132 Fleet Street

Engraving (coloured and uncoloured impressions) Sir Richard Worsley, wearing stag's antlers, stands outside a brick building, his back to the wall On his shoulders stands Captain Bissett, looking in at a window. Between Worsley and the wall is a wooden seat; on the r is a door over which is [T]HE BATH Worsley is saying *S——r [Seymour] B——ts [Bissets] looking at you*; words spoken by him according to the evidence at the trial His horns are inscribed, *L^d P——h, L^d D——st, M^r W——m, M· of G——m, M^r S——th,* see No 6105; see also Nos. 6106, 6108-12.

$8\frac{7}{16} \times 6\frac{1}{2}$ in.

6108 THE MAIDSTONE BATH OR THE MODERN SUSANNA.

Candaules invenit Gyges fecit. [Gillray?]

London Publish'd as the Act directs, March 12th 1782, N° 28 at the Ancient and Modern Print Warehouse, Hay Market.

Engraving (design in a circle) A stone building in which a bath is sunk in the floor. A young woman (Lady Worsley) stands in it, the water just above her knees. An attendant stands behind her holding a towel, both look up, the attendant with alarm, at the face of a man (Captain Bisset) looking through one of two oval apertures (r) high up in the wall In front of and below the bath is the upper part of a flight of spiral steps leading to high iron bars at right angles to the wall at the end of the bath, through which is seen Sir Richard Worsley holding Captain Bisset on his shoulders. This part of the design is in shadow.

The attendant is an attractive young woman wearing a hat The lady's clothes and hat are heaped on a chair behind her On the wall above the bath is a tap and below it a small basin built into the wall. The design has delicacy and charm in spite of its scurrilous intention See Nos. 6105-7, 6109-12

Diam. $10\frac{1}{4}$ in.

6109 SIR RICHARD WORSE-THAN-SLY, EXPOSING HIS WIFES BOTTOM; O FYE!

[Gillray.]

Pub^d 14th March 1782. by H Brown, Oxford Market

Engraving. The interior of a room in the floor of which is sunk a circular bath. A lady (Lady Worsley), holding a little drapery, steps into it. Through a window high in the wall behind her (l.) appear the head and shoulders of Captain Bisset Outside the building (l.) Sir R Worsley stoops down, his back to the wall, to support Bissett, who stands on his shoulders. Worsley, in cockaded hat and regimentals, looks towards the spectator, saying, *My Yoke is Easy & my Burden Light* Bisset is saying, *Charming View of the Back Settlements Sr Richard.* On the farther side of the bath (r.) stands a maid-servant of attractive appearance, holding her mistress's clothes; she holds up her r hand saying, *Good lack! My Lady the Captn will see all for Nothing.* On the back wall is nailed a *Map of the Isle of Wight* Worsley ceased to be Governor of the Isle of Wight in Apr. 1782. See No 6110, another version of this design See also Nos 6105–8, 6111, 6112. Grego, *Gillray*, p. 33, describing either this plate or No. 6110

12×9½ in.

6110 SIR RICHARD WORSE-THAN-SLY, EXPOSING HIS WIFES BOTTOM,—O FYE!

[Gillray.]

Pubd March 14th 1782 by W. Humphrey No 227 Strand

Engraving (coloured and uncoloured impressions) Another version in reverse, with several alterations, of No. 6109. The two women's figures are almost identical in both plates Worsley stands on tip-toe (l.) holding Bisset, who sits, instead of standing, on his shoulders; his hat is on the ground, and by it lies a paper inscribed *My Yoke is Easy & my Burden light.* The words spoken by Bisset and the maid are the same in both. In this design the ceiling of the room has a circle inset in the rectangle which may support a dome. A pair of mules stands beside the bath (r.). According-ing to a note on one impression, this plate was suppressed and is very rare. See also Nos 6105–8, 6111, 6112

11 15/16 × 8 13/16 in.

6111 LADY WORSLEY, DRESSING IN THE BATHING HOUSE.

[n d Feb –Mar. 1782]

Engraving. Probably an illustration from a book. Lady Worsley, dressed in an undergarment or dressing-gown, seated on a chair, is putting on her stockings. Part of a circular bath sunk in the floor is shown on the r An attendant stands behind her holding up a cloak or wrapper. The face of Captain Bisset (l.) looks in through a window over the door. On the wall (r.) is a framed picture probably intended to represent Susannah and the Elders See Nos. 6105, 6110, 6112.

5⅝×3¾ in.

6112 A PEEP INTO LADY ! ! ! ! ! Y'S SERAGLIO

[Gillray.]

Pubd April 29th 1782. by W. Humphrey No 227 Strand.

Engraving. On the r. is a bedroom, a man and woman embracing on a bed with a high tester draped with curtains. A man leaves the room by a door on the extreme r. On the l. is a staircase, descending from l. to r and ending in a door leading to the bedroom. On this stand, one behind the other, nine men. One is in military uniform, one is a bearded Jew, one is a fat parson in gown and bands. Labels inscribed with words issue from their mouths. Over the door is a picture, inscribed *Lucretia*, she is about to stab herself. Along the balustrade of the staircase is engraved, "*One lover to another still succeeds, Another & another after that —And the last Fool is welcome as the former· Till having lov'd his hour out he gives place, And mingles with the herd that went before him.*" *Rowe's Fair Penitent.*

The coarseness and scurrility of the subject are not reflected in its drawing. It is an incredibly libellous comment on the case of Sir Richard and Lady Worsley, see Nos. 6105-11.

$9\frac{3}{8} \times 13\frac{3}{4}$ in.

6113 FATHER D . . , LEAVING HIS CATHOLICK VOWS FOR THE JOYS OF THE FLESH.

[? Hixon][1]

Pub May 9th 1782 by T. Cornell.

Engraving. A man and woman riding (l. to r.) on the same horse along a country road. The woman sits in front, holding the reins and riding astride. She holds up a purse in her l hand saying, *This will pay you for your Trouble Honey.* The man sits behind, his feet in the stirrups, his l. hand on the woman's waist, he says, *Promise me that and I will never say another Mass.* The man wears ordinary riding-dress, the woman wears a feathered hat over a frilled cap, and a tight coat over a ruffled shirt.

Behind them (l) walks a young woman, wearing a cap of lace and ribbons; she holds her apron to her eye, saying, *The Old witch is carrying away my Director.* The words issue from the speakers' mouths on long scrolls. A sign-post on the road (r) points (l.) *To London* and (r) *To Newbury and Well Hall* In the foreground (l) is a tree; the background is an undulating landscape with a square church tower and the roofs of a village among trees.

$6\frac{5}{16} \times 9\frac{1}{4}$ in

6114 THE PORTLAND PLACE A——R. [ARCHER] DRIVING WITHOUT A BEAU TO R——D'S PERFUME WAREHOUSE P—LL M—LL.

Pubd as the Act directs June 18th 1782. by C. Clark No 6 Princes Street.

Engraving (coloured impression). Lady Archer in profile to the r. driving a very high gig, poised on high springs, with four horses, beside her sits a young girl. She wears a feathered hat and a coat of masculine cut. On the side of the gig is an *A* surmounted by a baron's coronet *A* also appears on the harness of the horses.

Behind the horses on the r. is the large glass window of a shop, the door also having glass panels Above the window on each side of the door is inscribed PERFUME WAREHOUS[E] Over the door is written *Italian Washes, Ivory Teeth, Mouse Eye Brows, &c* ; and *The Best French Roush* In the window various articles are exhibited. glass jars, one inscribed *Marsh*, switches of hair, a mask, and a fool's cap, &c. The shop is a corner one,

[1] Hixon has been written on the print by Mr Hawkins.

the glass window is of unusual size and appears to extend round the corner of the shop

Lady Archer was noted both as a whip and for painting her face, see No 5879.

$8\frac{7}{8} \times 13\frac{3}{8}$ in

6115 MONUMENTS LATELY DISCOVERED ON SALISBURY PLAIN

[Gillray]

Pub^d June 15th 1782 by H. Humphrey New Bond Street.

Engraving (coloured impression) A satire on the attentions of the Prince of Wales to Lady Salisbury In the foreground are four figures with numbers referring to explanatory notes in the margin On the right the Prince of Wales (*2*), wearing a ribbon and star, stands beside (*1*) (Lady Salisbury), holding her r. hand in his r., his l. arm is round her waist; she holds a fan in her l. hand. They are both in profile, looking towards each other; he says,

> *Oh let me thus . . .*
> *Eternally admiring, fix & gaze*
> *On those dear Eyes; for every glance they send*
> *Darts thro' my Soul —*

In the centre stand a man and a woman whose faces and limbs resemble blocks of stone, left unfinished by a sculptor; the man (*3*) is James, 6th Earl (afterwards 1st Marquis) of Salisbury (1748–1823), he clenches his fists, and stamps, his l leg raised, and saying, *Zounds S^r leave my Wife alone or I'll tell the Old Wig* [George III]. Rudimentary horns are sprouting from his forehead The lady (*4*), whose features are more defined than those of Salisbury, stands between, and slightly behind, Salisbury and the Prince of Wales. She holds out both hands in distress saying, *To leave me thus!* She is Mrs Robinson or Perdita, who had been deserted by the Prince of Wales. Behind and on the l two ladies and three men, holding hands, dance in a ring.

In the lower margin is etched, *The Figures N. 1 & 2 are Judged by Conoiseurs to have lately been animated with the Cælestial Fire—N° 3 is an unfinish'd resemblance of the Human Form, from the Vacancy of Countenance & roughness of the Workmanship this Figure cannot be supposed ever to have been intended as a companion to N° 1* [Lady Salisbury, whom he married in 1773; she was Mary Amelia, d of the 1st Marquis of Downshire] *N° 4 from the Attitude &c is supposed to represent some forlorn Dido or forsaken Ariadne of Quality &c &c &c*

The ladies in the middle distance may be intended for others to whom the Prince had paid attentions; his name was by Feb 1782 already associated with Lady Jersey and Lady Melbourne *Hist MSS Comm , Carlisle MSS* 1897, p. 575 According to Wraxall (*Memoirs*, 1884, v. 369 f), his attachment to Lady Melbourne was preceded (1780) by one for Lady Augusta Campbell, and followed by one for the Duchess of Devonshire, cf No 6263

For the Prince of Wales and Mrs. Robinson ('Florizel and Perdita') see No. 5767, &c. Reprinted *G W G* , 1830 Reproduced, Paston, pl clxv. Grego, *Gillray*, p 37

$8\frac{1}{8} \times 12\frac{11}{16}$ in.

6116 THE THUNDERER

[Gillray.]

Pub^d Augt 20th 1782 by E^k D'Achery St James's Street

Engraving. Colonel Tarleton as Bobadil stands holding out a drawn sword, his l hand on his hip boasting of his valour His plumed helmet caricatures that in Reynolds's well-known portrait of Tarleton On his r , behind his sword-arm, stands the Prince of Wales, with a plume of three ostrich feathers in place of a head, the centre feather having some resemblance to a face. He wears the garter ribbon, and very wide and wrinkled top-boots with small pointed feet; in his l hand is a riding-whip

Bobadil is saying, *They have assaulted me some Three, Four, Five, Six of them together, & I have driven them afore me like a Flock of Sheep,—but this is nothing, for often in a mere frolic I have challeng'd Twenty of them, kill'd them;—Challeng'd Twenty more, kill'd them,—Twenty more, killed them too,— & thus in a day have I kill'd Twenty Score; twenty score, that's two hundred; two hundred a day, five days a thousand; thats—a—Zounds, I can't number them half; & all civilly & fairly with this one poor Toledo!*

The Prince says, *I'd as lief as twenty Crowns I could talk as fine as you, Captn* (*Col^l* has been scored through and *Captn* added with a caret, probably to show that 'Captain Bobadil' is an officer with the rank of Colonel)

They are standing outside the door (r) of a dubious place of entertainment Over the door is inscribed THE WHIRLIGIG *Alamode Beef, hot every Night.* Above this is a branch, representing a bush, the sign that wine is sold, and on a projecting beam, the sign of the house· the figure of a courtesan seated with outstretched legs and arms saying,

> *This is the Lad'll kiss most sweet*
> *Who'd not love a Soldier?*

For the whirligig, a punishment for army prostitutes, see *Johnson's England*, ed. A S Turberville, p. 72

Beneath the title is engraved, *Vide; Every Man in his Humour, alter'd from Ben Johnson.*

Tarleton was very brave, and distinguished himself in the American War (though defeated at Cowpens), but was notoriously boastful Mrs Robinson (Perdita) lived with him after she had been deserted by the Prince of Wales See Nos 6085, 6221. Grego, *Gillray*, p 41. Wright and Evans, No 378 (Both identify Bobadil with Major Topham)

12½×9 in.

6117 PERDITO AND PERDITA—OR—THE MAN AND WOMAN OF THE PEOPLE

T. Colley Fe

Pub^d by W Richardson N° 68 high Holborn Decr 17. 1782

Engraving Mrs Robinson driving Charles Fox (r. to l.) in a phaeton or gig Only part of one wheel and the hind-quarters of a pair of horses appear in the print, the figures being on a large scale Fox, with the ill-dressed hair and the heavy 'gunpowder jowl' which are now beginning to characterize his satirical portraits, holds his hat in his l hand, showing C. F stamped inside the crown; he has a disconsolate expression Mrs. Robinson flourishes her whip in her r hand; she wears ringlets, a high-crowned hat trimmed with feathers, a short tight coat of masculine cut over a frilled shirt.

Her cipher, *M. R.*, in a wreath, appears on the side of the carriage. This, and the fact that she is driving, is intended to show that she is keeping Fox. On the upper margin of the print is engraved, "*I have now not fifty ducats in the World & yet I am in love*". They drive past the gateway and front of St. James's Palace, which forms the background

The title appears to be taken from a *mot* of George Selwyn: Walpole wrote (7 Sept. 1782) to Earl Harcourt, 'Charles Fox is languishing at the feet of Mrs Robinson. George Selwyn says, who should the *man of the people* live with, but with the *woman of the people*.' *Letters,* xii 328 A paragraph in the *Morning Herald,* 17 Sept. 1782, ran, 'In the late Phaetonic expedition of Perdita and the eloquent Patriot it is to be distinguished that the lady gives the gentleman the airing, and not, as usual, the gentleman the lady' Lady Sarah Napier writes 11 Sept. 1782, 'Charles *lives* with Mrs. Robinson, goes to Sadlers Wells with her, and is all day figuring away with her' *Life and Letters of Lady Sarah Lennox,* ii. 25. The name *Perdito* suggests the political and financial plight of Fox.

The amours of Mrs. Robinson, the Prince of Wales, Fox, and Col. Tarleton, were the subject of many newspaper paragraphs at this time. *The Morning Herald,* 16 Aug 1782, announced that Mr Fox has entirely chasséd the provincial Lieut.-Col. from the Suite of the amorous Perdita, who has now the felicity of driving the ex-minister in her pony drawn curricle for a daily airing to Turnham Green See No 5767, &c. and Nos. 6221, 6266, 6318, 6319, 6320

The manner suggests that it may be by Gillray imitating the style of Colley, see No. 6228, &c.

$8\frac{1}{2} \times 12\frac{11}{16}$ in.

6118 A CAUTION TO THE UNWARY.

Published May y^e 21 1782 by P. Dawe Goodge Street Tottenham Court Road.

Engraving One man (r.) in profile to the l leans over an E. O table Four others stand opposite him, conversing and pointing to the table. Another, in riding-dress (l.), leans against the wall of the room. One of the four wears the bag-wig, laced coat, and sword, which at this time were worn only on special occasions, another wears a clerical gown and bands. The table is lit by two candles, a lighted candle sconce hangs in the centre of the back wall Beneath the design is etched:

> *As Various Fish do Various baits require*
> *So different men, some different Games admire,*
> *Here Sharpers meet, in Combination[1] Wait,*
> *And hold to every fool, his favorite Bait.*
>
> *Some fond of Billiards, Some to Hazard go,*
> *And some, Get quicker ruin'd at E. O.*
> *Here Tradesmen Come, but do perhaps forget*
> *It is their Creditors, that risk the Bett*

For the game of E O. see No 5928, and for the campaign against the game see also Nos. 6119, 6120.

$6\frac{11}{16} \times 7\frac{5}{8}$ in

[1] i e conspiracy, see *O E D*

6119 JUSTICE WRIG——TS A COMING OR SECRETARY E O. ALIAS REYNARD PUT TO FLIGHT.

[T. Colley?]

Pub^d by T. Colley Augt 19 1782. Rolls Building fetter lane

Engraving (coloured impression) Gamblers at an E O. table disturbed by a peace-officer with a stick who attempts to force open a door (r.) which a man inside tries to hold shut. The circular table and two overturned chairs are the only furniture of the room. Fox, as a fox, wearing a coat and wig and with human hands, stands by the table (r.) looking over his shoulder at the door, saying, *what's the Devil coming for me before my time.* The peace-officer says, *Open the door you Gamblers*; the man holding it shut looks round saying, *be quick Gents I'm over power'd.* On the farther side of the table are three men: next Fox, an officer wearing a cockaded hat and epaulettes says, *O Reynard the Hounds are after you in full cry.* The other two are running in profile to the l., the foremost saying, *by Jupiter open the back door the Justice is here* In front of the table and on the l. a short stout gambler in profile to the r. holds his ground, his hands on the table, saying, *pray help gentlemen.* On the floor at his feet lies a candle-stick, the candle broken but still burning.

As a result of a petition from the justices of Middlesex and Westminster, on the great number of E.O. tables in public gaming-houses in Westminster, the harm which they did and the ineffectiveness of the laws against gaming to deal with the game of E. O, a Bill was brought in 'to prevent gaming', after which the justices immediately raided gaming-houses and destroyed tables, apparently acting on the orders of Townshend, the Secretary of State. See *Parl. Hist.* xxiii, pp. 110–13, and cf. Wraxall, *Memoirs*, 1884, ii, pp 14 f. See also Nos. 5928, 6118, 6120.

$6\frac{1}{8} \times 9\frac{1}{8}$ in.

6120 THE W—ST—R JUST-ASSES A BRAYING—OR—THE DOWNFALL OF THE E. O. TABLE.

[Gillray]

Pub^d Augt 26th 1782. by W. Humphrey N° 227 Strand.

Engraving (coloured and uncoloured impressions). An E. O. table lies in the street, outside a house, its legs already broken, its central mechanism damaged It is being further attacked with mallets and a poker by justices and constables of Westminster. The two Bow Street justices, Addington and Wright, and their clerk, Bond, have asses' heads Justice Addington (l), his head bleeding, is being chased from the open door of the house by a maidservant of meretricious appearance who holds a broom above her head as if to strike; she says, *Come out here! I'll Just-ass Addlehead you! what you'll open my Lock too, without a key will you?* Addington holds his hands over his head saying, *Help! Murder!—help—Fire! Thieves: Popery! help!* Justice Wright, wearing a bag-wig, stands over the table, his mallet raised above his head about to strike the table. A constable attempts to stop him, holding up both hands, saying, *O Lord, Mr Just-ass you'r not Wright!* [The W has been scored through] *they'll dite you on Magna-Charta for breaking open their Houses! & have you before the Judges.* Wright answers, *The Judges? damn the Judges! & Magna-Charta too! ! our Warrants above them both*—This constable wears a wig, a hat in whose upturned brim is a tobacco-pipe, a belted coat, a constable's staff terminating in a crown thrust through the belt. On the r of the table stand two other constables of disreputable appearance, one wields a poker, the other a large hammer; only the latter has a constable's staff protruding from his waistcoat pocket; his breeches are undone at the knee, his stockings ungartered. On the extreme l Bond, the clerk at Bow Street, stands on an upturned tub, his hands on his hips, saying, *Slap away Boys, slap away· I am* Bond *for all the mischief you do—I hope soon to be a Just-ass myself, for my Ears are now grown almost as long as Just-ass Addleheads—*

The background is the lower part of the house from which the E O. table has been taken, showing the door, part of two sash-windows. Plaster has fallen off in patches showing bricks

Below the title is engraved *N B The Jack-Asses are to be indemnified for all the mischief they do, by the Bulls & Bears of the City*

This satire is founded on a raid on 1 Aug on Dr Graham's, the quack, who had moved his Adelphi establishment, see Nos 5766, &c , 6325, to Schomberg House, Pall Mall, calling it the 'Temple of Health and of Hymen' [1] In a raid three days earlier the tables had been cut to pieces but the constables 'were not strong enough to take the company, for there were not less than 300 persons present' On this occasion Justices Hyde, Wright, and Addington broke two tables, 'Mr. Addington was very severely hurt by a stroke of a bludgeon on his head—an enormous crowd gathered round the house, report having spread that Mr Addington was killed' The allusion to 'Bulls and Bears' was probably inspired by the statement that the laudable activity of the justices was caused 'by an application from the Directors of the Bank to Mr Secretary Townshend, stating that they had suffered considerably by this public practice of gaming in the Metropolis, and requesting, 'on behalf of themselves, and the Public, that the laws now in being against gaming, might be extended as far as possible . . .' *London Chronicle,* 30 July–1 Aug , 1–3 Aug 1782

The satire is also a characteristic attack on the methods and personnel of the Bow Street office, which Gillray followed up in No. 6121 Addington (see No 5415) and Wright had been Bow Street magistrates under Sir John Fielding, who died in 1780 Bond was the very capable Bow Street clerk, see No 5599, afterwards made a magistrate See also Nos 5928, 6118, 6119. Grego, *Gillray,* p. 43.

$9 \times 13\frac{3}{8}$ in

6121 SAMPSON OVERCOME BY A PHYSITIAN.

[Gillray n.d , after 1st Oct. 1782.]

Invented by a Theif!   *Engrav'd by a Pickpocket!*

Publishd by Bonde *at the Thieftakers office Bow Street.*

Engraving. Sampson Wright sitting in an arm-chair behind a small square table He shrinks back, holding up his hands, as a man standing in front of the table thrusts his fist towards his face, saying, *You Rascal! I'll break every Bone in your Body.* A youth (r) standing behind the assailant says, holding up a handkerchief, *O Lord! O Lord! my poor Pap'll be killd!* At the

[1] Byng, M P for Middlesex, said on 5 June, 1782 'E O tables were now to be found in every part of the town . he did not doubt, but shortly the electric bed itself would be turned into an E. O. table.' *Parl. Hist* xxiii, p 110.

magistrate's r. hand stands (l) a man who appears disconcerted; he is probably Bond, the clerk

On the wall over Wright's head are two prints, one of a rat caught in a trap called *Trap'd*; the other of a bird. this resembles a cock standing on a vase or pot; and if so it may represent the brutal sport of cock-throwing practised on Shrove-Tuesday, which, thanks to the efforts of Sir John Fielding and the Bow Street magistrates, had been more or less stopped in London. Possibly some such print with a cautionary intention was actually exhibited at Bow Street. Perhaps, however, the bird represents a decoy, if so it would be more in keeping with the spirit of this satire On the table are writing materials and a purse inscribed *Dirty Shillings*, beside it lie coins

It was a recurrent calumny against the Bow Street magistrates from Henry Fielding onwards that they used 'Thieftakers' to decoy persons into crime for the sake of rewards to be gained by convicting them. This is implied by the print *Trap'd*, as well as by the term *Thief Taker's Office* in the imprint. *Bonde* is an allusion to Bond, the clerk at Bow Street A more recent accusation was that by their campaign against E. O. tables they had violated the liberty of the subject and 'Magna Charta', see No 6120.

Beneath the title is etched:

"*If e'er we want a very valiant Knight,*
"*Have we not Sampson—bold Sir*
                    Sampson Wright
                              Vide Beaut^s of Admin^n.

This Plate is humbly dedicated to the Magistrates of Westminster, as a grateful tribute to the unshaken integrity of a late Beknighted Justice, by their obliged Servant   On—slow—Dry—Butter.

Sampson Wright, who had been Sir John Fielding's clerk, then an assistant magistrate at Bow Street, and had succeeded Fielding as Chief Magistrate on his death in 1780, was knighted on 4 Sept 1782 The quotation (incorrect) is from a scurrilous political poem, the frontispiece to which, *Ecce*, dated 1 Oct. 1782, is No 6033. The lines (p. 27) are

When deep-laid plots of state, or war are plann'd,
Say are not N——th [North] and S——ch [Sandwich] both at hand?
And, if, to crown the whole you want a knight,
Have we not Sampson—hold—*Sir Sampson Wright?*

For Bond see No. 5599, and for another attack on the Bow Street magistrates by Gillray, No. 6120. Cf also No. 5197 Grego, *Gillray*, p. 43. 11¼ × 9¼ in.

6122 JUDGE THUMB, OR—STICKS OF A LAWFUL SIZE FOR FAMILY DISCIPLINE.

Pub by I Cooke, Temple Bar Novr. 21. 1782.   [? Hixon]

Engraving. Judge Buller in judge's wig and gown, walking, r to l, carrying in both hands a bundle of rods resting on his l shoulder He is saying, *Here's amusement for married gentlemen or, a Specific for a Scolding Wife; who buys of me.*

In the background (l.) a man has seized his wife by the arm, and raises a stick to beat her; she says: *Oh Murder! Murder! Oh cruel Barbarian.* He answers, *Cruel, ha! its according to Law, you Jazabel* Both are dressed in the fashion of the day; she wears a cap, a wide petticoat, and frilled apron.

This would appear to have suggested Gillray's well-known satire, No. 6123, which it closely resembles in design; see also No 6124. Reproduced, Paston, Pl. ccix.

$9\frac{5}{8} \times 7\frac{5}{8}$ in.

6123 JUDGE THUMB, OR—PATENT STICKS FOR FAMILY CORRECTION: WARRANTED LAWFUL[1]

[Gillray]

Pubᵈ Novʳ 27ᵗʰ 1782, by E. D'Achery, Sᵗ James's Street.[1]

Engraving (coloured and uncoloured impressions). Judge Buller, walking l. to r, in judge's wig and gown. He carries a bundle of rods on his l. shoulder, another bundle under his r arm He is saying, *Who wants a cure for a rusty Wife? Here's your nice Family Amusement for Winter Evenings! Who buys here.* His head is very fully characterized, and is, according to a contemporary note on one impression, 'a very striking likeness'.

In the distance, on the r., a screaming woman runs away from her husband, who raises his stick above his head with both hands She cries *Help! Murder for God's sake, Murder!* He says, *Murder, hay? its Law you Bitch! its not bigger than my Thumb!* They are dressed like working people. The background is a high stone wall, freely sketched, with clouds above it.

Buller (1746–1800) was reported to have said that a husband could thrash his wife with impunity provided that the stick was no bigger than his thumb. See Nos 6122, 6124. Grego, *Gillray*, pp 43–4; Wright and Evans, No 13.

$12 \times 8\frac{13}{16}$ in

A reduced copy (coloured) is in 'Caricatures', v, p. 6. B.M L. Tab. 524. a. Another reduced copy was published in *The Caricatures of Gillray* [1818] B.M.L 745 a 6

Both copies, $6\frac{3}{4} \times 5\frac{1}{16}$ in.

6124 MR JUSTICE THUMB IN THE ACT OF FLAGELLATION.
[1 Feb. 1782]

Engraving From *The Rambler's Magazine.* Judge Buller (r), in judge's wig and robes, is raising a stick above the shoulders of a woman, who cowers away from him, holding up her hands. He says *Tis no bigger than my Thumb.* She says, *Would I had known of this before Marriage.* She is dressed in a cap, a petticoat, and an under-bodice; her stays lie on a chair (l.) against which a cat is rubbing itself. A dog (r.) barks. Leaning against the wall is a large bundle of rods like those in Nos 6122, 6123 A partly-rolled document lies on the floor inscribed *A Husband may Chastize his Wife with a Stick the Size of his thumb Coke.*

$5\frac{1}{8} \times 3\frac{5}{8}$ in.

6125 A SUNDAY CONCERT.

[By C. Loraine Smith][2]

Pubᵈ 4ᵗʰ June 1782 by M. Rack London

Aquatint. Musicians are grouped round a piano. Their names (some mis-spelt) are written in the margin. The pianist sits in profile to the r. looking

---

[1] On one impression *W Humphry 227 Strand* has been substituted for *E D'Achery*   [2] Written on the print.

fixedly at his score; he is Ferdinando Bertoni, a Venetian composer who accompanied his friend Pacchierotti to England. The most prominent of the musicians is Pacchierotti, who stands behind the piano next the pianist, holding open a music book, but smiling at a lady, who sits (r.) on a bench among the performers She is Lady Mary Duncan, whose admiration for Pacchierotti's singing was the talk of the town, carried to the point of absurdity, and of discourtesy to other singers. (Walpole, *Letters*, xii 141, 3 Jan. 1782, and xv 16–17, 4 July 1791.) She is the largest figure in the design, out of scale with the other figures. She sits in profile to the r. holding up a closed fan, gazing intently at Pacchierotti Behind her stands the player of the bass, identified as Cariboldi Seated on the bench next her, on her r. hand and wearing spectacles, is a man playing the oboe, identified as Hayford. Seated in a chair in front of Lady Mary and on the pianist's r. hand is the cellist, Cervetto, evidently the younger Cervetto (1747–1837), who played at the professional concerts at the Hanover Square Rooms from 1780 Behind the piano stand (l. to r.) a violinist, identified as Salpietro, an oboist, J. C Fischer (1733–1800), who was a great attraction at the Bach-Abel and Vauxhall concerts, and another violinist, Langani or Langoni. To the r of the piano, blowing the French horn, stands Pieltain In the foreground (r.) in profile to the l. sits Miss Wilkes on a stool, her hands in a muff, smiling at Dr. Burney, who stands bending towards her, his hands held out. He wears a bag-wig and sword, and appears to be deep in conversation in spite of the singing of Pacchierotti, a fashionable habit much condemned by his daughter Frances, see *Cecilia* Behind Miss Wilkes on the r. stands another of the audience, holding his hat under his arm

A concert at Dr. Burney's. Reproduced, Burney, *Hist. of Music*, ed. F Mercer, 1934

$13\frac{1}{4} \times 16\frac{1}{4}$ in.

6126 THE RIVAL QUEENS OF COVENT GARDEN AND DRURY LANE THEATRES, AT A GYMNASTIC REHEARSAL!

[? *c.* Oct.–Nov. 1782]

Nº 66 Drury Lane [1]

Engraving A pugilistic encounter between Mrs Siddons (l) and her rival (r), who face each other with outstretched arms and clenched fists Behind Mrs Siddons (l) stands her backer, evidently her husband, holding out a lemon with an anxious expression A fool's cap is held above her head by a satyr-like creature wearing a fool's cap who leans upon a cloud; in his l. hand is a watchman's rattle. Behind her opponent stands her backer, probably her husband, a man wearing a hat, smiling, his hands on his hips. From a cloud above his head a man of dignified appearance with rays projecting from his head holds a laurel wreath over the head of the combatant. Both the actresses are wearing the adaptation of contemporary dress then worn on the stage by tragedy queens, Mrs. Siddons's breast is bare but her rival is decorously clothed On the extreme l is a group of five spectators, standing below the level of the stage. In the lower margin phrases are etched which are evidently intended to be spoken by the four principals. William Siddons says, *Sweet wife! you have seen cruel proof of this woman's strength I beg of you for your own sake to embrace your own safety and give over this attempt.* Mrs Siddons says, *Nay, an thou'lt mouth, I'll rant as*

[1] The address of Holland

well as thou. Her opponent says, *I will fight with her upon this throne untill my eyelids will no longer wag* Her backer says, *Keep it up Nan! Devil bury me but the Goddess will soon do her over!*

This appears to be the print advertised in a 'Catalogue of Books, Pamphlets and Prints, to be had at W Holland's Museum of Genius, No 50, Oxford-Street . .' in Jordan's *Elixir of Life*, 1789, as 'The Rival Queens, or Mrs. S——dons, and Mrs. C—f—d Boxing for the Theatrical Laurel'. Mrs Crawford (1734–1801) or Mrs Ann Spranger Barry, like Mrs Yates and Miss Younge (see No 5202), was a rival of Mrs Siddons. Boaden, *Memoirs of Mrs Siddons*, i 300 The original title, however, suggests the rivalry between Mrs. Siddons at Drury Lane and Mrs. Yates (Mary Ann, known as Anna Maria) at Covent Garden during the season 1782–3, when both played the part of Euphrasia in Murphy's *Grecian Daughter*, and an anonymous critic, probably her husband, supported the claims of Mrs Yates. Mrs Yates played Euphrasia for the first time on 21 Oct. 1782, Mrs. Siddons on 30 Oct. with her husband as Evander Ibid. i. 309, 339

$8\frac{7}{8} \times 13\frac{1}{4}$ in.

6127 THE RESURRECTION OR AN INTERNAL VIEW OF THE MUSEUM IN W—D-M—LL [WINDMILL] STREET ON THE LAST DAY

[? Rowlandson.]

Pub as the Act directs Feby 6th 1782 by H. Humphrey N° 18 New Bond Street

Engraving (coloured impression). The interior of a large circular building, the roof supported by two tiers of columns This is the anatomical museum of William Hunter (1718–83), who in 1770 built a house with a lecture-theatre, dissecting-room, and museum for his anatomical and pathological collections. A row of figures extends across the foreground: in the centre is William Hunter in a tie-wig, saying, *O what a smash among my Bottles and Preparations! never did I suppose that such a day could come* The other figures, those of specimens, either nude figures or skeletons, are (l. to r). a man saying, *My wife risen again!—that's one Rib more than I wish'd to find.* Next, a man turning his head to the r. holds out a leg, his own l. leg having been amputated above the knee, saying, *What this! arrah be easy my Dear Devil burn me if it be not my own I know it by the lump on the Shin here.* His neighbour, whose l. leg is also missing, says to him, *Damn me Sir that's my Legg.* A headless man addresses Hunter saying, *Where's my Head*

On Hunter's l hand an old woman with a stick says to him, *Restore to me my Virgin-honor did I keep it inviolated 75 Years to have it corked up at last.* Next are two skeletons shaking hands with each other one says, *Prodigously oblig'd to you Sweet Sir*, the other says, *My dear Madam I hope you are well I am over-joyed to see you.* A fat man in profile to the r. says, *Lack a day! did nobody see an odd large Stomach O what shall I do if I have lost my Stomach* (Cf. No 5751.)

Behind is a small hunchback, ringing a bell and shouting. Under the colonnade in the distance are minute figures. a demon, two persons embracing, and a gesticulating figure. Under the upper colonnade stands another demon (r.) In the foreground at the feet of the figures are a jar, a skull and bone, a bag (?) and an arm.

The anatomical collections here satirized are now in the Hunterian Museum of Glasgow University. For Hunter see No. 5119.

$6\frac{3}{8} \times 11\frac{7}{8}$ in.

6128 THE LAWYERS LAST CIRCUIT

[?After Rowlandson.]

Publish'd April 25 1782 by J. R. Smith N° 83 opposite the Pantheon Oxford Street London

Stipple. Four skeletons riding (r to l.) on skeleton horses, carrying off a fat lawyer. The two foremost horses are galloping almost neck and neck apparently towards a gulf The lawyer sits back to back with the rider of the near horse, to whom he is bound. He is shouting and struggling to get free; the skeleton holds up a bone. Behind him (r) ride two other skeletons on skeleton horses, the foremost holding up a scourge A sign-post (r) points the *Road to Hell* Two skulls (r) lie in the foreground Beneath the title is engraved ·

Where be his quiddits now? his quillets? his cases? his tenures? and his tricks? Why does he suffer this rude knave to knock him about the sconce with a rotten jaw-bone, and will not tell him of his action of battery? . . .

Hamlet.

This resembles in manner some of the plates for *The English Dance of Death*, 1815–16

A reduced version (coloured), dated 1806, is No 1, Pl. 7 in a series issued by Fores 'Caricatures', x, p 223, B M L Tab 524

A later print with the same title (n d.) by J Baker, published by E King, Chancery Lane, appears to have been imitated from this, though with very considerable alterations A coloured impression is in B.M L. Tab. 524, iv, p 125.

$4\frac{5}{8} \times 9\frac{3}{4}$ in.

6129 HOGARTH'S CREST.

[R Livesay sc.][1]

Publish'd April 23ᵈ 1782, by Rᵈ Livesay at Mʳˢ Hogarths Leicester Fields

Engraving A scroll-work design enclosing the word *Cyprus* forms a pedestal to support the 'Cyprian cone', the symbolic form under which Venus was worshipped at Paphos This cone is in the form of a spiral or a pyramidal shell. It appears in *The Analysis of Beauty*, No. 3217 (1753), the spiral being 'the line of grace', 'represented by a fine wire properly twisted round the elegant and varied figure of a cone' It also appears in a medallion under *The Bathos*, No 4106 (1764)

The crest was designed for Hogarth by Charles Catton the coach-painter and was painted on his coach. A Dobson, *William Hogarth*, 1908, p. 150. It was done from ' a sketch in oil, now in the possession of Mr. Catton', *Sketches from Hogarth on fifteen plates: with the Descriptions, By Mr. Livesay*, 1788.

$12\frac{1}{2} \times 9\frac{3}{16}$ in.

[1] See A Dobson, *Hogarth*, 1898, p 150.

6130 THE VICAR AND MOSES

[T. Colley?]

Pub^d accord^s to Act 21 Jany 1782. by H. Humphrey N° 18 New Bond Street.

Engraving beneath which is engraved a song, 'The Vicar & Moses'. A fat vicar, wearing hat, gown, and bands, walks in profile to the r., taking the arm of his lean clerk, who holds out a lantern to light them towards a church which is seen among trees in the distance. In the vicar's r. hand is a box inscribed *Tobacco*; in his l., which is thrust through the clerk's arm, he holds a long pipe with a smoking bowl The clerk has lank hair, wide-brimmed hat, and clerical bands, his stockings are ungartered, the candle in the lantern is broken and guttering Both smile tipsily, the vicar sings *Tol de rol de rol ti dol*, the clerk, *di dol*, the refrain of the song engraved below. The clerk had come to fetch the vicar to bury an infant, had stayed to drink with him till past midnight, when both stagger out to go to the church

This subject was etched by Rowlandson above a similar but not identical song with the same title, the words by G. A Stevens,[1] published 8 Aug. 1784. Rowlandson's version closely resembles this (reversed) and must have been imitated from it, though drawn with far more ability. A mezzotint of the same subject with the same verses is No. 3771, ascribed to *c.* 1760, but published after Oct. 1784.

The popularity 'among the vulgar' of the print of "The Vicar and Moses' is deplored by V Knox· it is 'often hung up on the walls of farmhouses', and will inevitably diminish the respect for the clergy among those 'who from their infancy are accustomed to behold the parson an object of derision, a glutton and a drunkard', *Winter Evenings*, xxvii (1787); *Br. Essayists*, vol. xxxviii, p. 151.

$9\frac{11}{16} \times 9\frac{7}{16}$ in.

6131 THE PHYSICAL ERROR.

P. V. delin. J. Kent Fecit. [Gillray]

Publish'd Jan. 25. 1782 by W Humphrey. N° 227 Strand.

Engraving The interior of a doctor's surgery A stout butcher (l.) with a knife in his r. hand has seized the cravat of a grotesquely lean and terror-stricken doctor, who puts out his hands in terror. Behind the doctor appears the end of a table or bench (r) on which are arranged medicine phials, pill-boxes, a jar and a pestle. Behind the butcher is an open door Beneath the title is engraved:

> *Butcher. Prepare Sir—you poison'd my wife — — —*
> *and by Jupiter I'll Butcher you — — — —*
>
> *Doctor   Good Sir — — hear me — Indeed — —*
> *upon my Honor it was only? — — only only*
> *— — A Physical Error.*

$6\frac{3}{4} \times 6\frac{5}{8}$ in

---

[1] The words of the printed broadside, *The Vicar and Moses*, in the Roxburghe *Ballads*, iii 313, ascribed to Stevens in the B M L Catalogue, are those of the song on this plate, not the version illustrated by Rowlandson

6132 A MEETING OF UMBRELLAS.

P. V. delin. J Kent Fecit. [Gillray]

Pub^d Jan 25 1782 by W. Humphrey. 227 Strand.

Engraving Three men, each holding up an umbrella, meet and seem to find difficulty in passing. An officer, his hair in a long pigtail queue, walks (l. to r.), his umbrella held in his r. hand and resting on his l. shoulder. A lean man, holding his umbrella high, and with tasselled cane in his l. hand, advances from the r Between them, his umbrella resting on his r shoulder, a plainly dressed citizen stands full face, holding out his l. hand as if to prevent a collision between the other two A stone wall forms the background.

For the introduction of the umbrella see No. 5793.

Grego, *Gillray*, p. 32 Reproduced, Paston, Pl. xxix

$7\frac{1}{2} \times 6\frac{5}{8}$ in

6133 CROSSING A DIRTY STREET.

A. Grant del. [Gillray]

London. Pub^d March 28th 1782 by H Humphrey, N° 18 New Bond Street

Engraving (coloured and uncoloured impressions). A gentleman (l) hands a lady across the cobble-stones of a street, both are in back view. Between the stones are pools of mud or water The man wears a high three-cornered hat, his hair or wig has curls, with a small queue.

The lady with her r. hand lifts at the back her voluminous and draped petticoats showing her legs nearly to the knee. She wears a large hat, cloak, a lace-trimmed apron and long gloves For the signature A. Grant cf No 5929

Grego, *Gillray*, p 33 (reproduced)

$9\frac{1}{2} \times 7\frac{7}{8}$ in.

6134 SKIRMISHING TO THE REAR.

R. Bran sc.

[From an original drawing sketch'd in the Mess Room, by an Officer in Ld. S——ds Reg^t of Light Horse][1]   [1 Feb 1782][1]

Stipple. A camp scene a light dragoon has been unseated by his horse, which stands, head down, ears back, heels in the air; its rider clutches the mane and is about to fall over its head, his helmet is falling off. He is facing a ragged woman (l), with a child on her shoulders, who is laughing at him, her arms akimbo. The soldier's carbine has been discharged by the accident, it is firing at a sign-board which hangs from a post (r). This is the head and shoulders of the Duke of Cumberland holding a staff inscribed, *The Duke of Cumberland Suttling House* On the r is a row of tents from which soldiers and women look on with amusement.

Evidently the militia regiment of light dragoons (22nd Sussex) raised in 1779 by J. B. Holroyd (cr. Baron Sheffield in 1781), of which he was Colonel. G. E. C., *Complete Peerage*. See Wraxall, *Memoirs*, 1884, i. 243.

$9 \times 10\frac{3}{8}$ in

[1] The publication line has been cut off, it is supplied from a note by Mr. Hawkins

6135 TASTING.

I. Nixon Inv^t et del.

Publish'd May 21st 1782 by Wm Wells N° 132 (opposite Salisbury Court) Fleet Street London

Engraving. A civic feast· men sit on each side of a table whose ends are cut off by the margins of the print. Four men sit on a bench on the near side of the table a short man (l) in regimentals, his hair or wig in a long pigtail queue, probably an officer in the city militia, drinks from a tankard. Next him a man in bag-wig and laced coat is waggishly pouring the contents of a sauce-boat into the coat-pocket of the man on his r. hand, who, quite unconscious of this, is stuffing into his other pocket provisions abstracted from the table. The man on the extreme l. lifts his glass in his l. hand, looking across to the man at the opposite corner of the table, who stands to return his toast On the farther side of the table are six men. A waiter serves a stout man with wine. The wall of the room forms the background: in the centre is a chimney-piece, over which is the seated T.Q.L. portrait of a Lord Mayor wearing his civic chain and smoking a long pipe; his elbow rests on a table and on a document *Pro Magna Charta*. An open book is *Lord Littleton on Co[ke]*. On each side of the chimney-piece hang hats, one with a tasselled cane·

$7\frac{7}{8} \times 10\frac{7}{8}$ in.

6136 THE TAYLOR TURN'D SPORTSMAN.

[R. Dighton ?]

Published by R. Sayer, N° 53, Fleet Street, as the Act directs, 4 June, 1782.

Engraving. The tailor (l). drops his gun, which is going off, and staggers backwards, holding up both hands in alarm, his wig and hat are falling off. A tape-measure hangs from his coat-pocket Four birds fly away (r) In the middle-distance a man with a spade, his hands on his hips, is grinning at the sportsman In the foreground (r) is a tree, in the distance are bushes, a windmill, a thatched cottage, and a haycock Beneath the design is engraved:

> *There once was a Taylor a Shooting wou'd go,*
> *Who before had ne'er fir'd a Gun we well know,*
> *The Piece double charg'd hit him full on the Breast,*
> *And gave him the Attitude here as express'd*
> *The Gun left his Hand and the Birds flew away*
> *And the Taylor's been sick of the Sport to this Day.*

In Sayer's book of 'Drolls'.

$5\frac{7}{8} \times 8\frac{1}{2}$ in.

6137 SUMMER DRESSES

Johannes Joh^nstonus in lucem protulit

Published as the Act directs Septr 2^d 1782.

Engraving (coloured impression) Three ladies stand, two wearing light transparent dresses, through which their nude figures are visible. The third, who is partly concealed behind and between the other two, wears a tight coat unbuttoned to show ruffles. The other two wear lace fichus, frilled aprons, and frilled petticoats. All wear hats.

Beneath the design is engraved.

My dear fair Friends
For two great Ends
This Summer Dress is recommended
Your Health's secured
Sweet-Hearts insured
The happy Objects here intended.

$12\frac{7}{16} \times 9\frac{7}{16}$ in

6138 ST. GEORGES FIELDS, OR THE POSTS NOT WIDE-ENOUGH FOR FATTY.

Printed for R Sayer, and J. Bennett, Map & Printsellers, N° 53. Fleet Street, as the Act directs, 21 Sep 1782

Engraving. A very fat woman is squeezing with difficulty between posts through which goes a foot-path. She is being helped through by two men companions, one of whom pulls her, the other (l) pushes her from behind with his closed umbrella. All are dressed in the fashion of the day. Behind them is a board, extending over a gateway in a paling, inscribed *Half Way House Cottrell, From Old Slaughters Coffee House, dealer in Foreign Spirituos Liquors. Dinners Drest on the shortest Notice.* Behind are trees, through which appears the 'Half-way House'.

This is evidently the Half-way House from the Borough to Westminster Bridge, which was immediately south of the Restoration Spring Garden in St George's Fields, at one time rival of the neighbouring Dog & Duck. W. Wroth, *The London Pleasure Gardens of the Eighteenth Century*, 1896, p. 264.

$6\frac{5}{8} \times 8\frac{1}{2}$ in

A mezzotint of a similar subject, evidently imitated from this, called *Labour in Vain—or Fatty in Distress*, is No. 591 in Carington Bowles's series of mezzotints. [c 1786]

6139 FOUGHT ALL HIS BATTLES O'ER AGAIN
AND THRICE HE SLEW THE SLAIN.

Mr Bunbury del.   *Js Bretherton f*
Publish'd 1st Jany 1782.

Engraving. Design in an oval. An old military officer with a wooden leg describes his campaigns to two cronies. He is seated in a chair (r) in profile to the l. wearing regimentals and sword, his wig has a long loosely twisted pigtail queue, his wooden leg (r) projects horizontally from his chair. He holds a map or plan taken from the wall, and is showing it to a stout man sitting on his r., who looks at it through spectacles. The third man standing behind, his l arm on the back of the soldier's chair, looks over their shoulders at the map. At their feet a small dog lies asleep. Through the open street-door (l) a man is seen dancing along while he plays a fiddle.

10×9 in

6140 A MODERN SPREAD EAGLE.

Mr Bunbury del.   *J^s Bretherton f*

Publish'd 3^d Jany 1782.

Engraving. In front of the sign of the (Hapsburg) Spread Eagle on a vertical post, a lady and gentleman stand together in back view, their attitude
reflecting that of the bird with its two necks She stands (l.) slightly behind
him taking his arm and looking to the l , holding up a closed fan. He bends
to the r. holding out his hand as if to greet an acquaintance In the background (r) is the side of a building
    Two impressions, one '2^d Proof', one slightly aquatinted.

9×6⅛ in

WARLEY HO!   [See No 4761—23 Jan 1782]

J. Bretherton after Bunbury.

A militia officer and his wife riding to the camp.

6141 No. 14 CONVERSAZIONE.

H. Bunbury Esqr Delin^t   *W. Dickinson Excudit*

*London, Published Feby 11th 1782, by W Dickinson Engraver and Print-
    seller N° 158 New Bond Street.*

Stipple. Ladies and gentlemen seated in a semicircle, while a footman
holds a circular tray on which are tea-cups, &c. In the foreground a man
sits (c.) his bag-wig hanging over the back of his chair facing the semicircle.
On the extreme l. a man sits stiffly, hat under his r arm, tea-cup in his l.
hand, next is an elderly and ugly woman, holding a fan; then a stout man
seated uncomfortably on the edge of his chair Then a lean and ugly old
woman sitting very upright, with a fan. In the centre of the circle, full face,
holding a tea-cup in both hands and looking downwards, is a lady with
enormously wide petticoats, who appears to be the hostess Next stands
the footman, who is glaring with scorn at a French manservant who stands
behind the guests on the l holding a plate of bread and butter.
    The remaining guests are in a group on the r. A stout and ugly man,
in profile to the l , stretches out his hand, either in gesticulation, or to take
a cup of tea from the tray Next him is a plainly dressed man with an
enormous wig who is laughing and looking through a single eye-glass.
These two are the only guests who show the slightest animation, the others
sitting rigidly silent On the extreme r. sits a young lady of pleasing appearance, in profile to the l., looking down demurely at her fan. Behind her
(r.) appears the head of a good-looking young man, whose arm rests on the
back of her chair. Two oval pictures are indicated on the back wall of
the room.
    Another impression with publication line, &c. but without title.

14¾×20½ in.

ENGLISHMAN AT PARIS, 1767
                                            [See No. 4185—23 Feb. 1782]
J. Bretherton after Bunbury

Another impression, coloured, with the publication line,
Publish'd Feby 27th 1799, by J Harris, Sweetings Alley, Cornhill, London.

6142 D^R. DAWDLE IN A HURRY.

Mr Bunbury del.   *J^s Bretherton f. 1st March 1782.*

Engraving An elderly doctor, wearing a tie-wig, riding (r. to l) on a wretched cob, with shaggy fetlocks and long unkempt tail The rider, frowning fiercely, holds his whip as if about to slash the animal's head, while he is pulling hard at the reins.

Two impressions, one slightly aquatinted and without title

$8\frac{3}{8} \times 9\frac{3}{4}$ in.

6143 RICHMOND HILL.

H. Bunbury Esqr Delin^t   *W. Dickinson Excudit*

London, Publish'd March 1st 1782, by Wm Dickinson Engraver &
Printseller N° 158, New Bond Street.

Stipple. Holiday-seekers driving and walking along a high-road with a margin of grass, evidently the Sunday crowd of 'cits' so often described in contemporary satire The chief group is a high phaeton of fashionable shape, but attached to two miserable hacks, who refuse to move, though they are being dragged at the head by a man with a long whip. The driver, who wears a looped hat and top-boots, kneels in the phaeton leaning forward over the horses and raising his (broken) whip with an expression of fury His companions are two ladies of pleasure who sit one on each side of him The one on his **r** holds up the top of the broken whip, its lash streaming behind her. The other, smiling, holds his **l** arm as if to prevent his falling from the carriage in his excitement. On the panel of the phaeton are the initials *ON* This carriage-full has just been passed on the r. by a fashionably dressed man driving (r to l) a high-stepping horse in one of the new high two-wheeled gigs, see Nos 5933, 6146. He looks round at them laughing

Behind (r.) is a hackney coach (number *251*) driving from l. to r , the horse being cut off by the margin of the print A woman seated on the box holds the rein Through the window over the door (it has no side windows) is seen a man seated with his back to the horse A man sits on the roof looking through a telescope Riding in the same direction (l to r.) on the off-side of the hackney coach are an elderly man on a long-tailed cob or pony and a pretty young lady on a white horse. A spaniel runs behind them

In the foreground are pedestrians A man stands in back view, legs apart, gazing at the stationary phaeton On the extreme l. a dejected-looking man and his wife walk wearily along He wears a handkerchief tied round his head, under his hat, she holds his wig in her l. hand, her r. hand rests on the small of his back He is carrying his stick in one hand, in the other a large bouquet of flowers in a paper sheath. Two dogs approach each other. Behind the two pedestrians, a man on horseback is in difficulties, his reins are slack and he holds the mane of the horse, which appears to be about to advance across the road in front of the advancing gig. In the background is a park-paling with trees showing above it.

The drawing for this print was exhibited at the R A , 1781, and presented to H. Walpole; see his effusive thanks, *Letters*, xi. 434-5.

Reproduced, Paston, Pl cxxv.

$17\frac{1}{8} \times 29\frac{3}{4}$ in.

6144 A LONG STORY

Designed by H. W. Bunbury Esq

London publish'd april 25ᵗʰ 1782 by J R. Smith Nᵒ 83 opposite the Pantheon Oxford Street.

Stipple A number of men seated round a circular table over the wine manifesting sleepiness or exhaustion in different ways, while an officer in regimentals harangues them on some campaign. He sits over the table, in profile to the r , gesticulating with outstretched arms over a plan drawn on the table-cloth Two overturned wine-glasses lie in front of him, two empty bottles stand on the table. On the farther side of the table a man stands up, stretching and yawning violently His neighbour on his r also yawns, the man on his l supports his head on his hands, scowling at the speaker through half-closed eyes Next him (r) a man in profile to the l holding a wine-glass yawns widely Two others in profile to the r are asleep in attitudes of extreme weariness. A very fat man, sitting on the l turned away from the table, with outstretched legs in top-boots, yawns violently From the r enters a servant with tousled hair, wearing a striped jersey, he is bringing in a boot-jack and pair of slippers, he too is yawning violently. In the foreground are two dogs

Two impressions, in one the title and publication lines are etched, in the other engraved

11⅝ × 15³⁄₁₆ in.

6145 A HAIL STORM

Drawn by H. W Bunbury Esqʳ

London Publish'd April 19 1782 by J. R. Smith, Nᵒ 83, opposite the Pantheon, Oxford Street.

Stipple Three pedestrians are walking (r to l) into the teeth of a storm In front is a very stout man with a globular figure, the lower part of his tightly buttoned coat blows backwards He wears spurred top-boots, and his hands meet across his chest, holding a stick. He resembles caricatures of Captain Grose, see Nos 4683, 5511, 5787, 5802 The next man wears a cloak which streams behind him as does his wig, he has a laced coat and hat, with two large keys tied to his wrist A lean man (r) puts his head down grimacing as he hastens along, his hair, queue, cravat, coat and breeches all blowing in the wind; his hands are clasped in front holding a stick which rests on his shoulder Farther off, between the two foremost pedestrians, a man on horseback holds his nose, his bag-wig, cravat, and coat-tails blown by the wind In front of him (l) a short man is crouching in the lee of a bush, his hat and wig have blown off, a paper flutters from his hand. The clouds extending diagonally from the upper r corner of the design indicate driving hail

Another version, in reverse, etched and coloured (n.d) is in 'Caricatures', IX, p. 52. B M L Tab 524 a

10 × 12 in.

6146 SIR GREGORY GIGG.

Designed by H W. Bunbury Esqʳ

Publshd July 23ᵈ 1782 by J. R. Smith N 83 Oxford Street London.

Mezzotint. A young man driving (r to l) one of the new high two-wheeled gigs, see Nos 5933, 6143. Its small body is poised high on springs above the large wheels; the driver leans forward to whip his pair of high-stepping horses, which are about to descend a precipitous hill. He wears the plain high-crowned hat which was so great a novelty in 1781 (see Nos. 5931, &c) and top-boots On the panel of the gig is a draped escutcheon with monogram or cipher In the foreground are bushes and rough ground with a milestone, *Miles XXI*

'Sir Gregory Gigg, or the City Beau' is the title of a song in O'Keefe's *Son in Law*, played at the Haymarket 1779, the songs only being printed

Reproduced, Paston, Pl. cxxiii.

$11\frac{1}{8} \times 9\frac{3}{4}$ in

6147 A BORE.

C L S ['Charles Loraine Smith].

Publish'd April 6th 1782 by Chs Bretherton.

Engraving. Three men seated at a small round table. The one in the centre is the 'Bore'. His r hand rests on an *Ext——y Gazette* which lies on the table, which he is expounding to the man who sits on his l whom he is literally button-holing, holding the button of his coat with a fierce intent gaze. His companion on the other side lies back in his chair asleep, his mouth open, legs crossed, hands in his breeches pocket.

The word bore (or 'boar') was a new and fashionable word in 1766, 'for tiresome people and conversations'.[1]

$8 \times 10\frac{3}{8}$ in.

6148 MODERN LOVE, PLATE I
COURTSHIP

Engraved after an Original Picture of Mr John Collett, in the Possession of Mr Bradford.

J. Collett pinxit   *J. Goldar Sculpsit*

Publish'd June 24th 1782[2] by John Boydell Engraver in Cheapside London

Size of the Picture. 3ft by 2ft 4in

Engraving A lady in profile to the r. seated in a wood, while a man dressed as a military officer lying at her feet, kisses her l hand Behind (l) an old woman points out the couple to an elderly man, apparently the lady's father, who scowls at them. On a high pedestal (r) inscribed *Omnia Vincit Amor* is a statue of Venus, with Cupid beside her; he aims an arrow at the lovers, while he tramples on a crown at his feet. A dog licks the lady's left hand. Beside her on the ground is a flute and an open book of music on which are the words, *Affettuoso*

Each Art he tried the fair One's Heart to move
He sigh'd, & kist, & swore eternal Love

[1] Lady Sarah Lennox (Bunbury) in a letter of 9 Jan 1766 She instances the Dukes of York and Gloucester as serving 'for an example of a boar' *Life and Letters*, 1901, i, p 179 The *O E D* gives the word as meaning ennui in 1766, its extension to a tiresome person being dated 1812
[2] Painted 1765 - -D N B

Beside the book is a paper inscribed, *La Lettione del l'Amore A favourite Duet compos'd by Sig^r Pianissimo.*

A peacock (l.) pecks at a basket of grapes. One of a series of four prints, see Nos. 6149-51.

13½ × 17$\frac{1}{16}$ in.

6149 MODERN LOVE. PLATE II.
THE ELOPEMENT.

J. Collett pinxit.   *J. Goldar Sculpsit.*

Engraved after an Original Picture of Mr John Collett, in the Possession of Mr Bradford.

Publish'd June 24th 1782^1 by John Boydell Engraver in Cheapside London.

Size of the Picture, 3^{ft} by 2^{ft} 4^{in}

Engraving. A sequel to No. 6148 A young girl (r) is descending some steps by which she has crossed a high paling, her lover in profile to the r receives her in his arms. An old hag waits, standing (r) holding a purse in her l hand. These three figures are intended for those in Plate I, but the lady looks many years younger; she wears a wide-brimmed flat hat over a close-fitting hood and a cape, instead of the more elaborate dress of Pl I Her lover wears military dress, with aiguillettes on the shoulder denoting a dragoon. A post-chaise and pair waits (r) outside a low paling, on the panel is a coat of arms with the motto *Ready* The postilion and coachman stand near their master (l.) the former is lifting up a small corded trunk, while a dog worries his cap which is on the ground, the coachman examines the priming of a pistol. At the foot of the ladder is a rectangular box tied with ribbon, inscribed *For Miss Fanny Falsestep.* Behind the paling (r.) is a notice board. *Notice is hereby given that a Man Trap is set every Night within these Pales* In the lane where the post-chaise waits is a sign-post, pointing (l.) *To London* and (r.) *This leads to the Great Northern Road.* In the background are trees, a cottage with a dovecote, and the tower of a church, the clock pointing to seven minutes past five See Nos. 6148, 6150, 6151.

13½ × 17$\frac{1}{8}$ in

6150 MODERN LOVE. PLATE III.
THE HONEY-MOON.

J. Collett pinxit.   *J. Goldar Sculpsit.*

Engraved after an Original Picture of Mr John Collett, in the Possession of Mr Bradford.

Publish'd June 24th 1782^1 by John Boydell Engraver in Cheapside London.

Size of the Picture 3^{ft} by 2^{ft} 4^{in}

Engraving A sequel to Nos 6148, 6149 The young couple sit on a settee (r) by a circular table on which are an urn and tea-things with a pot of *Virgin Honey* She leans on his shoulder while she puts a lump of sugar into the cup which he holds A manservant enters from the l with

^{1} Painted 1765 —*D N.B.*

a plate whose contents fall to the ground as a monkey seated on a cabinet pulls his queue Three dogs and a cat are in the room

The room is panelled and is a good example of a well-furnished breakfast-parlour of the period Books and papers scattered about are inscribed with various allusions to matrimony. See also No 6151.

$13\frac{5}{8} \times 17\frac{1}{8}$ in.

6151 MODERN LOVE, PLATE IV.
DISCORDANT MATRIMONY.

Engraved after an Original Picture of Mr John Collett, in the Possession of Mr Bradford.

J. Collett pinx^t   *J Goldar Sculp^t*

Publish'd June 29th 1782^1 by John Boydell, Engraver in Cheapside, London.

Size of the Picture 3^{ft} by 2^{ft} 4^{in}

Engraving. A sequel to Nos. 6148, 6149, 6150. The interior of a parlour. The husband (r.) leans on a table looking towards a meretricious-looking maidservant (l) who has just brought in two children: a little girl whom she holds in her arms, and an older boy who drags across the floor a broken guitar which is harnessed to a toy horse The maid looks alluringly at her master, a paper hangs from her pocket inscribed *The Willing Maid.* The lady, who appears to be ill, is seated by a circular table, leaning her head on her hand She looks with an expression of distress towards her husband On the table is an open book inscribed *Inconstancy A Poem—Eternal Love Let no Man swear,* and medicine phials, one labelled *A Composing Draught.* A dog licks her hand. A black servant stands by the table holding two other phials; he watches the maidservant with a scowl.

The pictures on the walls, the books and the behaviour of the animals all indicate the inconstancy of the husband two dogs (r.) coupled by a chain snarl at each other, their fore-paws resting on a book, *On the legality of Divorces.* A monkey (r.) seated on a toy-drum on a chair holds an open book, *Paradise Lost Hail Wedded Love Mysterious Law.* A book falls from the table inscribed, *The Scene is Changed or the faithless Husband.* The children's toys include three dolls: a king in ermine robes, crown and sceptre, a bishop, and a Harlequin.

$13\frac{5}{8} \times 17\frac{3}{16}$ in.

6152 TAX ON POST HORSES

John Nixon Inv^t 1782   [Paul Sandby aquatint]

Aquatint A stout elderly man on a lean hack, riding (l to r) towards London. His servant rides behind him, but is falling over the head of his horse, which is on its knees, collapsing under its burden: saddle-bag, a portmanteau, a bundle topped by a three-cornered wig-box inscribed *Dr Drowsey.* His hat, wig, and riding-whip are on the ground. The doctor rides on, unconscious of the accident.

In the foreground (r.) is a high brick wall which a projecting sign shows to be the corner of a public-house. The sign appears to be the head of George III, on a cracked and damaged sign-board, from which the name,

---

^{1} Painted 1765.—D N B.

John Bull, has broken, and hangs suspended. A broom is placed over the sign. A magpie in a wicker cage is partly visible, hanging from the front of the house In the distance (r) are spires and towers of London with the dome of St Paul's. A sign-post (l) points *To Oxford* Behind the riders are trees.

A tax on wagons, as part of a tax on the carriage of goods, figured in North's budget for 1782, but not one on post-horses. Post-horses were taxed in 1780. *Parl Hist* xxii, p. 1159

$10\frac{11}{16} \times 17$ in.

6153 A JOURNEYMAN PARSON GOING ON DUTY.

R. Dighton delin.

Publish'd by R. Sayer, 53 Fleet Street.   [? 1782]

Engraving. A companion print to No 6154. A lean parson on a sorry-looking horse rides, r. to l , along a country road. He wears a gown and bands, with an ill-fitting wig partly concealing his hair. Under his arm is a portfolio inscribed *Sermon* He has just passed an inn door (r) in which stands a fat butcher holding a tankard, who grins complacently towards him. Two grinning yokels stand behind the butcher The sign of a harrow hangs from a projecting beam. See Nos 5799, 3754 (*c* 1782), 3756 (*c* 1785–6).

Reproduced, A. S. Turberville, *Men and Manners of the Eighteenth Century*, 1926, p 288.

In book of Sayer's 'Drolls'

$7\frac{1}{16} \times 8\frac{13}{16}$ in.

6154 A MASTER PARSON RETURNING FROM DUTY.

R Dighton delin.

Publish'd by R. Sayer 53, Fleet Street.   [?c. 1782].

Engraving A companion print to No. 6153 A fat parson riding (l. to r.) a handsome horse arrives at the high iron gate of his house, which is seen in the background. He points arrogantly to a groom in livery, who stands (r.) holding another horse whose head appears on the r. The groom raises his hat. A butler holding a bunch of keys stands in front of the gate In the distance among trees (l) is a church spire. See Nos 5799, 3753 (*c* 1782), 3755 (*c*. 1785–6).

Reproduced, A S Turberville, *Men and Manners of the Eighteenth Century*, 1926, p 288

In book of Sayer's 'Drolls'.

$7\frac{1}{4} \times 8\frac{7}{8}$ in.

Nine prints from the series of mezzotints published by Carington Bowles.[1]

6155 A LESSON WESTWARD—OR A MORNING VISIT TO BETSY COLE.

466 *Printed for & Sold by Carington Bowles, at Nᵒ 69 in Sᵗ Pauls Church Yard, London. Published as the Act directs, 2 Janʸ 1782.*

Mezzotint A girl, in profile to the l , seated on the box-seat of a four-

[1] No 3754 has the imprint of Bowles and Carver.

wheeled cart drawn by a pair of horses She is receiving a driving-lesson from a man who sits behind her on the edge of the cart in which is a sheaf of straw On the side of the cart is a board inscribed *Tom Longtrot's Academy for Young Ladies. Driving taught to an Inch, Ladies compleatly finish'd in a fortnight, for Gig, Whiskey, or Phaeton· Single Lesson half a Crown, Five for half a Guinea*

The girl holds whip and reins very awkwardly, the hind wheel passes over one of a litter of small pigs which is with a sow in the foreground A short stout citizen (l) clutches a post or mile-stone in alarm at the prospect of being run over The driver wears an elaborate hat with feathers and a muslin dress, very unlike the dress of the fashionable women-whips of the day, cf No 6114.

Beneath the title is engraved, *Hammersmith Turnpike* and,

> *When once the Women taken the Reins in hand,*
> *'Tis then too true, that Men have no command.*

Behind the cart the upper part of the toll-house appears, with the head of a grinning spectator, probably the toll-keeper By the toll is a large rectangular Georgian house with a square pillared porch inscribed WILL-SON. This is the inn, The Bell and Anchor, which still exists (1932), altered, at the corner of Blyth Road close to Olympia

A coloured impression is in 'Caricatures', i, p. 202 B M.L Tab. 524 $12\frac{7}{8} \times 9\frac{7}{8}$ in.

6156 CAPT JESSAMY LEARNING THE PROPER DISCIPLINE OF THE COUCH.

471. *Printed for & Sold by Carington Bowles, at his Map & Print Warehouse, No 69 in St Pauls Church Yard.*

Published as the Act directs [date erased, 1782]

Mezzotint (coloured impression) A young man, in military dress, of elegant and effeminate appearance, sprawls on a sofa, looking towards a young woman (r) who leans towards him. She is of meretricious appearance, and wears the quasi-military riding-dress fashionable at this time in connexion with the militia camps of Coxheath and Warley The room is luxuriously furnished A round table with a wine bottle and glass is partly visible on the extreme r.

Perhaps intended for Captain Bisset and Lady Worsley, see No 6105, &c For satires on militia camps see No 5523, &c. Similar in character to Nos 5950, 6157.

$12\frac{7}{8} \times 9\frac{3}{4}$ in   'Caricatures', i, p 173 B M L. Tab. 524

6157 NARCISSUS AND THE NYMPH ECHO

473 *Printed for & Sold by Carington Bowles, at his Map & Print Warehouse, No 69 in St Pauls Church Yard, London Published as the Act directs* [date erased 1782]

Mezzotint (coloured impression) A young military officer in full regimentals wearing a gorget and fringed sash, with a toupet-wig, lies on the grass admiring his reflection in a pool His hat and sword lie beside him A young woman, fashionably dressed, wearing a hat over a large frilled cap, stands behind a low bank (l) holding out her hands in surprise

Beneath the title is engraved, *Ye Fates what made me chance to stroll that way,—Where Young Narcissus self admiring lay.* The scene is a park, with trees and a circular temple (r) in the background. Similar in character to Nos. 5950, 6156

12⅞×9⅞ in.   'Caricatures', 1, p 83. B M.L. Tab. 524.

6158 THE BARBER RIDING TO MARGATE.

474. Printed for & Sold by Carington Bowles, at his Map & Print Warehouse, No 69 in St Pauls Church Yard, London. Published as the Act directs [20 May 1782].[1]

Mezzotint (coloured impression) Scene outside a posting inn   A man (r) riding r to l. clutches his horse round the neck, he has lost his stirrups and his hat flies off The horse is rearing, startled by the drum and fifes of a recruiting party in Guards' uniform led by an officer with a drawn sword, and followed by three recruits wearing ribbon favours in their hats. The rider is fashionably dressed in riding clothes, a pair of curling tongs falls from his pocket, a box which he was carrying has fallen to the ground, where various articles of the barber's trade have fallen from it tresses of hair, a packet of *Powder*, a comb, razor, &c

In the background is a three-storied inn, with bay-windows on all floors. Spectators watch from the windows. The sign is hung from a standard (r); behind (l) are outhouses inscribed *Licensed to [hire] post horses*, a coach stands in front of them.

12⅞×9⅞ in   'Caricatures', i, p 190. B M L Tab 524.

6159 THE SAILOR RIDING TO PORTSMOUTH.

475 Printed for & Sold by Carington Bowles, at his Map & Print Warehouse, No 69 in St Pauls Church Yard, London. Published as the Act directs [date erased, 1782].

Mezzotint (coloured impression)   A sailor wearing striped trousers is seated outside an inn on a horse which is kicking, because one of two small boys (l) is prodding him with a stick. The sailor holds a bowl of punch, which is being spilt as he loses his stirrups and clutches the animal's mane in alarm. In front of the horse (r) stands a countryman with a handful of hay. At the door of the inn is a fat landlady, and on her l. a military officer of foppish appearance. The door has a small pediment inscribed *M Hewson Neat Wines* Above the door is the sign, a crescent surrounded by a huntsman's horn

12¾×10 1/16 in   'Caricatures', 1, p. 191. B.M.L , Tab. 524

6160 A MORNING RAMBLE, OR—THE MILLINERS SHOP.

478 Printed for & Sold by Carington Bowles, at his Map & Print Warehouse, No 69 in St Pauls Church Yard, London. Publish'd as the Act directs [date erased, 1782].

Mezzotint (coloured impression)   Interior of a milliner's shop, the counter running across the print, behind it are three milliners, dressed in

---

[1] Date erased, but supplied from an impression belonging to Mr. W T Spencer of New Oxford Street (1932)

the fashion of the day with elaborately frilled muslin caps on their high-dressed hair Two fashionably dressed men are on the near side of the counter, intent on a flirtation One, wearing riding-dress, sits on the edge of the counter, his legs dangling, while he leans on his elbow and looks over his r. shoulder towards a pretty young woman who is sewing, seated in profile to the r The other visitor (r) lounges against the counter as he hands a *Masquerade Ticket* to a young milliner The third milliner stands; she is sewing at one of the elaborately frilled muslin head-dresses of the day.

The print shows the arrangement of a shop at this period The shop-window is partly visible on the l, with wares for sale suspended across it on cords. On the wall is an oval mirror in a carved frame, while on the r shelves fill a recess in the wall and support boxes, inscribed *Feathers, Love Coxcomb, Mode.* An arched-top coffer, such as milliners in street scenes are depicted as carrying, stands open on the counter, a piece of lace hanging from it. On the near side of the counter is a tall circular stool for customers. In the foreground is a Pomeranian dog.

$11\frac{3}{4} \times 9\frac{3}{4}$ in.   'Caricatures', i, p. 31. B.M L., Tab. 524.

A MASTER PARSON WITH A GOOD LIVING (480)

Cf. No 6154.   See No. 3753 —*c* 1782.

A JOURNEYMAN PARSON WITH A BARE EXISTENCE (481).

Cf No. 6153.   See No. 3754 —*c* 1782

6161 A RICH PRIVATEER BROUGHT SAFE INTO PORT, BY TWO FIRST RATES.

Printed for & Sold by Carington Bowles, at his Map & Print Warehouse, Nº 69 in Sᵗ Pauls Church Yard, London. Publish'd as the Act directs [1782]

Mezzotint (coloured impression). A jovial sailor in a brothel holding his hat which is full of guineas One gaily dressed woman (l.) in hat and cloak leans on his r shoulder dipping her r hand into the guineas Another woman on his r. holds a watch and seals, while she puts her l hand on his l arm Behind (l) a stout woman is bringing in a large bowl of punch. A fourth woman is partly visible on the r

Reproduced, C. N. Robinson, *The British Tar in Fact and Fiction*, 1909, p 218 (with date 1782)

Also an uncoloured impression, publication line cut off

$12\frac{7}{8} \times 9\frac{7}{8}$ in.   'Caricatures', i, p. 182 B M.L. Tab. 524.

POLITICAL SATIRES

6162 WONDERS WONDERS WONDERS & WONDERS

Dedicated to the wonderfull wonderfull wonderer

Sold by W Humphrey 1783[1]

Engraving. Couples of notorious enemies stand clasping hands in friendship In the foreground (c) is a group of three: Fox with a fox's head stands between Shelburne[2] (l) and Lord Denbigh (r), who has the body of a fox-hound. Fox holds Shelburne's r. hand, his l arm is on the shoulder of Denbigh, who puts his forepaws affectionately on his shoulder Fox says,

> *I now will play the Foxes Part,*
> *And gain a Secret from each Heart,*

Shelburne, smiling, says,

> *I should not have used you so ill,*
> *If I had not swallow'd a Scotch Pill.*

Denbigh says,

> *Through you & Burke I lost my Place,*
> *Yet I forgive the sad Disgrace.*

On the extreme l stands Britannia, holding her spear, her shield beside her, the head of the British lion, *couchant*, appearing from behind it. Her r. hand grasps that of America, who holds in her l hand a staff surmounted by the cap of Liberty She wears the feathered head-dress and kilt of a red Indian. Britannia says, *Come, Come, shake hands, and lets be Friends*, America answers, *With all my Heart, I've gain'd my Ends*

As a pendant to the pair stand Wilkes and George III on the extreme r. clasping hands, Wilkes holds up his l. hand saying,

> *Your M . y has been long deceiv'd*
> *And at your Subjects was much griev'd,*

The king answers,

> *Enough! my Fault I own, my Subject Loyal,*
> *And you much love, 'pon my Word Royal*

Between and slightly behind these three groups are two other couples · the Duke of Richmond (l.) takes the hand of Parson Bate, wearing gown and bands and holding the *Morn*[g] *[H]erald* Richmond says, *Parson I you forgive, I know youre Bate*. Bate answers *I did repent when it was too late* As a pendant to this pair, stand Sir Hugh Palliser and Keppel, both in naval uniform Palliser rests his r hand on a stick, Keppel grasps his l hand in both of his Palliser says, *By Twitcher's Arts I you accus'd*, Keppel answers, *And to forgive I ne'er Refus'd* Beneath the design is engraved ·

> *If Kat——to can Bring Such Wonders to pass*
> *He sure deserves the Honor to Kiss the Kings ——*

The title is taken from the advertisements which Katerfelto circulated

[1] Another publication line, a pendant to this (l.), appears to have been obliterated
Mr. Hawkins (MS index) gives the date as 9 Nov 1782
[2] This figure is not without a certain resemblance to North, but is more like
Shelburne, and the similarity to 6 in No 6173 by the same artist leaves no doubt
of his identity

broadcast in London at this time, see No. 6326, &c. For Fox and Shelburne see No 6022, &c They were eventually reconciled (c. 1796) by their joint opposition to Pitt. Russell, *Memorials & Correspondence of Fox*, 1854, iii. 129. For Denbigh's deprivation of the Mastership of the Fox-hounds see No 5976. The vendetta between Wilkes and George III was ended over the opposition to Fox's India Bill and their amity was the subject of carica-tures in 1784 For Keppel and Palliser see Nos. 5536, 5537, &c.; for Richmond and Bate, No. 5666. Similar in manner to No 6173

$8\frac{3}{4} \times 14\frac{3}{8}$ in

6163 THE RELIEF OF GIBRALTAR A CABINET COUNCIL

Devonshire Inv^t T. Colley In^s Richmond Fecit
Pub^d by Thos Colley Jany 1. 1783 London

Engraving On a rectangular table in false perspective stands the grotesque bust of a woman whose hair forms waves which support a British man-of-war in full sail In her breast is an open door She appears to symbolize Gibraltar. On each side of the table sits a lady, T Q L., in profile, perhaps intended for the Dukes of Devonshire and Richmond (cf Nos 5478–80 where men are represented as women). Devonshire (l) touches with a fore-finger the object on the table Her vis-à-vis (r) holds in both hands the model of the angle of a fort, flying the British flag, with cannon in its embrasures. Behind the table (c.) stands a lean man, wearing a bag-wig, his head turned in profile to the r

The intention of the satire is obscure: Keppel had been blamed by the king for negligence over the relief of Gibraltar, *Corr. of George III*, vi. 99, 11 Aug 1782, but it seems more probable that it relates to the discussions (Nov.–Dec) on the cession of Gibraltar, when Shelburne, the King, and Grafton were prepared to agree to an exchange, while Richmond and Keppel objected [1] Fitzmaurice, *Shelburne*, 1912, ii. 208. *Corr. of George III*, pp. 159, 169, 170, 183–4, 192 Romilly, *Memoirs*, 1840, i. 250–5. Richmond's absorption in the Ordnance Office may also be satirized. Walpole, *Last Journals*, 1910, ii 449–51 The Duke of Devonshire, though taking little part in politics, had a certain importance as the head of a great Whig family

$6\frac{3}{4} \times 11\frac{3}{4}$ in

6164 SECRET REFLECTION. OR THE STOOL OF REPENTANCE.

Pub^d 6th Jan· 1783 by W· Humpry [sic] N° 227 Strand London

Engraving. Fox, with a fox's head, seated in a latrine, a small erection like a sentry-box with folding doors whose roof is inscribed *The Gentlemens Garden* He looks down meditatively, a large label issues from his mouth inscribed.

> *Sh—b—e* [Shelburne] *is a corrupted Government Tool*
> *And I am a beshitten Independent Fool.*

One of many satires on the resignation of Fox on Rockingham's death, see No. 6010, &c.

$7\frac{1}{4} \times 5\frac{3}{4}$ in.

[1] The exchange of Gibraltar for Guadeloupe was agreed to at a Cabinet meeting on 3 Dec 1782, Richmond and Keppel being present, but on the following day both opposed the exchange at an interview with the King, *Corr of George III*, vi, pp 170–2. See Fox's speech protesting against cession, 5 Dec. 1782. *Parl. Hist.* xxiii. 238–42.

6165 A LONG PULL. STRONG PULL. AND A PULL ALL TO-GETHER

Pub Jan 9ᵗʰ 1783 by W Humphrey Nᵒ 227 Strand.

Engraving. Lord Shelburne (l) stands in the open doorway of the *Treasury*, his arms outstretched and pressing his hands against each side of the door, as he leans backwards to resist the efforts of four men who pull at a rope round his waist in order to drag him out of the building Dunning, in legal wig and gown, stands behind him, holding him round the waist and by his arm, to prevent his being dragged out. Shelburne's complacent expression suggests that he expects to keep his place The foremost of the men pulling the rope is Fox, who tugs hard, looking over his l. shoulder with an anxious expression towards Keppel immediately behind him Keppel, who is looking at Fox with a melancholy expression, disappointed Fox by not resigning on Shelburne's appointment, and kept his post as First Lord of the Admiralty till 24 Jan. Next comes Richmond, in profile to the r., holding the rope over his r. shoulder; he was Master of the Ordnance in Shelburne's administration, although on 23 Jan he told the king 'that disapproving of Lord Shelburne's assumption of too much power in the [peace] negotiation, he would go no more to Council' but would keep his post as Master of the Ordnance 'if the king desired it' At the end of the rope is Burke, straining hard

The defection of Keppel and Richmond is anticipated, they are rightly represented as adherents of Fox rather than of Shelburne. See No 6023

$8\frac{13}{16} \times 13$ in.

6166 THE FOX AND STORK

T. Colley Fecet [sic]

Pubᵈ by W Richardson Janʸ: 14 1783 Nᵒ 174 near Surry Street Strand

Engraving. The fox and stork in Æsop's fable are Fox and Shelburne The stork (r) is dipping his beak into a transparent long-necked jar, whose square base is inscribed *The Treasury Jar*, and taking the guineas which are at the bottom The stork's head is that of Shelburne, his chin is inserted in the jar, and he smiles triumphantly; over the stork's neck is suspended the Garter ribbon The fox (l), with bushy eyebrows, bulbous nose, and hairy chin of Charles Fox, stands on its hind-legs, its fore-paws resting on the jar, looking at the inaccessible guineas with a melancholy expression. See No 6010, &c, and for Shelburne No 6018, &c Possibly by an imitator of Colley's style. [? Gillray.]

$5\frac{13}{16} \times 8\frac{13}{16}$ in.

6167 THE SYMPATHIZING POLITICIANS

Pubᵈ by J Barrow Janʸ 21 1783. White Lion Bull Stairs Surry Side Black Friars Bridge.

Engraving. Charles Fox (l), with a fox's head, shakes hand with a taller and slighter man who has a stag's head, with antlers. The latter says, *Alas my Friend Fox, We are in the wrong Box.* Fox answers *Indeed my true Buck, We have very bad luck* Both wear bag-wigs and ruffled shirts. The man with the stag's head is probably Lord John Cavendish (a stag's head being the crest of the Cavendishes), who had been Chancellor of the Exchequer in the Rockingham ministry and had resigned with Fox on

POLITICAL SATIRES 1783

Shelburne's appointment as prime minister See No 6010, &c, and No 6075.
$6\frac{1}{4} \times 6\frac{1}{4}$ in.

6168 L——D SHEL——, [SHELBURNE] BEGGING MONSIEUR TO MAKE PISS OR P——E [PEACE]

Pub^d by J Barrow Jany 21. 1783. White Lion Bull Stairs Surry Side Black Friars Bridge

Engraving (coloured and uncoloured impressions) Lord Shelburne (l.) holds out a chamber-pot towards 'Monsieur', a tall, thin, foppishly dressed man personifying France Shelburne is wearing his Garter ribbon and star. Monsieur wears a high toupet-wig and long queue Shelburne says, *Monsieur, be so obliging as to make piss with us.* Monsieur answers, *By the House of Bourbon, with the War we'll go on* He stands in profile to the l., holding up his hands to ward off Shelburne's proposals and raising his l. leg to kick the proffered pot

Beneath the design is engraved:

> *He's no heart of Oak,*
> *But he 's fit for a joke,*
> *That will ask of a Frenchman a peace;*
> *And such is our fate*
> *That we have of late*
> *Been degraded by puppies and geese*

> *To Britons success,*
> *Against the Congress,*
> *On the Seas & all over the plain;*
> *May they boldly advance,*
> *Make a Monkey of France,*
> *And Asses of Holland & Spain*

For the unpopularity acquired by Shelburne over the peace negotiations see Fitzmaurice, *Shelburne*, 1912, ii. 210 ff. See also Nos 6009, 6171, 6172, 6182, 6184, &c.
$6\frac{1}{8} \times 8\frac{1}{2}$ in.

RAISING THE ROYAL GEORGE.

Boreas design'd it.   *twitcher sculp^t*

Pub 21st Jan. 1783, by W Humphrey N° 227 Strand.

A reissue, with a different publication line, of No. 6043

6169 THE NABOB RUMBLED OR A LORD ADVOCATES AMUSEMENT

[Gillray]

Political Characters & Caracatures of 1783. N° 1 Pub^d Jan 21. 1783 by E D'Achery. St James's Street.

Engraving (coloured and uncoloured impressions) Sir Thomas Rumbold, who stands, supported by his son, holding his r. hand to his forehead, vomits a shower of guineas into a large chamber-pot held by Dundas,

671

the Lord Advocate of Scotland The pot, which is ornamented with a thistle, is full of guineas, and stands on a three-legged stool Dundas (r.), in legal wig and gown, kneels beside it, clasping it in both arms; he is saying, *I weel tak them to Lochabar and wash them in the Brook*. Rumbold is shackled by two chains, one attached to each ankle, and at the other end to a large weight or clog inscribed *Sureties* Captain Rumbold, who wears regimentals with a gorget, holds his father's l hand and arm, saying *Ah! these dam'd Scotch Pills will kill poor Dad*.

In the distance (l.) a military officer with a long queue, probably Captain Rumbold, is galloping off (r to l) mounted on an elephant and seated on the back of a large double sack which forms a saddle and is inscribed *Roupees*. He is saying *I am off—I know good manners*. An Indian seated behind him on the back of the elephant holds a tall umbrella over his master's head; he says, *Me and Massa leave England He! He! He!*

Behind the elephant a few palm-trees give an oriental touch to the landscape, which is otherwise of English character

Rumbold was regarded as the typical nabob of fabulous and ill-gotten wealth His prosecution in the Commons by a Bill of pains and penalties was managed by Dundas (whose Scottish accent was notoriously harsh), it was brought in on 3 May 1782 and abandoned 3 Dec 1783. At the same time a Bill was brought in to restrain him from leaving the country, hence the clogs attached to his ankles. The charges against him broke down and were abandoned.

Captain Rumbold (d 1786), lieutenant and captain in the 1st Life Guards, had been A D C. to Sir Hector Monro at the siege of Pondicherry and had been sent home with dispatches and colours For the Rumbold case, 1781-3, see the documents, &c , in B M L. 583. h. 13, and *The real Facts concerning Sir Thomas Rumbold*, 1893 For contemporary opinion, Wraxall, *Memoirs*, 1884, ii. 376-81, iii 98-100 See also Nos 5341, 6256

An impression is in the possession of White's Club, apparently on account of the unauthenticated story that Sir Thomas Rumbold had been a waiter or even a 'black-shoe boy' at White's See [Boulton], *The History of White's*, 1892, ii. 143 ff., where the print is reproduced.

$6\frac{7}{8} \times 8$ in.

6170 THE COMFORTS—AND—CURSE OF A MILITARY LIFE

Colley Fec[t]

Pub by E Darchery S[t] James Street Jan[y] 31. 1783

Engraving. A design in two compartments, to contrast the lot of officers with and without political interest.

The design on the l is headed FULPAY *Borough Interest*. Two portly and jovial senior officers in uniform with hats, sit at a round table drinking wine. One (r.) turns to the other holding up a full glass and pointing with his forefinger to the r saying *Success to the Peace Makers*. The other sits with his l hand resting on the table holding a full wine-glass which stands on a paper inscribed *Promotions* His legs are crossed, his r. arm, which is over the back of his chair, holds a long tasselled cane. A bunch of grapes, a bottle labelled *Claret*, and a decanter are on the table A pampered-looking spaniel lies at their feet. The luxury of their room is indicated by carpet with an elaborate pattern which reaches to the wall, by the mouldings on the wall, and by two oval mirrors in carved frames

The other design (r.) is headed HALF PAY *Ingrata Patria* The officer
stands reflectively, in profile to the l., very upright, but with a wooden leg
In spite of a neat appearance, his coat is out-at-elbows, the fringe of his
epaulette is worn away. A little boy hangs to his coat-tails His wife,
plainly dressed in the fashion of the day, with a large hat, sits full-face (r.)
on the only chair. Behind is a square table on which is an enormous
tankard inscribed *Small Beer*. A little boy grasps it with both hands; a
smaller child in petticoats, wearing a wooden sword, holds the edge of
the table. The room is poverty-stricken, the boards are bare, and there are
holes in them Its only furniture besides the chair and table is a small stool,
a cask, and a broom A book lies on the ground and a hungry-looking cat
takes the place of the sleek spaniel. The plaster is coming off the wall, and
its only ornaments are the officer's hat and sword, the scabbard of which is
worn out, and a print, *The Soldier—Tire'd of war* (cf. No. 5784)· an
officer wearing a bag-wig raises a cane to strike an old soldier on crutches,
who holds out his hat to beg. Beneath the design is engraved:

To the Commander in Cheif and Secretary of War—Under all Administrations
Gent^m

*You have been ever found callous to the Meritorious claims of Veteran
Soldiers and remain heroically unmoved by their memorials unless accompanied
by a Bribe to your Secretarys or a Vote in a dirty Borough In hopes that the
pencil may Succeed where the pen has not these contrasted Situations are
humbly inscribed to you by an Injured Miles.*

$8\frac{1}{8} \times 13\frac{3}{16}$ in.

6171 SHELB——NS SACRIFICE

Invented by Cruelty.   *Engraved by Dishoner.*

Pub^d by E. Dashery [sic] Feb^{th} 10 [sic] 1783 St James Street.

Engraving Two Red Indians are slaughtering American loyalists, Shelburne looks on with satisfaction and is attacked by Britannia The figures
are dispersed over the design Beneath the title is engraved, *Or the recommended Loyalists, a faithful representation of a Tragedy shortly to be performed on the Continent of America*

Shelburne (r) stands full-face with his hands on his hips, smiling, he
says, *be not angry Madam, no peace, no place* Britannia (r), in profile to the
l., rushes towards him, holding up her spear to stab him to the heart, her
shield on the ground beside her. She says, *Inhuman smiling Hypocrite thus
to disgrace my unsullied fame* Shelburne is looking to the l towards an
Indian brave with a tomahawk who is about to murder a wounded loyalist
who lies on the ground. Behind the Indian (r.) a loyalist lies dead. Behind
Shelburne stands a butcher, his knife and steel hanging from his waist,
holding a handkerchief to his face, above him is engraved, *Even Butchers
weep.* Three loyalists (l) flee in terror; they are pursued by an Indian
wearing a head-dress of feathers which denotes personifications of America.
She (or he) has seized one of the loyalists by the coat-tail and raises a tomahawk to strike him down. He exclaims *Ungratefull Britons to Abandon thus
your Loyal friends* A few dwarf pine-trees indicate an American landscape.

The peace terms were much and unjustifiably attacked for leaving the
loyalists to the mercy of the Americans, see Nos. 6182, 6184, 6223
Wraxall, *Memoirs*, 1884, ii 416 ff

$8\frac{1}{4} \times 12\frac{3}{4}$ in.

6172 PEACE PORRIDGE ALL HOT | THE BEST TO BE GOT

*T Colley Eng*ᵈ·

*Pub by W Richardson Feb*ʸ *11 1783 near Surrey Street Strand.*

Engraving. Beneath are engraved the words of a song. Persons representing the powers negotiating peace stand holding basins of soup. France (l.) in profile to the r, in feathered hat, bag-wig, and ruffles, holds a smoking bowl, and smiles, saying, *By gar John English you have well Crumb'd my dish.*

Spain, full-face, in ruff, cloak, and slashed doublet, with jack-boots, says, *my peace soup is made very good by Stewing down Minorca & the Floridas.* England, stout, plainly dressed, with a large stick under his arm, stands in profile to the l, saying to France and Spain, *my loss is your gain for my Soup is very Thin* America, in the foreground (l), sits on a low bank, saying, *I rest Contented with a dish of Independant Soup.* She is an Indian woman with a head-dress and girdle of feathers. Holland, dressed as usual in a plain hat, short jacket, and wide breeches, stands (r) holding a smoking tobacco-pipe in his hand He turns away from a waiter (r) who offers him a bowl, saying, *I will not taste it yet as it is not relish'd to my mind.* The waiter (l) says, *Taste it Mynheer 'tis better than you deserve*

Preliminaries of peace were signed at Versailles between Britain, France, and Spain on 20 Jan 1783, preliminary articles for a separate peace having been signed between England and America on 30 Nov. 1782 After being violently attacked by Fox and North as a means to overthrow Shelburne, the terms were substantially accepted by the Coalition, see Nos. 6222, 6229. A truce was made with Holland at the same time, but the Dutch demands were refused and a definite peace was not made till 20 May 1784 on terms more favourable to England, see No 6292. For the peace see also Nos. 6009, 6171, 6173, 6174, 6175, 6176, 6182, 6184, 6188, 6212, 6223, 6267

Beneath the design the words of the SONG are engraved *Tune. Roast Beef of Old England* The first and last verses are.

> *The Frenchman & Spaniard are both Cock-a-hoop*
> *With America too they have got such nice Soup*
> *Yet a Blow or two more might have made them all Stoop*
>> *O! the rare Soup & the Cooks boys*
>> *And O! the rare Cooks & the Soup.*
>
> *Tho' things have gone Cross for a long time Confest*
> *Yet now to lament, is no more than a Jest*
> *But as well as we can out of Bad, make the best.*

6 × 8¾ in.

6173 A POLITICAL CONCERT; THE VOCAL PARTS BY

1 *Miss America*, 2. *Franklin*, 3. *F——x*, 4 *Kepp——ll*, 5 *M*ʳˢ *Brittania,*
6. *Shelb——n*, 7 *Dun—i—g*, 8. *Benidick Rattle Snake*

*Colley Ingra*ᵈ¹

Pub. by W. Richardson Feb 18. 1783 near Suroy St Strand.

Engraving A number of figures, sitting and standing, the words of their catch or song issuing in large labels from their mouths, their identity indicated by numbers referring to an explanation engraved beneath the title In the centre stand (1) *Miss America* (l) and (5) *M*ʳˢ *Brittania* (r.),

¹ A design in the manner not of Colley, but of No 6162

each with a hand on the staff of liberty, which is surmounted by a large Phrygian cap. America, wearing her head-dress of feathers and a draped kirtle with sandals, holds a sword, she sings, *Oh give me death or liberty O give me &c . .* and 'Mrs. Brittania' holding her shield and spear, sings, *Brittons never shall be Slaves.* On each side of these two is a seated figure: (2), Franklin (l) next America, and (6) Shelburne (r) next Britannia. Franklin, a dignified figure, wearing a fur cap, as in recent French portraits, his l hand thrust into his waistcoat, sings, *We'll return it untainted to heaven well [sic] return &c. .* Shelburne, with a more jaunty air and his inevitable smile, sings, *Oh what a charming thing a Battle, Oh &c &c.* Behind Shelburne (r), his hand resting on the back of his chair, and in profile to the l., stands (7) Dunning, in councillor's wig, gown, and bands, singing, *hum hum hum crick crack crick crack Cannons rattle Oh what a Charming thing a battle* Dunning was known as 'Orator Hum', see Nos 6042, 6091. Behind Dunning, on the extreme r, stands (8) *Benedick Rattle Snake*, a creature with a man's body, but a snake from the waist downwards and with the head of a snake. He wears the coat of a military officer, from the pocket hangs a paper, *dying Speech of Major Andre* He is singing, *Blood & plunder oh what a Charming thing a Battle* Over his head is suspended a hatchment, *Benedick Rattle Snake's Arms*, a gallows on the cross-beam of which sits a devil playing a fiddle He is Benedict Arnold, see No 5331, the American officer whose treacherous design to surrender West Point in 1780 involved the death of Major André as a spy. After serving as brigadier-general with the British, Arnold came to England in 1782. Behind Franklin (l) stands (4) Keppel, one hand thrust in his waistcoat, the other in his breeches pocket, singing, *Then a Crusing we will go then a Crusing we will go* On the extreme l., next Keppel, stands Fox, his hands in his breeches pockets, singing *Give Peace America with you & war with all the World.*

At this time the Ministry of Shelburne was falling, the terms of the peace were being attacked, he had made unsuccessful overtures, first to Fox and then to North, who had clearly been drawing together, and at the debate on the Address on the Peace in both Houses on 17 Feb. it appeared that a coalition between North and Fox was an established fact On 18 Feb it was reported that Shelburne was to resign immediately. Fitzmaurice, *Shelburne*, 1912, ii 230 ff.

Another impression, Richardson's imprint erased, *Pubd by W. Humphrey 227 Strand London* [n d.].

$8\frac{9}{16} \times 13$ in

6174 BLESSED ARE THE PEACEMAKERS

Pub by E Dachery Feby 24 1783 St James's Street

Engraving A procession of the late belligerent powers walking, r. to l., along a country road The leader is Spain, holding a large sword as if it was a walking-stick, and pointing up a hill to a building inscribed *Inquisition*, to which he is leading the procession. He is not dressed as the usual Spanish don, but wears a coat and breeches of modern cut Next, his r. hand on Spain's shoulder, is France, holding the end of a rope tied round the neck of George III, who follows him. The king is walking under a gateway formed of two vertical spears with a horizontal spear as cross-bar, from which the crown, lion, and unicorn are falling. Behind the king walks Shelburne, his attitude and dress repeating that of the king, but while

George looks concerned, he has his usual smile, in his r hand he carries a large rolled document inscribed *Preliminaries*. Next comes America, a lean man, with short lank hair, wearing a sleeved waistcoat and breeches He raises above his head a scourge with many lashes inscribed *America*, and appears about to strike Shelburne and the king In his l. hand he holds the end of a rope, which is round the neck of Holland, a sulky boor, who turns full-face, his hands thrust into his breeches pockets, smoking a pipe. All the others are walking in profile to the l , Spain and France capering with satisfaction. For other satires on the peace negotiations see No 6172, &c , and 6175.

$13\frac{1}{8} \times 8\frac{3}{4}$ in.

6175 THE PRELIMINARY SOLOMONS SURPRIZED BY THE GHOST OF JOHN HANGEMCHOP ESQ^R

Pub^d by J Barrow Feby 24th 1783. White Lion Bull Stairs Surry Side Black Friars Bridge.

Engraving (coloured impression) Seven members of the Ministry (l) headed by Shelburne shrink back in alarm at the entry from the r. of 'John Hangemchop', a Jack Ketch, whose head is a headsman's axe in the blade of which is an eye. A rope is coiled round his l arm, he holds out his r hand towards the alarmed ministers, saying, *How durst you make so vile a peace? Look at me & see what you deserve.* Shelburne, holding out both hands to fend off the apparition, says *I will never more dabble in Politicks.* The Duke of Richmond says *Monsieur has actually outwitted us.* Two other ministers say, *Oh that we had left Lord North to his fate,* and, *I hope it will not be Block and Block with us* The heads of three other ministers appear over the heads of the four spokesmen; their legs have been omitted by the artist. Between the ghost and the ministers is a small round table, on which lies a document *Preliminaries*   a pen in an ink-pot stands beside it Two chairs stand behind the table; in the foreground is an over-turned chair.

The Preliminaries of Peace were signed in Paris on 20 Jan , and were attacked in Parliament on 17 Feb. in order to overthrow Shelburne, see No. 6172, &c. The terms were more justly evaluated by the king, who wrote, 24 Jan. 1783, 'When I reflect on the Want of Soldiers and Sailors to enable us to carry on . the War against so many enemies   the more I thank Providence for having through so many difficulties, among which the want of Union and Zeal at home is not to be omitted, enabled so good a Peace with France, Spain and I trust soon the Dutch to be concluded ' *Corr. of George III,* vi. 222.

$6\frac{1}{4} \times 8\frac{7}{8}$ in.

6176 SHELB———N BADGERED & FOXED,

[? Gillray]

Pub: by E D'Achery Feb 28. 1783. St James Street.

Engraving A sequel to No. 5964 Lord Shelburne, seated on a chair in a landscape, holding up a document inscribed *Preliminaries*   , is being violently attacked by a fox (l) and a badger (r). The fox and the badger resemble those in No 5964 The fox (Fox) is tearing at Shelburne's leg with his paws, and at the *Preliminaries* [of Peace] with his teeth, while he is excreting and urinating against Shelburne with great violence. Shelburne looks over his l shoulder at the badger (North), who is rushing at him from the r and has seized his coat in his teeth

In the background (l) is a little circular temple, its domed roof supported on two columns. On a pedestal in its centre stands a minute figure of Shelburne, three peers wearing coronets kneel at his feet, he holds out to them two documents, one inscribed *Preliminaries*. The temple is inscribed *Corruption*; on the apex of the roof is a coronet, above it is engraved *the Idol of the Lords*, it resembles the temple in No 5606, &c On the horizon (r) is a gallows by which stands a minute figure of Britannia, her head irradiated; she points to the gallows, saying, *Impeach*. Beneath the title is engraved, *To the Virtuous Majority of the Commons who Voted for the Amendment to the Address on the memorable 18th of Feby 1783*

The attack on the Preliminaries of the Peace which revealed unmistakably the coalition of Fox and North against Shelburne took place on 17 not 18 Feb. In the Commons the Ministry were defeated by 224 to 208, in the Lords they had a majority of 13, though the terms of Peace were much attacked *Parl Hist* xxiii 435–98, Walpole, *Last Journals*, 1910, ii. 481; Fitzmaurice, *Shelburne*, 1912, ii. 235 ff. The first of many satires on the Coalition. Overtures to bring Fox and North together began in December and had been anticipated in July Fitzmaurice, *op. cit*, ii 231, *Corr of Lord Auckland*, 1861, pp. 7 ff The theme of the fox and the badger was developed by Rowlandson in *The Loves of the Fox and the Badger, or the Coalition Wedding*, 7 Jan. 1784 See also Nos 5964, 6186, 6196, 6204

$7\frac{7}{8} \times 12\frac{1}{2}$ in.

6177 OVER WITH HIM

Pubd by E. D. Achery. Feb. 28. 1783 St James Street.

Engraving. Fox, with a fox's head, tumbling Lord Shelburne out of a wheelbarrow. Shelburne, arms and legs outstretched, lies on his back in the barrow, which Fox (l.) is tilting on its side From clouds above Fox's head appears the head of Lord North as Boreas directing a blast from his mouth at Shelburne's face

Beneath the title is inscribed, *The Devil can't Stand against a Double force. Vide the Votes of H: C. on ye 18 of Feby 1783.* This is a reference to the adverse vote of 17 Feb , see No. 6176, where the same mistake is made. After a second adverse vote on the terms of peace on 21 Feb. due to the combined attack of Fox and North, Shelburne resigned on 24 Feb., and there was a ministerial interregnum until 2 April Walpole, *Last Journals*, 1910, ii 487 ff.; *Ann Reg.*, 1783, pp. 168 ff See also Grafton, *Autobiography*, 1898, pp 363 ff , Fitzwilliam, *Shelburne*, 1912, ii, chap. vii, Romilly, *Memoirs*, 1844, i. 270–5.

$11\frac{5}{8} \times 8\frac{1}{2}$ in

6178 A COALITION OF PARTIES

[? Gillray.]

Pub E D. Achery Feb 28. 1783 St James St

Engraving North (l) and Fox (r) hanging back to back, each in a noose, from a stout post At the top of the post is a large oval shield (?) with a double St. George's cross. Nails are fixed in the shield, and to these the ropes are attached. North's arms hang limply at his side; Fox's hands are clasped, he has a fox's head. Beneath the title is engraved, *Give Justice her claims* A freely sketched landscape with clouds forms the background.

See Nos 6176, 6177, also satires on the joint attack of North and the Foxites on the Peace terms which revealed the Coalition

$11\frac{7}{8} \times 8\frac{1}{2}$ in.

6179 THE COALITION. [c Feb 1783]

Yearac [Carey] *Cuisit & Hac* . [1]

Engraving. North and Fox stand, bound together by a ribbon round their shoulders inscribed *Tie of Interest* The l arm of North (l.) is on the l. shoulder of Fox, he says to him,

> *Though you are a Fox by name & nature*
> *I hope to me you will prove no traitor*

Fox answers,

> *While you can give me Place & Pension*
> *Your neck need never fear Extension.*

Under North's hand, and resting on Fox's shoulder, is a paper inscribed *Vicar of Bray*. Fox's l hand rests on a table (r) against which he leans; he is holding a paper inscribed *Debts of honour to my Lord Cog—150 1700.* On the table are cards and dice, with a paper inscribed *Plan for disarming the I——h V——rs* [Irish Volunteers]

On the wall which forms the background are two oval bust portraits, one (l) behind North, of North in clerical bands and gown, inscribed *Vicar of Bray*, the other (r) behind Fox, a portrait of Fox with a rope round his neck inscribed *Sergius Cataline*, indicating that Fox is the treacherous conspirator, North the corrupt time-server. Above the portraits are three prints On the l. an execution scene· the cart has just moved off leaving two figures dangling from a gibbet In the centre is a ship in full sail, being blown by a blast inscribed *Boreas* The water on which it sails is the *Stream of Corruption* The frame is inscribed *State Vessel* On the r is a print of a fox running off with a goose On the ground (l) is a large sack inscribed *Budget* Beneath the design is engraved

> *Believe me friend quoth North to Fox,*
> *While we together scratch and Box,*
> *And in the House, incessant splutter,*
> *Ourselves bedaubing with state gutter,*
> *Like Æsop's Bear and Lion quar'ling,*
> *We lose the prey for which we're snarling;*
> *By mutual Interest bound, lets try*
> *To make this doughty Shelburne fly,*
> *If he's for war why zounds he's mad,*
> *If he's for Peace 'tis all as bad,*
> *When once we've got the treas'ry chest,*
> *You're much in debt—mum for the rest.*

Another satire on the joint attack of North and the Foxites on the peace terms which revealed the Coalition, see Nos 6176–8 For North as Vicar of Bray see also No 6235 For North appealing to Fox for protection from

[1] Clipped. The signature follows the verses.

the scaffold, see No 6282. R Lucas, *Lord North*, 1913, II 208 ff, contends that North's motive in joining Fox was fear of impeachment. See No. 5969, &c

7 × 6⅞ in

6180 THE F——X, GOOSE AND PRIMIER.   [I Mar 1783]

Engraving. From the *Rambler's Magazine*, Feb. 1783.[1] Shelburne (1) seated in an arm-chair near an ornate table, on which are coins At his feet kneel Burke and Fox with a fox's head. Neither Shelburne nor Burke is recognizably drawn, but they are indicated by the title and the words spoken. Burke says, *By Ja——s what a fool was I to turn myself out before I got in—That d——n'd F——x has made a Goose of me* Shelburne answers, *Very sublime and beautiful! but you are fallen like Lucifar [sic] never to hope again* Fox says, *Tho' you have stolen the Peace out of my Pocket, forgive me and henceforth Command me*

This is entirely contrary to the political situation of Feb. 1783, which is more correctly represented in Nos 6176-9

4¹³⁄₁₆ × 3¹⁄₁₆ in.

6181 THE WASHERWOMAN, UP WITH THE JESUIT

Pub^d. March 1st, 1783 by A Killingbeck Down Street

Engraving A pair of scales, in one, which rests on the ground, sits Lord North, in profile to the l, in the other, in the air, sits Lord Shelburne, in profile to the r., dressed as a monk. North is the same fat old washerwoman with a bag-wig as in No. 5975 by the same artist. Shelburne, wearing his Garter ribbon, holds in his l hand a money-bag inscribed *Blessings of Peace*, his r. is raised as if in admonition A fox (Charles Fox) runs along the beam of the scales weighing it down so that North completely outweighs Shelburne; he says, *My Weight for the People* Under the scale on which Shelburne sits is a tombstone inscribed, *I have met with the fate my Duplicity deserved, had I acted with Integrity to the man who had the full Confidence of the People, my Abilities might have done Honor to myself and served my country. PW. ob^t 1783.*

The allusion is to the premiership obtained in July 1782 to the chagrin and disappointment of Fox The initials probably stand for William Petty reversed

This satire, with No. 6232, is exceptional as a direct apology for the coalition between Fox and North, see Nos 6176-9, &c. But cf also the attacks on the peace terms, No. 6172, &c., which are indirect justifications of the joint attack on Shelburne by which the Coalition came into existence, and Nos 6274, 6277, 6291

8¼ × 7⅛ in.

6182 THE SAVAGES LET LOOSE, OR THE CRUEL FATE OF THE LOYALISTS

March 1783.

Sold by W Humphrey N° 227 Strand.

Engraving (coloured impression) American loyalists are being murdered

---

[1] Note by Mr Hawkins There is no copy of this magazine in the British Museum All other prints from the magazine are so annotated

by Red Indians. An Indian (l.) seizes by the hair a loyalist lying on the ground, and holds up a knife saying *I'll scalp him* Another Indian (r.) raises a tomahawk in both hands above a loyalist who kneels on one knee, saying *O cruel Fate! is this the Return for our Loyalty* The Indian says, *I'll tomahawk the Dog.*

A third Indian (l.) pulls a rope attached to the ropes by which four loyalists hang by the neck to the branch of a tree, inscribed *Recommended to Congress by lord S——e* [Shelburne] He is saying *I have them all in a String*

The Indians all wear tall feather head-dresses and kilts of feathers. Of the six loyalists, two of those hanging from the tree are dressed as military officers, the others as civilians.

Beneath the design is engraved:

> *Is this a Peace, when Loyalists must bleed?*
> *It is a Bloody Piece of work indeed.*

The chief danger to the loyalists was not from Red Indians, but from penal legislation, confiscation of property, and personal molestation at the hands of Americans, who, however, are perhaps represented by the Indians. The provision for loyalists in the peace terms was resented by American loyalists and denounced by many Englishmen, sometimes factiously, sometimes sincerely. To quote a contemporary squib·

> Tis an honor to serve the bravest of nations
> And be left to be hanged in their capitulations.

But 'England had gotten for the loyalists the utmost attainable in the treaty and, later, proved honorable and generous in the highest degree by compensating the Loyalists out of her own treasury'. Van Tyne, *The Loyalists in the American Revolution*, 1902, p. 288. See Nos. 6171, 6184, 6223.

$8\frac{3}{8} \times 13\frac{1}{8}$ in.

6183 A COALITION MEDAL STRUCK IN BRASS

Js ff. [Sayers]
Published 3ᵈ March 1783 by Edwᵈ Hedges

Engraving A medallion on which are the heads, in profile to the l, of Fox and North, as if in relief, that of Fox superimposed on that of North. The artist has brought out both the contrast and an unexpected similarity in the two faces, both fat, both with prominent eyebrows The expression of Fox suggests satisfied cunning, that of North bewilderment and dismay. Round the upper edge of the medallion is inscribed *Par nobile Fratrum.* Beneath the title is inscribed

> *N.B. The Reverse may be expected in a few days*

One of two famous and similar satires by Sayers, see No 6234 The 'medal' appears in No. 6219. Cf. also No. 6198 For the coalition see Nos 6176–9.

Diam. $6\frac{1}{4}$ in.

6184 THE NIGHT MARE OR HAG RIDDN MINISTER.

IB [J. Boyne].

London Publshed as the Act Direct [sic] *March 4 1783 by R Rusted*
N° 3 Bridge St¹ Ludgate Hill

Engraving Lord Shelburne lying at full length, asleep, supported on two
parallel rows of sharp pinnacles, representing the articles of the peace
treaty Dunning (l), now Lord Ashburton, in counsellor's wig and gown,
crouches behind his head, in profile to the r , holding a smelling-bottle to
his nose, and saying, *take comfort my Lord, for you I will be allways Dunning*
On Shelburne's prostrate body stands Fox, with his own face, but the body
of a fox; he urinates against Shelburne's face and tears at him with his fore-
paws, saying *If he opens his mouth I will be down his Throat.* North's head
(r.), suspended in space, is saying *the North fog Rot Him* On the nearer
row of sharp pinnacles, on the points of which Shelburne is so painfully
lying, is inscribed (l to r.), *It shall be Recomend* [sic] *to Congress to Cut the*
Loyalists .   16 Artic¹, 14 Art¹, 10 Art¹ᵉ, 6 Art¹ᵉ, 11 Art¹ᵉ, 7 Art¹ᵉ,
4 Art¹ᵉ. There is a background of minute zigzag lines or shading.

For the attack on the different preliminary articles of the peace by
North (17 Feb.) see *Parl. Hist.* xxiii 443 ff.; by Fox (21 Feb), pp 526 ff.
The Articles are printed on pp. 346 ff. See also Nos. 6168, 6171–7, 6181,
6182, 6199

Reissued, 29 March, with a different title.

6⅞ × 10 in.

6185 [GEORGE III HOLDING THE BALANCE]

Pub: March 6ᵗʰ 1783 by T. Connell, Bruton Street.

Engraving George III seated on a low square stool, each leg of which rests
on one of four pinnacles on the four corners of the roof of a building
inscribed *St Stephens Chapel 1783* In his l. hand he holds up a small pair
of empty scales, equally balanced. Beneath the design is engraved.

> *I'm above all! I yet Rule the Roast!*
> *As I please the Balance shall preponderate!*

This was published during the ministerial interregnum which followed
the resignation of Shelburne owing to the joint attack on the peace treaty
by Fox and North. The satirist's suggestion that the king could hold the
balance between Fox and North was unfounded, his unsuccessful attempts
early in March to induce North to break with Fox, by interviews, first with
Lord Guilford, North's father, and then with North on March 2nd and 3rd,
may have inspired this satire. *Corr. of George III*, vi 257–8, 259–60. The
king indeed on 7 March still contemplated resistance to the Coalition,
'a desperate Faction in whose hands I will never throw myself'. *Ibid.*,
vi 262 See also pp 265–8. George III, so far from 'ruling the roast',
contemplated abdication See Walpole, *Last Journals*, 1910, ii. 494 f.[1]
Cf. No. 6205.

---

[1] George III prepared two draft messages to the House of Commons, one
calling on 'those who feel for the spirit of the Constitution to stand forth to his
Assistance' against the Coalition, the other, announcing his intention to resign the
Crown to the Prince of Wales and retire to Hanover Both are conjecturally dated
28 March by Sir J Fortescue *Corr. of Geo III*, vi 314 ff See also Wraxall,
Memoirs, 1884, ii 35 f

6186 A COALITION BETWEEN THE FOX & THE BADGER, OR THE HONEY MOON OF THEIR HAPPY UNION

Pub^d according to act by W. Humphrey N° 227, Strand. 6th March 1783

Engraving. Fox (r) and North (l) embracing, Fox, about to kiss North on the mouth, says *I perfectly agree with your Lord Ship*, he is taller and less fat than North, and has an expression of cunning, North, one of perplexed alarm Under a tree (r.) a fox and a clumsy dog, its collar inscribed North, sniff at each other. In the distance (l.) stands Shelburne, a small figure, who points at Fox and North smiling and saying *Risum teneatis Amici*.

Dundas, on 17 Feb 1783, had spoken of the coalition of North with the Foxites, as revealed in the debate of that day, as 'the honeymoon of their loves', and Sheridan's comment had been that if there was a coalition it was 'rather to be called the wedding day'. *Parl. Hist.* xxiii. 469, 483 See also Nos. 6189, 6193 For Fox and North as fox and badger see Nos. 5964, 6176, 6196, 6204.

A coloured impression in B.M L , Tab. 524 a, iv, p 58

$8\frac{1}{4} \times 13$ in.

6187 WAR.

[Gillray.]

Pub 9th March 1783, by H. Humphrey N° 51 New Bond S^t

Engraving (coloured and uncoloured impressions). A companion print to No. 6188 A scene in the House of Commons, a characteristic attack by Fox and Burke on North during North's ministry. The figures of Fox and Burke are rising from clouds, as if to suggest a vision of past debates. The H L. figure of the Speaker in his chair (l) is faintly sketched, North (l.) stands below him on solid ground All are in attitudes characteristic of the speakers: North, his back to the spectator, his r. arm raised, is saying, *want of candor, Illiberality our misfortunes entirely owing to Opposition.*

Fox, standing full-face, and looking towards North, raises his r arm, his fist clenched, saying, *I shold hold myself Infamous if I ever form'd a connection with him!—deserve the Ax!—disgrace! infamy!—shame! incapacity ignorance! corruption!—love of place! blunders, wants, weaknesses, gross stupidity hardly conceivable that so much Pride Vice and Folly can Exist in the same Animal*

The words of the speakers are etched beneath them

Burke (r) stands in profile to the l., bending forward and gesticulating violently, both hands raised with clenched fists above his head.

A composite selection from Fox's speeches, including the famous speech of 8 March 1782, *Parl Hist* xxii 1139, to show the monstrous nature of the Coalition, an anticipation of the method used so effectively in the pamphlet, *The Beauties of Fox, North, and Burke selected from their Speeches . . . 1784.* See also Nos. 6207, 6265

Grego, *Gillray*, p. 45. Wright and Evans, No 15. Reprinted, *G.W G*, 1830.

$5\frac{7}{16} \times 7\frac{7}{16}$ in. (pl.)

6188 NEITHE [*sic*] WAR NOR PEACE¹

[Gillray.]

Pub 9ᵗʰ Mar 1783 by H. Humphrey Nº 51 New Bond Street.

Engraving (coloured and uncoloured impressions) A sequel to No. 6187.
Fox and Burke are in similar attitudes, but Fox is gesticulating still more
violently and Burke stands nearer Fox North now stands with the other
two (r), below them as before, his l arm raised instead of his r. The
Speaker is in his chair as before. The place of North in the other print is
taken by a long scroll of *Preliminary Articles of Peace*, crowned by leaves,
which hangs from the upper part of the design (l) and rests on the floor
From beneath it a dog appears barking, *Bough Wough* Beneath the design
is etched,

The astonishing Coalition.

Instead of an attack by Fox and Burke on North, the three combine to
attack Shelburne and the articles of the peace. While North was making his
attack on 17 Feb a dog began to bark and set all the members in a roar.
Lord North laughed heartily, and when the House was restored to order,
he threw it again into the loudest fit of laughter, by jocosely addressing the
chair, 'Sir, I was interrupted by a new Speaker, but as his argument is
concluded I will resume mine ' *Parl Hist* xxiii. 455, cf No 6192

These Preliminary Articles which had been so much abused were substantially accepted by the Coalition Ministry, see No 6267.

Grego, *Gillray*, p. 45. Wright and Evans, No. 16 Reprinted, *G.W G*,
1830

$5\frac{7}{16} \times 7\frac{7}{16}$ in. (pl.).

6189 THE UNION

[E. T.?]

Pub by Mʳˢ D Achery Sᵗ James Street March 11 1783.

Engraving (coloured and uncoloured impressions) The devil officiates at
the wedding of North and Fox. North stands in profile to the r. holding
out a ring in his l hand towards a corpulent fox, wearing a coat, who stands
on his hind-legs facing him, with a sly expression North's profile expresses
bewilderment. Between them, a hand on the shoulder of each, stands the
Devil capering, one eye closed, with a diabolical grin He is a nude man
with horns, tail, and the legs of a satyr. On the ground between Fox and
North is an open book, inscribed *Marriage Ceremony*. Beneath the title is
engraved *"Whom —— has Join'd, let no Man put asunder!"*

On 21 Feb Pitt denounced the 'unnatural coalition . . if this ill-omened
marriage is not already solemnized, I know a just and lawful impediment,
and, in the name of the public safety, I here forbid the banns'. *Parl Hist.*
xxiii 552. See also Nos 6186, 6193.

$5\frac{11}{16} \times 9$ in.

6190 THE TEA-TAX-TEMPEST—OR OLD TIME WITH HIS
MAGICK-LANTHERN.

Pubᵈ March 12. 1783 by W Humphreys [sic] Nº 227 Strand

Engraving A reduced and altered copy of No 5490, evidently by an
English artist It is less heavily shaded, and the details are clearer The
chief alteration is a large white label issuing from the mouth of Time,

covering much of the upper r corner of the design, and inscribed, *There you see the little Hot Spit Fire Tea pot that has done all the Mischief—There you see the Old British Lion basking before the American Bon Fire whilst the French Cock is blowing up a Storm about his Ears to Destroy him and his young Welpes—there you See Miss America grasping at the Cap of Liberty— There you see The British Forces be yok'd and be cramp'd flying before the Congress Men—There you see the thirteen Stripes and Rattle-Snake exalted —There you see the Stamp'd Paper help to Make the Pot Boil—There you See &c &c &c*

The scene thrown on the curtain by the lantern is copied with fair accuracy, except that the coffee-pot with its three legs and hinged lid has become an English tea-pot, its detached lid flying into the air. In place of the two books on the ground at Time's feet there is one book open at an illustration which represents a man (l) aiming with a cross-bow at a man on horseback, perhaps intended for George III, riding from l to r.; there are three standing figures and in the air is what appears to be a crown.

For the snake emblem on the American flag see No. 5973 &c. For other references to the Stamp Act see No. 5487, &c

$8\frac{7}{8} \times 12\frac{7}{8}$ in.

6191 BLUE & BUFF OR REYNARD IN HIS CLOSET, AT HIS WITS END

Pub: by D. Achery. March 16. 1783 St Jame's Street

Engraving. Fox, with a fox's head, stands looking up at the Devil, whose head appears from clouds in the upper r. corner of the print. He holds in his r hand a pistol, in his l a dagger and a noose. On a table (l.) beside him is a cup inscribed *Poison*. Behind it is a gallows, the upright constructed of playing-cards, the horizontal of dice, while a curved strut supporting the angle is the segment of an EO table (see No 5928), the letters *O* and *E* (for odd and even) alternating. The Devil's head is in profile looking downwards; he has twisted goat's horns, satyr's ears, and a beard, and is saying

I have presented you with the Choice of Four,
Dagger, Pistol, Halter Poison and no more,
make haste! decide, they'll either suit you well,
then to your seat below—the Red Hot Nyche in Hell.

Fox says,

O let me spare the tale!—
Tis full of Horror—Dreadfull was the sight!
The Hungry Lions greedy for their Prey—
devoured each place and pension—
——twixt me and death—

Beneath the title is engraved·

——Suicide
thou Balmy friend to Disappointed pride.

The spoken words are on large labels.

At this date the fruits of office were within sight, and Fox's financial position was correspondingly improved; this print would have had more point during Shelburne's ministry, cf Nos. 6015, 6020, &c.

$11\frac{13}{16} \times 9\frac{7}{16}$ in.

6192 [NORTH WHITEWASHING FOX]

Fred O'Daub fecit. [J Sayers]

Published 17ᵗʰ March 1783 by Edwᵈ Hedges Cornhill

Engraving A scene in the House of Commons. Fox has taken Lord North's l hand in both his, while North, applying a paint-brush to his face, has made a white patch on its swarthiness Fox (l.), full-face, with an inscrutable expression, is descending the lowest step below the tiers of seats. North stands in profile to his l looking at Fox with anxious frown. Behind are rows of members, their heads sketchily indicated. A dog looks up at North, cf No 6188 Beneath the design is etched,

—*Qui Color ater erat nunc est contrarius atro*

Translated for the Country Gentlemen.
I have found him a warm Friend a fair though formidable Adversary

The English is a paraphrase of North's praise of Fox and attempted justification of their relations on 21 Feb. 1783: 'When I had the happiness to possess his confidence and friendship, I always found him open, manly and sincere, I knew his Temper to be warm, but his nature is generous . . . As an enemy I have always found him formidable.' *Parl Hist* xxiii. 558. See Nos. 6186–9, &c, and p. 694 n

$9\frac{7}{8} \times 7\frac{3}{4}$ in

6193 ST JAMES'S PARK. [1782¹]

[? After Bunbury or C. L Smith.]

Engraving. Frontispiece from *The Coalitional Rencontre Anticipated.* 'Carlo Khan' (Fox) meets the fair Northelia by assignation in the Mall. North, dressed as a woman, looks round at Fox who has come up behind him, and addresses him with outstretched hand. They stand in a formal avenue of leafless trees which recedes in perspective behind them. North wears a cloak over a dress which trails on the ground, his hands are in a muff and a flat ribbon-trimmed hat is perched on his high coiffure. A large masculine foot protrudes from his petticoat, and he draws back coyly at the sight of Fox. Beneath the design are engraved Fox's words:

But why so soon abroad, my dear,
At this dull season of the Year?
Why meet this early chilling, breeze?
Why stroll amongst these leafless trees?

For similar ridicule of the Coalition, see Nos. 6186, 6189, 6197.

$8\frac{3}{4} \times 7\frac{5}{16}$ in.

6194 [FOX AND NORTH AS HEROD AND PILATE]

[Gillray]

Pubᵈ March 20ᵗʰ 1783 by H Humphrey Nᵒ 51 New Bond Street.

Engraving (coloured and uncoloured impressions). Fox and North, as Herod and Pilate, contemplating the execution of Shelburne, who for this occasion takes the part of Christ. All three have the beards of Jews, the

¹ This print should have been placed after No 6276 (December 1782), since Fox is called 'Carlo Khan' in the text W Sichel, *Sheridan*, ii 28 n The book does not appear to be in the B M L

countenance and appearance of Fox, but not of the others, being Jewish. Fox stands full-face, pointing backwards with his r thumb at Shelburne (l), who stands with downcast eyes, his wrists crossed as if tied together, leaning against a gallows North (l.) stands by Fox putting his r hand on Fox's left shoulder and holding his l. hand. North and Shelburne wear bag-wigs and their Garter ribbons Fox looks unkempt, with rough hair, his waistcoat partly unbuttoned, the empty pockets hanging inside out.

Beneath the design is etched, *And Herod and Pilate were made Friends together that same Day; for before they were Enemies one to another. Luke Chap 23, Ver. 12.*

Richard Hill, M P. for Shropshire, had compared the Coalition to an alliance between Herod and Pontius Pilate. R. Lucas, *Lord North*, ii 226 See Nos 6176-9, &c.

Reprinted, *G.W G.*, 1830

$7 \times 6\frac{13}{16}$ in

6195 THE LOAVES AND FISHES

J H inv^t

Pub by E^d Achery March 24. 1783 St James Street

Engraving. George III presides at a rectangular table at which sit past and prospective ministers, grasping at the loaves and fishes which lie on the table. On the l side of the table and on the king's r sit Shelburne and his supporters, on the opposite side sit those who have ousted them. The king sits in an ornate chair, on his r. sits Shelburne putting his arm on the shoulder of Dunning, who sits on his other side Shelburne says *I must submit!—may it prove Poison to them say I.* Dunning answers *Never mind my Lord—give them rope enough, and they will hang themselves* The king turns to Fox and North, who sit on his l hand, and says, pointing to the table, *pray help your selves Gentlemen* Fox, who has a fox's head, has seized a loaf in each hand, saying *An't please your Maj——ty I'll have these for me & my friends.* The loaf under his l hand is inscribed *Treasury*, North, who sits on Fox's l., says, *hold Charley, that 's more then comes to your Share* The other two on the r. side of the table are Keppel and Burke. Keppel, who is next North, puts his r hand on a loaf, in his l. he holds a fish from whose mouth go lines attached to two other fish and another loaf, he is saying *I'm fond of Sea fish* A naval officer opposite him hugs a loaf and grasps the tail of one of the fish on Keppel's line. He is identified in a contemporary hand as Palliser, but is more probably Lord Howe, who was First Lord of the Admiralty from 29 Jan. 1782 (after Keppel's resignation) till 8 April, when he was replaced by Keppel. He is in *profil perdu* but his figure and a black eyebrow suggest Howe

On Keppel's l , and at the r. corner of the table, sits Burke grasping a loaf in his r. hand, a fish in his l He is saying *Rhetorick is of no use here! tis catch that catch can* In the foreground (r), at Burke's side, two dogs laden with money-bags are running off to the r. Over them is inscribed *Pay Office Clerks* and (smaller) *Fulham.* On the money-bag of one is £200.000, on that of the other £100 000 Burke became paymaster-general under Rockingham, resigned office with Fox on Shelburne's appointment, and was again (on 7 April) to become paymaster. On returning to office he reinstated two clerks, Powell and Bembridge, who had recently been dismissed by Barré for malversation, for which he was attacked in parliament on 24 April and 19 May 1783 *Parl. Hist* xxiii, pp. 900 ff; Wraxall, *Memoirs*, 1884, iii. 77–86.[1]

Opposite Burke, at the near l corner of the table, sits Conway, the Commander-in-Chief, in general's uniform, grasping a fish in one hand, a lobster in the other. He is saying, *I fear they'll not leave me one poor lobster* He had disappointed Fox by not resigning on Shelburne's appointment, he did not however lose office till after the dissolution of Parliament in 1784, when he resigned. In the centre of the table are three unclaimed loaves, the one nearest the king is inscribed *Secretary of State.*

A representation of the uncertainties and jealousies of the political situation during the ministerial interregnum between the resignation of Shelburne on 24 Feb and the appointment of the coalition ministry under the nominal leadership of the Duke of Portland on 2 April See Walpole, *Last Journals*, 1910, ii. 487–509, Wraxall, *Memoirs*, 1884, iii. 25 ff. For the attitude of the King see No. 6185 On 14 April the Duke of Chandos, attacking the Coalition said that 'his Majesty's closet had been assailed by force and that parties fought now for the loaves and fishes only'. *Parl Hist* xxiii 755 Cf. Nos. 6223, 6240, 6248.

$8\frac{1}{2} \times 12\frac{13}{16}$ in.

6196 COALITION
THE FOX & BADGER BOTH IN A HOLE.
Pub W Richardson March 27. 1783 near Surry St Strand

Engraving An opening or cave in the side of a hill inside which sit facing each other, on their hind-legs, a corpulent badger (l) and a fox (r) The badger is adorned with a wide Garter ribbon, a shirt-frill, and a black bow which indicates the 'bag' which was the appendage to a wig. The front of the cave is wreathed with vines bearing many bunches of grapes. The badger (North) says,

> *The grapes which round this Cavern grow in plenty*
> *My new Friend Fox will prove to each a dainty.*

The fox (Charles Fox) says,

> *Tho once I stunk you from your Hole*
> *You now are welcome in upon my Soul*

Outside the cave (l) stands the Devil with horns, wings, satyr's legs, and a tail. He points at the couple within with his r hand, holding up his l and saying

> *He he he ——— he*
> *They both are for me*

On 22 March 1782 a satire by Gillray had been published called *Changing places; alias, Fox stinking the Badger out of his Nest.* See No. 5964, see also Nos 6176, 6186, 6204.

$8 \times 12\frac{11}{16}$ in

6197 COALITION MINUET
Pub: by E Dachery March 29 1783 St James Street

Engraving (coloured and uncoloured impressions). Design in an oval.

---

[1] Possibly the dogs were added in a later issue of the print, as they seem to refer to the scandal over Powell and Bembridge Powell committed suicide, Bembridge was tried and sentenced

Fox, r. (full-face), dances a minuet with Lord North (l.) dressed as a lady with enormous hooped petticoats and hair decorated with feathers, but wearing a Garter ribbon They hold hands, Fox holding his hat in his l. hand In the background (r.) the Lord Chancellor, Thurlow, sits playing a set of bagpipes, while he holds out his l. hand to Britannia, who sits near him (r.) in profile to the l., and hands to him a bag of money, saying *I pay the Piper.*

Thurlow was retained as Lord Chancellor during the ministries of Rockingham and Shelburne at the king's wish, and on Shelburne's resignation the king used him as an intermediary in attempts to form a ministry that should exclude Fox. *Corr. of George III*, vi. 257-8, 263-4, 269-72 On the formation of the Coalition ministry, Fox insisted on Thurlow's resignation and on 9 April the Great Seal was put in Commission with Lord Loughborough as Chief Commissioner. The bag of money which he is receiving is probably an allusion to the pension granted to Thurlow together with the reversion of a tellership of the exchequer, attacked in the House of Commons on 5 March *Parl. Hist.* xxiii. 583-4.

$6\frac{1}{4} \times 9\frac{1}{2}$ in.

THE NIGHT MARE, OR PRIME MINISTER HAG-RIDDEN

Pub^d 29th March 1783 by W Humphrey N° 227 Strand

A reissue (coloured) of No 6184 A later state.

6198 THE COMPOUND MEDALLION [*c.* March 1782]

Engraving. The heads of George III, Lord North, and Fox superimposed, in profile to the r., the King's lowest, Fox uppermost, in relief, within a circle representing a medallion Round the edge is engraved, *To Govern with Goodness, to Amuse with Falacy, to Abuse with Words*, indicating the parts played respectively by the three men.

An imitation of Sayers' *Coalition Medal struck in brass*, see No. 6183, but drawn with more competence, the effect of a medal in relief being more skilfully rendered.

Diam. 6 in.

6199 PUKE—ATION IN ANSWER TO THE LATE STATE OF THE NATION.

Pub^d by E Hedges N° 92 Cornhill April 1. 1783

Engraving. Candidates for office in the ministry (which was not formed till 2 April), most of them vomiting and grasping posts (cf No 5984) A devil with widespread bat's wings hovers over their heads, saying, *These Posts my dears are temporal I have Posts below which you Shall have Eternal.* The two central posts are *Treasury* (r.) and *Admiralty* (l.), a man, difficult to identify, kneeling on one knee and leaning forward, clasps the *Treasury* post with both hands He says, *Let me handle the stivers* Behind him, holding his forehead and resting his l. elbow on the *Admiralty* post, is Keppel, vomiting and saying *Tis a Damnable Peace!* Behind the *Treasury* post and to the r. stands Lord John Cavendish resting his elbow on the post, vomiting and saying *So we'll tell the Game* He was to be Chancellor of the Exchequer On the r. are the two Secretaries in the new ministry:

Fox is seated on the top of a post inscribed *Secretary*. He bends forward, in profile to the r., vomiting, and holding the hand of North who stands facing him, also vomiting, with one hand resting on the top of the post inscribed *Northern Department*. Fox says, *I'll join hands with you in Damning the Peace*, North says, *by God 'tis Froth*. On the l. a man, presumably the Duke of Portland, stands behind a tall post inscribed *P Minister Pst*, both hands clasped round it, vomiting and saying *It is not worth a groat*. On the extreme l., his l. hand resting on a lower *Post*, stands Burke, saying *This Peace sticks in my Throat*.

Through a little window in the extreme upper l. corner of the print looks the face of Shelburne, one finger laid to his nose, saying *I have sickend them all*.

A large scroll or document covering the ground on which they are vomiting is under the feet of the aspirants to office. On it is written *Preliminary Articles for restoring Tranquillity between the Powers at War. that they may all take a little Breath & then —— at it again Pell-Mell.*

Beneath the design is inscribed ·

> *But a short time ago, the Great Folks of the Nation*
> *The Doctors declar'd, was in a Purgation*
> *The case now is alter'd—such Shiting must cease*
> *Since now all the great ones are spewing on Peace*
> *In War or in Peace then you find out that Brittain*
> *Must some how or other be Pukeing or Shitting*

These lines and the title appear to refer to the print, *The State of the Nation*, see No. 5479, &c Shelburne had resigned owing to the combined attack of Fox and North on the Preliminary Articles of peace, see Nos. 6184, 6188, &c.

$8\frac{1}{4} \times 12\frac{7}{8}$ in.

6200 POOR OLD ENGLAND. [? *c.* Feb.–March 1783]

Criofogo (?) fecit Frizz Crump Exc. *Lillecompoop sculp*

Mezzotint. Design in an oval, the title being etched across the back of an ornamental arm-chair in which George III is seated His face is distorted and he is scarcely recognizable, but *G R* surmounted by a crown, on a corner of his shirt which hangs over his breeches, shows his identity. The design is confused and the details difficult to decipher Beneath the oval is etched ·

A Section of a Magnificient & Superb Water Closet, with an exact front view of a Little Personage bound up by excruciating evils endevouring by main force of straining & distortion to Irradicate & exterminate by laborious perseverance those hard bound racking & growing Evils that have for a long Series of time burnt up those interiors which are most Succeptable of pain.
                              send him a good deliverance

Above the back of the chair is a confused design resembling a coat of arms On a medallion a man with a sword pursues a smaller figure who from his pigtail queue and top-boots is probably a Frenchman. Above the medallion are writhing serpents, probably signifying Discord or Faction, and above these a bird which may be intended for a phoenix. The supporters are a fox and a goose.

The king clutches a paper in his l. hand, on it is *American* . . . The words on a paper beside him are in reverse and almost illegible, except for the word *America* His l. foot rests on a foot-stool, a crown or fragment of a crown is on the ground at his feet. Two court-officials stand behind his chair, each with a wand of office. Curtains are draped on each side of the chair, and a glass dome is indicated as the roof.

The date is probably before the formal peace with America, perhaps during a ministerial interregnum, since the blank space in the inscription may have been left for the names of new ministers.

$4\frac{11}{16} \times 4$ in.

6201 A NEW ADMINISTRATION; OR—THE STATE QUACKS ADMINISTRING.

[Gillray]

Pub^d April 1st 1783, by W. Humphrey N° 227 Strand

Engraving. Britannia, in profile to the r , kneels on the ground, bending forward with an expression of angry distress She supports herself on her spear, the upper part of which rests against her r shoulder Her shield, broken, lies on the ground, her knee resting on it. Behind her (l.) are the two 'State Quacks', Fox and North, Fox, with a fox's head, sitting on the ground, lifts Britannia's petticoats in both hands North, very stout and fat, stands (l.) in profile to the r , holding a large syringe. A mountainous landscape, with clouds, forms the background.

One of many satires on the Coalition of Fox and North. Published on the eve of the appointment of the Ministry. Cf. Nos. 6176-9, &c

There is a coloured impression in 'Caricatures', iv. 32. B.M.L Tab 524.

$8\frac{13}{16} \times 12\frac{7}{8}$ in.

6202 M^RS GENERAL WASHINGTON, BESTOWING THIRTEEN STRIPES ON BRITANNIA. [1 April 1783]

Engraving. From the *Rambler's Magazine.* Britannia (r.), holding her shield as if trundling it, tries to escape from Washington, who holds her by a lock of her short hair, flourishing a scourge with thirteen knotted lashes. Behind Washington walk France and Spain, followed (l) by Holland Washington wears a military coat, hat, sword, gorget, and a petticoat France is the conventional *petit-maître* dressed in the French manner, he holds a drawn sword in his r hand and points with the other at Britannia. Spain wears a feathered hat and ruff. Holland is a plainly dressed Dutch burgher with short jacket and bulky breeches Britannia says, *Is it thus my Children should treat me.* Washington answers, *Parents Should not behave like Tyrants to their Children* France says, *Encore mon Amy Encore.* Spain is saying, *Me wish you Stripe her well* Holland, behind the others, and on the extreme l , says, *Minheer deserves to be Striped for a Fool.*

$4\frac{13}{16} \times 3\frac{1}{16}$ in.

6203 THE MONSTER. 1783

[J. Boyne?]

Pub. April 2^d 1783 by W Humphrey N° 227 Strand, near Temple Bar.

Engraving (coloured and uncoloured impressions) A monster representing the new ministry, which was not actually formed until 2 April, the date of publication Its body is that of a fox, standing on one hind-leg It has eight heads in a group and no fore-legs, two other heads are below the tail. The central and uppermost head is that of the Duke of Portland, on the l is the Duke of Richmond, on the r. is Keppel. Below these there are four heads: l and in profile to the l is perhaps Lord Stormont; next probably William Eden, next Lord Carlisle; and, in profile to the r , Burke wearing his spectacles. Below these, and in profile to the l , is Lord John Cavendish From below the upraised tail issues a blast inscribed *Coalition*; beneath this are the heads of North and Fox.

Above the monster is inscribed:

The Beast that thou sawest Was and Is Not, and shall ascend out of the Bottomless Pitt, and go into Perdition, and they that dwell on the Earth shall wonder when they behold the Beast that Was & is Not & yet Is.

Rev. c. 17 v. 8.

Beneath the design is etched ·

This many-headed Monster of the Land
At present on one Leg is seen to stand,
Sometimes 'tis in, and sometimes it is out,
And like a Weather Cock it shifts about,
Fair Speeches and some Bribes it throws away,
To gain the Ascendancy,—perhaps a Day,
Stability and Permanency it mocks
The Head is [Portland] *and the Tail a Fox*
Each different Mouth bawls loudly for itself,
Yet all agree in one thing, Snack the Pelf.

One of many satires on the Coalition, cf Nos. 6176–9, 6195, &c. $9\frac{3}{4} \times 8\frac{13}{16}$ in.

A WARM BIRTH FOR THE OLD ADMINISTRATION

[Gillray]

Pub⁴ April 2ⁿᵈ 1783 by W. Humphrey

A reissue of No 5970 with an altered publication line.

6204 THE LORD OF THE VINEYARD.

[Gillray]

Pub⁴ April 3ᵈ 1783 by W. Humphrey N° 227 Strand.

Engraving (coloured and uncoloured impressions) Fox and North stand outside a high door under a stone arch, stretching out their arms to receive an enormous bunch of grapes which the Duke of Portland, who looks over the door, is handing down to them. He is saying *Take it between ye.* On the keystone of the arch is *Portland Place* [1]

Fox (l) has a fox's head with bushy eyebrows. He has grasped the bunch in both hands and is taking a great bite at the grapes; North (r) stands on tip-toe but is not touching the grapes.

---

[1] Portland Place is, of course, a punning allusion to Portland, the new prime minister It was then recently built, having been designed by the Adam brothers about 1778 Lord Stormont, President of the Council in the new ministry, was living at No. 15.

Beneath the title is etched:

> *Says the Badger to Fox,*
> *We're in the right Box,*
> > *These grapes are most charming & fine;*
> *Dear Badger you're right,*
> *Hold them fast squeeze them tight,*
> > *And we'll drink of political Wine.*

One of many satires on the Coalition, see Nos. 6176–9, &c For Fox and North as fox and badger see Nos. 5964, 6176, 6186, 6196

Grego, *Gillray*, pp. 46–7. Wright and Evans, No. 12. Reproduced, A. L. Simon, *Bottlescrew Days*, 1926, p 44

$12\frac{1}{4} \times 9$ in.

6205 COALITION DANCE.

[Gillray.]

Pub⁴ April 5ᵗʰ 1783 by W. Humphrey, 227 Strand.

Engraving (coloured and uncoloured impressions). North, Fox, and Burke, holding hands, dance round a terminal surmounted by a bust whose face is covered by a closed book, the *Whole Duty of Man* An owl perches on the head of the bust, round the terminal is a scroll inscribed *K. Wisdom 3ᵈ*, to show that the bust is that of George III Seated at the foot of the terminal on a stone is a demon, grinning diabolically and playing a fiddle Fox capers behind the demon, his r. hand holding North's l., his l. hand takes that of Burke, who is dressed as a jesuit as in No. 6026, but wearing a high biretta below which his wig and queue hang down. A cross and rosary are in his belt and he wears sandals over bare feet His head is turned in profile to the l., wearing spectacles, in his r. hand is an open book, *Little Red Riding Hood* Fox and North gaze sentimentally at each other, cf. No. 6193, &c The background is a mountainous landscape with clouds. Beneath the design is engraved:

> "*Let us dance & Sing, —— God bless the King, —— For he has made us merry Men all.*"

A satire on the king's prolonged resistance and unwilling surrender to the Coalition, cf. No. 6185. The title of Burke's book is apparently an allusion to his speech of 9 July 1782 on Fox's resignation, when he warned Conway against Shelburne, whom he compared first with the wolf in sheep's clothing who deceived Red Riding Hood and then with Borgia and Catiline. *Parl. Hist.* xxiii. 183. See also No. 6249.

$8\frac{7}{8} \times 12\frac{11}{16}$ in.

An earlier state (coloured) without the title but having publication line and inscription.

6206 THE ONLY BOOTH IN THE FAIR—PORTLAND & CO *late Shelburne*

J Boyne Invᵗ & excᵗ

London Published as the Act Directs Nᵒ 2 Shoe Lane Fleet Sᵗ April 9 1783

Engraving. A stage in front of a show booth, in the upper part of the design, below, spectators are gazing up at the performance On a stair leading up to the stage (r.) stands Shelburne, leaning on the bar across the front of the platform, and pointing at North who stands on the stage, ladling out guineas to Fox, who appears (l) looking over a barrier in which is a slit inscribed *American Letter Box*. Fox, who has a human face and the body of a fox, is wearing a fool's cap inscribed *Vox Populi* His fore-paws rest on the barrier, his hind-paws and the end of his brush appear through a semicircular aperture at the bottom of the barrier He is represented as a performing animal at a fair North holds in his r hand a receptacle filled with guineas inscribed *Treasury Bucket*. With an insinuating expression he holds out to Fox a large ladle filled with guineas, inscribed *Coalition Pay*

Through a door, inscribed *Treasury*, at the back of the platform (r), the head and outstretched l arm of Portland appear. He is saying *Charly now you have Baul'd Enough come round the Back way to Portland*. Shelburne, standing on the step, holding a money-bag in his r hand, points at North, saying, *A man may smile & be a Villian [sic] at least its so in England*. Shelburne himself has the half-closed eyes and sly smile with which he is usually drawn.

In front of the platform is inscribed *Tricks on the Cards by the Noted Charly with many New Shuffles by the Rest of the Company*. The heads and shoulders of seven spectators gazing up at the platform fill the lower part of the design.

One of many satires on the Coalition, see Nos. 6176–9, &c.

$10\frac{3}{4} \times 9$ in.

6207 AN ANALYSIS OF MODERN PATRIOTISM
PERFORMED BY PUBLIC OPINION & DISPLAYED BY PUBLIC INDIGNATION

PH [erased]; *AW Sc*[t]

Pub[d] *Accor*[g] *to Act, Aprill y*[e] *9 1783 by T Cornell Print Seller Bruton Street*

Engraving. A design in two compartments contrasting the politics of Fox in and out of office.

On the left Fox, with a fox's head, is seated before a fire-place with a blazing fire, to which he has just consigned *An Essay on Public Spirit [sic]*. From his coat-pocket protrudes a document inscribed *A Panegyric on Lord North*. At his r. hand (r) is a round table on which are four books and an inkstand with pens The books are inscribed *Soame Jennings [sic]* and *Tucker*. The table is almost covered by a large document to which Fox is pointing· *I do Firmly believe that Lord North is an able & upright Minister —That the American War was pursued on Wise and Virtuous Principles— that the Perogative [sic] of the Crown is too Confined—the liberties of the People too Extensive That the house of Commons ought to be the tool of the Minister—that y*[e] *Public Money is Well Applied in Purchasing that hon: House that a parliamentary Reform is A dangerous and Factious Measure— that I ought to do Anything to get into Place.*

In the foreground (l) is a monkey playing with an open book, *The True Principle of the Constitution* On the r four large volumes are tied up and labelled *To be Sold*; they are *Macauley, Locke, Sydney*. The books indicate that Fox has overthrown his constitutional and radical principles, and therefore disposes of the works of Mrs. Catherine Macaulay (see index),

Locke, and Sydney, while he studies those of Soame Jenyns and Dean Tucker, miscellaneous writers, intended to typify supporters of the prerogative. Cf. Tucker's *Treatise concerning Civil Government*, 1781, and Soame Jenyns's *Disquisitions on several Subjects*, 1782. For Tucker see No 5125

In the other compartment of the design (r), Fox, out of office, is haranguing the mob. He stands on a platform, r. hand raised, his hat in his l hand, surrounded on two sides by a crowd of plebeian appearance, two of whom wave their hats In front of the platform stands Jeffery Dunstan with his sack over his shoulder, see No 5637, &c ; he says, *Thank Heaven the People have Such a Friend.* Fox is saying, *Gentlemen Lord North deserves the Axe—Lost an Empire Burthened you with Taxes—plunged you into Debt—Gentlemen your virtue alone can Save the Kingdom—he Butchered your American Bretheren Gentlemen—Ought to be impeached We must clip the power of the Crown Gentlemen—the King is your Servant—Each of you Gentlemen Ought to have a Voice in the House of Commons.*[1]

See also Nos. 6187, 6208, 6215, 6225.

$8\frac{3}{8} \times 11$ in.

Another impression (n.d) with a different title,

6207A VOX POPULI IN PRIVATE. VOX POPULI IN PUBLICK.

London, Sold by W. Humphrey, 227 Strand

6208 THE WONDERFUL PATRIOT, OR M^R FOX—AND—GOOSE.

Pub^d by J. Barrow April 9. 1783 White Lion Bull Stairs Surry Side Blackfriars Bridge.

Engraving. Fox, standing meditatively with two heads, one of a fox (l.), one of a goose. A pen is thrust behind one of the fox's ears, indicating that he is now again a Secretary of State. His hands are thrust into the front of his waistcoat. He stands on ground which is covered, or patterned, with vine branches bearing many bunches of grapes The fox's head says *My goose head once led me from the Grapes; but Fortune kinder than I am wise hath me restor'd.* For Fox's misgivings on his resignation in July 1782, see his letter to Grenville, 5 July, Russell, *Life and Times of Charles Fox,* i. 327. Cf No. 6010, &c.

$6\frac{1}{2} \times 4\frac{3}{4}$ in.

---

[1] Fox, when haranguing the electors of Westminster or the members of the Westminster Association, was reputedly more violent than in the House of Commons, but on 13 May 1779 he said, 'when such men [Administration] grew insolent and abusive, urged their claims of merit, for which they deserve an axe, . to see a lump of deformity and disease (looking at Lord North), of folly and wickedness, of ignorance and temerity, smitten with pride, immediately breaks all measures of patience; it being hardly conceivable that so much pride, vice and folly, could exist in the same animal' *Parl Hist* xx 631 (where the words 'looking at Lord North' do not appear), quoted in *Beauties of Fox, North and Burke,* 1784 Cf also Loughborough to Eden 2 Aug. 1782, 'I think it would be of use to insist that Charles Fox should keep out of Westminster Hall, as a test that he wishes for a Coalition, and it would be a great gain to himself if he could detach himself from his mug-house friends'. *Corr of Lord Auckland,* 1861, i. 17 Cf Nos. 6213, 6216, 6225, 6230, 6235, 6265, 6287.

6209 BALAAM,—OR THE MAJESTY OF THE PEOPLE.

[Gillray]

Pub^d April 10th 1783 by W. Humphrey N° 227. Strand.

Engraving. Design in an oval. A satire on tithes and the clergy. A tall, thin military officer, wearing a hat, gorget, and sword, carries on his shoulders an enormously fat parson dressed in gown and bands. The officer, who walks from l to r , his head in profile to the r , is saying, *I am an Independent Country Gentleman & Col^l of Militia.* The parson, with a complacent expression, holds over his r shoulder a scourge with three lashes, one, ending in a snake's head, is inscribed *Pious Fraud,* the second is *English Statutes,* the third, ending in beads and a cross, is *Popish Canons.* Under his l arm he holds a basket labelled *Tithes,* in it are visible chickens and a sucking-pig. Behind the parson walks a dejected-looking farmer in a smock-frock, holding his hat in one hand, a branch in the other, he says, *We farmers have our Bodys Eat up, for the good of our Souls.* Behind the farmer (l.) are sheaves of corn, in one of which is a branch similar to that which he holds The landscape background is mountainous. After the title is inscribed, *The Lord opened the Mouth of the Ass &c.*

One of many satires on the clergy and on tithes, cf No. 4951 This attack on the Anglican Church as Popish is reminiscent of the seventeenth century.

$8\frac{7}{8} \times 12\frac{1}{2}$ in.

6210 THE TIMES, ANNO 1783.

[Gillray.]

Pub^d Apr^l 14th 1783. by W. Humphrey, N° 227 Strand.

Engraving (coloured and uncoloured impressions) Figures personifying England, France, Spain, and Holland represent the international situation. England (r.), a John Bull, stout and plainly dressed, holds up his hands, with a melancholy expression, exclaiming *Tis lost! Irrecoverably lost.* By his side (r) lies a broken anchor, and above his head a demon flies off, holding up a partly-rolled map of *America,* he has bat's wings, and is clad in ragged breeches, he excretes a puff of smoke inscribed *Poor John Bull! Ha! Ha! Ha!* France, in profile to the r , a *petit maître* of exaggerated leanness, offers John Bull a snuff-box, and takes a pinch himself, saying, with a grimace, *Ah Ah. me Lord Angla, volez vous une pince de Snuff, for de Diable will not give you back de Amerique.* Spain, the Spanish don of pictorial satire, wearing a long sword, stands, his l hand on the shoulder of France, the r. arm outstretched, saying, *See Gibraltar! See Don Langara! by S Anthony you have made me the Laughing Stock of Europe* Behind him is Gibraltar, a rock with fortifications flying the British flag, in front small vessels are exploding in smoke, evidently the floating batteries which suffered such damage in the futile attack on Gibraltar of 13 Sept. 1782, see No. 6035, &c. Don Langara had been captured by Rodney in his victory of 16 Jan 1780, see Nos 5646-8, 5658. On the extreme l is Holland, a stolid burgher wearing baggy breeches and a hat like an inverted flower-pot. He is in T.Q back view, looking to the r and saying *De Donder take you Monseuur [sic] I think I have paid the Piper.* Clouds above a low horizon form the background, with Gibraltar (l.) and a naval engagement (r) in the distance.

Spain had been induced by France to enter the war by an undertaking that Gibraltar should be recovered, see terms of the Convention of Aranjuez, 12 April 1779 Doniol, *Hist. de la Participation de la France à l'Établissement des États-Unis*, III. 810; cf. No. 6025. For the United Provinces and the war see No. 6292.

Grego, *Gillray*, p. 47.

$9\frac{1}{4} \times 13\frac{1}{2}$ in.

6211 THE WESTMINSTER ELECTORS CHAIRING THEIR FAVORITE CANDIDATE

Pub by Mrs Darchery April 16. 1783 St James Street.

Engraving (coloured and uncoloured impressions). Fox, with a fox's head, is chaired from l. to r. by men with asses' heads In front of the procession walk a flock of geese holding in their beaks threads which are attached to the front of the poles which support the chair; bystanders with asses' heads huzza. Fox is seated in an elaborately carved chair, he holds up his l hand addressing the electors. Four men with asses' heads hold the poles on which the chair rests. Behind (l.) the front of a procession appears, headed by a banner on which are a fox and the words *the Man of the People*. A woman with an ass's head behind Fox is selling a ballad; she holds up *A new Song the Fox & Wes^tr Geese*. Another stands (r) holding Fox's election address, a paper inscribed *To the Worthy Electors*. . . . Hats with favours inscribed *Fox* are being waved. Men with asses' heads and the geese shout *Huzza* and *Fox for ever*. The branch of a tree (r.) stretches over the foremost part of the procession, on this sit three owls. Beneath the title is engraved:

> "*Whilst Folly clap'd her hands, & Wisdom Stared*"
> "*Rosciad*"

Fox was re-elected unopposed for Westminster on 7 April, after taking office as Secretary of State, see No. 6215 For the Westminster geese see No. 5843, &c.

$8\frac{3}{4} \times 12\frac{3}{4}$ in.

6212 THE BLESSINGS OF PEACE.

[? After Viscount Townshend.]

Publish'd according to Act of Parliament, by M. Smith in Fleet Street. April 16th 1783.

Engraving (coloured and uncoloured impressions). Kings, ministers, and politicians in conference on both sides of the Atlantic, their identities indicated by numbers referring to notes engraved below the design. On the extreme l., beyond a piece of water inscribed *Atlantic*, a young girl dressed in feather head-dress and girdle, her name *America* inscribed over her head, sits between the kings of France (2) and Spain (3), giving a hand to each. Behind them, l , stands (1) *Dr Franklin*, supporting himself on his stick, and placing a wreath on America's head A dog, probably Holland, sits in front of this group, which is in the middle distance

On the English side of the water the sun is setting (r.) behind a hill, its rays are inscribed *England's Sun Setting*. In the distance groups of sailors and others are fighting with bludgeons; a soldier fires at an unarmed man who is running away. This probably represents the mutiny among the sailors at Portsmouth in March 1783 which was put down by Lord Howe. *Ann. Reg.*, 1783, p. 199; Walpole, *Last Journals*, 1910, ii 498.

A group of standing figures fills the foreground of the design. In the centre is the king (9, *The* ——); he holds out both hands, saying, *my Lords and Gentlemen, what should I do.* He wears one top-boot, the other lies on the ground in front of him This is an allusion to the supposed influence of Lord Bute. The boot had been the subject of innumerable satires early in the reign. See, e.g., No 3860 On each side of him is a judge: (8), *Lord Thurlow*, in profile to the r , says *Follow the Voice of the People.* (This was not the general interpretation of Thurlow's advice to the king) (10), *Lord Mansfield*, in profile to the l , to whom the king turns, says, *Fallo your own Inclanation Ye can do no wrong.* He wears a judge's wig and bands, with a kilt and tartan socks On the l. stand four persons addressing the king. (4), *Charles Fox*, stamping and gesticulating violently, fists clenched, r arm raised, says, *Keep Peace on any Terms* (5), *D of Richmond*, says *I have made 10,000 Saving in Sand Bags & Wheel Barrows.* (He was Master of the Ordnance under Rockingham and Shelburne, and prided himself on his energy in introducing economies Cf Walpole, *Last Journals*, ii. 450.) (6), *L*^d *Shelburne*, stands behind the group with a complacent air, saying, *I found ye in a Ruinous State and will quito you so.* (7), *Edmund Burke*, stands foremost of this group, addressing the king with outstretched forefinger, saying *nothing but deminishing your Expences and discarding old Servants, Will Save this Kingdom*, in his l. hand he holds a book, *B——k on Œconomy.* This illustrates the unpopularity which followed the execution of Burke's scheme of economical reform, more especially since it was accompanied by pensions to Barré and Dunning. Walpole, *Last Journals*, 1910, ii. 456–7.

The foremost of the group to the r of the king is (12) *Lord North*, in profile to the l. saying, *I thought to have had America at our Feet, but I see tis Otherwise.* Behind him stands (14) *Lord Nugent*, bending forward, his hat under his arm, saying *Give the Old Rat of the Constitution leave to offer a few words* (See Nos 6059, 6255.) (11), *M*^r *Sheridan*, turns towards (13) *M*^r *Pitt*, who looks like a boy; he is saying, *The next play I write, intend giving you a place in the Character of the Angry School Boy.* (The allusion is to a speech on 17 Feb. in answer to one by Pitt attacking Sheridan for theatricality; Sheridan said, 'if ever I again engage in the compositions he alludes to, I may be tempted to an act of presumption, to attempt an improvement on one of Ben Jonson's best Characters—the character of the Angry Boy in the Alchymist'. *Parl. Hist.* xxiii. 491.) (15), *Lord Keppel*, turning his head in profile to the r. says, *If the French had Stay'd till I drub'd them, this Bustle never would have happend*, an ironical allusion to the Battle of Ushant, cf. Nos. 5570, 5992, &c , and to the recent naval mutiny. (16), *Lord Ashburton* (Dunning) answers, *Hem, Hem, aye my lord the 27*th *of July 1778, might have done you Immortal Honor.* (Dunning was known as 'Orator Hum', see No. 6091.) In the distance, but in front of the distant fighting, is a group of figures on a small scale: (17), *Lord Amherst* addresses old soldiers with wooden legs, crutches, &c., saying *Gentlemen we have no further occasion for you.*

In the sky, riding on a broom-stick, is a witch in a cloak and steeple-crowned hat, behind her are black clouds, across which streams a label coming from beneath her petticoats, inscribed PEACE——PEACE—— P—E—A—C In the foreground (l.) a thistle is growing, to signify the baleful influence of Scottish advisers. Beneath the design is engraved, *Alas poor Country, almost afraid to know itself—Macbeth.*

For the peace see N° 6172, &c.

This print is exceptional, perhaps unique, in printing in full the names of the characters, with the exception of George III, who is *The ——*

$10\frac{1}{2} \times 13\frac{1}{8}$ in.

6213 THE COLE-HEAVERS.

[Gillray]

Pubᵈ April 16ᵗʰ 1783. by W Humphrey, N° 227, Strand.

Engraving. Fox and North, as coal-heavers, stand shovelling guineas into a sack. Fox (l.), in profile to the r., with a fox's head and brush, holds open the mouth of the sack which is nearly full. North (r) stands full-face, holding a long shovel in both hands from which guineas pour into the sack. At his feet are piles of guineas. He is saying *Pretty Pickings Charley.* The sack is inscribed *For Private Use.* On a rope stretched along the wall behind them hang a number of empty sacks inscribed *M T.* (empty) and *D°*, implying that the Treasury has been raided. Over these sacks is a scroll inscribed *For the use of the Publick.*

The slovenly dressing for which Fox was already noted is caricatured: he wears a shirt and waistcoat, his breeches are unbuttoned at the knee, his stockings ungartered, his shoe is unfastened, his brush comes through his torn breeches. His fox's head, with open mouth, protruding tongue, and great display of teeth, has an expression of greedy satisfaction. North, enormously fat, wears a ruffled shirt and breeches, with his Garter ribbon Beneath the title is etched:

> "*Two Virtuous Elves,*
> "*Taking care of Themselves*"

Cole was a slang term for gold or money. See also Nos. 6216, 6225, 6235, 6257

A print with this title and the same theme was issued in 1756, the 'cole heavers' being Newcastle, Hardwicke, Anson, and Fox, Charles Fox's father, as a fox holding out a sack. See No. 3423.

$8\frac{3}{16} \times 12\frac{7}{16}$ in.

Also a coloured impression in 'Caricatures', iv. 33 B.M L, Tab. 524.

6214 THE UP & DOWN OR WHEEL OF ADMI——RATION [ADMINISTRATION]

Pub by E Dachery April 17 1783 Sᵗ Jame's Street

Engraving. The 'Wheel' which stands in the centre is of the nature of a dredger, four oblong receptacles pivot on a bar supported by two posts and worked by a crank It is large in proportion to the figures The crank is being turned by the Devil, he stands on the bent shoulders of George III, who is saying *I've got the Devil & all upon my Back.* The Devil says, *ay never mind George'e lad we shall have a rare Crew in at last*

A group of small figures (l) stand in consultation, their identity indicated by numbers referring to notes below the design. (3), *F——x* and (2) *Nor——h* stand arm in arm, holding reins which are attached to the nose of (4) the *Duke of Port——and*, showing that the nominal prime minister is led by the nose by the two Secretaries of State. North (in back view) says, *Well Well Charley Ill help you and you shall hold me fast in my Place* Fox, who has a fox's head, answers, *But what can I do? my late tumble hath Crippled me quite & I have not got money enough to buy a pair of Crutches* (5), *Kep——ll*, in naval uniform, stands watching Fox and North; while, running towards them, in profile to the r., with outstretched hand, his r. hand in a sling is (6) *Bur——e*, saying, *Zooks I can no longer suffer Hungary Guts & empty Purse fol de rol*. Behind (l.) is a ballad-singer, pregnant, and holding out a ballad in each hand, while she sings *Sing Tantarara Rogues all*.

To the r. of the wheel and in the distance are three minute figures, representing the late Ministry: (1), *Lord Shel——ne*, his Garter ribbon very conspicuous, sits on the ground, saying, *Look what a crush a Pretty decent Tumble*. A man lying prone (probably Barré) says *Im almost kil'd*; the third, sitting, who, in spite of the minute scale, resembles Lord Ashburton (Dunning), says, *its all over with us my Lord*.

In the background, the front of a building is indicated by two mounted sentries and by the bills which are posted on its wall. It probably represents the Treasury. The bills are inscribed, *The Tower of Babel with Confusion of —— to be seen without loss of Time or Let at a moderate rent not a mile from Westminster Hall.* . On a torn placard is inscribed *Wanted 100 good recruits for a new regiment just. . . .* The third is illustrated by three figures the devil (c.) with a pitchfork, a skeleton (r.), and Fame (l.) blowing her trumpet, beneath in large letters is inscribed *Wonders Wonders Wonders . . . Astonish . . . World*. This last is taken from the advertisements of the quack Katerfelto, cf. No. 6162

One of many satires on the Coalition, see Nos. 6171–9, &c. The new ministry was formed on 2 April and on the 7th Burke was given his old post of Paymaster. Cf. No. 6281.

$5\frac{1}{4} \times 9\frac{1}{8}$ in.

6215 THE RE-ELECTING OF REYNARD, OR FOX THE PRIDE OF THE GEESE

I. Porter fec^t

Pub by Wm Richardson Aprill 19 1783. Strand.

Engraving (coloured impression). The electors of Westminster as geese, chairing Fox on his re-election, which his appointment as Secretary of State made necessary. Fox (r.), with a fox's head, in profile to the l., is seated in a chair resting on poles, which a number of geese are supporting on the points of their beaks He holds up a purse containing guineas in his r. hand, saying, *Gentlemen, I will be of Either side for or against is Aqualy alike to me so as I get the Chink*. Inside the crown of his hat, which he holds in his l. hand, are the initials C F. The back of his chair is inscribed *Fill'd with [de]ceit*. In front of the chair a procession of geese-electors marches with banners, staves, and musical instruments They all wear hats with election favours. In front (l.) two geese support between them on two poles a square fringed and tasselled banner inscribed *The Man of the People*. At the back of the procession on a triangular banner, also fringed and tasselled, is *Fox for ever*.

The scene is evidently 'the piazzas' of Covent Garden Above an arcade is a line of sash-windows, from which geese stretch their necks, saying (l. to r.) *A Deceiver of the World, no Coalition; hiss hiss of with him he his* [sic] *a Deceiver of the Geese, Fox for ever; and O, that Deceitfull F——x*

Fox's re-election took place on 7 April without opposition but not without clamour and hisses, which, Fox claimed, proceeded, not from the electors 'but from the lowest class of society'. He said, 'To diminish the influence of the Crown in Parliament and to increase the influence of the people, he assured the Electors had ever been, and ever should be, his great object, and he hoped his past conduct had gained their confidence'. He was chaired and taken to Wood's Hotel for the election dinner. *London Chronicle*, 5–8 April 1783. Walpole, *Last Journals*, ii. 513. See No. 6211. For Fox's geese see Nos. 5843, &c.

$8\frac{7}{16} \times 13$ in.

6216 THE BOWER OF BLISS OR, PARADISE REGAIN'D.

Pub^d April 21. 1783. by W. Wells, N° 132 Fleet Street.

Engraving. Fox and North sit under a vine-trellis covered with bunches of grapes, roses grow beneath the vines. Each sits facing the other in a small arm-chair, behind them is a table on which are money-bags Behind the table is a small temple, or pavilion, the folding doors of which are open Over the door is the bust in an oval of *Portland* The building is inscribed *Treasury*. North (l) turning in profile to the r , takes Fox's r hand, and is about to place in it a money-bag, saying *Now Reynard the whole Vineyard is our own, Therefore Let us be busy.* Fox (r.), holding up his l hand deprecatingly, says, *That is my Sole aim, but what will the People say.*

On the upper and lower margins of the print is engraved:

> *Gold—will make things the most opposite in*
> *Nature, start from extremes & bind together.*
> *Oh Sacred hunger of pernicious Gold!——*
> *What bands of Faith can impious Lucre hold?*

See also Nos. 6213, 6225, 6235, 6257.

$7\frac{7}{8} \times 11\frac{1}{8}$ in.

6217 RAZOR'S LEVÉE, OR Y^E HEADS OF A NEW WIG AD——N ON A BROAD BOTTOM.

J.S.f.[Sayers.]

Published 21st April 1783 by Thomas Cornell Bruton Street.

Engraving. The interior of a barber's shop At one side (l) stands the barber, a fierce, angry-looking man in an apron, washing his hands in a bowl, which appears to be attached to a double wig-stand. Opposite him, at the other side of the room, Sam House, with a bewildered frown, sits in an arm-chair, holding a foaming tankard on which *Sam House* is just legible. He wears a hat with a cockade inscribed *Fox*, as worn by Fox's supporters at Westminster elections. On the floor stand wig-blocks, each supported on a tall slender post of varying height with a circular base, the heads of which are those of members of the new ministry. The double stand, next the barber, has the heads of North and Fox North in a bag-wig, T.Q. face, with a frown of distress, Fox, in profile to the l., with rough hair, and a smile of satisfaction. The other heads, all in profile to the l , are (l. to r.) the Duke of Portland, in a bag-wig; Lord John Cavendish in a small close-fitting wig, Lord Stormont, Lord Carlisle, and Keppel, these three all in bag-wigs. Apart from and behind the others, behind Sam House and on the extreme r. of the print is Burke, frowning, as if dissatisfied with his place; he wears his customary small pig-tail queue. On the ground (l.), behind the barber, lie three heads, they are those of the Duke of Grafton, of Dundas, and Lord Shelburne.

Although Dundas lost his office of Treasurer of the Navy on the accession of the Coalition he remained Lord Advocate of Scotland until Aug. 1783.

On the shelves on the wall are wigs and wig-boxes. On a high shelf (r.) are the heads of Lord Ashburton, full-face, and of Lord Grantley in profile to the l These two, though once associated with Fox and Burke, are now shelved. Between them is a judge's wig in back view.

The satire is emphasized by the decorations of the back wall of the room. Immediately behind the heads of Fox and North is a large poster or playbill headed with the royal arms, and inscribed, *By his Majesty's Servants this day will be presented A new Way to pay old Debts. . .* Above it are two H L. portraits of Charles I and Cromwell, each holding out his arms as if in friendship to the other, a parallel to the unnatural alliance between North and Fox. For other comparisons of Fox with Cromwell see No. 6239, &c. Over the fire-place is a large map, *A new Map of Great Britain and Ireland*; the piece on which Ireland should be, hangs down and is almost torn off Behind Keppel's head a ballad is posted, headed by a design of two ships in full sail. This is *Rule Britannia Set to a new Tune . . . 27ᵗʰ July.* Cf. No. 5992, &c. Behind the barber (l.) is a wall, in which is a lattice window; a mirror and hat hang on the wall. Against it is a table on which are the materials of his trade (hair strung between two bobbins, a comb, and scissors) and two papers: *Westminster Association your desir[ed] . . .* and *Quintuple Alliance, The Favour of your Company is reques[ted] . . .* The Quintuple Alliance was an association of patriots of the City, Westminster, Southwark, Middlesex, and Surrey, with objects similar to those of the Westminster Association, the chief being parliamentary reform Cf. *The Remembrancer*, 1783, Part II, p. 7 See also No. 6247.

This appears to represent the dismay caused to the patriots of the metropolis by the formation of the Coalition Ministry 'When political reasons made it necessary for Mʳ Fox to unite with Lord North, Sam's confidence in Mʳ Fox was shook to the centre.' *Life and Political Opinions of the late Sam House*, 1785, p. 24 The barber is probably also a character well known at the time.

Walpole calls this the best of the deluge of satiric prints against the Coalition. 'It is better composed than ordinary and has several circumstances well imagined.' *Letters*, xii. 436, 25 April 1783. For the Coalition see Nos. 6176–9, &c.

10⅛ × 15 9/16 in.

6218 THE LEVEE

E T. fecet.

April 21. Pub· by E Dachery Aprill 21 1783. St. James Street

Engraving Ministers stand round a pole on the top of which is a head. This is turned from the spectator and is unrecognizable, but is evidently the king The pole is being held up by Fox and North; North, in profile to the l., very stout and wearing an enormous Garter ribbon, holds it with his r. hand Fox stands behind it, scowling downwards, legs astride, his l. hand stretched upwards against the pole An enormously tall man, with sword and *chapeau bras*, stands in profile to the r. holding a long staff of office. He is probably the Earl of Hertford, who again became Lord Chamberlain, a post which he lost on the fall of North, see No 5966.

Two men run towards the pole from the l , and two from the r., they are much caricatured and cannot be identified. Rays come from a sun with a smiling face in the upper r corner of the print. Beneath the title is engraved, *Good Morrow to your Night Cap!*

For the attitude of the Ministry and especially Fox to the Crown see No 6239, &c

By the same artist as No. 6189.

$6 \times 9\frac{3}{16}$ in.

6219 BONUS MELIOR OPTIMUS
  OR THE DEVIL'S THE BEST OF THE BUNCH.

[Gillray.]

Thos Pether inv^t

Pub^d April 22^d 1783 by W. Humphrey N° 227 Strand.

Engraving (coloured and uncoloured impressions). The Devil (r.) squats on a low circular stool before a fire which he blows with bellows to heat a cauldron hanging from a hook He says,

> *God save great George our King*
> *God bless our noble King,*
> *God damn the Broth it will never Boil.*

'God' (three times), 'George', and 'damn' have been scratched through but left fully legible.

Behind and on the l. sit North (l) and Fox (r.), Fox with his r arm round North's shoulders, North offering him a spoonful from the dish which he holds on his knees, at which (as Boreas) he is blowing. North is sitting on a cylindrical roll inscribed *Budget*. Fox, who has a fox's head, sits on a chest inscribed *Pandora's Box* Fox says, *Blow hot! Blow cold! He! He! He! with the self same Breath my Lord—give me a sup of your soup—I have often cool'd your Porridge my Lord! Hay? He! He! He!* North says, *My dear Reynard you are welcome to a Spoonfull!—Be cautious!—a little of my Broth goes a great way—'tis d——d high seasoned—look at my Cook he & my Freind hum! . . . with the consent of the . . hum, did both . . . hum the Nation.* Over the fire-place is an oval medallion of the heads of North and Fox, called COALITION MEDAL. This is a free rendering of Sayers's print of that name, see No. 6183.

The words of the title are placed under the three characters: North is BONUS, Fox MELIOR, the Devil OPTIMUS.

An adaptation of Æsop's fable of the Satyr and the Traveller: Fox as the Satyr approves instead of blaming the Traveller for blowing hot and cold with the same breath since his only desire is for gain. One of many satires on the Coalition, see Nos 6176–9, &c.

Grego, *Gillray*, p. 47

$8\frac{1}{2} \times 12\frac{7}{8}$ in.

6220 THE COALITION.

[Gillray.]

Pub⁴ Apr¹ 25ᵗʰ 1783, by G. Humphrey, N⁰ 48 Long Acre.

Engraving North (l.) and Fox (r.), back to back, excreting into a pan bearing the Royal Arms which stands between them. The Devil stands, crouching, with one foot on the bent back of each; he holds a long shovel in his r. hand, with which he stirs the mixture in the pan; with his l hand he holds his nose. He is a characteristic Gillray devil with bat's wings, a human torso, satyr's ears and legs, and the feet of a beast of prey. A disk or cup supported on a point, rests on his head.

The scene is outside a closed door in a stone wall. Over the doorway is a scroll, inscribed, CATAPLASMA BELLI ET PACIS, VEL COMPOSITIONE INFERNALIS. Under this scroll is the inscription, *To be used as the universal* SALVE-*ation of this Kingdom* | *By the* KINGS ROYAL LETTERS PATENT, | *The Original Warehouse* —— *by* —— *Messʳˢ Reynard & Boreas.*

Below this and on the architrave of the door is a framed print, *The Fox & Geese.* A fox standing on his hind-legs plays the fiddle to a row of geese, who stretch their necks and cackle. Prints of fox and geese, the geese representing the Westminster electors, were common See No. 5843, &c.

This coarse design is powerfully drawn. North, wearing a nightcap and his Garter ribbon, is in profile to the l. He is much caricatured and has an expression of sulky melancholy Fox, T Q. face, with his unkempt hair, bushy eyebrows, and 'gunpowder jowl', has a more sinister scowl.

12⅞×8⅞ in.

6220 A JUNCTION OF PARTIES.

[Gillray.]

N⁰ 1. Pub⁴ Apr¹ 25ᵗʰ 1783, by G Humphrey, N⁰ 48 Long Acre.

The same plate (coloured impression) as No. 6220 with an altered title. The wording of the scroll above the doorway has been altered by the substitution of the word COALITIO for COMPOSITIONE.

6221 SCRUB AND ARCHER

IB [J Boyne]

London Publish'd as the Act Directs Ap 25 1783 by I Boyne N⁰ 2 Shoe Lane Fleet Sᵗ

Engraving (coloured and uncoloured impressions) Fox (l.) as Scrub, and North (r.) as Archer, sitting on two upright chairs in close consultation as in Farquhar's play, *The Beaux' Stratagem*, Act III Behind (r), listening to their conversation, is Mrs. Robinson (Perdita) as Gipsey, the lady's-maid. Fox sits full-face wearing an apron, his hands on his knees, with an expression of puzzled melancholy. North, in toupet-wig, ruffled shirt, and Garter ribbon, in profile to the l , is talking to him with the insinuating smile of the gentleman playing the part of the gentleman's gentleman Perdita, her arms folded, wearing a frilled cap, low-cut bodice, wide hooped petticoats with an apron, looks coyly at them over her r. shoulder.

On the wall (centre) is a full-length portrait of Col. Tarleton, one foot on a cannon, a horse's head and the muzzle of a cannon indicated in the background This is a free rendering of Sir Joshua Reynolds's portrait, of which a mezzotint by J. R. Smith was published in 1782, the background, but not the figure, being reversed. The frame is inscribed *C Tarlton.*

Beneath the design is engraved:

ARCH *And this Col· I am Afraid has Converted the Affection of your Perdita*

SCRUB *Converted; ay and perverted my dear Friend for I am Afraid he has made her a Whore &c*

This is a slightly altered quotation from the play, the scene being that in which Archer and Scrub agree to be 'sworn brothers'. A satire on the Coalition and on the attachment of Fox to Mrs. Robinson, see No. 6117, &c For her relations with Col Tarleton see No. 6116. For the Coalition see Nos. 6176–9, &c. Similar in manner to No. 6231.

Reissued 1 Aug 1783.

$7\frac{5}{16} \times 6\frac{7}{8}$ in.

6222 A JOINT MOTION OR THE HONEY-MOON OF THE COALITION. [*c.* April 1783]

Porter fec^t

Sold by W. Humphrey. N° 227 Strand.

Engraving. A street scene, the background being the lower part of the stone wall of a building beneath which is an archway (r.). Under the archway crouch Fox and North clasping each other round the neck, and holding between them a paper inscribed *Preliminaries* Both are excreting, North looks with a pained expression at Burke, who stands opposite them, in profile to the r , as an apothecary holding a large syringe inscribed *Œconomy* Fox looks at North. Behind Burke, and in profile to the l, stands Lord John Cavendish holding a medicine bottle labelled *Reform* which he is pressing on a man standing under a recessed alcove in the wall This man, wearing the court suit and sword which denoted office, stands stiffly, holding a similar bottle inscribed *Office* and apparently rejecting *Reform.* The street is *Cleveland Row* (close to St. James's Palace and Park). Above the design is inscribed:

What Rhubarb Senna or what Purgative Drug
Will scower these English hence? Sc 3 Act 5th Macbeth

The Coalition Ministry was at last appointed on 2 April; Burke's appointment as Paymaster was on 7 April. It is suggested that its attitude to the Peace Preliminaries, Economy, and Reform has changed since its members were in opposition See Nos 6176–9, 6184, &c., and No. 6229.

$8 \times 12\frac{1}{2}$ in.

6223 AMUSEMENT FOR JOHN BULL & HIS COUSIN PADDY, OR, THE GAMBOLS OF THE AMERICAN BUFFALO IN S^T JAMES'S STREET.

Published 1st May 1783, by I Fielding, Pater-noster Row.

Engraving From the *European Magazine,* iii. 296. Ministers and would-be ministers are scrambling for the loaves and fishes which have been scattered in the street from the baskets of a baker and a fish-wife which lie on the ground The fall of the baskets has been occasioned by a buffalo, whose head and shoulders appear on the r.; in front of him the fish-wife lies prone. The background is intended for the lower part of the front of St James's Palace, the king, smiling, looks from a window over the gateway.

Two ministers kneel facing each other picking up loaves and fishes· Portland, in profile to the l, says *I am thankful to you, my Lord, for this large fish, you shall have as good a one soon from Portland*, the other, probably Lord John Cavendish, Chancellor of the Exchequer, says, *Our Windsor Acteon in the window, seems highly tickled with his Cabinet Hounds.* Behind Portland stand North and Fox stooping forward; Fox is kicking at a judge who stands behind him, and says, *This American Buffalo, has occasioned glorious sport. Keep off Bigwig* The judge, probably Thurlow, on whose resignation of the Chancellorship Fox had insisted, see No. 6197, says, *I will have a loaf & a fish, or the Wool-sack may go to the Devil.* North says, *Kick him off Charley, that Bloodhound must not come in, he'd devour the whole.*

Behind Cavendish two men stand wrestling; one (l.) is Keppel, who says, *This is fighting Yard-arm and Yard-arm my Lord, which you know I love* (an ironical allusion to the battle of Ushant, 27 July 1778. See No 5992, &c). His opponent, who is probably Shelburne, answers, *I'll share what I get among the Loyalists, if I dont change my mind.* Shelburne had been much attacked for failing to secure better terms for the American Loyalists, see No 6182, &c A man, running forward from the l, says, *I am as deep as a Pit, when any thing of this kind is going forward.* Probably Thomas Pitt (1737–93), who played an important part in negotiations during the ministerial interregnum, and was offered a Secretaryship of State by the king Possibly William Pitt.

The persons are poorly characterized, and can as a rule be identified only by their words.

One of many satires on the Coalition, see Nos. 6176–9, &c. See also Nos. 6195, 6240, 6248, &c.

$3\frac{7}{16} \times 5\frac{15}{16}$ in

6224 THE UNNATURAL CONNECTION.　　　[1 May 1783]

Engraving From *The Rambler's Magazine* Fox and North stand in a library grasping each other by the hand. Fox has a fox's head, both wear court-suits A table (r) is covered with coronets, a mitre, the insignia of orders of knighthood, a mace, money-bags, and papers inscribed *Pension* A dog, his collar inscribed *Thurlo*, barks at the two ministers, *Bow! wow! wow.* Fox says to North, *When I talk'd of impeaching you I was but in jest.* North says (pointing to the table) *Let us hang together & all those honours & Emoluments will be at our disposal.*

On the wall is a book-case and a map of *Little Britain, once Great Britain*, which appears to represent London and the district north of London. A heavily festooned curtain partly conceals the books.

One of many satires on the Coalition, see Nos 6176–9, &c. For Thurlow see Nos. 6197, 6223, &c

$5\frac{1}{2} \times 3\frac{7}{16}$ in.

6225 THE R^T HON^{BLE} CATCH SINGERS.

[Gillray.]

Pub^d May 2^d 1783 by W. Humphrey N° 227 Strand

Engraving (coloured and uncoloured impressions) Fox and North seated on an alehouse bench, singing a rollicking song, holding between them a two-handled tankard of beer. Fox (l) sits full-face looking towards North; in his r. hand is a pen, his l holds one handle of the tankard. North (r.) sits behind a solid oblong table on which are writing materials, he flourishes a rolled paper inscribed *Express . . .* in his l. hand, his r. holds the tankard. He turns his head in profile to the l, blowing a borean blast at the froth on the tankard, making it run down the pot, obscuring the crown and the *G* of the *G.R* inscribed on it. The froth falls on to a *Westminster Petition* which lies on the table.

The words of the catch are in labels issuing from the mouths of the singers Fox sings,

> *Bring every Flow'r that can be got*
> *Pinks Hyacynths & Roses,*
> *We two will drink out of one Pot*
> *And Fuddle both our Noses.*

North sings,

> *With Treasury Juice the Pot shall Foam*
> *For Reynard & for N——h*
> *The People still may wish for some*
> *And they shall have — the Froth.*

Fox is laughing and carefree, North scowls with the effort of blowing at the froth.

One of many satires on the Coalition, see Nos 6176-9, &c. Walpole records (7 May) that the Westminster Association (for parliamentary reform, &c.) had lately assumed a menacing tone, and had voted that they would not be content under their full demand. *Last Journals*, 1910, ii 516 Their petition and the demands of 'the People' are here treated with contempt by the new ministers. Cf. Nos 6207, 6213, 6216, 6230, 6235

Grego, *Gillray*, p. 48.

$8\frac{9}{16} \times 12\frac{3}{8}$ in.

6225 A A copy (coloured impression), reduced, without date or publication-line, in which 'hon^ble' is written 'hon^dle'.

$5\frac{1}{4} \times 7\frac{1}{4}$ in.

6226 [THE COALITION STAGE COACH]

J S f. [Sayers.]

Published 5th May 1783 by Thomas Cornell Bruton Street

Engraving. A stage coach, drawn by two wretched hacks, is being driven (r to l.) in the direction of a signpost (l.) which points *To Bulstrode thro' Bushy Park*, Bulstrode being a country house of the Duke of Portland, Bushy Park that of Lord North Portland and Fox sit side by side on the box. Portland, with an expression and in an attitude of anxiety, is being taught to drive by Fox, who leans across him holding both reins and whip, his mouth twisted, his eyes half-shut. At the back of the coach, in the boot or basket, stands Lord North in the place of a footman, holding straps; he wears a bag-wig and his hat is under his arm He watches the pair on the box with an expression of anger and anxiety. The coach has no windows except for oval panes let into the upper panels of the door On the door is inscribed *The New Fly | From St James's Street. | To the Land's End |*

performed (if God permit) by [names erased] *& Co.* On each panel is a ducal coronet surmounting the initial *P* ; on each coronet sits a fox. The road is covered with large boulders The near front wheel has been broken, apparently in passing over a rock inscribed *Loan.* An irregularity in the road is inscribed, *Per varios praeceps Casus rota volvitur Ævi* On the extreme r , just in front of the horses, a boulder is inscribed *Reform Bill*

The terms of the loan, proposed by Lord John Cavendish, the Chancellor of the Exchequer, were attacked by Pitt on 16 April On 6 May (a rock just ahead, at the date of this print) was the debate on parliamentary reform *Parl. Hist.* xxiii. 767 ff. and 826 ff. The Westminster Association had voted that they would not be content under their full demand for reform Walpole, *Last Journals*, 1910, ii. 516–17 Cf No 6225.

Beneath the design is etched, *Such was the love of Office of the noble Lord, that finding he would not be permitted to mount the Box,* | *He had been content to get up behind vide the Duke of C——— s's Speech Morning Chronicle 15ᵗʰ April* This was a speech by Chandos on the Irish Judicature Bill, 14 April, violently attacking the Coalition: 'he particularly arraigned the conduct of Lord North, and said that not being able to get again upon the state coach-box, he had been content to get up behind.' *Parl. Hist.* xxiii. 755

One of several satires on Portland as the puppet of Fox, see Nos. 6228, 6233, 6256.

$11\frac{1}{4} \times 16\frac{7}{8}$ in.

6227 A BLOCK FOR THE WIGS—OR, THE NEW STATE WHIRLI-GIG.

[Gillray.]

Pubᵈ May 5ᵗʰ 1783, by W Humphrey Nᵒ 227 Strand

Engraving A merry-go-round in violent action, ministers seated on the horses, &c , fixed on a circular platform which is supported on a short central beam This beam is held in place by three blocks or wedges inscribed *Treasury, Navy, Army.* In the centre of the platform, on a tall pedestal, a continuation of the supporting beam, is a bust of the king in profile, the features blank, the head bald, a bob-wig being supported on a pole above his head ; from this pole floats a ragged British flag The king, the centre of the structure, is represented as a wig-block, or a block for the Whigs. The foremost figure on the merry-go-round on the extreme r is Fox, seated in a chair, in back view, with a fox's head and brush; he holds up a large money-bag in his left hand, looking over his shoulder at his followers with a jeering expression, his large brush flies out behind him. Behind him, riding a galloping horse whose legs are cut off at the knees, is North, his wig flying from his head with the violence of the motion [1] Behind him is Burke, on a similar horse, dressed as a jesuit, wearing a large biretta as in No 6205 He is in profile to the r., wearing spectacles, and reading from a book he holds open before him, inscribed *Sublime & Beautiful* (in allusion to his *Philosophical Enquiry* .. , 1756). His leg is that of a skeleton, probably to indicate the character of his policy of economical reform. Behind Burke is Keppel, in naval uniform, riding on an ass with its legs folded beneath it. He is saying *Dam'd rough Sailing this, I shall*

[1] A great meeting of the Electors of Westminster on 6 March was repeatedly interrupted by a heckler asking 'How long has Lord North been a Whig?' *Remembrancer*, 1783, i 211.

never be able to keep my Seat till the 27ᵗʰ July, another allusion to the battle of Ushant Cf No. 5992, &c Behind Keppel, seated on a throne inscribed *President*, full-face and smiling, is a man with bare knees, short turban, breeches, and tartan stockings. From the crown which decorates the back of his throne hang two large thistles He wears the ribbon of an order, and represents Scottish influence personified possibly in Bute, probably in Lord Stormont, who was President of the Privy Council in the Coalition Ministry and K.T. The rim of the merry-go-round opposite Keppel, Burke, and North respectively is inscribed *Balaam, Œconomy, Secretary*

The round-about is outside an inn, part of which appears on the l On the sign-board, which swings from a beam inscribed *Crown & Royal Bob*, is a crown, above which is a bob-wig like that suspended above the king's head Beneath is written *John Bull Good Entertainment* A clock-face on the wall points to 12 15. From an upper window a man reaches out to take a large bundle which is being handed to him by a man on a ladder Above, on the upper margin of the print, is inscribed *Poor John Bull's House plunder'd at Noon Day*

On a low stool outside the inn sits a lame man, with swathed legs and closed eyes, his crutches beside him, he holds a pipe in one hand, a tankard in the other He sings, *Tis Liberty Tis Liberty, Dear Liberty alone*, signifying how easily John Bull is plundered and bemused by talk of liberty. One of many satires on the Coalition, see Nos 6176-9, &c.

Grego, *Gillray*, p 48

8⅞ × 13 in.

6228 A PETRIFIED LUSUS NATURAE
LATELY DISCOVERED IN THE RUINS OF A TEMPLE ONCE DEDICATED TO LIBERTY BY THE BRITONS

T C [? T. Colley]

Pub. by M Thomas. Princes Street. Mayᵗʰ 6 1783.

Engraving A large rock stands in a landscape, carved in the rock are busts in relief of Portland, Fox, and North, numbered respectively *1, 2, 3* The king (r) stands inspecting them through a single eye-glass He wears court-dress and a sword He is saying, *my friend Je—kinson shall write a desertation on this Phenomenon*

The centre head, in full face, superimposed on the other two, is that of Fox, his bushy eyebrows and 'gun-powder jowl' much stressed On the l , looking to l , is the Duke of Portland; on the r , in profile facing the king, is North Numbers refer to notes engraved below the title:

Nº 1 [Portland] *Supposed to be the head of a Patrician on close examination, Lennaeus was of opinion it never contained much Brain he vainly Accepted a Situation in the common Wealth that exposed him to his fellow Citizens as he was known to be a mere tool in the hands of others*

2 [Fox] *The head of a turbulent and factious Tribune of great abilities which he exerted occasionally for and Against Government as he happened to be in or out of Power in the Senate he cared not what falsehood he advanced to carry a Question against a Consul.*

3 [North] *The head of a Tribune of Patrician Ancestors who had been Consul and much admired for his Wit eloquence and knowledge, he had the Art to impose himself upon the People for an honest disinterested man, he was remov'd from the Consulate by a faction* [sic] *Whose conduct he declared would run the State, yet rather than lose the emoluments of Office he joined his enemies, and Submitted to hold under them a Subordinate office in the Republic, his conduct in this instance was much censured by the People and gave rise to many witty Pasquinades*

The supposed secret and great influence over the king of Jenkinson, afterwards 1st Earl of Liverpool, had made him very unpopular, see Walpole, *Last Journals*, 1910, ii 503, 504, 506, 508 March 1783 See also No 6256. For Portland as the puppet of others see No. 6226, &c

This satire appears to be an imitation of No 3417, *Lusus Naturae* (1756), in which the petrified heads were those of the Duke of Newcastle, Stone, the Duke's secretary, and Henry Fox.

Either by Colley or by an imitator of his style, perhaps Gillray, the head of Fox resembles that in No 6117

$7\frac{7}{10} \times 12\frac{15}{16}$ in.

6229 THE (ASS)-HEADED AND (COW-HEART)-ED MINISTRY MAKING THE BRITISH (LION) GIVE UP THE PULL.

Pub by J Barrow May 8 1783 White Lion Bull Stairs Surry Side Black Friars Bridge

Engraving. The words in brackets in the title are represented by small objects as in a rebus. The four enemy powers represented by animals are harnessed to the British lion and attempt to drag him into a circular pit. Four ministers with asses' heads drag at the lion to impede his efforts to save himself. The animals resemble those in No 6004 by the same artist. The pit, which is in the centre of the design, is *The Pit of ruin* on its farther side, watching the struggle, is the double-headed (? Russian) eagle, one head turned (r) towards the four powers saying *I am an armed Neutral*, the other turned (l) towards the British lion saying *Gratitude oft prompt me on to help thee, yet I refrain'd.*

The lion is on the l of the pit, his harness terminates in a large hook, which holds three chains attached to the harness of the four enemy powers who are on the r. The ass-headed ministers stand behind the lion, dragging at a rope attached to his head. The foremost, Keppel, in a naval coat, says, *He shall neither ramble nor roar in America, to disturb Congress; he shall only stand on the Defensive*, one of many allusions to Keppel's lack of enterprise in the battle of Ushant, see No 5992, &c. The next, who from his paunch and Garter ribbon must be intended for North, says, *He shall make peace before Count de Estaing [sic] goes on his dreadful Expedition*, an allusion to North's Conciliatory Propositions, see No. 5473, &c The third says, *My head is in a Labyrinth when I think on War, so Monsieur must have his terms.* The last says, *I hope the peace will be approv'd of, then we shall keep our places.*

From the lion's mouth come verses, engraved in the upper l. part of the print:

My honour'd Sirs, who me pretend to lead,
Tis plain the office does not sute your head.
Your hearts like mine all dangers should engage,
The more my foes, the more enflam'd I rage
Who leads a Lion, should himself be bold,
But you are Dastards, and it shall be told
By France I'm injured, yet you ask them peace,
What shall I call you? puppies, sheep, or geese?

To know you're such, go ask each British Tar,
Which would a Frenchman ask to end a war.
O'er the Atlantic, in the martial field,
You held me in, and now you make me yield;
And tho' I'm able to maintain my State,
I fall by Goose-caps, and by Fox's prate
I want the brave to lead me on to fight,
To scorn a Peace, till I have all my right,
But you're scarce fit to lead me out to sh——
How hard my fate that such should me control,
Who realy are without a British Soul,
For ever blush, for all the wise can see,
You are but Asses and make one of me.

The enemy powers, who are harnessed to the chains dragging at the lion by rigid bars attached to their collars, strain neck and neck at the lion The Spanish hound says, *He is stronger than Gibralter, but happy for us he is intangled by his leaders* Next him, and of approximately the same size, is the Gallic cock, saying *The old Raskel's Roast Beef keeps him too strong for us all, but his leaders are Asses* Next, the American rattlesnake, his tail stretching in front of the pit and almost reaching the lion, says, *The harangues of the British Patriots help me more to Independancy than 40000 Men* The fourth animal, nearest the spectator, is a pug-dog representing Holland, a pipe thrust through his collar; he says, *I wish I could have stood Jack on both sides and smok'd my pipe*, implying that to Holland neutrality had been profitable, war disastrous. Cf. Nos. 5557, 5827, 6292, &c.

Beneath the title is engraved

This Plate is designed for a Memorial of the Strength of the British Constitution, being able to cope with four Powers. and also to truly represent a Set of frantic, sophistical Patriots, who when they had wrangled themselves into Ministry, found themselves intirely incapable of the Task, Therefore very suddenly made very humiliating Concessions to France, to obtain a Peace, to the great Mortification of every true Briton, (the British Lion being in full Strength and had just obtain'd some glorious victories over the French and Spaniards) Thus by a desponding Ministry America got Independency, and France attain'd all her perfidious ends

The peace preliminaries denounced by North and Fox in Feb 1783, see No. 6172, &c , were accepted by the Coalition with only trifling readjustments One of the few attacks on the Patriots for their attitude to the war, cf. No 5334, &c., and No. 6065

$8\frac{11}{16} \times 15\frac{3}{8}$ in

6230 THE POLITICAL WEATHERCOCK

Pub by T. Colly May 10 1783 London

Engraving Charles Fox as a weathercock. He lies prone and rigid, his waistcoat resting on a pinnacle which rises from a castellated tower from whose embrasures project cannon. His l arm and l. leg are outstretched; in his l hand is a large money-bag inscribed £*12·000 for making a noise* On his back rests another bag inscribed, £*11 000 for holding my Tongue*; on the mouth of this bag rests a pack of cards showing the deuce of spades, across this lies a dice-box. This represents the upper part of the pivot of the weathercock.

His r. hand is thrust in his shirt frill, his r. leg is raised vertically from the knee, and receives the blast of *North wind* directed at the weather-cock from the mouth of Lord North, whose head appears among clouds in the upper r. corner of the print. Fox's face, much caricatured, is turned to the spectator; on one side are the words *Against the People*, on the other *for the people*. The four points of the compass are indicated by dice. Only the summit of the stone tower is visible, and the title is engraved across it.

Cf. also No. 6207, &c. In the manner of Colley or of his imitator. See No. 6117.

$5\frac{1}{8} \times 6\frac{3}{4}$ in.

6231 FALSTAFF & HIS PRINCE.

IB [J. Boyne.]

London Publishd as the Act Directs May 16 1783 by J. Boyne N° 2 Shoe Lane Fleet S^t

Engraving Fox (r.), as Falstaff, takes the hand of the Prince of Wales, who stands, slim and good-looking, in riding-dress. The prince is in profile to the r., his l hand behind his back holding a riding-whip. His wide double shirt-frill, cutaway coat, dangling bunches of seals, close-fitting breeches, and boots are in the height of the most recent fashion, cf No. 6233. Fox is in Elizabethan dress, with a thick curling beard, feathered hat, ruff, slashed doublet and cloak, wide wrinkled boots He smiles, his l. hand in his breeches pocket.

Beneath the design is engraved·

PRI. *There is a Gentlewoman in this Town her Name is* ——

FAL. *Master George I will first make bold with your Money next give me Your hand & Last as I am a Gent^n you shall if you will Enjoy* —— *Wife.*

For the influence of Fox over the Prince of Wales see Walpole, *Last Journals*, 1910, ii 496–7; Wraxall, *Memoirs*, 1884, iii. 152–3. See also Nos 6237, 6266. Similar in manner to No 6221.

$7\frac{1}{4} \times 6\frac{7}{8}$ in

6232 THE TRUE STATE OF THE JUNCTION; OR MEN OF ABILITIES CALL'D FOR

London, Publish'd May 20th 1783 by I Freeman Strand

Engraving. Design in an oval. Fox and North stand together in consulta-tion (l). Fox, holding the r. hand of North who stands on his r., points with his l. hand towards Britannia (r.), who has been thrown to the ground, and is being maltreated by Shelburne Her shield and broken spear lie beside her Shelburne has seized her by the hair and is tearing off her upper garments, he smiles saying, *I smile at the feeble efforts of them single.* Britannia looking towards Fox and North cries, *Help! tis only your united strength can save me* Pitt, young and slim, stands beside Britannia, his arms folded, looking down at her and saying *I see her danger, yet, better she should perish than I join the Man I hate.* Fox is saying to North, *Forgetting all our former disputes Quick! let us join to save her.* In the foreground lies a large scroll, inscribed, BRITANIA *rescue'd from the wicked designs of an artfull* ——, the last word hidden by a curl of the scroll.

This and No. 6181 are the only direct apologies for the Coalition. See also No. 6291, in which the fall of the Coalition is ascribed to the devil.

$5\frac{1}{4} \times 6\frac{11}{16}$ in.

6233 PUNCH AND THE JUGGLERS.

Pub by M^{rs} D Archery: May 20. 1783. St Jame's Street

Engraving. Lord Shelburne holds open the door to two gentlemen who enter from the r., pointing out to them a puppet on a low platform (l.) worked by strings held by North and Fox, whose heads and arms appear over a screen. The figure on the platform is the Duke of Portland, dressed as Punch, lifting his legs and arms stiffly as the strings are pulled. The two spectators appear to be the King and the Prince of Wales, tall and slim, in fashionable riding-dress, wearing a short waistcoat with two pendent bunches of seals, and tight riding-boots with long tops, cf. No. 6231. Behind him is the king, stout and shorter than his son. Both smile at the spectacle; Shelburne, wearing his Garter ribbon, says, *walk in Gemmen and see the shew, two secretaries of State in the Characters of Jugglers working a Prime Minister in the character of a Punch, the first Exhibition of the kind ever seen in this kingdom has had the honor of being performed before both Houses of Parliment with great Applause pray walk in Gemmen*

Punch's face is quite expressionless. North (l.) holds the strings attached to his r. foot and l. hand; Fox holds the other two strings. North, turning to Fox, says, *We are good men and true*; Fox says, looking at Punch, *Sing doodle doodle do. . . .* Behind the platform on a flight of steps on the extreme l. sit two demons, little nude imps with horns, long ears, one with bat's wings. One blows a pair of pipes with great vigour; the other, crouching above his head, points round the screen at Punch. A print is nailed to the wall over Shelburne's head: North, smiling and wearing his Garter ribbon, dances between a fox on its hind-legs and Punch. Over the door, in profile to the r., is a bust of George III. Beneath the title is engraved, *A Pantomical performance now exhibiting in the Cabinet at S^t Ja—ss.*

One of several satires on Portland as the puppet of Fox, cf. Nos. 6226, 6256. In the manner of Colley, resembling No. 6228, perhaps by Gillray, of whom the imps are characteristic; see also Nos. 6117, 6237, 6252, &c.

$8\frac{1}{2} \times 13\frac{3}{8}$ in.

6234 THE MASK

J S f. [Sayers.]

Published 21st May 1783 by H. Bretherton New Bond St.

Stipple. A composite mask, a full-face formed of the faces of Fox and North divided by a vertical line down the centre. Fox (l.) with black hair, swarthy complexion, drooping half-closed eye and cynical smile; North (r.) with powdered wig, fair complexion, and puzzled frown. Above the mask is engraved FRONTI NULLA FIDES. See also Nos. 6183, 6257.

$10\frac{1}{2} \times 7\frac{1}{2}$ in (pl.). Subject, $5\frac{1}{8} \times 5\frac{7}{8}$ in.

6235 THE SIPHON^s OR TALE OF A TUB

Pub· May 24 1783 by Thos Snoozel at the Cock & Bottle Maiden Head Thicket

Engraving Fox and North, as two cellarmen, are filling casks from *The Treasury Tub* which lies on a wooden stand in the centre of the design. A siphon inscribed *Premier* is inserted in the top of the cask, from which branch a number of curving pipes, or cocks; through these the cellarmen divert its contents to receptacles for their own use The *National Tub* which stands under the tap of *The Treasury Tub* (or cask) is empty. Fox sits on the l. in profile to the r., with a fox's head, curled wig, and long bushy queue, holding a jug on his knee and leaning forward, he says, *The cask sounds empty & well it might be my Lord for we & our Friends have long been drawing from it* The cocks which extend towards him from the siphon are inscribed, *C Fox's Cock, Cock Royal,* and *This Cock for Private Services* A cask at his side, in allusion to his gambling habits, is inscribed, *For C. Fox to be left at the Rattle Box Hazard Row till called for*. North (r.), very stout, in profile to the l., leans backwards pouring liquor from a jug through a funnel into the mouth of his cask, which is inscribed, *For Mr Deputy Secretary to be left at the Vicar of Bray'[s] Head—Bushy Park,* indicating that he is a turn-coat and a mere deputy to Fox The pipes which extend towards him from the siphon are described *Lord No . . .h's Cock; Election Bribe & Pension Cock* and *Admiralty*. His lips are pouted towards his own cock and he is saying (in the metre of the Vicar of Bray):

> *A Plenum in my Cask I shew,*
> *with Plus & Plus behind Sir;*
> *and now that Cask runs minus low*
> *A Vacuum some will find Sir.*

The figure of North appears to have been copied from No 6225. Cf. also No. 6213, and for North as Vicar of Bray, No. 6179.

8⅝ × 12 1/16 in

6236 PATENT SADDLES INVENTED SOLELY FOR THE EASE OF BOREAS AND REYNARD

Pub^d by T Colley May 29 1783 London

Engraving Fox and North riding (l. to r.) on clumsy horses in the direction of a sign-post (r.) pointing *To St James 5 Miles*. The seats of the saddles are covered with large projecting spikes. North (r.) has lost his stirrup, and is bouncing on the spikes with a face of anguish. Under his arm is a document inscribed, *Taxation* The rapidity of the horse's trot is indicated by his streaming wig and coat-tails His breeches, like those of Fox, are covered with cobwebs Fox is turning round in the saddle to face the spectator, having dropped the reins, one hand rests on the horse's shoulder, the other on its hindquarters Under his arm is a document inscribed *Coalition*. Beneath the design is engraved.
A true Englishmans toast; a hard trotting Horse, a Porcupine Saddle, a Cobweb Pair of Breeches, for the Enemies of Great Britt—an [1]

One of many satires on the Coalition, see Nos. 6167-9, &c The style resembles that of Nos 6117, 6228, &c. Perhaps by Gillray imitating Colley.

8 × 13¼ in.

[1] This, *mutatis mutandis,* was a toast of the Fellowship Club, Newport, Rhode Island, in December 1773 Belcher, *First American Civil War* 1911, i 120

6237 OUT OF THE FRYING PAN INTO THE FIRE

Colley. [?]

Pub⁴ by D archery May. 30. 1783. St James' Street.

Engraving. On a wooden platform a goose wearing a crown rests its neck on a block; the executioner, a fox, stands in front of him in profile to the l. holding up his axe. Two men caper with joy at each end of the scaffold. A slim young man (r.) with a high hat, in back view, sings,

> *Oh what Joy's will abound*
> *When the Goose is laid in Ground.*

North (l.), also in back view but showing an upturned cheek, sings,

> *& Ill sing fal de ral tit tit fal de ra. . . .*

This appears to represent the Prince of Wales and North exulting at the execution of the king by Fox.

For the association between Fox and the Prince of Wales see Walpole, *Last Journals,* ii. 496 ff. (March 1783): 'The Prince of Wales had of late thrown himself into the arms of Charles Fox, and this in the most indecent and undisguised manner . . . Fox's followers . . . were strangely licentious in their conversation about the king. At Brookes's they proposed wagers on the duration of his reign. . . .' See also Nos. 6231, 6266, and No. 5979, &c.

Possibly by Gillray, imitating the manner of Colley, see Nos. 6117, 6233, &c.

$6\frac{3}{8} \times 9\frac{7}{16}$ in.

6238 THE PORTLAND SHARKS, OR THE MINISTRY UPON A BROAD BOTTOM.   [1 June]

Engraving. From the *Rambler's Magazine.* Lord North, in bag-wig and court-suit, lies prone on the ground looking through his spy-glass at a ship, the *Britannia,* stranded and heeling over; three small figures walk away from her carrying their plunder in sacks. North says, *I knew the Britannia could not pass the Needles—Pillage her my Boys.* Four men stand on the back of North, who forms a 'broad bottom' for the ministry. Each clasps a large money-bag. Fox (l.) says, *We stand upon a broad bottom & are perfectly safe.* Portland, next him, says, *I am but a make weight amongst you.* The third figure [? Stormont] says, *I was always for a Good benefit.* Burke says, *By my Shoul these are true flowers of Rhetoric.* On the r., just behind North, stands 'Sir' Jeffery Dunstan, the street trafficker in old wigs, three times elected Mayor of Garratt. He holds out a tie-wig to North, saying *Old Whigs and Sham Whigs,* see No. 5637. In the distance, behind the pillagers of the *Britannia,* is a triangular gallows from which hang seven nooses, inscribed *To be Let.*

A cutting from the *Rambler* explains the print, as the dream or vision of a citizen who went to bed after 'punch port and politics' and meditations on a 'late unnatural alliance'. One of many satires on the Coalition, see Nos. 6176–9, &c.

$3\frac{3}{16} \times 5\frac{3}{16}$ in.

6239 A SUN SETTING IN A FOG, WITH THE OLD HANOVER HACK DESCENDING.

[Gillray]

*Pub⁴ June 3ᵈ 1783, by J Williams, Strand Nᵒ 227*¹

Engraving. Fox riding (l. to r.) the old white horse of Hanover, symbolizing the king, from a level plain down the sides of a ravine In the valley (r.) behind heavy dark clouds the sun is setting, in the sun's disk sits the figure of Britannia. Behind the horse (l) is a sign-post, with the expressive hands characteristic of Gillray's sign-posts: a hand (r) in a frilled cuff points downwards *To the Valley of Annihilation*; the other hand, with upturned palm, points *from the Pinacle of Glory*. Fox, who is less gross-looking than in most satires of this period, guides the animal with a rope halter, his reins are broken and trail on the ground, his stirrup is broken, moisture drips from the horse's eye and mouth; he flourishes a whip with a triple lash, saying *Aut Cromwell aut Nihil—so come up Old Turnips*. Puffs of smoke come from the animal's fundament inscribed *Heigh-Ho*.

Fox rides with a pair of open saddle-bags in front of him from which project a money-bag inscribed *Louis* [*sic*] *d'or*, and documents: *French Commiss*[*ion*], *Spanish Annuity*, *Settlement*, *Pʳ Annu*[*ity*] The bag is inscribed *Enjoyments*. A fleur-de-lys hangs from a ribbon on his waist-coat. His wide wrinkled boots are inscribed *Spanish Leather* Behind him, resting on the hind-quarters of the horse, is a basket labelled *Hopes & Expectations* containing a head of the king wearing a laurel wreath supported on a pike; on the top of the head stands a Gallic cock, decorated with a fleur-de-lys and crowing *Cock-a-doodle-doo*; a crown thrust through with a sword, a torn document is inscribed *Magna C*[*harta*].

One of several satires in which Fox is compared to Cromwell, see Nos. 6217, 6290. See also No. 5979, &c., and No 6271, &c He is here supposed to be acting in the interests of France and Spain.

Grego, *Gillray*, p. 48, where it is dated 8 June.

9 × 13⅜ in.

6240 THE COALITION GARLAND, OR THE STATE SWEEPS

Delin'g'd by Long heads   *Executed by Broad bottom*

Pub⁴ June 3. 1783 by W. Dent. Nᵒ 116. Strand.

Engraving. North and Fox as chimney-sweeps, each holding a shovel and brush, caper in front of a pyramid on a circular base, inscribed *Ways & Means*. The pyramid is formed of three fish whose heads converge and are surmounted by a crown. Between the fishes' tails are loaves. The whole is decorated with sprays of roses. This 'Garland' appears to represent the 'Jack in the green', a pinnacle covered with green leaves round which sweeps danced in London streets on May Day, or perhaps the milk-maids' garland, a pyramid of silver plate, round which chimney-sweeps also danced Here it symbolizes the loaves and fishes of office. Fox has an expression of cunning satisfaction; North looks expectantly towards him.

The drawing is crude. The two men are much caricatured and are heavily shaded to indicate their black condition The Garland stands upon gently rising ground, and on this is written in an old hand 'Constitution hill'. See also Nos 6195, 6223, 6248.

8⅞ × 12⅞ in.

¹ The address of W Humphrey.

6241 THE STATE WINDMILL.

Published 10 June 1783 by J. Wallis Nº 16. Ludgate Street.

Engraving (coloured impression). A windmill with four sails, two sinking
to the l., one from an almost vertical, the other from an almost horizontal
position, one being near the ground, the other in the air, the other two
opposite these and rising to the r. The body of the mill, a small timber
building, rests on a tripod of three beams springing from a low stone-
built cylinder on a small mound. Politicians are climbing about the mill
and others are inspecting it from the ground; they are identified by
numbers referring to names engraved below the print. On the summit of
the highest sail (which tilts downwards to the l.) sit (1) *Lord N——h*
and (2) *C. F——x* (r.); they hold hands. North says, *By G—d I am too
heavy my dear friend Charley.* Fox answers, *Hush my gentle Boreas, stick
fast & we'll support one another—The summer approaches and we shall have
easy weather.* (3), *Mʳ B——ke* hangs suspended in front of the sail holding
on to a leg of North and a leg of Fox, saying *My conscience bears me
up*; he wears a jesuit's biretta, as in No. 6205, &c. On the sail on the r.,
which is rising out of the horizontal, four men sit, gazing upwards. (4), *Lord
S——y* [Surrey] holds up both arms, saying *Here we go up! up! up!* (5),
Lord M—h—n [Mahon] says *Up we go!* his r. arm is across the shoulder
of (6) *Gov J——ne* [Johnstone], who says *Huzza for a fresh gale.*
Next him is (7) *Lord K—p—l* [Keppel] looking up. Commodore or
Governor Johnstone, a supporter of Sandwich and Sir Hugh Palliser
against Keppel (cf. Wraxall, *Memoirs*, 1884, ii. 68–70), seems out of place
among these Foxites. Clinging to the end of the opposite sail (l.) is (8)
The late C——r [Chancellor], Lord Thurlow, in judge's robes, his wig
falling from his head, saying *By G—d I can hold no longer What a d--m--d
bluster this is.* Beneath him, falling head downwards, is (9) *Lord Sh——ne*
[Shelburne] saying, *Lord what a fall.* On the ground at his side is (10)
T. T—s—d. Townshend, cr. Baron Sydney, 6 March 1782, for his
defence of the Shelburne Ministry and the peace against the attacks of
Fox and North. He is saying, *What a sudden change. I'll pledge myself
that by Christmas next we shall be up or down,* a prophecy which was literally
fulfilled by the dismissal of the Coalition and the formation of the Pitt
Ministry on 22 Dec., with Sydney as one of the Secretaries of State. The
next three figures are engaged in repairing (or demolishing) the foundations
of the windmill. (11), *Lord A——te* (Dundas, the Lord Advocate of
Scotland) stands in legal robes holding a saw across his shoulder, saying,
It wants mending—but the foundation is good. (12), *Mʳ S—d—n* [Sheridan]
stands at the foot of a ladder leading to the door of the mill, holding a
beam, and saying to Pitt, *Take care rash young man.* (13), *Mʳ P—tt* stands
on the ladder wielding an axe; he says, *We must make a new Machine this
is rotten & half the corn is devoured by lurking vermin.*

On the opposite (r.) side of the base of the mill, four figures (unspecified)
cling to the lowest sail, which is a mere ladder-like framework. Four men
stand on the r. gazing up at Fox and North on the summit of the windmill.
One, looking through a small telescope, says, *These Stars have a black
Aspect*; his neighbour, waving a larger telescope, says, *Past their Meridian
Altitude.* A man using a sextant says, *Two degrees of North declination*; his
neighbour on the extreme l., looking through a single eye-glass, says, *An
Owl & a Magpie by Jasus.*

At this time, though Fox had lost his popularity, the Ministry appeared firmly established, with an unshakable majority in the House of Commons Cf Wraxall, *Memoirs*, 1884, III 115 ff Pitt's activities against the 'vermin' represent his motion for Parliamentary Reform, and his Bill for a reform of abuses in public offices, see *Parl Hist* XXIII. 827 ff (7 May); pp 945 ff. (2 June) For Sheridan and Pitt cf No 6212

$9\frac{7}{8} \times 8\frac{5}{8}$ in.

6241A

A later state (uncoloured), having the same date and publication line with additions · rats run up the lowest sail of the mill A bearded Jew sits on the ground in front of the mill holding a document inscribed *Bond £10,000 Ch$ Fox to Moses Mordecai*, he says, *I must have my monies before Sharles's Tax on Receipts* The receipt tax was announced in Lord John Cavendish's budget speech, 26 May, was petitioned against by the City of London, and was the subject of a debate in the House of Commons on 11 June, see Nos. 6243, 6244 North says after 'Charley', *I wish I had some of my whip cord to keep me steady*, showing that the date of the reissue is after 17 June, see No 6254 Keppel says, *This gale is nothing to the storm of the 27th of July, and no danger of a Lee Shore* Cf No. 5992, &c

6242 STATE PROSTITUTION

[J. Boyne]

London Publish'd as the Act Directs June 12 1783 by J. Boyne N° 2 Shoe Lane Fleet S^t

Engraving (coloured and uncoloured impressions). Britannia, wearing her helmet, sits astride an animal with tail, legs, and mane of a lion, the head and ears of an ass, which symbolizes the British lion In round panniers on each side of the animal sit Fox (l) and North (r) clasping hands across Britannia, who has an arm on a shoulder of each, looking towards Fox Britannia, with her low-cut bodice, and skirts raised above the knee, has a meretricious appearance Her shield and broken spear lie on the ground, under the feet of the British lion, who is partly transformed into an ass. The animal's large clumsy head is bent to the ground, and partly hidden by an enormous flowing mane which covers its neck and shoulders like a cloak. Beneath the title is engraved:

> Here let my Sorrow give my Satyr Place
> To raise New Blushes on the British Race
> > Dryden

Similar in character to No 6243

$7\frac{1}{4} \times 6\frac{15}{16}$ in

6243 THIS REPRESENTATION OF A PARLIMENT CUR WITH HIS DOG LIKE COMPARISION IS DEDICATED TO THE IN-SULTED MERCHANTS TRADERS & DEALERS OF GREAT BRITIAN [sic]

[J. Boyne]

London Publish'd as the Act Directs June 13 1783 by J Boyne N° 2 Shoe Lane Fleet S^t

Engraving A dog, with human arms, and wearing the coat of a naval officer, stands between a sheep (l.) and a wild boar appearing from the r., its body partly cut off by the margin of the print. Round the dog's neck is a collar inscribed *I am a Govenor* [*sic*], indicating that he is Governor (or Commodore) Johnstone, M.P. for Lostwithiel. In his r. hand is a long knife with which he cuts the throat of the perfectly placid sheep which lies on the ground. The knife is inscribed *Five S[hillings] in the Poun[d]*. In his l. hand he holds out to the boar a *Tax on Receipts*. The boar, round whose neck is a collar inscribed *Comerce*, advances snarling ferociously.

Beneath the title is a quotation from a speech by Johnstone which explains the print: *Speaking of Taxation he said there were but two Objects the Commercial & the Landed Interests, the first of these he Compared to the Hog saying if you but touch his Bristles with your finger he'll grunt & begin to roar Whereas the other was like the Sheep you might Shear his Wool & even Cut his Throat & yet he'd make no resistance nor any Noise* (*vide Govr John——e on the Receipt Tax*). See debate on the Receipt Tax, 11 June. *Parl. Hist.* xxiii. 997. Johnstone was quoting 'an old member of that house'.

The Receipt Tax (2*d.* on sums from £2 to £20, and 4*d.* on sums over £20) was very unpopular, and became a cry against Fox at the Westminster election of 1784. The sheep is placidly submitting to a land tax of 5*s.* in the £, the maximum rate being 4*s.* See Nos. 6241A, 6244. For the country gentlemen as sheep cf. No. 6287.

Similar in character to No. 6242.

$6\frac{13}{16} \times 7\frac{1}{8}$ in.

6244 TAX ON RECEIPTS

T. Colley Fec^t [?]   *W. D.* [Dent] *Inv^t*

Pub: June 14th 1783 by W. Dent. N° 116 Strand

Engraving. Four men stand in a row protesting to Lord John Cavendish, the Chancellor of the Exchequer, against the tax on receipts. He turns away from them, holding in his hand a large document inscribed *Tax on Receipts*, to speak to a man wearing a court-suit, bag-wig, and sword who stands (r.) in profile to the l., saying *Persevere my dear Lord, don't mind the Canaille—the Tax won't affect me*. From his pocket hangs a paper, *Memoirs of a fine Gentleman*. He is perhaps intended for the Prince of Wales. Cavendish answers *so Charly Says*. Next Cavendish (l.) is a shoe-maker, out-at-elbows, wearing a cap and apron, holding a last and a rope, his stockings ungartered and his shoe unbuckled. He says, *My Lord it will throw Trade in Confusion*. A stout alderman in a furred gown, the most prominent figure of the design, holds out both hands saying, *Aye, and if this is allowed, Perhaps next year you'll stamp the whole Compting house apparatus—Tax receipts—Zounds! you might as well Tax Venison & Turtle*. Next him is a butcher in his apron, his steel dangling from his waist, a knife at his side. In his hat is stuck a candle. He says, *What if I make my Mark —I must pay for it*. On the extreme r. is the well-known figure of Jeffery Dunstan, knock-kneed, with his ragged clothes, open shirt, and sack over his shoulder as in No. 5637. He says, *I suppose, as how, you'll Tax compli-mentary Cards, by and by!* The print is *Humbly Dedicated to Sir Cecil Wray, Bar^t*.

Wray, whose candidature for Westminster had been supported by Fox, but who opposed the Coalition Ministry, led the opposition to the Tax on Receipts *Parl Hist* xxiii. 998, 1010. The tax is said to have been suggested by Sheridan, Sichel, *Sheridan*, ii. 36, an origin which invited satire For the Receipt Tax see Nos. 6241A, 6243, 6260

The profile head of Cavendish, a good portrait, is delicately drawn in a different manner from that of the rest of the design.

Perhaps by an imitator of Colley's manner, cf. No. 6233.

$8\frac{7}{8} \times 12\frac{7}{8}$ in.

6245 THE STATE VINTNERS.

Pub^d June 18th 1783 by W. Wells, N° 132 Fleet Street London.

Engraving. The interior of a punch-house. In an alcove or bar (r.), behind a counter, stand North and Fox mixing punch Over the alcove is inscribed *Pro bono Publico | The Coalition Punch-house by Charles & Co.* North (l.) holds a kettle in his r. hand, in his l a ladle with which he mixes the contents of the bowl. He says, *Gentlemen I can supply you with accid having had 6 or 7 years constant practice in making of it for 3 kingdoms & 13 provinces* Fox (r.), his r. hand resting on a wine-bottle, his l. outstretched, says *Gentlemen tho' I have enlarged my connections I can still serve you with good Liquor & give you Good Words as usual & if that wont please you may go & be Dm—d* Each has an expression of anxiety mixed with defiance, anxiety the more prominent in North, defiance in Fox

The guests sit on low benches in front of narrow tables, their backs to the punch-makers. Immediately in front of the bar sits a stout man in a bob-wig holding up his bowl and saying, *Coalition Punch do you call it? Phow! tis nauseous as Salts or Jalap* Next him (r) is a tall, thin military officer, wearing a cockaded hat and epaulettes and holding a tasselled cane. He holds a bowl in his l hand, saying, *Aye Friend they that drink it must take it down at a Gulph* Three men sit at a table on the l · a roistering buck wearing the fashionable riding-dress of the day, a favour in his hat, stands up, legs astride, holding out a bowl in his r. hand, the contents spilling, he says, *Right sort Charley Damme!* Next him a man with a melancholy expression leans his elbows on the table, supporting his head in his hands and saying *You may say poisonous indeed for it has thrown the whole Nation in a fermentation & by the addition of that cursed C^o he will loose all his good old Customers.* Next him, and on the extreme l., a trim-looking citizen smoking a long pipe, his bowl on the table, says *When Charles was on his own bottom, he sold wholesome tipple, but now C^o is added to his name we get a poisonous Compound*

One of many satires on the Coalition, see Nos 6176–9, &c.

$7\frac{3}{8} \times 9\frac{3}{4}$ in.

[SIR CECIL WRAY IN THE PILLORY]

Publish'd as the Act directs June 26th 1783 by H. Humphreys N° 51 New Bond Street.

In spite of the date, this print, relating to the Westminster Election of 1784, cannot have been issued in 1783. Another impression is dated 7 May 1784, and it is so catalogued.

6246 THE CONSTITUTIONAL SOCIETY

W D. [Dent.]

Designed by Caution   *Executed by F111 mness*

Pub by W Dent N° 116 Strand, June 27. 1783

Engraving. Three prominent members of the 'Society for Constitutional Information' (often called the Constitutional Society) dining off roast beef at a circular table Beneath the title is engraved:

> *Dedicated to all great Corporations*
> *Search* SURREY, *& all England over,*
> *In each* HOUSE *Beef & Porter sure*
> *Are* TOWERS *of strength, and best Tend,*
> *The* CONSTITUTION *to defend*

The persons of the satire are here indicated Dr Towers sits full-face, carving a sirloin of beef which is labelled *Extract from John Bull.* He wears a clerical wig and spectacles, a napkin is tucked into his coat On his r. sits Lord Surrey, the 'Jockey of Norfolk', raising a piece of beef to his mouth on a fork On Towers's l. sits Sam House, the Wardour Street publican, in his invariable dress. bald head, open shirt, breeches unfastened at the knee, see No 5696, &c He is eating beef with his knife. The knife blades of the three men are inscribed respectively *Resolved* (Towers), *Nem Con* (Surrey), and *Amen* (House) All three are stout, with 'great corporations' Behind Sam House, a waiter enters walking in profile to the l. He is very thin, and, unlike the other three, fashionably dressed with curled wig and ruffled shirt He carries on a salver a great foaming tankard inscribed *S H Wardour Street*, suggesting that the dinner is at Sam's public-house. He points at the table saying, *How the poor Men do labour for the good of the* CONSTITUTION

On the wall which forms the background are two framed pictures. That on the l. is *A Pastoral Dialogue·* a fat parson resembling Towers sits by a round table smoking a long pipe On the table is a steaming punch-bowl, two glasses, and papers inscribed *Magna Cha[rter]* and *Bill of Rights*, a small thin man addresses him, hat in hand On the r. is *The Decoy*, a man-of-war at sea, on her stern in large letters is LOWTHER. This is evidently an allusion to the offer in Sept 1782 of Sir James Lowther (noted for his miserliness) to equip a 74-gun ship at his own expense for the war which he had opposed during North's Ministry. (See *The Remembrancer,* 1782, Part II, p. 258) The peace (then in negotiation) made the offer otiose

The Society for Constitutional Information was formed in 1780[1] chiefly through the exertions of Major Cartwright; its objects were parliamentary reform and annual parliaments They printed and distributed gratis propaganda for reform, &c. Towers (1737–99) was a pamphleteer and presbyterian minister, and an active member of the Society which ordered extracts from his *Vindication of the Political Principles of M' Locke* to be entered in their books in 1782 See *Society for Constitutional Information.* B M L , E 2101/1 He was also 'a very convivial man'. G. B Hill in *Johnson Club Papers*, 1899, p. 79.

---

[1] It is often confused with the earlier Constitutional Society which replaced the Society for supporting the Bill of Rights when the latter was dissolved owing to quarrels between Wilkes and Horne, see No. 4861, &c

The satire seems to suggest that three republicans are devouring John Bull and attacking the Constitution, cf. No. 5979, &c.

$8\frac{7}{8} \times 13\frac{1}{8}$ in.

6247 THE QUINTUPLE ALLIANCE. [1 July 1783]

Engraving From the *Rambler's Magazine*, June 1783. The five partners in this 'alliance' are typical mountebanks, quacks, and persons of small repute. Astley, the famous equestrian, of Astley's Amphitheatre, stands on his head on the saddle of his horse, firing a pistol and saying *I and my Horse levy Contributions upon Asses.* Dr Graham (l.), notorious for his Celestial Bed, holds a cylinder labelled *Divine Balsam for the Ladies*, it resembles his electrical appliances, see No. 6325. Behind him stands Jack Ketch, the hangman, holding up a rope and saying *I am Doctor Katch & this is a sovereign Remedy for a sore throat.* Katerfelto (r) faces Graham, *saying Begar Me make de fine Puffs & de English swallow dem* He points to a black cat, which stands beside him, saying *I am old Scratch.* This is the black cat which usually sat on Katerfelto's shoulder and which he pretended to consult, see No 6327

Evidently a gibe at the Quintuple Alliance, one of the many political associations of the day, composed of the radicals of London, Westminster, Southwark, Middlesex, and Surrey, in the interests of parliamentary reform and annual parliaments. Cf. No. 6217.

$5\frac{1}{16} \times 3\frac{3}{8}$ in

6248 THE TREASURY LADDERS, OR, POLITICAL GAPERS

Pub^d by E. Rich July 5 [1]783 N° 55 Fleet Street.

Engraving (coloured impression) A man wearing the order of the Garter, probably intended for Portland (who had no order, cf No 6251), stands with his arms folded within an open bow window, a yoke across his shoulders, from each end of which hang bunches of grapes To this window two long ladders ascend, at the top of which stand Fox (l) and North (r), both grasping at the grapes Below them on the ladders are others gaping for the spoils of the Treasury. Below Fox stands Sheridan, gaping for the excrement which falls from Fox, this process is repeated by each climber on the ladders Fox says, *Gape wide Sherry* Sheridan says, *This is better than the School for Scandel.* The man below Sheridan says, *These are golden Drops.* North says, *I have still a Finger in the Pye.* The man below him says, *Shite away my Lord, my mouth is open*, and the man below again says, *I shall never have a Belly full.*

At the bottom of the design the ladders are supported by groups of men (H.L), who gape upwards for their share of the spoil The ladders stand against a high brick wall, across which is engraved *Treasury*, every brick being indicated.

Beneath the design is etched:

> *Some people may think this a comical Farce is,*
> *To see them a gaping at each others A——s,*
> *Tho' strange it may seem, its the trick of them all,*
> *For one still to catch what another lets fall.*

Such is the Oeconemy of our wise nation
Yet dunces will grumble about reformation;
The people may stare, but in spite of their wishes,
State Vultures will eat both the loaves and the fishes.

See also Nos 6195, 6223, 6240, 6251.

$11\frac{11}{16} \times 9$ in.

6249 [BURKE]

WD. [Dent].

Pub. by W Dent July 11th 1783 N° 116. Strand

Colley.

Engraving. Burke stands in profile to the r. dressed as a jesuit. He clasps to his breast a small female figure or doll, wearing a hat with a feather, perhaps intended to represent Little Red Riding Hood (see No. 6205), he is dressed as in that print. He is wearing spectacles and his wig appears beneath the biretta. His belt is inscribed *Friendship*, through it, in place of the cross, is a dagger on which are letters. This is attached to a rosary made of guineas

Although *Colley* is engraved below the publication line, it is not in his manner, but in that of Dent.

$8\frac{1}{8} \times 6\frac{1}{4}$ in

6250 JACK A' BOTH SIDES!

[Gillray.]

Pub^d July 11th 1783 by W. Humphrey N° 227 Strand

Engraving North balances himself on his l. toe on the centre of the beam of a pair of scales, his r. leg poised in the air. He stands so that the scale (r.) on which Fox is standing rests on the ground, while that on which Shelburne stands is in the air His attitude suggests that he could, if he liked, weigh down the scales on Shelburne's side. Fox, enormously obese, stands looking upwards with a cunning and satisfied smile, saying *Damn the Tories!!!* Shelburne, with an expression of disgust, is stamping and clenching his fists; he says, *Oh! Damn the Wigs!* North is excreting against Shelburne a blast of smoke inscribed *Anathema* which swells into a cloud. From dark clouds in the upper l. corner of the design the king's head (back view) and r. arm appear. He holds over North's head an enormous wig which envelops his head and shoulders. A crown is poised above the king's head, and he is blindfolded by a tartan bandage indicating Scottish influence

This seems to imply that the king had connived at the Coalition by converting North into a Whig in order to ruin Shelburne, an allegation with no support in common report or fact.

Grego, *Gillray*, pp. 48–9. Wright and Evans, No. 14.

13×9 in.

A coloured impression with Humphrey's publication line scored through but legible, and that of Fores added:

Pub Jan 1. 1794 by S. W. Fores N. 3 Piccadilly.

6251 THE GOLDEN-PIPPIN BOYS, ON THE BRANCHES OF STATE

Pub^d by J. Barrow. July 24. 1783. White Lion Bull Stairs. Surry side Black Friars Bridge.

Engraving. A symmetrical apple-tree, on the branches of which sit or stand ministers of state gathering the apples. They are poorly characterized. Against the trunk stands a ladder, inscribed *The Ladder by which the noble Lads ascend.* Each rung has an inscription: *Conceit, Lying, Swearing, Pretention, Assurance, Harangue, Flattery, Bribery, Interest, Money, Ambition, Title.* The topmost and centre figure is that of the Duke of Portland, standing; he says, *I hope there will be no Searching pockets when we come down.* He wears (inaccurately) a Garter ribbon, cf. No. 6248. Below him sit Fox (l.) and North (r.) Fox says, *They may call us what they please so they call us not—To Account* North says, *I will serve my self, my friends, and my Country.* Below these are Keppel (l.) and an unidentified minister (r.), perhaps Lord John Cavendish, Chancellor of the Exchequer. Keppel says, *This is the best Yard-arm that I ever crost.* The other says, *I shall follow the old Precedent—fill my Coffers.* Of the two lowest apple-gatherers, one (l.) has a vague resemblance to Burke, he says, *Apple stealing began at old Adam, and will only die with old Time.* The other (r.) says, *A few will never be missed.*

In front of the tree is a circular railing within which stand two grenadiers holding bayoneted muskets, as in the sentry-boxes outside the Treasury.

Beneath the design is etched:

> *Now, all you that stare*
> *And grumble, and swear,*
> *And wish that all Thieves had their whippings;*
> *Come, don't be so mad,*
> *Because a poor Lad,*
> *Will pocket a few Golden Pippins.*

> *No longer I blame,*
> *Or wish to reclaim*
> *The Statesman, because that he grapples;*
> *For coul'd I ascend,*
> *My self, and my Friend,*
> *I'd serve, with the sweet, golden Apples.*

See also No. 6248, &c.

11¾×8⅜ in.

6252 WAR ESTABLISHMENT.

T Colley fec^t [?].

Pub: by D. Archery July ^th [sic] 1783 St Jame's Street

Engraving. A pugilistic encounter between Lord Thurlow (l.) and Fox (r.), who face each other with clenched fists, stripped to the waist Behind each stands a second wearing a bag-wig; that of Thurlow (l) is a stout man wearing a laced coat and sword, with some resemblance to Rigby. Fox's second, probably Sheridan, holds out a lemon.

Thurlow, his judge's wig lying at his feet, says *I'll have the Patent with the War fees, or break every bone in your Body.* Fox says *I hate Imposters.*

A notice board on a post (r.) is inscribed *The Grant of a Tellership*. Beneath the title is engraved, *Vide the Debate on Lord T—r—ws Grant of a Tellership*

This debate took place on 4 and 7 July, *Parl. Hist* xxiii. 1061–95. A Bill was brought in to regulate the fees of Exchequer Officers, and especially to change the existing practice by which the Tellers of the Exchequer received annually something over £2,500 in peace time and nearly £8,000 in war. A proposal was thereupon made by Rigby to exempt Lord Thurlow from the operation of the Bill, on the ground that his promise of the reversion of a tellership had been first made in 1778 before the reform was thought of This exemption was supported by North and opposed by Fox and others, notably Sheridan. See Walpole, *Last Journals*, 1910, ii. 529.

For the signature see No. 6233, &c.

$8\frac{1}{2} \times 13\frac{1}{8}$ in.

6253 EVE'S TOLL-GATE OR THE NEW THREE-PENNY TURN-PIKE [1 Aug. 1783]

Engraving From the *Rambler's Magazine*. A lady in bed (l.) hands a coin to an official with a book under his arm, while a spectacled doctor hurries away (r) carrying an infant in his arms The official holds a paper inscribed *Rec^d Three Pence for admitting a Child into the World. J. Cavendish.*

This is an allusion to the tax of 3d. on the registration of Births, Marriages, and Deaths introduced into the budget of 1783 by Lord John Cavendish, see *Parl. Hist.* xxiii. 935–6. See also No. 6256.

$5\frac{5}{8} \times 3\frac{7}{16}$ in.

SCRUB & ARCHER

Pub 1st Aug 1783, by W Humphrey, N° 227 Strand.

A reissue of No. 6221.

6254 THE E. O. TABLE. [1 Aug. 1783]

Engraving From the *Rambler's Magazine*. Seven players standing round an E.O. table. On the l stand Fox and North, holding hands, both having secured the greater part of the money at stake. Fox, with a fox's head, holds a money-bag, saying, *My Noble Friend this is Coalition money.* North says, *This is better then Dealing in Whipcord* The other figures are poorly characterized and cannot be identified. Behind Fox a man partly visible (? the Earl of Surrey) says *I'll back you up Charley.* A man with a melancholy expression looks at North, saying, *Is it thus you Keep up your Corporation* A cheerful-looking man, with a money-bag and a pile of guineas (the only other player who has secured a share of the winnings), says, looking to two despairing players on the r., *You should have gone North about* They say, *I am Undone! I am Undone!* and *D—m E.O. and all the Vowels in the Alphabet* The last speaker resembles the Duke of Grafton.

Beneath the circular E O. table crouches the Devil, saying *I have play'd for you all & have won you all.*

On 17 June, Pitt, in bringing forward his Bill for Reform of Abuses in Public Offices, instanced the waste of stationery in the Treasury under

North, the bill for whipcord in 1781 being £340, see *Parl. Hist.* xxiii 953; Wraxall, *Memoirs*, 1884, iii. 458, see also Nos. 6241, 6257. For E O. see No. 5928.

$5\frac{9}{16} \times 3\frac{1}{2}$ in.

6255 THE OLD RAT OF THE CONSTITUTION ELOQUENCE.

W D. [Dent].

Pub^d Augt 6th 83 by W. Dent. Strand.

Engraving. W.L. portrait of Lord Nugent, in profile to the r. He bends forward, his l hand on his breast, as if making a speech. He holds up his coat-tails, uncovering his posterior, from which a blast issues, inscribed *my Son in Law* This was George Nugent Temple-Grenville, Earl Temple (1753–1818), cr. Marquess of Buckingham, 1784.

For Nugent see Nos 6059, 6212, 6256. He had 'all the garrulity of old age sustained by a sort of unblushing facility of utterance which might pass for a species of eloquence'. Wraxall, *Memoirs*, 1884, iii. 305.

$6\frac{1}{4} \times 4\frac{3}{8}$ in. (pl.).

6256 ALL ALIVE OR THE POLITICAL CHURCHYARD.

Pub according t Act by B. Pownall N° 6. Pallmall. Aug. 9 1783.

Engraving. A church and churchyard, with the graves of politicians and others, whose heads look from behind their respective tombstones The church is on the l with a square tower (r); on the r are conventional trees. The three central tombstones in the foreground are those of Burke (l.), North (c), and Fox (r.). On Burke's is inscribed, *Here Lieth Ed^d Burke Oeconomist Extraordinary to his Majesty. To Save his breath He welcom'd death.* On North's is *Here Lieth L——d N——H. I'm gone to realms below, To find more Cause for woe.* On that of Fox is *Here Lieth C——s F—x, The game I have play'd, I have lost by a Spade, My partner was wrong For he shuffl'd to long.* In the foreground on the extreme l is a flat stone inscribed, *Here Lieth G——l C——y* [Conway] *So fickle in his pliant mind He for a Change his life resignd.* In a corresponding position on the r is a rectangular brick tomb, inscribed, *Here Lieth his Grace the D——e of R——D* [Richmond] *Since he on Earth no good coul'd find, He is at last to death resign'd* Slightly behind and to the l. of Burke's tomb is that of the king: *Here Lieth G. K——g. I govern'd all with —— decree But now alas; Death governs me.* Behind and to the r of Fox's tomb is that of a peer: *Here Lieth L——d T——e Behold him now laid the Grave in Who noughty man —— L——y C——N* [Lady Craven]. He is perhaps intended for Lord Temple, the king's agent in the rejection of Fox's India Bill in Dec. 1783, cf. No. 6255.

The remaining tombs are described as they are placed, l. to r , some being in front and others behind. A rectangular upright tombstone is inscribed, *Here Lieth C——s J——N* [Charles Jenkinson] *To your advice we ruin owe; Go then, and council fiends below* (See No. 6228) More prominent is a rectangular brick tomb *Here Lieth L——d K——* [Keppel]. *This Gallant Admiral is no more, Behold him Stranded on Death's Lee Shore* (cf No 5992, &c). Behind Keppel's tomb is that of General Eliott, cr. Lord Heathfield for his defence of Gibraltar *Here Lieth G——l E——T.*

Who could bear Fire so well Cannot feel Pain in hell. To heav'n let him rise, Since he the Devil defies (see No. 6035, &c.). Next, and in the background is that of Lord John Cavendish, Chancellor of the Exchequer: *Here Lieth L——d J. C——H. He woul'd have tax'd our breath Had it not been for death.* An allusion to the tax on the registration of births, deaths, marriages, see No. 6253. Portland is next: *Here Lieth His G——e the D——e of P——d. An easy man of keen command, He ruled a State At Second hand* (cf. No. 6233, &c.). The tombstone of Shelburne is immediately behind that of the king: *Here Lieth The E——l of S——N. I made my peace on Earth, And why in heav'n Should not I hope to be forgiv'n.* Pitt's tomb is more elaborate, a rectangular stone tomb surmounted by a pyramid and surrounded by a railing: *Here Lieth The Honble Wm Pitt. Thou cov'rest Earth Unequall'd Worth.* The grave of Governor Johnstone is next: *Here Lieth G——r J——N. So fond of Snarling it is own'd, At Death he grinn'd But never Groan'd.* (He was a notorious duellist, cf. No. 5474.) Next and more prominent is the rectangular brick tomb of Sheridan: *Here Lieth R. B. S——N. He had great merit But woul'd you know it Look not for Politicks in a Poet.* Behind this, and inconspicuous, is Lord Nugent's tombstone: *Here Lieth L——d N——T An old Rat* (see No. 6255, &c.). Mansfield's tomb is more prominent: *Here Lieth L——d M——D. Stop says the Judge, while I my Ballance fix, Death kick'd his Breech and Sent him o'er the Styx.*

Behind are two stones commemorating Lord George Germain (Sackville) and Lord George Gordon. *L——d G. G——N. Alas how came I here, For Death was all my fear* (an allusion to his supposed cowardice at Minden). *Here Lieth L——d G. G——N. For religion, Od rot him. The Devil has got him* (see No. 5694, &c.). More prominent, and next to Mansfield, lies Dundas, the Lord Advocate of Scotland: *Here lieth the L——d A——E. The cause of damnation he gaind with such ease, He is gone to the Devil to ask for his fees* (see No. 6169). Behind is a minute stone: *Sir T—— R——d* [Thomas Rumbold] *His peculation has left no more.* (Rumbold was, perhaps unjustly, regarded as a typical nabob of the worst kind, see No. 6169, &c.) Sir Cecil Wray's tomb is in the form of an obelisk: *Here Lieth Sir Cecil W——y Honesty in him innate is, Then Let him pass; old Charon gratis.* (He was enjoying a short-lived popularity for his opposition to the tax on receipts, see No. 6244, &c. Also, though M.P. for Westminster as Fox's nominee, he had not supported the Coalition.) The last tombstone on the extreme r. is that of Lord Loughborough, Chief Justice of the Common Pleas: *Here Lieth L——d L——H. Tir'd of hanging he was grown, Till Death in Pity cut him Down.* Inscriptions on the wall of the church commemorate three more notables, the first (l.) being David Hartley (son of the more famous David Hartley), M.P. for Hull, and at this time the emissary of Fox for peace negotiations with America): *Underneath Lieth D——d H——y Esq' A man that all coul'd calculate Except the Sands which told his fate.* Next is Sir Charles Turner: *Below Lieth S—r C——S T——R An honest Man.* (Turner, M.P. for the City of York, see No. 6073, was classed with Sir George Savile, as pre-eminent for 'independence of character and zeal for public liberty'. Oldfield, *Representative History of Great Britain*, 1816, v. 279.) Savile's inscription is beside that of Turner: *Nigh this place Lieth S—r G—— S——E. Such humourous Satire mark'd his Fame, He made the Culprit smile in Shame.* (Both were supporters of the Yorkshire movement for Parliamentary Reform, see No. 5657, &c.)

No 6263 is a companion print; both perhaps imitate Sir Herbert Croft's very popular *Abbey of Kilkhampton*, 1780, &c , a collection of satirical epitaphs.

$8\frac{15}{16} \times 13\frac{1}{4}$ in.

6257 THE COALITION DISSECTED.

W D. [Dent].

Pub^d by W. Dent N° 116 Strand Augt 12th 1783

Re-pub^d by J. Cattermoul N° 376 Oxford Street Decr 15th

Engraving. A W L. figure divided vertically, half (l.) representing North, the other half Fox.

The head appears to be copied from Sayers's *Mask*, see No. 6234, reversed. The figure is nude except for a pair of short breeches, and the organs of the body from the neck to the waist are exposed Common to both is the inscription, *Pro privato lucro* across the forehead, and the protruding tongue inscribed *Truth* in reversed or looking-glass characters. North's hand holds a bag inscribed *Whipcord* (see No. 6254, &c) On his arm, as if tattooed, are guineas and the word *Finance* On Fox's arm are a dice-box and two dice inscribed *Industry*. Fox's hand, inscribed *Goodwill*, pulls at a cord labelled *Anodyne Necklace*; this comes from the lungs of the body, which are inscribed *Oratorical* (r), *Lungs* (l.). The Anodyne Necklace was a much advertised object supposed to prevent the convulsions and teething disorders of infants (cf Johnson, *Idler*, No 40). North's ribs are inscribed respectively *Place, Pension, Sinecure, Contract, Loan, Title, &c. &c.* Those of Fox are *13 Stripes* in allusion to his attitude to the American war, cf. Nos 6207, 6229 Each side has a heart inscribed *Union*, and other organs inscribed *Touch-Wood, Love, Honesty*. The central artery common to both is *Self-interest*, branches from this deviate into the respective breeches-pockets of the monster. On both sides of these are inscribed *East India Bill* and *P—— of W——'s Establishment*. The pockets into which these conduits debouch are full of guineas and are inscribed *Pickings*.

The debate on the Prince of Wales's establishment took place on 23, 25, and 26 June, when it appeared that Fox was in favour of a grant of £100,000 a year to the Prince by parliament; the king, with the approval of Lord John Cavendish, having proposed to allow the prince £50,000 a year from the Civil List, a disagreement which shook the Ministry *Parl Hist* xxiii 1030 ff Wraxall, *Memoirs*, 1884, iii. 108 ff., see Nos. 6258, 6259. Fox's India Bill was not brought in until 11 November, so that the inscriptions relating to India must have been added for the reissue in December A globe, in place of the stomach, common to both partners, is inscribed *Indostan*, and (below) *Great* (in reversed or looking-glass characters) *Britain*, to indicate (as in the case of the tongue inscribed *Truth*), that Britain was the reverse of Great.

The sides of North and Fox which partly cover the exposed ribs are inscribed *Green Fat*. North's foot, inscribed *Affection*, tramples on a fox which is excreting. Across his leg (l.) is written *Hypocrisy*, across that of Fox (r), *Prostitution*. See also No. 6213, &c. For the India Bill see No. 6271, &c.

$13 \times 9\frac{3}{4}$ in. (clipped).

6258 THE ROYAL MIDSHIPMAN OR PRINCE W^M HENRY'S
LEVEE.   [1 Sept. 1783]

Engraving. From the *Rambler's Magazine*. Prince William in naval uniform, wearing his Garter ribbon, stands (l.) on a dais under a canopy,
addressing a group of sailors. He says, *Had I £60,000, my Boys you
should have it all* (an allusion to the sum of £60,000 given to the Prince of
Wales on coming of age (Aug. 1783) for forming an establishment, in
addition to his allowance of £50,000 a year, see Nos. 6257, 6259. The
foremost sailor says, *I should like to be Archbishop of Canterbury, tis a
d——nd good See.* A sailor with one wooden leg says, *Make me Master of
the Ceremonies.* A third says, *Suppose as how you give us the Great Seal
among three of us.* A fourth, arm-in-arm with a meretricious-looking
woman, says *I wish your Worship would make my Moll a maid of Honour.*
A sailor with crutches seated on the ground says, *I should like a Birth at the
Exchequer da——me.*

Prince William's service as a midshipman during the war had made him
very popular, see No. 5677.

$5\frac{3}{4} \times 3\frac{5}{8}$ in.

6259 THE NEW VIS-A-VIS, OR FLORIZEL DRIVING PERDITA.
                                                             [1 Sept. 1783]

Engraving. From the *Rambler's Magazine*, Aug. 1783. The Prince of
Wales drives (l. to r.) a coach drawn by a pair of goats. Inside sits Mrs.
Robinson (Perdita) with three ostrich feathers in her hair. She looks from
the window, and stretches out her hand towards a man standing at the
back of the coach in the footman's place, who is handing to her a paper
inscribed *Grant of £60,000.* He is her husband; a paper, probably a bill
or cheque, protrudes from his coat-pocket. On the roof of the coach Lord
North lies on his back asleep, his arms folded; his head rests on a pillow
inscribed *Royal favor.* On Perdita's lap is a man's three-cornered hat.

This is an allusion to the grant of £60,000 to the Prince of Wales for
forming an establishment on coming of age (Aug. 1783), which was given
to him in addition to £50,000 a year and the revenues (c. £13,000) of the
Duchy of Cornwall. Mrs. Robinson was in the habit of driving about
London 'in an absurd chariot with a device of a basket likely to be taken
for a coronet, driven by the favoured of the day, with her husband and
candidates for her favour as outriders'. L. Hawkins, *Memoirs*, ii. 24. The
liaison with the Prince of Wales had been broken off for some time. See
No. 5767, &c., and for the Prince's establishment Nos. 6257, 6258. For
Perdita and Lord North see No. 6266. For the *vis-à-vis* cf. No. 5373.

$3\frac{3}{10} \times 5\frac{15}{16}$ in.

6260 DUTY ON <u>DISCHARGES</u>, OR A COMPANION TO THE
RECEIPT TAX.

WD. [Dent.]

Pub^d by W. Dent N° 116 Strand Sepr 2^d 1783.

Engraving. A row of four latrines, in each of which a person is seated.
Through a door (l.) Lord John Cavendish is entering followed by North
(l.) and Fox (r.). Cavendish, the Chancellor of the Exchequer, is writing

on a large scroll held in his hand, *Resources, Breathing, Eating, Drinking, Shit——* North says, *Set it down Johnny, it will be very productive.* Fox says, *Aye, Productive & salutary, for it will strike at the very* <u>*bottom*</u> *of luxury.*

The first seated figure (l) is that of a fat alderman in a furred gown. He is saying *If the* <u>*Great Houses*</u> *should stamp the* <u>*little houses*</u> *it will fall heavy on me, for my maw is always craving and must have its fill* A letter at his feet is addressed to *W. Leatherhead Esqʳ Aldⁿ of F——ward.* He is evidently Alderman Kitchin, of Farringdon Within, apparently a noted guzzler, see No 6314. The next figure is a man wearing spectacles and a parson's gown and bands In his hand is a newspaper, the *Morning Chronicle,* with the word *Taxes* in large characters He is saying *The Constitutional Society shall know of this and they will —— publish some Resolves.* At his feet is an open volume, *British Biography.* He is Dr. Towers, see No. 6246. Next him is a stout man, evidently intended either for one of the noted quacks of the day, or for a doctor whom the artist designed to pillory Above his head is a placard, *Quacks annihilated. Grand Restorer of human nature* He is saying *If this is the Case who'll take my bolus, pill, potion, lotion —— we may now throw Physic to the dogs indeed*

The last figure is a woman, a notorious brothel-keeper. She is saying *Good heaven help me! or next the fl—c—ng* <u>*Collution*</u> *will stamp my dear, sweet, pretty, little Girls —— playthings. —— spare them Charley, for Perdita's sake.* In her hand is an open book, *Rambler's Mag . . Taxes,* while she is befouling the *Christian Magᵉ.* At her feet is a paper inscribed *Mother Windsor King's place,* notorious for its houses of ill-fame Above the two central latrines is a scroll inscribed *Water —— Closets.*

Beneath the title is etched :

> *From Stamps, so sharp, and so strange, there's no stealth,*
> *They touch if you die, or Physic for health;*
> *The Coalition strange, our mettle to damp*
> *Likewise bid Johnny birth and marriage to stamp,*
> *And, stranger still, our Commerce for to vamp,*
> *They wisely Receipts confound with a stamp;*
> *To prove they all others at stamping surpass,*
> *Perhaps, they'll next order a stamp for the A——.*

Lord John Cavendish in his budget speech (25 May) proposed to increase the stamp duties and to tax 'quack medicines', i e. those sold by persons who were not 'bred to the profession of doctors, &c' *Parl. Hist* xxiii 935. For the tax on the registration of births see No. 6253, and for the Receipt Tax Nos. 6241A, 6243, 6244.

7⅛ × 13⅜ in.

6261 THE STATE GOOSE-CATCHER, OR A Sᵀ JAMES'S MARKET-MAN

Pubᵈ by J. Barrow Sepʳ 11. 1783. White Lion, Bull Stairs, Surry Side Black Friars Bridge.

Engraving Fox, with a fox's head, riding in profile from r. to l He holds a goose by the neck over his l. shoulder, another goose is tied by its feet to the horse's neck, the heads and necks of seven other geese project from two pair of saddle-bags. He is saying *I have Burgoyn'd the Geese at last by coming North about.* The horse says *I blush for my Master because he cannot blush for himself.* Beneath the design is engraved:

Ye politic Wolves, that watch for the Fleece,
And sophistic Foxes, that long for the Geese,
When bluster, and storm, and harangue is all vain,
Turn, like F—x your brave leader, and then you'll obtain.

The geese represent, as in No. 5843, &c., the electors of Westminster (or other persons deluded by Fox), whom Fox has 'Burgoyned' or (as at Saratoga) surrendered to the enemy, by joining North. One of many satires on the Coalition, see Nos. 6176-9.

$9\frac{1}{4} \times 8\frac{11}{16}$ in.

6262 THE SAILOR'S RETURN, OR BRITISH VALOR REWARDED.

S.B.

Pub^d by W. Dent Sep^t 20th 1783 N° 116 Strand.

Engraving. Two maimed sailors support themselves on crutches on the irregular cobble-stones of a London street. One (l.), full-face, holds his hat in his l. hand as if begging, a crutch under his arm; his l. leg has been amputated, his r. arm, which is without a hand, is raised towards his face; his r. eye is bandaged. The other (r.), in back view, has lost his r. leg, and supports himself on two crutches. Beneath the title is etched:

"Some, for hard Masters, broken under Arms,"
"In battle lopt away, with half their Limbs"
"Beg bitter bread, thro' realms their Valor sav'd"—
Young's Night Thoughts.

$7\frac{1}{4} \times 8\frac{7}{8}$ in.

6263 THE LADIES CHURCH YARD

Publish'd 22 Septr 1783 by B. Pownall N° 6 Pall Mall

Engraving. A companion print to No. 6256. The scene is reversed, the church being on the r., the trees on the l. From behind the tombstones appear the busts of women. The central grave in the foreground, however, is that of the Prince of Wales, a rectangular tomb, surmounted by a truncated pyramid, above which appear the head and shoulders of the Prince. He appears perhaps in response to Perdita's appeal (see below). The tomb is ornamented at the corners with ostrich plumes. *Here lies The P——s^e [sic] of W——s. How happy cou'd I be with Either Were the other Dear Charmer away But while you both Tease me togeather The Devil a word Will I say Tal de Ral.*

On each side of this is a flat tomb: on the l.: *Here lieth L——Y M—B—E* [Melbourne]. *Tho on my back Death Has me laid I might remain For him A Maid.* On the r. *Here lies the D——s of D——RE* [Duchess of Devonshire] *Cease Kissing Death You stop my Breath.* For the prince's attachment to Lady Melbourne and the Duchess of Devonshire see Wraxall, *Memoirs*, 1884, v. 370-2, and cf. No. 6115. The other tombs in the front row are (l. to r.): *Here lies L——Y G——R* [Grosvenor] *A lover ne'er I Thought to lack While I so long lay on my Back* (see No. 4844, &c.). The Queen has a rectangular tomb with a superstructure: *Here lies Her M——y Virtue on earth No more is seen For here she lies With Britains Queen; Here lies the*

730

D——ss of R——d [Rutland] *Tho beauteous she Was forced to Yield Death shook his Dart & won ye field.*

The other (less prominent) tombs (l to r) are: Catharine II: *Here lies the E—R—S of R——A How could you death This Empress slay For her one life she would a Million Pay*; Marie Antoinette: *Here lies y Q——N o F——CE Death has placed her on her Rump To play her cards Till the last Trump.* Behind, *Here lies Miss V——N* [Vernon] *I did not like the P——E of Ws for fops like him Might oft tel Tales* For the three Miss Vernons, daughters of Richard Vernon, the second husband of the Countess of Upper Ossory, half-sisters of Lady Shelburne, see Walpole's poem *The Three Vernons, Works,* 1798, iv 388. Next is the Duchess of Cumberland (Anne *née* Luttrell), *D——s of C—L—D Fair Lady you deserve rebuke Who could for Death desert a Duke.* Next, *H* [*sic*] *Lies M^rs S—H—N* [Sheridan] *To Heavn'n would you find a path Go follow this Fair Maid of Bath* (an allusion to Foote's play on Miss Linley). Behind is, *Death like the Scandalous of Tongue You neither Spare The old nor Young, Miss Y——g* [Young] Next is the tomb of an old woman, *Here Lieth L——y F——h Her loss why should another Weep Who doz'd Before now's fast Asleep Here lies D——s of G——R* [Gloucester, Maria Walpole] *If charms and Virtue could life Save She neer had been within the Grave.* Next, and immediately behind the Prince of Wales, is *M^rs M——N So cold a Lover neer was known Death lies upon Me like a Stone* She is of meretricious appearance, and is probably Mrs Mahon, see Nos 5868, 5948, who did her best to attract the Prince of Wales Bleackley, *Ladies Fair and Frail,* pp. 279-81 Next is Mrs Siddons with a rectangular brick tomb: *Here lies M^rs S—D—NS Her fate weep not Whom her survive For in our mem'ry She's alive.* Behind, with a pyramidal tomb, is the Queen of Spain, *Q——n of S——N I die resigned in spight of Foes Since I have Scrached Britannias Nose.* Next is the Princess Royal· *Here lieth The P——ss R——L. Here lies the Mildest of ye fair She was too good for Heaven to spare* Next is Perdita: *Here lies M^rs R——N* [Robinson] *If with thee You'd have me dwell Go Death & Bring me Florizel* (see No. 5767, &c) Behind her is the tomb of Miss Farren, *Here lies Miss F——n O Death from you This ought to far be* [*sic*] *To take poor Joan Without her Derby* (see No 5901) On the extreme r is Lady Archer. *L——y A——R Beneath lies the blooming Archer Q—sb—y D——e* [Queensbury Duke] *Neer Seem'd more starcher* (see No 5879). On the church wall is inscribed *Below lieth L——y W—s—y* [Worsley] *I ne'er before was sick of love I prithee Death a little move*; see No. 6105, &c.

$8\frac{3}{16} \times 13\frac{5}{8}$ in

6264 MR F—X MOVING ALL HIS PLATE & FURNITURE FROM ST JAMES'S PLACE TO WIMBLEDON. [1 Oct. 1783]

Engraving From the *Rambler's Magazine.* A procession of domestic servants walking (r. to l) carrying a very small quantity of household goods, indicative of Fox's poverty Two porters (l) carry between them a small stretcher on which are dice, playing-cards, a book, *Hoyle* [on whist], a small box of *Title Deeds,* a candlestick, small jug, and two salt-cellars A maid-servant with a broom walks beside it They are followed by a man carrying a bundle and a pair of tongs, a maid-servant with a mop and pail, a man with a bundle, gridiron, and pair of bellows

At this time Parliament was not sitting and there was no reason to anticipate the speedy fall of the Coalition Ministry, which seems to be here foreshadowed

A sale and removal of Fox's furniture by bailiffs in 1781 is described by Selwyn, *Hist. MSS. Comm.*, *Carlisle MSS.*, 1897, pp. 488-9, and another in 1784 by Wraxall, *Memoirs*, 1884, IV. 71.

$3\frac{7}{16} \times 5\frac{13}{16}$ in

6265 PROTEUS YE 2D IN SEVERAL AMONG HIS MANY PUBLICK CHARACTERS.

Pub^d as the Act directs (Octr 9) 178(3) by B Pownall N° 6. Pall Mall.[1]

Engraving. Fox in a number of contrasted situations. In the upper l. corner he is declaiming from the hustings His supporters appear below waving their hats; among these Sam House is conspicuous A flag is inscribed *A Man of the People*. A lady on horseback in profile to the r. is among the crowd, her horse inscribed *Chatsworth*, to show that she is the Duchess of Devonshire Fox is saying, *Gent^s & Ladies I will never Consent to any additional Taxes I will support the Majesty of the people*.

Beneath is the contrasting picture Fox and Lord John Cavendish drinking wine together, seated much at their ease, one on each side of a round table Fox, in profile to the l., says, *Tax away L^d C——h let the plebeians pay the piper I say* Behind Cavendish (l) is inscribed, *Intended Taxes by F. N C* [Fox, North, Cavendish] *& Co On Sense—On Speech—On all Victuals &c &c. &c. &c.*

In the upper r quarter of the print are two full-length figures of Fox declaring one (l), says, *Distraction what make peace when the Kingdom is so Flourshing*, the other says, *Make peace on any Terms The Kingdom is ruin'd*.

Below are two other representations of Fox In one (r) he says, *I pledge my honor I will never act in conjunction with the man That has ruin'd his Country* In the other, Fox and North stand facing one another, Fox saying *My dear Lord 'am your Sincere Friend*

One of several satires which anticipate *The Beauties of Fox, North, and Burke*, 1784. Cf. also Nos. 6187, 6188, 6192, 6207

8×14 in

6266 FLORIZEL AND PERDITA

Pub^d as the act directs (Octr 16) 178(3)[2] *by B. Pownall N° 6 Pall Mall*

Engraving. A bust portrait divided vertically by a line down the centre of the face, one half (l) representing the Prince of Wales, the other Mrs. Robinson, or Perdita The Prince wears the ribbon and star of the Garter; half of his pleated shirt-frill is visible. Perdita's softly curled hair, with ringlets falling on her shoulder, is framed by a light hood with a curious jagged edge She also wears a shirt-frill, it surrounds her breast, which is bare In the lower l. corner of the print is a small profile head of the king looking towards the prince with a melancholy expression, he says, *Oh! My Son My Son*. On his head is the front half of a crown Above are the Prince

---

[1] The figures in brackets have been inserted in ink in a contemporary hand, a space having been left in the publication line.

[2] The parts of the date in brackets have been added in ink in a space left by the engraver

of Wales's feathers with his motto *Ich Dien* On the r., by Perdita's shoulder, is the head of her husband, with branching stag's horns and animal's ears; *King of Cuckolds* and *R—N—S—N* being engraved beneath The horns support a shelf on which stand the busts of three men believed to be lovers of Perdita: Colonel Tarleton (r) in the plumed helmet which had been popularized by Reynolds's portrait, see No. 6116; Fox (c), see No. 6117, &c., and Lord North (l.) who looks at her through a single eye-glass, see No. 6259. For the attitude of the king to his son and Fox see Walpole, *Last Journals*, 1910, ii. 496, and Nos. 6231, 6237. For 'Florizel and Perdita' see No. 5767, &c.

$7 \times 9\frac{3}{16}$ in.

6267 PROCLAMATION OF PEACE

Pub^d Octr 21st 1783, by W. Wells, N° 132, Fleet Street.

Engraving. Peace, blowing a trumpet, and holding an olive-branch, flies above the heads of five standing figures representing the ex-belligerents; attached to her trumpet is a banner inscribed, *Peace proclaimed Octr 6th 1783.* America, on the extreme l., is a man, nude, except for a pair of striped breeches, his head decorated by a tuft of three feathers He capers, waving a tomahawk in his l. hand, and holding in his r the staff of liberty surmounted by a Phrygian cap, from the staff floats the striped American flag; a short length of chain lies at his feet. He says, *I have got my Liberty and the Devil Scalp you all.* France, next him, turns towards Spain, whose l hand he holds, saying, *Vat for do you mind dat now Diego, here be ver good man, will let you have de nice Tobacco to make you amends* (cf. No. 5859); he points to America with his r. hand. He is dressed as a French *petit-maitre* and has a long pigtail queue Spain, in cloak, slashed doublet, and feathered hat, looks away from France towards John Bull or England, he says, with his r. hand on his breast, *Ah me Signior! your Balls dat be all fire make me Shiver & cry for peace,* see No. 6035, &c. England is a burly sailor, wearing short wide trousers, holding a club in his r hand He turns away from Spain towards Holland, whom he holds by the neckcloth, saying, *Damme but you shall make peace Myneer, or never know the taste of Spice again* Holland, a stout plainly dressed burgher wearing baggy breeches, clasps his hands in distress, saying, *Vat Rob me & cut my troat too Myneer English!*

Beneath the design is inscribed:

> *Peace! Peace! says Monsieur, before Hood again calls;*
> *Spain Welcomes the sound, dreading Eliotts hot Balls;*
> *Return but my Gelt, Holland roars out in fear,*
> *I too will make peace; Indeed! will you Myneer!*
> *Aye Sink me you shall, and for you Miss revolt*
> *The time may yet come, to repent of your fault.*

Peace was signed on 2 and 3 Sept, and was formally proclaimed in London on 6 Oct., see Nos. 6336, 6351 Peace was not formally made with Holland till 1784, see No. 6292. The preliminary peace-terms which had been so much abused and the occasion of the coalition against Shelburne, see No 6172, &c., were substantially those accepted by the Coalition Ministry, and were not unpopular See Fitzmaurice, *Life of Shelburne,* 1912, ii 268, cf. Nos 6268, 6274. Contrast with this print No. 6291.

$11\frac{1}{8} \times 9\frac{1}{4}$ in.

6268 THE BRITISH TAR'S TRIUMPH

Published Oct'r 22ᵈ 1783 by W. Richardson 174 near Surry Street, Strand.

Engraving. Figures representing the four European ex-belligerent nations. A Jack Tar (c) rides on the shoulders of Holland, a Dutch burgher, Spain (l) and France (r.) shout recriminations at one another. Jack England, as he is called in similar prints, wears wide striped trousers, from one leg of which protrudes a wooden leg; he flourishes like a whip a long stiff pigtail queue cut from the head of France, and with his l. hand holds Holland by the nose, saying *Didn't you Splinter my Leg, between ye, you Bouger.* Holland is a clumsy figure in baggy breeches and steeple-crowned hat, a tobacco-pipe thrust in his hat, another protruding from his breeches pocket, he supports Jack submissively, holding his legs. Spain, running towards the l, with a face of terror, looks over his l. shoulder towards France, holding out a purse and a long sword, saying *By Sᵗ Jago I'll give up my Tolido & Run away.* France (r.), in profile to the l., holds out his r. hand towards Jack England, in his l. is part of a broken sword; he says *Begar he has taken away de best part of mine Head, wich is mine Tail.* France and Spain are dressed in the conventional manner of English caricature, both wear high boots.

Beneath the design is engraved:

The English Tar Triumphant Rides Mynheer.
And Bangs him with the Tail of Cropt Monsieur.
The Dutchman, does but gloomy looks Afford
While the Affrighted Spaniard gives his Sword

Such were the Scenes, when Britain's Navy Hurld
Her dreaded Vengeance o'er the astonish'd World
That glory fix'd the rage of War must Cease
And rougher Arts, give way to gentle Peace.

See Nos. 6267, 6274.

$5\frac{13}{16} \times 8\frac{15}{16}$ in.

6269 A CURIOUS COLLECTION OF WILD BEASTS.

[1 Nov. 1783]

Engraving. From the *Rambler's Magazine.* On a platform over which is inscribed *Bartholomew Fair,* are politicians in the guise of performing animals. Fox, a fox with a human face, standing on his hind-legs, leads by a chain a performing bear, with the head of Lord North (l). On a cushion (r) sits on its haunches a lion with the head of George III. Beside him squats a monkey, with a head intended to be that of Burke, who clips the nails of the paw which the lion meekly extends. Burke sits on two steps inscribed *Prerogative* and *Reform of the Household.* Beneath the platform appear the heads of six spectators.

One of many satires on the Coalition Ministry, see Nos 6176-9, &c, the allusions here being to its designs on the Prerogative, cf. No. 6239, &c., and to Burke's Bill of Economical Reform carried during the Rockingham Ministry.

$3\frac{1}{4} \times 5\frac{3}{8}$ in.

734

6270 THE PROTECTOR OF FREEDOM OF ELECTION.

Liberty Pinx^t   *Independance Sculp.*

Freedom excu^t

London Nov. 11. 1783 Publish'd as the Act directs

Engraving. A candidate stands in the foreground, his r hand extended, l. in his breeches pocket. Two groups of electors stand in the middle distance; those on the r. are a compact body, the three foremost of whom stand with linked arms, hats are thrown up with the shout *Galway for ever*. The group on the l consists of three figures only standing by a sign-post which points *To Helmsley* The names of the persons are written on the print in pencil. The candidate is 'Lord Galway', i e Robert Monckton Arundel, 5th Viscount Galway (1752–1810), M.P. for Pontefract 1780–3, elected for York 1783 on the death of Sir Charles Turner This evidently represents the by-election at York city caused by the death of Sir Charles Turner on 26 Oct. 1783.

The group on the l. consists of a man holding up his arms exclaiming *Oh! Oh! I shall be reduced to Whalebone*; on the ground at his feet is a pair of stays; he is identified as 'Kitson, Stay Maker'. Next him is a man of plebeian appearance, a yard measure round his neck, 'Wm Siddal Esqr Ld Mayor & Taylor'; he says to the third of the group, *You have not paid for your freedom*. This man, 'Mr Duncombe', answers, *make me your member then* (Henry Duncombe had been elected M.P. for Yorkshire in 1780) The three figures with linked arms who are leading a procession of Lord Galway's supporters, are 'Mr Martin Frobisher Stationer', '——Coupland, Cutler', and 'Richard Garland, Butter factor'. They are evidently all freemen of York In the background (r.) are buildings, including a Gothic church and part of the cathedral.

York was noted for independence in the exercise of its electoral rights, the electors being the freemen of the city. Oldfield, *Representative History*, v. 272.

5¾×6 in.

6271 A TRANSFER OF EAST INDIA STOCK.

JS f. [Sayers.]

Published 25th Novr 1783 by Thomas Cornell Bruton Street

Engraving. Fox carries on his shoulders the East India House and runs with it towards an arched gateway on the r. surmounted by a crown, and resembling the gateway to St James's Palace He looks round to the l. with a complacent smile, from his coat-pocket protrudes a paper, *New Arrange-[ment] Seven Emperors Eight Governors 8000 Deputy G[overnors] 10000 Collec[tors] of the Revenue.* Under his l. foot is a *List of Directors*, under the r a paper inscribed *Resolved That the Influence of the Crown has increased is incre[asing] ough[t to be] dim[inished]* Papers flutter from the India House to the ground inscribed *[Ea]st India Stock 115, India Bonds 54 to 55*

On 18 Nov. Fox moved for leave to bring in two East India Bills, one for vesting the affairs of the Company in seven Commissioners, brought in 20 Nov., the other for the better government of the territorial possessions of the Company, brought in on 26 Nov. This satire, though less effective than the more famous *Carlo Khan*, see No. 6276, is a brilliant summary of the attacks on the Bill (of 20 Nov.). its transference of patronage and the sovereignty of India from the Crown and the Company to Fox and the Coalition; its attack on chartered rights and depreciation of India stock See *Parl Hist.* xxiii 1210 (18 Nov), 1223 ff. (20 Nov), 1255 ff (27 Nov), 1306 ff (1 Dec) Wraxall writes of this print and *Carlo Khan*, 'it is difficult to conceive the moral operation and wide diffusion of these caricatures through every part of the country'. *Memoirs*, 1884, iii. 254. This print was referred to in an attack on the Bill by Sir Richard Hill on 27 Nov. *Parl. Hist.* xxiii. 1289 Fox had already been traduced as Cromwell, see No 6239, &c For the Bills see also Nos. 6257, 6275-83, 6285, 6286, 6287, 6289, 6290 For Dunning's famous resolution on the influence of the Crown see No. 5659.

$11\frac{3}{8} \times 8\frac{7}{8}$ in.

6272 THE IRISH PATRIOTS.

[Gillray.]

Published according to Act of Parliament, Nov. 25, by M. Smith; and sold at N° 46, in Fleet Street.   *Price one Shilling*

Engraving. A scene in the Irish House of Commons, Grattan and Flood, caricatured, exchanging abuse during the debate of 28 Oct 1783 In the foreground stands Grattan (l), in profile to the r , holding out his hat, his r. fist clenched, scowling at Flood. Flood (r), his l. hand resting on a cane, his r. in his breeches pocket, looks over his r shoulder at Grattan with an expression of angry contempt In the background is the rotunda of the Irish House of Commons, with the Speaker sitting at the head of the table, members seated and standing on each side On the r is a crowded gallery filled with spectators among whom ladies are conspicuous; these figures are freely drawn on a minute scale. Below and in front of the gallery seated and standing members or spectators watch the antagonists. Beneath the title extracts from the debate are printed in two columns.

G——N.

Sir, your talents are not so great as your Life is infamous.—You might be seen hovering about the Dome, like an ill-omened Bird of Night, with sepulchral Notes, a cadaverous Aspect, and broken Beak, ready to stoop and pounce upon your Prey —The People cannot trust you, the Ministry cannot trust you: You deal with the most impartial Treachery to both.—I therefore tell you, in the face of your Country, before all the World;—nay, to your Beard, you are not an honest Man!

F——D

I have heard a very extraordinary Harangue indeed, and I challenge any Man to say that any Thing, half so unwarrantable, was ever uttered in this House.—'The Right Honourable Gentleman set out with declaring, he did not wish to use Personality, and no sooner has he opened his Mouth, than forth issues all the venom that Ingenuity and disappointed Vanity, for Two Years brooding over Corruption have produced; BUT IT CANNOT TAINT MY PUBLIC CHARACTER!'*—As for me, I took as great a part with the first Office of the State at my Back, as ever the Right Honourable Gentleman did, with Mendicency behind him*

For this famous quarrel see *Ireland, Parliamentary Register,* ii 35 ff , and *D.N B.* (Flood) A duel was only prevented by the arrest of both on the way to an encounter, when they were bound over to keep the peace The quotations here given are abridged from the debate of 28 Oct. 1783, on Sir H. Cavendish's motion for retrenchment of public expenses, which was printed in the London newspapers, e g *Lond. Chronicle*, 6–8 Nov.

Grego, *Gillray*, p. 49

$8\frac{3}{4} \times 11$ in.

6273 A WADDLEING PROCESSION FROM THE STOCK EX-CHANGE, OR THE BULLS AND BEARS MAKING LONG FACES.

[1 Dec. 1783]

Engraving. From the *Rambler's Magazine* A procession of four ducks with human heads, wearing hats, walk (r to l), followed (r.) by a bull and a bear, also with human faces, and holding handkerchiefs to their eyes The heads of four persons, with melancholy expressions, much caricatured, appear at a window. The two foremost 'lame ducks' (a term for defaulters on the Stock Exchange, see No. 5835) have Jewish beards; the first says, *Me no pay 70,000 Guinea ven de Law vill not oblige Me*; the next says *You be vise Man a second Solomon.* The third duck, who wears a wide-brimmed hat, says, *The Spirit moveth Me to depart hence* The fourth, who wears clerical bands, says, *They must be Saved by Faith alone.*

On the approach of peace there had been much speculating in the Stocks in anticipation of a rise which did not occur. The first lame duck is Nathan Solomon, a great Jew broker who, according to the *London Chronicle* (26 Sept), sent on the 25th Sept. 'a letter to the Stock Exchange declaring himself a Lame Duck; and that his intention was never more to return to that house He complains of a confederacy formed against him by the Brokers, and that he therefore thought it his duty to take care of himself. It is said, he had bought near one million of Scrip, and that his differences were very considerable. By this letter the whole body of speculators in the funds were thrown into confusion and two or three other Brokers of inferior note waddled out of the Alley ' This settling day was said to have been marked by perhaps the greatest confusion since the institution of the Stock Exchange, five principal brokers having defaulted

$3\frac{5}{16} \times 5\frac{3}{4}$ in.

6274 DOMINION OF THE SEAS

Pub^d by E. D'achery St James's Street, Decr 1st 1783.

Engraving. Britannia (l) sits in a small boat moored by a rope among wavelets inscribed *Portland Road* (in allusion to the Portland Ministry). In her r. hand is an olive branch, in her l. she holds a flagstaff, from which float two British flags, the upper a long pendant which streams across the design By her side are her spear and sword. On the prow of the boat sits a small animal intended for a fox (Charles Fox), but with more resemblance to a badger. Facing Britannia, on the r., the four ex-enemy powers, each in a small boat, dip their national flags in the water in homage Holland (l.), plainly dressed in baggy breeches with a tobacco-pipe stuck through his hat-band, dips a flag with five stripes Spain, whose boat is hidden by those of France and America, in a high feathered hat and slashed clothes, dips a flag with three castles. France, with a long pigtail queue, dips the fleur-de-lys flag. America (r.), wearing a head-dress of erect feathers, dips a flag with thirteen stripes. Beneath the title is engraved:

BRITANNIA *on board the* FOX *safe Moor'd in* PORTLAND-ROAD—*As Mistress of the Sea, she receives Homage from the whole World. NB A distinction contended for by our present Peace Makers.*

See also Nos. 6267, 6268

$7\frac{1}{4} \times 11\frac{3}{16}$ in.

6275 THE POLITICAL BALLOON; OR, THE FALL OF EAST INDIA STOCK.

Pub. Dec 4 1783 by W Wells N° 132 Fleet Street

Engraving Fox, seated on a globe, looks down at three men who fall head-long from it On the globe is sketched a map, intended to represent India On it are marked, *Gold Mines* and *Madras*, and, to the south, *Indian Ocean.* Fox holds up in his l hand his *Bill to Reform India[n] Affairs* He is saying, *Thanks to my Auspicious Stars, for now I see, the Gold & Silver mines before me; 'tis this I am Soaring for* The central of the men falling head downwards wears a coat with military facings, his wig has fallen from his head, he says, *What my Government gone ere I had made or unmade one Nabob? Oh perdition Seize that wiley Fox* He is perhaps intended for Hastings The man falling on the l., evidently a Director, is saying, *If the Nation knew his Treacherous heart as well as me, the directors wou'd be prefer'd* The man on the r. says, *Must I for ever be hurl'd from such pretty pickings? wou'd I cou'd grapple in my fall the author of it* Coins are falling from the pockets of all three men.

The East India Company petitioned against Fox's India Bill on 24 Nov ; the East India Directors and the City of London petitioned on 25 Nov. *Parl Hist* xxiii 1247, 1248, 1255. One of many satires on the Bill, see No 6271, &c.

The first of many applications of the balloon, see No. 6333, &c, to political satire.

$12\frac{11}{16} \times 9\frac{1}{8}$ in.

6276 CARLO KHAN'S TRIUMPHAL ENTRY INTO LEADENHALL STREET.

J. S. f. [Sayers] plate 2ᵈ

Published 5ᵗʰ Decʳ 1783 by Thomas Cornell Bruton Street

Engraving Fox seated astride an elephant which is being led through Leadenhall Street towards the India Office, one door of which appears on the l. He is dressed as an oriental prince, wearing a jewelled turban; his elbows are akimbo and he looks down with a triumphant smile. At his side is a flag on which *The Man of the People* has been erased and *ΒΑΣΙΥΕΥΣ ΒΑΣΙΛΕΩΝ* (king of kings) substituted The elephant has the face of North, with an expression of pained anxiety, from his mouth protrudes a small snake-like trunk Burke (r), dressed as an oriental, leads the elephant by a rope, his head is turned in profile to the r and he is blowing a trumpet to which is attached a fringed banner on which is a map of India inscribed *C F* [Charles Fox], it shows *Bengal*, the *Bay of Bengal*, the *Ganges*, extreme north *Delhi* and in the extreme south *Tanjeour* and *F[ort] S George.*

738

In the background the houses of the street recede in perspective, on a chimney on a roof (l) a raven bends ominously towards Fox, beneath it is etched, *The night Crow cried foreboding luckless Time. Shakespeare.*

A sequel to No 6271, which is presumably Pl 1st, and Sayers' most famous satire Fox is said to have called it the most effective blow at his India Bill, its effect was multiplied by pirated copies and imitations. T. Wright, *Caricature History of the Georges*, p. 373, see also Wraxall, *Memoirs*, 1884, iii 254. Burke leads the elephant to show that he is the draftsman of the India Bill and the reputed inspirer of Fox's Indian policy, see No 6277, &c. Nos. 6285, 6286 are sequels to this print. For the India Bill see No 6271, &c. At this time the Coalition, having staked their existence on the passing of the Bill, regarded themselves as firmly established See *Corr. of Lord Auckland*, 1861, i 63 (letter of 9 Dec.)

Copy by F W. Fairholt, T. Wright, *op et loc cit.* Reproduced, A. S. Turberville, *Men and Manners of the Eighteenth Century*, 1926, p. 464. $11\frac{1}{4} \times 8\frac{7}{8}$ in.

6276 A A copy with the same title but without signature or publication line
$11\frac{3}{4} \times 8\frac{3}{4}$ in.

6277 CONFUCIUS THE SECOND; OR, A NEW SUN RISING IN THE ASIATIC WORLD[1]

Pubd according to the Act by Willm Holland No 66 Drury lane Dec. 12 1783

Engraving. Fox as the rising sun, his head, smiling, satisfied, fills the circle of the sun, whose rays are shed over the sky, and fall upon two groups of persons divided by the River Ganges. On the nearer side (r.) a group of Indians make obeisance to the sun with gestures of ecstatic gratitude: a kneeling prince with a feathered turban, bends low with his hands on his breast; he is *The unfortunate Prince, Cheit Sing* (words etched on the lower margin) Next him are four kneeling women, three young, one old, they hold out their arms with expressions of gratitude towards Fox; the most prominent turns to point out their benefactor to two young children who kneel at her side They are *The plundered Princesses, the Begums of Oude.* Behind them (r.) an Indian bows his head to the ground He is the foremost of a crowd whose arms are stretched out towards Fox, the faces of some being Nubian in type. Behind and approaching this group is a procession headed by Burke and North each on an elephant Burke (l), dressed as a jesuit, as in No. 6205, points at Fox, looking towards North, who stretches out his r arm towards the rising sun; in his l hand he holds a book, *Sublime and Beaut[iful]*, to show that he is the author of *A Philosophical Enquiry. . .* The howdah cloth of North's elephant is inscribed *Plunder restored 1[7]83*, on the animal's back is a bale of goods Behind Burke and North, apparently mounted on elephants, stand two men blowing trumpets to which are attached fringed banners, as in No 6276, one inscribed *The Trumpet shall soun'd in the East and man shall be called to judgment.*

On the farther side of the river a procession of 'plunderers', officers of the East India Company, being led by a man with an axe on his shoulder, he holds a chain which is attached to the wrists of the victims They are *Plunderers doomed to Execution when the new Sun [Fox] gains his Meridian*

An exceptional print in its (apparent) defence of the India Bills; the dress of Burke, and Fox as the sun ascending, suggest an ironical intention. Cf. No. 6239, &c. It is based on Burke's speech of 1 Dec., which he had printed (Walpole, *Letters*, xiii 118, 1 Feb. 1784), in which (*inter alia*) he expounded the wrongs of the Begums of Oude and of 'Cheit Sing', and attacked Hastings, describing the rule of the East India Company's servants 'as oppressive, irregular, capricious, unsteady, rapacious, and peculating despotism, with a direct disavowal of obedience to any authority at home and without any fixed maxim, principle or rule of proceeding to guide them in India . . .' *Parl. Hist.* xxiii 1312–86 For the India Bill see No. 6271, &c.

$9\frac{1}{8} \times 13\frac{1}{16}$ in.

6278 THE TEMPTATION IN THE WILDERNESS.

Pub^d Decr 12. 1783. by H. Humphrey. New Bond Street.

Engraving In the centre of the design is the summit of a mountain or rocky mound on which stands the small figure of Fox, who is addressing a number of geese who stand on the rock beneath him at different levels He points towards an oriental landscape on the l. of the design. undulating ground dotted with palm-trees, and in the distance a bay in which are four ships at anchor protected by a fort, inscribed *Madras*. Over this a small circular sun sheds its rays. On the extreme r. of the plate appears part of the India House, inscribed *Leadenhall Street*, falling into ruins On its broken cornice is a crown

Beneath the design is inscribed *Then Reynard taketh them into an exceeding huhg [sic] Mountain, and Shewed them all the Kingdoms of the East and the Glory of them, Saying all these will I give ye, if ye will fall down and Worship me.*

For Fox's India Bill see Nos 6271, &c For Fox's geese cf. No. 5843, &c.

6279 EAST INDIA REFORMERS OR NEW WAYS & MEANS.

Pub^d as the act directs Dec^{br} 81 [sic] 1783 by T. Wiggins N° 9 Founders Court Lothbury.

Engraving North, Fox, and Burke in a room in the India House, the wall of which is inscribed *Committe [sic] Room*. They stand in front of a long table behind which is a tall arm-chair inscribed *President's Chair*. Fox (c.) squats over a torn paper on which he is excreting, inscribed *[East] India Com[pa]ny's Charters*. North, standing on Fox's r., hands him another torn paper, *Rights & privileges . . . Honourable East India Company*. From Fox's l. pocket projects a *List of Commissonor[s] [sic]* Under North's r. arm is a large bundle of papers, some inscribed *100000*, Stock, and *000*, his r. hand is in his coat-pocket Burke (r.), in profile to the r., is kicking and pushing out of the door two East India Directors, one, whose wig has fallen off in the struggle, looks round over his shoulder at Burke, who says, *I will direct ye* On the r., in very incorrect perspective, are what appear to be two chests full of coins, one is inscribed *Dollars*. On the ground beside them are money-bags inscribed *Rupees* and *a Lack* [lakh] with a label, *100000*. In the centre of the floor in front of North and Fox is a heap of coins

On the table are torn papers inscribed *accounts*, *India Bonds*, coins, a book inscribed *Ledge[r]*, and an ink-stand On the wall (l) is a framed picture of two small figures in a room, one intended for Fox; it represents a foul and scurrilous tale told of Fox (according to which he bets upon a certainty), which is related in *The Gamblers*, 1777, pp. 43-4, a poem, published anonymously, by Theophilus Swift. It was the subject of a print, *The Gamesters*, 13 May 1784

One of many attacks on Fox's India Bill, see No 6271, &c.

$8\frac{1}{16} \times 12\frac{3}{4}$ in.

6280 S——TE [STATE] MINERS

Pub^d as y^e act directs Decr 21 1783 by E. D'Archery St James's Street

Engraving. Fox and North, as miners, are undermining the rock of the constitution, which by their efforts has been reduced to a circular platform supported on an irregularly shaped and jagged pillar which dwindles as it reaches the ground On the summit sit George III and Britannia. The king (l.) leans back in an arm-chair, his eyes closed, with an angry expression Britannia, with a melancholy expression, her eyes closed, rests her head on her l hand; her r rests on her shield, her spear is broken and the cap of liberty falls from it Over the king is poised an inverted crown on which stands a fox using it as an urinal The rock (reading from the summit to the base) is inscribed *Constitution, Trade, Justice, Laws, Charters*. North (r) is digging at the foundation of the rock with a spade inscribed *Craft*. Fox (l.) swings above his head a pick-axe inscribed *Oratory*. He wears a sleeved waistcoat, the sleeves rolled up, his breeches pocket is inscribed *Full*

Behind, on a very small scale, three riders bestride the muzzled British lion In front, wielding a scourge, is Burke, distinguished by his jesuit's dress and spectacles, see No 6205, &c. Holding to his waist is a man wearing a Garter ribbon, probably intended for Portland, see No 6248; a third rider sits behind him.

Between the two words of the title is a shield on which is a fox, apparently hanging by its neck from a noose. The Devil, holding a headsman's axe, sits cross-legged on the shield

A satire on the Coalition, see Nos 6176-9, &c , and on the India Bill as an attack on chartered rights, see No. 6271, &c For Fox as the assailant of the Crown see Nos. 5987, 6239, &c.

$12\frac{1}{8} \times 8\frac{7}{8}$ in.

6281 BANDITTI

I. B. [J. Boyne]

Published by E. Hedges N° 92 Cornhill Dec. 22. 1783.[1]

Engraving (coloured and uncoloured impressions) Ministers, as bandits, grouped round a table, drinking and dividing their spoil. The two most prominent figures, facing each other, are North and Fox. North (l), very stout, with a good-humoured expression of satisfied repletion, sits at the corner of the rectangular table, one hand on his breast, the other grasping a goblet which stands on the table He is dressed in Roman armour, with buskins and bare legs, but over this is a cloak and his ribbon and star. He

[1] The publication line (on the upper margin of the print) is almost obliterated.

741

wears a bag-wig. Fox (r.) is dressed as a Roman centurion. The front of his plumed helmet is decorated with a fox running with a goose in its mouth; his short sleeve is ornamented with a fox's head. He leans across the table, the fingers of his r. hand stretched across three dice, inscribed *Madras, Bombay, Bengal*, his l. hand grasps a large dice-box. Behind him is Keppel, wearing a voluminous cloak and a plumed helmet, ornamented with an anchor and the words *July 27* (cf. No. 5992, &c.). Behind North is Burke, leaning across the table dressed as a jesuit (cf No. 6205) wearing spectacles and reading intently his *Plan of oeconomy* [sic]. In the centre of the farther side of the table is the Duke of Portland, looking to the r He wears a ducal coronet, and a Garter ribbon over a furred robe (cf. No. 6248) Two keys hang from a ribbon round his neck On his r. shoulder leans Lord John Cavendish, his head turned in profile to the r Portland, the pay-master, looks away from Cavendish towards Lord Carlisle, who has a wallet attached to the front of his belt, and who lays his l. hand on the table to take coins which Portland is counting out to him Between Carlisle and Keppel, his eyes fixed on the money, is Sheridan, Treasury Secretary, wearing a turban inscribed *School for Scandal* He has an animal's [ass's?] ears, a beard, and a Jewish profile.

Under the table are the dead bodies of Dunning (Baron Ashburton, d. 18 Aug 1783) and Shelburne, enemies routed by the Coalition, see No. 6214, &c Under Fox's seat lies a fox On the table is a punch-bowl. The shaded background indicates that the bandits are seated in the mouth of a cave The title is etched across the foreground.

One of many satires on the Coalition, see Nos. 6176–9, &c., and on Fox's India Bill, see No 6271.

$10\frac{1}{16} \times 13\frac{1}{2}$ in

Two earlier states before the design was reduced along the upper margin:
1. *Publish'd as the Act directs* [erasure] *Decr 20* [?][1] *1783*, to which is added in ink, 'by E^d Hedges No 92 Cornhill' The title engraved below the design, publication line below the title
$11\frac{1}{8} \times 13\frac{1}{2}$ in
2. *Publish'd by E Hedges N° 92 Cornhill Decr 22 1783.* Title and size as above.

6282 LORD N——S [NORTH'S] SUPPLICATION TO M^R FOX

[*c.* Nov –Dec 1783][2]

Engraving North, in profile to the r, kneels in supplication to Fox (r), who stands with arms extended, feet apart, dressed as an oriental potentate. He wears a turban, ornamented with a crescent and aigrette, a long robe over a frogged tunic, girt with a sash. North kneels near the edge of a pit (l); a round sack or bag hangs at his back, inscribed *Nation's Plunder*, ropes are attached to his arms and are being pulled by a Devil who appears from the pit behind North, from which flames are ascending North is weeping, his handkerchief raised to his eye, he says, *They are going to prosecute me for the American War, Charles take me under your protection and I will promise to be Gratefull* Fox answers, *I would Protect you But your promise I cannot rely upon! How many poor people have you ruined by promiseing what*

[1] The 'o' is written in ink over another figure, perhaps a '2'
[2] Publication line perhaps cut off.

you never intended to perform. Witness the Author of this, Blush, Honor, Blush. The Devil says, *This is my Fav'rite¹ one that has dureing his whole Ministry Obey'd and made others Obey my Laws & Rules. He shall be my Prime Minister.*

The date must be before the fall of the Coalition on 18 Dec.; Fox's oriental dress shows that it is after the introduction of his India Bill on 11 Nov., cf No. 6179. See also No. 6207. For the India Bill see No 6271, &c
$7\frac{11}{16} \times 8\frac{3}{4}$ in.

6283 GREAT CRY AND LITTLE WOOL.

[Rowlandson]

Published 22 Dec' 1783 by Humphrys Strand.

Engraving (coloured and uncoloured impressions) Fox (r) attempting to flee from the Devil, who has firm hold of him and is shearing his hairy chest with a large pair of scissors. The Devil is a satyr-like creature with a beard, goat's horns, and hairy legs; his fingers are talons, his feet are those of a bird of prey, he has a forked tail. He clutches Fox by the r. leg, which is bare, and fixes the talons of his l. foot in Fox's l leg Fox is naked except for breeches, and one stocking and shoe; he clutches his hair and looks round at the Devil, who holds the *India Bill* under his r. arm.

In the background (l) is the *India House* Outside it a fox is tied to a stake round which burns a fire A circle of men holding hands dance round the fire in exultation; they evidently represent the City and East India interests which had petitioned against the Bill. The smoke from the bonfire, drifting to the r , forms a background to the figures of Fox and the Devil.

On 17 Dec , owing to the influence of the king conveyed through Lord Temple, the India Bill was rejected in the Lords, and on 18 Dec. the two secretaries were dismissed and the Ministry fell, see *Corr of George III*, vi 476 f (the king writing to Lord North at 10 43 p m. on 18 Dec to return the seals); *Life and Letters of Sir Gilbert Elliot*, i. 89–91; Wraxall, *Memoirs*, 1884, iii. 186 ff. For the India Bill see No 6271, &c.

Grego, *Rowlandson*, i. 109.

$8\frac{1}{4} \times 12$ in.

6284 THE AEROSTATICK STAGE BALLOON.

Hanibal Scratch del

Pubᵈ Dec' 23 1783 by Wᵐ Wells Nᵒ 132 Fleet Street

Engraving. A balloon about to rise from the ground encircled by three tiers of galleries or narrow platforms, protected by railings Behind the railings sit the passengers In the highest tier are three ladies notorious at that time for their amours (see index)· Grace Elliott or Eliot, *née* Dalrymple, known as 'Dally the tall', she holds a fan, turning her head in profile to the l , towards Perdita (Mary Robinson), who clasps her hands ecstatically, Lady Worsley sits on the r.

In the centre gallery sit ex-ministers· North (l) and Fox (r) in the centre, North's arm on Fox's shoulder, Fox turns his head to North with an expression of satisfaction. Each rests his r. hand on the railing in front of him, and these hands hold an inconspicuous thread which is attached to the nose of the Duke of Portland (l), who turns in profile to the r. On the r., a little apart, sits Burke dressed as a Jesuit (see No 6205) looking in profile to the r. towards the Pope, who stands on the gallery, emerging from behind the curve of the balloon. He wears furred robes and his triple crown; as a pendant to him on the extreme l is the Devil looking towards the ministers with a pleased expression, over his arm he holds a net

In the lowest gallery sit celebrated quacks and other London characters. These are (l to r) 'Vestina', the goddess of Health who advertised the virtues of the celestial bed (incorrectly said to have been Lady Hamilton), sits next her employer, Dr. Graham; they look at each other; she holds a sceptre wreathed with a garland. Jeffery Dunstan, Mayor of Garrat, stands, knock-kneed, with his sack over his shoulder in his accustomed attitude when calling 'old wigs' Sam House sits resting a foaming tankard of porter on the railing in front of him, the tankard inscribed *House Ward[our] Stre[et]* Katerfelto, turned in profile to the r , gazes up at the moon through his telescope; in his l hand is a paper, *Wonders, Wonders Most Wonderfull Wonders*, the usual heading of his advertisements, cf. No. 6162. His black cat sits on the railing facing him, saying, *are there Mice in the Moon Master* In the upper r corner of the design is the moon, a crescent-shaped profile inset in a circle, looking down at the balloon.

The balloon is encircled longitudinally by eight ropes which meet in a knot beneath it and are there attached to four stouter ropes attached to the four corners of a platform which rests on the ground, from which the balloon appears about to ascend. On this platform is a tub inscribed *Vanity*, bubbling over with soapsuds inscribed *Froth*. Beside the platform (r.) stands a Frenchman capering on one leg and flourishing a knife. He says, *Oh Begar dis be von fine Cargo*

Beneath the title is etched, *Setts out from Swan with two Necks Lad Lane every Monday Mor*ᵍ

In the background are the roofs and spires of London, St. Paul's being prominent on the l , the Monument on the r Beneath the design is inscribed:

> *Who choose a journey to the Moon*
> *May take it in our Stage Balloon.*
> *Where love sick Virgins past their prime*
> *May Marry yet and laugh at time,*
> *Perdita—W——sley Fillies free,*
> *Each flash their Lunar Vis a Vis,*
> *There N——th may realize his Dreams,*
> *And F—x pursue his golden schemes*
> *And Father B——ke may still absolve 'em*
> *Howe'er the Devil may involve them;*
> *The Pope may plan his Machinations*
> *With Panders Quacks & Polititions.*
> *Sam House enjoy his Tankard there*
> *And Old Wigs still be Garrats May'r*
> *Great Katerdevil work his Wonders*
> *Spruce Gr—ham launch Electric thunders*
> *Vestina too—nor fear a fall*
> *Sʳ Satans Net shall catch ye all*
> *So said Monseiur in broken Brogue*
> *And up they mounted W——e and R——e*

One of many satires on balloon ascents, see No 6333, &c , here combined with a satire on the Coalition, or on politicians, who are associated with mountebanks and women of damaged reputation.

$12\frac{13}{16} \times 9\frac{11}{16}$ in

6285 THE RETREAT OF CARLO KHAN FROM LEADENHALL S^r

[J. Boyne.]

Publish'd by E Hedges N° 92 Cornhill, Dec. 24. 1783

Engraving. A sequel to No 6276 Fox, seated cross-legged on an ass, his head facing the tail, holds his head in both hands while he vomits into his feathered turban. The ass has the face of Lord North, in his mouth is a bridle, the bit being represented by a crown; it is led by a draped woman (l) representing the City of London. On the animal's hind-quarters are the letters *L N* [Lord North]. She wears a mural crown and, as a brooch, the City Arms. In her l. hand she holds up a whip, the lash of which is a narrow banner or scroll inscribed *Public Resentment* Large saddle-bags hang across the ass's back, one (l) containing rolled documents. Burke (r.), dressed as a jesuit, see No 6205, follows the ass barefooted. He reads from a book, *Sinners Guide.* Instead of the biretta covering a wig in which he is usually depicted, he is bald-headed, which accentuates his expression of senile melancholy

On the r. of the street is the India House, along which is inscribed *Business done as usual.* George III leans out of an upper window flourishing a cap of liberty on a staff; a symbol of the 'liberation' of the Crown and the East India Company and protection of chartered rights Over the window sill hangs a document *India Bill*, the words scored through to signify the defeat of the Bill, see No 6283 Over the roof of the house the sun is appearing, surmounted by a crown, and sending out rays which are dispersing the clouds. In the sun's circle is a face

For the India Bill see No 6271, &c , and for its defeat No 6283 and No. 6286, also a sequel to No. 6276.

$12\frac{5}{16} \times 9$ in

6286 THE FALL OF CARLO KHAN

Published as the Act Directs 24 Decr 1783 by D Brown.

Engraving. A sequel to No. 6276, and an imitation of that print by another artist The elephant with North's head is being chased by a group (r.) of opponents of Fox's India Bill Conspicuous among these is the king, wearing a hat, his star indicated on his coat; he prods the animal's near hind-leg with a spiked stick, drawing blood. On his l hand, and on the extreme r of the design, walks Thurlow, on whose advice the king had informed the peers through Temple of his desire for opposition to the Bill On the king's r is a judge, probably Lord Camden, who spoke vehemently against the Bill, *Parl. Hist* xxiv. 190 f Next is Dundas, the Lord Advocate of Scotland, also in legal robes, who opposed the Bill as 'highly unconstitutional', ibid , p. 51. Behind Camden is Lord Shelburne blowing a horn although he had in fact abstained from voting Behind the king, and waving his hat, is Lord Mahon, who vehemently opposed the Bill (ibid., pp. 202-3) Behind Thurlow is the Duke of Richmond (ibid , pp. 134, &c.).

Fox is falling head-downwards from his seat on the elephant, his head is about to strike the *East Ind[ia] Bill*, which lies on the ground and is being befouled by a small dog From his mouth issue the words, *Secret Influence*. Burke (l) has dropped the rope by which he was leading the elephant and is running away, turning to look over his l. shoulder, a large bundle, *Plans of Oeconomy*, lies on the ground beside him Fox's turban and Burke's banner also lie on the ground, both are dressed as in No. 6276.

One side of Leadenhall Street forms a background, the India House, on the extreme l., has been shored up by Pitt with two large beams, one of which he is placing against the façade.

For the Bill see No. 6271, &c., and for its defeat No. 6283 and No. 6285, also a sequel to No. 6276.

$8\frac{5}{16} \times 11\frac{1}{8}$ in

6287 TWO NEW SLIDERS FOR THE STATE MAGIC LANTHERN.

[Rowlandson]

Pub 29ᵗʰ Decʳ 1783 by W. Humphrey 227 Strand.

Engraving (coloured and uncoloured impressions) Two horizontal strips each divided by vertical lines into rectangular compartments of varying width, numbered 1–5 and 6–10, depicting the Coalition and its fall.

1 VOX POPULI OUT OF DOORS Fox (r.). as a fox wearing a coat, stands on a platform haranguing the mob, a small crowd of men and women (l). His platform is little more than a large four-legged stool, behind him stands a man dressed like the zanies who accompanied the quack doctors who hawked their wares in public places, such as Dr Bossy, who used to put up his platform in Covent Garden, the scene of Fox's oratory The background is part of the portico of Covent Garden Church, the scene of Westminster elections.

$3\frac{1}{2} \times 2\frac{3}{8}$ in.

2. FIRST COALITION North (l) and Fox, with a fox's head (r.), stand in profile facing each other, clasping hands. North's l hand is held behind his back, in it he holds strings attached to the neck of sheep standing behind him; these are *Country Gentlemen*, cf. No 6243 Fox similarly holds in his r. hand the strings attached to a flock of geese, inscribed *Wesʳ Geese*, representing the electors of Westminster or the populace, cf. No 5843, &c.

$3\frac{1}{2} \times 3\frac{1}{4}$ in

3 VOX POPULI—IN DOORS. Fox (l.), with a fox's head, haranguing with clenched fists an audience (r) seated under the pillars supporting the roof of a rotunda On the roof minute figures stand or lean over to see the orator.

$3\frac{1}{2} \times 2\frac{1}{2}$ in.

4. EMBLEM OF LIBERTY Fox, with a fox's head and brush, kneels on one knee before a fire which he is feeding. In its centre is a stake, on the top of which is a cap of liberty. Attached to the stake is a large rolled document with a pendent seal inscribed *India Charter*. See also No 6207

For the India Bill see No 6271, &c.

$3\frac{1}{2} \times 2\frac{1}{4}$ in.

5. NEW STATE IDOL. North (l.) and Fox (r.) stand pressed together on a low rectangular pedestal inscribed POWER Fox is depicted as a fox; the

coat which Fox has worn in the first four designs is buttoned round both of them, the sleeves hanging limp. On the ground (r) is a crown and sceptre.

$3\frac{1}{2} \times 2\frac{5}{16}$ in.

6. POLITICAL MONTGOLFIER. A parti-coloured balloon suspended in the air, from its summit protrudes the head of a fox. Below is the word *Ascending*. For balloons see No. 6333, &c.

$3\frac{1}{2} \times 2\frac{1}{4}$ in.

7. HIS FALL INTO THE PITT. From a balloon, the lower part only of which is visible, a fox is falling headlong. Beneath him on the ground is a circular hole, representing the ministry of Pitt which is about to engulf him.

$3\frac{1}{2} \times 2\frac{1}{4}$ in

8 THE COALITION CANDIDATES REJECTED Britannia seated (r.), with her spear and shield, turns her head from Fox and North who stand together (l.), North's r arm round Fox's shoulders. Fox has a fox's head, brush, and hind-legs By Britannia is a bust of George III She points in disdain to the couple, who seem to be appealing for her support On the sky-line (l.) behind Fox is a gibbet Above Britannia's head is a sun sending out rays.

$3\frac{1}{2} \times 3$ in.

9. LAST COALITION. Fox, in the shape of a fox (l.), North (c), and Burke (r) seated together in a cart under a gallows with two uprights, one on each side of the cart. An executioner sits astride the cross-beam arranging three nooses The figures are minute but very expressive. Burke, wearing his spectacles, turns his head away from his companions with an expression of melancholy.

$3\frac{1}{2} \times 2\frac{1}{2}$ in.

10. TANTALUS . IXION . SYSIPHUS. A scene in Hades; water on the l., from which rises a rock or mountain (r); the background is composed of flames, in the smoke of which is the figure of a minute demon The head and shoulders of Burke (l.) as Tantalus appear from the water Fox (a fox) as Ixion is bound to the centre of a wheel North as Sisyphus climbs up the rock, pushing before him a spherical boulder.

For the fall of the Coalition see No. 6283, &c

Attributed by Grego to Gillray (*Gillray*, p. 51) It is similar in manner and design as well as in spirit to Rowlandson's *The Loves of the Fox and the Badger*, 7 Jan. 1784; they were probably companion prints

$7\frac{15}{16} \times 12\frac{13}{16}$ in.

6288 ORIGINAL AIR BALLOON   Nᵒ 8

Pubᵈ as yᵉ act directs Decʳ 29. 1783 by G Humphrey, Nᵒ 48 Long Acre.

Engraving. The ascent of a circular balloon, inscribed *America*, is watched by spectators, there are two passengers in its basket The names of the persons are shown by numbers referring to notes in the upper margin

(1), *Spain* and (2) *France* stand (l) bound together by a chain held by a padlock inscribed *family Compact*. France, lean and elegant, though grotesque, rests his r. elbow on Spain's shoulder, he points upwards at the balloon, saying, *T'will be ours Soon*, within the label containing these words is a small butterfly. On the r stands (3) *Dʳ F- k n* [Franklin] wearing dark spectacles; in his r. hand he holds up a knife inscribed *Sedition*, in the l is an oval mask, probably symbol of duplicity. He says *I've cut the bands that have long restraind my Ambition as poor Richard says*, evidently implying that the ropes which held down the balloon America have been cut by him The ground at Franklin's feet is inscribed, *Once British Colonys But now to be lett on Fighting Leases*; in front of him are the ends of two broken 'bands' cut by him, inscribed *Loyalty* and *Friendship*. Behind Franklin (r.) is (4) *Holland*, a clumsy Dutch burgher; he gazes at the balloon saying *I will profit by your inexperiance Mynheers*, from his pocket three small devils are emerging

A stream divides these four persons in the foreground from groups on a much smaller scale (5) and (6), *Chas F—x* and *L—— N——th* dance together hand-in-hand, signifying the Coalition Beside them, piping for their dance, is the Devil capering on one hoof, he is (7) *Director General* A group (l) of prostrate and despairing figures on a minute scale is weighted down by a rectangular block inscribed *Oppression, Taxes*. On this block a gallows stands, from which hang three corpses inscribed respectively *Trade, Wealth, Liberty* On the cross-beam of the gallows stands a small figure, (8), *Military Force of G^t B——n*, who appears to be sending up small oval balloons or bladders, he stretches out his arms towards the large balloon, America, a label issues from his mouth inscribed *G——E H—WE C—T—N, B—G—E &c* , evidently Gage, Howe, Carleton, Burgoyne

To the balloon is attached a basket in which are two passengers. on the l. (10), *Genl W—h—t—n* [Washington] stretches out his arms towards (11) *The Ghost of O Cromwell*, who emerges from clouds on the l. wearing armour and holding out a crown cut in half and a headsman's axe. Washington has two faces, one in profile to the l. facing Cromwell, the other in profile to the r. On the r. of the basket is (9) *Silas D——ne* [Deane] covering his face with his hands at (12) the ghost of *John ye Painter* emerging from clouds on the r. and holding out a gallows. Deane's hair is rising in horror

'John the Painter' was James Aitken, who set fire to the rope-house in Portsmouth dockyard (Dec. 1776) and to a warehouse at Bristol (Jan. 1777) His aim was to destroy the shipping and dockyards of England to ensure victory for America. He propounded his scheme to Silas Deane, the American envoy in Paris, and obtained some encouragement from him and a false French passport. He was executed at Portsmouth on 10 March 1777. A pamphlet in doggerel verse, *John the Painter's Ghost*, was published in 1777 attacking Lord Temple for his share in obtaining a confession from Aitken Deane afterwards acted as a British agent (1781), see *Corr. of George III*, v 200, &c.

The only unfavourable representation of Washington in the collection, and one of the few satires hostile to the Americans, cf. Nos. 5329, 5401

For balloons see No 6333, &c.

11¼×8 in.

6289 THE EAST INDIA AIR BALLOON.

W D. [Dent]

Designed by Boreas The Figures by Le Roi Exec^d by Reynard.

Pub^d by J Cattermoul N° 376 Oxford Street Decr 30th 1783

Engraving (coloured and uncoloured impressions) Fox hangs by the neck from a rope attached to the 'East India Air Balloon', a globe on which is depicted the East India House in Leadenhall Street On the ground beneath are two larger figures, George III (l.) and North (r). The king is dressed as a woman in pseudo-classical draperies, wearing a laurel wreath and the ribbon and star of the Garter. He holds in his r. hand a pair of scales, equally balanced, on the l scale half a royal crown, on the r the word *America* He stands on a solid stone dike or mound, with a broad base, under one foot is a paper inscribed *Coalition*, under the other is the *East India Bill* The mound is inscribed *Auspicium melioris ævi*. The king looks towards Fox, raising a narrow bandage which has been tied over his eyes, from his mouth he directs a blast which strikes and bends the rope by which Fox is suspended Fox holds in his hand a paper inscribed [Bill of] *Pains and Penalties*; a large fox's brush hangs from his person, inscribed *The Man of the People* Behind his head is a horizontal scroll inscribed, *Harm Watch—Harm Catch* North, with an expression of acute distress, kneels towards the king, his hands together in an attitude of prayer, saying *Sire—let me be in the Closet, even the Water Closet, rather than out of office.* He kneels in a mountainous landscape evidently representing the wilderness of opposition, in front of him is a *Letter of Dismission*, cf the king's letter to him on 18 Dec. *Corr. of George III*, vi 476 [1] Beneath him is etched, *Quid feci?* Above the balloon clouds are indicated

For the India Bill see No. 6271, &c , and for its defeat No 6283 On 17 Dec. a motion was carried that to report an opinion of the king in order to influence votes in parliament was 'a high crime and misdemeanour'. *Parl. Hist* xxiv. 199

$12\frac{5}{8} \times 9\frac{9}{16}$ in.

6290 THE TIMES OR THE DOWNFALL OF MAGNA FAR—TA BY CARLO CROMWELL ESQ[R]

Scott Fecit.

Engraving (partly coloured) A man-of-war is being raised by three balloons each fastened by a cord to the top of a mast Beneath the ship five sailors haul at ropes attached to her, they are on a small island or sandbank near the coast; the figures are on a very small scale. Lord North is climbing up one of these ropes which is held by a sailor who says, *this Destroys the Coalition* North says *I am going for More airy Promises*, a paper falls from him inscribed *Ch——s [Fox] is a curse on Coalitions* The other four sailors are saying, *Avast hauling There*; *Take Ch——s with you*; *D——n my Eyes bring her Back*, *I'll be damn'd if She goes* In the upper r corner of the print a head with demon's wings appears from clouds, directing at the balloons a blast of air inscribed *No Boreas here*. A winged imp or demon is flying from the balloon (r) saying, *A Paris*

On the shore (l.) stand three spectators: a man looking through a telescope says *Dont go N——th*; he wears a ribbon and is probably the Duke of Portland; a lady who says, *His other Half is Behind*; a fox on his hind-legs (Charles Fox), holding a scourge, with a paper inscribed *Pains & Penalties*. (Cf. No. 6289)

On the edge of a rock overhanging the sea (l) on the horizon is Britannia, with her shield, holding a broken spear, she is about to fall into the water. A label issues from her inscribed *Britania Æterna*. A ship at anchor, a ship's boat, &c , show that the scene is a harbour.

[1] '. . . I choose this method as Audiences on such occasions must be unpleasant.' 'm 43 past 10 P.M.'

In the lower part of the print, encroaching on the foreground, are small inset designs of irregular shape. On the r. is *India scourg'd*, a confused representation of a monster with wings and three heads, an angel with a sword, a number of prostrate and fleeing figures, and smoke. It is *Cap 9*, which appears to be a reference to *Revelation*

Below it is a design inscribed *Revelations Cap 13*; a monster with seven heads is rising out of the sea Four figures wearing crowns kneel before it, one of these has an animal's head and is perhaps intended for Fox A beast with horns resembling an ox rises from the ground behind

To the r of this design is seated Fox in oriental dress, with animal's legs, he holds a sceptre in his r hand, a sword (?) in his l He is seated on a placard or paper inscribed *My Power will last 42 Months* Fox's India Bill vested the government of the East India Company in the seven directors named in the Bill for 48 months, but 42 was the duration of the power of the Beast in the Apocalypse. A winged devil, wearing legal bands, says to him, *it is only a Bit of Wax C——s*, an allusion to the much-quoted speech of John Lee, Attorney General in the Coalition, who asked (3 Dec), 'what was the consideration of a charter, a skin of parchment with a waxed seal .. compared to the happiness of thirty millions of subjects ..'. *Parl Hist* xxiv. 49 Wraxall, *Memoirs*, 1884, iii. 182

On the r., and in the lower r corner of the design, is the India House, partly ruined, is falling; across part of the house is the Company's Charter with a large seal. On this charter, the Beast, a four-footed monster with wings and tail, wearing the papal crown, plants its four feet; the charter is inscribed, *India Charter Well Done Man of My People*. Beneath is inscribed *The India House Falling*

On the extreme l. is a small design of Fox and a winged devil standing (l.) on a cliff, below (r) is a rectangular enclosure surrounded by a wall in which are gates. Above is inscribed *Bengal* and *Cap 21*, a reference to the *Book of Revelation*, that is, to the revelation by an angel to John of 'the holy Jerusalem' lying foursquare.

Below the design is engraved, *The Air Balloon Carrying up the Royal George and Lord N——th &c* , apparently an allusion to the sinking of the *Royal George* at Spithead in Aug. 1782

An elaborate and confused attack on Fox's India Bill. Fox is here, as often, represented as a Cromwell, usurping the prerogatives of the Crown, see No. 6239, &c

The allusions to the Apocalypse are based on a speech of Scott, afterwards Lord Eldon, in the debate on the third reading of the East India Bill (8 Dec) in which he read verses from the *Book of Revelation* comparing Fox to the Beast and Dragon, and the fall of Babylon to the fall of the East India Company. This is indicated by the signature *Parl Hist*. xxiv. 34–5. Wraxall, *Memoirs*, 1884, iii. 169–70. For the India Bill see No 6271, &c., and for its defeat No 6283 For balloons see No 6333, &c.

$12\frac{1}{2} \times 7\frac{1}{8}$ in.

6291 TO DAY DISLIKED, AND YET PERHAPS TOMORROW AGAIN IN FAVOUR SO FICKLE IS THE MIND OF R—Y—L—TY.!!! [After 18 Dec 1783]

Yerac del^t & Sculp^t [? W. P. Carey.]

Engraving. Fox, North, and Burke hurled to the ground from a pedestal on which sits the king. On each side of the design is a large rectangular pedestal with a projecting base That on the l supports a bust of George II, that on the r the seated figure of George III, in profile to the l, blowing a bubble, *R—y—l favour*, through a long-stemmed pipe. In his l hand he holds a large scroll inscribed *Starvation, a poem written from feeling in the shades, by T. Chatterton of Bristol The tears of genius, or merit in distress, an elegy by the Same Rowly's poems &c.*[1] Under his arm is a book *Calhpedia* (or *Callipaedia*)

At the king's feet a platform or shutter is falling; it is inscribed, *New Methed [sic] of executing criminals Fall of the leaf.*.   It is this which has caused the fall of the three ministers in the central part of the design between the two pedestals The uppermost is Burke, staggering to the l, he holds in his hand a paper inscribed *Fall of Longinus The Sublim[e and the Beautiful]* Beneath him is North falling head downwards, he holds up in his l. hand a pouch inscribed *Budget* from which are falling papers inscribed *Tax on Honesty, List of Opposition, Tax on maids, Disarming the Irish* Fox has already reached the ground and kneels with composure on his l knee He is saying, *Truth, Honour, Justice, Warring on my side against Oppression, Cruelty & Avarice, I fall to rise more glorious* In his l hand he holds out a paper inscribed *The cries of blood & injured in - Inocence [sic], being an account of the rapacious cruelty committed in India by the I—d—a C—mp—y*

The bust of George II (l), crowned with a laurel wreath, is in profile to the r, irradiated by a star-shaped glory; the pedestal is inscribed:

The 2nd—— | *The Father of his People* | *British Meridian A D 1760. Just & necessary wars with natural & perfidious enemies; crownd with victory & success. The admirals Hawk, Boscawen, Warren, Anson, Watson, Pocock & Saunders destroying the Enemies fleets in every quarter of the Globe while our Generals drove them entirely out of America, and dispossess'd them of their cheif Settlements in India War concludes with a glorious, honourable & advantageous peace · Great Britain look'd up to as the Arbitress of Europe, fear'd by all the world, Sovereign of the Sea and possessed of a greater extent of Territory than Rome in the zenith of her glory!!!——*

> *Immortal wreaths for G——ge fair fame shall twine,*
> *And Britain's tears bedew his msacred [sic] shrine*
> ——*Yerac.*

The pedestal on which George III sits is inscribed:

——*The 3rd——* | *The Father of his — Children!* | *British Sunset 1783* ——* | *Annals of the Reign of —— By Positive Telltruth, & Impartial Justice, Historians to the People Stamp Act. Boston Port Bill American Remonstrance disregarded—177— Irish awake 177— Start up & 177— look about them Peace broken at Concord Battle [of] Lexington—of Bunker's Hill Riots in Lon[don] Irish begin to think, —— for themselves—Trenton, Saratoga Cornwallis taken. Drawn Battles at sea, in the East & West Indies, Europe & Am*

Lose the Empire of the Sea Hyder Ally defeats Col. Baily. Anarchy, Confusion & Destruction in East In[dies] War concludes with an exhausted Treasury, distracted Councils, divided Senate decay'd Fleet, Enfeebled Army, discontented People & America not only for ever, ever lost to England, but

---

[1] George III had nothing to do with Chatterton (d 1770), but the Rowley-Chatterton controversy was active 1781-3.

thrown into the arms of our natural enemies!!! Oh!!! Oh!!! Oh!!! unhappy
——!!!

Tempora mutantur. . . . Sic transit gloria Mundi.

The head and talons of the Devil appear from behind this pedestal threatening the falling ministers and saying *So perish all who seek to disturb my empire*

At the top of the design the winged figure of Fame, in profile to the l., appears from clouds. She faces the bust of George II, blowing a trumpet inscribed *Good* In her l. hand is a trumpet pointing towards George III inscribed *Evil* From its mouth come the words *disgrace!! How lost!!! How fallen!!*

The only allusion to Hyder Ali (d. 1782) in these satires.[1] Col. William Baillie was defeated 10 Sept. 1780 by Hyder Ali, wounded and captured after a heroic defence, dying in captivity 1782 The much more important series of defeats inflicted on Hyder Ali by Sir Eyre Coote, 1781–2, is characteristically omitted.

At this time the early return to power of the Coalition was confidently expected, but not through royal favour. Cf also Nos. 6181, 6232, which are apologies for the Coalition. For other references to the Stamp Act see No. 5487, &c., and for the Boston Port Act No 5230 Contrast with this print Nos. 6267, 6268, 6274

$8\frac{9}{16} \times 8\frac{3}{8}$ in.

6292 DE VREEDE VAN ANNO 1783.   [1783]
[THE PEACE OF 1783]

Engraving. A Dutch satire on the Peace between England and the Dutch Republic Figures arranged in disconnected groups on the sea-shore, with numbers referring to a printed *Verklaring* pasted on the back of the print, here translated and abridged.

(1), 'The Dutch Maid', in profile to the l., wearing a plumed helmet, holding the hat of liberty on a staff, sits behind a low palisade of broken wicker-work. She is approached by (2) Peace, who is urged forward by an Englishman, to whom is attached a small scroll inscribed *Negapatam*. He is followed by 'Envy', a man with snakes for hair blowing a horn, and by 'Duplicity', a woman holding a mask

The Dutch Maid 'is sitting in her garden which has been grievously despoiled; she says, "what will become of me? Until now I have remained unharmed by my enemies, now I am shamefully treated by my friend! By my so-called ally and co-religionist. Heaven punish the people of the Netherlands who have lent a hand to this". Peace, . . shows the Dutch Maid a withered sheaf in place of the horn of plenty, and shackles in place of love branches ' The Dutch Maid is also addressed by two men wearing short cloaks They are (3) 'Two notorious clergymen (*predikanten*) with orange favours in their hats, busy helping to ruin the Maid's garden' They say, 'even if it should be to the destruction of our Fatherland, we will stand firm in saying that England justly inflicted the war upon us, and that his Highness in a very Christian way is carrying on the war as feebly as possible, against our ally and co-religionist. .'

A plainly dressed man (4) addresses four men in military uniform (5)

[1] A French satire, an aquatint by Borel, *Hyder Ali, corrigeant les Anglois, un Soldat Francois lui presente les Verges*, is No. 1193, *Collection de Vinck* (reproduction).

(r), with a large banner with the seven arrows of the United Provinces inscribed *Voor Vryheyd en Vaderland*. He holds out to them a large scroll inscribed, *De militare jurisdictie en het begeven Van de Ampten Aan de Moff enverntitigt* He is (4) 'a statesman full of zeal, busy cleansing the oppressed Fatherland of many corrupt monsters, showing the destruction of military jurisdiction and the abolition of the bestowal of office upon foreigners "Henceforth will offices be bestowed on you my fellow-countrymen and natives of the free commonwealth, no foreigner will be superior to you" ' They are 'the citizens who take up arms to support, and the statesmen who execute his orders'.

Figures 1–5 fill the foreground of the design. Behind are a number of smaller figures on the sea-shore. Four persons (6) (r.) run in single file (r. to l) They are 'the foreigners [Germans] who seeing now no more chance of obtaining office return to their country with bag and baggage' They say, in very bad semi-Germanized Dutch, 'who the devil would have expected this! The war has caused it all . .'

On the extreme l. is a cross-beam supported on posts beneath which stand three naval officers (8), pointing to ships with furled sails which are chained to the beam Two men stand (r.) pointing at the ships, one (7) holds the end of another chain attached to a ship. He is 'an august person with his mentor [the Stadtholder with the Duke of Brunswick], with one hand ordering the fleet to sail for Brest, while holding a chain with the other. He says, "Ha Ha Ha! I thought rightly that the time would come when I should do my cousin [George III] a great favour . make as if I meant to give orders that the ships should sail to Brest, though the officers might be so well instructed that in any case they would refuse to sail". The officers (8), ordered to Brest, have not departed, giving the deceitful pretext of lack of provisions . .' Ten Dutch vessels refused to sail to Brest to join the French fleet, Sept 1782, saying they were not ready, causing a storm of protest and attacks on the Stadtholder Edler, *The Dutch Republic and the American Revolution*, Baltimore, 1911, p 204.

The central group in the background is Louis XVI (9), crowned and standing on a square pedestal inscribed *Vivae Louis*, Fame blowing a trumpet holds a wreath over his head. Four men surround the pedestal, hat in hand, with gestures of acclamation, he holds out to them a paper inscribed, *Alles vry te rug* He is 'in a generous way giving everything freely to Holland, he says "see there, in spite of envy and slander I give you all freely back—my soldiers have taken up arms for you, my powder and lead is used in your service, my fleet has reconquered your lost places Yes, my subjects have offered their lives for you, and now I give you everything freely ". Some Dutchmen (10), showing their gratitude, say, "For ever should we acknowledge your affection . . and we will always show ourselves grateful to you who helped us".'

From the clouds (l.) appear the heads and shoulders of (11) 'Tromp and Ruyter who are calling down vengeance on a fleet of English ships (12), which is passing along the Dutch coast without sufficient convoy They say, "Oh times, Oh times how are you changed! It seems as if Holland is no longer Holland . ."'

A truce was made with the United Provinces in Jan. 1783, a preliminary treaty was signed on 2 Sept 1783, and the final peace on 20 May 1784, on terms which were less favourable to the Republic than could have been secured earlier (cf. No. 6014) The basis was mutual restitution, except that England retained Negatapam and the Dutch were forced to allow British freedom of commerce in the Eastern Seas. See Edler, op. cit., Chap IX. The prophecies of the party opposed to war with England, see No 5712, had been fulfilled The Stadtholder had been dilatory in war, cf No 6038, and was accused of treachery. The French navy had recovered the Dutch W India Islands and the settlements in Guiana, had saved the Cape of Good Hope, and recaptured Trincomalee This had encouraged the 'Patriots' who were opposed to the House of Orange; the men with the banner (5) represent the corps of uniformed militia, the Patriotic Free Corps which sprang up in Dutch towns in 1783. The *predikanten* (3) are conjecturally identified (Van Stolk) as Hofslede and Barueth, the statesman as Van der Kemp, the leader of the Patriots. The Duke of Brunswick left the Republic in October 1784 owing to the activities of the Patriots.

For the loss of prestige, naval and diplomatic, to the United Provinces by the war, see F. P Renaut, *Les Provinces-Unies et la Guerre d'Amérique*, Paris, 1932, pp. 233 ff. For the decadence of the Dutch navy see the same author's *Le Crépuscule d'une Marine*, Paris, 1932. For the cumbrous naval administration and the position of the Stadtholder as Admiral-General without effective powers, see ibid., pp. 239 ff.

Van Stolk, No 4461. Muller, No. 4516

$6\frac{9}{16} \times 9\frac{7}{8}$ in.

PERSONAL AND SOCIAL SATIRES

6293-6305

Series of Tête-à-tête portraits

6293 Nᵒ XXXIV. MISS C——M.
  Nᵒ XXXV THE BON VIVANT.

London, Publish'd by A. Hamilton Junʳ Fleet Street Janʸ 1; 1783,

Engraving. *Town and Country Magazine*, xiv 625. Two bust portraits in oval frames illustrate 'Histories of the Tête-à-Tête annexed '. This appears to be an account of Bamber Gascoyne, but Sir C—— G——[Crisp Gascoyne], his father, is here alluded to as his grandfather. There are allusions to his services as a Commissioner of 'a certain great board' (the Admiralty), and to the hospitality of his villa in Essex [Bifrons].

 Miss C——m is said to be the natural daughter of a late Irish peer of that name, educated at a capital boarding school in Kensington, and to have been drugged and seduced by Lord B. When she was about to be discarded, she met the Bon Vivant who made her a settlement.

Ovals, $2\frac{5}{8} \times 2\frac{3}{16}$ in.   B.M.L , P P 5442 b.

6294 Nᵒ XXXVII THE ENTHUSIASTIC WIDOW.
  Nᵒ XXXVIII. THE POPULAR PREACHER.

London, Publish'd by A Hamilton Junʳ Fleet Street, Janʸ 15; 1783.

Engraving. *Town and Country Magazine*, xiv 681 (supplement) Two bust portraits in oval frames illustrate 'Histories of the Tête-à-Tête annexed, .' An account of a Scottish divine, with two livings in or near London, who is LL D of Aberdeen, an authority on Botany and also on Chemistry. He has much fame as a pulpit orator, and is in great request for charity sermons. He has managed to divest himself of his Scottish accent.

 'Mʳˢ Deborah Dubious', daughter of a bankrupt drysalter of London, married an unfrocked Irish Jesuit, who had eloped from Douai with a nun. She takes a great interest in theology and their association may be platonic

Ovals, $2\frac{5}{8} \times 2\frac{3}{16}$ in.   B.M L., P.P. 5442 b

6295 Nᵒ II Mʳˢ W——N.
  Nᵒ III. THE GENEROUS GALLANT.

London. Publish'd as the Act directs by A Hamilton Junʳ Fleet Street, Febʸ 1783

Engraving *Town and Country Magazine*, xv 9 Two bust portraits in oval frames illustrate 'Histories of the Tête-à-Tête annexed, .' An account of Lord Hinchinbroke, afterwards 5th Earl of Sandwich, who has the musical and social qualities of his father without his political aptitudes. He is said to have been generous to 'impures of the ton' including Mrs Armistead and the Bird of Paradise (Mrs. Mahon). He now devotes himself to Mrs W——n, really Adc——k She is Mrs. Wilson or Warton *née* Adcock, d. 1786, see *D N B*, here said to have been brought up as an actress by her father, an itinerant actor.

Ovals, $2\frac{5}{8} \times 2\frac{1}{4}$ in   B.M L , P P 5442 b

6296 Nº IV. MISS G—D—N.
    Nº V. THE JUVENILE FINANCIER

London. Publish'd by A. Hamilton Jun' Fleet Street, March 1; 1783.

Engraving *Town and Country Magazine*, xv 65 Two bust portraits in oval frames illustrate 'Histories of the Tête-à-Tête annexed, or Memoirs of the Juvenile Financier and Miss G—dw—n ' An account of William Pitt He 'seldom makes his appearance in public places . . has never exchanged a syllable with Perdita, the Bird of Paradise, the Gold-finch or the Swan' An economical liaison with his laundress while in chambers has now been followed by one with a milliner, Miss G——, the daughter of an officer, who had been decoyed and ravished, identified by H. Bleackley as Miss Goodwin.

Ovals, $2\frac{5}{8} \times 2\frac{3}{16}$ in.   B M.L., P.P. 5442 b.

6297 Nº VII MISS GR——HILL.
    Nº VIII THE SUSPICIOUS HUSBAND

London, Publish'd by A. Hamilton Jun' Fleet Street, April 1, 1783.

Engraving *Town and Country Magazine*, xv. 121 Two bust portraits in oval frames illustrate 'Histories of the Tête-à-Tête annexed; . . ' An account of Lord —— who married Lady C—— [*sic*] in 1764, had many children, till in 1773 they separated He then reverted to his former intercourse with courtesans, until he wished to marry, when he attempted to get a divorce, on the ground of his wife's intimacy with a young musician, but was unsuccessful. He has therefore made an arrangement with Miss G——, a noted courtesan

He is Edmund Boyle, Earl of Cork (1742–98). He m. Anne Courtenay, the marriage was dissolved in 1782 G E C , *Complete Peerage.*

The lady is Miss Greenhill, known as the Greenfinch. H. Bleackley, *Ladies Fair and Frail*, p. 285

Ovals, $2\frac{5}{8} \times 2\frac{3}{16}$ in.   B.M.L., P.P. 5442 b.

6298 Nº X. MRS W—LL—MS
    Nº XI THE NAUTICAL CORNUTER.

London, Publish'd by A. Hamilton Jun' Fleet Street 1 May 1783

Engraving. *Town and Country Magazine*, xv. 177 Two bust portraits in oval frames illustrate 'Histories of the Tête-à-Tête annexed, . ' An account of Captain Joseph Peyton, who was the occasion of the divorce of Mrs. W., *née* M——h, married 1774, and separated from her husband in Oct. 1780. He paid damages of £1,000, and is now living with Mrs Williams

Ovals, $2\frac{5}{8} \times 2\frac{3}{16}$ in.   B.M.L., P.P. 5442 b

6299 Nº XIII. LADY B—NT—N.

Nº XIV THE IRRESISTIBLE CAPTAIN.

London. Publish'd by A. Hamilton Jun' Fleet Street June 1, 1783.

Engraving. *Town and Country Magazine*, xv. 233 Two bust portraits in oval frames illustrate 'Histories of the Tête-à-Tête annexed, . .'. An account of John Allen Cooper, nephew of Andrew Bayntun, the occasion of a suit of *crim con.* brought by Andrew Bayntun against his wife, Lady Maria, and of Lady Maria Bayntun, daughter of Lord Coventry by his wife Maria Gunning, and of the circumstances which led up to the divorce. In the printed account of the trial (B M L , 518. c 15 /2) is an engraving of a dinner-table scene, *Lady Maria Bayntun returning her Wedding-Ring to her Husband.*

Ovals, $2\frac{5}{8} \times 2\frac{3}{16}$ in.   B M.L , P. P. 5442 b.

6300 Nº XVI. MRS II——Y.

Nº XVII THE DORKING HERO.

London, Publish'd by A. Hamilton Jun' Fleet Street July 1; 1783.

Engraving *Town and Country Magazine*, xv. 389 Two bust portraits in oval frames illustrate 'Histories of the Tête-à-Tête annexed, . ' An account of Turner Straubenzee, Lt -Col. 52nd Foot, the occasion of a suit of *crim. con.* brought by John Hankey against his wife, and of the wife, Elizabeth Hankey, daughter of Andrew Thomson They eloped together from Brighton to Dorking, where Straubenzee's regiment was quartered. The *Trial of Mrs. Elizabeth Hankey* recounts the facts here alluded to. (B.M.L., 518 c. 15/5.)

Ovals, $2\frac{5}{8} \times 2\frac{3}{16}$ in   B M L., P P. 5442 b.

6301 Nº XIX. MISS CHARLOTTE F——R.

Nº XX. THE PATRIOTIC ORATER [*sic*]

London, Publish'd Aug¹. 1; 1783, by A Hamilton Jun' Fleet Street.

Engraving *Town and Country Magazine*, xv. 345 Two bust portraits in oval frames illustrate 'Histories of the Tête-à-Tête annexed, . ' An account of Lord ——, descended from an ancient family which has never been conspicuous His speeches on 'Irish affairs, and the late proclamation for confining the trade of America of [*sic*] England' show that he speaks from conviction not interest. Conjecturally identified by H Bleackley with Lord Sheffield (Baker Holroyd), this is supported by his speech on 15 April 1783 *Parl. Hist.* xxiii. 762-4.

Miss Charlotte Fisher (the name has been written in) is a well-known courtesan, the name Fisher assumed because it 'had been an excellent travelling appellation in the line of the impures'—an allusion to Kitty Fisher.

Ovals, $2\frac{5}{8} \times 2\frac{1}{16}$ in.   B M L., P.P. 5442 b.

6302 Nº XXII. MRS W——N.

Nº XXIII THE CAREFUL COMMANDER

London, Publish'd by A. Hamilton Jun' Fleet Street, Sep', 1, 1783

Engraving *Town and Country Magazine*, xv. 401 Two bust portraits in oval frames illustrate 'Histories of the Tête-à-Tête annexed; . .' The man wears a ribbon and star An account of the military career of Sir Guy Carleton (1724–1808) (then in New York), K.B.1776.[1] Mrs. W. was a Miss J—mes, who married Mr. W. and went with him to New York, where he went in 'a public capacity', and died there. She then accepted a proposal made her by the Careful Commander.

Ovals, $2\frac{5}{8} \times 2\frac{1}{8}$ in.   B M L., P.P. 5442 b.

6303 N° XXV. THE CAPTIVATING MISS B——
      N° XXVI THE AMERICAN NEGOTIATOR.

London, Publish'd by A. Hamilton Jun' Fleet Street, Oct' 1; 1783.

Engraving *Town and Country Magazine*, xv. 457 Two bust portraits in oval frames illustrate 'Histories of the Tête-à-Tête annexed, .'. An account of Silas Deane, said to have carried on a correspondence with the late ministry, and therefore to have been obliged to quit France, and of his alleged association in Paris with Mlle Ro——lle, the mistress of a deceased farmer-general He is said to be residing in a private manner in London.

Miss B is a courtesan, the daughter of a farrier in the Borough, who eloped to escape from marriage with her father's apprentice For Deane see No 6288.

Ovals, $2\frac{5}{8} \times 2\frac{1}{16}$ in.   B.M L , P P 5442 b.

6304 N° XXVIII THE ENGAGING M^RS G——R.
      N° XXIX. THE ACCOMPLISHED PEER.

London, Publish'd by A. Hamilton Jun' Fleet Street Nov' 1; 1783.

Engraving. *Town and Country Magazine*, xv. 513. Two bust portraits in oval frames illustrate 'Histories of the Tête-à-Tête annexed; . . .'. An account of a peer who is a captain in the Dragoon Guards, and succeeded his uncle. He is George Evelyn Boscawen who succeeded his uncle Lord Falmouth (the Lord Pyebald of this series) in 1782

Mrs. G——r was a Miss H—r—s, who was induced to elope by her dancing-master G——r [? Garnier] from a polite boarding school in Kensington under a promise of marriage, and has had a succession of lovers.

Ovals, $2\frac{5}{8} \times 2\frac{1}{16}$ in.   B M L , P P. 5442 b.

6305 N° XXXI THE ELEGANT M^RS O——N.
      N° XXXII THE APPROVED MAGISTRATE.

London Publish'd by A Hamilton Jun' Fleet Street. Dec' 1; 1783

Engraving. *Town and Country Magazine*, xv 569. Two bust portraits in oval frames illustrate 'Histories of the Tête-à-Tête annexed; . . ' An account of a Lord Mayor of London, M P for 'one of the most respectable cities of the world', presumably London, who is said to have refused a knighthood on presenting a congratulatory address. He received the thanks of the Corporation at the close of his year of office. Probably Nathaniel Newnham, M P for the City, 1780–90, and Lord Mayor 1782–3, who received the thanks of the Corporation in Oct 1783 *Ann Reg* , 1783,

---

[1] The identification is clear; he is, however, identified by H Bleackley as Robert Monckton

p 219 M P. Ludgershall 1793–6 Master of the Mercers Company, 1786, d. 1809 Founded, 1785, the banking firm of Newnham, Everett, Drummond, &c, afterwards Everett and Co. Beaven, *Aldermen of London, City Biography*, 1800, p 26

Mrs O——n was Miss S——n, who married a rich young merchant who became bankrupt and died. The Magistrate is said to have gained her affections by presenting her with a snuff-box containing his portrait and a £500 note. He now makes her an allowance

Ovals, $2\frac{5}{8} \times 2\frac{1}{16}$ in   B M L., P P. 5442 b.

6306 A HOP MERCHANT.

Pub 14 Jan. 1783 by Cornell, Bruton Street, near Bond Street.

Engraving (coloured and uncoloured impressions) Bust portrait of a man in profile to the l, his hair in black bag His small eye, large blunt nose, and coarse mouth, combined with a backward tilt of the head, give him an expression of arrogance and stupidity. Perhaps a dancing-master.

$4\frac{3}{8} \times 3\frac{1}{4}$ in (pl)

6307 THE GOLDEN PIPPIN.

Pub: 9th Feby 1783 by H. Humphrey No 51 New Bond Street.

Engraving (coloured and uncoloured impressions) Head of an old woman in profile to the l, tilted upwards She wears a cap which conceals her hair. 'Betty' is written on the print in an old hand,[1] she is evidently the Betty of the famous fruit shop in St James's Street, the 'patriot Betty' of Mason's *Heroic Epistle*, 1773 'Betty's' was a fashionable 'lounge' and centre of gossip, often mentioned by H Walpole and others. She was Elizabeth Munro or Neale, 1730–97, called 'the Queen of apple-women' by the *Gentleman's Magazine* (obituary).

A burletta, 'The Golden Pippin', was first played 1772–3. *Genest*, v 364

$3\frac{15}{16} \times 3$ in (pl.).

6308 [UNIDENTIFIED PORTRAIT.]

Pub 14th Feb 1783 by H Humphrey, No 51 New Bond St

Engraving Head of a man in profile to the r wearing spectacles, with a very long beak-shaped nose.

$4\frac{5}{16} \times 3\frac{5}{8}$ in (pl)

6309 [MRS HEXETER?]

Pub: 25 Feb. 1783 by H Humphrey 51 New Bond St

Engraving Bust portrait of an elderly lady of demure appearance in profile to the r Her hair is dressed with two side curls, partly covered by a cap. The shoulders and bust are small in proportion to the head. She is identified by Mr. Hawkins as 'Mrs Hexeter'.

$3\frac{1}{4} \times 2\frac{3}{8}$ in. (pl.).

[1] Mr Hawkins expands this into 'Mrs Humphrey's Betty', but in 1796, the date of Gillray's *Twopenny Whist*, she was a much younger woman than this Betty in 1780, to whom she bears no resemblance. A resemblance is traceable (the ravages of time allowed for) to the mezzotint of 'Betty' by J. Dixon after Falconer, 1750. Chaloner Smith, p 213

6310 [UNIDENTIFIED PORTRAIT]

Pub 25 Feby 1783 by H Humphrey N° 51 New Bond S^t

Engraving Bust portrait of a man in profile to the l. with a whip under his l arm. He is plainly dressed; his hair is brushed forward over his forehead and arranged in small curls on the neck.

$3\frac{9}{16} \times 3$ in (pl.).

6311 [J. KEMBLE]   [n d ? c 1783]

Engraving Bust portrait in profile to the r. of John Philip Kemble (1757–1823) (identified by Mr Hawkins). Kemble did not appear on the London stage till 1783 when he played Hamlet at Drury Lane.

$2\frac{3}{4} \times 1\frac{7}{8}$ in.

6312 [UNIDENTIFIED PORTRAIT.]

Pub ^{1}Feb. 1783 by H Humphrey N° 51 New Bond Street.

Engraving Sketch of an old man seated, turned three-quarters to the r. In his r. hand he holds a candle-stick in which is a lighted candle; in his l. what may be a print. He is drawn as far as the waist, below which his crossed legs from the knee downwards are sketched. He wears a cocked hat, the points over the ears, spectacles, and a plain coat buttoned to the chin. On a small round table (r.) are tea-things. Perhaps a portrait of a connoisseur.

$4\frac{7}{8} \times 3\frac{1}{8}$ in. (pl).

6313 THE RIGHT HON^{BLE} CHARLES JA^S FOX.   [n.d. 1783?]

[After Bunbury.]

Stipple. A copy of No 5878 Probably published while Fox was Secretary of State.

$5\frac{1}{4} \times 4\frac{1}{4}$ in

6314 CITY COALITION.

WD. [Dent.]

Pub by W Dent N° 116 Strand July 11. 1783.

                                                                    Colley.

Engraving (coloured impression) A stout alderman, standing T Q to the l , clasps to his chest a turtle, whose mouth he is kissing. He wears a long furred alderman's gown over a laced coat and waistcoat Beneath the title is engraved:

> *Of all Life's Dainties, says K—tch—n,*
> *Turtle is the most bewitching.*

Henry Kitchin of Berners Street was alderman of Farringdon Within, elected in 1774. He was sheriff in 1778–9, d. 1786 Was twice Master of the Curriers' Company. Beaven, *Aldermen of London*, ii 136 See *City Biography*, 1800, p. 119. See No 6260.

$8\frac{1}{4} \times 6\frac{7}{16}$ in

                    ^{1} Date illegible

6315 THE ITALIAN POET.

WD. [Dent.]

Pub^d by W. Dent. Octr 10th 1783. N° 116 Strand.

Engraving. Portrait of a man walking in profile to the r stooping forwards From his pocket project a book, *Flames of Newgate*, and two papers or letters inscribed *King of Sardinia* and *Empress of Russia* A jagged strip also hangs from his pocket which resembles a parchment indenture; this is inscribed *Lancet*. He is saying, *Ven I vos in Rome de Boys vos call me de little Pope*

The profile has a certain resemblance to portraits of Alfieri (1749–1803) Alfieri visited London in 1768, 1770–1, and 1783–4, when, however, he did not, according to his *Autobiography*, reach England till December

7×5 in (pl)

6316 [WOODFORD RICE ESQ]¹ [1783]

Engraving. Portrait of a man W L. and full-face, wearing a coat with military facings and epaulettes He stands with his r. hand on his hip; in his l he holds out an open book, on the r. hand page is inscribed *The Rutland Volunteers*, on the l. is the portrait of himself here described A chair (l) and a table (r) are behind him, on the chair are a cockaded hat and a sword, on the table writing-materials and papers, one inscribed *Ode*. On the wall is a plan showing two camps divided by a river inscribed *Villa Velha Ford* The camp on the north of the river is *The Combined Army of France & Spain consisting of 40000 Men at 3 Miles distance*. Between this camp and the river is the *Spanish Military Camp*. South of the river is *Genl Burgoynes small Brigade 3000 men*

Woodford Rice published a satirical poem in 1783 called *The Rutland Volunteer influenza'd or a receipt to make a Patriot, a Soldier or a Poet* (Kearsley) This print appears to have been designed as its frontispiece, but is not in either of the B M.L. copies of the book. On p. 5 are the lines

> Valentia's Plains shall tell the story,
> Villa-Velha-Ford will sound the glory.

To this is appended a lengthy note describing the storming of the camp of Villa Velha which closed the campaign in Portugal in 1762 'Capt Rice had the honour of contributing to the glory of that night, and received his share of the plunder . . Capt Rice has no objection to wear a red ribband, get a higher rank in the army, or be appointed to an Irish Government '

9×8 in

6317 [MRS WELTJE IN HER SHOP IN PALL MALL.]

['*Capt Hays del* '² n.d. ? 1783]

Ch^s Bretherton. Published as the Act Directs.

Engraving The interior of a shop showing the window (l.) and a semi-circular counter or bar behind which sits a buxom lady (r) in a chair, her

¹ Written on the print.
² A MS. note by Miss Banks, who has also written 'Mrs Weltje Fruit Shop Pall-Mall' On the back of another impression is written in an old hand 'next door neighbour to Mr Neville Pall Mall'

761

head in profile to the l On the narrow counter are pears, apples, and three dishes of fruit Displayed in the window are pine-apples, pottles of fruit, glasses, &c., and a plant in a pot. Bunches of grapes hang in front of the window-panes; rows of glasses, glass bottles, and jars stand on narrow ledges across the divisions between the panes of glass. On three shelves (r) above Mrs. Weltje's head are ranged jelly glasses, &c For Weltje see No 5888

$7\frac{1}{8} \times 10\frac{11}{16}$ in.

6318 FLORIZEL GRANTING INDEPENDENCY TO PERDITA.

[1 Feb. 1783]

Engraving From the *Rambler's Magazine*, Jan 1783 Mrs Robinson (Perdita) seated on a settee (r), her head in profile to the l, checks with her r. hand the advance towards her of the Prince of Wales, in her l she holds a document. He says, *Submit to my Royal Will*; she answers, *Declare me Independent and then* ——. On the wall is a framed picture of Danaë receiving the shower of gold; Danaë resembles Perdita, but all the heads are poorly characterized The Prince's sword lies on the floor, his hat, cloak, and writing materials are on a circular table (l) A small dog barks at the Prince. A festooned curtain (r) and a patterned carpet make part of the design.

About this time Perdita, whose relations with the Prince had been broken off, was induced to return to him his bond to pay her £20,000 on coming of age, it was valueless, but she threatened to enforce it. Charles Fox acted as an intermediary and secured her an annuity of £500 a year D N.B., Huish, *Memoirs of George IV*, i. 77. See Nos. 5767, &c., 6117, 6221, 6266, 6319, 6320.

$5\frac{7}{16} \times 3\frac{5}{8}$ in

6319 PARIDISE REGAIN,D

SB [? Gillray].

London Publish'd as the Act directs Feby 20 1783 by J. Langham in the Great Piazza Covent Garden.[1]

Engraving. Design in an oval. Fox (c.) making addresses to Mrs Robinson (Perdita) who stands demurely (r) with her arms folded. The Prince of Wales (l) watches with amusement from behind a tree Fox's hands are clasped in an attitude of prayer, he is saying, *Sweet Robenet your Eyes Jet your Teeth are lilly White your Cheeks are Roses Lips are Poses and your Nose is Wonderous Bright* Perdita wears a small cap of muslin and lace, ringlets rest on her neck, her petticoats are voluminous and adorned in front with a wide frilled apron The Prince, who wears his star, clasps the trunk of the tree behind which he stands, saying *Ha! Ha! Ha! Poor Charly.* Trees (r and l) are indicated in the background.

For Perdita, the Prince, and Fox see Nos 5767, &c., 6117, and 6318, &c.

$7\frac{1}{4} \times 11\frac{1}{4}$ in

6320 [MRS ROBINSON AND FOX]

[? c 1783]

Engraving. Fox and Perdita dancing together, she as a bacchante, he as Bacchus or perhaps Falstaff. She (l) holds out a glass in her r hand, a

[1] Beneath this is an almost obliterated publication line showing the word *Sep.*

garland of leaves hangs over her l shoulder. Fox is wearing a ruff, tunic, breeches, and shoes with rosettes and has a garland of leaves round his hips, he holds a long wand in his l hand. Both are crowned with leaves. An open book is on the ground On the wall which forms a background are two framed portraits (T.Q.L.): a man with horns (l.) and a woman holding an open book (r), probably Mr and Mrs Robinson

For Mrs. Robinson see No 5767, &c , and for her association with Fox, Nos. 6117, 6221, 6266, 6318, 6319

$4 \times 6\frac{3}{8}$ in

6321 THE ROYAL ADONIS

['E. T '?]

March 14, 1783 Pub. by Mrs D Archery St James Street

Engraving. Caricature portrait of one of the royal dukes, probably of William Henry, Duke of Gloucester, 1743–1805 He stands in profile to the l wearing a sword and bag-wig, his hat under his l arm. His coat has a fur collar and the star of the Garter; over it he wears the Garter ribbon. His features and the arrangement of his hair are caricatured The open mouth, double chin, and thick neck, the recession of the hair on the temples, which are here conspicuous, are noticeable even in the mezzotint by Earlom (1771) after Hamilton ,

$6\frac{7}{8} \times 4\frac{1}{2}$ in.

6322 LES CAPRICES DE LA GOUTE (LINE OF MUSIC), BALLET ARTHRITIQUE.

[P Sandby.]

Published as the Act directs Jany 1 1783 by P Sandby St George's Row, Oxford Turnpike.

Aquatint. A room in the establishment of Abraham Buzaglo, whose treatment of the gout by 'muscular exercises' is here satirized Men with their limbs strapped into wooden cases are performing exercises A stout man whose arms are extended by a wooden frame or jacket strapped across chest and arms, his thighs similarly encased and extended, capers on one leg, the other is swathed in a stocking (perhaps one of the 'bootikins' described by Horace Walpole, *Letters*, x 342, 30 Oct. 1778, &c.). On each side of him is a man in a contorted attitude, with legs or leg encased (the other leg being swathed) Each wooden case is inscribed *Buzaglo*.

In the background (l.) Buzaglo himself, apparently, stands in profile to the l superintending his assistant, who is strapping the leg of a patient into a case; the other leg is already encased; his crutches are beside him Against the centre of the back wall is an elaborate stove, inscribed *Buzaglo*. On the wall (r and l) hang two pairs of leg-cases.

In front of the design, as if decorating the front of a stage, is a placard nailed above a pair of crossed crutches.

PATENT MUSCULAR HEALTH-RESTORING EXERCISE

I. *It takes off within the hour all Pains from the Shoulders, Elbows, Sides, Back, Knees, Calves & Ancles.*

763

II. *It radically cures the Cramp, dissipates callous Swellings round the Knees & Ancles originating from the Gout.*

III. *It restores wasted Calves to their former state of fullness of Flesh.*

IV. *It greatly facilitates the Discharge of the Gravel.*

Abraham Buzaglo, a Jew (d. 1788), first attracted notice as an inventor of heating apparatus, then set up as a gout doctor, professing to cure by muscular exercises only. He advertised extensively and was considered a quack. Walpole, *Letters*, x. 168–9 and n. A. Buzaglo, *A Treatise on the Gout*, 3rd ed., 1778.

Cf. Anstey's *Election Ball* 1776, probably an allusion to Buzaglo:

No—I'd have thee to know that I walks pretty stout
Zince I'v vound an invallible cure for the Gout
Vor the Doctor I've try'd has with Wedges and Pegs
Zo stretched out my zinews and hammer'd my Legs,
Zo zuppl'd the Joint by Tormenting the Tendon
My Heel I can raise, and my Toe I can bend down.

A humorous handbill advertising the print calls it 'a companion to *Jason & Medee, Ballet Tragique*', see No. 5910.

$14\frac{3}{4} \times 18\frac{1}{16}$ in.

6323 THE DOCTER HIMSELF POURING OUT HIS WHOLE SOUL FOR 1s

I B [J. Boyne.]

London Published as the Act Directs Feby 12 1783 by R. Rusted N° 3 Bridge St Ludgate Hill

Engraving. Dr. James Graham, the famous quack, stands on a small platform or pedestal, addressing an audience of both sexes who sit and stand in front of him. He stands rather to the r. of the design looking l., his r. hand raised, his left holding a rolled paper as in No. 6324. He wears a bag-wig and ruffled shirt. Those of the audience whose faces are visible are probably portraits, but only Fox, Wilkes, and (?) Perdita Robinson can be identified. Three persons sit on a raised seat immediately under the lecturer and with their backs towards him: a young man puts his arm round a lady who draws back with a coy expression; the third is Fox who sits gloomily impassive, his head supported on his hand, perhaps annoyed at the way in which Mrs. Robinson looks towards the man standing next her, who stands on the extreme r. in profile to the l. He is slim and wears the fashionable riding-dress but is very ugly. Two rows of people sit on forms facing the lecturer. Others stand on the l. Wilkes is in profile to the r., an elderly beau with receding hair, sunken eyes, and broken teeth.

The lecture in question may be that on 'Generation &c.' satirized in the *Rambler's Magazine*, where it was, according to the Doctor, 'a poor nonsensical mutilated jumble of stuff full of false facts and representations, and not one fourth part of the matter or size of the real original lecture as I delivered it and as it is here printed'. Preface to 'A Lecture on the Generation Increase and Improvement of the Human Species! . . . with a glowing, brilliant and supremely delightful Description of the Structure and most irresistibly Genial Influences of the CELESTIAL BED!!!'.

764

Beneath the title is engraved·

> *How Fluent Nonsense Trickles from his Tongue*
> *How Sweet his Lectures neither S^d nor Sung*
>
> *Pope*

For Graham see Nos 5766, 6120, 6324–7. For Fox and Perdita see No. 6117, &c

$10\frac{3}{8} \times 9\frac{1}{8}$ in

6324 THE DOCTOR HIMSELF.   [1 Mar. 1783]

Woodcut From the *Rambler's Magazine*, Feb 1783. Portrait (H L) in an oval of James Graham, the quack doctor, looking to the r He wears a bag-wig in the prevailing fashion with horizontal side curls, and a ruffled shirt as in No. 6323. His r. hand is partly visible holding a bulky rolled MS. evidently the text of one of his lectures

Beneath the portrait is an inscription in which the arrangement, division of words, punctuation, and use of capitals is such as to make it appear at first sight to be in some unknown language It begins, *Tot-* | *Hele, Ar n Edsci, Ent . . .* | It runs, i e [*To the learned, scientific, ingenious, celestial, rhetorical, whimsical, satyrical and moving Doctor, this head is most submissively dedicated by an admirer of his talents, a lover of his warm doctrines, and his most obedient humble servant The Rambler.* Feb 1783]

See Nos 5766, 6120, 6323, 6325, 6326, 6327.

$3\frac{3}{4} \times 3\frac{1}{8}$ in

6325 THE QUACKS

Pub^d March 17 1783 by W. Humphrey N° 227 Strand.

Engraving The two notorious quacks of the period, Graham and Katerfelto, demonstrating their marvels, one against the other, each standing on a stage Graham (l), in profile to the r, is on a stage shaped like an E O table, circular and surrounded by the letters E O (Graham's establishment in Pall Mall was used for gambling, and E.O tables there were broken by the Westminster Justices on 1 Aug 1782, see No 6120) He stands astride a long cylinder, supported on a vase-shaped pillar inscribed *insulated*; each foot rests on a circular stool supported on a vase-shaped pillar, these are the glass insulators which he used in his electrical demonstrations The cylinder is inscribed *Prime conductor Gentle restorer Largest in the World* In his l hand he holds up a phial or cylinder inscribed *Medicated tube*, he points at Katerfelto, saying, *That round Vigour¹ that full-toned juvenile Virility which Speaks so cordially and so Effectually home to the Female Heart, Conciliating its Favour & Friendship, and rivetting its Intensest Affections away thou German Maggot killer, thy Fame is not to be Compar'd to mine* (probably a quotation from one of his lectures) He wears a physician's full-curled wig, a ruffled shirt, and laced waistcoat.

At his feet stands a duck, on a label coming from its beak are the words *Quack Quack Quack.* and a thistle indicating Graham's Scottish origin Other objects on the platform are the model of a cannon inscribed *Cœlestial Musick* and two jars, one inscribed *Leyden Vial Charg'd with Load Stones Aromatic Spices, &c. &c. &c.*; the other *Tin foil or Antidote*

Above the farther side of the platform (l.) appear the heads and shoulders of the two gigantic porters who were part of his establishment, see Nos. 5766, 6346. One (l.) labelled Gog stands full-face, a placard round his neck· *Temple of Health & of Hymen*, the name of the establishment at Schomberg House, Pall Mall, in allusion to his 'celestial bed' for the cure of sterility. The other footman, *Magog*, is in profile to the r. Attached to the wall above their heads is a stuffed alligator inscribed *Cured of the Dropsey & Gout in the Stomach*. Beneath this is a shelf, on it are a pestle and mortar, a bust, perhaps of Galen, and a monkey seated in profile to the r. holding up a phial in imitation of Graham.

Graham had lived for two years in Philadelphia and had learned something of Franklin's experiments in electricity.

Katerfelto's stage is a flimsy rectangular structure supported on thin planks, with cross planks, one decorated with a skull and cross-bones, the other by insects, &c (a butterfly, centipede, moth, and worm). He crouches over a cylindrical conductor supported on a pillar, similar to, but not identical with, that of his rival, it is inscribed, *Positively Charg'd*, his feet rest on the base of its pillar, a trident on its other end touches a barrel-shaped cylinder or grindstone which is being turned by the Devil, who says, *away with it my Dear Son I'll find fire eternally for you* Katerfelto embraces his cylinder with one arm, while his r hand points at Graham, sparks come from his thumb and forefinger, from a spike on the front of his cylinder, and also drop from his chin. He is saying *Dare you was see de Vonders of the Varld, which make de hair Stand on tiptoe, Dare you was see mine Tumb and mine findgar, Fire from mine findger and Feaders on mine Tumb—dare you was see de Gun Fire viddout Ball or powder, dare you was see de Devil at mine A——e— O Vonders! Vonders! Vonderfull Vonders!*

The chain of sparks from Katerfelto's chin drops on to the touch-hole of a toy cannon at his feet so as to fire it in the direction of Graham His attitude and profile express intense excitement, and his whole person appears charged with electricity; the hair on his forehead stands up, his long pigtail queue flies out behind him as do his coat-tails. Other objects on his platform, besides the electrical appliance which he is grasping, the devil's cylinder and the cannon, are a Leyden jar, a small rectangular box inscribed *Arcanum sublimum, Mask'd Battery*, a toy windmill, a square bottle inscribed *Tinct' Aurum Vivae*, a small pent-house supported on a stick inscribed *Thunder House*, a bag or small sack inscribed *Aurora Borealis*, and an insect resembling a scorpion. Beneath the platform is a *Reservoir for Dead Insects destroy'd by D' Katterf[elto]*; insects are faintly indicated as if seen through a screen.

Graham was a compound of quack, fashionable doctor, and visionary, see Nos. 5766, 6284, 6323–7 Katerfelto, who appeared in London about 1782, was quack, conjurer, and travelling showman, see No 6326 Both made great use of advertisement, in handbills, placards, and in the newspapers. Graham also published a number of pamphlets.

$8\frac{5}{8} \times 13\frac{7}{16}$ in

6326 THE WONDERFUL MOST WONDERFUL DR KATE—HE—FELT—HO, HAVING PACK'D UP HIS ALLS IS TRUDGING AWAY WITH HIS FAMILY & ALL HIS LITTLE NECESSARY APPENDICES TO HIS OWN DEAR COUNTREY—WEEP ENGLAND! WEEP! OH!

Pub 31 March 1783 by H. Humphrey N° 51 New Bond Street

Engraving Katerfelto walking rapidly, in profile to the r, leaning forward

under the weight of a peep-show or magic lantern strapped to his shoulders
He wears military uniform, his hat decorated with the skull and cross-
bones of the Death's Head Huzzars in which he claimed to have served At
his l side hangs an enormous sabre, its scabbard inscribed *100000000000
Caterpillars slain in one year*. In his hat is a curious erection, three folds
of which are visible, inscribed respectively, *Geography, Opticks*, and
Astronomy Below the first is a hemisphere or circular map, below the
second, three pairs of double eye-glasses, below the third another map in
a circle. In his r hand he carries an electrical implement like that which
he clasps in No 6325, but smaller. It is inscribed *Gentle Restorer* In his
l hand is a bag inscribed *5000 English Guineas* His magic lantern is
inscribed *Lady Catarena*, from its lens rays are spreading, inscribed
Wonders, Wonders, Wonders; the rays strike on three insects of fantastic appearance, probably representing the objects which he was accustomed to show
through his microscope (In an advertisement in the *Morning Post*, July
1782, he says, that by its aid those insects which caused the late influenza
will be seen as large as a bird; and in a drop of water the size of a pin's
head will be seen 50,000 insects. Sampson, *Hist. of Advertising*, p. 404)
Other rays project behind him from his coat-tails and his hat, the former
inscribed *Physic & Philosophy*, the latter *Fire* He is saying, *Galante Show,
here be de Death of Philosophy & de Glory of Legerdemain, here be de Vonders
of all the Kings in Europe, Asia, Africa & America*

He is followed by his wife and children, who are on a smaller scale The
woman holds a doll-like little girl in each arm, a little boy walks behind
her clutching at her garments All four have small horns growing from
their foreheads and cloven feet The woman, who is plainly dressed, says
Be good children, & you shall both go to Germany & ride in the Coach The
two children say *Aynt my Daddy a Cunning Man, Mammy?* and *Ayn't de
Englishmen great Fools Mammy?* The little boy says *Is my Daddy a Devil,
Mammy?*

See No 6325

$8\frac{1}{4} \times 12\frac{7}{16}$ in

6327 THE WEST COUNTRY PUFFING FAMILY.

Published by J. Mills, April 9, and to be had at N° 51, Bond-Street.

Engraving, heading to a song printed in three columns Five heads, much
caricatured, arranged in two pairs, facing each other, in profile, the centre
head being full-face and superimposed upon the two heads which are
back to back On the l, in profile to the r., is 'honest old Coward' who faces
'Squire Richard'. On the r. 'Dick Howard', in profile to the r , faces 'Miss
Bridget'. In the centre is an old woman wearing spectacles, 'Goody Gobble
Cock'. The song is 'To be sung in character, to the Tune of an "Old
Woman cloathed in Grey"'. The song relates the efforts of all to rekindle
a candle with a glowing wick by blowing or 'puffing' at it The first and
last verses are:

I.

'A Family lived in the West,
Of whom I this Story indite,
Whose Mouths were the drollest confest
That ever gave Mirrh [*sic*] or Delight.

VIII.

Thus Puffing 's become now the Trade,
Of *Katerfelto** and *Graham** well known,
Whose Mouths confessedly are made,
For nought else but *Puffing* alone.

* Two Travelling Philosophers.'

'This *Song* is dedicated to those *Princes* of *Puffs*, who exist at their *Wholesale Puff* a de *Puff Warehouses*, the Sign of the *Devil* and *Black Cat*, Piccadilly; the *Temple* of *Health*, *Pall Mall*, the *Brazen Head*, *St Stephen's Chapel* [the House of Commons]; and those numourous *Tribe* of *Puffs* whose Names are on the Back Door, with Lamps in the Passage, &c. &c.

By their most humble Servant, LIVY PUFF, Jun[r] '

A satire on the advertisements so lavishly circulated in handbills, placards, and the newspapers by Katerfelto, who professed to receive advice from a black cat, and Dr Graham at Schomberg House, Pall Mall See Nos. 6325, 6326, &c.

$3\frac{1}{8} \times 12$ in

6328 APOLLO AND THE MUSES, INFLICTING PENANCE ON D[R] POMPOSO, ROUND PARNASSUS.

[Gillray.]
Pub[d] July 29th 1783 by   Holland N[o] 66 Drury Lane.

Engraving Dr Johnson, a rope round his neck, is being driven from l. to r by Apollo and the nine muses, who follow him with uplifted scourges and birch rods. Johnson is clad only in breeches, shoes, and stockings; on his head is a dunce's cap shaped like a four-sided pyramid, on this is inscribed the names of poets whose lives he had written· *Milton, Otway, Waller, Gray, Shenston[e], Lyttelton, Gay, Denman, Collins &c. &c &c* Over his shoulder he carries a placard inscribed, *For defaming that Genius I could never emulate, by criticism without Judgment,—and endeavouring to cast the beauties of British Poetry into the hideous shade of oblivion* A tear falls from his eye and he is saying, *I acknowledge my transgressions, and my sins are ever before me*; an asterisk indicates a note in the margin· *Vide The Last Sermon at St Dunstans* Apollo and the Muses wear classical draperies and laurel wreaths, Apollo holds the end of the rope which is round Johnson's neck, his head is surrounded by a halo. Above the ground by Johnson (r.) are two books, each with a pair of wings, in full flight· *An Essay on the Milk of Human kindness dedicated to D[r] Johnson as a Man*, and *An Essay on Envy dedicated to D[r] Johnson as an Author*

Clouds and a rocky mountain form the background On the summit of the mountain is a small circular temple behind which is the sun; Pegasus flies near the summit

This is the print which was being discussed at Sir Joshua Reynolds's when Johnson entered, and being told of the caricature, said to Dr. Farr: 'Sir I am very glad to hear this. I hope the day will never arrive when I shall neither be the object of calumny or ridicule, for then I shall be neglected and forgotten.' *Johnsonian Miscellanies*, ii 419-20 Churchill had called Johnson Pomposo in *The Ghost*, 1762 See also No 6103.

This print (presumably) appears, price 2s., in the 'Catalogue' appended to Jordan's *Elixir of Life* . published by W. Holland, 50 Oxford Street, 1789 as 'Apollo and the Muses whipping Dr Johnson round Parnassus'. $9\frac{7}{8} \times 12\frac{1}{8}$ in.

6329 THE CUCKOLDS REEL. [1 April 1783]

Engraving From the *Rambler's Magazine*, Mar. 1783. Three men, each with a pair of long horns, dance holding hands On the r , in profile to the l , is a man in judge's wig and long gown He says *What Monsters our Wives have made of us Sir R——d¹ who would be an Advocate for Matrimony.* The centre figure, evidently Sir Richard Worsley, see Nos. 6105-12, is dressed as a military officer with a gorget round his neck He answers, *Never Mind¹ Caesar & Pompey were both of them horn'd.* The man on the l , facing the judge, is dressed as a naval officer and holds a telescope in his r hand. He says *A sailor who Marries deserves to be a Cuckold. While an Admiral is at Sea his Frigate at home must be mann'd.*

Two animals seated on brackets on the wall supply the music for the dance An ape (l.) plays a flute; a very ill-drawn goat (r) plays a fiddle $5\frac{3}{8} \times 3\frac{3}{8}$ in.

6330 [A COURTSHIP]

Pub^d April 17th 1783 by H Humphrey New Bond Street.

Engraving. The interior of a well-furnished parlour or drawing-room An elderly lady stands (l.) turning her head in profile to the r. towards a man who bends towards her, clasping his hands on his breast in an attitude of supplication, his hat under his l arm. She holds a long stick in her l. hand. The heads of two servants peep through a partly-open door in the back wall Against this wall (r.) appears part of a settee on the back of which two monkeys are crouching. Above it is a framed picture of a man, back view, wearing a hat and long cloak. On the l. wall is an oval mirror in front of which, on a bracket, sits a parrot The floor is covered by a carpet with an arabesque pattern Beneath the design is etched ·

> *Refulgent shine*
> *Goddess benign,*
> *With looks divine,*
> *Tell me thou'rt mine,*
> *Or ah! with Grief I pine.*

Apparently a satire on the courtship of an elderly and wealthy widow. $5\frac{13}{16} \times 4\frac{7}{8}$ in.

6331 THE ROBIN HOOD SOCIETY.

Pub^d May 25. 1783 by W Humphrey. N° 227 Strand.

Engraving. A meeting of this well-known debating society The chairman, on the extreme r , leans over a rostrum looking down at the speaker, Jeffery Dunstan, who stands below him on a low three-legged stool, holding up his l. hand in his wonted attitude, as if crying 'old wigs', knock-kneed, his sack over his l shoulder, with his ragged clothes, open shirt, ungartered stockings, and unlatched shoes, see No 5637 The audience (l) sit or stand facing the chairman in tiers, one above the other. They are all caricatured, and of plebeian appearance, their expressions are either imbecile, sly, or saturnine. On the side of the rostrum is engraved, *Q. to be Debat,d. next Thursday Eve* '*How Far is it from the 1ˢᵗ of Augᵗ to the foot of Westminster Bridge.*

A panelled wall forms the background. In the centre of this is a framed portrait of Jeffery Dunstan, his r. hand raised, wearing a civic chain, and holding a mace, the emblems of his mayoralty of Garrat. The frame is decorated with the arms of the City of London.

This debating society was for long a subject of ridicule, see Nos. 3260, 3539, and 4860, the common accusation being that the members were ignorant, atheistic, and factious tradesmen.

6¼ × 8¼ in.

6332 A SCENE IN GLASGOW, OR—SIR DONALD DICTATE IN THE DUMPS

Pubᵈ Octʳ 17ᵗʰ 1783 by W. Wells, Nᵒ 132 Fleet Street.

Engraving (coloured and uncoloured impressions). A procession of men moving slowly from l to r led by a stout, plainly dressed man holding a thread which is attached to the noses of some of those who follow him, the others being onlookers, except for a man immediately behind the leader. The labels from the mouths of the characters are a prominent part of the design.

The leader, 'Sir Donald', in profile to the r on the extreme r. says, *Damn that mad Fellow I was in hopes he was half way at America by this time, he'll cut my leading strings as sure as a Gun, I'll never medle with a Scotch thistle again aw my Life; I'll lead as lang as I can tho', I have good connections I'll take care none of our house shall give him Consignments, and as his Backs turn'd I'll do everything to hurt him the Edinʳ & Paisley Bank are twa severe cuts also, I wish the Stocks at the Devil· we had no Buissiness we them*
The man behind him, also in profile to the r, holds up the thread, which he is about to cut with a knife. His coat is of military cut. He says, *Poor souls I'll set em all loose I shall always Glory in serving the Town I received my existance in—Damn all Norlands. I fancy he never felt before*

The foremost man with the thread attached to his nose walks with a stick under his arm, saying *I mun een follow him, he set me up here & is my Brother in Law, I have often thought of cutting the string we the knife I got in Virginia. & have thro' necessity kept ever since.* The next man on the string holds out his r. hand saying, *Truth her nain sell man* [? mun] *gang we the Cheild I'm obliged to do every thing he bids me, tho' I could do muckle better without him: I wish he would mind his ayn Bank, he has an excelent house & Sallary, for walking the Cross four hours every Forenoon· I hope ne body ill tell him what I have said: tho' its true* The next man on the thread is thin and lank, his arms hang beside him, the hands thrust in the pockets of his coat, he says *God Folks man* [? mun] *Just do in this World as ether Folks does.*

The last three of the procession walk together, a joint label issuing from all three mouths they say, *Altho' we are convinced he is possessed of no merit sufficient to entitle him to lead mankind, we must at present humor his dictaterial inclination, other way he won't discount our Bills Best hope the day is almost at hand, when his fall will be more rapid then his Rise Memento Paisley Bank Donald* [1]

[1] The four last words in large letters.

Behind the procession stand three spectators. The first (r.), immediately behind the man with the knife, says, *By the Lord Tam I give you credit for that*. A short stout man between (but standing behind) the second and third of those led by the nose, says *Hem Hum A Hem*. The third, near the back of the procession, points with his r forefinger towards 'Sir Donald'. He wears a civic chain round his neck and is saying, *True he has a long Arrangement of followers, I have many more, but do not expose them so much, I flatter their different humours· but he wants the Graces it gives me infinite pleasure that cutting fellow is gone, he had like to have give me a home slice last year; but all blew over when I was in London. Damn the Glasgow Journals*

Beneath the design is inscribed:

> *In pride in reasoning pride his Error lies,*
> *He quites his sphere & rush into the Skies;*
> *Pride is still aiming at the Blest abodes,*
> *Bankers would be Merchants, Merchants, Lords.*
>
> *Who knows but he whose hand the Lightning forms,*
> *Who heaves old Ocean, & who wings the Storms;*
> *Pours fierce ambition, in a Caesars mind;*
> *Or turns young Amon loose, to scourge Mankind.*[1]

$8\frac{3}{8} \times 13\frac{1}{4}$ in

6333 THE MONTGOLSIER [*sic*], A FIRST RATE OF THE FRENCH AERIAL NAVY.

Observator del.   *Recordum Sculpt*

Pub by E. Dachery N. 11 St James Street, the 25 of October 1783

Engraving. A Frenchman, in profile to the l, seated on a globe To the globe are fixed vertical rods, the upper ends of which terminate in four smaller globes which are thus supported above the principal one; chains link these four globes to a fifth globe above, and slightly longer than, the other four On this fifth globe is a child from whose bare posteriors six balls are being projected. On two (r.) of the four globes are the heads of an ass, and of a man wearing a fool's cap; to their jaws are attached reins which are held by the Frenchman whose r hand is extended in the attitude of an orator On the third globe is a monkey's head, which more resembles that of a sheep, the fourth globe is blank The intention of the satire is explained by the inscription beneath the title, *A F——t —— An Ass —— A Fool —— A Monkey —— A Nothing.*

On the large globe on which the aeronaut sits is a cannon, its muzzle projecting upwards and to the l. beyond the contour of the globe. In the centre is the winged head of a bald and bearded man in profile to the l Below is the stern and part of the side of a man-of-war, with cannon projecting from port-holes

This is apparently the first reaction of an English caricaturist to the possibilities of aerial navigation[2] (the phrase was used immediately after the experiments of the brothers Montgolfier, see *Scots Magazine*, 1783, p. 651)

---

[1] It appears strange that so elaborate a print on a matter of, apparently, local interest only should have been published in London. The London newspapers for Oct 1783 throw no light on its subject.

[2] Prints in a similar spirit were issued in France and in Germany, see F. L. Bruel, *Collection de Vinck*, pp. 403 ff., where they are catalogued under 'Les folies du jour'

The first experiment was made at Vivarais on 5 June 1783. This caricature probably relates to the ascent of a balloon from Versailles on 10 Sept. with a wicker cage attached to it in which were a sheep, a cock, and a duck. Faujas de St. Fond, *Description des Expériences de la Machine Aerostatique*, Paris, 1783.

See also Nos 6334, 6335, and for applications of the balloon to political satire,[1] Nos 6275, 6284, 6287, 6288, 6289, 6290.

$11\frac{3}{4} \times 8\frac{5}{8}$ in

6334 THE ASCENT OF THE AERIAL BALLOON

Jn° Lodge sc.

Engraved for the European Magazine
Published Novr 1st 1783, by I. Fielding, Pater Noster Row.

Engraving From the *European Magazine*, iv 272 A completely circular globe to which is attached the handle of a shallow basket containing a cock, a sheep, and a duck It is watched by a group of French spectators, one of whom, a tailor, kneels on the ground holding a pair of shears with which he has just cut the cord of the balloon One man (l.) looks through a telescope, a *petit-maître* (r) looks through an eye-glass. A monk, a jesuit, and a man in a furred robe and cap resembling a magician or quack are among the spectators From a circular tower (r) an ape looks through a telescope, on his r. is an owl wearing bands, on his l. a man wearing a mortar-board cap and bands

In the background small figures run up a hill-side. The print illustrates a paragraph which expresses scepticism of reports that animals and even the inventor, Montgolfier, had ascended into the air See No 6333, &c.

A sequel, *The Descent of the Air-Balloon* (1 Dec), faces p 353 of the *European Magazine*.

$6 \times 3\frac{3}{4}$ in.

6335 THE AIR BALLOON OR A TRIP TO THE MOON.

Publish'd 02th [sic] Novr by W. Humphrey N° 227 Strand.

Engraving. A circular globe floating in the air just above the heads of three standing spectators A witch on a broom-stick (l.) flies with her back to the balloon at which she directs a blast, labelled *Inflammable Air*, from her posteriors; she is suckling a cat which sits on the broom-stick A man standing below (l.) holds a torch in the 'Inflammable Air' saying *How blue it burns* On the r two men look up at the balloon. One, in profile to the l., wearing pigtail queue, looped hat, and ruffled shirt, says *We shall now have a Lunatick Journal* The letters F R S inscribed at his feet show that he is a Fellow of the Royal Society. Behind him is a more plainly dressed man wearing a bob-wig and no hat; he holds up a card saying *I've a card for y^e Georgium Sidus*; he is A S S.

One of a number of satires on balloon-ascents, see No. 6333, &c

The 'Georgium Sidus' was the planet (afterwards renamed Uranus) discovered by Sir W Herschel in 1781 and so named by him in honour of George III. *D.N.B.*

$8\frac{5}{8} \times 13\frac{5}{16}$ in

[1] Ascents to the moon by a kite had been an earlier subject of satire, see No. 4163, *P[itt] and Proteus or a Political Flight to the Moon*, 1766, and No 4212, *A New Flying Machine . . . 1769*.

6336 THE BLESSINGS OF PEACE, OR, PROCLAMATION UPON PROCLAMATION. [1 Dec. 1783]

Engraving. From the *Rambler's Magazine*. A street scene showing some of the noises of a London street In the centre stands a man who appears to have been chased from his house by a virago, who threatens him with a long ladle; on one of his shoulders sits a parrot, on the other a magpie; a child at the woman's side is crying A dustman ringing a large hand-bell shouts *Dust hoa!* A mechanic sharpens a two-handled saw A fish hawker (l.) with one basket of fish on his head and another under his arm calls *Come buy my flounders* A young woman (r) turns the handle of a hurdy-gurdy or vielle which she holds under her arm In the foreground (l) two large dogs are fighting.

Peace was proclaimed in London on 6 Oct., see Nos. 6267, 6351.

$3\frac{1}{2} \times 5\frac{13}{16}$ in.

6337 THE CRIES OF THE CURATES, OR THE GROWING EVIL. [n d *c*. 1783]

Roulette mezzotint A satire on the taking of orders by ex-army officers at the close of the American War. A man stands full-face, dressed half as a military officer, half as a parson His hat, his hair, his shirt, his waistcoat, his breeches, are military on his r. side (the l. side of the print). The darker shading of the dress on his l side indicates a clerical black His r. breeches pocket hangs inside out to show that it is empty. In his r hand he holds a spear, in his l. a book A long label issues from each side of his head; that on the r of the print encloses the words, *Hear me O Lord for I am poor & needy*; that on the l., *and in peace I jogg on to the Devil* By his r side is inscribed *The modern call*, and beneath his feet, *The Reverend Captain Pennyless & many others half dyed and left unfinish'd 178   by   .*

He stands in a landscape between two buildings. on the l is a prison inscribed *Kings Bench*. On the extreme r the corner of a plain four-storied house appears; from the highest window hangs out a flag or sign inscribed, *Dying in all its Branches. The worst Reds dyed Black: or any Colour be it ever so bad; Enquire at the Key and Crook, in S*^{t} *As   h, & at the three Cats-Heads in He . . ford* In the distance (r) among trees is a church, inscribed *Dernier resort*.

On the military side of the soldier-parson is a large paper or scroll obscuring part of the prison; it is inscribed ·

> *No saucy remorse*
> *Intrudes on my course,*
> *Nor impertinent notions of evil,*
> *So there's Claret in store,*
> *In peace I've my Whore*

On the other side (r) an open book, *Trusler's Sermons*, lies on the ground. The Rev John Trusler, see No 5200, published sermons in engraved script to resemble handwriting which could be read in the pulpit and so save the clergy the trouble of either composition or transcription. These were regarded with great disfavour Beneath the title is engraved *To the Most Rev*^{d} *His Grace the Arch-Bishop of Canterbury*.

Beneath the print verses are engraved

With spear & scarlet I'm now deck'd,
And sing a jolly song,
But pennyless I must be wreck'd,
On Limbo's rocks e'er long

But hope I spy from Bishops kind,
Like Lighthouse placed high,
If for to change, I heart can find,
Catches, for Psalmody.

My scarlet coat I then will doff,
For qeue a grizzle wear;
The outward man I will put off,
And prim as Bawd appear.

Away let Oxford Curates trudge
And starve with learning great:
For Bishops ne'er can wrongly judge
Who've palm'd my empty pate.
I Sternhold.

For an explanation of the origin of this print see No. 6338

8×7⅝ in

6338 THE CHURCH MILITANT. [n d , not before 1793]

Engraving, partly mezzotinted and coloured A copy of No 6337, with certain alterations. The label running from the soldier-parson on his r side (the l. of the print) is inscribed *Come Jolly Bacchus God of Wine!*
On the large scroll, in place of 'No saucy remorse ', is a tailor's bill:

March 10th 1783

Sir . . . put off three times . due now near six years, besides two new suits . . bear it no longer . . . not paid by Tuesday next . . will arrest you . . . go to goal for you
Yrs Thos Thimble
To Captn Squander

On the sign, in place of the words St. As - - h, three Cats-Heads, and H - - ford, are marks of cancellation Under the title, in place of the dedication is engraved *See Mr Pennant's literary life P. 21.*
This work, an autobiography, was not published till 1793. In the passage referred to Pennant writes, 'I am a sincere well-wisher to the Church of England . Now and then complaint has been made against the unguarded admission of persons of the most discordant professions into the sacred pale, who, urged by no other call than that of poverty, do not prove either ornamental or useful in their new character. To check the progress of a practice injurious to the Church, and highly so to those who had spent their fortune in a course of education for the due discharge of their duties, I sent a sarcastic, but salutary print into the world. at which even bishops themselves have deigned to smile.'
This passage identifies the 'sarcastic print' with No. 6338
The allusions to St Asaph also indicate Pennant, who took a prominent part in the local affairs of Flintshire, coming into contact with Shipley, Dean of St. Asaph
8×7⅝ in.

6339 MOSES.

Mr Bunbury del.   *J^s Brethertonf*

Publish'd 23^d Jany 1783.

Engraving. A stout, complacent-looking man rides a small horse in profile to the l. He has a very bad seat and is pulling hard on the curb; the animal puts down its head A servant on a rough-looking pony canters behind him, carrying a basket of hay and a triangular box or package (perhaps his master's hat-box) under his l. arm. The scene is a country road, with a signpost (l) pointing *To Hackney, To Islng[ton]*, and (down a turning on the r. of the riders) to *Shoredi[tch]* The post stresses the idea conveyed in the drawing, that this is a citizen riding to or from his country-box in the suburbs

    A companion print to No 6340. See also Nos 5914-17.

$9\frac{1}{4} \times 14$ in

6340 SYMPTOMS OF REARING.

Mr Bunbury del.   *J^s Brethertonf*

Publish'd 23^d Jany 1783

Engraving An elderly country parson, in profile to the r , on a horse which rears almost vertically, he clasps the animal round the neck, and is seated on his hind-quarters, having lost his stirrups and slipped from the saddle His whip flies through the air behind him, his coat-tails fly out, and the sheets of his sermon inscribed *IOB* protrude from his pocket A small dog (l) rushing towards the animal's hind-legs and barking furiously appears to have caused the 'symptoms of rearing'

    The parish clerk, with two large volumes under his arm, beside the horse, looks over his r. shoulder and stoops or runs to escape being trampled on Trees and a church steeple are indicated in the background (r). A similar subject to Nos 5914-17, also by Bunbury.

    A companion print to No 6339

$9\frac{3}{8} \times 14$ in.

6341 ALL FOURS

Design'd by H W Bunbury Esqr [? Rowlandson f.]

Publish'd Mar^h 14th 1783 by J. R Smith N° 83 Oxford Street London

Engraving (coloured and uncoloured impressions). Design in an oval Two men playing cards at a small round table. The man on the r. pulls out an ace of spades from the five cards in his hand and shows it with a grimace of satisfaction His opponent (l), in profile to the r , looks at it with an expression of consternation, frowning and opening his mouth wide. The pack and other cards lie on the table The men are probably portraits The successful player is middle-aged, plainly dressed, with a bob-wig; the other is younger, very thin, and more fashionably dressed, with a long pigtail queue.

    The etching resembles the manner of Rowlandson

$12\frac{5}{8} \times 15\frac{1}{4}$ in

6342 FRONT, SIDE VIEW, AND BACK FRONT, OF A MODERN FINE GENTLEMAN.

[? J. R. Smith *sc.*] *Designed by H. W. Bunbury Esq*

London Publish'd Mar 24*th* 1783 by J. R. Smith N 83 opposite the Pantheon Oxford Street

Crayon engraving. A W.L. satirical portrait of a slim and foppish young man, in three positions. He stands (l.) in profile to the l., his r. hand resting on the head of a high cane and holding a large three-cornered hat. In the centre he stands in back view, his hat under his l. arm, his cane in his r. hand. On the r. he stands full-face, in a rather swaggering pose, cane in his r. hand, hat in his l.

The three attitudes show the fashion of the day. Hair loose and full over the forehead, a horizontal side curl below each ear, and a tightly-bound pig-tail queue. A fitting coat double-breasted at the chest, cut away to show the lower part of a waistcoat ending at the waist; its special feature is an elongated and narrow lapel projecting beyond the shoulders. A ruffled shirt, closely fitting breeches, and low-heeled shoes. In the foreground buildings are indicated.

In a contemporary hand is written on an impression in the Banks Collection, 'Col¹ Gardner vel Col¹ Phipps'. A William Gardiner (1748–1806) was gazetted Lt.-Col. in the 45th Foot on 29 June 1778. Col. Phipps was the Hon. Henry Phipps (1755–1831), gazetted Lt.-Col. of the 88th Connaught Rangers 4 Oct. 1780, afterwards first Earl of Mulgrave. These are the only two colonels of those names in the Army List of 1783 (*Royal Kalendar*), both being men of note, see *D.N.B.*

A companion print to No. 6343.

Frankau, p. 102.

$8\frac{7}{16} \times 9\frac{3}{4}$ in.

6343 THE INFLEXIBLE PORTER. A TRAGEDY.

Design'd by H. W. Bunbury Esq

London Published Mar 24*th* 1783 by J. R. Smith N 83 opposite y^e Pantheon Oxford Street

Crayon engraving. The roofed gateway of a great man's house. In front of an archway (l.) through which appears a staircase, an obese porter stands in profile to the r., lifting up both hands to show the impossibility of access to his master. He is addressing a would-be visitor, middle-aged and stout, who faces him with an insinuating smile, hat in hat, pointing with his r. hand towards his companion, a slim young man (r.), who stands full-face, his r. hand in his breeches pocket. The young man is dressed like, and resembles, the *Modern Fine Gentleman* in No. 6342, a companion print. His r. hand is in his breeches pocket, his l., holding his hat, rests on the head of his tall cane.

$8\frac{1}{2} \times 9\frac{1}{2}$ in.

6343 A A later impression with the additional publication line:

London pub by S. W. Fores 41 Piccadilly

6344 ST JAMES'S PARK

[After Bunbury.]

*London Publish'd as the Act directs Nov' 30ᵗʰ 1783 by J Wallis Nᵒ 16
Ludgate Street & E Hedges Nᵒ 92 under the Royˡ Exchange Cornhill
Price 2ˢ 6ᵈ plain.*

Engraving. The humours of a promenade in St James's Park · a number
of figures, walking under trees. The central group consists of those watching a lady meeting an elderly beau. She walks in profile to the r. followed
by a little black boy carrying one of her dogs, another, lifting a paw, gazes
up at the beau. She walks with a cane and is dressed in masculine fashion,
with round hat, cut-away coat, showing a shirt-frill, and a plain skirt. He
bows low, holding his hat in his hand, and wears a sword. A young woman
holding up a small parasol, stands between them. Other walkers stare and
point at the lady, an elderly man (r), with an ugly old woman hanging to
his arm and scolding violently, looks through his glass.

On a seat (l.) a fat citizen is asleep, his wife sitting next him has two
children on her lap. At the other end of the bench is a young man reading
a book. On the extreme l a stout man carrying his wig and suffering from
the heat, walks in profile to the r. In the foreground (l.) some children play
with a peg-top. On the extreme r. a bare-footed little boy begs from a man
who raises his cane in a threatening manner

Reproduced, Paston, Pl xxxii.

14½×24⅞ in.   Crace Collection, Portfolio xii, No 94.

6345 A TRIP TO SCARBOROUGH

Jˢ Bretherton f.

Publish'd 3ᵈ March 1783. by James Bretherton.

Engraving. A group of people, strung out in a line, standing on the cliffs
at Scarborough

On the extreme edge of the cliffs (r.) stand two gentlemen gazing at the
view, the nearer holds his hat in his hand, and looks up as if absorbing the
sea air. Slightly behind are two ladies, one with an arrangement of lace
and ribbons on the summit of a very high pyramid of hair, the other with
a calash hood concealing her equally high head-dress. Next come two
quite young ladies talking to each other, one with a calash hood, the other
with a large hat tilted forwards on her pyramid of hair. Next are two
children a very little girl stands between the older child and the young
lady with a hat, reaching up an arm towards each.

The next couple are an elderly lady in a calash hood and a pretty young
lady elaborately dressed, who looks coyly down and away from the addresses
being paid her by a man who stands behind the elder of the two children.
Another man, apparently a disappointed rival, turns his back. Behind, on
the extreme l, are a gentleman and lady, both in riding-dress, her arm
through his, with discontented expressions.

The landscape shows the line of the bay with cliffs and rising moor behind
—no building is visible. For the calash hood see No. 5433, &c

Apparently unconnected with Sheridan's play of the same title

7⅛×16⅛ in

6346 WHITSUNTIDE HOLIDAYS.

Printed for & Sold by Carington Bowles, N⁰ 69 in St Pauls Church Yard, London.

Published as the Act directs, 4th June, 1783.

Engraving. A large coach, the roof overcrowded with passengers, is driven (r to l.) along a country road The coach is a double one with two sets of doors and windows but four wheels, somewhat resembling the earliest railway carriages Each door-panel is inscribed *Greenwich to Charing Cross.* The inside passengers are relatively quiet, the outside ones noisy and rollicking, many of them poised precariously on the edge of the roof. An elderly woman in the front part of the coach holds a cord attached to the neck of a dog which she drags along the road, the animal trying to resist and planting its four feet on the ground, this amuses the other inside passengers who look out of the window at the dog

Sixteen people are visible on the roof of the coach, among them a recruiting party: a man wearing epaulettes and a feathered hat stands up, holding out a paper, *All able bodied Men willing to serve King George*; in his l. hand is a sabre. One of Dr. Graham's gigantic porters, see No 5766, wearing the well-known large laced hat, holds out towards the recruiting officer one of Graham's hand-bills, inscribed *Dr Graham* in large letters. His profile resembles that of 'Magog' in No 6325 Other soldiers are playing instruments: a man seated behind the driver blows a horn, a man sitting next him plays the fiddle, a man seated on the edge of the coach, his legs dangling over the windows, plays the fife; another on the back edge of the roof beats a drum A sailor holds up a rough flag tied to a pole, inscribed *Rodney for Ever* Another sailor, on the extreme edge of the coach, fondles a woman who sits beside him A woman, dangerously balanced, attends to an infant which is held across her lap. A man loses his hat. A young boy, sitting on the front of the coach, leans over to embrace a woman seated on the box seat beside the driver. On a platform between the back wheels a man seated on a trunk is taking a pinch of snuff.

The coach is drawn by three horses, heavily-built animals, but very small in proportion to the coach On the road, which has a foot-path with posts to protect pedestrians, stands a beggar (l.) supported on crutches and holding out his hat towards the coach; the driver flicks at him with his whip. A man in naval uniform sits by the road-side, holding a bundle and a knotted stick. Clouds of dust rise from the wheels and the horses' hoofs. In the middle distance, on the extreme l , is a toll-gate by which stand a man on horseback and a pedestrian Two sailors, wearing trousers and round hats, canter towards the gate on a small horse or pony A rural landscape of undulating ground with trees forms the background

$12\frac{5}{8} \times 18\frac{11}{16}$ in.

THE RAPACIOUS QUACK (N⁰ 2)   See No 3798—[c 1783-8]

Stipple by J. Baldrey after a picture by E Penny exhibited at the Royal Academy in 1782 Not a copy of No. 3797.

A companion design to No. 6347.

6347 THE BENEVOLENT PHYSICIAN.   [*c.* 1783][1]

E Penny Pinxit   *J. Baldrey Sculpsit*

Stipple   After a picture exhibited by E. Penny at the Royal Academy,
1782. A companion design to No 3798. The interior of an artist's studio
showing no sign of poverty   The physician, a young man, is walking from
the room (l to r) followed by the artist's wife, a well-dressed and comely
middle-aged woman, who offers him a coin which he refuses to take.
Through a door (l) is seen an inner room, with a man seated, leaning his
elbow on a table on which are a phial of medicine and a bowl. On the lintel
of the door is a classical bust   On an easel behind the doctor is a canvas
with a sketch (H.L) of a woman holding an infant. Canvases stand against
the wall (r.); a portfolio leans against a chair. Two pictures are hung high
on the r wall

   Cf No. 6350.

11¾×9½ in   'Caricatures', iii 183. B.M.L. Tab 524.

Seven prints from the series of mezzotints published by
Carington Bowles.

6348 INTELLIGENCE ON THE CHANGE OF THE MINISTRY.

[? After R. Dighton.]

477. *Printed for Bowles & Carver, at their Map & Print Warehouse,
    N° 69 in S* *Paul's Church Yard, London. Published as the Act
    directs,* [date erased, *c* April 1783]

Mezzotint (coloured impression). Interior of a poorly-appointed barber's
shop. The barber (l) is shaving a customer who sits in profile to the l.
facing the window, he holds his razor carelessly, to his customer's alarm,
while looking eagerly towards another customer, who sits (r.) on a stool in
profile to the l., reading from the *Morning Chronicle*. The barber's assistant
or apprentice, a small ragged fellow, gapes up at the reader, he straddles
across the stand of a barber's block on which is the wig which he is combing.
Two other customers listen intently, both wear aprons, one of them is a
shoemaker with a last under his arm. The man reading is shown to be
a tailor by the yard-measure which hangs from his coat-pocket.

   On the wall hang coat, hat, wig, a broken looking-glass, a ballad, a
roller-towel   In the window wigs are suspended   On the floor are two
wig-boxes (l), inscribed *M* *Deputy Grizzle* and *M* *Snipp*, a barber's
bowl, and a night-cap

   The Coalition is evidently under discussion. One of the many satires
on the intense interest taken by mechanics and tradesmen in politics. Cf.
No 6351, a companion print.

12⅞×9⅞ in.   'Caricatures', i. 52 B M.L , Tab 524.

6349 TWO PRIVATEERS ATTACKING A MAN OF WAR.

482. *Printed for & Sold by Carington Bowles, at his Map & Print
    Warehouse, N° 69 in S* *Pauls Church Yard, London Published as
    the Act directs* [date erased, *c.* 1783]

Mezzotint (coloured impression). A military officer in uniform, in profile

_____
[1] The publication line appears to have been cut off.

to the l., between two courtesans, each of whom holds him by an arm. He wears a gorget, riding-boots, and spurs The women are elaborately dressed in the fashion of the day, wearing large hats over muslin caps. Trees form the background, with an elderly man (r) walking in profile to the r. On the l is the back of a seat, behind which is an officer in back view The scene is perhaps St. James's Park, where such encounters were said to be common.

$12\frac{15}{16}\times9\frac{2}{8}$ in.   'Caricatures', i. 19. B.M.L., Tab. 524

6350 THE BENEVOLENT PHYSICIAN.   [1783]

486. Printed for & Sold by Carington Bowles at N° 69 in St Paul's Church Yard, London

Published as the Act directs [date erased]

Mezzotint (coloured impression). The interior of a room showing no trace of actual poverty. The invalid, a man, fully dressed but wearing a night-cap, sits in an upholstered arm-chair by the fire. A little girl stands at his knee; at his side on a tray or table are two bowls and a medicine bottle labelled *as before*

The physician, a well-dressed man wearing a bag-wig, is about to leave the room (r), he puts coins into the hand of a young woman holding an infant

The room is papered, a half-tester bed with curtains stands against the wall. Tea-things are ranged along the chimney-piece, over which is a framed picture of a Biblical (?) subject

Beneath the title is engraved:

> *The Benevolent Physician takes no Fee.*
> *Of those that need him much in Poverty.*
> *To Poor distress'd, and those of small estate*
> *He Money gives, takes only of the great.*

A companion design to No 3797.
The subject and the title are probably imitated from Nos. 6347, 3798 There is, however, no similarity in design

$12\frac{3}{4}\times9\frac{3}{4}$ in   'Caricatures', i 58 B.M L , Tab. 524.

THE RAPACIOUS QUACK (487)   See No 3797—[1783]

6351 INTELLIGENCE ON THE PEACE.

[? After R. Dighton.]

495 Printed for & Sold by Carington Bowles, at his Map & Print Warehouse, N° 69 in St Pauls Church Yard London. Published as the Act directs, [date erased, c. Oct. 1783]

Mezzotint (coloured impression). A London street, a cobbler reading the *Gazette* to a group of intent listeners. He stands outside his bulk or stall, which is protected by a penthouse projecting from the stone wall of a building on which are pasted a number of placards, conspicuous among which is one headed *Proclamation of Peace*, and ending *God Save the King* A street-lamp projects from the wall on a bracket, against this rests a ladder (l.) on which stands a man who is about to insert the oil-container

and wick which his assistant below is supposed to be filling The latter, however, is watching the cobbler so intently that he pours the oil on to the ground instead of into the lamp Facing the cobbler and looking up at him is a little chimney-sweep, his bag and brushes over his shoulder. A short stout man, carrying a basket, puts out his tongue at the reader. The other listeners are a baker with a cylindrical basket of bread on his back, a barber carrying a wig-box inscribed *Mr Thos Tipple*, and a scowling man whose head and shoulders only are visible. The cobbler has a pair of top-boots and another boot tucked under his arm, lasts and boots are hung up over his stall, over which is a board inscribed, TRISTRAM AWL *Boote & Showe Maćer Likewise Corns Cut in the neteest manner at home & abrode.* The placards over the stall include an advertisement of Katerfelto, see No. 6326, &c., which is headed by a print (torn) of a rider on horseback below an angel and a devil, a notice of the *Royal Circus* with *Mr Hughes* in large letters; a *Cock Fighting* placard headed by a design of two cocks fighting, a proclamation headed by the royal arms, and a notice offering a *Reward.*

The theme is the favourite one of the illiterate working man who concerns himself with State affairs to the neglect of his business, cf. No. 6351, a companion design The print is a good representation of a London street scene, and shows the lamp-lighting method of the period The lamplighter standing below the ladder has a large can on the ground, a small can for filling the lamps, a bunch of lamp-wicks, and a pair of scissors tucked into his belt. In the background (r.) are high brick houses and a church spire

The *Gazette* containing the announcement that peace had been signed was that of 6–9 Sept. 1783 Peace was formally proclaimed in London on 6 Oct., after which the proclamation was 'stuck up in divers parts'. *London Mag*, 1783, p. 363. See also Nos 6267, 6336.

12⅞×9¹³⁄₁₆ in.   'Caricatures', i. 53. B.M.L., Tab. 524.

Another impression, uncoloured, publication line cut off.

6352 A REAL SCENE IN St PAULS CHURCH YARD, ON A WINDY DAY.

[After R. Dighton]

504. Printed for & sold by Carington Bowles, No 69 in St Pauls Church Yard, London Published as the Act directs [date erased, c. 1783]

Mezzotint (coloured and uncoloured impressions) Street-scene, outside the print-shop of Carington Bowles. Foot-passengers are having their hats and wigs blown off, their garments blown violently, by a gust of wind In the foreground a boy wearing an apron has fallen to the ground, his tray of fish is under the feet of a lady who walks from r. to l , holding her hat, a muff in her l hand, her hair, cloak, and petticoats streaming behind her A stout woman in profile farther to the r tries to catch her wig and hat which have blown from her head, she wears a cloak trimmed with ermine. Other walkers clutch and lose their hats with expressions of anger

Behind (l.), each of twenty-eight panes of the shop-window is occupied by a print, as in No. 3758 (1774), another view of this shop, the margins being displayed, and the titles almost legible The top row consists of seven prints of divines, in which, as in 3758, well-known mezzotint portraits of John Wesley and Whitefield are conspicuous. The other prints are humorous, among them are Nos. 3753, 3754 (1782), 5953 (these three are partly cut off by the l margin of the print), 5951, 5952, 5954, 5955, 5956, 6348

Over the shop window, partly cut off by the upper edge of the design, is the name of the shop, [. . *Map & Prin]t Warehouse*, in large letters.

On the r appears the door of the adjoining house, inscribed *68*, with its railings and part of the front of the house

The original water-colour for this is in the Victoria and Albert Museum, reproduced E B Chancellor, *The Eighteenth Century in London*, 1920, frontispiece.

13×9⅞ in.   Crace Collection. 'Caricatures', i. 30, Tab. 524.

THE CONTRAST (507)   See No 3757—[*c.* 1783-4]

[After R. Dighton.]

A Frenchman and an Englishman disputing over the outcome of the recent war.

ADDENDA TO VOL. V

PERSONAL SATIRES

6353 [SUB-PORTER & LAMP-LIGHTER OF TRIN. COLL. CAMB
1771][1]

Topham fecit 1771

Engraving. A man walking in profile to the r. carrying a ladder resting
horizontally on his l shoulder. In his r hand is an oil-can.
$7\frac{3}{8} \times 5\frac{1}{4}$ in.

6354 [CREAM-WOMAN OF TRIN. COLL. CAMBR.] [1771][1]

Topham fecit

Engraving. A stout and ugly woman walking (l. to r.) in profile carrying
in her r. hand a pot or pail. She wears a flat wide-brimmed hat over a hood,
and an apron (torn).
$4\frac{1}{16} \times 2\frac{5}{8}$ in. (pl).

6355 [A CAMBRIDGE WOMAN-SERVANT?] [*c.* 1771]

Topham inven: et fecit

Engraving. W L portrait, slightly caricatured, of a woman similar in type
to No 6354. She walks (l to r), holding in her r. hand a pair of unlatched
shoes without buckles, in her l a pot, perhaps a blacking-pot, similar to
that of the cream-woman, but smaller.
$7\frac{7}{16} \times 5\frac{3}{8}$ in. (pl.)

6356 [VOCAL AND INSTRUMENTAL MUSIC IN A CHURCH]
[*c.* 1777.]

Mortimer del   L Bates fec[t]

Engraving. The musicians' gallery of a large church, the vocalists being
divided by a barrier from the instrumentalists who sit below and in front
of them. The musicians, whose heads and shoulders only are visible, are
probably caricature-portraits. Thirteen vocalists, crowded together, are
singing from music-books. The instrumentalists are lettered to show their
nationalities: a man, wearing a hat and holding a horn, who sits farthest l
is inscribed *Prussia*. Next him a stout elderly man holding a 'cello or double-
bass is *Ger*, he is possibly intended for Abel. Next are an oboist and a
flautist blowing their instruments. Between them is the head of an elderly
man wearing spectacles. Music-books in front of these three are inscribed
Ital and *Swiss*. Farthest r. is an old man in profile to the r., who appears
to be seated at a harpsichord which is not shown. He is *Engl*, and his
profile suggests that he is Dr. Arne.
  Behind the vocalists the pipes of an organ are indicated, and on the
extreme l sits a parson or clerk asleep. In the background (r) is the body
of the church: the heads of a male congregation are indicated, behind and

---

[1] Written on the print in an old hand

783

above them is a gallery in which are seated rows of ladies, their hair in the exaggerated inverted pyramid fashionable 1776–8, cf. No. 5370, &c. The design probably satirizes (*inter alia*) the employment of foreign musicians, a favourite theme. Apparently a companion print to No. 6357.

$8\frac{1}{2} \times 11$ in.

6357 [GROUP OF SATIRICAL PORTRAITS.]   [*c.* 1777]

Mortimer del. L. Bates fec[t]

Engraving. Figures grouped on each side of a central post or terminal which supports a small circular platform. The summit of the post is decorated with the heads of Comedy in profile to the l., of Tragedy in profile to the r.; between them is the head of a satyr. On the platform a kneeling female figure supports a large medallion with the head of Shakespeare (or perhaps Ben Jonson) in relief.

The two central figures are an elderly man (l.) seated with his legs crossed, fingers held together, who resembles Dr. Johnson. On the r. of the post sits a stout and aged man, in gown and bands, without a wig; he is asleep and is inscribed *A Fellow of Maudlin*. Farthest r., and in profile to the r., is an elderly man holding a large volume under his arm; he wears a handkerchief or turban twisted round his head, and may be intended for an artist. These three are T.Q.L. figures. Behind them fourteen other persons are grouped, whose heads or heads and shoulders alone are visible. All are men except for one sharp-featured elderly woman in profile to the r., wearing a frilled cap. One man clutches his forehead and may be intended for an actor; another reads a book with a scowl of concentration.

Apparently a companion print to No. 6356. The figure of Dr. Johnson resembles a figure in No. 4247, *The Reviewers Cave* (1768), which is also in the manner of Mortimer, and is inscribed in an old hand 'etch'd by Mortimer'; it is, however, attributed by Mr. Stephens to de Loutherbourg.

$11\frac{1}{16} \times 8\frac{1}{2}$ in.

6358 [NO TITLE.]

J. H. Mortimer del[t] Sam[l]: Ireland fecit.   [n.d.]

Engraving. Two figures perhaps associated accidentally from juxtaposition on the page of a sketch-book. A grotesquely obese nude man (l.) pushes, l. to r., a wheelbarrow which supports his stomach. He wears a turban with an aigrette, and has a Semitic profile. This was a traditional subject in caricature, see No. 5433.

An oafish-looking youth (r.) wearing the exaggerated buttons fashionable in 1777, see No. 5432, &c., stands looking towards the man with the wheelbarrow. He holds a round hat in his l. hand, a cane or riding-whip is under his r. arm. His dress, though fashionable, is slovenly, his coat is wrinkled, his hair ill dressed, and his attitude is slouching. His feet are cut off by the lower margin of the print.

Prints after Mortimer (d. 1779) were etched by S. Ireland between 1780–5.

$6\frac{7}{8} \times 9$ in.

6359 A PUFF OFF. [? 1781]

[J. Sayers]

Engraving. Eliza Farren (l.) as Almeida, and Bensley as Omar (r.), in 'The Fair Circassian' face each other in profile. She bends towards him, clasping her hands; he stands erect holding out his r. hand towards her. He holds in his l. hand the end of a chain which is attached to his r. wrist. Almeida's body from the waist upwards is not attached to her voluminous petticoats. Omar has a beard, he wears a feathered hat or turban and an ermine-bordered robe over a tunic. Beneath the figures are etched the words spoken by them· Almeida says,

> *Omar methinks I rose above my sex*
> *Now Almoran half the human form is thine*
> *I'm off*

Omar answers,

> *Puff'd off you mean for God's sake Miss go on*
> *Don't take such tragic flights but mind your Cue*

Beneath the title is etched, *To the greatest of all great Tragedy Writers This rude sketch of a new scene for the Fair Circassian is most respectfully offerered by his most obed hble Serv[t] JS*

S. J Pratt's tragedy of 'The Fair Circassian', founded on Hawkesworth's novel, *Almoran and Hamet*, was first played at Drury Lane on 27 Nov. 1781, with Eliza Farren and Bensley as Almeida and Omar. See Genest, vi 214-15, and *Town and Country Magazine*, xiii, pp. 619 ff.

11 × 14¼ in.

6359A. A later impression: the plate reduced along the lower edge removing the inscription. Across the upper part of the design is etched:

> *A moving Scene in the Fair Circassian*
> *a woeful Tragedy written by Mr. Pratt*
> *So Bensley stared with all his Might*
> *E'en till his Eye-ball started*
> *So Farren flew to meet his Sight*
> *But she had laced herself so tight*
> *Her Top and Bottom parted.*

A detached eye, representing Bensley's r eye, has been added to the l. of his profile.

6360 [UNIDENTIFIED PORTRAIT] [n d.]

Engraving (coloured impression). Bust portrait of a man in profile to the l. His mouth is open, and he has a long upper lip and small receding chin. Similar in character to No 6306. Cropped

3⅞ × 3⅛ in. (pl).

APPENDIX

KEY TO THE DATES OF THE SERIES OF MEZZOTINTS ISSUED BY CARINGTON BOWLES[1]

THE dates have in general been erased from the prints; in reissues by Bowles and Carver they appear to have been burnished from the plate. As the series was numbered consecutively impressions which are both numbered and dated are a guide to the approximate dates of the rest of the series.

In many cases reduced versions of these prints were issued, also in a numbered but shorter series. The dates of these are sometimes identical with those of the larger version, sometimes later and occasionally earlier

Bowles's No.	Date	Title	Catalogue No.	
248	17 Apr. 1772	English Gentleman at Paris	4516	Vol. IV
260	19 Nov 1772	How d'ye like me?	4522	,,
273	19 Jan 1773	Docking the Macaroni	4527	,,
283	29 May 1773	Irish Peg in a Rage	4531	,,
286	13 July 1773	Old Beau in an Extasy	4532	,,
293	8 Feb 1774	Portrait of Harriet Lady Grosvenor, engr. Dickinson	—	—
300	25 June 1774	Spectators at a Print Shop	3758	Vol. III, Part II
306	12 Oct 1774	New Method of Macarony Making. Not in B M., see under	5232	Vol. V
—	20 Oct. 1774	Exhibition of Wild Beasts	4580	Vol IV
—	2 Jan. 1775	Unexpected Levee for a new married couple	4581	,,
323	3 Aug. 1775	Portrait of George III	—	—
332	20 Oct. 1775	Search the World . . .	4542	Vol. IV
344	25 Oct. 1776	Sleight of Hand by a Monkey	4546	,,
352	25 June 1777	Six Weeks after Marriage	4549	,,
365	10 Nov. 1777	Bachelor's Fare	4553	,,
366	10 Nov. 1777	Amorous Thief	4554	,,
368	10 Nov. 1777	Father Paul Disturbed . . .	3782	Vol. III, Part II
370	1 Jan. 1778	Miss Wicket and Miss Trigger	4666	Vol IV
373	1 Jan. 1778	Morning Visit	5532	Vol. V
393	1 Jan. 1779	Summer	4565	Vol. IV
395	1 Jan. 1779	Winter	4567	,,
308	15 Sept. 1779	Church Militant	3752	Vol. III, Part II
413	6 Jan 1780	Contemplative Charmer	5815	Vol. V
416	25 Mar. 1780	Morning Frolic (not in B M)	—	—

[1] See pp 48, 104–7, 158–9, 191, 215, 245, 278–9, 316–17, 366–7, 489–93, 551–6, 664–7, 779–82

Bowles's No.	Date.	Title.	Catalogue No.	
417	12 Apr. 1780	Pleasures of Skaiting	5818	Vol V
418	12 Apr 1780	Pretty Waterwoman . . .	5819	,,
422	15 May 1780	Triple Plea	3761	Vol. III, Part II
428	2 Sept. 1780	Foolish Woman	5824	Vol. V
433	1 May 1781	Fielding's Myrmidons ..	5947	,,
465	9 Nov. 1781	Fleet of Transports	5957	,,
466	2 Jan. 1782	Lesson Westward	6155	,,
474	20 May 1782	Barber riding to Margate	6158	,,
495	After 6 Oct. 1783	Intelligence on the Peace	6351	,,
542	9 Nov. 1784	Pit Door		(Vol. VI)

To be continued in Vol VI.

INDEX OF PERSONS

Persons depicted, mentioned or alluded to in the prints are included, but not persons mentioned only in the explanatory notes (other than conjectural or alternative identifications). An asterisk denotes a foreign print.

---

[1] Date uncertain

[1] Date uncertain
[2] Probably not a personal caricature but merely an illustration to *Tristram Shandy*

[1] Date uncertain.

¹ Date uncertain.

[1] Date uncertain

[1] Date uncertain

[1] Date uncertain

[1] Date uncertain.

[1] Date uncertain.

3 F

[1] Date uncertain

[1] Date uncertain.

[1] Date uncertain

[1] Date uncertain.

[1] Date uncertain.

INDEX OF TITLES

For portraits where the title is the name of the subject see Index of Persons
An asterisk denotes a foreign print

INDEX OF SELECTED SUBJECTS

Political events are not indexed; they will be found under the appropriate dates and by the cross-references there given.

AMERICA 1770: 4839, 4842. 1771: 4864. 1772: 4964.[1] 1774. 5225, 5226, 5227, 5228, 5530, 5231, 5232, 5236, 5238, 5241, 5242, 5244 1775: 5281, 5282, 5283, 5284, p 196, p. 197, 5285, 5286, 5287, 5288, 5289, 5290, 5291*, 5292, 5292 A*, 5292 B, 5293, 5294, 5295, 5296, 5296 A*, 5297, 5298. 1776 p. 216, 5328, 5329, 5330, 5331, 5331 A*, 5332, 5332 A*, 5333, 5334, 5335, 5336*, 5337*, 5338, 5339*, 5340, 5342, 5343. 1777: 5397, 5399, 5400, 5401, 5402, 5403, 5404, 5405, 5405A*, 5406, 5406A*, 5407*, 5408. 1778: 5469, 5469 A*, 5470, 5472, p. 286*, 5473, 5474, p 288, 5475, p. 289, pp 289–90*, 5476, 5477, 5482, 5483, 5485, 5486, 5487, 5490*, 5491*, 5492, 5493, 5494, 5495, 1779: 5540, 5541, 5548, 5549, 5557, 5567, 5568, 5569, 5573, 5574, 5578, 5579, 5580, 5581*, pp 349–50*, 5603, 5613, 5614. 1780: 5624, 5629, 5631, 5636, 5640, 5641, 5644, 5645, 5647, 5649, 5653, 5659, 5663, 5667, 5675, 5691*, 5699, 5704, 5706, 5707, 5711*, 5715*, 5716*, 5719,* 5721*, 5724*, 5725*, 5726*, 5726 A*, 5726 B*, 5726 C*, 5727*, p 451*, 5728*, 5729*, 5731*, 5732*, 5733* 1781: 5827, p 496*, 5828, 5831, 5832, 5833, 5834, 5837, 5839*, 5850, 5853, 5855, 5856, 5857*, 5858*, 5859*, 1782: 5961, 5973, 5982, 5984, 5985, 5986, 5987, 5988, 5989, 6004, 6008, 6009, 6024, 6029, 6039, 6040, 6047, 6048*, 6049*, 6050, 6051. 1783 6162, 6168, 6171, 6172, 6173, 6174, 6182, 6184, 6190, 6200,[1] 6202, 6206, 6207, 6207 A, 6210, 6212, 6223, 6229, 6257, 6267, 6274, 6282, 6288, 6291 *See* PAUL JONES, LAFAYETTE

ART · Artists, architects, connoisseurs and antiquarians 1771: 4632, 4683, 4685, 4601, 4770. 1772: 4692, 5031, 4701, 4771, 5089, 4582, 4520. 1773: 5157, 5159, 5160, 5166, 5220, 4772. 1774: 2008, 3758 1775: 5318. 1776: 5367, 4621 1780: 5757, 5770. 1781: 5897, 5898, 5903, 5912, 5921 1782: 6102, 6104, 6129 1783: 6352

AUCTIONS AND AUCTIONEERS 1771: 4770. 1772: 5001, 5066. 1773: 5171. 1780: 5651 (political). 1781: 5842 (political) 1782: 6101

AUSTRIA 1771: 4388 1772: 4957. 1774: 5222, 5229 1780: 5643, 5711*

BALLOONS 1783: 6275, 6284, 6287(6), 6288, 6289, 6290, 6333, 6334, 6335

BILLIARDS 1773: 4667. 1780: 5795, 5803 1781: 5913

CAMBRIDGE· University, Colleges, &c. 1771: 6353, 6354, 6355. 1772: 4999, 4723, 4725 1773: 5187, 5188, 5189, 4728, 4726. 1774: 4727 1777: 4729. 1778: 5510. 1780. 5804. 1781: 5893

CARD PLAYING 1773: 4728, 4824. 1777: 5453 1778: 5515. 1779: 5617. 1781: 5889. 1782: 6098. 1783: 6341. *See* GAMBLING

CLERICAL the church and clergy 1771: 4866. 1772: 4944, 4948, 4951, 4972, 4997, 5003, 5021, 5068, 5070, 5075, 4725, 3789. 1773: 5107, 5125, 5161, 5188, 5189, 5193, 4827, 4611, 4726, 4533. 1774: 5228, 5233, 4618 1775: 3784, 3760, 3785 1776: 5343 [1] 1777: 5400, 6356,[1] 5447, 5465 1778: 5492,[1] 5496, 5520, 4780 1779:

[1] Date uncertain

¹ Date uncertain. ² Direct satires on costume

[1] Date uncertain.

[1] Date uncertain.

¹ Date uncertain.

[1] Date uncertain.

INDEX OF ARTISTS

No distinction is made between draughtsman and engraver. Doubtful and conjectural attributions are included.

A , I. or J. 1772: 5060

A——o. H. 1781: 5934

ADAMS, Francis Edward[1] 1774: 4783

ASTLE, Daniel 1776· 5366

AUSTIN, William[2] (1721–1820) 1773: 5112, 5113, 5114, 5115, 5116, 5117, 5118, 5119, 5120, 5121, 5122, 5123. 1778: 5528. 1780: 5772, 5773, 5774, 5775, 5776, 5777[3]

B., E. 5793[3]

B., Eliz 1772: 5009. *See* GULSTON, Elizabeth

B , I or J. *See* BOYNE

B., S. 1782: 6020, 6044 *See* GILLRAY

B., S. 1783: 6262, 6319

BALDREY, Joshua Kirby (1754–1828) 1780: 5673. 1781: 5878, 5918. 1783: 3798, 6347

BAMFYLDE, Coplestone Warre (d 1791) 1776: 5385, 5386, 5387, 5388, 5389, 5390

BANNERMAN, Alexander (b. *c.* 1730, d. after 1780) 1771: 4600

BARROW, J [4] *See* index of publishers No. 6278 (1783) is by the same artist

BARTOLOZZI, Francesco (1727–1815) 1771: 4870, 4871, 4872, 4873 1780: 5769. 1781: 5905, 5906, 5910, 3799. 1782: 5983, 6005

BATES, L. 6356,[3] 6357[3]

BLAND 1771: 4864

BONNOR, T. (worked *c.* 1763–1807) 1772: 4941

BOYNE, John[1] (1750–1810) 1783: 6184, 6203, 6206, 6221, 6231, 6242, 6243, 6281, 6285, 6323

BRAN, R. 1780: 5694. 1782: 6134

BRANDOIN, Michel-Vincent (Charles) (1733–90) 1771: 4922, 4601, 4923, 4924, 4925, 4931, 4932, 4933. 1772: 5081, 4603, 5082, 5089, 5091

BRETHERTON, Charles[1] (1760–July 1783) 1772: 4739, 4740, 4756, 4722, 5087. 1780: 5759[3] 1781: 5879, 5880, 5881, 5882, 5883, 5884, 5885, 5886, 5887, 5888, 5889. 1782: 5960, 6090, 6091, 6092, 6093. 1783: 6317[3]

BRETHERTON, James[1] (b. *c.* 1750) 1772: 4649, 5083, 4757, 4738, 4753, 4669, 4712, 4713, 4725, 4723, 4755, 4714, 5084, 5085, 5086. 1773: 5213, 5214, 5215, 5216, 5217, 5218, 4758, 4759, 4728, 4726, 4716, 4721, 4748, 4749, 4762. 1774: 5279, 4727, 4747, 4735, 4741, 4720 1777: 4719, 4717, 4730, 4731, 4729 1778: 5510, 4732. 1779: 4736, 4737,[3] 4760. 1780· 5802 1781: 5913, 5925, 5926, 5927. 1782: 6094, 6139, 6140, 4761, 4185, 6142. 1783: 6339, 6340, 6345

BROOKSHAW, Richard (*c* 1736–1800) 1779· 5561

BUNBURY, Henry William (1750–1811) 1771: 4668, 4670, 4673, 4913, 4674, 4675, 4677, 4782, 4679, 4680, 4681, 4918, 4919, 4764, 4633, 4920, 4921,[3] 4767. 1772: 4648, 5056, 5083, 4757, 4738, 4753, 4669, 4712, 4713, 4725, 4723, 4755, 4714, 5084, 5085, 5086, 4715, 4739, 4740, 4756, 4722, 4742, 4734, 4752, 5087. 1773: 5213, 5214, 5215, 5216, 5217, 5218, 4758, 4759, 4728, 4726, 4716, 4721, 4748, 4749, 4762. 1774: 5279, 4727,

---

[1] See Index of Publishers.
[2] See Index of Persons.
[3] Date uncertain
[4] John Barrow, jeweller, b 1758, drew and scraped a self-portrait to illustrate *Poems*, 1813 (B. M. L 993 b. 3.) The rambling account he gives of his life makes his identity with J Barrow unlikely.

4747, 4735, 4741, 4720. 1775: 5313 1777: 4719, 4717, 4730,[1] 4731,[1] 4729. 1778: 5511, 4732. 1779: 4736, 4737,[1] 4760, 4765, 5620.[1] 1780: 4766, 5802, 5803, 5804, 5805,[1] 5806[1] 1781: 5878, 5901, 5913, 5914, 5915, 5916, 5917, 5918, 5919, 5920, 5921, 5922, 5923, 5924, 5925, 5926, 5927. 1782: 6139, 6140, 4761, 6141, 4185, 6142, 6143, 6144, 6145, 6146. 1783: 6193, 6313, 6339, 6340, 6341, 6342, 6343, 6344

BURNET (? political pseudonym), *see* K. B.

CALDWALL, James (1739–1819) 1771: 4923, 4925, 4595, 4599, 4600, 4932. 1772: 4603, 4602, 5082, 4612, 4605 1773: 4607. 1774: 4616

CAMPBELL, Alexander (fictitious) 1775: 5290, 5291. *c.* 1776: 5338

CAREY, P. or W. P. 1780: 5685, 5707. 1783: 6179, 6291

COCHIN, Charles Nicolas, jun. (1715–90) 1777: 5407

COLE, I. or James 1774: 5280

COLLET, John (*c* 1725–80) 1771: 4606, 4595, 4599, 4600, 4433. 1772: 4608, 4612, 4605. 1773: 4609, 4607, 4611. 1774: 4613, 4614, 4615, 4616. 1778: 4555, 4556, 4558, 4559, 4560, 4561, 4562, 4563. 1779: 5566, 5621, 4564, 4565, 4566, 4567, 4569, 5622, 3752. 1780: 5816, 5817, 5818, 5819, 3761, 5822 1781: 5946, 5947, 3786, 3787. 1782: 6148, 6149, 6150, 6151

COLLEY, Thomas[2] 1780: 5627, 5628, 5649, 5674, 5706, 5786. 1781: 5842, 5848, 5862,[1] 5933. 1782: 5967, 5968, 5971, 5984, 5989, 5991, 5993, 5994, 6000, 6008, 6035, 6036, 6037, 6038, 6040, 6043, 6051, 6119, 6130. 1783: 6163, 6170, 6172, 6173

COLLEY or an imitator of his manner,

perhaps Gillray 1782: 6117. 1783: 6166, 6228, 6230, 6233, 6236, 6237, 6244, 6252. Cf. 6249

'CORBUTT, C.' (?R. Purcell, *c.* 1736, supposed d. *c.* 1766) 1775: 5292, 5292 A, 5292 B, 5293, 5294, 5296. 1776: 5331, 5331 A, 5332, 5336. 1777: 5405, 5405 A, 5406, 5406 A. 1778: 5469, 5469 A, p. 286. 1782: 6034

COSWAY, Richard (1742–1821) 1780: 5770

COURTENAY, William, 2nd Viscount (1742–88) 1782: 6100[1]

CRAVEN, Elizabeth (Berkeley), Baroness (Margravine of Anspach from 1791) (1750–1828) 1775: 5325

CROSLAND, George 1772: 5070

DANCE, Nathaniel (1735–1811) 1781: 5905, 5906, 5910

DARLY, Mathina (?Mary) 1777: 5441

DARLY, Matthew[3] 1771: 4919, 4628. 1772: 5011, 5056, 5063, 5064. 1774: 5264, 5270. 1776. 5370, 5371, 5373. 1777: 5436, 5437, 5439, 5440, 5442, 5444, 5445, 5446, 5447, 5448, 5449. 1778: 5473, 5482, 5483

DAWE, Philip[2] (*c.* 1750–85) 1772: 4583, 5096. 1773: 4584, 5221, 4772. 1774: 5241, 5284, p. 196, p. 197. 1775: 4542. 1776: 5393, 5394, 5395, 4621, 5396. 1777: 5466, 5467 1778: 5533

DE FERRARS of Chartley, George Townshend, Baron (b 1753, cr Earl of Leicester 1784, succ. 1807 as 2nd Marq. Townshend, d. 1811) 1780: 5763, 5763 A

DE LOUTHERBOURG, Philippe-Jacques (1740–1812) 1776: 5361. 1780: 5769

DENT, William. 1783: 6244, 6246, 6249, 6255, 6257, 6260, 6289, 6314, 6315

DICKINSON, William (1746–1821)[4]

---

[1] Date uncertain [2] See Index of Publishers.
[3] See Index of persons, Index of publishers. He probably engraved the greater number of the prints which he published.
[4] See Index of Publishers, probably the engraver as well as publisher of these prints.

1779: 4765. 1780: 4766, 5803, 5804 1781: 5914, 5915, 5916, 5917, 5921, 5922, 5923, 5924. 1782: 6141, 6143

DIGHTON, Robert (c. 1752–1814) 1772: 4520. 1774: 5237. 1778: 5530. 1779: 5597 1780: 5778, 5783, 5784, 5795,[1] 5796,[1] 5799[1] 1781: 5900, 5939, 5957 1782: 6136, 6153,[1] 6154.[1] 1783: 6348, 6351, 6352, 3757

DIXON, John (b c. 1720–30, d. 1804) 1774. 5225, 5230

DUTSMAN, P. 1781: p 494

E., B 5793[1]

EARLOM, Richard (c. 1742–1822) 1772: 5089, 5091, 4520

G., T. P. 1781: 5835

GILLRAY, James (c. 1757–1815) 1775: 5326 1777. 5465. 1778: 5489, 5523, 5524. 1779: 5553, 5603, 5604, 5605, 5606, 5607, 5608, 5609, 5610, 5611, 5612, 5614, 5616 1780: 5623, 5624, 5625, 5634, 5635, 5646, 5667, 5678, 5679, 5695, 5748, 5749, 5750, 5750 A, 5751, 5751 A, 5752, 5779, 5790. 1781: 5837, 5845, 5846, 5876, 5877, 5911, 5912, 5938. 1782: 5964, 5966, 5970, 5972, 5973, 5978, 5987, 5990, 5992, 5996, 5997, 6001, 6003, 6006, 6007, 6012, 6013, 6015, 6018, 6019, 6020, 6021, 6022, 6025, 6026, 6027, 6031, 6032, 6033, 6041, 6044, 6095, 6096, 6097, 6098, 6103, 6104, 6108, 6109, 6110, 6112, 6115, 6116, 6120, 6121, 6123, 6131, 6132, 6133 1783: 6169, 6176, 6178, 6187, 6188, 6194, 6201, 6204, 6205, 6209, 6210, 6213, 6219, 6220, 6225, 6227, 6311, 6239, 6250, 6272, 6328 See under COLLEY and E T. (Topham)

GODFREY, J. B. 1771: 4931

GOLDAR, John (1729–95) 1771: 4789. 1772: 4604. 1773: 4609, 4611. 1774: 4613, 4614, 4615 1782: 6148, 6149, 6150, 6151

GRANT, A. 1781: 5929. 1782: 6133

GREEN, James 1779: 5576[2]

GRIGNION, Charles (1716–1810) 1771: 4895, 4896, 4897, 4898, 4899, 4900, 4901, 4902, 4922, 4601, 4924, 4606, 4933. 1772: 5088

GRIMM, Samuel Hieronymus (1734–1806) 1771: 4857, 4784, 4785, 1772: 4604, 4602. 1773: 4533. 1774. 4536, 4537, 4786

GROSE, Francis[3] (c 1731–91) 5757[1]

GULSTON, Elizabeth Bridgetta née Stepney (d. 1780) 1772: 5009 1780: 5807[1]

GUTTENBERG, Carl (1744–90) 1778: 5490. 1779: 5565

H., J.[4] 1777: 5452, 5453, 5455, 4778

H., J.[4] 1781: 5893

H., J.[4] 1783: 6195

H., T. 1773: 5190. 1779: 5598

HALL, C (?Charles Hall, c. 1720–83) 1781: 5840

HAMILTON (?John, 1765–86) 1780: 5686

'HANNIBAL SCRATCH' (?John Nixon) 1783: 6284

HASSEL, William 1776: 5386, 5387, 5388, 5389, 5390

HAYS, Captain 1783: 6317

HIXON, J.[5] 1782: 5998, 5999, 6113, 6122

HOLMAN 1771: 4864

HONE, Nathaniel (1718–84) 1772: 4474

HOOK 1783: 6271 A. Cf 6276 A

HUMPHREY, G.[6] 5756[1]

HUMPHREY, William[6] (c. 1740–1810) 1775: 5295. 1777: 5454, 5456, 5457, 5465. 1778: 4779, 5523. 1781: 5912

'HYDER, E.' 1782: 6044. See GILLRAY

'HYDER, H.' 1782: 6033 See GILLRAY

IBB., Hen. 1777: 5451

IRELAND, Samuel (d. 1800) 6358[1]

J , H. 1778: 5514, 5517, 5521

JOHNSTON, John 1782: 6137

---

[1] Date uncertain   [2] Reissue of pl published 1754.
[3] See Index of Persons.
[4] There is nothing to suggest that these initials denote the same person.
[5] See J. NIXON and 'HANNIBAL SCRATCH'.   [6] See Index of Publishers.

[1] See Index of Publishers
[2] Signed J. N. but resembling the manner of Gillray.
[3] Date uncertain.

843

S., C. L, *see* SMITH, Charles Loraine

S., G L. 1777: 5428

S., J ¹ 1772: 5017   1776: 5335. 1780: 5638

S., P. 1777: 5463

S., R ² 1777: 5452, 5453, 5455, 4778. 1778: 4779

S., R. 1780: 5665

S., R. 1781: 5827

SAM SHARP-EYE ('Bunbury) 1772: 5083

SANDBY, Paul (1725-1809) 1781: 5903, 5908, 5909, 3799. 1782: 6152. 1783: 6322

SANDERS or SAUNDERS, John (1750-1825) 1772: 5090

SAYERS, James (1748-1823) 1781: 5882, 5883, 6359.³ 1782: 6011, 6028, 6052, 6053, 6054, 6055, 6056, 6057, 6058, 6059, 6060, 6061, 6062, 6063, 6064, 6065, 6066, 6067, 6068, 6069, 6070, 6071, 6072, 6073, 6074, 6075, 6076, 6077   1783: 6183, 6192, 6217, 6226, 6234, 6271, 6276

SHARP, William (1749-1824) 1780: 5641

SHERIDAN, Richard Brinley, *see* RICHARD SNEER, and R. S

SHERWIN, John Keyse (1751-90) 1782. 5977

SIMPSON, John (? fictitious) 1779: 5573

SMITH, A 1771: 4927

SMITH, B T. 1781: 5890

SMITH, Charles Loraine 1772: 4742, 4734, 4752. 1782: 5983, 6125, 6147   1783· 6193

SMITH, John Raphael⁴ (1752-1812) 1772: 5090   1773: 5220.   1774: 3758   1776: 4543, 4544   1780: 5814, 5820, 5820 A, 5823, 5824. 1781: 5949. 1783: 6342

SMITH, W. 1777: 5459

SPARROW, S (worked c. 1782-1806) 1770: 4843

STEPHANOFF, N Fileter 1781: 5851

STUBBS, George Townley (1756-1815) 1780: 5770

T., E. (? Topham or perhaps Gillray imitating his manner) 1783: 6189, 6218, 6321

T , J. 1777: 5433

TAGG, Thomas 1780: 5689

TAYLOR, J. (?Isaac Taylor sen. b 1730, or jun. b. c. 1750) 1772: 5066

TERRY, G ⁴ (worked 1770-88) 1772: 5069   1774: 5233, 5238, 5243, 5244, 5275

THOMLINSON or Thomlinsen (? fictitious) 1775: 5296. 1777: 5404

THORNTON 1780: 5686

TOPHAM, Edward (1751-1820) 1771: 4671, 6353, 6354, 6355. 1772: 5011, 5012, 4701   1773: 5171. 1775: 5317. 1777: 5438 *See* E. T.

TOWNSHEND, George, 4th Viscount Townshend (cr. Marquis 1786) (1724-1807) 1772: 4944. 1780: 5645. 1781: 5850. 1782: 5961, 5988, 6005. 1783: 6212

TRINGHAM, William⁵ 1772: 5079, 5080

V., P. 1782: 6131, 6132

'VAN GROG' 1773. 5195, 5196

VAN SHROETER, J. 1781: 5845. *See* GILLRAY

VINCENT, Christian 1779: 5536

W , A. 1783: 6207

W , I. or J. 1772: 4997

WALE, Samuel (1720-86) 1771: 4895, 4896, 4897, 4898, 4899, 4900, 4901, 4902. 1772: 5066, 5088

WATSON, Thomas⁴ (1743-81) 1774: 4786

WELLS⁴ 1781· 5830

WHITE, Charles (1751-85) 1772: 4781

WIGSTEAD, Henry (d. 1793) 1774: 5273, 5274

---

¹ Probably three persons.
² Perhaps identical with 'Richard Sneer'.
³ Date uncertain.
⁴ See Index of Publishers
⁵ Called by H. Bleackley, the well-known book-plate engraver, he was employed by Wilkes to engrave a title-page for the *Essay on Woman*, Wilkes, 1917, p. 67. See Index of Publishers.

WILKINSON, John (probably fictitious) 1775: 5292, 5292 A, 5292 B, 5294. 1777: 5408. *See* 'CORBUTT'

WILL or WILLE, Johann Martin[1] 1775: 5291, 5292 A, 5296 A 1776: 5331 A, 5332 A, 5336, 5337, 5339. 1777: 5405 A, 5406 A, 5407. 1779: 5582 1782: 6034

WILLIAMS, J.[2] 1771: 4852

WOODING (worked *c.* 1780–3) 1781: 5841

YERAC or YEARAC, *see* CAREY

[1] Probably engraver as well as publisher of these prints.
[2] See Index of Publishers

[1] See Index of Artists   [2] With Hedges.

[3] All the prints published by Barrow are by the same artist, perhaps himself.

[4] No address.

[5] On the death (intestate) of Carington Bowles 1793, his son Carington carried on the business as Bowles and Carver. Plomer, *Dict of Booksellers and Printers,* 1932

[6] See Index of Artists, he may have published the plates etched by himself in 1781 and 1782

6056, 6057, 6058, 6059, 6060, 6061, 6062, 6063, 6064, 6065, 6066, 6067, 6068, 6069, 6070, 6071, 6072, 6073, 6075, 6076, 6077, 6147 1783: 6317[1]

BRETHERTON, H.,[2] New Bond Street 1783: 6234

BRETHERTON, James, 134 New Bond Street 1772: 4649, 5083, 4757, 4738, 4753, 4669, 4712, 4713, 4725, 4723, 4755, 4714, 5084, 5085, 5086, 4715, 4739, 4740, 4756, 4722, 4742, 5087. 1773: 5213, 5214, 5215, 5216, 5217, 5218, 4758, 4759, 4728, 4726, 4716, 4721, 4748, 4749, 4762. 1774: 5279, 4727, 4747, 4735, 4741, 4720 1777: 4719, 4717, 4729. 1778: 4732. 1779: 4736, 4737,[1] 4760. 1780: 5802[3] 1781: 5913. 1782: 6139, 6140, 4185. 1783: 6345[3]

BROWN, D. 1783: 6286

BROWN, H, Oxford Market 1782: 6109

BROWN, W. 1782: 5970

BROWNING, J., Oxford Street 1782: 5966

BRYER, Henry, London[4] c. 1771: 4892, 12 Stephen Street, Tottenham Court Road 1773: 4788

C., T. M. 1780: 5643

CATTERMOUL, J., 376 Oxford Street 1783: 6257, 6289

CLARK, C., 6 Princes Street 1782: 6114

COLLEY, Thomas,[5] Clare Market, London 1780: 5627; 288 Strand 5674; Strand 5706; 288 Strand 5786; 1781: 288 Strand 5848; High Holborn 5850; 257 High Holborn 5854; 1782: Rolls Buildings, Fetter Lane or Acorn Court, Rolls Buildings 5967, 5989, 5993, 6000,[3] 6008, 6035,[3] 6037,[3] 6038,[3] 6040,[3] 6043,[3] 6119. 1783: 6163,[3] 6230,[3] 6236[3]

COOKE, I., Temple Bar 1782: 6122

CORNELL, T., Bruton Street 1780: 5650, 1781: 5854, 5887. 1782: 5976, 6113.[3] 1783: 6185, 6207, 6217, 6226, 6271, 6276, 6306

DARCHERY (or D'Archery) Elizabeth, St. James's Street or 11 St. James's Street 1780: 5659. 1782: 5969, 5979, 5980, 5987, 5992, 5996, 6006, 6015, 6018, 6022, 6026, 6031, 6032, 6041, 6106, 6116, 6123. 1783: 6169, 6170, 6171, 6174, 6176, 6177, 6178, 6189, 6191, 6195, 6197, 6211, 6214, 6218, 6233, 6237, 6252, 6274, 6280, 6321, 6333

DARENY, M S, Opposite to the King's Head, Strand 1779: 5569

DARENY, Ja[8] (same address) 1780: 5629

DARLING, W., Great Newport Street 1771: 4767. 1772: 4948

DARLY, Mary[6] 1772: 4752. 1776: 5369

DARLY, Matthew,[6] 39 Strand 1771: 4879, 4632, 4710, 4668, 4670, 4671, 4672, 4673, 4913, 4675, 4677, 4782, 4679, 4914, 4634, 4680, 4681, 4915, 4916, 4682, 4917, 4683, 4684, 4685, 4686, 4687, 4711, 4918, 4764, 4635, 4636, 4639, 4641, 4919, 4633, 4920, 4305, 4628.[7] 1772: 4985, 4986, 4987, 4988, 4989, 4990, 4991, 4692, 4693, 4992, 4993, 4994, 4995, 4996, 4997, 4704, 4998, 4694, 4697, 4999, 5000, 5001, 5002, 5003, 5004, 5005, 5006, 4690, 4647, 5007, 5008, 5009, 5010, 4705, 5011, 5012, 5013, 5014, 4648, 5015, 5016, 4695, 4696, 4698, 4652, 5017, 4653, 5018, 4700, 5019, 5020, 5021, 4691, 5022, 5023, 5024, 5025, 5026, 5027, 4709, 4654, 5028, 5029, 5030, 5031, 5032, 5033, 4656, 5034, 5035, 4657, 5036, 5037, 5038, 5039, 4658, 4660, 5040, 5041, 4661, 5042, 5043, 5044, 5045, 4662, 5046, 4663, 4664, 5047, 5048, 5049, 4659, 5050, 5051, 5052, 5053, 5054, 4665, 5055, 5056, 4703, 5057, 5058, 4701, 5059, 5060, 5061, 4637, 4706, 4699,

---

[1] Date uncertain.   [2] H is perhaps an engraver's error   [3] No address.
[4] Engraver. pupil and partner of William Wynne Ryland, they were printsellers at 27 Cornhill until Dec. 1771, when they became bankrupt Bryer again had a Cornhill address in 1776. Died before 1783 D N.B s v Ryland, Chaloner Smith, 1, pp. lii, 123–4.   [5] See Index of Artists
[6] See Index of Persons, Index of Artists   [7] With R Sayer.

4829, 4640. **1773:** 4666, 4707,
5149, 5150, 5151, 5152, 5153, 4667,
5154, 5155, 5156, 5157, 5158, 4688,
5159, 5160, 5161, 5162, 5163, 5164,
4689, 5165, 5166, 5167, 5168, 5169,
5170, 4642, 5171, 5172, 5173, 4643,
5174, 5175, 4644, 4645, 4646, 5176,
5177, 5178, 5179, 5180, 5181, 5182,
5183, 5184, 5185, 5186. **1774:**
5261, 5262, 5263, 5264, 4651,
5265, 4650, 5266, 5267, 5268,
5269, 5270, 4708, 4655. **1775:**
5312, 4638, 5313, 5314, 5315,
5316, 5317. **1776:** 5335, 5368,
5369, 5370, 5371, 5372, 5373, 5374,
5375, 5376, 5377, 5378 **1777:**
5397, 5400,[1] 5429, 5430, 5431,
5432, 5433, 5434, 5435, 5436,
5437, 5438, 5439, 5440, 5441,
5442, 5443, 5444, 5445, 5446,
5447, 5448, 5449, 5450, 5451.
1778: 5473, 5474, p. 288, 5475,
p. 289, 5482, 5483, 5511, 5513,
5514, 5515, 5516, 5517, 5518, 5519,
5520, 5521, 5522. **1779:** 5551,[2]
5599, 5600, 5601, 5602, 5603, 5606,
5607 **1780:** 5652, 5654, 5661,
5662, 5665, 5669; 159 Fleet Street
5670, 5671, 39 Strand 5675, 5682,
5688, 5700, 5701, 5753, 5754, 5785.
1781: 159 Fleet Street 5835.
5860,[3] 5897

DAWE, P.,[4] [15] Goodge Street, Tottenham Court Road 1782: 6118

DENT, W.,[4] 116 Strand 1783: 6240, 6244, 6246, 6249, 6255, 6257, 6260, 6262, 6314, 6315

DICKINSON, William,[4] 158 New Bond Street[5] 1781: 5921, 5922, 5923, 5924. 1782: 6141, 6143

EVANS, T., Oxford Street 1782: 5968

EWART, T, the Corner of Hudson's Court near St. Martin's Lane Strand 1781: 5861

FIELDING & WALKER, [20] Paternoster Row (booksellers) 1779: 5548, 5618. 1780: 5684

FIELDING, John, [23] Paternoster Row (bookseller) 1781: 5844. 1783: 6223, 6334

FORES, S. W., 41 Piccadilly, 1783: 6343 A[6]

FREEMAN, I. or J., Strand 1783: 6232

GEHAGAN, Patrick, Oxford Road (probably fictitious) 1778: 5489 A

GUNDRY, Thomas 1781: 5940

HALL,[4] 2 Grafton Street, Soho 1781: 5840

HAMILTON, A. jun.,[7] near St. John's Gate, Publisher of the *Town and Country Magazine*, his imprint is on all *Tête-à-tête* plates from No. 5250. *See* Index of Titles

HARRIS, John, 3 Sweetings Alley, Cornhill 1771: 4764. 1780: 5636, 5637, 5640, 5673, 5694, 5699,[8] 5705. 1782: 6019

HART, Thomas, London (? fictitious) 1775: 5292 B, 5294. 1776: 5331, 5331 A, 5332, 5332 A, 5336, 5337, 5338, 5339. 1777: 5404, 5408

HAWKINS, I. or J., Strand, London 1779: 5547

HEDGES, Edward, 92 Under the Royal Exchange, Cornhill, or 2 Under the Piazzas, Royal Exchange, or 92 Cornhill 1780: 5627, 5628, 5645,[9] 5649, 5651, 5708.[10] 1781: 5838, 5842, 5843, 5878,[11] 5933. 1782: 5959, 6009. 1783: 6183, 6192, 6199, 6281, 6285, 6344[12]

HINTON, W., 12 Corner of Bell Yard, Grace Church Street (copper plate printer) 1779: 5558

HITCHCOCK, William, 5 Birchin Lane 1777: 5401, 5464

HOGG, Alexander, The King's Arms, 16 Paternoster Row (bookseller) 1780: 5686. 1781: 5841

---

[1] 120 New Bond Street and 39 Strand.
[2] No address
[3] No publication line, see print
[4] See Index of Artists.
[5] See Watson and Dickinson.
[6] Date uncertain.
[7] Son of Archibald Hamilton (1736-93), printer, d 1792. Plomer, *Dict of Booksellers*, 1932
[8] With Mitchell.
[9] With Kearsley.
[10] With Kearsley and Stockdale
[11] With Baldrey
[12] With J. Wallis.

HOLLAND, William, 50 Oxford Street 5480,[1] 5787,[1] 5794,[1] 1782: 6036
—— 66 Drury Lane 1782: 6126.[1] 1783: 6277, 6328
HOLT, Mrs., 111 Oxford Street, London 1779: 5539
HONE, Mr,[2] St James's Place 1772: 4474
HOOPER, S., 25 Ludgate Hill 1771: 4864, 4865, p 18, 4791, 4931. 1772: 5081. 1773: 5108; Corner of Arundel Street, Strand 1782: 6033
HUMPHREY, G,[2] 48 Long Acre 1783. 6220, 6220 A, 6288
HUMPHREY, H. [Hannah] or Mrs. [Miss], Bond Street 1774: 5273, 5274
—— 18, New Bond Street 1779: 5596, 5602 A, 5603 A. 1780: 5630,[3] 5633,[3] 5646, 5648,[3] 5662 A, 5682 B, 5683, 5690, 5748, 5749, 5756,[4] 5761 1781: 5725, 5892, 5894, 5929, 5930, 5936, 5937, 5938. 1782: p. 559, 5963, 5972,[5] 5974, 5981,[6] 5990, 5997, 6001, 6003, 6020, 6025, 6044, 6050,[6] 6095, 6096, 6098,[8] 6101, 6102, 6104, 6105, 6115, 6127, 6130, 6133
—— 51 New Bond Street 1783: 6187, 6188, 6194, 6278, 6307, 6308, 6309, 6310, 6312, 6326, 6330
—— St. James's Street, 5481,[7] 5812[7]
HUMPHREY, William,[2] St. Martin's Lane 1772: 5096, 4775. 1773: 4772. 1774. 5280, 4776
—— Gerrard Street, Soho 1775: 5295. 1776: p. 216, 5357, 5380, 4777[9]
—— 227 Strand 1777: 5402, 5452, 5453, 5454, 5455, 4778, 5456, 5457.[10]

1778: 5489, 4779,[10] 5523,[10] 5524,[10] 5525[10]
—— 70 St. Martin's Lane 1778: 4780
—— 227 Strand 1779: 5553,[9] 5555, 5570, 5579, 5604,[9] 5605,[9] 5608, 5609, 5610, 5614, 5616 [9] 1780: 5623, 5624, 5625, 5630,[11] 5633,[11] 5633 A, 5635, 5648,[11] 5664, 5676, 5678, 5695, 5707, 5779, 5790. 1781: 5831 A, 5837, 5906. 1782: 5964, 5965, 5971, 5973, 5978, 5989, 5994, 6007, 6012,[9] 6016, 6036, 6051, 6110, 6112, 6120, 6131, 6132. 1783: 6162,[9] 6164, 6165, p. 671, 6173, 6182, 6186, 6190, p 688, 6201, 6203, p. 691, 6204, 6205, 6207 A, 6209, 6210, 6213, 6219, 6222, 6225, 6227, 6250, p 724, 6283, 6287, 6325, 6331, 6335
HUMPHREY, Mrs., St. Martin's Lane 1778: 5526
JOHNSON, G. 1778 · 5487
JONES, C., Brewer Street, Golden Square 1780. 5703
JONES, J,[12] Gerrard Street 1777: 5422
JONES, J,[12] 103 Wardour Street, Soho 1780: 5696, 5697 [13] 1781: 5856[9] Cf. 5904
JONES, J.,[12] Hayes's Court, Soho 1781. 5907. See ASSEN, F.
KEARLY, J., Stafford Street, Old Bond Street 1780: 5645[14]
KEARSLEY, George.[15] 1772: Ludgate Street (bookseller) 4970,
—— 1780: 46 Fleet Street 5692, 5708 [16] 1782: 6005
KENT, J (? fictitious) 1781: 5845, 5846

[1] Date uncertain.   [2] See Index of Artists   [3] With W. Humphrey
[4] Date uncertain, pub at Old Bond Street
[5] 118 New Bond Street.   [6] Pub at Bond Street
[7] Copy of an earlier plate
[8] Pub at 51 New Bond Street, several of the plates of 1782 have the address New Bond Street without a number, but in or before Nov 1780 H Humphrey seems to have moved from 18 to 51   [9] No address
[10] No address, cf Nos 5526, 4780.
[11] 227 Strand or 18 New Bond Street (address of H. Humphrey).
[12] Perhaps the same person, possibly John Jones, the engraver in mezzotint and stipple, d 1797   See also Nos. 5904, 5907   [13] With Rowlandson
[14] With Hedges.   [15] See Bleackley, Wilkes, 1917, pp. 94–5, &c
[16] With Stockdale and Hedges.

KILLINGBECK, A., Down Street 1783: 6181

KNIGHT, C., Berwick Street 1781: 5876, 5877

LANGHAM, J., St Bride's Passage, Fleet Street 1781: 5941. 1782: 5976, 5998, 5999; 84 Dorset Street 6042
—— The Great Piazza, Covent Garden 1783: 6319

LAURIE, Robert,[1] 17 Rosomon's Row, Clerkenwell[2] 1780: 5657

LEATHERHEAD, P J. (? fictitious) 1782: 6013

LIVESAY, Rd ,[2] at Mrs. Hogarth's, Leicester Fields 1782: 6129

LOCKINGTON, J , Shug Lane, Golden Square 1776· 5378, 5379. 1777: 5458, 5459, 5460, 5461

LONG, D 1780: 5639

LOW, T. 1780: 5626

MACINTOSH, W. (? fictitious) 1780: 5644

MACKLIN, Thomas, 1 Lincoln's Inn Fields 1779: 5559

MEADOWS, R 1781: 5903

MILLS, I or J., 1 Ratcliff Row near the French Hospital, Old Street 1780: 5647, 5653. 1783: 6327[3]

MITCHELL or MITCHEL, P., North Audley Street, Grosvenor Square 1780: 5673,[4] 5699,[4] 5766. 1781: 5844.[5] With J. Fielding 1782: 5991

MORRIS, John, Rathbone Place (? fictitious) 1777: 5405, 5405 A, 5406, 5406 A 1778: 5469. 1782: 6034

NEALE, S. J., 352 near Exeter 'change, Strand 1782: 6097

NICOLL, William, [51] St. Paul's Church Yard (bookseller) 1775: 5319, 5320, 5321, 5322, 5323, 5324

OWEN, R., Fleet Street 1782: 5961

PETHER, T.,[6] Berwick Street, Soho 1772: 5195, 5196

PHELPS, W. 1780: 5788. 1781: 5834

POWNALL, B., 6 Pall Mall 1783: 6256, 6263, 6265, 6266

RACK, Mr., or M., London. 1782: 5983, 6125

RENIGALD or RENEGAL, W. 1780: 5666, 5667

RENNIE, W. 1782: 6103

RICH, E The Little Print Shop facing Anderton's Coffee House, Fleet Street or 55 Fleet Street 1782: 5985, 5986 1783: 6248

RICHARDSON, W., 68 High Holborn 1778: 5484, 5527 1779: 5550, 5555, 5613. 1780: 5642, 5658, 5677, 5702, 5723, 5792. 1781: 5831. 1782: 5984, 6004, 6117. 1783: 174 Near Surrey Street, Strand 6166, 6172, 6173, 6196, 6215, 6268

ROBERTS, J., St. Martin's Lane 1772: 5068

ROWLANDSON, T ,[2] & JONES, J., 103 Wardour Street, Soho 1780: 5697, 5764, 5765

RUGENDAS, Johann Lorenz, Augsburg[2] 1779: 5561 A

RUSTED, R., 3 Bridge Street, Ludgate Hill 1783: 6184, 6323

RYLEY, C. R [2] 1780: 5780, 5781

SANDBY, P.,[2] St. George's Row, Oxford Turnpike 1781: 5909. 1783: 6322[7]

SAYER, Robert, 53 Fleet Street[8] 1771: 4922,[9] 4601,[9] 4923,[9] 4924,[9] 4925,[9] 4606,[9] 4595,[9] 4599,[9] 4600,[9] 4628,[10] 4932,[10] 4933.[10] 1772: 5056,[11] 5060[11], 4603,[9]

---

[1] See Index of Artists He was connected with Sayer, to whose business he succeeded in partnership with Whittle Chaloner Smith, ii, p. 796.
[2] See Index of Artists
[3] No address, 'to be had at 51 Bond Street' [? H. Humphrey's].
[4] With Harris. [5] With J Fielding.
[6] Probably Thomas, a wax-modeller who exhibited portraits in wax with the Free Society from 1772 to 1781. D N B , s v Abraham Pether
[7] Advertised as 'To be had at Mr. Sandbys' . . . [ut s.]; and of G Kearsley, at No. 46, in Fleet Street'.
[8] 'The Golden Buck' till c. 1771. Also a bookseller, see Plomer, Dict. of Booksellers, 1932. [9] With John Smith. [10] With Darly. [11] Date uncertain.

4604,[1] 4602,[1] 5082,[1] 4608,[1] 4612,[1] 4605,[1] 5089, 5091, 5097.[2] **1773:** 5172,[2] 5173,[2] 5176,[2] 4609,[1] 4607,[1] 4611.[1] **1774:** 5261 A,[2] 5265.[2] **1778:** 5511 A.[2] **1780:** 5795,[2] 5796,[2] 5797,[2] 5798,[2] 5799 [2] **1782** 6136, 6153,[2] 6154.[2] *See* SAYER & BENNETT

SAYER, R & BENNET OR BENNETT, J , 53 Fleet Street **1774:** p. 169, 5241, 4613, 4614, 4615, 4616, 4618, 4619, 4620. **1775·** 5284, p. 196, p 197, 4622. **1776:** 5361, 5391, 5393, 5394, 5395, 4621, 4629, 4623, 5396, 4624, 4610. **1777:** 5463, 5467, 5468, 4625. **1778:** 4626, 4631. **1779:** 5562. **1780:** 5783 [1] **1781:** 5828,[1] 5900,[1] 5939 [1] **1782:** 6138

'T SCRATCHLEY' **1771·** 4782 *See* DARLY, Matthew

SEAGO, J., High Street, St. Giles, London **1777·** 5428

SHARPE, I or J. **1782:** 6024

SHEPHERD, C. London (? fictitious) **1775:** 5290, 5291, 5292, 5292 A, 5293, 5296, 5296 A

SHEPPARD, C., Lambeth Hill, Doctors' Commons **1778:** 5477

SLEDGE, S. (or Mrs), Henrietta Street, Covent Garden **1771:** 4857, 4784, 4785 **1773:** 5187, 5188, 5189 **1774:** 5234,[3] 4786. **1777·** 5462

SMITH, John,[4] Cheapside **1771:** 4922,[5] 4601,[5] 4923,[5] 4924,[5] 4925,[5] 4606,[5] 4595,[5] 4599,[5] 4600,[5] 4932,[5] 4933 [5] **1772:** 4603,[5] 4604,[5] 4602,[5] 5082,[5] 4608,[5] 4612,[5] 4605 [5] **1773:** 4607,[5] 4609,[5] 4611 [5] **1778:** 5530. **1779:** 5597. **1780:** 5783 [5] **1781:** 5828,[5] 5847,[5] 5900,[5] 5939[5]

SMITH, J. R.,[6] 83 Oxford Street· **1781:** 5901, 5919, 5920. **1782:**

6128, 6144, 6145, 6146. **1783:** 6341, 6342, 6343

SMITH, M , Fleet Street **1783:** 6212, 6272[7]

STATON, J. & JONES, J , 13 Parliament Street, London **1781:** 5904

STOCKDALE, John, 181 Piccadilly (bookseller) **1780:** 5708[8]

SWAN, Mr., facing Norfolk Street, Strand **1774:** 5234[9]

TERRY, G.,[6] Pater Noster Row[10] **1772.** 5069 **1774·** 5233, 5238, 5243, 5244, 5275

THANE, J , Rupert Street, Haymarket **1782:** 6099 *See* TORRE & THANE

THOMAS, M , Princes Street **1783:** 6228

TOMLINSON, James, Oxford Street (? fictitious) **1779:** 5573

TORRE, 44 Market Lane[11] **1781:** 5905

TORRE, A., & THANE, J , Ancient and Modern Print Warehouse, 28 Haymarket **1781:** 3799 **1782:** 6108[14]

TRINGHAM, William,[6] under St. Dunstan's Church, Fleet Street **1772:** 5079, 5080

TURNER, Frame-maker and Printseller, 40 Snow Hill **1772:** 4787. **1782:** 5985

WALKER, J , 13 Parliament Street **1776:** 5381

WALLIS, J., 16 Ludgate Street **1783:** 6241, 6241 A, 6344[12]

WATSON & DICKINSON,[13] 158 New Bond Street. **1779:** 4765. **1780:** 4766, 5803, 5804. **1781:** 5914, 5915, 5916, 5917

WELLS, W ,[6] 132 Fleet Street (the address, c 1768, of T. Bradford, *see* No 4256) **1779:** 5568. **1780:** 5632,[14] 5660, 5668, 5680,[15] 5782,

---

[1] With John Smith
[2] Date uncertain.
[3] With Mr Swan
[4] See Index of Persons
[5] With Sayer or Sayer & Bennett
[6] See Index of Artists.
[7] Sold at 46 Fleet Street (address of Kearsley)
[8] With Hedges and Kearsley
[9] With Mrs Sledge.
[10] G Terry & Batley were engravers at 29 Paternoster Row in 1770. Chaloner Smith, iii, p 1362
[11] Torre & Brothers were Merchants at Market Lane, Pall Mall, 1784 Lowndes, *London Directory*
[12] With Hedges
[13] See Dickinson.
[14] Address only, no name.
[15] Address only, 132 Fleet Street.

[1] Address only, no name
[2] He succeeded to the business of John Bowles. Plomer, *Dict. of Booksellers and Printers*, 1932.
[3] Whether two, three, or all are identical is not clear. One at least is probably the John Williams who was pilloried for his share in the *North Briton*, Bleackley, *Wilkes*, 1917, p 170. His address was Next the Mitre Tavern 1763-74, his subsequent history unrecorded. Plomer, *Dict. of Printers*, 1932, p 265.
[4] The address of W. Humphrey.

PRINTED IN GREAT BRITAIN AT THE UNIVERSITY PRESS, OXFORD
BY JOHN JOHNSON, PRINTER TO THE UNIVERSITY

Lightning Source UK Ltd.
Milton Keynes UK

171022UK00004B/8/P